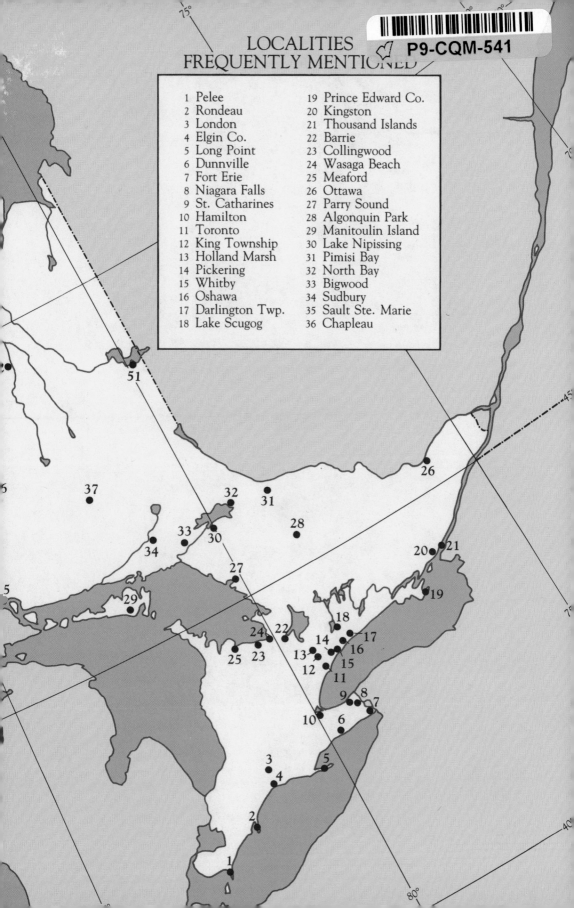

## LOCALITIES
## FREQUENTLY MENTIONED

| | |
|---|---|
| 1 Pelee | 19 Prince Edward Co. |
| 2 Rondeau | 20 Kingston |
| 3 London | 21 Thousand Islands |
| 4 Elgin Co. | 22 Barrie |
| 5 Long Point | 23 Collingwood |
| 6 Dunnville | 24 Wasaga Beach |
| 7 Fort Erie | 25 Meaford |
| 8 Niagara Falls | 26 Ottawa |
| 9 St. Catharines | 27 Parry Sound |
| 10 Hamilton | 28 Algonquin Park |
| 11 Toronto | 29 Manitoulin Island |
| 12 King Township | 30 Lake Nipissing |
| 13 Holland Marsh | 31 Pimisi Bay |
| 14 Pickering | 32 North Bay |
| 15 Whitby | 33 Bigwood |
| 16 Oshawa | 34 Sudbury |
| 17 Darlington Twp. | 35 Sault Ste. Marie |
| 18 Lake Scugog | 36 Chapleau |

# BIRDS OF
# ONTARIO

# BIRDS OF ONTARIO

## J. Murray Speirs

NATURAL HERITAGE/NATURAL HISTORY INC.

**Canadian Cataloging in Publication Data**

Speirs, J. Murray (John Murray), 1909-
  Birds of Ontario

Bibliography: p.
Includes indexes.
ISBN 0-920474-38-1 (v. 1).   ISBN 0-920474-39-4 (v. 2)

1. Birds – Ontario. 2. Birds – Ontario –
Identification. 3. Bird populations – Ontario.
4. Bird populations – Ontario – Maps. I. Title.

QL685.5.05S67 1985   598.29713   C85-099423-3

DESIGNERS: Derek Chung Tiam Fook/Gail Ferreira Ng-A-Kien
MAP ILLUSTRATOR: Julian Cleva
TYPESETTING: Q Composition Inc.
Printed in Canada by D. W. Friesen

85 86 87 88 89 DWF 5 4 3 2 1

# CONTENTS

# INTRODUCTION

When I was a lad, I served a term as "Joe Boy" at the Wildlife Research Camp in Algonquin Park. I was seventeen years old and very excited by all of the contact, not only with the wilderness, but with all the naturalists and scientists who were exploring its mysteries. One day, word spread through the camp that Murray and Doris Speirs had arrived for a visit. Everyone greeted the news with pleasure. In the thirty-eight years since that time everyone that I know who knows them, has the same reaction towards the Speirs.

There are many reasons for this, but I am sure that it is due in large part to their intelligence, knowledge, sense of discovery and enthusiasm. I usually think of the Speirs as a unit. They are one of the most inspiring team relationships I know. This wonderful work on Ontario birds is Murray's book, but I know that the help and inspiration of Doris has been interwoven in the years of effort and experiences.

My most vivid memory from that 1947 day in Algonquin Park was the auspicious flock of evening grosbeaks which lifted off from the central open area of the camp just as the Speirs arrived. The enthusiastic exclamations of Doris were my first insight into the decades of study of that bird, by Doris and Murray. I was flattered to have the same delighted reaction to my sketch book which include several evening grosbeak studies. Incidentally, I am proud to say that they were among the first to purchase my paintings.

Through the years, I learned their great depth of skill in research and timeless efforts in learning more of these birds and other birds in Ontario. As I grew older and became involved with organizations such as the Federation of Ontario Naturalists, I observed the great esteem which all of the top people in natural history and conservation had and still have for Murray Speirs. When he spoke, you knew that you were listening to a voice of wisdom.

It is the qualities of Dr. Speirs as a scientist and a man which has made possible his own work and his co-operation with others to produce this very worthwhile book.

*Robert Bateman*

# INTRODUCTION

I have often been asked "Which is your favourite bird?' I have to confess that I have many favourites, not one.

When I am walking through Lynde Shores woodlot and a Black-capped Chickadee confidently comes to my hand for sunflower seeds, who could resist this and not get a glow of pleasure? When a Hermit Thrush sings its ascending hymns to the wilderness, who could not be spellbound? Which is our most colourful bird? Is it the jaunty Blue Jay, or the Cardinal against a snowy background, or the garrulous Evening Grosbeaks arguing on your winter feeder? How can one express the admiration for a flock of Oldsquaws riding out a winter storm on the rough waves off Toronto's waterfront? When the flocks of shorebirds gather on the mudflats during the "doldrums" of late August when other birds are skulking out of sight during moult, they delight the birdwatcher, and excite the imagination wondering about their origin in our Arctic and their destination in South America. The joy of summer in northern Ontario is the great variety in plumage and song of the warbler hordes. And then there is the September flypast of the hawks, with its "kettles" of spiralling Broad-wings, the great tilting Turkey Vultures, the rare glimpse of a majestic Bald Eagle or the spectacular plunge of Peregrine Falcon. How can the shorebirds know that it is a Peregrine before we even see the bird coming? The winter gatherings of secretive owls is a challenge, drawing bird watchers from all over North America. How can anyone have one favourite bird species? Anyone who has studied any species in detail will know the endless satisfaction that is derived from learning about the behaviour, the migrations, even the great variety in plumage and structure that go to make up a single species.

The purpose of this book is to give a picture of each of the birds that have been known to occur in Ontario up to the end of 1984, where they have been found, when they have occurred at each season, some of the things that have been discovered in studies by banders and other students. Although we have attempted to find a photograph of each species, some have eluded us, mostly the very rare species in our province. This is not primarily a guide for identification: there are already many excellent field guides available: the Peterson guides, the guide by Robbins, Bruun & Zim, the various Audubon guides and many others. No guide can possibly illustrate more that a few representative plumages, as a glance at a tray of museum specimens will quickly reveal.

In the seasonal accounts the material is arranged from south to north, except for the autumn accounts which are arranged from north to south. The winter account is always introduced with a summary of the Christmas count findings for the period 1968-1977, which has been illustrated by a map of the findings, if any. In these summaries the regions in which more than 100 individuals have been found per 100 party-hours have been designated as common, where more than 10 have been found as fairly common, more than one as uncommon and less than 1 as rare. Similarly the summer accounts have been introduced by a summary of the findings from the Breeding Bird Surveys made from 1968-1977, Here more than 10 birds per 50 stops has been called common, more than 1 as fairly common more than 0.1 as uncommon and less than that as rare. The results of the Breeding Bird Surveys have also been illustrated with maps, where pertinent.

Another method of measuring abundance has been the use of quadrats, where the number of territories on 10 hectares (or some other size) has been found by a series of daily walks through the study area during the breeding season. For species that have faint songs or that avoid highways (such as Bay-breasted Warblers and Henslow's Sparrows) these give a better picture of abundance than do the roadside counts used for the Breeding Bird Surveys. Birds such as waterfowl and birds of prey that are not found by roads or have very large territories are not well censused by either method and we have to be satisfied by general statements of their abundance. For the more common species we have used mainly the accounts of local lists, but for the less common species we have gone into somewhat more detail though the available literature is too great to have found all the references for even the less common species. Our intent has been to give a picture of each species and its distribution in space and time throughout Ontario.

J.Murray Speirs

# ACKNOWLEDGMENTS

This book is dedicated to my wife, Doris Louise, for her enthusiastic support and companionship on travels throughout Ontario (and other parts of the world), for meticulous attention to detail when proofreading the manuscript, and for her gift of making friends wherever we have gone.

My interest in birds I can trace back to the time when my brother, Gordon, won as a prize for violin playing, a copy of Neltje Blanchan's "Bird Neighbors," which enabled me to identify a Ruby-crowned Kinglet as it passed through our city garden in migration. From that moment I was "hooked" on birds and I prowled the Don Valley and other Toronto oases with a copy of Reed's "Bird Guide" in pocket. My parents at first merely tolerated my interest but later became most supportive. Various friends and relatives invited me to their country retreats: I particularly remember the visits to my Aunt Margaret's farm near Lowbanks and the summer spent at the Hodges' cottage near Whalen's Island, Georgian Bay. Murray Scott and Lester Beldan were sometimes companions on these early expeditions, as were members of the family and relatives.

As a teenager I found some friends with similar tastes, among them Hubert Richardson, who lived near J. H. Fleming. Mr. Fleming had a fabulous library and collection of birds, and fostered my interest in ornithology. Although I have never collected birds myself (except those found dead as road kills, or window casualties) the staff of the Royal Ontario Museum, particularly James L. Baillie, Clifford Hope, Terrence Shortt and L. L. Snyder, and more recently Ross James and others shared their knowledge and enthusiasm. No bird book can give any adequate idea of the great individual variation in plumage, with age, sex and degree of feather wear, that is evident at a glance at a tray of museum specimens: or with the intimacy that develops when a person studies living birds in detail in the field. Doris and I have found, in our detailed studies of Evening Grosbeaks, American Robins and Lincoln' Sparrows, that much of what has been written in books has been copied from author to author without adequate checking, so that many statements were merely perpetuated errors. Any compilation (including this work) depends upon the accuracy of its sources.

During my university days I was blessed with much understanding from helpful staff and students. Prof. J. R. Dymond and the staff of the Royal Ontario Museum were supportive, as I compiled information from their file of checking cards and literature sources to produce my MA work on fluctuations in the numbers of birds in the Toronto region. At the University of Illinois Dr. S. Charles Kendeigh supported my studies on the movements of the American Robin in regions east of the Rocky Mountains, and I benefited from the close proximity of such distinguished fellow graduate students as "Ted" Black, Reed Fautin, Eugene Odum and Frank Pitelka.

Returning to the University of Toronto, Prof. Alan Coventry, Prof. John MacArthur and his sons John and Robert were particular sources of inspiration. Prof. E. M. Walker was perhaps the most erudite naturalist I have ever encountered. Fellow students, too numerous to mention, shared field expeditions far and near at that time, but particular mention must be made of the group that formed the Toronto Intermediate Naturalists (to bridge the gap between junior and senior members of the Toronto Field Naturalists). This group included Frank Banfield, the Boissonneau sisters and brother, Andrew Lawrie, Douglas Miller, the Riddell sisters, etc., with the inspirational assistance of James L. Baillie *et al.* This group was most helpful in my studies of daily robin roost movements and the pioneer study on the York Downs quadrat (then on the northern edge of Toronto).

During our stay at Ancaster, in the early part of the war years, I came to admire the field work of George North in the Hamilton vicinity, scanning every bird in big flocks of waterfowl, with his patience often rewarded by exciting finds. George also helped in organizing data, as did William Mansell with his fine printed forms.

After graduation, my early field work included the quadrat studies at Eaglehead Lake, north of Lake Superior, studying the effects of DDT on bird populations in a pristine spruce forest, following a similar study the previous year by S. Charles Kendeigh at Black Sturgeon Lake, both studies under auspices of the Ontario Dept. of Lands & Forests. There followed studies on Beausoleil Is. and Beckwith Is. in Georgian Bay, the first sponsored by Dr. Harrison Lewis of the National Parks Service and the second by Dr. David Fowle of the Dept. of Lands & Forests.

Work with the International Great Lakes Fisheries Commision took me to the shores of Lake Superior for several years in the 1950's. Dr. F. E. J. Fry was in charge of this project. The Atkinson family and Aarne Lamsa, a fellow worker, stimulated part time work on the birds of this fascinating area and I was aided by the long time experience in the area of Dr. A. E. Allin and Keith Denis. During one summer, Robert R. Taylor, now a well-known bird photographer, was our field assistant at Dorion.

Returning to full time work at the University of Toronto in the late 1950's, Professors Bruce Falls, F. E. J. Fry and Frederick Ide made life there most interesting. Many students helped with my work on the birds of Ontario County during the 1960's. Among these, Christopher Amos, Barry Kent MacKay, Ronald Orenstein and Ronald Tozer shone. David Spratt, and some of the above, helped with the quadrat studies in the University of Toronto forest, near Dorset, for four years. Many of Dr. Bruce Falls' students studied this forest in late summers, adding interesting information on other forms of life there. David Elder, Donald Hughes, Dann Lee and Donald Price helped with quadrat studies in northern Ontario, while John Frank, Erica Nol, Christopher Risley *et al* helped in such studies in southwestern Ontario.

While attending the International Ornithological Congress at Helsinki, Finland, in 1958, we heard Dr. E. Sutter's pioneer paper on the use of radar to study bird migration, and in 1960 we visited him in Switzerland to learn more about this work. Dr. W. W. H. Gunn began making radar films in connection with bird strikes near airports and kindly made available one of his films for analysis, of goose migration near Thunder Bay: Jaqui Kanitz, John Novak and James M. Richards helped with this work.

Chandler Robbins devised the method of using roadside counts to census bird populations during the breeding season and Dr. Martin Edwards set up the Ontario grid and coordinated the work until I took over. Leonard Hanna, Miles Hearn, Donald Hughes, Sheldon McGregor, Robert Nisbet and Steven Price have given me field support, running my personal routes, and a great many volunteers have helped out throughout Ontario (as far as roads occur). I am particularly indebted to Laura Howe and Jean Wallace for hospitality during our northern Ontario work as well as the Frank LeVay family at Kapuskasing. In the Kingston area, Kenneth and Mary Edwards and Helen Quilliam have extended hospitality, and provided many records of interest. The results of the first full ten years of this work have been used in this book to suggest regional variations in abundance of birds in Ontario during the summer season.

The Christmas counts mapped in this book were first summarized in tables by Dennis Rupert and I am indebted to him for the use of these tabulated summaries.

The seasonal accounts have been compiled from local lists prepared by numerous authors, listed in the "Literature Cited" and from seasonal reports in such works as the Federation of Ontario Naturalists' Bulletin, Audubon Field Notes and its successor, American Birds. James L. Baillie, Clive Goodwin and James Woodford did much of the work compiling these reports. Peter Iden, Bruce Parker and Ken Walton compiled reports for the Toronto region. Muriel Grant provided me with a typed copy of L. Beamer's records covering a period of 20 years in the Meaford region. Although I have not used newspaper reports I am grateful for Peter Whelan's column in the Globe & Mail and reports from other newpapers for up to date information on sightings as they occur.

For data compilation and secretatial help I am particularly grateful to Dianne Friesen, Peggy Gillespie, Anne-Liis Ots, Holly Petrie, Steven Price and his mother and to Kaia Toop. For banding information I am grateful to Erica Dunn, David Hussell, Pat and James Woodford, the Canadian Wildlife Service, and the authors of publications mentioned in the text.

Members of our immediate families have been most supportive. Barbara Hearn gave secretarial assistance and Iris Weir helped in many practical ways. Miles Hearn and Margaret and Reid Wilson have been most helpful in the field. Adèle Koehnke helped with proofreading. My brother Rae and his children, David, Gordon and Rosemary shared some of our expeditions and gave encouragement.

Finally, this work could not have been made without the army of bird observers throughout Ontario and the many who compiled their observations, especially Arnold Dawe and more recently, Bruce Parker, for the Toronto Ornithological Club (TOC) and for the many writers I have quoted in the text and in the "Literature Cited" section.

For help in the actual production of the book, the librarians at the Royal Ontario Museum have been very helpful checking references and the librarians at the University of Toronto, Rare Books Section, kindly gave access to the diaries and other original writings of James L. Baillie. Dr. D. V. "Chip" Weseloh, and his wife Linda, read the section on gulls and offered helpful suggestions.

Most of the colour photographs illustrating the book were provided by Victor Crich, FRPS. Additional photographs were contributed by Ken Carmichael, Phillip Holder, Bruno Kern, Betty Pegg, James M. Richards, Dr. George K. Peck, Mark K. Peck and the author. The publisher, Barry L. Penhale, has been a tower of strength throughout the preparation and he has been ably supported by Heather Wakeling, Gail Ferreira Ng-A-Kien and Derek Chung Tiam Fook.

# BIRDS OF
# ONTARIO

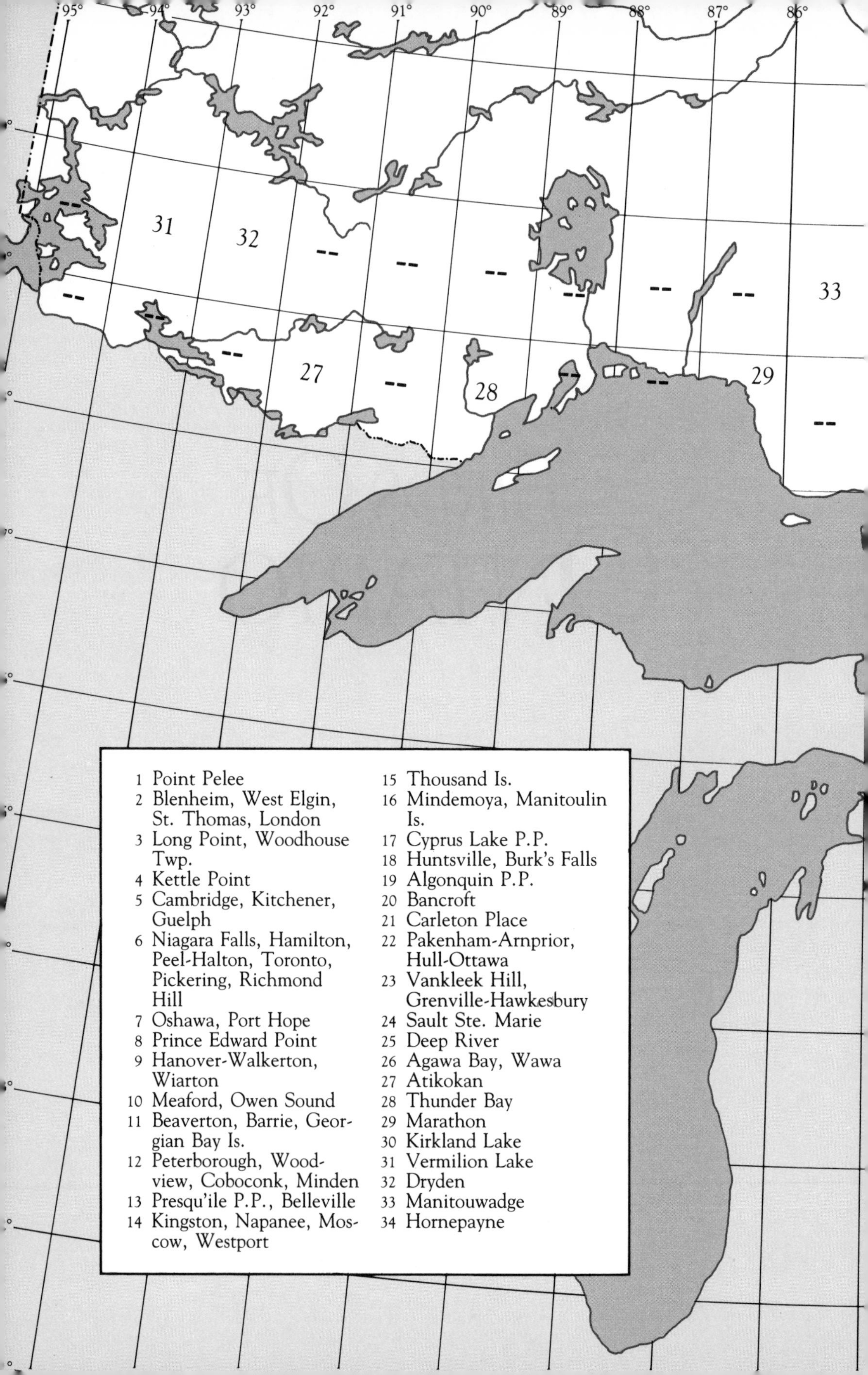

31

32

--

--

--

--

33

27

--

--

28

--

--

29

--

--

| | | |
|---|---|---|
| 1 | Point Pelee | |
| 2 | Blenheim, West Elgin, St. Thomas, London | |
| 3 | Long Point, Woodhouse Twp. | |
| 4 | Kettle Point | |
| 5 | Cambridge, Kitchener, Guelph | |
| 6 | Niagara Falls, Hamilton, Peel-Halton, Toronto, Pickering, Richmond Hill | |
| 7 | Oshawa, Port Hope | |
| 8 | Prince Edward Point | |
| 9 | Hanover-Walkerton, Wiarton | |
| 10 | Meaford, Owen Sound | |
| 11 | Beaverton, Barrie, Georgian Bay Is. | |
| 12 | Peterborough, Woodview, Coboconk, Minden | |
| 13 | Presqu'ile P.P., Belleville | |
| 14 | Kingston, Napanee, Moscow, Westport | |
| 15 | Thousand Is. | |
| 16 | Mindemoya, Manitoulin Is. | |
| 17 | Cyprus Lake P.P. | |
| 18 | Huntsville, Burk's Falls | |
| 19 | Algonquin P.P. | |
| 20 | Bancroft | |
| 21 | Carleton Place | |
| 22 | Pakenham-Arnprior, Hull-Ottawa | |
| 23 | Vankleek Hill, Grenville-Hawkesbury | |
| 24 | Sault Ste. Marie | |
| 25 | Deep River | |
| 26 | Agawa Bay, Wawa | |
| 27 | Atikokan | |
| 28 | Thunder Bay | |
| 29 | Marathon | |
| 30 | Kirkland Lake | |
| 31 | Vermilion Lake | |
| 32 | Dryden | |
| 33 | Manitouwadge | |
| 34 | Hornepayne | |

# CHRISTMAS COUNT MAP

Note that in the blank degree-blocks there
were either no roads or observers available
to run a route.

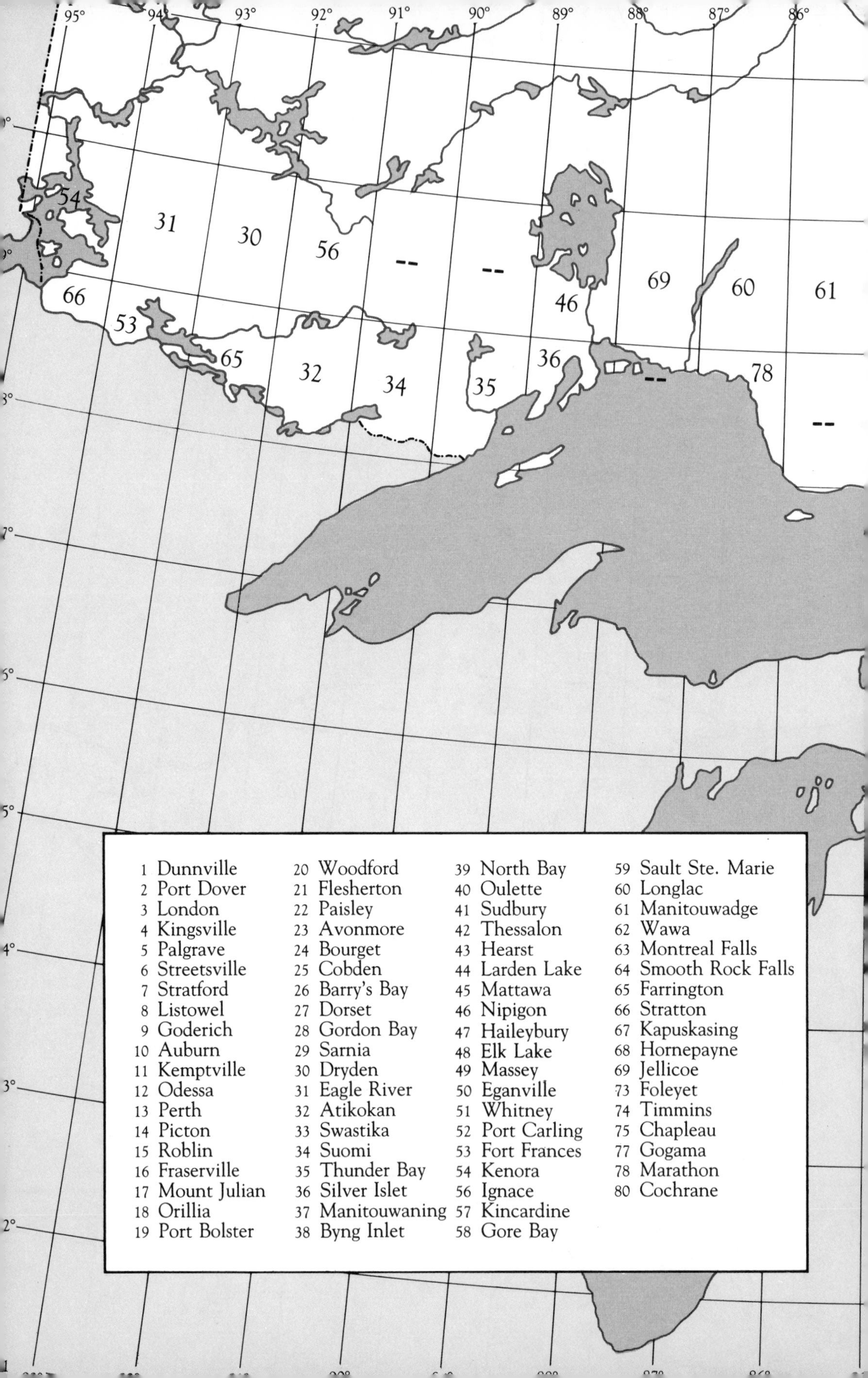

95° 94° 93° 92° 91° 90° 89° 88° 87° 86°

54

31 30 56 -- --

66 69 60 61

46

53 65 36

32 34 35 -- 78

--

# BREEDING BIRD SURVEY ROUTES

Note that in southern Ontario there are usually two routes within a degree-block, while in northern Ontario there is only one route per block. In the blank degree-blocks there were either no roads or observers available to run a route.

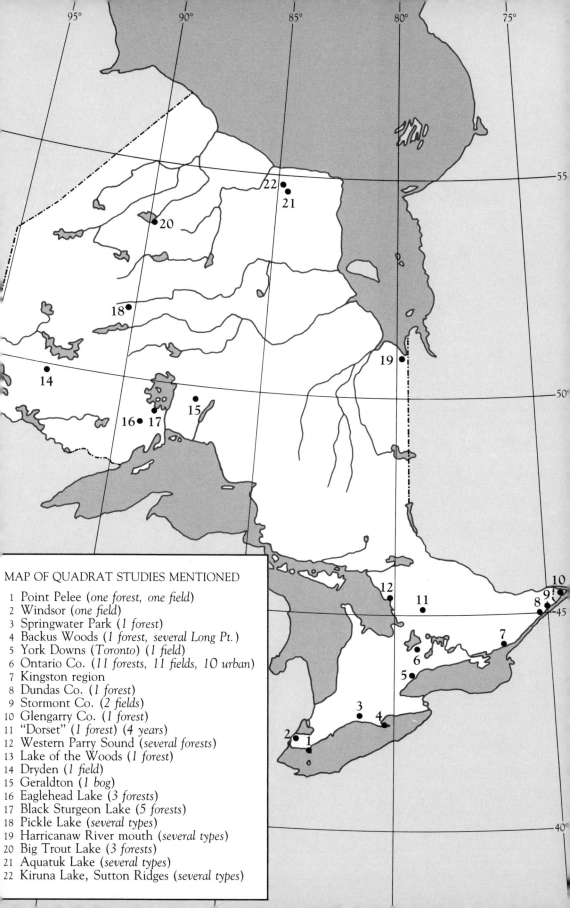

MAP OF QUADRAT STUDIES MENTIONED

1 Point Pelee (*one forest, one field*)
2 Windsor (*one field*)
3 Springwater Park (*1 forest*)
4 Backus Woods (*1 forest, several Long Pt.*)
5 York Downs (*Toronto*) (*1 field*)
6 Ontario Co. (*11 forests, 11 fields, 10 urban*)
7 Kingston region
8 Dundas Co. (*1 forest*)
9 Stormont Co. (*2 fields*)
10 Glengarry Co. (*1 forest*)
11 "Dorset" (*1 forest*) (*4 years*)
12 Western Parry Sound (*several forests*)
13 Lake of the Woods (*1 forest*)
14 Dryden (*1 field*)
15 Geraldton (*1 bog*)
16 Eaglehead Lake (*3 forests*)
17 Black Sturgeon Lake (*5 forests*)
18 Pickle Lake (*several types*)
19 Harricanaw River mouth (*several types*)
20 Big Trout Lake (*3 forests*)
21 Aquatuk Lake (*several types*)
22 Kiruna Lake, Sutton Ridges (*several types*)

# RED-THROATED LOON   *Gavia stellata*   (Pontoppidan)

This trim little loon with slender "snooty" upturned bill is not common anywhere in Ontario. It is essentially a bird of circumpolar tundra ponds, wintering normally on salt water along both coasts, but rarely straying inland. Such strays may occur anywhere in Ontario and have occurred at all seasons.

IDENTIFICATION: Adults in summer, with the red patch on the lower throat, light gray crown and face and side of the neck and the striped hind neck are unmistakable in good light. At a distance the slender uptilted bill is diagnostic at all seasons. In winter the white of the face tends to extend above the eye so that only the crown is dark, and the back is prominently white spotted. In poor lighting conditions this species may be confused with small individuals of the Common Loon and the Red-necked Grebe, both of which are more likely to be seen in most localities.

WINTER: Individuals have been noted on Christmas counts at Pelee, Niagara Falls, Barrie and Ottawa. Stirrett (1973a: 13) had one winter record for Pelee on Dec. 23, 1956 and Kelley (1978: 9) had another southwestern Ontario record on Dec. 24, 1971. Saunders & Dale (1933: 165) cited two winter records for Middlesex Co.: one on Feb. 21, 1885 and another in January, 1898. A. R. Muma picked up Niagara Falls casualties on Dec. 27, 1948 and Jan. 3, 1954 (Sheppard, 1960: 2). Speirs (1938: 53) listed a Dec. 9 record for Toronto. Long (1968b: 13) observed one at Pickering Beach on Dec. 4 and 28, 1966. A female was found alive on a road near Uxbridge on Dec. 24, 1959 by William Murray and ended up as a specimen in the Royal Ontario Museum (Speirs, 1979: 3). Quilliam (1965: 19) had two winter records for Kingston: Jan. 3, 1955 and Dec. 18, 1959. Devitt (1967: 24) had only one winter record for Barrie, on Dec. 3, 1953.

SPRING: Stirrett (1973b: 13) called it rare and irregular at Pelee from Apr. 25 to May 28. Saunders & Dale (1933: 165) saw one two miles SW of London on the Thames River on May 5, 1902 and noted another taken in the spring of 1881. Sheppard (1945: 152) had only one record for Niagara Falls, one collected on March 26, 1888 by Walter Brett. Fleming (1906: 441) called it a regular and not uncommon migrant at Toronto, with one in winter plumage as early as March 14, 1899 and birds in breeding plumage from Apr. 28 to June 3. Speirs (1938: 39) gave March 3 as the earliest spring date for Toronto and J. Theberge noted one at Oshawa as early as March 9 (Tozer & Richards, 1974: 57). Quilliam (1965: 19) had only one spring record for Kingston, on Apr. 25, 1954. Devitt (1967: 23) had one early spring record for Simcoe Co., at Wyebridge on March 7, 1938.

SUMMER: Strays have been reported through the summer in southern Ontario; e.g. one in southwestern Ontario on Aug. 2, 1952 (Kelley, 1978: 9); at Toronto on July 1 and Aug. 29 (Speirs, 1938: 45 and Saunders, 1947: 359); several summer reports from Pickering to Oshawa (Speirs, 1979: 3) and one on June 20, 1951 at Kingston (Quilliam, 1965: 19). W. E. Saunders reported a female taken in a fish net at Rossport on June 20, 1911 and L. S. Dear found a nest with 2 eggs at Thunder Cape, Lake Superior, on July 1, 1913 (Baillie & Harrington, 1936: 5). Manning (1952: 15) identified 15 from June 13 to July 7 along the west coast of James Bay (and found one nesting just outside Ontario waters): he also noted 8 along the Hudson Bay coast between Little Cape and Fort Severn from Aug. 3 to 15, 1948. Simkin (1968: 49) photographed two adults with two downy young at 55°7' N and 82°43' W on July 29, 1966 and flushed an adult from a nest with

2 eggs on Aug. 3, 1962 at 55°15′ N and 84°W. (both east of Winisk near the Hudson Bay coast). Schueler, Baldwin & Rising (1974: 142) took a specimen at Winisk but considered the species uncommon there. Hope saw two at Fort Severn on July 1, 1940 and collected one there on July 5.

AUTUMN: Nicholson (1972: 11) gave three fall records for Manitoulin: on Nov. 14, 1968, Sept. 13, 1970 and Nov. 6, 1971. Most of the 10 fall records for Simcoe Co. given by Devitt (1967: 23-24) were October reports, but 4 were seen in Collingwood Harbour as early as Sept. 18, 1938. Most "Ontario Co." records were in October and November, with the earliest on Sept. 20, 1960 at Whitby, and the latest on Nov. 28 at Pickering (Speirs, 1979: 3). Fleming (1906: 441) had fall records at Toronto from Oct. 6 to Nov. 30. Saunders and Dale (1933: 165) reported one immature taken in a strawberry bed on Nov. 11, 1898. Stirrett (1973d: 15) had one fall record of 3 birds at Pelee on Oct. 20, 1956.

**MEASUREMENTS:**
*Length:* 24 to 27 ins.
(Palmer, 1962: 49)
*Wingspread:* 42 to 45 ins.
(Palmer, 1962: 49)
*Weight:* 1.6 to 2.0 kg.
(Palmer, 1962: 51).

**REFERENCE:**
Simkin, Donald W. 1968
Red-throated Loon nesting
in northern Ontario. Can.
Field-Naturalist,
82: (1): 49.

# ARCTIC LOON  *Gavia arctica*  (Linnaeus)

This is another circumpolar breeder, wintering chiefly in Pacific waters and very rare in the interior and Atlantic waters. In Ontario it may be expected only along the Hudson Bay shores in summer: records in other parts of Ontario are very few and its status "accidental". It tends to use larger ponds and lakes than the Red-throated Loon and non-breeders are often found on salt water. (My best views of this black-throated diver were in some of the lakes of Sweden where it is fairly common.)

IDENTIFICATION: Adults in summer with their slender straight bill, pearly gray crown and back of neck, black throat bordered with black and white stripes and checkered back are quite easily separated from other loons (and grebes). The slender, straight bill is the best field mark in winter when adults differ from other loons in their blackish, unmarked back but young have "scaly backs" like Common Loons but tend to be more brown and less gray. Red-necked Grebes in winter plumage might be confused with winter plumaged Arctic Loons but usually show the knobby "crest" and somewhat dumpier body.

WINTER: Kelley (1978: 9) cites a report of one at Pelee on Dec. 17, 1974 by Morin.

SPRING: Speirs (1979: 2) documented two sightings for the Pickering waterfront: one on May 15, 1952 and the other on Apr. 13, 1968. McIlwraith (1894: 32) described an encounter with one in Hamilton Bay in April, when there was still ice in the bay.

SUMMER: Stirrett (1973c: 13) reported one at Pelee on June 23, 1962. Manning (1952: 15) identified two between Moosonee and Fort Albany on June 13, 1947 and five at Cape Henrietta Maria between July 20 and 25. He collected two downy young and three adults at Little Cape on the Hudson Bay coast on July 29 and noted 13 more between there and Fort Severn from July 19 to Aug. 15. C.E. Hope collected four at Fort Severn between July 3 and 12, 1940.

AUTUMN: Skeel and Bondrup-Nielsen (1978: 15) saw one in summer plumage at Pukaskwa on Sept. 18, 1977. Kelley (1978: 9) cited a record by Rider and Rupert at Kettle Point from Oct. 28 to 31, 1973. Keven McLaughlin found one in the ship canal under the Burlington Skyway on Nov. 8, 1980, later seen by many others.

**MEASUREMENTS:**
*Length:* 23 to 29 ins.
(Godfrey, 1966: 11)
*Wingspread:*
*Weight:* 1.2 to 2.6 kg.
(Palmer, 1962: 43)

**REFERENCE:**
Peck, George K. 1970 First Ontario nest records of Arctic Loon (*Gavia arctica*) and Snow Goose (*Chen hyperborea*). Ont. Field Biologist, No. 24: 25-28. This mentions an adult male attending young, collected 10 miles off Cape Henrietta Maria on Aug. 16, 1944 by R.H. Smith. W.P. Geraghty found 6 nests at Radar Site 416 at the Cape, all with 2 eggs, between June 23 and July 2, 1970, with a photograph of an incubating adult on a nest on June 29.

# COMMON LOON   *Gavia immer*   (Brünnich)

This is the most important bird of Ontario's lake country, its haunting cry the very symbol of our wilderness. Lakes must be lengthy enough to allow for the long take-off run required for flight but small enough that wave action does not flood the nest from which the incubating bird can slip directly into the water. Power boating on small lakes may also flood the lakeside nests and harass adults with young: this is probably the chief cause of the loss of our breeding population from southern Ontario lakes and the more populous lakes in the cottage country. Traditional hunting of the species has reduced the population in the vicinity of northern Indian communities.

IDENTIFICATION: The adults in summer, with their checkered back, white "necklace", big black head with long pointed bill and long, slim silhouette in the water, are quite distinctive (see illustration). See Yellow-billed Loon and Arctic Loon for differences compared with these rare species. However the young and winter adults with their dark gray back and white underparts are sometimes confused with other loons, grebes and mergansers. In good seeing conditions the mergansers can be eliminated by their reddish heads and slim, hooked beaks and somewhat smaller size. Red-throated Loons have small, uptilted bills and when close can be seen to have a spotted rather than a scaly back pattern. Adult Arctic Loons have black, unpatterned backs while the young have brownish backs rather than gray. Red-necked Grebes have whiter cheeks and a hint of a knobby crest. In flight the loons stretch their necks downward and forward and tend to fly with their pointed bills partly open, frequently calling in early morning lake-to-lake flights on their breeding grounds and sometimes uttering their laughing call even in migration. The wailing or yodelling call and high-pitched screaming call so often heard on TV programs are usually uttered from the water. When their curiosity is aroused they often swim in close with occasional barking "hah" calls.

WINTER: A few sometimes linger in the larger lakes and rivers as long as open water is available and have been reported on Christmas counts as far north as Deep River and Sault Ste. Marie. (See map.) The great majority migrate to winter along the Atlantic coast. One seen off Whitby on Jan. 29, 1967 by G. Bellerby *et al* is an interesting midwinter record (Iden, 1967b: 1).

SPRING: At Pelee a few may show up as early as late February, e.g. one there on Feb. 24 (Stirrett, 1973a: 13) but the peak is not until late May (Stirrett, 1973b: 13). I usually see the first ones flying over Pickering in mid-April, but numbers build up until late May or even early June in some years (Speirs, 1979: 3). Louise Lawrence heard one flying over Pimisi Bay, near North Bay, as early as Apr. 20, 1945, an unusually early spring, but our first 6 on Lake Nipissing in 1944 were seen on Apr. 28 (Speirs and Speirs, 1947: 24). Denis (1961) gave Apr. 12, 1959 as earliest and Apr. 25 as average at Thunder Bay. Elsey (1950 MSS) reported the arrival of loons at the junction of Asheweig and Winisk Rivers on May 28, 1950.

SUMMER: Breeding Bird Surveys have indicated that this is still a fairly common species on routes in the Precambrian country with greatest numbers between Thunder Bay and the Manitoba border. (See map.) None have been reported on Breeding Bird Surveys in southwestern Ontario though they formerly did breed (Macoun, 1900: 9) and non-breeding birds still occur around Pelee in summer (Stirrett, 1973c: 13). The only recent evidence of breeding along the Lake Ontario shore was the sighting of an adult with downy young near Whitby on June 2, 1974 (Tozer and Richards, 1974: 309) though adults are not infrequently noted in summer. Some are still seen in the small kettle lakes of the Interlobate Moraine in summer but the lakes of the Precambrian country is their chief breeding area. Manning (1952: 14) identified 16 Common Loons between Moosonee and Cape Henrietta Maria and six between there and Fort Severn in the summer of 1947: he considered these to be non-breeders. Schueler, Baldwin and Rising (1974: 141) collected a female with eggs in her oviduct at Hawley Lake on June 30, 1962: they found loons common there and at Winisk, present at Moosonee and Attawapiskat but not seen at Fort Albany. Todd (1963: 77) has no actual nest record north of Lake Temagami in Ontario. Cringan (1950) noted them as widespread but not common (due to hunting by Indians) in the Nikip Lake region in 1950 and Lee (1978: 18) found a similar status at Big Trout Lake in 1975.

AUTUMN: Todd (1963: 77) cited late fall dates for northern localities: Oct. 19, 1943 at Moose Factory by Stirrett and Oct. 27, 1914 by Murie; and Nov. 3, 1935 at Timmins by Speirs. Large flocks sometimes gather on lakes in the fall: e.g. 80 on Lake Nipissing on Sept. 14, 1944 (Speirs & Speirs, 1947: 24) and 400 on Lake Ontario between Pickering and Whitby on Oct. 8, 1965 (Speirs, 1979: 1). At Pelee numbers increased until mid-November but were smaller than in spring (Stirrett, 1973d: 15).

**MEASUREMENTS:**
*Length:* 690 to 768 mm.
(Baillie & Hope, 1943: 4).
Wingspread: 1180 to 1360
mm. (Baillie & Hope,
1943: 4).
Weight: 1.6 to 8 kg.
(Palmer, 1962: 25).

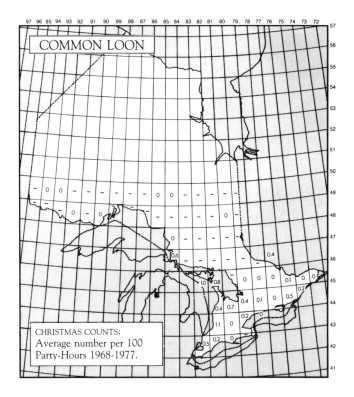

COMMON LOON

CHRISTMAS COUNTS:
Average number per 100
Party-Hours 1968-1977.

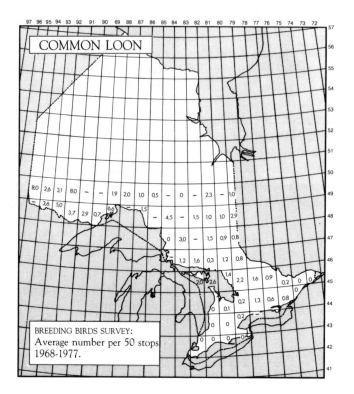

COMMON LOON

BREEDING BIRDS SURVEY:
Average number per 50 stops
1968-1977.

# YELLOW-BILLED LOON   *Gavia adamsii*   (Gray)

This is a bird of the barren lands of northern Canada and Siberia, usually migrating no farther south than Alaska, sometimes to British Columbia. In Ontario it is of hypothetical or accidental occurrence.

IDENTIFICATION: Adults in breeding plumage (which have not yet been reported from Ontario) differ from the Common Loon in somewhat larger size with a relatively long, uptilted ivory-coloured bill and with larger, more rectangular white "checkers" on the back and with more purple and less green in the head gloss. Immatures and adults in winter plumage differ chiefly in bill shape and upward head tilt. Both have much white in the bill in winter but the upper part of the bill in the Common Loon is generally dark but still whitish in this species. The culmen in this species is essentially straight, but curved down toward the tip in the Common Loon. The mandible (lower part of the bill) in this species has a chisel-shaped profile instead of tapering gradually to a point as in the Common Loon. Shape and carriage of the head in this species more resembles that of the much smaller Red-throated Loon.

WINTER: An oil-soaked bird was first noted off Port Credit, Lake Ontario, on Dec. 5, 1956 and collected on Dec. 9, 1956 (ROM No. 76360) (Gunn, 1957: 263). This was first thought to be a Yellow-billed Loon. Donald Gunn reported another similar bird there on Dec. 10 (Beardslee & Mitchell, 1965: 80). Several authorities examined the specimen and concluded that it was either a hybrid with the Common Loon or an unusual variation of the Common Loon and "There is no satisfactory record of the Yellow-billed Loon for Ontario according to L.L. Snyder . . ."
(Woodford & Lunn, 1962: 328).

SPRING: Donald Gunn showed one to James L. Baillie and Bill Smith at Fort Erie on May 11, 1957 and John Crosby sketched one at Pelee on May 25 (Beardslee & Mitchell, 1965: 80). R. Curry reported one off Grimsby on Lake Ontario on May 4, 1967 and another was reported at Ottawa on May 19, 1980 (James, 1983: 8) but the Ottawa record was later rejected (James, 1984: 63).

SUMMER:

AUTUMN:

**MEASUREMENTS:**
*Length:* 30 to 36.5 ins.
(Palmer, 1962: 35)
Wingspread: to 55 ins.
(Palmer, 1962: 35)
Weight: to 14 lb. or more
(Palmer, 1962: 35).

# PIED-BILLED GREBE    *Podilymbus podiceps*    (Linnaeus)

While most of the other grebes favour open water this little fellow seems to prefer weed-choked ponds and occurs in such places throughout most of North and South America. The nest is a pile of water plants and may be floating or attached to the bottom. Unless flushed unexpectedly the eggs are covered when the adult leaves the nest so that the nest looks like any other pile of weeds. The young frequently ride on the parent's back (as indeed do the young of other waterfowl).

IDENTIFICATION: This is a brown bird, about the size of a small duck, with a bill shaped like that of a hen (not sharp-pointed like other grebes). In breeding dress it has a black throat (whitish in winter) and the blueish bill has a black band midway to the tip (hence *pied*-billed). Coots and gallinules also have similar shaped bills but these birds are dark blue to dark gray in colour, not brownish. The loud "kow'kow'kow——kow-ugh-ugh-kow-ugh" call is distinctive.

WINTER: It has been reported on Christmas counts north to Ottawa and Manitoulin Island but is rare in Ontario in winter. Stirrett (1973a: 13) had one at Pelee as late as Dec. 31. William Girling saw one at London on Dec. 26, 1931 (Saunders and Dale, 1933: 167). Sheppard (1960: 3) reported one on the Niagara River on Dec. 8, 1938, and a specimen found below the falls on Dec. 10, 1949. Saunders (1947: 359) gave a Dec. 14 record for Toronto. George A. Scott saw two at Oshawa on Dec. 12, 1948 (Speirs, 1979: 8). Quilliam (1965: 22) mentioned four Christmas count records for Kingston and one seen there on Jan. 1 and Feb. 28, 1954. Devitt (1967: 26) noted three at Barrie on Dec. 28, 1957. Lee (1978: 18) described the most unusual finding of one at Big Trout Lake in February, 1975.

SPRING: Stirrett (1973b: 13) had a spring peak of 21 on May 9 at Pelee. Saunders and Dale (1933: 167) gave Apr. 7 as their 17-year average arrival date for London, with the earliest on Mar. 25, 1911. Baillie (in Saunders, 1947: 359) gave Apr. 13 as his 23-year average arrival at Toronto, with his earliest on Mar. 26. Speirs (1938: 43) had Apr. 27 as the spring peak for Toronto. Long (1969: 17) reported one at Pickering Beach as early as Mar. 3, 1969 but George A. Scott's median arrival date at Oshawa was Apr. 3 (Speirs, 1979: 8). Quilliam (1965: 21) gave Mar. 17 as her 14-year average arrival date at Kingston, while Devitt (1967: 26) had his 21-year average at Barrie on Apr. 16 with the earliest on Mar. 18, 1963. Nicholson (1972: 12) reported them arriving in Manitoulin in early April with 11 on Apr. 9, 1971 as his recent maximum. Baillie and Harrington (1936: 7) reported a female taken at Moose Factory on May 23, 1930 by S. Waller. Denis (1961: 2) gave Apr. 3, 1952 as the earliest and Apr. 17 as average for arrivals at Thunder Bay.

SUMMER: Small numbers have been reported on Breeding Bird Surveys from Lake Erie north to Longlac, Dryden and Eagle River. Stirrett (1973c: 13) had records through the summer at Pelee and gave it nesting status there. Tozer and Richards (1974: 60) cited several breeding records for Cranberry and Scugog marshes, and Quilliam (1965: 21) had breeding records for Kingston. Devitt (1967: 25) called it a common breeder in Simcoe Co. (with F. S. Cook he found 17 nests at Matchedash Bay on June 16, 1939). I saw 4 downy young with adults at Timmins on Sept. 3, 1935, while J. Satterly saw 2 immatures on Twin Lakes near Matheson on July 22, 1951 and two others near Dyment on Aug. 8

and 17, 1958. Baillie and Harrington (1936: 7) reported young taken at Lac Seul on Aug. 26, 1919. James, McLaren and Barlow (1976: 8) called it a common summer resident north to Sandy Lake and Fort Albany.

AUTUMN: On Oct. 27, 1935 at Timmins I saw three flying a great deal "as if practicing for the trip south" and these were the last seen there that fall. Nicholson (1972: 12) noted a return movement through Manitoulin during Sept. and Oct. Quilliam (1965: 22) gave Oct. 30 as the 12-year average departure date from Kingston. George A. Scott's median departure date from Oshawa is Oct. 27 (Speirs, 1979: 8). The fall peak at Toronto was given as Oct. 3 (Speirs, 1938: 51). Saunders (1947: 359) gave Nov. 6 as his 13-year average departure date from Toronto. Stirrett (1973d: 15) had a peak of 40 at Pelee on Oct. 16.

**MEASUREMENTS:**

*Length:* 12 to 15 ins. (Godfrey, 1966: 18)
*Wingspread:* 23 ins. (Pough, 1951: 12)
*Weight:* ♂ 138-146 g. ♀ 119-132 g. (Palmer, 1962: 106).

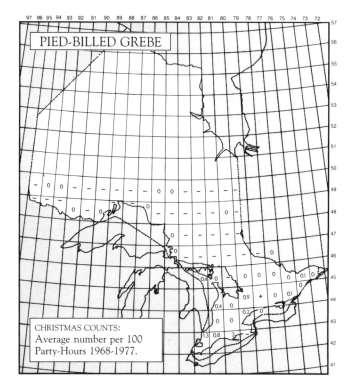

PIED-BILLED GREBE

CHRISTMAS COUNTS:
Average number per 100
Party-Hours 1968-1977.

10

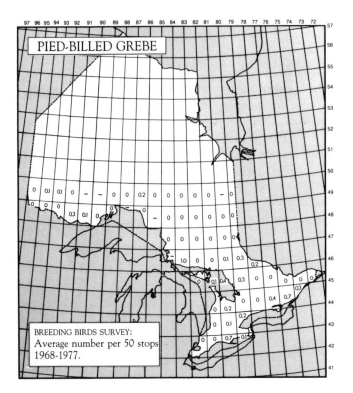

PIED-BILLED GREBE

BREEDING BIRDS SURVEY:
Average number per 50 stops
1968-1977.

# HORNED GREBE   *Podiceps auritus*   (Linnaeus)

This small grebe is mainly a prairie breeder wintering on both coasts but sometimes does breed in Ontario, especially in the west, and is fairly common in migration. A few have wintered in southern Ontario. They are more apt to occur on small lakes and ponds than the Red-necked Grebe but also are found on the Great Lakes.

IDENTIFICATION: In breeding dress the black head, with fiery red eyes and jaunty golden "horns" running back from the eyes to the angle where crown and nape come together, is quite distinctive. The somewhat similar Eared Grebe is a prairie bird, exceedingly rare in Ontario waters and differs from the Horned Grebe in having a black neck (not red), a more diffused patch of orange extending well below the eye and a more slender upturned bill. In winter plumage it may be distinguished from the Red-necked Grebe by its much smaller size (smaller than most of the winter ducks) and from the Eared Grebe by its much whiter cheeks and front of the neck (which tend to be gray in the Eared Grebe). Again the bill shape is distinctive.

WINTER: A few have been seen in winter as far north as Manitoulin and Ottawa. It is fairly common at Pelee in winter and good numbers (36 and 46) have occurred rarely at Wiarton and Blenheim on Christmas counts. Stirrett (1973a: 13) had one at Pelee as late as Feb. 10. Saunders and Dale (1933: 165) noted one seen near London on Dec. 22, 1917. Speirs (1979: 5) gave several early winter records for Ontario County, the latest on Jan. 8, 1967. Quilliam (1965: 21) reported that they are frequently seen on Christmas counts at Kingston and she had 4 records extending into January. Devitt (1967: 25) noted that they occurred on 4 Christmas counts at Barrie and cited a find on Feb. 23, 1963 at Stroud by Frances Westman.

SPRING: Stirrett (1973b: 13) had 18 at Pelee as early as Mar. 20 with a peak of 124 on Apr. 13 and the latest one on May 23. Saunders and Dale (1933: 165) noted one in an opening in the river, before breakup, on Mar. 18 and 25, 1916 and on p. 167 they give the 17-year average for arrival at London as Apr. 12: 125 were counted on two local ponds on May 1, 1929. On Apr. 21, 1929 William Girling saw one patter along the pavement, take off and fly to the river some blocks away: this unusual observation was in London, Ont. Sheppard (1945: 152) saw about 50 at Niagara Falls on Apr. 18, 1937 and called them common to abundant there in spring. Speirs (1938: 43) gave Apr. 23 as the spring peak date for Toronto and Saunders (1947: 359) cited a late record on May 30 by J.L. Baillie. In Ontario County the earliest spring records were on Mar. 12, with George A. Scott's median arrival date on Apr. 12, while in the late April peak as many as 100 may be found in good years (Speirs, 1979: 5). Quilliam (1965: 21) gave Apr. 4 and May 1 as average arrival and departure dates at Kingston with extremes on Mar. 21, 1954 and May 26, 1963. Devitt (1967: 25) gave Apr. 18 as the 22-year average arrival date for Barrie with the earliest on Apr. 1, 1957. Nicholson (1972: 11) gave mid-April to mid-May as their time of arrival on Manitoulin. Denis (1961: 3) gave Apr. 25, 1953 as the earliest and May 7 as the average for arrivals at Thunder Bay.

SUMMER: None have shown up on any of the Breeding Bird Surveys in Ontario. Baillie and Harrington (1936: 6) cite several possible breeding records from as far east as Leeds Co., as far south as Lake St. Clair and as far northwest as the Severn River but considered them all in need of confirmation. Stirrett (1973c: 13) had three summer records for Pelee—on June 13, July 16 and Aug. 21. There are several summer records for Ontario County (including reports of young at Eastbourne and an adult at Cedar Point, Lake Simcoe on July 2 and 7. 1962) (Speirs, 1979: 5). C.E. Hope noted two at Fort Severn on July 2, 1940. Manning (1952: 15) cited records by others at the mouths of the Moose, Albany and Severn Rivers but apparently saw none himself in 1947.

AUTUMN: Nicholson (1972: 11) had Manitoulin records from early Sept. to early Dec. with a recent maximum of 220 on Oct. 17, 1970. Devitt (1967: 25) wrote that they arrive in Simcoe Co. about Sept. 10 and stay until mid-November. Quilliam (1965: 21) gave Oct. 23 as the average date for fall arrival at Kingston, with peak in late October or early November and some lingering into early winter. In Ontario Co. Speirs (1979: 5) had fall records as early as Sept. 7 and as late as Nov. 21 with George Scott's median departure date on Nov. 5 and peak count of 60 on Oct. 27, 1957. Stirrett (1973d: 15) had one at Pelee as early as Sept. 12 with a peak of 500 on Nov. 6.

**MEASUREMENTS:**
*Length:* 12.5 to 15 ins.
(Godfrey, 1966: 16).
*Wingspread:* 24 ins.
(Robbins *et al*, 1966:21).
*Weight:* ♂ 432 to 485g. ♀
351 to 433 g. (Palmer,
1962: 73), i.e. about 1 lb.

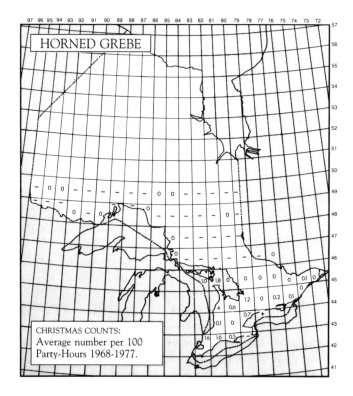

HORNED GREBE

CHRISTMAS COUNTS:
Average number per 100
Party-Hours 1968-1977.

# RED-NECKED GREBE   *Podiceps grisegena*   (Boddaert)

This big grebe has been a bird of surprises, unpredictable and delightful. Sometimes years have gone by when I saw none, then for a few years hundreds have gathered off the Pickering shore in migration. For a few years some accepted floating shallow boxes anchored behind the breakwater at Burlington as nesting sites but when we began to take them for granted they moved elsewhere and we found them nesting up near Cochrane, or one summer found young on South Bay on Manitoulin. Most of my early records were of winter birds along the Toronto waterfront but recently it has been a very rare bird in winter. Essentially a prairie breeder, wintering on both Atlantic and Pacific waters, in Ontario this is a "fringe benefit".

IDENTIFICATION:   The long, stiffly upright neck and pointed beak and tailless appearance proclaim this as a grebe. In winter it looks like a big edition of the Horned Grebe but has a relatively long, yellowish bill (dark in the Horned Grebe): both are dark above, light below with whitish cheeks and hint of a crest: the cheeks of the Horned Grebe are whiter: in the Red-necked the front of the cheek may be gray while the back extends as a whitish crescent behind the gray and in young of the year the cheeks are all gray. Red-throated Loons and female mergansers are superficially similar but both are more elongate and the bill shapes are very different, uptilted in the loon and hooked in the mergansers which also have reddish heads. Adult Red-necked Grebes present no problem with their reddish brown necks and white cheeks (Horned Grebes also have reddish necks but have black cheeks and yellowish "horns". ) In migratory flocks you may hear the characteristic raspy chattering whinny.

WINTER:   On Christmas counts they have occurred as far north as Ottawa and Manitoulin Island. Stirrett (1973a: 13) recorded one at Pelee on Dec. 16, 1952. Saunders and Dale (1933: 166) had two winter records for Middlesex County: on Jan. 18, 1910 and Feb. 16, 1929. Sheppard (1945: 152) mentioned a male taken at Niagara Falls on Dec. 8, 1888. Speirs (1979: 4) cited half a dozen winter records for Ontario County. Quilliam (1965: 20) gave two January records for Kingston: Jan. 16, 1929 and Jan. 1, 1963.

SPRING:   Stirrett (1973b: 13) reported only two spring records for Pelee; on Mar. 22 and Apr. 12. Saunders and Dale (1933: 166) gave the average arrival date for London as Apr. 20 with the earliest on Apr. 14, 1925. Sheppard had just one spring record for Niagara Falls. Saunders (1947: 359) gave Apr. 10 as his 11-year average arrival date for Toronto while Speirs (1938: 43) gave Apr. 25 as the spring peak date there. Spring numbers along the Ontario County waterfront varied from 0 some years to a maximum of 120 on Apr. 13, 1968 (Speirs, 1979: 4). Quilliam (1965: 20) had a few spring records for Kingston between Mar. 10 and Apr. 30: all single birds except one record of two. Devitt (1967: 24) gave the average date of spring arrival for Barrie over 15 years as Apr. 22 with the earliest on Apr. 4, 1945. Denis (1961) gave Apr. 26, 1945 as earliest and May 7 as average for Thunder Bay.

SUMMER:   On Breeding Bird Surveys they have been noted several times at Manitowaning on Manitoulin Is. as well as at Eagle River and Ignace. In the 1940's large numbers (100 or more) summered on Lake Ontario and some nested at Burlington and Lorne Park (Gunn, 1951: 144). A few have been seen off Pickering and Whitby in recent years (Speirs, 1979: 4). Quilliam (1965: 20) reported one seen at Wolfe Is., near Kingston, on June 5, 1950. Devitt (1967: 24) mentioned one collected at Orillia on June 6, 1902 and one at Barrie on Aug. 22, 1949, while J.L. Baillie saw two there on July 19, 1943: I noted from one to ten there from Aug. 5 until we left in October, 1945. D.B. Ferguson found a nest with 6 eggs at Bass Lake, Manitoulin, on June 12, 1976 (Nicholson, 1981: 50). Baillie & Harrington (1936: 6) gave a nest record for Lake of the Woods and three for Whitefish Lake, Thunder Bay. I saw a bird at Sioux Lookout on June 27, 1971. Smith (1957: 165-166) saw 30 or more at the well-known colony on Lillabelle Lake, near Cochrane, on Aug. 8, 1954. James, McLaren & Barlow (1976: 7) called this a common summer resident in western Ontario north to Sandy Lake.

AUTUMN: Smith (1957: 165) saw one on Porcupine Lake near Timmins, on Sept. 5, 1953. Nicholson (1981: 50) observed a loose raft of 300 at Lynn Point, Manitoulin, on Oct. 1, 1977 and 55 at West Bay as late as Nov. 22, 1978: I sketched a stripe-faced young at South Bay on Oct. 11, 1947. Devitt (1967: 24) reported 300 at Barrie on Nov. 1, 1948 and 500 near Wasaga Beach on Oct. 13, 1966. Quilliam (1965: 20) had a few fall records at Kingston from Oct. 15 to Dec. 6. Very large flocks sometimes occur on Lake Ontario in fall. Harold Reeve estimated 3000 off Willow Beach (Port Britain) on Sept. 6, 1945 (Gunn, 1951: 144). A flock of 541 was counted off the mouth of Duffin Creek, Pickering, on Sept. 27, 1952, but some years there have been none there (Speirs, 1979: 4). Saunders (1947: 359) gave Oct. 29 as his 10-year average departure date from Toronto, while George A. Scott's median departure date from Oshawa was Nov. 8. Kelly (1978:10) had a maximum of 63 at Ipperwash Beach, Lake Huron, on Oct. 11, 1973. Stirrett (1973d: 15) had only one fall record for Pelee (3 seen on Oct. 11, 1948).

**MEASUREMENTS:**
*Length:* 18 to 20.5 ins.
(Godfrey, 1966: 15).
*Wingspread:* 32 ins.
(Robbins *et al*, 1966: 21)
*Weight:* 6 averaged
1023 g. (Palmer,
1962: 65).

**REFERENCE:**
Gunn, W.W.H. 1951 The changing status of the Red-necked Grebe in southern Ontario. Can. Field-Naturalist, 65: (4): 143-145.

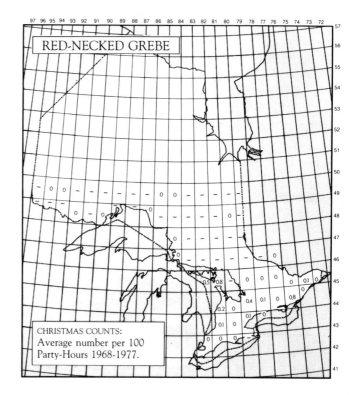

RED-NECKED GREBE

CHRISTMAS COUNTS:
Average number per 100
Party-Hours 1968-1977.

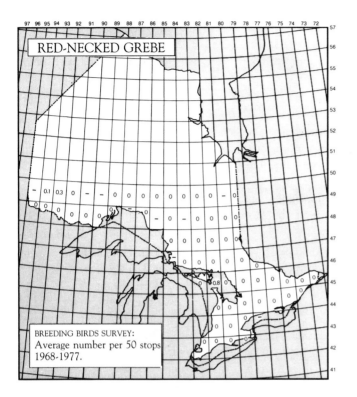

RED-NECKED GREBE

BREEDING BIRDS SURVEY:
Average number per 50 stops
1968-1977.

# EARED GREBE   *Podiceps nigricollis*   Brehm

This is a bird of prairie and intermontane lakes, very rare east of Manitoba with only a few stragglers in Ontario.

IDENTIFICATION: The Eared Grebe is about the size of a Horned Grebe, or slightly smaller. In breeding plumage the head, neck and much of the breast is black, except for the patch of tawny plumes radiating back from the eye both above and below it. The black crest is usually raised, giving the head a triangular outline. (In the Horned Grebe only the head is black, with the neck and breast brown and the yellow crest above the eye, not below it.) The beak of the Eared Grebe is relatively broad, but not as deep as in the Horned Grebe, and appears slightly upturned toward the tip. In winter plumage the cheeks are gray, not white as in the Horned Grebe, and the same is true of the foreneck.

WINTER: Beardslee & Mitchell (1965: 85) recorded two specimens from Niagara Falls, the first found by Roy Muma on Feb. 6, 1950 (ROM No. 77014) and the other by R.F. Andrle on Jan. 1, 1958 (Buffalo Soc. Nat. Hist. No. 4090).

SPRING: Stirrett (1973b: 13) had two spring records for Pelee: one on Apr. 16-17, 1960 and another on May 11, 1965. Kelly (1978: 10) had 3 records for southwestern Ontario: one at Ipperwash Beach by D. Ruppert on Apr. 26 to 29, 1969; one at Rondeau on Apr. 27, 1971 and one at Wheatley on May 6, 1974. Beardslee & Mitchell (1965: 85) noted two records from Morgan's Point, Lake Erie, on May 7, 1950 and May 4, 1952, both in full breeding plumage. Tozer & Richards (1974: 59) reported one seen by J.L. Baillie at Whitby Harbour on May 31, 1958 and by D. Perks on June 3. Baillie and J. Keenleyside saw one there on May 22, 1961, which Perks observed on May 30. George A. Scott noted one at Oshawa on May 23, 1971. Weir & Quilliam (1980: 3) observed one at Prince Edward Point on May 4, 1976.

SUMMER: D. Perks reported one off Cranberry Marsh, Whitby, on July 28, 1959 (Speirs, 1979: 6).

AUTUMN: Weir & Quilliam (1980: 3) reported one close to shore at Prince Edward Point from Oct. 17 to 26, 1979. J. Dales, D.R. Gunn and D. Perks reported one at Whitby Harbour between Oct. 19 and 25, 1959 (Speirs, 1979: 6). Two were noted near Fort Erie by B. Nathan *et al* on Nov. 24, 1957 and one there on Nov. 26, 1959 (Beardslee & Mitchell, 1965: 85). Kelley (1978: 10) reported birds at Sarnia Bay on Nov. 15, 1970 and Nov. 25, 1973; at Rondeau on Oct. 25, 1972 and at Pelee on Oct. 28 and 29, 1974.

MEASUREMENTS:
*Length:* 12 to 14 ins.
(Godfrey, 1966: 17)
*Wingspread:* 22.5 ins.
(Pough, 1951: 10)
*Weight:* 7 averaged 297 g.
(218 to 375 g.) (Dunning,
1984: 1).

# WESTERN GREBE   *Aechmophorus occidentalis*   (Lawrence)

This is the swan of the grebe world, with long graceful neck and noble bearing. In Ontario it is a rare straggler, breeding chiefly in the prairies and intermontane lakes and wintering along the Pacific coast.

IDENTIFICATION:  A large grebe with long, slender neck. The white face and foreneck contrasts strikingly with the black crown and black stripe down the back of the neck. The bill is more slender than that of the Red-necked Grebe and often appears slightly upturned. The fiery red eye is most striking when the bird is close.

WINTER:

SPRING:  Stirrett (1973b: 13) had Pelee records for May 19-20, 1951 (2 birds) and one on May 11, 1968. J.L. Baillie had a May 23-24 record for Toronto (Saunders, 1947: 359). Speirs (1979: 7) cited over a dozen spring records in the Oshawa-Pickering portion of Lake Ontario between Mar. 27, 1949 and May 11, 1969. Many of these were at the mouth of Duffin Creek in company with the large flocks of Red-necked Grebes which gathered there in the 1960's.

SUMMER:  Nicholson (1972: 10) reported a record by W.R. Lowe at Providence Bay, Manitoulin, on Aug. 13, 1961.

AUTUMN:  There are two fall records from Lake Simcoe: one by J. Satterly at Cedar Point on Nov. 6, 1975 and the other by E.L. Brereton on Kempenfeldt Bay on Oct. 25, 1944 (Devitt 1967: 25). Speirs (1979: 7) cited several records along the north shore of Lake Ontario between Whitby and Squires Beach, Pickering, as early as Sept. 15 and as late as Nov. 15. Kelley (1978: 10) reported one seen by Reynolds at Pelee on Oct. 25, 1949.

**MEASUREMENTS:**
*Length:* 22 to 29 ins.
(Godfrey 1966: 18)
*Wingspread:* 30 – 40″
(Pough, 1951: 11)
*Weight:* average 52 oz
(Palmer, 1962: 95)

# NORTHERN FULMAR   *Fulmarus glacialis*   (Linnaeus)

This is a bird of the open oceans, usually coming to shore only to breed. Very rare in Ontario.

IDENTIFICATION:   In flight it looks superficially like a gull with a white head, grey back and yellow bill, but the manner of flight and details of build are very different. It usually flies with wing stiffly outstretched, taking advantage of updrafts off waves to glide for long periods, then flapping rapidly when it runs out of uplift and settling on the water to wait for a breeze in calm weather. Its bill is short and stout with conspicuous tubes on top near the base. Dark phase birds have dark head and neck: these are white in light phase birds: both show a white flash in the wing between the bend and the tip.

WINTER:   K. Charles and J.B. Miles picked up an exhausted bird, being harassed by ravens, near Manitouwadge on Dec. 11, 1970 (Goodwin, 1971: 50). Prevett (1975: 462) detailed the discovery of one disoriented in snow near Moosonee on Dec. 8, 1974.

SPRING:   The first Ontario specimen was taken on a minnow-baited fish line where the Madawaska River empties into the Ottawa (Lake des Chats), near Arnprior, on May 3, 1924 (Gormley, 1924: 470-471). Baillie (1951: 253) reported one seen by Thomas Swift at Port Credit on May 13, 1951.

SUMMER:   No record.

AUTUMN:   Snyder (1929: 376) reported the second specimen from Ontario, taken at Ottawa on Nov. 15, 1928. Beamer (1937: 200) forwarded a specimen to the Royal Ontario Museum, the bird found dead by William Lin west of Cape Rich about 10 miles north of Meaford. It had a 3 inch fish hook in its throat and was all entangled in fishing line when found on Nov. 20, 1936. Goodwin (1974: 45) reported one seen by A. Rider off Kettle Point, Lake Huron, on Oct. 31, 1973 (a fall with many pelagic reports).

**MEASUREMENTS:**
*Length:* 17-20 ins.
(Palmer, 1962: 141)
*Wingspread:* to 42 ins.
(Palmer, 1962: 141)
*Weight:* ♂ 725 g;
♀ 577 g. (Palmer, 1962: 143)

**REFERENCES:**
Beamer, L.H. 1937 Fulmar at Meaford, Georgian Bay, Ontario, Auk, 54: (2): 200.
Gormley, A.K. 1924 First Ontario record for *Fulmarus g. glacialis*. Auk, 41: (3): 470-471.
Prevett, J.P. 1975 Fulmar from southern James Bay in December. Can. Field-Nat., 89: (4): 462-463.

Snyder, L.L. 1929 Second Ontario record for *Fulmarus g. glacialis*. Auk, 46: (3): 376.

# BLACK-CAPPED PETREL   *Pterodroma hasitata*   (Kuhl)

This is a bird of Guadeloupe and other islands of the West Indies, just a storm waif in Ontario.

IDENTIFICATION:  This is a large long-winged petrel with distinctive dark-bordered white underwings, with elongated triangular white rump patch and pure white belly. It has a pale nape and collar, white face and black cap.

WINTER:

SPRING:

SUMMER:  One specimen, now in the Royal Ontario Museum, was picked up dead on Aug. 21, 1955, following Hurricane Connie on Aug. 13, by Alice Ulrich at Morgan's Point on Lake Erie near Port Colborne (Baillie, 1955: 375 and Beardslee and Mitchell, 1965: 87).

AUTUMN:  One specimen was picked up dead on Oct. 30, 1893, on Toronto Is. by George Pierce (Brown, 1894: 11) and another was found near Oakville about the same time (Fleming, 1906: 443). Both are now in the Royal Ontario Museum (Baillie, 1955: 375).

**MEASUREMENTS:**
*Length:* 14 to 18 ins.
(Palmer, 1962: 203).
*Wingspread:* 38 ins.
(Pough, 1951: 18).
*Weight:* One weighed
278 g. (Dunning, 1984: 1).

**REFERENCES:**
Brown, H.H. 1894
*Aestralata hasitata* taken at
Toronto. Biol. Rev. Ont.,
1: 11.

# AUDUBON'S SHEARWATER   *Puffinus lherminieri*   (Lesson)

This is typically a bird of tropical seas, breeding rarely north to Bermuda, accidental in Ontario.

**IDENTIFICATION:**   This is a small, rich brown shearwater with white underparts and a white spot above the eye, rather fluttering flight.

**WINTER:**

**SPRING:**

**SUMMER:**

**AUTUMN:**   One was found dead by J. Stuart McGiffin on his lawn about 3 miles north of Almonte, Lanark Co. on Sept. 8, 1975. It is now Specimen No. 62529 in the National Museum (Godfrey, 1976: 494).

**MEASUREMENTS:**
*Length:* about 12 ins.
(Palmer, 1962: 198).
*Wingspread:* 26 ins.
(Robbins *et al*, 1966: 25).
*Weight:* 78 averaged
168 g. (128-211 g.)
(Dunning, 1984: 2).

**REFERENCE:**
Godfrey W. Earl 1976
Audubon's Shearwater, a
species new for Canada.
Can. Field-Naturalist, 90:
(4): 494.

# WILSON'S STORM-PETREL   *Oceanites oceanicus*   (Kuhl)

This Antarctic breeder is sometimes common off the Atlantic coast of U.S. in our summer. In Ontario it is accidental.

**IDENTIFICATION:**   This is a swallow-sized blackish-brown tube-nosed marine bird with white rump and yellow webs on its long, dangling legs. It tends to flutter along the sea surface, with toes sometimes dipping in the water.

**WINTER:**

**SPRING:**   Some boys picked one up at Gull Lake, Muskoka, in spring of 1897 (Baillie, 1955: 375) the specimen is in the Royal Ontario Museum.

**SUMMER:**

**AUTUMN:**   One was picked up dead on Long Beach, Lake Erie, on Aug. 14, 1955, the day after Hurricane Connie struck the area, by Eric Bastin and Glenn and George Meyers and later seen by several members of the Buffalo Ornithological Society and ultimately sent to the Royal Museum (Beardslee and Mitchell, 1965: 89).

**MEASUREMENTS:**
*Length:* about 7 ins.
(Palmer, 1962: 243).
*Wingspread:* 15 to 16½
ins. (Palmer, 1962: 243).
*Weight:* about 1¼ oz.
(Palmer, 1962: 243).

# LEACH'S STORM-PETREL
*Oceanodroma leucorhoa* (Vieillot)

This is a bird of the Atlantic (and Pacific) Oceans, coming to shore at night to its breeding burrows in offshore islands. In Ontario they are storm waifs.

IDENTIFICATION: Seen in flight off the Newfoundland coast, they reminded me of nighthawks in size and manner of flight, with frequent turns and glides, here low over the ocean waves. The general colour is very dark brown, almost black, with contrasting lighter wing coverts and forked tail. At close range the white rump with dark median stripe is a good field mark.

WINTER:

SPRING:

SUMMER: There are two specimens from Ontario. On July 19, 1939, one was picked up by A. Burrelle two miles below Cornwall on the St. Lawrence River. Recognizing it as unusual (actually the first record for Ontario) he mounted it and it is now in the Royal Ontario Museum (Toner, 1940: 124). The other was picked up alive by Mrs. Harold Patry on Aug. 16, 1955, at Loughboro Lake, near Kingston, following the passage of Hurricane Connie (Baillie, 1955: 375): this is now in the ROM also.

AUTUMN:

**MEASUREMENTS:**
*Length:* 8 ins. (Palmer, 1962: 225).
*Wingspread:* to 19 ins. (Palmer, 1962: 225).
*Weight:* Kent Is. breeders 40.1 to 57.3 g. (av. 48.4 g.) young up to 90 g. (Palmer, 1962: 226).

**REFERENCE:**
Toner, G.C. 1940 Leach's Petrel in Ontario. Wilson Bull., 52: (2): 124.

# BAND-RUMPED STORM-PETREL
## Oceanodroma castro   (Harcourt)

This was an accidental in Ontario: it is normally a bird of the tropical eastern Atlantic.

**IDENTIFICATION:** This is a dark brown bird similar to the more common Leach's Storm-Petrel, but with white rump patch complete both above and below the tail and a more shallowly forked tail. The white rump feathers are tipped with black but do not have a dark median line as in the Leach's.

**WINTER:**

**SPRING:**

**SUMMER:** A female was picked up alive but helpless by the Rideau River in Ottawa by some boys who took it home, kept it overnight and found it dead in the morning, when they took it to the National Museum: the find was on Aug. 28, 1933 (Taverner, 1934: 77). The identity was confirmed by R.C. Murphy, the expert on birds of the Atlantic.

**AUTUMN:**

**MEASUREMENTS:**
*Length:* 7.75 to 8.10 ins.
(Godfrey, 1966: 26).
*Wingspread:* 18" (Palmer,
1962: 236).
*Weight:*

**REFERENCE:**
Taverner, P.A. 1934 The
Madeira Petrel in Ontario.
Auk, 51: (1): 77.

# NORTHERN GANNET   *Sula bassanus*   (Linnaeus)

This is a bird of the Atlantic coast and Gulf of St. Lawrence. In Ontario a few immatures have appeared briefly.

IDENTIFICATION:   These are large birds. In the immature plumage they are brownish with white speckling, long pointed wings and long pointed beak. The white adults, with cream-coloured heads and black wing tips, have not yet appeared in Ontario but are a great tourist attraction at Bonaventure Is. on the Gaspé coast and at Cape St. Mary's in Newfoundland.

WINTER:   Brooman (1954: 6) reported one seen by Lionel Cromwell over Lake Erie about 17 miles off Port Stanley on Dec. 9, 1947. On Jan. 29, 1950, two were seen by several members of the Buffalo Ornithological Society near Point Abino (Beardslee and Mitchell, 1965: 93). Fleming (1913: 225) reported an immature male found floating on Lake Ontario outside Toronto on Dec. 19, 1908. B.M. DiLabio reported 4 or 5 at Ottawa between Nov. 29 and Dec. 3, 1983, all immatures (Weir, 1984: 196).

SPRING:

SUMMER:

AUTUMN:   Fleming (1913: 225) reported two taken at Ottawa, including one immature on Oct. 14, 1909. Speirs (1979: 10) reported two occurrences in Ontario County, 100 years apart: one collected in 1861 at Oshawa by A. Dulmage and another immature found at Whitby on Oct. 21, 1961 by Gerry Norris and Don Pace and probably the same bird seen flying east past Oshawa the next day by George A. Scott. K. McLaughlin *et al* reported two immatures at Hamilton from Oct. 29 to Nov. 29, 1983 (Weir, 1984: 196). One was picked up dead about 10 miles southwest of Welland during the last week of November, 1907, by Joseph Gilmore (Fleming, 1908: 486). Harold D. Mitchell *et al* observed one at Fort Erie on Nov. 4, 1933 and on Oct. 19, 1947 an immature in flight was seen over Lake Ontario west of the Niagara River by Bernard Nathan, Dr. and Mrs. Harold Axtell and John Filot (Beardslee & Mitchell, 1965: 92). F.W. Johnson saw one off Port Stanley on Nov. 16, 1947 (Brooman, 1954: 6). One was sighted at Pelee on Nov. 25, 1973 by Kleiman, Greenhouse and Wilson (Kelley, 1978: 11).

**MEASUREMENTS:**
*Length:* 35 – 40 ins.
(Palmer, 1962: 304)
*Wingspread:* 5½ to 6 ft.
(Palmer, 1962; 304).
*Weight:* 6 – 7 lbs.
(Palmer, 1962: 304).

# AMERICAN WHITE PELICAN
*Pelecanus erythrorhynchos*   Gmelin

There is a good breeding colony at Lake of the Woods where some may be found feeding around the shores or soaring in majestic flight in its vicinity. Elsewhere in Ontario it is a rare visitor.

**IDENTIFICATION:** This is a very large bird, white with black wing tips, with a long hooked beak and large pouch in the throat region.

**WINTER:**

**SPRING:** McIlwraith (1894: 63-64) wrote about two specimens from a flock of five in Hamilton Bay, shot by John Dynes in May, 1864 and another flock of five there on Mar. 13, 1884 observed by Mr. Smith of the Ocean House: these flew off to the east when shot at. Fleming (1930: 66) reported a male shot off Whitby on May 25, 1881. Devitt (1967: 26) noted one seen at Matchedash Bay as reported in the Globe and Mail of May 17, 1944. Fleming (1900: 177) told of a male shot by an Indian boy at Lake Nipissing on May 27, 1899 which was mounted by O. Spanner for G. W. McFarland of Cache Bay.

**SUMMER:** Stirrett (1973c: 13) had one summer record at Pelee from July 5 to 7. Ussher (1965: 2) had a June 18 record at Rondeau. In J.L. Baillie's journal there is a report of one seen at Port Perry on Aug. 2, 1942 (Speirs, 1979: 9). On July 4, 1953 one was seen on Amherst Is. by A.J. Erskine, Herbert and Dorothy Blades (Quilliam, 1965: 23). Devitt (1967: 26) had two summer records from Simcoe Co.: two seen at Orr Lake on Aug. 23, 1944 by Alfred Benham and one seen at Cook's Bay by Harold van Wyck on June 26, 1959. One spent the summer on Lake Mindemoya, Mànitoulin, during the late 1940's according to D.B. Ferguson (Nicholson, 1972: 12). On July 19, 1944, one weighing 45 lbs. was killed by lightning at Lake Chebogamog, 11 miles NE of Sturgeon Falls: this was picked up by Reg. Corbett, Pat Quinn and Geo. Spencer and mounted for exhibition in North Bay (Hewitt, 1945: 45). In June, 1947, five were seen at Shoal Lake, Lake of the Woods (Snyder, 1953: 49). Peck (1976: 9) collected two addled eggs on Three Sisters Is., Lake of the Woods, on July 6, 1976 to establish it as a nesting bird. Denis (1961: 6) called it an occasional, very rare summer visitant to Thunder Bay. Lewis (1944: 304-305) reported one found dead at Hannah Bay by Samuel Hardisty in late June, 1943. Esear Thomas, an Indian chief, found the decomposing carcass of one at Fort Severn on June 8, 1955, and gave the head, radius and ulna to Lumsden (1955: 168).

**AUTUMN:** Cringan (1950: 2) reported one at Round Lake, described by James Sakchekapo, seen in Sept., 1947 or 1948. One was shot in Victoria Harbour by W.N. Ball and reported in the Mail and Empire of Oct. 27, 1930 (Devitt, 1967: 26). Three were seen at Lake Scugog on Sept. 23, 1944 by K. Sands and R. Nesbitt and one weakened bird was captured there and sent to Riverdale Zoo later that fall on Oct. 20 by C. Bowerman (Tozer and Richards, 1974: 61). I saw one circling over Corner Marsh, Pickering, with a mob of gulls up to get a closer look at this stranger, on Sept. 7, 1975: this bird was observed by many others later the same day and the following day (Speirs, 1979: 9). On Oct. 5, 1894, one was shot by James Savage on the Niagara River (Sheppard, 1945: 154). On Sept. 28, 1889, a female was shot near Dunnville, at the mouth of the Grand River (McIlwraith, 1894: 64). A.R. Muma found one in Port Colborne harbour on Sept. 28,

1957: it was photographed there the next day (Sheppard, 1960: 3). Ussher (1965: 2) had an Oct. 6 date for Rondeau while two were seen at Pelee as late as Sept. 24, 1969 (Stirrett, 1973d: 15).

**MEASUREMENTS:**
*Length:* 50-65 ins.
(Palmer, 1962: 265).
*Wingspread:* 8-9 1/2 ft.
(Palmer, 1962: 265).
*Weight:* 10-30 lbs.
(Palmer, 1962: 265)
*but see above - 45 lbs.*

**REFERENCES:**
Hewitt, Oliver H. 1945 Recent occurrences of the White Pelican in northern Ontario. Can. Field-Nat., 59: (1): 45.
Lewis, Harrison F. 1944 White Pelican at James Bay, Canada. Auk. 61: (2): 304-305.
Lumsden, H.G. 1955 Ruff and White Pelican at Fort Severn. Can. Field-Nat., 69:(4): 168.

# BROWN PELICAN   *Pelecanus occidentalis*   Linnaeus

This is a familiar bird to those who winter along subtropical shores but it is very rare in Ontario.

**IDENTIFICATION:**   A very large brownish bird with long hooked beak and prominent throat pouch.

**WINTER:**

**SPRING:**

**SUMMER:**   Lloyd Beamer had two notes on Brown Pelicans during the summer of 1937: one was reported by Wm. Pillgrem who saw it catching fish at the Bustard Islands in Georgian Bay and identified for him by visitors from the southern U.S.A. familiar with the species: the other (perhaps the same bird) was noted at Oliphant by Mrs. W. Dowkes of Owen Sound.

**AUTUMN:**   One was photographed at Waverly Beach (between Ft. Erie and Point Abino on the northeast shore of Lake Erie) by P.M. Benham on Sept. 25, 1971 (Goodwin, 1972: 597).

**MEASUREMENTS:**
*Length:* 42-54 ins.
(Palmer, 1962: 271).
*Wingspread:* to 7 1/2 ft.
(Palmer, 1962: 271).
*Weight:* to 8 lbs. (Palmer, 1962: 271).

# GREAT CORMORANT   *Phalacrocorax carbo*   (Linnaeus)

This cosmopolitan species is quite rare in Ontario but may be overlooked because the similar Double-crested Cormorant is much more likely to be found here during the warmer months. In winter this is the common species on the Atlantic coast and wintering cormorants in Ontario should be carefully examined with this in mind.

IDENTIFICATION: In spring this species often shows white flank patches and white feathers on the throat behind the gular pouch and may show some white on the back of the crown and nape: the Double-crested lacks these white feathers. In winter the young often have a white belly (the light area in young of the Double-crested is less extensive and higher on the breast). This is a larger bird and has a relatively stouter bill than the Double-crested.

WINTER: One in immature plumage was found at Port Credit on Jan. 15, 1978 by David Broughton, Herbert Elliott and Harry Kerr and was frequently observed by many observers until last seen there on Mar. 25, 1978. With A.L. Beldan, I saw it there on Mar. 13, 1978 and noted the white breast and belly and whitish chin. John Kelley was the last to see it there according to records of the Toronto Ornithological Club. Perhaps the same bird was noted the following winter on the Peel-Halton Christmas count on Dec. 17. 1978 (Eric Nasmith, compiler). Derrick Marven, Doris Speirs and I had a good view of one on Lake Ontario off Squires Beach, Pickering, on Feb. 1, 1984. One was also noted on the Prince Edward Point Christmas count of Dec. 15, 1979 (Ron Weir, compiler).

SPRING:

SUMMER:

AUTUMN: Fleming (1906: 443) wrote about one male taken Nov. 21, 1896 at Toronto: "This bird was in an extremely exhausted condition when found, and is the only one I have seen from anywhere on the Great Lakes."

**MEASUREMENTS:**
*Length:* 34-40 ins.
(Godfrey, 1966: 31).
*Wingspread:* 61 ins.
(Pough, 1951: 32).
*Weight:* 5-11 lbs. (Palmer,
1962: 316).

# DOUBLE-CRESTED CORMORANT
*Phalacrocorax auritus*    (Lesson)

In Ontario I have seen these birds perched on pound net poles off Pelee, perched on piles in the Dundas Marsh, swimming with typical uptilted beak in the North Channel off Thessalon and drying their outstretched wings on rocky islets at various other localities. Because of supposed competition with fishermen, it is not a common bird in Ontario. I believe that their persecution is short-sighted, as the guano from such birds is the natural fertilizer that initiates the food chain upon which fishes ultimately depend.

IDENTIFICATION: The only species with which this big, black waterbird might be confused are the closely related Great Cormorant and the Anhinga, both very rare in Ontario (see the accounts of these species for distinctions).

WINTER: Not seen on any of the map period Christmas counts (1968-1977). However, Kelley (1978: 11) reported eight December records in SW Ontario, one as late as Dec. 26, 1973 at Pelee. John Lamey noted one off Squires Beach, Pickering, on Dec. 9, 1973. Sheppard (1960: 4) noted one collected below Niagara Falls on Dec. 14, 1948 by A.R. Muma. One was seen on the Georgian Bay Islands Christmas count on Dec. 28, 1978 and two were reported on the 1979 counts: one at Blenheim on Dec. 16 and another at Hamilton on Dec. 26.

SPRING: Stirrett (1973b: 13) had a spring record for Pelee as early as Mar. 10 with the peak of 40 to 70 birds there in mid-April. Kelley (1978: 11) reported 13 nests on the Chicken Islands in Lake Erie on May 22, 1954. Baillie (in Saunders, 1947: 359) gave Apr. 11 as his earliest date at Toronto with May 11 as his 10-year average. Speirs (1979: 12) had about 20 spring records for Ontario Co., the earliest on Apr. 13, 1969 and the largest number, 13, seen "flying single file" over Oshawa on Apr. 26, 1959 by George A. Scott. Quilliam (1965: 25) gave the average arrival at Kingston as May 3 with the earliest on Apr. 16, 1955. Dennison (1980: 14) cited a May 28 spring date for Sault Ste. Marie. Denis (1961: 3) gave Apr. 19, 1954 as the earliest at Thunder Bay with the average arrival on May 3. D.H. Elder noted his first at Marmion Lake near Atikokan on May 24, 1978 and May 15, 1979.

SUMMER: None were seen on Breeding Bird Survey routes in the 1968-1977 map period. Stirrett (1973c: 13) cited several summer dates for Pelee of 1 to 8 birds. A few strays have been seen off Whitby in summer (Speirs, 1979: 12). Quilliam (1965: 24-25) summarized nesting data for small islets off Kingston where they succeeded in 1949 to 1956 and attempted again in 1962 and 1963. Chip Weseloh told me that good numbers nested on eastern Lake Ontario islets in 1980 as well as in Lake Erie and Georgian Bay localities. Snyder (1928: 253-254) noted 19 nests on an island in Lake Nipigon on June 18, 1924 and he had a count of 1432 nests for Lake of the Woods in the summer of 1947 (Snyder, 1953: 49). Dear (1940: 123) noted 20 pairs with nests at Black Bay, Lake Superior on June 3, 1933. Skeel and Bondrup-Nielsen (1978: 152) gave a few summer records for Pukaskwa and mentioned nest records for Agawa Bay and other Lake Superior localities. Smith (1957: 166) reported one at Remi Lake on June 24, 1953 and 7 nests in Lake Abitibi on June 15, 1953. Cringan (1950: 2) saw one flying over Lake Opakopa on June 16, 1956 (about 200 miles north of Sioux Lookout). Manning (1952: 16) mentioned one collected by Hugh Conn at Ft. Severn as a great rarity there.

AUTUMN: Devitt (1967: 26-27) had several Simcoe Co. records, as early as Sept. 15, 1937 and as late as Nov. 2, 1931. Quilliam (1965: 25) listed 7 fall records for Kingston, the earliest on Sept. 16, 1958 and latest on Oct. 24, 1964. Speirs (1979: 12) had 12 fall records for Ontario Co., the earliest Sept. 10, 1978 and latest Nov. 14, 1948; some from Lake Simcoe and Lake Scugog but most from the Whitby-Oshawa area. Baillie (in Saunders, 1947: 359) gave Nov. 24 as his latest date for Toronto. Stirrett (1973d: 15) had a fall peak of 135 at Pelee on Oct. 29.

**MEASUREMENTS:**
*Length:* 29-35 ins.
(Godfrey, 1966: 32).
*Wingspread:* 51 ins.
(Pough, 1951: 33).
*Weight:* 1670 to 2100 g.
(Palmer, 1962: 328).

**REFERENCE:**
Baillie, James L., Jr.
1947: The Double- crested
Cormorant nesting in
Ontario. Can. Field-Nat.,
61: 119-126.

# ANHINGA   *Anhinga anhinga*   (Linnaeus)

This is normally a bird of the cypress swamps of southern U.S.A. There are just two old specimen records for Ontario.

**IDENTIFICATION:** Superficially it resembles the cormorants, but differs in having a sharp pointed (not hooked) beak, a relatively long tail and much white in the plumage of the back. In the water it often swims with most of the body submerged so that only the snake-like long neck and beak show above the surface. In flight they frequently soar high in the air, looking like black crosses silhouetted against the sky.

**WINTER:**

**SPRING:**

**SUMMER:**

**AUTUMN:** One was shot by an Indian, Billy Brant, at West Lake, Prince Edward County, on Sept. 7, 1904, and identified by Wm. Carrell. Further details are given by Snyder (1941: 28-29).

A female was shot by an Indian at Garden River, near Sault Ste. Marie, "about 1881," possibly in late summer or early autumn. The bird was obtained by Patrick E. Roach, a contractor building the first lock at Sault Ste. Marie in the year when this bird was taken. The lock opened on Sept. 1, 1881. Roach sent the bird to Charles Dury of the Cincinnati Society of Natural History whence it was sent as exchange material to the University of Michigan Museum of Zoology, where it resides as No. 91960 in their bird collection.

**MEASUREMENTS:**
*Length:* 34-36 ins.
(Godfrey, 1966: 34).
*Wingspread:* 48 ins.
(Pough, 1951: 36).
*Weight:* 1326 g. ♂
Palmer, 1962, 359).

**REFERENCE:**
Van Tyne, J. 1950. Old record of *Anhinga anhinga* taken on St. Mary's River, Ontario. Auk, 67: (4): 508-509.

# MAGNIFICENT-FRIGATE BIRD
## *Fregata magnificens* Mathews

This tropical pirate was an accidental visitor to Ontario.

**IDENTIFICATION:** This big, but lightly built bird, with its W-shaped wings and deeply forked tail might only be confused with the equally rare Swallow-tailed Kite. The kite has a wingspread of only about 4 ft. while this frigate-bird has a 7 to 8 ft. wingspread. The kite differs in having white under wing coverts, dark in the frigate-bird. Adult male frigate-birds are all black, females have a white breast and young have both white breast and head (in which they most resemble the kite).

**WINTER:**

**SPRING:**

**SPRING:**

**AUTUMN:** Baillie (1950: 200) wrote:"The occurrence of a Magnificent Frigate-bird, Oct. 16, [1949] at Port Rowan (Hanson Ferris) - a new Ontario record - was reported to James Savage."

**MEASUREMENTS:**
*Length:* 37-45 ins.
(Palmer, 1962: 367).
*Wingspread:* to 8 ft.
(Palmer, 1962: 367).
*Weight:* to 2 1/4 lbs. and
1587 g. (Palmer, 1962:
367-369).

# AMERICAN BITTERN   *Botaurus lentiginosus*   (Rackett)

Saunders and Dale (1933: 170) wrote: "their well-known pumping is a characteristic sound from marsh and bog" and indeed most observations are based on this "plum puddin" sound. Early in spring when cover is scarce they may be seen around marsh edges with beak pointed skyward, looking in silhouette like a broken stump or snag. In summer you may flush one from a roadside puddle and note its two-toned wings as it flaps away—taffy brown at the base with slaty, dark tips. Young night-herons are superficially similar in flight but have more uniformly coloured wings, with white spots (if you are close enough to see them).

WINTER:  On Christmas counts from 1968 to 1977 individuals were noted once at Pelee and Niagara Falls and three times at Long Point, not elsewhere. Stirrett (1973a: 13) noted five winter records for Pelee: single birds on Dec. 2 and 16, Jan. 20 and 25, and on Feb. 15. George A. Scott had one on the Oshawa Christmas count on Dec. 22, 1957 and another at Oshawa on Dec. 20, 1970 (Speirs, 1979: 23). Tozer and Richards (1974: 68) reported a sighting in Darlington Twp. on Dec. 6, 1970 by R. Henry. W.H. Robb found an injured one at Abbey Dawn near Kingston on Jan. 6, 1932, which was sent as a specimen to the Royal Ontario Museum (Quilliam, 1965: 32).

SPRING:  Stirrett (1973b: 13) noted one as early as Mar. 6 at Pelee and observed eight there on Apr. 25. Ussher (1965: 3) found his earliest at Rondeau on Apr. 7 with a 12-year average on Apr. 25. Saunders and Dale (1933: 170) had a 17-year average arrival at London on Apr. 15 with the earliest on Mar. 28, 1925. Baillie (in Saunders, 1947: 359) gave May 1 as his 24-year average arrival at Toronto with the earliest on Apr. 7. Naomi LeVay noted one at Cranberry Marsh, Whitby, as early as Apr. 1, 1973 with plenty of records after mid-April (Speirs, 1979: 23). Quilliam (1965: 31-32) gave Mar. 30, 1960 as the earliest date for Kingston with Apr. 14 as her 15-year average. The 15-year average for Barrie arrivals was Apr. 26 with the earliest on Apr. 12, 1967. Beamer saw one perched *in a spruce tree* in Meaford as early as Apr. 9, 1944. Our earliest record for North Bay was on May 21, 1945 (Speirs and Speirs, 1947: 24). Denis (1961: 3) gave Apr. 19, 1953 as the earliest arrival at Thunder Bay and May 7 as the average arrival date. Cringan saw one at Kasabonika Lake on May 28, 1953, two days after the ice went out.

SUMMER:  On Breeding Bird Surveys, 1968-1977, it was noted in small numbers on most routes north to Kapuskasing and Dryden. Baillie and Harrington (1936: 10-11) documented nesting from Pelee north to Lake Nipigon and from Ottawa west to Lake of the Woods. David Elder found a nest with 4 young and one egg on our Geraldton bog plot on June 21, 1971 which held five downy young the following day. C.E. Hope heard one pumping near Favourable Lake on June 18, 1938 and collected two and noted others at Ft. Severn between June 17 and July 10, 1940. Lee (1978: 19) encountered young at Big Trout Lake in August, 1975. Manning (1952: 17) flushed 13 in four hours at North Point on James Bay, near Moosonee, on June 3-4, 1947 and found them in all suitable country along the James and Hudson Bay coasts, except in the barrens around Cape Henrietta Maria. Schueler *et al* (1974: 142) found them abundant at Moosonee, common at Ft. Albany and Attawapiskat and uncommon at Hawley Lake and Winisk.

AUTUMN:  Beamer noted one at Epping, near Meaford, as late as Nov. 9, 1942. Devitt (1967: 31) gave Oct. 15, 1965, as the latest Simcoe Co. record, at Wye Marsh by Bartlett. Quilliam (1965: 32) gave Oct. 4 as the average last date for Kingston with the latest on Oct. 30, 1956. Ron Tozer noted one as late as Nov. 9, 1975, at the West Causeway, Scugog (Speirs, 1979: 23). Baillie (in Saunders, 1947: 359) had a latest date of Nov. 1 at Toronto with his 24-year average departure date on Sept. 24. Ussher (1965: 3) gave Nov. 6 as his latest date for Rondeau. Stirrett (1973a: 13) had one at Pelee as late as Nov. 27 and had a fall maximum of 12 on Oct. 30 (1973d: 15).

**MEASUREMENTS:**
Quilliam (1965: 31) gave the following for one shot near Kingston by Hadfield on Sept. 12, 1857:
*Length:* 23 1/2"
*Wingspread:* 3 ft. 4 ins.
*Weight:* 1 1/2 lbs.
C.E. Hope collected a female at Favourable Lake on July 13, 1938 that weighed 532 g.

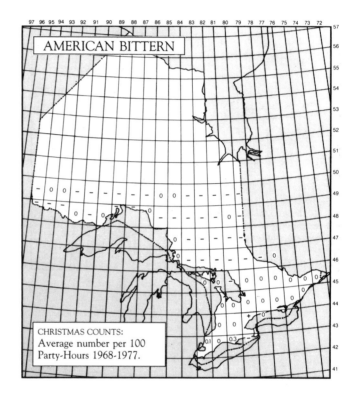

AMERICAN BITTERN

CHRISTMAS COUNTS:
Average number per 100 Party-Hours 1968-1977.

34

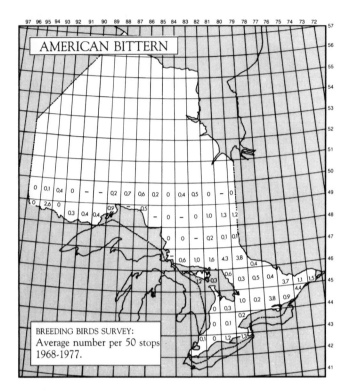

AMERICAN BITTERN

BREEDING BIRDS SURVEY:
Average number per 50 stops
1968-1977.

# LEAST BITTERN   *Ixobrychus exilis*   (Gmelin)

It is always a "red letter day" when I chance across one of these secretive little denizens of cattail marshes, usually as it flies across an opening, only to drop down into cover on the other side and promptly disappear.

IDENTIFICATION: This tiny rich brown bittern is not likely to be confused with any other bird if seen at all well. The call:"coo-coo-coo-coo—-" should alert observers to watch for it in the cattails.

WINTER:

SPRING: Stirrett (1973b: 13) gave Apr. 19 as his earliest Pelee record. Ussher (1965: 3) gave May 7 as the earliest date for Rondeau with May 14 as the 10-year average. Saunders and Dale (1933: 171) had May 18 as their 7-year average for arrival at London with the earliest on May 2, 1923. Baillie (in Saunders, 1947: 360) gave May 2 as his earliest date for Toronto with average arrival in mid-May. George A. Scott's earliest at Oshawa was on May 1, 1976 with the median arrival on May 20. Quilliam (1965: 31) had her earliest at Kingston on May 13, 1956 with May 21 as her 8-year average arrival. Beamer had one as early as May 7, 1943 at Meaford.

SUMMER: On the Breeding Bird Survey, 1968-1977, it showed up once on the Picton, Woodford, Cobden and Byng Inlet routes, not elsewhere. Stirrett (1973c: 13) listed this as a nesting species at Pelee and noted as many as 25 there on Aug. 20. Long (1968b: 13) found two pairs in the 44-acre Shoal Point Marsh, Pickering, in 1968. Tozer and Richards (1974: 67) listed 7 nests with eggs in the Oshawa-Lake Scugog area between June 12 and July 17. Quilliam (1965: 30-31) had a few breeding records in the Kingston region. Devitt (1967: 30-31) cited numerous nest records for Simcoe Co. between June 3 (1936) and July 13 (1942). Beamer had 3 June records at Meaford in 1940 and 1941. Baillie and Harrington (1936: 11) reported a set of 3 eggs collected by D. Chitty on June 24, 1934 at West Bay, Lake Nipissing. I found a highway casualty about 5 miles east of Thessalon where Hwy. 17 runs through a cattail marsh, on June 26, 1976. Snyder (1942: 12) collected a female at MacLennan on June 20, 1931 and Harry Graham found a nest with 5 eggs at Maskinonge Bay on July 7, 1941 (both localities a few miles SE of Sault Ste. Marie). A.E. Allin reported a Least Bittern at Fort William on June 10, 1963 (Woodford, 1963: 457).

AUTUMN: J.L. Baillie and John Crosby observed one at Holland Marsh as late as Sept. 13, 1942 (Devitt, 1967: 31). Quilliam (1965: 31) gave Sept. 1, 1956 as her latest date for the Kingston area. George A. Scott's latest date for Oshawa was Sept. 26, 1965 (Speirs, 1979: 22). Fleming (1906: 447) had an exceptionally late individual at Toronto on Nov. 28, 1894, where he regarded it as common until mid-Sept. Saunders and Dale (1933: 171) reported a specimen taken by A.A. Wood at Coldstream as late as Sept. 13, 1917. Ussher (1965: 3) had a Sept. 19 date for Rondeau. Kelley (1978: 14) had one as late as Oct. 10, 1954 at Bradley's Marsh. Stirrett (1973d: 15) gave Sept. 30 as his latest date for Pelee.

MEASUREMENTS:
*Length:* 11-14 1/2 ins.
(Palmer, 1962: 491).
*Wingspread:* 16-18 ins.

36

(Palmer, 1962: 491).
*Weight:* 1 1/2 to 4 oz.
(Palmer, 1962: 491).
*Note:* Fleming (1906: 447)
listed several specimens of
Cory's Least Bittern from
Ashbridge's Bay, Toronto.
This dark race was then
considered a distinct
species. The birds were
taken between May 18
(1890) and Sept. 8 (1899)
with young from Aug. 3 to
17 and a nest on June 25,
1898.

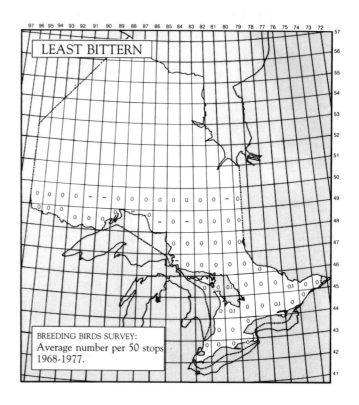

LEAST BITTERN

BREEDING BIRDS SURVEY:
Average number per 50 stops
1968-1977.

# GREAT BLUE HERON   *Ardea herodias*   Linnaeus

This is the most conspicuous large wader in Ontario waters, waiting patiently at the edge of marshes for an unwary fish or frog to come its way, or flapping ponderously to its nest high in a treetop heronry in some secluded woodlot often miles from the feeding marsh. After the nesting season, herons spread out in all directions and this species may be joined by some of its smaller relatives that have bred south of the border.

IDENTIFICATION: This big, blue-gray bird stands about 4 ft. high. It is often called a crane but cranes fly with the head outstretched, not folded back so that the neck forms an S-curve as in the case of herons. Adult cranes have a bare red patch on the forehead while the heron has a white face and usually sports a long black crest, shorter in the immatures. Cranes are very rare in Ontario.

WINTER: This species has occurred on Christmas counts at most localities in Ontario north to the Thousand Islands and Wiarton with outliers north to Deep River and Manitoulin. It is rare north of the Lake Erie marshes and uncommon even there.

SPRING: These big birds arrive back early at their heronries: one of my most vivid memories is the sight of several sitting dejectedly on the ice of Lake Simcoe waiting to occupy the Thorah Island heronry. Kelley (1978: 12) wrote that the large Lake Erie island colonies may be occupied as early as mid-March. Stirrett (1973b: 13) had his earliest Pelee record on Mar. 16 with a peak of 17 on Apr. 27. Saunders and Dale (1933: 168) gave Mar. 29 as their 10-year average for spring arrival at London with the earliest on Mar. 19, 1910. Baillie (in Saunders, 1947: 359) gave Apr. 11 as his 14-year average arrival date at Toronto. Speirs (1979: 13) had an Ontario Co. record as early as Mar. 4, 1969, with the spring peak in the second week of April, while J. Satterly's earliest date at Cedar Point, Lake Simcoe was Apr. 5, 1953. Quilliam (1965: 26) had her 14-year average for arrivals at Kingston on Apr. 1 with the earliest on Mar. 22, 1961. Devitt (1967: 28) gave Apr. 4 as the 22-year average arrival date for Barrie with the earliest on Mar. 21, 1953. Dennison (1980: 14) gave Apr. 12 as the spring date for Sault Ste. Marie. Skeel and Bondrup-Nielsen (1978: 152) saw their first migrant at Pukaskwa on Apr. 10, 1977. Denis (1961: 2) gave Apr. 5, 1954 as earliest and Apr. 18 as average arrival at Thunder Bay. Cringan noted an arrival at Sioux Lookout on Apr. 24, 1953.

SUMMER: They have shown up as fairly common to rare on most Breeding Bird Surveys north to Cochrane and Kenora with the greatest numbers just north and east of Georgian Bay. Smith (1957: 66) was shown a 17-nest colony on an island in Lake Abitibi on July 13, 1953 by E. Nelson. Manning (1952: 16) mentioned one collected at Moose Factory on Aug. 29, 1860, possibly a post-breeding stray. Ross James noted one frequently from May 30 to June 11 at Pickle Lake in 1977. Hope (1938: 7) reported one young-of-the-year bird collected at Favourable Lake on Aug. 22, 1938, and one seen by J. Satterly at Sandy Lake on Aug. 14, 1937. Lee (1978: 18) gave a report of a heronry 24 miles south of Bearskin Lake. Cringan (1950: 2) detailed the finding of a nest at Nikip Lake. Schueler, Baldwin and Rising (1974: 142) reported this species only at Fraserdale, nowhere along the Hudson or James Bay coasts, but a single adult was seen at Cape Henrietta Maria on Aug. 16, 1948 by the ROM field party (Peck, 1972: 337).

AUTUMN: Manning (1952: 16) reported that Hewitt saw one at Ship Sands (near

Moosonee) on Sept. 25, 1947. Skeel and Bondrup-Nielsen (1978: 152) had their last sighting at Pukaskwa on Oct. 9, 1977. Quilliam (1965: 26) had her 11-year average departure date from Kingston on Nov. 5. Speirs (1979: 13) gave late Sept. as the peak for Ontario Co. with George A. Scott's median departure date on Nov. 26. Saunders (1947: 359) gave Oct. 25 as his 13-year average departure date from Toronto. Stirrett (1973d: 15) had a peak of 100 at Pelee on Sept. 17 but some lingered on into mid-winter there.

**MEASUREMENTS:**
*Length:* 43-52 ins.
(Godfrey, 1966: 36)
*Wingspread:* 70 ins.
(Pough, 1951: 40)
*Weight:* 5 to 8 lbs.
(Palmer, 1962: 393)

**REFERENCE:**
Gray, Paul A., James W. Grier, George D. Hamilton and D. Paul Edwards 1980 Great Blue Heron colonies in northwestern Ontario. Can. Field-Nat., 94: (2): 182-184. Gives a map showing colonies north to 54°12′N, 91°23′W.

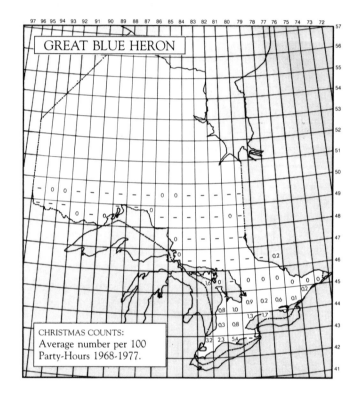

GREAT BLUE HERON

CHRISTMAS COUNTS:
Average number per 100
Party-Hours 1968-1977.

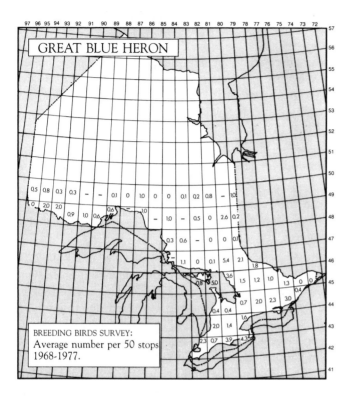

GREAT BLUE HERON

BREEDING BIRDS SURVEY:
Average number per 50 stops
1968-1977.

# GREAT EGRET   *Casmerodius albus*   (Linnaeus)

This is the tallest of the Ontario white herons and the most likely to be seen at the present time. It sometimes nests with other herons, particularly on the western Lake Erie islands and along its north shore. Elsewhere in Ontario it is largely a post-breeding wanderer.

IDENTIFICATION: Its large size, yellow bill and black legs distinguish it from other white herons in Ontario (but note that the young of the small, stocky Cattle Egret have somewhat similar colouration). In breeding plumage, long white filamentous plumes extend from the back beyond the tail (the former aigrettes of commerce): these are shed after the breeding season.

WINTER: One was reported on the Pelee Christmas count on Dec. 24, 1978. On Jan. 5, 1952, one was found dead in the ice of Talbot Creek, Elgin Co., which had been seen alive there about a week previously (Brooman, 1954: 7).

SPRING: Kelley (1978: 13) noted an occupied nest on East Sister Island, Lake Erie, on May 10, 1953. Stirrett (1973b: 13) called it a "fairly common vagrant" at Pelee, with the earliest on March 28 and 8 there on May 23. Ussher (1965: 3) had a March 25 record at Rondeau and 8 there on Apr. 20. Sheppard (1945: 154) reported a sighting by J. Savage at Frenchman's Creek, Niagara, on May 15, 1935. Fleming (1906: 447) had one in his collection from Port Union, taken on May 24, 1895: he also reported "a pair bred regularly many years ago (about 1870) at Port Union" according to Wm. Brodie. Speirs (1979: 17) had over a dozen spring records for Ontario Co., the earliest on Apr. 1, 1973. On Apr. 30, 1908, one was taken at Orillia, mounted and later presented to the ROM: on May 25, 1963. O.E. Devitt photographed one near Angus (Devitt, 1967: 29). H. McConnell noted one along the Beaver River on May 23, 1954, according to L. Beamer. Weir & Quilliam (1980: 32) gave Apr. 21 as a 5-year average arrival date at Kingston.

SUMMER: J.L. Baillie, J. Livingston and J. Woodford found 6 nests on East Sister Is. on June 10, 1957 (Gunn, 1957: 402). Peck (1976: 10) photographed nestings on East Sister Is. and Pelee Is. in June, 1975. Stirrett (1973c: 13) had a maximum of 20 at Pelee on July 28. Smith (1964: 59-60) located nests near Amherstburg in the summers of 1959 and 1960. Ussher (1965: 3) noted 7 at Rondeau on Aug. 12. W.E. Saunders collected one on Aug. 19, 1882, a few miles below Middlemiss on the Thames River (Saunders & Dale, 1933: 168). Sheppard *et al* (1936: 97) saw two on the Niagara River shore about 15 miles down from Ft. Erie on Aug. 8, 1933 and W.E. Hurlburt saw one at Wainfleet Marsh on Aug. 15, 1928. There have been several summer records for the marshes between Pickering and Oshawa (Speirs, 1979: 17). One seen with R.J. Rutter on June 5, 1932, at Weller's Bay, Prince Edward Co., stayed until the first week of September (Townson, 1933: 94). Quilliam (1965: 28) had 6 August records from Kingston, one involving 7 birds. Devitt (1967: 29) detailed the summer records from Simcoe Co. L. Beamer noted two flying along the shore east of Meaford on Aug. 13, 1953. I saw one in a swamp near Stokes Bay, Bruce Co., on July 19, 1941.

AUTUMN: L. Beamer had four fall records, including one shot 4 miles NW of Owen Sound (see measurements below) and one as late as Oct. 25, 1941, near Oliphant. Devitt (1967: 29) cited various September records for Simcoe Co., and four birds near Gilford on or about Oct. 5,1953. Weir & Quilliam (1980: 32) gave Sept. 24 as the latest Kingston record. One lingered at Oshawa's Second Marsh as late as Nov. 23, 1963, when it was seen by Ron Tozer and George A. Scott (Speirs, 1979: 17). Saunders & Dale (1933: 16) noted one near London as late as Sept. 27, 1930. Ussher (1965: 3) had 6 at Rondeau on Sept. 15 with one as late as Sept. 28. Stirrett (1973d: 15) had a peak of 20 at Pelee on Sept. 19 with 2 there as late as Oct. 10. Smith (1964: 59-60) gave Oct. 15, 1960, as the latest date for Lake Erie marshes.

**MEASUREMENTS:**

*Length:* 35 ins. (Beamer). 37-41 ins. (Palmer, 1962: 406).
*Wingspread:* 52.5 ins. (Beamer) to about 55 ins. (Palmer, 1962: 406).
*Weight:* 12 ♂ averaged 935 g. 9 ♀ averaged 812 g. (Dunning, 1984: 3).

**REFERENCES:**

Smith, Winnifred 1964 Common Egrets nesting near Amherstburg, Ontario. Can. Field-Naturalist, 78: (1): 59-60.
Townson, John. 1933 American Egret in eastern Ontario. Auk. 50: (1): 94.
   *Notes:* James, McLaren & Barlow (1976: 10) mentioned late summer records at Sault Ste. Marie, Kapuskasing and Winisk, without details.
   Seton (1885: 336) reported one shot at Lake Nipissing in 1883 (no date): according to Ricker & Clarke (1939: 4) this specimen ended up in the Old Mill on the Humber at Toronto.

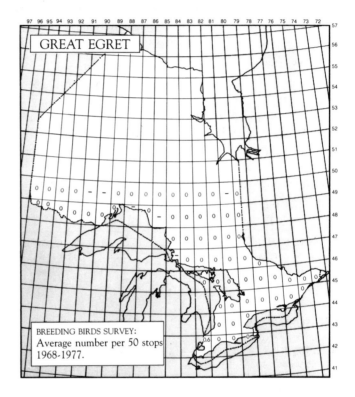

GREAT EGRET

BREEDING BIRDS SURVEY: Average number per 50 stops 1968-1977.

# SNOWY EGRET   *Egretta thula*   (Molina)

This dainty little egret is quite common in Atlantic coastal marshes as far north as Maine but is still quite rare in Ontario.

**IDENTIFICATION:** This is a small white heron with slender black bill, black legs and "golden slippers". It often erects a white crest. In breeding plumage it sports white, upturned lacy back feathers. Young of the year may have rather dull greenish yellow feet instead of gold and the back of the legs may be green or dull yellow instead of black.

**WINTER:**

**SPRING:** Stirrett (1973b: 13) had one spring record for Pelee, on May 16, 1957. Kelley (1978: 13) reported two at Rondeau on May 6, 1970. Speirs (1979: 18) cited records of five birds in Ontario County marshes, one as early as Apr. 10, 1977 at Corner Marsh seen by Edgerton Pegg. Quilliam (1965: 29) gave details of a bird found on Galloo Is., Lake Ontario, on May 21, 1964 by Robert Rainault. One was found at Purbrook Marsh, Conc. 3, Orillia Twp. on Apr. 25, 1965; verified by several observers on May 1 and later photographed by W.E. Cattley, the original discoverer (Devitt, 1967: 29-30).

**SUMMER:** George A. Scott and others saw one at Oshawa's Second Marsh on June 10, 1956 (Tozer and Richards, 1974: 66).

**AUTUMN:** George A. Scott had two fall sightings at Oshawa's Second Marsh: on Sept. 1, 1974 and Sept. 30, 1975 (Speirs, 1979: 18). Stirrett (1973d: 15) had two fall records for Pelee: Sept., 1904 and Sept. 11 to 13, 1937. Kelley (1978: 13) reported two at Bradley's Marsh, Lake St. Clair, on Sept. 5, 1970.

**MEASUREMENTS:**
*Length:* 22-26 ins.
(Palmer, 1962: 456).
*Wingspread:* to 38 ins.
(Palmer, 1962: 456).
*Weight:* to 13 oz. (Palmer, 1962: 456).

# LITTLE BLUE HERON   *Egretta caerulea*   (Linnaeus)

This is one of many species of heron that wanders north after breeding in the United States and may get as far as the southern Ontario marshes, where it thrills the rarity-seeking bird watchers.

IDENTIFICATION: Young birds in their white plumage superficially resemble egrets. From these it may be distinguished by its two-toned bill, the basal portion pale while the terminal part is almost black: in the Great Egret the bill is yellow while in the Snowy Egret it is black. The greenish gray legs are also a good mark (again yellow or black in most egrets). Adults are very dark blue and appear almost black in flight. The long, thin neck distinguishes it from the chunky Green-backed Heron.

WINTER:

SPRING: Stirrett (1973b: 13) noted three between late April and May 2, 1971 at Pelee and single birds there on May 11, 1957 and May 17, 1942. On May 22, 1955, an adult was seen south of Dunnville at the base of Rockhouse Point by W. Brockner and Bernard Nathan (Beardslee & Mitchell, 1965: 96). An early bird was seen by D. Scovell at Whitby on Apr. 10, 1983 (James, 1984: 54). Tozer & Richards (1974: 64) reported two adults at Oshawa's Second Marsh, one on May 7, 1961 and the other on May 10, 1968. Devitt (1967: 28) reported a white bird taken in a muskrat trap on the Simcoe Co. side of the Atherley Narrows by George Moase on March 28, 1929. Nicholson (1972: 12) reported an adult found at Ice Lake, Manitoulin, on Apr. 14, 1960: this was forwarded to the ROM and confirmed.

SUMMER: Stirrett (1973c: 13) noted 4 on Aug. 6; 7 on Aug. 13 and 2 on Aug. 20 at Pelee. I saw one at Wheatley on Aug. 26, 1954 and again there on Aug. 30, 1956. Ussher (1965: 3) had Aug. 16 and Aug. 21 dates for Rondeau. Saunders & Dale (1933: 169) reported a white one at Komoka on Aug. 2 and 3, 1930 and 3 on the Thames River below Byron on Aug. 9, 1930: they also mentioned a Port Bruce record that summer. My first acquaintance with a Little Blue Heron was seeing a white one in the Second Marsh up the Humber River, Toronto, using a newly purchased telescope on Aug. 11, 1933. Speirs (1938: 53) also had an Aug. 25 date for Toronto. Naomi Le Vay and others saw a white one at Cranberry Marsh on Aug. 24, 1952 and two there from Aug. 4 to 23, 1955 (Speirs, 1979: 15). Henry H. Barston saw a white one on an island in West Lake, Prince Edward Co. at least twice during August, 1937 (Snyder, 1941: 30).

AUTUMN: A "real wanderer" turned up as late as Nov. 7-8, 1970 at Thunder Bay where it was seen by Keith Denis and others (Goodwin, 1971: 50). The 1952 bird at Cranberry Marsh, Whitby, was seen as late as Sept. 4 by Naomi Le Vay (Speirs, 1979: 15). An immature was seen at Rockhouse Point, Lake Erie, on Sept. 4, 1960, by Schaffner, Clark and Brownstein (Beardslee & Mitchell, 1965: 96). One was reported at Bradley's Marsh on Sept. 5, 1970, by W.R. Jarmain and G. Clements (Goodwin, 1971: 50). Stirrett (1973d: 15) noted single birds at Pelee on Sept. 10 and 20, Oct. 1 and 8.

MEASUREMENTS:
*Length:* 20 to 29 ins.
(Godfrey, 1966: 38)
*Wingspread:* to 41 ins.

44

(Palmer, 1962: 428)
*Weight:* 11 ♂ averaged
364 g. 8 ♀ averaged
315 g. (Dunning, 1984: 3).
*Note:* James, McLaren &
Barlow (1976: 9) reported
other sightings, north to
Ottawa, Sudbury and
Winisk, without details.

# TRICOLORED HERON  *Egretta tricolor*  (Müller)

This is normally a bird of coastal salt marshes, where I have seen it north to Maine. It is a rare straggler in Ontario.

**IDENTIFICATION:** This is a strikingly beautiful smallish heron, with unstreaked white belly and white rump, contrasting with the dark slaty-blue upperparts. There is often a rusty red border to the white foreneck. The combination of dark blue, white and rusty red gave it its name *tricolor*. Note that the young Great Blue Heron has a whitish belly but it is heavily streaked and the bird itself is much larger and much paler than the Tricolored Heron.

**WINTER:**

**SPRING:** One was photographed at Rondeau on Apr. 21, 1974 (James, McLaren and Barlow, 1976: 10). Kelley (1978: 13) summarized previous sightings at Rondeau: on May 18, 1957; May 1, 1959; May 14, 1970 (2); and May 22, 1971. Pauline Higgins found one at Long Point on May 6, 1959 (Baillie, 1969: 34). Clive Goodwin observed one at Corner Marsh, Pickering, on May 10, 1974 and another was reported there on Apr. 24, 1976 by Peter Whelan, William W. Smith *et al* (Speirs, 1979: 19). Gordon Bellerby found one at Cranberry Marsh, Whitby, on May 12, 1974, which was seen by many others there until May 19 (Tozer and Richards, 1974: 309)—this may have been the same bird noted earlier at Corner Marsh in 1974. T. Hince found one at Marathon on May 19, 1983 (James, 1984: 54-55).

**SUMMER:** Chesterfield (1969: 43) reported one at Bradley's Marsh, Lake St. Clair, photographed by Alfred Rider (copy of photo to R.O.M.): this bird also seen by James L. Baillie and Roy Poulter and Norman Chesterfield. Tozer and Richards (1974: 66) found one at Cranberry Marsh on July 17, 1972, which was seen there subsequently by several other observers until July 28. Joanne Dean and R. Doug McRae saw an adult at Prince Edward Point on June 5, 1979 (Weir & Quilliam, 1980: 4).

**AUTUMN:**

**MEASUREMENTS:**
*Length:* 24-28 ins.
(Palmer, 1962: 465).
*Wingspread:* to about 36
ins. (Palmer, 1962: 465).
*Weight:* to 11 oz. (Palmer,
1962: 465).

**REFERENCE:**
Chesterfield, Norman
1969. A Louisiana Heron
photographed in Ontario.
Ont. Field Biol., 23: 43.

# CATTLE EGRET   *Bubulcus ibis*   (Linnaeus)

This small, stocky egret is a recent newcomer from Africa, first reported in North America about 1941 in Florida, and in Ontario in 1956. In Africa it follows elephants and other big grazing animals picking off insects they kick up—in America cattle serve this purpose. Although differing in food habits from our other herons, it frequently nests in their heronries.

IDENTIFICATION: Our other white herons are slim, long-necked birds: the Cattle Egret is comparatively short in neck and legs. In breeding dress it sports buffy plumes in patches about the head and neck and has yellowish-orange bill and legs. The immatures with pale yellow bill and very dark green (almost black) legs might be confused with Great Egrets in colour, but not in size and build.

WINTER:

SPRING: Godfrey (1966: 38) gave Port Rowan on May 4-6, 1956 as the first Ontario record, with one at Lake St. Clair on May 26, 1956 and one at Port Dover on May 1, 1959 as subsequent sightings. Stirrett (1973b: 13) had records for Pelee on Apr. 2, 1967 and May 13, 1964. One was seen near Byng on May 13, 1962 by Schaffner and Clark (Beardslee & Mitchell, 1965: 96). The first report from Ontario County was at Frenchman Bay in early May, 1963 when one was spotted by David O'Brien and Alf. Bunker. There are about six additional spring records there, one as early as Apr. 7, 1966 at Lynde Creek Marsh, Whitby (Speirs, 1979: 16). Quilliam (1965: 28) had records of one near Westport on May 11-12, 1962 and one near Harrowsmith on May 16, 1962. Mrs. Gerry Shemilt found the first one in Simcoe Co. a few miles north of Angus on May 22, 1960 which was photographed on May 24 by Donald Gunn; another was photographed on May 10, 1964 near Collingwood by Alf. Mitchener (Devitt, 1967: 29). One was reported in Otter Cove, Pukaskwa on Apr. 27, 1977 by Elwyn Richardson (Skeel and Bondrup-Nielsen, 1978: 153).

SUMMER: "In the summer of 1974 the species was found to nest on Pelee Island" by Campbell (Kelley, 1978: 12). Speirs (1979: 16) had five summer records for Ontario Co. including one 7 miles south of Brechin by J. Satterly on June 6, 1973. Tozer and Richards (1974: 65) noted one at Lake Scugog south of Caesarea on June 13, 1963. Godfrey (1966: 39) gave the first nestings for Canada at Presqu'ile and Luther Marsh in 1962. The first Kingston record was at Black Ant Island on June 25, 1960: other summer records there were on Aug. 2, 1962 when two were seen on Wolfe Is. and June 1, 1964 with one on Pigeon Is. (Quilliam, 1965: 27). One was noted near Little Current, Manitoulin, in late June, 1971 by W.G. Allan (Nicholson, 1972: 12).

AUTUMN: W. Broughton and E. Taylor found one at Dorion on Oct. 23, 1982. George A. Scott and others saw two on the Beaton farm by Oshawa's Second Marsh on Sept. 12, 1965 and one there as late as Oct. 9, 1977 (Speirs, 1979: 16). (James, 1983: 9). Stirrett (1973a: 13 and 1973d: 15) reported one at Pelee from Nov. 15 to 17, 1967.

**MEASUREMENTS:**
*Length:* 19-21 ins.
(Palmer, 1962: 438).
*Wingspread:* 36-38 ins.

(Palmer, 1962: 438).
*Weight:* to about 12 oz.
(300 to 400 g.) (Palmer, 1962: 438-439).

# GREEN-BACKED HERON    *Butorides striatus*    (Linnaeus)

You may hear a cough in the sky and looking up see a bird about the size and the manner of flight of a crow but with long, dangling yellow legs and a sharp pointed bill. In my experience Green-backed Herons seldom look green, usually a dusky blue back and brownish purple face and neck are the general impression, but they do have a green gloss in good light on the wings and back. They are often seen leaning forward from a rock or stump at the water's edge, raising the crest and flicking the tail, patiently waiting for dinner to come by. I have found nests low in deciduous trees and high in dense cedars, sometimes solitary and then again in small groups.

IDENTIFICATION:    This is a small, crow-sized, stockily built heron, with other special characteristics noted above, not likely to be confused with any other species. The young are more streaked below than the adults and have green rather than orange-yellow legs.

WINTER:    Not seen on the 1968 to 1977 Christmas counts, but one was reported on the Long Point Christmas count held on Dec. 26, 1964 and studied by 2 parties at 15 yards (Miles, 1965: 93).

SPRING:    Stirrett (1973b: 13) noted his earliest at Pelee on Apr. 16 with a peak of 7 in mid-May. Saunders and Dale (1933: 169) gave Apr. 28 as their 17-year average arrival date at London with the earliest on Apr. 20, 1917. Speirs (1938: 39) had an early Apr. 18 record for Toronto. Saunders (1947: 359) gave May 8 as his 13-year average for arrivals at Toronto. Speirs (1979: 14) noted two Apr. 18 dates by Calvert at Oshawa but his median arrival date was May 8 and the spring peak during the third week of May. Quilliam (1965: 27) gave May 4 as the 13-year average arrival date for Kingston with the earliest on Apr. 25, 1960. Devitt (1967: 28) had May 6 as the 14-year average for Barrie with the earliest on Apr. 23, 1960. Beamer's earliest two at Meaford were seen on May 16, 1948 but his only breeding evidence, the discovery of a dead, pin-feathered young at the entrance of a fox den on May 23, 1954 evidenced an earlier arrival. Louise Lawrence noted one near Rutherglen on May 20, 1945 (Speirs and Speirs, 1947: 24).

SUMMER:    On Breeding Bird Surveys this was a fairly common to rare species, from the southern edge of Ontario north to Mattawa and Manitoulin Island. Baillie and Harrington (1936: 9) cited Taverner's June 18, 1918 record in Grenville Co. as their northernmost outpost for this species as a breeder. Devitt (1967: 28) had nesting records in Simcoe Co. north to Collingwood (by A. J. Mitchener) and Beamer had several summer records from the shoreline east of Thornbury as well as the young noted above. Nicholson (1972: 12) considered it an "occasional summer resident" on Manitoulin.

AUTUMN:    Beamer noted one east of Thornbury on Sept. 7, 1941. Devitt (1967: 28) gave Sept. 24 as his latest date for Barrie. Quilliam (1965: 27) gave Sept. 21 as the 8-year average departure date from Kingston with the latest on Oct. 6, 1956. Speirs (1979: 14) had a fall peak in mid-Sept. in the Whitby-Oshawa area with one very late bird noted by E. Pegg on Nov. 14, 1971. Saunders (1947: 359) gave Sept. 14 as the 10-year average departure date from Toronto with the latest on Oct. 15. Ussher (1965: 2) had a Nov. 15 record for Rondeau but his 7-year average departure date was Oct. 8. Stirrett (1973d: 15) had a fall peak of 13 on Sept. 14 at Pelee with the latest on Oct. 2.

**MEASUREMENTS:**
Length 16-22 ins.
(Godfrey, 1966: 37).
*Wingspread:* "to about 26
ins." (Palmer, 1962: 415)
*Weight:* 34 averaged
212 g. (Dunning, 1984: 3).

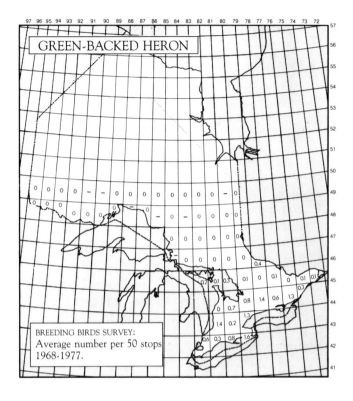

GREEN-BACKED HERON

BREEDING BIRDS SURVEY:
Average number per 50 stops
1968-1977.

# BLACK-CROWNED NIGHT-HERON
*Nycticorax nycticorax*    (Linnaeus)

As the name implies these are birds of crepuscular habits, becoming active as night begins to set in and hiding from view as the dawn brightens. They are gregarious nesters, usually at lower elevations than the Great Blue Herons, but sometimes in the same heronry. At Pelee I found them in a grove of hackberry trees but frequently they use old willow trees.

IDENTIFICATION: The adults of this medium-sized, rather squatty heron are quite distinctive with their black back, white underparts and light gray wings. At close range the bright red eyes and white plumes dangling from the black crown are striking features. The young, especially in flight, might be confused with the American Bittern, but are a dull, gray-brown rather than rich yellowish brown of the bittern, which shows much contrast between the almost black wing tips and pale brown of the rest of the wing. The shorter, less pointed bill of the night heron contrasts with the long, dagger-like bill of the bittern.

WINTER: On the 1968-1977 Christmas counts, individuals showed up in 1974 at Blenheim and Hamilton, and in 1975 at Pelee, Toronto and Meaford. Stirrett (1973a: 13) had Pelee records for Dec. 1, 14 and 18. Ussher (1965: 3) listed a Dec. 22 report for Rondeau. One was reported by Doyle at Point Abino on Dec. 4, 1941 (Beardslee & Mitchell, 1965: 100). Saunders (1947: 359) noted one as late as Dec. 8 at Toronto. One was observed at Amos Ponds, Pickering, by A. Reid on Dec. 5, 1965 (Speirs, 1979: 20).

SPRING: Stirrett (1973b: 13) had one at Pelee as early as March 28 and a peak of 100 there on May 17. Ussher (1965: 3) gave Apr. 10 as the 15-year average for arrivals at Rondeau with the earliest on March 20. One was seen near London on May 21, 1924 and on several subsequent days (Saunders & Dale, 1933: 170). Sheppard (1945: 155) noted 30 at Niagara-on-the-Lake on May 24, 1938. Saunders (1947: 359) had his earliest at Toronto on Apr. 18 and his 6-year average arrival on May 5. George A. Scott's earliest date for Oshawa was March 31, 1962: he saw 25 on Apr. 27, 1975 and his median arrival date was May 7 (Speirs, 1979: 20). Weir & Quilliam (1980: 32) gave March 29 as the earliest Kingston date with Apr. 17 as the 24-year average arrival. Devitt (1967: 30) gave May 11, 1954 as his earliest date for Collingwood. L. Beamer had only one record for Meaford, on May 15, 1949.

SUMMER: On Breeding Bird Surveys they have appeared only at Sarnia, Kingsville, Stratford and Port Dover. J.L. Baillie, J. Livingston and J. Woodford found 300 nests on East Sister Is., Lake Erie on June 10, 1957 (Gunn, 1957: 402). Stirrett (1973c: 13) reported nesting at Pelee and had a peak of 60 birds there on July 28. Kelley (1978: 13) recorded 4 active nests at Bradley's Marsh on July 15, 1951. Saunders & Dale (1933: 170) had five summer records in Middlesex Co., including one collected on Aug. 24, 1892, by W.A. Balkwill. Seeber estimated 630 nests in a colony at Port Weller in 1948 (Beardslee & Mitchell, 1965: 100). J.M. Richards found 10 nests at Oshawa's Second Marsh on June 26, 1977 (Speirs, 1979: 20). Devitt (1967: 30) *et al* found 11 nests on Clarke's Is. off Collingwood on June 11, 1967, the first for Simcoe Co. Quilliam (1965: 30) mentioned a heronry of about 20,000 birds on Wolfe Is., about 1954 and another of about 100 nests on Pigeon Is. on June 6, 1961. MacLulich (1938: 4) saw an immature near Brule Lake,

Algonquin Park, on July 29 and Aug. 17, 1938 and reported a heronry observed by Mark Robinson at Blackbear Lake in 1913, that was destroyed by fire in May, 1914. C.E. Garton noted one at the Slate Is., Lake Superior, in summer, 1957 (Gunn, 1957: 402).

AUTUMN: Louise Lawrence saw one at Pimisi Bay on Sept. 7, 1945, our only record for the North Bay region (Speirs & Speirs, 1947: 24). Devitt (1967: 30) gave Sept. 13, 1942 at Holland Marsh as his latest Simcoe Co. record. Quilliam (1965: 30) gave Oct. 5 as the average departure date from Kingston, with the latest record on Nov. 25, 1958 by George Stirrett. George A. Scott had a maximum of 50 at Oshawa on Sept. 14, 1957: his median departure date was Sept. 30 and my latest date for Whitby was Oct. 29, 1977 (Speirs, 1979: 20). This species was tallied on 30 of 35 field days of the Toronto Ornithological Club held in the Pickering-Whitby area. Saunders (1947: 359) gave Sept. 25 as his 9-year average departure date from Toronto. Stirrett (1973d: 15) had one at Pelee as late as Nov. 1 (as well as the three December dates noted above).

**MEASUREMENTS:**
*Length:* 23-26 ins.
(Palmer, 1962: 472).
*Wingspread:* to 45 ins.
(Palmer, 1962: 472).
*Weight:* 26 to 36 oz.
(Palmer, 1962: 472).

**REFERENCES:**
Middleton, A.L.A. 1978 Feeding at a trap-net by Black-crowned Night Herons. Can. Field-Nat., 92: (2): 196. Five flew out to trap nets set in Lake Huron off Sarnia on the evenings of July 10 and 11, 1971.
Richards, James M. 1978 Black-crowned Night Heron (*Nycticorax nycticorax* nesting in the Regional Municipality of Durham, Ontario. Ont. Field Biologist, 32: (1): 45-46. On June 26, 1977, 11 nests were found at Oshawa's Second Marsh by JMR.
Sheppard, R.W. 1944 Black-crowned Night Heron nesting in Lincoln County, Ontario. Can. Field-Nat., 58: (2): 31-33. About 500 nests in a heronry near Port Weller was visited on July 1, 1943. This account gives a graphic description of activities of young and fishing methods of adults,

BLACK-CROWNED NIGHT-HERON

CHRISTMAS COUNTS:
Average number per 100
Party-Hours 1968-1977.

50

as well as a summary of
other Ontario colonies
known at that time (at
Bradley's Marsh, Walpole
Is., Pelee, Byron (near
London), Hamilton,
Toronto, Beverley Lake
(Leeds Co.), and Ottawa).

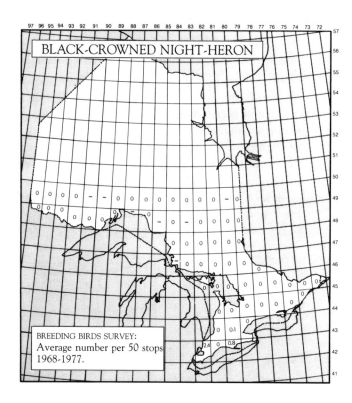

BLACK-CROWNED NIGHT-HERON

BREEDING BIRDS SURVEY:
Average number per 50 stops
1968-1977.

# YELLOW-CROWNED NIGHT-HERON
## *Nycticorax violaceus*   (Linnaeus)

This is an exceedingly rare straggler in Ontario. The immatures are so similar to the young Black-crowned Night-Heron that they may be overlooked (or misidentified).

IDENTIFICATION: Adults with their black head, contrasting with the yellowish white crowns and cheeks are quite distinctive. The young are very similar to the young of Black-crowned Night-Herons but differ chiefly in shorter, stouter bill and longer legs—the whole foot and part of the tarsus project beyond the tail in flight, not just the toes as in Black-crowned young.

WINTER:

SPRING: Lawrence E. Hicks saw an adult near a nest on East Sister Island in Lake Erie on May 23, 1954 (Baillie, 1955: 254). One was reported at Wheatley by Norman Chesterfield and Wilfred Botham from Apr. 13 to 15, 1964 (Kelley, 1978: 14). The 1974 Check-List of Rondeau Birds lists this as rare there in spring. An adult was seen at McNab near Lake Ontario, on May 7, 1950 by the Axtells, Nathan and Seeber (Beardslee & Mitchell, 1965: 101).

SUMMER: An immature was studied at rest and in flight near Wainfleet on July 27 and Aug. 24, 1952 and perhaps the same bird at Mud Lake on Aug. 10 and 18, 1952 (Beardslee & Mitchell, 1965: 101). Movies were made of it. Fleming (1906: 447) recorded a specimen taken near Toronto by John Maughan on Aug. 15, 1898, an immature birds . . . see Auk, 23: 220. 1906. George A. Scott watched an adult in full breeding plumage at Oshawa on June 5, 1977 (Speirs, 1979: 21).

AUTUMN: A documented sighting of an immature was made at Amos Ponds, Pickering, on Sept. 13, 1964 during a field day of the Toronto Ornithological Club (Speirs, 1979: 21). Another was reported on the TOC field day on Sept. 16, 1945. Sally Thompson reported one at Holiday Beach, Essex Co., from Sept. 22 to Oct. 1, 1964 (Kelley, 1978: 14).

**MEASUREMENTS:**
*Length:* 22 to 28 ins.
(Palmer, 1962: 484).
*Wingspread:* 40 to 44 ins.
(Palmer, 1962: 484).
*Weight:* 8 ♂ averaged
716 g. 7 ♀ averaged
649 g. (Dunning, 1984: 3).

# WHITE IBIS  *Eudocimus albus*  (Linnaeus)

This is normally a bird of coastal swamps from the Carolinas south to Florida and west to Texas (and southward). It is an accidental in Ontario.

IDENTIFICATION: The adults are white with red legs, face and downcurved bill and black tips to the wings, unlike any other North American bird. The young are similar in shape but are dark brownish gray above with white belly, very similar to young of the Scarlet Ibis but with more whitish speckling on the head.

WINTER:

SPRING:

SUMMER: James, McLaren and Barlow (1976: 11) mention a summer, 1965 specimen from Long Point.

AUTUMN: Two were seen at Clayton, Lanark Co. on Oct. 13, 1955. One of these was shot and became a specimen in the collection of A.E. Bourguignon of Ottawa (Baillie, 1957: 2). One was seen at Pelee on Sept. 27, 1970 by G. Van Vliet, J.P. Kleiman and others (Goodwin 1971: 50).

**MEASUREMENTS:**
*Length:* 21 1/2 to 27 1/2
ins. (Palmer, 1962: 522).
*Wingspread:* to 38 ins.
(Palmer, 1962: 522).
*Weight:* to 2 lb. (Palmer,
1962: 522).

# SCARLET IBIS   *Eudocimus ruber*   (Linnaeus)

This is a bird of tropical swamps of northern South America, accidental anywhere in North America, including Ontario.

IDENTIFICATION: Similar in size and shape to the White Ibis of Florida swamps, but bright scarlet, if adult, and dirty brown if immature.

WINTER:

SPRING:

SUMMER:

AUTUMN: Stirrett (1973d: 16) reported one at Pelee from Sept. 13 to Oct. 2, 1937. He included it as a hypothetical species, not because of any doubt as to its proper identity but because it may have been an escape from some aviary. He pointed out however that another was reported from Ridgefield Lakes, Conn. the previous week (Sept. 5, 6, 1937 . . . see Bird-Lore, 39: (6): 469 by Ed. Sullivan.

**MEASUREMENTS:**
same as White Ibis          *Length:*
(Palmer, 1962: 530).        *Wingspread: Weight:*

# GLOSSY IBIS  *Plegadis falcinellus*  (Linnaeus)

Palmer (1962: 515) considered the Glossy Ibis and White-faced Ibis just subspecies with the white-faced subspecies typical of western North America while the glossy is almost world-wide in occurrence. It will be considered as one species here and usually quite rare in Ontario.

IDENTIFICATION: At a distance it looks like a big, black curlew, flying with neck and legs outstretched, alternating direct flapping flight with long glides, then dropping down into marshy cover.

WINTER:

SPRING: Kelley (1978: 14-15) reported two in Lake St. Clair marshes, one on May 22, 1954 and one May 18 to 22, 1960; single birds in 1967 at Pelee on May 20 and at Bradleys' Marsh on May 21, with a maximum of 18 at Bradley's from May 4-10, 1971. Stirrett (1973b: 13) had single birds at Pelee on Apr. 9, 1966, May 13, 1962, and May 13, 1963 and 18 from May 9 to 13, 1971. One was seen at Dunnville Marsh on May 25, 1947 by Nathan, Filor and Pause (Beardslee and Mitchell, 1965: 104). Tozer and Richards (1974: 68-69) cited several interesting records in the Whitby, Oshawa, Bowmanville area: the earliest on May 8, 1965 when I saw three at Lynde Creek Marsh, Whitby: the big year was 1971 when George A. Scott saw 11 at Oshawa's Second Marsh on May 23 and Paul Bridges saw 7 at Bowmanville on May 30: Ron Tozer with Edgerton Pegg had found 30 at Stein's Marsh, near Pelee on May 8 the same spring. Speirs (1979: 24) gave several spring records from Cranberry Marsh, Whitby, by Naomi LeVay and others and one as far north as Gamebridge on May 30, 1970 by Gordon Bellerby. David Elder found one in a flooded field a few miles north of Angus on May 1, 1960; seen by others until May 8 (Devitt, 1967: 32). Lloyd Beamer and others saw one in a grassy pool at Meaford on May 15, 1940 after a violent thunderstorm the night before. T. Hince reported one at Marathon on May 19, 1983 (James, 1984: 55).

SUMMER: Naomi LeVay had several summer sightings at Cranberry Marsh: with Alf Bunker I photographed one of these there on Aug. 11, 1962 and the most recent sighting there was by G. Graves on July 30, 1978 (Speirs, 1979: 24).

AUTUMN: Two were shot in late October or early November 1828 at the Narrows at the north end of Lake Simcoe by an Indian and eventually sent to Charles Fothergill who wrote a detailed description of them (Devitt, 1967: 31-32).

**MEASUREMENTS:**
*Length:* 19-26 ins.
(Palmer, 1962: 516).
*Wingspread:* to about 38
ins. (Palmer, 1962: 516).
*Weight:* to about 28 oz.
(Palmer, 1962: 516).

# WOOD STORK   *Mycteria americana*   Linnaeus

The only true stork in North America, breeding from the coast of Georgia south into South America. Accidental in Ontario.

**IDENTIFICATION:** Adults are white, except the flight feathers and tail which are black, and the bald head and beak which are blackish. The beak is stout, downturned at the tip. Young are gray, rather than white.

**WINTER:**

**SPRING:**

**SUMMER:** Barlow (1966: 183) mentioned three late summer birds, two of them specimens: a sight record concerned a bird wounded at Port Huron, Michigan, which apparently flew across the river to Sarnia where it was seen, probably in August, some time prior to 1912. A dead bird was found at Dorcas Bay, Bruce Co., by Keith Quirk on Aug. 4, 1965 and is preserved as a skeleton at ROM (95204). The other specimen (ROM 76069) was collected by A. Strang at Apple Hill, Glengarry Co., on Aug. 2, 1948.

**AUTUMN:** Fleming (1913: 226) reported a fall record based on a drawing of a dead bird, shot near Simcoe in November, 1892. W.E. Hurlburt observed one at Hamilton on Nov. 9, 1950 (Baillie, 1951: 13). Following Hurricane "Carol" one was found on Sept. 1, 1954 at Little Cataraqui Marsh, near Kingston, by John Cartwright and W.H. Moulton: it remained there until Sept. 12 and was seen by many members of the Kingston Field Naturalists (Quilliam, 1965: 32).

**MEASUREMENTS:**
*Length:* 35 to 45 ins.
(Palmer, 1962: 509)
*Wingspread:* to 66 ins.
(Palmer, 1962: 509)
*Weight:* 9 ♂ averaged
2702 g. one ♀ weighed
2050 g. (Dunning,
1984: 3).

# FULVOUS WHISTLING-DUCK
## *Dendrocygna bicolor* (Vieillot)

This is a semitropical species found in North America chiefly from southern California through Mexico and Louisiana to Cuba: accidental in Ontario.

IDENTIFICATION: This is a long-legged, long-necked species. The *bicolor* in its specific name refers to the chiefly yellowish or buffy brown body with very dark brown flight and tail feathers. A blackish stripe extending from the crown down the back of the neck, a whitish stripe along the sides below the wings and whitish tail coverts add class to the otherwise obscure plumage. In flight the slow, gooselike wingbeats and the long legs extending beyond the tail are good field marks.

WINTER: One was shot at the Big Point Club, south of Mitchell's Bay, Lake St. Clair, by L.E. Roberts on Dec. 8, 1960 and later presented to the Royal Ontario Museum by W.H. Carrick (Barlow, 1966: 184).

SPRING: R.D. McRae and A. Wormington saw one at Pelee from May 3 - 10, 1979 (James, 1984: 55). One was found at Fanshaw Lake, near London, on Apr. 7, 1963 by Brian Hobbs and Jack Laughton and was seen by others until early May (Woodford, 1963: 400).

SUMMER:

AUTUMN: Two were photographed at Yacht Harbour, Welland Co. (now Niagara R.M.) on Aug. 20, 1962 (Barlow, 1966: 184). Three were seen at Frenchman Bay, Pickering, on Nov. 27, 1962, by Tom Klein and one of these was collected, mounted and presented to the Royal Ontario Museum (Speirs, 1979: 32).

**MEASUREMENTS:**
*Length:* 17 1/2 to 20 ins.
(Palmer, 1976: 15).
*Wingspread:* to 37 ins.
(Palmer, 1976: 15).
*Weight:* seldom reaches 2
1b. (Palmer, 1976: 15).

# TUNDRA SWAN   *Cygnus columbianus*   (Ord)

In Ontario most observers connect this species with the great springtime concentrations at Long Point and elsewhere along the north shore of Lake Erie. North of this migration corridor this species is generally uncommon to rare.

IDENTIFICATION: It is smaller than the Mute Swan and carries its head atop a stiffly erect neck (when not grubbing for food on the bottom, under water). It has a black bill, usually (but not always) with a yellow spot at its base. Normally all white, the head and neck may be stained brown. Young birds are brownish-gray with pinkish base to the bill, very similar to young Mute and Trumpeter Swans.

WINTER: They are fairly common from Pelee to Long Point in early winter (until freezeup); rare along the shores of lakes Ontario and Huron, with three as far north as Sault Ste. Marie on the 1971 Christmas count, on Dec. 18. Stirrett (1973a: 13) gave Dec. 12 as his latest date for Pelee when 18 were noted but four were found there on the Dec. 24, 1970 Christmas count. One was found on the TOC Waterfowl Inventory on Jan. 7, 1979. Speirs (1979: 26) detailed four winter records for the Whitby-Oshawa waterfront. Quilliam (1965: 34) had only one winter record for Kingston (on Jan. 1, 1952). Devitt (1967: 33) cited 4 winter records for Simcoe Co. Sheppard (1945: 156) wrote that swans have occurred on the Niagara River as late as Dec. 24 and as early as mid-January, but this is rare.

SPRING: Stirrett (1973b: 14) reported 100 at Pelee as early as Mar. 7, a peak of 200 there on Mar. 21 and 8 at late as May 22. Kelley (1978: 15) estimated 23,000 at Wallaceburg in late March, 1974. Fleming (1930: 66-67) wrote about the spring flights at Kingsville in the 1920's, usually arriving about Mar. 22 (but as early as Mar. 11, 1927) and leaving between Apr. 5 and 10. Sheppard (1945: 155) stated that swans are most apt to appear on the Niagara River between Mar. 10 and 25 when several hundred may occur. Beardslee and Mitchell (1965: 108-110) gave a vivid account of swan kills at Niagara Falls chiefly in late March and early April, which has been going on since the time of the early explorers. On the Lake Ontario waterfront of Ontario Co. the largest spring flock of 58 was seen on Frenchman Bay on Mar. 23, 1968 by Charles Long (Speirs, 1979: 26): most years none are seen. Quilliam (1965: 33) gave her 17-year average for arrivals at Kingston as Apr. 5 and the largest number as 6. Devitt (1967: 33) gave Mar. 30 as the average arrival date at Barrie with the earliest on Mar. 10, 1957 and the largest number as 14 at Matchedash Bay on Apr. 18, 1964. Beamer's largest flock at Meaford was 27 on Mar. 28, 1951: his earliest there 9 on Feb. 24, 1952 and his latest one on Apr. 19, 1954. Dennison (1980: 14) gave Apr. 24 as the time of spring passage at Sault Ste. Marie. Skeel and Bondrup-Nielsen (1978: 153) reported two at Otter Cove, Pukaskwa, on May 1, 1975. Denis (1961: 2) gave Apr. 15, 1945 as the earliest arrival at Thunder Bay and Apr. 27 as the average. Lee (1978: 19) arrived at Big Trout Lake on May 29, 1975, too late to see swans, which were reported to be common spring migrants there by local residents.

SUMMER: Not recorded on any of the Breeding Bird Survey routes. There are about 8 records of one to five birds seen during the summer months between Pickering and Oshawa (Speirs, 1979: 26). On July 31, 1949 an injured bird was found near Alliston by J.S. Ellis and another bird was seen June 3, June 4 and July 9, 1967 by three observers between Marl Lake and Kempenfeldt Bay (Devitt, 1967: 32-33). Skeel and Bondrup-

Nielsen (1978: 153) had two sightings at Pukaskwa, single birds on July 21 and Aug. 15, 1973. Cringan (1953: 1) reported a June 3 observation at Sioux Lookout by J. Macfie. Peck (1976: 10) cited two Ontario breeding records: at Cape Henrietta Maria on July 22, 1973 (Lumsden) and Hudson Bay at mouth of Niskibi River, west of Ft. Severn, in Aug. 1974 (Prevett), both photographed.

AUTUMN: Beamer noted one at Meaford on Nov. 19, 1940 and reported that E. Durkin saw four or five about the same time at Craigleith. Quilliam (1965: 34) noted 2 near Kingston on Oct. 16, 1953 and 4 there on Nov. 19, 1961. Tozer and Richards (1974: 70) had two fall records for Lake Scugog: Sept. 30, 1908 and Oct. 9, 1965. There are fall sightings from the Pickering, Whitby and Oshawa marshes from Sept. 8 to the end of November with the largest flock (26 or 27) at Frenchman Bay on Nov. 15, 1975 by David O'Brien. Saunders and Dale (1933: 171) reported several flocks over London in early November and suggested an increase in numbers during the 1920's. Ussher (1965: 3) gave earliest, average and latest fall dates for Rondeau as Oct. 12, Nov. 1 and Dec. 8. Stirrett (1973d: 16) reported four at Pelee as early as Aug. 16 and a maximum of 10 on Nov. 9.

**MEASUREMENTS:**
*Length:* 47 to 54 ins.
(Palmer, 1976: 72).
*Wingspread:* 83 ins.
(Pough, 1951: 63).
*Weight:* usually 12-18 lb.
(Palmer, 1976: 72).

**REFERENCE:**
Lumsden, Harry G. 1975
The Whistling Swan in
James Bay and the
southern region of Hudson
Bay. Arctic, 28: (3): 194-
200.

# TRUMPETER SWAN   *Cygnus buccinator*   Richardson

This is a western species, now breeding from the Cypress Hills of Saskatchewan west to B.C. and north to Alaska: not found in Ontario in this century, until the recent introductions.

IDENTIFICATION: Distinguished from the Mute Swan by its black bill (orange in adult Mute Swans and dark purplish gray in young) and lack of knob on bill and straight "ramrod" neck posture. From the Tundra Swan it differs in having no yellow at base of bill (usually present in Tundra Swan) and in straight (not dished in) profile of bill and forehead. Young birds have gray rather than white plumage and pinkish bill as in other species but often have yellow webs in the feet (not black as in the young of Tundra Swans). Note that some Tundra Swans lack the yellow spot at the back of the beak. See Godfrey (1966: 46-47) for positive identification of dead specimens.

Fleming (1906: 446) wrote: "There are no recent records, but Prof. Hincks described in 1864 a new swan *Cygnus passmori* taken here, which was really a young Trumpeter: and between 1863 and 1866 he was able to get six local birds to examine.[1] There are two specimens in the collection at Toronto University that were no doubt taken here."

WINTER:

SPRING:

SUMMER:

AUTUMN:

**MEASUREMENTS:**
*Length:* to 59 ins. (Palmer, 1976: 55).
*Wingspread:* 85 ins. (Palmer, 1976: 55).
*Weight:* usually 18-27 lbs. (Palmer, 1976: 55).

*Note:* The Ontario Ministry of Natural Resources, under the direction of Harry Lumsden, started a programme to re-introduce Trumpeter Swans to Ontario in 1982. Mute Swans have been used to act as foster parents, incubating eggs flown in from western Canada and put in their nests to replace the Mute Swan eggs. Young were raised at Ontario Place, Toronto, and at Cranberry Marsh, Whitby. These have been seen along the Lake Ontario lakefront from Whitby to Port Credit in fall and two marked birds migrated to Chesapeake Bay where they wintered, remaining there as late as Apr. 5, but seen back in Ontario by Apr. 7. One was found dead at Burgessville, Oxford Co. Ont., on May 24. Margaret Wilson and I saw one with wing tag #23 at Whitby Harbour as recently as Nov. 19, 1984. This very tame bird had been raised at Ontario Place in 1982.

**REFERENCES:**
Proc. Linnaean Society of London, Zoology, VIII, 1864. 1-7 and IX, 1868. 298-300.
Alison, R.M. 1975 Some previously unpublished records of Trumpeter Swans in Ontario. Can. Field-Nat., 89: (3): 311-313. This cites several sight and specimen records from Hudson and James Bay and the region between Toronto and Lake St. Clair, all prior to 1900, suggesting former abundance.
Lumsden, Harry G. 1984 The pre-settlement breeding distribution of Trumpeter, *Cygnus buccinator*, and Tundra Swans, *C. columbianus*, in eastern Canada. Can. Field-Naturalist, 98: (4): 415-424.

# MUTE SWAN   *Cygnus olor*   (Gmelin)

Mute Swans have been introduced from the Old World and are now breeding in several cattail marshes in southern Ontario. They build massive nesting platforms with a ramp leading down to the water.

IDENTIFICATION:   This is a large swan that carries its head on an S-shaped neck and in the adult has an orange bill with conspicuous knob on it: on the immatures the black knob is missing and the bill is grayish purple. Some cygnets have white down and others gray (even in the same family); they accompany the adults for several months.

WINTER:   On the 1968-1977 Christmas counts they were found as far north as Presqu'ile and Kettle Point but were rare except in western Lake Ontario. George A. Scott found one along the Oshawa waterfront as early as Dec. 6, 1953 (Speirs, 1979: 35). On the midwinter waterfowl inventories along the Toronto waterfront this species was first reported in Jan., 1964: numbers were less than 10 until 1977 when 15 showed up: they increased to 37 in 1979. Single birds were seen on the 1968 Christmas counts at Toronto and Long Point: in 1969 they appeared at Hamilton and Peel-Halton and in 1971 at Pickering. Some remain all winter if open water is available.

SPRING:   Kelley (1978: 15) reported a pair with 5 cygnets at Bradley's Marsh on May 25, 1969. Stirrett (1973b: 13) mentioned only one spring record for Pelee: Apr. 9 to the end of May, 1965. Two were seen at Rockhouse Point, Lake Erie, on May 10, 1962 by Rosche, Able *et al* (Beardslee and Mitchell, 1965: 107). J.L. Baillie noted one at Oshawa as early as May 24, 1954 (probably the same bird seen by Scott the previous winter). On Mar. 12, 1975 we counted 14 off Whitby (Speirs, 1979: 25). W. Geiger reported one as far north as Lake Scugog on Mar. 31, 1973 (Goodwin, 1973: 766). Peck (1966: 43) photographed eight 10-day old cygnets at Georgetown on May 24, 1958, the first published breeding record for Ontario.

SUMMER:   None were tallied on any of the Breeding Bird Surveys from 1968-1977. However, feral birds have been breeding in southern Ontario marshes since at least 1958 (Peck, 1966: 43). Stirrett (1973c: 13) noted one through the summer of 1965 at Pelee. Long (1972: 40) saw five young with adults in marshes at the mouth of Duffin Creek. Pickering, during the summer of 1972 and they have nested there frequently since that time. C.M. Sharpe reported three on Lake Scugog during August, 1970 and one there in mid-July, 1971 (Tozer and Richards, 1974: 69).

AUTUMN:   T. Cheskey reported the species at Lake Superior Prov. Park, Algoma from Sept. 2-4, 1982 (James, 1984: 55). During the breeding season the birds are highly territorial but aggregations occur in the fall: on Oct. 29, 1977 we counted 20 in a flock off Cranberry Marsh, Whitby (Speirs, 1979: 25). Stirrett (1973d: 16) had three fall records for Pelee, one as late as Nov. 7.

**MEASUREMENTS:**
*Length:* 54-62 ins.
(Palmer, 1976: 38)
*Wingspread:* 82-94 ins.
(Palmer, 1976: 38)
*Weight:* 18-24 lbs. usually

(Palmer, 1976: 38). one ♂
49.5 lbs.

**REFERENCE:**
Peck, George K. 1966 First
published breeding record
of Mute Swan for Ontario.
Ontario Field Biologist,
No. 20: 43.

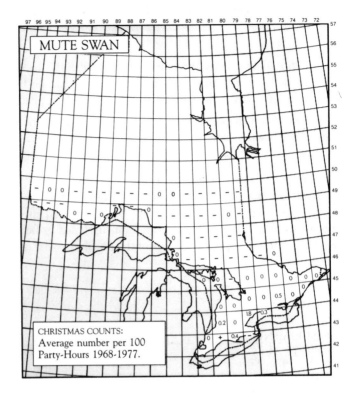

MUTE SWAN

CHRISTMAS COUNTS:
Average number per 100
Party-Hours 1968-1977.

# BEAN GOOSE   *Anser fabalis*   (Latham)

This is normally a goose breeding from Spitzbergen to eastern Greenland, wintering in the British Isles: in Ontario it may occur as an escape from domestic stock or as a very rare straggler. This is the Pink-footed Goose of European authors.

IDENTIFICATION: A small grayish goose with dark neck, with pink feet and bicoloured bill, black at the tip and base with a pinkish midsection.

WINTER:

SPRING: James Savage and Harold Mitchell identified three in Port Colborne Harbour on Apr. 9, 1933 in company with 60 "Whistling Swans" and a "Blue Goose", with which they flew off when disturbed. Savage took moving pictures of them and compared with specimens in the Royal Ontario Museum. Included in Beardslee and Mitchell (1965: 120) as a "hypothetical" species because of the possibility that they were feral birds from domestic stock.

SUMMER:

AUTUMN:

**MEASUREMENTS:**
*Length:* 24-35 ins.
(Palmer, 1976: 111)
Wingspread:
*Weight:* 1.90-3.35 kg. (av.
2.77 for 750 ♂) (Palmer,
1976: 113).
1.81-3.15 kg. (av. 2.52 for
796 ♂) (Palmer,
1976: 113).

# GREATER WHITE-FRONTED GOOSE
*Anser albifrons* (Scopoli)

This is a circum-polar breeder, wintering in Mexico and the Gulf States, rare in Ontario at any season.

IDENTIFICATION: Adults have white forehead (hence the name white-fronted) and grey belly splotched with black (hence the nickname "speckle-belly"). Look also for pinkish bill and orange feet. Young of the year lack both the white forehead and splotched belly, are olive coloured except for whitish belly, have orange-yellow to gray bill and dingy yellow feet.

WINTER: George A. Scott watched one feeding with Black Ducks at Oshawa's Second Marsh on Feb. 4, 10, 17 and 18, 1962 (Speirs, 1979: 29), noting the white forehead, pink bill, speckled belly (Tozer and Richards, 1974: 73). One was reported at Sault Ste. Marie during the Christmas count period in 1973 (Dennison, 1980: 14).

SPRING: Stirrett (1973b: 14) had a Mar. 20 record from Pelee and one was observed at Jack Miner's sanctuary from Mar. 20 to 28, 1971 (Kelly, 1978: 16) D.V. Weseloh reported one at Whitby on Apr. 9-10, 1982 (James, 1983:9). Two were taken at Port Perry on Apr. 15, 1884, one of them examined by J.H. Fleming (Fleming, 1906: 453). Weir & Quilliam (1980: 32) gave an Apr. 16 date for Kingston. Denis (1961: 2) gave Apr. 12, 1945 as the earliest date for Thunder Bay and Apr. 27 as the average arrival date there.

SUMMER:

AUTUMN: James, McLaren and Barlow (1976: 11) reported one on the Moose River on Oct. 1, 1966. One turned up at Jack Miner's sanctuary on Oct. 11, 1970 (Kelley, 1978: 16). M. Oldham and A. Wormington reported 2 adults at Kingsville from Nov. 13-27, (James, 1984: 55). There are also two undated records: McIlwraith (1894: 97) had an imm. ♂ in this collection shot at St. Clair flats and another was shot by F. Orford on Barrie Island in 1969, now in the Laurentian University collection (Nicholson, 1972: 13).

**MEASUREMENTS:**
*Length:* 25-34 ins.
(Palmer, 1976: 89).
*Wingspread:* 50-65 ins.
(Palmer, 1976: 89): few greater than 58".
*Weight:* 4 1/2 to 9 lb.
(Palmer, 1976: 89): few greater than 7 lb.

# SNOW GOOSE   *Chen caerulescens*   (Linnaeus)

This is a bird with two distinct colour morphs, formerly considered two species (Snow Goose and Blue Goose). They are tundra breeders and are much more common to the west and east of Ontario than here. However, the numbers breeding in the vicinity of Cape Henrietta Maria are increasing rapidly and we may expect more migrants to appear in the south.

IDENTIFICATION:   The Snow morph with its all white plumage, except for black wing tips, is unlike any other wild goose but might be confused with escapes of some white domestic geese, which however lack the black wing-tips and have orange bill and legs (not pink as in adult Snows). The Blue morph has a white head and neck, topping a gray-blue body. Young are a "dirty gray" with varying amounts of white.

WINTER:   On the 1968-1977 Christmas counts, they were seen north to Deep River and Sault Ste. Marie in numbers less than 10 per 100 party-hours. Ussher (1965: 3) had a Dec. 8 record for a Snow at Rondeau. Speirs (1979: 30-31) documented several winter sightings for the Ontario County waterfront: eight (1 Blue adult, 2 Snow adults and 5 immatures) were still present on Cranberry Marsh, Whitby, on Dec. 1, 1980. Quilliam (1965: 36) reported two near Kingston on Dec. 1, 1963. A.J. Mitchener saw one Blue at Collingwood on Dec. 4, 1960 (Devitt, 1967: 35). Beamer had 8 Snows at Meaford on Dec. 16, 1948.

SPRING:   Stirrett (1973b: 14) had the earliest (9) at Pelee on Mar. 16 and the latest one on May 9. One Snow was taken on May 1, 1887 at Hyde Park, near London, by J. Wallis (Saunders and Dale, 1933: 172). Ussher (1965: 3-4) had Rondeau records from Mar. 6 to May 6. Earl Lemon saw one flying with 11 swans near West Lorne on Apr. 2, 1949 (Brooman, 1954: 8-9). One was photographed at Port Colborne on Apr. 9, 1933 by James Savage (Beardslee and Mitchell, 1965: 122). Speirs (1979: 30-31) had spring records for Ontario Co. for Snows from Mar. 12 to May 23 and Mar. 1 to May 16 for Blues. Quilliam (1965: 35) had 6 spring records for Kingston, 20 as early as Mar. 15, 1960 and one as late as May 3, 1958. Devitt (1967: 34-35) reported a light movement through Simcoe Co. between Apr. 5 (1958) and May 2 (1938). Beamer had a few in spring at Meaford, one Snow as early as Mar. 24, 1938, a maximum of 12 Snows on Apr. 20, 1940 and one Blue as late as May 14, 1949. Denis (1961: 2-3) gave Apr. 16, 1952 as the earliest arrival at Thunder Bay with the average for Blues on Apr. 24 with Apr. 18, 1953 and Apr. 25 as the corresponding dates for Snows. J. Satterly saw 30 at Jaab Lake (50°10' N. 82°08' W) on May 30, 1949. Manning (1952: 20) wrote that large numbers arrive in James Bay from Apr. 25 to 30 before departure for Winisk: he saw 300 Snows and 400 Blues at Shipsands Is., near Moosonee, on May 31, 1947. Cringan (1953) reported that both morphs were first seen at Sioux Lookout by Joe Wesley on Apr. 30, 1953. Cringan (1950: 3) called it an abundant spring migrant in the Nikip Lake area, arriving at Round Lake in late Apr. or early May, appearing later in May in great numbers on the ice. He quoted Elsey who gave May 13 as the arrival date in the Asheweig area with a peak on May 20, 1950. Lee (1978: 19) was told by the inhabitants of Big Trout Lake that it is an abundant spring migrant there but they had all gone by the time he arrived there in late May.

SUMMER:   Speirs (1979: 30-31) had four June records for the Whitby-Oshawa marshes.

J. Satterly observed a lone bird at Dinorwic Lake on June 8, 1940 (Snyder, 1953: 50). Smith (1957: 167) flushed an immature bird from the grassy edge of Porcupine Lake, near Timmins, on June 19, 1953. Manning (1952: 21) saw about 20 flightless Snows and the same number of Blues swimming in the sea off Cape Henrietta Maria on July 26, 1947. Peck (1972: 337) documented breeding there and cited H. Lumsden that the flock had increased to about 40,000 birds by 1970. Schueler, Baldwin and Rising (1974: 142) found none at Moosonee or Hawley Lake, had some at Attawapiskat and Winisk and found them common at Fort Albany in summer.

AUTUMN: Manning (1952: 20) saw about 600 in 9 hours at Shipsands Is. on Sept. 9 and 11, 1950 and he quoted Kelsall and Stirrett's estimate of 40,000 between Moose Factory and Attawapiskat on Oct. 3, 1948. I saw at least 40 Snows flying south over Timmins on Oct. 26, 1935. D.H. Elder saw his first fall birds at Atikokan on Oct. 6, 1978 and Oct. 7, 1979. A very tame Blue was noted at Eau Claire from Nov. 11-15, 1944 by Dorothy MacKenzie and Louise Lawrence (Speirs and Speirs, 1947: 26). Nicholson (1972: 14) reported 1670 on Oct. 19, 1969 at Manitoulin. Beamer noted large numbers at Meaford most years from 1938 to 1955: the earliest were 18 Blues on Oct. 3, 1945; the maximum estimate was 6400 on Nov. 7, 1945 and the latest was one Blue on Nov. 24, 1938. Devitt (1967: 34-35) had Simcoe Co. records from Oct. 9 (1951) to early November. Weir & Quilliam (1980: 32) gave Sept. 6 as the earliest fall date for Kingston with Oct. 12 as the average arrival date. There are fall records from Sept. 14 to the end of November in Ontario Co. including a flock of 60 Blues over Brock Twp. on Nov. 5, 1967 (Speirs, 1979: 30-31) and over 200 at the mouth of Duffin Creek from Nov. 20-27, 1970 (Long, 1972: 40). Snyder and Shortt (1936: 175-177) described the 1935 flight through Ontario as "unprecedented" with many thousands over Toronto on Oct. 26; 14,000 at Hamilton, leaving Nov. 1 according to George North, "myriads" at Niagara Falls, etc. Beamer (1935: 137) had a big flight at Meaford that year from Oct. 16 to Nov. 1, mainly on Oct. 27-28 after a northerly gale on the 27th. Beardslee and Mitchell (1965: 121, 123) estimated 10,000 Blues and 1000 Snows above Niagara Falls on Oct. 27, 1935. Sheppard (1945: 156) also mentioned this big flight and a group of about 1000 at Niagara Falls on Oct. 18, 1936. Brooman (1954: 8-9) cited several records for Elgin Co., including a flock of 72 Blues and 3 Snows on Oct. 16, 1952 near West Lorne and 8 Blues off New Glasgow on Nov. 13, 1949. Saunders and Dale (1933: 172) had two fall records for London, a Blue shot Nov. 15, 1888 and two Snows (one shot) on Nov. 1 or 2, 1887. Ussher (1965: 3-4) had Rondeau records from Oct. 19 to Nov. 30 and considered it uncommon and irregular there. Stirrett (1973d: 16) had the earliest flock of 22 at Pelee on Oct. 7, a maximum of 100 on Nov. 3 and the latest one on Nov. 11.

**MEASUREMENTS:**
Length: 26-30 ins.
(Palmer, 1976: 122).
Wingspread: 53-64 ins.
(Palmer, 1976: 122).
Weight: usually 6 1/2 to
10 lb. (♂ av. 10 lb.)
(Palmer, 1976: 122).

**REFERENCES:**
Beamer, L.H. 1935 Great
migration of Snow Geese
in the neighbourhood of

Meaford, Ontario. Can.
Field-Nat., 49: (8): 137.
 Snyder, L.L. and T.M.
Shortt 1936 A summary of
recent events pertaining to
the Blue and Lesser Snow
Goose. Auk, 53: (2): 173-
177.

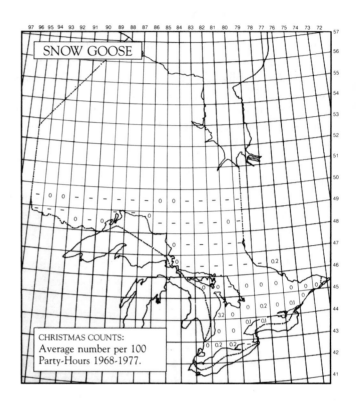

SNOW GOOSE

CHRISTMAS COUNTS:
Average number per 100
Party-Hours 1968-1977.

# ROSS' GOOSE   *Chen rossii*   (Cassin)

This tiny white goose appears to be increasing along the Hudson Bay coast of Ontario, probably breeding at Cape Henrietta Maria among the Snow Geese (H. Lumsden, pers. comm.).

**IDENTIFICATION:**   This is a Mallard-sized goose, with stubby bill without a "grinning patch" (as in Snow Geese): breeding adults have warty outgrowths at the base of the upper mandible. Plumage is white except black tips to the wings. Legs and feet are pink: bill varies seasonally from scarlet with greenish warts to pink with grayish warts.

**WINTER:**

**SPRING:**

**SUMMER:**   Peck (1976: 10) reported the capture, photographing and banding of a pair and three pre-fledging juveniles on July 29, 1975 at the mouth of the Brant River at Hudson Bay by Prevett and Johnson.

**AUTUMN:**

**MEASUREMENTS:**
*Length:* 21-26 ins.
(Palmer, 1976: 154).
*Wingspread:* 47-53 ins.
(Palmer, 1976: 154).
*Weight:* usually 2 1/4 to 3
1/4 lbs. (Palmer,
1976: 154).
*Note:* Palmer (1976: 154)
calls it *Anser rossii* Cassin.
He also includes the Snow
Goose in the genus *Anser*.

# BRANT  *Branta bernicla*  (Linnaeus)

Brant usually winter along the Atlantic and Pacific coasts and breed in the high Arctic. They are usually uncommon to rare in Ontario waters but large numbers may be seen, often well offshore on the Great Lakes, on a few occasions, and stragglers may occur at any season. They tend to be late migrants in spring, probably because their Arctic breeding grounds are frozen until well into June.

IDENTIFICATION:  They superficially resemble small Canada Geese but lack the white cheeks and chin, showing only a diffuse white marking high on the neck. They have rather stubby beaks and tend to mass tightly together in offshore rafts.

WINTER:  On the 1968-1977 Christmas counts there were records of four per 100 party-hours at Blenheim in 1968, one at Toronto in 1975 and five at Kingston in 1977, none elsewhere. Beardslee and Mitchell (1965: 118) reported one at Crystal Beach as late as Dec. 7, 1953. Frances Westman saw two at Allandale on Dec. 5, 1956 and one there on Dec. 4, 1960 (Devitt, 1967: 34).

SPRING:  Beardslee and Mitchell (1965: 116-117) cited four May records for Ontario waters, one as early as May 4, 1958 at Morgan's Point. Naomi LeVay saw one at Eastbourne, Whitby, as early as Apr. 1, 1951 and over 500 there on May 14, 1960 (Speirs, 1979: 28). Saunders (1947: 162-163) recounted observations of a pair at Toronto's Eastern Gap on May 26, 1946. Quilliam (1965: 35) reported about 2000 off Kingston on May 13, 1955 and May 19, 1960 with good-sized flocks in intervening years: she gave May 14 as her 11-year average arrival date with some staying until the end of June. Frances Westman saw ten on Kempenfeldt Bay for several weeks in May, 1953 (Devitt, 1967: 34). Beamer noted 31 at Meaford as early as Mar. 26-27, 1949 and one there as late as May 31, 1950. Smith (1957: 167) reported two seen near Gogama at the end of April, 1954 by M. Loucks and 94 there from May 18-25: on May 27, 1954 W.K.W. Baldwin and W. John Smith counted 250 on a grassy field by Lake Timiskaming while A.N. Boissoneau saw 20 in late May, 1954 near Cochrane: that same spring F. Cowell observed some near Timmins on May 1. Manning (1953: 19) noted 50 at Shipsands Is., near Moosonee, on May 31, 1947.

SUMMER:  Ussher (1965: 3) gave a June 4 date for Rondeau. Beardslee and Mitchell (1965: 116-117) reported 30 eating carrot tops in a field near Port Weller from June 6-14, 1946 and 13 at Gull Is., Ont. on June 18, 1950 and a straggler at Windmill Point on July 27, 1953. Edgerton Pegg saw 20 at Frenchman Bay as late as June 26, 1972 and Rob Nisbet showed me a straggler at Ajax on Aug. 8, 1977 (Speirs, 1979: 28). Devitt (1967: 34) reported two that browsed a cottage lawn by Lake Couchiching from June 22 to mid-July, 1967. Speirs and Speirs (1947: 26) observed three at North Bay on June 5, 1945. Baillie (see Smith, 1957: 167) reported that 18 spent the summer at Kelly Lake, Copper Cliff, in 1954 and Frank Fielding observed a pair there with five young from Aug. 12 to Sept. 29. Smith (1957: 167) noted that about 2000 arrived in late May, 1953 on Lake Abitibi and about 100 survived Indian hunting until August: he saw seven there on July 13 and described a possible nest site on a rocky island (specimens sent to ROM and NMC). H. Lumsden watched a flock of 157 west of Cape Henrietta Maria on July 12, 1957 (Peck, 1972: 337).

AUTUMN:  Beamer noted 10 at Meaford as early as Oct. 16, 1938: on Nov. 14,

1948 he counted 234 in 11 flocks with 69 in 10 flocks until Nov. 28 there. A.J. Mitchener estimated 200 on Nottawasaga Bay on Nov. 2, 1953 (Devitt, 1967: 34). Quilliam (1965: 35) reported 50 on Wolfe Is. as late as Nov. 19, 1953 with Oct. 21 as her 4-year average fall arrival date at Kingston. George A. Scott saw one at Oshawa as early as Sept. 8, 1968 and had a maximum number of 35 at Whitby on Oct. 29, 1967, while John Miles saw eight at Port Bolster as late as Nov. 11, 1977 (Speirs, 1979: 28). Fleming (1906: 446) had two Toronto specimens: one taken Nov. 12, 1899, the other on Dec. 2, 1895. A.R. Muma found one dead below Niagara Falls on Nov. 7, 1955 (Sheppard, 1960: 6). Kelley (1978: 16) reported a maximum of 180 at Ipperwash Beach on Oct. 23, 1971. "One alighted among Canada Geese in Jack Miner's ponds at Kingsville, Ontario on Oct. 27, 1918. It was seen by W.E. Saunders on November 4, and I saw it a year later at Mr. Miner's" (Fleming, 1930: 66). Stirrett (1973d: 16) noted single birds at Pelee on Oct. 22, 1967 and Oct. 25, 1960.

**MEASUREMENTS:**

*Length:* to about 24 ins. (Palmer, 1976: 244).
*Wingspread:* to 45 ins. (Palmer, 1976: 244).
*Weight:* to almost 5 lb. but usually 2 1/2 to 3 1/2 (Palmer, 1976: 244).

**REFERENCE:**

Sheppard, R.W. 1949 The American Brant on the lower Great Lakes. Can. Field-Nat., 63: (3): 99-100.This gives details of the Brant invasion of the carrot field at Port Weller in the late spring of 1946 and 19 photographed at Wiarton on May 19, 1946 (at about the same time). It also summarizes the Lake Ontario and Lake Erie records up to that time (from 1866 to 1946).

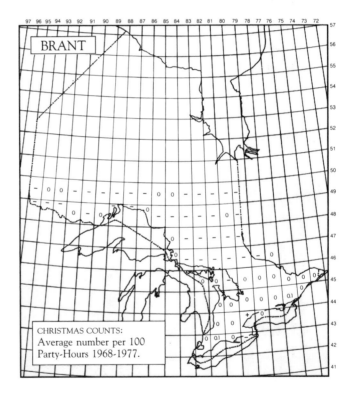

BRANT

CHRISTMAS COUNTS:
Average number per 100
Party-Hours 1968-1977.

# BARNACLE GOOSE  *Branta leucopsis*  (Bechstein)

This beautiful goose is normally a bird of the Old World Arctic, breeding from Greenland east to Spitzbergen, wintering in Ireland and Scotland and other parts of northern Europe. A few stragglers, or escapes from waterfowl breeders, have shown up in various parts of North America.

IDENTIFICATION:  The white forehead, face and chin distinguish it from Brant and Canada Goose. The back is gray with black bars, rather than brown as in Brant and Canada Goose and the breast is black, not whitish as in Canadas.

WINTER:  Reid Wilson saw two with a large flock of Canada geese at the Exhibition waterfront at Toronto on Jan. 18, 1980: later the same day I went with Margaret Wilson to see and photograph the pair, both at rest on the grass and in flight. Although not as approachable as the Canadas, we had excellent views with binoculars, noting all the identification features mentioned above, and obtained a few photographs.

SPRING:

SUMMER:

AUTUMN:  The first Ontario record was on Oct. 27, 1955 when a group of five turned up at Jack Miner's sanctuary at Kingsville (Speirs, 1956: 31).

**MEASUREMENTS:**
*Length:* to 28 ins. (Palmer, 1976: 235).
*Wingspread:* 52-56 ins. (Palmer, 1976: 235)
*Weight:* usually about 4 lb.. to above 5 lb. (Palmer, 1976: 235).

# CANADA GOOSE   *Branta canadensis*   (Linnaeus)

Until the mid-1960's we knew them only as spring and fall migrants, and thrilled to see the migrating V's and hear the "ow-ah" honkings from gray October and early April skies. About that time a breeding population became established at various points in southern Ontario and encouraged by winter feeding and gleaning from mechanically harvested corn fields they have wintered in ever increasing numbers.

IDENTIFICATION: The black head and neck with white cheeks and chins are distinctive. The smaller Brant shares the same general colouration but lacks the white cheeks and chin, having only a rather diffuse white area on the upper neck.

WINTER: Goodwin, Freedman and McKay (1977: 3-5, 8-9, 14) had none on the mid-winter watefowl inventory and only one on Toronto Christmas counts until the mid '60's, after which the inventory number reached 1788 by 1975 and the Christmas count reached 1909 at Toronto in 1976. A few winter at Pelee (Stirrett, 1973a: 13) and many at Jack Miner's sanctuary at Kingsville (Kelley, 1978: 15). Beamer had a few winter records at Meaford: one lingered until Jan. 10, 1940 and another was shot as early as Feb. 12, 1945. They have been seen on 12 of 25 Christmas counts at Sault Ste. Marie, mainly at Bellevue Park (Dennison, 1980: 22).

SPRING: Migrants returning from the south reach peak numbers from late March to early May as open water becomes available. Stirrett (1973b: 14) found them common in March and April at Pelee with a peak in mid-April and a few lingering into May. Speirs (1938: 43) gave the spring peak for Toronto as Mar. 25 while early April was the peak period in Ontario Co. (Speirs, 1979: 27). Quilliam (1965: 34) gave the average arrival date at Kingston as Mar. 24, with peaks in late April and early May and most gone by mid-May. Devitt (1967: 33) reported the 18-year average for arrivals at Collingwood as Apr. 4. Beamer saw them regularly in spring at Meaford, the first usually seen during the last 10 days of March, with peak numbers in mid-April and a few lingering into early May. At Sault Ste. Marie the spring date is given as Apr. 25 (Dennison, 1980: 14). Denis (1961: 2) gave Mar. 31, 1953 as the earliest date for Thunder Bay with Apr. 16 as the average. Manning (1952: 18) gave Apr. 6 as the earliest, Apr. 18 as average and May 1 as the latest for arrivals at Fort Albany. Lee (1978: 17) arrived at Big Trout Lake on May 29, 1975, too late for the spring migration but local residents considered it a very common spring migrant there. Elsey (in Cringan, 1950: 3) gave May 3 as the 1950 arrival date in the Asheweig area but thought Apr. 22 was more usual). Resident birds in the south of Ontario are nesting in April and downy young are seen with parents by early May.

SUMMER: Stirrett (1973c: 13) had only one June record for Pelee. Kelley (1978: 15) reported some breeding in Kent Co. Breeding in southern Ontario was formerly a rare event but is now regular and increasing, so much so that the birds are sometimes a problem because of droppings polluting (and fertilizing) the lawns of public parks. Skeel and Bondrup-Nielsen (1978: 153) noted 22 in summer along the Lake Superior shore of Pukaskwa. Schueler, Baldwin and Rising (1974: 141) saw them in summer at Moosonee, Attawapiskat and Winisk, with breeding evidence for Hawley Lake and 30 miles north along the Sutton River. Manning (1952: 18-19) found it rare in summer along the James and Hudson Bay coasts. Cringan (1953: 1) saw one or two near Kasabonika Lake on June

4, 1953, suggestive of local breeding. Hope noted 200 on June 30, 1940 at Ft. Severn and collected adults and young there during July.

AUTUMN: The goose hunt in Hudson Bay Lowlands ceases abruptly after the first severe freezeup. Radar studies (Speirs et al, 1971: 172) suggest that geese leaving the Ft. Severn area may fly south to santuary lakes in Wisconsin in one long "hop" at this time. Some flocks were a mile high as they passed over Ft. William on Oct. 3, 1965 when some 5000 flocks were detected within 60 miles of the radar there. The average ground speed was about 50 knots, representing an air speed of about 35 knots. Although headed SW the flocks travelled almost due south as they allowed for wind drift. The total number of geese involved in this radar display may have approached half a million birds yet few were reported by ground observers: many passed too high to be detected.

Skeel and Bondrup-Nielsen (1978: 153) reported a few fall flocks over Pukaskwa flying SE from Sept. 18 to Oct. 12, 1977, often very high and sometimes at night. Speirs and Speirs (1947: 26) had fall flocks on Oct. 21 and 27, 1944 near North Bay. Nicholson (1972: 13) reported return migrants on Manitoulin from mid-Sept. to mid-Oct. Beamer, at Meaford, noted a few as early as mid-Sept. with peak numbers in the latter half of October and a few lingering into December. Quilliam (1965: 34) indicated that the peak of the fall flight at Kingston was in mid-Oct. with the earliest fall record on Sept. 21, 1953. Speirs (1979: 27) found that the peak of the fall flight through Ontario Co. was in early October. Saunders (1947: 360) gave Nov. 1 as his average departure date for Toronto. Ussher (1965: 3) gave earliest and latest dates for Rondeau as Sept. 8 and Dec. 11 with average arrivals and departures on Sept. 26 and Nov. 24. Stirrett (1973d: 16) reported it as a fairly common transient at Pelee from Sept. 21 to Nov. 7 with a peak in late October while Kelley (1978: 15) rated it as abundant during October and November in SW Ontario.

**MEASUREMENTS:**
*Length:* 23-43 ins.
(Palmer, 1976: 183).
*Wingspread:* 43-72 ins.
(Palmer, 1976: 183).
*Weight:* 2-20 lbs. (Palmer, 1976: 183).
Note the great variation between the large "giants" and the tiny Mallard-sized "Hutchins" types. Both occur in Ontario.

**REFERENCES:**
Hanson, Harold C. and Robert H. Smith. 1955. Canada Geese of the Mississippi flyway with special reference to the Illinois flock. Bull. Ill. Hist. Survey, 25: (Art. 3): 67-210.

Speirs, J. Murray; J.J.C. Kanitz and J. Novak 1971 Numbers, speeds and directions of migrating geese from analysis of a radar display at Fort

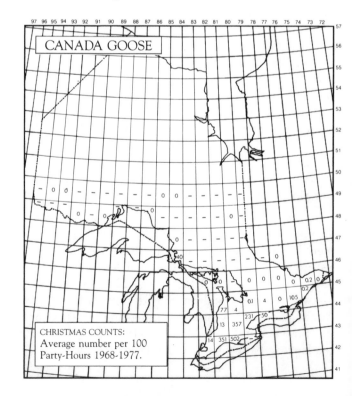

CANADA GOOSE

CHRISTMAS COUNTS:
Average number per 100
Party-Hours 1968-1977.

William, Ontario. Can.
Wildlife Service, Rept. Ser.
No. 14: 69-76. (Studies of
bird hazards to aircraft).

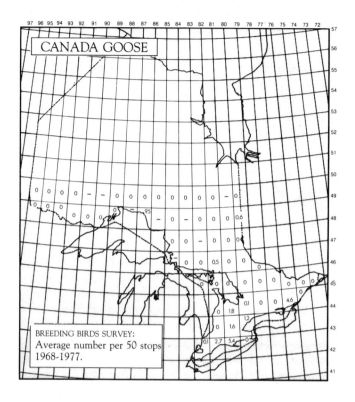

# WOOD DUCK   *Aix sponsa*   (Linnaeus)

This is a species to gladden the eye, considered by many to be the most beautiful of our ducks. For a time in the early 1900's it was considered an endangered species but it has responded well to more enlightened hunting policy and, although still not common, it graces many a marsh and swamp in southern Ontario. It breeds high in trees in large holes or in Wood Duck boxes suitably placed.

IDENTIFICATION: At close quarters the beautiful male is unmistakable with its greenish crest, white face, dark blue wings, partly red bill and yellowish buff sides. The female also has a bit of a crest but the "spectacles" around the eyes are its best field mark. In flight the absence of conspicuous white on the wings and the big head are suggestive. When flushed in its breeding swamps it goes off with loud squeals, unlike the note of any other duck.

WINTER:   On Christmas counts it has occurred in small numbers south of a line from Ottawa to Wiarton. On the Guelph counts numbers frequently exceeded 100 per 100 party-hours. Stirrett (1973a: 13) had a Pelee record on Dec. 13. The few winter records for Ontario Co. were documented in Speirs (1979: 41): and Wood Ducks banded at Oshawa were found to winter mainly along the Atlantic coast from Connecticut south to northern Florida but a few went down the Mississippi valley to Alabama and Mississippi. Quilliam (1965: 42) had one winter record for Kingston, on Jan. 2, 1964. (Weir & Quilliam (1980:33) gave another winter date for Kingston on Feb. 14.) Beamer noted a female at Meaford on Jan. 27, 1952. Dennison (1980: 148) listed two seen on a Christmas count at Sault Ste. Marie.

SPRING:   Stirrett (1973b: 14) noted two at Pelee as early as Mar. 10, with a peak of 30 on Apr. 30. Ussher (1965: 5) had his earliest sighting at Rondeau on Mar. 15 with the 14-year average arrival on Apr. 2. Saunders & Dale (1933: 177) had a few London records in the latter half of April, beginning in 1925. Saunders (1947: 360) gave Apr. 21 as the 10-year average arrival date for Toronto with the earliest on Mar. 21. George A. Scott's median arrival date for Oshawa was Mar. 31 with some early sightings in mid-March and spring peak in mid-April (Speirs, 1979: 41). Weir & Quilliam (1980: 33) gave Mar. 24 as the 28-year average arrival date for Kingston with the earliest on Mar. 4. Devitt (1967: 41) gave Apr. 13 as the average arrival date for Barrie with the earliest on Mar. 20, 1964. Skeel & Bondrup-Nielsen (1978: 156-157) saw up to four at Pukaskwa from Apr. 23 to June 4. Denis (1961: 3) gave May 2 as the average arrival date for Thunder Bay with Apr. 20, 1958 as the earliest record.

SUMMER:   On Breeding Bird Surveys it has been well respresented on most routes north to North Bay and Thessalon, rare or absent north of this line. Saunders & Dale (1933: 177) indicated that this species was abundant near London until about 1890, becoming rare or absent for the next 30 years, with a gradual increase in the 1920's. Tozer & Richards (1974: 83) gave an interesting account of the past scarcity and recent increase in the Oshawa-Scugog region, while Devitt (1967: 40) and Quilliam (1965: 40-42) attributed the early decline to overhunting and loss of habitat and the recent increase to closed seasons from 1918 to 1941 and improvement in habitat due to increasing beaver populations. Smith ( 1957: 168) reported them as not uncommon at Timmins and Goganda. Robert Rybczynski saw four on Aug. 19, 1972 about two miles west of Clute,

Cochrane District (Schueler, Baldwin & Rising, 1974: 145). I saw one at Jellicoe on June 24, 1980. David Elder saw individuals near Atikokan on June 1, 1978 and June 10, 1979. Todd (1963: 158) gave details of several stragglers in northeastern Ontario from North Bay north to Moose Factory.

AUTUMN: Smith (1957: 168) saw one six miles south of Matheson on Sept. 4, 1953. Escott saw two at Marathon on Sept. 5, 1976 (Skeel & Bondrup-Nielsen, 1978: 157). Nicholson (1972: 15) had Manitoulin records to mid-Oct. Devitt (1967: 41) had his latest record for Simcoe Co. on Nov. 15, 1963. Weir & Quilliam (1980: 33) gave the 24-year average for departure from Kingston as Oct. 17 but Helen saw two very late migrants on Wolfe Is. with Ken Edwards on Nov. 26, 1957 (Quilliam, 1965: 42). From my records the fall peak in Ontario Co. was in the latter half of Sept. while George A. Scott's median departure date from Oshawa was Oct. 24 (Speirs, 1979: 41). Saunders (1947: 360) gave Oct. 6 as the 10-year average fall departure date from Toronto with the latest on Oct. 30. Ussher (1965: 5) had his latest Rondeau record on Dec. 6 with the 7-year average departure on Nov. 10. Stirrett (1973d: 16) had a fall peak of 300 at Pelee on Aug. 30 with a few lingering into late Nov.

**MEASUREMENTS:**
*Length:* 17-20 ins.
(Palmer, 1976: 252).
*Wingspread:* to 29 1/2 ins.
(Palmer, 1976: 252).
*Weight:* about 1 1/2 lb.
(Palmer, 1976: 252).

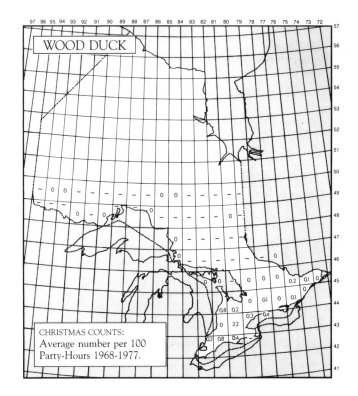

WOOD DUCK

CHRISTMAS COUNTS:
Average number per 100
Party-Hours 1968-1977.

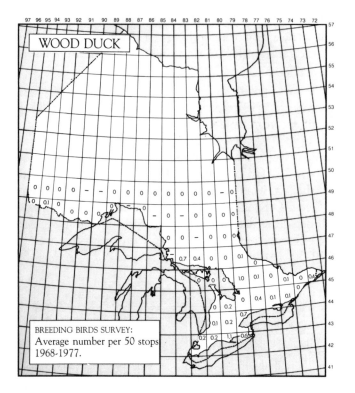

WOOD DUCK

BREEDING BIRDS SURVEY:
Average number per 50 stops
1968-1977.

# GREEN-WINGED TEAL  *Anas crecca*  Linnaeus

This is our smallest "puddle duck" and, at least in the Toronto region, it is often found slithering around on exposed mud flats: most of our ducks prefer to float in the water or sun themselves on drier ground.

IDENTIFICATION:  The small size distinguishes it from other ducks, except other teal and Buffleheads and Ruddy Ducks. The white in the head of the Bufflehead and its habit of frequent diving distinguish it. The Ruddy Duck is also a frequent diver and at close quarters shows some white in the head also. Blue-winged Teal always show much blue-white on the fore part of the wing in flight while the Green-wing shows little or no colour on the wing in flight. Both have a green speculum but it is usually more prominent in the Green-wing when at rest on the water. Females at rest on the water are often indistinguishable from female Blue-wings, but *late* fall birds and "mud-grubbers" usually turn out to be Green-wings. The only safe way to identify females is to flush them and look for the wing pattern. Males of the Eurasian subspecies lack the white crescent in front of the wing but have a white stripe high on the side.

WINTER:  This duck has been uncommon to rare on Christmas counts from lakes Ontario and Erie north to Kingston and Barrie. Kelley (1978: 17) had five winter records, including 33 at Ipperwash Beach on Dec. 26, 1970. Stirrett (1973a: 13) noted one at Pelee as late as Dec. 5. Speirs (1979: 37) cited several winter records for Whitby and Oshawa. Quilliam (1965: 39) noted one for the Dec. 22, 1956 Christmas count at Kingston and gave a Jan. 20 record as the latest there (Weir & Quilliam, 1980: 33).

SPRING:  Stirrett (1973b: 14) called it a common and regular transient at Pelee from Mar. 14 to June 1 with the largest number (50) on Apr. 2. Kelley (1978: 17) recorded a male of the Eurasian subspecies at Pelee from Mar. 22-30, 1971 seen by several observers. Ussher (1965: 4) had his earliest at Rondeau on Mar. 16 and latest spring departure on May 16 with averages Apr. 5 to Apr. 24. Saunders & Dale (1933: 1976) gave the average arrival date for London as Apr. 5 with the earliest on Mar. 31. George A. Scott's median arrival date for Oshawa is Mar. 28 with his earliest on Mar. 11, 1973 and largest number (65) on Apr. 20, 1974: by May they are generally uncommon in Ontario Co. (Speirs, 1979: 37). Weir & Quilliam (1980: 33) had a 30-year average arrival date for Kingston as Mar. 26 with the earliest on Mar. 18: she gave 130 as a peak number noted on Apr. 20, 1955 (Quilliam, 1965: 39). Devitt (1967: 38) gave Apr. 5, 1963 as the earliest date for Barrie with the 19-year average arrival as Apr. 15 and latest (except for 3 summer records) on May 14. Beamer had spring records from Mar. 24 to May 3 at Meaford: on Apr. 22, 1952, a flock of 10 passed him when he was travelling 55 MPH in a car (no mention of wind condition). Nicholson (1972: 14) wrote that it arrives from mid-Apr. to early May in Manitoulin. Dennison (1980: 15) gave Apr. 17 as the spring date for Sault Ste. Marie. Denis (1961: 2) gave Apr. 20, 1957 as the earliest date for Thunder Bay with the average arrival on Apr. 27. D.H. Elder had his first in 1979 at Atikokan on Apr. 22. Apr. 20 was his earliest spring date at Geralton (Elder, 1979: 29). Cringan (1953: 2) saw one at Sioux Lookout on May 12, 1953.

SUMMER:  On the Breeding Bird Surveys this species has been noted fairly commonly on the Sudbury route and uncommonly to rarely at Fraserville, Manitowaning, Hornepayne, Atikokan and Eagle River, not at all in southeastern or southwestern Ontario.

However, Kelley (1978: 17) gave a breeding record for Rondeau (adult with 5 young on July 21, 1970) and mentioned several summer records there. Sheppard (1945: 158) reported a breeding record for Strawberry Is. in the Niagara River. Beardslee & Mitchell (1965: 139) cited several summer records for Dunnville Marsh and Mud Lake. Speirs (1979: 37) mentioned several recent breeding records for Ontario Co. Quilliam (1965: 38) noted several summer records and some breeding cases for Kingston. Devitt (1967: 38) had 3 summer records for Simcoe Co. Nicholson (1972: 14) called it a regular summer resident on Manitoulin. Four were flushed near Favourable Lake on June 27, 1938 (Hope, 1938: 8). Cringan (1950: 5) called this the second commonest of the pond ducks in the Nikip Lake area and found two broods of young during the summer of 1950. Schueler, Baldwin & Rising (1974: 142) found it common at Moosonee, Ft. Albany and Winisk, uncommon at Attawapiskat and uncommon but breeding at Hawley Lake. Manning (1952: 25) called it the second commonest surface feeding duck along the south Hudson Bay coast. Peck (1972: 338) called it one of the commonest ducks in the region of Cape Henrietta Maria. C.E. Hope had 2 July records at Ft. Severn (one collected).

AUTUMN: Smith (1967: 168) saw one near South Porcupine on Sept. 6, 1953. Fall records for North Bay ranged from Aug. 31 to Oct. 26 in 1944 (Speirs & Speirs, 1947: 26). Beamer had fall records from Meaford from Sept. 8 to Oct. 19. Devitt (1967: 38) gave the latest date for Simcoe Co. as Nov. 4, 1940 (at Holland River). Quilliam (1965: 39) wrote that numbers in the Kingston area begin to build up in late August and some remain into the first two weeks of November. She gave Nov. 6 as the 26-year average departure date (Weir & Quilliam, 1980: 33). By September this species is numerous in Ontario Co. with 1000 estimated at Oshawa on Sept. 22, 1957: from my records the fall peak is generally in the first week of November with many staying until freezeup (Speirs, 1979: 37). Ussher (1965: 4) had the earliest and latest fall dates for Rondeau as Aug. 2 and Dec. 8 with average arrival on Aug. 16 and departure on Nov. 14. This is a common fall migrant at Pelee from Aug. 28 to early Dec. with the largest number (500) noted on Nov. 7 (Stirrett, 1973d: 16).

**MEASUREMENTS:**
*Length:* 14 1/2 to 15 1/2
ins. (Palmer, 1976: 347).
*Wingspread:* to 26 ins.
(Palmer, 1976: 347).
*Weight:* ♂ 11-14 oz. ♀ 9-
12 oz. (Palmer,
1976: 347).

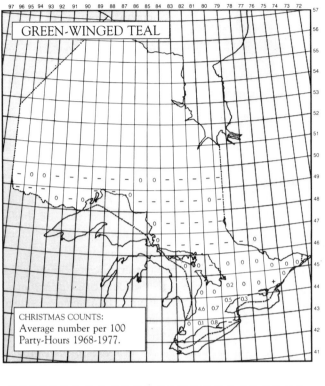

GREEN-WINGED TEAL

CHRISTMAS COUNTS:
Average number per 100
Party-Hours 1968-1977.

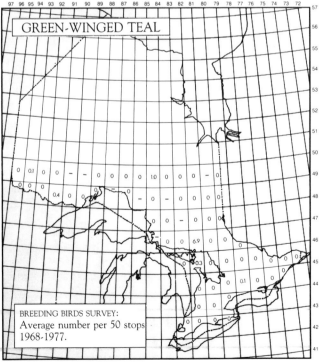

GREEN-WINGED TEAL

BREEDING BIRDS SURVEY:
Average number per 50 stops
1968-1977.

# AMERICAN BLACK DUCK   *Anas rubripes*   Brewster

This was the most important "puddle duck" in Ontario until eclipsed by the Mallard in the 1960's. The population of Black Ducks appears to be holding its own fairly well but it has had to yield first place to the prettier and more trusting Mallard in recent years. In captivity the two species hybridize frequently and hybrids are sometimes found in the wild populations as well.

IDENTIFICATION: This is a big black duck with pale cheeks. The female Black Scoter has somewhat similar colouration but is a smaller, chunkier bird, often seen with other scoters farther from shore than most Black Ducks. In flight the brilliant white underwing is a good field mark, contrasting with the otherwise black plumage. Female Mallards are brown rather than black and have the blue speculum bordered with white: the blue in the Black Duck has no white border. White-winged and Surf Scoters are the other black ducks but usually show white in the wing or about the face and lack the scoop-shaped "puddle duck" bill shape.

WINTER: On Christmas counts this is a common duck in open water around the lower Great Lakes with smaller numbers as far north as Deep River and Sault Ste. Marie. The numbers of Black Ducks on Toronto Christmas counts have not changed significantly from 1944 to the present, the year to year variation reflecting changes in observing conditions (Goodwin, Freedman and McKay, 1977: 8-9). Many Ontario birds migrate to Chesapeake Bay and Tennesee to winter with a few south as far as Georgia and Louisiana (Speirs, 1979: 34, map).

SPRING: Stirrett (1973b: 14) had his largest spring count at Pelee on Mar. 14. Saunders and Dale (1933: 174) gave the 17-year average arrival at London as Mar. 28. The arrival of migrants from the south is masked by the large wintering population in the marshes north of Lake Ontario but a notable increase in numbers is apparent in late March and early April as winter ice leaves the ponds (Quilliam, 1965: 36-37 and Speirs (1979: 34). Devitt (1967: 37) gave the 16-year average for arrivals at Barrie as Apr. 6. The median arrival date at Meaford (from Beamer's records) was Mar. 26 (17 years). Ten were noted at Pimisi Bay on Mar. 31, 1945 by Louise Lawrence (Speirs & Speirs, 1947: 26). This was the most common dabbling duck at Pukaskwa from Apr. 11 to May 24, 1975 (Skeel and Bondrup-Nielsen, 1978: 155). Denis (1961: 2) gave Apr. 4, 1958 as his earliest date for Thunder Bay with average arrival on Apr. 14. D.H. Edler saw his first at Atikokan on Apr. 19, 1978. Cringan (1953b:2) saw his first in 1953 at Sioux Lookout on Apr. 28. Todd (1963: 148) reported an arrival at Moose Factory as early as Apr. 17, 1930 (Sam Waller). Elsey (in Cringan, 1950: 4) gave May 17, 1950 as the arrival date in the Asheweig area.

SUMMER: On Breeding Bird Surveys they were noted as far north as Kapuskasing and Nipigon, with the greatest numbers on the Port Dover and Sudbury routes. Baillie & Harrington (1936: 13) called this "the most common and most widely distributed of the ducks" in Ontario (but this was before the recent increase in the Mallard population). Smith (1957: 167) called it the most common resident dabbling duck of the Clay Belt. Ross James found a nest near Pickle Lake in June, 1977. Cringan (1953: 1) saw two on May 28 and three on June 4, 1953 near Kasabonika Lake and he had only two June records in the Nikip Lake region (Cringan, 1950: 4): much less common than the Mallard at both locatities. Todd (1963: 148) reported the finding of a nest with 10 freshly incubated eggs at Moose Flats on June 15, 1912 (by Preble). Manning (1952: 22) saw 3 adult and 5 downies at Ship Sands (near Moosonee) on June 17, 1949. Peck (1972: 338) reported fairly large numbers in the Cape Henrietta Maria region. C.E.Hope saw 10 on July 11, 1940 and collected one the following day at Ft. Severn. Schueler, Baldwin & Rising (1974: 141) found them common at Moosonee, Ft. Albany and Hawley Lake but uncommon at Attawapiskat: they found pairs with 3-week-old young on July 9 and July 12, 1964 at Aquatuk Lake (70 mi. SSE of Winisk).

AUTUMN: Manning (1952: 22) noted about 200 feeding on the edge of the tide flats at Ship Sands (near Moosonee) on Sept. 9 and 11, 1950. The main fall migration at Pukaskwa was from Aug. 12 to Sept. 6, 1975 but one was noted as late as Oct. 3 (Skeel & Bondrup-Nielsen, 1978: 155). Three were seen at Pimisi Bay as late as Oct. 23, 1944 by Louise Lawrence (Speirs & Speirs, 1947: 24). Beamer noted large numbers at Meaford as early as Sept. 2 (500 in 1939) and as late as Nov. 25 (20 in 1944) with a few lingering into December some years. Numbers at Kingston peaked in November (Quilliam, 1965: 37). Fleming found it plentiful at Toronto in October and November with one as late as Dec. 6, 1897 (Fleming 1906: 444). Stirrett (1973d: 16) had his highest count at Pelee on Oct. 13.

**MEASUREMENTS:**
*Length:* 22-26 ins.
(Palmer, 1976: 321).
*Wingspread:* 33-37 ins.
(Palmer, 1976: 321).
*Weight:* ♂ 2 1/2 to 3 1/4
lb. ♀ 2 1/4 to 2 3/4 lb.
(Palmer, 1976: 321).

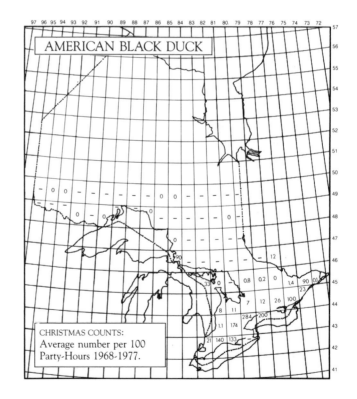

AMERICAN BLACK DUCK

CHRISTMAS COUNTS:
Average number per 100
Party-Hours 1968-1977.

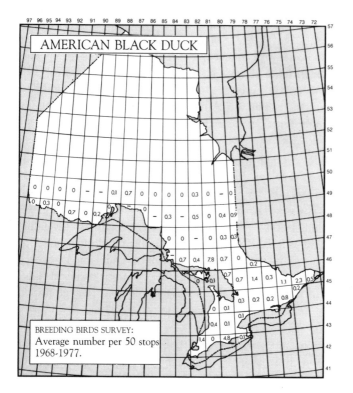

AMERICAN BLACK DUCK

BREEDING BIRDS SURVEY:
Average number per 50 stops
1968-1977.

# MALLARD   *Anas platyrhynchos*   Linnaeus

This is a handsome duck, the males with green heads and curly tails and the females with bright blue speculum, bordered fore and aft with white. It is the ancestor of most domestic varieties. When protected it soon becomes trusting and tame but where it is hunted it has a reputation as one of the wildest of wild ducks: it has learned to get along with all kinds of men so is widespread and common in most of the northern hemisphere.

IDENTIFICATION:   Both sexes of the Northern Shoveler resemble Mallards but differ in having the huge broad bill which unfortunately spends much of its time underwater. In flight shovelers have a big patch of light blue on the fore part of the wing (as in Blue-winged Teal) while the blue speculum of the Mallard is in the hind edge of the wing. The breast of the shoveler is white while the sides are chestnut brown: in the Mallard this is reversed with brown breast and white sides. The recurved black tail coverts of the Mallard are distinctive. Females are best distinguished by the size of the bill, when not underwater.

WINTER:   On Christmas counts in the 1968-1977 period Mallards were common to abundant around the shores of the lower Great Lakes, north as far as Sault Ste. Marie and Kingston: rare to uncommon along the Ottawa valley, north to Kirkland Lake with intermediate numbers wherever open water was present inland north to the Thousand Islands and Manitoulin. It was formerly very rare in the Toronto region (none on Christmas counts before 1944) increasing to hundreds in the 1950's and thousands in the 1960's (Goodwin, Freedman & McKay, 1977: 4-5): it is now the most numerous duck wintering in the Toronto region. Banding indicates that many Ontario Mallards winter to the south along the Atlantic from Chesapeake Bay to South Carolina, with a few as far south as central Florida and west to Mississippi and Arkansas (see maps in Speirs, 1979: 33 and Buckalew, 1980: 104).

SPRING:   Stirrett (1973: 14) called it a fairly common transient at Pelee with a maximum of 43 on Mar. 14. Saunders & Dale (in 1933: 173) considered it "rather rare" near London but in more recent times Kelley (1978: 16) called it a common migrant in southwestern Ontario. Speirs (1979: 33) found the spring peak in Ontario Co. to be in late March or the first week of April at the time of the spring breakup while George A. Scott found a nest with 12 eggs at Oshawa as early as Apr. 17. Quilliam (1965: 36) indicated that the peak of the spring flight at Kingston was about Apr. 20. Devitt (1967: 36) gave the average date of spring arrival at Barrie as Apr. 5 (15 years) with the earliest on Mar. 20, 1966. Beamer generally reported the first Mallards at Meaford in mid-April but saw 9 there as early as Mar. 22 in 1953. Skeel and Bondrup-Nielsen (1978: 154) had records from mid-April to the end of May at Pukaskwa. Elder (1979: 29) gave Apr. 15 as the earliest spring date for Geraldton. D.H. Elder sighted his first at Atikokan on Apr. 15, 1979. Cringan (1953) saw his first at Sioux Lookout on Apr. 23, 1953. Elsey (in Cringan, 1950) gave May 5, 1950 as the arrival date in the Asheweig area. Denis (1961: 2) gave Mar. 24, 1946 as the earliest date for Thunder Bay with Apr. 14 as the average arrival date.

SUMMER:   Mallards now breed commonly in marshes north of the lower Great Lakes and in smaller numbers inland as far north as Longlac and Kenora (see Breeding Bird Survey map). North of this Smith (1957: 167) saw about 30 on Lillabelle Lake, near

Cochrane on Aug. 18, 1954 and one on Ogoki Lake on Aug. 13, 1954. Parties from the Royal Ontario Museum found them present, but not common, in the Favourable Lake area in 1938 while in June, 1977 Ross James saw them frequently in the Pickle Lake area. Seven pairs were noted near Kasabonika Lake in late May and early June, 1953 by Cringan (1953b: 1). Cringan (1950: 4) called this the commonest pond duck in the Nikip Lake area, with 35 seen on June 24, 1950, with two nests with 5 and 7 eggs found on July 5 as well as a predated nest, and a brood seen in late August. Lee (1978: 19) saw a pair at Big Trout Lake in the summer of 1975. C.E. Hope saw two (collected one) at Fort Severn in 1940. Manning (1952: 21-22) called it "rather scarce" in James Bay, citing a few records from Moosonee around the coast to Ft. Severn. Schueler, Baldwin and Rising (1974: 142) found them common at Moosonee, Ft. Albany, Attawapiskat, Winisk and Hawley Lake. Peck (1972: 338) saw one near Cape Henrietta Maria on June 22, 1970.

AUTUMN: In the fall a few were noted at Pukaskwa from Sept. 2 to Oct. 16 (Skeel and Bondrup-Nielsen, 1978: 154). Louise Lawrence saw one at Eau Claire as late as Oct. 27, 1944 (Speirs & Speirs, 1947: 26). L.H. Beamer's largest flock at Meaford was seen on Oct. 24, 1948, when 200 were noted. Devitt (1967: 36) stated that the largest fall flights in Simcoe Co. occur between Sept. 25 and Nov. 1. The fall peak in Ontario Co., when thousands may be seen in the lakefront marshes, is generally in October but large numbers remain until freezeup (Speirs, 1979: 33). Early in the century Fleming (1906: 444) considered it a rare migrant at Toronto, with a few November records only. Stirrett (1973d: 16) called it a fairly common transient in fall at Pelee, with a maximum of 500 on Oct. 13.

**MEASUREMENTS:**
*Length:* about 24 ins. (21-28). Palmer, 1976: 275.
*Wingspread:* about 35 ins. (31-40). Palmer (1976: 275).
*Weight:* 2 1/2 to 3 lbs. Palmer (1976: 275, details p. 281).

**REFERENCE:**
Buckalew, John M. 1980. Distribution of Mallards. North American Bird Bander, 5: (3): 104.

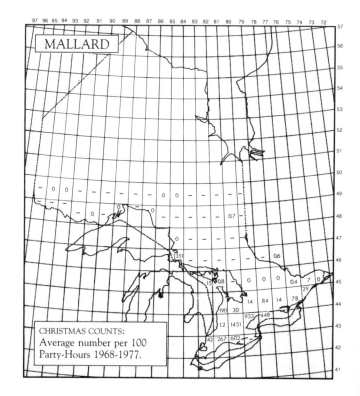

MALLARD

CHRISTMAS COUNTS:
Average number per 100
Party-Hours 1968-1977.

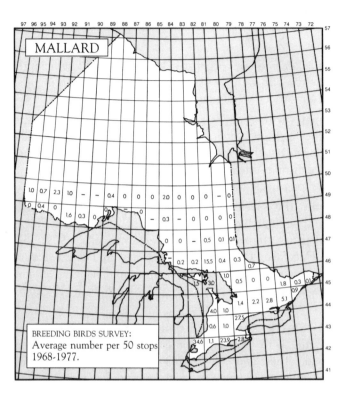

MALLARD

BREEDING BIRDS SURVEY:
Average number per 50 stops
1968-1977.

# NORTHERN PINTAIL  *Anas acuta*  Linnaeus

An elegant duck. Although large flocks sometimes occur, the Pintail is usually sufficiently uncommon to excite the interest of the bird watcher. I associate it with early spring and late fall among large congregations of other "puddle ducks."

IDENTIFICATION: Breeding males with their dark chocolate heads with the white stripe running down the side of the neck and long central tail feathers are unmistakable: only the Oldsquaw has such long tail feathers among our ducks. The females are long, slim ducks, also with longish spiky central tail feathers: they have long slender necks and a creamy brown head. In flight the long neck and pointed tail is distinctive.

WINTER: On Christmas counts this species has been uncommon along the north shores of lakes Erie and Ontario, and rare north to Ottawa and Barrie. A few have shown up on about 20% of the counts in the western Lake Ontario region (Speirs, 1979: 36). Most winter records are for early December (lingering fall migrants) and late February (early spring migrants) but there are some mid-winter reports in mild winters. A few overwinter on the Niagara River above the falls (Sheppard, 1945: 158). Quilliam (1965: 38) had a few winter records for Kingston (two in mid-winter).

SPRING: Stirrett (1973b: 14) considered it to be a common and regular transient at Pelee with Mar. 7 as an early date, with a peak in mid-March and two lingering as late as June 5. Ussher (1965: 4) had earliest and latest spring dates at Rondeau on Mar. 6 and May 24 with average arrival on Mar. 22 and departure on Apr. 27. Saunders and Dale (1933: 175-176) had only about half a dozen records for Middlesex Co., all in spring. Sheppard (1945: 158) reported a male killed going over Niagara Falls in fog about Apr. 19, 1937. Fleming (1906: 444) gave Apr. 6 as his only spring record for Toronto. George Scott's median arrival date for Oshawa was Mar. 26 with a maximum of 125 there on May 1, 1960 (Speirs, 1979: 36). Weir & Quilliam (1980: 32) gave Mar. 17 as the 30-year average arrival date for Kingston with the earliest on Feb. 10. Quilliam (1965: 38) mentioned a flock of 500 at Kingston on Apr. 7, 1964 as a maximum. Devitt (1967: 37) wrote that the spring peak in Simcoe Co. occurs in late April or early May, with 15-year average arrival date at Barrie on Apr. 10 and the earliest on Mar. 19, 1966. Beamer had a few spring records from Meaford between Mar. 22 and May 6. Six were noted on Lake Nipissing on Apr. 28, 1944 (Speirs & Speirs, 1947: 26). Skeel & Bondrup-Nielsen (1978: 155) saw a few at Pukaskwa between Apr. 14 and 27, 1975. D.H. Elder saw one at Atikokan on May 19, 1979. Cringan (1953a: 2) noted his first at Sioux Lookout on Apr. 23, 1953. Elsey (in Cringan, 1950: 5) gave May 18 as the 1950 arrival date in the Asheweig area.

SUMMER: On the Breeding Bird Survey a few have shown up on the Ottawa and Sudbury routes, none elsewhere. Stirrett (1973c: 14) had only two summer records for Pelee, but Kelley (1978: 17) cited six breeding records from Kent Co. marshes. Beardslee & Mitchell (1965: 127) cite several breeding records from Gull Is., off Rockhouse Pt., Lake Erie. There are a few breeding records for Ontario Co. at Pickering Beach and Cranberry Marsh (Speirs, 1979: 36 and Tozer and Richards, 1974: 78). Quilliam (1965: 38) wrote that the Pintail is increasing in the Kingston area and cited several breeding records since 1949. Nicholson (1972: 14) called it a regular summer resident on Manitoulin. Baillie & Harrington (1933: 13-14) cited nest records from Erieau and from the west coast of James Bay, north of the Albany River. Beamer saw a male at Meaford on June 26,

1949. Smith (1967: 168) saw only one in the Clay Belt during two summers - on Long Lake on Aug. 12, 1954. Cringan (1950: 5) saw 40 near Nikip Lake on June 24, 1950. C.E. Hope collected 35 at Ft. Severn on July 12, 1940, including 20 young. Schueler, Baldwin & Rising (1974: 141-142) called it common at Moosonee, Attawapiskat and Winisk and uncommon at Ft. Albany, with nest records for Winisk. Peck (1972: 338) called the Pintail "easily the most abundant surface-feeding duck" in the Cape Henrietta Maria region, and cited nest records.

AUTUMN:    Five were seen at North Bay on Sept. 13, 1944 (Speirs & Speirs, 1947: 26). Beamer noted a few at Meaford between Sept. 19 and Nov. 7. Devitt (1967: 37) said that southward migrants appear in Simcoe Co. in early Sept. and remain in small numbers until mid-Oct.: his latest record was one at Midland on Oct. 30, 1965. Quilliam (1965: 38) wrote that they begin to show up at Kingston in late August and stay until late November. Weir & Quilliam (1980: 32) gave Dec. 6 as the 27-year average departure date from Kingston. In Ontario Co. the fall peak was in early to mid-October with good numbers remaining until freezeup (Speirs, 1979: 36). Fleming (1906: 444) had Toronto records from Oct. 20 to Dec. 6. Ussher (1965: 4) had extreme fall dates for Rondeau from Aug. 7 to Nov. 27 with average arrival and departures on Aug. 29 to Nov. 11. Stirrett (1973d: 16) called it an uncommon fall transient from Aug. 29 to Nov 11 with peak numbers in late October at Pelee.

**MEASUREMENTS:**
*Length:* ♂ 24-29 ins. ♀
20-24 ins. (Palmer,
1976: 437).
*Wingspread:* ♂ to 37 ins.
♀ to 35 ins. (Palmer,
1976: 437).
*Weight:* ♂ 1 3/4 to 2 1/4
lb. ♀ 1 1/2 to 2 lb.
(Palmer, 1976: 437).

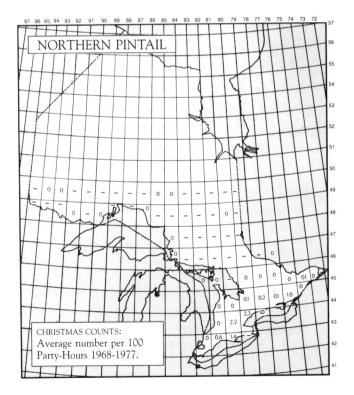

NORTHERN PINTAIL

CHRISTMAS COUNTS:
Average number per 100
Party-Hours 1968-1977.

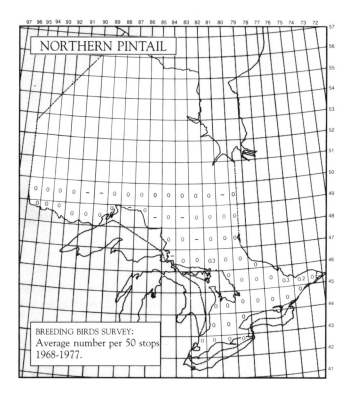

NORTHERN PINTAIL

BREEDING BIRDS SURVEY:
Average number per 50 stops
1968-1977.

## BLUE-WINGED TEAL   *Anas discors*   Linnaeus

This is the common breeding teal of most of Ontario, a jaunty little duck, late to arrive and early to depart, and migrating far south to the Caribbean and northern South America.

IDENTIFICATION:  The males have a distinctive white crescent in front of the eye on a bluish head. The big pale blue patch on the front of the wing distinguish both sexes from all but the very rare (in Ontario) Cinnamon Teal and the much larger Northern Shoveler. Males of these two species present no problems. The large size and very big bill of the female Northern Shoveler should identify it. Female Cinnamon Teal cannot be safely distinguished from female Blue-winged Teal in the field, but are unlikely to occur in Ontario.

WINTER:  This is a very rare bird in Ontario in winter. Lingering strays have shown up on Christmas counts at Sault Ste. Marie, Kingston, Pickering, Hamilton and Long Point. Most banding recoveries are from tropical American regions (see map in Speirs, 1979: following p. 38).

SPRING:  Stirrett (1973b: 14) gave Mar. 20 as his earliest date for Pelee with the peak number on Apr. 16. Ussher (1965: 4) had his earliest sighting on Mar. 15 at Rondeau with the 19-year average arrival on Mar. 30. Saunders & Dale (1933: 176) gave Apr. 16 as the 10-year average for arrivals at London with the earliest on Mar. 26, 1925. Saunders

(1947: 360) gave J.L. Baillie's earliest date for Toronto as Mar. 28, with Apr. 23 as the average for arrivals there. George A. Scott had one very early arrival at Oshawa on Mar. 1, 1959 but his median arrival date there was Mar. 31: my spring peak for Pickering has been in the third week of April (Speirs, 1979: 28). Quilliam (1965: 39-40) documented the recent increase in numbers in the Kingston region and gave Mar. 30 as her 31-year average for arrivals with the earliest on Mar. 17 (Weir & Quilliam, 1980: 33). Devitt (1967: 39) gave Mar. 31, 1962 as the earliest arrival date for Barrie with Apr. 15 as the 16-year average. Beamer's median arrival date for Meaford was Apr. 22 with the earliest on Apr. 11, 1948. Dennison (1980: 15) gave Apr. 17 as the spring date for Sault Ste. Marie. Skeel & Bondrup-Nielsen (1978: 155) saw a few at Pukaskwa from Apr. 14 to May 29 with peak in late April. Denis (1961: 3) gave Apr. 19, 1954 as the earliest date for Thunder Bay with Apr. 30 as the average arrival date. Elder (1979: 29) gave Apr. 23 as his earliest date for Geraldton: he saw one at Atikokan on Apr. 25, 1979. Lee (1978: 19) reported one on the local sewage pond at Big Trout Lake on May 31, 1975.

SUMMER: On the Breeding Bird Surveys the Blue-winged Teal was found as far north as Larder Lake and Dryden and was most numerous on the Dunnville and Manitoulin routes. Stirrett (1973c: 14) listed this as a nesting bird at Pelee. It is a common nesting species in Ontario Co. (Speirs, 1979: 38). Quilliam (1965: 39) gave some breeding records for Kingston and called it "one of our commonest ducks". A nest with six eggs was found by L.A. Prince near Favourable Lake on June 22, 1938 (Hope, 1938: 89). Cringan (1950: 5) saw this species once in the summer of 1950 in the Nikip Lake area. Schueler, Baldwin & Rising (1974: 142, 145) found it uncommon at Moosonee, Attawapikat, Ft. Albany and Winisk and reported a flightless juvenile collected near Ft. Albany on Aug. 31, 1964: they suggest a recent increase into northern Ontario.

AUTUMN: Skeel & Bondrup-Nielsen (1978: 155) saw 7 on Sept. 2 and one on Oct. 15 at Pukaskwa. Beamer's latest report for Meaford was on Sept. 27, 1939, when he called them plentiful. Weir & Quilliam (1980: 33) gave Oct. 21 as the 29-year average departure date for Kingston with the latest on Dec. 17. George A. Scott's median departure date from Oshawa was Oct. 13 with his latest on Nov. 1, 1970 but Don Perks saw one as late as Dec. 7 at Whitby (Speirs, 1979: 38). Saunders (1947: 360) gave his latest fall date for Toronto as Nov. 10 but Baillie's latest date was Oct. 19. Ussher (1965: 4) gave his 7-year average departure date from Rondeau as Nov. 1. Stirrett (1973a: 13) gave Dec. 10 as his latest fall date for Pelee with fall peaks on Aug. 30 and Oct. 10.

**MEASUREMENTS:**
*Length:* 14-16 1/4 ins.
(Palmer, 1976: 463).
*Wingspread:* 22-25 ins.
(Palmer, 1976: 463).
*Weight:* 12-14 oz.
(Palmer, 1976: 463).

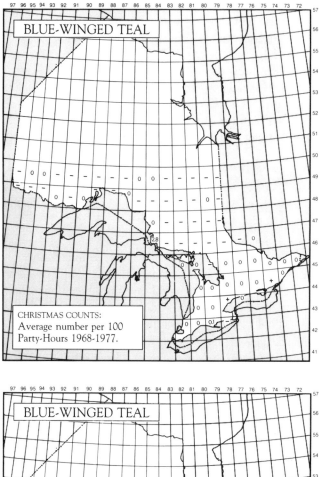

BLUE-WINGED TEAL

CHRISTMAS COUNTS:
Average number per 100
Party-Hours 1968-1977.

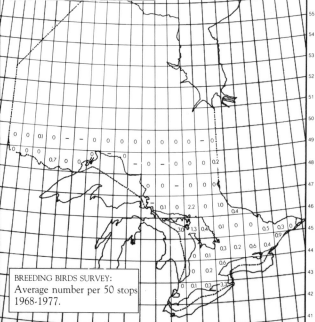

BLUE-WINGED TEAL

BREEDING BIRDS SURVEY:
Average number per 50 stops
1968-1977.

# CINNAMON TEAL   *Anas cyanoptera*   Vieillot

This is normally a bird of the southwestern U.S.A. (and southern South America), accidental in Ontario.

IDENTIFICATION: Females are too much like female Blue-winged Teal to be safely identified in the field, but the handsome cinnamon-red males are distinctive. Fully adult Ruddy Ducks are somewhat similar in size and colour but have white cheeks. Both the Blue-winged Teal and Northern Shoveler share the big pale blue patch on the leading edge of the wing but lack the reddish colour of the whole body. The Northern Shoveler does have chestnut sides but is much bigger and has a green head and white breast.

WINTER:

SPRING:   Two were seen at Turkey Point on May 5, 1963 by Don Baldwin, J. Olmsted and Dan Strickland (Woodford, 1963: 457). A male was reported at Hamilton by G. North from Apr. 15-19, 1973 (Goodwin, 1973: 766). A male was sighted at Prince Edward Point on May 3-4, 1980 by A. Bell, Ken and Mary Edwards *et al* (Weir & Quilliam, 1980: 5): this was a very wary bird so considered a wild bird.

SUMMER:   A.R. Muma and Capt. C. Keech has a close study of a male as it perched on a rocky islet near the Maid-of-the-Mist landing dock below Niagara Falls on Aug. 1, 1953 (Sheppard, 1960: 9). T. Sprague observed a very tame bird (possibly an escapee) on Big Island, Prince Edward Co. in June, 1966 (Weir & Quilliam, 1980: 5).

AUTUMN:   John Murray, caretaker of the Osler reserve on Lake Scugog, reported a pair there during a fall "prior to 1940": another bird, a male, was shot at Whitby "prior to 1950" and viewed by S. Hockett (a duck bander): both these records from Tozer & Richards (1974: 81). Naomi LeVay observed a male at Cranberry Marsh, Whitby, on Oct. 2, 1976 (Speirs, 1979: 39). E.A. Roberts and L.E. Roberts shot three from a flock of five at Mitchell's Bay, Lake St. Clair in Oct., 1939: one of these was mounted and loaned in 1948 to the Chatham-Kent Museum (Wood, 1948: 125). Another male was shot nearby at Big Point Marsh on Nov. 14, 1953 (Godfrey, 1966: 62).

**MEASUREMENTS:**
*Length:* 15-17 ins.
(Palmer, 1966: 483).
*Wingspread:* 23-26 ins.
(Palmer, 1966: 483).
*Weight:* usually under 1
lb. (Palmer, 1966: 483).

**REFERENCE:**
Wood, A.A. 1948 The
Cinnamon Teal in Ontario.
Can. Field-Nat., 62; 125.

# NORTHERN SHOVELER   *Anas clypeata*   Linnaeus

This is essentially a bird of the prairies, sufficiently rare in Ontario to delight the bird watcher when discovered, but common enough that some are usually discovered each year. They winter in Mexico, the Gulf States and West Indies, with a few stragglers farther north.

IDENTIFICATION:   The oversize "Donald Duck" bill is the best field mark, especially for the females which much resemble female Mallards when at rest on the water. In flight the females look like big Blue-winged Teal with the prominent blue-white patches at the bend of the wing. The males in breeding plumage are beautiful ducks with their green heads, chestnut sides, white breast and black back. When feeding they have a bad habit of keeping their diagnostic bills under water and so out of sight for so long that you wonder if they are ever going to bring them up into view: this is almost a good field mark!

WINTER:   On Christmas counts it has been uncommon at Long Point, rare in the western end of Lake Ontario and at Kingston and absent elsewhere in Ontario. Stirrett (1973a: 13) noted two at Pelee on Dec. 10 and two on Feb. 28. Kelley (1978: 18) mentioned six winter records for SE Michigan and SW Ontario, without details. Speirs (1979: 42) detailed several early Dec. records for the Lake Ontario marshes between Pickering and Oshawa, but none later than Dec. 11.

SPRING:   Stirrett (1973b: 14) called it a very common transient at Pelee, the earliest on Mar. 7, a maximum of 200 on Apr. 2 and the latest seven on June 1. Ussher (1965: 4) had earliest and latest dates for Rondeau on Mar. 15 and May 25 with average arrivals on Apr. 1 and departures on May 4. Saunders & Dale (1933: 176-177) considered it "one of the rarest of Middlesex ducks" and detailed only three spring records between Apr. 13 and Apr. 18. A.R. Muma retrieved a male from the Niagara River below the falls on Apr. 26, 1953 (Sheppard, 1960: 9). The earliest record for Ontario Co. was at Cranberry Marsh on Mar. 17, 1973, by Naomi LeVay: George A. Scott's median arrival date for Oshawa was Apr. 16 and his earliest on Mar. 29 (Speirs, 1979: 42). Weir & Quilliam (1980: 33) gave the 26-year average arrival date for Kingston as Apr. 10 with the earliest on Mar. 23. Devitt (1967: 40) gave the average arrival date for Barrie as Apr. 16 with the earliest on Mar. 30, 1963. Beamer had just three spring records for Meaford: one on Apr. 18, 1948, four on Apr. 20, 1949 and a male that was spotted on June 1, 1938 and remained for several days. Nicholson (1972: 15) considered it an uncommon spring migrant on Manitoulin from mid-Apr. to late May. Skeel and Bondrup-Nielsen (1978: 156) considered it a scarce spring migrant at Pukaskwa with a few records between May 10 and 17, 1975. Denis (1961: 3) gave May 8 as the average for spring arrival at Thunder Bay with the earliest on Apr. 23, 1957. Elder (1979: 29) considered it a rare spring migrant at Geraldton with the earliest on May 7: he also saw one at Atikokan on May 7, 1979.

SUMMER:   Kelley (1978: 18) gave details of four breeding records from Kent Co., including one nest with 7 eggs at Devon Marsh as early as May 28, 1966: she also cited six summer records of single birds in July and Aug. Stirret (1973c: 14) had two early August records at Pelee. C.A. MacCallum saw adults with young in 1886 and 1887 on the Grand River, near Dunnville, the only breeding record in Baillie & Harrington (1936: 15). Beardslee & Mitchell (1965: 133) suggest that they may still breed in the Dunnville marshes as well as the Wainfleet Marsh and Mud Lake in Niagara R.M. R.

Charles Long found a nest with incubating female in the Lynde Creek Marsh, Whitby, as early as May 23, 1967 while on July 2, 1961 Naomi and John LeVay saw a female with 14 downy young on nearby Cranberry Marsh: the first Toronto region breeding record (Speirs, 1979: 42). The first breeding record for the Kingston region was on June 25, 1961 at Horseshoe Is. where a female with 7 or 8 young was observed (Quilliam, 1965: 41). Devitt (1967: 40) has a few summer records for Simcoe Co., some suggesting breeding. T.M. Shortt saw one near Cape Henrietta Maria on Aug. 16, 1948 (Peck, 1972: 338). Schueler, Baldwin & Rising (1974: 144-145) found them uncommon at Ft. Albany and saw two males on June 23 and 28, 1971 about 4 miles east of Winisk.

AUTUMN: Skeel & Bondrup-Nielsen (1978: 156) called it an early and scarce fall migrant, from July 22 to Sept. 2, at Pukaskwa. Nicholson (1972: 15) had only one fall record for Manitoulin, shot during the 1968 hunting season. Devitt (1967: 40) had just three fall (Sept.) records for Simcoe Co. Weir & Quilliam (1980: 33) gave Oct. 25 as the 13-year average departure date from Kingston. George A. Scott's median departure date from Oshawa was Nov. 7 (Speirs, 1979: 42). Saunders & Dale (1933: 176) had only one fall record for the London region, one shot near Duncrief in Oct., 1916 by Roger T. Hedley. Ussher (1965: 4) had earliest and latest fall dates at Rondeau on Aug. 17 and Dec. 14, with average arrivals on Sept. 25 and departures on Nov. 11. Stirrett (1973d: 16) considered this an uncommon fall transient at Pelee from August through to a maximum of 50 on Nov. 5.

**MEASUREMENTS:**

*Length* ♂ 18-21 ins. ♀ 17-20 ins. (Palmer, 1976: 498)

*Wingspread:* ♂ 29-33 ins. ♀ 27-31 ins. (Palmer, 1976: 498)

*Weight:* ♂ about 1 1/2 lb. ♀ about 1 1/4 lb. (Palmer, 1976: 498)

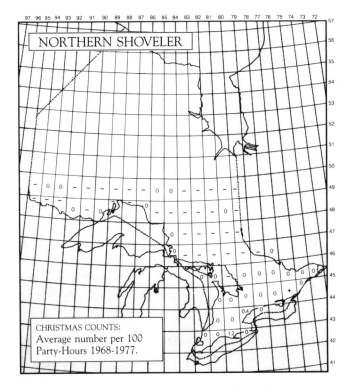

NORTHERN SHOVELER

CHRISTMAS COUNTS:
Average number per 100
Party-Hours 1968-1977.

# GADWALL  *Anas strepera*  Linneaus

This was essentially a prairie duck and very rare in Ontario until quite recently: in my early birding days it was always a red letter day when a Gadwall was spotted among the more common puddle ducks. Nowadays it is not unusual to find 100 in favourable localities such as Lynde Creek marsh in autumn or the New Toronto waterfront in winter.

**IDENTIFICATION:** Males in breeding plumage are gray with black rear ends. Females look like somewhat smaller female Mallards, but like the males with a spot of white where the Mallard has its blue speculum bordered with white along the rear edge of the wing. Sometimes this white spot does not show when they are at rest on the water, but when it does show it is diagnostic. The gray bill *bordered with orange-yellow along the sides* is also characteristic.

**WINTER:** it is now fairly common in western Lake Ontario in winter but uncommon to rare elsewhere. It has shown up on Christmas counts north to Wiarton and the Thousand Islands. Goodwin, Freedman and McKay (1977: 4-9) documented the spectacular increase in numbers in recent winters in the Toronto region from one in 1941, the next in 1960, but continous and increasing numbers since 1965 (with 294 tallied on the mid-winter inventory in 1976). Sheppard (1945: 157) wrote that two or three occurred with several hundred Black Ducks and Mallards near Navy Island, Niagara Falls, since 1931-32. Devitt (1967: 37) had just one mid-December record from Barrie.

**SPRING:** Stirrett (1973b: 14) called it a common and regular transient at Pelee, with the earliest on Mar. 23, the peak on Apr. 7 and latest on May 22. Ussher (1965: 4) considered it uncommon at Rondeau, with the earliest on Mar. 20, the 12-year average arrival on Apr. 8 and latest on May 24. Saunders & Dale (1933: 124) had only six spring records for the London region, the first on May 6, 1924 by E.M.S. Dale. Beardslee and Mitchell (1965: 126) reported one at Erie Beach on May 23, 1957 by R.D. Coggeshall. Migrants appear in the Toronto region during the latter half of March with peak numbers in early May, e.g. R.G. Tozer noted 150 at Cranberry Marsh on May 10, 1977 (Speirs, 1979: 35). Weir & Quilliam (1980: 32) gave Mar. 24 as the 14-year average arrival date for Kingston. Devitt (1967: 37) had only four scattered records from Simcoe Co. from late Apr. to early June. Nicholson (1972: 14) reported a few recent records from late Apr. to late May at Manitoulin.

**SUMMER:** Beardslee & Mitchell (1965: 126) reported a pair at Dunnville Marsh on June 27 and Aug. 24, 1948 and two at Rockhouse Point on Aug. 30, 1947 (by Wright). The first breeding record for the Toronto region was on July 6, 1969 at Cranberry Marsh when G. Norris and R. Wood flushed a female from a nest with 6 eggs (Speirs, 1979: 35); several broods of young have been seen there in more recent years. Quilliam (1965: 37) had two mid-August records for the Kingston area. Beamer reported one flying past the Meaford shore on aug. 24, 1948. Nicholson (1972: 14) cited an observation of a female with 7 ducklings at Hensley Bay by R.R. Tasker, as the only summer record for Manitoulin. James. McLaren & Barlow (1976: 12) list the Gadwall as a common summer resident north to Orangeville and Ottawa, with sightings to James Bay and Thunder Bay, while Baillie & Harrington (1936) had no records of this species breeding in Ontario up to that date.

AUTUMN: A few have been noted at Manitoulin in late Sept. (Nicholson, 1972: 14). Beamer mentioned two at Meaford on Spet. 24, 1949. Quilliam (1965: 37) had two mid-Oct. records for the Kingston region but now gives Dec. 17 as the 15-year average departure date (Weir & Quilliam, 1980: 32). On the fall outings of the Toronto Ornithological club the first was noted in 1957 with increasing numbers in most subsequent years. R.G. Tozer estimated 225 at Shoal Point Marsh, Pickering, on Nov. 9, 1975. Fleming (1906: 444) reported a male at Toronto on Nov. 2, 1901, as a notably rare find. Beardslee & Mitchell (1965: 126) reported three at Ft. Erie on Sept. 8, 1946 (by R.F. Andrle and E.L. Seeber). Saunders & Dale, 1933: 174-175) had only one fall record for the London region, on Sept. 27, 1930. Ussher (1965: 4) gave earliest and latest dates for Rondeau as Sept. 22 and Nov. 28, with average arrival and departure dates on Sept. 25 and Nov. 14. Stirrett (1973d: 16 and 1973a: 13) called it an uncommon fall transient at Pelee from Oct. 2 to Nov. 26.

**MEASUREMENTS:**
*Length:* 18-23 ins.
(Palmer, 1976: 380).
*Wingspread:* to 35 ins.
(Palmer, 1975: 380).
*Weight:* ♂ about 2 lb. ♀
about 1³/₄ lb. (Palmer,
1976: 380).

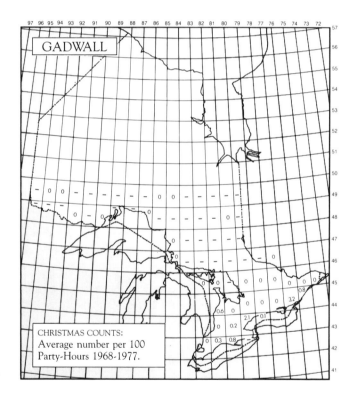

GADWALL

CHRISTMAS COUNTS:
Average number per 100
Party-Hours 1968-1977.

# EURASIAN WIGEON   *Anas penelope*   Linneaus

This is the Eurasian counterpart of the American Wigeon (or Baldpate as it was formerly called). Palmer (1976: 402) gave it the appropriate name of Eurasian Wigeon, as it is just as common across Siberia as it is in northern Europe. In North America it is a red letter day when you spot one among the flocks of Baldpates or other puddle ducks.

IDENTIFICATION: The creamy crown atop a fiery red head is the most striking field mark. The sides are gray rather than wine-coloured (as in the Baldpate). In flight both have conspicuous white patches near the leading edge of the wing near the body, but the wing linings are grayish rather than pure white as in the Baldpate. Females are too similar to female Baldpates for easy identification in the field.

WINTER: Kelley (1974: 18) published a report of one at Rondeau on Dec. 30, 1967. The 1974 check-list of Rondeau birds lists it as a rare spring and fall migrant. John Crosby found one in Toronto's Humber Marsh No. 3 on Dec. 5, 1943 which was seen again there on Dec. 8 by R.M. Saunders (1947: 343, 345). Sheppard (1945: 158) reported one seen at Goat Island, Niagara Falls, by James Savage on Dec. 25, 1924.

SPRING: Kelley (1974: 18) had 14 records from SW Ontario in spring. Stirrett (1973b: 14) had four records from Pelee between Apr. 2 and May 20. Brooman (1954: 9) reported one found by Field in Conc. 6, Yarmouth Twp. Elgin Co., on Apr. 21, 1952. Saunders (1947: 96) described his delight at finding one at Hamilton on Mar. 31, 1935: he mentioned other sightings on Apr. 23, 24 and May 28 and 30 (Saunders, 1947: 360). There are records of two beautiful males seen at Cranberry Marsh, Whitby (Speirs, 1979: 40): the first seen from Apr. 19 to May 7, 1971 and the other from Apr. 20 to May 1, 1973, both by many observers including myself (details in Tozer & Richards, 1974: 81). Quilliam (1965: 40, 195 and 1980: 5, 33) detailed records for the Kingston area, the earliest Apr. 5 and the latest May 19: I well remember seeing one of these on Apr. 25, 1965 with Ken. Edwards *et al* from Wolfe Island. Denis (1961: 3) gave records for May 1, 1954 and another May 6 record for Thunder Bay.

SUMMER: George A. Scott with K. and O. Sands saw a male at Oshawa's Second Marsh on July 3, 1955 (Speirs, 1979: 40).

AUTUMN: Quilliam (1965: 40) mentioned two shot during the hunting season of 1952 near Kingston by R. Fray, identified by H.W. Curran. Saunders (1947: 360) had two fall records for the Toronto region, on Oct. 8 and 15. Kelley (1974: 18) had a report from Rondeau on Nov. 11, 1967.

**MEASUREMENTS:**
*Length:* ♂ to 20 ins., ♀ to 19 ins. (Palmer, 1976: 402).
*Wingspread:* to about 32 ins. (Palmer, 1976: 402).
*Weight:* ♂ about 1³/₄ lb., ♀ about 1¹/₂ lb. (Palmer, 1976: 402).

# AMERICAN WIGEON   *Anas americana*   Gmelin

I rather like the old name, Baldpate, although the pate (top of the head) is not really bald, but white or whitish, as in the Bald Eagle. My most vivid memory of these sprightly ducks is of the flocks that gathered in Hamilton Bay in early spring, often among the groups of "Whistling Swans," but it was the Baldpates that were whistling, not the swans.

IDENTIFICATION: Look for the white, or cream-coloured, crown of the males above the dark green sides of the head. In the rare European Wigeon the whole head is red. The female is best distinguished by her vinaceous (wine-coloured) sides. The whistling voice of the male "whee'whee'whee" should alert the observer to look for Baldpates. The big white wing-patches in flight are also suggestive of this species.

WINTER: On Christmas counts they have been fairly common near Long Point and the west end of Lake Ontario but uncommon to rare elsewhere north to the Thousand Islands and Pelee, with single birds on two counts at Sault Ste. Marie. Stirrett (1973a: 13) gave three winter records for Pelee. Goodwin, Freedman & McKay (1977: 4-9) illustrated the recent increase in numbers wintering in the Toronto region from zero on early counts to dozens in the 1970's. Devitt (1967: 39) had only one winter record for Simcoe Co., on Dec. 12, 1964 at Allandale by Frances Westman. Weir & Quilliam (1980: 33) had Jan. 20 and Feb. 13 records for Kingston.

SPRING: Stirrett (1973b: 14) had his earliest Pelee record on Mar. 7 with the peak of 500 on Apr. 17 and last seen on June 1. Ussher (1965: 4) gave Mar. 6 and May 25 as earliest and latest spring dates for Rondeau with average arrivals on Mar. 18 and departures on Apr. 29. Saunders & Dale (1933: 175) remarked that a male shot about 1880 was the only Middlesex record for about 40 years but that since 1921 they had become almost common in late March through April. George A. Scott's median arrival date for Oshawa was Apr. 1 with his earliest on Mar. 13, 1947 and the spring peak during the first week of April (Speirs, 1979: 41). Weir & Quilliam (1980: 33) gave the average stay at Kingston from Mar. 22 to May 6, with a few staying until the end of May. Devitt (1967: 39) gave the 15-year average for arrivals at Barrie as Apr. 16, with the earliest on Mar. 27, 1961 and the heaviest flights in May. Beamer, at Meaford, had spring records as early as Mar. 30, 1938 and as late as May 21, 1949. Nicholson (1972: 15) noted the spring passage through Manitoulin from mid-Apr. to late May. Skeel & Bondrup-Nielsen (1978: 156) found it scarce at Pukaskwa from Apr. 14 to May 29. Denis (1961: 2) gave Apr. 14, 1955 as the earliest date for Thunder Bay with Apr. 26 as the average arrival date. Elder (1979: 29) had his earliest spring record for Geraldton on Apr. 24: his earliest record for Atikokan in 1979 was on May 5. Dick Van Vliet saw one at Perrault Falls on May 8, 1953 (Cringan, 1953: 2). Elsey gave May 27, 1950 as the arrival date in the Asheweig area (Cringan, 1950: 5). J. Satterly saw one at South Porcupine on May 30, 1949.

SUMMER: On the Breeding Bird Surveys individuals have shown up on the Sudbury, Atikokan and Dryden routes, none elsewhere in Ontario. Stirrett (1973c: 14) had just one summer record for Pelee: 4 birds on Aug. 7. Baillie (1960: 16-17) detailed breeding records for Toronto (the first on Aug. 19, 1934 when a nest with 3 eggs was found at Ashbridge's Bay by H.H. Southam); at Mud Lake near Pt. Colborne where 2 adults and 4 young were seen on June 8, 1951 by members of the Buffalo Ornithological Society; at Fort William where N. Denis saw an adult with 6 young on July 5, 1957; at Nikip Lake where Alec Cringan noted two broods in Aug., 1951 and at Fort Severn where C.E. Hope and W.B. Scott saw young on July 9, 10 and 21, 1940 (some of these collected for the ROM). There are recent summer records for the Pickering and Whitby marshes but no breeding evidence to date (Speirs, 1979: 41). Devitt (1967: 39) cited several summer records for Simcoe Co. but no breeding reports. Quilliam (1965: 41) had only one summer record for Kingston, on June 25, 1961. James, McLaren & Barlow (1976: 13) mentioned summer records for Luther Marsh, Cornwall, Owen Sound and Sandy Lake, in addition to others documented here. Smith (1957: 168) saw four males at South Porcupine on June 20, 1953 and one at Lillabelle Lake, Cochrane, on Aug. 18, 1954. Elder (1979: 29) called it a scarce summer resident at Geraldton. Cringan (1953: 1) saw at least 3 pairs at Kasabonika Lake in late May-early June, 1953. A downy young was collected about 20 miles south of Cape Henrietta Maria on July 26, 1948, by T.M. Shortt (Peck, 1972: 338). Schueler, Baldwin & Rising (1974: 145) found them common at Moosonee, Attawapiskat, Winisk and Hawley Lake but not seen at Ft. Albany: they collected young at Winisk and Hawley Lake on July 1, 1971 and July 16, 1964 respectively.

AUTUMN: Nicholson (1972: 15) noted fall migrants on Manitoulin from late Aug. to late Sept. Beamer had three fall records from Meaford: Sept. 7, 1939 (6), Sept. 25, 1949 (36) and Oct. 10, 1938 (1). Devitt (1967: 39) mentioned just four fall birds (including two specimens) all from Little Lake, Barrie. Quilliam (1965: 41) noted a fall peak of 500 on Nov. 8, 1953 and gave Sept. 22 and Nov. 23 as average arrival and departure dates for Kingston (Weir & Quilliam, 1980: 33) Tozer & Richards (1974: 82) reported 1000 on Lake Scugog on Oct. 11, 1969. Speirs (1979: 41) found the fall peak in late October in the Whitby region, with George Scott's median departure date for Oshawa on Nov. 12. Baldpates banded in the Longlac, Montreal and Fredericton, N.B. areas were taken in fall in the Toronto region (Speirs, 1979: 41). Saunders & Dale (1933: 175) mentioned just one fall record for Middlesex Co., on Oct. 5, 1924. Ussher (1965: 4) had the earliest and latest fall migrants at Rondeau on Aug. 17 and Dec. 14 with average arrivals on Sept. 16 and departures on Nov. 20. Stirrett (1973d: 16) found them common in fall at Pelee from late Aug. to mid-Nov. with a peak of 1000 in early Nov.

**MEASUREMENTS:**
*Length:* ♂ 19-22 ins.
♀ 18-20 ins. (Palmer,
1976: 414).
*Wingspread:* ♂ to 35 ins.
♀ to 33 ins. (Palmer,
1976: 414).
*Weight:* ♂ about 1³/₄ lb.
♀ about 1¹/₂ lb. (Palmer,
1976: 414).

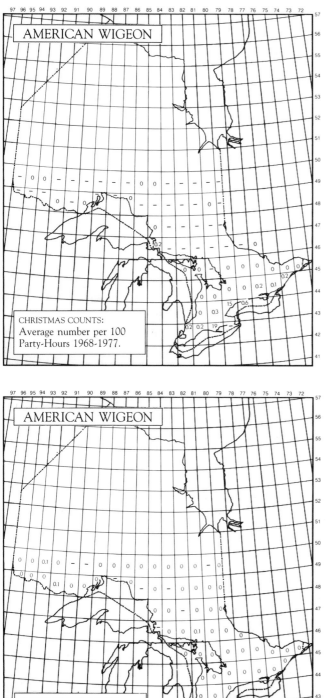

AMERICAN WIGEON

CHRISTMAS COUNTS:
Average number per 100
Party-Hours 1968-1977.

AMERICAN WIGEON

BREEDING BIRDS SURVEY:
Average number per 50 stops
1968-1977.

# CANVASBACK   *Aythya valisineria*   (Wilson)

This is essentially a prairie breeder and readers are referred to Hochbaum's delightful monograph "The Canvasback on a prairie marsh" for the story of its life history. In Ontario we look for it in migration and at a few favoured wintering localities.

IDENTIFICATION:   The long sloping head and bill profile is diagnostic. The very white back separates it from the somewhat similarly coloured Redhead at a distance.

WINTER:   On Christmas counts it has been common at Niagara Falls, Long Point and sometimes at Blenheim, with small numbers north to Ottawa and Wiarton. Kelley (1978: 19) reported large numbers wintering in St. Clair and Detroit Rivers. Stirrett (1973a: 17) had 100 at Pelee on Dec. 26 and a few January and February records. Sheppard (1945: 159) mentioned 130 near Fort Erie on Jan. 28, 1943 (90% males) while Mitchell reported 1000 near Grand Island on Feb. 25, 1940. Goodwin, Freedman & McKay (1977: 8-11) showed a gradual increase in numbers wintering in the Toronto region, with none in most winters before 1956, increasing to 36 on the 1977 Christmas count. This is a rare wintering duck along the Pickering-Oshawa waterfront (Speirs, 1979: 46). Quilliam (1965: 45) had several records throughout the winter at Kingston, with 400 there on Dec. 30, 1961. Devitt (1967: 42) had just three winter records for Barrie.

SPRING:   They diminish in the St. Clair-Detroit River areas through April with most gone by mid-May (Kelley, 1978: 19). It is a common spring migrant at Pelee with a peak of 450 on Mar. 25 (Stirrett, 1973b: 14). Ussher (1965: 5) had some winter records for Rondeau but average arrival date there was Mar. 22 and departure on Apr. 23 with the latest noted on May 16. Saunders & Dale (1933: 178-179) documented an increase at London beginning about 1924 with spring records as early as Apr. 10, 1931 and as late as May 25, 1924. Saunders (1947: 361) gave the average arrival date for Toronto as Apr. 16 with May 31 the latest spring date. The spring peak at Pickering is usually in early April with maximum numbers about 30 (Speirs, 1979: 46). Quilliam (1965: 45) found the peak at Kingston in late March, with a maximum estimate of 1500 on Mar. 30, 1959, with most leaving by mid-April and May 3, 1955 the latest date. Devitt (1967: 42) gave Apr. 17 as the average spring arrival date at Barrie with Apr. 11 as the earliest. Beamer had two spring records for Meaford: Mar. 19, 1938 (4) and Apr. 5, 1953 (2). Nicholson (1972: 15) called it an occasional visitor with only a few recent reports on Manitoulin. Denis (1961: 3) gave Apr. 12, 1953 as the earliest record for Thunder Bay with the average arrival date on Apr. 29.

SUMMER:   Baillie (1962: 10-11) cited five breeding records for Lake St. clair (in Lambton Co. and Kent Co.) There have been also recent scattered summer records at Lake St. Clair (Kelley, 1978: 19) and in the Oshawa-Whitby area (Speirs, 1979: 46) but no recent breeding evidence. Beardslee & Mitchell (1965: 137) cite two summer records for the Niagara region by Arthur Schaffner: one at Mud Lake on July 22, 1954 and five at McNab on July 2, 1957. R. Badger reported a female with downy young at Luther Marsh during the summer of 1965 (Goodwin, 1965: 539).

AUTUMN:   This is just an occasional visitor to Manitoulin in fall (Nicholson, 1972: 15). Beamer had only one fall record for Meaford, when 50 were seen along the eastern shoreline on Sept. 2, 1949. Devitt (1967: 42) called it an uncommon fall transient at Barrie, mainly in late October and early November. Quilliam (1965: 44-45) called it a common fall transient at Kingston, with 2000 estimated on Nov. 8, 1927 (by Beaupré). It is an uncommon fall migrant in the Pickering-Oshawa area, most numerous in early November (Speirs, 1979: 46). Saunders (1947: 361) gave the earliest fall date for Toronto as Sept. 30, with his 6-year average fall arrival date as Oct. 11 (but Baillie's 8-year average not until Nov. 6). Saunders & Dale (1933: 179) had only one fall record for London, on Nov. 2, 1924. Ussher (1965: 5) had his earliest fall record for Rondeau on Oct. 1, with average arrivals on Oct. 19 and departures on Nov. 28. Fall migrants arrive at Lake St. Clair in early Oct. and are abundant by the end of the month (Kelley, 1978: 19). Stirrett (1973d: 16) considered it fairly common at Pelee with a peak of 350 on Nov. 2.

**MEASUREMENTS:**

*Length:* ♂ 19¹/₂ to 23 ins.
♀ 19-22¹/₂ ins. (Palmer, 1976: 137)
*Wingspread:* ♂ to 35¹/₂ ins. ♀ to 33¹/₂ ins. (Palmer, 1976: 137)
*Weight:* ♂ 3 lbs.
♀ 2¹/₂ lbs. (Palmer, 1976: 137)

**MONOGRAPH:**

Hochbaum, H. Albert 1944 The Canvasback on a prairie marsh. Washington, D.C. American Wildlife Institute: i-xii; 1-207.

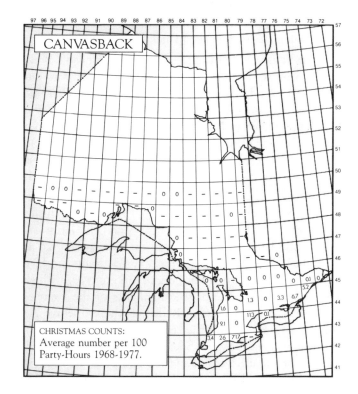

CANVASBACK

CHRISTMAS COUNTS:
Average number per 100 Party-Hours 1968-1977.

# REDHEAD   *Aythya americana*   (Eyton)

My most vivid memory of this species is of the great rafts in late March on Long Point Bay at the time of ther "Whistling" Swan migration. Previous to this visit I had always thought of the Redhead as an uncommon bird, one of the special highlights of the spring waterfowl show, but here were Redheads from close up to as far as the eye could see.

IDENTIFICATION: Males are most likely to be confused with Canvasbacks, though the Canvasbacks are bigger, with long, sloping foreheads and much whiter backs. Females are almost indistinguishable in the field from female Ring-necked Ducks and are best recognized by the male companions associated with them. Godfrey (1966: 66) suggests that the female Ring-necked Duck has a more distinct white eye-ring than the Redhead.

WINTER: On Christmas counts the Redhead has been common at Long Point, fairly common in western Lake Ontario and uncommon to rare at other localities north to the Thousand Islands, Wiarton and Sault Ste. Marie. Kelley (1978: 19) reported an aerial count of 8500 in Feb. 1950, on Lake St. Clair and western Lake Erie. Stirrett (1973a: 14) had no record at Pelee between Dec. 1 when 7 were noted and Feb. 25 when 14 were tallied. Fleming (1906: 444) reported a flock wintering at Toronto in 1901-1902, that left Mar. 15 Speirs (1979: 44) documented the recent increase in the Pickering-Oshawa lakefront, perhaps associated with warm water effluents from the Pickering Nuclear Plant and Lasco Steel.

SPRING: Stirrett (1973b: 14) gave Mar. 12 as his earliest Pelee record, with a maximum of 500 from Mar. 18 to Apr. 3 and the latest on May 31. Ussher (1965: 5) had earliest and latest spring dates at Rondeau on Feb. 26 and May 11, with average arrival date Mar. 23 and departure on Apr. 23. Saunders & Dale (1933: 178) had an 8-year average for spring arrivals at London on Apr. 10, with the earliest on Mar. 21, 1914. As mentioned above, one of the highlights of the swan excursions to Long Point in late March are the great rafts of Redheads there. George A. Scott's median arrival date for Oshawa is Mar. 13 and the spring peak in the Pickering-Oshawa region is generally in late March or early April (Speirs, 1979: 44). Quilliam (1965: 43) wrote that they appear on the Cataraqui River at Kingston almost as soon as open water appears, peak about the end of March and leave, on the average, about Apr. 18. Devitt (1967: 41) had Simcoe co. records as early as Apr. 8, 1955 and as late as June 3, 1967 (both on Georgian Bay) with the 7-year average for arrivals at Barrie on Apr. 18. Skeel & Bondrup-Nielsen (1978: 157) noted only one at Pukaskwa, on May 22, 1975. Denis (1961: 3) gave Apr. 16, 1949 as the earliest date for Thunder Bay with average arrival date as Apr. 27.

SUMMER: Kelley (1978: 19) wrote that no broods or nests have been reported since 1954 in the Lake St. Clair marshes, though summer sightings were still made there as well as at Pelee. J. Kamstra reported an adult female with four young in the Scugog marshes in early Aug., 1971 (Tozer & Richards, 1974: 84) and there are a few other summer records from Ontario Co. marshes (Speirs, 1979: 44). Fleming (1906: 444) reported a small flock of non-breeding birds at Toronto in the summer of 1906. Smith (1957: 168) saw a male at Lillabelle Lake, Cochrane, on July 12, 1953. Three were noted in the Pickle Lake area on June 17,1977 by Ross James et al. Elder (1979: 29) had only one record at Geraldton, on June 4, 1966, when a pair was observed.

AUTUMN: David Elder saw one at Atikokan on Oct. 14, 1979. Devitt (1967: 41) considered them uncommon in Simcoe Co. from early Oct., with some on Kempenfeldt Bay as late as Dec. 15, 1961 (Frances Westman). Weir & Quilliam (1980: 33) gave the 24-year average for arrivals at Kingston as Oct. 10, while hundreds were noted on Oct. 20, 1957 (Quilliam, 1965: 43). George A. Scott's median departure date from Oshawa is Nov. 20 and I usually find the peak at Cranberry Marsh, Whitby, just before the November freezeup (Speirs, 1979: 44). Ussher (1965: 5) had his earliest and latest fall dates for Rondeau on Aug. 10 and Dec. 4 with average arrival on Oct. 8 and departure on Nov. 21. Stirrett (1973d: 16) called it a common fall transient at Pelee from an early arrival on Sept. 3 to a maximum on Oct. 17 and latest on Dec. 1.

**MEASUREMENTS:**

*Length:* ♂ to 20½ ins. ♀ to 19½ ins. (Palmer, 1976: 162).

*Wingspread:* ♂ to 32 ins. ♀ to 30½ ins. (Palmer, 1976: 162).

*Weight:* ♂ usually about 2¼ lb. ♀ 2 lb. (Palmer, 1976: 162).

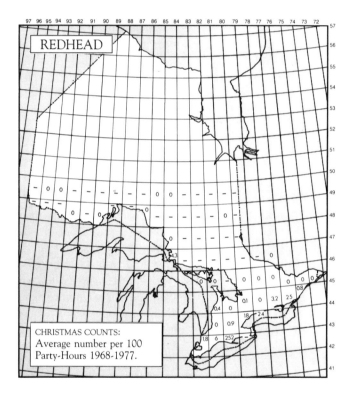

REDHEAD

CHRISTMAS COUNTS:
Average number per 100
Party-Hours 1968-1977.

# RING-NECKED DUCK    *Aythya collaris*    (Donovan)

About a mile north of the Geraldton station the road forks and in the angle between the south and east forks lies a pool of black water, an acre or two in extent, rimmed with black spruce and tamarack. Here I often saw a pair of Ring-necked Ducks in a setting that they often choose for breeding in the spruce-moose biome of northern Ontario.

IDENTIFICATION: Males look a bit like scaup ducks but have black backs and a prominent white crescent on the sides in front of the wings. Females are very similar to female Redheads but lack the prominent white about the bill typical of female scaups and share the white ring around the bill with the female Redheads. (See Redhead).

WINTER: This is a rare duck on Christmas counts, north to Ottawa and Manitoulin: one showed up on the Thunder Bay count in 1976. Saunders & Dale (1933: 177) had only one winter record for London, through Dec., 1931. Edward Reinecke saw one in Feb., 1899, near Niagara Falls (Sheppard, 1945: 158). Speirs (1979: 45) cited seven records of birds seen during the winter months along the Oshawa to Pickering lakeshore. Quilliam (1965: 44) had three Christmas count records and three January reports for Kingston. Devitt (1967: 42) reported three winter records for Barrie. Beamer had one in Meaford harbour on Dec. 8, 1945. An unusual northern record was one that wintered on Pearl Lake, Schumacher, for two winters according to F. Cowell (Smith, 1957: 169). Banding returns suggest that our birds winter mainly in the Carolinas, some going south to Florida and Louisiana (Speirs, 1979: 45 and Todd (1963: 159).

SPRING: Stirrett (1973b: 14) called it a common and regular transient at Pelee from Mar. 16 to May 20, with a peak of 100 on Mar. 27-28. Ussher (1965: 5) gave earliest and latest spring dates for Rondeau as Mar. 6 and Apr. 28 with average arrivals on Mar. 22 and departure on Apr. 21. Saunders & Dale (1933: 178) gave the 8-year average for spring arrivals at London as Aprl 10, with the earliest on Mar. 27, 1925. Saunders (1947: 361) listed Baillie's 16-year average for Toronto arrivals as Mar. 29, with most departures by late April and May 23 as the latest spring date. George A. Scott noted four at Whitby as early as Mar. 5, 1961, but his median arrival date for Oshawa was Mar. 29 and the spring peak is Apr. 4 (Speirs, 1979: 45). Tozer & Richards (1974: 84) reported about 100 on Cranberry Marsh, Whitby, on Apr. 17, 1971. Weir & Quilliam (1980: 33) gave Mar. 16 as the 31-year average arrival date for Kingston with the average departure date on Apr. 28. Quilliam (1965: 44) mentioned a maximum spring count for Kingston of 400 to 500 on Apr. 27, 1962. Devitt (1967: 42) gave the 14-year average arrival for Barrie as Apr. 10 with the earliest on Mar. 30, 1967. Beamer saw them at Meaford as early as Mar. 26, 1938 and as late as Apr. 30, 1939. Nicholson (1972: 15) had Manitoulin records from early Apr. to early May. Spring arrivals at North Bay were noted on Apr. 28, 1944 and Apr. 20, 1945 (Speirs & Speirs, 1947: 26). Skeel & Bondrup-Nielsen (1978: 157) saw their first at Pukaskwa on Apr. 20. Denis (1961: 2) gave Apr. 15, 1955 as the earliest date for Thunder Bay with average arrival on Apr. 25. Elder (1979: 29) had his earliest spring sighting at Geraldton on Apr. 25; he noted one at Atikokan on Apr. 27, 1979. Dick VanVliet saw one at Perrault Falls on May 8, 1953 (Cringan, 1953: 2).

SUMMER: On Breeding Bird Surveys they showed up occasionally south to Eganville and Sudbury, north to Longlac, Suomi and Dryden, and more frequently at Smooth Rock Falls, Atikokan and Kenora. Beardslee & Mitchell (1965: 136) mentioned a drake seen on several occasions during the summer of 1951 on Mud Lake (Niagara R.M.). There are a few June and Aug. records for Ontario Co. but no evidence of breeding (Speirs, 1979: 45). Devitt (1967: 41) mentioned several summer records from Simcoe Co. Nicholson (1972: 15) called it a regular summer resident on Manitoulin. Skeel & Bondrup-Nielsen (1978:157) documented three broods at Pukaskwa. J. Satterly had numerous records near Matheson, including a pair with 11 downy young at TwinLakes on July 3, 1948 and 5 young there on July 10, 1949 and a pair with 7 small young there on June 29, 1952. Smith (1957: 168) had other records near Matheson, as well as from Kapuskasing, Hearst and Cochrane. Baillie & Harrington (1936: 16) had breeding records from Lac Seul (Kenora) and Whitefish Lake (Thunder Bay) with a summer record from Lake Abitibi. Hope (1938: 9-10) considered it the commonest breeding duck of the Favourable Lake region, with three broods noted on July 24, 1938. Ross James also found it to be the most common duck near Pickle Lake in 1977. Cringan (1953: 1) saw two males and a female near Kasabonika Lake on June 3, 1953. Lee (1978: 19) quoted Keith Reynolds to the effect that "this was the most abundant duck seen on Hawley Lake in late July. Many had broods of young." James, McLaren & Barlow (1976: 13) called it a summer resident north to Ft. Severn, Attawapiskat, and south to Luther Marsh, Peterboroughj and Ottawa.

AUTUMN: Skeel & Bondrup-Nielsen (178: 157) saw their last at Pukaskwa on Sept. 29, Nicholson (1972: 15) had fall records from Manitoulin from mid-Sept. to late Nov. Beamer had only one fall record from Meaford, shot on Oct. 15, 1948. Devitt (1967: 41-42) had fall records from Simcoe Co. from mid-Sept. to Nov. 11. Weir & Quilliam (1980: 33) gave average arrival and departure dates for Kingston as Oct. 23 and Dec. 11, respectively. George A. Scott's median departure date from Oshawa was Nov. 7 and his latest Nov. 24, 1963: this species is generally much less common in fall than in spring there; one exception was a flock of 350 reported by Ron Tozer at Scugog on Nov. 12, 1977 (Speirs, 1979: 45). Saunders (1947: 361) had an early fall record for Toronto on Aug. 17, but his average fall arrival date was Oct. 67, with average departure at the end of October. Saunders & Dale (1933: 178) mentioned only one fall record for London, a female taken on Oct. 3, 1921 by A.A. Wood. Ussher (1965: 5) had earliest and latest fall dates for Rondeau on Sept. 1 and Nov. 28, with the average arrival on Oct. 3 and departure on Nov. 13, Stirrett (1973a: 14 and 1973d: 16) considered it uncommon at Pelee in fall, from Sept. 23 to Nov. 16.

**MEASUREMENTS:**
*Length:* ♂ 16 to 18 ins.
♀ 14-18 ins. (Palmer,
1976: 185).
*wingspread:* ♂ to 29¹/₂
ins. ♀ to 28 ins. (Palmer,
1976: 185).
*Weight:* ♂ 1.6 lb. ♀ 1.5
lb. (Palmer, 1976: 185).
4 ♀ averaged 603 g. at
Favourable Lake (Hope,
1938: 10).

**MONOGRAPH:**
Mendall, Howard L. 1958
The Ring-necked Duck in
the Northeast. Univ. Maine
Bull., 2: (16): xv; 1-317.
24 plates, figs. maps.

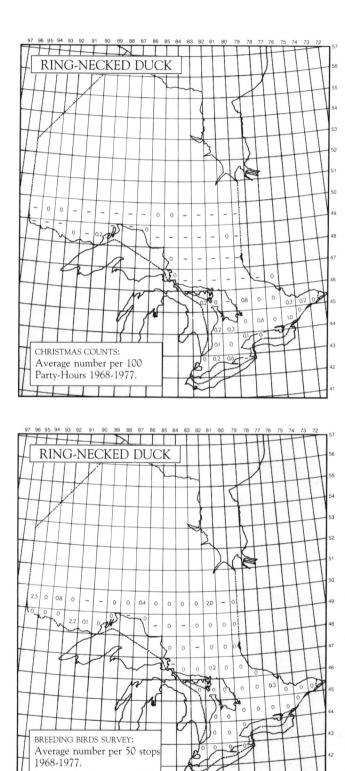

RING-NECKED DUCK

CHRISTMAS COUNTS:
Average number per 100
Party-Hours 1968-1977.

RING-NECKED DUCK

BREEDING BIRDS SURVEY:
Average number per 50 stops
1968-1977.

# TUFTED DUCK   *Aythya fuligula*   (Linnaeus)

The Tufted Duck is normally an Old World duck, rarely seen in North America.

IDENTIFICATION:  Males resemble Greater Scaup males but have black rather than gray backs and show a pronounced drooping crest. Females resemble female scaups but have less white on the face.

WINTER:  D. Gardiner, K. McLaughlin and A. Wormington observed a male at Oakville from Jan. 23 to Feb. 9, 1983 and at Hamilton from Feb. 27 into spring. With Phillip Holder, I watched the Oakville bird on Feb. 1, 1983 among a huge flock of scaups.

SPRING:  The Hamilton bird remained until Apr. 24, 1983.

SUMMER:

AUTUMN:

**MEASUREMENTS:**
*Length:* 17 ins. (Peterson,
Mountfort & Hollom,
1954: 37)
*Wingspread:*
*Weight:* ♂ 1.0 to 1.4 kg.
♀ 1.0 to 1.15 kg.
(Johnsgard, 1978: 310).

# GREATER SCAUP   *Aythya marila*   (Linnaeus)

This is one of the most numerous wintering ducks on the lower Great Lakes, where great "rafts" form in favoured localities. They breed along the Hudson Bay coast of Ontario, north to the Northwest Territories and Alaska.

IDENTIFICATION:  Scaups are ducks that are black at both ends and white in the middle. Females are dark brown and white around the bill. The best way to distinguish Greater Scaups from Lessers is by the wing stripe, which extends well beyond the bend of the wing towards the tip in the Greater Scaup but stops at the bend in Lewsser Scaups. Unfortunately for the observer scaups spend a lot of time on the water, not flying. The gloss on the head of the Greater Scaup tends to be green while on the Lesser it tends to be purple. The crown of the Greater Scaup is generally less puffed up than in Lesser Scaups. In most parts of Ontario most wintering scaups are Greaters, while in summer they are usually Lessers. Ring-necked Ducks, Redheads and Canvasbacks look a bit like scaups at a distance and often associate with them, so it is well to look over the flocks carefully, looking for the red heads of Redheads and Canvasbacks and the black backs and white crescent in front of the wing of the Ring-necked Ducks, and absence of white around the base of the bill in females.

WINTER:  On Christmas counts this is an abundant, but local, wintering duck at Long Point, western Lake Ontario and Kingston, with a few as far north as Deep River and Sault Ste. Marie. Kelley (1978: 20) reported large numbers wintering in Lake St. Clair, Detroit River and western Lake Erie. Stirrett (1973a: 14) had Dec. records at Pelee but mentioned none in Jan. or Feb. Goodwin, Freedman & McKay (1979: 11) stated that many thousands winter in the Toronto region where it is frequently the most numerous wintering duck (surpassed sometimes by Oldsquaw and in recent years by Mallard). Sheppard (1945: 159) called it one of the commonest winter ducks on the Niagara River, especially near Fort Erie. Large numbers winter near Kingston wherever open water is available (Quilliam, 1965: 47). Devitt (1967: 45) gave three Dec. records for Simcoe Co. Dennison (1980: 23) remarked that only 7 of the 31 scaups reported on the Sault St. Marie Christmas counts were given as Greater Scaup, the others as Lessers.

SPRING:  Stirrett (1973b: 14) called it a very common, regular transient at Pelee, with large flocks in late March, generally more numerous than Lesser Scaup before mid-April but less common in late April, with May 18 as the latest record. Saunders & Dale (1933: 129) had only three definite records of this species near London (while Lesser Scaups were abundant there). Ussher (1965: 5) gave average arrival and departure dates at Rondeau as Mar. 25 and May 6, with the latest sighting on May 24. I saw about 1000 at Whitby on Mar. 1, 1970 with 450 still there on Mar. 28; by mid-May they have usually become scarce but Charles Long noted this species at Pickering Beach as late as May 28, 1967 (Speirs, 1979: 47). Quilliam (1965: 45-47) gave this as a very numerous spring migrant near Kingston, with peak numbers (up to 40,000 estimated) in early April. Devitt (1967: 43) called it a fairly common spring transient at Barrie, and cited 6 specimens taken between Apr. 15 and May 2, all males. Nicholson (1972: 15) considered it an uncommon migrant at Manitoulin (in contrast with the Lesser Scaup which he considered common). Denis (1961: 3) had his earliest report for Thunder Bay on Apr. 18, 1945 with Apr. 27 as the average arrival date. D.H. Elder saw his first at Atikokan on May 5, 1978.

Cringan (1953a: 2) noted this species at Ear Falls on May 14, 1953, and he saw two to ten daily on Kasabonika Lake from May 27 to 29, 1953 (Cringan, 1953b: 2).

SUMMER: None have been reported on any of the Breeding Bird Surveys in Ontario. Sheppard (1945: 159) reported solitary males on the Niagara River in early June. Speirs (1979: 47) had two July records for the Whitby region. Quilliam (1965: 47) had two summer records for Kingston. Fleming (1906: 445) reported a small flock at Toronto during the summer of 1906. Two groups of downy young with adult females were collected at Cape Henrietta Maria by C.E. Hope during the summer of 1948 to establish the first breeding record for Ontario: there are several subsequent observations from this area (Peck, 1972: 338). Hope collected both species of scaup at Ft. Severn in summer, 1940, but noted more Greater Scaup than Lessers there.

AUTUMN: Devitt (1967: 43) called it a fairly common fall transient in Simcoe co. (much less abundant than the Lesser Scaup). Weir & Quilliam (1980: 33) gave Sept. 20 as the 27-year average arrival date at Kingston. This species has been reported a few times on the TOC Fall Field Days during the second week in September on the Pickering-Whitby lakefront but it is generally late October before they become numerous (Speirs, 1979: 47). Wainio et al estimated 5000 off Whitby on Nov. 7, 1970 (Tozer & Richards, 1974: 85). Ussher (1965: 5) gave average fall dates at Rondeau from Oct. 4 to Nov. 13, but a few sometimes winter there. Stirrett (1973d: 16) had his earliest fall record for Pelee on Aug. 31 with a maximum of 350 on Oct. 16.

BANDING: Birds banded in the Toronto region have been taken in winter in Virginia and in summer in Manitoba (Speirs, 1979: 47). Devitt (1967: 43) mentioned that one banded at Cayuga Lake, N.Y. on Feb. 23, 1923 was taken at Barrie on May 3, 1925.

**MEASUREMENTS:**
*Length* ♂ 17-20 ins. ♀ 16-19 ins. (Palmer, 1976: 232)
*Wingspread:* ♂ to 32½ ins. ♀ to 31 ins. (Palmer, 1976: 232)
*Weight:* ♂ usually under 2½ lb. ♀ about 2 lb. (Palmer, 1976: 233).

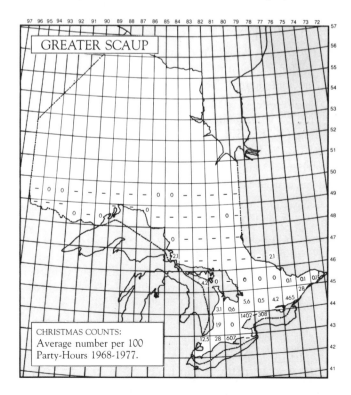

GREATER SCAUP

CHRISTMAS COUNTS:
Average number per 100 Party-Hours 1968-1977.

# LESSER SCAUP   *Aythya affinis*   (Eyton)

This is chiefly a prairie breeder, south of most of the Greater Scaups, wintering south to the Gulf states. It is mainly a bird of passage in Ontario, though a few may be found in summer and winter. I have found it mainly in shallow, marshy habitat, not in deep water where the Greater Scaup is often seen in great rafts.

IDENTIFICATION: From the Greater Scaup it is most readily distinguished by the short white wing stripe in flight and on the water at close range by the purple gloss on the head and somewhat more puffy head shape. See comparison under Greater Scaup.

WINTER: On Christmas counts it has appeared fairly commonly near Long Point, and rarely north to Ottawa and Sault Ste. Marie, in much smaller numbers than the Greater Scaup except at Sault Ste. Marie. Kelley (1978: 20) suggested that they may outnumber Greater Scaup in extreme SW Ontario in winter also. Stirrett (1973a: 14) reported two at Pelee as late as Jan. 18. In contrast with the Greater Scaup, this species is listed as only an incidental winter visitor in the Toronto region (Goodwin, Freedman & McKay, 1977: 26).

SPRING: Stirrett (1973b: 14) called it a very common transient at Pelee with a peak of 250 on May 6 and the earliest on Mar. 18. Ussher (1965: 5) gave Mar. 24 to May 16 as the average spring period at Rondeau, with the latest on May 29. Saunders & Dale (1933: 179) called this "one of our most abundant ducks" in the London region, with the 17-year average arrival on Apr. 5, the earliest on Mar. 16, 1921 and some lingering to end of May or early June. Saunders (1947: 361) gave the 13-year average for arrival at Toronto as Apr. 12 with the earliest on Mar. 26. George A. Scott's median arrival date for Oshawa Apr. 1 and his largest spring flock of 250 was on May 8, 1960 (Speirs, 1979: 48). Quilliam (1965: 47) wrote that this species is generally much less common and later in appearing at Kingston than the Greater Scaup, comprising less then 5% of the scaups seen there and with none identified during some seasons. Devitt (1967: 44) gave the 15-year average arrival date for Barrie as Apr. 14, with the earliest on Apr. 3, 1963, and flocks of 200 to 500 from mid-April to the first week of May. Nicholson (1972: 16) considered it common on Manitoulin from mid-Apr. to mid-May. Skeel & Bondrup-Nielsen (1978: 157) saw a few at Pukaskwa from Apr. 20 to May 10. Denis (1961: 2) gave Apr. 9, 1958 as the earliest Thunder Bay record with Apr. 22 as the average arrival date there. D.H. Elder saw his first at Atikokan on May 5 in 1979. Cringan (1953a: 2) had his first at Sioux Lookout on May 6 in 1953.

SUMMER: On Breeding Bird Surveys they have shown up on the Larder Lake, Swastika and Atikokan routes, not elsewhere in Ontario. Stirrett (1973c: 14) had two summer records from Pelee. Kelley (1978: 20) reported some at Ipperwash Beach in summer. Baillie & Harrington (1936: 16) reported breeding records from Walpole Is. (Lake St. Clair), Toronto, Frenchman Bay and the Haliburton-Hastings area. McIlwraith (1984: 81) wrote "Dr. Macallum states that some still breed in the marsh near Dunnville". Small numbers are sometimes seen in the Lake Ontario shore marshes in summer (Speirs, 1979: 48). Devitt (1967: 43-44) detailed breeding evidence for the northern part of Simcoe Co. Ross James *et al* saw some in early June, 1977, near Pickle Lake. Cringan (1953b: 2) saw a few at Kasabonika Lake from June 1 to 4, 1953 and Cringan (1950: 5) had a few thought to be this species in the Nikip Lake region in June, 1950. Manning (1952: 26) collected three from a flock of 200 at the mouth of the Moose River on May 31, 1947 and four were seen there on June 8 by Kelsall and Lemieux. Peck (1972: 338) saw small groups of both sexes at Cape Henrietta Maria on 6 of 9 days between June 22 and 30, 1970 and mentioned that Young made a collection there on Aug. 11, 1968. Schueler, Baldwin & Rising (1974: 142) found it uncommon at Winisk but common at Hawley Lake. C.E. Hope collected one at Ft. Severn on June 24, 1940.

AUTUMN: Manning (1952: 26) quoted observations by Lewis and Peters at the mouth of the Albany river in mid-September and at the mouth of the Moose River in Sept. and early Oct. Wm. Goddard secured four specimens from Indians near Favourable Lake between Oct. 12 and Nov. 5, 1938 (Hope, 1938: 10). Smith (1957: 169) saw 20 on Pearl Lake, Schumacher, on Sept. 6, 1953. Skeel & Bondrup-Nielsen (1978: 157) noted 11 on Sept. 4, 1975 in two Lake Superior coves at Pukaskwa. Nicholson (1972: 16) gave 350 as the recent maximum on Manitoulin in fall. Devitt (1967: 43) reported that the main flight through Simcoe Co. was in the first half of October: he noted over 1000 during one hour at Wasaga Beach on Oct. 13, 1940. Weir & Quilliam (1980: 33) gave Oct. 16 and Dec. 7 as average arrival and departure dates from Kingston. Flocks of up to 200 have been reported in Ontario Co. in late Oct. and early Nov. (Speirs, 1979: 48). Fleming (1906: 445) had extreme fall dates for Toronto from July 21, 1890 to Oct. 29, 1895 but Saunders (1947: 381) gave the 8-year average departure date for Toronto as Oct. 28 with the latest on Dec. 7. Ussher (1965: 5) gave Aug. 5 to Nov. 20 as fall extremes for Rondeau, with a few sometimes wintering. Stirrett (1973d: 16) had a peak of 200 on Nov. 1 at Pelee and Kelley (1978: 20) considered them numerous in SW Ontario in fall.

BANDING: Birds banded in Alberta, Maryland and New Jersey have been taken in the Toronto region (Speirs, 1979: 48).

**MEASUREMENTS:**
*Length:* ♂ 16½ to 18½
ins. ♀ 15-17¾ ins.
(Palmer, 1976: 213)
*Wingspread:* ♂ 27-31 ins.
♀ 27-30½ ins. (Palmer,
1976: 213)
*Weight:* ♂ slightly under
2 lb. ♀ about 1¾ lb.
(Palmer, 1976: 213).

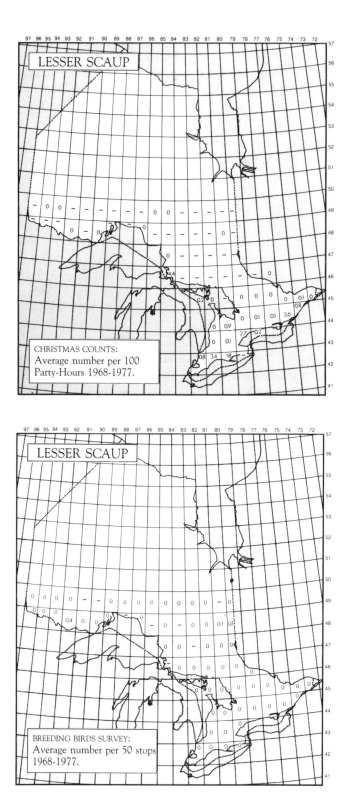

LESSER SCAUP

CHRISTMAS COUNTS:
Average number per 100
Party-Hours 1968-1977.

LESSER SCAUP

BREEDING BIRDS SURVEY:
Average number per 50 stops
1968-1977.

# COMMON EIDER   *Somateria mollissima*   (Linnaeus)

This is essentially a marine species which I have seen mostly along rocky seacoasts in such places as Maine, the Gulf of St. Lawrence and Scandinavia. In Ontario it is a rare duck.

IDENTIFICATION: Adult males with their black caps and bellies, otherwise white (except for some green on the nape) are unmistakable. These are very big ducks. The females are mostly likely to be mistaken for King Eiders but are heavily barred on the sides while King Eiders have crescent shaped black marks on the sides. The bill profile in this species is long and flat (as in a Canvasback), while in the King Eider it is dished in (concave). The feathering on the side of the bill in this species comes farther forward than the feathering on the culmen (mid line of the upper mandible). In the King Eider the feathering on the side of the bill is about the same length as the culmen feathering: i.e. they project about the same distance forward. Most eiders seen in southern Ontario in winter have been King Eiders.

WINTER:   McIlwraith (1894: 89) mentioned one shot at Toronto Island on Dec. 6, 1890 by William Cross. George A. Scott saw two females (with long sloping profiles) in Oshawa Harbour on Dec. 2, 1956 (FON Bull. 75: 30). A.J. Mitchener, Frances Westman *et al* identified one at Collingwood on Jan. 2, 1961 (Devitt, 1967: 46). Weir & Quilliam (1980: 6) reported two adult males at Wolfe Is. on Dec. 31, 1974, seen by George Finney and a female or immature male at Prince Edward Point on Dec. 17, 1977, identified by Bob Stewart, on a Christmas count. Individuals were also reported on Christmas counts at Kingston in 1970 and Guelph in 1976.

SPRING:

SUMMER:   Macoun (1900: 105) citing R. Bell called it "Common from a short distance north of Moose Factory to Richmond Gulf, June, 1896". Manning (1952: 28) estimated 145 along the Hudson Bay shore from Cape Henrietta Maria to Winisk in the summer of 1947: of these he collected a few. H. Lumsden found them common in this same area ten years later (Peck, 1972: 339).

AUTUMN:   McIlwraith (1894: 89) reported one young male taken at Ottawa on Nov. 7, 1889 by George R. White and a young male in his collection which he shot at Hamilton (no date given). Devitt (1967: 46) reported a female at Barrie from Nov. 14 to 30, 1953, seen by J.L. Baillie and many others. Weir & Quilliam (1980: 6) noted a female or immature at Prince Edward Point on Oct. 19, 1978, identified by Helen Quilliam and Roger Etcheberry, and two at Amherst Is. on Nov. 29, 1978 seen by John Nicholson. C. Blomme discovered the remains of an eider near Bowmanville on Nov. 21, 1970, identified as this species at the Royal Ontario Museum (Tozer & Richards, 1974: 89). Speirs (1979: 54) reported one seen at Whitby on Nov. 13, 1949, by Doug Scovell, Tom Swift and David West (from J.L. Baillie's journal). On Nov. 25, 1936, three were seen off Navy Island in the Niagara River, and one specimen was taken by N.G. Anderson and brought to R.W. Sheppard (1937: 59) . . . a young male. A female was collected in the Niagara Gorge on Sept. 25, 1960, by H. Axtell (Beardslee & Mitchell, 1965: 146). Kelley (1978: 21) cited three records for SW Ontario: Nov. 13, 1966 at Sarnia by D. Rupert; Nov. 20, 1967 again at Sarnia by Rupert and Lamb and one off Point Pelee on Nov. 24, 1968 by Kleiman.

114

## MEASUREMENTS:

*Length:* ♂ av. 24 ins. ♀
av. 22.8 ins. (Kortright,
1942: 386)
*Wingspread:* ♂ av. 40.2
ins. ♀ av. 38.8 ins.
(Kortright, 1942: 386)
*Weight:* ♂ av. 4 lb. 6 oz.
♀ 3 lb. 6 oz. (Kortright,
1942: 386)

## REFERENCES:

Sheppard, R.W. 1937 The
American Eider on the
Niagara River. Can. Field-
Nat., 51: (4): 59.
  Snyder, L.L. 1941 On the
Hudson Bay Eider. Occ.
Pap. Roy. Ont. Mus.
Zool., No. 6: 1-7.

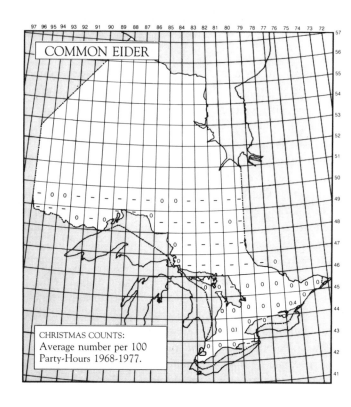

COMMON EIDER

CHRISTMAS COUNTS:
Average number per 100
Party-Hours 1968-1977.

# KING EIDER  *Somateria spectabilis*  (Linnaeus)

Although more numerous than the Common Eider, this is still a rare species in southern Ontario, most often seen in late fall or early winter. Alison (1975: 445) estimated that there are no more than 200 pairs nesting in Ontario from Cape Henrietta Maria to the Manitoba border.

IDENTIFICATION:  Adult males in breeding plumage present no difficulty, with their white foresection and black rear, and distinctive yellow, knobby bill. However, this plumage is very seldom seen in southern Ontario, where most of those seen are females or immature males, which superficially look a bit like very dingy female Mallards, without the white-bordered blue speculum of the Mallards. See Common Eider for distinctions between these similar species. If you are close enough to see the bill well, the feathering on the side of the bill does not extend forward to the nostril in this species whereas it does in the Common Eider.

WINTER:  On the 1968-1977 Christmas counts King Eiders were noted at Pelee (1970), Blenheim (1973), Niagara Falls (1973), Hamilton (1970, 1973 and 1976), Toronto (1968), Oshawa (1970) and Kingston (1977). One was seen off Wheatley on Dec. 24, 1970 (Kelley, 1978: 21) and two at Pelee the same day (Stirrett, 1973a: 14). H. Axtell reported up to 15 on the Niagara River during Dec., 1956, (Beardslee & Mitchell, 1965: 148). Fleming (1906: 445) gave a Feb. 4, 1889 date for Hamilton. Saunders (1947: 361) had Toronto records from Dec. 16 to Feb. 29. There have been a few winter records along the Pickering-Oshawa lakefront (Speirs, 1979: 55). Quilliam (1965: 50) mentioned one collected in Dec., 1896, at the Thousand Islands and two seen at Loughborough Lake on Dec. 10, 1948 by S. O'Neil. In recent years they have appeared almost every year near Kingston (Weir & Quilliam, 1980: 6). E.L. Brereton identified one off Big Bay Pt., Lake Simcoe, on Dec. 15, 1948 and H.B. Haugh saw one on Little Lake, Barrie, also in Dec., 1948 (Devitt, 1967: 46).

SPRING:  One was seen at Sombra on the St. Clair River, on Mar. 5, 1972 by Rupert and Wilson (Kelley, 1978: 21). Beardslee & Mitchell (1965: 147) gave several records including three on the Niagara River on Mar. 7, 1936 and one in the Niagara Gorge from May 8 into June, 1949 with individuals at Fort Erie and Pt. Abino on May 20, 1951 and May 25, 1952 respectively. Bruce Rattray and Ron Weir had the good fortune to find an adult male off Pt. Traverse, Prince Edward Point, which was seen by many others from Apr. 29 to May 21, 1978 (Weir & Quilliam, 1980: 6). Nicholson (1972: 16) identified one at Cape Robert, Manitoulin, on May 16, 1971.

SUMMER:  John Crosby and R.M. Saunders spotted one off Scarborough Bluffs with mergansers on July 16, 1942 (Saunders, 1947: 219). Manning (1952: 28, 29) collected females and young at Cape Henrietta Maria in July, 1947 and saw about 150 males at sea nearby: he also mentioned a male collected at Ft. Severn by Hugh Conn in June, 1932 as an unique occurrence there (Hope saw none there in 1940). Peck (1972: 339) cited H.R. Smith's collection of a female attending six young at Cape Henrietta Maria on Aug. 23, 1944, as the first Ontario breeding record: he also reported H. Lumsden's sighting of four males (one collected) and three females about 25 miles west of the cape in mid-July, 1957. Schueler, Baldwin & Rising (1974: 142) reported none at any of their northern Ontario sites (Moosonee, Ft. Albany, Attawapiskat, Winisk or Hawley Lake).

AUTUMN: L. Roy shot one at Little Current on Nov. 10, 1970 (Nicholson, 1972: 16). A female was taken by H.B. Haugh at Little Lake, Barrie, on Nov. 1, 1926 (Devitt, 1967: 46). Weir & Quilliam (1980: 33) gave Nov. 16 as the earliest fall date for Kingston, with Nov. 20 as the 6-year average for arrivals there. There are several fall records from Whitby and Oshawa, among which was one found by George A. Scott at Oshawa on Oct. 25, 1959 and shown to me and others on Nov. 1 (Speirs, 1979: 55). Fleming (1906: 445) reported a fully adult male taken at Toronto on Nov. 18, 1895 by C.W. Nash as unusual, though young males were "not uncommon in November and December". J.B. Williams reported that "A fine male specimen of *Somateria spectabilis* was collected in Toronto Bay, November 25", 1889. "This is the first positive record of the species for the Province." (Proc. Can. Inst., 25: (153): 199. Dec. 10, 1889.) Saunders & Dale (1933: 181) reported one taken near London on Nov. 24, 1900. Two were seen in the Niagara Gorge as early as Sept. 5, 1949 by Andrle, Nathan and Vaughan (Beardslee & Mitchell, 1965: 147). Ussher (1965: 6) had two records for Rondeau: on Nov. 9 and Nov. 16. One was shot at Mitchell's Bay on Nov. 16, 1950 and another was photographed at Kettle Pt. on Nov. 30, 1973 by Rider (Kelley, 1978: 21).

**MEASUREMENTS:**
*Length:* ♂ av. 22.7 ins. ♀ av. 21.1 ins. (Kortright, 1942: 386)
*Wingspread:* ♂ av. 36.5 ins. ♀ av. 36.4 ins. (Kortright, 1942: 387)
*Weight:* ♂ av. 4 lbs. ♀ av. 3 lbs. 10 oz. (Kortright, 1942: 386: 387).

**REFERENCE:**
Alison, R.M. 1975 The King Eider in Ontario. Can. Field-Nat., 89: (4): 445-447. He mapped the specimen records for southern Ontario, from Erieau and Niagara in the south to Ottawa and Manitoulin in the north.

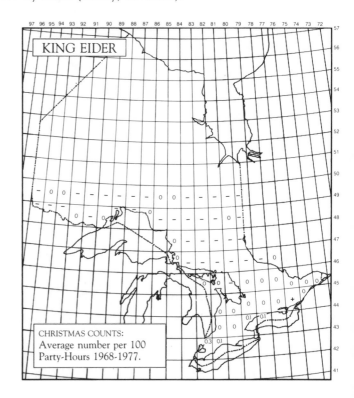

KING EIDER

CHRISTMAS COUNTS:
Average number per 100
Party-Hours 1968-1977.

# HARLEQUIN DUCK  *Histrionicus histrionicus*  (Linneaus)

The histrionic scientific name of this species was no doubt inspired by the improbable disruptive pattern of the male, with its slashes of white on a body mainly blue above and purplish red below. Actually in its habitat of river rapids and windblown bays the outlandish costume renders the bird hard to see against the blue water with small whitecaps. Like Barrow's Goldeneye this is primarily a bird of the west coast, with a shadow population on the east coast and a few stragglers in Ontario, chiefly along the lower Great Lakes.

IDENTIFICATION: The male with its wild pattern mentioned above, is unmistakable. The female is a small dark brown duck, somewhat like a smaller version of the female Surf Scoter, but usually with three white spots on the side of the head (two in the Surf Scoter). The small size and short bill separate it from the scoters and lack of white in the wing from other small dark ducks except female Ruddy Ducks which have indistinct stripes on the face rather than the prominent white spots of the Harlequin (usually 3, but sometimes only 2 spots).

WINTER: Denis Rupert found two at Kettle Point, Lake Huron, on Dec. 28, 1971 (Kelley, 1978: 21). A fine male wintered in Toronto Harbour in recent years, where it was admired and photographed by many (I saw it there on March 4, 1978). Harlequins showed up on several other Christmas counts in southern Ontario: at Blenheim in 1969, on several counts at Hamilton, Peel-Halton and Toronto, on the 1974 count at Port Hope-Cobourg, on the 1971 and 1975 Ottawa counts and the 1978 count at Sault Ste. Marie. Beardslee & Mitchell (1965: 144-145) cited several records of birds wintering on the Niagara River. Sheppard (1945: 160) reported a young male taken on the Niagara River in Jan., 1902, and three seen in the Canadian rapids above the falls on Dec. 23, 1933: he also mentioned a female retrieved below the falls on Jan. 3, 1954 (Sheppard, 1960: 11). Ken. Edwards saw a male at the Lennox Generating Station, near Kingston, on Feb. 21, 1978: this was seen by many others until Mar. 18 (Weir & Quilliam, 1980: 6). Devitt (1967: 45) gave details of two seen at Collingwood from Dec. 27, 1958 for about a week, and a male seen there on Jan. 2, 1961 and again on Mar. 4. On Dec. 20, 1970, Nicholson (1972: 16) saw one at Wolsey Lake, Manitoulin.

SPRING: Kelley (1978: 21) reported a male on the Detroit River at Windsor on Mar. 16, 1969. A.R. Muma retrieved an immature male below Niagar Falls on Apr. 14, 1949 (Sheppard, 1960: 11). McIlwraith (1894: 88) mentioned a pair seen at Hamilton in spring and a pair collected at Toronto by Wm. Loane in the spring of 1865. Speirs (1979: 53) had three spring records for Ontario Co.: a pair at Whitby on Apr. 14, 1955; a female on Mar. 6, 1955 and another female on Mar. 9, 1969. Just yesterday, Mar. 3, 1981, another female was seen off Cranberry Marsh, Whitby. Another female, apparently imprinted on a group of 8 Common Goldeneyes, was seen with them off Whitby from May 9, 1980, until early Sept. There are several recent records of individuals and couples in Toronto, one pair as late as May 17, 1980. Ron Weir *et al* found a female on Amherst Is. on May 22 and 23, 1976 (Weir & Quilliam, 1980: 6). D.H. Elder had a mid-May record for Atikokan.

SUMMER: George W. North observed a male near Oakville at frequent intervals during the summer of 1959 (Speirs & Speirs, 1960: 31). R. Nisbet *et al* noted one frequently during the summer of 1980 off Cranberry Marsh, Whitby (Wilson, 1980: 117). C. Drexler secured a specimen at the mouth of the Moose River on June 5, 1860 (Todd, 1963: 176). Manning (1952: 28) mentioned another specimen (in the U.S. National Mus.) taken in James Bay on Aug. 3, 1860.

AUTUMN:   Nicholson (1972: 16) saw two at Murphy Point, Manitoulin, on Nov. 8, 1970. Martin Edwards and Ron Weir saw one at Prince Edward Point on Nov. 5, 1977 (Weir & Quilliam, 1980: 6). Tozer & Richards (1974: 88) mentioned one seen at Whitby on Sept. 28, 1963 and another off Oshawa from Aug. 20 to Sept. 13, 1967. McIlwraith (1894: 88) mentioned a female collected at Toronto by Wm. Loane during the fall of 1881, while Fleming (1906: 445) told of a female taken at Toronto on Oct. 20, 1894. The female that summered off Cranberry Marsh, Whitby, I saw on Sept. 7, 1980. The Oakville bird noted by George North during the summer of 1959 was found dead on Nov. 8 by Jack Sherrin. Kelley (1978: 21) gave two fall records near Sarnia and Port Franks on Nov. 18 and 23, 1973, respectively.

**MEASUREMENTS:**
*Length:* ♂ to 17 1/2 ins. ♀ to 16 1/2 ins. (Palmer, 1976: 323).
*Wingspread:* ♂ to 26 1/2 ins. ♀ to 25 ins. (Palmer, 1976: 323).
*Weight:* ♂ usually about 1 1/2 lb. ♀ 1 1/4 lb. (Palmer, 1976: 323).

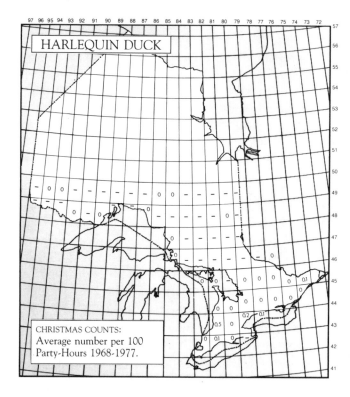

HARLEQUIN DUCK

CHRISTMAS COUNTS:
Average number per 100
Party-Hours 1968-1977.

# OLDSQUAW   *Clangula hyemalis*   (Linneaus)

This has always been my favourite duck, riding out the storms on wintry Lake Ontario in great numbers, diving to great depths for little pea clams, flying back and forth through the gaps between the lake and Toronto Bay, and talking constantly: "Ow—ow—oo—ah" as befits a bird with a name like Oldsquaw.

IDENTIFICATION:   This is a mainly black and white duck: some black on a mostly white body and head in winter, and some white on a mostly black background in summer, with a few touches of colour on the beak and back. The long thin tail distinguishes it from all other males except the Pintail (which has a long, almost swanlike neck, brown head and long white stripe on the side of the neck, very different from the low profile, black and white Oldsquaw). The very fast flight, low over the water, rolling from side to side as they fly, is also characteristic.

WINTER:   On Christmas counts it has been abundant along the north shore of Lake Ontario and uncommon to rare elsewhere north to Ottawa and Sault Ste. Marie. Stirrett (1973a: 14) had several maxima of 500 at Pelee during the winter months. Saunders & Dale (1933: 180) had few inland records near London but mention that thousands are sometimes drowned in gill nets set for fish in the Great Lakes. Saunders (1947: 3-4) gave a graphic picture of the thousands that gathered at the Eastern Gap on Jan. 1, 1945, calling and flying into Toronto Harbour when disturbed. With the help of Frank Beldan, I timed the speed of some of these flocks as they sped through the gap at 60 MPH or better (with a helping tail wind) (Speirs, 1945: 135-136). Several thousands generally have been reported on the Midwinter Waterfowl Inventory in the Toronto region (a maximum of 11,886 estimated on the Jan. 1960, survey, when it was by far the most abundant duck reported: in recent years its numbers have often been eclipsed by Mallard and Greater Scaup but it is still one of our most numerous ducks (Goodwin, Freedman & McKay, 1977: 4-5). Numbers are usually much smaller both east and west of Toronto, often quite scarce at Hamilton and Pickering, but regular in small numbers at Oshawa Harbour. Devitt (1967: 45) reported a few winter records at Barrie up to early January. Beamer noted two individuals at Meaford on Christmas counts and two as late as Jan. 8, 1939. Skeel & Bondrup-Nielsen (1978: 159) called it an uncommon winter resident at Pukaskwa.

SPRING:   According to Kelley (1978: 20) most leave SW Ontario by the end of April but her latest date was May 29, 1968. Stirrett (1973b: 15) had his maximum of 50 at Pelee on May 13 with the latest two on June 7. Ussher (1965: 6) gave Mar. 17 and May 23 as extreme spring dates for Rondeau with average arrival on Apr. 6 and departure on May 9. Sheppard (1945: 159) reported a spring peak in late April or early May on the Niagara River. Saunders (1947: 361) gave the average departure date from Toronto as May 31 but "occasionally summers". Weir & Quilliam (1980: 33) gave May 21 as the 28-year average for departure from Kingston. Devitt (1967: 45) considered this a very rare spring migrant at Barrie with the earliest on Apr. 19 and 5-year average departure date on May 4. Nicholson (1972: 16) wrote that large flocks move west off the south shore of Manitoulin during late May. Dennison (1980: 15) gave Apr. 30 as the spring date for Sault Ste. Marie. Speirs & Speirs (1947: 26) noted a female on Lake Nipissing as late as June 4, 1944. This was a common spring migrant at Pukaskwa from Apr. 3 to May 29

(Skeel & Bondrup-Nielsen, 1978: 159). Denis (1961: 2) gave Mar. 9, 1950 as the earliest date for Thunder Bay with average arrival on Apr. 15. Cringan (1953b: 2) saw a male and two females on Kasabonika Lake on May 27 and a female on June 1 on the Asheweig River.

SUMMER:    The only ones reported on the Breeding Bird Survey have been on the Swastika route; 3 in 1968 and 2 in 1971, probably lingering migrants. Speirs (1979: 52) cited several summer records of birds seen during the summer months on Lake Ontario off the Pickering-Oshawa shores. Quilliam (1965: 50) had two summer records for the Kingston region. Devitt (1967: 45) had only one summer record from Simcoe Co., a female at Singhampton on June 5, 1967. W. Wyett et al noted Oldsquaw at Pukaskwa on June 17, 1975 and Aug. 2, 1974 (Skeel & Bondrup-Nielsen, 1978: 159).

Manning (1952: 27) had records from the mouth of the Moose River and from Cape Henrietta Maria, where two nests were found with eggs. Peck (1972: 338) found this to be the most common species of waterfowl near Cape Henrietta Maria and cited other nesting evidence for the region. Schueler, Baldwin & Rising (1974: 142) noted Oldsquaws only at Moosonee, none at Fort Albany, Attawapiskat, Winisk or Hawley Lake. Hope reported none from Ft. Severn in 1940 and Lee (1978) had none at Big Trout Lake. Snyder (1957: 76) considered this the most widely distributed breeding bird of the Arctic, and included only the Cape Henrietta Maria portion of Ontario as within its breeding range.

AUTUMN:    Nicholson (1972: 16) considered it a common migrant at Manitoulin from mid-Oct. to mid-Nov. Beamer had a few fall records from Meaford, the earliest on Oct. 26, 1938 and one taken dead from a gill net on Nov. 16, 1944. The main fall flight at Barrie was in late October and early November (Devitt, 1967: 45). Weir & Quilliam (1980: 33) gave Oct. 20 as the 24-year average for fall arrivals at Kingston while Quilliam (1965: 50) mentioned a maximum of 1000 at Amherst Is. on Nov. 28, 1950. Saunders (1947: 361) gave Oct. 9 as the average arrival date for Toronto. Ussher (1965: 6) gave Oct. 27 as his earliest fall date for Rondeau with the latest on Dec. 28. Kelley (1978: 20) regarded it as uncommon in fall in SW Ontario, with the earliest on Oct. 21 and a maximum of 275 at Pinery Park on Nov. 4, 1967.

BANDING:    One banded at Presqu'ile Provincial Park on Mar. 8, 1972 was shot there on Nov. 25, 1972 by J. Pawlowski less than 200 m. from the banding site (Alison, 1974: 188).

**MEASUREMENTS:**
Length: ♂ 19-22 ins. (incl. 7-10 in. tail) ♀ 15-17 ins. (Palmer, 1976: 345).
Wingspread: ♂ to 31 ins. ♀ to 29 ins. (Palmer, 1976: 345).
Weight: ♂ usually about 1 3/4 lb. ♀ 1 1/2 lb. (Palmer, 1976: 345).
Palmer (1976: 354 presented a table showing seasonal weight variations, heaviest in mid-winter

(Feb.) and May before migration (data from over 1000 birds taken from Lake Michigan gill nets).

**REFERENCES:**

Alison, R.M. 1974 Oldsquaw homing in winter. Auk. 91: (1): 188.

Speirs, J. Murray 1945 Flight speed of the Oldsquaw. Auk, 62: (1): 135-136.

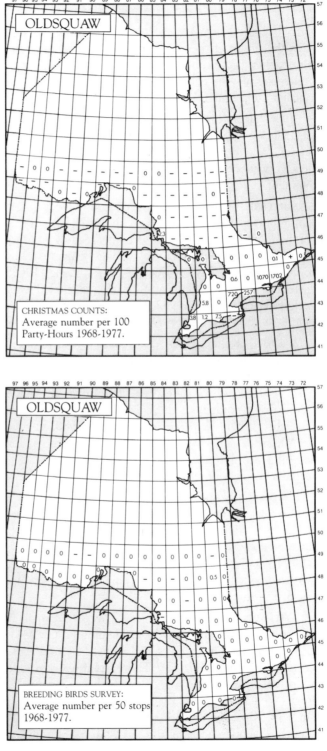

OLDSQUAW

CHRISTMAS COUNTS:
Average number per 100
Party-Hours 1968-1977.

OLDSQUAW

BREEDING BIRDS SURVEY:
Average number per 50 stops
1968-1977.

# BLACK SCOTER   *Melanitta nigra*   (Linnaeus)

When the bustle of the spring and fall warbler migrations and the breeding bird studies are past, then is the time to scan the chill, dark waters of Lake Ontario for Black Scoters. A telescope may be called for as small groups sometimes gather on the lake just out of binocular range and a telescope is needed to tell them from Black Ducks or other scoters.

IDENTIFICATION: Females and immatures, which are the ones usually seen, resemble Black Ducks with their black bodies and silver-gray cheeks. Black Ducks have longer necks and a longer, slimmer silhouette and do not dive for long periods below the surface. The silvery cheeks should distinguish them from other scoters. The black males with their prominent yellow bills should present no problems.

WINTER: There are Christmas count records as far north as Carleton Place and Manitoulin, south to Pelee where the only large flock was reported (in 1971). Kelley (1978: 22) reported only three December records from SW Ontario. Sheppard (1945: 160) noted a fine adult male on Dec. 4, 1943 below Niagara Falls. Saunders (1947: 355) saw two at Frenchman Bay on Dec. 24, 1944. Long (1968b: 14) saw a female at Pickering Beach on Jan. 6, 1968. Speirs (1979: 58) mentioned records by George A. Scott at Ontoro Beach on Dec. 7 and 26, 1969. Devitt (1967: 47) cited records by Frances Westman from Dec. 14 to 16, 1956 and on Dec. 7, 1961, on Kempenfeldt Bay, near Barrie.

SPRING: Kelley, (1978: 22) had four records of one or two birds from late April to mid-May in SW Ontario. Stirrett (1973b: 15) considered them fairly common at Pelee: the earliest on Apr. 11, the latest on May 18 and a maximum of 40 on May 11. Saunders (1947: 361) had spring dates from Toronto from May 8 to May 23. There are about a dozen spring records from the Lake Ontario shore of Ontario Co. from Apr. 21 to May 27 (Speirs, 1979: 58). Weir & Quilliam (1980: 33) had Kingston records for 13 of 33 years, from the earliest on Mar. 22 to one as late as June 6. Devitt (1967: 47) had just one spring record from Simcoe Co., a male at Tollendal on Apr. 18, 1954, seen by Frances Westman. Four were seen on Kasabonika Lake on May 29, 1953 (Cringan, 1953b: 2).

SUMMER: Schueler, Baldwin & Rising (1974: 142) noted this species at Moosonee and Hawley Lake and found them uncommon at Winisk. Manning (1952: 30) considered this the most common species of scoter along the west James Bay and south Hudson Bay coasts: he collected two from a flock of 300 mixed scoters midway up the James Bay coast on July 15, 1947 and one midway between Winisk and Ft. Severn on Aug. 15, 1947 from a flock of about 100. (Peck, 1972) reported none at Cape Henrietta Maria and Hope saw none at Ft. Severn in 1940.

AUTUMN: Nicholson (1972: 17) reported small numbers on Manitoulin annually between early Oct. and early Dec. Fleming (1906: 446) reported a male in full plumage taken at Havelock in Oct. 1900. Fall records from Simcoe Co. ranged from Oct. 1 into December (Devitt, 1967: 47). The 15-year average for arrivals at Kingston was Oct. 14 and for departures was Nov. 25, with the earliest on Sept. 14 and some lingering into winter (Weir & Quilliam, 1980: 33). Speirs (1979: 58) had fall records from Ontario Co. from Sept. 7 to Nov. 25 with a maximum of 40 seen at Whitby on Nov. 5, 1949 by R.M. Saunders. Saunders (1947: 361) gave fall dates from Toronto from Sept. 17 to Oct. 30 but Speirs (1938: 53) had a Nov. 18 Toronto record. Saunders & Dale (1933: 181) had two specimen records from Middlesex Co.: one on Oct. 16, 1891 and the other on Nov. 13, 1901. Ussher (1965: 6) had only one record for Rondeau, on Sept. 2. Kelley (1978: 22) considered them fairly common in fall in SW Ontario, with flocks of up to 350 at Kettle Point in 1972. Stirrett (1973a: 14 and 1973d: 17) found them to be uncommon at Pelee, with the earliest on Oct. 20 to the latest on Nov. 27.

**MEASUREMENTS:**
*Length:* ♂ to 21 ins. ♀ to 19 ins. (Palmer, 1976: 308)
*Wingspread:* ♂ to 36 ins. ♀ to 33 ins. (Palmer, 1976: 308)
*Weight:* ♂ usually about 2.4 lb. ♀ about 1.8 lb.

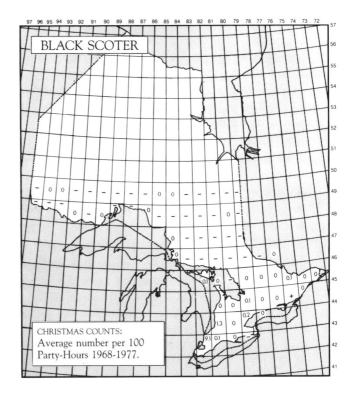

BLACK SCOTER

CHRISTMAS COUNTS:
Average number per 100
Party-Hours 1968-1977.

# SURF SCOTER   *Melanitta perspicillata*   (Linnaeus)

Like the White-winged Scoter this is mainly a northwestern breeder in Canada, most likely to be seen in Ontario during migration and, in my experience, not common even then.

IDENTIFICATION:   Adult males, with their colourful bulbous bill and big white patches on the forehead and nape, are distinctive. Females and juveniles look very much like White-winged Scoters but lack the white wing patch of that species: this is little consolation when they sit on the water for long periods without flapping. Black Scoters also have all black wings (or very dark brown in the case of females and young) but the yellow bill of the male Black Scoter and the white cheeks of the females and young will separate them when the seeing is good.

WINTER:   On Christmas counts this is generally a rarity but has been reported from Pelee north to Napanee and Barrie. Kelley (1978: 21) had one winter report from Lambton Co. on Feb. 8, 1968. The Axtells saw one at Chippewa on Feb. 22, 1954 (Beardslee & Mitchell, 1965: 149). Speirs (1979: 57) had only one January record (on Jan. 11, 1976) and five December records from Oshawa to Ajax. Devitt (1967: 47) reported three December records from Simcoe Co.

SPRING:   Stirrett (1973b: 15) had a few records at Pelee from Apr. 21 to May 19. Ussher (1965: 6) had only three spring records at Rondeau, from Mar. 17 to May 10. Saunders (1947: 361) had spring dates for Toronto from Mar. 22 to May 3. Speirs (1979: 57) had about 30 spring records of up to 10 individuals along the Ontario Co. shore, from Mar. 12 to May 22. Tozer & Richards (1974: 90) reported two males over Lake Scugog on Apr. 14, 1963. Weir & Quilliam (1980: 33) had Kingston records from Apr. 12 to May 20 on 9 of 33 years. Quilliam (1965: 51) cited an old record by Merriman at Kingston on May 22, 1922. Cringan (1953b: 2) saw 27 on May 28, 10 on May 29, three on June 1 and one on June 4 near Kasabonika Lake.

SUMMER:   Beardslee & Mitchell (1965: 149) reported one seen by Filor and Nathan in the Niagara Gorge on July 13, 1946. Baillie noted one as early as Aug. 18 (Saunders, 1947: 361). The only summer record for Ontario Co. was one seen off Beaton's Point, Oshawa, from Aug. 11 to 20, 1967 (Speirs, 1979: 57). Manning (1952: 29) cited a few summer reports from the vicinity of Moosonee. Lee (1978: 20) noted four at Big Trout Lake on June 8, 1975. Schueler, Baldwin & Rising (1974: 142) found none at Moosonee, Ft. Albany or Attawapiskat, considered them uncommon at Winisk in 1965 and saw none there in 1971 and found them uncommon at Hawley Lake in 1964 but common there in 1965. The only actual breeding record for Ontario is based on a female and one 1/3 grown downy young collected near Winisk by Michael Hunter and Donald W. Simkin on Aug. 3, 1960: there were also five other young in the brood (Simkim, 1963: 60).

AUTUMN:   Skeel & Bondrup-Nielsen (1978: 159) saw a flock of 29 at Pukaskwa on Sept. 29 (some were taken in a fisherman's net) and the last one was seen there on Oct. 16. I observed one near North Bay on Oct. 5, 1944 (Speirs & Speirs, 1947: 26). Nicholson (1972: 16-17) called it a regular fall migrant on Manitoulin, mostly of single birds in October, but C.T. Bell reported a flock of 162 on Oct. 3, 1971. Devitt (1967: 47) had a few fall records from Simcoe Co. from Oct. 1 to Oct. 28. The average arrival date at

Kingston was Oct. 14 and the largest number reported was about 20 on Oct. 28, 1961 (Quilliam, 1965: 51). Ontario Co. records from Lake Ontario, Lake Scugog and Lake Simcoe ranged from Sept. 27 to Nov. 11, mostly of one to a dozen birds but one flock of 45 was seen at Scugog on Oct. 26, 1976 by Ron. Tozer (Speirs, 1979: 57). Saunders (1947: 361) gave early and late fall dates for Toronto from Sept. 13 to Nov. 14. Saunders & Dale (1933: 181) recorded two specimens from Middlesex Co., one on Nov. 16, 1891 and the other on Oct. 8, 1901. A.R. Muma collected one below Niagara Falls on Oct. 27, 1952 (Sheppard, 1960: 12). Ussher (1965: 6) had only one fall record for Rondeau, on Oct. 3. Most reports from the Lake Huron shore of Lambton Co. ranged from mid-Oct. to early Dec. (Kelley, 1978: 21). Stirrett (1973d: 17 and 1973a: 14) had four fall records from Pelee from Oct. 16 to Nov. 22.

**MEASUREMENTS:**

*Length:* ♂ 20-21 ins. ♀ 18-19 ins. (Palmer, 1976: 297)
*Wingspread:* ♂ to 31 1/2 ins. ♀ to 29 1/2 ins. (Palmer, 1976: 297)
Weight:♂ about 2 1/4 lb. ♀ about 2 lb. (Palmer, 1976: 297).

**REFERENCE:**

Simkin, Donald W. 1963 A Surf Scoter nesting record for northwestern Ontario. Can. Field- Nat., 77:(1): 60.

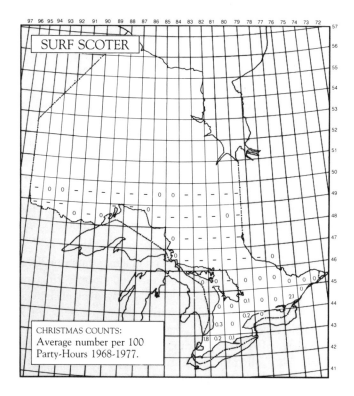

SURF SCOTER

CHRISTMAS COUNTS:
Average number per 100
Party-Hours 1968-1977.

# WHITE-WINGED SCOTER   *Melanitta fusca*   (Linneaus)

This is mainly seen as a migrant in Ontario. I fondly remember seeing long strings of them flying low over Lake Ontario when I sought out the privacy of Cherry Beach (then called Fisherman's Island) to study for final exams in early May. These flights still occur as the birds migrate from the Atlantic coast to their breeding areas in northwestern Canada.

IDENTIFICATION:   This is the largest of the three scoters found in Ontario and usually the most common. On the water, at a distance, they all appear as dark, even black, rather chunky ducks. The Black Duck, in comparison, appears to have a longer neck and tail, presenting a longer, slimmer silhouette and in flight it shows a prominent white wing lining, absent in the scoters. The White-winged Scoter differs from the other two by showing white wing patches: these are often concealed when resting on the water and you have to wait until one sits up and flaps its wings to determine the species. At close range the single white "tear-drop" patch around the eye of the male is distinctive. In early September, when male Common Eiders are moulting from their brown summer plumage to the winter white, they pass through a stage where they resemble White-winged Scoters, with their white wing patches on a dark brown background. This is more apt to be a problem on the Atlantic coast where both are common, than in Ontario.

WINTER:   On Christmas counts it has been common at Pelee in some years, and uncommon to rare at other Great Lakes localities north to Ottawa, Manitoulin and Sault Ste. Marie (where individuals were reported in 1977 and again in 1979 acc. to Dennison (1980: 149). Stirrett (1973a: 14) had maximum numbers of 200 at Pelee on Jan. 18 and 24. Speirs (1979: 56) documented winter sightings in the Pickering, Whitby and Oshawa region, mostly of one or two individuals (maximum of six). One was noted at Collingwood as late as Jan. 15, 1967 by A.J. Mitchener (Devitt, 1967: 46).

SPRING:   Kelley (1978: 21) had a maximum of 200 in SW Ontario on May 13, 1965. Ussher (1965: 6) considered it an uncommon spring migrant at Rondeau from Mar. 17 to May 15. F. Bodsworth reported seeing over 30 hauled up in fish nets from a depth of at least 50 ft. off Port Burwell during the spring of 1937 (Brooman, 1954: 11-12). Sheppard (1945: 160) saw 11 near Chippewa on the Niagara River on May 6, 1939. Saunders & Dale (1933: 181) had just one spring record near London, on May 7 and 8, 1931. Fleming (1906: 446) called it common from Mar. 1 to May 11 at Toronto, usually in full plumage. My peak date for Toronto was May 17 (Speirs, 1938: 43). Ken Adcoe and Charles Long counted 2309 passing Pickering Beach on May 23, 1966 (Speirs, 1979: 56). At Kingston they also fly west over Lake Ontario, with a peak number of 200 reported on May 13, 1957 (Quilliam, 1965: 81). The largest spring flock for Simcoe Co. was 80 noted over Bradford on May 27, 1942 (Devitt, 1967: 46). Nicholson (1972: 16) has noted this species commonly off the south shore of Manitoulin during late May. Skeel & Bondrup-Nielsen (1978: 159) saw 15 on Apr. 16 and 9 on May 2 at Pukaskwa. Denis (1961: 4) gave May 3, 1953 as the earliest record for Thunder Bay with May 18 as the average spring arrival date. F. Cowell saw this species at Timmins on May 16, 1954 (Smith, 1957: 169). D.H. Elder saw his first at Atikokan on May 18, 1979. Cringan (1953b: 2) saw from one to 34 per day, with a peak in late May, at Kasabonika Lake.

SUMMER:   One was seen on June 10, 1952 at Ipperwash Beach (Kelley, 1978: 21) and Stirrett (1973b: 15) also had one at Pelee on June 10 (which he considered a late spring record). Saunders (1947: 361) gave June 10 as his latest spring date for Toronto and Aug. 1 as his earliest fall date. Rob. Nisbet saw 15 northbound at Thickson's Point, Whitby, on June 13, 1977 and a returning bird as early as Aug. 4, 1979 at Simcoe Point, Ajax (Speirs, 1979: 56). Quilliam (1965: 51) had spring migrants at Kingston as late as June 19 and one was reported by Bell on July 1, 1959. Devitt (1967: 46) reported Simcoe Co. birds as late as June 13 in spring and as early as Aug. 5 in fall. Skeel & Bondrup-Nielsen (1978: 159) had several summer sightings at Pukaskwa. Five were noted at Ombabika Bay, Lake Nipigon, on June 18, 1924 (Snyder, 1928: 256). J. Satterly found adults common at Ney Lake on the Manitoba border and photographed downy young there on Aug. 8, 1936, the first breeding record for Ontario (Baillie, 1939: 130). The only other breeding record for Ontario has been at Hawley Lake (James, McLaren & Barlow, 1976: 15). Manning (1952: 29) found several hundred summering on the west James Bay and southern Hudson Bay coasts during the summer of 1947 and cited several previous records for these areas. Schueler, Baldwin & Rising (1974: 142) found them uncommon at Winisk in 1965 and missed them there in 1971: they noted them at Hawley Lake in 1964 but not in 1965: they saw none at Moosonee, Ft. Albany or Attawapiskat. Peck (1972: 339) saw pairs at Cape Henrietta Maria from June 22 to July 1, 1970. Lee (1978: 20) saw 18 fly west over Big Trout Lake as late as June 29, 1975 and Hope in 1940 saw 100 at Ft. Severn on June 29.

AUTUMN: Skeel & Bondrup-Nielsen (1978: 159) saw a few flocks off Pukaskwa from Sept. 26 to Oct. 18. Nicholson (1972: 16) found that they return through Manitoulin from mid-Oct. to early Nov. Devitt (1967: 46) suggested that the fall peak in Simcoe Co. is in early October: the one specimen was taken on Nov. 13, 1939 at Orr Lake. Weir & Quilliam (1980: 33) gave Oct. 7 as the 20-year average for fall arrivals at Kingston with the earliest on Aug. 31. Most fall sightings in the Whitby area are of fewer than 10 birds but LGL (1974: 49) reported 300 there on Oct. 18, 1973. Saunders (1947: 361) gave Sept. 25 and Nov. 9 as his average fall arrival and departure dates for Toronto. Saunders & Dale (1933: 181) had two fall specimens for London and one sight record on Nov. 10-11, 1923. This was an uncommon fall migrant at Rondeau from Oct. 3 to Dec. 26 (Ussher, 1965: 6). Stirrett (1973d: 17) had two at Pelee as early as Oct. 5 and a peak of 50 on Oct. 30.

**MEASUREMENTS:**
*Length:* ♂ to about 23 ins.
♀ to 22 ins. (Palmer,
1976: 280).
*Wingspread:* ♂ to about
39 ins. ♀ to 37 ins.
(Palmer, 1976: 280).
*Weight:* ♂ 2 1/2 to 4 lb.
♀ 2-3 lb. (Palmer,
1976: 280).

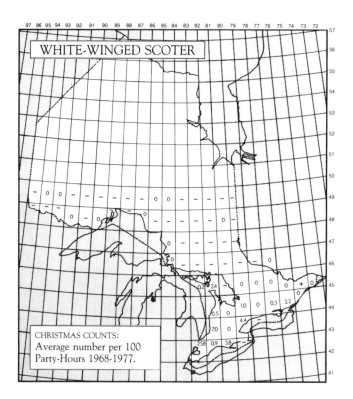

WHITE-WINGED SCOTER

CHRISTMAS COUNTS:
Average number per 100
Party-Hours 1968-1977.

# COMMON GOLDENEYE  *Bucephala clangula*  (Linnaeus)

This is a widespread diving duck, occurring wherever there are tree cavities in which it may nest, and wintering as far north as open water may be found, coming south only when freezeups demand that it move and leaving in spring as soon as open water is available in the north. One of the great joys upon purchase of a telescope was seeing the detailed delicacy of the black and white tracery on the upper sides, the green gloss on the head and the bright golden eye, and the yellow-tipped pinkish bill of the reddish-headed female. The mating display of the male in late winter is fascinating to watch, as it throws back its head until it touches its back, opens its beak and emits a note like a toy horn. The final joy was seeing the dapper little ducklings, black with startling white cheeks and little patches of white on the wings: ducklings of other species which I have seen have been of various shades of golden brown.

IDENTIFICATION:  Like the much smaller Bufflehead the first impression is of a mainly white duck, with black head, back and tail. The large roundish white spot in front of the yellow eye is diagnostic of adult males. When young males are first acquiring this spot it may go through a stage when it resembles the crescent shape of a Barrow's Goldeneye. Adult females are greyish ducks with reddish heads and a prominent white wing patch and yellow-tipped pinkish bill. In female Barrow's the bill is largely all yellow but at a distance are considered indistinguishable from the Common Goldeneye by most observers.

The Barrow's male has less white on the wing than the Commons and has a more rounded head profile, rather puffy in the Common. Buffleheads are much smaller, the male has a distinctive triangular white patch on the head and the female has a "feather in its cap" white patch above the eye. All goldeneyes have a distinctive whistling flight note.

WINTER: On Christmas counts this was a common species on open waters of the Lower Great Lakes and north as far as Ottawa and Wiarton, with smaller numbers north to Deep River, Marathon, Thunder Bay and Atikokan. Stirrett (1973a: 14) had a winter peak of 800 at Pelee on Dec. 30 and Kelley (1978: 20) called it an abundant winter bird in SW Ontario. Sheppard (1945: 159) called it the most abundant duck on the Niagara River. Goodwin, Freedman & McKay (1972) ranked this species third among the wintering diving ducks in the Toronto region, behind the Greater Scaup and Oldsquaw, with numbers in the hundreds rather than the thousands. Speirs (1979: 49) stated "this is usually our most widely distributed and numerous winter duck in Ontario Co." Quilliam (1965: 48) called it one of the commonest wintering ducks at Kingston with Christmas counts in the high hundreds. Devitt (1967: 44) had numerous winter records for Simcoe Co. Beamer saw them most winters at Meaford; e.g. 25 on Jan. 24, 1942 and 20 on Feb. 1, 1947. Louise Lawrence saw four near Rutherglen on Dec. 24, 1944 (Speirs & Speirs, 1947: 26). Dennison (1980b: 146) included this among the reliable Christmas birds at Sault Ste. Marie, averaging 56 per count over the past 25 years. Skeel & Bondrup-Nielsen (1978: 158) gave a few winter records from Pukaskwa and Marathon. Cringan (1953a: 2) listed this as resident at Sioux Lookout 1952-53.

SPRING: Stirrett (1973b: 14) had a peak of 200 at Pelee between Mar. 8 and 14, with the latest noted on May 24. Speirs (1938: 41) indicated that this species may be expected at Toronto until May 3. Ussher (1965: 5) gave Apr. 23 as his 12-year average departure date from Rondeau with the latest sighting on May 25. George Scott's median departure date from Oshawa was Apr. 25, with May 21, 1972 his latest record (Speirs, 1979: 49). Weir & Quilliam (1980: 33) gave May 12 as the 31-year average departure date from Kingston. Devitt (1967: 44) gave the 18-year average for arrivals at Barrie as Apr. 4. Beamer saw large flocks at Meaford in mid-April, but his latest record was May 1, 1943, when he noted several. Nicholson (1972: 16) called it a common migrant on Manitoulin in early April with his peak count of 190 on Apr. 11, 1970. Skeel & Bondrup-Nielsen (1978: 158) called it a common spring migrant at Pukaskwa, with peak numbers about May 12 at smelt spawning time. D.H. Elder saw his first at Atikokan on Apr. 19, 1978. Elsey (in Cringan, 1950: 5) reported the first in the Asheweig area on May 29, 1950.

SUMMER: On the Breeding Bird Surveys it has been absent or rare in southern Ontario becoming frequent but uncommon on the northern routes. Baillie & Harrington (1936: 16-17) documented breeding records as far south as Honey Harbour, north to Hudson Bay between which "this is one of the most common . . . breeding ducks". Kelley (1978: 20) reported five at Pelee on July 8, 1953. A few have been seen in the Whitby area in summer (Speirs, 1979: 49). Quilliam (1965: 48) cited three summer records for Kingston. Devitt (1967: 44) had two summer records for northern Simcoe Co. Beamer's only summer record was of two at Owen Sound on July 18, 1939. Nicholson (1972: 10) considered it a resident on Manitoulin but gave no summer data. Skeel & Bondrup-Nielsen (1978: 158) reported broods at Pukaskwa. Two broods were noted during budworm surveys at Eaglehead Lake in 1946: one brood of 7 tiny young was found on the river on June 4 by Mark Cressman and J. Cross; this was reduced to 4 young by June 29 and two by July 1: I saw another brood of five on the lake on June 9. J. Satterly saw groups of one to four on lakes near Matheson from June 15, 1946 to Sept. 5, 1949, and Smith (1957: 169) called it the common breeding duck of the Clay Belt (53% of all ducks noted). Hope (1938: 11) saw a few in summer near Favourable Lake and James *et al* saw them frequently near Pickle Lake in June, 1977. Cringan (1953b: 2) saw them daily in numbers up to 20 near Kasabonika Lake in late May and June, 1953. He also found them common in the Nikip Lake area and found a female with 7 downy young there on July 18, 1950. Flocks of up to 25 were seen at Big Trout Lake in June, 1975 (Lee, 1978: 19) but Hope did not report any at Ft. Severn in the summer of 1940. Schueler, Baldwin & Rising (1974: 142) found them common at Ft. Albany, Winisk and Hawley Lake, uncommon at Moosonee and none at Attawapiskat. Manning (1952: 26-27) called this a fairly common duck along both the west James Bay and southern Hudson Bay coasts with flocks up to 100 noted in July. Peck (1972: 338) reported that non-breeders were fairly common at Cape Henrietta Maria in summer.

AUTUMN: Wm. Goddard secured two young of the year on Oct. 9, 1938, from Indians near Favourable Lake (Hope, 1938: 11). Skeel & Bondrup-Nielsen (1978: 158) considered this the most common fall waterfowl migrant at Pukaskwa, but with fewer than in spring. Nicholson (1972: 16) found that the main movement through Manitoulin took place from late Oct. to mid-Nov. Beamer's earliest fall record at Meaford was 20 seen on Sept. 25, 1949 and his only large flocks were seen on Oct. 29, 1944. The biggest fall flights in Simcoe Co. are in late Oct., remaining common into Dec. (Devitt, 1967: 44). Weir & Quilliam (1980: 33) gave the 26-year average for arrivals at Kingston as Oct. 18, while Quilliam (1965: 48) gave Oct. 6, 1963 as the earliest fall record there. George A. Scott's median arrival date for Oshawa was Nov. 7 after which they rapidly increase to winter numbers: his earliest fall record was Sept. 18 (Speirs, 1979: 49). Speirs (1938: 49) indicated that this species should be expected in Toronto waters by Nov. 5. Ussher (1965: 5) had his earliest fall sighting at Rondeau on Oct. 3, with Oct. 26 as the 10-year average arrival date. Stirrett (1973d: 16) considered this an uncommon fall transient at Pelee with the earliest record on Oct. 28, but Kelley (1978: 20) has a SW Ontario record as early as Sept. 17, 1949.

**MEASUREMENTS:**
*Length:* 17-19 ins.
(Palmer, 1976: 378).
*Wingspread:* 28 1/2 ins.
(Pough, 1951: 100).
*Weight:* 58 ♂ av. 2.2 lb.,
max. 3.1 lb. 53 ♀ av. 1.8
lb., max. 2.5 lb. (Palmer,
1976: 377).

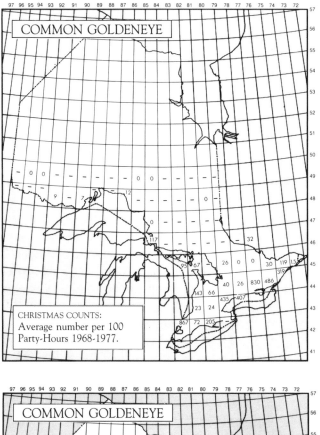

COMMON GOLDENEYE

CHRISTMAS COUNTS:
Average number per 100
Party-Hours 1968-1977.

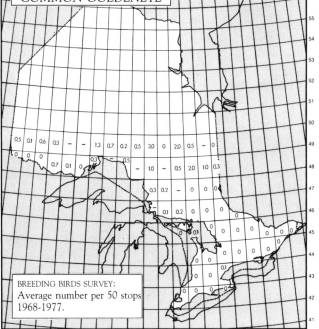

COMMON GOLDENEYE

BREEDING BIRDS SURVEY:
Average number per 50 stops
1968-1977.

# BARROW'S GOLDENEYE   *Bucephala islandica*   (Gmelin)

This is mainly a bird of the Rocky Mountain region, though some breed in Labrador. In Ontario it is a rare winter visitor.

IDENTIFICATION: The usual field mark for distinguishing this from the Common Goldeneye is the shape of the white spot in front of the eye, circular in the Common Goldeneye and crescent-shaped in this species. But note that young male Commons may show a crescentic shape when changing from immature to adult plumages. This species shows much less white on the sides than does the Common Goldeneye, the white being broken up into distinct spots or bars, instead of by the thin black lines as in the Common. In flight this species has a black bar crossing the big white wing patch while there is no such black bar in the male Common (it is present in the females of both species).

WINTER: On Christmas counts it has been a rare duck, chiefly in western Lake Ontario, southern Georgian Bay, Ottawa and Presqu'ile. Kelley (1978: 20) recorded single birds at Sarnia on Dec. 14, 1966; Dec. 30, 1967; Feb. 14 to Mar. 1, 1970 and Jan. 22 to Mar. 1, 1972 (by Rupert *et al*): there were also two on Lake Huron in Lambton Co. on Dec. 31, 1967. Sheppard (1960: 11) reported a male retrieved below Niagara Falls by A.R. Muma on Dec. 20, 1956 and sent to the Royal Ontario Museum for confirmation: this turned out to be a hybrid with the Common Goldeneye according to Beardslee & Mitchell (1965: 141): these authors also mentioned a male found above the falls and carefully identified by Andrle, the Axtells and Coggeshall on Jan. 3, 1959 and another there from Jan. 1 to Feb. 21, 1960 seen by many observers. The first for the Hamilton Christmas count was found on Dec. 26, 1980: none has yet been found on the Toronto Christmas count, although it was reported on the Midwinter Waterfowl Survey for the Toronto region on Jan. 3, 1971, Jan. 9, 1972 (when two were reported). Jan. 7, 1973 and Jan. 6, 1974, all at Oakville, identified by A. Dawe, C. Goodwin *et al*. Naomi LeVay reported a male at Cranberry Marsh, Whitby, on Dec. 2 and 3, 1972 and Feb. 2 and Dec. 26, 1973. John Crosby showed me a fine male at Ottawa on Jan. 2, 1961, which had been seen by many others for the preceding two weeks. There have been several other winter reports from Ottawa. A male was closely observed by Aubrey May and R.J. Rutter at Huntsville on Jan. 1 and 2, 1951 (Rutter, 1951: 158).

SPRING: Kelley (1978: 20) reported one at Wheatley on Apr. 10, 1971 (also mentioned by Stirrett, 1973b: 14). Fleming (1906: 445) reported one that was shot by Chas. Pickering at Toronto on Apr. 18, 1885 and confirmed by Ernest T. Seton. D. Gunn reported an immature male at Oakville on Mar. 10, 1958, while J. (Red) Mason noted one at Port Credit on Apr. 10, 1976 (TOC records). Quilliam (1965: 48-49) cited a Kingston report for Apr. 14, 1950 by Orville Brown but considered the record somewhat hypothetical. Weir & Quilliam (1980: 5) gave another record of an adult male sighted by M. Runtz and Mark Gawn near Amherst Is. on Mar. 12, 1979, as the first Kingston record for the Canadian side of the river.

SUMMER:

AUTUMN: Saunders & Dale (1933: 180) corrected the specimen record for London as a misidentified Common Goldeneye and pointed out that the crescent shape of the face spot is not a good field mark (see above). D. Perks saw one of the Oakville birds as early as Nov. 1, 1970. D. Curry and D. Pace discovered a male at Toronto Is. on Nov. 19, 1967 which was collected for the Royal Ontario Museum on Nov. 22 to constitute the first confirmed specimen for the Toronto region (but see Fleming, 1906 above). Quilliam (1965: 49) wrote that there were several unconfirmed reports by hunters in the Kingston region, while Weir & Quilliam (1980: 56) mentioned 3 shot in the N.Y. section of the Kingston region on Nov. 27, 1960. Rutter (1951: 158) reported one seen at Weller's Bay, Northumberland Co. on Nov. 21, 1913 by John Townson and one taken near Prescott on Oct. 9, 1900 (specimen in the Mus. Comp. Zoology, Cambridge, Mass.).

**MEASUREMENTS:**
*Length:* 16.5 to 20.5 ins. (Godfrey, 1966: 70).
*Wingspread:* 28 1/2 ins. (Pough, 1951: 102).
*Weight:* 3 ♂ av. 2.4 lb. 7 ♀ av. 1.6 lb. (Palmer, 1976: 403).

**REFERENCE:**
Rutter, R.J. 1951 Barrow's Golden-eye at Huntsville, Ontario. Can. Field-Nat., 65: (4): 158.
*Note:* I am indebted to Arnold Dawe for a number of records from the Toronto Ornithological Club (TOC records above): some have not been used if they did not add information to that already reported.

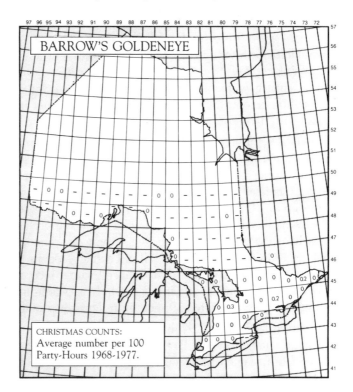

BARROW'S GOLDENEYE

CHRISTMAS COUNTS:
Average number per 100
Party-Hours 1968-1977.

# BUFFLEHEAD  *Bucephala albeola*  (Linnaeus)

Because of its constant activity, this tiny black and white duck is a joy to watch. It is fairly common in open waters in southern Ontario in winter but is very scare anywhere in Ontario in summer, though some non-breeders may turn up almost anywhere.

IDENTIFICATION:  This is a small diving duck, about the size of a teal, with much white both when floating high on the water and when in flight. The male, with its puffy black head with white triangle wedging from the crown in towards the eye, is easily identified. The female appears darker but wears a white "feather in its cap" and is usually associated with one or more males. Some Ruddy Ducks look a bit like the female but generally look whiter on the cheeks and darker on the sides: Ruddy Ducks are known for their "sticky up tails" but Buffleheads also have been known to stick up their tails. A close look is sometimes required to distinguish the two, but the white patch behind the eye and slightly below it, in the Bufflehead, may usually be seen farther than the whitish cheek, with dark horizontal line through it, of the Ruddy female.

WINTER:  Buffleheads have usually been common on Christmas counts near Kingston and western Lake Ontario, fairly common elsewhere along the north shores of Lake Ontario and Lake Erie, becoming rare north to Deep River and Sault Ste. Marie. They have steadily increased in numbers in the Toronto region: less than 10 were noted on Christmas counts up to 1937, less than 100 to 1955, while recent counts have been in the hundreds (Goodwin, Freedman & McKay, 1977: 8-9). Stirrett (1973a: 14) had records at Pelee throughout the winter, in numbers less than 20. Saunders & Dale (1933: 180) had only three winter records for London, all in February. Devitt (1967: 45) cited only four winter records for Simcoe Co. Beamer had several winter records for Meaford, with 6 on Jan. 8, 1939 his largest number. It winters regularly at Manitoulin (Nicholson, 1972: 16). Dennison (1980: 148) reported 39 seen on 6 Christmas counts at Sault Ste. Marie.

SPRING:  Stirrett (1973b: 15) had spring records at Pelee up to May 21 with his maximum number on Apr. 3. Ussher (1965: 5) gave Mar. 8 and June 5 as extreme spring dates for Rondeau, with average arrival on Mar. 23 and departure on May 5. Sheppard (1945: 159) reported for the 14 seen near Chippewa on May 6, 1939, as an exceptionally large number for the Niagara River. Saunders & Dale (1933: 180) gave the 17-year average arrival date for London as Apr. 10, with the earliest on Mar. 22, 1926. Saunders (1947: 361) gave May 30 as his latest spring record for Toronto, with May 8 as the 13-year average departure date. The spring peak in Ontario Co. was in the first week of April with my latest date on May 26, 1969 while George A. Scott's median departure date from Oshawa was May 9 (Speirs, 1979: 51). Numbers peaked at Kingston from late March to mid-April, but most leave by the end of April and the latest noted was on May 19, 1963 (Quilliam, 1965: 46). At Barrie the 15-year average arrival date was Apr. 12, but one was seen at Collingwood as early as Mar. 16, 1953 (Devitt, 1967: 45): he gave May 19 as the latest spring date. Beamer's earliest spring record for Meaford was on Mar. 16, 1946, with peak numbers in the latter half of April and the latest spring record on Apr. 30. It usually arrived on Manitoulin from mid-April to mid-May (Nicholson, 1972: 16). Louise Lawrence observed a pair at Pimisi Bay from Apr. 9 to 13, 1945 (Speirs & Speirs, 1947: 26). Dennison (1980: 15) gave Apr. 2 as the spring date for Sault Ste. Marie. Denis (1961: 2) has his earliest at Thunder Bay on Apr. 11, 1945 with Apr. 25 as the average arrival date there.

This was a common spring migrant at Pukaskwa from Apr. 24 to May 30, with the peak about May 10 (Skeel & Bondrup-Nielsen, 1978: 158). D.H. Elder saw his first at Atikokan on Apr. 27 in 1978, while Apr. 23 was his earliest spring date at Geraldton (Elder, 1979: 30). Cringan (1953a: 2) noted his first at Sioux Lookout on May 5 in 1953.

SUMMER: The only one reported on the Breeding Bird Survey was probably a lingering migrant seen on the Mount Julian route in 1968. Kelley (1978: 20) had a few July records for Rondeau and Ipperwash Beach. I had two summer records: one at Corner Marsh, Pickering, on July 3, 1969 and seven at Whitby on July 13, 1965 (Speirs, 1979: 51). James et al saw one near Pickle Lake on June 6, 1977. Hope (1938: 11) reported two broods of young near Favourable Lake on July 24, 1938. Manning (1952: 27) cited a report by Kelsall and Lemieux of seven on June 9 and two on July 4 near the estuary of the Moose River. Peck (1972: 338) saw a male and three females near Cape Henrietta Maria on June 30, 1970. Schueler, Baldwin & Rising (1974: 142) found them to be uncommon at Ft. Albany and Winisk and saw none at Moosonee, Attawapiskat or Hawley Lake, nor even at Cochrane. As this is a tree nesting species, those seen beyond the limit of trees would be non-breeders, as was probably the case for the ones seen in southern Ontario. Actual breeding records in Ontario are very few.

AUTUMN: Hope (1938: 11) reported that they stayed at Favourable Lake until ice formed. Lumsden saw two males and 15 females near Cape Henrietta Maria on Oct. 16, 1971 (Peck, 1972: 338). Todd (1963: 168) mentioned one shot by one of his guides about 10 miles from the mouth of the Abitibi River on Oct. 23, 1912. They were seen on four days between Aug. 26 and Oct. 27 at Pukaskwa (Skeel & Bondrup-Nielsen, 1978: 158). Southbound birds were noted on Manitoulin from late October to mid-Nov. at Manitoulin (Nicholson, 1972: 16) and during the same period in Simcoe Co. (Devitt, 1967: 44). Beamer had few fall records for Meaford, the earliest on Oct. 10, 1938. Weir & Quilliam (1980: 33) gave the 24-year average for arrivals at Kingston as Oct. 25 with the earliest on Oct. 11. My earliest fall records for Ontario Co. were on Sept. 3, but George A. Scott's median arrival date for Oshawa was Oct. 19 and the fall peak is in mid-November (Speirs, 1979: 51). Saunders (1947: 361) gave Aug. 30 as his earliest fall arrival at Toronto, but his 12-year average was Oct. 22. Ussher (1965: 5) gave Oct. 8 and Dec. 7 as extreme fall dates for Rondeau, with the average arrival date on Oct. 25 and departure on Dec. 1. Stirrett (1973d: 17) had one at Pelee as early as Sept. 20 with the maximum of 100 on Nov. 5.

BANDING: One banded in Maryland on Feb. 24, 1956 was shot in the Toronto region on Nov. 17 the same year. Devitt (1967: 44) reported one banded at Branchport, N.Y. on Apr. 6, 1972 and found drowned in a fish net at Collingwood on Apr. 17 (just 11 days later).

**MEASUREMENTS:**
*Length:* ♂ to 15 1/2 ins. ♀
to 14 1/4 ins. (Palmer,
1976: 426).
*Wingspread:* ♂ to 24 ins.
♀ to 23 ins. (Palmer,
1976: 426).
*Weight:* 2 ♂'s: 433.5 and
517 g. ♀ 313.6 g. (Hope,
1938: 11) all at Favourable
Lake.

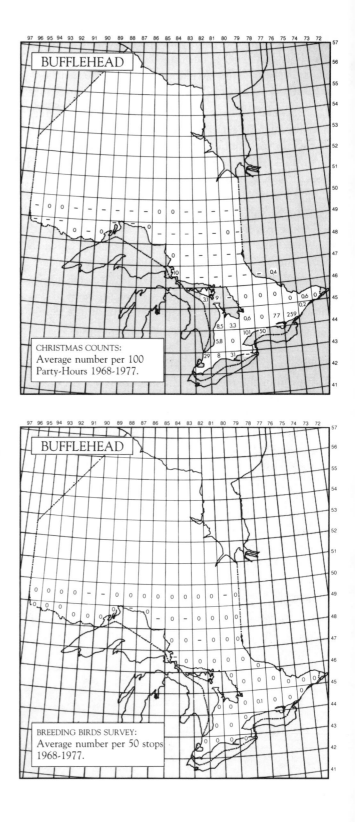

BUFFLEHEAD

CHRISTMAS COUNTS:
Average number per 100
Party-Hours 1968-1977.

BUFFLEHEAD

BREEDING BIRDS SURVEY:
Average number per 50 stops
1968-1977.

# SMEW  *Mergellus albellus*  (Linnaeus)

This is an accidental visitor from northern Europe and Asia, with only two Ontario records.

IDENTIFICATION:  The white-tipped brown secondary flight feathers distinguish it from other small mergansers in all plumages. Those seen have been females or immature males which have white cheeks and throat, reddish brown crest and back of the neck, shading to black on the forehead and lores, the back gray and breast white. Adult males are mainly white, with several streaks of black (about the eye, crest, breast and back).

WINTER:  Beardslee & Mitchell (1965: 153-154) described in detail the discovery by R.D. Coggeshall of one in Buffalo Harbour on Jan. 17, 1960 and seen there until Jan. 22 when it vanished until redisovered on the Niagara River by J.L. Baillie *et al* on Feb. 21. Donald R. Gunn took excellent colour photos of it (two reproduced in black & white on p. 154). Another female or young male was identified at Normandale Fish Hatchery on Dec. 9-10, 1973 by J. Olmsted *et al* and extensively described and photographed (Goodwin, 1974: 633).

SPRING:  The Niagara River bird was last noted by Brockner *et al* on Mar. 30, 1960 (Beardslee & Mitchell, 1965: 154). Ontario observers who saw the bird included J.L. Baillie, D.R. Gunn, Rosemary Gaymer, John and Joan Keenleyside, Lucie McDougall and William W. Smith. Godfrey (1966: 84) gave the dates of Gunn's photos as Feb. 26 and Mar. 6, 1960.

SUMMER:

AUTUMN:

**MEASUREMENTS:**
*Length:* ♂ 15-16 ins. ♀
about 15 ins. (Palmer,
1976: 446).
Wingspread:
*Weight:* ♂ 540-935 g. ♀
515-560 g. (Johngard,
1978: 348).

# HOODED MERGANSER  *Lophodytes cucullatus*  (Linnaeus)

The males are noted for their fancy crests and the females for their demure dress and hole-nesting habits. They are not as numerous as the larger mergansers but are not really rare, and are usually found in sheltered bays, rivers and ponds rather than on the open waters of the Great Lakes favoured by the larger mergansers.

IDENTIFICATION: The long, low profile marks them as mergansers. The males with their large fan-shaped white crests, bordered with black, and their reddish sides and white breasts crossed by the black vertical stripes, are easily identified. At a distance the chunky males of the Buffleheads might be mistaken, but the different shape of both bird and crest should separate them easily. The females are very demurely dressed, with tan-coloured crests on a dark body, the crests usually depressed: notably inconspicuous birds.

WINTER: On Christmas counts it has been uncommon to rare on open waters north to Deep River and Sault Ste. Marie. Stirrett (1973a: 14) had records from Pelee for all winter months, with a maximum of 25 in early December. Speirs (1979: 60) reported seeing individuals in Ontario Co. in seven of 30 winters. Quilliam (1965: 52) had four January and two February records for Kingston as well as those seen on Christmas counts. Devitt (1967: 48) found it common at Barrie well into December, with one at Collingwood as late as Jan. 20, 1953. Beamer had three winter records for Meaford: Jan. 14, 1939; Jan. 12, 1941 and Dec. 27, 1952.

SPRING: Stirrett (1973b: 15) had his largest spring count of 32 at Pelee on Apr. 21 with his latest record on May 21. Ussher (1965: 6) gave earliest and latest dates for Rondeau as Mar. 12 and May 2, with Mar. 22 and Apr. 16 as average arrival and departure dates. Saunders & Dale (1933: 182) gave Mar. 23 as the 16-year average arrival date for London with the earliest on Mar. 13, 1915, and some remaining into May. They were most common on the Niagara River in March but one stayed as late as May 7 (Sheppard, 1945: 161). Baillie (in Saunders, 1947: 361) gave his 18-year average for arrivals at Toronto as Apr. 11. Speirs (1979: 60) has noted good numbers in Ontario Co. from late March to early May with peak numbers in the first week of April. Weir and Quilliam (1980: 33) gave Mar. 15 and Apr. 21 as average arrival and departure dates for Kingston. Devitt (1967: 48) gave Apr. 4 as the 17-year average for arrival at Barrie, with the earliest on March 12. Beamer had spring records for Meaford as early as Mar. 29 and as late as Apr. 30. Nicholson (1972: 17) called it a regular spring migrant at Manitoulin from mid-April to early May. Louise Lawrence saw them on Pimisi Bay from Apr. 2 to 11, 1945 (Speirs & Speirs, 1947: 26). Dennison (1980: 15) gave Apr. 28 as the spring date for Sault Ste. Marie. Cringan (1953b: 2) saw three on May 31 near Kasabonika Lake. Cringan (1953a: 2) saw his first in 1953 at Sioux Lookout on Apr. 28. Denis (1961: 2) gave Apr. 25 as the average spring arrival date for Thunder Bay with the earliest on Apr. 4, 1958. D.H. Elder saw his first in 1979 on Apr. 19 at Atikokan. He gave Apr. 20 as his earliest date for Geraldton (Elder, 1979: 30).

SUMMER: On Breeding Bird Surveys it has been found, but rarely, in a band from Barry's Bay to Fort Frances, north of the agricultural south and south of the coniferous forest of the north. Baillie & Harrington (1936: 17) gave breeding records as far south as Simcoe Co., north to Thunder Bay. Saunders & Dale (1933: 182) reported a female on the river near Delaware on May 31, 1930 and a young bird nearby on Aug. 15, 1930.

There are several summer records from Ontario Co. and one documented breeding record (in a chimney!) at Uxbridge (Speirs, 1979: 60). Devitt (1967: 48) detailed five breeding records from Simcoe Co. Nicholson (1972: 17) called it an uncommon summer resident on Manitoulin. Skeel & Bondrup-Nielsen (1978: 160) had two summer records for Pukaskwa and cited a nest record for Lake Superior Provincial Park. Ross James *et al* noted this species at intervals near Pickle Lake during June, 1977. Smith (1957: 169) reported a female with 6 to 8 young near Kapaskasing on June 27, 1953 and a female with 6 young near Gogama on July 24, 1954. J. Satterly saw a male and two females on Twin Lakes, near Matheson, on June 3, 1950. Manning (1952: 31) reported a fully grown juvenile collected near Ft. Albany on July 31, 1947 by Harold Hanson (one of two seen there that day).

AUTUMN: Skeel & Bondrup-Nielsen (1978: 160) noted six females off Pukaskwa on Sept. 18. Fall records from North Bay ranged from Aug. 31 to Oct. 30, 1944 (Speirs & Speirs, 1947: 26). Nicholson (1972: 17) wrote that it returns in good numbers on Manitoulin from late Sept. to late Oct. Beamer had just one fall record from Meaford, on Oct. 31, 1948. Weir & Quilliam (1980: 33) gave Sept. 24 and Nov. 23 as average arrival and departure dates for Kingston. George Scott's median departure date from Oshawa was Nov. 26, with a peak in the first week of November and frequent records through October until freezeup (Speirs: 1979: 60). Saunders (1947: 361) gave Nov. 26 as his 13-year average departure date for Toronto. Sheppard (1945: 161) found them most common on the Niagara River in November but noted one as early as Aug. 23. Ussher (1965: 6) gave extreme fall dates for Rondeau as Aug. 15 and Dec. 8 with the average arrival on Oct. 31 and departure on Nov. 27. Stirrett (1973d: 17) had his earliest at Pelee on Sept. 20 and a maximum of 200 on Nov. 5.

**MEASUREMENTS:**

*Length:* ♂ about 18 ins. ♀ about 17 ins. (Palmer, 1976: 448)

*Wingspread:* ♂ to 26 ins. ♀ to 24 1/2 ins. (Palmer, 1976: 448)

*Weight:* ♂ about 1 1/2 lbs. ♀ about 1 1/4 lbs. (Palmer, 1976: 448).

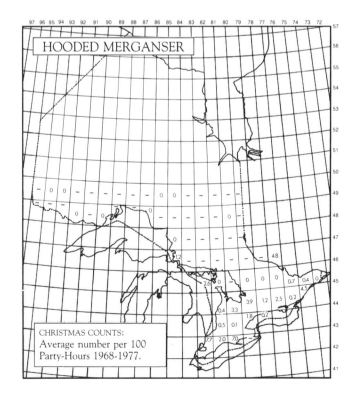

HOODED MERGANSER

CHRISTMAS COUNTS:
Average number per 100
Party-Hours 1968-1977.

140

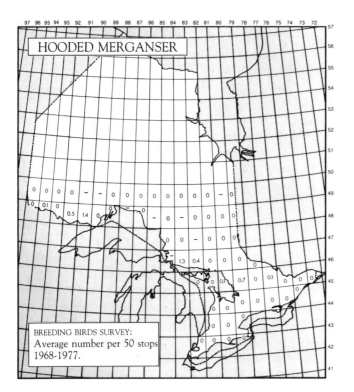

HOODED MERGANSER

BREEDING BIRDS SURVEY:
Average number per 50 stops
1968-1977.

# COMMON MERGANSER   *Mergus merganser*   Linnaeus

If you see a long, low, slim duck with an impossibly large brook of young hurrying along a rocky shoreline in summer, it is likely to be this species. Aggressive females "kidnap" youngsters from less aggressive mothers, so that broods of 30 or more are accumulated. At most localities and in most seasons this *is* the common merganser in Ontario, although the Red-breasted Merganser may outnumber it at the height of their spring and fall migrations.

IDENTIFICATION:   The long, low profile and "sawbill" beak identify it as a merganser. Females look a good deal like female Red-breasted Mergansers but are somewhat larger, have a less shaggy crest and may be distinguished by the round white spot on the chin, contrasting with the reddish head and neck. Males lack the shaggy crest of the Red-breasted Merganser and show more white when resting on the water. In spring the white breast is suffused with a salmon pink "blush".

WINTER:   On Christmas counts this has been a common species north to the Thousand Islands and Manitoulin, abundant at Pelee, and present at Marathon and Thunder Bay. Like the Common Goldeneye it is likely to be found wherever there is open water. Stirrett (1973a: 15) gave 15,000 on Dec. 30 as his winter maximum at Pelee. Ussher (1965: 6) wrote that it usually winters at Rondeau. Saunders & Dale (1933: 182) said that they are usually found in open places along the Thames River, near London. This has been a common wintering duck in the warm water off the Pickering Nuclear Plant, where 312 were noted on the 1977 Christmas count (Speirs, 1979: 61). Goodwin, Freedman & McKay (1977: 13) documented the increase in this species in the Toronto region during the 1970's, which they attributed to the warm effluent from the Hearn Generating Plant. They have been seen on most of the Kingston Christmas counts, with a high of 725 on Dec. 30, 1960. It appeared on 9 Christmas counts at Barrie (Devitt, 1967: 48). Beamer had many records for all winter months at Meaford (about 150 on Jan. 7, 1939) and recorded a Snowy Owl seen carrying and later eating one on Jan. 2, 1946. Nicholson (1972: 17) had a peak of 800 on Dec. 19, 1971 on Manitoulin. Dennison (1980: 146) listed this among the species always seen on Christmas counts at Sault Ste. Marie (averaging 10 on 25 counts). Skeel & Bondrup-Nielsen (1978: 160) reported two at Pukaskwa on Jan. 10.

SPRING:   Stirrett (1973b: 15) gave 125 as his spring maximum for Pelee on Mar. 18, with June 8 as his latest spring date. Ussher (1965: 6) gave Mar. 14 to Apr. 20 as average arrival and departure dates for Rondeau. Speirs (1938: 43) gave Mar. 8 as the spring peak at Toronto, while Fleming (1906: 443) had his latest spring sighting there on May 11, 1891. George A. Scott's median departure date from Oshawa is May 11. Devitt (1967: 48) said the peak of the spring flight in Simcoe Co. is about Apr. 7 and the 16-year average for arrivals at Barrie is Apr. 4, Weir & Quilliam (1980: 33) gave Apr. 22 as the 30-year average departure date from Kingston. Beamer saw several as late as May 24, 1947 at Meaford. Speirs & Speirs (1947: 26) noted a pair on Lake Nipissing as early as Mar. 29, 1945. Skeel & Bondrup-Nielsen (1978: 160) called this "about the most common" migrant waterfowl at Pukaska up to mid-May. Denis (1961: 2) gave Apr. 18 as the average arrival date at Thunder Bay. Elder (1979: 30) gave Apr. 19 as his earliest spring date for Geraldton, and he saw his first at Atikokan on Apr. 19 in 1979. Cringan

(1953a: 2) saw his first at Sioux Lookout on Apr. 26 in 1953. Elsey (in Cringan, 1950: 6) had his first in the Asheweig area on May 19, 1950.

SUMMER: On Breeding Bird Surveys it was noted from Dorset and Manitoulin, north to Kapaskasing and Eagle River, with the greatest numbers in the Georgian Bay area. Kelley (1978: 22) mentioned females with downy young at Kettle Point in 1950 and 1951. Ussher (1965: 6) said that it has nested at Rondeau. Summer records have been scarce in Ontario Co., though Speirs (1979: 61) had a few records from Lake Ontario, Lake Simcoe and Lake St. John. Quilliam (1965: 53) had old nest records from the Kingston area and recent reports of females with young. Devitt (1967: 48-49) detailed several breeding records from Simcoe Co., from Barrie north to Georgian Bay. Beamer reported several young (two of them 3/4 grown) on July 6, 1941 at Meaford and a family of 19 on July 20, 1947. On June 24, 1944 a female with 11 downy young was seen on Lake Nipissing (Speirs & Speirs, 1947: 26). Skeel & Bondrup-Nielsen (1978: 160) saw three broods at Pukaskwa. Baillie & Harrington (1936: 18) detailed breeding records from Frontenac Co. north to Kapuskasing and Thunder Bay. J. Satterly saw a female with 8 ducklings on Munro Lake on July 11, 1951 and five large young in McCool Twp, on Aug. 11, 1951, both near Matheson. Smith (1957: 169) saw one near Timmins on June 21, 1953 and several on Lake Timiskaming on July 31, 1953. James *et al* saw them frequently in June, 1977, near Pickle Lake. Cringan (1953b: 2) saw them near Kasabonika Lake in early June, 1953. He found them regularly during the summer of 1950 in the Nikip Lake area and found a nest with 9 eggs on July 5 (Cringan, 1950: 5-6). Lee (1978: 20) had just two records for Big Trout Lake, both in early June. Peck (1972: 339) cited two mid-July records for Cape Henrietta Maria. Schueler, Baldwin & Rising (1974: 142) found them common to abundant at Hawley Lake, and uncommon to rare at Moosonee, Atawapiskat and Winisk.

AUTUMN: Skeel & Bondrup-Nielsen (1978: 16) found it to be an uncommon fall migrant at Pukaskwa up to Oct. 8. Five were seen on Lake Nipissing on Nov. 10, 1944 (Speirs & Speirs, 1947: 26). Ron Tozer saw about 3000 on Lake Scugog on Nov. 12, 1972 and gave a vivid account of their co-operative fishing techniques and their harassment by gulls who tried to pirate their catch (Tozer & Richards, 1974: 92). George A. Scott's median arrival date for Oshawa was Nov. 8 though there are a few September records and they sometimes become common by late October (Speirs, 1979: 61). Speirs (1938: 51) gave Nov. 10 as the fall peak at Toronto. Sheppard (1945: 161) called them exceedingly common on the Niagara River from November to April. Ussher (1965: 6) gave Sept. 16 as the earliest fall date for Rondeau with average arrival there on Oct. 23. Kelley (1978: 22) reported fall migrants by Sept. 8, becoming numerous in SW Ontario by early November. Stirrett (1973d: 17) gave 2000 on Oct. 19 as his fall maximum for Pelee.

**MEASUREMENTS:**

*Length:* ♂ to 27 ins. ♀ to 25 ins. (Palmer, 1976: 480).

*Wingspread:* ♂ to 36 ins. ♀ to 34 ins. (Palmer, 1976: 480).

*Weight:* ♂ usually about 3 1/2 lb., ♀ about 2 1/2 lbs. (Palmer, 1976: 480).

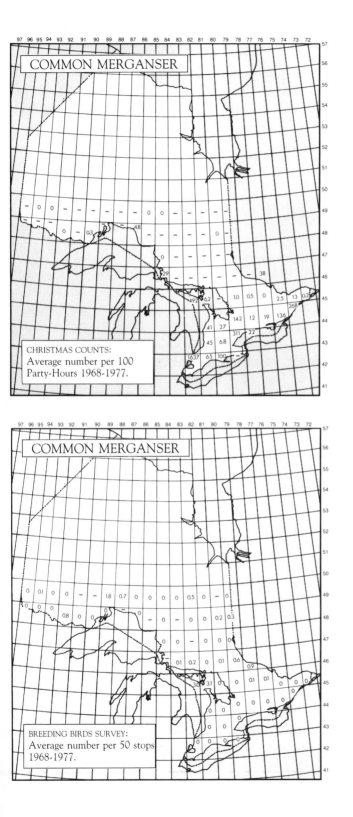

COMMON MERGANSER

CHRISTMAS COUNTS:
Average number per 100
Party-Hours 1968-1977.

COMMON MERGANSER

BREEDING BIRDS SURVEY:
Average number per 50 stops
1968-1977.

# RED-BREASTED MERGANSER   *Mergus serrator*   Linnaeus

In migration, as I usually see them, they always strike me as high-spirited fowl, "having a ball", diving, chasing, flying to a new fishing area, "necking" and having great fun. "Anthropomorphism" you may object, but just watch them and see for yourself.

IDENTIFICATION:   Males differ from male Common Mergansers in their rakish crests, and with spotted, reddish upper breasts and generally darker overall appearance. Females lack the sharply marked off white chin of the female Common Merganser.

WINTER:   This species is generally much less frequent than the Common Merganser in winter, except perhaps at Pelee, where hundreds or even thousands have shown up on Christmas counts. On other Christmas counts it has been uncommon to rare, north to Ottawa and Sault Ste. Marie. A few sometimes winter along the Lake Ontario shoreline (Speirs, 1979: 62) but it frequently requires a telescope to pick them out from the much more abundant Common Mergansers. It showed up on only one of the Barrie Christmas counts: on Dec. 18, 1965 (Devitt, 1967: 49). Beamer had records for four winters in the Christmas-New Year's period at Meaford. Seven individuals were tallied on three Christmas counts as Sault Ste. Marie over the past 25 years (Dennison, 1980: 148).

SPRING:   Stirrett (1973b: 15) had a peak of 6000 at Pelee on May 11. Ussher (1965: 6) gave Mar. 21 and June 14 as extreme spring dates for Rondeau, with average arrival on Mar. 25 and departure on May 14. Saunders & Dale (1933: 182) called it decidedly rare in Middlesex Co., with only a few records in the period from Mar. 28 to Apr. 27. Saunders (1947: 361) gave average departure dates from Toronto as May 19 (RMS) and May 22 (J.L. Baillie). The peak of the spring flight at Toronto is about Apr. 30 (Speirs, 1938: 43) when Lake Ontario seems full of their westward-moving flocks, with courting parties scattered here and there on the water. George A. Scott's median departure date from Oshawa was May 17 (Speirs, 1979: 62). Weir & Quilliam (1980: 33) gave Mar. 29 as the average arrival date at Kingston and May 12 as the average departure date. At Barrie the earliest date for spring arrival was Apr. 6, 1932, the 14-year average was Apr. 17 and the latest spring date was May 27, 1956 (Devitt, 1967: 49). Beamer has several spring records for Meaford between Mar. 22 and May 11. Sheppard (1945: 161) called them abundant on the Niagara River from mid-April to early May. It arrives on Manitoulin from late April to late May (Nicholson, 1972: 17). Twelve were noted on Lake Nipissing on Apr. 28, 1944 (Speirs & Speirs, 1947: 26). Denis (1961: 2) gave Apr. 19, 1953 as the earliest date at Thunder Bay with average arrival on Apr. 26. Skeel & Bondrup-Nielsen (1978: 161) called it an abundant spring migrant at Pukaskwa from Apr. 22 onwards. Elder (1979: 30) considered it uncommon at Geraldton with the earliest on May 2. He saw his first at Atikokan on May 5 in 1978. Cringan (1953: 2) saw his first at Sioux Lookout on May 3, 1953. He saw up to 20 on Kasabonika Lake in late May and early June, 1953 (Cringan, 1953b: 2).

SUMMER:   On Breeding Bird Surveys a few showed up on the Mattawa, Wawa, Atikokan and Kenora routes. Small numbers (less than 10) were reported through the summer at Pelee (Stirrett, 1973c: 14). Rob. Nisbet saw a pair with 10 juveniles at Eastbourne, Whitby, on July 30, 1977 and J.A. Edwards found two nests on Thorah Is., Lake Simcoe, both with 9 eggs, one on July 9, 1926, the other on June 20, 1929 (Speirs, 1979: 62). Quilliam (1965: 54) cited two breeding records for the Kingston area and noted a group of 14 there on Aug. 5, 1961. On July 16, 1952, A.J. Mitchener *et al* saw a pair with at least six young near Jack's Lake, Simcoe Co. (Devitt, 1967: 49). According to Nicholson (1972:17) it is an occasional summer resident on Manitoulin. A female with five downy young was found on Smith Lake, near Rutherglen, on June 19, 1945 (Speirs & Speirs, 1947: 26). This is by the far the most common duck at Pukaskwa in summer, with 14 records of nests or broods (Skeel & Bondrup-Neilsen, 1978: 161). Dear (1940: 124) reported a nest with 8 eggs found on June 22, 1932 about 8 miles east of Port Arthur, Thunder Bay. Cringan (1950: 6) found them reguarly in small numbers in the Nikip Lake area during the summer of 1950. Scheuler, Baldwin & Rising (1974: 142) found them uncommon at Moosonee, common at Hawley Lake and noted at Winisk, not seen at Ft. Albany or Attawapiskat. Peck (1972: 339) had a few records for Cape Henrietta Maria, including one collected by Hope in July, 1948. They were seen regularly in summer at Big Trout Lake, with a maximum of 14 on June 29, 1975 (Lee, 1978: 20). C.E. Hope saw three at Ft. Severn on June 29, 1940.

AUTUMN: Skeel & Bondrup-Neilsen (1978: 161) found this to be the most common fall duck at Pukaskwa up to Oct. 16. It returned to Manitoulin from early Oct. to early Nov. (Nicholson, 1972: 17). Beamer mentioned only one fall record at Meaford, on Nov. 2, 1947. The fall migration through Simcoe Co. was from the last week of Sept. to mid-Nov. (Devitt, 1967: 49). Weir & Quilliam (1980: 33) gave Oct. 17 as the 25-year average for fall arrivals at Kingston. George A. Scott's median arrival date for Oshawa was Oct. 16 (Speirs, 1979: 62). LGL (1974: 54) had a peak of 3920 on their waterfront survey near Toronto on Nov. 5, 1973. Saunders (1947: 361) gave Aug. 17 as the earliest fall arrival for Toronto but average arrival dates of Oct. 28 (RMS) and Nov. 3 (JLB). Stirrett (1973d: 17) had a peak of 5000 on Nov. 1 at Pelee. Ussher (1965: 6) had extreme dates at Rondeau of Sept. 16 and Dec. 8 with average arrival on Oct. 22 and departure on Nov. 23.

**MEASUREMENTS:**
*Length:* ♂ to 26 ins. ♀ to about 23 ins. (Palmer, 1976: 461).
*Wingspread:* ♂ to 34 ins. ♀ to 33 ins. (Palmer, 1976: 461).
*Weight:* ♂ about 2 1/2 lb. ♀ about 1 3/4 lb. (Palmer, 1976: 461).

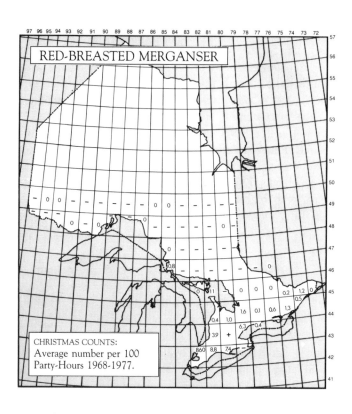

RED-BREASTED MERGANSER

CHRISTMAS COUNTS:
Average number per 100
Party-Hours 1968-1977.

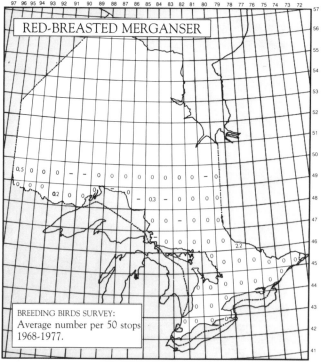

RED-BREASTED MERGANSER

BREEDING BIRDS SURVEY:
Average number per 50 stops
1968-1977.

# RUDDY DUCK   *Oxyura jamaicensis*   (Gmelin)

This is another prairie breeder, usually rare in Ontario. It breeds in cattail marshes, but many sometimes can be found loafing offshore on the Great Lakes at other seasons.

IDENTIFICATION:   The jaunty little males, with their sky blue bills, white cheeks, black caps and generally ruddy plumage, are unmistakable. The spiky "sticky-up" tail, from which they received their scientific name, is a suggestive, but not entirely diagnostic field mark (Buffleheads, and some other diving ducks, sometimes cock their tails up in a similar fashion). Females and males out of breeding plumage might be mistaken for female Buffleheads at a distance but lack the single white patch behind the eye of that species, having instead grayish cheeks with dark horizontal stripe (or stripes).

WINTER:   On Christmas counts they have occurred from Pelee to Kingston along the north shore of Lake Erie and Lake Ontario, usually in very small numbers, except for one very large flock at Pelee in 1972 and moderate numbers there and at Blenheim in 1974.

SPRING:   Kelley (1978: 22) found them from mid-March to mid-May in SW Ontario, sometimes very numerous in the lower Detroit River. Stirrett (1973b: 15) gave Mar. 25 as his earliest record for Pelee, with a maximum count of 622 on Apr. 24 and the latest on May 17. Saunders & Dale (1933: 181) gave the 11-year average arrival date for London as Apr. 20, with the earliest on Apr. 13, 1918. Ussher (1965: 6) gave the earliest and latest dates for Rondeau as Mar. 24 and May 10 with Apr. 4 and May 1 as average dates for arrival and departure there. On Mar. 23, 1938, a female was salvaged as a specimen for the ROM below Niagara Falls (Sheppard, 1945: 16). Saunders (1947: 361) had spring dates at Toronto from Apr. 21 to May 17. George A. Scott's median arrival date for Oshawa was Apr. 14 (Speirs, 1979: 59) and LGL (1974: 50) reported as many as 54 on their Apr. 10 waterfront survey. Quilliam (1965: 52) considered this species very rare in the Kingston area with sightings between Mar. 16 and Apr. 30. Devitt (1967: 47) had spring dates for this rare duck in Simcoe Co. from Apr. 26 to May 26. Nicholson (1972: 17) had recent records of small numbers on Manitoulin during May.

SUMMER:   Kelley (1978: 22) reported nine nests near Walpole Is., Kent Co., in 1954. Stirrett (1973b: 15 and 1973c: 14) had individuals at Pelee on June 10 and 16. Baillie (1962: 1-3) gave details of the breeding status in Ontario at that time, including more Lake St. Clair nestings; nestings at Mud Lake, Welland Co. where Gertrude Selby found an adult with 4 downy young on June 26, 1947; nestings at Luther Marsh where G.F. Boyer and O.E. Devitt found nests with eggs in June, 1958 and at Thunder Bay where the Rydholms observed young on June 23, 1957, he also gave summer records north as far as Deep River where C.H. Millar saw one in July, 1960. Saunders & Dale (1933: 181) had one summer record at London, on July 8, 1928. The first evidence of breeding at Cranberry Marsh, Whitby, was on June 16, 1972, when J.M. Richards saw a female with 7 young there (Tozer & Richards, 1974: 91) but there are several subsequent breeding records there including a nest with eggs and young on July 17, 1976 (Speirs, 1979: 59). Richards (1977: 45-47) updated the nesting status in Ontario with much detail on the Cranberry Marsh nestings. With Bob Taylor, I saw two on Lillabelle Lake, Cochrane, on July 17, 1957.

148

AUTUMN: Devitt (1967: 47) considered it rare in Simcoe Co. but had a few fall records from the second week in October to Dec. 6. Weir & Quilliam (1980: 33) gave Nov. 14 as the 10-year average departure date from Kingston. George A. Scott's median departure date from Oshawa was Nov. 28 (Speirs, 1979: 59). Fleming (1906: 446) reported one at Toronto on Oct. 16, 1895, and called it a regular fall migrant, "all examined are immature". Saunders (1947: 361) gave fall dates at Toronto from Oct. 8 to Nov. 6. Ussher (1965: 6) had extreme Rondeau dates from Oct. 1 to Dec. 26 with Oct. 11 and Nov. 19 as the average fall arrivals and departure dates. Stirret (1973d: 17) gave Sept. 12 and Nov. 25 as extreme fall dates for Pelee with a maximum of 100 on Oct. 16.

BANDING: Speirs (1979: 59) gave details of two banded in summer, in Minnesota and Wisconsin, and shot during the subsequent hunting season in the Toronto-Oshawa area.

**MEASUREMENTS:**
*Length:* ♂ av. (of 23) 15.4 ins. ♀ av. (0f 15) 15.1 ins. (Kortright, 1942: 388)
*Wingspread:* ♂ av. (of 11) 22.5 ins. ♀ av. (of 8) 22.4 ins. (Kortright, 1942: 388)
*Weight:* ♂ av. (of 8) 1 lb. 5 1/2 oz. ♀ av. (of 13) 1 lb. 2 oz. (Kortright, 1942: 388)

**REFERENCE:**
Richards, James M. 1977 A summary of nesting records for Ruddy Ducks, *Oxyura jamaicensis*, in Ontario, with particular reference to the Regional Municipality of Durham. Ont. Field Biol., 31: (2): 45-47.

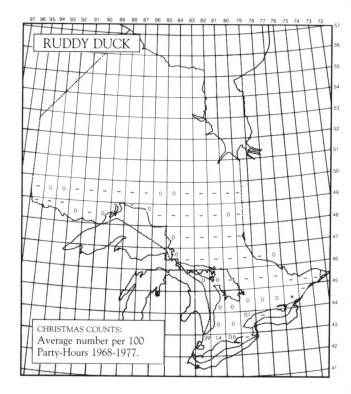

RUDDY DUCK

CHRISTMAS COUNTS:
Average number per 100
Party-Hours 1968-1977.

# BLACK VULTURE   *Coragyps atratus*   (Bechstein)

This is a common scavenger in the southern U.S.A. but very few make their way north to Ontario.

IDENTIFICATION:   The naked, black head distinguishes it from adult Turkey Vultures, which have red heads, but young Turkey Vultures also have black heads. In flight it reminds one more of a young Golden Eagle than of a Turkey Vulture, because of the white wing flashes and relatively short, broad wings, carried horizontally when soaring, not in a V as in Turkey Vultures. It flaps much more and soars less than a Turkey Vulture, and the short square tail, contrasts with the long, rounded tail of the Turkey Vulture.

WINTER:   D. Shepherd and T. Woodrow reported one at Long Point Provincial Park on Feb. 16-17, 1984 (Weir, 1984: 311).

SPRING:   On May 6, 1948, a pair was seen at Pt. Rowan by W.H. Carrick and H.M. Halliday (Baillie, 1948: 174). George North documented a sighting on May 28, 1961, at the Halton County Forest, Campbellville (Woodford & Burton, 1961: 407).

SUMMER:   A. Wormington *et al* observed one at Pelee on Aug. 17, 1981 (Goodwin, 1982: 172). A.L. Patterson found one in east Lambton Co. on July 29, 1982 (Weir, 1982: 971). The first one recorded in Ontario, an adult in worn breeding plumage, was taken on July 21, 1947, about 4 miles north of Niagara Falls (in Stamford Twp., Welland Co.) by Marion Miles, and forwarded to the Royal Ontario Museum by A.R. Muma (Hope, 1949: 81-82). One was reported at Cayuga by D.A. Smith on Aug. 24, 1974 (Goodwin, 1975: 49). R. Curry reported another north of Milton in Halton Co. on July 1, 1962 (Woodford, 1962: 473). The farthest north and east was one reported at Kaladar by W.E. Edwards about June 23, 1949 (Baillie, 1950: 13).

AUTUMN:   Brooman (1954: 12-13) reported one seen on Oct. 15, 1953, by Marshall Field, over Pinafore Park, St. Thomas, circling very low so that all indentification markings could be checked.

**MEASUREMENTS:**
*Length:* 25 ins. (Pough, 1951: 124)
*Wingspread:* 57 ins. (Pough, 1951: 124)
*Weight:* 4 1/2 lbs. (Pough, 1951: 124) Note this is more than for the Turkey Vulture!

**REFERENCE:**
Hope, C.E. 1949 First occurrence of the Black Vulture in Ontario. Auk, 66: (1): 81-82.

# TURKEY VULTURE   Cathartes aura   (Linnaeus)

In most parts of Ontario it is a rare sight to see these big, red-headed vultures soaring aloft with scarcely a wingbeat, tilting from side to side.

IDENTIFICATION: Of the hawk-like birds only the eagles surpass the Turkey Vulture in wingspread and they soar with the wings held horizontally, not well above the horizontal to form a wide V as in this species. Marsh Hawks also fly with wings above the horizontal as do Red-tailed Hawks in a high wind: the large size and black colour suffice to distinguish the vulture from these smaller predators. Note the two-toned pattern on the underwing, black near the body with paler flight feathers. For differences between this species and Black Vultures see that species.

WINTER: On the 1968-1977 Christmas counts, Turkey Vultures showed up along the north shores of Lake Erie and Lake Ontario from Pelee to the Thousand Islands, in small numbers. Stirrett (1973a: 14) noted individuals at Pelee on Dec. 6 and Dec. 27. On Jan. 2, 1952, one was seen flying over Aldborough Twp., Elgin Co., by Harold Lancaster (Brooman, 1954: 12). Weir & Quilliam (1980: 33) had a Dec. 17 record for Kingston. John Comer observed one at Orillia on Dec. 23-24, 1953 (Devitt, 1967: 50). L. Beamer had two records for the Christmas season at Meaford, on Dec. 27, 1948 and Dec. 28, 1954. R.M. Saunders and R.W. Trowern saw one on Feb. 18, 1969, at Eels Creek, Peterborough, (Goodwin, 1969: 474).

SPRING: Stirrett (1973b: 15) had the earliest two at Pelee on March 28 and a maximum of 9 on Apr. 21. Ussher (1965: 7) gave Apr. 13 as the 16-year average for arrival at Rondeau, with the earliest on Mar. 27 and latest on May 24. Saunders & Dale (1933: 183) gave Apr. 24 as the 9-year average for arrival at London, with Apr. 8 as the earliest; they reported nests found in hollow logs on May 18, 1919 near Coldstream and on May 24, 1927 near Kerwood. Saunders (1947: 361) gave Apr. 20 as his earliest Toronto record. The earliest Ontario Co. record was one seen by George A. Scott near Oshawa's Second Marsh on Mar. 13, 1949 (Speirs, 1977: 1). Weir & Quilliam (1980: 33) gave Apr. 7 as the 20-year average arrival date for Kingston, with the earliest on Mar. 25. Devitt (1967: 50) gave Apr. 17 as the 12-year average arrival date at Barrie with the earliest on Mar. 31, 1963. Beamer's median arrival date for the Meaford area was Apr. 10, with the earliest on Feb. 27, 1948 by Lloyd Moore. Mills (1981: 31) gave Apr. 12, 1968, as the earliest Muskoka date (near Bala). Fred Warburton reported one at Sault Ste. Marie on May 22, 1948 (Baillie, 1948: 205). Elder (1979: 30) saw one on May 12, 1971, at Cavers Hill between Schreiber and Nipigon.

SUMMER: On Breeding Bird Surveys this species was uncommon, even in southwestern Ontario, and rare north to Thessalon and Suomi, none in the east and northeast. Stirrett (1973b: 15) had 11 at Pelee on June 6. Brooman (1954: 12) called it a common summer resident in Elgin Co. Sheppard (1939: 74) visited John G. Trafford on Aug. 18, 1938, and was shown two young taken as downies 6 weeks or more prior to his visit, about a mile NW of Pt. Rowan. Speirs (1977: 1) reported them as rather rare in the southern part of Ontario Co. but more common in the northern half. Devitt (1967: 50) gave details of nesting near Singhampton. Beamer reported that Vincent Miller shot a female from a nest with 2 eggs near Walter's Falls in late June, 1932, while Lloyd Moore found another nest in a crevice in the escarpment south of Meaford on June 10, 1942 (these eggs hatched on June 12 and June 14). Mills (1981: 30-31) cited several summer records for Muskoka and Parry Sound, including one flock of 30 near Go Home Lake in late August reported by B. Falls. Nicholson (1972: 17) stated that "it almost certainly breeds" on Manitoulin. R.W. Trowern saw an immature on Aug. 12, 1950, 16 miles south of Elk Lake (Baillie, 1950: 273). Snyder (1953: 52-53) gave many records of Turkey Vultures summering in Lake-of-the-Woods, Kenora and one flock of 12 feeding on fish offal at Sydney Lake, about 60 miles north of Kenora. Cringan (1953a: 2) reported one at Perrault Falls on June 16, 1953. Manning (1952: 32) cited two summer records from the far north: one killed at Moose Factory in June, 1898 and examined by Newnham (Fleming, 1903: 66) and one collected at Ft. Severn in Aug. 1931, by Hugh Conn (Norris-Elye, 1932: 142).

AUTUMN: Cringan (1950: 6) quoted an Indian guide who told him of "a large, black eagle with no head feathers" at Nikip Lake in November (he thought). Nicholson (1972: 17) gave 17 seen on Sept. 11, 1971, by Chris Bell and John Lemon as the maximum count for Manitoulin. Mills (1981: 30) reported one collected on Oct. 2, 1954, at Blackstone Lake, Parry Sound. Beamer had a few fall records for Meaford, three seen as late as Nov. 8, 1946 by Lloyd Moore. Weir & Quilliam (1980: 33) gave Oct. 18 as the 18-year average departure date from Kingston. Speirs (1977: 1) found a fall peak in Ontario Co. during the second week of October, with one very late record by Edgerton Pegg on Nov. 27, 1976 in Pickering Twp. Saunders (1947: 361) gave Sept. 29 as his latest fall record for Toronto but Speirs (1938: 53) had a Nov. 17 record. One was taken on Oct. 26, 1936 by A.R. Muma in the Niagara region (Sheppard, 1960: 14). Ussher (1965: 7) had fall records at Rondeau from Aug. 26 to Oct. 20. Kelley (1978: 23) reported a count of 1128 during a hawk watch at Holliday Beach in the fall of 1974. Stirrett (1973a: 14) had one at Pelee as late as Nov. 23 and a maximum of 31 on Oct. 23 (Stirrett, 1973d: 17).

**MEASUREMENTS:**
*Length:* 26.5 to 32 ins.
(Godfrey, 1966: 85)
*Wingspread:* 70 ins.
(Pough, 1951: 123)
*Weight:* 3 1/2 lbs. (Pough, 1951: 123)
*References:* Fleming, J.H. 1903 Turkey Vulture at Moose Factory, James Bay. Auk, 20: (1): 66.
  Norris-Elye, L.T.S. 1932 A few records from the Arctic. Can. Field-Nat., 46: (6): 142.
  Sheppard, R.W. 1939 Turkey Vulture nesting in Norfolk County, Ontario. Auk, 56: (1): 74-75.

152

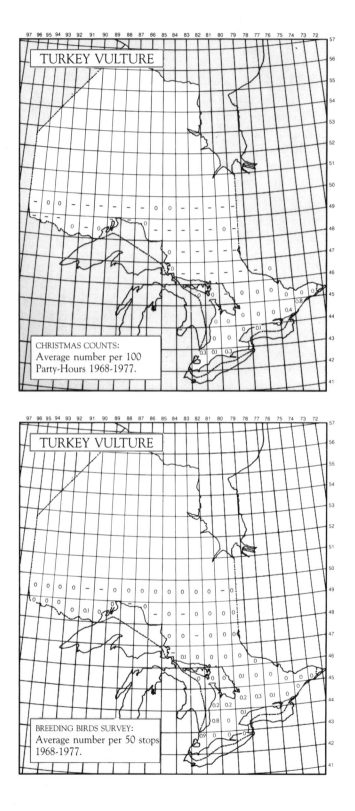

TURKEY VULTURE

CHRISTMAS COUNTS:
Average number per 100
Party-Hours 1968-1977.

TURKEY VULTURE

BREEDING BIRDS SURVEY:
Average number per 50 stops
1968-1977.

# OSPREY   *Pandion haliaetus*   (Linnaeus)

Bald Eagles sometimes bully Ospreys into dropping their fish, then stop to grasp it before it hits the water (or ground). One of my most vivid memories involved this interaction. I was startled to hear a roar of wings overhead and looked up to see an Osprey, which had evidently been pirated of its catch, diving at the offending eagle and then pulling up at the last moment as the eagle dropped its prize and rolled over presenting an armament of talons to the oncoming Osprey, which swerved upward to safety. The result of this episode was that neither bird got the fish. I did, as the big sucker hit the ground near me.

IDENTIFICATION: The first impression of an Osprey is often that a very big gull is winging overhead, with long, slender wings, swept back at the wrists where there is a dark blotch, very white below and dark above. Then you notice the dark mark behind the eye and the conspicuous white "eyebrow". The wingspan approaches six feet (about a foot less than the eagles). When not disturbed they will build their bulky nests atop big, tall trees or poles, sometimes quite close to human habitations. Some will accept platforms provided for them mounted on tall poles near or over water.

WINTER: This is a very rare bird in winter in Ontario. On Christmas counts they have been reported at Thousand Is., Kingston and Guelph. Weir & Quilliam (1980: 34) had Kingston records as late as Dec. 18 and as early as Feb. 15.

SPRING: Stirrett (1973b: 15) had a few spring records at Pelee from Apr. 8 to May 22. Ussher (1965: 8) had Rondeau records from Apr. 15 to May 28. Saunders & Dale (1933: 187) gave Apr. 20 as the 12-year average arrival date for London, with records as early as Apr. 11, 1947 and as late as June 2, 1930. Saunders (1947: 362) had spring dates for Toronto from Apr. 12 to May 15, while Speirs (1938: 44) suggested the third week of April as the spring peak. Speirs (1977: 12) had a spring record for Ontario Co. as early as Apr. 8. Allin (1940: 95) reported a very early record for Darlington Twp. on Mar. 5, 1881, by Dutton. Weir & Quilliam (1980: 34) gave Apr. 13 as the 26-year average arrival date for Kingston. Devitt (1967: 56) gave Apr. 19 as the 12-year average arrival date for Barrie, with the earliest on Mar. 30, 1967. Beamer's median arrival date for Meaford was Apr. 23, with the earliest on Apr. 11, 1948. Mills (1981: 40-41) gave arrival dates for the cottage country from Apr. 11 to May 5. Nicholson (1981: 86) gave Apr. 16 as the 12-year average for Manitoulin, the earliest on Apr. 6, 1980. Skeel & Bondrup-Nielsen (1978: 164) had only one spring date for Pukaskwa: May 8, 1977. Denis (1961: 3) gave Apr. 28 as the average date for arrival at Thunder Bay with the earliest on Apr. 15, 1955. Bondrup-Nielsen (1976: 42) gave May 8 as his earliest sighting near Kapuskasing in 1975 and reported a nest with nearby adult on May 29. Elder (1979: 31) gave Apr. 30 as his earliest date for Geraldton. Cringan (1953a: 2) saw his first at Sioux Lookout on May 20: his only observation at Kasabonika Lake was on May 28 (Cringan, 1953b: 2). Ross James noted one at Pickle Lake on May 30, 1977.

SUMMER: Although widespread in summer in Ontario they are not at all common. On Breeding Surveys they were noted only on the Kingsville, Whitney, Byng Inlet and Silver Islet routes. Ussher (1965: 8) had one at Rondeau on July 24. Fred Bodsworth saw one at St. Thomas on June 20, 1942 (Brooman, 1954: 15). From July 15 to 29, 1956, one or two were seen near Pt. Abino, Lake Erie (Beardslee & Mitchell, 1965: 178). Saunders (1947: 362) had Toronto observations on June 17 and Aug. 6. Speirs (1977: 12) had several summer records for Ontario Co. but no nest records, but since that time nests had been found in Thorah and Mara Twps. Quilliam (1965: 63) cited several nest records for the Kingston region. Devitt (1967: 55-56) gave several old nest records for Simcoe Co., the latest about 1924. Beamer reported nesting near Irish Lake, Grey Co. Mills (1981: 41) gave details of several nestings in the Muskoka-Parry Sound region. Nicholson (1981: 86) gave details of three of seven nests for Manitoulin: his high count of birds was eight at Gore Bay on Aug. 2, 1977. Skeel & Bondrup-Nielsen (1978: 164) had Pukaskwa records for June 14 and July 11, 1977 and Aug. 14, 1973. Smith (1957: 17) cited several summer records for the Clay Belt. Snyder (1953: 54-55) had several nest records from the region between Minaki and Kenora east to Dinorwic Lake. Snyder (1928: 260) reported a nest at Lake Nipigon. Dear (1940: 126) reported nests with eggs near Thunder Bay on May 30, 1929 and June 5, 1931. Hope (1938: 13) reported that three immatures (2♂, 1♀) were taken by Indians near Favourable Lake on Aug. 12, 1938. Todd (1963: 234, 236) summarized the literature for the area between North Bay and James Bay and reported a nest at the mouth of the Opazatika River (50°24'N, 82°22'W) on June 23, 1908. Manning (1952: 35) cited an old nest record for Moose Factory and personal sightings there: he also gave records for the Ft. Albany region. Schueler, Baldwin & Rising (1974: 142) noted Ospreys at Moosonee, Attawapiskat, Winisk and Hawley Lake, with evidence of nesting at Hawley Lake. Harry Lumsden saw Ospreys near the mouth of the Brant River on July 14 and Aug. 2, 1969 (Peck, 1972: 339). Cringan (1950: 7) reported a nest in the Nikip Lake area. Lee (1978: 20) saw an Osprey on June 12, 1975 at Big Trout Lake and reported a nest at a nearby lake: he also saw one at Ft. Severn on June 19, 1975 where Cliff Hope had collected one of several seen in July, 1940.

AUTUMN:    Along the Lake Superior shore of Pukaskwa, individuals were noted on Sept. 18, 20, 30 and on Oct. 2 (Skeel & Bondrup-Nielsen, 1978: 164). Nicholson (1981: 86) gave Oct. 17, 1973 as a late date for Manitoulin. Mills (1981: 41) wrote that the autumn migration through the Parry Sound-Muskoka region is primarily in Sept. and Oct. and cited one Huntsville record as late as Nov. 10, 1969. Beamer had Meaford records from Sept. 5 to Oct. 4. Frances Westman saw one near Barrie as late as Oct. 12, 1945 (Devitt, 1967: 56). Weir & Quilliam (1980: 34) gave Oct. 11 as the 21-year average departure date from Kingston. Speirs (1977: 12) suggested that the third week of Sept. was the fall peak in Ontario Co., though his maximum count of 11 was on Sept. 23, 1951: Doris H. Speirs saw one as late as Nov. 14, 1970 at Pickering. Saunders (1947: 362) gave Oct. 22 as the latest Toronto date. Beardslee & Mitchell (1965: 177-178) reported Ospreys in Canadian waters as early as Aug. 10, 1946 (at Chippewa) and as late as Oct. 30, 1943, with a maximum of 10 on Sept. 4, 1937 near Long Beach. Field & Field (1979: 11) had a daily maximum of 36 at Hawk Cliff on Sept. 21, 1977, with one as early as Aug. 27 and one as late as Oct. 12. Ussher (1965: 8) gave Sept. 4 as the 13-year average arrival date in fall at Rondeau and noted one there as late as Nov. 25. Stirrett (1973d: 17 and 1973a: 15) had Pelee records from Aug. 21 to Nov. 26, with a maximum of five on Sept. 27.

**MEASUREMENTS:**

*Length:* 23 ins. (Pough,
1951: 160)
*Wingspread:* 68 ins.
(Pough, 1951: 160)
*Weight:* 3 1/2 lbs. (Pough,
1951: 160)
Beamer reported
wingspreads of 62 ins., 64
ins. and 6 ft. for three
taken near Meaford.

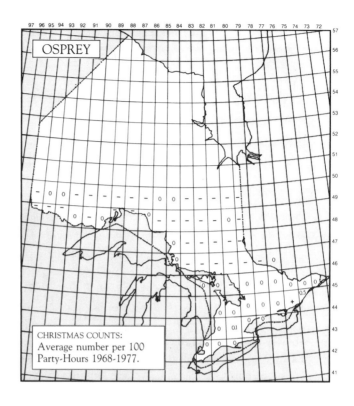

OSPREY

CHRISTMAS COUNTS:
Average number per 100
Party-Hours 1968-1977.

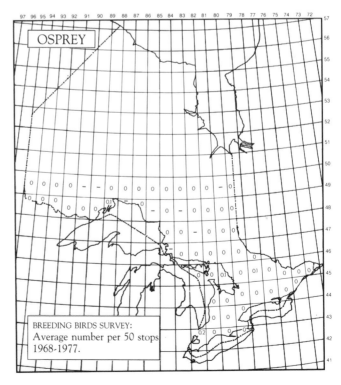

OSPREY

BREEDING BIRDS SURVEY:
Average number per 50 stops
1968-1977.

# AMERICAN SWALLOW-TAILED KITE
*Elanoides forficatus*    (Linnaeus)

The only place that I have encountered this beauty was on it normal breeding territory in the Carolinas but a few have strayed north to Ontario to delight those fortunate enough to have seen them.

IDENTIFICATION:  With its deeply forked tail, white body and black wings and tail this bird is unmistakable: it is a medium-sized bird of prey.

WINTER:

SPRING:   D. Jackson and C. Urquhart observed and photographed one at Pelee on May 15 and May 22, 1978 (Goodwin, 1978: 998). Howard Snelgrove saw one by Hwy. 2, between Bowmanville and Newcastle on Apr. 14, 1953 (Baillie, 1953: 270).

SUMMER:   Many observers saw one near Buckhorn Lake, Peterborough region, between June 14 and June 24, 1982: this bird was photographed on June 17 by A.G. Carpentier (Weir, 1982: 971-972). G. and V. Hanna observed one at Wakami Lake Provincial Park on July 17, 1983 (Weir, 1983: 983).

AUTUMN:   There have been several old sightings without specific dates, including: "a pair of hawks with forked tails" that stayed all summer about 8 miles northwest of London, reported by Mr. Vernor prior to 1882 (Saunders & Dale, 1933: 183); a specimen taken near Toronto "many years ago" in the Fleming collection (Fleming, 1907: 87) and one seen at the Rideau Rifle Range, near Ottawa, "prior to 1881" (Lloyd, 1923: 151).

**MEASUREMENTS:**
*Length:* 24 ins. (outer tail
feathers project 8 ins.
beyond middle ones
(Godfrey, 1966: 86).
*Wingspread:* 48 ins.
(Pough, 1951: 127).
*Weight:* 2 averaged 475 g.
(Dunning, 1984: 6).

# MISSISSIPPI KITE   *Ictinia mississippiensis*   (Wilson)

The Mississippi Kite is primarily a bird of the southern United States, very rare in Ontario.

IDENTIFICATION:   The Mississippi Kite is a smallish hawk, about the size of a Merlin, but with relatively long wings. Adults, with their white heads and black tails, are easily identified. The young are streaked with brown and have banded tails and might be mistaken for young Merlins, but for their relatively long tails and very buoyant flight.

WINTER:

SPRING:   There have been three reports from Pelee: the first noted on May 21, 1971 was rejected by the Ontario Ornthological Records Committee (Goodwin, 1972: 35); the second on May 16, 1979, was photographed by Alan Wormington and seen by many others from May 16 to May 20—observers included M.J. Bronskill and K.A. Quickert (Goodwin, 1979: 766); M. Gawn reported another at Pelee on May 9, 1983 (Weir, 1983: 864). T.W. Weir gave a good description of one seen at Wainfleet on May 28, 1977 (Goodwin, 1977: 994).

SUMMER:

AUTUMN:   Ron. Scovell reported an immature bird at High Park, Toronto, on Sept. 19, 1951 (Baillie, 1952: 14).

**MEASUREMENTS:**
*Length:* 14 ins. (Pough, 1951: 129)
*Wingspread:* 35 ins. (Pough, 1951: 129)
*Weight:* 14♂ averaged 248 g.; 6♀ averaged 314 g. Dunning, 1984: 6).

# BALD EAGLE   *Haliaeetus leucocephalus*   (Linnaeus)

Eagles are impressive birds. Nineteen Ontario lakes are listed in the Gazeteer of Canada as Eagle Lake, and some forty other localities have names starting with eagle. I can recall searching for the nest which gave Eagle, Ont. its name and spending part of a summer at Eaglehead Lake, north of Thunder Bay. I recall the odd sight of a hummingbird dashing at a young eagle riding the updraft along the shore cliff near Port Ryerse, Lake Erie. During the fall hawk flights over our home in Pickering, we have sometimes seen a lone eagle cruising along with the Broad-wings.

IDENTIFICATION:   The adult with its white head and tail poses no problem for the bird watcher. Immatures might be mistaken for young Golden Eagles (see that species for the distinctions).

WINTER:   A few have shown up on Christmas counts, as far south as Pelee and north as far as Dryden and Deep River. Stirrett (1973a: 15) listed several winter records for Pelee, with a maximum of six on Jan. 24. Sheppard (1960: 15) described the former abundance along the Niagara River: "eight or ten being shot nearly every winter". Thompson (1890: 182) mentioned one seen by Hubert H. Brown at Victoria Park, Toronto, on Jan. 1, 1889. Speirs (1977: 10) cited several winter records between Ajax and Oshawa. Beamer had several December and February records for Meaford and recounted an encounter between an eagle and a dog at nearby Mountain Lake on Jan. 18-19, 1939. Mills (1981: 39) reported specimens taken at Port Loring in Jan. 1902 and at Dunchurch on Dec. 20, 1897 and in Jan., 1896. Nicholson (1981: 85) noted that eagles have been seen quite frequently along the souther shore of Manitoulin in winter. Dennison (1980: 147) listed this species as occurring on six of 25 Christmas counts at Sault Ste. Marie. Elder (1979: 31) reported them feeding on discarded coarse fish at Onaman Lake in winter.

SPRING:   Saunders & Dale (1933: 186) saw three adults together at Komoka on Mar. 16, 1930. Beardslee & Mitchell (1965: 175) noted an adult turning the eggs in a nest on Navy Island on Mar. 16, 1946 and also reported nests at Mohawk Point and Port Maitland. Speirs (1938: 46) gave May 21 as the latest spring date for Toronto. Doris H. Speirs saw one over our Pickering home on Apr. 14, 1955 and Naomi LeVay observed one flying west over Cranberry Marsh on May 26, 1962 (Speirs, 1979: 10). Charles Fothergill noted that "Bald eagles are paired" on Apr. 9, 1821, at Rice Lake (Black, 1934: 145). Quilliam (1965: 61-62) documented several former nestings in the Kingston area and expressed concern over the recent decline in numbers. Beamer noted individuals over Meaford almost every spring from 1938 to 1953. Mills (1981: 39) gave arrival dates for Port Sydney on May 3, 1901 and for Huntsville from Apr. 8 to 19. Ricker & Clarke (1939: 7) mentioned one seen at Frank's Bay, Lake Nipissing, as early as Apr. 29, 1934, by F.E.J. Fry. I saw one drifting west as it circled over the North Bay airport on May 23, 1945 (Speirs & Speirs, 1947: 27). Skeel & Bondrup-Nielsen (1978: 163) saw an immature at Pukaskwa on Apr. 25 and 29. Denis (1961: 2) gave Apr. 5 as the average arrival date at Thunder Bay, with the earliest on Mar. 2, 1956. Dear (1940: 125) reported two nests from the Thunder Bay region, one with two eggs on Apr. 13, 1936 and the other with three young on May 18, 1934. Cringan (1953a: 2) noted his first in 1953 on May 15 at Perrault Falls.

SUMMER:   On Breeding Bird Surveys they have been noted only on the Kingsville, Suomi and Atikokan routes. Kelley (1978: 25-26) listed only three pairs nesting in recent years in southwestern Ontario, down from 14 in the summer of 1951. Ussher (1965: 7) listed it as a nesting species at Rondeau: one of my fondest memories is of observing these great birds there. Brooman (1954: 14) gave several breeding records for Elgin Co. Speirs (1977: 10) gave three summer records from Pickering (June 1 to July 2). Charles Fothergill shot one at Rice Lake on June 18, 1821 (Black, 1934: 145). Snyder (1941: 43-44) stated that two or three pairs were nesting in Prince Edward Co. during the summer of 1930. Paul Harrington saw individuals at Wasaga Beach on June 12 and July 16, 1919 (Devitt, 1967: 55) and Beamer saw two over Meaford on July 3, 1943 and had several June records in subsequent years. Jas. H. Fleming reported three nests at Lake Rosseau, Muskoka, in the summer of 1888 (Thompson, 1890: 185) and Mills (1981: 38-39) cited several other nest records for the Muskoka-Parry Sound region. Nicholson (1981: 85) reported a nest with two young at Beaver Is., Manitoulin, in July, 1961 as the latest Manitoulin nesting, though two young with adults were seen at Clapperton Is. in July and August, 1972. A.F. Coventry found a nest with one young at Frank's Bay, Lake Nipissing, on July 10, 1930 (Ricker & Clarke, 1939: 7) and I saw one pursued by an irate Osprey nearby on Aug. 5, 1944 (Speirs & Speirs, 1947: 27). MacLulich (1938: 9) gave several summer records for Algonquin Park. One was seen at Pukaskwa on July 7, 1973 (Skeel & Bondrup-Nielsen, 1978: 164). Snyder (1928: 259) took an almost fully feathered young from a nest at East Bay, Lake Nipigon. He cited several nest records from the Lake-of-the-Woods region (Snyder, 1953: 54). Smith (1957: 170) gave several summer records from the periphery of the Clay Belt area but stated that it does not nest near its center. T.F. McIlwraith saw one at Moose Factory on Aug. 29, 1931 (Baillie & Harrington, 1936: 23). Schueler, Baldwin & Rising (1974: 142) saw this species only at Hawley Lake (in 1964). Cringan (1950: 6) saw an adult on June 13 along the North Caribou River. Lee (1978: 20) reported nest and young at Big Trout Lake (from reports by local residents).

AUTUMN:   Skeel & Bondrup-Nielsen (1978: 163-164) noted immatures at Pukaskwa as late as Oct. 12 and 13. Katherine Ketchum had October sightings at Pointe au Baril from 1951 to 1958 (Mills, 1981: 39). Beamer had fall sightings as early as Sept. 5 at Meaford, but records were scarce compared with spring. One was taken on Nov. 12, 1890 at Waubaushene (Devitt, 1967: 55). J. Satterly watched one fishing at Cedar Point, Lake Simcoe, with a flock of Bonaparte's Gulls on Oct. 28, 1951 and I have seen individuals over Pickering as early as Sept. 3, 1958 and as late as Nov. 10, 1952 during the fall *Buteo* flights (Speirs, 1977: 10). James R. Thurston received at his store, one shot on the 5th. Conc. West, York Co., on Oct. 24, 1889 (Thompson, 1890: 197). Speirs (1938: 48) gave Sept. 5 as the earliest fall date for Toronto. Brooman (1954: 14) mentioned that up to 21 had been seen in Elgin Co. in a day but in 1977 Field & Field (1979: 11-13) listed only two individuals in the fall flight at Hawk Cliff, on Sept. 19 and Nov. 24. Stirrett (1973d: 17) had his maximum fall count of four at Pelee on Sept. 21.

**MEASUREMENTS:**
*Length:* ♂ 34 ins. ♀ 36
ins. (Pough, 1951: 157)
*Wingspread:* ♂ 80 ins. ♀
85 ins. (Pough, 1951: 157)
Fleming (1907: 73) gave
lengths of ♀ from 33 to
34.75 ins. wingspreads of
♀ from 83 to 88.25 ins.
(adults larger than
immatures, no ♂
measured).
*Weight:* ♀ 13 lbs. (Pough,
1951: 157)
35 ♂ averaged 4124 g.; 37
♀ averaged 5244 g.
(Dunning, 1984: 6).

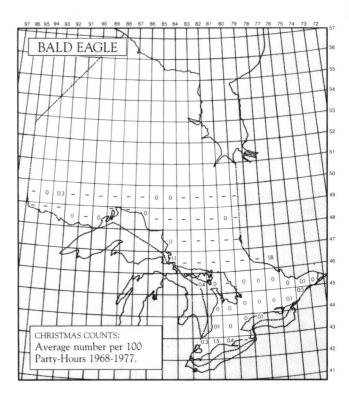

BALD EAGLE

CHRISTMAS COUNTS:
Average number per 100
Party-Hours 1968-1977.

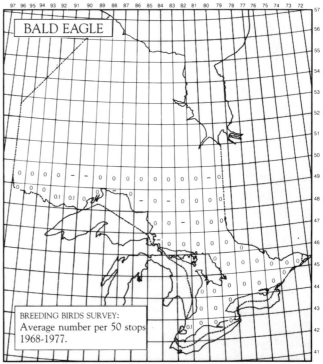

BALD EAGLE

BREEDING BIRDS SURVEY:
Average number per 50 stops
1968-1977.

# NORTHERN HARRIER   *Circus cyaneus*   (Linnaeus)

Although frequently seen quartering over cattail marshes, they often breed in upland old fields, far above any open water. In Europe this species is known as the Hen Harrier.

IDENTIFICATION:   This is one of the most easily identified hawks, with its long slender wings held above the horizontal and white rump at the base of its long tail. Adult males are a lovely blue gray above, females and young are brown. The young are orange-brown below. In the spectacular mating flight they do 50 ft. "push ups" rising vertically high in the air, then plunging down, only to rise again and again. They usually hunt very low over field or marsh searching for mice. If they should pass by a prospective meal, they may do a loop and come back over it again . . . altogether a joy to watch.

WINTER:   On Christmas counts they have been fairly common along the north shore of Lake Erie and uncommon to rare from the north shore of Lake Ontario to Meaford and Moscow, Ont. Stirrett (1973a: 15) reported them regularly at Pelee in numbers from 1 to 6, with one astounding estimate of 90 on Dec. 21. Saunders & Dale (1933: 186) found them especially abundant during the winter of 1931-32, with five noted on the afternoon of Dec. 12. On the Pickering Christmas counts, the maximum of 20 was found on the Dec. 26, 1965 count, while on some other counts none were found (Speirs, 1977: 11). Quilliam (1965: 62) noted that although they had been seen on 10 of the Kingston Christmas counts, she had only three February records. Devitt (1967: 55) gave only two December records and one February observation for Simcoe Co.

SPRING:   Stirrett (1973b: 15) had his maximum count of 15 at Pelee on Apr. 22. Ussher (1965: 7) gave Mar. 21 as the 13-year average arrival date for Rondeau. Saunders & Dale (1933: 186) also had Mar. 21 as their 17-year average for arrivals at London, with the earliest on Feb. 26, 1922. Saunders (1947: 362) gave Apr. 5 as his 13-year average arrival date at Toronto while Speirs (1938: 44) had Apr. 20 as the spring peak date at Toronto. Speirs (1977: 11) considered that the third week of April was the time of the spring peak in the Pickering-Oshawa area. Weir & Quilliam (1980: 33) gave Mar. 16 as the 29-year average arrival date for Kingston. Quilliam (1965: 62) described a multiple display on Wolfe Is. in which five birds participated: she noted an early nest with 5 eggs taken on May 11, 1924 by E. Beaupré at Cataraqui. Devitt (1967: 55) gave Mar. 27 as the 15-year average arrival date for Barrie. Beamer's median arrival date for Meaford was Mar. 25 with the earliest on Mar. 16, 1948: he called them "plentiful" there on Apr. 22, 1943, during a mouse plague. Mills (1981: 40) gave Apr. 7 as the 10-year average arrival date for Huntsville with the earliest on Mar. 20, 1966. Nicholson (1981: 85) gave Mar. 28 as the 12-year average arrival date for Manitoulin with the earliest on Mar. 9, 1974 and a peak of 13 on Apr. 14, 1979. Speirs & Speirs (1947: 27) noted one at North Bay as early as Mar. 24, 1945 and gave evidence of breeding in that region. Skeel & Bondrup-Nielsen (1978: 164) considered it rare at Pukaskwa with only two personal spring records, on Apr. 19 and 23, 1977: an earlier observer saw one there on May 16, 1973. Denis (1961: 2) found Apr. 6 to be the average arrival date at Thunder Bay, with the earliest on Mar. 24, 1953. Bondrup-Nielsen (1976: 42) saw his first near Kapuskasing on May 5, 1974. Elder (1979: 31) gave Apr. 25 as his earliest date for Geraldton. Cringan (1953a: 2) saw his first in 1953 on Apr. 12 at Dryden. James (1980: 85) saw only one at Pickle Lake, on May 30, 1977.

SUMMER:   On Breeding Bird Surveys it has been widespread but rather rare, north as far as Haileybury and Dryden. Stirrett (1953c: 15) listed this as a nesting species for Pelee, with as many as 15 seen on Aug. 20. Brooman (1954: 14-15) mentioned two nests in Elgin Co., each with six eggs from which three young were actually reared: he called it "the commonest of our summer hawks". Saunders & Dale (1933: 186) gave details of several sets of eggs found near London. Speirs (1977: 11) detailed several nestings in Ontario Co., from May 12 into the summer months. Allin (1940: 95) listed several nest records for Darlington Twp. Devitt (1967: 55) cited several breeding records for Simcoe Co. where he considered it to be "our commonest large hawk". Beamer, near Meaford, noted a nest with four downy young and one egg on June 17, 1938; a nest with three eggs on June 20, 1940; and a nest with four young and one infertile egg on June 26, 1941. Mills (1981: 40) summarized breeding evidence for the Muskoka-Parry Sound regions. Snyder (1942: 125) noted young out of the nest near Sault Ste. Marie as early as June 24, 1931. He collected a nest with four eggs and a newly hatched young at Lake Nipigon on June 22, 1924 (Snyder, 1928: 259). Baillie & Hope (1943: 7) observed courtship flight at Peninsula on June 18, 1936. Dear (1940: 125) found two nests near Thunder Bay, one with six eggs on May 24, 1924 and one with four eggs on May 24, 1935. Smith (1957: 171) called it "well distributed throughout the Clay Belt". Snyder (1953: 54) found it to be widely distributed but not common in western Ontario. Cringan (1953b: 2) saw one on June 4, 1953 at Kasabonika Lake and he noted some along the North Caribou River in the summer of 1950 (Cringan, 1950: 6). Hope saw a juvenile on July 31, 1938 near Favourable Lake. Manning (1952: 34) reported it as "fairly generally distributed along the west coast of James Bay and southern coast of Hudson Bay" citing several several records to support this view. Schueler, Baldwin & Rising (1974: 142) found them common at Moosonee and Fort Albany, uncommon at Attawapiskat and Winisk and just noted at Hawley Lake. Peck (1972: 339) gave summer records for the Cape Henrietta Maria region. Hope saw this species frequently during the summer of 1940 at Fort Severn, with a maximum count of 10 on July 1.

AUTUMN:   Manning (1952: 34) cited several fall records for the James Bay region, one as late as Oct. 2, 1948 at Ship Sands Is. Skeel & Bondrup-Nielsen (1978: 164) saw single birds at Pukaskwa on Sept. 20 and 30. One was seen at North Bay as late as Oct. 22, 1944 (Speirs & Speirs, 1947: 27). Nicholson (1981: 86) had a maximum of nine on Sept. 21, 1978 on Manitoulin and the latest on Dec. 1, 1979. Mills (1981: 40) gave Nov. 12, 1959 as the latest date for Huntsville. Beamer noted "about a dozen" on Oct. 18, 1952 at Meaford. Devitt (1967: 55) noted 32 over Holland Marsh on Sept. 20, 1952. Quilliam (1965: 63) saw a flock of Snow Buntings give chase to a Marsh Hawk cruising along by the Cataraqui River. Speirs (1977: 11) found that the third week of September was the time of the fall peak in the Pickering-Oshawa area. Saunders (1947: 362) gave Nov. 22 as his 13-year average departure date from Toronto while Speirs (1938: 52) had Sept. 25 as the peak date there. Field & Field (1979: 10) had a maximum of 140 at Hawk Cliff on Sept. 11, 1977, banded 60 there during the fall migration that year. Stirrett (1973d: 17) had a maximum of 30 on Sept. 20 at Pelee.

BANDING:   Brooman (1954: 15) reported that a nestling banded by Field at St. Thomas on June 9, 1948 was shot at Covington, La. on Oct. 17, 1948. Field & Field (1979: 24) banded one at Hawk Cliff on Oct. 4, 1977 and recovered at Tunica, Miss. on Nov. 4, 1977.

**MEASUREMENTS:**
*Length:* ♂ 19 ins. ♀ 22
ins. (Pough, 1951: 159)
*Wingspread:* ♂ 42 ins. ♀
49 ins. (Pough, 1951: 159)
*Weight:* 90 ♂ averaged
350 g.; 97 ♀ averaged
531 g. (Dunning, 1984: 6).

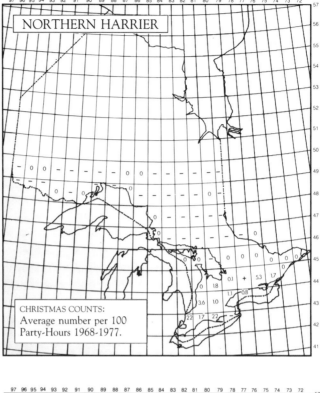

NORTHERN HARRIER

CHRISTMAS COUNTS:
Average number per 100
Party-Hours 1968-1977.

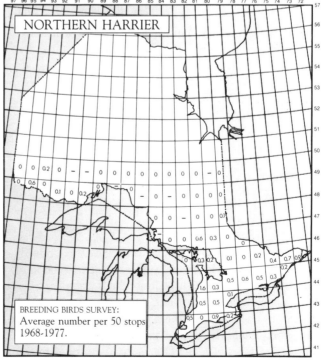

NORTHERN HARRIER

BREEDING BIRDS SURVEY:
Average number per 50 stops
1968-1977.

# SHARP-SHINNED HAWK  *Accipiter striatus*  Vieillot

The small birds "freeze" or vanish into the shrubbery when one of these beauties with red-barred breast and blue back comes to perch on a winter day in the lilac over our bird feeder or when the striped young ones pause to circle low overhead in their southward passage in mid-September.

IDENTIFICATION:  The short rounded wings and long barred tail mark this as one of the *Accipiter* hawks. The small size and square-ended tail separate this from the somewhat larger Cooper's Hawk which has a rounded tail (but the Sharp-shinned Hawk's tail will also look rounded when it is fanned when circling overhead). A large female Sharp-shinned Hawk may approach the size of a small male Cooper's Hawk but in general the Sharp-shin is a pigeon-sized bird while the Cooper's is crow-sized. In the breeding season the Sharp-shin is usually found in coniferous forest while the Cooper's prefers deciduous woodland.

WINTER:  On Christmas counts this is a rare species north to Ottawa and Meaford and uncommon along the north shores of Lake Ontario and Lake Erie. Stirrett (1973a: 14) had December and February records of individuals at Pelee. Beamer had several winter reports of individuals at Meaford chasing birds from the size of chickadees to Blue Jays from feeders: one immature shot on Feb. 22, 1943 was 12 1/2 inches in length. Nicholson (1981: 81) had only one winter record for Manitoulin on Dec. 22, 1968.

SPRING:  Spring migrants seem to follow the south shores of the Great Lakes whereas in fall they are most numerous along the north shores. Stirrett (1973b: 15) considered it uncommon at Pelee with a maximum of four in mid-May. Beardslee & Mitchell (1965: 163) mentioned a spring route around the west end of Lake Ontario: "a good vantage point for observing this flight being the lake shore near Port Weller, Ontario." Recent observers have preferred the top of the escarpment near Grimsby. Weir & Quilliam (1980: 33) gave Apr. 8 and May 14 as average spring arrival and departure dates at Kingston. Devitt (1967: 51) gave Apr. 22 as his 12-year average arrival date for Barrie, with the earliest on Mar. 24, 1949. Beamer noted up to 30 birds per day at Meaford during the first two weeks of May. Mills (1981: 33) reported that it returned to Muskoka and Parry Sound in mid-April. Nicholson (1981: 79) gave Apr. 24 as the 12-year average for arrival on Manitoulin (with the earliest on Apr. 3, 1972). One was noted flying NW over North Bay on Apr. 26, 1944 (Speirs & Speirs 1947: 26). Skeel & Bondrup-Nielsen (1978: 162) saw 11 on 8 days between Apr. 24 and May 14 along the Lake Superior shore of Pukaskwa. Denis (1961: 3) gave Apr. 25, 1959 as the earliest date for Thunder Bay with average arrival on Apr. 27. Elder (1979: 30) gave May 3 as his earliest date for Geraldton. Cringan (1953a: 2) had his earliest Sioux Lookout sighting in 1953 on Apr. 28.

SUMMER:  On Breeding Bird Surveys there have been scattered records of individuals from Farrington, Montreal Falls and Deep River south to London. Stirrett (1973c: 14) had a few summer records of individuals at Pelee. Saunders & Dale (1933: 184) reported five nests with eggs from the London region, as early as May 23, 1904 and as late as June 27, 1905. There are two nest records from Ontario Co., one at Glen Major and one at Pickering (Speirs, 1977: 3). Weir & Quilliam (1980: 7) cited two recent nest records from Kingston. Devitt (1967: 51) gave five nesting records from Simcoe Co. Beamer reported a nest about 25 ft. up in a cedar by the Meaford shoreline on July 10, 1952. Mills (1981: 32) gave two nest records for Parry Sound District and some additional breeding evidence. J. Tasker found a nest with 4 young on Manitoulin on July 13, 1975 (Nicholson, 1981: 80). Skeel & Bondrup-Nielsen (1978: 162) mentioned a nest record from Marathon. Snyder (1928: 259) took an adult female at Macdiarmid, Lake Nipigon, on July 22, 1923. Smith (1957: 170) saw a family on an island in Lake Timiskaming on July 24, 1953 and one "vigorously attacking an adult Bald Eagle on July 30 at Kapuskasing Lake." Synder (1953: 53) reported several summer records from western Ontario, at High Lake, Ingolf, Kenora, Wabigoon and Malachi. James (1980: 85) had summer records for Pickle Lake. Hope (1938: 12) took an adult male at Favourable Lake on July 28, 1938. Cringan (1953b: 2) saw one at Kasabonika Lake on June 3, 1953, and noted this species as far north as Nikip Lake during the summer of 1950 (Cringan, 1950: 6). Manning (1952: 33) gave two records from the vicinity of Moose Factory. Lee (1978: 20) saw one at Big Trout Lake on June 6, 1975. James, McLaren & Barlow (1976: 16) reported a summer straggler at Lake River south of Cape Henrietta Maria.

AUTUMN: Nicholson (1981: 80) noted 350 passing Great Duck Is. south of Manitoulin in Lake Huron, on Sept. 22, 1978, approaching from the north and leaving to the southeast. Mills (1981: 33) reported a count of 166 at Beausoleil Is. on Sept. 17, 1976, by Donald Sutherland: his latest personal sighting was one at Magnetewan on Oct. 14, 1979. Weir & Quilliam (1980: 33) gave Sept. 9 and Oct. 26 as the average arrival and departure dates for Kingston: their maximum count at Prince Edward Point was 510 on Sept. 21, 1975. The peak of the fall flight over Pickering is about Sept. 22 (Speirs, 1977: 3). James R. Thurston reported them as very abundant at Toronto on Oct. 1, 1889 with "stomachs of nearly all—full of grasshoppers" (Thompson, 1890: 195). Brooman (1954: 13) reported a count of 631 at Hawk Cliff, Lake Erie, on Sept. 24, 1949 while Field & Field (1979) summarized the 1977 sightings there (a maximum estimate of 2737 on Sept. 28 with 325 banded on Sept. 11). Recoveries of birds banded at Hawk Cliff came from as far south as Miami, Florida, Louisiana and even Guatemala and from as far north as Whitefish Point, Michigan and Rouyn, Quebec. Large numbers congregate at Pelee in mid-September, e.g. 1000 estimated on Sept. 17 (Stirrett, 1973d: 17).

**MEASUREMENTS:**
*Length:* ♂ 10-12 ins. ♀ 12-14 ins. (Godfrey, 1966: 87). Imm. at Meaford on Feb. 22, 1943 - 12 1/2 ins.
*Wingspread:* ♂ 21 1/2 ins. ♀ 26 ins. Pough (1951: 133).
*Weight:* Adult ♂ at Favourable Lake July 28, 1938 - 97.7 g.

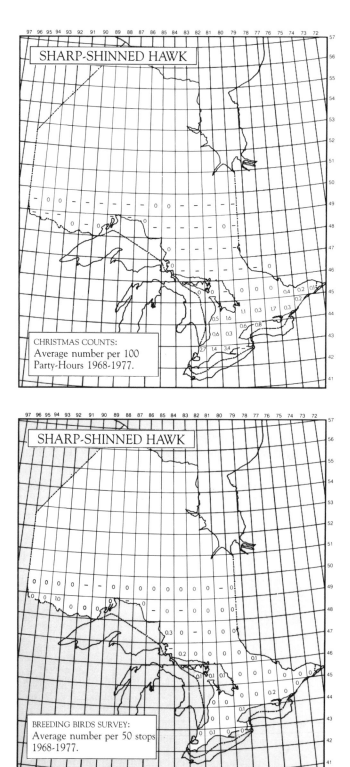

SHARP-SHINNED HAWK

CHRISTMAS COUNTS:
Average number per 100
Party-Hours 1968-1977.

SHARP-SHINNED HAWK

BREEDING BIRDS SURVEY:
Average number per 50 stops
1968-1977.

# COOPER'S HAWK   *Accipiter cooperii*   (Bonaparte)

One of my most exciting bird watching experiences involved this species. A pigeon rose up from the roof of a barn and took off in alarm. A Cooper's Hawk emerged from the Altona Forest and overtook the pigeon in a long fast glide with apparent ease, coming up from below at the last moment. There was a puff of feathers and all was over for the pigeon.

IDENTIFICATION: This is a crow-sized *Accipiter*, bigger than a Sharp-shin and smaller than a Goshawk, though some small male Cooper's approach the size of a large female Sharp-shin and some large females approach the size of a small male Goshawk. The rounded tail is a useful field mark, separating this species from the square tailed Sharp-shin. Adult Cooper's with their red-barred breast are easily separated from the gray-breasted adult Goshawk. Young Goshawks have a prominent white line over the eye, lacking in Cooper's. Cooper's are birds of deciduous forest, so are seldom seen in the coniferous forests of northern Ontario.

WINTER: This species has been uncommon to rare on Christmas counts north to Ottawa and Barrie, with one outlying report from Sault Ste. Marie. Three were reported at Pelee on Dec. 14 with individuals sighted there through the winter months (Stirrett, 1973a: 14). Tozer & Richards (1974: 98) gave two accounts of individuals with prey both at Oshawa; one carrying a Red Squirrel on Feb. 18, 1956 (John Theberge) and one eating a male Kestrel on Jan. 5, 1964 (George A. Scott). Beamer had February records for Meaford in 1940, 1949 and 1951 as well as several December records: one was observed by telescope by a whole school class as it perched in a tree near the school on Dec. 14, 1945. Mills (1981: 34) cited winter records for Huntsville, Bala and Honey Harbour. Nicholson (1981: 81) had two winter records for Manitoulin (Dec. 16, 1978 and Feb. 25, 1978).

SPRING: Stirrett (1973b: 15) considered it uncommon but regular in spring at Pelee, with a maximum of seven on May 19. Saunders & Dale (1933: 184) indicated that Apr. 4 was about the usual arrival time at London. Weir & Quilliam (1980: 33) gave Mar. 30 and May 10 as average arrival and departure dates for spring at Kingston. Devitt (1967: 52) gave Apr. 22 as the 8-year average for arrival at Barrie, with the earliest on Mar. 29, 1942. Chas. Jenkins trapped an 18" bird on Apr. 1, 1944 which had been feeding on his Meaford pigeons for weeks: according to L. Beamer; migrants often arrived by mid-March there with a spring peak about mid-May. Nicholson (1981: 81) gave Apr. 11 as the 9-year average for Manitoulin arrivals. Speirs & Speirs (1947: 27) had two spring records for the North Bay area in 1945, one on May 11, the other on May 14. Skeel & Bondrup-Nielsen (1978: 162) had five spring records for Pukaskwa, from Apr. 24 to May 28. Denis (1961: 3) gave May 7 as the average arrival date for Thunder Bay, with the earliest on Mar. 23, 1947. Elder (1979: 30) gave May 29 as his earliest date for Geraldton.

SUMMER: On Breeding Bird Surveys they have been reported in the east as far north as Avonmore and Dorset: in western Ontario at Thunder Bay and Suomi. Stirrett (1973c: 14) gave this as a nesting species for Pelee. Brooman (1954: 13) cited nest records south of St. Thomas: Marshall Field banded three young from one of these on July 1, 1950. Saunders & Dale (1933: 184) gave details of five nestings near London, the earliest on May 6, 1901 and the latest on JUne 11, 1908. Beardslee & Mitchell (1965: 164-165) mentioned a nest with three eggs found in Burgoyne Woods, Lincoln Co., by Clout on June 26, 1938 while Sheppard (1960: 14) cited a set of eggs collected by A.R. Muma of Niagara Falls in May, 1936. Speirs (1977: 4) gave details of several nests in Ontario Co., one with three eggs as early as Apr. 29, 1959, others with young well into June. Devitt (1967: 52) cited details of two June nests in Simcoe Co. Beamer followed a nesting 40 ft. up in a maple in Meaford from the time of its discovery on May 16 until early July when two young left: in 1949 they nested about 100 yards south of this nest but in 1950 they nested again in the 1948 nest. Mills (1981: 33) reported nest records for Pt. Sydney and Doe Lake in the Muskoka-Parry Sound cottage country, both with eggs in May. Nicholson (1981: 81) had a few summer records for Manitoulin but no nests reported. Snyder (1942: 124) observed one near Sault Ste. Marie on July 24, 1931. Skeel & Bondrup-Nielsen (1978: 162) had one summer sighting at Pukaskwa, on June 25. Dear (1940: 125) took a set of three eggs at Thunder Bay on May 15, 1927. Snyder (1953: 53) saw one near Dryden on July 5, 1937.

AUTUMN: Manning (1952: 33) cited records for the Albany River estuary on Aug. 25, 1920 and at Attawapiskat on Oct. 4, 1948, probably post-breeding wanderers this far north. Smith (1957: 170) with F. Cowell, saw two about four miles north of Timmins on Sept. 6, 1954. Speirs & Speirs (1947: 27) reported one over the French River, near Lake Nipissing on Sept. 14, 1944. Nicholson (1981: 81) had a maximum of seven at Mississauga Light, Manitoulin, on Sept. 22, 1974. Beamer gave details of various birds raiding poultry pens near Meaford in autumn. Weir & Quilliam (1980: 33) gave Sept. 8 and Nov. 1 as average fall arrival and departure dates for Kingston. The peak of the fall flight over Pickering is generally in the third week of September (Speirs, 1977: 4). James R. Thurston reported the first Toronto record: a male "disabled by flying against the wires in the city" on Oct. 12, 1889 (Thompson, 1890: 196). Field & Field (1978: 17) had a maximum of 119 observed at Hawk Cliff on Oct. 17, 1976. Stirrett (1973d: 17) had maxima of 150 at Pelee on Sept. 26 and Oct. 13.

**MEASUREMENTS:**
*Length:* Four shot at Meaford measured 16, 16 1/2, 18 and 18 ins. Beamer.
*Wingspread:* ♂ 28 ins. ♀ 33 ins. (Pough, 1951: 135)
*Weight:* 51 ♂ averaged 349 g.; 57 ♀ averaged 529 g. (Dunning, 1984: 6)
*Banding:* Field & Field (1978: 24) reported recoveries of birds banded at Hawk Cliff from Kingston and Port Carling, Ont. and near Farmersville, Ohio.

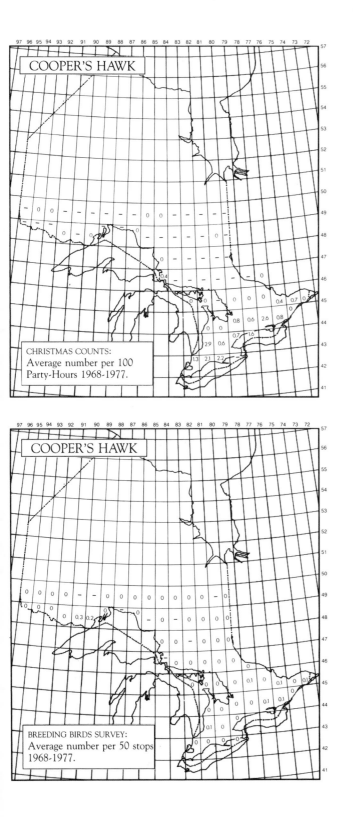

COOPER'S HAWK

CHRISTMAS COUNTS:
Average number per 100
Party-Hours 1968-1977.

COOPER'S HAWK

BREEDING BIRDS SURVEY:
Average number per 50 stops
1968-1977.

# NORTHERN GOSHAWK  *Accipiter gentilis*  (Linnaeus)

Whoever named this bird *gentilis* has surely not experienced the wrath of the female defending her nest and young. When Edgerton Pegg visited a nest with young in Uxbridge Forest, he just turned his back when the female dove at him, and received a cut on his back from her talons: I was more fortunate—I ducked behind a tree as she whizzed by me and just felt the rush of air as she passed. When one chased a Mourning Dove into a plate glass window in Cherrywood, the beautiful male was stunned by the impact and I was pleased to be able to caress this really gentle bird before it revived and flew away.

IDENTIFICATION:  The adult with its breast barred in gray, with its black cap over the white eyebrow and fiery red eye, is a joy to behold and easy to identify. The young with brown streaked breast is very similar to young Cooper's Hawk, but somewhat larger and with a more definite white stripe over the eye.

WINTER:  On the 1968-1977 Christmas counts they occured in small numbers at most localities north to Deep River and Sault Ste. Marie with outliers at Marathon and Thunder Bay. Stirrett (1973a: 14) had several records of single birds during the winter months at Pelee. Fleming (1907: 72) mentioned a great migration into the Toronto area from Oct. 26 to Dec. 20, 1896: he personally examined 35 taken. Speirs (1938: 93) suggested that peak influxes occurred at 9 to 11 year intervals in the Toronto region. Devitt (1967: 50) gave supporting evidence of this cycle in the Barrie area. Beamer reported that one took 15 pigeons near Meaford before it was shot about Feb. 2, 1945: another molesting poultry was killed with a pitchfork when the farmer defending his poultry was also attacked by the hungry bird. Louise Lawrence saw single birds at Pimisi Bay on Jan. 5 and Dec. 22, 1944 (Speirs & Speirs, 1947: 26). Skeel & Bondrup-Nielsen (1978: 161) had three winter records at Pukaskwa.

SPRING:  Stirrett (1973b: 15) gave only three spring records for Pelee; on Apr. 11, May 5 (2) and May 25. A. Schaffner observed one at close range at Ft. Erie on Mar. 17, 1954 (Beardslee & Mitchell, 1965: 162). Saunders (1947: 362) gave Mar. 13 as his 6-year average departure date from Toronto, one as late as May 28. Speirs (1968: 38-39) reported the first nesting for the Toronto region, in the Altona Forest behind our home, where a nest with three eggs was photographed by J.M. Richards on May 6, 1967. Baillie & Harrington (1936: 20) mentioned a set of eggs taken at Sharbot Lake, Frontenac Co., on May 10, 1900 by C.J. Young and a nest with three eggs found by L.S. Dear at Thunder Bay on May 2, 1935. Weir & Quilliam (1980: 33) gave Apr. 20 as the 21-year average departure date from Kingston. Beamer's latest spring record for Meaford was one reported by F. Barr, Jr. on Apr. 23, 1943. B. Ranford found a nest with 3 eggs on May 13, 1964, about 75 ft. up in a yellow birch near Huntsville (Mills, 1981: 31). Skeel & Bondrup-Nielsen (1978: 161) saw one at Pukaskwa on May 17, 1973. Bondrup-Nielsen (1976: 42) noted one near Kapuskasing on Apr. 13, 1974.

SUMMER:  On the 1968-1977 Breeding Bird Surveys individuals showed up only on the Palgrave, Odessa and Roblin routes. Stirrett (1973c: 14) had two summer records for Pelee: on June 20 and Aug. 6. A nest with three young was found by J. Brown east of Mallorytown Landing on June 10, 1961 (Quilliam 1965: 55). Mills (1981: 31) reported several nest records for Muskoka and Parry Sound. Snyder (1942: 124) noted one on St. Joseph's Is. on June 22, 1931. Baillie & Harrington (1936: 20) reported that W.B. Rubridge had taken a female and nestling at Anima, Timiskaming on July 10, 1906. Skeel & Bondrup-Nielsen (1978: 161) had several summer sightings at Pukaskwa. Denis (1961: 5) reported a nest with young at Thunder Bay on June 16, 1959. Snyder (1953: 53) reported an adult at Savanne on July 14, 1937 and another at Malachi on July 19, 1947. Smith (1957: 170) had two summer records near Kapuskasing: one on June 30, 1953 and another on Aug. 7, 1953. D.H. Baldwin photographed a nest 35 ft. up in a poplar on June 12, 1964, found near Aquatuk Lake, with one young visible from the ground (Schueler, Baldwin & Rising, 1974: 145).

AUTUMN: E.S. Covell collected a juvenile male at the mouth of the Moose River on Nov. 6, 1935 (Manning, 1952: 32). Elder (1979: 30) had fall dates for Geraldton from Sept. 13 to Oct. 26. Ricker & Clarke (1939: 7) reported single birds near North Bay on Sept. 7, 1925 and Nov. 10, 1924. Beamer's earliest fall record for Meaford was noted on Oct. 11, 1940 by F. Barr, Jr. and another shot on Oct. 31, 1938 had a "field mouse" in its stomach. Devitt (1967: 50-51) reported several fall birds taken in Simcoe Co. and gave the earliest fall date as Sept. 9, 1966 when Frances Westman saw one at Little Lake, Barrie. Weir & Quilliam (1980: 32) gave Oct. 7 as the 19-year average arrival date for Kingston. Saunders (1947: 362) gave Sept. 28 as his 8-year average arrival date for Toronto, with one as early as Sept. 9. Stirrett (1973d: 17) had several fall records for Pelee with a maximum of 4 on Oct. 6, but Kelley (1978: 23) reported 31 (mostly at Pelee) during the "flight year" of 1973.

**MEASUREMENTS:**
*Length:* Beamer measured 5 immatures shot near Meaford: 20" to 25 1/2"
*Wingspread:* a 22" imm. had a wingspread of 40" (Beamer).
*Weight:* Beamer gave 3 weights: 839 g; 880 g and 1150 g. Hope (1938: 12) gave 870 g. for a ♂ and 1257 g. as the average for 3 ♀ taken at Favourable Lake (Nov.-Dec.).

**REFERENCE:**
Speirs, J. Murray 1968 First nesting of Goshawk (*Accipiter gentilis*) in the Toronto region. Ont. Field Biologist, No. 21: 38-39.

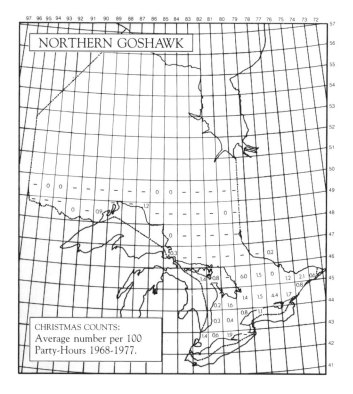

NORTHERN GOSHAWK

CHRISTMAS COUNTS:
Average number per 100 Party-Hours 1968-1977.

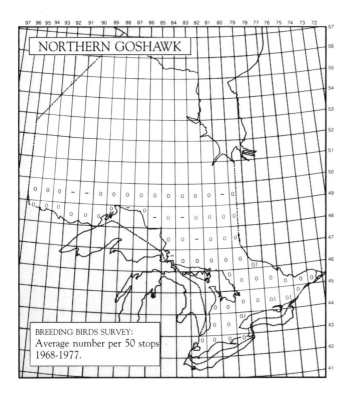

NORTHERN GOSHAWK

BREEDING BIRDS SURVEY:
Average number per 50 stops
1968-1977.

# RED-SHOULDERED HAWK   *Buteo lineatus*   (Gmelin)

Each spring, in late March, we look forward to the return of the pair that makes the Altona Forest its summer home. Our resident Blue Jays have learned the "kee-yah" call and appear to anticipate the arrival of the hawks, so that it is only by the greater volume and loudness of the real thing that we know when to look up to see the hawk circling over the forest or doing spectacular power dives to celebrate their return (or to impress the mate). During April they call loudly to show their disapproval of intrusion on their territory but by May when nesting is underway they are usually very silent except when the local Red-tail invades their air space and has to be shown off. By late summer the young are awing and add their food calls to the local medley of bird voices. The forest would be a poorer place without these beautiful hawks.

IDENTIFICATION:   The adult with its strikingly barred black and white tail, barred reddish breast and red shoulders is easily identified. The translucent whitish patch, like windows in the wing, at the base of the flight feathers is a field mark that many look for (though this is also present in some Broad-wings). The relatively longer tail and smaller size help to distinguish all ages from Red-tails. The call, mentioned above, is very difficult from the raspy, guttural call of the Red-tail and from the high-pitched whistle of the Broad-wing.

WINTER:   On Christmas counts this has been an uncommon hawk at Pelee and Long Point, and rare elsewhere north to Kingston and Meaford. Stirrett (1973a: 15) had individuals at Pelee through the winter months, with a maximum of four on Dec. 13. Quilliam (1965: 57) had only three winter records for Kingston, one for each of the winter months.

SPRING:   Stirrett (1973b: 15) saw single birds at Pelee through the spring. Ussher (1965: 7) gave Mar. 22 as his 7-year average arrival date for Rondeau. Saunders & Dale (1933: 185) had nest records in the London region as early as Apr. 18, 1903 and as late as May 6, 1901 for eggs, while A.A. Wood and C.H. Zavitz found one incubated egg in the nest of a Great Blue Heron on May 10, 1901 (the hawk having been ousted upon return of the herons). Speirs (1938: 44) gave Mar. 29 and Apr. 12 as peak periods for Toronto, while at our home in Pickering Mar. 24 has been the median arrival date for our local Red-shoulders (Speirs, 1977: 6). Spring migrants usually appear in Simcoe Co. during the first half of April (Devitt, 1967: 53) but one was seen at Bradford as early as Mar. 10, 1946. Weir & Quilliam (1980: 33) gave Apr. 7 as the 26-year average for arrivals at Kingston. Beamer's earliest spring records for Meaford were on Apr. 6, in both 1940 and 1941. Mills (1981: 36) gave dates from Apr. 10 to 15 for arrivals in Muskoka and Parry Sound. Nicholson (1981: 82) had his earliest Manitoulin arrival on Apr. 3, 1976. Louise Lawrence noted one near Rutherglen on May 1, 1944 (Speirs & Speirs, 1947: 27).

SUMMER:   On Breeding Bird Surveys this has been a rare bird, north to Barry's Bay, Port Carling and Thessalon. Stirrett (1973c: 14) gave this as a nesting species for Pelee. Brooman (1954: 14) cited two nesting records for Elgin Co. Tozer & Richards (1974: 100) reported several nests in the Oshawa region, with eggs from Apr. 24, to May 20 and with young in the nest until the end of June. Allin (1940: 95) considered it a common summer resident of Darlington Twp. at that time and cited nest records. Formerly the most common breeding hawk in the Kingston area but none were found nesting since June 18, 1950, when George North located a nest. Mills (1981: 35) gave several nest records for the Muskoka-Parry Sound cottage country but believed that the species has declined in numbers since Fleming considered it "fairly common" in 1901. Chris. Bell found a nest at Pike Lake on May 7, 1971, the only known nesting record for Manitoulin (Nicholson, 1981: 82). Smith (1957: 170) cited summer records for Timmins and Lake Abitibi, in the Clay Belt.

AUTUMN: Louise Lawrence reported one at Pimisi Bay on Sept. 11, 1944 (Speirs & Speirs, 1947: 27). The latest Manitoulin date was Oct. 15, 1978 (Nicholson, 1981: 82). Fall migrants were reported from Parry Sound and Muskoka from Sept. 18 to Oct. 18 (Mills, 1981: 36). Beamer reported only one fall sighting at Meaford, on Oct. 1, 1948. Weir & Quilliam (1980: 33) gave Oct. 26 as the 20-year average departure date from Kingston. James R. Thurston received a specimen from Toronto on Oct. 22, 1889 (Thompson, 1890: 197). Beardslee & Mitchell (1965: 167) reported three in migration at Mud Lake, near Niagara Falls, as early as Aug. 24, 1952. Brooman (1954: 13-14) mentioned a maximum count of 29 at Hawk Cliff on Oct. 12, 1953. Stirrett (1973d: 17) had a maximum of 50 at Pelee on Oct. 30.

**MEASUREMENTS:**
*Length:* ♂ 18 to 23 ins. ♀ 19 to 24 ins. (Godfrey, 1966: 90)
*Wingspread:* ♂ 38 ins. ♀ 45 ins. (Pough, 1951: 140)
*Weight:* 2 to 3 lbs. (Forbush, 1929, II: 129). Note that length and weight are similar to Red-tail but wings are much shorter.

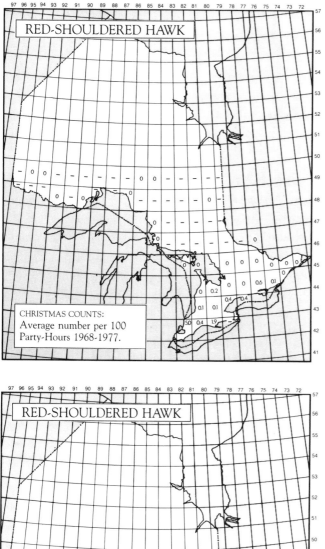

RED-SHOULDERED HAWK

CHRISTMAS COUNTS:
Average number per 100
Party-Hours 1968-1977.

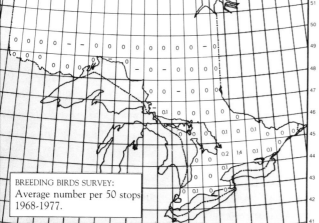

RED-SHOULDERED HAWK

BREEDING BIRDS SURVEY:
Average number per 50 stops
1968-1977.

# BROAD-WINGED HAWK   *Buteo platypterus*   (Vieillot)

This is the common hawk of Ontario's cottage country in summer. In southern Ontario it is known chiefly for spectacular mass migrations, along the south shores of the Great Lakes in spring and along the north shores in autumn. Thousands may be seen on a good day at Hawk Cliff and hundreds at certain points near Toronto in mid-September when NW winds produce thermals capped with cumulus clouds. The hawks gather in swirling "kettles" and ride the thermals up until binoculars may be needed to see them, then they peel off to the SW to find another thermal and repeat the process. To the hawk-watcher this looks like a fun way to migrate from Ontario to Colombia where many spend the winter.

IDENTIFICATION: They are about the size of a crow and shaped like a Red-tailed Hawk. The few broad white bars on the dark tail of the adult are diagnostic. On the breeding ground the high-pitched whistle "psee-eeeee" is distinctive. The young look like small Red-tails. Do not let the mustache mark delude you into thinking it is a Peregrine!

WINTER: Saunders (1947: 362) gave Feb. 13 as J.L. Baillie's earliest record and Dec. 16 as his latest. Any self-respecting Broad-wing winters in the tropics, not in Ontario.

SPRING: Stirrett (1973b: 15) noted a few spring individuals at Pelee from Mar. 25 to June 7. Marshall Field saw 320 at St. Thomas on Apr. 27, 1951, but spring numbers there are usually small (Brooman, 1954: 14). Saunders & Dale (1933: 185) gave Apr. 23 as the 17-year average for arrivals at London with the earliest Apr. 14, 1918 and a maximum of 100 on Apr. 27, 1903: they reported two nestings in Middlesex Co., one in late May and one pair that nested in 1896 and 1897, the latter followed from Apr. 15 to May 24 when two downy young were seen in the nest. Saunders (1947: 362) gave Apr. 20 as the average arrival date for Toronto, with his earliest on Mar. 21. Speirs (1977: 7) gave Apr. 4 as the earliest date for Ontario Co. and documented various nests, from the earliest on Apr. 28, 1974 through the summer. Weir & Quilliam (1980: 33) gave Apr. 19 as their 26-year average for Kingston arrivals with the earliest on Mar. 31. Devitt (1967: 53) gave Apr. 20 as the 15-year average for arrivals at Barrie, with the earliest on Mar. 27, 1962. Beamer counted 227 (and 25 probables) at Meaford on May 1, 1954, and had good flights in early May in other years. Mills (1981: 36) gave Apr. 18 as the 7-year average for arrivals at Huntsville, with the earliest on Mar. 28, 1976. Nicholson (1981: 82) had an 11-year average for Manitoulin arrivals on Apr. 24, with the earliest on Apr. 15, 1979. Ricker & Clarke (1939: 7) had one at North Bay as early as Apr. 12, 1924. Denis (1961: 3) noted his earliest at Thunder Bay on Apr. 17, 1954 with May 2 as the average arrival date there. Elder (1979: 30) gave Apr. 29 as his earliest date for Geraldton. Cringan (1953a: 2) gave May 6 as his 1953 arrival date at Sioux Lookout.

SUMMER: On Breeding Bird Surveys they have been noted as far south as Stratford and as far north as Hearst and Kenora, with the greatest number from North Bay over to Thessalon. Kelley (1978: 25) reported a nest found in Lambton Co. on June 3, 1971 which contained 3 eggs. Tozer & Richards (1974: 101) documented several nestings in the Oshawa region. Quilliam (1965: 58) had only one nesting record for the Kingston region. Devitt (1967: 53) mentioned some nest records for Simcoe Co. Mills (1981: 36) called it "certainly our most common breeding hawk" in the Muskoka-Parry Sound cottage country: he cited several specific records from an adult on a nest as early as May 2 to young leaving the nest on July 14. Ron. Tasker found a nest with two fledged young at Ice Lake, Manitoulin on July 26, 1972 (Nicholson, 1981: 82). With Louise Lawrence we noted scolding adults at a nest near Rutherglen, which contained two downy young on July 13 (Speirs & Speirs, 1947: 27). Skeel & Bondrup-Nielsen (1978: 163) found this to be the most common summer hawk at Pukaskwa (from May 4 to Sept. 24). Smith (1957: 170) gave several records from the Clay Belt, as far north as Lake Abitibi. Bondrup-Nielsen (1976: 46) found a nest with two downy young near Kapuskasing on July 13, 1974. Elder (1979: 70) considered them to be common in summer at Geraldton. Snyder (1928: 259) called it the most common hawk in the Lake Nipigon region. Baillie & Harrington (1936: 23) cited two nest records for Thunder Bay. Snyder (1953: 54) saw a nest near Wabigoon on June 17, 1937. James (1980: 85) saw one daily in the Pickle Lake region. Manning (1952: 53) cited two old records from the Moosonee region (Spreadborough considered it common on the Moose River). Lee (1978: 20) had sightings at Big Trout Lake on June 25 and July 29, 1975.

AUTUMN: One was noted at Pimisi Bay on Sept. 11, 1944(Speirs & Speirs, 1947: 27). Nicholson (1981: 83) gave 1040 as his high count for Manitoulin, at Mississauga Light, on Sept. 18, 1976. Mills (1981: 36) had fall records from Parry Sound and Muskoka from Sept. 1 to Oct. 13, with a maximum of 502 at Beausoleil Is. on Sept. 17, 1976. Devitt (1967: 53) reported a maximum of 125 on Sept. 21, 1952 at Holland Marsh with Sept. 23, 1959 as his latest date. Weir & Quilliam (1980: 33) gave Sept. 27 as the 19-year average departure date from Kingston, with the latest on Nov. 7. Speirs (1977: 7) noted fall migrants over Ontario Co. from Aug. 17 to Nov. 8, with a maximum of 3735 over the Altona Forest on Sept. 20, 1949. Saunders (1947: 362) gave Sept. 29 as his average departure date from Toronto, with his latest on Oct. 26. Beardslee & Mitchell (1965: 169) mentioned eight seen as late as Oct. 30, 1943 by Andrle, along the Canadian shore of Lake Erie with other migrating hawks. Field & Field (1979: 10-11) summarized the 1977 Broad-wing flight at Hawk Cliff from Sept. 3 (58 birds) to Oct. 13 (15 birds) with a maximum of 1979 on Sept. 11. Brooman (1954: 14) estimated 50,000 passing along the Lake Erie shore of Elgin Co. on Sept. 20-21, 1952. Stirrett (1973d: 17) had a maximum of 400 at Pelee on Sept. 17, with the earliest two on Aug. 13 and latest two on Nov. 20. Kelley (1978: 25) reported 34,700 over Holiday Beach on Sept. 16, 1970.

**MEASUREMENTS:**
*Length:* ♂ 13.5 to 16.5
ins. (Godfrey, 1966: 90).
*Wingspread:* ♂ 35 ins. ♀
37 ins. (Pough,
1951: 141).
*Weight:* 14 ♂ averaged
420 g.; 13 ♀ averaged
490 g. (Dunning, 1984: 6).

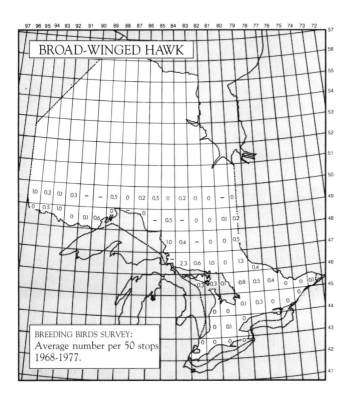

BROAD-WINGED HAWK

BREEDING BIRDS SURVEY:
Average number per 50 stops
1968-1977.

# SWAINSON'S HAWK   *Buteo swainsoni*   Bonaparte

This is essentially a prairie hawk, very rare in Ontario.

**IDENTIFICATION:** Typical adults have white throats contrasting with the brownish band across the upper breast. Compared with Red-tails the wings are long but narrow and tend to be carried above the horizontal as do Marsh Hawks (but some Red-tails also soar with wings above the horizontal). Look for the white *sides* to the rump in flight.

**WINTER:**

**SPRING:**   D.G. Cox reported one at Rosedale, Toronto, on May 3, 1890. Fleming (1907: 72) listed a female specimen taken near Toronto on May 22, 1894, an almost black individual. Stirrett (1973b: 15) had only one Pelee record, noted on Apr. 27, 1968; this was identified by Joseph P. Kleiman according to Kelley (1978: 25). Nicholson (1981: 83) mentioned a dark phase bird identified in Burpee Twp., Manitoulin, on May 19, 1976 by Ron Tasker and his wife.

**SUMMER:**

**AUTUMN:**   Nicholson (1981: 83) reported a light phase adult at Mississagi Light, Manitoulin on Sept. 11, 1977. A male was taken Sept. 5, 1890 at the Don Flats by W. Cross: Fleming (1907: 72) describes this bird as black, the breast mottled with buffy yellow. Other old Toronto records include an immature at the Humber on Sept. 3, 1897 by J.H. Samuel, one at Fisherman's Island (now Cherry Beach) on Sept. 22, 1916 by Townson and Pickering, a dark phase bird specimen taken to O. Spanner on Oct. 16, 1909; and one at Well's Hill on Nov. 27, 1896 by George Pearce and J.H. Samuel. Allan Brooks also had a dark phase bird in Oct., 1883 in Halton Co.

There are also specimens taken at Ottawa (noted in Godfrey, 1966: 92) and at Moose Factory, the latter in 1881 with no date. Regarding the Moose Factory bird Manning (1952: 33) noted that "An unsexed adult . . . in the dark plumage collected at Moose Factory by Haydon in 1881 is in the United States National Museum (Preble, 1902, p. 106)."

**MEASUREMENTS:**
*Length:* ♂ 18.75 to 20.6 ins. ♀ 18.9 to 22.0 ins. (Godfrey, 1966: 91)
*Wingspread:* ♂ 49 ins. ♀ 52 ins. (Pough,, 1951: 143)
*Weight:* 5 ♂ averaged 908 g.; 7 ♀ averaged 1069 g. (Dunning, 1984: 6)

# RED-TAILED HAWK   *Buteo jamaicensis*   (Gmelin)

This is the common *Buteo* of the southern farmland of Ontario, usually seen soaring in lazy circles high overhead, or perched conspicuously on a big dead tree in the midst of a farm field. Occasionally you may see one hovering over a field, then folding its wings to make a spectacular plunge upon some luckless mouse. Most enlighted farmers now encourage this bird as a prime aid in rodent control and leave its big stick nests strictly alone. Sometimes one will take up residence in the city, where its rodent and pigeon control may also be appreciated.

IDENTIFICATION:   The ample wingspread and fan-shaped tail and soaring flight mark it as a *Buteo*. The adults are easily identified by their rufous-red tail and white underside of the wings in flight. The immatures have dark-brown tails with rather fine black bars, but their large size and white wing-linings also identify them. The other large open country *Buteo* is the Rough-legged Hawk which has conspicuous black patches at the bend of the wing. Both of these are larger than a crow. The Red-shouldered Hawk is a forest bird and has a relatively long, narrow tail, conspicuously barred in black and white: it is about crow size or slightly larger. The other Ontario *Buteo*, the Broad-winged Hawk is shaped like a Red-tailed Hawk but is much smaller and is uncommon in southern Ontario except during migration: the prominent broad black and white bars on the tail of adults are distinctive. See also the descriptions of these other Buteos. The harsh guttural scream of the Red-tail is a good means of identification when once learned.

WINTER:   On Christmas counts this hawk is common in southwestern Ontario, becoming rare north to Ottawa, Manitoulin and Sault Ste. Marie. Stirrett (1973a: 14) reported a maximum of 40 at Pelee on Dec. 27. Numbers on the Pickering Christmas count increased from only two in 1961 to 131 on the 1976 count (Speirs, 1977: 5). Quilliam (1965: 56) reported very few on counts at Kingston before 1955 increasing to 78 on the 1962 count. Mills (1981: 35) had winter records for Parry Sound District as late as Jan. 2. C. Bell reported one on Manitoulin as late as Jan. 21, 1979 (Nicholson, 1981: 82).

SPRING:   Stirrett (1973b: 15) had a maximum of six at Pelee on May 24. Saunders & Dale (1933: 184) cited nest records for the London region with eggs as early as Mar. 30 (fresh) and as late as May 6 (about to hatch). Speirs (1938: 43) gave Mar. 23 as the spring peak date at Toronto. Devitt (1967: 52) gave Apr. 3 as the 15-year average for arrival at Barrie, with the earliest on Mar. 17, 1945. Mar. 30 was Beamer's median arrival date for Meaford: he reported "about 70" going over on Apr. 4, 1951. Mills (1981: 34) had a Muskoka record as early as Mar. 26, 1961 and gave Apr. 11 as the 9-year average for spring arrivals at Huntsville. C. Bell observed a nest near Sheguiandah, Manitoulin, from May 20 until the end of June, 1974 (Nicholson, 1981: 82). I saw one as early as Mar. 24, 1944, at the North Bay airport (Speirs & Speirs, 1947: 27). Denis (1961: 2) gave Apr. 19 as the average arrival date at Thunder Bay, with the earliest on Mar. 30, 1953. Elder (1979: 30) gave Apr. 22 as his earliest date for Geraldton, and considered it a fairly common migrant there. Bondrup-Nielsen (1976: 42) saw his first at Kapuskasing on Apr. 25, 1944. Cringan (1953a: 2) noted his first at Dryden, on Apr. 9, 1953. Elsey (in Cringan, 1950: 6) saw his only Red-tail in the Asheweig area on May 17, 1950.

SUMMER: On Breeding Bird Surveys it has been uncommon in southwestern Ontario, then rare but regular north to Ottawa and Manitoulin, then rare and scattered north to Larder Lake and Kenora. This decrease in abundance reflects the decrease in amount of open country suitable for this species as one proceeds northward in Ontario. Although they usually nest in large trees near open country, they will accept such sites as Hydro towers (I saw such a nest a few days before writing this, in Whitby). Stirrett (1973c: 14) considered this a rare summer resident at Pelee (he had no July record there). Tozer & Richards (1974: 98) cited several nest records for the Oshawa-Scugog region. Devitt (1967: 52) gave details of four nestings in Simcoe Co. L. Beamer saw one young on the side of a nest near Meaford on June 26, 1938. Mills (1981: 34-35) described several breeding records for the Muskoka-Parry Sound cottage country. Smith (1957: 170) called it "not uncommon" in the Clay Belt and cited a few specific records. Dear (1940: 125) found several nests with eggs near Thunder Bay: one with three on May 20, 1929 and one with two on May 24, 1928 (and seven other nests). Snyder (1953: 53-54) gave several summer records from western Ontario from Ingolf and Kenora east to Savanne, one specimen referable to *krideri* the whitish prairie race. Manning (1952: 33) cited old records for Moosonee and the Albany River estuary. Cringan (1950: 6) called it the "most frequently observed hawk of the area" (Nikip Lake). James (1980: 85) reported three June nests near Pickle Lake. Schueler, Baldwin & Rising (1974: 142) reported it as "uncommon" at Hawley Lake and saw none along the sites visited on the James and Hudson Bay coasts. Lee (1978) saw none at Big Trout Lake and Hope saw none at Ft. Severn during his summer there in 1940.

AUTUMN: Hope (1938: 13) reported an immature female taken near Favourable Lake on Sept. 4 by Goddard. Louise Lawrence noted one at Rutherglen as late as Oct. 24, 1944 (Speirs & Speirs 1947: 27). Nicholson (1981: 82) reported a maximum of 13 flying NW past Great Duck Is. in Lake Huron on Oct. 8, 1978. W. Linn told Beamer of seeing "hundreds" on Oct. 16, 1943 near Meaford while F. Richardson reported seeing about 75 on Nov. 5, 1952 on the Bruce Peninsula. Thompson (1890: 196) mentioned one taken in Oct., 1889 at Toronto with its stomach containing "several field mice". Speirs (1938: 51) gave Oct. 27 as the fall peak for Toronto and the third week of October as the usual fall peak in Ontario Co. (Speirs, 1977: 5). The maximum count at Hawk Cliff in the fall of 1977 was 652 on Nov. 12, a day when 57 were banded there (Field & Field, 1979: 12). Stirrett (1973d: 17) had a maximum of 50 at Pelee on Oct. 12.

**MEASUREMENTS:**
*Length:* ♂ 19-22 ins. ♀
21-24 ins. (Godfrey,
1966: 89)
*Wingspread:* ♂ 48 ins. ♀
53 ins. (Pough, 1951: 136)
*Weight:* ♂ 2 lbs. ♀ 2 3/4
lbs. (Pough, 1951: 136).
*Banding:* Field & Field
(1979: 23) had one of their
hatching-year Hawk Cliff
birds banded on Nov. 1,
1976 recovered on Jan.
23, 1977 at Atlanta,
Georgia. Most of their

recoveries were from Ontario, however.

**REFERENCE:**

Duncan, Bruce W. 1983 Red-tailed Hawks banded at Hawk Cliff, Ontario: 1971-1982. Analysis of data. Maps show recoveries south to northern Florida in winter and some found as far south as Alabama in summer!

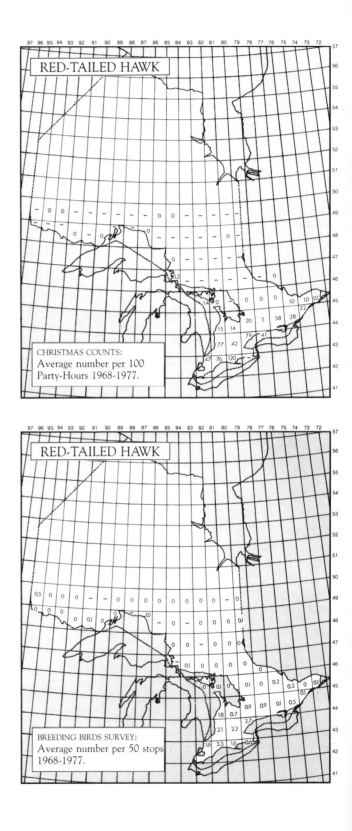

RED-TAILED HAWK

CHRISTMAS COUNTS:
Average number per 100
Party-Hours 1968-1977.

RED-TAILED HAWK

BREEDING BIRDS SURVEY:
Average number per 50 stops
1968-1977.

# ROUGH-LEGGED HAWK   *Buteo lagopus*   (Pontoppidan)

They usually arrive in southern Ontario in late fall, and winter in areas where the snowfall is light where they may hunt their favourite prey, the meadow mouse. They have remarkably small feet for such a large predator, well adapted for grasping small prey, like mice. When the excitement of the warbler and shorebird migrations has faded, it is good to look forward to the arrival of our wintering birds, among which the Rough-leg is one of those most sought out.

IDENTIFICATION:   Compared with the usually more abundant Red-tail, this is a hawk with relatively longer wings and tail, making it look somewhat larger. The dark phase birds are strikingly beautiful with the white undersides of the flight feathers contrasting with the generally blackish plumage. Other dark phase Buteos lack these white flight feathers. Light phase Rough-legs (usually the more common phase) have a large black patch at the bend of the wing (wrist) on its underside and the basal part of the tail is whitish on the upper side: the white is not on the rump as it is on the Marsh Hawk. They frequently hunt by facing into the wind; flapping vigorously, so that they hover over one spot in the manner of a hunting Kestrel or Kingfisher. (Red-tails sometimes hunt in this manner too, but not as frequently as do Rough-legs.) At close range you may see that Rough-legs are feathered to the toes while Red-tails have yellowish, unfeathered lower legs (tarsi). On perched birds look for the black belly and creamy breast. When Red-tails show black below it is on the lower breast, not the belly.

WINTER:   On Christmas counts they have been fairly common in the agricultural southwestern part of Ontario, becoming rare north to Ottawa, Manitoulin and Sault Ste. Marie. Numbers vary considerably from year to year, sometimes being almost as common as Red-tails while in other winters it is hard to find one (Speirs, 1939: 413-414). Stirrett (1973a: 15) had a maximum winter count at Pelee of 49 on Dec. 13 but Kelley (1978: 25) reported 67 following the Kent Co. shore on Dec. 28, 1970. Thompson (1890: 186-187) gave an interesting account of Rough-legs hunting mice at Toronto Marsh on Jan. 25, 1889. At Pickering the maximum Christmas count was 38 on Dec. 26, 1965, but the average count is about 8 (Speirs, 1977: 8). Mills (1981: 37) mentioned one winter record for Parry Sound, on Dec. 25, 1974 (Campbell).

SPRING:   Stirrett (1973b: 15) had records of individuals at Pelee up to May 7. Ussher (1965: 7) gave Apr. 25 as the 6-year average departure date from Rondeau, with the latest on May 7. Saunders (1947: 362) gave Apr. 5 as his 9-year average departure date from Toronto, the latest on May 19 (Baillie). Speirs (1977: 8) saw two dark phase birds north of Oshawa as late as May 22, 1965. Weir & Quilliam (1980: 33) gave May 3 as the 23-year average departure date from Kingston. Devitt (1967: 54) gave Apr. 7 as the 9-year average arrival date at Barrie, with one as late as May 27, 1957 (Hughes). Beamer had Meaford records as early as Mar. 18 and as late as May 31 (on which date in 1950 a total of 42 were noted). Mills (1981: 37) gave spring dates for Muskoka ranging from Mar. 31 to May 18. Nicholson (1981: 84) found that the majority moved through Manitoulin in mid-April but had records as early as Mar. 10, 1974 and as late as May 27 in 1976. Skeel and Bondrup-Nielsen (1978: 163) had just two spring records from Pukaskwa, one on Apr. 14 and one on June 1. Denis (1961: 2) gave Apr. 22 as the average arrival date at Thunder

Bay, with the earliest on Apr. 3, 1949. Elder (1979: 31) had his earliest Geraldton record on Apr. 22.

SUMMER:    Fleming (1907: 73) reported a female taken at Toronto on Aug. 25, 1894. My most unexpected sighting of this species was one which I saw on June 21, 1969, near a slaughter house north of Manilla (Speirs, 1977: 8). Naomi LeVay had two August sightings near Whitby, one on Aug. 19, 1956 and one on Aug. 22, 1958 (Tozer & Richards, 1974: 103). Weir & Quilliam (1980: 33) noted July 18 and Aug. 11 observations for Kingston. J. Livingston and D. MacDonald saw one on the Magnetawan River west of Ahmic Harbour on Aug. 5, 1945 (Mills, 1981: 38). On June 14, 1979 I was surprised to find one hunting behind my motel at Timmins. Dear (1940: 125) observed a pair repeatedly in one locality near Thunder Bay during June, 1931 but failed to find a nest. Schueler, Baldwin & Rising (1974: 142) noted them in summer at Moosonee, Attawapiskat and Winisk. Peck (1972: 339) gave several summer records for Cape Henrietta Maria and mentioned a possible nest record, but it was not until July, 1976, that nesting was confirmed when Prevett photographed young in the nest there (Goodwin, 1977: 40). Hope saw one at Ft. Severn on June 17, 1940. This is generally an Arctic breeder.

AUTUMN:    Manning (1952: 33) saw ten hunting over the Ship Sands barrens near Moosonee on Sept. 8, 1950, and cited records by others as late as Oct. 8 in that vicinity. Skeel & Bondrup-Nielsen (1978: 163) had fall records for Pukaskwa as early as Sept. 6 and as late as Oct. 16 when a northwesterly flight of 68 was noted. We noted one at North Bay on Oct. 17, 1944 and three there on Oct. 22 (Speirs & Speirs, 1947: 27). Nicholson (1981: 83) gave Oct. 4 as the 11-year average arrival date for Manitoulin, the earliest on Sept. 14, 1975 (Bell): he described a big flight in Oct., 1977 of the hawks moving west to northwest - 86 on Oct. 16, 82 on Oct. 22 and 45 on Oct. 23. Mills (1981: 37) gave records as early as Sept. 18 at Go Home Bay and as late as Nov. 12 at Magnetawan. Beamer had fall records for Meaford as early as Oct. 1, 1948 and as late as Nov. 2, 1940,when 15 were noted. The peak of the fall flight at Barrie has been in the latter half of October with some seen in early Sept. and about 200 estimated on Oct. 26, 1948 moving west (Brereton) according to Devitt (1967: 54). Weir & Quilliam (1980: 33) gave Oct. 8 as the 26-year average arrival date at Kingston. Naomi LeVay had two records as early as August near Whitby, one as early as Aug. 19, 1956: I counted 162 over our Pickering home moving west, some very high, on Oct. 18, 1948 (Speirs, 1977: 8). Speirs (1938: 52) gave Oct. 25 as the fall peak for Toronto, while Saunders (1947: 362) gave Oct. 13 as his 11-year average for arrivals there, with Sept. 5 as the earliest. Fleming (1907: 73) reported an immense flight at Toronto from Oct. 26 to 29 (about 50 *specimens* were brought to him). Field & Field (1979: 12-13) noted their first four at Hawk Cliff on Oct. 16 in 1977 and had high counts of 44 on Nov. 12 and 45 on Dec. 10. Ussher (1965: 7) gave Oct. 28 as the 7-year average arrival date at Rondeau. Stirrett (1973d: 17) had one as early as Aug. 25 at Pelee and a maximum of 41 on Nov. 2 there.

**MEASUREMENTS:**
*Length:* ♂ 19.5 to 22 ins.,
♀ 21.5 to 23.5 ins.
(Godfrey, 1966: 93).
*Wingspread:* ♂ 50 ins. ♀
54 ins. (Pough,
1951: 148).

*Weight:* 11 ♂ averaged 1027 g.; 17 ♀ averaged 1278 g. (Dunning, 1984: 6).

**REFERENCE:**
Cade, Tom J. 1955 Variation of the Common Rough-legged Hawk in North America.
   Condor, 57: (6): 313-346.
This describes in considerable detail the great variation in plumages in this species. Females and juveniles tend to have black bellies while in adult males the belly tends to be finely barred.

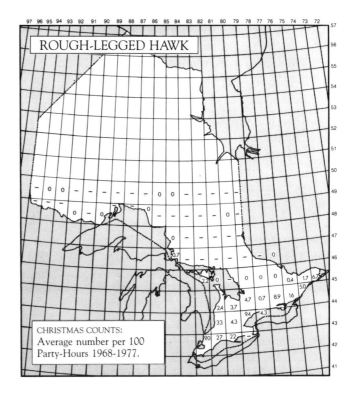

ROUGH-LEGGED HAWK

CHRISTMAS COUNTS:
Average number per 100
Party-Hours 1968-1977.

# GOLDEN EAGLE   *Aquila chrysaetos*   (Linnaeus)

It is a red letter day when one of these magnificent eagles is spotted in Ontario. A few are observed annually by some fortunate bird watcher, but such encounters are so few as to call for special celebration. In the Rocky Mountains sightings are more frequent.

IDENTIFICATION:   The large size should distinguish it from other birds of prey, except for immature Bald Eagles: both have wingspread of six to seven feet, while the Rough-legged Hawk which somewhat resembles the immature Golden Eagle in pattern has only about 4 foot wingspread. Adult Golden Eagles are brown with a golden gloss on the head and neck. Immatures have a white base to the flight feathers of wing and tail: immature Bald Eagles may also show some white but it tends to be patchy. The Golden Eagle is shaped more like a Red-tailed Hawk with wings broad from front to rear, while the Bald Eagle has wings more or less the same width over much of their expanse, usually held horizontally, while the Golden Eagle often holds its wings above the horizontal when soaring. Both eagles have big heads and beaks, but the neck is especially prominent in Bald Eagles. If you are close enough you may see that Golden Eagles have fully feathered feet, to the toes, while Bald Eagles have scaly tarsi.

WINTER:   On Christmas counts they have been noted at Algonquin Park, Cambridge, Long Point, Blenheim and Point Pelee. Stirrett (1973a: 15) had individuals at Pelee on Dec. 17, 23, 25 and Jan. 21. Marshall Field noted one east of Union on Dec. 6, 1953 (Brooman, 1954: 14). Field & Field (1979: 13) noted one at Hawk Cliff on Dec. 10 and six there on Dec. 11, 1977. Saunders & Dale (1933: 186) reported one found wounded on Dec. 1, 1900 (later to become a specimen in the WES collection) and another seen near Byron on Feb. 14, 1929 by Eli Davis. Sheppard (1960: 15) mentioned an adult male shot in the winter of 1890 near Queenston by James Sheppard and mounted. Fleming (1907: 73) reported one taken at Toronto on Dec. 15, 1904. Grace Eves noted one on Amherst Is. from Jan. 1 to 8, 1978, when it died from porcupine quills in its face and stomach (this female is now a specimen in the National Museum, Ottawa): another adult was seen at Prince Edward Point by Art. Bell on Jan. 6, 1980 (Weir & Quilliam, 1980: 7). Devitt (1967: 54) cited one seen by A.V. Mason at Creemore on Feb. 9, 1964. Mills (1981: 38) gave several winter records for Muskoka; some of these taken in traps set for wolves.

SPRING:   Stirrett (1973b: 15) had but one spring record for Pelee, on Mar. 22, 1940. Beardslee & Mitchell (1965: 172) mentioned one seen at Port Weller on May 1, 1949, by Seeber and another at Niagara-on-the-Lake on May 21, 1950 by Beardslee and Verrill. Saunders (1947: 118) described the thrill of finding one just north of Aurora on Apr. 26, 1942. An immature was reported on Apr. 25 at Sydenham by Shirley Treganza and an adult at Gould Lake on May 31 by Bruce Lyons, both in 1980 (Weir & Quilliam, 1980: 7). Macoun (1903: 243) listed one shot at Loring about Mar. 1, 1897, and three more (1♂, 2♀) shot there in Mar., 1898, as well as two females taken at Dunchurch the same month. Nicholson (1981: 84) saw one near Evansville, Manitoulin, on May 22, 1980. One was taken alive on Mar. 5, 1930, at Powassan (Ricker & Clarke, 1939: 7). Elder (1979: 31) told of an injured bird taken at Nakina on Mar. 17, 1972, nursed back to health and released.

SUMMER:   Stirrett (1973d: 17) had Pelee records for Aug. 15 and 18. Quilliam

(1965: 60) summarized old records for the Kingston area, including two possible nest sites. An adult was seen near Joyceville from July 28 to Aug. 21, 1976 (Weir & Quilliam, 1980: 7). Mills (1981: 38) referred to a Muskoka specimen taken in August, 1889. Baillie & Hope (1943: 7) observed a Golden Eagle at Peninsula on June 20, 1936: they also mentioned an old nest record from Thunder Cape. Douglas Mair reported an occupied nest on Pipestone Lake, about 30 miles north of Emo, in late spring, 1927 (Snyder, 1949: 40). On June 5, 1942, Shortt and Hope observed a Golden Eagle at Cockispenny Point, between Moosonee and Ft. Albany (Snyder, 1949: 40) Schueler, Baldwin & Rising (1974: 142) noted this species only at Hawley Lake (in 1964).

AUTUMN:    Elder (1979: 31) salvaged an injured bird at Terrace Bay on Oct. 16, 1972 and released it when it recovered. Nicholson (1981: 84) had eight fall records for Manitoulin; one as early as Oct. 14 and another as late as Nov. 23. Beamer gave a good description of one seen near Meaford on Nov. 3, 1944. Devitt (1967: 54) detailed three November records for Simcoe Co. (two collected and one seen). Weir & Quilliam (1980: 7) cited several recent fall records for the Kingston region, from Sept. 16 to Nov. 19. Tozer & Richards (1974: 104) had fall dates from the Oshawa-Scugug region from Oct. 2 to Nov. 6. Speirs (1977: 9) had fall records from the Pickering-Whitby area as early as Sept. 19 and as late as Nov. 17. Charles Fothergill received a pair shot near his home on Rice Lake by Indians on Oct. 13, 1820. Macoun (1903: 243) reported one shot near Ottawa on Oct. 30, 1883 and another killed at Lake Scugog on Oct. 20, 1897. Fleming (1907: 73) reported Toronto specimens taken Oct. 24, 1896 and Oct. 24, 1903. Saunders (1947: 362) gave fall dates for Toronto from Sept. 22 to Oct. 28. Brooman (1954: 14) gave several fall records from Elgin Co., including a specimen (now in the Royal Ontario Museum) taken on Nov. 30, 1950. Stirrett (1973d: 17 and 1973a: 15) had a few Pelee records from Oct. 1 to Nov. 19.

**MEASUREMENTS:**
Length: ♂ 33 ins. ♀ 38 ins. (Pough, 1951: 154)
Wingspread: ♂ 79 ins. ♀ 87 ins. (Pough, 1951: 154)
Weight: ♂ 9 lbs. ♀ 12 lbs. (Pough, 1951: 154)

**REFERENCE:**
Snyder, L.L. 1949 On the distribution of the Golden Eagle in eastern Canada. Can. Field- Nat., 63: (1): 39-41.

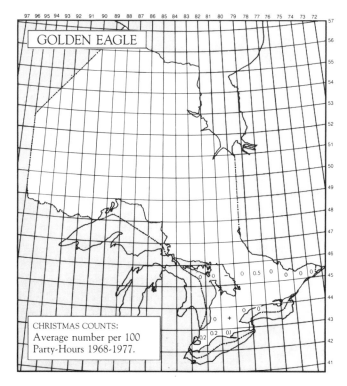

GOLDEN EAGLE

CHRISTMAS COUNTS:
Average number per 100
Party-Hours 1968-1977.

# AMERICAN KESTREL   *Falco sparverius*   Linnaeus

This is a very colourful little falcon, frequently seen perched on roadside wires or hovering on rapidly beating wings over open country, looking down for a mouse or grasshopper. Although these seem to be the usual foods they will sometimes take larger prey when these are scarce. I saw one male Kestrel take a male Evening Grosbeak at our feeder one cold wintry day, which was almost as heavy as it was and which it was only able to carry for a short distance.

IDENTIFICATION: The male, with its blue wings, reddish body and black vertical stripes before and behind its white face, is easily identified. The female is larger and has reddish brown wings. Even the young have the black and white face pattern. The reddish back and tail separate it from the much less common Merlin, a stouter bird with blue or brown back and barred tail.

WINTER: On Christmas counts it has been fairly common north to Kingston and Wiarton, with a few north as far as Ottawa and Manitoulin. Stirrett (1973a: 15) had records of one to four throughout the winter months at Pelee. Snyder (1941: 46) mentioned one seen by Frank Brimley on Feb. 9, 1912 in Prince Edward Co. Nicholson (1981: 89) cited two January records and one on Feb. 16, 1975 on Manitoulin.

SPRING: Saunders & Dale (1933: 187) gave Mar. 22 as the 15-year average arrival date for London and gave details of four sets of eggs for May, one set of four as early as May 8. Speirs (1938: 44) gave Apr. 12 as the peak of the spring migration at Toronto. In Ontario Co., two peaks were suggested by Speirs (1977: 16), one on Apr. 4, and another on Apr. 19. C. Christy found a nest with five eggs as early as Apr. 15 in 1963 near Oshawa (Tozer & Richards (1974: 110). Quilliam (1965: 66) reported nesting as early as Apr. 26 at Kingston. Devitt (1967: 58) gave Apr. 11 as the 8-year average arrival date at Barrie. Beamer's median arrival date at Meaford was Apr. 2 with the earliest on Mar. 22, 1938: he gave several cases of Kestrels nesting in the hay in barns, entering through knot holes in the outer walls. Mills (1981: 44) reported the 14-year average arrival date for Huntsville as Apr. 6, the earliest on Mar. 15, 1974. Nicholson (1981: 89) gave Mar. 23 as the 11-year average arrival date for Manitoulin, the earliest on Mar. 9, 1974. Ricker & Clarke (1939: 8) saw one as early as Apr. 6, 1934 at North Bay. Denis (1961: 2) gave Apr. 14 as the average arrival date at Thunder Bay, with the earliest on Apr. 5, 1956. Bondrup-Nielsen (1976: 42) had his earliest at Kapuskasing on Apr. 20, 1974, where they become common later in spring and summer (Smith, 1957: 171). The earliest Geraldton record was Apr. 15 (Elder, 1979: 31). Cringan (1953a: 2) had his earliest at Sioux Lookout on Apr. 10 in 1953. Sam Waller reported its arrival at Moose Factory on Apr. 10 in both 1929 and 1930 (Todd, 1963: 248).

SUMMER: On Breeding Bird Surveys it has shown up on almost all routes as uncommon to rare but somewhat more numerous in the north than in the south. Stirrett (1973c: 14) had records through the summer months at Pelee but no definite breeding record. Devitt (1967: 58) documented nesting in Simcoe Co. Mills (1981: 44) had only one nesting record for Muskoka: a nest with 5 eggs found on June 18, 1917 at Port Sydney by L. Snyder. A nest with four eggs was found at Providence Bay, Manitoulin, on June 5, 1976 (Nicholson, 1981: 89). Speirs & Speirs (1947:27) saw a flying young at North Bay on June 7, 1945. Harry Graham reported finding a nest with young at Maskinonge

Bay, near Sault Ste. Marie, on July 16, 1939 (Snyder, 1942: 126). Baillie & Hope (1943: 8) collected a set of five fresh eggs at Rossport on May 29, 1936 in an old Flicker hole only five feet up in a telegraph pole. Snyder (1928: 260) collected a male at Lake Nipigon on June 21, 1924, that was attempting to pick up a downy young Ruffed Grouse, nest holes were also located there. Dear (1940: 126) found two nests, both with five eggs, near Thunder Bay in 1927, one on May 29 and the other on June 5. James (1980: 86) found a nest with four eggs at Pickle Lake on June 20, 1979. Hope (1938: 14) found evidence of breeding at Favourable Lake where he considered it "the commonest hawk of the region". Snyder (1928: 22) collected an incompletely feathered young near Lowbush, Lake Abitibi, on Aug. 3, 1925. D.A. MacLulich saw adults entering a nest hole on May 29, 1935, at Smoky Falls (Baillie & Harrington, 1936: 27). Manning (1952: 36) had a few records for Moosonee including one he saw on June 24, 1950. Schueler, Baldwn & Rising (1974: 142) found it common at Cochrane and noted some at Hawley Lake, but not at any of the coastal stations visited on James Bay and Hudson Bay. Hope had one record during his stay at Ft. Severn in 1940, one on July 20.

AUTUMN: Louise Lawrence saw one at Pimisi Bay as late as Oct. 11, 1944 (Speirs & Speirs, 1947: 27). Ron. Tasker reported 100 on Manitoulin on Sept. 12, 1971, at the peak of the fall migration (Nicholson, 1981: 89). Beamer's latest fall mention of one at Meaford was on Sept. 30, 1939. Peak numbers during the fall migration to the southwest parallel to the Lake Ontario shore are usually in the third week of September (Speirs, 1977: 16). Speirs (1938: 52) gave Sept. 9 as the fall peak at Toronto. The highest daily count at Hawk Cliff during the fall of 1977 was 624 on Sept. 28 (Field & Field, 1979: 11). Stirrett (1973d: 18) had a maximum of 17 at Pelee on Sept. 14 while "in the fall of 1974 about 1,040 were counted at Holiday Beach" (Kelley, 1978: 27).

BANDING: Individuals banded at Hawk Cliff have been taken in winter as far south as Duck Key, Fla., Morgan City, La. and Goliad, Texas (Field & Field, 1979: 24, 26).

**MEASUREMENTS:**
*Length:* ♂ 8.75 to 10.65 ins. ♀ 9 to 12 ins. (Godfrey, 1966: 103)
*Wingspread:* ♂ 21 ins. ♀ 24 ins. (Pough, 1951: 171)
*Weight:* 3 ♂ averaged 102.5 g. 3 ♀ averaged 128.5 g. (Hope, 1938: 14)

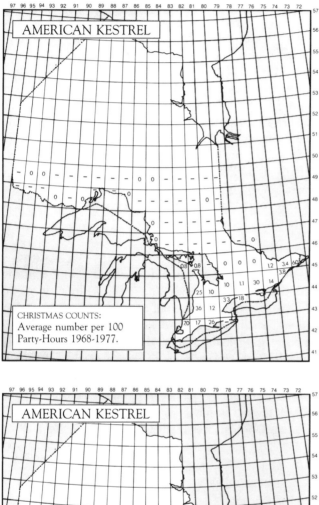

AMERICAN KESTREL

CHRISTMAS COUNTS:
Average number per 100
Party-Hours 1968-1977.

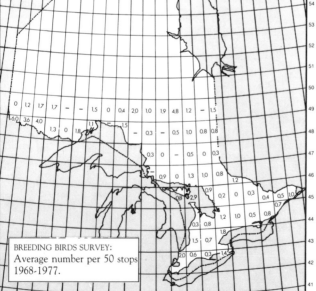

AMERICAN KESTREL

BREEDING BIRDS SURVEY:
Average number per 50 stops
1968-1977.

# MERLIN  *Falco columbarius*  Linnaeus

Although not much larger than a Kestrel, they weigh about twice as much, looking somewhat like a pigeon in flight, hence the former name Pigeon Hawk. Their presence is often noted by shorebirds, that scatter in alarm before I can even see the speck on the horizon that comes in on a gentle glide at great speed to easily overtake any small bird that it desires. Yet Louise Lawrence found that small birds nested with impunity close to the nest that she studied at Rutherglen, where the Merlins hunted at a distance from their nest, not molesting their neighbours.

IDENTIFICATION: This is a stout pigeon-sized falcon with barred tail and streaked breast, lacking the contrasting face pattern of the Kestrel. Adult males have blue backs where the females and young are brown. The yellow cere is often quite conspicuous.

WINTER: Although several years may intervene between records, individuals have shown up at most localities on Christmas counts in the triangle between Long Point, Kingston and Manitoulin, with more frequent sightings at Thunder Bay. Field & Field (1979: 13) noted one at Hawk Cliff on Dec. 31, 1977. Beardslee & Mitchell (1965: 181) mentioned a Niagara River record for Dec. 27, 1931. Saunders (1947: 362) gave Dec. 24 and Feb. 7 records for Toronto. Tozer & Richards (1974: 109) cited several winter records from Oshawa and Darlington. A.J. Mitchener noted one at Collingwood on Jan. 24, 1954 (Devitt, 1967: 57). V. Heron reported seeing one catch a Chickadee by the Fox Point Road, Lake of Bays, on Feb. 10, 1973 and another at Huntsville in early January, 1980 (Mills, 1981: 44). R. Young saw one that spent the month of January, 1976 at Providence Bay, Manitoulin (Nicholson, 1981: 89).

SPRING: A few have been seen at Pelee from Mar. 28 to May 19 (Stirrett, 1973a: 16). Ussher (1965: 8) had Rondeau records from Apr. 23 to May 28. Saunders & Dale (1933: 187) reported one taken at London on Apr. 17, 1885. One was reported at Fort Erie as late as May 30, 1944 (Beardslee & Mitchell, 1965: 181). Speirs (1977: 15) cited Ontario Co. records between Mar. 5 and May 22. Beaupré shot one at Kingston on May 5, 1896 (Quilliam, 1965: 66). Devitt (1967: 57) had spring records for Simcoe Co. from Mar. 23 (1940) to May 11 (1941). Beamer had Meaford records from Apr. 10 to May 22. Mills (1981: 43-44) gave spring dates from the cottage country from Apr. 13 (1934) to May 23 (1954). Nicholson (1981: 88) gave Mar. 16, 1974 as the earliest spring date for Manitoulin. MacLulich (1938: 11) reported Apr. 30, 1932 as an arrival date for Algonquin Park. Speirs & Speirs (1947: 27) noted one at North Bay on Apr. 19, 1945. Baillie & Hope (1943: 8) saw one miss catching a Barn Swallow at Rossport on May 27, 1936. Denis (1961: 2) gave Apr. 20 as the average arrival date at Thunder Bay. Elder (1979: 31) gave Apr. 24 as his earliest date for Geraldton. Todd (1963: 246-247) saw one near Mattice on May 25, 1926 and one by the Missanabie River at 49°50′ N on May 27: he also reported one taken at Moose Factory on May 1, 1930 and another that he collected there on May 31, 1941. Ross James noted one at Pickle Lake on May 29, 1977.

SUMMER: On Breeding Bird Surveys a few have been noted as far south as Deep River and Montreal Falls and north to Smooth Rock Falls and Eagle River. There have been three August records for Pelee, the earliest on Aug. 5 (Stirrett, 1973c: 14). Beardslee & Mitchell (1965: 181) gave a July 31, 1949 record for Windmill Point, Lake Erie. Tozer & Richards (1974: 109) cited records by Naomi LeVay at Cranberry Marsh on June 29,

1968; Aug. 1, 1956 and Aug. 3, 1953. Weir & Quilliam (1980: 34) gave July 13 and Aug. 15 dates for Kingston. Devitt (1967: 57) reported a speciment taken at Collingwood on Aug. 17, 1880. Beamer reported one at Blantyre on July 9, 1947. The most southerly breeding records have been those cited by Mills (1981: 43) for the Muskoka and Parry Sound regions. Nicholson (1981: 89) gave two breeding records for Manitoulin, on June 13, 1974 and July 6, 1980. Lawrence (1949: 15-25) gave an excellent account of nesting at Pimisi Bay including the effect on neighbouring birds. Dennis Chitty took a pair at West Bay, Lake Nipissing, on June 24, 1934 and noted another pair at the Goose Islands three days later (Ricker & Clarke, 1939: 8). Snyder (1942: 126) noted one at Lake George, near Sault Ste. Marie, on July 9, 1931. Skeel & Bondrup-Nielsen (1978: 164) had observations suggestive of nesting at Pukaskwa. Baillie & Harrington (1936: 27) mentioned a nest on Lynx Island, Temagami, observed by A.F. Coventry during the summer of 1930. Smith (1957: 171) saw this species near Gogama on July 26 and Aug. 3, 1954. Snyder (1928: 260) took several specimens at Lake Nipigon and found a nest there with two downy young on July 2, 1924. Dear (1940: 126) found nests at Whitefish Lake, Thunder Bay, one with four eggs on June 15, 1929 and another with 5 eggs on July 3, 1938. Snyder (1928: 22) took two young from a nest on an island in Lake Abitibi on July 25, 1925. He collected a yearling male at Wabigoon and saw individuals at Kenora, Ingolf and Malachi during the summer of 1937 (Snyder, 1953: 55). T.M. Shortt took an adult and four young at Fraserdale on June 19 and one at Genier on June 1 in 1939 (Todd, 1963: 247). Hope (1938: 14) had only one record near Favourable Lake, on July 31, 1938. Schueler, Baldwin & Rising (1974: 145) noted territorial birds at Aquatuk Lake on July 12, 1964 and at Winisk on June 26, 1971. Lee & Speirs (1977: 50, 52) reported Merlins on two of the three quadrats studied near Big Trout Lake during the summer of 1975. In 1940 Hope found a nest with five eggs at Fort Severn on June 20 and another with four eggs on July 7.

AUTUMN: Manning (1952: 36) cited records from the vicinity of Moosonee on Sept. 23, 1947 and Sept. 10, 1950. Skeel & Bondrup-Nielsen (1978: 164) noted a few migrating along the Lake Superior shore during September. One was seen frequently in North Bay from Aug. 18 to Oct. 4, 1944 and "When it appeared great flocks of English sparrows would form a big whirling ball of birds high above the buildings" (Speirs & Speirs, 1947: 27). MacLulich (1938: 11) has one at Algonquin Park as late as Nov. 28, 1908. Beamer had Meaford records from Sept. 3 to 11, 1946 and Sept. 23-24, 1950. Devitt (1967: 57) had Simcoe Co. records from Sept. 3 (1934) to Nov. 16 (1962). Weir & Quilliam (1980: 34) gave Sept. 13 and Nov. 2 as average arrival and departure dates for Kingston. J.L. Baillie saw one at Wellers Bay on Oct. 24, 1932 (Snyder, 1941: 45). Speirs (1977: 15) had Ontario Co. records from Aug. 28 to Nov. 8 and gave two accounts of predation on shorebirds. Thompson (1890: 196: 198) mentioned one collected by Hubert H. Brown at Toronto on Oct. 7, 1889 and one seen darting after a flock of Pine Siskins on Oct. 28, 1889. Fleming (1907: 73) called it a regular but not very common migrant at Toronto from Sept. 1 to Dec. 6. Saunders (1947: 362, 264) gave dates for Toronto from Aug. 22 to Oct. 28 and described one eating a House Sparrow on Sept. 11, 1942. On Sept. 20, 1942 Saunders (1943: 50) counted 27 at Hawk Cliff, while Field & Field (1979: 10-12) had 17 records there during the fall of 1977 from Aug. 31 to Nov. 6 and banded ten during this period. Ussher (1965: 8) reported Rondeau birds from Aug. 22 to Oct. 17. Kelley (1978: 27) considered the 22 tallied during the fall of 1964 at Pelee and Holiday Beach as unusually numerous. Stirrett (1973d: 18) had Pelee records from August until Nov. 1.

**MEASUREMENTS:**

*Length:* ♂ 10 to 10.6 ins.
♀ 12 to 13 ins. (Godfrey, 1966: 102)
*Wingspread:* ♂ 25 ins. ♀ 26 ins. (Pough, 1951: 169)
*Weight:* ♂ 6 oz. ♀ 8 oz. (Pough, 1951: 169)

**REFERENCES:**

Lawrence, Louise de Kiriline 1949 Notes on nesting Pigeon Hawks at Pimisi Bay, Ontario. Wilson Bull., 61: (1): 15-25.
Saunders, W.E. 1942 A huge migration of hawks in Ontario. Can. Field-Nat., 57: (2&3): 49-50.

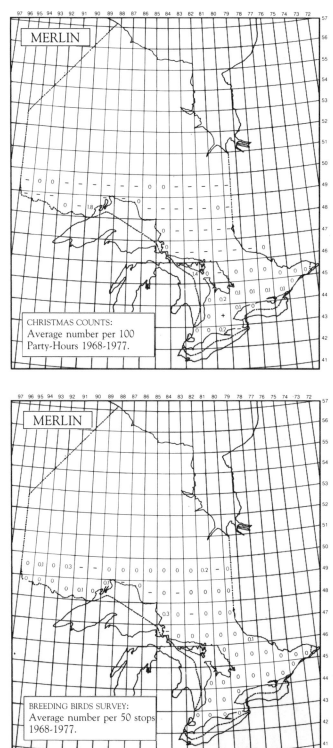

MERLIN

CHRISTMAS COUNTS:
Average number per 100
Party-Hours 1968-1977.

MERLIN

BREEDING BIRDS SURVEY:
Average number per 50 stops
1968-1977.

# PEREGRINE FALCON  *Falco peregrinus*  Tunstall

As a predator at the end of its food chain, this was always a rare bird. With the advent of the persistent insecticides it was almost wiped out, accumulating DDT in its tissues from every infected prey consumed until its egg shells thinned and produced no viable young. With the banning of DDT and introductions from less contaminated areas it appears to be making some comeback.

IDENTIFICATION: This is a crow-sized falcon with dark brown or blue back and prominent blackish "mustache" markings on its face. When perched, Broad-winged Hawks may look very similar but they lack the toothed beak of a falcon. In flight the pointed wings and great speed of the Peregrine is evident as is its effect on gulls, ducks and pigeons that fly up and scatter in alarm when the Peregrine is just a speck on the horizon.

WINTER: On Christmas counts individuals have been observed as far south as Blenheim and north to Ottawa. Beardslee & Mitchell (1965: 180) had three February records: one at Erie Beach on Feb. 12, 1946; one at Niagara Falls on Feb. 15, 1947 and one at Wainfleet on Feb. 16, 1947. Saunders (1947: 362) reported Dec. 22 and Feb. 9 dates for Toronto. Tozer & Richards (1974: 108) had three winter records: one on the Oshawa Christmas count (at Columbus on Dec. 22, 1957) and two at Cranberry Marsh, on Jan. 16, 1950 and Jan. 20, 1951 (Naomi LeVay). Weir & Quilliam (1980: 34) mentioned a Jan. 5 observation at Kingston. Dennison (1980: 149) reported one on the Sault Ste. Marie Christmas count in 1958.

SPRING: Stirrett (1973b: 16) had a few at Pelee from Mar. 28 to May 20. Ussher (1965: 8) had Rondeau records from Apr. 7 to May 17. Saunders & Dale (1933: 187) cited records for Middlesex Co. on Apr. 14, 1885 and Apr. 5, 1930. Beardslee & Mitchell (1965: 180) had a Port Colborne record for May 27, 1945. Fleming (1907: 73) reported a female at Toronto on May 23, 1892. Saunders (1947: 362) gave spring dates for Toronto from Apr. 13 to May 31. Speirs (1977: 14) had spring records from Ontario Co. from Mar. 15 to May 29. Allin (1940: 96) had only one old record from Darlington Twp., on Apr. 16, 1881 (Dutton). Quilliam (1965: 65) gave two spring records for Kingston: Apr. 24, 1949 and May 2, 1955, while Weir & Quilliam (1980: 34) gave Mar. 8 as the earliest spring date for Kingston. Beamer followed the fortunes of the Redwing eyrie from 1938 to 1949 where they arrived as early as Feb. 27 in 1944 though the median arrival date was Mar. 23. Mills (1981: 43) cited Mar. 19, 1964 as an early date for Huntsville. Nicholson (1981: 88) had 12 spring records from Manitoulin from Apr. 28 to May 25. Ricker & Clarke (1939: 8) had one spring record near North Bay on May 17, 1924 and one was seen near Rutherglen on May 14, 1945 (Speirs & Speirs, 1947: 27).

SUMMER: On Breeding Bird Surveys one was reported at Thessalon in 1969 and one at Cobden in 1972. Stirrett (1973c: 14) had one record at Pelee on Aug. 12, 1911. Beardslee & Mitchell (1965: 180) cited a record at Rockhouse Point, Lake Erie, on June 26, 1958 by A. Schaffner and the Brownsteins. Maughan (1897: 2) took one at Ashbridge's Bay, Toronto, on June 25, 1894. Saunders (1947: 362) had an Aug. 1 date for Toronto. Naomi LeVay reported one at Cranberry Marsh, Whitby, on July 27, 1955 (Tozer & Richards, 1974: 108). Quilliam (1965: 64-65) detailed the fortunes of three eyries in Frontenac Co. from 1901 to 1929: prey items ranged from the size of Meadow Mice to Black Ducks. Mills (1981: 42-43) listed several former nest sites for Muskoka and Parry

Sound. Nicholson (1981: 88) cited a few former nestings around the fringes of Manitoulin. Snyder (1942: 125) saw one at Rydalbank on June 30, 1931 and a pair along the Garden River (both near Sault Ste. Marie). Dear (1940: 126) mentioned an eyrie near Thunder Bay that contained four small young on June 4, 1933 and three eggs on May 15, 1934. Denis (1961: 5) noted another Thunder Bay nest which contained three eggs on June 1, 1950. Manning (1952: 35) mentioned that Macpherson collected a female on June 23, 1949 at Middleboro Is., near Moosonee, "with a bell and leather strap on its foot".

AUTUMN: Manning (1952: 35) cited two fall records at Ship Sands Is., near Moosonee; on Sept. 24, 1947 and Sept. 9, 1950. Speirs & Speirs (1947: 27) observed one at Rutherglen on Sept. 11, 1944. Nicholson (1981: 88) had 26 fall sightings on Manitoulin as early as Aug. 28 and as late as Oct. 20. Beamer had one as late as Nov. 28 near Meaford after the Redwing pair had raised two broods in 1945. Devitt (1967: 56-57) gave several fall records from Simcoe Co. between Aug. 22 and Oct. 20. Tozer & Richards (1974: 109) listed records from the waterfront between Bowmanville and Whitby from Aug. 31 to Nov. 21. James R. Thurston commented that one collected at Toronto on Sept. 25, 1889, had its "stomach distended with grasshoppers", a most unusual prey for this species (Thompson, 1890 195). Fleming (1907: 73) reported young birds at Toronto from Sept. 18 to Oct. 20. Saunders (1947: 362) gave fall dates from Toronto from Sept. 15 to Oct. 21, while Speirs (1938: 52) suggested Sept. 27 as the peak of the fall flight there. Beardslee & Mitchell (1965: 180) saw one along the Canadian shore of Lake Erie on Oct. 25, 1936. Sheppard (1960: 16) saw one as late as November in 1947, chasing pigeons along the Niagara Gorge. Field & Field (1979: 10-12) listed five individuals at Hawk Cliff in 1977 between Sept. 17 and Oct. 9. Ussher (1965: 8) had fall records from Rondeau between Sept. 3 and Oct. 30. Stirrett (1973d: 18) had fall records at Pelee from Aug. 28 to Nov. 1 with a maximum count of six on Oct. 3. Kelley (1978: 27) mentioned a fall total of 24 at Pelee in 1965.

BANDING: A hatching year male banded near Limbour, Que. on July 25, 1977 was recovered at Hawk Cliff on Sept. 17, 1977 (Field & Field, 1979. 26).

**MEASUREMENTS:**
Length: ♂ 15 to 18 ins. ♀ 18 to 21.4 ins. (Godfrey, 1966: 102)
Wingspread: ♂ 40 ins. ♀ 45 ins. (Pough, 1951: 167)
Weight: ♂ 1 lb. 4 oz. (Beamer)
Note: Beamer took measurements of one killed by K. Kerr on Oct. 2, 1941, which had been chasing pigeons and chickens, probably a young male: Length 16 1/4 ins. Wingspread: 38 ins. and weight as above. The one taken by Maughan at Toronto on June 25, 1894, probably a female, was 19 1/2 ins. long with a wingspread of 44 3/4 ins.

196

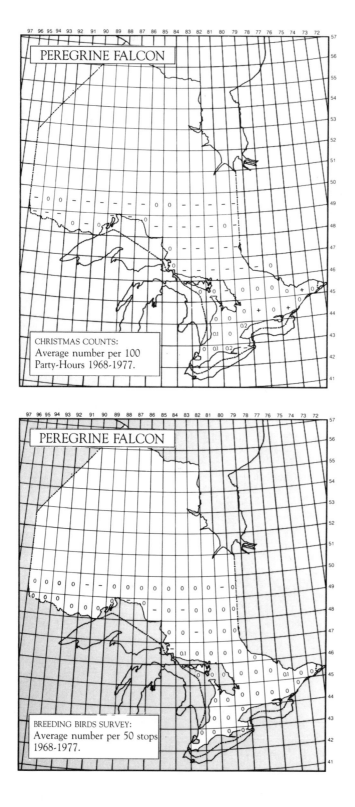

PEREGRINE FALCON

CHRISTMAS COUNTS:
Average number per 100
Party-Hours 1968-1977.

PEREGRINE FALCON

BREEDING BIRDS SURVEY:
Average number per 50 stops
1968-1977.

# GYRFALCON   *Falco rusticolus*   Linnaeus

Although ducks and pigeons are its usual prey in southern Ontario, I saw one make a pass at Canada Geese in Toronto Harbour and George Scott reported seeing one chase a swan at Oshawa. Most observers are impressed by its great speed. Seeing one in southern Ontario has been a once in a lifetime experience, although sightings have been more frequent in recent years. The Toronto Harbour bird mentioned above came to roost regularly on a waterfront warehouse where birders from all over North America gathered to see it arrive at sunset. I saw it Feb. 15 and Mar. 8, 1978.

**IDENTIFICATION:**  Its pointed wings proclaim it to be a falcon and the large size (Red-tail size) eliminate other falcons except perhaps a large female Peregrine, from which it may be distinguished by its last of pronounced facial pattern, chunkier build and more uniform colouration. The white phase birds are patterned somewhat like Snowy Owls but the different build and manner of flight should easily distinguish it from that species. The gray and dark phase birds are most like Peregrines.

**WINTER:**  On Christmas counts it has been reported at Ottawa and Kingston. Saunders & Dale (1933: 248) reported two white-phase birds; the first in Dec. 1889 about 25 miles west of London and the second on Jan. 9, 1932 some 5 miles west of London. Sheppard (1960: 16) saw one over Niagara Falls on Dec. 17, 1943. Speirs (1977: 13) cited five winter records for Ontario Co.: Dec. 10, 1964 (white - R.C. Long ); Dec. 27, 1964 (black - George Scott and Dennis Barry); Jan. 11 and 20, 1967 (white - Audrey Russ); and Jan. 21, 1976 (gray - Edgerton Pegg, *et al*); since that time a dark phase bird was seen by many observers including myself at Whitby during the 1980-81 winter. Weir & Quilliam (1980: 7) listed several recent sightings near Kingston: Jan. 28 and Feb. 18, 1973; Dec. 21, 1975; Dec. 3, 1978; Feb. 17 to Mar. 3, 1979 and Jan. 12, 1980. Devitt (1967: 56) reported a white-phase bird seen by Alf. Mitchener at Collingwood on Dec. 17, 1952. Craig Campbell saw a single bird near Parry Sound on Dec. 21 and 22, 1974 (Mills, 1981: 42). Elder (1979: 31) mentioned a dead light gray-phase individual brought into his Geraldton office on Feb. 18, 1969.

**SPRING:**  Stirrett (1973b: 16) had only one record for Pelee, on May 4, 1958, conservativley labelled "hypothetical". A.F. Bell had a brief glimpse of a white-phase bird on Mar. 27, 1960, near Kingston (Quilliam, 1965: 14) and Ken Edwards saw a gray-phase bird on Wolfe Island on Mar. 23, 1980 (Weir & Quilliam, 1980: 7-8). Beamer reported a sighting on May 4, 1947 in Meaford by George Irving, of a white-phase bird perched on a sign from the base of which he observed the bird with 6x binoculars. On Mar. 26, 1956, one was watched as it fed at the Limberlost Lodge feeding station, and on Apr. 4, 1974, Robin Morgan spotted a light-phase bird near Huntsville (Mills, 1981: 42). Nicholson (1981: 87) noted a white-phase bird near the Barrie Island causeway on Apr. 13, 1969, and Ron. Tasker saw a dark-phase bird in Burpee Twp., Manitoulin, on May 15, 1975.

**SUMMER:**  On June 22, 1935, Williams (1942: 73) saw a gray-phase bird that occupied a "granite" hill on the Cloche Peninsula and "repeatedly darted at us" (a most unusual observation in time and place for this high-Arctic breeder). Manning (1952: 35) cited old references for Moosonee, Ft. Albany and Severn River, but no recent sightings.

AUTUMN: Nicholson (1981: 87) gave eight fall records for Manitoulin, as early as Sept. 25 and as late of Nov. 24. E.L. Brereton observed a white-phase bird near Barrie on Oct. 26, 1948 and Jack Westman saw a dark-phase bird there on Nov. 3, 1953 (Devitt, 1967: 56). Alden Strong had a brief glimpse of one near Westport on Oct. 27, 1957, cited by Quilliam (1965: 64) as hypothetical. Speirs (1938: 54) had only one record of this species for Toronto: a white-phase female taken at Fisherman's Is. on Nov. 20, 1905 by Frank Otto (see also Fleming, 1907: 73). Saunders (1947: 272-273) described his elation at finding a black-phase bird on Oct. 14, 1945, near the Malton airport: he also gave Oct. 26 and Oct. 27 dates for Toronto without comment (on p. 362). Harold Lancaster saw a dark-phase bird flying west over his Elgin Co. farm on Oct. 9, 1952 (Brooman, 1954: 15). Kelley (1978: 26) had just two records for SW Ontario: a dark-phase bird at Kettle Point on Oct. 29, 1967 and a gray-phase bird there on Oct. 27, 1971.

**MEASUREMENTS:**
*Length:* ♂ 21 to 22.5 ins.
♀ 22 to 24.5 ins.
(Godfrey, 1966: 100)
*Wingspread:* 48 ins.
(Pough, 1951: 164)
*Weight:* 4 lbs. (Pough, 1951: 164)

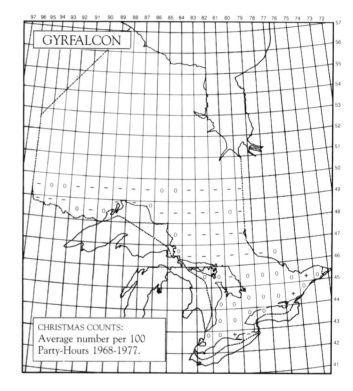

GYRFALCON

CHRISTMAS COUNTS:
Average number per 100
Party-Hours 1968-1977.

# PRAIRIE FALCON   *Falco mexicanus*   Schlegel

In Canada this is a bird of the western provinces, from Saskatchewan to B.C. Those seen in Ontario may be escapes from falconers or wandering individuals far out of their normal range.

IDENTIFICATION:   This is a crow-sized falcon, about the size of a Peregrine but with pale brown upperparts with contrasting dark brown flanks and axillars.

WINTER:   One was reported on the Long Point Christmas count in 1976.

SPRING:

SUMMER:

AUTUMN:   "Jack Livingston, Jim Baillie, Bill Smith and John Keenleyside observed a prairie falcon at Point Pelee in a big hawk flight on September 20, 1958. The only previous report of a prairie falcon in Ontario was one seen by George W. North at Hamilton on September 15, 1944, according to Mr. Baillie." (Speirs, 1958: 32). "Prairie falcon Hamilton (GWN doc.) 2, Sept. 15; 1 Sept. 30." (Goodwin, 1962: 25).

**MEASUREMENTS:**
*Length:* ♂ 16.8 to 18 ins.
♀ 18.5 to 20 ins.
(Godfrey, 1966: 101)
*Wingspread:* 42 ins.
(Pough, 1951: 165)
*Weight:* 2 lbs. (Pough,
1951: 165)

# GRAY PARTRIDGE   *Perdix perdix*   Linnaeus

The Gray Partridge is our only true partridge in Ontario and it is a "foreigner" having been introduced from Europe as a game bird. The Ruffed Grouse is often improperly called "partridge" although they belong to different families of birds. The Gray Partridge does better than many introduced game birds, especially in the fields of southeastern Ontario.

IDENTIFICATION:   This is a medium-sized fowl, smaller than our native grouse but larger than the Bobwhite. When flying away the brown outer tail feathers are conspicuous and when facing the observer the brown belly patch of the male is outstanding (females lack this patch in most cases). The diagonal brown flank stripes contrast with the general gray underplumage. Another foreign gamebird, the Chukar, has black flank stripes, a conspicuous black face stripe and conspicuously reddish legs and beak: it seldom survives our winters and has not become established in the Ontario avifauna.

WINTER:   On the 1968 to 1977 Christmas counts they were fairly common in southeastern Ontario, as far west as Carleton Place and Napanee, with a few ouliers at Hamilton, Waterloo, Long Point and St. Thomas and away west at Thunder Bay. Sheppard (1960: 17) considered it rare in the Niagara region. Saunders (1947: 15) flushed a covey of eight on the Hamilton mountain on Jan. 26, 1941 that "shot away squeaking like an unoiled piston" over the open fields there. They used to come into the fields behind our home at Ancaster, in winter about the same time. A male, collected by A.E. Armstrong near Uxbridge on Jan. 25, 1947, was donated to the Royal Ontario Museum (Speirs, 1977: 22). Quilliam (1965: 69) considered this a fairly common resident of the Kingston area and reported as many as 75 on the Dec. 30, 1961 Christmas count there. Devitt (1967: 61) gave some details of introductions in Simcoe Co., some successful but many not (due to bad winters). Following a 1936 release, Beamer reported them in the Meaford vicinity every winter from 1938 to 1952: on Jan. 17, 1938, a Snowy Oil was shot while chasing a flock. Snyder (1942: 127) cited newspaper reports at Sault Ste. Marie about Jan. 13, 1931 and Dec. 2, 1933, following releases there on May 1, 1930. Denis (1961: 5) mentioned that they survive the Thunder Bay winters near the grain elevators there, along the railroad tracks. Todd (1963: 278) cited releases near Haileybury and R.W. Trowern saw eight on the New Liskeard Christmas count in 1950 (Audubon Field Notes, 5: (2): 47, Apr., 1951).

SPRING: Kelley (1978: 28) reported three seen near Wheately on May 11, 1950. Beardslee & Mitchell (1965: 190) noted two seen on Mar. 30, 1947, north of Dunnville and two at Rockhouse Point on May 23, 1953, since when yearly reports have come from these areas as well as from Lowbanks, McNab and South Cayuga, becoming suffiently common that an open season was declared from Sept. 24 to Nov. 19 in 1960. Speirs (1977: 22) reported one found dead on the beach at Whitby on May 13, 1939 by F.S. Dingman and sent to the Royal Ontario Museum, and two seen at Oshawa by George A. Scott, on Apr. 22, 1946 and May 2, 1948. Allin (1940: 96) saw two on Apr. 21, 1935 and cited other Darlington sightings since March, 1932.

SUMMER: Only in the southeastern Ontario stronghold have they shown up on the Breeding Bird surveys, on the Avonmore and Kemptville routes. Tozer & Richards (1974: 115) reported a covey near Oshawa during the summer of 1942 and a single bird there in June, 1947. Baillie & Harrington (1936: 30) reported very young birds seen by A.E. Allin at Darlington in August, 1934 and young with adults at Woodville seen in 1934 by F. Starr. Beamer reported a nest with 10 eggs broken by a mowing machine, in the summer of 1940 and another nest with 25 eggs in July, 1940, as well as a nest with 20 eggs in the summer of 1941, all near Meaford. Skeel & Bondrup-Nielsen (1978: 167) reported as "accidental" a sighting at Otter Is., near Pukaskwa, on July 3, 1975 by Elwyn Richardson, the lighthouse keeper there. Baillie & Harrington (1936: 30) mentioned a release near Huntsville and a sighting at Minaki, Kenora District, but these do not seem to have persisted. James, McLaren & Barlow (1976: 19) mention Cochrane as a northern limit.

AUTUMN: H.G. Lumsden has a road-killed specimen in his collection, found on Sept. 10, 1966 near Bondhead (Devitt, 1967: 61).

**MEASUREMENTS:**
*Length:* 12 to 13 ins.
(Godfrey, 1966: 118)
Wingspread:
*Weight:* 13 oz. (Pough,
1951: 182)

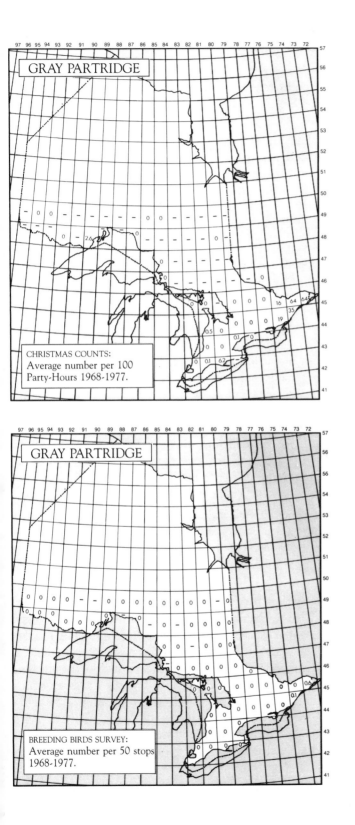

GRAY PARTRIDGE

CHRISTMAS COUNTS:
Average number per 100
Party-Hours 1968-1977.

GRAY PARTRIDGE

BREEDING BIRDS SURVEY:
Average number per 50 stops
1968-1977.

# RING-NECKED PHEASANT   *Phasianus colchicus*   Linnaeus

This is a favourite game bird in southwestern Ontario, particularly on Pelee Is. where they thrive. Elsewhere in Ontario they have been frequently introduced but populations tend to crash during winters of prolonged deep snow.

IDENTIFICATION: They are about the size of a domestic hen, but have a very long, slim tail, usually cocked up as they dash across a road or from one bit of cover to another. The males are brilliantly coloured in a variety of hues, with a red face and usually a white collar. They utter a hoarse "uh-ah" accompanied by wing flutter and stamping feet. Females and young are dull brown.

WINTER: On Christmas counts they have been common at Pelee, fairly common along the north shores of Lakes Erie and Ontario, becoming uncommon to rare north to Ottawa and Meaford, with one sighting at Thunder Bay in 1970. Stirrett (1973a: 15) had a maximum count of 84 at Pelee on Dec. 31. I witnessed a fascinating confrontation of a male pheasant with a Snowy Owl on Jan. 29, 1976 at Whitby, in which the pheasant stood his ground in a group of burs which he was eating, and escaped unharmed. (Speirs, 1976: 10). Quilliam (1965: 68) reported a male and a female taken near Kingston on Feb. 3, 1941, and recounted their great abundance during the mild winter of 1933-1934. Devitt (1967: 61) reported a female taken at Little Lake, Barrie, on Feb. 1, 1931: but most Simcoe Co. winters are too severe for pheasants which must be frequently reintroduced to maintain a huntable population. Beamer had a few winter records for Meaford and Thornbury: one killed by a dog on Feb. 7, 1949 was measured (see below). One was reported at Huntsville on Jan. 9, 1972 and other sightings were made there on Feb. 29 on Mar. 1, 1976 (Mills, 1981: 49). D.A. MacLulich reported one killed during the winter of 1934-1935 at Frank's Bay, Lake Nipissing and others were seen just south of North Bay in 1935 (Ricker & Clarke, 1939: 8). Denis (1961: 5) noted that it "survives only when able to forage in farm yards during winter" at Thunder Bay.

SPRING: The maximum spring count at Pelee was 30 on May 9 (Stirrett, 1973b: 16). Ken Carmichael found a nest with 6 eggs as early as Apr. 30, 1966 at Dunbarton (Speirs, 1977: 21). Devitt (1967: 61) reported a nest with 14 eggs found at Bradford on May 16, 1939 by R.A. Smith. Ross Lowe saw 15 at Mindemoya, Manitoulin, on May 13, 1961 (Nicholson, 1981: 92).

SUMMER: On Breeding Bird Surveys they have been fairly common at Kingsville, and uncommon to rare elsewhere north to Ottawa and Meaford. Stirrett (1973c: 15) gave 12 on Aug. 6 as his high summer count at Pelee. Ussher (1965: 8) called it a rare resident at Rondeau. J.A. Edwards found a nest at Beaverton with 12 eggs, as late as Aug. 28, 1926 (Speirs, 1977: 21). Tozer & Richards (1974: 114) gave a short history of the pheasant in Ontario from its introduction at Niagara-on-the-lake in 1897 and the first open season in 1910 until 1932 when the first hunting was allowed in Darlington (Allin, 1940: 96). Devitt (1967: 61) reported young in Simcoe Co. on June 9, 1938 and Aug. 14, 1937. Beamer reported two half-grown broods of young in 1938, one near Meaford on July 17 and one near Thornbury on Aug. 10. Snyder (1942: 127) found them well established on St. Joseph's Island in 1931.

AUTUMN: Beamer saw one in Meaford on Oct. 30, 1946 following a release that summer. Devitt (1967: 61) reported males taken at Little Lake on Nov. 15, 1931 and at

Bradford on Sept. 11, 1937. Quilliam (1965: 68) reported a female taken near Kingston on Nov. 13, 1939, following introductions beginning about 1920. Stirrett (1973d: 18) had an autumn maximum of four at Pelee on Oct. 30.

**MEASUREMENTS:**
*Length:* ♂ 32.5 to 36 ins.
♀ 18 to 22.5 ins.
(Godfrey, 1966: 116)
Beamer gave 36 ins.
Wingspread:
*Weight:* 2 1/2 to 4 1/2 lbs.
(Pough, 1951: 186)
Beamer gave 2 1/2 lbs.

**REFERENCE:**
Speirs, J. Murray 1976 A
confrontation. Toronto
Field Naturalists Club, No.
298: 10.

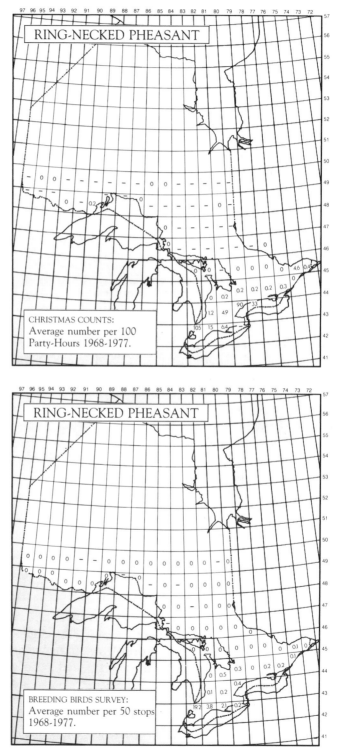

RING-NECKED PHEASANT

CHRISTMAS COUNTS:
Average number per 100
Party-Hours 1968-1977.

RING-NECKED PHEASANT

BREEDING BIRDS SURVEY:
Average number per 50 stops
1968-1977.

# SPRUCE GROUSE   *Dendragapus canadensis*   (Linnaeus)

Most of those that I have seen have been along Highway 11 between Hearst and Jellicoe: some of these were hens with chicks. On Sept. 4, 1959 my wife drew my attention to a group on the highway just east of Klotz Lake. A fine male was strutting with tail erect like a peacock in display, circling around to show off the striking black undertail coverts, each tipped with white and the brown-tipped tail feathers, evidently intended to impress the three females and oblivious to the risk of being run down by passing traffic. May is the normal time for such displays and arenas in the forest the normal place. In Roberts' Birds of Minnesota there are fine photographs of the display.

IDENTIFICATION: This is a small grouse, a bird of the spruce forest. The male with his black breast and throat and bluish back and the shower of stars tipping his undertail coverts is distinctive. A few of the larger Blue Grouse have been introduced north of Lake Superior but have not thrived: they have orange "eyebrows" whereas the Spruce Grouse has red ones when displaying. The females look a bit like small Ruffed Grouse but have black bars across the back rather than lengthwise streaks as in Ruffed Grouse: the latter can always be distinguished by its ruffs on the neck and the large fan-shaped tail with broad subterminal black bar in flight.

WINTER: On Christmas counts it has been found, usually in groups of five to ten, from Dryden and Manitouwadge, south to Algonquin Park. At the present time it is seldom seen south of Algonquin Park but there are several old records much farther south. Baillie & Harrington (1936: 28) reported one shot in Caledon Twp., Peel Co., about 1908. James R. Thurston saw one in Melancthon Twp., Grey Co. in 1887 as well as several freshly killed specimens and considered it "quite common" there at that time (Thompson, 1890: 182). Tozer & Richards (1974: 111) cited records from Manvers Twp., Durham Co., in 1875 and in the Lindsay area about 1885. Devitt (1976: 58) gave old records from Simcoe Co., the latest about 1910 at Collingwood. Mills (1981: 45-46) listed 7 Muskoka and 11 Parry Sound specimens in the Royal Ontario Museum and reported one seen near Huntsville as recently as Dec. 18, 1960. Snyder (1942: 126) reported a few from Rydal Bank and the Goulais River, near Sault Ste. Marie. Elder (1979: 31) called it a common year-round resident at Geraldton.

SPRING:

SUMMER: On Breeding Bird Surveys it has been reported only at Larder Lake and Fort Frances. (You usually have to get off the highways to see this species in June when the surveys are run.) Baillie & Harrington (1936: 28) cited nest records for Algoma, Cochrane, Nipissing, Parry Sound, Sudbury and Thunder Bay Districts. Fleming (1907: 87) reported a covey seen on July 29, 1904 by E.F. Handy near Zephyr, Ontario Co., far south of its present range. Saunders (1947: 202) reported a family of Spruce Grouse seen by Cliff Hope and Dalton Muir on July 4 in Algonquin Park. Ricker & Clarke (1939: 81) cited several records for the North Bay region, including breeding reports. Baillie & Hope (1943: 8) collected several at Amyot and found five newly hatched young in the stomach of a Red-tailed Hawk collected there. Skeel & Bondrup-Nielsen (1978: 165) had six breeding records (adults with young) at Pukaskwa in the summer 1977. Baillie & Hope (1947: 6) collected a female and downy young at Biscotasing and reported one near Chapleau. Snyder (1928: 258) collected seven, including male, female and young, at Lake

Nipigon during the summer of 1924. Denis (1961: 5) reported a nest with 8 eggs at Thunder Bay on June 4, 1950. On June 3, 1946, I flushed a female from a nest with five eggs on one of the Eaglehead Lake study quadrats: she returned to the nest while I watched and did not flush again until my hand was about a foot over her: she was still on her nest in the black spruce forest on June 9. Smith (1957: 171) considered it fairly common in the Clay Belt, but Bondrup-Nielsen (1976: 42) reported it as rare near Kapuskasing in 1974 and 1975 and Snyder (1928: 21) reported only one near Lake Abitibi, seen near Lowbush by J.R. Dymond and A.L. Pritchard on July 20, 1925. Snyder (1953: 55-56) collected 4 adults and 2 young between Ingolf and Savanne in western Ontario from 1937 to 1949. Hope (1938: 14) listed a dozen collected near Favourable Lake between June 30 and Dec. 11, 1938: he saw newly hatched young for the first time on June 30. James (1980: 86) saw small numbers regularly in the Pickle Lake region during the summer of 1977. Cringan (1950: 7) observed Spruce Grouse throughout the summer in the Nikip Lake area. Lee (1978: 21) encountered a female with three flying young on one of the three quadrats studied at Big Trout Lake, on July 6, 1975. Cliff Hope collected several at Fort Severn during the summer of 1940. Manning (1952: 36) cited old records along the James Bay coast as far north as the Raft River. Schueler, Baldwin & Rising (1974: 142), however, found none at any of the James Bay or Hudson Bay sites visited, but reported them inland (hens with young) at Aquatuk Lake and Smooth Rock Falls in early July.

AUTUMN:   James R. Thurston received two from Haliburton during the fall of 1889, one on Oct. 19 and another on Oct. 26 (Thomspon, 1890: 197). Mills (1981: 45) gave two Rebecca Lake records: one on Sept. 3, 1944 by W. Mansell and another on Nov. 5, 1972 by J. Welsh. Nicholson (1981: 90) cited a few fall records from Manitoulin.

**MEASUREMENTS:**
15 to 17 ins. (Godfrey, 1966: 107)
*Wingspread:* 23 to 24 ins. (Roberts, 1955: 543)
*Weight:* ♂ 1.25 lbs. (Roberts, 1955: 543)

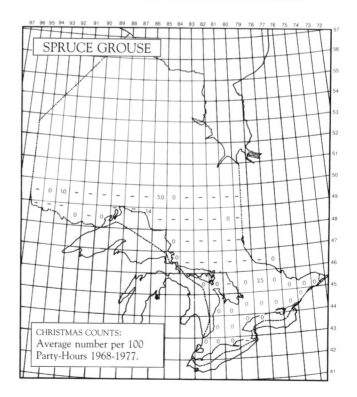

SPRUCE GROUSE

CHRISTMAS COUNTS:
Average number per 100
Party-Hours 1968-1977.

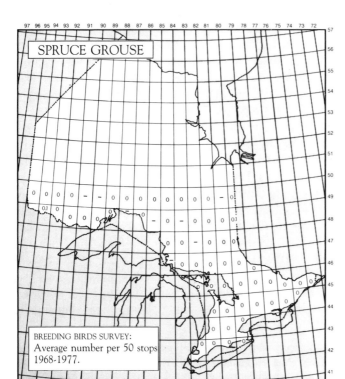

SPRUCE GROUSE

BREEDING BIRDS SURVEY:
Average number per 50 stops
1968-1977.

# WILLOW PTARMIGAN   *Lagopus lagopus*   (Linnaeus)

This is an Arctic breeder, occurring in Ontario in summer only along the narrow tundra zone bordering Hudson Bay and northern James Bay. In winter a few stragglers have come south, one as far south as Whitby. I have never seen one.

IDENTIFICATION:  The feathered feet and toes identify it as a ptarmigan. It is somewhat larger (and much more likely to be seen in Ontario) than the very similar Rock Ptarmigan, adult males of which have a black line from the beak to the eye which is lacking in the Willow Ptarmigan. Females and young have to be distinguished from Rock Ptarmigan by their larger size and heavier bill.

WINTER:  Fleming (1907: 71) mentioned a major southerly movement during the winter of 1896-97, when he recorded them as far south as Lake Nipissing: he also cited old records from Whitchurch Twp., York Co., and from the townships "back of Darlington". Two were shot at Callander in Dec., 1896, and two others were taken at Cache Bay during the same winter (Ricker & Clarke, 1939: 8): one of the latter found its way into the collection of J.H. Fleming. Smith (1957: 171) reported sightings near Cochrane and Elsas during a very severe winter about 1932 or 1933. Elder (1979: 31) recorded them at Geraldton during the winters of 1968 and 1969 when there was a major southerly influx of Sharp-tailed Grouse. Cringan (1950: 7) called it a regular winter visitor, sometimes abundant, in the Nikip Lake area. The local inhabitants of Big Trout Lake considered it to be a regular winter visitor there (Lee, 1978: 21). Manning (1952: 37) mentioned thousands wintering in the Fort Severn region.

SPRING:  Fleming (1907: 71) mentioned a specimen taken near Whitby on May 15, 1897. This was shot about 4 miles north of Whitby by Mr. Gold and later donated to the Royal Ontario Museum by J.H. Ames (Tozer & Richards, 1974: 113). Elsey (in Cringan, 1950: 7) noted a northward movement in the Asheweig region beginning April 7, 1950 and largely over by Apr. 22, with a few injured birds noted until May 11.

SUMMER:  Schueler, Baldwin & Rising (1974: 142, 145) saw none at Cochrane and none at stations along the James Bay coast, but collected a pair 54 miles north of Hawley Lake by the Sutton River on June 24, 1962 (the female contained an ovum and had a brood patch): they also noted the species at Winisk. Peck (1972: 340) found eight nests containing one to 12 eggs per nest at Cape Henrietta Maria between June 23 and 29, 1970 and wrote that they were seldom out of sight or hearing during his entire stay there. Hope collected seven and saw five others at Fort Severn between June 18 and July 23, 1940.

AUTUMN:

**MEASUREMENTS:**
*Length:* 14 to 17 ins.
(Godfrey, 1966: 110)
*Wingspread:*
*Weight:* 18 oz. (Pough,
1951: 177)

# ROCK PTARMIGAN   *Lagopus mutus*   (Montin)

The Rock Ptarmigan is a circumpolar high Arctic breeder, usually in rocky tundra regions. In Ontario they have occurred in winter along the Hudson Bay coast and to a limited extent further south in the Hudson Bay lowlands, usually in severe winters.

IDENTIFICATION:   The Rock Ptarmigan averages smaller than the Willow Ptarmigan. In winter plumage they generally have a black bar between the bill and the eye, lacking in Willow Ptarmigans. The summer plumage lacks the reddish tones of the Willow Ptarmigan, being more gray and more finely barred.

WINTER:   Lumsden (1964: 164-165) reported a small flight during the winter of 1960-61 when Michel Hunter shot about 15 as far south as the region of Shagamu Lake. A major flight occurred during the following winter, 1961-1962 when Joseph Morris saw a flock of about 30 ten miles north of Sherman Lake, about 180 miles south of the Hudson Bay coast. Seven specimens were preserved from this 1961-1962 flight: 2 males and one female killed on March 25, 1962 by Michel Hunter at Winisk and 3 males and a female taken at Fort Severn on March 25, 1962 by Elijah Stoney. Xavier Sutherland reported birds present at Cape Henrietta Maria during both the 1960-1961 flight and the 1961-1962 flight.

SPRING:   Some birds have lingered into March, as noted above.

SUMMER:

AUTUMN:

**MEASUREMENTS:**
*Length:* 12 3/4 to 15 1/2
ins. (Godfrey, 1966: 111)
Wingspread:
*Weight:* 90 averaged
425 g. (Dunning, 1984: 7)

**REFERENCE:**
Lumsden, Harry G. 1964
The Rock Ptarmigan,
*Lagopus mutus rupestris*, in
Ontario and Manitoba.
Can Field-Naturalist,
78: (3): 161 167.

# RUFFED GROUSE  *Bonasa umbellus*  (Linnaeus)

This is the bird that explodes ahead of you and whirrs off, recklessly banging into small branches, as it twists its way through the forest. In the spring you may hear the males "drumming", sounding like cold motors that finally warm up:"thump-thump-thump-thump-thrrr". Clarke (1936) wrote about the cyclic fluctuations in its populations, averaging peaks every nine or ten years. He indicated that diseases of the young during the summer were the chief cause of the declines. The usual territory size in unpastured forest he found to be about five to ten acres, with a minumum size of two acres in heavily populated areas.

IDENTIFICATION:  The blackish "ruffs" on the neck and blackish subterminal bar on the fanned tail are the essential field marks.

WINTER:  On Christmas counts this has been fairly common at most localities in southern Ontario (except at Pelee) and has been somewhat less common in northern Ontario. Stirrett (1973) had no record for Pelee at any season. Saunders & Dale (1933: 187) reported one seen in London on Dec. 28, 1915. From 1938 to 1951 Beamer reported from one to 12 on each of the Christmas counts as Meaford, he cited Wm. Linn who found a dead one on Feb. 20, 1943 with its crop stuffed with buds from apple and "Balm-of-Gilead" trees. Mills (1981: 47) reported that Ruffed Grouse were seen on every Christmas count at Huntsville since 1959 in numbers from one to 27 (average 4 or 5). Dennison (1980: 147) reported from one to 15 on 14 of 25 Christmas counts at Sault Ste. Marie (averaging 3.4 for the years present). Skeel & Bondrup-Nielsen (1978: 166) encountered small numbers regularly throughout the winter at Pukaskwa. Hope (1938: 15) listed one collected on Dec. 6, 1938 at Favourable Lake.

SPRING:  Fred Bodsworth found a nest with 12 eggs two miles east of Port Burwell on May 4, 1941 (Brooman, 1954: 15). Saunders & Dale (1933: 188) recorded four sets of eggs for Middlesex Co., containing from 9 to 13 eggs, found as early as Apr. 9, 1897 and as late as June 6, 1890. Fleming (1907: 71) called it "formerly abundant, not now common" at Toronto and reported a Toronto nest for May 23, 1893. Speirs (1977: 18) reported nests in Ontario Co. one as early as May 3 with 9 eggs and one as late as June 2 with 7 eggs. Fothergill noted the first drumming of the season at Rice Lake on Apr. 7, 1821 (Black, 1934: 145). Quilliam (1965: 67) cited an early nesting near Kingston, found by Beaupré on Apr. 20, 1896, Devitt (1967: 59) gave May 2, 1945 as his earliest nest record for Simcoe Co. found by E.L. Brereton at Shanty Bay. On May 22, 1942 three nests were reported by Beamer at Meaford, with 7 to 12 eggs per nest. J. Goltz found a nest with two eggs at Bala as early as Apr. 29, 1979 (Mills, 1981: 46). Denis (1961: 5) reported a nest with 10 eggs at Thunder Bay on May 24, 1952, where Dear (1940: 126) found 11 eggs on May 18, 1930.

SUMMER:  On Breeding Bird Surveys this species has been lacking on routes along the north shore of Lake Erie and well distributed but uncommon to rare elsewhere in Ontario. Ussher (1965: 8) called it a "scarce resident" at Rondeau. Brooman (1954: 15) saw a covey of half-grown young at Springwater Pond on July 10, 1949, but called it "uncommon" in Elgin Co. Snyder (1931: 177) found none on Long Point in 1927 or 1928 but mentioned a nest with 14 eggs found by H. Fulcher at nearby Fisher's Glen on May 3, 1931. Allin (1940: 96) saw broods of young in Darlington Twp. on June 12 and 22, 1930. Nicholson (1981: 90) saw an adult with six young at Ice Lake, Manitoulin, on July

12, 1969. Ricker & Clarke (1939: 8) reported a nest with 10 eggs at Frank's Bay on June 1, 1932 and the earliest young on June 6, 1933. Skeel & Bondrup-Nielsen (1978: 166) detailed nine breeding records for Pukaskwa, the earliest a nest with seven eggs on June 5. Snyder (1942: 127) collected male, female and four young near Sault Ste. Marie in the summer of 1931 and found nests with eggs as late as June 16. A female at Chapleau on June 8, 1937 had ten small downy young and "attacked Mr. Hope spiritedly" (Baillie & Hope, 1947: 6). Snyder (1928: 258-259) took 17 specimens at Lake Nipigon in June and July of 1923 and 1924. Baillie & Hope (1943: 8) noted a brood of newly-hatched young with the female at Amyot on June 27, 1936, while a female collected at Rossport had its stomach full of birch leaves and contained five eggs, one almost ready to be laid. Snyder (1938: 185-186) collected several in western Rainy River District in 1929 and described the drumming, which continued there until the end of June. Snyder (1953: 56) reported the first brood of the year at Kenora on June 9, 1949 and cited several records for other parts of western Ontario. Smith (1957: 177) considered this a common breeding species in the Clay Belt. On July 12, 1974 a female with flightless young was seen near Kapuskasing (Bondrup-Nielsen, 1976: 46). Snyder (1928: 21) considered them scarce at Lake Abitibi during the summer of 1925 but collected four adults and five young there. Hope (1938: 15) noted the first young at Favourable Lake on June 22 in 1938: he collected four males, four females and three young there. James (1980: 86) gave four breeding records for the Pickle Lake region, including a nest with 10 eggs on June 17, 1979. Cringan (1950: 7) often heard grouse drumming in the Nikip Lake region in early summer, 1950, but only one was actually seen. Manning (1952: 37) saw three near Moosonee between June 15 and 29, 1949 and heard them drumming as early as May 28. Schueler, Baldwin & Rising (1974: 142) found them common at Cochrane, noted some at Moosonee and Hawley Lake but had none along the coast at Fort Albany, Attawapiskat or Winisk. Peck (1972) had none at Cape Henrietta Maria. Lee (1978) had no record of them at Big Trout Lake and Hope found none at Ft. Severn in 1940.

AUTUMN: W. Wyett heard one drumming at Pukaskwa as late as Sept. 8, 1971 (Skeel & Bondrup-Nielsen, 1978: 167). Snyder (1942: 126) reported that one shot near Sault Ste. Marie on Oct. 3, 1932, had eaten a 14-inch Garter Snake. M. Hill saw a group numbering 18 at Solitaire Lake, Muskoka, during the autumn of 1958 (Mills, 1981: 47).

**MEASUREMENTS:**
*Length:* 16 to 19 ins.
(Godfrey, 1966: 109)
*Wingspread:* 23.5 to 24
ins. (Roberts, 1955: 542)
*Weight:* 4 ♂ averaged
602.5 g. 4 ♀ averaged
460 g. (Hope, 1938: 15)

**REFERENCES:**
Clarke, C.H. Douglas 1936
Fluctuations in numbers of
Ruffed Grouse, *Bonasa*
*umbellus* (Linné), with
special reference to
Ontario. Univ. Toronto
Studies, Biological Ser.

No. 41: 1-118.
Snyder, L.L. and T.M.
Shortt 1946 Variation in
*Bonasa umbellus* (Linné),
with particular reference to
the species in Canada east
of the Rockies. Can. Journ.
Res., D. 24: 118-133.
(Contr. Roy. Ont. Mus.
Zool. No. 27.)

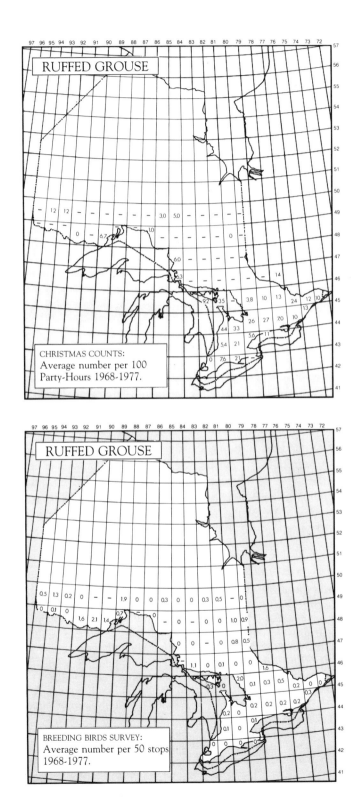

RUFFED GROUSE

CHRISTMAS COUNTS:
Average number per 100
Party-Hours 1968-1977.

RUFFED GROUSE

BREEDING BIRDS SURVEY:
Average number per 50 stops
1968-1977.

# GREATER PRAIRIE-CHICKEN
## Tympanuchus cupido    (Linnaeus)

My one experience with this interesting species in Ontario was in the Manitoulin region, watching the birds fly in to the Gore Bay airstrip at dawn. Here they performed their ritual dances with heads and wings lowered, neck tufts directed stiffly upward and orange neck sacs expanded like balloons when uttering their characteristic booming hums. They shared this display area with Sharp-tailed Grouse which had very similar displays but had pinkish-purple neck sacs, sharp-pointed tails, v-shaped dark tips to their breast feathers instead of the heavy barring of the prairie chickens. The two species hybridized with the sharp-tailed dominant, so that the population of prairie chicken dwindled and is now probably extirpated there.

IDENTIFICATION:  This is an open country bird, slightly larger than Ruffed Grouse from which it is distinguished by its erectile neck "pinnae", very different from the dark "ruffs" on the neck of the Ruffed Grouse, which is essentially a forest bird. From the Sharp-tailed Grouse it is distinguished as indicated above.

WINTER:  This bird is resident wherever found, so general references will be given here. Godfrey (1966: 113) mentioned former occurrences in Essex Co. from 1824 to 1880; in Kent Co. to 1897 and on St. Joseph's Is. from 1925. Baillie (1947: 49) reported a specimen in the Royal Ontario Museum that was shot by a railroad worker about 50 miles NW of Fort William (Thunder Bay).

SPRING:  McIlwraith (1894: 179) saw one that had just been picked up after being shot at Burlington Beach in the first week of May, 1886. Nicholson (1981: 91) gave some background relating to the arrival of this species on Manitoulin in the late 1920's or early 1930's, from Michigan by way of the chain of islands between St. Joseph's Is. and Manitoulin: also the subsequent extirpation due to hybridization with the Sharp-tailed Grouse. Five hybrids with orange sacs, but with pointed tails, were observed as recently as April and May, 1970 at Barrie Island. Denis (1961: 6) listed this as a casual, very rare visitant to Thunder Bay.

SUMMER:

AUTUMN:  John Turner shot two at the Holland River Marsh about 1875 and Edwin Sandys flushed one there about 1889 (Baillie, 1947: 49).

**MEASUREMENTS:**
Length 16 1/2 to 18 3/4 ins. (Godfrey, 1966: 113) *Wingspread:* 28 ins. (Pough, 1951: 179) *Weight:* 2 lbs. (Pough, 1951: 179)

**REFERENCES:**
Baillie, James L., Jr. 1947 Prairie Chickens in Ontario, Sylva, 3: (1): 49-51. Hamerstrom, Frances 1980 Strictly for the chickens. Iowa State Univ. Press: i-x; 1-174. This is a light-hearted but informative story of the fight to preserve this species in Wisconsin.

# SHARP-TAILED GROUSE
*Tympanuchus phasianellus*   (Linnaeus)

At dawn on April 14, 1959, Alen McCombie and I visited the Gore Bay airstrip on Manitoulin Island to watch the ritual dances of Greater Prairie Chickens and Sharp-tailed Grouse. They pirouetted around with heads and wings lowered, tails cocked and rapidly stamping feet. Three appeared to be good Prairie Chickens (heavily barred birds, with dark fan-shaped tails, orange resonating sacs, long "ear tufts" and saying "ooh-gloo-ooaah". Five looked like good Sharp-tailed Grouse, with black-arrow-tipped breast feathers, purple-lilac resonating sacs, no ear tufts, inverted V-shaped tails, and voices like a hen that has just laid an egg "ke-dac-ca-ca-ca-aa". Three seemed to be hybrids, with short ear tufts, indistinct breast barring and uttering single "glooh" notes. Others, probably females, could be seen in the rough, bordering the runway. The sharp-tails seemed to be more aggressive than the chickens (feathers sometimes flew in combats) but both kinds generally backed off after running up to opponents, content with a ritual combat. On the previous afternoon we had seen a sharp-tail sparring with a "chicken". On these occasions we had used the cars as a blind and had no trouble driving up to the birds and watching with telescope and binoculars while they paid us scant attention. When we returned with Bob Taylor on Apr. 21, 1962, the birds were much more skittish and flushed as we drove up, so Bob had to erect his photographic blind well before dawn to watch them the next morning: now the ratio was about two "chickens" to about a dozen "sharp-tails". In recent years the "chickens" appear to have been wiped out by the dominant "sharp-tails", and even they are getting hard to find.

IDENTIFICATION: The whitish, dark-tipped, spiky tail readily identifies this species from other Ontario grouse.

WINTER: Some introduced birds were seen at Prince Edward Point on Jan. 1, 1974 and Dec. 17, 1976 (Weir & Quilliam, 1980: 8). Dennison (1980: 148) noted a total of 12 on three Christmas counts of the 25 held at Sault Ste. Marie up to that time. Hazel Petty saw one near Callander on Jan. 20, 1959 (Mills, 1981: 48). The National Museum of Canada has seven specimens taken at Cochrane on Dec. 7, 1932 at the time of a major influx from the north (Smith, 1957: 171). Elder (1979: 31) reported flocks containing hundreds of birds near Geraldton during another such influx in the winters of 1968 and 1969. Goddard took one at Favourable Lake on Dec. 10, 1938 (Hope, 1938: 16). At Big Trout Lake the local inhabitants considered them regular winter visitors, in varying numbers (Lee, 1978: 21).

SPRING: Quilliam (1965: 67) recorded an unsuccessful introduction in 1949 and another on Apr. 18, 1950, at Barriefield near Kingston, while Weir and Quilliam (1980: 8) detailed further introductions in the region and observed dancing leks on May 8, 1975 and on May 22, 1977. One was shot at Bracebridge during the third week of March, 1933 following the influx of 1932 (Mills, 1981: 48). On May 27, 1956, I saw one at Dorion, noting the spiky tail and lack of bars on the breast. Elsey (in Cringan, 1950: 7) saw one in the Asheweig area on Apr. 23, 1950.

SUMMER: On June 9, 1974, a dancing lek and a nest with half-shells were found near Prince Edward Point (Weir & Quilliam, 1980: 8). Nicholson (1981: 92) reported an adult with five young, seen near Kagawong, Manitoulin, on July 2, 1977. Dear (1940: 127) mentioned a nest with nine infertile eggs taken by J. Jacob about 60 miles SW of Thunder Bay (no date given). Snyder (1938: 186) took two femals and a juvenile on June 24, 1929, and a set of five eggs was collected near Emo, Rainy River District on June 9, 1929, by Douglas Mair. Snyder (1953: 56) made a few summer observations near Kenora in 1949 and reported a young bird at Redditt on Aug. 3, 1952. James (1980: 86) saw one each summer near Pickle Lake and found three predated eggs on June 15, 1977. Baillie & Harrington (1936: 29) reported half-grown young seen on Aug. 25, 1930 by D.R. Derry between 53° and 54° N on the Manitoba boundary: they also noted chicks observed on July 24, 1925, at Twin Falls near Lake Abitibi. Todd (1963: 276) came across a party of 2/3 grown chicks "as tame as chickens" near Cochrane on Aug. 5, 1941 and cited a record of an adult with half-grown chick seen by William C. Baker near Coral Rapids on July 10, 1951. They appear to be rare or absent from the Hudson and James Bay coasts; Schueler, Baldwin and Rising (1974) reported none at any of their stations from Moosonee to Hawley Lake and Winisk: Peck (1972) had no record from Cape Henrietta Maria and Hope observed none at Fort Severn in 1940.

AUTUMN: Manning (1952: 38) noted one at Attawapiskat on Oct. 13, 1948; five at Moosonee on Sept. 27 and hundreds between there and Cochrane between Sept. 27 and Oct. 26 during this 1948 flight. Snyder (1935) mapped the major 1932 flight fanning out from Moosonee where birds were noted coming in from north and east, and as far south as Gravenhurst. Todd (1963: 277) saw a large flock near Coral Rapids on Oct. 15, 1930, and on page 275 mapped his known records for the region between Moosonee and North Bay. Goddard collected one at Favourable Lake as early as Oct. 20 and several others later (Hope, 1938: 16). Snyder (1953: 56) mentioned an autumn specimen in the Royal Ontario Museum from the Kenora area. Some 60 were reported to K.P. Morrison between Oct. 14 and 18, 1973, from Billings Twp., Manitoulin (Nicholson, 1981: 92). Mills (1981: 47-48) reported several influxes into Parry Sound and Muskoka including one in Oct. 1896 (birds shot Oct. 16 and 17 at Beaumaris, Bracebridge on Oct. 12 and Huntsville the same day and some at Emsdale) and on Oct. 13, 1949 Paul Harrington saw one at Restoule Lake. Some of the birds released near Kingston in the spring of 1972 were shot in November, 1972 and Oct. 1973 in Prince Edward Co., and one was shot on Sept. 30, 1974 at Westbrook (Weir & Quilliam, 1980: 8).

**MEASUREMENTS:**
*Length:* 16.4 to 18.5 ins.
(Godfrey, 1966: 113).
*Wingspread:* 27 ins.
(Pough, 1951: 181).
*Weight:* one ♂ 806 g.; 4 ♀ averaged 699.5 g.
(Hope, 1938: 16)

**REFERENCE:**
Snyder, L.L. 1935 A study of the Sharp-tailed Grouse. Univ. Toronto Studies, Biol. Ser. N0. 40: 1-66 (Cont. Roy. Ont. Mus. Zool. No. 6).

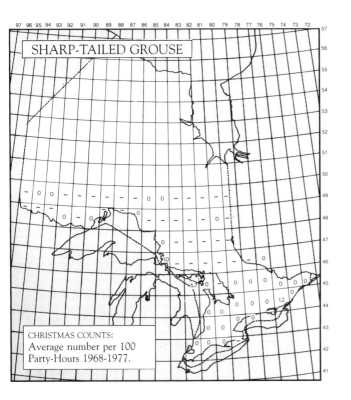

97 96 95 94 93 92 91 90 89 88 87 86 85 84 83 82 81 80 79 78 77 76 75 74 73 72

SHARP-TAILED GROUSE

CHRISTMAS COUNTS:
Average number per 100
Party-Hours 1968-1977.

# WILD TURKEY  *Meleagris gallopavo*  Linnaeus

At present the only place in Ontario where you may expect to see this species in the wild is the vicinity of the Ivy Lea bridge between Canada and the U.S.A. Introductions in other parts of southern Ontario have done well for a few years, then petered out.

IDENTIFICATION:  Turkeys are large fowl, well known as domestic birds. The wild birds differ from the domestic form (a Mexican race) in having a brown tip to the tailfeathers (white in the domestic forms), in having a bronzy irridescence on the body and in possessing a much warier disposition.

WINTER:  On the 1968-1977 Christmas counts there were fairly common on the Thousand Is. counts, uncommon on the Pickering counts (none after 1971) and seen in 1974 only on the Meaford count; all from introduced stock. Kelley (1978: 28) mentioned a release of six birds in Lambton Co. in 1950, and a subsequent count of 25 there, but no recent sightings. Ussher (1965: 8) called it a former resident of Rondeau, now extinct there. Saunders & Dale (1933: 188) wrote that it was formerly abundant near London, now extirpated.

SPRING:  A nest with 13 eggs was found in Delaware Twp., near London, in 1878 (Saunders & Dale, 1933: 188). Quilliam (1965: 69) reported the purchase of 100 chicks from which the flock at the Ivy Lea bridge originated, in April, 1960; and gave some account of their subsequent survival and spread.

**SUMMER:**   Speirs (1977: 23) gave details of two introductions by William Newman, one during the summer of 1961 from which some nested and survived unti 1967 near the Claremont Conservation Area, while some of the others survived near Glen Major until June, 1972. Devitt (1967: 61) cited archaeological and historical evidence for their former occurrence in Simcoe Co.

**AUTUMN:**   Nicholson (1981: 92-93) mentioned recent introductions on Manitoulin but held out little hope for their survival. In early September, 1954, the Toronto Anglers and Hunters Association released 56 in Clarke Twp., Durham Co., and J. Graham saw two in neighbouring Darlington Twp. during Sept., 1957 (Tozer & Richards, 1974: 116). The last birds heard of near London, were near Arva in the fall and winter of 1885 (Saunders & Dale, 1933: 188). The last one shot in Elgin Co. was taken in Nov., 1889 by Charles Axford near Eagle but great numbers occurred there in the early 1800's (Brooman, 1954: 16).

**MEASUREMENTS:**
*Length:* 36 to 48 ins.
(Godfrey, 1966: 118)
*Wingspread:* ♂ 60 ins.
(Pough, 1951: 188)
*Weight:* ♂ 15 to 20 lbs. ♀
9 lbs. (Pough, 1951: 188)

**REFERENCE:**
Clarke, C.H.D. 1948 The
Wild Turkey in Ontario.
Sylva, 4:(6): 5-12, 24.
Originally abundant in
hardwood forests adjacent
to Lake Erie, and some as
far east as York Co.
Populations declined with
the cutting of forests. There
was still good hunting as
late as 1874. The last in
Kent Co. was taken in
1900 and there were still
some in Essex Co. in 1902.

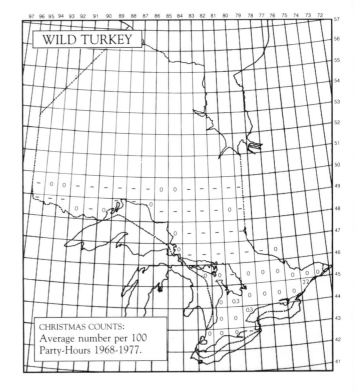

WILD TURKEY

CHRISTMAS COUNTS:
Average number per 100
Party-Hours 1968-1977.

# NORTHERN BOBWHITE   *Colinus virginianus*   (Linnaeus)

This lovely little quail with its cheery "Bob-why-it" whistle is now restricted to a few southwestern counties in Ontario. Frequent introductions into the remainder of southern Ontario seldom survive more than one winter. Clarke (1954) suggested that these failures are due to lack of proper food, adequate cover and suitable greens to provide needed vitamins. Many of the introduced birds have been from southern stock, not as resistant to cold as native stock, and which by interbreeding reduce the hardiness of native birds (or their hybrid offspring).

IDENTIFICATION: This is a plump brownish bird with a prominent white throat and white "eyebrows" (buffy in the young and females), looking not much larger than a meadowlark as it perches on a roadside fencepost. The diagnostic whistle may guide you to the bird perched conspicuously on a fencepost, or may be given in dense cover. Because our Starlings often learn to imitate this whistle on their winter sojourn in the Midwest, identification based on song alone should be viewed with some reserve.

WINTER: On Christmas counts they have been common at West Elgin, fairly common at London, St. Thomas and Blenheim, uncommon at Kettle Point, and rare to absent elsewhere in Ontario. Stirrett (1973a: 15) reported as many as 30 in winter at Pelee, but none were noted there on Christmas counts from 1968 to 1977. A covey of 11 was noted by A. Slyfield on the Oshawa-Columbus Christmas count on Dec. 26, 1946 and one came to a feeder in Oshawa from Dec. 21 to 26, 1970 (Speirs, 1977: 20). Tozer & Richards (1974: 114) cited a few recent records of birds in the Darlington and Bowmanville region. Allin (1940: 96) considered it extinct in Darlington Twp. but quoted former residents who considered it quite plentiful, coming into barnyards in winter for shelter. Devitt (1967: 60) cited from 1822 to 1910 in Simcoe Co.

SPRING: Stirrett (1973b: 16) considered it uncommon at Pelee with a maximum spring count of four on May 9.

SUMMER: On Breeding Bird Surveys they have been fairly common at Sarnia and London, uncommon at Kingsville, and absent on other routes except for one at Auburn in 1977. Stirrett (1973b: 16) had one count of 25 on June 2, but most of his summer records were of one or two birds, at Pelee. Ussher (1965: 8) called it a rare resident at Rondeau. Brooman (1954: 15) cited a record of a nest with 18 eggs taken at Aylmer by R.T. Anderson and sent to the Royal Ontario Museum: he considered it an uncommon resident of Elgin Co. Saunders & Dale (1933: 188) reported a nest with 12 eggs seen near London on June 6, 1890. Sheppard (1960: 17) wrote that it was not uncommon near Niagara many years ago but that it had practically disappeared in spite of repeated introductions. Beardslee & Mitchell (1965: 186-187) reported that about 250 were released in Lincoln Co. during the early summer of 1961 and also mentioned that two were seen near St. Catharines on June 9, 1957. Tozer & Richards (1974: 114) noted observations in Aug., 1968 and July, 1969 of birds in Clarke Twp., Durham Co. Mills (1981: 48) reported one singing in Muskoka on June 12, 1968, possibly a survivor of an introduction at Fairy Lake in 1966.

AUTUMN: Nicholson (1981: 92) mentioned releases on Manitoulin in the 1940's but knew of no survivors. Mills (1981: 48) noted one seen near Huntsville on Sept. 23,

1974. Beamer had a few reported to him from Meaford, Clarksburg and Thornbury between Sept. 21, 1941 and Dec. 2, 1946. Fleming (1907:71) wrote that "The Quail was at one time found along the north shore of Lake Ontario, certainly as far east as Port Hope . . ." Kelley (1978: 29) reported a very late nest, with 13 eggs, at Wallaceburg on Sept. 14, 1950. Stirrett (1973a: 18) had a maximum count of 20 at Pelee in fall but considered it an uncommon species there.

**MEASUREMENTS:**
*Length:* 9.5 to 10.6 ins. (Godfrey, 196: 115)
*Wingspread:* 14 1/2 to 15 1/4 ins. (Roberts, 1955: 540)
*Weight:* 7 oz. (Pough, 1951: 184)

**REFERENCE:**
Clarke, C.H.D. 1954 The Bob-White Quail in Ontario. Fed. Ont. Naturalists Bull. 63: 6-16. This details the spread following settlement, peaking in the 1840's and 1850's, when it occurred from Kingston to Georgian Bay, and the subsequent decline during cold winters with deep snows and the advent of tidy farming, until the present status was attained with native stock in southwestern Ontario and sporadic temporary sightings elsewhere following introductions.

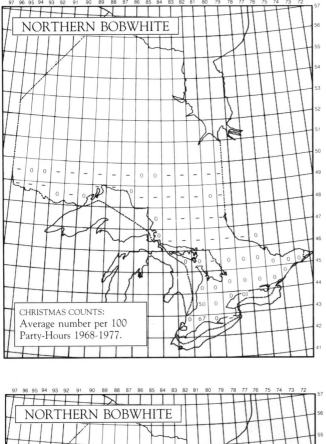

NORTHERN BOBWHITE

CHRISTMAS COUNTS:
Average number per 100
Party-Hours 1968-1977.

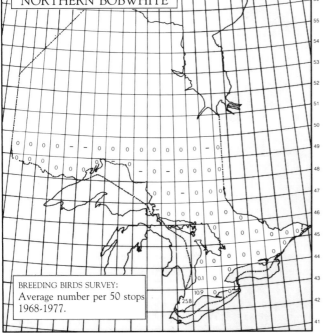

NORTHERN BOBWHITE

BREEDING BIRDS SURVEY:
Average number per 50 stops
1968-1977.

# YELLOW RAIL   *Coturnicops noveboracensis*   (Gmelin)

My first experience with this elusive rail was at a meeting of the Toronto Ornithological Club, where F.H. Emery produced one to demonstrate how the expression "skinny as a rail" may have originated. The bird passed easily between two books set up on a table about an inch apart. His account of how be came upon the bird was equally amazing. He was tapping two stones together to simulate the bird's "didi-dididi" call on a dark wet night by a cat-tail marsh when he felt something hit his raincoat and fall into his pocket. He was able to produce the rail to corroborate this improbable story! My second experience was of one picked up by a Scarborough schoolboy on his way home from school and kept alive for a few days until given to Barry MacKay.

IDENTIFICATION:   This is a tiny yellowish brown rail, looking like a small quail except for its big feet. It is usually identified by its white wing patch when flushed or by its "two-three" stone-tapping type of call.

WINTER:

SPRING:   One was banded by W.W.H. Gunn at Pelee on May 12, 1956 (Kelley, 1978: 30). Ussher (1965: 9) had a May 11 date for Rondeau. Saunders & Dale (1933: 190) reported one calling at London on May 19 and 20, 1920, found by John A. Morden. Fleming (1906: 448) had only one spring record for Toronto: a male taken by C.W. Nash on Apr. 24, 1899. Saunders (1947: 363) gave May 17 and May 25 dates for Toronto. Weir & Quilliam (1980: 9) reported several spring records from Prince Edward Point between May 16 and May 23, in the period 1973 to 1980. Devitt (1967: 64) cited records from the Holland Marsh from May 24 into the summer months. Nicholson (1981: 95) reported three Manitoulin observations, on May 17, 1970 and May 3 and 25, 1980.

SUMMER:   Fleming (1906: 448) had a Toronto record for Aug. 5, 1896. H.K. Gordon reported one at Oshawa on Aug. 30, 1934 (Tozer & Richards, 1974: 119). Devitt (1967: 64) found a nest with 7 eggs at the Holland Marsh on June 12, 1938. Snyder (1953: 57) heard them calling at Wabigoon Lake on June 2, 24 and July 4, 1937. Manning (1952: 40) saw one at Shipsands on June 17, 1949, and reported one collected there the same day by Macpherson: he cited other summer records indicating that Yellow Rails are fairly common in the Moosonee region. Schueler, Baldwin & Rising (1974: 145) found them common in sedge-grass marshes at Attawapiskat, where they collected two on June 15, 1971 and found a nest with 6 eggs on June 20, and also at Winisk where they collected one on June 27, 1971. Peck (1972: 340) reported that T.M. Shortt collected a male at Cape Henrietta Maria on July 8, 1948, and found egg shells there. C.E. Hope collected one at Ft. Severn on July 17, 1940 and estimated 100 there on the same day.

AUTUMN:   On Sept. 25, 1947, Hewitt saw one at Ship Sands (near Moosonee) (Manning, 1952: 40). G.R. White collected specimens at Rockland (east of Ottawa) on Oct. 22, 1895 and Oct. 20, 1909 and had sight records there as early as Sept. 1 in 1920 (Lloyd, 1923: 126). C.W. Nash collected a male in the Holland Marsh on Sept. 19, 1908 (Devitt, 1967: 64). Maughan (1897: 2) took a specimen at Centre Is., Toronto, on Oct. 6, 1894. Fleming (1906: 448) considered it a rare but regular fall migrant at Toronto, between Sept. 12 and Oct. 15. Speirs (1938: 54) gave Oct. 25 as the latest Toronto record. Norval G. Jones and J.C. Higgins found one dead on Sept. 21, 1908 a mile east of London and gave it to W.E. Saunders. Another was killed on Oct. 11, 1906 at Grand Bend on Lake Huron (Saunders & Dale, 1933: 189-190).

**MEASUREMENTS:**
*Length:* 6.5 to 7.7 ins.
(Godfrey, 1966: 124)
*Wingspread:* 12 ins.
(Pough, 1951: 201)
*Weight:* 2 1/4 oz. (Pough, 1951: 201)

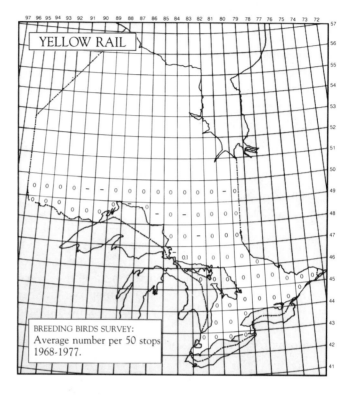

YELLOW RAIL

BREEDING BIRDS SURVEY:
Average number per 50 stops
1968-1977.

# KING RAIL   *Rallus elegans*   Audubon

This large rail has been a rare inhabitant of cat-tail marshes in southern Ontario.

IDENTIFICATION: Except for its much larger size and buffy face and cheeks, it greatly resembles the much more common Virginia Rail.

WINTER: One was reported on the Long Point Christmas count in 1976. Kelley (1978: 29) mentioned one that was caught in a muskrat trap in Dover Twp., Kent Co. on Feb. 25, 1953. Stirrett (1973a: 15) had four December records for Pelee, one as late as Dec. 31. Saunders & Dale (1933: 189) collected one on Dec. 20, 1921 near London. One was seen at Pt. Abino on Jan. 11, 1945 (Beardslee & Mitchell, 1965: 195). Fleming (1930: 67) reported one taken on Dec. 25, 1919 at Frenchman Bay. Quilliam (1965: 71) cited a specimen taken at Kingston in Dec., 1899.

SPRING: Baillie & Harrington (1936: 32) noted that a female and 13 eggs were collected at St. Anne's Is., Lambton Co. by W.E. Saunders in May, 1882. Stirrett (1973b: 16) observed two as early as Apr. 22 at Pelee. Ussher (1965: 9) had one at Rondeau as early as Apr. 3. Brooman (1954: 16) had two spring records for Elgin co., both by Harold Lancaster, one on May 22, 1946 and another on May 14, 1950. Beardslee & Mitchell (1965: 194) mentioned a nest with 10 eggs found by Ottomar Reinecke at Pt. Abino on May 30, 1894 in a swamp that has since been drained: they also had records from Rockhorse Pt. on May 25, 1952; at Lowbanks on May 14, 17 and 24, 1953 and three at Stromness on May 25, 1952. Speirs (1938: 40) had only one spring record for Toronto, on Apr. 24. The earliest Ontario Co. report was one seen on Apr. 21, 1973 at Port Perry by R.G. Dingman and J.L. Baillie (Auk, 57: 109-110). One was collected by William Carrell near Wellington, Prince Edward Co. on Mar. 28, 1917, and sent to C. W. Nash of the Ontario Provincial Museum for confirmation. Beamer mentioned a sighting of two near Bognor on May 21, 1941, by Ernie Durkin.

SUMMER: Kelley (1978: 29) reported an adult with three downy young at Pelee on Aug. 1, 1965. Harold Lancaster flushed an immature bird at his sanctuary in Aldborough Twp. Elgin Co., on Aug. 15, 1951 (Brooman, 1954: 16). Saunders & Dale (1933: 189) had three rather unsatisfactory summer records from Middlesex Co. Baillie & Harrington (1936: 32) mentioned young seen in 1921 by C.K. Rogers at Port Rowan. Sheppard (1960: 17) had a few summer reports from the Niagara region. One was noted in the Dunnville marsh on June 16, 1946 (Beardslee & Mitchell, 1965: 195). Speirs (1977: 25) reported several summer observations at Cranberry Marsh, Whitby, including a nest with eggs in May photographed by Ken. Carmichael and downy young seen on July 12, 1962 by Naomi LeVay: young were also noted there in 1970 and 1971. Ron. Weir flushed one at Prince Edward Pt. on July 15, 1973 (Weir & Quilliam, 1980: 9). Baker (1932: 100-101) had a good view of one that was also calling loudly, at Crane Lake, Bruce Peninsula, on July, 31, 1931.

AUTUMN: Lloyd (1923: 126) reported one "shot at Billing's Bridge by May and identified by G.R. White" and perhaps the same bird seen by J.H. Fleming in a local taxidermy shop (Ottawa). Devitt (1967: 62) mentioned one killed by A.D. Henderson on Nov. 9, 1896, on the Nottawasaga River. Young were seen in Oshawa's Second Marsh on Sept. 20, 1960 by A.A. Wood and on Sept. 14, 1963 by R. and A. Foster (Tozer &

Richards, 1974: 117). Fleming (1906: 447) gave three Toronto records, one taken in Sept., 1903. Speirs (1938: 54) gave a Sept. 1 date for Toronto. Ussher (1965: 9) noted one at Rondeau on Sept. 14. Stirrett (1973a: 15) had one on Nov. 20 at Pelee.

**MEASUREMENTS:**
*Length:* 15.5 to 19 ins.
(Godfrey, 1966:
122)
*Wingspread:* 24 ins.
(Pough, 1951: 196)
*Weight:* 3/4 lb. (Pough,
1951: 196)

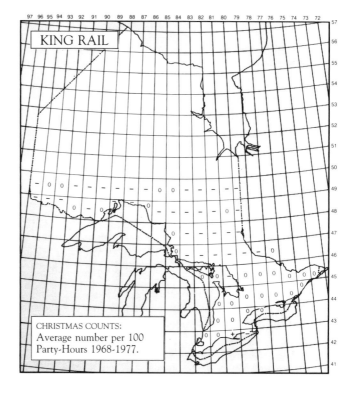

KING RAIL

CHRISTMAS COUNTS:
Average number per 100
Party-Hours 1968-1977.

# VIRGINIA RAIL   *Rallus limicola*   Vieillot

This denizen of cat-tail marshes is more frequently heard than seen. It utters a variety of notes, including a diagnostic "n'yek,n'yek", a deep gutteral "thump, thrump, thrump" (a little higher-pitched than a similar note of the King Rail) and a staccato "ka-dick, ka-dick, ka-dick" (which has been confused with the call of the Yellow Rail (even on Cornell records). Adults are sometimes glimpsed as they poke around the edges of marshes at dawn or dusk, while the downy blackish young may dash across roads through marshes at any time of day or night and may give rise to some false identifications as Black Rails.

IDENTIFICATION: The adult, with its lengthy down-curved bill, black and white barred flanks and rich cinnamon-brown breast, much resembles the much larger (and less common) King Rail, but has a bluish-gray face and crown (brownish in King Rail) and reddish base to the lower mandible (yellowish in King Rail). The calls and the blackish downies are most apt to be noted (see above).

WINTER: They have been noted on Christmas counts from marshes along the north shores of Lake Ontario and Lake Erie, most frequently at Long Point and Pelee. Speirs (1977: 26) cited about a dozen winter records from the Whitby and Oshawa marshes. Quilliam (1965: 72) gave two winter records for Kingston: Jan. 14 to Feb. 13, 1960, photographed by Martin Edwards and another from Dec. 31, 1961 to Jan. 7, 1962.

SPRING: Stirrett (1973b: 16) gave Apr. 15 as his earliest Pelee record. Ussher (1965: 9) had one at Rondeau as early as Apr. 3. Saunders & Dale (1933: 189) gave Apr. 29, 1913 and the earliest record for Middlesex Co., and cited two nest records: one with 10 eggs on May 24, 1915 and another with 9 eggs on May 25, 1916. Speirs (1938: 40) had a Mar. 14 record for Toronto. My earliest personal record was one seen at the Baseline Marsh, Whitby, on Apr. 19, 1971 (Speirs, 1977: 26). Weir & Quilliam (1980: 34) gave Apr. 24 as their 30-year average arrival date for Kingston. Devitt (1967: 63) gave May 1, 1941 as the earliest spring record for Barrie. Beamer told about one captured in a Meaford garage on May 6, 1943, and later released. Nicholson (1981: 94) reported one on Manitoulin as early as Apr. 26, 1980, with May 5 as his 11-year average arrival date.

SUMMER: This skulker is seldom reported on Breeding Bird Surveys, but there are a few reports from Long Point in the south to Manitouwadge in the north. Stirrett (1973b: 16) called it a common and regular summer resident at Pelee. Harold Lancaster found a nest with eggs on his sanctuary in Elgin Co. on June 6, 1938 (Brooman, 1954: 16). Beardslee & Mitchell (1965: 195-196) cited a record of an adult with young on June 5, 1953 at Cook's Mills, near Welland. Fleming (1906: 447) gave July 6, 1891 as a breeding date for Toronto, and reported young from July 7 to Aug. 27. Speirs (1977: 26) cited several breeding records from Ontario Co., including J.A. Edward's nest and 10 eggs as far north as Thorah Is. on May 24, 1931. Quilliam (1965: 71-72) also gave several breeding records for Kingston, and Devitt (1967: 63) had a few breeding records from Simcoe Co. Mills (1981: 50) had summer records as far north as Byng Inlet in the cottage country and reported a road kill of a downy young on July 22, 1954 at Foote's Bay found by C. Proctor. Beamer reported a nest with two eggs found near Meaford on June 17, 1941, and one brought in alive from a farm on the Owen Sound road near Meaford on June 12, 1947. I saw two adults with 5 young at South Baymouth, Manitoulin, on Aug. 5, 1934. Snyder (1942: 127) collected a downy young with its parents at McLennan, near Sault

Ste. Marie, on June 29, 1931. Denis (1961: 6) called it an occasional, very rare visitant at Thunder Bay. A.N. Boissonneau saw one at Slaughterhouses Lake, near Cochrane, on June 18, 1950 (Smith, 1957: 171). Elder (1979: 32) heard one calling from the Longlac marshes on July 18, 1970. Snyder (1953: 57) collected a male that was incubating a nest with 6 eggs, four miles north of Wabigoon, on June 30, 1937 "the most northern breeding record" for Ontario.

AUTUMN: Nicholson (1981: 94) noted three on Manitoulin as late as Oct. 2, 1976. Beamer reported one near Meaford on Sept. 5, 1949. A.J. Mitchener noted one at Collingwood as late as Nov. 14, 1954 (Devitt, 1967: 63). Weir & Quilliam (1980: 34) gave Sept. 20 as the 17-year average departure from Kingston. Speirs (1938: 54) gave Nov. 10 as the latest Toronto date. Ussher (1965: 9) gave Nov. 3 as his latest Rondeau record. Stirrett (1973a: 15) had one at Pelee as late as Nov. 23.

**MEASUREMENTS:**
*Length:* 8.9 to 10.2 ins.
(Godfrey, 1966: 122)
*Wingspread:* 14 ins.
(Pough, 1951: 198)
*Weight:* 2 1/2 oz. (Pough,
1951: 198)

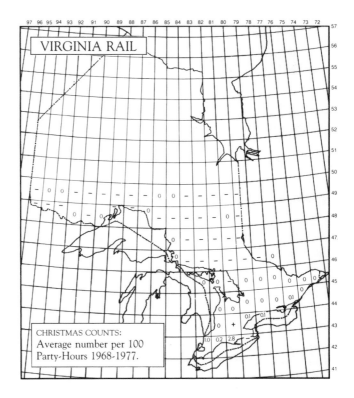

VIRGINIA RAIL

CHRISTMAS COUNTS:
Average number per 100
Party-Hours 1968-1977.

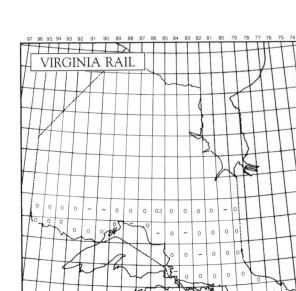

VIRGINIA RAIL

BREEDING BIRDS SURVEY:
Average number per 50 stops
1968-1977.

# SORA   *Porzana carolina*   (Linnaeus)

Soras look a bit like baby chicks that have just begun to get feathers. They move about on tip toes, enormously long toes, alertly darting this way and that, along the fringes of cat-tail marshes. They are more often heard than seen, sometimes uttering a plaintive "ker-weeee"; frequently an explosive, staccato whinny. They respond readily to play-backs of recorded calls. Like other rails they are crepuscular in habit, most active at dawn and dusk. They may be found in suitable cat-tail marshes throughout Ontario.

IDENTIFICATION: These are small rails (baby chick size), with bills shaped like chicken beaks (not long as in Virginia Rails). In adults the yellow beak contrasts strikingly with the black face and blue-gray breast and neck. Immatures lack the black face and are yellowish buff creatures (looking like big Yellow Rails, but lacking the white wing patch of that species).

WINTER: On the 1968-1977 Christmas counts they were noted only in some of the Lake Erie marshes, at Long Point, Blenheim and Pelee. Quilliam (1965: 72) reported one seen at Kingston from Jan. 15 to 18, 1961.

SPRING: Stirrett (1973b: 64) gave Apr. 25 as the earliest date for Pelee. Ussher (1965: 9) had his earliest at Rondeau on Mar. 24 and gave Apr. 17 as the 8-year average arrival date there. Saunders & Dale (1933: 189) had May 5 as the 16-year average arrival date at London, with the earliest on Apr. 26, 1915. Snyder (1931: 163) noted that one was picked up dead by the Long Point lighthouse on Apr. 17 or 18, 1930. Beamer's only spring record was at Cooksville on Apr. 15, 1941. Speirs (1938: 40) gave Mar. 14 as the earliest Toronto record, with a peak on May 17. Long (1968b: 15) noted one as early as Apr. 14, 1966 at Shoal Point Marsh, Pickering. Cyril Peake found a nest with 4 eggs on May 14, 1960 at Pickering (Speirs, 1977: 27) Weir & Quilliam (1980: 34) gave Apr. 29 as the 25-year average arrival date at Kingston, with the earliest on Apr. 14. H.P. Bingham collected a set of 6 eggs near Barrie as early as May 7, 1938: this and other nest records were given by Devitt (1967: 63): the earliest spring record there was on Apr. 27, 1957. A. Kay collected one at Lake Muskoka on May 15, 1928 (Mills, 1981: 50). Nicholson (1981: 95) gave May 7 as the 11-year average arrival date for Manitoulin, with the earliest on Apr. 24, 1977. Skeel & Bondrup-Nielsen (1978: 167) had only one record for Pukaskwa, on May 29, 1974. Denis (1961: 3) gave May 17 as the average arrival date for Thunder Bay, with the earliest on May 4, 1939. Cringan (1953a: 2) noted one at Dryden on May 16, 1953.

SUMMER: On Breeding Bird Surveys this secretive species has been rare but well distributed, from Pelee in the south to Dryden in the north. Saunders & Dale (1933: 189) cited two nest records for the London area: one with 15 eggs in two layers on May 29, 1916 and another with 7 eggs on June 24, 1902. Snyder (1931: 163) found a partially destroyed nest on Long Point on June 17, 1928: the one egg recovered was heavily incubated. Speirs (1977: 27) cited several breeding records from Ontario Co., including a nest with 10 eggs on Thorah Is., Lake Simcoe, found by J.A. Edwards on May 24, 1931. Quilliam (1965: 72) saw an adult with young at Kingston on July 13, 1958 and cited a set of 10 eggs taken by E. Beaupré on May 29, 1898. C.E. Garneau collected a nest with 12 eggs at Ottawa on July 16, 1900 (Lloyd, 1923: 126). A young bird was collected at Pickerel Lake on July 22, 1936 (Mills, 1981: 50). A young bird was collected at Pickerel

Lake on July 22, 1936 (Mills, 1981: 50). A nest with 9 eggs was found on July 12, 1970 at Bass Lake, Manitoulin (Nicholson, 1981: 95). Ricker & Clarke (1939: 9) had three early June records for Lake Nipissing. Snyder (1942: 127) reported two that were shot near Sault Ste. Marie: one on June 29, 1931 and another on Aug. 30, 1860. Dear (1940: 127) found a nest with 12 eggs at Thunder Bay on June 16, 1927. Snyder (1938: 186-187) flushed a female from a nest with 8 eggs near Emo, Rainy River, on June 21, 1929. Snyder (1953: 57) had other western Ontario records from Ingolf to Wabigoon (where a predated nest was found). Smith (1957: 171) heard Soras on June 19, 1953 at Porcupine Lake, in late July near Cochrane and on Aug. 15, 1954 at Longlac. Snyder (1928: 20) collected a male on July 3, 1925 at Lake Abitibi. Hope (9138: 16) found a nest with 10 eggs on June 16, 1938 near Favourable Lake and another with five eggs and one newly-hatched young on June 27. Ross James noted Soras at Pickle Lake on June 2 and 4, 1977. On June 3 and 4, 1947 Manning (1952: 39) saw three Soras (two collected) at North Point, on James Bay not far north of Moosonee, and he cited a nest with 10 eggs found near there by Spreadborough on July 10, 1904. A female was collected on July 9, 1948 about 20 miles south of Cape Henrietta Maria (Peck, 1972: 340). Our most northerly record is one noted at Ft. Severn on July 8, 1940 by C.E. Hope.

AUTUMN: MacLulich (1938: 13) saw one in juvenile plumage on Sept. 28, 1930 at Brent. Nicholson (1981: 95) had records to Sept. 22 on Manitoulin. In October, 1901, one was picked up alive at Emsdale and sent to J.H. Fleming (Mills, 1981: 50). Beamer's latest date for Meaford was Oct. 1, 1939. R. Tilt found one as late as Oct. 28, 1952 in the Holland Marsh (Devitt, 1967: 63). Weir & Quilliam (1980: 34) gave Sept. 19 as the 14-year average departure date from Kingston. J.M. Richards saw one as late as Oct. 19, 1963, at Whitby (Tozer & Richards, 1974: 118). Speirs (1938: 52) gave Sept. 11 as the fall peak date for Toronto, with the latest on Nov. 8. Snyder (1931: 163) reported one seen by Townson at Long Point on Oct. 14, 1927. Ussher (1965: 9) gave Oct. 21 at his latest date for Rondeau. Stirrett (1973d: 18) had a maximum count of 25 at Pelee on Sept. 15 and his latest date on Oct. 31.

**MEASUREMENTS:**
*Length:* 8.0 to 9.5 ins.
(Godfrey, 1966: 123)
*Wingspread:* 13 1/2 ins.
(Pough, 1951: 200)
*Weight:* one ♂ - 79 g. av.
of 3 ♀ - 84 g. (Hope,
1938: 16)

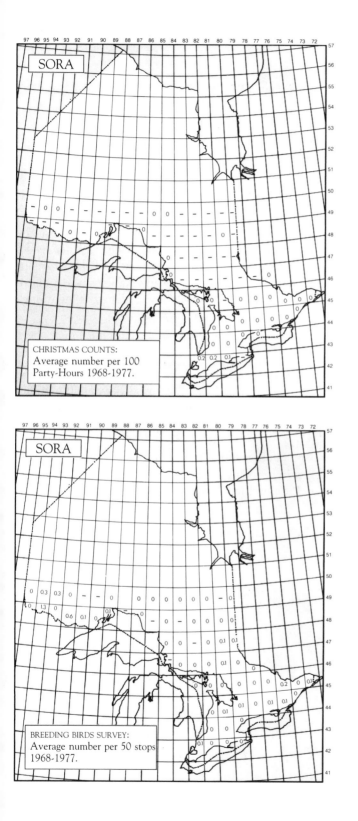

SORA

CHRISTMAS COUNTS:
Average number per 100
Party-Hours 1968-1977.

SORA

BREEDING BIRDS SURVEY:
Average number per 50 stops
1968-1977.

# PURPLE GALLINULE  *Porphyrula martinica*  (Linnaeus)

The purple Gallinule inhabits dense waterlilly growth in marshes throughout the warmer parts of North and South America, but rarely comes as far north as Ontario.

**IDENTIFICATION:**  The Purple Gallinule is about the size and build of the Common Moorhen but is a more colourful beauty, with purple-blue underparts and greenish upperparts and a distinctive blue-gray frontal shield. Its legs are yellow rather than greenish as in the Common Moorhen, and it lacks the white "waterline" of the Common Moorhen. The undertail coverts are all white, lacking the black central feathers of the moorhen.

**WINTER:**

**SPRING:**  Fleming (1906: 448) reported one that was collected at the mouth of the Rouge River, some 20 miles east of Toronto, on Apr. 8, 1892. One visited a garden feeder in Cobourg and was seen by many observers, including G. Bellerby and Mrs. H. Knapper, from Apr. 22, 1974, until captured, banded and released at nearby Willow Beach marsh on Apr. 28 (Goodwin, 1974: 796). James, McLaren & Barlow (1976: 20) mentioned other southern Ontario records between Apr. 2 and May 21.

**SUMMER:**  J. Major, G. Smith and R. Smith observed one at Pelee on July 8, 1891 (Goodwin, 1981: 935).

**AUTUMN:**  Harry Lumsden reported a juvenile female, picked up alive at Moosonee by an Indian on Oct. 18, 1971 and turned over to Lands & Forests personnel: it subsequently died and the specimen was sent to the ROM (Goodwin, 1972: 56). Weir & Quilliam (1980: 29) watched an immature bird at Kingston on Oct. 17, 1980. G.J. Clout reported two at Jordan Harbour on Sept. 11, 1937 (Beardslee & Mitchell, 1965: 199). James, McLaren & Barlow (1976: 20) had other southern Ontario records up to Oct. 27.

Godfrey (1966: 126) mentioned two old, undated records for Ontario: One was killed by a boy at the St. Clair flats about 1883 and identified by J.H. Garnier. Another was taken at Guelph about 1894.

**MEASUREMENTS:**
*Length:* 12 to 14 ins.
(Godfrey, 1966: 125)
*Wingspread:* about 22 ins.
(Terres, 1980: 755)
*Weight:* 20 ♂ averaged
257.g., 8 ♀ averaged
215 g. (Dunning, 1984: 8).

# COMMON MOORHEN   *Gallinula chloropus*   (Linnaeus)

This is the Moorhen of the Old World, where it frequents the lawns about pools in parks and estates. Our bird is less tolerant of man and is a denizen of cat-tail marshes, along with herons and rails, etc. In late summer, families may be seen, swimming like clockwork ducks or racing along mudflats by the edge of marshes.

IDENTIFICATION: The scientific name suggests that they look like "little hens with green feet", but omits the fact that their green "stockings" are embellished with "red garters". Adults with their flashy vermilion frontal plates and bills (tipped with yellow) are unmistakable. At a distance the white "water line" that separates the wings from the feathers of the sides, distinguishes them from the white-billed American Coots. The feathered young lack the brilliant bill and frontal plate of the adults but can still be told from coots by the white water lines (the sides of young coots are dark gray, lacking the white lines along the sides). Babies of both are blackish downies, with red bills and "bald as a coot". Young moorhens have a spur at the bend of the wing (a reminder of their reptilian ancestry). Downy young coots have reddish fuzz on their upper parts, especially about the face while young moorhens have whitish "beards".

WINTER: On the 1968-1977 Christmas counts they were tallied once at Blenheim and once at Long Point, not elsewhere. J.L. Baillie had a Toronto record as late as Dec. 7 (Saunders, 1947: 363). Speirs (1977: 30) reported two winter records for Whitby: one on Jan. 2, 1953 by J.M. Barnett and the other on Dec. 9, 1967 by Tom Hassall. Weir & Quilliam (1980: 34) gave a Feb. 4 record for Kingston, while Quilliam (1965: 73) mentioned one seen there on the 1956 Christmas count by K.F. Edwards.

SPRING: Stirrett (1973b: 16) gave Apr. 13 as the earliest Pelee record, with a peak of 18 on May 17. Kelley (1978: 30) mentioned a nest with eggs at Pelee as early as May 9, 1973. Ussher (1965: 9) gave Apr. 21 as the 12-year average arrival date for Rondeau, with the earliest on Apr. 1. Brooman (1954: 16) gave Apr. 20, 1948 as the earliest Elgin Co. observation. Saunders & Dale (1933: 190) gave May 13 as the 8-year average arrival date at London, with the earliest on May 1, 1914: he considered it rare there as did Brooman in Elgin Co. Saunders (1947: 363) gave Apr. 27 as his 13-year average for Toronto arrivals, with the earliest on March 7. Speirs (1938: 44) gave May 8 as the spring peak date for Toronto. Audrey Ross saw one at Whitby as early as March 27, 1967 and Cyril Peake found a nest with 3 eggs as early as May 15, 1960 on Duffin Creek (Speirs, 1977: 30). Quilliam (1965: 73) gave Apr. 21 as the 14-year average arrival date for Kingston, the earliest on Apr. 6, 1955. Devitt (1967: 65) gave May 1, 1941 as the earliest Barrie date. Nicholson (1981: 95) had just two spring records for Manitoulin: one by R.R. Tasker in Burpee Twp. on May 24, 1969 and two at Spring Bay by Donald B. Ferguson in spring, 1968.

SUMMER: On Breeding Bird Surveys, they were seen only on the routes near Lake Erie and in southeastern Ontario, with the greatest numbers on the Perth and Picton routes. Stirrett (1973d: 18) had a peak of 40 at Pelee on Aug. 25. Snyder (1931: 164) found three nests at Long Point, one with 13 eggs on June 10, 1927. Fleming (1906: 448) reported a downy young taken at Toronto on June 6, 1895. Tozer & Richards (1974: 120) had a nest with six young as early as June 6, 1970 at Oshawa's Second Marsh. Allin (1940: 97) found a nest with 8 eggs on June 14, 1926 in Baker's Bog, Darlington Twp.

Snyder (1941: 48) collected a set of fresh eggs on May 31, 1930 at Hallowell, Prince Edward Co. and noted downy young there on June 27. W.E. Saunders took a nest with 7 eggs at Kars (near Ottawa) on July 9, 1890 and P.A. Taverner found a nest with 3 hatching eggs and one downy young in mid-June, 1918 at the mouth of Kemptville Creek (Lloyd, 1923: 126). Devitt (1967: 64-65) gave details of several nest in Simcoe Co., one set of eggs as early as June 2, 1918 at Barrie. On June 16, 1978, one was seen from Hwy 69 between Rock Island Lake and Still River, Parry Sound District (Mills, 1981: 51). Nicholson (1981: 95) saw one at Bass Lake, Manitoulin, on June 20, 1970: his only summer record. F.W. McKee collected one at the mouth of the Sturgeon River, Lake Nipissing, about 1921 (now in the Royal Ontario Museum according to Baillie & Harrington, 1936: 33). Denis (1961: 6) called it a casual, very late, visitant to Thunder Bay. Schueler, Baldwin & Rising (1974: 142) listed it as present at Winisk in 1965, *without comment!*

AUTUMN:   On Sept. 11, 1974, W. Mansell reported one seen near Huntsville (Mills, 1981: 51). Atkinson collected one as late as Oct. 23, 1890, at Holland Marsh (Devitt, 1967: 64). Wier & Quilliam (1980: 34) gave Oct. 24 as the 25-year average departure date from Kingston. Snyder (1941: 48) reported nine on Sept. 14, 1931 in Prince Edward Co. Tozer & Richards (1974: 120) had one as late as Nov. 26, 1970 at Oshawa's Second Marsh. Speirs (1938: 52) gave Sept. 17 as the fall peak at Toronto, while Saunders (1947: 363) gave Oct. 14 as his 13-year average departure date with the latest on Oct. 29. Sheppard (1960: 18) suggested that some linger near Niagara as late as the first week of November. Brooman (1954: 16) noted one at St. Thomas on Sept. 22, 1940. Ussher (1965: 9) had one as late as Oct. 31 at Rondeau, but his 7-year average departure date was Sept. 17. Kelley (1978: 30) noted an adult with several small young at Big Creek, Essex Co., as late as Sept. 19, 1964. Stirrett (1973d: 19) gave Oct. 23 as his latest Pelee record.

**MEASUREMENTS:**
*Length:* 12 to 14.8 ins.
(Godfrey, 1966: 126)
*Wingspread:* 21 ins.
(Pough, 1951: 204)
*Weight:* 14 oz. (Pough, 1951: 204)

**CLUTCH SIZE:**
In Ontario Co. 62 sets totalled 451 eggs (about 7 per set): the largest set contained 18 eggs (Speirs, 1977: 30).

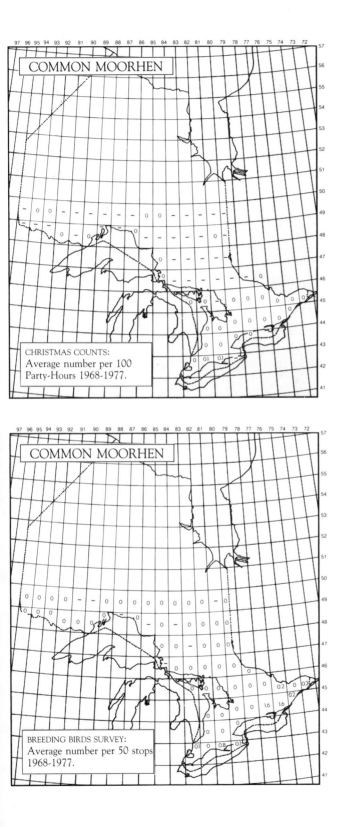

COMMON MOORHEN

CHRISTMAS COUNTS:
Average number per 100
Party-Hours 1968-1977.

COMMON MOORHEN

BREEDING BIRDS SURVEY:
Average number per 50 stops
1968-1977.

# AMERICAN COOT   *Fulica americana*   Gmelin

Tennyson noted that brooks may arise in marshes, the "haunts of coot and hern" but coots and herons are even more plentiful in the larger estuarial marshes where rivers empty into lakes. Several writers have noted recent increases in the numbers in Ontario, where large flocks gather in fall and linger until freezeup.

IDENTIFICATION: Coots look a good deal like Common Moorhens but have lobed toes (useful for swimming but seldom seen). They lack the vivid colours and the white "water line" of the moorhens. Their white beaks can be seen at great distances and are perhaps their best field marks.

WINTER: On the 1968-1977 Christmas counts they were common at Blenheim and Long Point, becoming rare north to Ottawa and Meaford. Stirrett (1973a: 15) had Pelee records to Dec. 31, and 32 were there on Feb. 10. Ussher (1965: 9) had a Dec. 8 date for Rondeau. Speirs (1977: 31) cited several winter records for the Lake Ontario marshes between Pickering and Oshawa. Weir & Quilliam (1980: 34) mentioned a Feb. 4 record for Kingston. Nicholson (1981: 96) had winter records for Manitoulin on Dec. 26, 1971 and two there on Feb. 9, 1980, one of which remained until Feb. 24.

SPRING: Kelley (1978: 30) reported a nest with 8 eggs as early as May 15, 1953 at St. Luke's Marsh, Kent Co. Stirrett (1973b: 16) had a peak count of 750 at Pelee on Apr. 15, with the earliest one on March 7. Ussher (1965: 9) gave March 22 as the 15-year average arrival date at Rondeau with the earliest on March 5. Saunders & Dale (1933: 190) gave Apr. 20 as the 11-year average arrival date at London, the earliest on March 27, 1916. Bent (1926: 368) gave earliest spring records for Ontario as March 15, 1885 at Dunnville and March 16, 1884 at Port Rowan. A.R. Muma found 22 dead below Niagara Falls between Apr. 24 and May 1, 1949 and one as early as March 7 (Sheppard, 1960: 18). Several observers from Buffalo saw three young on May 17, 1953 at Dunnville Marsh and five young the same year at Mud Lake on May 24 (Beardslee & Mitchell, 1965: 201). Speirs (1938: 44) gave Apr. 27 as the spring peak date for Toronto, while Saunders (1947: 363) had Apr. 14 as his 10-year average arrival date. The earliest spring record for Ontario Co. was on March 6, 1971 when Dave Calvert found one at Whitby Harbour: the spring peak is about Apr. 20, and Ron Tozer found downy young at Cranberry Marsh as early as May 26, 1969 (Speirs, 1977: 31). Snyder (1941: 48) had Prince Edward Co. records from March 28 to May 22. Weir & Quilliam (1980: 34) gave March 22 as the 23-year average arrival date at Kingston and May 11 as the corresponding spring departure date. Devitt (1967: 65) reported the 8-year average arrival date for Barrie as Apr. 23, with one at Collingwood as early as March 27, 1960. Beamer's earliest date for Meaford was Apr. 11, 1948. Mills (1981: 51) had only one spring record for Muskoka, on May 10, 1980 at Bala. The earliest Manitoulin record was on March 27, 1976 (Nicholson, 1981: 96). Skeel & Bondrup-Nielsen (1978: 167) had just two spring records for Pukaskwa, one on Apr. 21, 1977 and one on Apr. 25, 1974.

SUMMER: On the 1968-1977 Breeding Bird Surveys they were noted several times at Port Dover, once at Dunnville and once at Atikokan. Stirrett (1973c: 15) had no June record for Pelee but a few in July and August. Snyder (1931: 165) had only two summer records for Long Point. G.R. White reported coots nesting near Ottawa (Lloyd, 1923: 126). Devitt (1967: 54) cited several nest records for Simcoe Co. between June 16 and July 14.

A. Kay noted breeding at Port Sydney, Muskoka (Baillie & Harrington (1936: 34). Nicholson (1981: 96) had just one summer record for Manitoulin, on June 11, 1977. J.W. Aldrich saw one at Fish Bay. Lake Nipissing in mid-June, 1938 (Ricker & Clarke, 1939: 9). Baillie & Hope (1947: 7) cited summer records for Sudbury District, but saw none themselves. Morris Green listed this species for Franz in June, 1924 (Baillie & Hope, 1943: 8). Smith (1957: 171) heard two near Hearst on June 2, 1954 and flushed one at Lillabelle Lake, Cochrane, on Aug. 18, 1954. Dear (1940: 127) found two nests (with 7 and 8 eggs respectively) at Whitefish Lake, Thunder Bay, on May 25, 1931. Snyder (1953: 57) reported a mid-summer observation near Kenora in 1930. Baillie & Harrington (1936: 34) reported one taken at Moosonee in 1926 by Sam Waller. Hugh Conn took one at Fort Severn but considered it very rare there (Manning, 1952: 40). James, McLaren & Barlow (1976: 21) noted summer occurences north to Lake River, Kapuskasing and Red Lake.

AUTUMN: Goddard collected a male at Favourable Lake on Sept. 17, 1938 (Hope, 1938: 17). Smith (1957: 171) reported them as common at Gogama in fall. Skeel & Bondrup-Nielsen (1978: 168) noted one seen at Marathon on Oct. 10, 1976. Ricker & Clarke (1939: 9) reported one taken in the West Arm of Lake Nipissing during Sept. 1925. A. Kay took one at Port Severn on Sept. 18, 1900, the latest fall record for Muskoka (Mills, 1981: 51). Beamer reported one killed at Meaford as late as Nov. 12, 1938. Devitt (1967: 65) noted that one was taken at Barrie on Nov. 10, 1962. Weir & Quilliam (1980: 34) gave Sept. 28 as the 22-year average fall arrival date at Kingston, and Quilliam (1965: 73) mentioned an unusually large raft of 500 there on Nov. 8, 1953. Snyder (9141: 48) had fall records from Prince Edward Co. from Aug. 30 to Nov. 22 (when 20 were seen). On Sept. 10, 1967, I saw three small downy young at Corner Marsh, Pickering: the fall peak there is in the first week of November (Speirs, 1977: 31). Speirs (1938: 52) gave Oct. 22 as the fall peak for Toronto where Saunders (1947: 363) had Nov. 19 as his 13-year average departure date. Townson saw "hundreds" on Oct. 28, 1927 in Long Point Bay (Snyder, 1931: 165). Ussher (1965: 9) gave Nov. 19 as his 8-year average departure date from Rondeau. Stirrett (1973a: 15) had a maximum of 3000 at Pelee on Nov. 26. Kelley (1978: 30) saw an adult with two downy young in the Big Creek marshes, Essex Co. on Sept. 10, 1966.

**MEASUREMENTS:**
*Length:* 13 to 16 ins.
(Godfrey, 1966: 127).
*Wingspread:* 26 ins.
(Pough, 1951: 205).
*Weight:* 1 1/4 lbs. (Pough,
1951: 205).
*Note:* In Ontario Co. 53
sets contained 361 eggs
*averaged* 7 per set but the
*mode* was 9 per set.
(Speirs, 1977: 31).

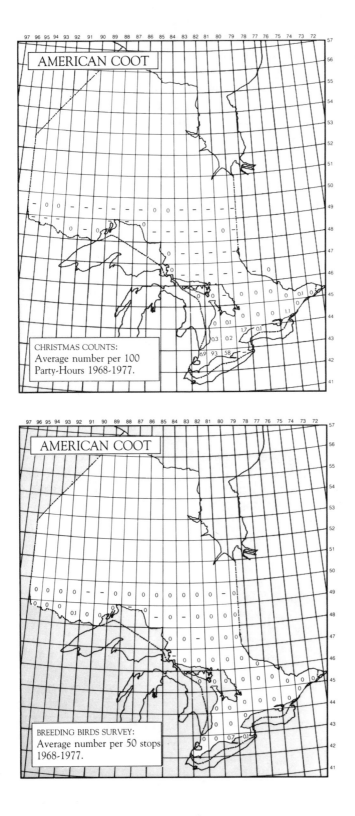

AMERICAN COOT

CHRISTMAS COUNTS:
Average number per 100
Party-Hours 1968-1977.

AMERICAN COOT

BREEDING BIRDS SURVEY:
Average number per 50 stops
1968-1977.

# SANDHILL CRANE   *Grus canadensis*   (Linnaeus)

Sandhill Cranes have been very rare birds in Ontario during the past century but more frequent sightings in recent years suggest some increase in their population. They breed in several places in Michigan and a small breeding group west of James Bay in Ontario has recently been discovered.

**IDENTIFICATION:** This is a large gray wader with a red crown and droopy tail, distinguished from the much more common Great Blue Heron (often misnamed "crane") by its manner of flight with neck stretched out (not folded in an S-curve as in herons). Cranes have a faster wing beat than herons and frequently soar high in the heavens. Unlike the simple "grauk" of the Great Blue Heron, the voice of the crane is a thrilling "rrrooo-rrrooo-rrrooo", with a definite Scottish "burr", perhaps even a suggestion of Spanish castenets.

**WINTER:** William Rapley saw one at the Metro Zoo during the Toronto Christmas count on Dec. 28, 1980. This bird wintered there, flying out to some unknown destination each evening and returning to spend the day with the zoo's waterfowl and various "free-loading Mallards and Canada Geese" that came to enjoy the free meals. I saw it there on Jan. 26 and again on Feb. 18, when Dr. Rapley took my wife Doris to see it. For many Toronto bird watchers this was their one opportunity to see a wild crane.

**SPRING:** Stirrett (1973b: 16) gave only two Pelee records: one on May 12, 1967, the other on May 15, 1968. Kelley (1978: 29) mentioned one at Wallaceburg from Mar. 31 to Apr. 15, 1973. Ussher (1965: 8) called it a very rare migrant at Rondeau, between Apr. 10 and May 16. George A. Scott watched one soaring over fields near the Oshawa Second Marsh on May 8, 1955 (Tozer & Richards, 1974: 116). Stuart Peters saw two on Wolfe Is. in 1953 (Quilliam 1965: 70). Weir & Quilliam (1980: 8) gave two records from Prince Edward Point, one on May 18, 1979 and one on Apr. 19, 1980 and another record from South Bay, near Kingston, by Kenneth Edwards on May 9, 1980. Nicholson (1981: 93) cited several recent sightings from Manitoulin between Apr. 15 and May 24. Three were seen at Pukaskwa on May 5, 1977 (Skeel & Bondrup-Nielsen, 1978: 167). I saw three circling over the eastern outskirts of Sault Ste. Marie on May 19, 1954 and three flying over Highway 17 near Pancake Bay on May 25, 1978. Bruce Atkinson reported to me seeing and hearing one migrating over the Dorion hatchery on May 14, 1971. Elder (1979: 31) called this a rare and irregular spring and fall migrant over Geraldton. Elsey (in Cringan, 1950: 8) saw his first on May 9, 1950, in the Asheweig area. Manning (1952: 39) gave evidence that they arrived at Ft. Severn in May and bred there in the late 1700's. Schueler, Baldwin & Rising (1974: 145) noted one at Shipsands Is. near Moosonee on May 31 and June 3, 1972. Lumsden (1971: 288-291) reported one at Kinoje Lake as early as Apr. 21, 1968 and flushed one from a nest with one egg on May 7, which contained two eggs when revisited on May 9.

**SUMMER:** Baillie (1958: 4) cited a report of a pair with two young, seen during the summer of 1862 at Murphy's Landing, Lake St. Clair, Kent Co. Mills (1981: 49) mentioned an old specimen from Beaumaris, Muskoka, now in the National Museum of Canada and cited a report by R. Harris of one seen on Aug. 11, 1972 near Parry Sound. Nicholson (1981: 93-94) reported breeding on islands near Manitoulin since 1977 and two adults seen at an inland lake on the island during June and July, 1978. Cringan (1950: 7-8) heard cranes on June 30, 1950, on the Petownikip River; he saw two concerned individuals on Aug. 3 in a tamarack muskeg, and heard two at the mouth of the Windigo River, all in the Nikip Lake area: he also cited a report by Hawkins in June, 1950, from the Wawa Lakes north of Kapuskasing. Lee (1978: 21) reported that cranes summered in the Big Trout Lake region (based on reports by local hunters). Lumsden (1971) summarized and mapped the records from northern Ontario, with records as far south as Longlac and north to Ft. Severn east of Moosonee near the Quebec boundary and west of Sandy Lake near the Manitoba boundary, with breeding evidence from the region west of James Bay in the drainages of the Moose, Albany and Attawapiskat Rivers: he made his studies at Kinoje Lake in this area.

AUTUMN: Lumsden (1971: 285-286) cited two fall records from northern Ontario: four seen as late as Sept. 26, 1958 at Bearhead Lake on the Winisk River by R. Malloch and three or four seen as late as Sept. 11, 1965 at Pitikupi Lake (about half way between Moosonee and Longlac). Nicholson (1981: 93) had Manitoulin records between Sept. 11 and Oct. 7. Devitt (1967: 62) reported that they were common in the cornfields of the Huron Indians in the early 1660's (four bones from a site near Coldsteam are in the ROM): a more recent sighting by Dale Nash in Oct., 1960, concerned one seen with his cattle for two weeks, in Conc. 6, Orillia Twp., Simcoe Co. Betty Hughes and Mary L'Estrange photographed one at Black River, near Kingston, on Oct. 5, 1978 (Weir & Quilliam, 1980: 8). One frequented fields near Maple during October, 1977 and was seen by many observers: Doris and I saw it on Oct. 19 as it flew north just west of Hwy. 400. Saunders & Dale (1933: 189) cited a report from a London newspaper of one taken in fall, 1876. Ussher (1965: 8) mentioned an October record for Rondeau. Stirrett (1973d: 18) had one fall record for Pelee, on Oct. 5, 1957.

**MEASUREMENTS:**
*Length:* 40-48 ins.
(Roberts, 1955: 547)
*Wingspread:* 80-90 ins.
(Roberts, 1955: 547)
*Weight:* 7 3/4 to 12 3/4 lbs. (Roberts, 1955: 547) Some Ontario specimens belong to a smaller race for which Roberts quotes Forbush, giving average measurements of:
*Length:* 36.4 ins.
*Wingspread:* 73.72 ins.

**REFERENCES:**
Lumsden, Harry G. 1971 The status of the Sandhill Crane in northern Ontario. Can. Field-Nat., 85: (4): 285-293. This has a map on p. 286 showing the distribution in northern Ontario of sight records, breeding records and specimen records. There are also photographs of two nests, showing habitat and close-ups of the nests and eggs. There are tables giving measurements of the eggs and of some specimens.
Walkinsaw, Lawrence H. 1949 The Sandhill Cranes. Cranbrook Inst. Sci., Bull. No. 29; i-x; 1-202.

# WHOOPING CRANE   *Grus americana*   (Linnaeus)

These magnificent birds may have been common in the early 1660's in Ontario, but are now an endangered species even in their prairie stronghold. James, McLaren & Barlow (1976: 19) mentioned sight records from Toronto prior to 1887.

**IDENTIFICATION:**  This was our largest (tallest) bird, somewhat larger than the Great Blue Heron. It has white plumage, except for black wing tips and the red face and crown. The long legs and neck are held straight out in flight. The rusty-tinged young might be confused with the smaller Sandhill Crane, but are white below, not gray or brown as are the Sandhills.

**WINTER:**

**SPRING:**  Mills (1981: 49) cited J.H. Fleming's note that "A pair were seen by Mr. Handy at Emsdale in 1895;—" and reported a more recent report by Mrs. J. Coons who "saw one white bird among four Blue Herons on Fish Lake east of Novar. Much larger than the Blue Herons. When in flight it showed black under the wings. It also had red on the face." This was on Apr. 23, 1975 after strong gales.

**SUMMER:**  L.J. Boughner reported one at Long Point ["Long Island - Lake Erie"] on June 29, 1898, without comment or description (Snyder, 1931: 222).

**AUTUMN:**  Quilliam (1965: 70) cited Champlain's mention of "cranes white as swans" in Sept., 1615 and a more recent, but still old record of "white cranes" near Loughborough Lake, on Oct. 28, 1815, both near Kingston. She also gave details of the only Ontario specimen: during the autumn of 1871, one frequented a small shallow lake in Camden Twp., Addington Co., and was finally shot by Wesley Potter on Sept. 27, 1871. The bird was mounted and loaned to Queen's University by Mrs. John Ewart about 1914. It is still in their collection.

**MEASUREMENTS:**
*Length:* 49 to 56 ins.
(Roberts, 1955: 547)
*Wingspread:* 76 to 92 ins.
(Roberts, 1955: 547)
*Weight:* 8 3/4 to 12 lbs.
(Roberts, 1955: 547)

# BLACK-BELLIED PLOVER   *Pluvialis squatarola*   (Linnaeus)

This is the Gray Plover of the Old World, an apt description of the fall and winter birds. When lake levels are low in Ontario, exposing broad beaches and mud flats, we often see good numbers, but in years of high water they may be hard to find. Seldom do we see in Ontario the large flocks found on some Atlantic coast beaches. They pass through very quickly in late May to breed in the Arctic but may linger for weeks or months on their way south to Central and South American beaches.

IDENTIFICATION:   This is the largest of our plovers, noticeably bigger than a Killdeer. In flight look for the black axillars, the best field mark in any plumage. In spring, the black throat and breast contrast strongly with the pearly gray crown and the white undertail coverts. The three-syllabled "tee-ooh-ah" whistle is diagnostic.

WINTER:   Beardslee & Mitchell (1965: 208) reported one found on Dec. 10, 1941 on the Canadian shore of Lake Erie by Doyle.

SPRING:   Stirrett (1973b: 16) reported 10 on Apr. 24 as the earliest Pelee record with one as late as June 4. Kelley (1978: 32) mentioned a flock of about 1500 in Essex Co. on May 13, 1973. Ussher (1965: 10) had Rondeau records from May 7 to May 30, but the average stay there was from May 18 to May 26. Brooman (1954: 17) had very few spring records from Elgin Co., between May 11 in 1952 and May 23 in 1948. Saunders & Dale (1933: 191) called it "very rare in both spring and fall" near London with 7 on May 26, 1924 as the largest number seen. Snyder (1941: 171) had two at Long Point as early as May 7, 1928. Speirs (1938: 40, 44) gave May 1 as the earliest Toronto record with a peak on May 27. Harry Kerr saw six at Squires Beach, Pickering, on May 1, 1976, but the peak there is usually about May 26 (Speirs, 1977: 36). Snyder (1941: 49-50) reported 25 on May 29 and one on June 4 in 1930, in Prince Edward Co. Weir & Quilliam (1980: 34) gave Apr. 29 as the earliest Kingston record, with the 26-year average arrival date on May 17. Devitt (1967: 68) gave May 25 as the 8-year average arrival date at Wasage Beach, the earliest on May 16, 1940 at Barrie and the latest spring record on June 6, 1953. Beamer had only one spring record at Meaford, on May 22, 1949. K. Ketchum saw one on Leland Is., off Pointe au Baril, on May 20, 1962, the only spring report for the cottage country (Mills, 1981: 53). Nicholson (1981: 98) had spring records from Manitoulin from May 6 (1972) to May 29 (1971), with a 12-year average arrival date on May 20 and a high count of 50 on May 27, 1974. Baillie & Hope (1943: 9) collected a female at Rossport on May 29, 1936. Denis (1961: 4) gave May 23 as the average arrival date for Thunder Bay, with the earliest on May 12, 1955. Manning (1952: 43) saw 50 in 3 hours on May 27, 1947 near Moosonee, 65 in 6 hours at North Point from June 2 to 6, 1947, 80 in 7 hours at Big Piskwanish from June 9 to 12, 1947 and 65 in 5 hours at Long Ridge Point from June 14-15, 1947: he considered these to be northbound migrants. Hope (1938: 18) collected a male at Favourable Lake on May 31, 1938. Lee (1978: 22) saw only one at Big Trout Lake, on June 1, 1975.

SUMMER:   Stirrett (1973c: 15) had two returning birds at Pelee on July 29 with the largest group of 10 on Aug. 26. J.P. Kleiman *et al* noted one at Pelee as early as July 4, 1971 (Goodwin, 1971: 852). Ussher (1965: 10) had the earliest Rondeau record on Aug. 2, with the average arrival on Aug. 17. Snyder (1931: 171) reported one at Long Point on June 16, 1927. Beardslee & Mitchell (1965: 205) reported one at Rockhouse Point,

Lake Erie, on June 16, 1957, seen by R.F. Andrle *et al.* J.L. Baillie (in Saunders, 1947: 364) had a June 25 record at Toronto and a returning one as early as Aug. 6. Fleming (1906: 451) reported one at Toronto as early as July 23, 1890. Naomi LeVay had northbound birds at Cranberry Marsh as late as June 10, 1950 and returning birds as early as July 24, 1960 (Tozer & Richards, 1974: 124). Weir & Quilliam (1980: 34) had northbound birds as late as June 17 at Kingston and returning birds as early as July 30. Devitt (1967: 67) reported southbound migrants at Wasaga Beach as early as Aug. 1, 1936. Nicholson (1981: 98) reported one on Aug. 8, 1971, as the earliest return to Manitoulin. Schueler, Baldwin & Rising (1974: 142) reported them as common at Moosonee and noted the species at Attawapiskat and Winisk. C.E. Hope and T.M. Shortt saw a few migrants between Ft. Albany and Big Piskwanish between July 15 and 25, 1944 (Manning, 1952: 42).

AUTUMN: Stirrett saw 16 at Attawapiskat as late as Oct. 10 (Manning, 1952: 42). Elder (1979: 32) called it a fairly common fall migrant at Geraldton. Skeel & Bondrup-Nielsen (1978: 169) had only one Pukaskwa sighting, on Sept. 19, 1977. Speirs & Speirs (1947: 28) had fall sightings at North Bay from Aug. 29 to Oct. 22 in 1944, with 15 there on Sept. 13. The 12-year average fall arrival on Manitoulin was Sept. 19 and the latest record on Nov. 8 (Nicholson, 1981: 98). Mills (1981: 53) had several fall records from the cottage country between Aug. 20 and Oct. 8. Beamer had just three fall records from Meaford: 10 on Aug. 28, 1948, and single birds on Sept. 5, 1943 and Oct. 28, 1948. Devitt (1967: 67) reported a sighting of 200 by Frances Westman at Edenvale on Sept. 25, 1966 and the latest fall sighting at Collingwood on Nov. 12, 1960 by Alf. Mitchener. C.E. Johnson saw four at Galetta, near Ottawa, on Nov. 4, 1920 (Lloyd, 1923: 127). Weir & Quilliam (1980: 34) gave Nov. 6 as the 26-year average departure date from Kingston, with the latest on Nov. 21. John Townson saw flocks of six to 40 in Prince Edward Co. from Sept. 13 to Oct. 29 in 1931 (Snyder, 1941: 50). George A. Scott saw one at Oshawa as late as Nov. 24, 1957, but the peak of the fall flight is generally in mid-October (Speirs, 1977: 36). Speirs (1938: 52, 54) gave Oct. 5 as the fall peak at Toronto with the latest on Nov. 13. Ussher (1965: 10) gave Oct. 26 as the average departure date from Rondeau, with one as late as Nov. 7. Stirrett (1973d: 18) gave Nov. 16 as the latest date for Pelee.

**MEASUREMENTS:**
*Length:* ♂ 274-295 mm.
♀ 274-307 mm. (Snyder,
1931: 172)
*Wingspread:* 22 to 25 ins.
(Roberts, 1955: 569)
*Weight:* ♂ 170-202 g. ♀
169-258 g. (Snyder,
1931: 172).

# LESSER GOLDEN-PLOVER   *Pluvialis dominica*   (Müller)

These delightful long distance migrants tend to come north from their South American wintering grounds via the Mississippi Valley and go south from their Arctic breeding areas via the Atlantic, missing most Ontario birdwatchers on both passages. However, some pass through the western parts on their way north and a few strays turn up southbound. Seeing these is one of the highlights of the migration seasons.

IDENTIFICATION: These greatly resemble the much more plentiful Black-bellied Plovers but lack the black axillars ("armpits") of that species and have a two-syllabled "twa-weet" instead of the three-syllabled "tee-ooh-ah" of the Black-bellied. The Golden also lacks the white rump of the Black-bellied, has a more delicate bill, and sports a blackish cap (gray in the Black-bellied). In spring and summer plumage the Golden has black undertail coverts (white in the Black-bellied).

WINTER: One was reported on the Long Point Christmas count in 1973.

SPRING: Stirrett (1973b: 16) called it a common spring migrant at Pelee, from 50 seen on Apr. 14 to one as late as May 28. Kelley (1978: 31) mentioned a group of 2000 in a field in Dover Twp., Kent Co. on Apr. 24, 1954. Ussher (1965: 10) had Rondeau records from Apr. 6 to May 28, with a 12-year average arrival on Apr. 28. Brooman (1954: 17) had a few spring records in Elgin Co. from Apr. 26 (1948) to May 8 (1953). Beardslee & Mitchell (1965: 207) reported 16 at Lowbanks on Apr. 22, 1954 and six at Rockhouse Point on May 20, 1956. Tozer & Richards (1974: 124) reported an early one seen by several observers at Oshawa on March 24, 1968: there were other reports later that spring and I saw one at Whitby on May 25 and 28, 1974 (Speirs, 1977: 35). Weir and Quilliam (1980: 34) had a few spring records at Kingston between May 11 and May 28. Nicholson (1981: 98) had Manitoulin records from May 10 (1970) to May 26 (1975) and a high count of 150 on May 12, 1978 near Tehkummah. Denis (1961: 4) gave May 25 as the average arrival date at Thunder Bay, with the earliest on May 21, 1960.

SUMMER: Beardslee & Mitchell (1965: 206-207) reported one at Point Abino on July 24, 1955 and six at Ridgeway on Aug. 6, 1949. I saw eight at Audley, Pickering Twp. in a wet, harvested pea field on Aug. 9, 1976 and forty were there by Aug. 15. Weir & Quilliam (1980: 34) had returning birds at Kingston as early as Aug. 10. Peck (1972: 340, 341 (photo)) discovered the first Ontario nest, with 4 eggs, at Cape Henrietta Maria on June 23, 1970: he cited several other summer records for that region.

AUTUMN: Manning (1952: 42) cited several records near Moosonee from Sept. 9 (1950) to Sept. 24 (1947) and three at Attawapiskat on Sept. 17, 1940. Elder (1979: 32) called it a common fall migrant at Geraldton, with up to 50 on open grassy areas. Smith (1957: 172) cited Timmins records by F. Cowell on Sept. 23, 1954 and Sept. 27, 1953 (specimen in National Museum of Canada) and also an autumn report from Gogama. Skeel & Bondrup-Nielsen (1978: 169) considered it the third most common non-resident shorebird in fall at Pukaskwa, from Sept. 4 to Oct. 13. Speirs & Speirs (1947: 28) saw one at North Bay on Sept. 26 and 29, 1944. Nicholson (1981: 98) had returning birds on Manitoulin between Aug. 28 (1971) and Nov. 1 (1970), with a high count of 250 near Gore Bay on Oct. 14, 1974. Devitt (1967: 67) gave Sept. 3, 1934 and Nov. 9, 1958 as extreme fall dates for Simcoe Co., with the 7-year average arrival date at Wasaga Beach on Sept. 19 and the largest flock of 75 at Edenvale on Sept. 25, 1966 by A.J. Mitchener and Frances Westman. Lloyd (1923: 151) reported an "immense flight" at Ottawa about Sept. 1, 1885 with "no such flight since." Weir & Quilliam (1980: 34) gave Aug. 26 as the 22-year average arrival date in fall at Kingston and Oct. 19 as the 25-year average departure date, with the latest on Nov. 20. Snyder (1941: 49) cited records for Prince Edward Co. on Oct. 13, 1934 and Oct. 12, 1935. The largest fall group at Whitby was 175 on Sept. 7, 1958 and one lingered there until Nov. 15 in 1959 (Speirs, 1977: 35). Speirs (1938: 48, 52) had Toronto records from Aug. 24 to a peak on Sept. 25 and John Edmonds collected one at Ashbridge's Bay, Toronto, on Nov. 9, 1889 (Thompson, 1890: 199). Beardslee & Mitchell (1965: 207) reported 27 at Mud Lake on Sept. 18, 1948 and 68 at Homer on Sept. 20, 1959. Snyder (1931: 173) cited reports by John Townson at Long Point on Oct. 7 and 14, 1927. Saunders & Dale (1933: 191) had a few fall records for London until Sept. 19, 1904 when two were taken at Duncrief by Roger T. Hedley. Brooman (1954: 17) had only one fall record for Elgin Co., of 7 birds seen by Harold Lancaster on his farm. A late bird was seen at Strathroy by many observers on Oct. 30, 1971 (Goodwin, 1972: 56). Ussher (1965: 10) considered it rare in fall at Rondeau, with records from Aug. 12 to Nov. 7. Stirrett (1973d: 18) considered it uncommon at Pelee in fall, from two as early as Aug. 17 to two seen as late as Oct. 16 and a maximum of 100 on Sept. 9.

**MEASUREMENTS:**
*Length:* 9 3/4 to 11 ins.
(Godfrey, 1966: 135)
*Wingspread:* 21 to 23 ins.
(Roberts, 1955: 570)
*Weight:* 5.36 to 8.75 oz.
(Roberts, 1955: 570).

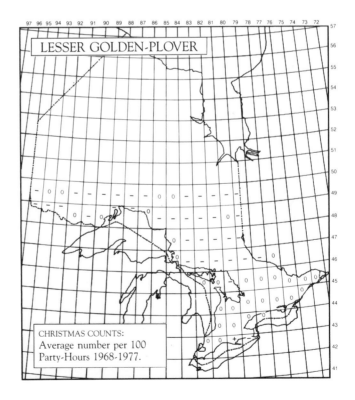

LESSER GOLDEN-PLOVER

CHRISTMAS COUNTS:
Average number per 100
Party-Hours 1968-1977.

## MONGOLIAN PLOVER   *Charadrius mongolus*   Pallas

This is normally an Old World plover, nesting in Siberia and wintering south to Australia, accidental in Ontario.

IDENTIFICATION: This is a small plover, about the size of a large Semipalmated Plover, with a distinctive reddish crown and breast, unlike any other Canadian plover, when in breeding plumage. In non-breeding plumage the black ear patches on white face and the blackish crown are suggestive of this species.

WINTER:

SPRING: R.D. McRae photographed one at Presqu'ile Provincial Park on May 4, 1984 (Weir, 1984: 904). This bird was also seen by many other observers on the same day.

SUMMER:

AUTUMN:

MEASUREMENTS:
*Length:* 7 1/2 ins. (Falla,
Sibson & Turbott
(1966: 126)
*Wingspread:*
*Weight:*

## SNOWY PLOVER   *Charadrius alexandrinus*   Linnaeus

This tiny Old World plover also has a population in southern and western United States. It favours dry sand and alkali flats which form backgrounds matching its colours. There are just two old Ontario records.

IDENTIFICATION: It looks like a small edition of the Piping Plover but has a slender black bill and gray legs (yellow in Piping Plover).

WINTER:

SPRING: One taken at Toronto in May, 1880, by J. Foreman, was identified by Ernest Seton. (Fleming, 1906: 452).

SUMMER: Another, taken at Toronto, on July 6, 1897 is now in the Royal Ontario Museum, from the J.H. Ames collection (Fleming, 1906: 452).

AUTUMN:

MEASUREMENTS:
*Length:* 5 3/4 ins. to 6 3/4
ins. (Godfrey, 1966: 133)
*Wingspread:* 13 1/2 ins.
(Pough, 1951: 212)
*Weight:* 37 to 49 g.;
average 41.4 g. (Dunning,
1984: 8).

# WILSON'S PLOVER   *Charadrius wilsonia*   Ord

This is a bird of southern coasts of the United States and central and South America, with just two sight records in Ontario.

IDENTIFICATION:   It looks like a Semipalmated Plover with a very big all black bill and dusky pink legs. It is somewhat larger than a Semipalmated Plover and a bit paler. The breast band is broader also.

WINTER:

SPRING:   One was seen and well described by George A. North *et al* from May 17 to May 20, 1966 at Hamilton (Goodwin, 1966: 503). Stirrett (1973b: 16) listed one the following spring at Pelee on May 8, 1967.

SUMMER:

AUTUMN:

**MEASUREMENTS:**
*Length:* 7.0 to 8.1 ins.
(Godfrey, 1966: 133)
Wingspread:
*Weight:* 55.8 to 64.2 g.,
average 60.5 g. (Dunning,
1984: 8).

# SEMIPALMATED PLOVER
## *Charadrius semipalmatus*   Bonaparte

This dainty little plover is a bird of passage through most of Ontario breeding only along the James Bay and Hudson Bay coasts. It winters along the seacoasts from southern United States, south around the coasts of South America to Patagonia. It is found chiefly on the beaches of the larger lakes in migration, but sometimes on mudflats with other shorebirds. The spring passage is very rapid, mostly between mid-May and May 25 but the fall migration is more leisurely, with adults arriving before the young, as is the case with many northern shorebirds.

IDENTIFICATION:   This looks very much like a small edition of the familiar Killdeer but has only one dark breast band instead of two. The "tur-wee" call is distinctive. From the very similar Old World Ringed Plover it may be distinguished (in the hand) by the greater extent of webbing between the toes (hence its name).

WINTER:

SPRING:   Stirrett (1973b: 16) had a maximum count of 32 at Pelee on May 12, with the earliest record on May 2. Ussher (1965: 9) had Rondeau records from May 7 to May 28, with May 15 as the 17-year average arrival date and May 25 as the 8-year departure average. Earl Lemon had his earliest Elgin Co. sighting on May 6, 1935 (Brooman, 1954: 17). Saunders & Dale (1933: 190) gave 20 as the maximum count for Middlesex Co., noted on May 22, 1927 at Lambeth. Snyder (1931: 173) saw and collected his first at Long Point on May 7, 1928 and the latest on May 30, 1927. Thompson (1890: 191) cited an Apr. 27 record for Toronto, while Speirs (1938: 40) had an even earlier one on Apr. 21 and gave May 23 as the Toronto peak date. Naomi LeVay noted one at Whitby as early as May 10, 1958 and the spring peak there was about May 22 (Speirs, 1977: 32). Snyder (1941: 49) noted three at Hallowell on May 28, 1930. At Kingston the earliest record was on May 5, 1968; the average arrival on May 15 and average departure on May 25 (Weir & Quilliam, 1980: 34). Devitt (1967: 66) gave May 25 as the 7-year average arrival date at Wasaga Beach, with the earliest Simcoe Co. record on May 11, 1959 at Collingwood. Beamer had only one spring record near Meaford: 10 on May 15, 1949. K. Ketchum saw one off Pointe au Baril on May 24, 1958 (Mills, 1981: 52). Nicholson (1981: 96) gave May 17 as the 10-year average for arrivals on Manitoulin, with the earliest on May 10, 1979, a high count of 22 on May 23, 1976 and the latest on June 3, 1972. Speirs & Speirs (1947: 27) noted four at North Bay on May 31, 1944. Skeel & Bondrup-Nielsen (1978: 168) considered this the most common non-resident shorebird at Pukaskwa between May 14 and May 22 (they saw 17 on four days). Denis (1961: 4) gave May 20 as the average arrival date at Thunder Bay, with the earliest on May 14, 1956. Elder (1979: 32) gave May 22 as the earliest date for Geraldton. Manning (1952: 41) saw about 100 on May 31, 1947 at Shipsands near Moosonee. Cringan (1950: 8) saw one at Nikip Lake on June 5, 1950 and reported one on May 25, 1950 in the Asheweig area seen by Elsey. Lee (1978: 21) noted one at Bearskin Lake on May 29, 1975 and noted them at Big Trout Lake from June 1 to June 8.

SUMMER: Stirrett (1973c: 15) had a northbound bird as late as June 14 at Pelee and four returning migrants as early as June 26, with 25 there on Aug. 13. Ussher (1965: 9) had a July 16 observation at Rondeau, with Aug. 12 as his 11-year average for arriving fall migrants. W.E. Saunders saw two at Long Point on June 7 or 8, 1925 and Snyder noted the first returning birds there on July 22, 1927 (Snyder, 1931: 173). Beardslee & Mitchell (1965: 203-204) gave several June records for Rockhouse Point, Lake Erie. Tozer & Richards (1974: 121) cited a record by Dennis Barry of two at Whitby as late as June 9, 1964. Long (1965: 34) noted returning birds at Pickering Beach on July 2 and 5, 1963. Weir & Quilliam (1980: 34) had northbound birds at Kingston as late as June 15 and returning birds as early as July 15, with the average arrival on Aug. 1. Devitt (1967: 65) had spring records to June 9, 1940 in Simcoe Co., with the earliest returning birds on July 26, 1942 at Wasaga Beach. Beamer saw one east of Thornbury on Aug. 17, 1941. K. Ketchum saw fall migrants at Pointe au Baril as early as July 4, 1956 and there are several August records for Muskoka and Parry Sound Districts (Mills, 1981: 51-52). Nicholson (1981: 96) gave July 15, 1976 as the earliest record for returning migrants on Manitoulin. MacLulich (1938: 14) saw five at the mouth of the Little Nippissing River on Aug. 23, 1930. Speirs & Speirs (1947: 27) saw one at North Bay on Aug. 22, 1944 and J.L. Baillie saw four at Callander on Aug. 14, 1934 (Ricker & Clarke, 1939: 9). Skeel & Bondrup-Nielsen (1978: 168) saw one at Pukaskwa as late as June 14, with fifty there on 11 days between Aug. 18 and 28. Baillie & Hope (1943: 9) collected a migrant male at Rossport on June 1, 1936. J.L. Baillie saw five on Sable Is., Lake-of-the-Woods on Aug. 8, 1929 (Snyder, 1938: 187). Todd (1963: 288) mapped the distribution around the Labrador peninsula coasts, including one breeding record near Moosonee, and gave an interesting account of behavior on the breeding grounds. Manning (1952: 40) reported nesting at Big Piskwanish by Kelsall and Lemieux on June 24, 1947: Manning saw about 200 including 15 young at Cape Henrietta Maria from July 20 to 24, 1947, and reported smaller numbers at Little Cape and Shagamu River on the Hudson Bay coast from July

31 to Aug. 14. Peck (1972: 340) further documented the abundance of this species in the Cape Henrietta Maria region. Schueler, Baldwin & Rising (1974: 145) found a nest at the tree line on the Sutton River on June 23, 1962, a nest with eggs at the north end of Hawley Lake on July 5, 1962 and one twenty miles from Winisk on the Winisk River on June 16, 1965. Lee (1978: 21) had the first returning migrants at Big Trout Lake on Aug. 1, 1975 and small flocks there to Aug. 10. C.E. Hope collected several nests with eggs at Fort Severn from June 16 to July 9, 1940 and saw as many as 35 adults there on July 1, 1940.

AUTUMN: Skeel & Bondrup-Nielsen (1978: 168) saw their latest at Pukaskwa on Oct. 6. Speirs & Speirs (1947: 27) observed one at North Bay on Sept. 13, 1944. Nicholson (1981: 96) gave Sept. 24, 1978 as the latest fall date for Manitoulin. K. Ketchum saw one off Pointe au Baril on Sept. 6, 1971 (Mills, 1981: 52). Frances Westman saw one at Allandale as late as Oct. 28, 1957 (Devitt, 1967: 65). Beamer had several records at Meaford between Sept. 1 and 21, and 10 near Thornbury on Sept. 8, 1940. Weir & Quilliam (1980: 34) gave Oct. 5 as the 25-year average departure date from Kingston, with the latest on Nov. 8, 1959. Snyder (1941: 49) saw four in Prince Edward Co. on Sept. 13, 1931. Long (1969: 18) had a very late one at Pickering on Nov. 15, 1969. Speirs (1938: 52) had fall peaks on Aug. 7 and Sept. 1 at Toronto, with the latest on Nov. 13. Beardslee & Mitchell (1965: 203-204) reported one as late as Nov. 5, 1944 at Yacht Harbour. Ussher (1965: 9) gave Oct. 9 as the 8-year average departure date from Rondeau, with the latest on Oct. 27. Stirrett (1973d: 18) gave Oct. 29 as his latest Pelee sighting, but A.J. Maley saw one there on Nov. 1, 1971 (Goodwin, 1972: 56).

**MEASUREMENTS:**
*Length:* 6.5 to 7.7 ins.
(Godfrey, 1966: 132)
*Wingspread:* 14 to 16 ins.
(Roberts, 1955: 568)
*Weight:* 1.06 to 1.62 oz.
(Roberts, 1955: 568).

# PIPING PLOVER   *Charadrius melodus*   Ord

This melodious little plover is an inhabitant of broad sandy beaches and sand dunes, which are rather restricted in distribution in Ontario and have become very popular with sunbathers and offroad vehicles, so that this is now an endangered species in Ontario. In my early birding days it was still seen regularly on the Lake Ontario and Lake Erie beaches. For example, in 1931, I saw one at Ashbridge's Bay shore, Toronto, on May 17 and 25, and on May 31 there was one at Lowbanks, Lake Erie.

IDENTIFICATION:  This looks like a very pale sandy brown version of the Semipalmated Plover, frequently with an incomplete dusky band between the breast and neck. As its name suggests, it utters a very musical, piping whistle.

WINTER:

SPRING:  W.E. Saunders took two sets of 2 eggs each at Point Pelee on May 24, 1906 (Baillie & Harrington, 1936: 35). Stirrett (1973b: 16) gave Apr. 4, 1953 as the earliest Pelee date, with 45 there on May 13, 1905, but now rare. Ussher (1965: 9) gave May 10 as the earliest Rondeau date. Fred Bodsworth saw one at Port Burwell on May 24, 1942 and others saw two there on May 25, 1952 (Brooman, 1954: 16). Snyder (1931: 174) cited several nest records for Long Point, including a nest with 4 eggs on May 14, 1928. I saw one there on the same date in 1975 but Hussell (1980: 1) bemoaned the loss of this species as a nesting species on Long Point, perhaps its last stronghold in Ontario: he blamed predation by Raccoons and harrassment by Ring-billed Gulls as the probable cause of their decline. G.W. Knechtel saw a nest with 4 eggs at Turkey Point on May 30, 1924 (Baillie & Harrington, 1936: 35). Beardslee & Mitchell (1965: 204) reported one at Sherkston, Lake Erie, as early as Apr. 17 in 1938; a nest there on May 17, 1934: the last nests found there were on May 28 and 30, 1944 and the last sighting there on May 25, 1947: they also had a sighting at Cedar Bay on May 26, 1929. Speirs (1938: 40) gave Apr. 7 as the earliest Toronto record, with a *peak* on May 25 (those were the days!): and J.L. Baillie found two nests, each with 4 eggs at Fisherman's Island, Toronto, on May 24, 1928. Speirs (1977: 33) gave just four Ontario Co. spring records: Apr. 25, 1964 at Whitby, May 7, 1974 and May 9, 1966 at Pickering Beach and May 16, 1964 at Frenchman Bay, but I had an earlier sighting at Frenchman Bay on Apr. 20, 1930. Snyder (1941: 49) collected a pair near Wellington, Prince Edward Co., on May 24, 1930 and reported a set of eggs collected by E. Beaupré at Consecon on May 26, 1926. Bruce Lyons photographed one on Amherst Is. on May 13, 1976 and another was seen at Prince Edward Point on May 21, 1979 (Weir & Quilliam, 1980: 9). Devitt (1967: 66) gave May 16 as the 9-year average arrival date at Wasaga Beach with the earliest on Apr. 27, 1941: the earliest complete set of eggs was found on May 4, 1933: with the advent of motorized vehicles on the beach these have now gone. Ron. Tasker saw one in Burpee Twp., Manitoulin from May 13-21, 1967 and others have been reported from Carter Bay from May 23, 1970 to May 23, 1976 (Nicholson, 1981: 96-97). J. Lemon and J. Nicholson saw a single bird at Kelly Lake, Sudbury, on May 10, 1971 (Goodwin, 1971: 737).

SUMMER:  E.M.S. Dale took a set of two eggs on Pelee Is. on June 5, 1933 (Baillie & Harrington, 1936: 35). Kelley (1978: 31) reported a pair with two downy young at Ipperwash Beach on July 10, 1953, and mentioned former nestings at Pelee and Rondeau.

Beardslee & Mitchell (1965: 205) reported young birds at Sherkston on June 25, 1933 and a nest with 4 eggs at Crystal Beach on June 24,1934, as well as a nest at Crescent Beach on June 3, 1936 and young just out of the nest on July 31, 1938. George W. North saw a nest at Van Wagner's Beach, Burlington, in June, 1934 (Baillie & Harrington, 1936: 35) and G.H. Richardson found a nest with 3 downy young and one egg at Hanlan's Point, Toronto, on June 9, 1934. Fleming (1906: 452) reported one at Toronto on June 20, 1894 and remarked that all old specimens from Toronto were of the subspecies *meloda*, while those subsequent to the 1894 bird were of the subspecies *circumcincta*. Speirs (1977: 33) gave a few late August reports of returning migrants at Whitby and Pickering Beach. Quilliam (1973: 75) cited two old nest records for the Kingston region: a nest with 4 eggs near Rockport on June 18, 1894 and a set of eggs at Collins Lake on June 16, 1903. Devitt (1967: 66) saw ten at Wasaga Beach on July 21, 1935 and mentioned several nest records there: he also gave a sighting of three on Giant's Tomb Is. on June 11, 1937. Adults and a downy young were seen at Carter Bay, Manitoulin, on July 4, 1970, and the latest date was Aug. 16, 1971 at Lonely Bay (Nicholson, 1981: 96-97). Denis (1961: 6) listed it as a "sporadic, very rare, visitant" at Thunder Bay (with no details). J.L. Baillie collected two young of the year females at Sable Is., Lake-of-the-Woods, of eight seen there on Aug. 8, 1929 (Snyder, 1938: 187).

AUTUMN: Devitt (1967: 66) gave Sept. 16, 1939 as his latest date for Wasaga Beach. E. Beaupré shot two on Amherst Is. on Oct. 4, 1895 (Quilliam, 1973: 75). Speirs (1938: 54) gave Sept. 9 as the latest Toronto date. Snyder (1931: 174) gave Sept. 19, 1905 as the latest Long Point date. Beardslee & Mitchell (1965: 205) gave several fall sightings in Sept., 1960, along Lake Erie beaches, with one very late bird at Erie Beach collected on Nov. 8, 1959. One was seen at Port Burwell on Sept. 7, 1953 and another on Sept. 3, 1938 (Brooman, 1954: 16). Ussher (1965: 9) gave Sept. 12 as the latest Rondeau date. Stirrett (1973d: 18) gave Sept. 24 as the latest date for Pelee.

**MEASUREMENTS:**
*Length:* 6.0 to 7.7 ins.
(Godfrey, 1966: 132)
*Wingspread:* 14 to 16 ins.
(Roberts, 1955: 568)
*Weight:* 3 oz. (Roberts,
1955: 568).

**REFERENCES:**
Cartar, Ralph 1976 The
status of the Piping Plover
at Long Point, Ontario,
1966-1975. Ont. Field
Biologist, 30: (2): 42-45.
    Hussell, D.J.T. and R.D.
Montgomerie 1966 The
status of the Piping Plover
at Long Point, 1960- 1965.
Ont. Field Biologist,
20: 14-16.
    Hussell, David 1980 The
last of the Piping Plovers?
Long Point Bird
Observatory, Newsletter,
12: (2): 1-2.

# KILLDEER   *Charadrius vociferus*   Linnaeus

This is our most familiar shorebird, nesting along gravelly beaches, in gravel pits, on plowed fields and even golf courses and lawns. It is the best-known exponent of the "broken-wing trick" to lure potential predators, including people, away from its nest or young. It arrives with the first hint of spring and lingers until winter sets in.

IDENTIFICATION: This is a Robin-sized shorebird with two dark bands across the upper breast and neck, with a brown back and reddish-orange tail tipped with black and white and a red ring around its prominent, big eyes. The precocial downy chicks run around very soon after hatching, looking like miniature copies of their parents. The familiar "kill-dee-er" cry gives them their name: this is often abbreviated to "kill-dee" or to "dee-dee———." when they are alarmed.

WINTER: On Christmas counts they are rare, but have been seen north to Kingston and Wiarton. Most winter records are of birds lingering into December or returning in late February. Stirrett (1973a: 15) had Pelee records as late as Dec. 31 and as early as Feb. 24. Ussher (1965: 9) had records at Rondeau to Dec. 26 and as early as Feb. 24. Saunders & Dale (1933: 191) had an early arrival at London on Feb. 23, 1922. D. Sands noted one at the Oshawa Second Marsh outlet on Dec. 21, 1968 (Tozer & Richards, 1974: 124) and George A. Scott saw one along the Oshawa shore as early as Feb. 25, 1954 (Speirs, 1977: 34). Quilliam (1973: 75) reported two Dec. records for Kingston, three for January and two in February. Devitt (1967: 67) had two winter records for Simcoe Co.: Dec. 13, 1959 at Collingwood by A.J. Mitchener and Feb. 28, 1961 at Midland by Dan. Middleton. Beamer reported a sighting at Meaford on Dec. 25, 1940 and had three late February returns, one as early as Feb. 22, 1954. Mills (1981: 52) had a Huntsville record for Feb. 21, 1971 and one at Wasi Falls on Feb. 26 in the same year.

SPRING: Stirrett (1973b: 16) had a high count of 15 at Pelee on March 16. Ussher (1965: 9) gave March 17 as the 23-year average arrival date for Rondeau. F. Starr took a set of four eggs at Port Burwell on May 13, 1924 (Brooman, 1954: 17). Saunders & Dale (1933: 191) gave March 13 as the 17-year average arrival date for London and found a nest with four eggs as early as May 5, 1898. Baillie (in Saunders, 1947: 363) gave March 25 as his 27-year average arrival date for Toronto. The peak of the spring migration along the Ontario Co. shore was about Apr. 4 (Speirs, 1977: 34). Ron. Tozer found a nest with one egg near Oshawa as early as Apr. 11, 1963 and saw an adult with three downy young as early as May 10, 1968 (Tozer & Richards, 1974: 122). Weir & Quilliam (1980: 34) gave March 11 as the 32-year average arrival date for Kingston, and Quilliam (1973: 75) reported adults with downy young there as early as May 7, 1963. Devitt (1967: 67) gave March 24 as the 16-year average arrival date for Barrie, with one at Collingwood as early as March 11, 1921, while R.A. Smith found a nest with 4 eggs at Holland Marsh as early as Apr. 17, 1939. Beamer's 20-year average arrival date for Meaford was March 14, and the earliest nest (with 4 eggs) was reported by Ron Jolley on Apr. 14, 1953. Mills (1981: 52) gave March 26 as the 16-year average arrival date for Huntsville. Nicholson (1981: 97) gave March 22 as the 11-year average arrival date for Manitoulin, with the earliest on March 10, 1973 and a high count of 123 on Apr. 9, 1971. Speirs & Speirs (1947: 27) observed one at North Bay as early as March 22, 1945 and followed a nest with 4 eggs from May 15 to June 4, 1944. F.A.E. Starr found a nest with four eggs about ready to hatch, at Sudbury on May 25, 1935 (Baillie & Hope, 1947: 7). Denis (1961: 2) gave Apr. 14 as the average arrival date for Thunder Bay, with the earliest on March 15, 1957: Dear (1940: 123) found a nest with 4 eggs there on May 15, 1936. Bondrup-Nielsen (1976: 42) saw his first near Kapuskasing on Apr. 17, 1975. Elder (1979: 32) gave Apr. 15 as his earliest sighting at Geraldton. On May 27, 1947 Hewitt saw two as Ship Sands, near Moosonee, and Sam Waller found a nest with 4 eggs at Moose Factory on May 26, 1930 (Manning, 1952: 41). Cringan (1953a: 2) saw his first at Sioux Lookout on May 2, 1953, Cringan (1953b: 3) saw individuals at Kasabonika Lake on May 27 and June 5, 1953. Lee (1978: 22) saw them at Big Trout Lake beginning on May 31, 1975.

SUMMER: On Breeding Bird Surveys they have been common throughout the agricultural south and well distributed but uncommon to fairly common on northern routes (due to scarcity of suitable habitat). Stirrett (1973c: 15) found it nesting at Pelee and had a high summer count of 75 on Aug. 13. Beardslee & Mitchell (1965: 206) found a nest with 4 eggs as late as July 20 at Cedar Bay, Lake Erie. Snyder (1941: 49) collected 4 eggs on June 6, 1930 at Bloomfield, Prince Edward Co., and two downy young at Hallowell on June 11, 1930. Bruce Parker found a nest with one egg and three newly-hatched young in Mara Provincial Park on July 22, 1973 (Speirs, 1977: 34). Beamer reported that the fourth egg of a nest in his Meaford garden hatched on July 22, three weeks after it was laid. Mills (1981: 52) reported egg dates from May 2 to July 11 in the cottage country. Snyder (1942: 128) collected a downy male at Laird on June 7, 1931 and another downy at Maclennan on June 23. Baillie & Hope (1947: 7) collected 4 eggs ready to hatch at Biscotasing on June 21, 1937 and a downy young at Bigwood on July 24, as well as several adults at Bigwood, Biscotasing and Chapleau. Skeel & Bondrup-Nielsen (1978: 168) found a nest with 3 eggs at Pukaskwa on June 27, 1977: they also noted nests with 4 eggs on June 22, 1973 and June 22, 1975. Baillie & Hope (1943: 9) collected four newly-hatched young at Peninsula on June 21, 1936 (3 ♂, 1 ♀). Snyder (1928: 258) collected a juvenile female on June 20, 1924 at Lake Nipigon. Dear (1940: 128) reported a nest with 4 eggs on June 4, 1914 at Thunder Bay. Snyder (1938: 187) collected a juvenile female at Emo on June 15, 1929. Snyder (1953: 57) found them common from Ingolf to Wabigoon and reported several June nests in this part of western Ontario. Snyder (1928: 21) saw only one Killdeer at Lake Abitibi (on June 3 and 6, 1925) but Baillie & Harrington (1936: 36) reported that eggs had been taken there by A.V. Dukes: they also reported a nest with 3 eggs found at Kenora by L. Paterson on June 7, 1931. James (1980: 86) found a nest with 4 eggs near Pickle Lake on June 15, 1977. Manning (1952: 41) counted 23 at Moosonee on June 30 and July 1, 1949, of which four pairs seemed to be nesting: he also saw one adult at Shagamu River on the Hudson Bay coast on Aug. 8 which acted as if it had young nearby. Schueler, Baldwin & Rising (1974: 145) found nests with 4 eggs at Attawapiskat on June 18, 1971 and at Winisk on July 3, 1965. Peck (1972: 340) cited observations near Cape Henrietta Maria by C.E. Hope on Aug. 12, 1948 and by H. Lumsden on June 28, 1964. Hope (1938: 17) took a set of 4 eggs at Favourable Lake on June 14, 1938 and saw young there on June 29 and July 9. Lee (1978: 22) found a nest with 3 eggs at Big Trout Lake on June 12, 1975 and downy young there in mid-July. Hope had just three sightings at Fort Severn (on June 17 and 18 and on July 17, 1940).

AUTUMN: Skeel & Bondrup-Nielsen (1978: 168) saw their last at Pukaskwa on Sept. 5, 1977. Speirs & Speirs (1947: 27) saw one at North Bay as late as Nov. 11, 1944. Nicholson (1981: 97) had a high count of 400 at Manitoulin on Sept. 21, 1975 and the latest record on Nov. 14, 1974. Mills (1981: 52) saw three at Magnetawan as late as Oct. 8, 1973. Beamer's latest report for Meaford was on Oct. 19, 1940. Weir & Quilliam (1980: 34) gave Nov. 13 as the 27-year average departure date for Kingston. John Townson reported them as still present in Prince Edward Co. on Oct. 27, 1930 (Snyder, 1941: 49). The peak of the fall migration in Ontario Co. was in the second week of September (Speirs, 1977: 34). Saunders (1947: 363) gave Nov. 4 as his 13-year average departure date for Toronto, with the latest on Nov. 30. Brooman (1954: 17) reported 200 to 300 at the St. Thomas Reservoir on Sept. 4, 1949. Ussher (1965: 9) gave Nov. 9 as the 11-year average departure date from Rondeau. Stirrett (1973d: 18) had a peak of 200 at Pelee on Oct. 3.

**MEASUREMENTS:**
*Length:* 9 to 11 1/4 ins.
(Godfrey, 1966: 133)
*Wingspread:* 19.88 to
20.75 ins. (Roberts,
1955: 567)
*Weight:* 3.25 to 3.50 oz.
(Roberts, 1955: 567)
♂ 98.5 g. ♀ 84 g. (Hope,
1938: 17).

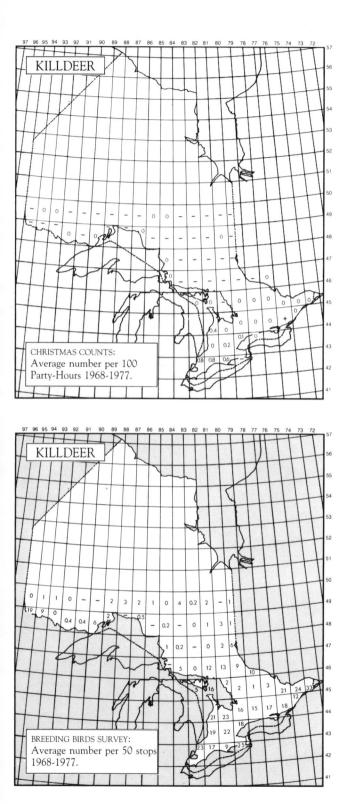

KILLDEER

CHRISTMAS COUNTS:
Average number per 100
Party-Hours 1968-1977.

KILLDEER

BREEDING BIRDS SURVEY:
Average number per 50 stops
1968-1977.

# AMERICAN OYSTERCATCHER
*Haematopus palliatus*   Temminck

This is now an uncommon resident of southern Atlantic coast beaches and is very rare indeed inland. All of the Ontario records probably refer to the same one bird.

IDENTIFICATION:   This is our largest shorebird (about the size of a Ring-billed Gull). It has a heavy, long (about 3 inch) bill, which is bright red, a striking black and white pattern in flight and when alarmed utters an interminable "peep, peep, peep. . . ." It has a black or brown back and white rump: the very similar European Oystercatcher has an all white back.

WINTER:

SPRING:   Clive Goodwin spotted one at the Western Gap, Toronto, on May 22, 1960. On the next day it was reported at Presqu'ile by Audrey Wilson and stayed there until last reported by Ron Scovell on June 4. Ken Edwards showed me a fine photograph he took of this bird and Donald Gunn also photographed it there on May 29.

SUMMER:   On July 2 it showed up at Thunder Bay, Lake Erie, where it was observed by George Letchworth and other observers from Buffalo. On July 21 it was collected for the Royal Ontario Museum by Ario Gatti and proved to be a male.

AUTUMN:

**MEASUREMENTS:**
*Length:* 17 to 21 ins.
(Godfrey, 1966: 130)
*Wingspread:* 30 to 36 ins.
(Terres, 1980: 674)
*Weight:* 495 to 625 g.
(Terres, 1980: 674)

**REFERENCE:**
Lunn, John 1961 An American Oystercatcher on the Great Lakes. Ont. Field Biologist, No. 15: 32-33. Most of the above records are from this account.

# BLACK-NECKED STILT  *Himantopus mexicanus*  (Müller)

Like the Avocet, the Stilt is a bird of western alkali marshes, but is of more southerly distribution, from Oregon and Colorado, south to South America.

**IDENTIFICATION:**  The very long, bright pink legs give it its name. It is black above with long slender black bill which is only slightly upturned. The face and underparts are white. The tail is white to gray. On the breeding grounds they are very noisy birds, uttering a constant "yip'yip'yip" or "yeep yeep yeep".

**WINTER:**

**SPRING:**

**SUMMER:**

**AUTUMN:**  Frances Bourne and Rita Seccombe described one seen at Frederickhouse Lake, near Timmins, on Sept. 1, 1955, probably carried north on the winds of Hurricane "Connie", as "size of (Common) Tern, perched on red legs to twice the height of the Ring-billed Gulls, solid black mantle, white tail and front and long straight bill" (Baillie, 1955: 376). G. Chapple and G.A. Novosel reported one at Smithville Sewage Lagoons on Oct. 14, 1979 (Goodwin, 1980: 157).

**MEASUREMENTS:**
*Length:* 13.5 to 15.5 ins.
(Godfrey, 1966: 166)
including 2 - 2 3/4" bill.
*Wingspread:* 26 to 30 ins.
(Roberts, 1955: 555)
*Weight:* 18 averaged
166 g. (Dunning, 1984: 8).
Legs 8 to 10 ins. long
(Terres, 1980: 37).

# AMERICAN AVOCET   *Recurvirostra americana*   Gmelin

The Avocet is a bird of alkaline and saline lakes of the prairies and southwestern U.S.A., wintering south to Guatemala. It is a rare straggler in Ontario.

IDENTIFICATION: With its slender black, upturned bill, fawn-coloured head and neck, sky blue legs, white breast and black and white back, the Avocet is a striking and unmistakable big shorebird.

WINTER:

SPRING: Stirrett (1973b: 17) had just one spring record for Pelee, on May 5, 1968 when 24 were seen (Kelley, 1978: 37 gave the date as May 4, 1968). Norman Chesterfield and Alan Wormington saw one at Pelee on May 2, 1974 (Goodwin, 1974: 796). One was reported at Port Rowan on May 14, 1977 by David Hussell *et al* (Goodwin, 1977: 995). R. Davis found one at Pickering on May 9, 1973 (Goodwin, 1973: 767). Audrey and J. Russ saw one at Ajax on May 23, 1963 and George A. Scott watched one near Oshawa on May 21, 1961 (Speirs, 1977: 65). Goodwin (1975: 846) reported one seen at Presqu'ile by many observers on May 29, 1975, and Peter Middleton noted one at Hepworth on May 7, 1976 (Goodwin, 1976: 834).

SUMMER: C.A. Campbell *et al* saw one on Pelee Is. on Aug. 9, 1974 (Goodwin, 1974: 897). D. Rupert and A. Rider reported one at Pelee on Aug. 27, 1972 (Goodwin, 1973: 52). One was seen at Long Point on Aug. 14, 1979 by J. Stewart, A.S. Weir and P.A. Woodliffe (Goodwin, 1980: 156). Beardslee & Mitchell (1965: 236) reported a sighting at Jaeger Rocks, Erie Beach, on Aug. 8, 1964 by three members of the Buffalo Ornithological Society. John Lemon noted one at Rodney, near Sudbury, from Aug. 20-22, 1978 (Goodwin, 1979: 173). James, McLaren & Barlow (1976: 25) reported a specimen taken at Geraldton on Aug. 29, 1974, sent to ROM by David H. Elder. D.H. Elder found three (with four Marbled Godwits) at the mouth of Rainy River from Aug. 2 to 4, 1980 (Goodwin, 1980: 891).

AUTUMN: Goodwin (1975: 50) mentioned a dead bird found at Longlac by T. Timmerman on Oct. 9, 1974 (the first for Thunder Bay District, according to K. Denis). Robert Orr found and photographed one at McDonald Is., near Gananoque, Sept. 5-12, 1980 (Weir & Quilliam, 1980: 12). Fleming (1906: 448) mentioned two Toronto specimens, one taken on Sept. 19, 1901 (no date given for the other). One was seen at Long Point on Sept. 1, 1974 (Goodwin, 1975: 50). Ten were noted at St. Luke's Marsh, Kent Co. from Sept. 24-27, 1974 (Kelley, 1978: 37). J.P. Kleiman, A.S. Weir, and P.A. Woodliffe noted three in southwestern Ontario from Oct. 25 to Nov. 6, 1979 (Goodwin, 1980: 157). Stirrett (1973d: 20) reported one seen at Pelee from Oct. 8-22, 1969.

**MEASUREMENTS:**
*Length:* 16-20 ins.
(Godfrey, 1966: 165) ♂
larger than ♀.
*Wingspread:* 27-38 ins.
(Roberts, 1955: 554)
*Weight:* 12 oz. (Pough,
1951: 252).

# GREATER YELLOWLEGS  *Tringa melanoleuca*  (Gmelin)

The pursuit of bird watching is greatly enhanced by such look-alike species as the Greater Yellowlegs and Lesser Yellowlegs. We look forward to the challenge they present each spring and fall as they migrate through Ontario.

**IDENTIFICATION:**  When you see the two kinds of Yellowlegs together, there is usually no problem in separating the big, boisterous beauty from the smaller, more sedate Lesser Yellowlegs. The long, bright yellow legs are shared, but the relatively longer, slightly upturned bill of the Greater, its resonant 3-syllabled whistle and its much larger size readily distinguish it from the Lesser. If no Lesser is present then look for a Killdeer - the Greater is much larger than a Killdeer while the Lesser is about the same size or smaller.

**WINTER:**  Stirrett (1973a: 15) had a few December records for Pelee, two as late as Dec. 31 (in 1966).

**SPRING:**  Stirrett (1973b: 17) reported spring migrants at Pelee from March 26 to June 5, with a maximum of 13 on May 6. Ussher (1965: 11) had Rondeau records from Apr. 9 to May 26, with average arrival on Apr. 19 and departure on May 22. Harold Lancaster reported a melanistic bird at Dunwich Marsh, Elgin Co., on Apr. 12 and 17, 1949 (Brooman, 1954: 18). Saunders & Dale (1933: 194) gave Apr. 21 as the 13-year average arrival date for London, with the earliest on Apr. 13, 1923. Speirs (1938: 40, 44, 46) had spring records at Toronto from March 20 to June 12, with a peak on Apr. 30. Baillie (in Saunders, 1947: 364) gave Apr. 21 and May 17 as average arrival and departure dates at Toronto. Long (1968b: 17) had his earliest record for Pickering Beach on March 27, 1968 and Speirs (1977: 46) the latest at Whitby on May 24, 1968, with the spring peak about May 10. Snyder (1941: 52) had spring dates for Prince Edward Co. from Apr. 29 (1933) to May 29 (1930). Weir & Quilliam (1980: 34) noted spring birds at Kingston from March 28 to May 27, with average arrival date on Apr. 18 and departure on May 15. Devitt (1967: 72) gave Apr. 20 as the 17-year average arrival date for Barrie, with the earliest on Apr. 11, 1967 and a peak during the first week of May, and the latest record on May 22, 1967 near Orillia. Beamer had his earliest Meaford record on Apr. 19, 1939 and latest on May 24, 1948. Mills (1981: 57) had only a few Muskoka records, between Apr. 24 and May 24. Nicholson (1981: 104) had Manitoulin records from Apr. 13 (1974) to May 26 (1973) with the 12-year average arrival date on Apr. 19 and a high count of 350 on Apr. 29, 1972. Speirs & Speirs (1947: 28) reported single birds at North Bay on May 6, 1944 and at Pimisi Bay on May 13, 1945. Skeel and Bondrup-Nielsen (1978: 171) had spring migrants at Pukaskwa from Apr. 19 to May 10, 1977. Denis (1961: 3) gave Apr. 30 as the average arrival date at Thunder Bay, with the earliest on Apr. 18, 1938. Elder (1979: 32) gave May 2 as the earliest date for Geraldton. Peruniak (1971: 16) had spring birds at Atikokan from Apr. 25 to May 14. Cringan (1953a: 2) saw his first in 1953 at Sioux Lookout on Apr. 27. Cringan (1953b: 3) saw one on June 3, 1953 and two on June 4, 1953 at Kasabonika Lake.

**SUMMER:**  Ussher (1965: 11) gave Aug. 7 as the 9-year average arrival of southbound birds at Rondeau, with the earliest on July 8. Snyder (1931: 170) noted the first returning group of four at Long Point on July 21, 1927. Naomi LeVay had an early record for returning birds at Cranberry Marsh, Whitby, on June 30, 1960 (Speirs, 1977: 46). Weir & Quilliam (1980: 34) had the earliest returning bird at Kingston on July 7, but Aug. 7

was the 31-year average. Mills (1981: 57) had two returning birds in Parry Sound District on July 1 (one at Franklin Is. and one at Killbear Park). Nicholson (1981: 104) reported one seen by Ron Tasker on Manitoulin Is. as early as July 9, 1978. Skeel & Bondrup-Nielsen (1978: 171) had returning birds at Pukaskwa from July 24 to Aug. 1, 1977. Snyder (1928: 257) saw a crippled bird at Lake Nipigon on June 15, 1924 which he considered "accidental" at that time. Ross James noted from one to six almost daily at Pickle Lake from May 31 to June 17, 1977. Hope (1938: 19) collected a male at Favourable Lake on Aug. 4, 1938. Manning (1952: 47) cited several summer records from the James Bay and Hudson Bay coasts, of which two at Lake River on July 17, 1947 "appeared to be a nesting pair": he saw 25 at Cape Henrietta Maria between July 20 and July 24, 1947 and 54 at Shagamu River between Aug. 8 and Aug. 14, 1947. Peck (1972: 341) cited several summer records from Cape Henrietta Maria including a juvenile collected by C.E. Hope during the summer of 1948. Schueler, Baldwin & Rising (1974: 145) saw territorial pairs south of Winisk on June 17, 1965 and collected a female with enlarged ova on June 17, 1964 at the north end of Hawley Lake: they also noted the species at Moosonee, Ft. Albany and Attawapiskat. Lee (1978: 22) saw his first at Big Trout Lake on June 27 and single birds thereafter to July 24, 1975. McLaren & McLaren (1981: 3) reported a nest with 2 eggs at Little Sachigo Lake on June 12, 1977. Nash & Dick (1981: 48) collected two flightless young at Aquatuk Lake, one on June 28, 1980 and flushed a female from a nest with 4 eggs on July 1, 1980. Ross James noted young at Kiruna Lake (54°30'N, 84°55'W) on July 4 and 15, 1981. C.E. Hope saw a few at Ft. Severn between July 11 and 24, 1940 and collected three there.

AUTUMN: Stirrett reported 20 at Attawapiskat between Oct. 10 and 13, 1948 (Manning, 1952: 47), who cited several earlier fall records from the James Bay coast. Peruniak (1971: 16) gave Sept. 13 as her only fall date for Atikokan. Speirs & Speirs (1947: 28) noted one at North Bay on Sept. 29, 1944. Nicholson (1981: 104) reported a high fall count of 8 on Manitoulin on Oct. 31, 1976 and the latest record on Nov. 9, 1978. J. Goltz saw one as late as Nov. 1, 1980 on Beausoleil Is. (Mills, 1981: 57). Devitt (1967: 72) gave Nov. 20, 1946 as the latest date for Barrie. Weir & Quilliam (1980: 34) gave Nov. 3 as the 24-year average departure date from Kingston, with the latest on Nov. 16. W.H. Lunn saw one in Prince Edward Co. as late as Nov. 21, 1937 (Snyder, 1941: 52). My latest records, at Whitby and Pickering, were on Nov. 22 and my maximum fall count of 20 was at Corner Marsh, Pickering, on Oct. 12, 1964 (Speirs, 1977: 46). Five were observed wading up to their breast feathers in still water around Dufferin Is., Niagara, on Oct. 19 and 20, 1952 (Sheppard, 1960: 20). Snyder (1931: 140) cited a Long Point record as late as Nov. 20. Ussher (1965: 11) gave Oct. 30 as the 10-year average departure date from Rondeau, with the latest on Nov. 9. Stirrett (1973d: 19) had a maximum of 25 at Pelee on Sept. 15.

**MEASUREMENTS:**

Length: 12.5 to 15 ins. of which 2 1/4 ins. is bill (Godfrey, 1966: 149)
Wingspread: 23 to 26 ins. (Roberts, 1955: 563)
Weight: 5 to 10 oz. (Roberts, 1955: 563): females bigger than ♂.

♂ 168 g. (Hope, 1938: 19).

**REFERENCE:**
Nash, Stephen V. and James A. Dick 1981 First documentation of Greater Yellowlegs breeding in Ontario. Ont. Field Biologist, 35: (1): 48.

# LESSER YELLOWLEGS   *Tringa flavipes*   (Gmelin)

If you are in any doubt about which species of Yellowlegs you are looking at, it is probably this species. They frequent the borders of marshes during migrations in late spring, late summer and autumn, often in company with Greater Yellowlegs.

**IDENTIFICATION:** See the account of Greater Yellowlegs, from which this species differs chiefly in its smaller size and relatively short, straight bill. The whistle of this species is less loud and is usually of two syllables, rather than the resonant 3-syllabled call of the excitable Greater Yellowlegs.

**WINTER:**

**SPRING:** Stirrett (1973b: 17) had two as early as March 27 and two as late as May 27 at Pelee, with a maximum of 15 on May 17. Ussher (1965: 11) had Rondeau records from March 28 to May 25, with a 16-year average arrival on Apr. 28. Saunders & Dale (1933: 194) found it quite rare in spring at London, with average arrival on May 4 and the earliest on Apr. 16, 1918. Baillie (in Saunders, 1947: 364) gave March 20 as his earliest Toronto date, with May 9 and June 4 as average arrival and departure dates there. Naomi LeVay saw one at Cranberry Marsh, Whitby, as early as Apr. 5, 1964 and Ron Tozer reported two at Scugog Causeway as late as June 14, 1963 (Speirs, 1977: 47). Weir & Quilliam (1980: 34) had Kingston reports from Apr. 22 to June 7, with average arrival on May 3 and departure on May 18. Devitt (1967: 73) gave May 3 as the 14-year average arrival date at Barrie, with the earliest on Apr. 18, 1959 and a maximum of 30 on May 5, 1939. Beamer had just two Meaford spring records, five on May 6, 1950 and one on May 22, 1949. Mills (1981: 57-58) had just two spring records for the cottage country: two near Huntsville on Apr. 29, 1961 and eight on May 18, 1973 on Gray Island, southern Georgian Bay. Nicholson (1981: 104) had Manitoulin records from Apr. 16 (1977) to June 1 (1974), with average arrival on Apr. 27 and a maximum of 160 on May 19, 1970. MacLulich (1938: 15) cited a record for Algonquin Park on May 4, 1932. Skeel & Bondrup-Nielsen (1978: 171) saw a few in spring at Pukaskwa from May 8 to May 25, 1977. Denis (1961: 3) gave Apr. 29 as the average arrival date at Thunder Bay, with the earliest on Apr. 18, 1955. Elder (1979: 32) gave May 5 as his earliest date for Geraldton. Peruniak (1971: 16) gave May 1 as her earliest date for Atikokan. Cringan (1953b: 3) saw five at Kasabonika Lake on June 3, 1953, his earliest sighting of this species that spring. Cringan (1950: 9) reported that Elsey saw his first in the Asheweig area on May 17, 1950. Dann Lee noted three at Big Trout Lake on May 31, 1975 and single birds there until June 7.

**SUMMER:** On Breeding Bird Surveys they were reported as rare at Fort Frances and Dryden (probably late migrants). Stirrett (1973c:15) had the earliest returning record at Pelee on July 5 and a maximum of 200 on Aug. 11. Ussher (1965: 11) gave July 29 as the average fall arrival date for Rondeau, with the earliest on July 8. Snyder (1931: 171) collected a male at Long Point on July 12, 1927 and saw 35 there on July 21. Beardslee & Mitchell (1965: 221-222) reported two at Mohawk Is., Lake Erie on June 18, 1939 and one there on June 23, 1946 and Rockhouse Point records on June 25, 1959 and June 30 the same year. Speirs (1938: 52) gave Aug. 5 as the fall peak for southbound birds at Toronto, while Baillie (in Saunders, 1947: 364) reported a June 25 date for Toronto but gave July 15 as his earliest date for returning birds and Aug. 12 as his average arrival date in fall. Naomi LeVay saw one at Cranberry Marsh on June 30, 1960, while J.L. Baillie recorded 132 at Whitby Harbour on Aug. 2, 1958 (Speirs, 1977: 47). Weir & Quilliam (1980: 34) had returning birds at Kingston as early as June 24 with the average arrival date from the north on July 15. Devitt (1967: 73) gave July 12 as the earliest returning record for Collingwood. FON summer campers saw this species at Franklin Is. as early as July 10, 1940 (Mills, 1981: 58). Nicholson (1981: 172) had the earliest returning bird for Manitoulin on June 28, 1980 and a high count of 80 on Aug. 5, 1974. Skeel & Bondrup-Nielsen (1978: 172) saw one on July 2 and two on July 27, 1977 at Pukaskwa. J.L. Baillie collected an immature female on Sable Is., Lake of the Woods, where he found them to be very common (Snyder, 1938: 188). Snyder (1953: 58) noted the "first autumn movement of the species" near Kenora on July 31, 1948. Hope (1938: 19) reported a nest with 2 eggs, found by G.M. Neal at Favourable Lake on June 4, 1938, and southbound birds there from July 12 to Aug. 6. Manning (1952: 48) reported from 20 to 210 at various James Bay and Hudson Bay coastal localities between June 10 and Aug. 1, 1947 and a total of 400 at Shagamu River, Hudson Bay, between Aug. 8 and Aug. 14, 1947 (mainly small groups of juveniles). Peck (1972: 342) saw an agitated adult at Cape Henrietta Maria on June 27, 1970. Schueler, Baldwin & Rising (1974: 145) collected two females with enlarged ovaries at Hawley Lake on June 14, 1962 and June 12, 1964, and saw territorial pairs south of Winisk on June 17, 1965: they also found them common at Ft. Albany. Cringan (1950: 9) found them in barren muskegs in the Nikip Lake region and noted defensive behaviour there on July 21, 1950. Dann Lee had returning birds at Big Trout Lake from July 2 until he left on Aug. 10. C.E. Hope collected one at Fort Severn on June 17, 1940 and young there on July 9 and 10, 1940: the maximum number he reported was 100 on July 16.

AUTUMN: Stirrett saw two at Attawapiskat on Oct. 7, 1948 (Manning, 1952: 48). Nicholson (1981: 104) gave Oct. 16, 1977 as the latest date for Manitoulin. The latest Muskoka record was on Sept. 19, 1931 at Port Sydney (Mills, 1981: 58). Devitt (1967: 73) gave Oct. 27, 1947 as the latest date for Barrie. Weir & Quilliam (1980: 34) gave Oct. 25 as the average departure date from Kingston, with the latest on Nov. 11. Speirs (1977: 47) cited a Whitby record as late as Nov. 19, 1966. Speirs (1938: 54) had Nov. 22 as the latest Toronto date, while Saunders (1947: 364) gave Sept. 30 as the average departure date. Ussher (1965: 11) gave Oct. 26 as the average departure date from Rondeau, with the latest on Nov. 5. Stirrett (1973d: 19) had a fall maximum of 250 at Pelee, and the latest on Oct. 15. D. Rupert saw one at Pelee as late as Nov. 7, 1971 (Goodwin, 1972: 56).

**MEASUREMENTS:**
*Length:* 9.3 to 11.1 ins.
(incl. 1.4 in. beak)
(Godfrey, 1966: 149).
*Wingspread:* 19 to 21.5
ins. (Roberts, 1955: 176).
*Weight:* 2 1/2 to 5 oz.
(Roberts, 1955: 176) ♀
larger than ♂.
   Imm. ♂ 78 g. imm. ♀
70.6 g. (Hope, 1938: 20).

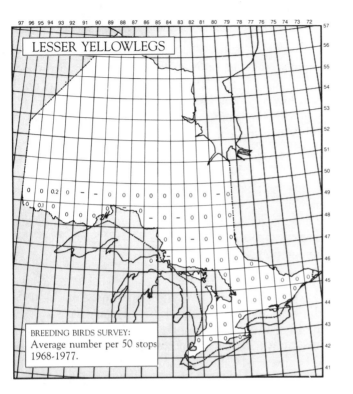

97 96 95 94 93 92 91 90 89 88 87 86 85 84 83 82 81 80 79 78 77 76 75 74 73 72

LESSER YELLOWLEGS

BREEDING BIRDS SURVEY:
Average number per 50 stops
1968-1977.

## SPOTTED REDSHANK *Tringa erythropus* (Pallas)

My only field experience with this beautiful wader was in Sweden. In North America it is purely accidental.

**IDENTIFICATION:** A black shorebird with white dots on its back and long red legs and a long, slender bill. Curry-Lindahl (1963: 328) has a fine colour illustration of one on its nest in northern Sweden. In flight look for the white rump and lower back (as in dowitchers). In winter the breast and lower back have a gray wash.

**WINTER:**

**SPRING:**

**SUMMER:** H.H. Axtell found one at St. Davids on July 25, 1976, also seen by others there (Goodwin, 1976: 950): carefully described.

**AUTUMN:**

**MEASUREMENTS:**
*Length:* 12 ins. (of which about 2 1/2 ins. is bill)
(Witherby *et al.* 4: 332)
*Wingspread:*
*Weight:*

# SOLITARY SANDPIPER   *Tringa solitaria*   Wilson

As the name suggests this bird is often seen alone, or in small groups. I have usually seen my first in the second or third week of May, but sometimes miss them on the way north and have to wait until they return in July. On their breeding ground in northern Ontario you may find the agitated parents proclaiming from the tops of dead spruces by roadside puddles. Unlike most sandpipers, they nest in trees.

IDENTIFICATION: I have often been alerted to their presence by their calls, which resemble the "wheet-wheet-wheet" whistles of the Spotted Sandpiper but given at a much higher pitch. They are a little bigger than "Spotties", darker in colour, with black-barred white outer tail feathers and prominent "spectacles" (white eye rings, with white lines running forward from these). The different manner of flight (see Spotted Sandpiper) and the white dots on the dark back also distinguish them from the Spotted Sandpiper, with which they often associate during migration.

WINTER: Stirrett (1973a: 15) reported one at Pelee on Feb. 26.

SPRING: Stirrett (1973b: 17) had Pelee records from the earliest on Apr. 14, 1954 to May 31, with a maximum of three on May 14. Ussher (1965: 11) gave May 9 as the 18-year average arrival date for Rondeau, with the earliest on Apr. 20 and latest on May 23. Saunders & Dale (1933: 194) gave May 6 as the 14-year average arrival date at London with the earliest on Apr. 21, 1923. Snyder (1931: 171) took a male at Long Point on May 6, 1928. Fleming (1906: 450) had a very early Toronto record on March 16, 1902, but Baillie (in Saunders, 1947: 364) gave May 12 as his 15-year average arrival date there with his latest on May 31: Speirs (1938: 44) gave May 19 as the peak of the spring migration at Toronto. Speirs (1977: 44) gave Apr. 19, 1976 as the earliest spring record for Ontario Co. with the peak on May 18 and latest on May 28, 1949. Snyder (1941: 52) found them in Prince Edward Co. from May 12 to June 1, 1934. Weir & Quilliam (1980: 34) gave May 8 and May 21 as the average spring arrival and departure dates at Kingston, with the earliest on Apr. 20 and latest on June 1. Devitt (1967: 71) gave May 7 as the 11-year average arrival date for Barrie, with the earliest on May 1 and latest on June 4, 1928. Beamer had only one spring record for Meaford: 3 on May 18, 1947. C. Harris saw one as early as May 4, 1977 at Go Home Bay (Mills, 1981: 56). Nicholson (1981: 103) gave Apr. 23, 1977 as the earliest Manitoulin record with May 6 as the 12-year average, a maximum count of 21 on May 10, 1970 and latest spring bird on May 31, 1975. MacLulich (1938: 15) cited a May 27, 1934 record for Algonquin Park. Ricker & Clarke (1939: 10) had four May records for Lake Nipissing between May 19 (1924) and May 24 (1925). Skeel & Bondrup-Nielsen (1978: 171) cited Pukaskwa records from May 29 to June 1, 1974. Denis (1961: 3) gave May 13 as the average arrival date at Thunder Bay, with the earliest on May 4, 1958. Bondrup-Nielsen (1976: 42) saw his first at Kapuskasing on May 15, 1974. Elder (1979: 32) gave May 9 as his earliest Geraldton date. Peruniak (1971: 16) gave May 11 as her earliest Atikokan record. Cringan (1953a: 2) saw his first in 1953 at Perrault Falls on May 7. Hewitt saw one near Moosonee on May 27, 1947 (Manning, 1952: 46). Cringan (1953b: 3) noted single birds in 1953 at Kasabonika Lake on June 2 and 4, and eight there on June 3.

SUMMER: On the Breeding Bird Surveys they were found only in the north, at Larder

Lake and Silver Islet and across the most northern routes from Smooth Rock Falls to Ignace; uncommon on all routes. Stirrett (1973c: 15) had returning birds at Pelee from July 15 to a maximum of 15 on Aug. 13. Ussher (1965: 11) had his earliest returning bird at Rondeau on July 16 and gave Aug. 8 as the average date for fall arrivals there. Speirs (1977: 44) gave July 9 as his earliest returning bird at Corner Marsh, Pickering. Snyder (1941: 52) had a returning bird in Prince Edward Co. on July 14, 1930. Weir & Quilliam (1980: 34) gave July 6 as the earliest returning bird at Kingston, with Aug. 3 as the average. E.G. White saw two adults with young 2/3 grown at South March, near Ottawa, during July, 1905 (Lloyd, 1923: 127). Southbound migrants were noted at Barrie by Frances Westman as early as July 20, 1959 (Devitt, 1967: 71). Beamer's early fall record for Meaford was on July 17, 1938. I saw one returning bird at Bella Lake, Muskoka, on July 13, 1940 (Mills, 1981: 51). Nicholson (1981: 103) had summer records for Manitoulin on June 13 and 20, 1920 and June 17, 1973 (suggesting the possibility of breeding there) and returning birds as early as July 22, 1972. MacLulich (1938: 15) cited several records for returning birds in Algonquin Park, the earliest on July 14, 1931. On June 19, 1973, K. Boshcoff found a nest on the Reagan Road, north of Pukaskwa (Skeel & Bondrup-Nielsen, 1978: 171): they saw returning birds there on July 10 and 24, 1977. Smith (1957: 172) collected a downy young near High Falls on the Frederick House River on June 20, 1953, and he saw two near Longlac on Aug. 12, 1954. Snyder (1938: 188) collected a female at Big Fork, Rainy River District, on July 24, 1929. Snyder (1953: 58) saw one at Kenora on July 31, 1931. Snyder (1928: 20) collected one at Lowbush, Lake Abitibi, on July 11, 1925. James (1980: 86) found one downy young with parents, 30 km. NE of Pickle Lake, on June 22, 1979. Hope (1938: 19) saw them at Favourable Lake from June 29 to July 29, 1938 and collected an immature male on July 29. Manning (1952: 46) collected two on July 13, 1947, at Raft River, James Bay, the male with an incubation patch. Schueler, Baldwin & Rising (1974: 142, 145) noted the species at Cochrane and Moosonee, but not at Ft. Albany, Attawapiskat or Winisk: they found a nest with 4 eggs, 6 1/2 ft. up in a 15 ft. spruce at Sutton Lake on June 28, 1964, and collected a juvenile at Hawley Lake on July 16, 1964. Cringan (1950: 9) noted one or two pairs in one mile of beaver meadow along the Petownikip River during June and July, 1950. Lee (1978: 22) noted them regularly at Big Trout Lake from July 10 to Aug. 10, 1975. C. Hope saw only two at Ft. Severn; on July 7, 1940.

AUTUMN: Peruniak (1971: 16) gave Sept. 24 as her latest Atikokan date. Nicholson (1981: 103) had a high fall count of 15 on Sept. 12, 1970 on Manitoulin and the latest record on Oct. 10, 1970. D. Sutherland saw four on Beausoleil Is. on Sept. 15, 1976 (Mills, 1981: 57). Beamer's latest Meaford record was on Sept. 17, 1938. Devitt (1967: 67) gave Oct. 28, 1952 as the latest date for Simcoe Co. (at Holland Marsh) and the maximum count of 8 at Barrie on Sept. 17, 1939. Weir & Quilliam (1980: 34) gave Sept. 23 as the average departure date from Kingston, with the latest on Nov. 4. Speirs (1977: 44) gave the second week of Sept. as the fall peak in Ontario Co., with one very late bird seen by Dave Calvert on Nov. 1, 1971 at Whitby. Speirs (1938: 54) gave Oct. 10 as the latest Toronto date. Ussher (1965: 11) had Rondeau records as late as Oct. 20. Stirrett (1973d: 19) had a few at Pelee in fall with the latest on Oct. 10.

**MEASUREMENTS:**
*Length:* 7 1/2 to 9 ins.
(Godfrey, 1966: 146)
*Wingspread:* 15 to 17 ins.
(Roberts, 1955: 574)
*Weight:* 2 ♂ averaged
47 g. 5 ♀ averaged 55 g.
(Hope, 1938: 19)

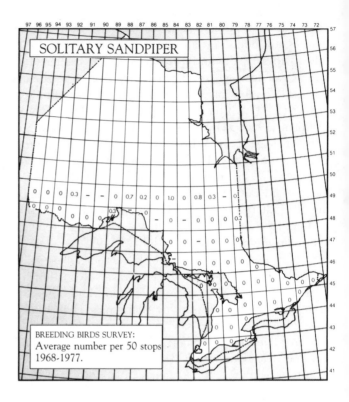

SOLITARY SANDPIPER

BREEDING BIRDS SURVEY:
Average number per 50 stops
1968-1977.

# WILLET   *Catoptrophorus semipalmatus*   (Gmelin)

This spectacular big, stout shorebird is rare in Ontario, preferring the salt marshes of the Atlantic coast and the margins of prairie lakes.

IDENTIFICATION: The broad white wing stripe, contrasting with the black flight feathers is diagnostic and the Willet has a habit of holding its wings aloft like flags for a few seconds after alighting from flight. Once it has settled down it tends to merge with its surroundings and looks rather like a stout Greater Yellowlegs but with *blue* legs and a heavier, *straight* bill and less contrasty body plumage. It's "pill-will-willet" call is also quite distinctive.

WINTER:

SPRING:  Stirrett (1973b: 17) gave five records of one or two birds at Pelee between May 2 and May 17. Kelley (1978: 34) reported seven at Pelee from May 5 to 17, 1968 and 23 at Stein's Marsh, near Pelee, on Apr. 28, 1974. Beardslee & Mitchell (1965: 219-220) reported single birds at Waverly Beach on Apr. 27, 1957; at Erie Beach on May 2, 1959 and at Point Abino on June 1, 1947. Long (1968b: 17) saw one as early as Apr. 13, 1968 at Shoal Point Marsh, Pickering, and another there on May 30, 1967: there were a few other Ontario Co. records between these dates (Speirs, 1977: 45). Walter Lamb saw one on Amherst Is., Kingston, on May 22, 1964 (Quilliam, 1973: 82). Devitt (1967: 72) reported two seen by A.B. Cockburn in Conc. 3, Oro Twp., Simcoe Co., on May 20, 1956 and one found near Collingwood during spring, 1958 by Aarne Lamsa. Nicholson (1981: 104) had Manitoulin records from May 4 (1975) to May 16 (1978).

SUMMER:  Stirrett (1973c: 15) had records of single birds at Pelee on June 17, Aug. 8, Aug. 14 and Aug. 25. J.P. Kleiman *et al* noted one at Rondeau on July 4, 1971 (Goodwin, 1971: 852). Wm. Girling reported one at Port Stanley, Lake Erie, on Aug. 17, 1940 (Brooman, 1954: 18). Beardslee & Mitchell (1965: 220) noted a maximum of six at Long Beach, Lake Erie, on Aug. 3, 1940. Baillie (in Saunders, 1947: 364) gave Aug. 7 and Aug. 23 dates for Toronto. Fleming (1906: 450) mentioned a Toronto specimen taken on July 20, 1898 (as well as four undated specimens). Naomi LeVay noted one at Cranberry Marsh on Aug. 17, 1969 (Tozer & Richards, 1974: 130). Bruce Falls and Jack Gates saw one on Amherst Is. on June 9, 1974 (Weir & Quilliam, 1980: 9): there were also three August records for the Kingston area: one on Wolfe Is. on Aug. 21, 1960 (Quilliam, 1973: 82); one on Amherst Is. from Aug. 9 to 12, 1979 and one at Prince Edward Point on Aug. 26, 1979 (Weir & Quilliam, 1980: 9). On July 27, 1963, Alf Mitchener and Frances Westman noted one at Collingwood (Devitt, 1967: 72). "A willet was identified at Kenora in August, 1932, by Dr. Hugh C. Keenan..." (Snyder, 1953: 58).

AUTUMN:  Ron Tasker saw one in Burpee Twp., Manitoulin, on Oct. 17, 1975 (Nicholson, 1981: 104). Devitt (1967: 72) saw one at Collingwood on Sept. 2, 1934 and Alf. Mitchener saw another there during October, 1944. Speirs (1977: 45) cited a few records for the first week of September in Pickering and Whitby marshes. Speirs (1938: 54) gave Sept. 8 as the latest Toronto record. Beardslee & Mitchell (1965: 220) reported one below Niagara Falls from Sept. 4 to 8, 1949.

**MEASUREMENTS:**
*Length:* 14 to 17 ins.
(Godfrey, 1966: 148)
*Wingspread:* 26 3/4 to 31
ins. (Roberts, 1955: 562)
*Weight:* 8 to 16 oz. ♀
larger than ♂ (Roberts,
1955: 562).

# WANDERING TATTLER  *Heteroscelus incanus*  (Gmelin)

This is normally a bird of the Pacific coast and islands, accidental in Ontario.

IDENTIFICATION: The Wandering Tattler is about the size and build of a Lesser Yellowlegs, but with shorter legs. The upper parts are uniform dark gray, except for a white line over and in front of the eye. In breeding plumage it is heavily barred below (like a Stilt Sandpiper, but lacking the white rump and scaly pattern above of that species). It has a habit of bobbing or teetering, like a Spotted Sandpiper.

WINTER:

SPRING:

SUMMER: Beardslee & Mitchell (1965: 218-219) gave detailed descriptions of the two Ontario sight records; both of birds in the distinctive breeding plumage, with heavily barred breasts. The first was seen about 2 miles west of Port Colborne on Aug. 1, 1948 by Mitchell, Harold Axtell and a dozen other observers. The second was found about five miles west of Ft. Erie at Windmill Park, Lake Erie, from July 12 to July 15, 1960, by Robert curry and confirmed by a dozen members of the Buffalo Ornithological Society during this period. A third was found at Windmill Point on June 8, 1977 by R.F. Andrle and stayed until June 13, where it was seen by many observers and photographed on June 12 by Alan Wormington (Goodwin, 1977: 1133).

AUTUMN:

**MEASUREMENTS:**
*Length:* 10.5 to 11.3 ins.
(Godfrey, 1966: 147).
*Wingspread:*
*Weight:* 146 g. (Terres,
1980: 786).

# SPOTTED SANDPIPER   *Actitis macularia*   (Linnaeus)

This is the familiar sandpiper that runs along the beach ahead of you, stopping to teeter up and down every few steps, and whistling as if calling your dog "wheet, wheet, wheet". Unlike most other sandpipers, which are birds of passage, the "spotty" breeds throughout Ontario, at the edge of lakes and streams, or even on ploughed fields.

IDENTIFICATION: With its plain, brown back, white breast (with big black spots in adults, but plain white in the young), its teetering habit (shared with the Solitary Sandpiper) and characteristic whistle, it is easily identified. The habit of circling out over the water on stiff, fluttering wings, separates it from the Solitary Sandpiper, which flies with the more usual direct, rowing flight of most other shorebirds.

WINTER: Stirrett (1973a: 15) had one record at Pelee as late as Dec. 18.

SPRING: Stirrett (1973b: 17) noted one at Pelee as early as Apr. 21, with a maximum of 24 on May 18. Ussher (1965: 10) gave Apr. 21 as the earliest Rondeau date, with May 1 as the 19-year average arrival date. Harold Lancaster gave Apr. 28 as the average arrival date in Elgin Co. (Brooman, 1954: 18). Saunders & Dale (1933: 193) gave Apr. 22 as the 17-year average arrival date for London, the earliest on Apr. 15, 1912. Speirs (1938: 40, 44) gave Apr. 15 as the earliest Toronto date, with the peak on May 9: J.L. Baillie gave May 3 as his 27-year average arrival date there (Saunders, 1947: 364). Audrey Russ noted one as early as Apr. 4, 1969 at Ajax, but the spring peak is about May 22 (Speirs, 1977: 43). Weir & Quilliam (1980: 34) gave Apr. 26 as the 30-year average arrival date for Kingston, the earliest on Apr. 7. Devitt (1967: 71) gave Apr. 25 as the 15-year average arrival date at Barrie, with the earliest on Apr. 11, 1956: J.C. Hall found a nest with 4 eggs as early as May 15, 1939 near Lisle, Simcoe Co. L. Beamer's earliest date for Meaford was Apr. 23, 1939 and his median arrival date was May 11: he found a nest with 4 eggs on May 23, 1943. Mills (1981: 56) gave Apr. 27 as the earliest record for the cottage country (at Huntsville). Nicholson (1981: 103) gave May 1 as the 12-year average arrival date for Manitoulin, with the earliest on Apr. 17, 1976. MacLulich (1938: 15) noted one at Algonquin Park as early as May 2, 1933. Ricker & Clarke (1939: 9) had a sighting at Lake Nipissing as early as Apr. 30, 1934. Skeel & Bondrup-Nielsen (1978: 170) saw their first at Puksaskwa on May 4, 1977. Denis (1961: 3) gave May 11 as the average arrival date at Thunder Bay, with the earliest on Apr. 29, 1941. Bondrup-Nielsen (1976: 42) had his earliest at Kapuskasing on May 15, 1975. Elder (1979: 52) gave May 11 as the earliest date for Geraldton. Peruniak (1971: 16) gave May 5 as the earliest date for Atikokan. Cringan (1953a: 2) saw his first at Sioux Lookout on May 3 in 1953. Cringan (1953b: 3) had his first at Kasabonika Lake on May 30 in 1953.

SUMMER: On Breeding Bird Surveys they were fairly common to uncommon on most routes from Lake Erie north as far as routes were run (Kapuskasing to Kenora). Stirrett (1973c: 15) had a maximum of 48 at Pelee on July 8. Kelley (1978: 33) reported three flying young with adults at Ipperwash Beach on Aug. 1, 1953 as a late breeding record. Brooman (1954: 18) reported two nests, each with 4 eggs, in Elgin Co.: one on June 2, 1939 and the other on June 5, 1949. Saunders & Dale (1933: 194) cited data for six sets (one with 3 eggs, five with 4 eggs), the earliest on May 26, 1914 and the latest on June 14, 1917, in the London region. Snyder (1931: 171) reported a set of eggs taken at Long

Point on June 1, 1927. R.F. Andrle found a nest with 4 eggs as late as July 11, 1943, at Crescent Beach, Lake Erie (Beardslee & Mitchell, 1965: 217). Speirs (1977: 43) summarized data from 20 sets totaling 76 eggs, in Ontario Co., the earliest nest with 4 eggs on May 21, 1956 and the latest which contained one egg and three tiny young on July 15, 1928. Quilliam (1973: 81) reported two nests, each with 4 eggs, at Kingston: the first was found on May 27, 1959 and hatched on June 16; the other still held 4 eggs on July 1, 1961. Lloyd (1923: 127) called this an abundant summer resident at Ottawa and reported one collected by C.L. Patch on June 5, 1916. On June 10, 1937, Devitt (1967: 71) found a nest with 2 eggs on Giant's Tomb Is.: on June 11 he observed a Fox Snake devouring the last remaining egg: he also reported a small flightless young as late as Aug. 2, 1936 at Duntroon, Simcoe Co. Beamer reported a nest with 4 young about a day old as late as July 12, 1940, at Meaford. Egg dates in the cottage country ranged from May 20 to July 23 and hatching clutches from June 25 to July 23 (Mills, 1981: 56). Nicholson (1981: 103) reported two Manitoulin nests; one on May 31, 1975 and one on June 10, 1912. Speirs & Speirs (1947: 28) saw a downy young with an adult at Trout Lake, near North Bay, on July 16, 1944 and Ricker & Clarke (1939: 9) noted three newly-hatched young at Frank's Bay, Lake Nipissing, on June 19, 1933. Snyder (1942: 128) reported complete clutches at Maclennan, near Sault Ste. Marie, on June 9, 10 and 11, 1931. Baillie & Hope (1947: 7) collected 4 downy young from a nest at Biscotasing on June 20, 1937 and two young, about 1/3 grown, at Bigwood on July 24, 1937. Skeel & Bondrup-Nielsen (1978: 170) wrote that this was the most common shorebird at Pukaskwa in summer. Baillie & Hope (1943: 9) found a nest with 4 eggs at Amyot on June 27, 1936, and a brood of 4 newly hatched young on July 4. Dear (1940: 128) reported nests with 4 eggs near Thunder Bay on June 10, 1922 and June 30, 1930. Smith (1957: 172) reported nests with eggs north of Timmins and south of Kapuskasing. Snyder (1928: 257) reported complete clutches at Lake Nipigon on June 19, 1923 and June 19, 1924. Snyder (1938: 188) collected an incubating male from a nest with 4 eggs at Aylesworth, Rainy River District, on June 25, 1929. Snyder (1953: 58) reported a nest with 3 eggs at Ingolf on June 5, 1937; a nest with 4 eggs at Kenora on June 18, 1930, and young at Dryden on June 20, 1939 and at Malachi on July 21, 1947. James (1980: 86) found four nests, each with 4 eggs, near Pickle Lake, on June 11, 1977, two on June 13, 1979 and one on June 15, 1979. Hope (1938: 18) collected a juvenile near Favourable Lake on July 28, 1938. Snyder (1928: 21) collected the incubating male from a nest with 4 eggs at Lake Abitibi on June 21, 1925. Manning (1952: 46) reported this species in summer of 1947 near Moosonee, Ft. Albany, Attawapiskat, and near the mouths of Raft River and Shagamu River. H. Lumsden noted three near the mouth of Brant River (Peck, 1972: 34) but none were found on the tundra near Cape Henrietta Maria. Schueler, Baldwin & Rising (1974: 142, 145) saw them at Winisk and reported six nests, each with 4 eggs, between June 17 and July 5, at Hawley Lake and vicinity. Cringan (1950: 8) found this to be the most frequently observed shorebird at Nikip Lake, with the maximum of 8 there on June 13, 1950. Lee (1978: 22) found a nest with 3 eggs on June 19, 1975 at Big Trout Lake and a downy young there on July 21: his maximum count was 9 on June 6. Hope had a maximum count of 20 at Ft. Severn on July 1, 1940, when he collected two juveniles: he found a nest with 4 eggs on July 9.

AUTUMN: Peruniak (1971: 16) gave Sept. 14 as the latest date for Atikokan. One was seen at Pukaskwa as late as Oct. 3, 1975 (Skeel & Bondrup-Nielsen, 1978: 170). Speirs & Speirs (1947: 28) saw one at North Bay as late as Oct. 20, 1944. Nicholson

(1981: 103) gave Oct. 14, 1973 as the latest Manitoulin sighting. Mills (1981: 56) had only two records later than Labour Day for the cottage country: one at Port Sydney on Sept. 8, 1894 and one at Bala on Oct. 5, 1980. Devitt (1967: 71) reported that they were rare in Simcoe Co. by Sept. 1, but that Frances Westman saw one at Barrie as late as Oct. 1, 1950. Weir & Quilliam (1980: 34) gave Sept. 26 as the 25-year average departure date from Kingston, with the latest on Nov. 7. The latest Ontario Co. record was on Oct. 25, 1952 when J. Satterly saw one at Cedar Pt., Lake Simcoe. Speirs (1938: 54) gave Nov. 11 as the latest Toronto date, and J.L. Baillie gave Sept. 12 as his 27-year average departure date (Saunders, 1947: 364). Beardslee & Mitchell (1965: 217) reported one as late as Nov. 1, 1947 at Crystal Beach, Lake Erie. Ussher (1965: 10) gave Sept. 14 as the 8-year average departure date from Rondeau, with the latest on Sept. 30. Stirrett (1973d: 19) had one at Pelee as late as Oct. 26, but most had left by Sept. 1.

**MEASUREMENTS:**
*Length:* 7 to 8 ins.
(Godfrey, 1966: 146).
*Wingspread:* 13 to 14 ins.
(Roberts, 1955: 578).
*Weight:* 1.5 to 2.0 oz.
(Roberts, 1955: 578) ♀
larger than ♂.
  ♀ 53.2 g. (Hope,
1938: 18).

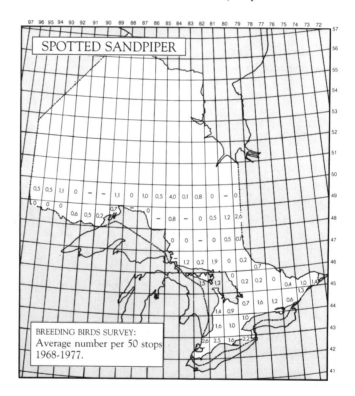

SPOTTED SANDPIPER

BREEDING BIRDS SURVEY:
Average number per 50 stops
1968-1977.

# UPLAND SANDPIPER   *Bartramia longicauda*   (Bechstein)

This is primarily a bird of pastureland. Since birdwatchers do not usually spend much time on large cattle ranches they may get the impression that this species is less common than it actually is.

IDENTIFICATION: This is a long-legged, long-necked, small-headed, brownish sandpiper, of medium size. Its fluttering flight is similar to that of the familiar Spotted Sandpiper (and unlike the swift, rowing flight of most sandpipers). It has a habit of holding its wings aloft after settling on a post or pole for a few seconds before folding them into the resting position. The calls are far carrying and diagnostic, once learned. In the breeding area it utters a rising, tremolo, followed by a deliberate descending whistle. In migration you may hear it high overhead giving a quavering call on one pitch.

WINTER:

SPRING: Stirrett (1973b: 17) had Pelee records from Apr. 21 to May 16, with a maximum of 15 on May 6. Brooman (1954: 18) reported a nest with 4 eggs taken on May 29, 1895 by R.T. Anderson of Aylmer, and a pair with 3 downy young seen by Fred Bodsworth and Donald Young near Aylmer on May 31, 1942. Saunders & Dale (1933: 193) gave Apr. 22 as the 14-year average arrival date near London, with the earliest on Apr. 17, 1915: A.A. Wood took sets of 4 eggs on May 21, 1926 and June 3, 1915. Beardslee & Mitchell (1965: 216-217) noted one at Ft. Erie as early as Apr. 1, 1951. Speirs (1938: 40) gave Apr. 19 as the earliest Toronto date. Speirs (1977: 42) suggested that the spring peak in Ontario Co. was in the fourth week of April, and the earliest was one seen by George A. Scott at Whitby on Apr. 14, 1963. Snyder (1941: 51) mentioned a nest with 4 eggs taken by C.J. Young at Allisonville, Prince Edward Co., on May 25, 1935. Weir & Quilliam (1980: 34) gave Apr. 23 as the 27-year average arrival date for Kingston, with the earliest on Apr. 12, 1952. Devitt (1967: 70) gave May 1 as the 10-year average arrival date for Barrie, with the earliest on Apr. 18, 1954. Mills (1981: 55) saw a pair near Burk's Falls on May 7, 1980. Nicholson (1981: 102) gave Apr. 30 as the 10-year average arrival date for Manitoulin, with the earliest on Apr. 23, 1977. Denis (1961: 3) gave May 13 as the average arrival date at Thunder Bay with the earliest on May 7, 1960.

SUMMER: On the 1968-1977 Breeding Bird Surveys they were common in extreme southeastern Ontario, then fairly common to rare north to Mattawa, Sudbury, Thunder Bay and Atikokan, with one outlier at Hearst on the 1976 survey. Stirrett (1973c: 15 and 1973d: 19) had a maximum of 4 at Pelee on Aug. 4 and the latest one there on Aug. 19. Beardslee & Mitchell (1965: 216) found a bird "hardly a week old" near Cedar Bay, Lake Erie, on July 27, 1929 "indicating a very late nesting". Frank Banfield saw two young on the Toronto Flying Field at York Downs on June 3, 1937 (Lawrie, 1937: 5). Tozer & Richards (1974: 129) cited several breeding records for Ontario Co., one nest with 4 eggs as early as May 19, 1956 near Oshawa, and young as late as July 29, 1962 in Whitby Twp. Snyder (1941: 52) collected 3 downy young, with well-developed pin feathers, at Mountain View, Prince Edward Co., on July 2, 1930. E. Beaupré took a set of 3 eggs on Simcoe Is., near Kingston, on June 25, 1896 (Quilliam, 1973: 80). W.W. Smith found a nest with 4 eggs on Big Cedar Point, Lake Simcoe, on June 14, 1942 and Devitt (1967: 70) cited a few other breeding records for Simcoe Co. Mills (1981: 55) cited a few June and July records for Muskoka and Parry Sound Districts and the latest on Aug. 8,

1979 near Ahmic Lake. Nicholson (1981: 102) gave Aug. 8th, 1972 as his latest date for Manitoulin: he cited a record by Ron Tasker, who saw 4 adults and a downy young in Burpee Twp. on July 12, 1980.

AUTUMN: This is a very early fall migrant. Devitt (1967: 70) gave Sept. 29, 1957 as the latest fall date for Simcoe Co., most having left by the end of August. Weir & Quilliam (1980: 38) gave Sept. 2 as the 21-year average departure date from Kingston, with an unusually late sighting on Oct. 13. Speirs (1977: 42) suggested that the peak of the southward flight through Ontario Co. was during the first week of August, with the latest observation on Sept. 25, 1974, over Pickering Twp. Speirs (1938: 54) gave Sept. 5 as the latest Toronto date.

**MEASUREMENTS:**
*Length:* 11.0 to 12.8 ins.
(Godfrey, 1966: 145)
*Wingspread:* 19 3/4 to 23
ins. (Roberts, 1955: 571)
*Weight:* 6.25 to 7.88 oz.
(Roberts, 1955: 571).

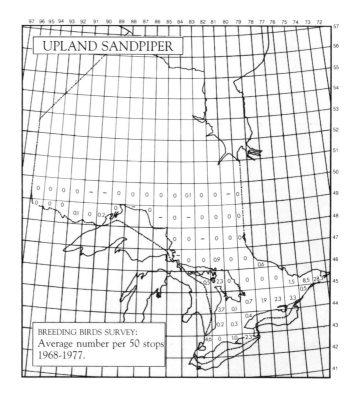

UPLAND SANDPIPER

BREEDING BIRDS SURVEY:
Average number per 50 stops
1968-1977.

# ESKIMO CURLEW   *Numenius borealis*   (Forster)

Although the old writers referred to this as the most numerous of the curlews (on the Labrador coast in fall and the Arctic breeding grounds in summer) I can find no evidence that it was ever plentiful in Ontario. It is now "virtually extinct".

IDENTIFICATION:   It was a smaller bird than the Whimbrel, with a shorter, less curved down bill. The only certain distinction is its unbarred outer primary (only the inner web of this feather is barred or "saw-toothed" in the Whimbrel).

WINTER:

SPRING:   Manning (1952: 103) cited the original description by Forster indicating that they visited Ft. Albany during April and early May.

SUMMER:   Forster wrote that they returned to Ft. Albany in August. Kathleen Anderson and Archie Hagar described two that flew by North Point, James Bay, on Aug. 15, 1976.

AUTUMN:   Forster wrote that they went away southward from Ft. Albany "the latter end of September". Fleming (1906: 451) reported that a specimen taken Oct. 10, 1873 at Wolfe Is. near Kingston, went to the British Museum. He also mentioned two specimens taken at Toronto Island in 1864, which went to the museum in Ottawa. McIlwraith (1894: 160) mentioned three specimens, one in his collection that he took at Hamilton and two taken by Macallum, presumably near Dunnville (no dates for any of these three).

**MEASUREMENTS:**
*Length:* 12 to 14 1/2 ins. (including 2 to 2 1/2 in. bill) (Godfrey, 1966: 144)
*Wingspread:* 26 to 30 ins. (Roberts, 1955: 558)
*Weight:* 1 lb. (Pough, 1951: 225).

**REFERENCE:**
Anderson, Kathleen and Archie Hagar 1976 Eskimo Curlew sighting. Am. Birds, 30: (4): 836. "two Black-bellied Plover-sized shorebirds with thin, decurved bills, flew past us, silently, not more than 80 feet away". Hagar had seen them in Texas in 1962 and identified them instantly.

# WHIMBREL   *Numenius phaeopus*   (Linnaeus)

In southern Ontario, the Whimbrels pass through very quickly in late May, often in good-sized flocks. In fall the migration is more prolonged but usually only stray individuals turn up, with other shorebirds on mudflats. If you miss the "big day" in spring you may have to wait another year before a chance to see them. Their passage is always a memorable event: the big brown, long-winged, birds approach in echelons along the lakeshore, sometimes passing over, sometimes circling around a bay, or settling on some promontory to rest. You may be first alerted to their approach by hearing the thrilling, bubbling trill.

IDENTIFICATION: Gull-sized shorebirds with long, downturned bills are usually Whimbrels. Other curlews are exceedingly rare in Ontario and Glossy Ibis are blackish, and are seldom seen along shores in May, more often with herons in marshes in summer.

WINTER:

SPRING: Stirrett (1973b: 17) had Pelee records from May 6 to June 2, with a high count of 400 on May 21. R. Simpson noted one at Rondeau as late as June 6, 1971 (Goodwin, 1971: 852). Ussher (1965: 10) had sightings at Rondeau from May 18 to May 28 with the 16-year average arrival date on May 22: Kelley (1978: 32) reported a maximum of 600 in that vicinity on May 23, 1970. Brooman (1954: 18) cited several Elgin Co. records between May 25 and May 29, with a maximum of 350 at Pt. Stanley on May 24. Saunders & Dale (1933: 193) had only one spring record for London: one flying over on May 24, 1927. Snyder (1931: 171) had Long Point records between May 24 and May 29, 1928. Beardslee & Mitchell (1965: 214) reported a maximum of 1575 along the Canadian shore of Lake Erie on May 25, 1957, mostly at Rockhouse Point. Speirs (1938: 40, 44, 46) had Toronto records from May 11 to June 5, with the spring peak on May 25. Speirs (1977: 41) had reports of spring migrants in Ontario Co. from May 15 to May 31, with a maximum of 470 between Whitby and Ajax on May 22, 1961. R.J. Rutter saw four in Prince Edward Co. on May 25, 1931 (Snyder, 1941: 51). Weir & Quilliam (1980: 34) had Kingston records from May 15 to May 30 with the 17-year arrival average on May 22: Quilliam (1973: 79) gave 130 as the largest spring flock, seen on May 24, 1969 on Amherst Is. R.A. Smith saw flocks of 200 and 350 flying north over Holland Marsh on May 27, 1942 (Devitt, 1967: 70). M. Austin found a flock of 31 at Skeleton Lake, near Huntsville, on May 27, 1968 (Mills, 1981: 55). Nicholson (1981: 101) had Manitoulin records from May 17 (1980) to June 2 (1974) with a maximum of 600 on May 23, 1980 and a 10-year average arrival date on May 22: he mentioned their "bubbling, lilting calls" as they passed westward along the southern shores. Denis (1961: 4) gave May 27 as the average arrival date at Thunder Bay, with the earliest on May 21, 1960. I saw about 55 on the beach at Dorion with 22 Hudsonian Godwits on May 23, 1956 and six there again on May 30 of the same spring. Dave Elder had an Atikokan record about June 1.

SUMMER: Stirrett (1973c: 15) had two summer records for Pelee: 50 on July 7, 1913 and one on July 22, 1914. Beardslee & Mitchell (1965: 215) reported 14 on Mohawk Is. on Aug. 5, 1950 as the fall maximum for the Buffalo region and one at Point Abino on July 9, 1940, as the earliest returning migrant. Fleming (1906: 451) wrote: "the old birds return early in July (July 4, 1904, July 17, 1906)" at Toronto. Long (1965: 35) had a northbound bird at Pickering Beach as late as June 12, 1965 and 13 returning migrants there on July 15, 1963. E. Beaupré had a Prince Edward Co. sighting on June 11, 1924 (Snyder, 1941: 51). Weir & Quilliam (1980: 34) had the earliest returning bird at Kingston on July 22. Devitt (1967: 70) gave records of returning birds at Wasaga Beach on July 14, 1935; at Cook's Bay on July 16, 1940; at Collingwood on Aug. 10, 1957 and one collected by E.L. Brereton at Wasaga Beach on Aug. 18, 1939. Beamer saw a northbound bird at Meaford on June 5 and 6, 1943. On June 4, 1897, a dead Whimbrel was found in a Peregrine Falcon's nest on Lake Muskoka by P.A. Taverner (Mills, 1981: 55). On July 17, 1947, Manning (1952: 45) collected a pair at Lake River, with three of the four downy young: he cited several other July records from the James Bay coast, mostly migrants going south (specimens collected were mainly adult males). Peck (1972: 340) reported two nests with eggs noted by C.E. Hope in the Cape Henrietta Maria region in the summer of 1948: Harry Lumsden found them abundant on the Hudson Bay coast. Schueler, Baldwin & Rising (1974: 142) found them common at Ft. Albany, uncommon at Winisk, and reported evidence of breeding along the Sutton River (they noted none at Moosonee, Attawapiskat or Hawley Lake). C.E. Hope collected one at Ft. Severn on July 3, and two of 4 seen on July 11, 1940: he noted 30 there on July 17 and one on July 21.

AUTUMN: M. Cryer saw one at Thunder Bay as late as Nov. 17, 1971 (Goodwin, 1972: 56). Nicholson (1981: 101) had only two records of returning birds on Manitoulin: two at Providence Bay on Aug. 26, 1973 and one at Quarry Point on Aug. 31, 1975. Beamer saw one on the shoreline below Thornbury on Sept. 8, 1940. Devitt (1967: 70) gave Sept. 4, 1949 as his latest record for Simcoe Co.: at Allenwood. Lloyd (1923: 127) cited G.R. White who took three specimens, with Golden Plover, at Ottawa about Sept. 1, 1885. Weir & Quilliam (1980: 34) gave Sept. 22 as the latest Kingston date. Snyder (1941: 51) noted a specimen collected at Weller Bay, Prince Edward Co., on Sept. 17, 1934. Long (1965: 35) observed two at Pickering Beach, on Sept. 11 and 19, 1964. Fleming (1906: 451) reported young birds at Toronto from Sept. 1 to Sept. 15 "but are very rare". Speirs (1938: 54) reported an exceptionally late bird at Toronto on Nov. 23. L.H. Smith shot one at Strathroy on Sept. 22, 1900, the only fall record for Middlesex Co. (Saunders & Dale, 1933: 193). Keith Reynolds reported nine migrating SW over Pt. Stanley on Sept. 24, 1949 (Brooman, 1954: 18). Ussher (1965: 10) had returning birds at Rondeau from Aug. 25 to Sept. 11. Stirrett (1973d: 19) had Pelee records from Aug. 26 to Nov. 10, with a maximum of nine on Nov. 5.

**MEASUREMENTS:**

*Length:* 15 to 18.8 ins. (including bill of 2 3/4 to 4 in.) Godfrey, 1966: 143. *Wingspread:* 31 to 33 ins. (Roberts, 1955: 559). *Weight:* to 1 1/4 lbs. (Terres, 1980: 787). 29 ♂ weighed 310 to 403 g. av. 354.8 g. 36 ♀ weighed 345 to 459 g. av. 403.9 g. birds live trapped at Churchill, Man.

**REFERENCE:**

Skeel, Margaret A. 1982 Sex determination of adult Whimbrels. Journ. Field Ornithology, 53: (4): 414-416.

# SLENDER-BILLED CURLEW
## *Numenius tenuirostris* Vieillot

This is another accidental species, normally a bird of the northern wet steppes of central Asia.

**IDENTIFICATION:** The lower breast and flanks have heart-shaped dark spots; the rump is white and as its name suggests, the bill is quite slender. There is a good photograph of the only Ontario specimen in Beardslee & Mitchell (1965: 213).

**WINTER:**

**SPRING:**

**SUMMER:**

**AUTUMN:** Beardslee & Mitchell (1965: 212-213) . . . gave details of the specimen, apparently shot at Crescent Beach, Lake Erie, by I.L. Terry about 1925, possibly in October or early November and subsequently mounted by Santerns. It is now in the Buffalo Museum of Science (BSNS 2092).

**MEASUREMENTS:**
*Length:* 15 to 16 ins. (incl.
3 in. bill) (Witherby *et al*,
1948: v. 4:179).
*Wingspread:*
*Weight:*

# LONG-BILLED CURLEW *Numenius americanus* Bechstein

This is essentially a prairie bird, accidental in Ontario.

**IDENTIFICATION:** This is a larger bird than the Whimbrel, with a relatively longer bill and it lacks the contrasting light and dark head stripes of that species. The general colouration is more buffy than the Whimbrel and the wings are pinkish buff with no barring on the axillars.

**WINTER:**

**SPRING:**

**SUMMER:**

**AUTUMN:** Jerry Norris photographed one at Ajax on Oct. 17 after observing it at close range. The bird was first reported by WIlliam G. Newman there, a few days earlier, in 1959 (Speirs and Speirs, 1960: 32).

**MEASUREMENTS:**
*Length:* 20 to 26 ins. (Roberts, 1955: 558).
(including 5 to 7 1/2 in. *Weight:* 1 lb. 12 oz. to 2
bill) Godfrey, 1966: 143. lb. 2 oz. (Roberts,
*Wingspread:* 36 to 40 ins. 1955: 558).

# HUDSONIAN GODWIT   *Limosa haemastica*   (Linnaeus)

Although it is not common, this is the godwit most likely to be seen in Ontario. It breeds along the Hudson Bay coast of Ontario and winters in southern South America. Large flocks may be seen along the James Bay coast during migration in late August and early September and smaller flocks on mudflats bordering the lower Great Lakes, but sometimes years go by when none are found there.

IDENTIFICATION: The large size and slightly upturned bill identify it as a godwit. The striking black and white tail pattern, white at the base and black at the tip, the white wing stripe and blackish axillars identify it as this species. In breeding plumage the breast is chestnut but young in fall are rather a uniform dull gray. The base of the bill is orange in spring and bright pink in fall (Hope & Shortt, 1944: 576).

WINTER:

SPRING: Stirrett (1973d: 17) had two spring records of single birds at Pelee: on May 13, 1905 and May 12, 1956: Kelley (1978: 36) reported another there on May 25, 1974. James Savage saw one at Point Abino, Lake Erie, on May 28, 1934 (Beardslee & Mitchell, 1965: 233). Fred Cooke reported one near Kingston on May 18, 1968 (Quilliam, 1973: 87) and Martin Edwards found one on Amherst Is. on May 19, 1974 (Weir & Quilliam, 1980: 11). Nicholson (1981: 109) had seven spring records for Manitoulin, the earliest on May 13 (1978) and the latest on May 30 (1974). Denis (1961: 4) gave May 18 as the average arrival date at Thunder Bay, with the earliest on May 9, 1959. I saw two there on May 30, 1955 and a group of 22 at Dorion on May 23, 1956, with 7 still in the vicinity on May 27. Elder (1979: 33) had just one spring record for Geraldton, on May 30, 1971.

SUMMER: Kelley (1978: 36) reported one at Erieau on June 20, 1970. J. Hughes Samuel saw one at Toronto on June 13, 1895, and a young bird was taken there on Aug. 20, 1898 (Fleming, 1906: 451). N. and M. Sherwood noted one at Whitby on July 28, 1962 according to J.L. Baillie's diary. Weir & Quilliam (1980: 11) reported a returning bird at Kingston as early as Aug. 7. Hope & Shortt (1944: 575-576) saw two at Big Piskwanish, James Bay, on July 20, 1942; on July 23 at least 1000 passed their camp there and 200 the next day: all that could be distinguished were adults: most of the flocks numbered 60 to 70, flew in flat V's or crescent formations at a height of about 200 ft., giving a modulated trill similar to Whimbrels. Manning (1952: 55) noted that most adults precede the young in migration: he saw 20 juveniles at Shagamu River on Aug. 11, 1947 and 30 there on Aug. 14 (on the Hudson Bay coast). Peck (1972: 343) saw one exhibiting territorial behaviour near Cape Henrietta Maria on June 25 and 26, 1970 and remarked that the ROM field party saw several hundred and collected 28 there in July and Aug., 1948: H. Lumsden noted 33 and collected two in the region from July 12-15, 1957 and observed numbers at the mouth of the Brant River in mid-July, 1969. Schueler, Baldwin & Rising (1974: 143) noted the species at Ft. Albany, Winisk and Sutton River. However, Peck (1981: 10) still had no definite nest record in Ontario.

AUTUMN: Nicholson (1981: 109) had only one fall record for Manitoulin, on Oct. 14, 1974 in Gordon Twp. Lloyd (1923: 127) listed a few Ottawa specimens taken between Sept. 21 (1874) and Oct. 20 (1900), but W.E. Godfrey *et al* saw 17 there on Oct. 17, 1971 (Goodwin, 1972: 57). Weir & Quilliam (1980: 11) reported that 46 were seen at the Amherstview Sewage Lagoons on Sept. 27, 1975 by Ron. Weir, and gave Nov. 12

as the latest Kingston date: 20 were banded at Amherstview. In 1973 one was seen at Corner Marsh, Pickering, from Aug. 23 to Sept. 23: there has been at least one fall record for 18 of the past 27 years, with a maximum of 10 noted at Whitby Harbour on Sept. 10, 1961 by Tom Hassall and the latest one noted on Nov. 11, 1974 when I saw one at Corner Marsh, with Miles and Penelope Hearn (Speirs, 1977: 62). Fleming (1906: 450) reported that two collected at Toronto on Sept. 25, 1894 were in winter plumage, while two taken on Oct. 20, 1890 were adults in changing plumage. One was reported at Sugarloaf Point, Lake Erie, on Sept. 7, 1958, seen by most observers on the shorebird count that day (Beardslee & Mitchell, 1965: 234). Ussher (1965: 12) called this a rare fall migrant at Rondeau, from Sept. 17 to Nov. 5. Stirrett (1973d: 19) noted one or two at Pelee from Sept. 8 to 10, 1955, while Goodwin (1972: 57) reported some there from Sept. 16 to Nov. 21, 1971.

**MEASUREMENTS:**
*Length:* 14.5 to 16.7 ins.
(including 2.7 to 3.2 in.
bill) (Godfrey, 1966: 163)
*Wingspread:* 25 to 28 ins.
(Roberts, 1955: 556)
*Weight:* 9 to 13 oz.
(Roberts, 1955: 556).
Females average larger
than ♂'s.

# MARBLED GODWIT   *Limosa fedoa*   (Linnaeus)

This big shorebird is relatively common in the prairie provinces but is rare in Ontario. It winters chiefly in Central America.

**IDENTIFICATION:**  This is a really big shorebird, almost as big as a Ring-billed Gull, with creamy brown general colouration and some cinnamon-brown in the wings in flight. It has a very long, slightly upturned bill and lacks the black and white tail pattern, the white wing stripe and blackish axillars of the more common Hudsonian Godwit.

**WINTER:**

**SPRING:**  Fleming (1906: 450) reported one taken at Toronto on May 30, 1895. Margaret Bain reported one at Corbett Creek Marsh, Whitby, on May 9 and 10, 1977. Weir & Quilliam (1980: 11) reported one seen by many observers at Amherst Is. from May 24 to 26, 1974 and another at Amherstview Sewage Lagoons from May 11-13, 1975. Devitt (1967: 76) noted one seen at Collingwood on May 27, 1961 by Alf. Mitchener and Frances Westman *et al.* Nicholson (1981: 109) had four spring records from Manitoulin: May 3-9, 1970 and June 1-2, 1974 in Gordon Twp., May 23, 1971 at Little Current and May 13-14, 1978 near Tehkummah. Denis (1961: 4) gave May 19 as the average arrival date at Thunder Bay, with the earliest on May 3, 1956: I saw two there on May 28, 1955 and one as late as May 30, 1955. I also noted one at Dorion on May 27, 1956 and one at Hurkett the same day.

SUMMER: Beardslee & Mitchell (1965: 233) reported one seen by Harold Axtell *et al* at Rockhouse Pt., Lake Erie, on July 22, 1956. Fleming (1906: 450) had one in his collection taken at Toronto on June 7, 1890. Speirs (1938: 48) had a Toronto record as early as Aug. 5. J.L. Baillie and Don. Burton saw one at Whitby Harbour on Aug. 2, 1958: B.B. Geale saw it there on Aug. 11 and 31 and with Doris H. Speirs I saw it there on Aug. 23: on Aug. 13, 1975 I found one at Corner Marsh, Pickering and saw two there on Aug. 24 (Speirs, 1977: 61). R.A. Smith reported one at Darlington Provincial Park on Aug. 1, 1972 (Tozer & Richards, 1974: 138). Kenneth Edwards, Betty Hughes, *et al* saw one from Aug. 4-15, 1976 at Amherstview Sewage Lagoons (Weir & Quilliam, 1980: 11). Lloyd (1923: 127) had just one Ottawa record: an injured bird captured alive at Britannia about June 4, 1902, and later seen by G.R. White at a taxidermist's. Alf. Mitchener saw one with its lower mandable missing, at Collingwood on July 27, 1963 (Devitt, 1967: 77). Morrison, Manning & Hagar (1976: 487-490) summarized and mapped records for the western James Bay breeding population: the first definite evidence of breeding was on July 4, 1975 when Manning's retriever found a 10-day old young north of Moosonee at North Point (now No. 63, 284 in the collection of the National Museum, Ottawa): Hagar saw 300 to 400 birds near Ft. Albany on July 24, 1964 and T.M. Shortt saw six flying overhead as far north as the ROM camp at Cape Henrietta Maria on July 27, 1948: other observers noted the species at various points along the west shore of James Bay to its southern extemity.

AUTUMN: Speirs (1977: 61) cited several fall records at Corner Marsh, Pickering, the latest on Sept. 27, 1975. Speirs (1938: 54) gave Sept. 20 as the latest Toronto date. Stirrett (1973d: 19) had only one fall record for Pelee: on Sept. 15, 1915.

**MEASUREMENTS:**
*Length:* 16.8 to 20 ins.
(including 3 to 5.5 in. bill)
(Godfrey, 1966: 162)
*Wingspread:* 6 ad. ♂ 29-
31.5 ins: imm. ♂ 's 28.5
& 29.5 ins:
   6 ad. ♀ 32 - 33.38
ins: imm ♀ 29 ins.
(Roberts, 1955: 557).
*Weight:* ♂ 11 1/4 oz.; 2
♀ 12 and 13 3/4 oz.
(Roberts, 1955: 557).

**REFERENCE:**
Morrison, R.I.G., T.H.
Manning & J.A. Hagar
1976
   Breeding of the Marbled
Godwit, *Limosa fedoa*, in
James Bay. Can. Field
Nat., 90: (4): 487-490.

# RUDDY TURNSTONE   *Arenaria interpres*   (Linnaeus)

It is always amazing to see how such a colourful bird will disappear against its stony background. In my early birding days I found it turning over flattened rusty cans on the Ashbridge's Bay dump and thought that Rusty Turncan might be a more appropriate name, but now that the dump has been grassed over they have reverted to turning stones again. They are much more abundant on sea beaches than on the fresh water shores in Ontario. We seen them only as migrants between their Arctic breeding grounds and their wintering shores, south to South America.

IDENTIFICATION: This is a stout, Robin-sized shorebird, with a ruddy back, a disruptive pattern of black and white on the foreparts, bright red legs and a harsh, chattering call. The immatures have more muted colours than the adults. The short, black, upturned bill is used to flip over stones and poke among piles of algae in search of their invertebrate food.

WINTER: One was reported on the Toronto Christmas count in 1977.

SPRING: Stirrett (1973b: 16) had Pelee records from 20 on May 6 to three on June 8, with a high count of 250 on May 31. Ussher (1965: 10) had Rondeau records from May 10 to June 2, with a 16-year average arrival date on May 21. Brooman (1954: 17) had a few Elgin Co. records between May 22 (1949) and May 29 (1952). Snyder (1931: 175-176) took Long Point specimens from May 14 (1928) to June 17 (1927). Beardslee & Mitchell (1965: 208-209) had spring records from the Canadian shores of Lake Erie from May 12 (1937) into June with a maximum of 500 on May 30, 1958. Speirs (1938: 40, 44) gave May 8 as the earliest Toronto record, with the spring peak on May 29, while Baillie (in Saunders, 1947: 364) gave May 25 as his 20-year average arrival date there. Speirs (1977: 37) reported spring dates from May 2 or 3 (1964) at Whitby to June 8 (1962) at Oshawa, with a high estimate of 220 at Pickering Beach on May 26, 1969. Snyder (1941: 50) reported sightings in Prince Edward Co. on May 24, 1930 and May 25, 1931. Weir & Quilliam (1980: 34) gave May 8 as the earliest arrival at Kingston, with the average arrival on May 21 and departure on June 1. The one seen by R. Pittaway at Britannia Bay on May 12, 1971 was the earliest on record for the Ottawa region (Goodwin, 1971: 737). Devitt (1967: 68) gave May 25 as the 12-year average arrival date for Wasaga Beach, with the earliest on May 18, 1953 and latest on June 7, 1928. Beamer saw two on May 21, 1949, his only spring record for Meaford. The only spring record for the cottage country was on May 24, 1958 when K. Ketchum reported the species off Pointe au Baril (Mills, 1981: 53). Nicholson (1981: 98) had Manitoulin records from May 14 (1978) to June 4 (1980). Denis (1961: 4) gave May 24 as the average arrival date at Thunder Bay, with the earliest on May 22, 1953. Lee (1978: 22) saw a migrant at Big Trout Lake on June 5, 1975.

SUMMER: Stirrett (1973c: 15) had six at Pelee as late as June 16 and one returning bird as early as July 27. Ussher (1965: 10) gave Aug. 15 as the earliest returning bird at Rondeau. Saunders & Dale (1933: 191) told about six killed by lightning at Lambeth, near London, on July 30, 1897, their only Middlesex Co. record. Beardslee & Mitchell (1965: 209) had June records as late as June 28, 1958 when two were seen at Rockhouse Point, Lake Erie. Speirs (1938: 46) had a June 19 record for Toronto, while Saunders

(1947: 364) gave July 27 as his earliest returning record for Toronto. J.L. Baillie saw one at Oshawa on July 26, 1963 and there were several other late July and early August records for the Ontario Co. shores (Speirs, 1977: 37). Snyder (1941: 50) cited a record by E. Beaupré in Prince Edward Co. on June 11, 1924. Weir & Quilliam (1980: 34) had northbound migrants at Kingston as late as June 21 and southbound birds as early as July 12. Skeel & Bondrup-Nielsen (1978: 169) saw one at Pukaskwa on Aug. 18 and 19, 1977. Elder (1979: 32) had only one record at Geraldton, on Aug. 20, 1970. Manning (1952: 43) reported them at several places on the James and Hudson Bay coasts in 1947: 10 in 6 hrs. on June 6 at North Point; 20 in 7 hrs. from June 9 to 12 at Big Piskwanish; 15 in 16 hrs. at Cape Henrietta Maria on July 23 and five in 7 hrs. at Shagamu River on Aug. 14: he cited other summer records for these coasts but had no breeding evidence. Schueler, Baldwin & Rising (1974: 142) reported the species at Moosonee and Winisk. Peck (1972: 340) cited several summer records for Cape Henrietta Maria but considered them all to be migrants.

AUTUMN: Skeel & Bondrup-Nielsen (1978: 169) saw three on an island in Lake Superior off the mouth of the Pic River on Sept. 6, 1977. Ricker & Clarke (1939: 9) had a Lake Nipissing sighting on Sept. 11, 1924. Nicholson (1981: 98) had just three fall sightings for Manitoulin: on Sept. 6, 1970; Oct. 7, 1979 and Oct. 15, 1974. Mills (1981: 53) found two specimen records for Go Home Bay: one taken on Sept. 20, 1902 ( ♀ in NMC) and the other taken 12 days earlier (juv. ♂ in ROM). Beamer had only one fall record for Meaford, on Sept. 5, 1943. Devitt (1967: 68) had fall records from Aug. 28 (1960) at Collingwood to Oct. 13 (1940) at Wasaga Beach. Weir & Quilliam (1980: 34) gave Sept. 24 as the average departure date from Kingston, with one as late as Nov. 8, 1970. Snyder (1941: 50) had fall sightings in Prince Edward Co. from Sept. 20 to Oct. 4, 1931. Doris H. Speirs and other members of the Margaret Nice Ornithological Club saw one at Frenchman Bay as late as Nov. 1, 1962 (Speirs, 1977: 37). Speirs (1938: 52) had fall peaks at Toronto on Aug. 7 and Sept. 13: with the latest Toronto record on Oct. 27 (Baillie, in Saunders, 1947: 364). Beardslee & Mitchell (1965: 208-209) had one as late as Nov. 7, 1954 at Waverly Beach, Lake Erie. Fred Bodworth saw two at Port Stanley on Sept. 17, 1942 (Brooman, 1954: 17). Ussher (1965: 10) gave Sept. 19 as his latest Rondeau record. Stirrett (1973d: 18) considered them uncommon at Pelee in fall and had two as late as Nov. 7, but Kelley (1978: 32) reported one unusual flock of 400 there on Sept. 25, 1962.

**MEASUREMENTS:**
*Length:* 8.0 to 9.9 ins.
(Godfrey, 1966: 138)
*Wingspread:* 16 to 19 1/2
ins. (Roberts, 1955: 579)
*Weight:* 100 to 124 g.
(Terres, 1980: 787).

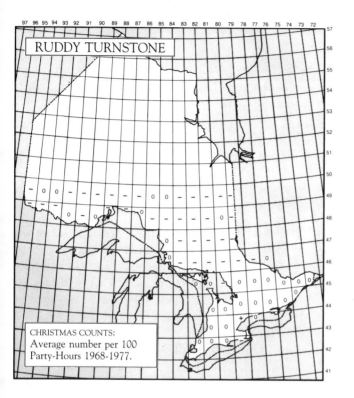

RUDDY TURNSTONE

CHRISTMAS COUNTS:
Average number per 100
Party-Hours 1968-1977.

# RED KNOT   *Calidris canutus*   (Linnaeus)

This is a circumpolar breeder in the high Arctic, wintering south to southern South America. In Ontario we see it in passage, chiefly in late May and early June going north and from July to October on the way south.

IDENTIFICATION: The Red Knot is a stout shorebird, about the size of a Killdeer, with a short, stout bill, rather pale gray scaly back pattern. In spring it has a pinkish or Robin-red breast but in the return flight many have lost this colour and have a grayish white breast and resemble oversize Sanderlings, and are often seen in similar habitat on sandy or gravelly beaches.

WINTER:

SPRING: Stirrett (1973b: 17) had Pelee records from May 14 to June 4, with a maximum of 8 on May 20. Ussher (1965: 11) had records at Rondeau from May 19 to May 23. Brooman (1954: 19) cited sightings at Port Stanley on May 27, 1933 and May 24, 1953 and one near West Lorne on June 1, 1952. Speirs (1938: 40, 44) gave May 20 as the earliest Toronto date, with a "peak" on May 25. Long (1970: 21) saw three at Shoal Point, Pickering, as early as May 16, 1970, while Speirs (1977: 48) reported two flocks of 50; one at Whitby on May 26, 1961, the other at Oshawa on May 27, 1953. Allin (1940: 98) had only one record for Darlington: 15 on May 31, 1936 at Hampton Pond. Weir & Quilliam (1980: 34) gave May 23 and May 29 as average arrival and departure dates for Kingston, with the earliest on May 4: a flock estimated at about 105 birds was seen on Amherst Is. on the evening of May 20, 1967 (Quilliam, 1973: 83). Devitt (1967: 73) gave May 30 as the 9-year average arrival date for Wasaga Beach, with the earliest on May 23, 1942. Nicholson (1981: 105) mentioned one seen by Ron Tasker in Burpee Twp., Manitoulin, on May 22, 1971 and four seen at Low Island on May 26, 1973. Ricker & Clarke (1939: 10) took one at Frank's Bay, Lake Nipissing, on May 28, 1932. Denis (1961: 4) gave May 25 as the average arrival date at Thunder Bay, with the earliest on May 20, 1956. With David and Mary Elder, I saw 11 at Longlac on May 24, 1971.

SUMMER: Stirrett (1973c: 15 and 1973d: 19) noted one at Pelee on Aug. 2, two on Aug. 25 and one on Aug. 29. Ussher (1965: 11) mentioned Aug. 14 and Aug. 28 dates for Rondeau. W.E. Saunders and E.M.S. Dale saw one at Port Stanley on Aug. 29, 1942 (Brooman, 1954: 19). Two were reported at Rockhouse Point, Lake Erie, on June 18, 1959 and one at Port Colborne on July 26, 1942 (Beardslee & Mitchell, 1965: 222). Speirs (1938: 46, 48) gave a June 26 date for Toronto and many records for the first week in June: he gave Aug. 1 as the earliest fall record. Tozer & Richards (1974: 132) saw one as late as June 14, 1972 at Oshawa, while Long (1966: 25) reported returning birds at Pickering Beach as early as July 1, 1964 and July 11, 1963. Charles Fothergill shot one on the shores of Rice Lake on Aug. 15, 1820 (Black, 1934: 147). Weir & Quilliam (1980: 34) had a record as late as June 7 and a returning bird as early as July 8 at Kingston, but the average fall arrival was on Aug. 17. Lloyd (1923: 127) mentioned six shot on June 4, 1890 at Ottawa by E.G. White. J.L. Baillie saw 26 at Wasaga Beach on June 6, 1929, while the earliest fall arrival there was on Aug. 26, 1942 (Devitt, 1967: 73). One was seen at Papoose Is., Manitoulin, on June 4, 1980, by Chip Weseloh (Nicholson, 1981: 105). Todd (1963: 322) saw one on June 6, 1912, while descending the Grand

Rapid on the Mattagami River. Hope & Shortt (1944: 574) saw huge flocks (up to 500 birds) on the west shore of James Bay at Big Piskwanish from July 20 to 25, 1942. C.E. Hope collected a juvenile at Cape Henrietta Maria on Aug. 14, 1948 (Peck, 1972: 342). Schueler, Baldwin & Rising (1974: 145) collected a male and a female, both with enlarged gonads, at the limit of trees along the Sutton River on June 22, 1962: they noted the species at Moosonee but not at the other localities along the James Bay and Hudson Bay coasts.

AUTUMN: Skeel & Bondrup-Nielsen (1978: 172) saw one at Pukaskwa on Sept. 18 and 19, 1977. Speirs & Speirs (1947: 28) saw single birds at North Bay on Sept. 19 and 21, 1944. Devitt (1967: 73) gave Oct. 4, 1941 as the latest date for Wasaga Beach. Weir & Quilliam (1980: 34) reported one as late as Oct. 29 at Kingston. Long (1968b: 17) saw one at Pickering Beach as late as Oct. 26, 1968. Speirs (1938: 52, 54) gave Sept. 1 as the fall "peak" at Toronto, with the latest on Sept. 25. In 1941, 18 were seen on Sept. 1; 15 on Sept. 7 and 19 on Sept. 14, all on the Canadian shore of Lake Erie: the latest was seen there on Oct. 25, 1936 (Beardslee & Mitchell, 1965: 222). Snyder (1931: 166) reported that one was shot at Port Rowan on Sept. 19, 1905, by W.D. Hobson. Marshall Field found one at Port Stanley on Sept. 9, 1951 (Brooman, 1954: 19). Ussher (1965: 11) had his latest Rondeau record on Oct. 6. Stirrett (1973d: 19) had fall records at Pelee from Sept. 3 to Oct. 3, with a maximum of 3 on Sept. 8.

**MEASUREMENTS:**
*Length:* 10 to 11 ins.
(Godfrey, 1966: 150)
*Wingspread:* 20 to 21 ins.
(Roberts, 1955: 573)
*Weight:* 4.0 to 6.5 oz.
(Roberts, 1955: 573).

# SANDERLING  *Calidris alba*  (Pallas)

The Sanderling is the endearing little sandpiper that has inspired writers as it chases retreating waves on the sandy sea shores, then beats a hasty retreat before the advancing combers, all the time gleaning morsels revealed by the ebb and flow. It is most numerous on sea beaches but a few patronize the shores of our larger lakes en route from their wintering areas from the southern tip of South America to their high Arctic breeding grounds.

IDENTIFICATION: The Sanderling is a whitish sandpiper about the size of our common Spotted Sandpiper with black bill, legs and "wrists". In fall it is immaculately white below and sandy white above, with the black wrists constrasting sharply with the rest of its plumage. In spring the head and foreparts are tinged with rust colour. The absence of a hind toe is diagnostic.

WINTER: On the 1968-1977 Christmas counts the only record was at Long Point on the 1973 count. Stirrett (1973a: 15) had Pelee records for the first three days of December. Ussher (1965: 12) had a Dec. 26 record for Rondeau. George A. Scott saw one on the Oshawa lakeshore on Dec. 12, 1954 (Speirs, 1977: 64).

SPRING: Stirrett (1973b: 17) noted two at Pelee as early as Apr. 25, with a maximum of 50 on May 25. Ussher (1965: 12) had the earliest Rondeau record on May 13, with the average stay from May 19 to May 25: he considered the Sanderling scarce in spring. Marshall Field found 300 at Port Stanley on May 29, 1952 (Brooman, 1954: 20). Snyder (1931: 169) saw one at Long Point on May 25, 1928 and collected a female there on May 30, 1927 and a male on June 4, 1927. Beardslee & Mitchell (1965: 235-236) reported five on the Canadian shore of Lake Erie as early as May 13, 1957. Fleming (1906: 450) considered it common at Toronto from May 21 to June 2. Speirs (1938: 40, 44) gave May 12 as the earliest Toronto date with a peak on June 1. Speirs (1977: 64) had spring records from the Pickering lakeshore from May 16 (1964) to June 1 (1965 and 1975) with a peak of 76 at Whitby on May 28, 1969. Weir & Quilliam (1980: 35) gave May 4 as the earliest date for Kingston, with average arrival on May 18 and departure on May 27. Devitt (1967: 77) gave May 23 as the average arrival date at Wasaga Beach, with the earliest on May 16, 1941. Beamer noted two at Meaford on May 15, 1949 and one there on May 16, 1948. Ron Tasker had records in Burpee Twp., Manitoulin, from May 14 to May 26, 1966 (Nicholson, 1981: 107). Denis (1961: 4) gave May 23 as the average arrival date at Thunder Bay, with the earliest on May 10, 1952.

SUMMER: Stirrett (1973c: 16) had four at Pelee as late as June 16 and noted the earliest returning bird on July 20, with 100 there on Aug. 15. Ussher (1965: 12) had a June 25 record at Rondeau, but gave Aug. 14 as the earliest returning bird. William Girling found 25 at Port Stanley on Aug. 17, 1940 (Brooman, 1954: 20). Snyder (1931: 169) collected a male from a pair at Long Point on July 17, 1927, and saw 40 there on July 21. Beardslee & Mitchell (1965: 235-236) noted one at Crescent Beach, Lake Erie, on June 19, 1953 and saw the first returning bird on July 11 at Rose Hill. Fleming (1906: 450) noted adults at Toronto from Aug. 24 to Aug. 28. J.L. Baillie (in Saunders, 1947: 365) had June 10 and July 20 records for Toronto: while Speirs (1938: 46) reported a June 18 record. Tozer & Richards (1974: 139) had a Lake Scugog observation on June 18, 1963 and the first returning bird, at Oshawa, on July 24, 1968. Quilliam (1973: 87) reported

16 very late spring migrants at Wolfe Is. on June 9, 1970 seen by Betty Hughes. Weir & Quilliam (1980: 35) noted the earliest returning bird for Kingston on July 19, with the average return on Aug. 9. Devitt (1967: 77) mentioned a female collected at Wasaga Beach as early as July 21, 1935. Beamer noted several at Meaford as early as July 8, 1940. R. Anderson collected a male and a female at Go Home Bay on June 10, 1903, while K. Ketchum noted the first returning bird on the South Limestones on Aug. 10, 1975 (Mills, 1981: 59-60). Nicholson (1981: 107) gave Aug. 16, 1970 as the earliest date for returning birds on Manitoulin. Speirs & Speirs (1947: 28) noted three at North Bay as early as Aug. 22, 1944. W. Wyett saw four at Pukaskwa from June 16 to 18, 1973 and one there returning on Aug. 14, 1973 (Skeel & Bondrup-Nielsen, 1978: 123). Snyder (1938: 188) collected one of three noted on Aug. 8, 1929 at Sable Is., Lake of the Woods. Hope & Shortt (1944: 576) saw flocks of several hundred passing Big Piskwanish, James Bay, from July 20 to 25, 1942: five adult males and one adult female in worn breeding plumage were collected. The 1948 ROM party collected eight near Cape Henrietta Maria and noted a flock of about 1000 on the beach on July 18, 1948 (Peck, 1972: 344). Lee (1978: 23) noted just one at Big Trout Lake, between Aug. 8 to 10, 1975. Schueler, Baldwin & Rising (1974) reported none at any of their James Bay or Hudson Bay stops and C.E. Hope noted none at Fort Severn during the summer of 1940.

AUTUMN: Oliver Hewitt saw several at Ship Sands, near Moosonee, from Sept. 22 to Sept. 25, 1947 and George Stirrett noted 25 there on Oct. 2, 1948 (Manning, 1952: 55). Skeel & Bondrup-Nielsen (1978: 173) noted the main passage at Pukaskwa from Sept. 14-23, 1977 and W. Wyett saw six there as late as Oct. 2, 1975. Ricker & Clarke (1939: 10) considered this the most common beach bird at Lake Nipissing, with flocks of 15 or 20 from Sept. 2 to Oct. 8, 1924. Nicholson (1981: 107) gave Nov. 1, 1980 as the latest date for Manitoulin. K. Ketchum saw Sanderlings off Pointe au Baril as late as Oct. 13, 1963 (Mills, 1981: 60). Beamer noted 20 at Meaford on Oct. 7, 1945 and one as late as Oct. 28, 1945. E.L. Brereton noted three at Wasaga Beach as late as Nov. 17, 1949 (Devitt, 1967: 77). Weir & Quilliam (1980: 35) gave Oct. 15 as the average departure date from Kingston, with the latest on Nov. 20: while Quilliam (1973: 87) reported over 100 at Prince Edward Point on Sept. 18, 1960. A flock of seven was noted in Prince Edward Co. as late as Nov. 5, 1930 (Snyder, 1941: 54), who also noted considerable numbers there from Sept. 23 to Oct. 4, 1931. Tozer & Richards (1974: 139) reported 58 at Darlington Provincial Park on Sept. 10, 1963. J.L. Baillie reported one at Ajax as late as Nov. 22, 1959 (Speirs, 1977: 64). Fleming (1906: 450) noted young at Toronto from Sept. 4 to Sept. 12: Speirs (1938: 52) gave Sept. 15 as the fall peak there, while J.L. Baillie (in Saunders, 1947: 365) had his latest observation there on Nov. 18. Beardslee & Mitchell (1965: 235-236) observed one at Crystal Beach on Nov. 30, 1941. John Townson saw three at Long Point as late as Oct. 23, 1927 (Snyder, 1931: 169). Saunders & Dale (1933: 197) had only one record of the Sanderling in Middlesex Co.: at Denfield on Sept. 1, 1930. Ussher (1965: 12) gave Aug. 28 to Nov. 4 as the average fall stay at Rondeau. Stirrett (1973a: 15 and 1973d: 20) had a Pelee record as late as Nov. 26 and a fall maximum of 100 on Sept. 17.

**MEASUREMENTS:**
*Length:* 7.1 to 8.7 ins.
(Godfrey, 1966: 164).
*Wingspread:* 14 to 16 1/4
ins. (Roberts, 1955: 581).
*Weight:* 2 to 3 oz.
(Roberts, 1955: 581).
Females average larger
than males.

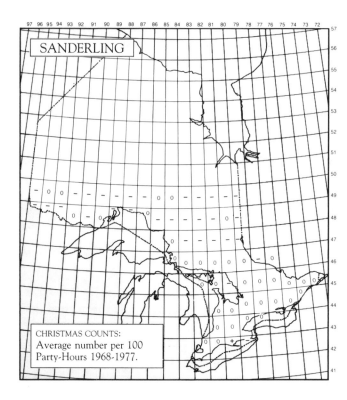

SANDERLING

CHRISTMAS COUNTS:
Average number per 100
Party-Hours 1968-1977.

# SEMIPALMATED SANDPIPER   *Calidris pusilla*   (Linnaeus)

The Semipalmated Sandpiper has much the same range and habits as the Least Sandpiper, breeding in the low Arctic and wintering from the southern U.S.A. to Brazil. However, it is more apt to be seen in large flocks and most of them pass through more quickly in migration. They also prefer sandier, less muddy shores.

IDENTIFICATION: The partial webbing between the toes gives it its name, but this is of limited use as a field mark unless you are very close. Its black legs separate it from the other common "peep" (the Least Sandpiper has greenish legs when clean). The Semipalmated has a stouter bill than the Least and lacks the fine, drooping tip of that species. It is generally more gray, less brown than the Least. The other possible "peep" in Ontario is the rare Western Sandpiper (see distinctions under that species).

WINTER:

SPRING: Stirrett (1973b: 17) had Pelee records from May 7 to June 7, with a maximum of 200 on May 30. Ussher (1965: 12) gave May 17 as his 15-year average arrival date for Rondeau, with the earliest on May 1. Saunders & Dale (1933: 197) gave May 19 as the average arrival date near London, with the earliest on May 6, 1922 and the largest flock of 25 on June 1, 1929. Snyder (1931: 168-169) collected 31 at Long Point between May 14 and June 16: the earliest was noted on May 8, 1928 and the latest on June 16, 1927. J.L. Baillie (in Saunders, 1947: 365) gave May 22 as his 22-year average arrival date at Toronto, with the earliest on May 11. Speirs (1938: 44) had spring peaks at Toronto on May 25 and June 1. R.M. Saunders saw one at Whitby as early as Apr. 26, 1964 but the spring peak there is about May 26 (Speirs, 1977: 58). Weir & Quilliam (1980: 35) gave May 18 and May 31 as average arrival and departure dates for Kingston, with the earliest on Apr. 25. Devitt (1967: 76) gave May 20 as the 10-year average arrival date for Barrie, with the earliest on May 10, 1964: well over 100 were noted at Wasaga Beach on June 1, 1939. Beamer's only spring record for Meaford was on May 15, 1949, when two were noted. Nicholson (1981: 107) gave May 22 as the 7-year average arrival date for Manitoulin, with the earliest on May 19 and the maximum count of 70 on May 31, 1969. Ricker & Clarke (1939: 10) reported one taken at Frank's Bay, Lake Nipissing, on May 28, 1932. Speirs & Speirs (1947: 28) noted 11 at North Bay on May 31, 1944 and one there on June 6, 1945. Skeel & Bondrup-Nielsen (1978: 173) had only one May record at Pukaskwa, on May 28, 1977. Baillie & Hope (1943: 9) noted two at Rossport on May 29, 1936 (one male collected). Denis (1961: 4) gave May 24 as the average arrival date for Thunder Bay, with the earliest on May 15, 1954. Cringan (1953b: 3) noted one at Kasabonika Lake on June 3 and 4, 1953. On May 26 and 28, 1947, Oliver Hewitt saw several at Ship Sands, near Moosonee (Manning, 1952: 53).

SUMMER: Stirrett (1973c: 16 and 1973d: 19) had strays at Pelee on June 22 and June 26, with the earliest returning birds on July21 and a maximum of 300 on Aug. 25. Ussher (1965: 12) had northbound birds at Rondeau to June 14 and the earliest southbound birds on July 19. Page & Bradstreet (1968: 84) found adults at Long Point from July 12 to Sept. 1, 1967, peaking on Aug. 17, while immatures first showed up on Aug. 12 and peaked on Aug. 31, 1967. Beardslee & Mitchell (1965: 230-231) reported one at Mohawk Is., Lake Erie, on June 18, 1939. Fleming (1906: 449) noted adults returning to Toronto as early as July 21, 1891, but the first young were noted on Aug. 24. Baillie (in Saunders, 1947: 365) had June 25 and July 4 dates for Toronto. Speirs (1977: 58) had northbound records as late as June 14, 1958 in Ontario Co. and the earliest returning bird on July 13, 1963. Weir & Quilliam (1980: 35) had June 18 and July 5 dates for Kingston, with the average arrival date for southbound birds on July 22. Devitt (1967: 76) noted seven on Giant's Tomb Is. on June 11, 1937 and strays in Simcoe Co. on June 20, 1937 and July 1, 1938. Beamer noted several at Meaford on July 31, 1941 and four east of Thornbury on Aug. 17, 1941. J.L. Baillie collected an adult male at Pickerel Lake, near Sundridge, on July 15, 1939, the earliest returning record for the cottage country (Mills, 1981: 59). Nicholson (1981: 107) noted one on July 1, 1974 at Cockburn Is., but Aug. 8, 1970 was a more usual date for returning birds on Manitoulin, with a maximum of 35 on Aug. 29, 1970. Speirs & Speirs (1947: 28) noted two at North Bay on Aug. 17, 1944. Skeel & Bondrup-Nielsen (1978: 173) had Pukaskwa records on June 14 and July 13, but the main passage was from Aug. 13 to 25, 1977 (88 on 11 days). Smith (1957: 173) noted 12 at Jackfish Bay, near Longlac, on Aug. 12, 1954 and three on Aug. 18, 1954 at Lillabelle Lake, near Cochrane. D. Strickland noted one on Aug. 31, 1964 at Atikokan (Peruniak, 1971: 16). Snyder (1938: 188) reported an immature female collected on Sable Is., Lake of the Woods, on Aug. 8, 1929. Manning (1952: 54) estimated 300 seen in 6 hours at North Point, James Bay, on June 6, 1947; 200 in 7 hours at Big Piskwanish between June 9 and 12, 1947; 450 in 5 hours from June 14 to 16, 1947 at Long Ridge Point; 400 in 16 hours at Cape Henrietta Maria from July 20 to 24 (of which the six collected had incubation patches); 30 in 8 hours from July 30 to Aug. 1 at Little Cape, Hudson Bay and 550 in 7 hours afield at Shagamu River (where one juvenile was collected) from Aug. 8 to 14,

1947. Hope & Shortt (1944: 575) noted flocks estimated to contain from 4000 to 5000 birds migrating along the James Bay coast between Ft. Albany and Moosonee, between July 15 and 25, 1942. Peck (1972: 343) found five nests at Cape Henrietta Maria: a nest with 3 eggs on June 24; two nests with 4 eggs on June 25 and two nests with 4 eggs on June 30, 1970. Schueler, Baldwin & Rising (1974: 145-146) found a nest with 4 eggs on June 24, 1962 at the mouth of the Sutton River and a nest with 4 eggs about 20 miles east of Winisk on June 25, 1965. Lee (1978: 23) noted 7 at Big Trout Lake on July 4, 1975: he also saw three on June 7 and 8 and one on June 11 northbound and from one to five daily from July 27 to Aug. 9 southbound. C.E. Hope noted two at Ft. Severn on July 1, 1940 and 10 there on July 17, 1940.

AUTUMN: Oliver Hewitt saw some at Ship Sands, near Moosonee, from Sept. 22 to 25, 1947 (Manning, 1952: 53). Skeel & Bondrup-Nielsen (1978: 173) saw their last at Pukaskwa on Sept. 5, 1977. Speirs & Speirs (1947: 28) noted five at North Bay on Sept. 13, 1944. Nicholson (1981: 107) gave Sept. 19, 1970 as his latest date for Manitoulin. The latest record for the cottage country was on Oct. 12, 1969 at Pointe au Baril by K. Ketchum (Mills, 1981: 59). Devitt (1967: 76) noted two at Wasaga Beach as late as Oct. 16, 1936. Weir & Quilliam (1980: 35) gave Oct. 9 as the average departure date from Kingston, with the latest on Nov. 20. The peak of the southbound flight in Ontario Co. was in the last week of September and the latest record, by Naomi LeVay at Cranberry Marsh, was on Nov. 11, 1950: Jno. Maugham collected an albino at Port Perry on Sept. 20, 1902 (Speirs, 1977: 58). Speirs (1938: 54) gave Nov. 22 as the latest Toronto record. Beardslee & Mitchell (1965: 230-231) noted their latest bird at Crystal Beach, Lake Erie, on Nov. 1, 1947. Page & Bradstreet (1968: 84) had their latest immature bird at Long Point on Oct. 7, 1967. Ussher (1965: 12) gave Oct. 27 as the average departure date from Rondeau, with the latest on Nov. 9. Stirrett (1973d: 19) had a fall maximum of 200 at Pelee on Sept. 15, and his latest record was on Oct. 27.

**MEASUREMENTS:**
*Length:* 5.5 to 6.8 ins.
(Godfrey, 1966: 159)
*Wingspread:* 11.14 to
12.80 ins. (Roberts,
1955: 583)
*Weight:* 10 to 44 g. (adults
averaged 29.8 g.;
immatures 25.7 g.)
   (Page & Salvadori,
1969: 53-54). Weight
influenced greatly by fat
deposits in migration.

**REFERENCES:**
See under Least Sandpiper.

# WESTERN SANDPIPER   *Calidris mauri*   (Cabanis)

This is primarily a bird of the Pacific coast, very rare in Ontario, and difficult to distinguish from our more common "peeps".

IDENTIFICATION: Its black legs and partly webbed toes distinguish it from the Least Sandpiper (which has green legs and unwebbed toes). In breeding plumage the Western Sandpiper differs from the Semipalmated Sandpiper by having V-shaped markings on the sides of its breast and more reddish brown in the upper parts. It generally has a longer, stouter bill than the Semipalmated, with a slight droop at the tip (but there is some overlap in bill size, which should not be used alone for identification: see Ouellet, McNeil & Burton, 1973: 291).

WINTER:

SPRING: H.H. Axtell reported two at Pelee on May 23, 1976 (Goodwin, 1976: 834). R. Curry noted five at Erieau on May 4, 1975 (Goodwin, 1975: 846). W.R. Jarmain had one at Strathroy on May 22-23, 1976 (Goodwin, 1976: 834). Beardslee & Mitchell (1965: 231) reported one seen at Mohawk Point, Lake Erie, on May 26, 1956. Saunders (1947: 365) had three spring observations at Toronto from May 10 to May 31. Doug. Sadler and D. McRae reported one at Lakefield, near Peterborough, on May 16, 1976 (Goodwin, 1976: 834).

SUMMER: Kelley (1978: 35) reported one near Sarnia from June 4-10, 1969. Fred and Margaret Bodsworth identified one by its long bill, at Port Stanley, on Aug. 14, 1945 (Brooman, 1954: 20). John Edmonds collected an adult female at Long Point on July 11, 1927 (Snyder, 1931: 169). A specimen was taken at Rockhouse Point, Lake Erie, on Aug. 10, 1954 by H.H. Axtell *et al* (Beardslee & Mitchell, 1965: 231). John Edmonds collected an adult female at Toronto on June 5, 1890 (Snyder, 1928: 207). Saunders (1947: 222, 365) reported one at Toronto on July 16, 1944 and others on Aug. 18 and Aug. 26 (Baillie). Gerry Bennett and J. Satterly reported one at Whitby on July 26, 1959 (Speirs, 1977: 59). Quilliam (1973: 86-87) reported one at Wolfe Is., near Kingston, on Aug. 18, 1970, also seen by Ron Weir the following day: the same observers had sightings at Prince Edward Point on Aug. 13, 1972 and Aug. 9, 1973 at Kingston's old dump (Weir & Quilliam, 1980: 10). I observed one at close range at North Bay on June 10, 1945 (Speirs & Speirs, 1947: 28).

AUTUMN: Ron Tasker reported two in Burpee Twp., Manitoulin Is., on Oct. 11, 1969 (Nicholson, 1981: 107). One was reported at Wasaga Beach on Oct. 8, 1941 by Barbara and L.E. Jaquith (Devitt, 1967: 76). Two were reported on Sept. 3 and three on Sept. 14, 1971 at Ottawa by many observers (Goodwin, 1972: 57). Fred Cooke had sightings on Amherst Is., near Kingston, on Aug. 30, 1969 and Sept. 1, 1968 (Quilliam, 1973: 86). Speirs (1977: 59) gave details of six fall records for the Oshawa-Pickering waterfront between Aug. 31 (1958) and Oct. 29 (1961). Hubert H. Brown collected an adult female at Toronto on Sept. 6, 1890 (Snyder, 1928: 207) and Saunders (1947: 365) gave Sept. 12 and Oct. 13 records for Toronto. Beardslee & Mitchell (1965: 231) noted one on Oct. 15-16, 1955 at Fort Erie where one was collected by James Savage during the first week of September in 1897: another specimen was taken at Crystal Beach by R.F. Andrle on Sept. 18, 1950. The first Ontario specimen was collected by W.E. Saunders at Port Franks, near Sarnia, on Sept. 5, 1883 (Snyder, 1928: 207). Stirrett (1973d: 19) had only one Pelee record, on Sept. 7, 1968.

**MEASUREMENTS:**
*Length:* 5.8 to 7.1 ins.
(Godfrey, 1966: 161)
*Wingspread:* 12 to 14 ins.
(Terres, 1980: 782)
*Weight:* 3/4 to 1 1/2 oz.
(Terres, 1980: 782).

**REFERENCES:**
Ouellet, Henri; Raymond McNeil and Jean Burton 1973 The Western Sandpiper in Quebec and the Maritime Provinces, Canada. Can. Field Nat., 87: (3): 291- 300. On p. 299 they concluded re *fall* sight records. "Sight records reported in the literature we regard as hypothetical".

Snyder, L.L. 1928 The Western Sandpiper in Ontario. Auk, 45:(2):207.

# LITTLE STINT   *Calidris minuta*   (Leisler)

The Little Stint is a Palaearctic breeder, from northern Norway to central Siberia, wintering from Africa to southern Asia, accidental anywhere in America (other North American sightings have been in Alaska, Bermuda and Antigua).

**IDENTIFICATION:**  The Little Stint is slightly smaller than the Semipalmated Sandpiper, with a more slender tapering bill (more like a Least Sandpiper in this respect). It has black legs but lacks the webs between the toes as in Semipalmated Sandpiper: Least Sandpipers have greenish legs. It has a rich orange-rufous wash on the head, sides of the neck and upper breast, but the throat is white (unlike the somewhat similar Rufous-necked Sandpiper). It has a V-pattern of light feathers on the back (especially prominent in the grayish fall plummage). The belly is pure white.

**WINTER:**

**SPRING:**

**SUMMER:**  Morrison (1980: 627) collected the first North American specimen (No. 68651 in National Museum of Canada) at North Point, James Bay, near Moosonee on July 10, 1979. It proved to be a male in full breeding plumage.

**AUTUMN:**

**MEASUREMENTS:**
*Length:* 5 3/4 ins.
(Witherby, Jourdain,
Ticehurst & Tucker,
1943: IV: 245)
*Wingspread:*
*Weight:* 24.5 g. (Morrison,
1980: 628).

**REFERENCE:**
Morrison, R.I.G. 1980 First
specimen record of the
Little Stint (*Calidris minuta*)
for North America. Auk,
97:(3):627-628.

# LEAST SANDPIPER   *Calidris minutilla*   (Vieillot)

The Least Sandpiper is a bird of passage in most of Ontario, breeding along the James Bay and Hudson Bay coasts and wintering in the Gulf States and southward. It frequently associates with the Semipalmated Sandpiper (collectively known as "peeps"). Tozer & Richards (1974: 134) and others have noted the tendency for the Least to feed in weedier, less open areas than the Semipalmated.

IDENTIFICATION: It is most apt to be confused with the Semipalmated Sandpiper, but it is a richer brown above, has a more slender bill with a slightly drooping tip and has greenish legs (black in Semipalmated). The Semipalmated tends to travel in larger flocks and to pass through more quickly in migration. "Adults have streaked breasts and upper wing coverts lacking buffy edges, juveniles have unstreaked breasts and buffy edges on the wing coverts" (Page & Bradstreet, 1968: 82).

WINTER:

SPRING: Stirrett (1973b: 17) had Pelee records from May 7 to June 3, with a maximum of 50 on May 22. Ussher (1965: 11) had spring records at Rondeau from May 1 to May 26, with average arrival on May 10 and departure on May 22. The largest number reported from Elgin Co. was 25, noted by Wm. Girling on May 27, 1933 at Port Stanley (Brooman, 1954: 19). Saunders & Dale (1933: 195) gave May 17 as the average arrival date for London, with the earliest on May 14, 1923. Snyder (1931: 167) collected a male at Long Point on May 4, 1928 and noted one there on June 2, 1927. Saunders (1947: 364) gave Apr. 23 as his earliest date for Toronto, and cited J.L. Baillie's average arrival on May 18 and departure on May 30. Tozer & Richards (1974: 134) reported a very early sighting by D. Calvert at Oshawa's Second Marsh, on Apr. 16, 1972. The Spring peak appeared to be about May 20 in Ontario Co. (Speirs, 1977: 53). Snyder (1941: 53) collected two females in Prince Edward Co.: on May 23, 1930 and May 25, 1931. Weir & Quilliam (1980: 35) had spring records at Kingston from Apr. 25 to June 2, with the average arrival on May 12 and departure on May 24. Devitt (1967: 75) gave May 17 as the 11-year average arrival date for Barrie, with the earliest on May 5, 1960 and "By June 1, all have moved on northward". Beamer had Meaford records from May 18 to May 29. Mills (1981: 58) had spring records from the cottage country from May 13 to May 24. Nicholson (1981: 106) had Manitoulin records from May 4 (1969) to June 1 (1969) with the 12-year average arrival date on May 11 and a high count of 48 on May 23, 1976. Skeel & Bondrup-Nielsen (1978: 172) noted one at Pukaskwa on May 16, 1977. Denis (1961: 4) gave May 20 as the average arrival date for Thunder Bay, with the earliest on May 12, 1955. Hewitt saw one at Ship Sands, near Moosonee, on May 27, 1947 and Manning collected one of 200 seen there on May 31, 1947 (Manning, 1952: 51).

SUMMER: Stirrett (1973c: 16) had 12 returning birds at Pelee as early as June 27, with small flocks through July and August. Ussher (1965: 11) gave July 11 as the earliest date for returning birds at Rondeau, with the average arrival on Aug. 5. Beardslee & Mitchell (1965: 226-227) had a June 15 record for Mohawk Is., Lake Erie. Least Sandpipers were first recorded at Long Point on July 2 in 1967 and July 4 in 1968 (Page & Salvadori, 1969: 52). Page & Bradstreet (1968: 84) noted adults at Long Point from July 3 to Aug. 12, but the young of the year came later, between July 30 and Sept. 20, with most of the overlap during the first week of August. C.W. Nash noted the species as early as June 28 at Toronto, while Fleming noted the early return of adults from July 4 on, with the young showing up from Aug. 10 to 24 (Fleming, 1906: 449). Saunders (1947: 364) had a June 17 record at Toronto. Tozer & Richards (1974: 134) saw four at the Scugog Causeway on June 13, 1963. Long (1966: 25) saw six at Pickering Beach on July 2, 1964. The peak for returning adults in Ontario Co. was about the fourth week of July, but for immatures it was about a month later (Speirs, 1977: 53). Snyder (1941: 53) cited a record by E. Beaupré in Prince Edward Co. on June 11, 1924. Weir & Quilliam (1980: 35) had the earliest returning bird at Kingston on July 1 and the average southbound arrival date on July 18: Quilliam (1973: 84) reported a maximum of 100 on July 17, 1950. Southbound migrants were noted as early as July 13, 1941 at Wasaga Beach (Devitt, 1967: 74). Mills (1981: 58) gave July 9, 1940 as the earliest date for returning birds on the South Limestones, Georgian Bay, but cited an earlier record by K. Ketchum off Pointe au Baril on June 26, 1960. Nicholson (1981: 106) gave Aug. 4, 1974 as his earliest sighting of returning birds on Manitoulin, with a maximum of 25 on Aug. 29, 1970. Speirs & Speirs (1947: 28) observed one at North Bay on Aug. 2, 1944. Snyder (1942: 128) collected a male at Laird on July 9, 1931 and saw two at Echo Bay on July 22, 1931. Skeel & Bondrup-Nielsen (1978: 172) saw one at Pukaskwa on June 29, 1977 but noted the "main passage" there from Aug. 17 to Sept. 1 (20 noted on 11 days). Snyder (1928: 257) collected a female at Lake Nipigon on July 26, 1923. D. Strickland saw one at Atikokan on Aug. 31, 1964 (Peruniak, 1971: 16). Snyder (1938: 188) reported an immature collected on Sable Is., Lake of the Woods, on Aug. 8, 1929. Hope (1938: 20) collected two immature females at Favourable Lake on Aug. 5 and 6, 1938 (averaging 19 g. in weight). Manning (1952: 51) collected four adults and two sets of young (4 and 3) at Cape Henrietta Maria on July 22, 1947 and saw about 85 there: at Shagamu River between Aug. 9 and 14, 1947 he saw about 300 in 7 hours, most of which were juveniles: he also collected individuals at North Point, Long Ridge Point and Lake River along the James Bay coast and at Little Cape on Hudson Bay. Peck (1972: 343) reported a nest with 4 eggs found by Hope's party on June 29, 1948 near Cape Henrietta Maria and he photographed a nest with 3 eggs that he found there on July 2, 1970. Schueler, Baldwin & Rising (1974: 145) collected a female with enlarged ova about 20 miles north of Hawley Lake on June 16, 1962 and found a nest with 4 eggs on June 22, 1962 about 54 miles NE of Hawley Lake (both along the Sutton River): they also found evidence of breeding at Winisk in 1965. Lee (1978: 3) found agitated adults on an island in Big Trout Lake on June 29, 1975, suggesting breeding there: he saw returning migrants from June 29 to Aug. 10 with a maximum of 10 on Aug. 2, 1975. Hope collected several at Fort Severn from June 22 to July 17, and noted a nest there with 3 eggs on July 1, 1940: his maximum count of 35 was on July 11, 1940.

AUTUMN: Hewitt saw some occasionally between Sept. 22 and 25, 1947 at Ship Sands, near Moosonee (Manning, 1952: 51). Nicholson (1981: 106) gave Sept. 19, 1970 as his latest date for Manitoulin. K. Ketchum saw one as late as Oct. 14, 1957 off Pointe au Baril (Mills, 1981: 59). Beamer's latest date for Meaford was Sept. 25, 1949. Devitt (1967: 74) gave Sept. 24, 1939 as his latest date for Simcoe Co. (at Allandale Station). Weir & Quilliam (1980: 35) gave Sept. 28 as the average departure date from Kingston, with a very late one on Nov. 1, 1969. W.H. Lunn saw one in Prince Edward Co. as late as Oct. 13, 1934 (Snyder, 1941: 53). Numbers in Ontario Co. dropped off sharply after mid-September, but J.L. Baillie noted a very late one at Whitby on Nov. 17, 1956 (Speirs, 1977: 53). J.L. Baillie (in Saunders, 1947: 364) gave Sept. 15 as his average departure date from Toronto, with his latest on Nov. 5. Speirs (1938: 54) gave Nov. 22 as the latest Toronto record. Beardslee & Mitchell (1965: 226-227) gave Oct. 31 as the latest fall date, when one was seen at Erie Beach. Least Sandpipers were not observed at Long Point after Sept. 21 (Page & Salvadori, 1969: 52). Ussher (1965: 11) gave Sept. 26 as the average departure date from Rondeau, with the latest on Oct. 25. Stirrett (1973d: 19) noted the latest two at Pelee on Nov. 11.

**MEASUREMENTS:**

*Length:* 5.0 to 6.8 ins. (Godfrey, 1966: 154)

*Wingspread:* 11.00 to 12.17 ins. (Roberts, 1955: 583)

*Weight:* 16 to 40 g. (Page & Salvadori, 1969: 53-54). Weights were influenced greatly by fat reserves: adults averaged 27.2 g. while juveniles were lighter, averaging 22.2 g.

**REFERENCES:**

Page, Gary and Michael Bradstreet: 1968 Size and composition of a fall population of Least and Semipalmated Sandpipers at Long Point, Ontario. Ont. Bird Banding, 4:(2):82-88.

Page, G. and A. Salvadori 1969 Weight changes of Semipalmated and Least Sandpipers pausing during autumn migration., Ont. Bird Banding, 5:(2):52-58.

# WHITE-RUMPED SANDPIPER   *Calidris fuscicollis*   (Vieillot)

This long-distance migrant breeds in the Canadian Arctic and winters in southern South America. In Ontario it is an uncommon or rare migrant, sometimes seen in puddles in ploughed fields, other times on mud flats. I have sometimes missed seeing it on both spring and fall flights. Some may linger throughout the summer on especially enticing mud flats and others often linger until freezeup in the fall in company with the more numerous Dunlins

IDENTIFICATION:   As the name suggests the best field mark is the white rump, especially in flight: it is often hidden by the long wings when not in flight. Once learned the very high-pitched "tic" call is also a good means of identification. The general impression is of a big "peep", with wings that project well beyond the tail (as in Baird's Sandpiper). It has a pronounced white line over the eye. In the fall when it is most likely to be seen it is grayer than other small sandpipers and has a heavily steaked breast (somewhat like a Pectoral but gray rather than brown). It has black legs and short bill (like a Semipalmated Sandpiper, but is noticeably bigger than that species). In spring plumage it looks like a big Least Sandpiper but the Least has greenish-yellow legs.

WINTER:

SPRING:   Stirrett (1973b: 17) saw his earliest at Pelee on May 8 and his maximum of two on May 30. Ussher (1965: 11) called it a scarce migrant at Rondeau from May 14 to May 31. Marshall Field noted one at Port Stanley on May 29, 1952 (Brooman, 1954: 19). Saunders & Dale (1933: 195) had only one record for Middlesex Co., one flushed by W.E. Saunders near Lambeth on May 15, 1929. W.E. Saunders saw two at the Long Point lighthouse on May 31, 1908 (Snyder, 1931: 107). Beardslee & Mitchell (1965: 225) noted a maximum of seven at Rockhouse Pt., Lake Erie, on May 30, 1958. Sheppard (1960: 21) cited reports of single birds at Mud Lake, Humberstone and Ft. Erie on May 25, 1952 by various observers from Buffalo. Speirs (1938: 40) gave Apr. 26 as the earliest Toronto record. Speirs (1977: 51) had Pickering and Whitby records from May 15 (1931) to June 3 (1961). D. Perks noted as many as 15 at Whitby on May 30, 1961 (Tozer & Richards, 1974: 133). R.J. Rutter saw one in Prince Edward Co. on May 25, 1931 (Snyder, 1941: 53). Weir & Quilliam (1980: 34) reported Kingston dates from May 14 to June 1. Devitt (1967: 74) had three records from Barrie between May 4 (1939) and May 26 (1956). Beamer had just one record of a single bird at Meaford, on June 3, 1948. Nicholson (1981: 105) had 17 spring records from Manitoulin between May 6 and May 30, with a high count of six. Ricker & Clarke (1939: 10) saw one at North Bay on May 27, 1925. Denis (1961: 4) gave May 19 as the average arrival date at Thunder Bay, with the earliest on May 12, 1955.

SUMMER:   Stirrett (1973b: 17; 1973d: 19) had late northbound birds at Pelee on June 8 and June 13 but the earliest southbound bird not until Aug. 28. Ussher (1965: 11) had the earliest returning bird at Rondeau on Aug. 8. Snyder (1931: 167) reported four at Long Point on June 18, 1927 (two females collected). R. Curry and A. Wormington suggested that birds of this species stayed through the summer at Long Point and Hamilton in 1975 (Goodwin, 1975: 965). Beardslee & Mitchell (1965: 224-225) reported one as late as June 23 at Rockhouse Point, Lake Erie, and a returning bird as early as July 21,

1946 at Windmill Point. Fleming (1906: 449) reported a June 21 bird at Toronto. Saunders (1947: 364) gave July 27 as his earliest fall arrival date for Toronto. J.L. Baillie saw one at Whitby on June 28, 1959 and Naomi LeVay had several July records for Cranberry Marsh, the earliest on July 11, 1962 (Speirs, 1977: 51). W.H. Lunn noted one near Hillier, Prince Edward Co., on Aug. 1, 1933 (Snyder, 1941: 53). George North reported one at Kingston on June 19, 1950 (Quilliam, 1973: 84): the earliest returning date there was July 22 (Weir & Quilliam, 1980: 34). Frances Westman saw one at Barrie as late as June 11, 1964 (Devitt, 1967: 74). W.E. Saunders noted one in Algonquin Park on Aug. 7, 1908 (MacLulich, 1938: 16). J. Nicholson reported 13 at Chelmsford on June 11, 1972 and one at Kelley Lake, on July 6, 1972 (Goodwin, 1972: 853), both near Sudbury. Manning (1952: 50) noted 65 in 16 hrs. between July 20 and 24, 1947 at Cape Henrietta Maria, and collected two females with incubation patches there: he reported 84 in 8 hrs. at Little Cape between July 30 and Aug. 1, 1947 and 420 in 7 hrs. at Shagamu River between Aug. 9 and 14, 1947. The ROM party collected 11, including two juveniles, near Cape Henrietta Maria on Aug. 15, 1948 (Peck, 1972: 343). Lee (1978: 34) observed an exhausted individual at Big Trout Lake on June 13, 1975.

AUTUMN: Hewitt identified several on Ship Sands, near Moosonee, between Sept. 22 and 25, 1947 (Manning, 1952: 50). Elder (1979: 33) had only one Geraldton record, on Sept. 29, 1970. Nicholson (1981: 105) had only four fall records from Manitoulin, between Sept. 10 (1967) and Nov. 11 (1972), both extreme dates by Ron Tasker in Burpee Twp. Devitt (1967: 74) had fall records from Simcoe Co. between Sept. 2 (1962) and Oct. 31 (1964), both these extreme dates by Frances Westman at Allandale. Lloyd (1923: 127) cited specimen records from Ottawa between Oct. 8 (1921) and Nov. 4 (1911). Weir & Quilliam (1980: 34) gave Oct. 26 as the average departure date from Kingston, with the latest on Nov. 12. Long (1968b: 17) reported one seen by J.L. Baillie at Shoal Point, Pickering, as late as Nov. 16, 1968. James R. Thurston collected one at Toronto on Sept. 24, 1889 (Thompson, 1890: 195) and Speirs (1938: 54) gave Nov. 14 as the latest Toronto record. Marshall Field and Wm. Girling saw two at Port Stanley on Sept. 10, 1950 (Brooman, 1954: 19). Ussher (1965: 11) gave Sept. 28 as his latest Rondeau record. Kelley (1978: 34) reported a late one at Kingsville on Nov. 12, 1967. Stirrett (1973d: 19) noted two at Pelee on Sept. 14 and the latest bird on Oct. 2.

**MEASUREMENTS:**
*Length:* 6.8 to 8.0 ins.
(Godfrey, 1966: 153)
*Wingspread:* 14 to 16 1/2
ins. (Roberts, 1955: 580)
*Weight:* 1.38 to 1.63 oz.
(Roberts, 1955: 580).

# BAIRD'S SANDPIPER   *Calidris bairdii*   (Coues)

Baird's Sandpiper is a high Arctic breeder, wintering in western South America mainly. In Ontario it is an uncommon to rare bird of passage.

IDENTIFICATION:   Baird's Sandpiper looks like the more common "Peeps" (Least and Semipalmated Sandpipers) but is noticeably bigger, with long wings, projecting well beyond the tail, with a scaly back pattern and "toast-coloured" head and breast. In breeding plumage you may have to flush it to distinguish it from a White-rumped Sandpiper (Baird's has a brown rump). In my experience Baird's tends to be an earlier fall migrant than the White-rump, and more partial to sandy (less muddy) shores. Sanderlings in breeding plumage resemble Baird's but have a much more prominent white wing stripe in flight (obscure in Baird's).

WINTER:   One was reported on the 1971 Christmas count at Blenheim.

SPRING:   Stirrett (1973b: 17) had just two spring records at Pelee: three on May 17, 1942 and two on May 29, 1950. Ussher (1965: 11) considered it rare at Rondeau, but had a few records from May 16 to May 28. Saunders & Dale (1933: 195) noted three at Lambeth on May 18, 1927 and two there on May 24, 1927: one was found near Delaware on May 31, 1930. Beardslee & Mitchell (1965: 225) cited a record of three at Rockhouse Point, Lake Erie, on May 25, 1946. Speirs (1938: 40, 46) gave May 21 as the earliests Toronto record and June 4 as the latest in spring. Speirs (1977: 52) had only six spring records from Whitby and Pickering, the earliest on May 16, 1969 and the latest on June 3, 1958. Weir & Quilliam (1980: 35) had spring records from May 8 to May 31 at Kingston. Nicholson (1981: 105) had just two spring records from Manitoulin: two on May 28, 1977 at Gore Bay and one on May 15, 1978 in Campbell Twp. Skeel & Bondrup-Nielsen (1978: 172) noted one at Pukaskwa on May 28, 1977. Denis (1961: 4) gave May 25 as the average arrival date for Thunder Bay with the earliest on May 19, 1956.

SUMMER:   Stirrett (1973c: 16 and 1973d: 19) noted three at Pelee on Aug. 14 and a maximum count of 25 on Aug. 25. W.E. Saunders shot one at Port Stanley on Aug. 17, 1886 (Brooman, 1954: 19). W.E. Saunders saw one at Long Point on June 7 or 8, 1925 (Snyder, 1931: 167). Thomas L. Bourne reported the species at Long Beach, Lake Erie, on July 15, 1939 (Beardslee & Mitchell, 1965: 225-226). C.W. Nash had a returning bird at Toronto as early as July 28 (Fleming, 1906: 449). Naomi LeVay had a returning bird at Cranberry Marsh on Aug. 2, 1968 and there have been a few other August records nearby. Weir & Quilliam (1980: 35) had a southbound bird at Kingston as early as July 13, but the average arrival was on Aug. 19. Devitt (1967: 74) gave Aug. 19, 1945 as the earliest date for Simcoe Co. (he had no spring record). Nicholson (1981: 105) had several August records from Manitoulin, the earliest on Aug. 4, 1974 and a high count of five on Aug. 31, 1974. Speirs & Speirs (1947: 28) noted four at North Bay on Aug. 17, 1944 and five there on Aug. 28, 1944. Skeel & Bondrup-Nielsen (1978: 172) reported this as one of the "more common shorebird migrants" at Pukaskwa, from Aug. 15 to early Sept., 1977. Hope & Shortt (1944: 574) saw a few between Ft. Albany and Moosonee, from July 15 to 25, 1942. T.M. Shortt saw two on Aug. 8, 1948 near Cape Henrietta Maria (Peck, 1972: 343).

AUTUMN:   This was one of the most numerous shorebirds that I noted near Timmins in the fall of 1935: from five on Sept. 2 to 10 on Sept. 15 (at nearby Connaught). Skeel & Bondrup-Nielsen (1978: 172) noted their last at Pukaskwa on Sept. 16, 1977. Stuart Thompson took a specimen from a flock at North Bay on Sept. 7, 1904 (Ricker & Clarke, 1939: 10). Nicholson (1981: 105) gave Ron Tasker's observation on Oct. 14, 1974 as the latest date for Manitoulin. Devitt (1967: 74) gave Sept. 1 as the 7-year average fall arrival date for Wasaga Beach, with the latest on Sept. 23, 1945. G.R. White collected one at Ottawa on Sept. 11, 1894, the only local record known to Lloyd (1923: 127). Weir & Quilliam (1980: 10, 35) suggested a "peak" at Kingston during the first week of September and the six seen on Sept. 2, 1974 at Amherst Is. was the largest number reported: the latest report was on Oct. 22. The "peak" of the fall flight in the Whitby area has been during the second week of September (when it has been reported on 16 of 35 fall field days of the Toronto Ornithological Club): the latest at Pickering was on Nov. 3, 1974, identified by Edgerton Pegg (Speirs, 1977: 52). Speirs (1938: 52, 54) gave Aug. 31 as the fall peak for Toronto, with the latest on Nov. 14. Thompson (1890: 195) collected two and saw several others at Ashbridge's Bay, Toronto, on Sept. 10, 1882 and one there on Sept. 16, 1889: another specimen was received by James R. Thurston on Sept. 24, 1889. Beardslee & Mitchell (1965: 225-226) reported two collected at Yacht Harbor on Sept. 24, 1950 and one at Ft. Erie on Aug. 31, 1954, and gave the latest date at Ft. Erie as Nov. 25, 1954. Ussher (1965: 11) had fall records at Rondeau from Sept. 4 to Nov. 1. Stirrett (1973d: 19) saw his latest two at Pelee on Oct. 15.

**MEASUREMENTS:**
*Length:* 7.0 to 7.6 ins. (Godfrey, 1966: 154)
*Wingspread:* 15 to 16 1/2 ins. (Roberts, 1955: 582)
*Weight:* ♀ 60.3 g (2.14 oz.) (Roberts, 1955: 582)
♀ slightly larger than ♂.

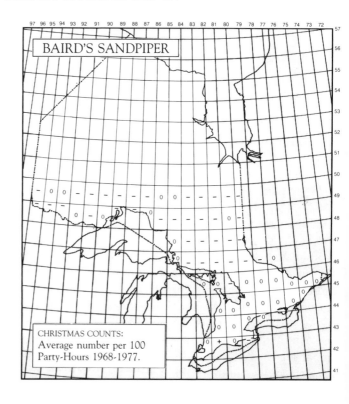

BAIRD'S SANDPIPER

CHRISTMAS COUNTS:
Average number per 100
Party-Hours 1968-1977.

# PECTORAL SANDPIPER  *Calidris melanotos*  (Vieillot)

For an Arctic breeder the Pectoral Sandpiper is rather an early migrant in spring and I have frequently missed them altogether until the return flight in late summer and autumn when they are usually quite common.

IDENTIFICATION: The most conspicuous field mark is the sharp break between the heavily streaked chest (pectoral region) and the white belly. From the rear it shows an inverted white V on its brown back, as does the Common Snipe. When flushed it flies off with a grunting "kruk" call and zigzagging flight, also somewhat like a snipe. Some of the old market hunters used to call them "Jack Snipe" or "Grass Snipe".

WINTER:

SPRING: Stirrett (1973b: 17) had records at Pelee from 100 seen on Mar 31 to 3 on May 30. Kelley (1978: 34) reported 400 at Bradley's Marsh on Apr. 21, 1968. Ussher (1965: 11) considered it scarce in spring at Rondeau but had records from March 28 to May 23, with a 9-year average arrival date on Apr. 19. Saunders (1932: 190-191) reported, as very unusual, a big spring flight at London from Apr. 10 to May 10, 1931, with a maximum of 125 on May 3. Speirs (1938: 40, 46) had spring records at Toronto from Apr. 7 to May 28. Edgerton Pegg, George A. Scott *et al* saw three at Oshawa as early as Mar. 24, 1968, and Naomi LeVay had a record at Cranberry Marsh, Whitby, as late as June 1, 1963 (Speirs, 1977: 50). Weir & Quilliam (1980: 34) gave Apr. 18 as the earliest and May 31 as the latest spring records for Kingston, with Apr. 26 and May 17 as average arrival and departure dates. Devitt (1967: 73) had only seven spring records for Simcoe Co., the earliest flock of 30 on Apr. 22, 1960 and the latest on May 22, 1967. Nicholson (1981: 105) had Manitoulin records from Apr. 25 (1970) to May 25 (1974) with a high count of 15 on May 14, 1970 by Ron Tasker. Denis (1961: 4) gave May 18 as the average arrival date at Thunder Bay, with the earliest on May 13, 1956. Elder (1979: 33) gave May 5 as the earliest Geraldton date. Hewitt saw two at Ship Sands, near Moosonee, on May 27, 1947 (Manning, 1952: 49).

SUMMER: Stirrett (1973c: 16) gave July 24 as the earliest returning record at Pelee, when he saw four. Ussher (1965: 11) gave July 10 as the earliest date for returning birds at Rondeau. Wm. Girling reported 50 or 60 at Union Pond, Elgin Co., on July 30, 1936 (Brooman, 1954: 19). Beardslee & Mitchell (1965: 224) reported two at Mohawk Is., Lake Erie, as late as June 9, 1946 and a returning bird at Crescent Beach as early as July 5, 1935 and a fall maximum of 75 along the Canadian shore of Lake Erie on Aug. 9, 1936. Saunders (1947: 364) gave July 4 as J.L. Baillie's earliest returning bird at Toronto. J.L. Baillie also noted one at Whitby as early as July 10, 1960 (Speirs, 1977: 50). Weir & Quilliam (1980: 34) gave July 19 as the earliest date for a returning bird at Kingston, with the average arrival date on Aug. 8. Devitt (1967: 73) reported the earliest returning bird at Wasaga Beach on July 22, 1934. J. Sherrin saw one on Franklin Is. on July 5, 1946 (Mills, 1981: 58). Nicholson (1981: 105) gave July 26, 1970 as the earliest date for returning birds on Manitoulin. Smith (1957: 172) saw 11 near Geraldton on Aug. 4, 1954, one near Longlac on Aug. 12 and one each at Ogoki Lake and Melchett Lake on Aug. 13. Snyder (1938: 188) reported five on Sable Is., Lake of the Woods, on Aug. 8, 1929 (one male collected). Schueler, Baldwin & Rising (1974: 142) reported the species at Cochrane, but at none of their James Bay or Hudson Bay stops. Two half-grown birds were collected near Cape Henrietta Maria by the ROM collecting party on July 5, 1948 (Peck, 1972: 342) but Peck (1981: 1) still listed this as one of Ontario's breeding species for which no nest has yet been found. Manning (1952: 50) saw 50 in three hours at Lake River on July 17, 1947: he collected a juvenile and a female with an incubation patch and saw about 1000 between July 20 and July 24 in 16 hours at Cape Henrietta Maria: he noted 700 in 8 hours from July 29 to Aug. 1, 1947 at Little Cape and 90 in 7 hours from Aug. 9 to 14, 1947 at Shagamu River, Hudson Bay. Lee (1978: 23) noted them frequently between July 7 and Aug. 9 at Big Trout Lake, with a maximum of six on Aug. 2, 1975. C.E. Hope saw 15 and collected two at Ft. Severn on July 17, 1940.

AUTUMN: Stirrett saw 150 at Ship Sands, near Moosonee, on Oct. 2, 1948 (Manning, 1952: 49). Skeel & Bondrup-Nielsen (1978: 172) had only one fall record at Pukaskwa, on Sept. 15, 1977. Ricker & Clarke (1939: 10) had Lake Nipissing records from Oct. 15 (1898) to Oct. 27 (1925). Speirs & Speirs (1947: 28) noted one at North Bay on Sept. 16, 1944. Nicholson (1981: 105) had a high fall count of 60 at Silver Lake, Manitoulin, on Oct. 31, 1976 and the latest on Nov. 7, 1976. K. Ketchum noted one as late as Oct. 13, 1974 at Pointe au Baril (Mills, 1981: 58). Devitt (1967: 74) cited the four seen by Frances Westman at Allandale on Oct. 31, 1964 as the latest Simcoe Co. report. Weir & Quilliam (1980: 34) gave Oct. 27 as the 24-year average departure date from Kingston, with the latest on Nov. 25. Tozer & Richards (1974: 132-133) estimated over 300 at Whitby on Oct. 18, 1964 and gave Nov. 22, 1964 as the latest sighting there. Speirs (1938: 54) gave Nov. 22 as the latest Toronto record. Ussher (1965: 11) gave Oct. 24 as the 8-year average departure date from Rondeau, with the latest on Nov. 6. Stirrett (1973d: 19 and 1973a: 15) had a fall maximum of 50 at Pelee on Sept. 22, and the latest two there on Nov. 16.

**MEASURMENTS:**
*Length:* 8.0 to 9.6 ins. ( ♂ larger than ♀ ) (Godfrey, 1966: 152)
*Wingspread:* 15.35 to 17.5 ins. (Roberts, 1955: 575)
*Weight:* 2 to 3 1/4 oz. (Terres, 1980: 778).

**REFERENCE:**
Saunders, W.E. 1932 Spring records of Pectoral Sandpiper at London, Ontario. Can. Field-Naturalist, 46:(8):190-191.

# SHARP-TAILED SANDPIPER
## *Calidris acuminata*   (Horsfield)

This bird is normally a breeding bird of northern Siberia, migrating south to Australia, and somewhat rarely along the British Columbia coast. Purely accidental in Ontario.

**IDENTIFICATION:**  This is the Siberian counterpart of our Pectoral Sandpiper and is about the same size and general appearance but lacks the definite cutoff between its pectoral (chest) striping and the white belly. The breast tends to be spotted rather than striped. The bird at Dundas Marsh had a "pronounced superciliary stripe, a strongly rufous crown and generally buffy appearance, fading towards the belly" (see illustration on p. 123 of Robbins, Bruun & Zim).

**WINTER:**  The Dundas Marsh bird was last noted on Dec. 5, 1975, when I missed seeing it by a few minutes.

**SPRING:**

**SUMMER:**

**AUTUMN:**  Chauncey Wood identified one at Dundas Marsh, Hamilton, which was seen by many observers (thousands on TV) from Nov. 26 to Dec. 5, 1975 (Goodwin, 1976: 61).

**MEASUREMENTS:**
*Length:* 8 1/4 to 9 1/4 ins.
(Terres, 1980: 780)
*Wingspread:* to 17 ins.
(Terres, 1980: 780)
*Weight:* about 2 1/2 oz.
(Terres, 1980: 780)

# PURPLE SANDPIPER   *Calidris maritima*   (Brünnich)

The Purple Sandpiper is another circumpolar Arctic breeder, but unlike many others in this category it winters along the North Atlantic coasts, not far to the south in South America. I associate it with drear November days on rocky promontaries or piers. Even then it is sufficiently rare in Ontario to be a cause for rejoicing when spotted.

**IDENTIFICATION:**  The Purple Sandpiper is a little bigger than a Spotted Sandpiper. When we see it here in the fall it is mainly dark slate gray (like the rocks on which it is often found), with a white belly and yellow to orange legs. In the breeding plumage (seldom seen in Ontario) it has a good deal of a scaly brown pattern on its back.

**WINTER:**  On the 1968-1977 Christmas counts, there were single reports at Kingston, Kettle Point and Long Point. Kelley (1978: 34) reported four at Rondeau on Dec. 4, 1974. Sheppard (1960: 21) mentioned a sighting near Niagara Falls in December, 1938 and two seen at Ft. Erie on Dec. 3, 1954. Beardslee & Mitchell (1965: 223) reported another at Ft. Erie on Dec. 23, 1945. Fleming (1906: 449) mentioned a Dec. 7 record for Toronto. Don Burton found one at Whitby on Dec. 4, 1966 (Speirs, 1977: 49). K.F. Edwards and party found one near Kingston on the Dec. 27, 1970 Christmas count (Quilliam, 1973: 83).

SPRING: One was reported at the Long Point Bird Observatory on May 28, 1971 (Goodwin, 1971: 737). Quilliam (1973: 83) cited a record on Wolfe Is. on May 28, 1961 by Art Bell, Anne Hutchison, Nora Mansfield and Gwen Woods.

SUMMER: Weir & Quilliam (1980: 34) gave an Aug. 13 date for Kingston (without comment).

AUTUMN: Lloyd (1923: 127) had only one Ottawa record: a specimen take by W. Forbes on Oct. 29, 1885. Quilliam (1973: 83) gave 25 as the maximum count for the Kingston region: these were noted at Prince Edward Point on Nov. 19, 1969. George A. Scott found one at Darlington Provincial Park on Nov. 10, 1957 (Tozer & Richards, 1974: 132). Speirs (1977: 49) cited several fall records from the Pickering shore of Lake Ontario, the earliest on Oct. 10, 1964 by Tom Hassall and the latest a female specimen in the collection of Barry Kent MacKay dated Nov. 19, 1966. Saunders (1947: 364) had fall records at Toronto on Oct. 23 and Nov. 16. James R. Thurston reported one shot at Toronto on Oct. 30, 1889, as the second Ontario record (Thompson, 1890: 198). Maughan (1897: 2) collected a male on Toronto Is. on Oct. 27, 1894, and gave several measurements. McIlwraith (1894: 138) reported the first Ontario record as one taken by K.C. McIlwraith at Hamilton on Oct. 3, 1885. Beardslee & Mitchell (1965: 235) had a maximum of 8 at Crystal Beach, Lake Erie, on Nov. 18, 1941: they also noted 5 at Point Abino on Nov. 28, 1948 and had their earliest record on Oct. 29, 1959 at Ft. Erie. Stirrett (1973d: 19 and 1973a: 15) had four Pelee records, all of single birds: Oct. 27, 1945; Oct. 30, 1948; Nov. 6, 1966 and one as late as Nov. 29.

**MEASUREMENTS:**
*Length:* 8.1 to 9.5 ins.
(Godfrey, 1966: 150).
*Wingspread:* 15 3/4 ins.
(Maughan, 1897: 2).
*Weight:* 2 to 3 oz. (Terres, 1980: 779).

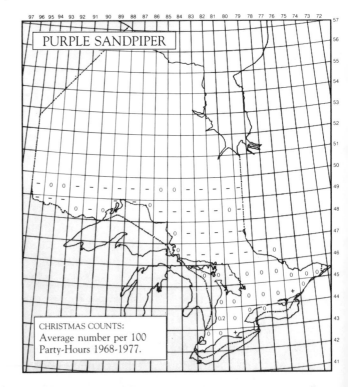

PURPLE SANDPIPER

CHRISTMAS COUNTS:
Average number per 100
Party-Hours 1968-1977.

# DUNLIN   *Calidris alpina*   (Linnaeus)

This Holarctic breeder usually passes rather quickly through Ontario in May but lingers on its southward journey to its wintering areas along the Atlantic and Gulf coasts of America. It is often the last of the shorebirds to be seen on the mudflats of the lower Great Lakes in fall.

IDENTIFICATION: The old names "Red-backed Sandpiper" and "Blackheart Sandpiper" were descriptive of the reddish brown upperparts and black patch on the white underparts of northbound migrants in spring but the present name "Dunlin" is more appropriate for the dun-coloured southbound birds. These are small sandpipers (though larger than the tiny "peeps") but have rather long bills, downturned near the tips, with which they probe the mudflats like small dowitchers.

WINTER: A few individuals have shown up on Christmas counts at Blenheim and Long Point. Stirrett (1973a: 15) noted individuals at Pelee as late as Dec. 10. Ussher (1965: 11) noted one at Rondeau as late as Dec. 2. J.L. Baillie (in Saunders, 1947: 365) had a Dec. 31 record at Toronto. There were four records of birds lingering into December along the Pickering-Oshawa lakefront, the latest on Dec. 16, 1963 (Speirs, 1977: 55).

SPRING: Stirrett (1973b: 17) noted the earliest at Pelee on Apr. 23, 1949 and a maximum of 75 on May 23. Ussher (1965: 11) had Rondeau records from May 1 to June 10, but his average arrival date was May 15 and departure date on May 26. Marshall Field noted 150 at Port Burwell on May 23, 1953 (Brooman, 1954: 19). Saunders & Dale (1933: 196) had just two spring records for Middlesex Co.: two on May 22, 1927 at Lambeth and one on May 24, 1931 at Wonnacott's farm. Snyder (1931: 168) collected 29 specimens at Long Point from May 12 (1928) to June 11 (1927). Beardslee & Mitchell (1965: 227) noted two at Rockhouse Point, Lake Erie, as early as Apr. 16, 1955 and about 1000 there on May 30, 1958. Speirs (1938: 44) gave May 23 as the spring peak date for Toronto. Saunders (1947: 365) noted one as early as Apr. 23 at Toronto but gave May 22 as his average arrival date. The earliest Ontario Co. date was one seen by George A. Scott at Whitby on Apr. 20, 1969, while the maximum count there was 500 by J.L. Baillie on May 22, 1962 (Speirs, 1977: 55). Snyder (1941: 54) collected three males at Hallowell, Prince Edward Co. on May 23, 1930 and saw some there until May 28 that year. Weir & Quilliam (1980: 35) gave May 10 as the average arrival date at Kingston, with Apr. 19 as the earliest and May 29 as the average departure date. Devitt (1967: 75) gave May 23 as the 9-year average arrival date at Wasaga Beach, the earliest on May 6, 1949 at Collingwood, and the maximum of 75 on May 27, 1956. Beamer had a Meaford record on May 22, 1949 and noted one at nearby Cape Rich on June 2, 1940. At Pointe au Baril, K. Ketchum had records from May 19 to May 24 (Mills, (1981: 59). Nicholson (1981: 106) had Manitoulin records from Apr. 25 (1971) to June 4 (1980), with the average arrival on May 11 and a high count of 600 on May 27, 1974. Speirs & Speirs (1947: 28) noted one at North Bay on May 17, 1944. Ricker & Clarke (1939: 10) took two at Frank's Bay, Lake Nipissing, on May 28, 1932. Skeel & Bondrup-Nielsen (1978: 173) saw three at Pukaskwa on May 25, 1977. Denis (1961: 4) gave May 20 as the average arrival date at Thunder Bay, with the earliest on May 4, 1958. Elder (1979: 33) gave May 22 as the earliest arrival date at Geraldton, for this uncommon migrant. On May 24, 1971 we watched a young Indian lad unsuccessfully hunting a flock of 80 at

Longlac (with a catapult). Hewitt found them common at Ship Sands, near Moosonee, from May 26 to 28, 1947 and Manning (1952: 52) estimated 1000 there on May 31, 1947.

SUMMER: Stirrett (1973b: 17; 1973c: 16) had two at Pelee as late as June 13, and two laggards on June 27, with the earliest returning birds on Aug. 9. Ussher (1965: 11) gave Aug. 22 as the earliest date for returning birds at Rondeau. Brooman (1954: 19) noted one at Port Stanley on Aug. 18, 1946. Snyder (1931: 168) had Long Point records to June 15, 1927 and reported two collected there by W.E. Clyde Todd on July 16, 1907. Beardslee & Mitchell (1965: 227) reported two on Mohawk Is. on June 18, 1950; one there on June 24, 1951 and one at Rockhouse Point on July 18, 1953. Speirs (1938: 46, 48) had a Toronto record on June 18 with the earliest returning bird on Aug. 6. Speirs (1977: 55) had Whitby records as late as June 17, 1972 and as early as Aug. 2, 1958. Weir & Quilliam (1980: 35) had June 21 and Aug. 25 dates for Kingston. Paul Harrington saw one at Wasaga Beach as late as June 12, 1928 (Devitt, 1967: 75). Manning (1952: 52) collected a brood of four downy young from a nest at Cape Henrietta Maria on July 21, 1947 and estimated seeing 900 there in 16 hours afield between July 20 and 24: he estimated 300 in eight hours at Little Cape; and 25 including two juveniles collected in 7 hours at Shagamu River between Aug. 11 and 14, 1947. Hope & Shortt (1944: 575) noted only small numbers between Ft. Albany and Moosonee from July 15 to 25, 1942: no great movement had yet begun. Peck (1972: 343) found two nests, each with 4 eggs, at Cape Henrietta Maria on June 27, 1970 (photo on p. 342). Schueler, Baldwin & Rising (1974: 143, 145) noted the species at Attawapiskat and laying females at Winisk: they found a nest with two eggs on June 24, 1962 at the mouth of the Sutton River and a nest with downy young there the same day. Lee (1978: 23) noted one on June 7 and three on June 8 at Big Trout Lake (his only summer records there). Hope reported none during the summer of 1940 at Ft. Severn.

AUTUMN: Skeel & Bondrup-Nielsen (1978: 173) saw one at Pukaskwa on Oct. 6, 1977. Ricker & Clarke (1939: 10) noted two at Lake Nipissing on Sept. 18, 1929. Nicholson (1981: 106) had returning birds on Manitoulin from Aug. 31 (1972) to Nov. 8 (1980), with a maximum of 50 on Oct. 25, 1970. Mills (1981: 59) had fall records from the cottage country from Sept. 23 to Oct. 13. Beamer saw a small flock at Meaford on Oct. 16, 1938 and one there on Nov. 7, 1948. Devitt (1967: 75) had Wasaga Beach records from Sept. 28 (1964) to Nov. 25 (1942) with a maximum of 100 on Oct. 15, 1936. Weir & Quilliam (1980: 35) gave Sept. 24 and Nov. 12 as average fall arrival and departure dates at Kingston, with the latest on Nov. 28. John Townson saw flocks in Prince Edward Co. from Oct. 3 to Oct. 29, 1931 (Snyder, 1941: 54). Dunlins are generally uncommon in the Whitby-Pickering area until the end of September, but I estimated 500 there on Oct. 29, 1969 and saw my latest on Nov. 23, 1974: Doug. Scovell saw a Merlin capture a Dunlin at Whitby on Nov. 8, 1959 (Speirs, 1977: 55). Speirs (1938: 52) gave Oct. 17 as the fall peak date for Toronto. A.A. Wood collected one of two seen at Coldstream on Oct. 15, 1917 (Saunders & Dale, 1933: 196). Brooman (1954: 19) noted one at Port Burwell as late as Nov. 11, 1951. Ussher (1965: 11) gave Sept. 13 as the average arrival date at Rondeau and Nov. 8 as the average departure date. Stirrett (1973d: 19) had maxima of 40 at Pelee on Oct. 1 and Oct. 20, but Kelley (1978: 35) reported 1500 at Bradley's Marsh in fall.

**MEASUREMENTS:**
*Length:* 7.5 to 9.3 ins.
(Godfrey, 1966: 155)
*Wingspread:* 14 1/2 to 15
3/4 ins. (Roberts,
1955: 572)
*Weight:* 1.5 to 3 oz.
(Roberts, 1955: 572).

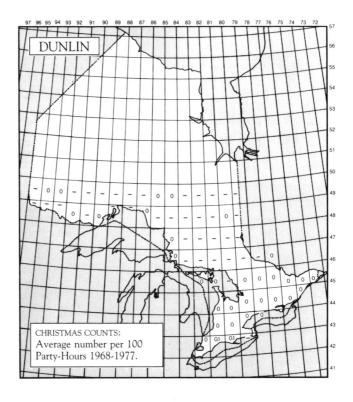

DUNLIN

CHRISTMAS COUNTS:
Average number per 100
Party-Hours 1968-1977.

# CURLEW SANDPIPER   *Calidris ferruginea*   (Pontoppidan)

This is an Old World shorebird, a very rare straggler in Ontario. My only personal experience with this red-breasted beauty was at a roadside puddle in Sweden on Aug. 22, 1966.

IDENTIFICATION:  In breeding plumage the brick-red underparts and longish down-curved beak are diagnostic. In the drab winter garb it looks like a white rumped version of a Dunlin, but with somewhat longer legs and with a bill that is more slender and more uniformly curved throughout its length. (Note that a Dunlin may often appear to have a white rump when at rest and seen from the side.)

Fleming (1906: 449) reported a specimen taken at Toronto by Wm. Loan about 1886. Most of the specimen was later destroyed, except the head, which finally reached the Fleming collection.

WINTER:

SPRING:  Goodwin (1980: 772) reported one seen at Bradley's Marsh by many observers on May 17, 1980. John H. Enns saw one in the distinctive breeding plumage in May, 1953 on the Crow Creek flood plain where it crosses Hwy 11 (about 9 miles E. of Mattice).

SUMMER:  N. Randall *et al* reported one at Blenheim on Aug. 22, 1976 (Goodwin, 1976: 171). R.F. Andrle *et al* found one at Waverly Beach, Lake Erie, on July 18-19, 1971 (Goodwin, 1971: 852-853). K.F. Edwards and son Kenneth observed one at Amherstview Sewage Lagoons, near Kingston, on July 20, 1974 (Weir & Quilliam, 1980: 10).

AUTUMN:  Tozer & Richards (1974: 134) detailed sightings of one found at Whitby on Oct. 21, 1961 by Tom Hassall, photographed by G. Norris and seen by J.L. Baillie *et al* during the next two days and last reported by A.A. Wood on Oct. 25. George W. North found one at Dundas which was seen from Oct. 11 to 13, 1954 and another was reported by A.J.V. Mason at Hamilton on Oct. 2, 1959 (Andrle & Axtell, 1966: 300). On Sept. 11, 1965 one was found at Grant Point, about 3.5 miles SW of Port Maitland on the Lake Erie shore by Daniel Salisbury and Adrian Dorst who collected the bird which proved to be a male in slightly worn fall plumage. There were several sightings during the previous 3 weeks (Andrle & Axtell, 1966: 300).

**MEASUREMENTS:**
Length: 7 to 9 ins.
(Godfrey, 1966: 155)
Wingspread: 14 1/2 to 16
1/2 ins. (Terres, 1980: 777)
Weight: 1 3/4 to 3 1/2 oz.
(Terres, 1980: 777).

**REFERENCE:**
Andrle, Robert F. and
Harold H. Axtell 1966
Curlew Sandpiper in
Ontario. Condor,
68: (3): 300-301.

# STILT SANDPIPER  *Calidris himantopus*  (Bonaparte)

This rather rare sandpiper sometimes rewards those who scrutinize the flocks of sandpipers along the borders of mud flats, where its long legs allow it to wade into the shallows and probe the bottom with a sewing machine action of its vertically held beak. They breed in the low Arctic and winter in South America.

IDENTIFICATION: The Stilt Sandpiper is a bit like a Lesser Yellowlegs in build, but has greenish yellow legs (not brilliant yellow as in the yellowlegs). It also has a white line over the eye and slightly drooping tip to the beak. The manner of feeding is also distinct (see above). In spring the heavily barred underparts are only matched by the Wandering Tattler, which lacks the white rump of the Stilt Sandpiper. Adults returning in summer may retain the barring but the immatures coming later lack this feature and are best identified by the manner of feeding, the white "eyebrows" and the long greenish legs. They look a bit like fall dowitchers and often associate with them, but in flight they lack the white stripe up the back of the dowitchers, have longer legs, shorter beaks and a more slender upswept rear end.

WINTER:

SPRING: Spring records are scarce. D. Rupert noted two at Steen's Marsh, near Pelee, on May 22, 1971 (Goodwin, 1971: 737). Harold Lancaster found one at Dunwich Marsh, Elgin Co., on Apr. 23, 1952 (Brooman, 1954: 20). Speirs (1938: 40) gave May 21 as the earliest Toronto record. George A. Scott saw one at Oshawa's Second Marsh on May 18, 1958 and Naomi LeVay had a sighting at Cranberry Marsh, Whitby, a week later on May 25, 1958 (Tozer & Richards, 1974: 136). R.B. Stewart found one at Prince Edward Point on May 11, 1972 (Quilliam, 1973: 86) and Ken Edwards *et al* observed one at Amherstview Sewage Lagoons from May 12 to May 27, 1979 (Weir & Quilliam, 1980: 10). Nicholson (1981: 108) had just one spring record for Manitoulin at Little Current on May 25, 1974. Denis (1961: 3) reported a very early bird at Thunder Bay on May 2, 1960 with the average arrival date on May 14.

SUMMER: Stirrett (1973c: 16) had one at Pelee on June 22 and 18 there on Aug. 1. Wm. Girling, W.E. Saunders and E.M.S. Dale identified one at St. Thomas on Aug. 25, 1934 (Brooman, 1954: 20). Saunders & Dale (1933: 196-197) noted one near London on Aug. 15-16, 1930 and another on Aug. 11, 1931. W.E. Clyde Todd collected two at Long Point on July 16, 1907 (Snyder, 1931: 166). W. Brockner and R. Hermes saw one in full spring plumage on Mohawk Is., Lake Erie on June 15, 1946: the first returning bird on the Lake Erie shore was seen on July 12, 1934; later flocks included 11 at Point Abino on July 25, 1959 and 20 along the Lake Erie shore on Aug. 16, 1963 (Beardslee & Mitchell, 1965: 229-230). Fleming (1906: 449) noted adults in full plumage at Toronto from July 18 to July 28 and young later from Aug. 9 into Sept. J.L. Baillie saw single birds at Whitby on July 25-26, 1959 (Speirs, 1977: 57). Weir & Quilliam (1980: 10, 35) gave July 10 as the earliest date for a returning bird at Kingston: a maximum of seven was noted on July 30, 1978 at Amherstview Sewage Lagoons by Fred Cooke. Devitt (1967: 76) had just four records for Simcoe Co.: one found near Barrie on Aug. 25, 1945 by E.L. Brereton and birds found at Collingwood by Alf Mitchener on July 24, 1957; July 17, 1960 and Aug. 6, 1961. Nicholson (1981: 108) gave Aug. 4, 1974 as the earliest date for a southbound bird on Manitoulin. Manning (1952: 53) saw five adults (4 males collected) and a half-fledged juvenile (also collected) at Cape Henrietta Maria from July 20-23, 1947 (the first breeding record for Ontario). The 1948 ROM party collected two downy young at Cape Henrietta Maria on July 9 and Peck (1972: 343) noted active courtship behaviour there from June 23 to 30, 1970. Schueler, Baldwin & Rising (1974: 145) collected one downy young from a brood of four at the mouth of the Sutton River, on June 24, 1962.

AUTUMN: Skeel & Bondrup-Nielsen (1978: 173) had only one record at Pukaskwa, on Sept. 23, 1977. Nicholson (1981: 108) reported one seen on Manitoulin by Ron Tasker on Oct. 12, 1980. Weir & Quilliam (1980: 35) gave Nov. 6 as the latest Kingston date. George A. Scott noted 35 in one group and 7 in another on Sept. 22, 1957 at Oshawa's Second Marsh: the latest Whitby bird was spotted by Rosemary Gaymer and Donald Gunn on Oct. 25, 1959 (Speirs, 1977: 57). Speirs (1938: 54) gave Oct. 16 as the latest Toronto record. James R. Thurston received three at his taxidermy store on Sept. 26, 1889 (Thompson, 1890: 195). The latest sighting along the Lake Erie shore was three seen on Oct. 17, 1948 (Beardslee & Mitchell, 1965: 229-230). Wm. Girling noted the species at St. Thomas on Oct. 5, 1947 (Brooman, 1954: 20). Stirrett (1973d: 19) gave Oct. 2 as his latest date for Pelee (two noted).

**MEASUREMENTS:**
*Length:* 7.5 to 9.3 ins.
(Godfrey, 1966: 159)
(beak: 38.6-41.9 mm.)
*Wingspread:* 15 1/2 to 17
ins. (Roberts, 1955: 573)
*Weight:* 2 to 2 3/4 oz.
(Roberts, 1955: 573) ♀
larger than ♂.

# BUFF-BREASTED SANDPIPER
*Tryngites subruficollis* (Vieillot)

This is a rare bird in Ontario. It breeds in the northwestern Canadian Arctic, winters in Argentina and migrates chiefly through the prairies. In Ontario it may be found in grassy fields with Upland Sandpipers, in grain stubble or harvested pea fields.

IDENTIFICATION: The buffy cheeks and underparts, yellow legs and short black beak identify this species. It is about the size of a Spotted Sandpiper or a Dunlin. The upright posture (like a small Upland Sandpiper) is also a helpful field mark.

WINTER:

SPRING: Stirrett (1973b: 17) reported three at Pelee on May 31, 1952, his only spring record. Speirs (1938: 40, 46) listed spring records from Toronto between May 19 and June 3.

SUMMER: Goodwin (1974: 46) noted one at Pelee as early as Aug. 20, 1973 and Stirrett (1973d: 19) gave Aug. 29 as his earliest record there. Speirs (1938: 48) gave Aug. 22 as the earliest date for southbound birds at Toronto. Tom Hassall discovered six in a harvested pea field near Shoal Point, Pickering, on Aug. 31, 1963, which stayed until Sept. 2 (Long, 1966: 26). George A. Scott noted one at Whitby Harbour on Aug. 28, 1966 (Tozer & Richards, 1974: 138). Weir & Quilliam (1980: 11) gave Aug. 21 as the earliest date for returning birds at Kingston, with a maximum of three seen by the Kenneth Edwards on the "plover fields" near Prince Edward Point on Aug. 31, 1980. E.G. White shot eight at Duck Is., near Ottawa, on Aug. 24, 1886 (Lloyd, 1923: 127). Unusually early birds were reported at Ottawa by R.A. Foxall and R. Pittaway on July 30, 1972 and S. O'Donell on Aug. 12 the same year (Goodwin, 1972: 853). Devitt (1967: 76) reported one seen by E.L. Brereton at Wasaga Beach on Aug. 28, 1949 and one photographed at Collingwood Harbour by A.J. Mitchener on Aug. 23, 1962. Skeel & Bondrup-Nielsen (1978: 174) saw one at Pukaskwa on Aug. 24, 1977. Elder (1979: 33) called this a rare fall migrant, with only three records during late August at Geraldton and Neys Provincial Park, east of Terrace Bay.

AUTUMN: According to Ross James, a specimen was taken at the mouth of the Moose River, near Moosonee on Sept. 7, 1974 and went to the collection in University of Western Ontario (James, McLaren & Barlow, 1976: 24). Denis (1961: 6) gave Sept. 4 as the average for three fall arrivals at Thunder Bay. Nicholson (1981: 108) had five records of single birds on Manitoulin: on Sept. 19, 1970, Sept. 14, 1975, Sept. 21, 1975, Sept. 10, 1977 and Sept. 18, 1977 (this last a casualty at the Great Duck Is. lighthouse). Weir & Quilliam (1980: 11) had eight fall records for Kingston, the latest on Sept. 20. Jack Gingrich found one at Whitby on Sept. 30, 1961 which remained until last seen by A.A. Wood on Oct. 19 (Speirs, 1977: 60). Tozer & Richards (1974: 138) mentioned one seen by J.L. Baillie at Whitby Harbour on Sept. 27, 1964 and another noted by George A. Scott at Oshawa on Oct. 4, 1964. Speirs (1938: 54) had fall records at Toronto to Oct. 26. Wm. Loane collected one at Toronto on Sept. 5, 1889 (Thompson, 1890: 195) and Fleming (1906: 451) considered it regular but rare there from Sept. 1 to Oct. 4. Beardslee & Mitchell (1965: 232) had a few fall records from the Canadian shore of Lake Erie near Buffalo: one on Sept. 7, 1932 at Ft. Erie; one at Rockhouse Point from Sept. 4 to 6, 1954 and another there on Sept. 8, 1956; one at Yacht Harbour on Sept. 7, 1959 and one at Erie Beach on Sept. 11, 1959. Stirrett (1973d: 19) had Pelee records to Oct. 13 while Kelley (1978: 36) reported a maximum of 35 there on Sept. 1, 1973.

**MEASUREMENTS:**
*Length:* 7.5 to 8.9 ins.
(Godfrey, 1966: 161)
*Wingspread:* 15.75 to
17.4 ins. (Roberts,
1955: 577)
*Weight:* 2.25 oz. (Roberts,
1955: 577).

# RUFF  *Philomachus pugnax*  (Linnaeus)

The Ruff is an Old World species but, in recent years, they have been reported almost every year somewhere in Ontario. The males are much larger than the females (known as Reeves) and have display arenas like Prairie Chickens and other lek species.

IDENTIFICATION: During the courting season the males develop colourful ruffs on the neck and head. These are exceedingly variable in colour and pattern. Ruffs are intermediate in size between Greater and Lesser Yellowlegs, with which they often associate on migration and somewhat resemble. However the Ruff has duller, more orange-yellow legs, shorter and stouter than those of the Yellowlegs; their bills are also stouter and the plumage more brown and less gray. The tail pattern with black central feathers bordered by big white oval patches is distinctive. Males, with their fancy ruffs are easily identified but rather seldom seen.

WINTER:

SPRING: Stirrett (1973b: 17) had just one Pelee record, on May 11, 1967. Two males were sighted in spring of 1973, one with a white ruff at Walsingham from Apr. 23-28 by D.R. Baldwin *et al* and one almost wholly black at Pelee from May 13-17 by D.R. Gunn *et al* (Goodwin, 1973: 767). Two males appeared at Bradley's Marsh in 1971: one on May 7 and 16 seen by J.B. Miles and D. Rupert and the other on May 9 seen by E. Knapp (Goodwin, 1971: 737 and Kelley, 1978: 37). Another showed up at Wheatley on May 12, 1967 (Kelley, 1978: 37). Goodwin (1972: 756) reported two in spring, 1972: one seen at Strathroy by W.R. Jarmain, Bill Girling and J. Tabak on May 7 and the other seen by many observers at Hepworth, Bruce Co., on Apr. 27 and 28. Fleming (1906: 450) reported a male in full plumage taken at Toronto Island in 1882 and Lumsden (1955: 168) indicated that this was collected in spring and also mentioned another taken in 1887. Rob Nisbet notified me about a male in winter plumage at Carr Marsh, between Port Hope and Cobourg, which I saw with Sheldon McGregor *et al* on Apr. 18, 1981. Weir & Quilliam (1980: 11) gave three spring records for the Kingston region: May 18, 1974 on Wolfe Is. by Fred Cooke *et al*; May 15, 1976 at Amherstview Sewage Lagoons by Kenneth and Ken Edwards and a male there again from May 2-19, 1979 (accompanied by a female on May 12-13), seen by Kenneth and Mary Edwards *et al*.

SUMMER: R. Curry *et al* saw one at Bradley's Marsh from July 22-26, 1973 (Goodwin, 1973: 865). Beardslee & Mitchell (1965: 234-235) gave details of four summer records from the Lake Erie north shore: the first from Aug. 6-10, 1956 at Rockhouse Point, the next there from July 20-22, 1957 was a male in nuptial plumage and George North saw a female there on July 21; a female was collected at Yacht Harbour on July 26, 1957 and on July 21, 1962 one was found at Erie Beach. Peter Iden reported one to me on the evening of July 28, 1967 at Claireville Dam, which I saw, with Ron Orenstein, the next day: this was a fine big male with reddish legs, much black on the belly and black-and-white barred ruffs. George A. Scott found a female at Oshawa Harbour on July 21, 1963 and showed the bird to Doris H. Speirs and me (Speirs, 1977: 63). Naomi LeVay reported two at Cranberry Marsh on Aug. 2, 1968 (Tozer & Richards, 1974: 139). Lumsden (1955: 168) wrote about a male with chestnut ruff, barred with black, that was shot by an Indian at Ft. Severn a few days before June 12, 1955 when the specimen was given to him by R. Still, the manager of the Hudson Bay post there.

AUTUMN: J. Nicholson *et al* reported one at Chelmsford from Sept. 12-17, 1972 (Goodwin, 1973: 52). One was seen by Edgerton Pegg and photographed by Harvey Medland at Whitby on Sept. 9 or 10, 1972 (Speirs, 1977: 63). A Ruff seen at Wildwood by E. Eligsen, M. Ross and I. Snider on Sept. 25, 1970, was the first Oxford Co. record (Goodwin, 1971: 52). Kelley (1978: 37) reported one at River Canard, Essex Co., on Sept. 27, 1969. Stirrett (1973d: 19) had just one fall record for Pelee on Sept. 13.

**MEASUREMENTS:**
*Length:* 8.5 to 11.5 ins. ♂ larger than ♀ (Godfrey, 1966: 164).
*Wingspread:*
*Weight:* 35 ♂ averaged 163 g. 185 ♀ averaged 95 g. (Dunning, 1984: 10).

**REFERENCE:**
Lumsden, H.G. 1955 Ruff and White Pelican at Fort Severn.
Can. Field Nat., 69:(4):168.

# SHORT-BILLED DOWITCHER
*Limnodromus griseus* (Gmelin)

This is the more common dowitcher in Ontario. One race breeds in northern Quebec and another in the northern prairies. They winter from the southern U.S.A. to central South America. We see them in migration in Ontario.

IDENTIFICATION: This is a stocky, medium-sized shorebird with a long, straight bill. In flight it is readily identified by the white median stripe from the rump up the middle of its back. In spring its rosy underparts distinguish it from the Common Snipe. The American Woodcock is a woodland bird with a much stouter bill than dowitchers which are birds of the mudflats. Immatures lack the rosy breast of adults and look a bit like fall Stilt Sandpipers, but have shorter legs and longer bills than that species.

WINTER:

SPRING: Stirrett (1973b: 17) had Pelee records from May 9 to May 25. Kelley (1978: 36) reported a high of 65 at Pelee on May 15, 1974. Ussher (1965: 12) had Rondeau sightings from May 7 to May 28, with the 10-year average arrival on May 18. Bob Lemon found 16 just west of Eagle on May 16, 1948 and 30 at Dunwich Marsh on May 23, 1948 (Brooman, 1954: 19). Saunders & Dale (1933: 196) were thrilled to find 26 at Lambeth on May 18, 1927. Snyder (1931: 165) collected a female on May 18 and a male and female on May 24, and saw another on May 25, in 1928 at Long Point. Speirs (1938: 40, 44, 46) gave May 13 as the earliest Toronto date and May 31 as the latest, with a peak on May 24. A.A. Wood had a very early record at Whitby on Apr. 28, 1960 (Tozer & Richards, 1974: 135) and the spring peak there has been about May 17 (Speirs, 1977: 56). Weir & Quilliam (1980: 35) gave May 10 as the earliest Kingston record with the average stay from May 17 to May 26. Lloyd (1923: 126) considered it rare at Ottawa and reported only one collected by G.R. White on May 9, 1890 and two by E.G. White on May 22, the same year. Devitt (1967: 75) gave May 10, 1964 as the earliest Barrie record: one was collected on May 24, 1963 by H.B. Haugh. H. Savage saw 43 (and collected four) on the South Limestone Is., Georgian Bay, on May 17, 1964 (Mills, 1981: 60). Nicholson (1981: 107) had Manitoulin records from May 7 (1977) to June 1 (1974), with a high count of 36 on May 16, 1970. Denis (1961: 4) gave May 19 as the average arrival date at Thunder Bay, with the earliest on May 16, 1953. Manning (1952: 53) mentioned an adult female collected at Moose Factory as early as May 17, 1930.

SUMMER: Stirrett (1973c: 16) noted eight at Pelee on Aug. 1. Ussher (1965: 12) gave July 16 as the earliest returning bird for Rondeau, with Aug. 1 as the 9-year average. Wm. Girling saw one at St. Thomas on Aug. 23, 1936 (Brooman, 1954: 19). Beardslee & Mitchell (1965: 228) had several records for Rockhouse Pt., Lake Erie: two as early as July 5, 1958 and three collected (on July 25, 1950, Aug. 11, 1950 and Aug. 24, 1954). Fleming (1906: 449) took one in full plumage at Toronto on Aug. 1, 1894, but young birds only on Aug. 24, 1891 and later. Speirs (1938: 52) noted a peak (presumably adults) at Toronto on Aug. 7. Saunders (1947: 365) had a June 13 sighting at Toronto, while J.L. Baillie had his earliest returning bird there on July 20. Tozer & Richards (1974: 135) reported one as late as June 17, 1963 at Scugog, and I saw two at Corner Marsh, Pickering, as early as July 9, 1975, with a peak in the first week of August (Speirs, 1977: 56). Weir & Quilliam (1980: 35) gave June 12 as the latest date for northbound birds at Kingston and July 6 as the earliest for southbound migrants, with July 26 as the average arrival date. Paul Harrington saw 30 at Wasaga Beach as late as June 6, 1927 (Devitt, 1967: 75). Nicholson (1981: 108) noted the earliest returning bird on Manitoulin on July 18, 1969. Elder (1979: 33) had only one Geraldton record; on Aug. 22, 1970. A male with an incubation patch was collected by C.E. Hope on July 16, 1942 on the Nettichi River, and R.T. Morris saw a number at North Point, James Bay, about Aug. 1, 1906 (Manning, 1952: 53). Peck (1972: 343) mentioned two juveniles collected near Cape Henrietta Maria on Aug. 14, 1948 by the ROM field party and "many" noted by H. Lumsden at the mouth of the Brant River on July 27, 1969. Schueler, Baldwin & Rising (1974: 143) noted this species at Winisk during the summer of 1965. Tuck (1968: 39) published the first evidence of breeding in Ontario: he caught and examined a young bird about five or six days old at Winisk on July 10, 1963, with its primaries and scapulars in the pin-feather stage and on July 23 he saw two juvenals barely able to fly there.

AUTUMN: Nicholson (1981: 108) gave Sept. 24, 1978 as the latest date for Manitoulin. The three photographed by A.J. Mitchener at Wasaga Beach on Sept. 5, 1959 constituted the latest Simcoe Co. record (Devitt, 1967: 75). Weir & Quilliam (1980: 35) gave Sept. 30 as the average departure date from Kingston, with the latest on Nov. 6. I saw two as late as Nov. 22, 1970 at Corner Marsh, Pickering (Speirs, 1977: 56). Fleming (1906: 449) collected a young bird at Toronto as late as Sept. 15, 1889; and Speirs (1938: 52, 54) had a second peak (presumably immatures) at Toronto on Sept. 1, with the latest on Sept. 30. H. Axtell collected one at Rockhouse Pt., Lake Erie, on Sept. 13, 1954 (Beardslee & Mitchell, 1965: 228). Saunders & Dale (1933: 196) reported two near London on Sept. 6, 1929. One was seen at Port Burwell, on Sept. 7, 1953 (Brooman, 1954: 19). Ussher (1965: 12) gave Oct. 27 as the average departure date from Rondeau, with the latest on Nov. 9. Stirrett (1973d: 19) had a maximum of 12 at Pelee on Sept. 7 with the latest record on Oct. 2.

**MEASUREMENTS:**
*Length:* 10 1/2 to 12 ins.
(including 2 to 2 1/4 in.
beak) (Godfrey, 1966: 157)
*Wingspread:* 19 ins.
(Pough, 1951: 241)
*Weight:* one ♂ 110 g. two
♀'s 113 and 114 g.
(Snyder, 1931: 166).

**REFERENCE:**
Tuck, Leslie M. 1968
Dowitcher breeding in
Ontario.
   Ont. Field Biologist,
21: 39.

# LONG-BILLED DOWITCHER
*Limnodromus scolopaceus*   (Say)

This species breeds near the mouth of the Mackenzie River and west to Alaska and Siberia, wintering in southern U.S.A. and Central America. It is apparently much less common in Ontario during migration than the Short-billed Dowitcher.

IDENTIFICATION: It is seldom safely identified from the very similar Short-billed Dowitcher under field conditions! Both dowitchers may have barred flanks, but in spring plumage the bars may extend forward on the breast in this species. The reddish underparts of the Long-billed Dowitcher extend back to the under tail coverts, which are white in the Short-billed. Bill lengths overlap slightly so this is not a good field mark.

WINTER:

SPRING: Weir & Quilliam (1980: 10) reported four spring records for the Kingston region, the earliest on May 1, 1971 at Amherst Is. by Fred Cooke and the latest on May 19-20, 1967 on Wolfe Is. by Cooke *et al* (Quilliam, 1973: 85). Fred Cooke also reported one on Amherst Is. on May 14, 1974 and Ken Edwards noted another on Amherst Is. on May 11, 1975.

SUMMER: Beardslee & Mitchell (1965: 229) reported two at Crystal Beach, Lake Erie, on Aug. 28, 1949 and one at Windmill Point on Aug. 19, 1956. Fred Cooke reported one at Amherstview Sewage Lagoons on July 30, 1978 (Weir & Quilliam, 1980: 10).

AUTUMN: Nicholson (1981: 108) noted one in a ploughed field near Gore Bay on Nov. 1, 1970 that was thought to be this species, based on the call note heard. Beardslee & Mitchell (1965: 229) reported one in the collection of James Savage that was taken on Strawberry Is., Niagara River, in October, 1892: Lawrence E. Hicks saw one at Fort Erie on Oct. 21, 1935: another was seen at Crystal Beach on Sept. 8, 1951, and one at Rockhouse Point on Sept. 7, 1958, where one was collected on Sept. 4, 1960.

**MEASUREMENTS:**
*Length:* 11 to 12 1/2 ins.
(including 2 1/4 to 3 in.
bill) (Godfrey, 1966: 158)
*Wingspread:* 18 to 20 ins.
(Terres, 1980: 771)
*Weight:* 4 to 5 1/2 oz.
(Terres, 1980: 771).

# COMMON SNIPE   *Gallinago gallinago*   (Linnaeus)

If on a May morning you hear spooky "whoo-whoo-whoo..."s emanating from the sky, it is probably a snipe up there, not one of the heavenly host. He will be flying high, in wide circles, and may take careful scrutiny to discern. When you do spot him, you will find that each series of "whoo-whoo-whoo..."s coincides with a fast, slanting descent away from the main flight path. After some minutes of this spectacular flight music, your performer will sideslip down to perch on a stump, or fencepost or utility pole where he will "yak-yak-yak" or "ke-dak, kedack, kedack" until inspired to go aloft again. Tuck (1972) has written an admirable monograph on the snipes which all students of these fascinating birds should read.

IDENTIFICATION: This is a long-billed shorebird, like the woodcock and dowitchers, but lacks their colourful breast and the white back stripe of the dowitchers, being dressed in drab grays and browns. It is a bird of muddy or grassy margins of marshes, not a forest bird like the woodcock.

WINTER: On Christmas counts they have shown up, but rarely, from Pelee north to Ottawa and Manitoulin. Stirrett (1973a: 15) had a Pelee record as late as Dec. 27. Ussher (1965: 10) had a Dec. 4 record at Rondeau. Brooman (1954: 17-18) cited records near St. Thomas on Dec. 13 and 19, 1953 and on Feb. 4, 1888. Saunders & Dale (1933: 192) mentioned London sightings on Jan. 13-20, 1923: Dec. 6, 1926; Feb. 17, 1929 and Dec. 28, 1929. Saunders (1947: 378) listed Christmas count sightings at Toronto in 1934 and 1937. Speirs (1977: 39) cited several winter records for Ontario Co. from Whitby and Ajax north to Chalk Lake. Weir & Quilliam (1980: 34) listed Jan. 13 and Feb. 20 dates for Kingston. Devitt (1967: 69) cited several winter records for Simcoe Co. A solitary snipe wintered at Blue Jay Creek, Manitoulin in 1966-67 and the following winter (Nicholson, 1981: 100). This species "has wintered in several years in the water below the dam" at Atikokan (Peruniak, 1971: 15).

SPRING: Stirrett (1973b: 17) gave Apr. 4 and May 18 as earliest and latest spring dates for Pelee. Ussher (1965: 10) had Rondeau records from March 3 to May 14 with the average stay from Apr. 2 to May 9. Harold Lancaster gave Apr. 6 as the average arrival date in Elgin Co., with the earliest on Mar. 27, 1946. Saunders & Dale (1933: 192) gave Apr. 22 as the 13-year average arrival date for London with the earliest on Mar. 27, 1925: one set of 4 eggs was taken at Duncrief on May 2, 1924 by A.A. Wood. Speirs (1938: 40, 44) gave Mar. 12 as the earliest Toronto date with a peak on Apr. 16, while Baillie (in Saunders, 1947: 364) gave Apr. 26 as the average arrival date there. Speirs (1977: 39) reported one as early as Mar. 6, 1966 at Whitby and a nest with 4 eggs found by Richard Robinson near Brechin on May 25, 1946. Tozer & Richards (1974: 127) cited two nest records for Darlington Twp., both with 4 eggs, on Apr. 24 and May 4, 1966: also an adult with young at Oshawa on May 23, 1965. Snyder (1941: 51) gave Apr. 6 as his earliest spring record for Prince Edward Co. and took a set of 4 eggs on May 14, 1938. Weir & Quilliam (1980: 34) gave Mar. 29 as the 29-year average arrival date for Kingston, and Quilliam (1973: 79) reported two nests, each with 4 eggs, on May 7, 1968 and May 15, 1972. C.H. Young found a nest with 4 eggs near Ottawa on May 26, 1897 (Lloyd, 1923: 126). Devitt (1967: 69) gave Apr. 13 as the 15-year average arrival date for Barrie and a nest with 3 eggs there as early as May 15, 1966. Mills (1981: 54) gave Apr. 13 as the 9-year average arrival date for Huntsville. Nicholson (1981: 100) gave Apr. 15 as the 12-year average arrival date for Manitoulin, earliest on Apr. 10, 1971. Speirs & Speirs (1947: 28) noted four at North Bay as early as Mar. 30, 1945. Skeel & Bondrup-Nielsen (1978: 170) noted their first at Pukaskwa on Apr. 18, 1977. Denis (1961: 3) gave Apr. 28 as the average arrival date for Thunder Bay, with the earliest on Apr. 11, 1949: Dear (1940: 128) reported a nest with 4 eggs there on May 22, 1935. Bondrup-Nielsen (1976: 42) found them common near Kapuskasing, with the earliest on Apr. 28, 1975. Elder (1979: 32) gave Apr. 25 as his earliest Geraldton record. Cringan (1953a: 2) gave Apr. 28 as his first record for Sioux Lookout in 1953.

SUMMER: On Breeding Bird Surveys they were noted on most routes, but were uncommon in southwestern Ontario and in Precambrian bedrock areas: they were common in southeastern Ontario and Rainy River, with moderate populations in the Clay Belt region. Stirrett (1973c: 15) had returning birds at Pelee from July 8 through August. Ussher (1965: 10) gave July 24 as the earliest returning date for Rondeau. Beardslee & Mitchell (1965: 210-211) reported one at Rockhouse Pt., Lake Erie, on July 19, 1946. On Aug. 29, 1918, P.A. Taverner flushed more than 50 at the Petrie Is., near Ottawa (Lloyd, 1923: 126). Mills (1981: 54) cited breeding records for the cottage country: a nest with 4 eggs on June 21, 1924 on the French River and young collected at Katrine and Pickerel Lake in July. D.V. Weseloh found a nest with 4 eggs at Manitowaning, Manitoulin, on June 4, 1980 (Nicholson, 1981: 100). Snyder (1942: 128) collected a juvenile female at Maclennan, near Sault Ste. Marie, on June 16, 1931 and saw six at Echo Bay on July 19. Baillie & Hope (1947: 7) had just one summer sighting in Sudbury District, at Biscotasing on June 26, 1937. Baillie & Hope (1943: 9) flushed one at Peninsula on June 13, 1936. Snyder (1938: 187) described the displays of a pair noted near Emo, Rainy River, on June 4, 1929. Snyder (1953: 57) had only one record for western Ontario, at Upsala on July 5, 1937. Hope (1938: 18) considered this to be the commonest shorebird near Favourable Lake: he saw young first on June 29. Ross James had four records of single birds at Pickle Lake from May 31 to June 17, 1977. Cringan (1950: 8) recorded them frequently in the Nikip Lake area in June and July, 1950, some calling from treetops, some winnowing, along the Windigo, North Caribou and Petownikip Rivers. Lee (1978: 22) heard them frequently in tamarack bogs at Big Trout Lake during the summer of 1975. Manning (1952: 44-45) listed several between Moosonee and Lake River, along the west coast of James Bay between June 1 and July 17, 1947. Peck (1972: 340) had a few summer records from Cape Henrietta Maria but no breeding evidence. Schueler, Baldwin & Rising (1974: 142) considered them to be uncommon at Hawley Lake, but common at Moosonee, Ft. Albany, Attawapiskat, Winisk and Cochrane: they found a nest with 4 eggs about 54 miles north of Hawley Lake on June 21, 1962. C.E. Hope saw them regularly at Fort Severn from June 17 to July 22, 1940 and collected a juvenile there on July 20.

AUTUMN: Manning (1952: 44) tallied 200 near Moosonee during 4 hours from Sept. 8 to 10, 1950. N.G. Escott reported one at Marathon as late as Nov. 28, 1976 (Skeel & Bondrup-Nielsen, 1978: 170). Ricker & Clarke (1939: 9) reported one collected at Sturgeon Falls on Oct. 15, 1898. Nicholson (1981: 100) gave 45 as the high count for Manitoulin, on Oct. 13, 1973. Mills (1981: 55) gave Nov. 4 or 5, 1961, as the latest sighting for the cottage country (by R. Rogers near Pointe au Baril). Beamer reported "great numbers" near Meaford on Oct. 18, 1952 and one near Thornbury as late as Oct. 29, 1944. Weir & Quilliam (1980: 34) gave Nov. 30 as the 24-year average for departures from Kingston. W.H. Lunn saw one at Pleasant Bay, Prince Edward Co. on Nov. 13, 1939 (Snyder, 1941: 51). The fall peak in Ontario Co. was usually in the second week of October, but I saw 19 at Pickering as late as Nov. 21, 1975 (Speirs, 1977: 39). Saunders (1947: 364) gave Oct. 14 as his average departure date from Toronto, while Fleming (1906: 448) gave Nov. 24, 1894, as his latest record there. Beardslee & Mitchell (1965: 210-211) reported two at Pt. Abino, Lake Erie, as late as Nov. 27, 1949. Ussher (1965: 10) gave Aug. 30 to Nov. 8 as the average stay at Rondeau in the fall. Stirrett (1973d: 19) had a maximum of 300 at Pelee on Oct. 15.

BANDING: Tuck (1972: 384-385) had 16 recoveries from 763 snipe banded at Partridge Creek, near Moosonee. Two were shot later the same fall as banded, in Guadeloupe, West Indies. Several adults were taken later from Florida north to Virginia in winter. There were also a few recoveries of southbound birds in New York and Quebec and of one returning bird in late March in New York.

**MEASUREMENTS:**
*Length:* 10.3 to 11.7 ins. (including 2 1/2 to 2 3/4 in. bill) (Godfrey, 1966: 142)
*Wingspread:* 13 to 17 3/4 ins. (Roberts, 1955: 562)
*Weight:* ♂ 2.25 to 4.62 oz. ♀ 4 to 5 oz. (Roberts, 1955: 562).
2 ♂ av. 97.5 g. 2 ♀ av. 114 g. (Hope, 1938: 18).

**REFERENCE:**
Tuck, Leslie M. 1972 The snipes: a study of the genus *Capella*. Can. Wildlife Service, Monograph Series, No. 5: 1-428.

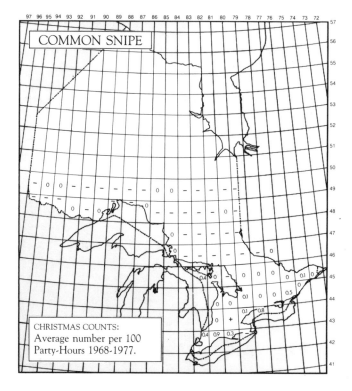

COMMON SNIPE

CHRISTMAS COUNTS: Average number per 100 Party-Hours 1968-1977.

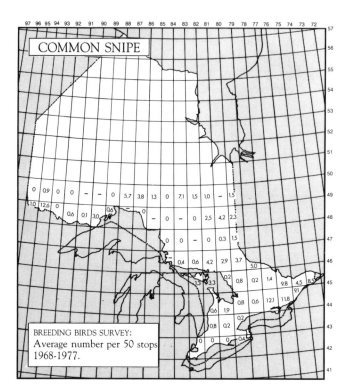

COMMON SNIPE

BREEDING BIRDS SURVEY:
Average number per 50 stops
1968-1977.

# AMERICAN WOODCOCK   *Scolopax minor*   Gmelin

One of the joys of spring is seeking out a meadow, surrounded by scattered young trees, at dusk, to listen to the ethereal flight music of the Woodcock. He rises on whistling wings and circles high overhead with crescendo "rrrrrr"s, followed by ecstatic whistles as he plunges back to the ground. After a few seconds you hear an interminable office-buzzer noise "bzzt-bzzt-bzzt————" which eventually stops and overhead the performance is repeated. Later in the season the nest may be found, a hollow in dead leaves that so match the colours of the sitting bird that you may almost step on it before it explodes to reveal the eggs. This is a forest dweller, not a typical "shorebird".

IDENTIFICATION:   This is a stocky "Robin-sized" bird with a tremendously long, stout bill, used for probing for earthworms in soft soil. The eyes are placed well back on the head so the bird can spot predators while probing in the mud. The Common Snipe is of somewhat similar build but prefers wetter habitat and is dressed in sombre checks, rather than the leaf browns and pinks of the Woodcock. Dowitchers are also somewhat similar in build but are seldom seen out of shallow water or away from mudflats or wet fields and wet lawns when resting.

WINTER:   On the 1968-1977 Christmas counts there were reports at London, Long Point, Peel-Halton and Meaford. One lingered at Pelee as late as Dec. 2 (Stirrett, 1973a: 15). Harold Lancaster reported one in north Aldborough Twp., Elgin Co., on Dec. 27, 1949 (Brooman, 1954: 17). One was noted on the Toronto Christmas count on Dec. 24, 1939 (Saunders, 1947: 379).

SPRING:   Stirrett (1973b: 16) gave Mar. 10 as the earliest Pelee arrival date. Kelley (1978: 32) reported a nest with eggs in Lambton Co. as early as Apr. 21, 1968. Ussher (1965: 10) gave Mar. 13 as his earliest Rondeau record, with Apr. 11 as the 11-year average arrival date of this nesting species there. Harold Lancaster had one as early as Mar. 14, 1936 in Elgin Co. (Brooman, 1954: 17). Saunders & Dale (1933: 192) gave Mar. 27, 1921 as his earliest London date and reported three nests: a set of 4 eggs on Apr. 14, 1890; a set of 4 eggs on May 10, 1915 and a set of 3 eggs on May 30, 1919: the adult on the May 10 nest allowed itself to be stroked on the head before leaving the nest. Charles Fothergill shot one on the banks of the Don River, Toronto, on Apr. 10, 1824 and considered them to be very common there and below the falls at Niagara (Black, 1934: 146). Speirs (1938: 40, 44) gave Mar. 17 as the earliest Toronto date, with a peak on Apr. 17. Long (1969: 19) gave Mar. 13, 1965 as his earliest record for Pickering Beach. Tozer & Richards (1974: 126) reported a nest with one egg as early as Apr. 5, 1967 near Oshawa, which held 4 eggs by Apr. 8. Snyder (1941: 50) reported taking a female at Bloomfield, Prince Edward Co., on Apr. 16, 1938. Weir & Quilliam (1980: 34) gave Mar. 8 as the earliest Kingston record, with Mar. 25 as the 30-year average arrival there. Quilliam (1973: 78) cited a few breeding records for the Kingston area between Apr. 15 (1964) and May 20 (1961). Devitt (1967: 68, 69) gave Apr. 8 as the 16-year average arrival date for Barrie, with the earliest on Mar. 24, 1963: he cited several breeding records for Simcoe Co. between Apr. 16 (1937) and May 26 (1940). Beamer's earliest record for Meaford was on Mar. 22, 1938 with the median arrival date on Apr. 6. Mills (1981: 53) gave Apr. 5 as the 17-year average arrival date for Huntsville, with the earliest on Mar. 15, 1964. Nicholson (1981: 99) reported Mar. 17, 1973 as the earliest Manitoulin date, while Grant Garrette found a nest with 4 eggs near Sheguiandah as early as Apr. 2, 1977. Speirs & Speirs (1947: 25) saw one at North Bay on Apr. 8, 1945 and V.E. Solman flushed an adult from a nest with 4 eggs there on May 23, 1945. Skeel & Bondrup-Nielsen (1978: 169) found one nesting at Pukaskwa on May 6, 1977. Denis (1961: 2) gave Apr. 22 as the average arrival date at Thunder Bay, with Apr. 3, 1942 as the earliest record. Dear (1940: 128) reported a nest with 4 eggs in Neebing Twp., Thunder Bay, on May 29, 1938. A.N. Boissonneau saw two near Cochrane on May 13, 1950 (Smith, 1957: 172). Elder (1979: 32) gave Apr. 30 as the earliest Geraldton date.

SUMMER: On Breeding Bird Surveys they were reported as far north as Thunder Bay and Swastika. Stirrett (1973c: 15) had records through the summer months at Pelee and listed it as nesting there. Snyder (1931: 165) reported a nest with 4 eggs at Long Point on June 2, 1927. Beardslee & Mitchell (1965: 209-210) reported a nest with two young at Wainfleet Marsh on June 16, 1946. Speirs (1977: 38) had summer observations from every township in Ontario Co. and twice witnessed the strange "hiccup dance" as birds of both sexes slowly and in single file crossed unpaved roads, pausing to rock back and forth before taking each step. Lloyd (1923: 126) reported a fully grown young found dead at Rockcliffe (Ottawa) on June 16, 1920. Mills (1981: 53-54) cited several breeding records from the cottage country. C. Ramsay found a nest with 4 eggs at North Bay on June 8, 1926 (Ricker & Clarke, 1939: 9). Snyder (1942: 128) noted three at Maclennan on June 5, 1931 and mentioned a few other summer reports from the Sault Ste. Marie region. Baillie & Hope (1947: 7) noted two to five daily at Bigwood, Sudbury Dist., between July 15 and 22, 1937. Skeel & Bondrup-Nielsen (1978: 169) had June and July records at Pukaskwa.

AUTUMN: J. Coyne saw single birds near Gogama during September in 1952 and 1953 (Smith, 1957: 172). Skeel & Bondrup-Nielsen (1978: 169) noted two at Pukaskwa on Sept. 19, 1977. Speirs & Speirs (1947: 28) noted one at North Bay on Oct. 19, 1944. Nicholson (1981: 99) gave Nov. 7, 1970 as the latest Manitoulin record. Mills (1981: 54) had several October records for the cottage country, the latest reported by G. Withers at Interlaken on Oct. 29, 1978. F. Mutrie reported one to L. Beamer seen as late as Nov. 15, 1938 at Stokes Bay, Bruce Co. Devitt (1967: 69) gave Oct. 31, 1962 as the latest date for Simcoe Co. Weir & Quilliam (1980: 34) gave Nov. 2 as the 16-year average departure date from Kingston, with the latest on Nov. 21. Snyder (1941: 50) reported a specimen taken in Prince Edward Co. on Nov. 6, 1937. Dave Calvert found one at Oshawa as late as Nov. 14, 1972 (Tozer & Richards, 1974: 127). Fleming (1906: 448) reported one as late as Nov. 11, 1896 at Toronto. Brooman (1954: 17) reported one at St. Thomas on Oct. 26, 1946. Ussher (1965: 10) gave Oct. 23 as the average departure date from Rondeau, with the latest on Nov. 2. Stirrett (1973d: 18) had reports at Pelee throughout the fall months with a high count of 50 on Oct. 1.

**MEASUREMENTS:**
*Length:* 10 to 12 ins.
(including 2 1/2 to 3 in.
bill) (Godfrey, 1966: 140).
*Wingspread:* 16.00 to
19.55 ins. (Roberts,
1955: 560).
*Weight:* ♂ 5 to 6 oz. ♀ 6
to 8 oz. (Roberts,
1955: 560).

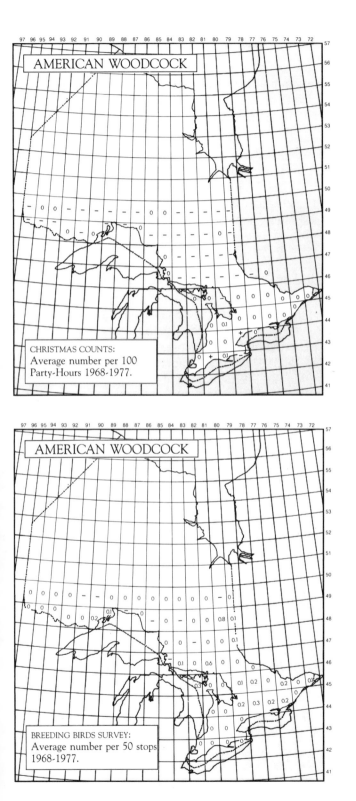

AMERICAN WOODCOCK

CHRISTMAS COUNTS:
Average number per 100
Party-Hours 1968-1977.

AMERICAN WOODCOCK

BREEDING BIRDS SURVEY:
Average number per 50 stops
1968-1977.

# WILSON'S PHALAROPE   *Phalaropus tricolor*   (Vieillot)

The dainty Wilson's Phalarope breeds in prairie marshes and increasingly in grassy ponds in Ontario, wintering in southern South America. The more colourful and larger females are content to lay the eggs and let the more demurely coloured males look after the incubation duties.

IDENTIFICATION:   As with other phalaropes it spins as it swims, jabbing at insects on the water surface. From other phalaropes it is distinguished by the lack of a white wing stripe in flight and by its relatively large size. From the somewhat similar Lesser Yellowlegs it is distinguished by its green or blackish legs and much whiter and less patterned appearance, and if in the water by its spinning activity. The long, needlelike bill separates it from the Red Phalarope.

WINTER:

SPRING:   Stirrett (1973b: 17) had one spring record at Pelee, on May 11, 1967. Earl Lemon reported them at Dunwich Marsh, Elgin Co., as early as Apr. 27, 1947 (Brooman, 1954: 20). Fleming (1906: 448) reported Toronto specimens taken on May 22, 1855 (♀), May, 25, 1890 (♀) and June 1890 (♂). Speirs, (1938: 40) had a May 15 record for Toronto. Speirs (1977: 67) reported spring birds at Pickering on May 12-13, 1976 (ad. ♀); two at Frenchman Bay on May 15, 1931; a ♀ at Cranberry Marsh on May 24-25, 1969; three (2♂, ♀) at Oshawa on May 24, 1972 and one at Corner Marsh, Pickering, on May 27, 1958. Weir & Quilliam (1980: 35) gave May 10 as the 11-year average arrival date at Kingston, with the earliest on Apr. 4, 1980 and a maximum of eight on May 12 at Amherstview Sewage Lagoons by Mary and Ken Edwards. One was noted at Wiarton by J.W. Johnson on May 29, 1974 (Goodwin, 1974: 796). Nicholson (1981: 110) gave May 10 as the 10-year average arrival date on Manitoulin, with the earliest on May 3, 1970 and latest on June 4, 1980, and a high count of nine at Little Current Sewage Lagoon on May 14, 1972. J. Reynolds and G. Thorn noted one in Algonquin Park on May 24, 1980 (Goodwin, 1980: 772). Skeel & Bondrup-Nielsen (1978: 174) reported one at Pukaskwa on May 17, 1977. M. and S. Gawn noted the species at Manitouwadge on May 13, 1980 (Goodwin, 1980: 772). Denis (1961: 4) gave May 23 as the average arrival date at Thunder Bay, with the earliest on May 18, 1958. Peruniak (1971: 16) saw one at Atikokan on May 26, 1959 and David Elder noted two there on May 6, 1977 (Goodwin, 1977: 995). Alan Wormington noted "up to 12" at Harris Hill, Rainy River, on May 19, 1974 (Goodwin, 1974: 796). Morrison and Manning (1976: 656-657) noted six at North Point, James Bay, on May 17, 1975 and eight there the next day (one collected).

SUMMER:   On the Breeding Bird Surveys it has been found only on the Stratton route, in Rainy River District. Kelley (1978: 37) reported the first nesting, at Kettle Point, Lake Huron, on July 23, 1967, when a nest with one newly-hatched young was found. Ussher (1965: 12) noted one at Rondeau on June 25, 1947. P.D. Pratt found a nest with 4 eggs at Blenheim on June 13, 1977 (Goodwin, 1977: 1133). Earl Lemon found a nest at Dunwich Marsh, Elgin Co. on June 10, 1934 (Brooman, 1954: 20). Sheppard (1960: 23) reported a female at Mud Lake, near Welland, on June 14, 1949. A nest with 3 eggs was found at Dunnville on June 9, 1879 by G.A. Macallum, who collected the male, 2 young and one egg the following day: a second nest, with 4 eggs, was found by R.F. Andrle and

H. Axtell on June 3, 1959 at Long Beach (Beardslee & Mitchell, 1965: 238). Fleming (1906: 448) reported a young ♀ taken at Toronto on Aug. 15, 1890. J.L. Baillie had a July 20 record for Toronto and R.M. Saunders noted one on Aug. 11 (Saunders, 1947: 365). Late spring migrants were seen at Whitby on June 3, 1959 and at Oshawa on June 5, 1960 (Speirs, 1977: 67). Tozer & Richards (1974: 140) listed a number of August records for the Lake Ontario marshes between Darlington and Whitby, the earliest on Aug. 5, 1967 at Oshawa. Weir & Quilliam (1980: 12) reported two nests with downy young on Amherst Is., near Kingston, one found on June 21, 1980 and the other on July 19, 1980, by Ron Weir *et al*. Devitt (1967: 78) detailed two breeding records for Simcoe Co.; two young at Holland River marsh, Bradford, on June 16, 1946 and one young on Aug. 3, 1947 at Marl Lake. J.W. Johnson reported two young at Wiarton on June 9, 1974 (Goodwin, 1974: 897) and he also noted two fully grown young at Isaac Lake, Bruce Co., on July 6, 1977 (Goodwin, 1977: 1133). Goodwin (1972: 57) reported one seen at Ottawa as early as July 16, 1971. J.L. Baillie collected a juvenile male at Pickerel Lake, near Sundridge, on July 30, 1936 (Mills, 1981: 60). Nicholson (1981: 110) had two summer records: a pair at Mindemoya on July 2, 1971 and one at Manitowaning on Aug. 3, 1980. J. Nicholson noted territorial behaviour at Kelly Lake, Sudbury, on July 27, 1980 (Goodwin, 1981: 177). Shirley Peruniak saw three near Atikokan on June 5, 1977 (Goodwin, 1977: 1133). Morrison and Manning (1976: 656-657) reported the first breeding in the James Bay region at North Point: they found a nest on June 10, 1975; this contained 4 eggs on June 24 but was found destroyed on June 26: three small downy young were located nearby on June 22 (one of which was collected).

AUTUMN:   Morrison & Manning (1976: 656-657) saw their last at North Point, James Bay, on Aug. 13 in 1974 and Aug. 5 in 1975. Weir & Quilliam (1980: 35) gave Sept. 1 as the 10-year average departure date from Kingston, with the latest on Sept. 29. Speirs (1977: 67) cited a few Whitby and Pickering records from Sept. 1 to Oct. 4. Saunders (1947: 365) reported one at Toronto on Sept. 30. Ussher (1965: 12) had one fall record for Rondeau on Sept. 15, 1964. Stirrett (1973d: 20) had one fall record for Pelee, on Sept. 7, 1963.

**MEASUREMENTS:**
*Length:* 8.4-10 ins. (♀ larger than ♂ ) (Godfrey, 1966: 167)
*Wingspread:* ♂ 14.5 - 15.0 ins. ♀ 15.0 - 17.38 ins. (Roberts, 1955: 566)
*Weight:* ♂ av. 1 3/4 oz. (50.17 g) ♀ av. 2 1/2 oz. (68.09 g.) (H hn, 1967: 222).

**REFERENCES:**
Hohn, E. Otto 1967 Observations on the breeding biology of Wilson's Phalarope (*Steganopus tricolor*) in central Alberta. Auk, 84:(2):220-244.

Morrison, R.I.G. & T.H. Manning 1976 First breeding records of Wilson's Phalarope for James Bay, Ontario. Auk, 93:(3):656-657.

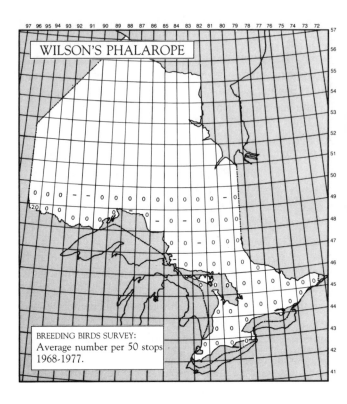

WILSON'S PHALAROPE

BREEDING BIRDS SURVEY:
Average number per 50 stops
1968-1977.

# RED-NECKED PHALAROPE   *Phalaropus lobatus*   (Linnaeus)

The slim little Red-necked Phalarope is a circumpolar breeder, wintering largely at sea, south of the equator.

IDENTIFICATION:  This dainty little phalarope is usually seen on shallow ponds, spinning rapidly around jabbing at unseen items of food on the water surface. From the Red Phalarope it is distinguished by its needle-like bill (much heavier in the Red Phalarope) and by its slimmer, more delicate appearance and somewhat darker back. From the much larger Wilson's Phalarope it is separated by the white wing stripe (absent in Wilson's but also present in the Red Phalarope).

WINTER:

SPRING:  There are several recent sightings at the Strathroy Sewage Lagoons: R. Coker saw one there on May 17, 1976 (Goodwin, 1976: 834) and W.R. Jarmain reported one there on June 3, 1971 (Goodwin, 1971: 737). Alan Wormington noted this species at Essex on May 25, 1978 (Goodwin, 1978: 999). George W. North saw one at Hamilton on June 4, 1971 (Goodwin, 1971: 737). Speirs (1938: 40) had a May 30 record for Toronto. The only spring record for the Kingston region was one seen by Fred Cooke on May 28, 1973 at Amherstview Sewage Lagoons (Weir & Quilliam, 1980: 12). L. Chambers reported one at Dorcas Bay on May 27, 1978 (Goodwin, 1978: 999). Goodwin (1975: 846) noted six at Ottawa from May 18-27, 1975. Chris. Bell and John Lemon saw one on Manitoulin at West Bay on May 20, 1973 (Nicholson, 1981: 111).

SUMMER:  Brooman (1954: 20) reported one seen by W.E. Saunders, E.M.S. Dale and Wm. Girling at St. Thomas on Aug. 25, 1934. W.R. Jarmain *et al* had an early sighting at Strathroy from Aug. 8-11, 1971 (Goodwin, 1971: 853). An adult was taken at Toronto on June 7, 1890 (Fleming, 1906: 448). Speirs (1977: 68) cited several August records, the earliest by J.L. Baillie at Whitby on Aug. 3 and 8, 1959. Weir & Quilliam (1980: 35) gave Aug. 3 as the earliest date for returning birds at Kingston, with the 12-year average on Aug. 25. Frances Westman saw one as late as June 9, 1960 off Barrie and one as early as Aug. 5, 1954 there (Devitt, 1967: 78). Goodwin (1972: 57) reported one at Ottawa as early as July 24, 1971 and 16 there on Aug. 24, 1971. Chris. Bell saw four at Little Current Sewage Lagoon on Aug. 27, 1977 (Nicholson, 1981: 111). J. Lemon noted 14 at Kelly Lake, Sudbury, on Aug. 22, 1976 (Goodwin, 1977: 171). Alan Wormington found one on Sable Is., Lake of the Woods, on June 1, 1978 (Goodwin, 1978: 1154). Leslie Paterson collected one near Kenora on Aug. 8, 1932 (Snyder, 1953: 58). Along the west shore of James Bay, Manning (1952: 56) listed 15 in 6 hours at Long Ridge Point on June 15, 1947; 120 in 16 hours at Cape Henrietta Maria from June 20-24, 1947; and along the Hudson Bay shore he noted 50 in 8 hours at Little Cape, where he collected 3 adults and 6 downy young from July 29-Aug. 1, 1947 and at Shagamu River he saw 25 in 7 hours between Aug. 9 and 11, 1947. Peck (1972: 344) reported five nests at Cape Henrietta Maria: two by the ROM field party (nests with 4 eggs on July 1 and July 21, 1948) and three by Peck on June 26, 27 and 29, 1970, all with 4 eggs. Schueler, Baldwin & Rising (1974: 143, 146) saw this species at Winisk and collected two females in breeding condition at the mouth of the Sutton River on June 24, 1962 (one with a shelled egg in its oviduct). C.E. Hope collected five at Ft. Severn from June 17 to July 17, 1940 and saw 20 there on July 17.

AUTUMN: John Nicholson reported six at Chelmsford, near Sudbury, on Sept. 1, 1971 (Goodwin, 1972: 57). Chris. Bell identified one at Little Current on Sept. 27, 1974 and one on Lake Mindemoya on Nov. 16, 1974 (Nicholson, 1981: 111). Lloyd (1923: 126) cited four specimens taken near Ottawa between Sept. 10 and Oct. 12, by E.H. White, G.R. White and A.G. Kingston. Devitt (1967: 78) gave Nov. 3, 1962 as the latest report for Simcoe Co., at Allandale. Kenneth Edwards saw the maximum of seven at Amherstview Sewage Lagoons on Sept. 16, 1972 and the latest Kingston region record was on Nov. 8 (Weir & Quilliam, 1980: 12, 35). Speirs (1977: 68) cited several fall records from the Lake Ontario marshes, the earliest on Sept. 1, 1964 and the latest at Whitby Harbour on Oct. 16, 1960 by Earl Stark and R.M. Saunders. Fleming (1906: 448) wrote that "young birds occur regularly" from Sept. 22 to Oct. 31 at Toronto. Speirs (1938: 48) had a Sept. 1 record for Toronto. Saunders (1947: 256-258) described in detail a sighting at Sunnyside, Toronto, by J.L. Baillie and himself. Sheppard (1954: 137-138) gave details of six seen at Niagara Falls on Sept. 26-27, 1947 and single birds there on Sept. 29, 1949; Sept. 26, 1950 and Sept. 12-13, 1953. Beardslee & Mitchell (1965: 239-240) reported 12 at Niagara Falls on Sept. 4, 1949 seen by R.F. Andrle, B. Nathan et al and one at Point Abino, Lake Erie, as late as Nov. 10, 1957. Saunders & Dale (1933: 197-198) described the excitement of finding one at Denfield, near London, on Sept. 20, 1930. Brooman (1954: 20) reported one seen at St. Thomas by W.E. Saunders, Wm. Girling et al on Nov. 11, 1949 and one at Pt. Stanley on Oct. 14, 1953, seen by Vern Smith and his wife. Ussher (1965: 12) had four Rondeau records between Sept. 5 and Oct. 14. Stirrett (1973d: 20 and 1973a: 16) had records at Pelee from Aug. 29 to Nov. 28, and a maximum count of 22 on Sept. 14.

**MEASUREMENTS:**
Length: 6.5 to 8 ins.
(Godfrey, 1966: 169)
Wingspread: 13 to 14.5
ins. (Roberts, 1955: 565)
Weight: 26.2 g. ♀ a little
larger than ♂ (Roberts,
1955: 565).

# RED PHALAROPE   Phalaropus fulicaria   (Linnaeus)

This is a high Arctic breeder in both North America and the Old World. The American birds migrate chiefly down the Atlantic and Pacific coasts and may be found riding the waves far out to sea. It is rare in Ontario, especially in spring and summer.

IDENTIFICATION: The easily recognized breeding birds, with rich red breasts are seldom seen in Ontario. Most are seen in late autumn when they look a bit like Sanderlings, but with black ear patch and habit of swimming. They are paler in colour than the other phalaropes, mostly white in autumn, with a distinct white wing stripe to distinguish them from Wilson's Phararopes and the much shorter and stouter bill to distinguish them from Northern Phalaropes.

WINTER: Brian Morin reported one at Pelee on Dec. 13-14, 1974 (Goodwin, 1975: 685) and Kelley (1978: 37). R. Snider saw one at Ipperwash on Dec. 11. 1971 (Goodwin, 1972: 598). One was noted at Niagara-on-the-Lake on Dec. 21, 1975 by A.E. Schaffner and R. Clark (Goodwin, 1976: 712).

SPRING: One was reported at Pelee by R. and M. Simard and J. Hardy on May 9, 1978 (Goodwin, 1978: 999). Speirs (1938: 40) reported a Toronto record on May 23.

SUMMER:

AUTUMN: Alfred Kay shot one at Port Sydney, Muskoka, on Oct. 24, 1937 (Mills, 1981: 60). Lloyd (1923: 126) cited five Ottawa specimens taken between Sept. 1 and Oct. 31 by E.G. White and G.R. White. B. MacTavish saw one at Ottawa as late as Nov. 9, 1972 (Goodwin, (1973: 52) and a maximum of 11 was noted at Richmond on Sept. 21, 1977 by R.M. Poulin and B.M. DeLabio (Goodwin, 1978: 198). Devitt (1967: 77) cited six fall records for Simcoe Co., the earliest at Wasaga Beach on Oct. 7, 1960 by Alf. Mitchener and the latest photographed there on Nov. 15, 1936 by A. Van. Weir & Quilliam (1980: 12) had Kingston records from Oct. 4 (1973) to Nov. 19 (1969). Ross Harris showed me one that was busy picking worms off the concrete embankment of Duffin Creek in Pickering on Oct. 8, 1974: possibly the same bird was seen at the mouth of the creek on Nov. 16 and 17, 1974 by David Maugham and Harvey Medland (Speirs, 1977: 66). George A. Scott found one on Nov. 10, 1957 at Oshawa: this bird was later shot and abandoned by hunters, and the remains were collected by Scott on Dec. 1: he found another there on Nov. 7, 1971 (Tozer & Richards, 1974: 140). Speirs (1938: 54) reported a Toronto record as late as Nov. 28. Fleming (1906: 448) considered it regular but rare at Toronto from Sept. 12 to Nov. 14 (all young birds "usually taken among duck decoys"). Maughan (1897: 2) took one on Toronto Island on Oct. 27, 1894 and published several measurements. E.C. Ulrich found one at the wading pool at Erie Beach on Oct. 6, 1935 and a very early one showed up at Niagara Falls on Aug. 31, 1947 (Beardslee & Mitchell, 1965: 237). Sheppard (1954: 137-138) reported two at Niagara Falls on Oct. 4-5, 1948 and one there on Oct. 7, 1948; two again on Sept. 29-30, 1949 and one there on Oct. 25, 1952. E. Leach and J.W. Leach reported one at Strathroy on Oct. 24, 1972 (Goodwin, 1973: 52). Marshall Field and Harold Lancaster found one at Port Burwell on Oct. 13, 1952 (Brooman, 1954: 20). Ussher (1965: 12) had only one Rondeau record, on Oct. 20, 1906. Kelley (1978: 37) reported single birds at Pelee on Oct. 15, 1970 and Nov. 16, 1969; at Wheatley on Oct. 18, 1970; at Rondeau from Oct. 23-26, 1973; at Ipperwash Beach on Nov. 2-3, 1965 and at Kettle Point on Nov. 16 and 23, 1974.

**MEASUREMENTS:**
*Length:* 7.7 to 9 ins. (♀
larger & brighter than ♂)
(Godfrey, 1966: 166).
*Wingspread:* ♂ 15 ins.
(Maughan, 1897: 2).
*Weight:* 1 1/2 to 2 1/4 oz.
(Terres, 1980: 686).

# POMARINE JAEGER   *Stercorarius pomarinus*   (Temminck)

Jaeger (in German) means hunter and the jaegers are the "falcons of the seas" where they pursue gulls and terns to rob them of their fish dinners. On the nesting grounds they eat lemmings, small birds, eggs and carcasses of larger animals. The Pomarine Jaeger is a high Arctic breeder, circumpolar, and winters mainly out on the oceans. In Ontario it is a rare, chiefly fall, migrant seen over the Great Lakes.

IDENTIFICATION: This is the largest and most heavily-built of the jaegers. In the dark phase, as generally seen here, it somewhat resembled a first year Herring Gull in colour and heavy bill, but the white flash in the wing and dashing flight and panic among gulls and terns distinguish it. Adults are easily identified by the blunt twisted tail streamers extending beyond the rest of the tail. Light phase birds may have a dark necklace (sometimes present in Parasitic Jaeger, but seldom in Long-tailed Jaeger).

WINTER:

SPRING: Chris. Blomme collected a badly decomposed specimen found near Bowmanville on the Lake Ontario beach on May 16, 1971 and identified it as this species at the ROM (Tozer & Richards, 1974: 141).

SUMMER:

AUTUMN: One was photographed by Alf. Mitchener at Wasaga Beach as it fed on a dead Canada Goose on Nov. 3, 1963 (Devitt, 1967: 78-79). Weir & Quilliam (1980:13) cited two observations on Lake Ontario during "pelagic" boat trips near Main Duck Island: 4 seen on Oct. 4, 1973 and one on Oct. 9, 1975: also a dead one was picked up on Amherst Is. on Oct. 31, 1976 and sent to the National Museum of Canada (Spec. No. 63936). R.M. Saunders spotted one off Simcoe Point, Pickering, on Aug. 29, 1958 (Speirs, 1976: 1). Tozer & Richards (1974: 141) mentioned two seen about 15 miles NW of Niagara-on-the-Lake on Sept. 15, 1968 and two seen off Hamilton on Sept. 23, 1973 during "pelagic" boat trips on Lake Ontario. A.R. Muma salvaged a Niagara Falls casualty on Oct. 30, 1957 and sent the specimen to the ROM (Sheppard, 1960: 24). Beardslee & Mitchell (1965: 241) reported one seen by B. Nathan *et al* on the Canadian shore of Lake Ontario on Oct. 12, 1958 and on Oct. 30, 1960, Harold Axtell collected an immature at Rockhouse Point, Lake Erie. Kelley (1978: 37-38) reported one seen at Pelee on Oct. 13, 1973 by Dennis Rupert; one at St. Lukes Bay, Kent Co. on Oct. 30, 1973 observed by Wm. Schlageter and two noted at Kettle Point on Nov. 9 by Alfred Rider.

**MEASUREMENTS:**
*Length:* 20-23 ins.
(including 2-4 in. tail
streamers) (GOdfrey,
1966: 170)
*Wingspread:* 48 ins.
(Terres, 1980: 830)
*Weight:* 1 lb. 6 oz. to 2
lb. 6 oz. (Terres,
1980: 830)

# PARASITIC JAEGER   *Stercorarius parasiticus*   (Linnaeus)

This is the only jaeger known to breed in Ontario (along the Hudson Bay coast). It is also the one most likely to be seen during migration, usually at the southern end of Lake Huron and the ends of Lake Ontario. In Europe this is known as the Arctic Skua and we found it fairly common off the northern Norwegian coast.

IDENTIFICATION: Adults, which come in light and dark phases, are known by the spiky, pointed central tail feathers that protrude 3 or 4 inches beyond the rest of the tail. Young are less heavily built than young Pomarines yet heavier than the buoyant Long-tailed Jaegers.

WINTER: Speirs (1938: 54) listed a Dec. 4 record for Toronto.

SPRING: Stirrett (1973b: 17) had three Pelee records: May 16, 1941; May 5, 1951 and May 9, 1959, all single birds.

SUMMER: The Axtells noted one at Morgan's Point, Lake Erie, on July 25, 1959 (Beardslee & Mitchell, 1965: 241-242). Fleming (1906: 441) reported a light phase adult taken at Toronto on June 20, 1891. Nicholson (1981: 111) observed one as it flew past Quarry Point, Manitoulin, on Aug. 9, 1975. Skeel & Bondrup-Nielsen (1978: 174) saw a jaeger at Pukaskwa on June 21, 1977. Schueler, Baldwin & Rising (1974: 143) observed this species only at Moosonee. Manning (1952: 57) saw three in six hours at North Point, James Bay, on June 3-6, 1947; two in 7 hours at Big Piskwanish on June 11, 1947; two in 8 hours at Long Ridge Point on June 14, 1947; three in six hours at Lake River on July 17, 1947; he collected two adults and one downy young found dead at Cape Henrietta Maria in 16 hours on July 22, 1947; and saw two in 13 hours at Little Cape, Hudson Bay on Aug. 1, 1947. Peck (1972: 344) photographed a nest with 2 eggs at Cape Henrietta Maria, with the two light-phased adults on June 25-26, 1970: he also mentioned 9 specimens collected there by the 1948 ROM party (including a half grown, flightless young on July 23).

AUTUMN: On Sept. 13, 1944, Doris H. Speirs and I were delighted to observe one "with its dashing flight and display of white in the wings" over Lake Nipissing off North Bay. Ricker & Clarke (1939: 10) also noted one on Lake Nipissing during two weeks in late Sept. and early Oct., 1923. Two flew past Great Duck Is., off Manitoulin, on Sept. 23, 1979 (Nicholson, 1981: 111). Lloyd (1923: 103) recorded a young bird collected near Ottawa on Sept. 4, 1909. Devitt (1967: 79) cited four Simcoe Co. records: Sept. 22, 1935 at Three Mile Point, near Wasaga Beach; three on Sept. 13, 1939, off Jackson's Point, Lake Simcoe; Oct. 2, 1949 at Allandale and Oct. 16, 1956 near Collingwood. Weir & Quilliam (1980: 13) reported three pale phase birds at Prince Edward Point on Sept. 6, 1975 and gave details of big flocks seen on the New York side of Lake Ontario, usually peaking in early October. Snyder (1941: 55) had just one Prince Edward Co. specimen, an immature taken Oct. 24, 1929 at Wellington. C. Christy found one at Darlington Prov. Park on Sept. 4, 1963 and Al. Wainio *et al* reported one off Whitby on Oct. 1, 1970 (Tozer & Richards, 1974: 141). Long (1968b: 18) watched one harassing shorebirds at Pickering Beach on Aug. 30, 1966 and Tom Hassall saw one off Simcoe Point, Pickering on Oct. 23, 1965 where R.M. Saunders had seen one on Nov. 8, 1959 (Speirs, 1976: 2). Saunders (1947: 365) listed Toronto records from Sept. 6 to Nov. 3.

Fleming (1906: 441) reported a light phase bird taken at Toronto on Oct. 20, 1894 as "not quite adult", five other local specimens were dark phase birds. Tozer & Richards (1974: 141) mentioned 18 counted during 3 "pelagic" trips in western Lake Ontario on Sept. 15, 21 and 28, 1968 and at least 7 on a boat trip off Hamilton on Sept. 23, 1973. George W. North *et al* have noted them in the fall off Hamilton quite regularly for many years. H. Axtell took a subadult specimen at Fort Erie on Nov. 26, 1960 (Beardslee & Mitchell, 1965: 242). On Oct. 16, 1886, "Dr. Macallum secured a young female, which was shot on the Grand River, near Dunnville, just after a severe storm" (McIlwraith, 1894: 41). Snyder (1931: 148) wrote about three specimens from the Long Point vicinity, of which one immature was killed at the Long Point lighthouse on Sept. 2, 1930. On Nov. 12, 1928 Eli Davis and W.E. Saunders saw one at Port Stanley (Brooman, 1954: 20). Ussher (1965: 13) had just two fall records at Rondeau, on Oct. 1 and 10. Kelley (1978: 38) had 14 recent records of 24 birds at Pelee, Rondeau and Kettle Point (since 1966). Stirrett (1973d: 20) had three Pelee records: Sept. 29, 1966; Oct. 1, 1915 and Oct. 1, 1916. Dennis Rupert *et al* have noted good flights during fall blows, between Sarnia and Kettle Point, in recent years.

**MEASUREMENTS:**
*Length:* 18-21 ins.
(including 2 1/2 - 3 1/2"
tail streamers (Godfrey,
1966: 171).
*Wingspread:* 36 ins.
(Terres, 1980: 829)
*Weight:* 1 lb. 2 oz. - l lb.
13 oz. (Terres, 1980: 830).

# LONG-TAILED JAEGER   *Stercorarius longicaudus*   Vieillot

This beauty is a high Arctic, circumpolar breeder, wintering at sea and quite rarely seen in Ontario during migrations.

IDENTIFICATION: With its jaunty black cap over yellow cheeks and collar, its very long pointed tail streamers and blue legs, this is the beauty of the jaegers. The Pomarine and Parasitic Jaegers have black legs and are much heavier birds.

WINTER:

SPRING:

SUMMER: On Aug. 4, 1968, D. Sands discovered one at Oshawa, confirmed later in the day by George A. Scott (Tozer & Richards, 1974: 142). R.B. Stewart saw one on June 10, 1955 near Snake Is. in Lake Ontario, noting the two long central tail feathers as it flew overhead (Quilliam, 1965: 88). On June 6, 1945, Bourguignon (1947: 117) went with Hoyes Lloyd to Lake Deschenes, near Ottawa, and managed to collect a light phase adult female. At Cape Henrietta Maria, the 1948 ROM party saw one on July 2 and collected one on July 14 (Peck, 1972: 344). Schueler, Baldwin & Rising (1974: 143) reported this species only at Winisk. At Fort Severn, C.E. Hope in 1940 saw five (of which three were collected) on June 20: he saw two there on July 1 and one on July 9.

AUTUMN: The first Ontario specimen was taken in Kempenfeldt Bay, off Innisfil Twp., in Nov., 1913 by W.E. Playter and sent to the ROM (Devitt, 1967: 79). In Sept., 1935 an immature came down in Fred Bodsworth's garden at Port Burwell, died a day or two later and was sent to the ROM (Brooman, 1954: 21). W.E. Saunders took two specimens at Rondeau on Oct. 2, 1900 (Fleming, 1906: 452). Stirrett (1973d: 20) had only one Pelee record: on Oct. 22, 1916.

**MEASUREMENTS:**
*Length:* 20-23 ins.
(including 5-9'' tail
streamers) (Godfrey,
1966: 172)
*Wingspread:* 30 ins.
(Terres, 1980: 829)
*Weight:* 8 1/2 to 13 oz.
(Terres, 1980: 829)

**REFERENCE:**
Bourguignon, A.E. 1947 A
Long-tailed Jaeger at
Ottawa, Ontario. Can.
Field-Nat., 61: (3): 117.

# GREAT SKUA   *Catharacta skua*   Brünnich

The skua is normally seen out on the open oceans, preying on small sea birds and pirating food from larger birds. Most breed in the Antarctic but some from Iceland eastward in the Old World.

**IDENTIFICATION:** The Skua is about the size of a Herring Gull, somewhat shorter but with longer wings. It is a dark brown bird with prominent white flashes in the wing (something like an overgrown Pomarine Jaeger young). Adults have yellowish-brown tips to the feathers of the head, neck and back but young are more uniform dark brown.

**WINTER:** Sheppard (1965: 24) reported a Niagara Falls casualty, picked up in the gorge below the falls on Dec. 3, 1915.

**SPRING:** Charles Linden collected one on the Niagara River during the spring, 1866 (Beardslee & Mitchell, 1965: 242).

**SUMMER:**

**AUTUMN:**

**MEASUREMENTS:**
*Length:* 21 ins. (Pough,
1951: 261)
*Wingspread:* 59 ins.
(Pough, 1951: 261)
Weight 2 1/2 lbs. (Pough,
1951: 261)
*Note:* Both specimens have
been lost and there is some
doubt as to which side of
the Ontario-New York
border they were taken.

# LAUGHING GULL   *Larus atricilla*   Linnaeus

This is a common gull of the southern Atlantic coast, but rare in Ontario.

**IDENTIFICATION:** Adults are known from other dark-hooded species by their dark mantle and wings. The wing tips are black with no white spots and the only white on the upper surface is a thin white trailing edge. In size they are intermediate between Ring-billed and Bonaparte's Gulls. Immatures are dark brown except for the white trailing edge to the wing, gray tail with black subterminal bar and white tip (looking a bit like young Ring-bills, but smaller in size).

**WINTER:** Reid Wilson spotted one in immature plumage at Frenchman Bay on the Pickering Christmas count on Dec. 26, 1978: this was seen by many others until the bay froze over: I saw it on Jan. 1, 1979. One was picked up at Winisk in Dec., 1955 according to Vince Crichton and the specimen sent to the ROM (Speirs, 1956: 29).

SPRING: The first Pelee sighting was apparently the one noted by R. Pittaway and A. Wormington on May 16, 1972 (Goodwin, 1972: 756) but there have been several other May observations there, with reports from Apr. 15 to May 25 in 1978 by J.A. Greenhouse et al (Goodwin, 1978: 999). Three were seen at Long Point on May 27, 1971 (Goodwin, 1971: 738) and one there on Apr. 24, 1975 (Goodwin, 1975: 846). One was seen at Morgan's Point, Lake Erie, on May 22, 1955 by R.F. Andrle and R.D. Coggeshall and one at Point Abino on May 26, 1958 (Beardslee & Mitchell, 1965: 251). A. Epp and K. McLaughlin had Hamilton sightings on May 29, and June 4, 1977 (Goodwin, 1977: 995). Fleming (1906: 442) had two Toronto specimens: a mature ♂ taken on May 23, 1890 and a female lacking the black hood on June 1, 1898. Speirs (1938: 96) mentioned a May 28 record for Toronto. Tom Hassall found an adult at Whitby Harbour on May 23, 1964 and, with Bruce Falls, I saw one there on May 15, 1976 (Speirs, 1976: 12). Margaret Bain and J. Burns saw one at Whitby on May 30, 1979 (Goodwin, 1979: 766). D. Sands found one at Oshawa on May 2, 1970, seen the following day by Dennis Barry and J.M. Richards (Tozer & Richards, 1974: 147). E. and H. Kerr saw one at Presqu'ile on May 29, 1978 (Goodwin, 1978: 999).

SUMMER: One was reported at Pelee on June 12, 1975 (Goodwin, 1975: 965). A. Rider reported one at Kettle Point on July 22, 1978 (Goodwin, 1978: 1154). One was seen at Point Abino, Lake Erie on Aug. 1, 1948 (Beardslee & Mitchell, 1965: 250-251). A. Epp noted one at Hamilton from July 14-25, 1976 (Goodwin, 1976: 950) and K. McLaughlin reported one there on July 1, 1977 (Goodwin, 1977: 1133). Saunders (1947: 366) listed a Toronto record on June 17. S. Forsythe had records at the Upper Canada Migratory Bird Sanctuary near Morrisburg on July 2 and 9, 1976 (Goodwin, 1976: 950).

AUTUMN: M. and S. Gawn reported one that appeared at Ottawa on Sept. 25, 1977 (Goodwin, 1978: 198). Speirs (1938: 48, 54) had Toronto records on Sept. 15 and Oct. 9 while Saunders (1947: 366) gave records on Sept. 7 and 28 and Nov. 14 for Toronto. Beardslee & Mitchell (1965: 250-251) cited Fort Erie records on Sept. 18, 1937 and Nov. 29, 1959. W.R. Jarmain et al saw one at Port Stanley on Oct. 10-11, 1970 (Goodwin, 1971: 52). Dennis Rupert et al noted one at Wheatley from Sept. 14 to Oct. 5, 1974 (Goodwin, 1975: 51). J. Greenhouse and J. Wilson saw one at Pelee on Oct. 16, 1976 (Goodwin, 1977: 171).

**MEASUREMENTS:**
Length: 15-17 ins.
(Godfrey, 1966: 183)
Wingspread: 42 ins.
(Terres, 1980: 461)
Weight: 39 averaged
325 g. (270 to 400 g.)
(Dunning, 1984: 10).

# FRANKLIN'S GULL   *Larus pipixcan*   Wagler

This is a common species in parts of the Prairie Provinces and flocks sometimes wander east to Lake of the Woods. Elsewhere in Ontario it is a rare straggler.

IDENTIFICATION: Of the black-hooded species, Franklin's Gull most resembles the Laughing Gull but is somewhat smaller, with a paler mantle and much white in the wing tips, though first year immatures lack the white in the wing tips and closely resemble a smaller, paler version of the Laughing Gull at the same age. The smaller and more abundant Bonaparte's Gull shows the white flash on the leading edge of the wing in all plumages.

WINTER: Dennis Rupert noted one at Sombra on Jan. 24, 1981 (Goodwin, 1981: 296). Beardslee & Mitchell (1965: 251) reported one along the Niagara River on Dec. 11, 1948 and more recently W.F. McKale *et al* saw one at Ft. Erie from Jan. 15-23, 1972 (Goodwin, 1972: 598). D.C. Sadler reported two at Toronto on Jan. 25, 1976 (Goodwin, 1976: 713).

SPRING: Stirrett (1973b: 18) reported nine at Pelee on Apr. 20, 1952 and singles there on May 11, 1957, May 8-10, 1966 and May 15, 1971. Clive Goodwin has cited a few subsequent sightings in that vicinity on May 11-15, 1974; May 15, 1976; May 6 and 10, 1978; May 7, 1979 and five seen at Leamington on May 15, 1980 by A. Wormington *et al* (Goodwin, 1980: 772). J.A. Kelley spotted one at Mimico on May 29, 1979 (Goodwin, 1979: 766). Speirs (1938: 46) gave a June 1 record for Toronto. Don Perks found one at Whitby on May 25, 1980 (Goodwin, 1980: 772). George A. Scott observed one at Oshawa on Apr. 25, 1965 (Speirs, 1976: 13). R.K. Edwards had sightings at Amherst Is. on May 23, 1976; May 20, 1979 and May 18, 1980 (Weir & Quilliam, 1980: 14-15). R.A. Foxall *et al* saw two at Ottawa on May 9, 1973 (Goodwin, 1973: 767): V. Humphries and R.M. Poulin saw two there again on May 18, 1976 (Goodwin, 1976: 834): another was found there on May 19, 1980 by R. Bracken, B.M. DiLabio and J. James (Goodwin, 1980: 772). Chris Bell spotted one near Tehkummah, Manitoulin, on May 13, 1978 (Nicholson, 1981: 113).

SUMMER: D. Morin saw one at Pelee June 8-9, 1975 (Goodwin, 1975: 965). P.A. Woodliffe noted one at River Canard in June, 1980 (Goodwin, 1980: 891). P.D. Pratt reported one at Erieau on June 19, 1977 (Goodwin, 1977: 1133). Kelley (1978: 40) wrote that one in breeding plumage was present at Rondeau through the summer of 1970. Goodwin (1975: 965) reported five at Long Point on July 6, 1975. Beardslee & Mitchell (1965: 251) had sightings at Rockhouse Pt., Lake Erie, on July 7, 1957 and July 4, 1959; also at Windmill Pt. on July 15, 1960: R.F. Andrle collected one at Morgan's Pt. on Aug. 23, 1958. K. McLaughlin observed one at Burlington on July 8, 1976 (Goodwin, 1976: 950). Goodwin (1971: 853) reported up to six at Hamilton with the first on June 13, 1971 and another there in July, 1973. Saunders (1947: 248-249) described his delight at finding one at Toronto on Aug. 31, 1942. George A. Scott saw one at Oshawa's Second Marsh on June 2 and 3, 1962, later photographed by W. Laird, and Naomi LeVay found one at Eastbourne, Whitby, on June 19, 1972 (Speirs, 1976: 13). George North reported an adult at Kingston on June 27, 1950 (Quilliam, 1965: 92) and another was found at Mallorytown Landing on July 28-29, 1973 (Weir & Quilliam, 1980: 14). J. Jones *et al* saw one at Ottawa on June 21, 1977 (Goodwin, 1977: 1133). Fred Cooke found one in a flock of Ring-tailed Gulls at Snow White's Lake, Manitoulin, on Aug. 29, 1972 (Nicholson, 1981: 113). J. Nicholson and J. Lemon found one at Garson, near Sudbury, from Aug. 14-16, 1977 (Goodwin, 1978: 198). There are several reports of flocks at Lake of the Woods: I saw 60 there on June 16, 1971: G. Holborn and A. Wormington estimated 525 on Sable Is. in the lake on June 18, 1978 (Goodwin, 1978: 1154); M. Robson and A. Wormington reported 200 adults on Sable Is. on July 1, 1979 (Goodwin, 1979: 859); D.H. Elder, T. Nash and A. Wormington estimated 3000 at Lake of the Woods, Aug. 3-5, 1978 (Goodwin, 1979: 173); D.H. Elder *et al* reported 15,000 there on Aug. 2, 1980 (Goodwin, 1980: 891) and A. Wormington *et al* estimated 900 on Sable Is. on Aug. 3, 1979 (Goodwin, 1980: 157). Snyder (1953: 59) saw a flock of seven at Ingolf as far back as June 13, 1937.

AUTUMN: M. Brigham and R. Pittaway had sightings at Ottawa on Sept. 8 and Oct. 10, 1970 (Goodwin, 1971: 52). Goodwin (1975: 51) had other Ottawa reports on Sept. 16, 1974 by S. O'Donnell and from Oct. 15-19, 1974 by many observers and on Sept. 10, 1976, R. Killeen reported two there (Goodwin, 1977: 171). Devitt (1967: 92) had three Simcoe Co. records: one he collected at Wasaga Beach on Aug. 31, 1936; one seen at Barrie from Oct. 26 to Nov. 20, 1948 by Jack Westman *et al* and one observed at Collingwood by A.J. Mitchener on Nov. 20, 1956. Weir & Quilliam (1980: 14-15) had Kingston records on Oct. 20, 1974 and Oct. 14, 1975 and two at Prince Edward Point on Nov. 6, 1977. E.R. McDonald saw Willow Beach's first ever on Oct. 4, 1971 (Goodwin, 1972: 57). F. Bakker reported one at Laurel on Oct. 11, 1970 (Goodwin, 1971: 52). Speirs (1976: 13) cited six fall records in Ontario Co. between Sept. 21 (1969) and Oct. 7 (1972). Wm. Cross observed that one was taken at Toronto on Nov. 11, 1889 (Thompson, 1890: 198) but Fleming (1906: 452) suggested that "recent records no doubt refer to *L. artricilla*". A. Epp and L.A. Grey noted seven at Dundas on Oct. 11, 1971 (Goodwin, 1972: 57). A. Epp and W. Smith estimated 20 at Hamilton on Sept. 29, 1974 (Goodwin, 1975: 51). P.M. Benham noted three at Queenston on Oct. 17, 1971 (Goodwin, 1972: 57): Beardslee & Mitchell (1965: 251) noted one at Ft. Erie on Oct. 17, 1937 and noted them in the vicinity almost yearly since that first sighting. T.R. Scovell *et al* reported one at Niagara from Nov. 11, 1979 (Goodwin, 1980: 157). Goodwin (1975: 51) reported six at Long Point from Aug. 28 to Sept. 15, 1974. D. Rupert reported 79 flying down the St. Clair River at Sarnia from Oct. 23-25, 1979 (Goodwin, 1980: 157). J.P. Kleiman *et al* noted up to five at Wheatley on Oct. 3, 1970 (Goodwin, 1971: 52). Stirrett (1973d: 20) noted two at Pelee from Oct. 6-8, 1967 and A.J. Maley had seven there on Oct. 16, 1971 (Goodwin, 1972: 57). Goodwin (1975: 51) had 20 reports from SW Ontario from Sept. 20-Nov. 6, 1974 and A.H. Kelley had up to 14 there in fall, 1976 (Goodwin, 1977: 171).

**MEASUREMENTS:**
*Length:* 13.5 to 15.5 ins.
(Godfrey, 1966: 183).
*Wingspread:* 34-38 ins.
(Roberts, 1955: 591).
*Weight:* 0.55 to 0.59 lbs.
(Roberts, 1955: 591).

# LITTLE GULL   *Larus minutus*   Pallas

I well remember our excitement when we found this striking little gull at Sunnyside, Toronto, on Sept. 18, 1938 (the first Toronto record). Scott (1962: 548-549) was equally elated to discover the first three nests for North America in Oshawa's Second Marsh on June 1, 1962. Since then sightings have been more frequent, but it is still a cause for rejoicing when one is found, usually in a flock of migrating Bonaparte's Gulls.

IDENTIFICATION: The best field mark for adults is the black wing lining. The small size and lack of white leading edge to the wings, helps to distinguish immatures (see illustration for Black-headed Gull). Scott (1963: 3) heard "kek-kek" notes from the nesting birds at Oshawa (quite different from the buzzy notes of Bonaparte's Gulls).

WINTER: J.P. Kleiman and P.D. Pratt observed one at Pelee on Dec. 6 and 24, 1980 (Goodwin, 1981: 296). J.P. Kleiman and R. Simpson saw four at Rondeau on Dec. 28, 1971 (Goodwin, 1972: 598) and one there on Dec. 26, 1972 (Goodwin, 1973: 609). Marshall Field and Harold Lancaster found one at Pt. Stanley on Dec. 6, 1953 with Bonaparte's Gulls and Harry Lumsden saw one at Pt. Burwell in January, 1949 (Brooman, 1954: 21). On the 1973 Christmas count at Long Point, 18 were tallied (Goodwin, 1974: 634). There have been sightings at Blenheim and Niagara Falls on several Christmas counts. Beardslee & Mitchell (1965: 254-255) reported one at Ft. Erie on Jan. 15, 1949 and another there on Feb. 12, 1950; also one at Queenston on Feb. 6, 1954. K.F. Edwards picked one out in a flock of Bonaparte's Gulls on Dec. 18, 1952 (the first Kingston record) (Quilliam, 1973: 93).

SPRING: Stirrett (1973b: 18) had records at Pelee from Apr. 8 to June 1 with a maximum of 7 on May 7. Goodwin (1971: 738) mentioned five immatures and two adults at Rondeau from May 29, 1971. Beardslee & Mitchell (1965: 254-255) noted one at Ft. Erie on May 2, 1953. Gus Yaki found one at Thorold as early as Apr. 8, 1973 (Goodwin, 1973: 767). Goodwin (1971: 738) reported five immatures and one adult at Hamilton from May 24, 1971. Saunders (1947: 142) found at Toronto on May 30, 1943 (the first spring sightings there). Six were noted at Cranberry Marsh, Whitby, on May 6, 1973 (Speirs, 1976: 15). Tozer & Richards (1974: 148) saw two at Oshawa as early as Apr. 24, 1964. Ron Tozer found two at Lake Scugog on May 21, 1977 (Goodwin, 1977: 995). Fred Cooke found one on Amherst Is. on May 18, 1969 (Quilliam, 1973: 94) and the only other spring record there was on May 19 (Weir & Quilliam, 1980: 35). Dave Fidler reported one at Tiny Marsh on May 31, 1974 (Goodwin, 1974: 796).

SUMMER: Kelley (1978: 40) reported three pairs nesting at Rondeau on July 12, 1970 and 35 summering there in 1974. A. Wormington reported 9 adults, 9 immatures and 19 young of the year at Long Point on June 29, 1975 (Goodwin, 1975: 965). Beardslee & Mitchell (1965: 254-255) reported one at Ft. Erie on Aug. 30, 1953. There were 14 at Hamilton in early July, 1971, but only one of these was an adult (Goodwin, 1971: 853). Saunders (1947: 248, 366) saw one at Toronto on Aug. 31, 1942 and another on June 16. Tozer & Richards (1974: 345-346) detailed the histories of Little Gull nestings at Oshawa's Second Marsh and Cranberry Marsh, Whitby (and Rondeau): there were 10 sets with 3 eggs each and one with two eggs: the first documented successful nesting was in 1971, though I saw a young begging from an adult at Oshawa Harbour, probably from George A. Scott's Second Marsh nest of June 8, 1963. Weir & Quilliam (1980: 35) listed an Aug. 8 record for Kingston. C.J. MacFayden saw one at Nottawasaga Bay on June 23-24, 1972 (Goodwin, 1972: 853). S. Gawn noted two at Ottawa from June 4-11, 1975 (Goodwin, 1975: 965). John and Margaret Catto found 4 adults on an island off Parry Sound on July 8, 1979, with one downy chick and K. Ketchum verified the identity of the adults on Aug. 4 (Mills, 1981: 64). The first breeding records for Ontario's north coast were established in 1984. P. Burke and A.G. Carpentier found a nest with one egg and two chicks near Attawapiskat on July 15,1984, while at Winisk adults with 4 young were found on July 24, by George Fairfield, P. Smith and Jim and Pat. Woodford (Weir, 1984: 1015).

AUTUMN: M. Gawn reported one at Nairn Is., Stormont Co., on Oc.t 28, 1979 (Goodwin, 1980: 157). A.E. Hughes had Kingston records on Nov. 8 and 22, 1970 (Goodwin, 1971: 52). Weir & Quilliam (1980: 35) gave Sept. 24 and Nov. 17 as 7-year average fall arrival and departure dates for Kingston. Devitt (1967: 83) had only one record for Simcoe Co., identified at Barrie on Oct. 26, 1957 by Miss A.M. Hughes. Goodwin, (1972: 57) mentioned two at Prince Edward Point on Nov. 20, 1971, and three at Toronto on Sept. 11. Saunders (1947: 277-278) described finding Toronto's second Little Gull at Sunnyside on Oct. 2, 1940. Beardslee & Mitchell (1965: 254) reported individuals along the Niagara River in fall almost every year since 1938: on Oct. 17, 1971 there were six at Queenston (Goodwin, 1972: 57). P.M. Benham noted 29 along the Niagara River on Nov. 4, 1973 (Goodwin, 1974: 47). The first Canadian record was at Pt. Stanley on Nov. 16, 1930 by W.E. Saunders: another was spotted there from Nov. 22-26, 1952 by Marshall Field (Brooman, 1954: 21). Stirrett (1973d: 20) had two fall records for Pelee: two on Sept. 18, 1961 and two again on Nov. 7, 1964: Goodwin (1972: 57) reported birds there on Oct. 23 and Nov. 7.

**MEASUREMENTS:**
*Length:* 11 ins. (Godfrey, 1966: 185)
Wingspread:
*Weight:* 11 averaged 120 g. (103 to 140 g.) (Dunning, 1984: 10).

**REFERENCES:**
Richards, James R. 1973 Little Gull nestings. Ont. Naturalist, 13: (2): 38-41. This has excellent photographs of the marsh habitat, adults on nests, eggs and chick.
  Scott, George A. 1963 First meeting of the Little Gull (*Larus minutus*) in Ontario and the New World. Auk, 80:(4) 548-549.
  Scott, George A. 1963 Second nesting of the Little Gull at Oshawa. Naturalist, 9: (6): 3.

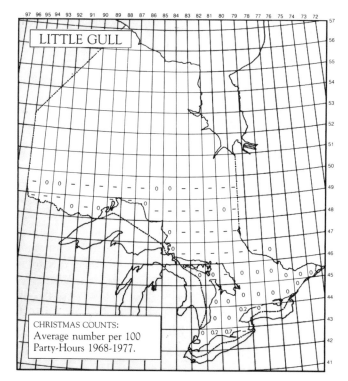

LITTLE GULL

CHRISTMAS COUNTS:
Average number per 100
Party-Hours 1968-1977.

# COMMON BLACK-HEADED GULL
## *Larus ridibundus* Linnaeus

On our visits to northern Europe, Black-headed Gulls often greeted us as we entered the ports. Later we saw them flying about downtown buildings in the cities, greatly enhancing the skies as they circled overhead. In Ontario they are rare stragglers.

IDENTIFICATION: They most resemble our common Bonaparte's Gulls with which they often associate and share with that species the white leading edge to the wings. Adults differ in having dark *brown* hoods (not black, in spite of their name). They are also considerably larger than Bonaparte's and have red bills (black in Bonaparte's). In winter plumage (see illustration) they are still distinguished by larger size and red bills. In flight the wing linings are gray, not black as in Little Gull or white as in Bonaparte's. Laughing Gulls also have the red bill and larger size, but have a very different wing pattern (very dark gray mantle with a narrow white trailing edge).

WINTER: H.H. Axtell, P.M. Benham *et al* reported one at Fort Erie to Jan. 2, 1971 (Goodwin, 1971: 572). H.D. Mitchell *et al* saw one at Queenston on Dec. 4, 1971 (Goodwin, 1972: 598). Another was seen along the Niagara River on Dec. 3, 1977 by H.H. Axtell, M. Parker and A. Wormington (Goodwin, 1978: 344).

SPRING: Kelley (1978: 39) cited two records for the tip of Pt. Pelee: one on May 6, 1960 by Paul Hamel and George Holland and the other seen by Dennis Rupert on May 18, 1973. On May 26, 1970 John Frank and I noted the brown hood and red bill of one seen in a flock of Ring-billed Gulls on a plowed field near the Lake Erie shore, about 7 miles east of Wheatley. P. Satterly and P.A. Woodliffe reported one at Rondeau on May 17, 1979 (Goodwin, 1979: 766). George North noted an adult in breeding plumage at Niagara-on-the-Lake on Apr. 12, 1959 (Beardslee & Mitchell, 1965: 249). One was spotted at Corner Marsh, Pickering, as early as Apr. 20, 1974 by B. Cruikshank (Speirs, 1976: 11) and Clive Goodwin (1974: 796) saw it there a week earlier. Several individuals have been seen at Whitby: one by Clive Goodwin on May 20, 1957 also seen the following day by J. Livingston and R.M. Saunders: and other records on May 25, 1958; May 27, 1966; May 29, 1966; May 14, 1967 and May 19, 1968 (Tozer & Richards, 1974: 146). Goodwin (1976: 834) reported another one at Whitby on May 14, 1976.

SUMMER: There have been several summer records at Hamilton: Goodwin (1971: 853) saw one there June 18 to 20 and July 5 to 10, 1971: J.B. Miles and W. Smith noted one there July 15-16, 1972 (Goodwin, 1972: 853): two were seen there by George North *et al* July 5-23, 1972 (Goodwin, 1973: 53): and one was seen by many observers there from June 28 to July 12, 1975 (Goodwin, 1975: 965). Goodwin (1973: 865) reported one at Bronte from June 28 to July 10, 1973 and saw another there on July 3, 1976 (Goodwin, 1976: 950). The first Ontario record was the one found at Sunnyside, Toronto, by George North on Aug. 1, 1935 and seen a few days later by John Crosby (Baillie, 1963: 98). Don Perks found an adult and an immature bird at Whitby on June 5, 1966 and showed it to J.L. Baillie on June 14 (Speirs, 1977: 11). Tom Hassall found one with Little Gulls and Bonaparte's Gulls at Oshawa Harbour on July 20, 1963,which I photographed the following day: this was collected by J.L. Baillie on July 29.

AUTUMN: Ottawa had its first Black-headed Gull from Sept. 27 to Oct. 1, 1975, seen by S. O'Donnel *et al* (Goodwin, 1976: 61). P.M. Benham reported one at Queenston on Nov. 21, 1970 (Goodwin, 1971: 52) and one at Niagara Falls on Nov. 5, 1972 (Goodwin, 1973: 53). Harold Axtell found an adult in winter plumage at Fort Erie on Nov. 22, 1959, later photographed by R.F. Andrle (Beardslee & Mitchell, 1965: 249-250).

**MEASUREMENTS:**
*Length:* 14 to 15 ins.
(Godfrey, 1966: 182)
Wingspread:
*Weight:* 324 averaged
284 g. (195 to 327 g.)
(Dunning, 1984: 10)

# BONAPARTE'S GULL   *Larus philadelphia*   (Ord)

Bonaparte's Gull is by far the most numerous of the pigeon-sized gulls to be found in Ontario. It nests in trees in northern Ontario. In migration large flocks may be found along the shores and harbours of the larger bodies of water in southern Ontario. Some linger along the north shore of Lake Erie until freezeup and well into the winter along the Niagara River, but most migrate south to the Gulf of Mexico.

IDENTIFICATION: Most black hooded gulls seen in Ontario are this species. After the breeding season the black hood is lost and replaced by "dirty ear" patches. In either plumage Bonaparte's Gulls can be identified almost as far as they can be seen in flight by the white flash in the leading edge of the wing. (The Black-headed Gull also shows this white leading edge but is seldom seen in Ontario and never in large flocks.)

WINTER: On Christmas counts they have been common from Pelee, along the north shore of Lake Erie and along the Niagara River, with singles at Oakville and Kingston; not elsewhere in Ontario. Stirrett (1973a: 16) had a winter maximum of 100 at Pelee on Dec. 18, with his latest three on Feb. 7. Fred Bodsworth reported 400 to 500 at Pt. Burwell on Dec. 28, 1948 (Brooman, 1954: 21). Fleming (1906: 442) gave Dec. 15, 1897 as his latest Toronto record. J. Satterly saw 100 at Cedar Point, Lake Simcoe, as late as Dec. 5, 1953 and I found one at Whitby Harbour on Dec. 12, 1970 (Speirs, 1976: 14). Weir & Quilliam (1980: 35) mentioned one at Kingston as late as Jan. 1. E.L. Brereton counted 102 at Barrie on Dec. 17, 1948 and A.J. Mitchener had a record at Collingwood on Dec. 1, 1962 (Devitt, 1967: 82).

SPRING: Stirrett (1973b: 18) saw his earliest flock of 20 at Pelee on March 24 and his largest flock of 2000 there on May 21. Saunders & Dale (1933: 199) considered it rare at London, with most records of single birds from Apr. 7 (1921) to May 6 (1924). Snyder (1931: 150) collected a female at Long Point on May 8, 1928 and males on May 26 and 29, 1927 and May 31, 1928: he suggested a peak about May 28. On Apr. 14, 1975, I estimated a huge flock at Long Point to contain at least 10,000 birds. Speirs (1938: 40, 44) gave Mar. 27 as the earliest date for Toronto, with the spring peak on May 22.

Saunders (1947: 366) gave Apr. 29 and May 28 as his average arrival and departure dates for Toronto (J.L. Baillie gave Apr. 26 and June 3). Speirs (1976: 14) gave Apr. 11, 1965 as the earliest Whitby date, with peaks in the first and third weeks of May. Tozer & Richards (1974: 148) reported a flock of 3500 off Cranberry Marsh, Whitby, on May 4, 1970. R.J. Rutter saw six in Prince Edward Co. as late as May 25, 1931 (Snyder, 1941: 56-57). Weir & Quilliam (1980: 35) gave Apr. 22 as the 18-year average arrival date for Kingston, with the earliest on Mar. 23 and average departure on May 25. Devitt (1967: 82-83) gave May 10 as the 8-year average arrival date at Barrie, with the earliest on Apr. 22, 1949 and two at Wasaga Beach as late as May 29, 1936. Mills (1981: 64) considered it a rare spring migrant in the cottage country, with records of 4 at Huntsville on May 17, 1970 and one at Magnetawan on May 24, 1947. Nicholson (1981: 114) had Manitoulin records from May 5 (1973) to May 29 (1971) with a maximum of 70 at Mississagi Light on May 15, 1978. Speirs & Speirs (1947: 29) saw four at North Bay on May 13, 1945 while Ricker & Clarke (1939: 11) noted flocks of 20 to 50 there each spring for about a week, arriving from May 19 to May 25. Denis (1961: 3) gave May 16 as the average arrival date at Thunder Bay with the earliest on May 5, 1942. J. Coyne saw four at Gogama from May 12-18, 1954 and A.N. Boissonneau saw one at Lillabelle Lake, Cochrane, in spring, 1953 (Smith, 1957: 173). Bondrup-Nielsen (1976: 42) gave May 10 as the arrival date near Kapuskasing in 1975. Elder (1979: 33) considered it a fairly common spring migrant at Geraldton, with the earliest on May 20. Oliver Hewitt saw 25 in the estuary of the Moose River on May 25, 1947 and Manning (1952: 59-60) saw four in 3 hours afield at Ship Sands on May 31, 1947. Elsey gave May 19, 1950 as his earliest recod for the Asheweig region (Cringan, 1950: 10).

SUMMER: On Breeding Bird Surveys they were reported only at Kapuskasing and Kingsville (the latter obviously a non-breeding straggler). Stirrett (1973c: 16) had one on June 16 at Pelee and a summer maximum of 1000 on July 31. Snyder (1931: 150) collected 11 (both adults and immatures) at Long Point from June 4 to July 19, 1927 and commented on the great variation in plumages. Beardslee & Mitchell (1965: 252-253) noted 20 at Ft. Erie as late as June 6, 1936. J. Satterly had summer records at Cedar Point, Lake Simcoe, in June, July and August, with 250 there on Aug. 24, 1959 (Speirs, 1976: 14). Lloyd (1923: 103) mentioned a specimen taken at Ottawa on June 9, 1885. Mills (1981: 64) cited a few late July and August records from the cottage country, with Franklin Is. records from June 25 to July 12, 1947. Ron Tasker saw one near Western Duck Is., off Manitoulin, on July 18, 1970 (Nicholson, 1981: 114). Smith (1957: 173) had summer records suggesting breeding in the Clay Belt: one on Frederickhouse Lake on June 22, 1953 and one near Moonbeam from June 24 to July 6, 1953 (which attacked a "Marsh Hawk" on June 28). Bondrup-Nielsen (1976: 42) noted the species near Kapuskasing on June 9, 1974. Snyder (1928: 19) saw two at Lake Abitibi on July 25 and one on July 28, 1925. I have seen them in summer, several times between Longlac and Lillabelle Lake, Cochrane. One was collected in summer, 1919 at Lac Seul and 9 were seen in June, 1939 at Remi Lake by Paul Harrington and Fred Starr (Baillie, 1960: 19). James (1980: 86) found three nests near Pickle Lake in 1977: one with 2 eggs on May 29; another with 2 eggs on June 4 and one with 3 eggs on June 13. Cringan (1950: 10) had June and early July records along the North Caribou River and in the Petownikip Marsh. Manning (1952: 60) saw six in 7 hours afield at Big Piskwanish June 9-11, 1947; one in 8 hours at Long Ridge Point and a flock of 15 at Attawapiskat on July 5, 1947: he also cited several records of birds collected by others between Moosonee and Ft. Albany in summer. Schueler, Baldwin & Rising

(1974: 143, 146) noted the species at Cochrane and Winisk and collected a female at Hawley Lake on June 12, 1964 with an unshelled egg in her oviduct. Lee (1978: 24) saw single Bonaparte's Gulls at Big Trout Lake on Aug. 2, 4 and 6, 1975 and cited reports by others from Sachigo Lake, Angling Lake and the mouth of the Fawn River. C.E. Hope collected four at Ft. Severn on June 17, 1940 and saw others there on June 16, 17 and 22, and one July 23.

AUTUMN: Smith (1957: 173) was shown four at Pearl Lake, Schumacher, on Sept. 6, 1953 by F. Cowell, who reported adults with young on this lake during the summer. MacLulich (1938: 16) saw several on Sept. 26, 1930 in Algonquin Park. Nicholson (1981: 114) gave Nov. 11, 1972 as the latest date for Manitoulin, with a maximum of 100 on Sept. 27, 1980 at West Bay. Chris. Harris noted 43 at Go Home Bay on Oct. 30, 1977 and 75 there on Oct. 1, 1976 (Mills, 1981: 64). Devitt (1967: 82) estimated 500 near Barrie on Nov. 7, 1948. Weir & Quilliam (1980: 35) gave Oct. 4 and Nov. 29 as the 30-year averages for fall arrivals and departures at Kingston. John Townson saw 50 or 60 in Prince Edward Co. on Sept. 20, 1931 (Snyder, 1941: 57). Tozer & Richards (1974: 148) reported 300 on Lake Scugog on Nov. 12, 1972. Saunders (1947: 366) gave Aug. 20 and Nov. 6 as average fall arrival and departure dates for Toronto (J.L. Baillie gave Aug. 19 and Nov. 4). Marshall Field estimated 5000 at Pt. Stanley on Nov. 22, 1952 (Brooman, 1954: 21). Stirrett (1973d: 20) had a fall maximum of 3000 at Pelee on Sept. 30.

**MEASUREMENTS:**
*Length:* 12.0 to 14.5 ins. (Godfrey, 1966: 184)
*Wingspread:* 32.0 to 33.5 ins. (Roberts, 1955: 592)
*Weight:* 8 oz. (Roberts, 1955: 592)

**REFERENCE:**
Beardslee, Clark S. 1944 Bonaparte's Gull on the Niagara River and eastern Lake Erie. Wilson Bull., 56:(1):9-14. Discussed seasonal changes in abundance and plumages in this region.
Dear, L.S. 1939 Bonaparte's Gull breeding in Ontario. Auk. 56:(2):186. Clare Watson found 2 nests of 3 eggs each 25 ft. up in black spruces by a muskeg lake near Rat Rapids on the Albany River on June 16, 1938. See also Baillie (1939: 130-131) for first breeding record for Ontario: On July 21, 1937, J.W. Britton and V.K. Prest found 3 flightless young and agitated adults at Ivan

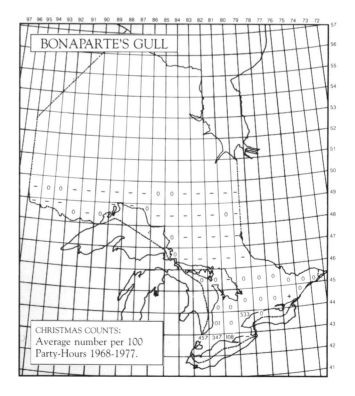

Lake, near Lake Mimiska,
about 100 miles north of
Lake Nipigon & 75 miles
east of Rat Rapids.

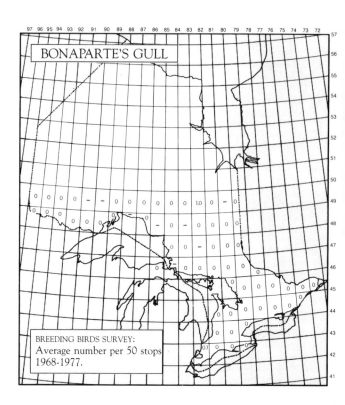

BONAPARTE'S GULL

BREEDING BIRDS SURVEY:
Average number per 50 stops
1968-1977.

# MEW GULL   *Larus canus*   (Linnaeus)

In America this is essentially a western species, accidental in the east. In northern Europe it is known as the Common Gull, though not nearly as numerous as the Herring Gull, even there.

**IDENTIFICATION:**   The American race has a very short, delicate bill, and has been called the Short-billed Gull for this reason. The Black-legged Kittiwake is similar in size and in its unmarked yellowish bill, but it has black legs, unlike the Mew Gull which has yellow-green legs like a Ring-billed Gull. In flight the conspicuous white bar across the black wing tips help to separate the Mew Gull from the larger Ring-billed Gull and much larger Herring Gull. The blue-gray mantle is somewhat darker than in those species. Young birds are best distinguished by the small delicate bill: this may have a black ring like young Herring and Ring-billed Gulls.

**WINTER:**

**SPRING:**

**SUMMER:**   Goodwin (1981: 177) reported that one had been seen at Amherst Is. on June 28, 1980.

**AUTUMN:**   Goodwin (1981: 177) cited a record by S. Gawn at Ottawa on Oct. 24, 1980. Mitchell & Andrle (1970: 5-6) reported two specimens taken by Robert Andrle, an adult at Port Weller on Oct. 24, 1967 and a first year bird at Thorold on Nov. 30, 1967. Both were first discovered by Daniel Salisbury, the Port Weller bird on Oct. 24 and the Thorold bird on Nov. 28, 1967.

**MEASUREMENTS:**
*Length:* 16-18 ins.
(Godfrey, 1966: 182)
Wingspread:
*Weight:* 96 ♂ averaged
432 g. (340 to 552 g.) 72
♀ averaged 375 g. (290 to
530 g.) (Dunning,
1984: 10).

# RING-BILLED GULL   *Larus delawarensis*   (Ord)

This is the gull that frequents shopping plazas, picnic grounds and the one that follows the plow. During the warmer months this is the most common gull around the southern Great Lakes but in the winter it is generally greatly outnumbered by the Herring Gull.

IDENTIFICATION:   From the larger Herring Gull it is distinguished by its smaller size, more dainty proportions and more trusting nature. Adults have greenish-yellow legs (Herring Gulls have pink legs). Adults have a black ring around the bill near its tip while adult Herring Gulls have a red spot on the lower mandible but clear yellow upper mandible but note that immature Herring Gulls have a very similar ring around the bill and may have pinkish legs like immature Ring-billed Gulls. The tail pattern is the best field mark to distinguish immatures: Immature Ring-bills have a narrow, blackish subterminal bar while immature Herring Gulls have a broad terminal bar. Young in juvenile plumage are very similar, except for the smaller size and more dainty proportions of the Ring-bill.

WINTER:   In most winters they have been common on Christmas counts along the shores of Lake Erie, southern Lake Huron and Lake Ontario, becoming uncommon to rare north to Deep River and Thunder Bay. In very cold Decembers they may be quite scarce. Stirrett (1973a: 16) had a winter maximum of 300 at Pelee on Dec. 23, with his latest 10 on Feb. 7. Ussher (1965: 13) called them "sometimes scarce in winter" at Rondeau. Speirs (1976: 10) wrote that they are generally scarce in Ontario Co. from mid-Dec. to mid-Feb.: none were seen on 6 of 15 Pickering Christmas counts and the maximum was 125: on the Oshawa counts none were seen on 5 of 21 and the maximum reported was 309: some 500 returning birds were seen on Frenchman Bay on Feb. 22, 1975. Quilliam (1973: 92) found them rare on Kingston Christmas counts and usually absent for about 2 1/2 months in winter, with Jan. 4 as the 30-year average for the last noted. Nicholson (1981: 113) gave the 10 seen at Providence Bay dump on Jan. 8, 1972 as the latest date for lingering Ring-bills on Manitoulin. Dennison (1980: 147) reported this species on 12 of 25 Christmas counts at Sault Ste. Marie, with a maximum of 34 in 1973.

SPRING:   Stirrett (1973b: 18) gave the 10 seen on Mar. 15 as his earliest returning date for Pelee, with a maximum count of 5000 on May 20. Saunders & Dale (1933: 198-199) cited a few spring records near London, the earliest on Mar. 29, 1929 and the latest on Apr. 18, 1926. Speirs (1938: 42, 44) gave Apr. 1 as the spring peak date for Toronto, not to be expected before March 10. Speirs (1976: 10) noted a spring peak for adults near Pickering in the second week of April, with an influx of immatures in the latter half of May. Weir & Quilliam (1980: 35) gave March 14 as the 27-year average arrival date at Kingston. Devitt (1967: 82) gave Mar. 30 as the 12-year average arrival date at Barrie. Mills (1981: 63) saw one at Magnetawan as early as Mar. 25, 1979. Nicholson (1981: 113) gave Mar. 10, 1974 as the earliest arrival date for Manitoulin. Speirs & Speirs (1947: 29) saw two at North Bay as early as Apr. 9, 1945. Skeel & Bondrup-Nielsen (1978: 175) saw their first at Pukaskwa in 1977 on May 17. Denis (1961: 2) gave Apr. 24 as the average arrival date at Thunder Bay, with the earliest on Apr. 4, 1958. Cringan (1953a: 2) noted his first at Sioux Lookout on Apr. 24 in 1953. Ross James noted two at Pickle Lake on May 29 and one there on May 30 in 1977.

SUMMER:   On Breeding Bird Surveys they have been common on routes near the big breeding colonies on Lake Erie, Lake Ontario and Georgian Bay, but uncommon to rare elsewhere north to Kapuskasing, Ignace, Dryden and Kenora. Stirrett (1973c: 16) had a summer maximum of 2000 at Pelee on July 31 and again on Aug. 12. Kelley (1978: 39) reported 11 occupied nests at Ipperwash Beach on July 5, 1964. Beardslee & Mitchell (1965: 248-249) summarized the increase in the Mohawk Island colony from about 50 nests in 1945 to about 2000 in 1960. Sheppard (1960: 25) reported that several hundred young were reared in a Niagara River colony in 1958 and a dozen pairs reared young near the brink of the falls in a tern colony there. Tozer & Richards (1974: 145) reported a gathering of about 5000 at Lake Scugog on Aug. 21, 1953. Although none are known to breed in Ontario Co. this was the most numerous species tallied on roadside counts in the County during the June counts in 1962, 1963 and 1965 (Speirs, 1976: 10). Quilliam (1973: 91-92) documented the increase in nesting populations on islands near Kingston, from two nests in 1927 to five or six thousand by the 1960's (and 100,000 or more on Little Galloo Is. in adjacent N.Y. waters). Devitt (1967: 81-82) gave some history of the breeding colony on Tiny Is. in Georgian Bay, Simcoe Co. from 1927 to 1967 and summarized results from banding done there by Herb. Southam and Gordon Lambert (see below). Mills (1981: 63) gave details of nesting colonies in the Muskoka-Parry Sound portion of Georgian Bay, the largest on the Limestone Islands where Cyril Peak estimated 7000 pairs in 1959. Nicholson (1981: 113) reported a nest with 3 eggs at Gertrude Is., Manitoulin, on June 2, 1979. Baillie & Hope (1947: 8) saw over 100 at Bigwood over cultivated farmland from July 18 to July 24, 1937. Peruniak (1971: 17) saw an immature bird at Atikokan on June 7, 1968. Hope (1938: 20) saw none at Favorable Lake during his stay but recorded an immature female collected there on Aug. 16 by Goddard. Ross James noted two at Pickle Lake on June 11, 1977 and one there the next day. Schueler, Baldwin & Rising (1974: 146) saw two about 4 miles east of Winisk in 1971 and others near Moosonee during the summers of 1971 and 1972.

AUTUMN: Oliver Hewitt saw one at Ship Sands, near Moosonee, on Sept. 24, 1947 (Manning, 1952: 59) and Alan Wormington saw from 20 decreasing to one, daily from Oct. 14 to 27, 1981 with a few at intervals until the last was noted on Nov. 5, at Netitishi Point at the south end of James Bay. Peruniak (1971: 17) saw two immatures at Atikokan on Sept. 7, 1964. Skeel & Bondrup-Nielsen (1978: 175) saw their last at Pukaskwa on Oct. 10 in 1977. Speirs & Speirs (1947: 29) saw one at North Bay as late as Oct. 22, 1944. Speirs (1976: 10) watched them catching flying ants in Pickering Twp. on Sept. 1, 1961, with fall peaks there in the second week of October and first week of November. Speirs (1938: 50, 52) gave Sept. 23 as the fall peak for Toronto, not to be expected after Nov. 29. Saunders & Dale (1933: 199) reported a specimen taken at Byron, near London, on Nov. 27, 1903. Harold Lancaster and Marshall Field noted about 4000 at Port Burwell on Oct. 13, 1952 (Brooman, 1954: 21). Stirrett (1973d: 20) had a fall maximum of 2000 at Pelee on Sept. 4.

BANDING: Herb. Southam and Gordon Lambert banded 359 young at Tiny Is. Georgian Bay on June 18, 1939 and 1300 there on June 23, 1940. Some of these had reached Prince Edward Co. by Aug. 15, Onondaga Lake, N.Y. by Aug. 25, with later recoveries in Pennsylvania, Virginia, South Carolina and Florida by late November. Two were recovered in Cuba, on Dec. 8, 1940 and June 9, 1941 (from the 1940 banding) and one in the Azores on Nov. 5, 1945 (Devitt, 1967: 81-82). One banded on the North Limestone Is. in Georgian Bay on June 22, 1968 was recovered at Miami, Florida on Jan. 27, 1971 (Mills, 1981: 64). Of 43 banded near Toronto from 1937 to 1969 and recovered out of

Ontario, most were recovered later to the east, from Quebec and Prince Edward Is. south to Florida, but 5 were taken in Ohio and one in Louisiana, no doubt following the Mississippi route. Of 77 banded elsewhere and recovered near Toronto from 1936 to 1970, 46 came from the west (Wisconsin and Michigan colonies) while only 31 came from banding areas to the southeast (27 from N.Y., 3 from Quebec and one from South Carolina). Alf. Bunker banded some at Weller's Bay, eastern Lake Ontario, from 1953 to 1956 and large numbers at the Bluff, Northumberland Co. from 1955 to 1970. Fifty were recovered in Florida as young in their first year, four as early as November and one lingering into May, with the peak of recoveries in December (16). Of 12 immatures (in their second year), one showed up in Florida in July and another in August and 4 were taken as late as the following March. Only six adults were recovered in Florida (one in Dec., two in Jan., two in Feb. and one in March). Other young of the year wandered as far afield as Cuba, Puerto Rica, Mexico, Brazil and one amazing one 50 km. SE of Cadiz, Spain (near the Strait of Gibraltar). Most of the young of the year recovered in late summer and early fall were found in N.Y. (one in July, 30 in Aug., 16 in Sept., 8 in Oct. and 3 as late as Nov.: two were taken on the return flight in March). Immatures (in their second year) were taken in N.Y. as follows: one in June, 3 in July, six in Aug., 1 in Sept. two in Oct. and 2 in Nov. and a returning bird in April. Adults taken in New York in fall were taken in July (2), Aug. (2) Sept. (4), Oct. (1) and returning birds in March (1) and May (2). Only two of this group were found in the Gulf states (one in Alabama in May and one in Louisiana in December. Some were recovered to the west in Ohio. Michigan and Wisconsin (mostly in late summer and fall) but the great majority went east to Quebec. New Brunswick and to all of the Atlantic coast states south to Florida. One banded on the Leslie St. Spit, Toronto, as a nestling on July 8, 1980 was recovered near the Ebro River near the southeast coast of Spain in January, 1981 (Toronto Bird Observatory Newsletter, 5:(1):2. March, 1982).

**MEASUREMENTS:**
*Length:* 18 to 20 ins.
(Godfrey, 1966: 180)
*Wingspread:* 46.5 to 50
ins. (Roberts, 1955: 589)
*Weight:* 14.65 to 19.25
oz. (Roberts, 1955: 589)

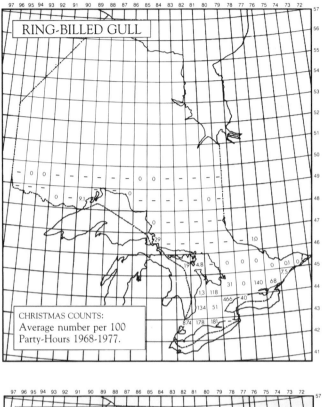

RING-BILLED GULL

CHRISTMAS COUNTS:
Average number per 100
Party-Hours 1968-1977.

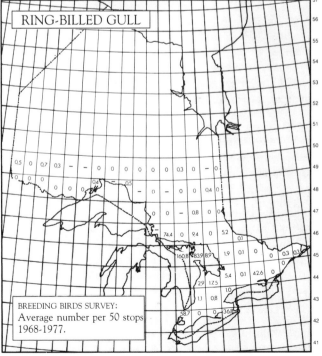

RING-BILLED GULL

BREEDING BIRDS SURVEY:
Average number per 50 stops
1968-1977.

# CALIFORNIA GULL   *Larus californicus*   Lawrence

Most California Gulls breed in prairie lakes east of the Rockies and winter along the Pacific coast south to Central America. They are accidental in Ontario.

**IDENTIFICATION:**   California Gulls are intermediate in size between Ring-billed and Herring Gulls. They have greenish-yellow legs like Ring-billed Gulls but lack the black ring around the bill. They have a red spot on the lower mandible, like Herring Gulls, but there is usually a black bar in front of this spot in California Gulls. They have dark eyes surrounded by a red eye ring, while Herring Gulls have yellow eyes.

**WINTER:**

**SPRING:**   Hans Blokpoel found a bird with a nest containing 2 eggs on the Leslie St. spit, Toronto, on May 14, 1981: the eggs did not hatch. On May 19, 1982 the bird was back again on a nest with one egg and J.E. Mason photographed the bird sitting on eggs on May 31, 1982 (James, 1984: 25).

**SUMMER:**

**AUTUMN:**

**MEASUREMENTS:**
*Length:* 20.5 to 23.0 ins.
(Godfrey, 1966: 180)
*Wingspread:* 48 to 54 ins.
(Terres, 1980: 458)
*Weight:* 101 averaged
609g. (486 to 775 g.)
(Dunning, 1984: 10).

# HERRING GULL   *Larus argentatus*   Pontoppidan

During the winter this is the most numerous gull in most parts of Ontario and it is the most widespread breeding gull, though the smaller Ring-billed Gull is much more common on the lower Great Lakes during the summer months.

**IDENTIFICATION:**   Adults differ from Ring-billed Gull adults in their larger size, pinkish legs (greenish-yellow in Ring-bills) and lack of black ring around the bill near the tip from which the Ring-bill gets its name. Note, however, that *immature* Herring Gulls do often have a black ring on the bill. Immature Herring Gulls differ from young Ring-bills in their larger size, and in having a broad dark band at the tip of the tail (young Ring-bills have a narrow, more contrasty band with a white tip). Young of the year in their first flight plumage are very similar except for size.

**WINTER:**   On Christmas counts, Herring Gulls have been abundant to common at all localities on the Great Lakes becoming rare to absent at inland localities. At Pelee, Stirrett (1973a: 16) had good numbers throughout the winter with a peak of 5000 on Dec. 30. Speirs (1976: 8) saw only one during the winter of 1954-55 at Pickering, while large numbers were seen almost daily during the winter of 1971-72: numbers generally peak in December, decline during the coldest part of the winter, and increase again in late February as the bays begin to open up. Quilliam (1973: 91) noted that the population at Kingston usually peaked in early December, with up to 4500 still present for Christmas counts but that most had departed by freezeup in mid-January. Mills (1981: 61-62) reported Christmas count records at Huntsville, Port Severn and Parry Sound with one at Fairy Lake on Feb. 22, 1975 and two at Skeleton Lake the same day. Nicholson (1981: 112) indicated that most have left Manitoulin by mid-December, but small numbers linger along the open waters of the south shore through the winter. Speirs & Speirs (1947: 29) saw two at North Bay as late as Dec. 7, 1944. Dennison (1981: 146) reported that this species had been found on all 25 Christmas counts at Sault Ste. Marie in numbers ranging from 2 to 396, averaging 83. Skeel & Bondrup-Nielsen (1978: 175) reported that this was usually the most numerous species found on Christmas counts at Marathon: they found 14 along the Pukaskwa coast on Jan. 10 and 41 on Feb. 19.

SPRING: Stirrett (1973b: 18) had a spring peak of 800 at Pelee on May 6. Saunders & Dale (1933: 198) gave May 25, 1925 as a very late date to see one migrating north over London. Speirs (1938: 44) gave Feb. 28 as the peak of the spring migration at Toronto. The peak of the spring flight at Pickering and Whitby is generally in the second week of March (Speirs, 1976: 8). Devitt (1967: 80) reported migrating flocks flying north over Simcoe Co. in late March and early April. Mills (1981: 61) gave March 10 as the 9-year average arrival date at Huntsville. Nicholson (1981: 112) noted that the southern influx at Manitoulin occurred from early March through April. MacLulich (1938: 16) gave arrival dates in Algonquin Park as Apr. 20, 1932; Apr. 14, 1933 and Apr. 10, 1934. Speirs & Speirs (1947: 29) noted one at North Bay as early as Mar. 16, 1945. Skeel & Bondrup-Nielsen (1978: 175) counted 2552 eggs in 900 nests along the Lake Superior shore of Pukaskwa on May 25-26, 1977. Denis (1961: 2) gave Mar. 19 as the average arrival date at Thunder Bay, with the earliest on Mar. 11, 1957. Dear (1940: 128) found a nest with 3 eggs near Thunder Cape on May 25, 1913 and another nest with 3 eggs at Thunder Bay on May 28, 1930. Elder (1979: 33) gave Apr. 13 as the earliest spring date for Geraldton. Peruniak (1971: 16) gave Mar. 21 as the earliest date for Atikokan: she considered it a common breeding bird there "subject to considerable predation by ravens and Bald Eagles". Cringan (1953a: 2) saw his first at Sioux Lookout on Mar. 29, 1953. Elsey gave May 6 as this 1950 arrival date in the Asheweig area (Cringan, 1950: 10). Manning (1952: 58) collected one on May 30, 1947 near Moosonee and saw 10 there on May 31.

SUMMER: On the 1968-1977 Breeding Bird Surveys, Herring Gulls were fairly common on routes in the Precambrian lake country but rare to absent in the farming districts of Ontario. Stirrett (1973c: 16) found them scarce at Pelee during June but returning birds gave him a count of 1000 on July 5 and 2000 by Aug. 17. Kelley (1978: 39) mentioned 15 occupied nests on Middle Sister Is. in Lake Erie on July 5, 1952; 40 nests on the Chicken Is. in 1954; two successful nests at Kettle Point, Lake Huron in 1968 and 3 newly-hatched young there on July 7, 1974. Beardslee & Mitchell (1965: 246-247) gave some history of the nestings on Mohawk Is., Lake Erie, from the discovery of two nests there in 1944 by Stanley Franklin to 13 nests on June 9, 1946: nests with eggs were found there from May 30 to June 26, 1949. Sheppard (1960: 25) reported seeing a downy young chick on a rock near the brink of Niagara Falls in a tern colony in the 1958 breeding season. Quilliam (1973: 90-91) documented the fortunes of Herring Gull colonies on

Pigeon and other islands near Kingston which showed increases into the 1960's when pesticides began to affect hatching success. Devitt (1967: 80) mentioned nesting colonies off Collingwood. Mills (1981: 61-62) reported several large nesting colonies in Georgian Bay and smaller ones in the interior lakes of Muskoka and Parry Sound. MacLulich (1938: 16) cited several nest records for Algonquin Park. Ricker & Clarke (1939: 11) reported eggs in Lake Nipissing-French River colonies from June 10 to June 30 and young from June 10 to July 11. Snyder (1942: 128-129) observed them regularly along the North Channel of Lake Huron with a large nesting colony off Thessalon. Baillie & Hope (1943: 10) reported nesting off Rossport and Peninsula, Lake Superior and Baillie & Hope (1947: 8) found them nesting in Wanapitei Lake, Sudbury. Snyder (1928: 18) found them nesting on a rocky island in the upper part of Lake Abitibi. Snyder (1928: 253) reported four nesting colonies on an island in Lake Nipigon from 1922 to 1924. Snyder (1953: 58-59) found summering birds throughout western Ontario with breeding colonies in northern Lake of the Woods and near Dryden. James (1980: 86) reported "As many as a dozen on a couple of large lakes" near Pickle Lake. Hope (1938: 20) found this species rare in the Favourable Lake region. Cringan (1953b:3) found two nests on June 4, 1953: one with 2 eggs and one with one egg, in the Kasabonika Lake region. Cringan (1950:10) reported 24 nests at Nikip Lake on June 25, 1950 (2 with eggs, 18 with 3 and 2 with 4): there were also smaller colonies on several nearby lakes. McLaren & McLaren (1981:3) found 10 nests on islets between North Caribou and Makoop lakes and 30 pairs in a small lake SE of Two River Lake. Lee (1978: 24) reported a small colony in Big Trout Lake in late July, 1975. Manning (1952: 47) saw this species at most localities visited from Moosonee north to Cape Henrietta Maria and west to Shagamu River on the Hudson Bay coast. Peck (1972: 344) found eight nests at Cape Henrietta Maria on June 25, 1970: he also reported other nests in the region found by other observers. Schueler, Baldwin & Rising (1974: 146) reported 5 nests along the Sutton River, one near Hawley Lake on June 23, 1962 and four near Winisk June 16-17, 1965. C.E. Hope observed from one to 75 near Ft. Severn from June 16 to July 23, 1940. Peck (1981:10) listed over 500 nest records for Ontario.

AUTUMN: Stirrett saw 10 at Attawapiskat as late as Oct. 10 and two at Ship Sands, near Moosonee on Oct. 2. (Manning, 1952: 47). Peruniak (1971: 16) gave Dec. 1 as the latest date for Atikokan. Speirs (1938: 52) gave Nov. 13 as the fall peak date for Toronto. Harold Axtell estimated 23,000 milling about Niagara Falls in November, 1958. Stirrett (1973d: 20) had a fall maximum of 4000 at Pelee on Sept. 1.

BANDING: Up to 1969 some 92 Herring Gulls banded in the U.S.A. were later recovered in the Toronto-Muskoka area: one from Minnesota, 14 from Wisconsin, 75 from Michigan, one from New York and one from Maine. Most of these were recovered in fall, some into December, 4 in January, one in February and 4 in April.

During the same period some 60 Herring Gulls were banded in the Toronto-Muskoka area and were recovered out of Ontario: 33 in Quebec, 3 in N.B., 2 in Newfoundland and one in P.E.I., one in Manitoba. Only 3 were taken in Michigan, the others going east and south to New York (5), Mass., Penna., N.J., Maryland, Delaware, Virginia (2), Florida (2). One went to Cuba.

**MEASUREMENTS:**
*Length:* 23 - 26 ins.
(Godfrey, 1966: 178)
*Wingspread:* 54 - 60 ins.
(Roberts, 1955: 588)
*Weight:* ♂ 2 lbs. 10 oz - 2
lbs. 12 oz. ♀ 2 lb. 5 oz.
(Roberts, 1955: 588).

**REFERENCE:**
Weseloh, D.V.; P. Mineau
and D.J. Hallet 1979
Organochlorine
contaminants and trends in
reproduction in Great
Lakes Herring Gulls, 1974-
1978. Trans. 44th North
American Wildl. and Nat.
Res. Conf.: 543-557.

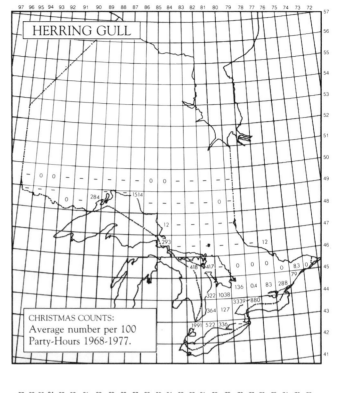

HERRING GULL

CHRISTMAS COUNTS:
Average number per 100
Party-Hours 1968-1977.

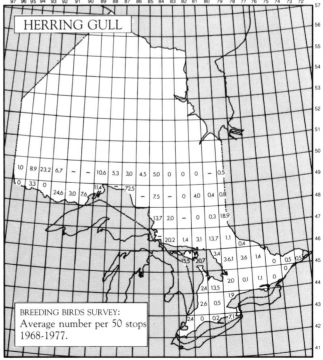

HERRING GULL

BREEDING BIRDS SURVEY:
Average number per 50 stops
1968-1977.

# THAYER'S GULL   *Larus thayeri*   Brooks

Formerly considered a race of the Herring Gull, this Arctic breeder is seldom identified in Ontario. Most winter on the B.C. coast.

IDENTIFICATION: Adults differ from Herring Gulls in having dark eyes (yellow in Herring Gulls) and have reddish or purplish eye rings (yellow in Herring Gulls). They also have more white in the wing tips and often have some gray in the feathers near the tips, where the Herring Gulls have black. Immatures may look intermediate between young of Herring Gull and Iceland Gull, some with quite pale wing tips.

WINTER:   Individuals have been reported on Christmas counts at Niagara Falls, Hamilton and Ottawa. Dennis Rupert gave a good description of one seen on Jan. 2, 1971 on the St. Clair River (Goodwin, 1971: 572) and saw two there up to Jan. 11, 1979 (Goodwin, 1979: 277). A well described Thayer's Gull was seen at Erieau by P.D. Pratt and C.A. Campbell on Dec. 8, 1974 (Goodwin, 1975: 685). Andrle (1969: 107) observed at least six possible Thayer's Gulls in the lower Niagara River, and with A.R. Clark collected three females, one on Dec. 11 and two on Dec. 17, 1967: he mentioned that R.D. Coggeshall had seen three at Niagara Falls in Dec., 1954 and Jan., 1955. Goodwin (1976: 713) mentioned that an adult was seen at Toronto during the winter of 1975-1976 by John Lamey and Don Perks. Goodwin (1974: 634) also mentioned that one had been seen at Ottawa during the winter of 1973-1974.

SPRING:

SUMMER:

AUTUMN:   Alan Wormington reported individuals at Netitishi Point, southern James Bay on Oct. 15 and 21 and Nov. 22, 1981 and one at Marathon, Lake Superior, on Oct. 10, 1980. R.J. Pittaway noted one at Dwight on Nov. 10, 1980 (Goodwin, 1981: 177). R.A. Foxall, R. Pittaway and R. Poulin identified in the field five first year birds at Ottawa between Oct. 3 and Nov. 22, 1974 (subsequently collected and identification confirmed): see photo by Tom Hince in Goodwin (1975: 51). Eleven were collected at Ottawa in the fall of 1975 (Goodwin, 1976: 61). Ottawa had 10 fall Thayer's gulls in 1976 from an early one on Sept. 7 (Goodwin, 1977: 171). Doug. McRae and A.G. Carpentier saw one at Peterborough on Nov. 27, 1978 (*fide* Ross James).

**MEASUREMENTS:**
*Length:* 22.5 to 25.0 ins.
(Godfrey, 1966: 179)
Wingspread:
*Weight:* ♂ 2 lbs. 4 1/2 oz.
to 2 lbs. 6 oz. (Terres,
1980: 464) ♀ 1 lb. 12 3/4
oz. to 2 lbs. 2 1/2 oz.
(Terres, 1980: 464).

**REFERENCES:**
Andrle, Robert F. 1969 "Thayer's" Gull in the Niagara Frontier Region. Auk. 86:(1): 106-109.

Lehman, Paul 1980 The identification of Thayer's Gull in the field. Birding, 12: (6): 198-210.

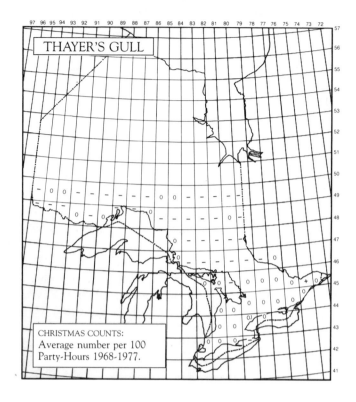

THAYER'S GULL

CHRISTMAS COUNTS:
Average number per 100
Party-Hours 1968-1977.

# ICELAND GULL   *Larus glaucoides*   Meyer

This is an Arctic breeder from south Baffin Is. east to Iceland where in, spite of its name, it is considered rare. It winters mainly along both coasts of the North Atlantic. In Ontario it has usually been considered a rare find. I have encountered it most frequently in late February and early March.

IDENTIFICATION:   The Iceland Gull is about the size of a Herring Gull, or slightly smaller, with short legs and long wings tipped with white. In the *kumlieni* race the white wing tips have some gray splotches. Breeding adults have a narrow red eye ring (yellowish in Glaucous Gull). For other distinctions from the larger Glaucous Gull see the account of that species.

WINTER:   On Christmas counts a few have shown up as far north as Ottawa and Sault Ste. Marie, but most sightings have been at localities near the Lake Ontario shores. Fred Bodsworth found one at Port Burwell on Dec. 30, 1948 (Brooman, 1954: 21). Fleming (1906: 442) had just one Toronto record, an immature female taken on Dec. 12, 1898, in the collection of J.H. Ames. Speirs (1938: 48) gave Dec. 2 as the earliest Toronto arrival date. Speirs (1976: 5) detailed several winter reports from the Lake Ontario shores from Frenchman Bay to Whitby Harbour: both good places to look for this species. Tozer & Richards (1974: 143) pointed out that this species was tallied only once in 19 Christmas counts in the Oshawa region (and that at Bowmanville on Dec. 28, 1969). Weir & Quilliam (1980: 35) gave Dec. 16 as the 19-year average arrival date at Kingston. A.J. Mitchener had two Collingwood sightings on Dec. 28, 1959 and in January, 1956 (Devitt, 1967: 80). Craig Campbell had several Parry Sound sightings between Dec. 23 and Jan. 9 (1966 to 1975): these included both races (Mills, 1981: 61). Nicholson (1981: 112) reported immature birds at the Little Current dump on Dec. 13, 1970 and from Jan. 2 to 8, 1972; and one at the Gore Bay dump on Dec. 20, 1970. Speirs & Speirs (1947: 28) observed one immature at the North Bay dump on Dec. 23, 1944. Dennison (1980: 149) reported one during the 1973 Christmas count period at Sault Ste. Marie. Denis (1961: 7) noted that there was an acceptable record for Thunder Bay (but gave no details).

SPRING:   Stirrett (1973b: 18) had two Pelee records: on May 5, 1968 and from May 9 to 13, 1962. W.E. Saunders observed one at Port Stanley on March 22, 1931 (Brooman, 1954: 21). Speirs (1938: 46) gave Apr. 5 as the latest Toronto sighting but J.L. Baillie noted one as late as May 23 (Saunders 1947: 365). Don Perks saw one at Whitby as late as May 27, 1958 (Speirs, 1976: 5). George A. Scott spotted one at Oshawa Harbour on May 21, 1961 (Tozer & Richards, 1974: 143). Weir & Quilliam (1980: 35) gave Apr. 13 as the 15-year average departure date from Kingston, with the latest on May 30. On Apr. 8, 1898, A. Kay collected an immature female *kumlieni* at Port Sydney, Muskoka (Mills, 1981: 61). Nicholson (1981: 111-112) saw one at Mississagi Light on Apr. 18, 1976 and reported one seen by Ron Tasker flying over Lake Huron toward Manitoulin on May 16, 1970.

SUMMER:   Kelley (1978: 38) had a Kettle Point record on June 8, 1969. Saunders (1947: 365) reported an Aug. 31 record for Toronto. Weir & Quilliam (1980: 35) listed a July 19 record for Kingston. R. and H. Simpson saw an immature near Parry Sound on June 28, 1973 (Mills, 1981: 61). Peck (1972: 344) wrote that the "remains of an Iceland Gull were collected on August 17, 1968" near Cape Henrietta Maria. James, McLaren &

Barlow (1976: 26) reported summer sightings on June 19, July 13 and Aug. 26, without details.

AUTUMN:   Weir & Quilliam (1980: 35) gave Nov. 10, as the earliest arrival date for Kingston. David O'Brien reported one at Frenchman Bay on Nov. 1, 1975 (Speirs 1976: 5). Beardslee & Mitchell (1965: 243-244) cited one seen at Yacht Harbour, Lake Erie, on Oct. 6, 1957.

**MEASUREMENTS:**
*Length:* 23 - 26 ins.
(Terres, 1980: 460)
*Wingspread:* about 50 ins.
(Terres, 1980: 460). 55
ins. (Pough, 1951: 265)
*Weight:* One weighed
557 g. (Dunning,
1984: 10)

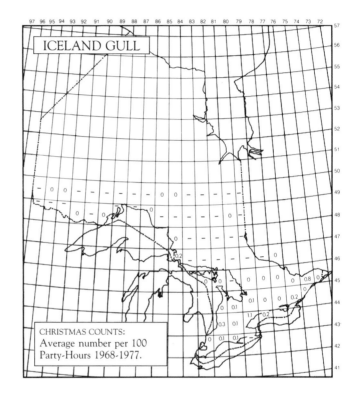

ICELAND GULL

CHRISTMAS COUNTS:
Average number per 100
Party-Hours 1968-1977.

# LESSER BLACK-BACKED GULL   *Larus fuscus*   Linnaeus

My experience with this beautiful gull has been largely in northern Europe, where it is commonly noted following ships and patrolling harbours.

IDENTIFICATION: Except for its yellow legs it is coloured much like the Great Black-backed Gull, but it is normally much smaller (about the size of a Herring Gull). In flight its more slender wings give it a more buoyant flight than the ponderous, big, pink-footed Great Black-backed Gull.

WINTER: One was seen along the Niagara River on Dec. 3, 1977 by Harold Axtell, Martin Parker and Alan Wormington (Goodwin, 1978: 344). Sightings were reported at St. Davids on Dec. 27, 1972 by R.F. Andrle and A. Clark and in Vaughan Twp. on Dec. 9, 1972 by Gerry Bennett (Goodwin, 1973: 609). Goodwin (1981: 296) saw one at Bronte on Jan. 31, 1981 and suggested that the one noted by Gerry Bennett and Don Perks at Port Credit in mid-January was probably a different bird.

SPRING: Gerry Bennett reported one at Bronte on March 22, 1980 (Goodwin, 1980: 772). J.A. Kelley saw one at Mimico between March 1-4, 1979 (Goodwin, 1979: 766).

SUMMER:

AUTUMN: M. Gawn *et al* noted one at Ottawa beginning Oct. 20, 1979 (Goodwin, 1980: 157) and four were reported there from Oct. 25 to Nov. 29, 1980 (Goodwin, 1981: 177). R. John et al reported one in the Cobourg area on Oct. 28, 1972 and there were other sightings west to Oakville that fall (Goodwin, 1973: 53). D.V. Weseloh saw one at the Whitby dump on Nov. 2, 1972 (Tozer & Richards, 1974: 144). C. Wood found one at Hamilton from Nov. 20-21, 1971 and the slides by P.M. Benham "authenticated the species for the Province" (Goodwin, 1972: 598). One was seen at Dundas from Oct. 25, 1978 to Nov. 11 by Alan Wormington *et al* (Goodwin, 1979: 173). P.D. Pratt and D.F. Brunton observed one at Niagara Falls on Nov. 11, 1973 (Tozer & Richards, 1974: 144). Goodwin (1977: 171) reported at least two, an adult and a first-year immature, along the Niagara River during October and November, 1976. One was seen along the Niagara River from Nov. 3 to 20, 1977 by R.F. Andrle *et al* (Goodwin, 1978: 198), and appeared the following year from Oct. 22 (Goodwin, 1979: 173), and again in Nov. 1979 (Goodwin, 1980: 157). H.H. Axtell reported two at Queenston Nov. 10 and 30, 1980 (Goodwin, 1981: 177), who also cited reportes at Port Stanley by Wm. Girling on Sept. 20 and at St. Clair River on Nov. 11 by Dennis Rupert.

**MEASUREMENTS:**
*Length:* 23 ins. (Pough, 1951: 267)
Wingspread:
*Weight:* 22 ♂ averaged 880 g. (770 to 1000 g.) (Dunning, 1984: 11). 31 ♀ averaged 755 g. (620 to 908 g.)

# GLAUCOUS GULL  *Larus hyperboreus*  Gunnerus

The Glaucous Gull is a circumpolar Arctic breeder, wintering chiefly on the Atlantic and Pacific coasts. Some may be found wintering with Herring and other gulls in Ontario and often going with them to feed at garbage dumps, returning to sheltered bays and breakwaters to rest.

IDENTIFICATION: Glaucous Gulls are large, mainly white gulls, with long, heavy bills. Because of their long legs they usually tower above associated Herring Gulls when standing but if not standing a telescope may be needed to pick out their white wing tips in a flock of Herring Gulls. The similar Iceland Gull has shorter legs and longer wings which protrude well beyond the tip of the tail. Both species have a creamy brown, barred, first year plumage, but most of the bill is black in Iceland gulls in this plumage, while only the tip is black in Glaucous Gulls. In the almost pure white second-year plumage the short legs and long wings of the Iceland Gull help to separate it from the long-legged, relatively short, broad wings of the Glaucous Gull. Adults of both have bluish-gray mantles, paler than in Herring Gulls, and again the leg and wings are the best means of separating the two species.

WINTER: On Christmas counts, Glaucous Gulls have been farily common at Marathon and Wawa, usually uncommon to rare at other localities bordering the Great Lakes, the St. Lawrence and Ottawa rivers. Saunders & Dale (1933: 198) had one record for Middlesex Co., a second year female shot by Will Elson on Feb. 1, 1901 near Hyde Park. A.R. Muma found one above Niagara Falls on Dec. 22, 1949 (Sheppard, 1960: 24). Fleming (1906: 442) called it a regular winter resident at Toronto from Dec. 23 to March 25. Speirs (1938: 44) gave Feb. 23 as the peak date for Toronto. They showed up on about half of the Christmas counts at both Pickering and Oshawa (Speirs, 1976: 4). Quilliam (1973: 89) noted that Kingston had the highest count (34) of Glaucous Gulls on the continent on the 1965 Christmas count, as it did on a few other counts about that time, but that numbers have decreased with better dump management. Devitt (1967: 79) had very few Simcoe Co. records (and these mainly at Barrie and Collingwood between Dec. 15 and Jan. 4). C. Campbell reported them at Parry Sound during winters from 1966 to 1974 with 18 there in December, 1974 (Mills, 1981: 60). Nicholson (1981: 171) reported five on Manitoulin on Dec. 20, 1970 and one as late as Jan. 8 in 1972. Dennison (1980: 149) had records during the Christmas count period for five of 25 years at Sault Ste. Marie, with a maximum of six in 1973. From two to 20 were tallied on the Marathon Christmas counts on each of the five counts held there (Skeel & Bondrup-Nielsen, 1978: 174). Elder (1979: 33) considered it an uncommon winter resident along the Lake Superior shore between Marathon and Terrace Bay, while Denis (1961: 6) found it to be an irregular, rare winter visitant at Thunder Bay.

SPRING: Stirrett (1973b: 18) had a few "vagrants" at Pelee between March 28 and May 21. W.E. Saunders *et al* identified one at Port Stanley on March 22, 1931 (Brooman, 1954: 21). Beardslee & Mitchell (1965: 243) reported one at Point Abino, Lake Erie, as late as May 27, 1945. A.R. Muma retrieved a Niagara Falls casualty on Apr. 14, 1949 (Sheppard, 1960: 24). A second year (all white) bird was shot at Toronto on March 25, 1889, and sent to W. Cross (Thompson, 1890: 190). Fleming (1906: 442) mentioned an immature male (all white) taken by John Maughan, Jr. at Toronto on May 4, 1893.

Saunders (1947: 365) gave Apr. 6 as the average departure date from Toronto. Weir & Quilliam (1980: 35) gave May 3 as the 28-year average departure date from Kingston and Quilliam (1965: 88) reported 100 there on Apr. 16, 1960. Lloyd (1923: 103) had a few Ottawa records between Apr. 10 and May 27. Lloyd Beamer and Howard Krug saw three just west of Collingwood on March 17, 1957. Nicholson (1981: 111) had seven Manitoulin records from March 27 (1976) to May 15 (1978). Speirs & Speirs (1947: 28) noted single birds at North Bay on Apr. 16 and Apr. 21, 1944. Ricker & Clarke (1939: 10) saw one near Lake Nipissing from Oct. 2-4, 1924. W. Wyett noted one at Pukaskwa on Apr. 3, 1975 and N.G. Escott saw 17 at Marathon on March 31, 1976 (Skeel & Bondrup-Nielsen, 1978: 174).

SUMMER: Stirrett (1973c: 16) had one at Pelee on June 22, 1933. Saunders (1947: 365) had a June 10 record for Toronto. George A. Scott saw a first year bird at Oshawa's Second Marsh on June 3, 1974 (Speirs, 1976: 4). Weir & Quilliam (1980: 35) had a June 17 and an Aug. 22, 1969 record for Kingston. Peck (1972: 344) reported that single birds were seen at Cape Henrietta Maria on July 3 and Aug. 17 by the 1948 ROM party.

AUTUMN: Speirs & Speirs (1947: 28) noted one on Nov. 10 and two on Nov. 12 1944, at the North Bay wharf. R. Rutter saw one at the Huntsville dump during November, 1964 (Mills, 1981: 60). Weir & Quilliam (1980: 35) gave Nov. 21 as the 30-year average arrival date at Kingston. A.A. Wood spotted one at Oshawa Harbour as early as Sept. 29, 1960 (Tozer & Richards, 1974: 142). Speirs (1938: 48) gave Sept. 26 as the earliest fall date for Toronto. John Townson saw one at Long Point on Oct. 23, 1927 (Snyder, 1931: 148). Kelley (1978: 38) gave Sept. 29, 1974 as an early record for Pelee.

**MEASUREMENTS:**
*Length:* 26 to 32 ins.
(Terres, 1980: 459)
*Wingspread:* 60 to 66 ins.
(Terres, 1980: 459)
*Weight:* 5 lbs. (Terres, 1980: 459)

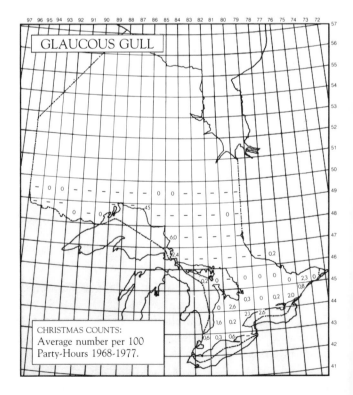

GLAUCOUS GULL

CHRISTMAS COUNTS:
Average number per 100
Party-Hours 1968-1977.

# GREAT BLACK-BACKED GULL   *Lanus marinus*   Linneaus

This handsome, big gull is a common breeder along the coasts of the Atlantic Provinces but is rather scarce in summer in Ontario. However, increasing numbers have been wintering around the Great Lakes in recent years and some lingering well into spring and a few have been found breeding.

IDENTIFICATION: Adults, with their great size, and jet black backs contrasting with snowy white head, tail and underparts, are distinctive. Immatures look a bit like similar-aged Herring Gulls but have whiter heads, massive black bills and a general "nattily dressed in checks" appearance, unlike the more sombre brownish appearance of young Herring Gulls. I have not seen recently fledged birds in Ontario, but in Maine those that I saw looked like recently fledged Herring Gulls, but "carried more sail", had more impressive beaks and, like their parents, had a more ponderous, deliberate flight than young Herring Gulls.

WINTER: On Christmas counts the Great Black-backed Gull has been fairly common from Pelee to the Thousand Islands, becoming rare north to Ottawa and Wiarton. Stirrett (1973a: 16) had records for Pelee throughout the winter, with a maximum of 20 on Dec. 23. Brooman (1954: 21) saw four or five among several hundred Herring Gulls at Port Stanley on Dec. 12, 1948. Maughan (1897: 2) took a male 8 miles out from Toronto "on an island in Lake Ontario" on Feb.8, 1894 and Thompson, (1890: 188) reported another male taken on Lake Ontario between Feb. 5 and 19, 1889 (L. 2 ft 7ins., WS 4 ft 7 ins.; wt. 4 1/2 lbs.). Speirs (1976: 6) noted a maximum of 35 on the 1974 Pickering Christmas count. Quilliam (1973: 89) gave 155 as the maximum count for Kingston on the Dec. 27, 1953 count. E.L. Brereton saw one at Barrie on Jan. 3, 1949 (Devitt, 1967: 80). Lloyd Beamer reported one on the Meaford Christmas count on Dec. 27, 1943 and one in the harbour there on Jan. 3, 1947.

SPRING: Stirrett (1973b: 18) had a few vagrants lingering at Pelee to May 24. Wm. Girling saw six at Port Stanley on March 21, 1937 (Brooman, 1954: 21). Beardslee & Mitchell (1965: 245) reported one at Rose's Point, Lake Erie as late as May 24, 1941. Fleming (1906: 442) gave May 26, 1897 as the latest Toronto date. Speirs (1976: 6) noted two at Whitby as late as May 31, 1972. Weir & Quilliam (1980: 35) gave Apr. 21 as the 26-year average departure date from Kingston. P. Harrington saw one at Wasaga Beach on Apr. 17, 1949 (Devitt, 1967: 80). Lloyd (1923: 103) reported sightings near Ottawa on May 2, 1885 and Apr. 9, 1906. Ron Tasker saw one in Burpee Twp., Manitoulin, on Apr. 23, 1972 and John Lemon watched one at Little Current on Apr. 13, 1972 (Nicholson, 1981: 112).

SUMMER: On the 1968-1977 Breeding Bird Surveys, this species was noted only at Silver Islet, in 1972 (one of the very few Lake Superior records). Stirrett (1973c: 16) had one summer record for Pelee: 2 seen on July 28, 1957. Beardslee & Mitchell (1965: 245) reported the 12 seen at Point Abino, Lake Erie, on July 26, 1958, as the maximum summer count near Buffalo. Speirs (1938: 46) had June 16 and Aug. 10 summer records for Toronto and Saunders (1947: 365) listed a July 30 Toronto date. Speirs (1976: 6) cited several summer sightings from the Lake Ontario shores of Ontario Co. Alf. Bunker and Gordon Lambert found a nest with 3 eggs at Presqu'ile on June 24, 1962, the first Lake Ontario nesting (Woodford, 1962: 474). Quilliam (1973: 90) mentioned a nest with 2 eggs on

Pigeon Is. as the first nesting for the Kingston region: Goodwin (1971: 853) gave the date of this find as June 1, 1971. Krug (1956: 559) banded two flightless young on Little Haystack Is. (about 15 mi. west of Wiarton in Lake Huron) on July 1, 1954 and another flightless young there on July 10 when three adults were seen, one scolding the banders: this was the first breeding record for Ontario. Snyder (1941: 55) cited summer records by E. Beaupré at Scotch Bonnet Is., Lake Ontario on June 7, 1927 and at Green Is. on July 6, 1927, but remarked that these were undoubtedly nonbreeding birds. Todd (1963: 375) considered this species absent from Hudson Bay, but an adult was reported by the 1948 ROM party at Cape Henrietta Maria on Aug. 14 (Peck, 1972: 345) and H. Lumsden has noted it at Attawapiskat and at Winisk (James, McLaren & Barlow, 1976: 26).

AUTUMN: Nicholson (1981: 112) had two fall records for Manitoulin: Nov. 19, 1972 and Sept. 24, 1979. Donald Sutherland saw an immature at Honey Harbour on Oct. 6, 1976 and a subadult there on Nov. 2, 1976 (Mills, 1981: 61). Krug (1956: 559) saw an immature at Wiarton on Nov. 28, 1954 (presumably one of the birds he had banded 15 miles to the west on July 1 or 10, 1954). R.M. Saunders saw two at Cook's Bay, Lake Simcoe, on Nov. 25, 1944 and A.J. Mitchener noted one at Collingwood on Nov. 20, 1964 (Devitt, 1967: 80). Weir & Quilliam (1980: 35) gave Sept. 7 as the 27-year average for fall arrivals at Kingston. Speirs (1976: 6) noted peak numbers during November along the Pickering-Oshawa waterfront. Fleming (1906: 442) gave Sept. 18, 1896, as the earliest Toronto date. Ussher (1965: 13) gave Oct. 18 as the earliest fall arrival date for Rondeau, with Nov. 17 as the 6-year average. Stirrett (1973d: 20) gave Oct. 1 as the earliest fall date for Pelee.

BANDING: A flightless young banded at Pilgrim Is., Kamouraska Co., Que. on July 6, 1952 by Alf. Bunker was recovered at Hamilton Beach on Dec. 22, 1952.

**MEASUREMENTS:**
Length: 28 to 31 ins.
(Godfrey, 1966: 176) 30 ins. (Maughan, 1897: 2)
Wingspread: 65 ins.
(Pough, 1951: 266) 69.5 ins. (Maughan, 1897: 2)
Weight: 4 1/2 lbs.
(Thompson, 1890: 188)

**REFERENCES:**
Angehrn, P.A.; M.H. Blokpoel and P.A. Courtney 1979 A review of the status of the Great Black-backed Gull in the Great Lakes area. Ont. Field Biologist, 33: (2): 27-33.
Krug, Howard H. 1956 Great Black-backed Gulls nesting on Little Haystack Island, Lake Huron, Auk. 73:(4):559.

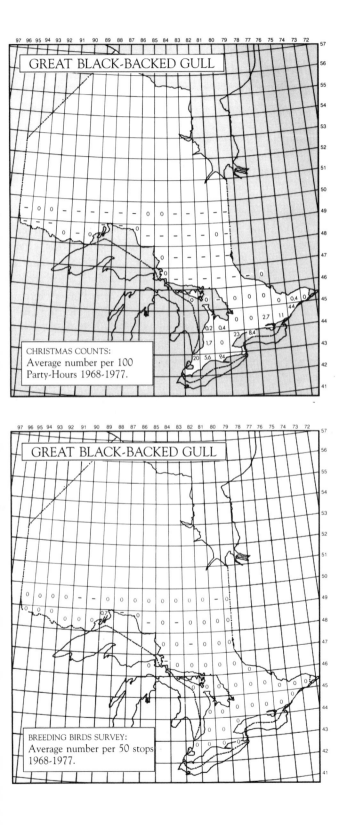

GREAT BLACK-BACKED GULL

CHRISTMAS COUNTS:
Average number per 100
Party-Hours 1968-1977.

GREAT BLACK-BACKED GULL

BREEDING BIRDS SURVEY:
Average number per 50 stops
1968-1977.

# HYBRIDS HERRING GULL X GREAT BLACK-BACKED GULL
## Larus argentatus × Larus marinus

Gulls with characters intermediate between those of Herring Gulls and those of Great Black-backed Gulls have been collected and sighted along the Niagara River, at Kingston and at Ottawa in recent years, since the advent of the Great Black-backed Gull as a breeding bird in Ontario. Foxall (1979: 838) has summarized these occurrences and out-lined some of the identification problems which have arisen.

IDENTIFICATION: The presumed hybrids have measurements intermediate between those of Herring Gulls (which are smaller) and the Great Black-backed (which are larger). Mantle colour was also intermediate, but dark enough to be confused with either Great Black-backed or Lesser Black-backed when in flight. The amount of dark streaking on the head was also intermediate (less than in typical Herring Gulls and more than in typical Great Black-backs). Typical Lesser Black-backs have a more slender bill than a Herring Gull, while the hybrids had a heavier bill. The hybrids were also larger than Herring Gulls (Lessers are generally the same size or smaller), had a paler mantle than typical Lessers and most had yellow eye rings (red in Lessers).

WINTER: Andrle (1972: 669-671) collected a probable hybrid about 2.5 km. up-stream from Queenston on Dec. 5, 1970, a female with measurements and colour inter-mediate between Herring Gull and Great-backed Gull. Godfrey (1973: 171-172) described one in the collection of the National Museum, Ottawa, which was taken at Kingston on Jan. 12, 1967 after observations by Fred Cooke and Eric L. Mills.

SPRING:

SUMMER:

AUTUMN: Godfrey 1973: 171-172) reported a sight record of a hybrid at Nepean Bay, Ottawa, on Nov. 23, 1972, of a bird carefully observed at close range by telescope by Roger A. Foxall and Ronald Pittaway. Roger Foxall observed a hybrid at Ottawa on Sept. 25, 1974 and saw a second one from Nov. 16 to 26 (Goodwin, 1975: 50). A hybrid was recorded at Ottawa from Nov. 22-29, 1975 by Roger Foxall and Bruce DiLabio (Goodwin, 1976: 61). R.M. Poulin noted a hybrid at Ottawa on Nov. 15, 1976 (Goodwin, 1977: 171). The bird collected by Andrle on Dec. 5, 1970 was first spotted by Arthur R. Clark et al on Nov. 22, 1970 at the place where it was eventually collected. Andrle (1973: 170) collected a similar hybrid at the same location upstream from Queenston on the Niagara River, on Nov. 22, 1971, after finding it there the previous day with Arthur R. Clark.

REFERENCES:
Andrle, Robert F. 1972 Another probable hybrid of Larus marinus and L. argentatus. Auk, 89: (3): 669-671.
Andrle, Robert F. 1973 A second probable hybrid of Larus marinus and L. argentatus on the Niagara River. Can. Field-Nat., 87:(2): 170-171.
Foxall, Roger A. 1979 Presumed hybrids of the Herring Gull and Great Black-backed Gull - a new problem of identification.
Am. Birds, 33:(6): 838.
Godfrey, W. Earl 1973 More presumed hybrid gulls: Larus argentatus x L. marinus. Can. Field-Nat., 87: (2): 171-172.

# BLACK-LEGGED KITTIWAKE   *Rissa tridactyla*   (Linnaeus)

Kittiwakes breed on cliffs along Canada's east coast from Percé, Que. north to the Arctic Islands. Unlike most so-called "sea gulls" which seldom stray far from the coasts, kittiwakes wander far out to sea and sometimes wander inland. In Ontario it is a rare bird.

IDENTIFICATION:   Adults are distinguished from other gulls with blue-gray mantle and yellow bills, by their black legs and black wing-tips with no white spots. They are also somewhat smaller than Ring-billed Gulls. Immatures have a dark W-pattern on the upper surface, a dark ear patch and a diagnostic black bar across the hind neck. The white tail has a black tip and may appear slightly forked (not distinctly forked as in Sabine's Gull). They lack the white flash in the leading edge of the wing as in young Bonaparte's and the white wedge on the trailing edge as in Sabine's Gull.

WINTER:   On Christmas counts, they have shown up at Hamilton in 1972 and 1975 and at Kettle Point in 1971. Dennis Rupert saw two at Sarnia on Dec. 9, 1978 (Goodwin, 1979: 278) and one there on Dec. 14, 1980 (Goodwin, 1981: 296). Several observers noted one at the Niagara Gorge from Dec. 24-26, 1955 (Beardslee & Mitchell, 1965: 257) and R.F. Andrle *et al* saw one there until Dec. 30, 1973 (Goodwin, 1974: 634). K. McLaughlin and P. Walker saw one at Hamilton on Jan. 2, 1976, probably the one seen there on the Christmas count on Dec. 26, 1975 (Goodwin, 1977: 327). Saunders (1947: 366) listed a Jan. 8 sighting for Toronto. Naomi LeVay saw an adult in flight over Eastbourne, Whitby, on Dec. 30, 1961 and another was seen there on Feb. 23, 1975 by Bruce Falls and Ronald Tasker (Speirs, 1976: 17). On Feb. 3, 1956 a dead kittiwake was found by a schoolgirl in Kingston and later made into a study skin by G.M. Stirrett (Quilliam, 1973: 94).

SPRING:   P.A. Woodliffe reported one at Rondeau on Apr. 3, 1979 (Goodwin, 1979: 766). M. Jennings and A. Wormington noted one at Long Point on Apr. 24, 1975 (Goodwin, 1975: 846). J. Satterly and Wm. Smith saw one at Niagara Gorge on Mar. 5, 1950 (Beardslee & Mitchell, 1965: 256). Wm. Cross, taxidermist, received two specimens at Toronto on Mar. 25, 1889 (Thompson, 1890: 190). Speirs (1938: 40) had a Mar. 28 date for Toronto. An adult was seen at Whitby Harbour on May 24, 1964 by George A. Scott *et al* and R. Charles Long found one at Pickering Beach on May 29, 1969 (Speirs, 1976: 17). An immature was reported at Providence Bay, Manitoulin on May 13, 1972 by D. Ferguson (Nicholson, 1981: 114).

SUMMER:   R. Curry noted one at Hamilton on Aug. 29, 1978 (Goodwin, 1979: 173). D. Ruch reported one at Whitby on June 7, 1980 (Goodwin, 1980: 891). S. Findlay reported one at Morrisburg on July 7, 1976 (Goodwin, 1976: 950).

AUTUMN:   D. McRae and A. Wormington noted single birds at Netitishi Point, James Bay on Nov. 6 and 21, 1981 and two there on Nov. 19. R.K. Edwards *et al* saw one from the Wolfe Is. ferry on Oct. 4, 1970 (Quilliam, 1973: 94). Weir & Quilliam (1980: 15) reported one at La Salle Causeway, Kingston, on Nov. 9, 1976 and one at Prince Edward Point on Nov. 6, 1977. Tozer & Richards (1974: 151) reported two found dead at Darlington Provincial Park: one on Sept. 13, 1967 and the other on Sept. 21, 1969. Freya and Sylvia Hahn found one dead at Eastbourne, Whitby, on Sept. 15, 1966 and D. Mann brought a dying immature to R. Charles Long at Pickering Beach on Nov. 26, 1965 (Speirs, 1976: 17). Fleming (1906: 442) wrote that several immatures were taken at Toronto from Oct. 31 into November, 1889. Speirs (1938: 48) had a Sept. 25 date for Toronto and R.H. Westmore saw one there on Sept. 4, 1971 (Goodwin, 1972: 57). R. Curry *et al* saw three at Clarkson on Nov. 6, 1972 (Goodwin, 1973:52). One was seen at Hamilton on Nov. 14, 1971 by R. Curry and two there on Nov. 22 by G.W. North and A. Wormington (Goodwin, 1972: 57): a boat trip off Hamilton on Nov. 4, 1972 yielded one (Goodwin, 1973: 52): H. & P. van Dyken saw one at Hamilton on Nov. 4, 1979 (Goodwin, 1980: 157). There have been several sightings along the Niagara River in November: on Nov. 9, 1939, Mrs. T.M. Kelly and Mrs. Lloyd Mansfield saw an immature near Bridgeburg: an adult was watched at the Niagara Gorge on Nov. 23, 1952: an immature was seen near Frenchman's Creek on Nov. 30, 1952: and in the fall of 1959, two immatures were seen at Ft. Erie from Nov. 24-Nov. 30 (Beardslee & Mitchell, 1965: 256-257). More recently, W. Klabunde *et al* saw one on Nov. 28, 1971 at Niagara Falls (Goodwin, 1972: 57): R.F. Andrle had sightings along the Niagara River on Nov. 24, 1972 (Goodwin, 1973: 52) and one or two there from Nov. 4-23, 1980 (Goodwin, 1981: 177). H. Axtell *et al* saw one at Ft. Erie on Nov. 27 and 29, 1970 (Goodwin, 1971: 52). W.E. Saunders saw one at Pt. Stanley on Nov. 10, 1924 (Brooman, 1954: 21). In the fall of 1971 A. Rider found three at Kettle Point (Goodwin, 1972: 57): in the fall of 1976 he reported 13 there (Goodwin, 1977: 171) and in the fall of 1980 he noted five there (Goodwin, 1981: 177). D. Rupert had one at Sarnia on Nov. 25, 1978 (Goodwin, 1979: 173); six there from Nov. 3-10, 1979 (Goodwin, 1980: 157) and 28 between Oct. 20 and Nov. 22, 1980 (Goodwin, 1981: 177). B. Morin *et al* had up to three at Wheatley from Oct. 29 to Nov. 27, 1974 (Goodwin, 1975: 51). One was noted at Pelee on Oct. 21, 1978 by D. Rupert (Goodwin, 1979: 173).

**MEASUREMENTS:**
*Length:* 16-18 ins.
(Godfrey, 1966: 186)
*Wingspread:* 36 ins.
(Pough, 1951: 280)
*Weight:* 11 1/4 oz.
(Terres, 1980: 465)

**REFERENCE:**
Richards, James M. 1970
First specimen record of
Black-legged Kittiwake
(*Rissa tridactyla*) for
Durham County, Ontario.
Ont. Field Biol., 24: 37.

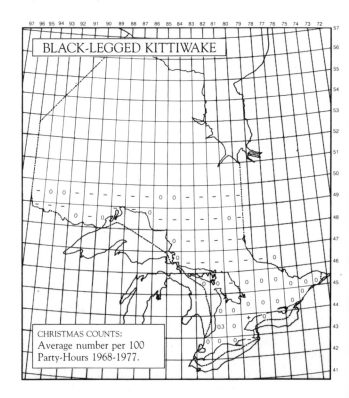

BLACK-LEGGED KITTIWAKE

CHRISTMAS COUNTS:
Average number per 100
Party-Hours 1968-1977.

# ROSS' GULL   *Rhodostethia rosea*   (MacGillivray)

With the recent nestings at Churchill, Man. (Chartier & Cooke, 1980: 839-841), interest in this normally high Arctic breeder has greatly increased. To date there have been just two Ontario records, but the Hudson Bay coast should be examined for this beautiful species.

IDENTIFICATION:   This is our only gull with a wedge-shaped tail. Adults with their rosy blush and thin black ring around the neck are unmistakable, though they lose these features in winter. Young resemble other small gulls but the wedge-shaped tail is diagnostic. Observers have remarked on its ternlike flight and its habit of nesting in Arctic Tern colonies, where they are protected from predators by the pugnacious terns.

WINTER:

SPRING:   Stirrett (1973b: 18) reported one at Pelee on May 24, 1957. Diana and Kenneth F. Abraham observed one at Moosonee from May 14-23, 1983: it was photographed there by A. Wormington on May 16.

SUMMER:

AUTUMN:

**MEASUREMENTS:**
*Length:* 12.5 – 14.0 ins.
(Godfrey, 1966: 187)
*Wingspread:*
*Weight:* 19 averaged
187 g. (170 to 210 g.)
(Dunning, 1984: 11).

**REFERENCE:**
Chartier, Bonnie and Fred Cooke 1980 Ross' Gulls (*Rhodostethia rosea*) nesting at Churchill, Manitoba, Canada. Am. Birds, 34: (6): 839-841.
The cover illustration of a bird on the nest and the nest with 2 eggs on p. 839 were by Robert R. Taylor. Note the black bill, dark eye, red legs and very long silvery wings. At least three pairs nested in June and July, 1980 at Churchill and again in 1981.

# SABINE'S GULL   *Xema sabini*   (Sabine)

Sabine's Gull is a high Arctic breeder usually migrating south along the Pacific coast to South America. In Ontario it has been rare, but most often seen near Hamilton or Sarnia, or on "pelagic" boat trips on the Great Lakes.

IDENTIFICATION:   This is our only gull with a distinctly forked tail. The wedge of white at the rear of the generally very dark wings is also distinctive in all plumages. Adults have a purplish-gray hood, narrowly bordered with black, a yellow-tipped black bill and black legs. Immatures have a black-tipped tail, brownish back and wing coverts, gray face and nape.

WINTER:   The Harold Axtells, Arthur Clark and Arthur Schaffner saw one at Ft. Erie until Dec. 3, 1959 (Beardslee & Mitchell, 1965: 258).

SPRING:   Stirrett (1973b: 18) had one spring record for Pelee on May 26, 1946.

SUMMER:   The 1948 ROM party collected one near Cape Henrietta Maria on July 19 (Peck, 1972: 344).

AUTUMN:   E. and H. Kerr saw two at the Wawa Sewage Lagoons on Sept. 4, 1975 (Goodwin, 1976: 61). One was photographed at Chelmsford and seen from Sept. 29 to Oct. 1, 1971 by J. Nicholson *et al* (Goodwin, 1972: 57). W.R. Lowe saw one at Lake Panache, Sudbury, on Sept. 12, 1972 (Goodwin, 1973: 53). Hector Bedard shot one midstream of the Ottawa River off Thurso, Que. on Sept. 25, 1933 and E.F.G. White identified the fresh mount (Lloyd, 1936: 144). Subsequent Ottawa sightings have been at Shirley's Bay from Sept. 18-21, 1974 by R.A. Foxall *et al* (Goodwin, 1975: 51); one on Sept. 7, 1975 by M. Brigham (Goodwin, 1976: 61); one on Oct. 6, 1976 by R. Gorham *et al* (Goodwin, 1977: 171) and one on Sept. 22, 1977 by B. DiLabio (Goodwin, 1978: 198). My only personal sighting was on Oct. 9, 1933 at Meaford, where an immature was fishing with a Common Tern for minnows in the harbour: I was impressed with its black-tipped forked tail and white wedge along the trailing edge of the wings. It uttered a high-pitched burry whistle and ternlike "krrr". R. Curry *et al* have spotted several in western Lake Ontario off Hamilton: four on Sept. 26, 1971 (Goodwin, 1972: 57): four or five on Sept. 22, 1974 (Goodwin, 1975: 51): one at Hamilton on Sept. 24 and one at Niagara on the Lake on Nov. 16, 1975 (Goodwin, 1976: 61) and one off Grimsby on Oct. 3, 1976 (Goodwin, 1977: 171). Beardslee & Mitchell (1965: 258) saw one at Ft. Erie on Oct. 3, 1937, found there earlier by Mrs. T.M. Kelly: another was seen by E.L. Seeber and Harold Axtell in the gorge at Niagara Falls on Sept. 30, 1958 and by many others on the following day: on Nov. 22, 1959 one was seen by B. Nathan *et al* at Ft. Erie. More recent sightings at Niagara have been by R.F. Andrle on Oct. 31, 1976 (Goodwin, 1977: 171) and by T.R. Scovell on Nov. 11, 1979 (Goodwin, 1980: 157). Dennis Rupert has had several recent sightings at Sarnia: one at Kettle Point on Oct. 22, 1976 (Goodwin, 1977: 171): two at Sarnia on Oct. 1, 1977 (Goodwin, 1978: 198): and in 1980, five on Sept. 26; one on Oct. 7 and two on Oct. 13 (Goodwin, 1981: 177). Brian Morin reported one at Pelee on Oct. 14 and 29, 1974 (Kelley, 1978: 40).

MEASUREMENTS:
*Length:* 13-14 ins.
(Godfrey, 1966: 187)

*Wingspread:* about 36 ins.
(Terres, 1980: 463)
*Weight:* ♂ 6 1/4 oz. ♀ 5
1/2 to 6 oz. (Terres,
1980: 463)

# IVORY GULL   *Pagophila eburnea*   (Phipps)

For most Ontario bird watchers this has been a once in a lifetime bird (if you were lucky). It breeds in the high Arctic. Ontario sightings have been few and generally in winter.

**IDENTIFICATION:**   The only one I have seen had a very pale blue-gray mantle (usually called pure white), with brown spots on the wing coverts and black tips to the primaries and tail feathers. It had a "dirty face" as do most immatures. I was impressed with its colourful bill; mostly purple-blue, but with a yellow-tip. Its legs were short and black. It flew strongly with shallow wing beats. Adults are "pure white", lacking the spots of the immatures with short black legs and with still a colourful bill, blue at the base, shading through green to yellow with small red tip.

**WINTER:**   The only one tallied on the 1968-1977 Christmas counts was seen at Oshawa on Jan. 3, 1971 by David Calvert and George A. Scott. Fred Bodsworth and Donald Young saw one that frequented the Port Burwell harbour from Dec. 28-31, 1948 (Brooman, 1954: 21). Another was observed at London from Dec. 19-27, 1973 by many observers (Goodwin, 1974: 634). Beardslee & Mitchell (1965: 255-256) reported one seen at Niagara Falls on Feb. 10, 1934 by W.C. Vaughan. Sheppard, Hurlburt & Dickson (1936: 131) reported another at Niagara Falls in Dec., 1924. M. Gustafson *et al* found one in Niagara Gorge on Dec. 22, 1980 (Goodwin, 1981: 296). Wm. Loane took an immature at Toronto on Dec. 25 (1887?) (Fleming, 1906: 442). McIllwraith (1894: 42) mentioned a "fine adult male" taken by fishermen on Lake Ontario (no date given). David Calvert found a second bird at Oshawa Harbour on Dec. 24, 1973, seen by several other observers until Jan. 1, 1974 (Tozer & Richards, 1974: 150). On Jan. 2, 1967 D. Sadler *et al* reported one at Presqu'ile Provincial Park (Goodwin, 1967: 414). Marnie & Geoff. Matthews saw one on Amherst Is. on Dec. 9, 1977 (Weir & Quilliam, 1980: 15). My only experience was seeing the one at Port Bolster, Lake Simcoe on Jan. 26, 1980: this bird was seen by many avid bird watchers for several days before and after this date as it visited ice fishermen for fish scraps. Snyder (1938: 279) reported a female in first winter plumage taken on Dec. 12, 1937 at Cameron Lake, near Oba, and sent to the Royal Ontario Museum. Atkinson (1894: 95) told of two brought in to him at Thunder Bay for mounting (no dates given). One was found dead at Ft. Albany, James Bay, in January, 1956 and sent to the Royal Ontario Museum (Speirs, 1956: 29).

**SPRING:**   David O'Brien saw a very small white gull on Frenchman Bay on Mar. 11, 1962, which he believed to be this species (Speirs, 1976: 16): he is quite familiar with Glaucous and Iceland Gulls, which frequent the bay at this time of year.

**SUMMER:**

**AUTUMN:**   Doug. McRae reported an adult at Netitishi Point, James Bay, on Nov. 13, 1981.

**MEASUREMENTS:**
*Length:* 15.5 to 19.3 ins.
(Godfrey, 1966: 185)
*Wingspread:* about 41 ins.
(Forbush, 1925: 60)
*Weight:* 8 averaged 616 g.
(Dunning, 1984: 11)

**REFERENCE:**
Snyder, L.L. 1938 Ivory
Gull from Oba, Ontario.
Auk. 55:(2):279.

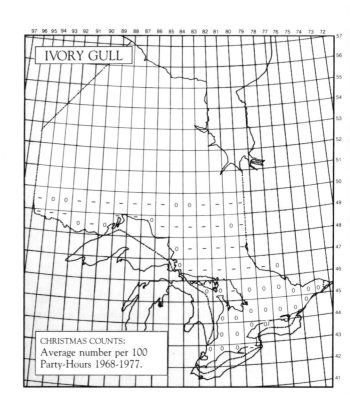

IVORY GULL

CHRISTMAS COUNTS:
Average number per 100
Party-Hours 1968-1977.

## CASPIAN TERN   *Sterna caspia*   Pallas

The Caspian Tern is a cosmopolitan species. We have seen it in New Zealand and in Europe as well as many parts of North America, but never in the large colonies of the smaller terns. In Ontario it often nests in colonies of other species of terns and gulls.

**IDENTIFICATION:** It is about the size of a Ring-billed Gull and, at a distance, looks much like one in flight, but lacks the black wing tips of the gull. At closer range the big red bill, black cap and forked tail identify it as a tern and its large size eliminates other Ontario terns. The harsh "krr-aak" call is distinctive. Young Caspian Terns, with their streaked foreheads and orange bills might be misidentified as Royal Terns but this bird of the southern American beaches has a much longer, more deeply forked tail reaching beyond the wing tips when at rest.

**WINTER:** D. Broughton and H. Howkins saw one at Niagara on Dec. 1, 1973 (Goodwin, 1974: 634).

**SPRING:** Stirrett (1973b: 18) gave Apr. 18 as the earliest Pelee date, with 11 on May 22 as the maximum count there. Ussher (1965: 13) had Rondeau records from Apr. 16 to May 28, with the 10-year average arrival date on Apr. 26. Saunders & Dale (1933: 200) had just one spring record for Middlesex Co., on May 3, 1926 at London. Brooman (1954: 22) cited a few records along the Lake Erie shore of Elgin Co, between Apr. 25 and May 30, 1953. Speirs (1938: 40, 44) listed the earliest Toronto record on

Apr. 8 with the peak there on May 1. The earliest sighting in Ontario Co. was on Apr. 11, 1954 at Cranberry Marsh by Naomi LeVay and the largest count of 100 was at Oshawa on May 11, 1958 by J.M. Richards (Speirs, 1976: 20). Weir and Quilliam (1980: 36) gave Apr. 17 as the 29-year average arrival date at Kingston, with the earliest on Apr. 6. Devitt (1967: 85) gave May 5 as the 9-year average arrival date at Wasaga Beach, with the earliest on Apr. 15, 1959 at Collingwood: he counted 73 at Wasaga Beach on Apr. 28, 1963. K. Ketchum saw this species as early as Apr. 20, 1973 off Pointe au Baril and C. Harris saw one at Go Home Bay on Apr. 16, 1976 (Mills, 1981: 66). Nicholson (1981: 115) gave Apr. 25 as the 12-year average arrival date for Manitoulin with th28.

SUMMER: On Breeding Bird Surveys they have been noted on routes near Georgian Bay, Manitoulin and at Ft. Frances. Stirrett (1973c: 16) had Pelee records throughout the summer, with a maximum count of 8 on Aug. 4. Snyder (1931: 150) collected tronto during the summer of 1976, the beginning of that colony (Goodwin, 1977: 171). Ron Tozer noted 50, including both adults and young, at Lake Scugog on Aug. 25, 1968 (Tozer & Richards, 1974: 154). C.J. Young found a nest with one egg in a Common Tern colony on Gull Bar near the False Duck Is. in eastern Lake Ontario on June 6, 1917 and E.S. McIlwain saw two birds at Weller Bay on Aug. 25, 1938 (Snyder, 1941: 58). Quilliam (1973: 96) followed the fortunes of the big Pigeon Is. colony in the Kingston region from the time of its discovery on June 6, 1961, when 50 or more nests were found to a peak of 375 nests in 1967. A set of two eggs was found on an island off Collingwood on June 11, 1967 (Devitt, 1967: 84). B. DiLabio found one at Ottawa on June 16, 1973 (Goodwin, 1973: 865). Mills (1981: 66) gave details on nestings in Georgian Bay, with 101 nests found on the South Watchers Is. in both 1974 and 1977 and 243 running young noted in 1977: on the Limestone Is. there were 339 nests in 1975, with smaller numbers in recent years. Baillie & Harrington (1936: 42) mentioned a small colony of about 10 pairs on Gull Is. off the east coast of Manitoulin, visited in 1933 and 1935 by Wm. I. Lyon and a set of 2 eggs taken from Sewell Is., west of Manitoulin, on July 2, 1891. Elder (1979: 34) saw three flying by Ney's Beach, Lake Superior, on June 16, 1971. J.L. Baillie saw one at Lake of the Woods on Aug. 8, 1929 (Snyder, 1938: 189). Snyder (1953: 59) saw from one to three, June 2-4, 1937 at Ingolf at Long Pine Lake. Manning (1952: 62) noted one seen at North Point, James Bay on June 18, 1947 by J.P. Kelsall and Louis Lemieux. Schueler, Baldwin & Rising (1974: 143) called them common at Ft. Albany but saw none elsewhere on their northern expeditions.

AUTUMN: Manning (1952: 62) noted one seen flying over Ft. Albany on Sept. 22, 1940 by Harrison Lewis and Harold S. Peters. Ricker & Clarke (1939: 11) saw two at Lake Nipissing in September, 1923. Nicholson (1981: 115) gave Sept. 25, 1968 as the latest date for Manitoulin. C. Harris saw one as late as Sept. 11, 1976 at Go Home Bay (Mills, 1981: 66). R. Pittaway saw two at Ottawa on Sept. 20, 1973 (Goodwin, 1974: 46). The latest sighting for Simcoe Co. was at Collingwood on Sept. 6, 1937 (Devitt, 1967: 84). Weir & Quilliam (1980: 36) gave Sept. 23 as the 26-year average departure date from Kingston, with the latest on Oct. 25, 1970. R. Charles Long and K. Adcoe saw three at Pickering Beach as late as Oct. 16, 1965 (Speirs, 1976: 20). Speirs (1938: 54) gave Nov. 20 as the latest date for Toronto. J.F. Calvert saw one at London on Sept. 15, 1916 (Saunders & Dale, 1933: 200). Ussher (1965: 13) gave Sept. 10 as his latest Rondeau record. Stirrett (1973d: 20) gave Oct. 16 as his latest Pelee record, with a maximum count of 200 on Sept. 1.

BANDING: One collected by Snyder (1931: 150) at Long Point on June 23, 1927, had been banded by Wm. I. Lyon as a young bird at Gravelly Is., Lake Michigan, on July 21, 1925. A young bird banded by J.P. Ludwig on Halfmoon Is. in Georgian Bay on June 23, 1968 was found dead on Scugog Causeway on Aug. 10, 1968 by Dennis Barry and J.M. Richards (Tozer & Richards, 1974: 154). A male banded by F.C. Lincoln at St. James, Mich. on July 19, 1925 was taken by J.L. Baillie at Wasaga Beach on June 3, 1928 (Devitt, 1967: 84).

Mills (1981: 66) summarized banding results from the Limestone Is. colony in Georgian Bay. One banded on June 23, 1949 was retaken there 18 years later on June 19, 1967. Another banded there on June 17, 1967 was recovered in Colombia on Sept. 3, 1970. Others were recovered in Sept. in Cuba, in October in Jamaica, in Nov. in Honduras, in December in Florida and Colombia, in Jan. in Haiti. One also went east to Nova Scotia.

## MEASUREMENTS:
*Length:* 19-23 ins.
(Godfrey, 1966: 193)
*Wingspread:* 50-55 ins.
(Terres, 1980: 467)
*Weight:* one weighed
644 g. (about 1 lb. 6 3/4
oz.) (Terres, 1980: 467)

## REFERENCES:
Ludwig,James Pinson 1965
Biology and structure of
the Caspian (*Hydroprogne
caspia*) population of the
Great Lakes from 1896 -
1964. Bird-banding
36:(4): 217-233. This gives
population estimates of
Great Lakes colonies
including some in Ontario
from 1959-1964 and maps
showing recoveries of
banded birds - mainly
down the Mississippi to
Louisiana and Colombia
but good numbers from the
Atlantic coast to Florida
and the West Indies.

Merriman, R. Owen 1932
Caspian Tern breeding on
Lake Ontario. Can. Field-
Nat., 46:(1):22. Four
adults seen on Salmon Is.,
near Kingston, and two
young banded (of three
seen). In large colony of
Ring-billed Gulls and
Common Terns.

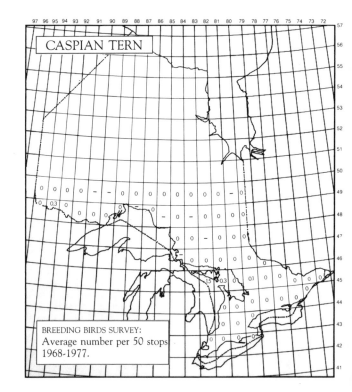

CASPIAN TERN

BREEDING BIRDS SURVEY:
Average number per 50 stops
1968-1977.

# ROYAL TERN   *Sterna maxima*   Boddaert

Bird watchers who have vacationed on oceanic beaches from South Carolina southwards will no doubt be familiar with Royal Terns.

IDENTIFICATION: Royal Terns resemble our more familiar big Caspian Terns but average somewhat smaller and have much more deeply forked tails and orange-red rather than blood-red bills. Caspian Terns in breeding plumage have completely black caps while Royal Terns have whitish foreheads and more conspicuously crested blackish napes. Caspian Tern young might be confused with Royal Terns, as they have orange bills and white-speckled foreheads.

WINTER:

SPRING:

SUMMER:   Robert Finlayson and Alan Wormington reported one at Cedar Beach, near Kingsville, Aug. 22-29, 1974 (Goodwin, 1975: 51): this record was rejected by the Ontario Records Committee because of the possibility of confusion with young of Caspian Terns, but was reinstated in Wormington and James (1984: 19).

AUTUMN:

**MEASUREMENTS:**
*Length:* 18 to 21 ins.
(Godfrey, 1966: 192)
*Wingspread:* 42 to 44 ins.
(Terres, 1980: 470)
*Weight:* 28 averaged
470 g. (Dunning,
1984: 11)

# SANDWICH TERN *Sterna sandvicensis* Latham

My only experience with this bird has been in Europe although it breeds along the southern U.S. coasts and southward. In Ontario it has been purely accidental.

**IDENTIFICATION:** The long black bill with yellow tip distinguishes this species from the Common Tern and other Ontario terns.

**WINTER:**

**SPRING:** McIlwraith (1894: 52) described the taking of the one specimen by J.H. Garnier at Lucknow, Bruce Co. McIlwraith saw the specimen and gave the date as "spring of 1882". Apparently there was a group of three.

**SUMMER:**

**AUTUMN:** Morden and Saunders (1883: 243) gave the time of collection as "autumn of 1881". Since the specimen ended up in Morden's collection this may be more accurate than the date given by McIlwraith. (The specimen is now in the ROM: it does not have any original data but has two labels, one in Fleming's writing following the McIlwraith date and one in J.L. Baillie's writing following Morden & Saunders.

**MEASUREMENTS:**
*Length:* 14 to 16 ins.
(Godfrey, 1966: 193)
*Wingspread:* 34 ins.
(Terres, 1980: 471)
*Weight:* 10 averaged
208 g. (193 to 238 g.)
(Dunning, 1984: 11).

# ROSEATE TERN   *Sterna doughallii*   Montagu

The Roseate Tern breeds on temperate and tropical seashores in both the Old World and in America. It is extremely rarely sighted in Ontario. My experience with it has been on the coast of Maine, where I have frequently seen it on sandbars at low tide with other species of terns.

IDENTIFICATION:   The long slender jet black bill and extremely long white tail with no black on the outer feathers are the most obvious field marks. The "chi-vee" call is also distinctive, very different from the calls of similar terns. I have not seen the rosy blush on the breast of spring birds, as we have gone to Maine in late summer.

WINTER:

SPRING:   Stirrett (1973b: 18) reported one at Pelee on May 12, 1917. Beardslee & Mitchell (1965: 261) mentioned two old sight records from the Niagara River: one by J.L. Davison on May 31, 1886 and the other on May 6, 1938 by T.L. Bourne.

SUMMER:   A report from Rondeau on June 17, 1971 was rejected by the Ontario Ornithological Records Committee (Goodwin, 1972: 35) as a possible Forster's Tern. Beardslee & Mitchell (1965: 261) saw individuals at Niagara Falls on Aug. 22, 1935 and June 22, 1937 (both from the N.Y. side of the river).

AUTUMN:

**MEASUREMENTS:**
*Length:* 14-17 ins.
(Godfrey, 1966: 191)
*Wingspread:* about 30 ins.
(Terres, 1980: 470)
*Weight:* 299 averaged
110 g. (Dunning, 1984:11)

# COMMON TERN  *Sterna hirundo*  Linnaeus

Common Terns occur in both the Old World and in America. In Ontario they breed on exposed shores from Lake Erie north to the northern limit of the Precambrian Shield. Banding has shown that our birds winter south to Ecuador in South America.

IDENTIFICATION: Adults are difficult to distinguish in the field from Forster's and Arctic Terns. For distinctions see these species. The combinations of red bill with black tip, white tail with thin black outer edges, the "tee-arrr" call are field marks of adults: the young have black napes. These three species are about the size of Bonaparte's Gull but have much more deeply forked tails and lack the black hood of adult Bonaparte's Gull.

WINTER: The only Christmas count record was at London, in 1973. A few have lingered into December but most are in the tropics by then. Harold B. Mitchell saw one at Ft. Erie on Dec. 3, 1971 (Goodwin, 1972: 598). Beardslee & Mitchell (1965: 259-260) gave a Dec. 3 record for Niagara Falls in 1935. D.G. Wake and M. Wake reported one at Fanshawe Lake, London, as late as Dec. 15, 1973 (Goodwin, 1974: 634). George W. North and Alan Wormington noted one at Oakville on Dec. 2, 1970 (Goodwin, 1971: 572).

SPRING: Stirrett (1973b: 18) had two at Pelee as early as March 29 and a peak of 1000 on May 20. Ussher (1965: 13) gave Apr. 28 as the 15-year average arrival date at Rondeau, with the earliest on Apr. 6. Saunders & Dale (1933: 199) considered it rare at London, with four spring records from May 16 (1930) to May 24 (1931). Harold Lancaster gave the average arrival date in Elgin Co. as May 6 (Brooman, 1954: 22). Snyder (1931: 150) saw his first at Long Point on May 1, 1928 and found them common by May 4. Beardslee & Mitchell (1965: 259-260) gave Apr. 6, 1952 as the earliest spring record in the lower Niagara River. Saunders (1947: 366) gave May 10 as the 13-year average arrival date at Toronto with his earliest on Apr. 20: Speirs (1938: 48) gave May 25 as the spring peak at Toronto. Long (1968b: 18) reported a very early one at Pickering Beach on Apr. 2, 1967; where the spring peak is about May 26 (Speirs, 1976: 19). On May 25, 1931, R.J. Rutter estimated three to five thousand were seen in Prince Edward Co. (Snyder, 1941: 57). Weir & Quilliam (1980: 35) gave May 3 as the 32-year average arrival date for Kingston, with the earliest on Apr. 21. Devitt (1967: 84) gave May 13 as the 19-year average arrival date for Barrie, with the earliest on Apr. 23, 1943. Chris Harris saw 12 at Go Home Bay as early as May 11, 1979 (Mills, 1981: 65). Nicholson (1981: 115) gave May 10 as the 11-year average arrival date for Manitoulin, with the earliest on May 4, 1969. Speirs & Speirs (1947: 29) saw two at North Bay on May 16, 1944, then frequently until June 6 when 60 were noted. Baillie & Hope (1943: 10) saw a flock of six at Rossport on May 30, 1936, their only record for the NE shore of Lake Superior. Elder (1979: 33) gave May 25 as the earliest date for Geraldton. Peruniak (1971: 17) saw her earliest at Atikokan on May 16. Cringan (1953b: 3) saw his first at Kasabonika Lake on May 28, 1953.

SUMMER: On Breeding Bird Survey counts they were most numerous on the Dunnville (Lake Erie) and Mantowaning (Manitoulin) routes but some appeared as far south as Kingsville and as far north as Dryden. Stirrett (1973c: 16) reported this as a nesting species at Pelee but had no more than 12 in June; increasing to 1000 by Aug. 10. Kelley (1978: 41) reported 13 nests with young or eggs at Kettle Point on July 6, 1974: A. Rider and D. Rupert watched 24,000 moving past Marentette Beach, Essex Co., on Aug. 27,

1972, with as many more in nearby fields. Snyder (1931: 150) noted nesting on the south beach of Long Point about two miles west of the lighthouse and described changing plumages of birds in their second year, which he collected there during June. Beardslee & Mitchell (1965: 259-261) documented the increasing population of nesters on Mohawk Is., Lake Erie, from 500 pairs on July 4, 1933, to 1800 pairs in 1946, decreasing to 130 nests in 1960 (due to increase in gulls nesting there): at Port Colborne pier the population increased from 50 pairs in 1950 to several hundreds "in recent years" with a few also nesting at Port Maitland. The colony at Leslie St. Spit, Toronto, peaked with about 1200 pairs in 1976 according to H. Blokpoel (Goodwin, 1977: 171 and 1133). There is generally a peak in numbers in the first week of August near Whitby (Speirs, 1976: 19). Tozer & Richards (1974: 153) gave details of nestings in the Lake Scugog marshes (unusual habitat for this species) with 21 nests (19 with eggs) as early as May 30, 1964 and flightless young as late as Aug. 27, 1962. The Presqu'ile colony was down to three pairs in 1978 from 16,000 pairs in 1970 (Goodwin, 1978: 1154). Snyder (1941: 57) reported colonies of 2500 on Gull Bar near the False Duck Islands visited by H. Southam on July 5-6, 1938; and 87 eggs on Green Is. on June 27, 1922 according to E. Beaupré; and an abandoned colony fronting Weller Bay (3 eggs taken By R. Rutter on June 7, 1931). Quilliam (1973: 94-95) detailed the changing fortunes of several colonies in the Kingston region, notably those on Amherst Is. and Pigeon Is. Devitt (1967: 83) noted nesting colonies off Collingwood; at Gull Is. in Tiny Twp.; at Wolfhead Is. in Sparrow Lake and probably on Giant's Tomb Is. Mills (1981: 65) detailed nestings on the Georgian Bay islands; some with several hundred nests in some years but unoccupied other years. Nicholson (1981: 115) mentioned 300 pairs nesting on a Georgian Bay island off Manitoulin in 1976 but by 1980 only 758 birds at 8 locations could be found by CWS personnel. Ricker & Clarke (1939: 11) reported a colony of 100 to 200 on an island in Lake Nipissing in 1929. Snyder (1942: 129) reported nestings off Thessalon and in the St. Mary River near Sault Ste. Marie on June 26, 1939. Skeel & Bondrup-Nielsen (1978: 176) found them rare at Pukaskwa from June 16-24, 1975 as did Denis (1961: 6) at Thunder Bay, Snyder (1928: 19) collected four young on Lake Abitibi and called them "fairly numerous" there: Smith (1957: 173) noted 25 pairs on an island in Lake Abitibi with several sets of eggs and some young on July 13, 1953. Snyder (1953: 59) noted nesting colonies in the Kenora-Dryden area from mid-June to mid-July, 1939 to 1947. J. Satterly found them nesting at Sandy Lake on July 12, 1937 (Hope, 1938: 21). Cringan (1950: 10) found two nests (with one and two eggs) on an island in Nikip Lake on June 25, 1950 and recorded daily maxima of 100 at times during the summer. Manning (1952: 60) reported one taken by Sam Waller at Moose Factory on June 7, 1928 and collected one himself at Long Ridge Point, James Bay between June 14-16, 1947. Schueler, Baldwin & Rising (1974: 143) noted the species at Hawley Lake but not at any of the coastal localities visited. Lee (1978: 24) found six nests, each with 2 eggs, on a rocky islet in Big Trout Lake on June 29, 1975; he also noted small numbers at Bearskin Lake and Kasabonika Lake. McLaren & McLaren (1981: 3) found a colony of about 60 birds at Little Sachigo Lake on June 11, 1977.

AUTUMN: Speirs & Speirs (1947: 29) saw 100 near North Bay on Sept. 13, 1944 and two as late as Sept. 16. MacLulich (1938: 16) saw one on Sept. 21, 1930 at Cedar Lake, Algonquin Park. Nicholson (1981: 115) gave Oct. 16, 1977 as the latest date for Manitoulin. Devitt (1967: 84) gave Nov. 3, 1957 as his latest sighting at Barrie with a general exodus of 175 from Wasaga Beach on Sept. 1, 1940. Weir & Quilliam (1980: 35) gave Oct. 3 as the 24-year average departure date from Kingston, with the latest on Nov.

15, 1966. Tozer & Richards (1974: 153) noted 12 as late as Oct. 3, 1965 at Lake Scugog and four as late as Oct. 6, 1963 at Darlington Provincial Park. Speirs (1938: 52) gave Aug. 23 and Sept. 12 as fall peaks for Toronto, while Saunders (1947: 366) had Sept. 22 as his 11-year average departure date, with J.L. Baillie's latest on Oct. 13. Ussher (1965: 13) gave Sept. 25 as the 8-year average departure date from Rondeau, with the latest on Oct. 14. Stirrett (1973a: 16) had six at Pelee as late as Nov. 16 and his fall maximum of 3000 on Sept. 7. J.P. Kleiman *et al* estimated 10,000 at Pelee on Sept. 19, 1971 (Goodwin, 1972: 57).

BANDING: Of 29 banded by Alf Bunker in eastern Lake Ontario colonies and re-covered out of Ontario, one was found in Quebec in July; one in Newfoundland in Oct., one in Minnesota in Sept.; six in New York between July and Oct.; one in Pennsylvania in Sept.; one in Virginia in Oct.; three in Florida (Oct., Nov. and Jan.); the rest were farther south in winter quarters: one in Cuba in Nov.; one in Mexico in Feb.; three in the Canal Zone (Nov. and Dec.); two in Panama (Nov. and Dec.); three in Trinidad (Nov., Apr. and May); one in Guyana in Jan.; two in Colombia in Nov. and one in Ecuador in Nov. One returned to the original banding site 9 years after banding.

Of 10 banded near Toronto and recovered out of Ontario; one was taken in Michigan in Nov.; one in N.Y. in Aug., one in North Carolina in Nov.; two in Florida in Nov.; two in Panama in Oct.; two in Colombia in Dec., and one in Ecuador, in the August one year following banding.

**MEASUREMENTS:**
*Length:* 13 to 16 ins. (Godfrey, 1966: 189)
*Wingspread:* 29 to 31.5 ins. (Roberts, 1955: 598)
*Weight:* 4 oz. (Roberts, 1955: 598). Hope (1938: 21) gave 136.3 g. as the average weight of two males.

**REFERENCE:**
Connors Peter G.; Victor C. Anderlini; Robert W. Risebrough; Michael Gilbertson and Helen Hays 1975 Investigations of heavy metals in Common Tern populations. Can. Field-Nat., 89:(2):157-162.
Heavy metals were not considered to be an imortant cause of low hatching success of Common Terns breeding in Hamilton Harbour.

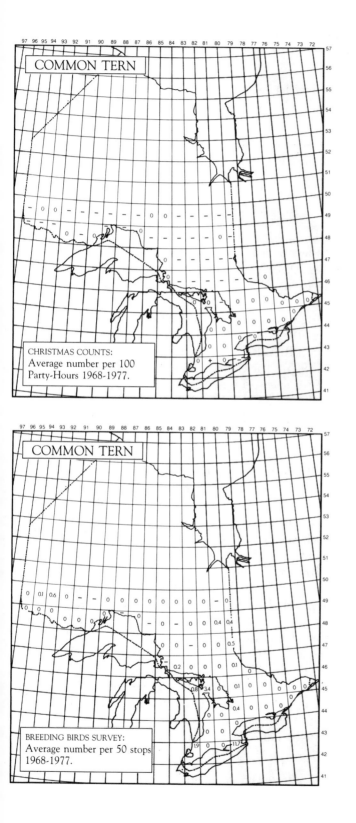

COMMON TERN

CHRISTMAS COUNTS:
Average number per 100
Party-Hours 1968-1977.

COMMON TERN

BREEDING BIRDS SURVEY:
Average number per 50 stops
1968-1977.

# ARCTIC TERN   *Sterna paradisaea*   Pontoppidan

The Arctic Tern is a circumpolar breeder, wintering south to Antarctica. In Ontario it breeds along the Hudson Bay coast and has seldom been seen in southern Ontario except in the vicinity of Ottawa.

IDENTIFICATION:   Arctic Terns are very difficult to distinguish from Common Terns except under ideal viewing conditions. When both are present and in breeding plumage the shorter legs of the Arctic, its blood red bill with no dark tip, its grayer underparts extending to the lower face and the long tail extending to the wingtips may be noted. In winter plumage only the shorter legs distinguish the Arctic.

WINTER:

SPRING:   Fleming (1930: 66) mentioned a Toronto specimen, labelled by J.B. Williams, taken in May, 1891. On May 20, 1979, Martin Edwards saw five terns on Amherst Is. with very short legs compared with nearby Common Terns and on the next day Doug McRae saw two at Prince Edward Point which he thought were Arctic terns (Weir & Quilliam, 1980: 15-16). C.W. Eifrig reported that a specimen was taken in the Ottawa region on May 30, 1909 (Godfrey, 1973: 51). B. McTavish noted three at Ottawa on May 25, 1973 (Goodwin, 1973: 767). R.A. Foxall *et al* saw up to 30 at Ottawa from May 26 - June 1, 1977 (Goodwin, 1977: 995). The earliest Ottawa record, by M. Bostock and B.M. DiLabio, was on May 18, 1980, when 35 were noted (Goodwin, 1980: 772). Sam Waller noted the arrival at Moose Factory on May 13, 1930 (Todd, 1963: 397). Manning (1952: 61) collected one of several seen in the Moose River estuary on May 29, 1947 and saw 50 at Ship Sands on May 31, 1947.

SUMMER:   G. Bennett *et al* reported two at Bronte from June 8-18, 1978 (Goodwin, 1978: 1155). On June 8, 1952, D.B.O. Saville and his wife saw eight at Ottawa (Saville, 1957: 33). In recent years there have been several sightings at Ottawa during the first half of June, with up to 40 reported there by Roger Foxall *et al* on June 11, 1972 (Goodwin, 1973: 53). R. Pittaway saw four at Pembroke on June 14, 1973 (Goodwin, 1973: 865). D. Gunn photographed one at Cochrane on June 19, 1965 (Goodwin, 1965: 539). Todd (1963: 396-397) cited several records from the Moosonnee region. Manning (1952: 61) saw about 250 along the James Bay and Hudson Bay coasts (probably including some Common Terns which he could not distinguish in flight) between North Point and Shagamu River from June 3 to Aug. 14, 1947: two Arctic Terns were collected at Long Ridge Point (June 14-16); one at Little Cape (July 29-Aug. 1) and one at Shagamu River (Aug. 9-14). The 1948 ROM party found two nests, each with 2 eggs, on June 29 at Cape Henrietta Maria and another nest on July 1: they also saw about 100 adults of which 25 were collected (Peck, 1972: 344). Schueler, Baldwin & Rising (1974: 146) found a nest with 2 eggs on June 23, 1962 at the limit of trees along the Sutton River and six nests (3 with one egg and 3 with 2 eggs) on an island in the Winisk River about 20 miles from Winisk on June 16-17, 1965. C.E. Hope frequently saw from one to 12 at Fort Severn from June 17 to July 23, 1940, and collected four there.

AUTUMN:

BANDING:   Shortt (1949: 50) collected an immature female about 25 miles south of

Cape Henrietta Maria on July 4, 1948, which was banded at Disko Bay, West Greenland, on July 22, 1947 as a nestling.

**MEASUREMENTS:**
*Length:* 14-17 ins.
(Godfrey, 1966: 190)
*Wingspread:* 29-33 ins.
(Terres, 1980: 466)
*Weight:* 3 1/2 to 4 1/4 oz.
(Terres, 1980: 466)

**REFERENCES:**
Godfrey, W. Earl, 1973. A possible shortcut spring migration route of the Arctic Tern to James Bay, Canada. Can. Field-Nat., 87:(1):51- 52.

Shortt, T.M. 1949, Arctic Tern banded in Greenland, recovered in Ontario. Bird Banding, 20:(1):50.

# FORSTER'S TERN   *Sterna forsteri*   Nuttall

This is a common breeding bird in prairie marshes and has recently been proven to be a rare breeder in certain marshes in southwestern Ontario, notably at Lake St. Clair, Rondeau and Long Point. They winter around the Gulf of Mexico.

**IDENTIFICATION:** The outermost tail feathers are dark on the inner webs, not on the outer webs as in Common Tern. Adults have deep red bills with black tip in Common Terns but orange-red in Forster's. These differences are usually difficult to discern in the field. In fall and winter the black ear patch of Forster's is distinctive (in Common Terns the black continues around the nape). The tail in Forster's is pale gray while in Common Terns it is white. Young Common Terns have a black bar on the leading edge of the wing from the bend to the body: this is lacking in Forster's.

**WINTER:**

**SPRING:** Stirrett (1973b: 18) had Pelee records from May 1 to June 1. D. Fidler and G. Bennett saw one at Bradley's Marsh on Apr. 22, 1972 (Goodwin, 1972: 756). A. Rider *et al* found at least 12 nests and saw 65 birds on Walpole Is., Lake St. Clair, from late May, 1976 and George K. Peck also reported nesting at Mitchell Bay (Goodwin, 1977: 1133). T.N. Hayman observed one at London on Apr. 30, 1980 (Goodwin, 1980: 772). Saunders (1947: 123) reported one at Hamilton on Apr. 30, 1941 and Alan Wormington found them present there from Apr. 19, 1972 (Goodwin 1972: 756). C. Wood noted them at Dundas as early as Apr. 16, 1973 and R. Curry as late as May 20 (Goodwin, 1973: 767). Fleming (1906: 442) reported a male taken at Toronto on May 22, 1894. Naomi LeVay reported two at Cranberry Marsh, Whitby, on May 15, 1971 and one there on May 31, 1969 (Tozer & Richards, 1974: 151). Goodwin (1978: 999) saw one at Whitby on May 13, 1978, while Margaret Bain and David Ruch noted one there on May 17, 1980 (Goodwin, 1980: 772). Weir & Quilliam (1980: 15) recorded observations at Prince Edward Point on Apr. 15-16, 1978 and on Apr. 27 and May 4, 1980. R. Bracken, T. Platch *et al* spotted one at Ottawa on Apr. 17, 1980 (Goodwin, 1980: 772). David Elder *et al* reported three at Steep Rock marsh on May 8, 1979 and six at Lake of the Woods May 12-13, 1979 (Goodwin, 1979: 767).

**SUMMER:** G. Agnew, R. Curry *et al* saw an adult feeding young at Pelee on July 12-13, 1975 (Goodwin, 1975: 965): J. W. Johnson noted an adult feeding young at Steen's Marsh, Pelee, in summer, 1977 (Goodwin, 1977: 1133). A. Rider found 25 nests on Walpole Is., Lake St. Clair in summer, 1979 (Goodwin, 1979: 859). D. Rupert reported 32 birds, about 50% immatures, at Sombra ferry dock on July 22, 1972 (Goodwin, 972: 853): on July 27, 1974 he noted 12 flying young with 7 adults at Port Lambton, while A. Rider saw 30, including several young, at Kettle Point on July 20 (Goodwin, 1974: 897). R. Simpson photographed an immature at Rondeau on June 21, 1970, saw up to four there from Aug. 1-14 and an adult feeding a young bird on Aug. 14 (Goodwin, 1971: 52). G. Muller saw one at Strathroy on Aug. 24, 1974 (Goodwin, 1975: 51). A. Wormington saw a group at Long Point on July 6, 1975, consisting of 8 adults, four immatures, and 12 young of the year (Goodwin, 1975: 965). A colony of some 50 pairs was found at Long Point from May 29-June 6, 1976, in which 28 nests were checked by Erica Dunn, M.H. Field and D.H. Hussell (Goodwin, 1976: 950). One was identified at Port Burwell on Aug. 24, 1952 by Marshall Field and Wm. Stewart (Brooman, 1954: 22).

Beardslee & Mitchell (1965: 258-259) reported one at Pt. Abino, Lake Erie on June 1, 1943 and one at Rockhouse Pt. on Aug. 13, 1958. R. Curry noted an immature at Toronto on June 7, 1974 (Goodwin, 1974: 897). Naomi LeVay reported two at Cranberry Marsh on Aug. 26,1961, while Tom Hassall saw one at Whitby Harbour in August, 1962 (Tozer & Richards, 1974: 151). George A. Scott saw one at Oshawa from Aug. 9, 1975 (Goodwin, 1976: 61). R.D. Weir noted one at Sandbanks Provincial Park on Aug. 4, 1980 (Goodwin, 1981: 177-178). A. Wormington *et al* noted them on Sable Is., Lake of the Woods, from Aug. 3-5, 1979 (Goodwin, 1980: 157).

AUTUMN: R.A. Foxall and R. Pittaway saw Ottawa's first from Sept. 20-29, 1974 (Goodwin, 1975: 51). B.M. DiLabio and J. Harris saw another at Ottawa on Sept. 21, 1978 (Goodwin, 1979: 173). E.L. Brereton observed one at Wasaga Beach on Oct. 4, 1941 (Devitt, 1967: 83). R.D. Weir noted one on Amherst Is. on Oct. 27, 1980 and B. White *et al* saw one at Presqu'ile Provincial Park on Sept. 5 (Goodwin, 1981: 178). Goodwin (1976: 61) mentioned one seen at Oshawa by George A. Scott to Sept. 5, 1975. J.L. Baillie *et al* saw an immature at Whitby on Sept. 10, 1960 and another was noted there as late as Oct. 18, 1959 by Tom Hassall *et al*: I saw one at Corner Marsh, Pickering, Sept. 7-8, 1975 (Speirs, 1976: 18). Fleming (1906: 442) cited a specimen taken at Toronto on Oct. 19, 1899: Saunders (1947: 366) listed Sept. 1 and Sept. 15 dates for Toronto. On Sept. 30, 1953 Arthur Schaffner and Harold Axtell saw 17, some of these at Ft. Erie (Beardslee & Mitchell, 1965: 259): R. Brownstein noted five there on Oct. 17, 1971 (Goodwin, 1972: 57). Sheppard (1960: 27) reported three where Frenchman's Creek empties into the Niagara River on Oct. 19, 1936.

**MEASUREMENTS:**
*Length:* 14-15 ins.
(Godfrey, 1966: 188)
*Wingspread:* 30.50 -
32.12 ins. (Roberts,
1955: 596)
*Weight:* 5 oz. (Roberts,
1955: 596)

# LEAST TERN   *Sterna antillarum*   Lesson

My experience with this tiny tern has been largely on its breeding grounds on the coast of Maine. There is one Ontario record.

IDENTIFICATION: The very small size (even smaller than the Black Tern) bright orange-yellow bill and legs, white forehead, black cap and black stripe between eye and base of bill, are diagnostic characters.

WINTER:

SPRING:

SUMMER: One was well observed at Erie Beach on June 26, 1958 after heavy rain on June 25 accompanied by strong SW gales by R.F. Andrle, Richard Brownstein and A.E. Schaffner (Beardslee & Mitchell, 1965: 262).

AUTUMN:

**MEASUREMENTS:**
*Length:* 8 1/2 to 9 1/2 ins.
(Terres, 1980: 469)
*Wingspread:* about 20 ins.
(Terres, 1980: 469)
*Weight:* 31.1 g. (about 1
oz.) (Terres, 1980: 470)

# SOOTY TERN   *Sterna fuscata*   Linnaeus

The Sooty Tern is normally a tropical oceanic island breeder: one blown up to Ontario on a hurricane.

IDENTIFICATION: Mainly white below and black above, but with white forehead and white band to top of eye; slightly larger than a Common Tern.

WINTER:

SPRING:

SUMMER: One was seen by David Hurrie and well described on Aug. 14, 1955 after Hurricane Connie, about 7 miles NW of Brockville (Baillie, 1955: 376).

AUTUMN:

**MEASUREMENTS:**
*Length:* 15 to 17 ins.
(Godfrey, 1966: 191)
*Wingspread:* 34 ins.
(Terres, 1980: 471)
*Weight:* 5 to 8 1/2 oz.
(Terres, 1980: 472)

# BLACK TERN   *Chlidonias niger*   (Linnaeus)

Black Terns breed in marshes in the Old World and in America, including much of Ontario. They are very aggressive in defending their cattail marshes: hard hats are recommended — or better still, just stay away. Since they often nest on floating debris, it is important not to make waves near their nesting colonies.

IDENTIFICATION: Black Terns are much smaller than Common Terns. Adults have black bodies, the only white being under the tail, when in breeding plumage. Flying young and winter adults are mainly white below and about the head, except for black on the nape and behind the eyes but are still much darker above than other terns. In this plumage they have sometimes been misidentified as Least Terns, but these southern terns are accidental in Ontario, and show much white at the base of the tail and on the trailing edge of the wing: adult Least Terns with their bright yellow beak and feet are distinctive.

WINTER:

SPRING: Stirrett (1973b: 18) gave Apr. 10 as the earliest Pelee date and had a maximum of 100 on May 22. Ussher (1965: 13) gave May 2 as the earliest Rondeau record with the 20-year average arrival on May 8. Saunders & Dale (1933: 200) had few records inland at London, from Apr. 30 (1902) to May 28 (1926). Harold Lancaster saw seven flying NW over his farm in Elgin Co. on May 26, 1947 (Brooman, 1954: 22). Snyder (1931: 151) first noted the species at Long Point on May 3, 1928 but they were not common until May 13. Beardslee & Mitchell (1965: 264-265) had early records from Morgan's Point on Apr. 20, 1960 and Mohawk Point on Apr. 21, 1958. J.L. Baillie had one at Toronto as early as Apr. 29 (Saunders, 1947: 366) who gave May 17 as his 11-year average arrival date there: Speirs (1938: 44) gave May 24 as the spring peak for Toronto. Tozer & Richards (1974: 154) saw one at Oshawa's Second Marsh as early as Apr. 26, 1964 and found nests with eggs there on May 31, 1970. Weir & Quilliam (1980: 36) gave May 5 as the 32-year average arrival date for Kingston, with the earliest on Apr. 21. Devitt (1967: 85) gave May 12 as the 20-year average arrival date for Barrie, with the earliest on May 5, 1967. E.G. White took six specimens on the Rideau near Ottawa on May 28, 1881 (Lloyd, 1923: 104). Barbara Wilkins saw one at Go Home Bay on May 24, 1954 and E.L. Brereton noted one at Lake of Bays about the same date in 1937 (Mills, 1981: 67). Nicholson (1981: 115) gave May 17 as the 12-year average arrival date for Manitoulin, with the earliest on May 8, 1977 and a high count of 50 on May 19, 1974. Ricker & Clarke (1939: 11) saw one at North Bay on May 27, 1924. Bondrup-Nielsen (1976: 42) saw his first near Kapuskasing on May 29, 1975. Peruniak (1971: 17) gave May 15 as the earliest date for Atikokan. James (1980: 86) found a nest with 2 eggs near Pickle Lake on May 31, 1977. Cringan (1950: 10) gave May 29, 1950 as the arrival date in the Asheweig area. Oliver Hewitt saw one at Ship Sands, near Moosoneee, on May 28, 1947 (Manning, 1952: 62).

SUMMER: On Breeding Bird Surveys they were seen wherever suitable marshes occurred near the BBS routes, from Port Dover and Dunnville, north to Dryden and Eagle River. Stirrett (1973c: 16) found them nesting at Pelee and had a maximum of 2000 there on Aug. 6, after the nesting season. Saunders & Dale (1933: 200) had one summer record near London, by John A. Morden on June 19, 1924. Snyder (1931: 151-153) detailed observations at three Long Point colonies, from courtship feeding on May 25, 1928 to fully-fledged young on July 11: most sets had 3 eggs, but some had 2 or 4: 25 specimens were collected and the changing plumages were described in some detail. Beardslee & Mitchell (1965:264) mentioned breeding in the Dunnville marshes for at least 30 years and estimated 6000 migrating near the Peace Bridge on Aug.31, 1948. J. Satterly reported the main exodus from Cedar Point, Lake Simcoe on Aug. 11, 1963 and saw his last there on Aug. 23 (Speirs 1976: 21). Allin (1940: 98) saw two small young on July 4, 1937 in Darlington Twp. and many immatures flying about on July 25, 1937. Snyder (1941: 58) found the species common in the Prince Edward Co. marshes and collected a male on July 14, 1930 at Huyck Bay. Weir & Quilliam (1980: 36) gave Aug. 18 as the 24-year average departure date from Kingston. Devitt (1967: 85) listed several breeding localities in Simcoe Co. from the Holland River marshes north to Collingwood. A nest with 2 eggs was found at Go Home Bay on June 22, 1971 by C. Harris et al (Mills, 1981: 67). Nicholson (1981: 115) gave Aug. 4, 1980 as the latest date for Manitoulin. Ricker & Clarke (1939: 11) saw three at North Bay on June 6, 1925 and cited a report by J.G. Oughton at Manitou Is. on June 14, 1932, while Speirs & Speirs (1947: 29) noted two there on Aug. 5, 1944. Denis (1961: 6) called it an "occasional rare, summer visitant" at Thunder Bay. F. Cowell has seen Black Terns near Timmins in the summer (Smith, 1957: 173). Elder (1979: 34) gave June 6 as his earliest date at Geraldton and called it locally common later in the summer. Peruniak (1971: 17) considered this a fairly common summer resident and breeder in the Atikokan region, but her latest date was Aug. 2. Snyder (1938: 189) found them common at Off Lake and Rainy River, and J.L. Baillie noted young with adults on Aug. 1, 1929. Snyder (1953: 59) found two occupied nests near Kenora on June 16, 1947 and reported breeding from there east to Wabigoon Lake, Dryden. Hope (1938: 21) found them to be abundant near Favourable Lake, where he located a number of nests with 3 eggs on June 8, 1938 and collected a downy young on June 27, 1938. Cringan (1953a: 2) noted the species on June 18, 1953 at Perrault Falls. Cringan (1950: 10-11) saw about 200 in the Petownikip marshes in June, 1950 and others along the North Caribou and Windigo Rivers, with the latest two on Aug. 28 in the Nikip Lake area. Manning (1952: 62) saw two at Ship Sands on June 17, 1949 and others saw one at Sandy Is. on June 13, 1947 (both near Moosonee): he also cited a breeding record some 9 miles south of Albany. Schueler, Baldwin & Rising (1974: 143) found them uncommon at Ft. Albany and saw none elsewhere in the north. McLaren & McLaren (1981: 3) saw four individuals between Severn River and Little Sachigo Lake, June 1-10, 1977.

AUTUMN:   Speirs & Speirs (1947: 29) saw three at Cache Bay, Lake Nipissing, on Sept. 4, 1944. On Sept. 16, 1902, an immature male was collected at Go Home Bay (Mills, 1981: 67). Devitt (1967: 85) wrote that practically all had left Simcoe Co. by Sept. 1, but E.L. Brereton took a late straggler near Elmvale on Oct. 4, 1945. Weir & Quilliam (1980: 36) gave Sept. 3 as the latest Kingston date. George A. Scott saw one at Oshawa's Second Marsh as late as Oct. 11, 1959 (Speirs, 1976: 21). Fleming (1906: 443) gave Sept. 5 as the latest Toronto date. Beardslee & Mitchell (1965: 264-265) estimated 5000 near the Peace Bridge on Sept. 19, 1953 and had records of single birds at Ft. Erie as late as Nov. 22, 1947 and Nov. 25, 1937. Ussher (1965: 13) gave Oct. 3 as the latest Rondeau record with the 11-year average departure date on Sept. 1. Stirrett (1973d: 20) had his latest two on Sept. 22 but there were 400 as late as Sept. 1 at Pelee.

**MEASUREMENTS:**
*Length:* 9 to 10 1/2 ins.
(Godfrey, 1966: 194)
*Wingspread:* 23 to 24 1/4
ins. (Roberts, 1955:
595)
*Weight:* 4 ♂ averaged
63 g. 3 ♀ averaged 58 g.
(Hope, 1938: 21)

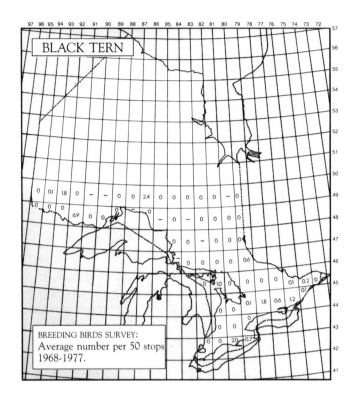

BLACK TERN

BREEDING BIRDS SURVEY:
Average number per 50 stops
1968-1977.

# BLACK SKIMMER   *Rynchops niger*   Linnaeus

This is a bird that I associate with warm, sandy ocean beaches in Florida and South Carolina. There have been three unexpected recent sightings in Ontario.

IDENTIFICATION: The peculiar red scissor-like beak, with lower mandible much longer than the upper, is diagnostic. Skimmers are largely black above and white below, with bright red feet. When feeding they skim the ocean surface with open beak, the lower mandible dipping in to catch unwary fish. Much of the time is spent with flocks resting on the sand facing into the wind, or doing flock aerobatics in the sky over the beach.

WINTER:

SPRING:

SUMMER: One was reported at Pelee on July 6, 1978 by M. and S. Gawn and J.C. Wilson (Goodwin, 1978: 1155).

AUTUMN: Josephine Burns and her mother noted an unusual bird at Whitby Harbour on Nov. 1, 1977 and had the presence of mind to photograph the bird and show the photograph to Margaret Bain who confirmed her identification and have the sighting established as the first Ontario record at the ROM (Bain, 1978: 33). Chip and Linda Weseloh saw the third bird at Erieau on Sept. 15, 1981, several days after it was first seen there.

**MEASUREMENTS:**
*Length:* 16 to 20 ins.
(Godfrey, 1966: 195)
*Wingspread:* 42 to 50 ins.
(Terres, 1980: 826)
*Weight:* 13 ♂ averaged
344 g. 8 ♀ averaged
255 g. (Dunning,
1984: 11).

**REFERENCE:**
Bain, Margaret 1978 First
sighting of a Black
Skimmer in Ontario. Ont.
Field Biologist, 32: (2): 33.

# DOVEKIE   *Alle alle*   (Linnaeus)

The Dovekie is a common breeder on Greenland and northern parts of the Old World. It winters at sea along the Atlantic coasts. The Ontario records are probably due to wind-blown waifs following violent NE storms.

**IDENTIFICATION:**   Dovekies are much smaller than the Murres but somewhat similarly patterned, with black back, white below and white cheeks (in winter). The one that I saw impressed me with its rapidly beating wings, stout body and size smaller than a Killdeer, as well as the pattern noted above. Two birds collected in Ontario and at first identified as Dovekies have turned out to be Ancient Murrelets, a somewhat larger west coast relative, so sight records should be treated with some reservations.

**WINTER:**   Baillie (1951: 202) mentioned one that I saw in Toronto Bay on Jan. 14, 1951. George A. Scott found one swimming in a weakened condition in Oshawa Harbour on Feb. 8, 1955 (Speirs, 1976: 24).

**SPRING:**

**SUMMER:**

**AUTUMN:**   Fleming (1930: 65) reported one taken during the last week of October, 1924 at Mississippi Lake, near Carleton Place, and identified by P.A. Taverner and E.F.G. White. Another one was shot by a hunter at Mississippi Lake on Nov. 11, 1959 *fide* W.E. Godfrey (Speirs & Speirs, 1960: 33). One taken at Cornwall on Nov. 19, 1963 is in the ROM (Spec. No. 93840). One was noted at Toronto on Nov. 25, 1950 (Baillie, 1951: 202) at the time of one of the influxes of Thick-billed Murres.

**MEASUREMENTS:**
*Length:* 7.5 to 9 ins.
(Godfrey, 1966: 198)
*Wingspread:* 13.86 to
15.50 ins. (Forbush, 1925,
v.1:46)
*Weight:* 3 1/4 to 5 7/8 oz.
(Terres, 1980: 26) ♀
smaller than ♂.

# THICK-BILLED MURRE   *Uria lomvia*   (Linnaeus)

These birds nest in great colonies on ledges of towering cliffs in the Arctic and bordering the North Atlantic and normally spend the winter at sea. Sometimes, after NE gales a few have shown up in Ontario waters.

IDENTIFICATION: Apart from bill shape this species looks much like the Razorbill and very much like the Common Murre (which has yet to be found in Ontario). In breeding condition the Thick-billed Murre has a pale blue line along the cutting edge of the upper mandible: this is lacking in the Common Murre. The Thick-billed Murre has a pointed wedge of white running up from the breast towards the throat: this is a very broad wedge in the Common Murre. In winter plumage the Common Murre has a heavy black line running back from the eye on the white face: in the Thick-billed Murre there is only a dark smudge in this area.

WINTER: One specimen was secured at Pelee on Dec. 10, 1907, from several seen on Lake Erie (Stirrett, 1973a: 16). Ussher (1965: 13) had one Rondeau record: on Dec. 18, 1896. Saunders & Dale (1933: 200) reported one collected by J. Hevey on the Thames River in London on Dec. 10, 1894. Sheppard (1960: 28) reported Niagara Falls records for Dec. 23, 1896 and Dec. 1, 1907: and 13 were retrieved below the falls between Nov. 29 and Dec. 7, 1950 and sent to the ROM. Fleming (1906: 441) reported them off Toronto "increasing in numbers through December" from 1893 to 1903. O.E. Devitt found one dead at Frenchman Bay on Dec. 10, 1950 donated to the ROM: George A. Scott saw one alive at Oshawa on Dec. 3, 1950 and found another dead (Speirs, 1976: 23). Quilliam (1973: 97-98) cited several records for the Kingston region: two men killed 40 near Rockport in Dec. 1896: two were shot near Portsmouth on Dec. 30, 1950: E. Beaupré killed one with a stick on Dec. 13, 1926 on Amherst Is.: W.E. Saunders reported one that was picked up dead on Dec. 15, 1932: K.F. Edwards noted two along the Bath Road from Dec. 9-13, 1952 and R.B. Stewart picked up one alive by Hwy. 15 on Dec. 21, 1952 which later died and went to the ROM. E.L. Brereton found eight off Big Bay Pt., Lake Simcoe on Dec. 15, 1948, where R.J. Robinson took one during the 1896 flight (Devitt, 1967: 85). Lloyd (1923: 103) cited Ottawa records to Dec. 21, in 1894: flocks of 20 to 100 from 10 a.m. to 3 p.m. on Dec. 12, 1897: also some the previous and following days in 1897: a male taken Dec. 13, 1901: another taken Dec. 29, 1907: six seen Dec. 1, 1908 as well as 400 to 500 seen Dec. 19, 1908 and one taken Dec. 11, 1909. A. Kay shot one at Pt. Sydney, Muskoka on Dec. 21, 1894 and found a dead female there on Dec. 18, 1896 which was sent to the ROM: another was shot at Parry Sound in Dec., 1897 and another was reported from Beaumaris in Dec., 1897 (Mills, 1981: 67). Levi Smith found a male in dying condition on the upper end of Lake Timiskaming in December, 1908, which he sent to Alfred Kay to be mounted (Kay, 1910: 43).

SPRING: Saunders (1947: 137-138) described one he saw at Toronto on May 27, 1943, later also seen by Bruce Falls. One was taken at Ottawa on March 23, 1903 (Lloyd, 1923: 103).

SUMMER: Saunders (1947: 138) mentioned July sightings off Van Wagner's Beach, Hamilton, by George North. One was found alive near Kingston on July 8, 1897 by Chas. M. Clarke and two others by E. Beaupré about a week later: Jean Argue noted one at

Amherst Is. on June 8, 1952 and Tony Bidwell saw one at Snake Is. on June 22, 1952 (Quilliam, 1973: 97-98).

AUTUMN: One bird reached Matheson and was picked up on Nov. 30, 1950 (Baillie, 1951: 14). Lloyd (1923: 103) cited several Ottawa records: five were taken from a flock of 20 on Nov. 19, 1893: large flocks were noted from Nov. 13-15, 1901: a flight took place from Nov. 15-21, 1903: arrival was noted on Nov. 25, 1907: and one was taken on Nov. 25, 1908. A.D. Henderson shot six and saw a number of others on Nov. 21, 1896 at Barrie and Frances Westman saw one there on Nov. 8, 1948 (Devitt, 1967: 85). At the end of November, 1950, ten were shot between Adolphustown and Gananoque and inland to Kingston Mills and about 20 to 30 were seen near Amherst Is. (Quilliam, 1973: 97). George A. Scott saw about 25 off Oshawa Harbour on Nov. 28, 1950 (Speirs, 1976: 23): this was part of a major flight that year following a severe NE gale (Baillie, 1951: 12-14). Naomi LeVay reported one off Cranberry Marsh, Whitby, on Oct. 12, 1953 (Tozer & Richards, 1974: 156). Fleming (1906: 441) wrote that considerable numbers entered Lake Ontario in 1893, the first at Toronto on Nov. 29: they then occurred annually for the next ten years. During the big 1950 flight in late November, 140 were counted flying west between Pt. Credit and Burlington by W.W.H. Gunn and George W. North (Baillie, 1951: 14). Beardslee & Mitchell (1965: 267) published a photograph of one taken at Niagara Falls in November, 1950.

**MEASUREMENTS:**
*Length:* 17-19 ins.
(Godfrey, 1966: 197)
*Wingspread:* 24.5 - 32 ins.
(Forbush, 1925: Vol. 1:40)
*Weight:* 964.4 g. (about 2
lb. 2 oz.) (Terres,
1980: 28).

**REFERENCE:**
Kay, Alfred 1910 Brunnich
Murre, *Uria lomvia.*
Ottawa Nat., 24:(2):43.

# RAZORBILL  *Alca torda*  Linnaeus

The Razorbill is a bird of the stormy North Atlantic coasts, often associated with the more common Murres. It is accidental in Ontario.

IDENTIFICATION: The Razorbill is a chunky fowl about the size of a Common Goldeneye. It is white below and black above except for a narrow white wingbar. As its name implies the bill is flattened from side to side: it is black except for a diagonal white stripe when in breeding condition: the bill shape serves to distinguish it from the murres which have pointed (carrot-shaped) bills.

WINTER: Maughan (1897: 2) collected one at Hamilton Bay on Dec. 9, 1893. Wm. Cross reported a specimen taken in Toronto Bay on Dec. 10, 1889 (Thompson, 1890: 200).

SPRING: One was seen at Hamilton from Mar. 12-31, 1972 by R. Curry *et al* (Goodwin, 1972: 598). One of a flock of 30 was decapitated by an aeroplane propeller at Toronto Is. on May 6, 1971 and the remains are now a skeleton specimen in the ROM. George A. Scott saw an alcid off Oshawa on May 10, 1959 that he considered to be this species (Speirs, 1959c: 29).

SUMMER: Donald Gunn reported one off Lorne Park, Lake Ontario, on June 19, 1956.

AUTUMN: One was collected in Lanark Co. on Oct. 14, 1950 (James, McLaren & Barlow, 1976: 28). An immature female was caught in a fish net off Consecon, Prince Edward Co., on Nov. 24, 1948 and turned over to the ROM by H. Townson: it weighed 575 g. A specimen was shot off Hamilton in November, 1891 (McIlwraith, 1894: 39).

**MEASUREMENTS:**
*Length:* 16-18.5 ins.
(Godfrey, 1966: 196)
*Wingspread:* 27 1/8 ins.
(Maughan, 1897: 2)
25 5/8 ins. (Thompson, 1890: 200)
*Weight:* 575 g. (see above).

# BLACK GUILLEMOT   *Cepphus grylle*   (Linnaeus)

One of the joys of a visit to the Atlantic coast is seeing some of these black and white beauties with their unbelievably scarlet feet. In Ontario our northern seacoast is the only place you are likely to see them.

IDENTIFICATION: They are about the size of a small duck, black with large white wing patches and bright red feet. The bill is pointed. Young and winter adults are mainly white with dark brown barring on the back.

WINTER: There have been two Toronto specimens, a female taken on Dec. 19, 1895 (Fleming, 1906: 441) and a male taken on Dec. 11, 1920 (Fleming, 1930: 65). K.F. Edwards saw one at Kingston on Jan. 8, 1954 (Quilliam, 1973: 98).

SPRING: In the ROM is a specimen picked up by an Indian in Apr., 1940, 40 miles west of Ft. Severn (Lumsden, 1959: 54).

SUMMER: E. Beaupré saw one at Kingston on June 10, 1904 (Quilliam, 1973: 98). Schueler, Baldwin & Rising (1974: 143) noted this species only at Hawley Lake. Manning (1952: 62) saw two about 15 miles south of Cape Henrietta Maria on July 19, 1947 and one about 30 miles west of the cape on July 27, 1947. R.L. Peterson and L. Walden collected two of about 50 seen about ten miles south of Cape Henrietta Maria on July 6, 1948 (Peck, 1972: 344). H.G. Lumsden provided the first proof of breeding in Ontario when he found a hatched egg and collected two adults with brood patches (of about 80 seen) some 22 miles west of Cape Henrietta Maria (Peck, 1972: 345). Indians at Ft. Severn described to C.E. Hope on June 26, 1940 what must have been this species there and Manning also mentioned an early record from Severn House.

AUTUMN: Doug. McRae and Alan Wormington saw one or two on five days between Oct. 23 and Nov. 14 at Netitishi Point, James Bay in 1981.

**MEASUREMENTS:**
*Length:* 12 to 14 ins.
(Godfrey, 1966: 198)
*Wingspread:* about 23 ins.
(Terres, 1980: 31)
*Weight:* about 1 lb. 1 1/3
oz. (Terres, 1980: 31).

**REFERENCE:**
Lumsden, H.G. 1959
Mandt's Black Guillemot
breeding on the Hudson
Bay coast of Ontario. Can.
Field- Nat., 73:(1):54-55.

# ANCIENT MURRELET   *Synthliboramphus antiquus*   (Gmelin)

This species breeds around the north Pacific Ocean, wandering south along both coasts in winter. It is accidental in Ontario.

IDENTIFICATION: In winter plumage it looks a great deal like the smaller Atlantic species, the Dovekie and both specimens taken in Ontario were first identified as Dovekies. The larger size and pale bill appear to be the best distinctions from the Dovekie.

WINTER:

SPRING:

SUMMER:

AUTUMN: A female taken at Toronto on Nov. 18, 1901 by John Maughan Jr. and originally called a Dovekie, proved to be this species (Fleming, 1906: 441). The first Ontario specimen was found by Everett P. Wheeler at Crystal Beach (about 7 miles east of Buffalo on the Canadian shore of Lake Erie), on Nov. 15, 1908 and was originally identified as a Dovekie, but subsequent inspection by J.H. Fleming proved it to be an Ancient Murrelet (Fleming, 1912: 387-388).

**MEASUREMENTS:**
*Length:* 9.5 to 10.5 ins.
(Godfrey, 1966: 200)
*Wingspread:*
*Weight:* about 8 oz.
(Terres, 1980: 29).

**REFERENCE:**
Fleming, J.H. 1912 The
Ancient Murrelet
(*Synthliboramphus
antiquus*) in Ontario. Auk,
29:(3):387-388.

# ATLANTIC PUFFIN   *Fratercula arctica*   (Linnaeus)

Puffins, with their clownlike painted faces and bills, are the darlings of bird watchers along our Atlantic coast. There is only one Ontario record.

IDENTIFICATION: The huge laterally compressed bill is diagnostic at all seasons, though somewhat more subdued in colour in winter than during the breeding season.

WINTER:

SPRING:

SUMMER:

AUTUMN: Lloyd (1923: 103) reported one specimen taken at Ottawa during October, 1881. The specimen was made up by E.G. White, but has since been missing.

**MEASUREMENTS:**
*Length:* 11.5 to 13.5 ins.
(Godfrey, 1966: 203)
*Wingspread:* 21 to 24 ins.
(Terres, 1980: 31)
*Weight:* about 1 lb. 1 1/2
oz. (Terres, 1980: 31).

# ROCK DOVE   *Columba livia*   Gmelin

The Rock Dove is the ancestor of our domestic pigeons and many live in the wild state, nesting under bridges, on ledges of buildings, in abandoned barns as well as on cliff ledges. Now they usually are found in proximity to man and his buildings and sources of waste grain.

IDENTIFICATION: The typical Rock Dove is dark gray, with black bars on the wing coverts, a white rump and pink feet. They are often joined by white or brown semidomestic stock and a great variety of other colours but are usually recognizable as "pigeons". It was formerly not fashionable to "count" these as wild birds and many of the older lists do not mention them, but they do make up an important element of our avifauna, particularly in urban habitats where much bird watching is done, so recent counts have included the species.

WINTER:   On Christmas counts they have been common throughout the agricultural southern part of Ontario as well as at Sault Ste. Marie and Thunder Bay, becoming uncommon to rare or absent on the most northerly counts. Devitt (1967: 86) noted that eight pigeons were sent to the Jesuit Fathers at Sainte Marie, near Midland as a New Year's gift in 1647! Mills (1981: 67-68) considered it uncommon to rare in winter in towns in Muskoka and Parry Sound Districts. Dennison (1980: 146) listed this among species always present on Christmas counts at Sault Ste. Marie, with 72 on the 1979 count.

SPRING:   Stirrett (1973b: 18) called it a common permanent resident at Pelee, with 32 there on Apr. 4. George A. Scott found a dead young under a bridge in Oshawa as early as Apr. 1, 1972 and there are several records of nests with eggs (usually 2) during April (Tozer & Richards, 1974: 157). Pigeons roosting under the narrow's bridge at Huntsville attracted the attention of a Gyrfalcon on Apr. 4, 1974 (Mills, 1981: 67).

SUMMER:   On Breeding Bird Surveys they were common in the agricultural southern part of Ontario, becoming uncommon to absent on northern routes. Beardslee & Mitchell (1965: 269) reported them nesting on ledges on the steep cliffs bordering Niagara Gorge. Saunders (1947: 131) noted that a pair had hatched young on a ledge of the Spadina viaduct in Toronto on May 6, 1941. Breeding populations varied from 16 to 64 birds per 100 acres in urban quadrats in Ontario County (Speirs, 1976: 26). Snyder (1941: 58) found them nesting about farm buildings in Prince Edward Country. Mills (1981: 68) cited a few summer records for the cottage country. Nicholson (1981: 116) considered it a fairly common resident on Manitoulin. Smith (1957: 173) called it common about farms and settlements along the railroads in the Clay Belt. Snyder (1953: 60) found feral pigeons breeding around Kenora. Schueler, Baldwin & Rising (1974: 143) found them to be uncommon at Cochrane and did not find them at other localities around James and Hudson Bay.

AUTUMN:   Mills (1981: 68) cited Sept. 9, 1943 and Sept. 15, 1979 records for Magnetawan (and Parry Sound records throughout the year).

**MEASUREMENTS:**
*Length:* 11 to 13.5 ins.
(Godfrey, 1966: 207)
*Wingspread:*
*Weight:* 10 to 16 oz.
(Terres, 1980: 731)

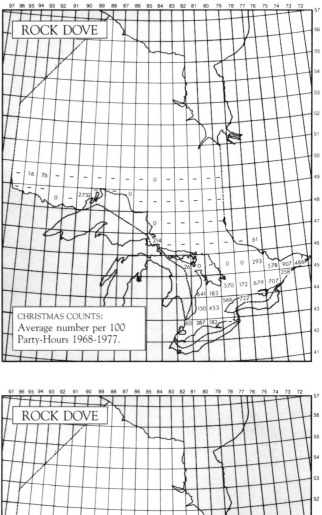

ROCK DOVE

CHRISTMAS COUNTS:
Average number per 100
Party-Hours 1968-1977.

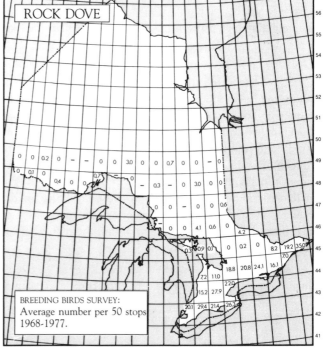

ROCK DOVE

BREEDING BIRDS SURVEY:
Average number per 50 stops
1968-1977.

# BAND-TAILED PIGEON    *Columba fasciata*    Say

This is a bird of the coast forest of British Columbia: accidental in Ontario.

**IDENTIFICATION:**    This is a large pigeon: somewhat larger than the Rock Dove and most domestic pigeons. Its tail has a narrow black band near the middle and a broad pale terminal portion. The feet and base of the bill are yellow, not dark as in the Rock Dove which has pink feet. Adult Band-tailed Pigeons have a white mark across the back of the neck. They lack the black bars on the wing coverts and white rump patch of Rock Doves.

**WINTER:**

**SPRING:**

**SUMMER:**

**AUTUMN:**    One was photographed at Dorion by A. Maki on Oct. 20, 1978 (Goodwin, 1979: 173). One was collected at Port Hope by J. Mulvey on Oct. 8, 1970 and is now in the ROM (Goodwin, 1970: 17). Gus Yaki carefully examined one near Pickering on Oct. 31, 1973 (Speirs, 1976: 25). Another was carefully identified at Rondeau on Sept. 6-7, 1930 by Melba and W.D. Bates, C.C. Bell and J.H. Smith using 8x binoculars at about 20 ft. range (Bell, 1941: 13).

**MEASUREMENTS:**
*Length:* 14.2 to 15.5 ins.
(Godfrey, 1966: 206)
*Wingspread:*
*Weight:* 280 - 350 g.
(about 10-12 oz.) (Terres,
1980: 733)

**REFERENCE:**
Bell, C.C. 1941 Unusual
bird records for Kent
County, Ontario - Band-
tailed Pigeon *Columba
fasciata* Say. Can. Field
Nat., 55:(1): 13.

# WHITE-WINGED DOVE   *Zenaida asiatica*   (Linnaeus)

This is normally a subtropical or tropical dove, breeding from southern U.S.A. south to northern South America. In Ontario it is accidental.

IDENTIFICATION:   It looks a bit like a Mourning Dove in size and general colour but has a rounded tail (not a long tapering tail as in the Mourning Dove). The tail has conspicuous white corner tips and there are large white wing patches.

WINTER:   R.S. Morphy photographed one at a feeder in Belleville on Dec. 14-19, 1975 (Goodwin, 1976: 713).

SPRING:

SUMMER:   An adult male was shot by an Indian at Ft. Albany on James Bay, on June 17, 1942 and given to T.M. Shortt and C.E. Hope. It is now Spec. No. 67776 in the ROM. (See Shortt & Hope, 1943: 449-450).

AUTUMN:

**MEASUREMENTS:**
*Length:* 285 mm. (Shortt & Hope, 1943: 449-450)
*Wingspread:* 460 mm. (Shortt & Hope, 1943: 449 450)
*Weight:* 131 g. (Shortt & Hope, 1943: 449-450)

**REFERENCE:**
Shortt, T.M. and C.E. Hope, 1943 White-winged Dove in Ontario. Auk. 60:(3): 449-450.

# MOURNING DOVE   *Zenaida macroura*   (Linnaeus)

This is the common resident dove of Ontario. In recent years it has increased in numbers and spread northward. Most early writers reported it arriving in March or early April and departing for the south in October, but large numbers now winter, patronizing bird feeders.

IDENTIFICATION:   The Mourning Dove is larger than a Robin but smaller than the Rock Dove (domestic pigeon). It is mostly gray, with iridescent pinks and greens around the neck, a long, tapering white-bordered tail and blackish blotches on the wing coverts. The mournful call "ooh-ah-ooo-ooo-ooo" is a familiar sound in its suburban and rural haunts.

WINTER:   On Christmas counts the Mourning Dove has been common along the north shores of Lake Erie and Lake Ontario, becoming rare north to Ottawa, Manitoulin, Sault Ste. Marie, Thunder Bay and Dryden. The increase in recent years is well shown by the Pickering Christmas counts, where none were seen on four counts in the early 1960's while on the 1974 count there were 672 (Speirs, 1976: 27).

SPRING:   Stirrett (1973b: 18) had a maximum of 50 at Pelee on Apr. 22 and May 20. Saunders & Dale (1933: 201) had egg dates for London from Apr. 23 (1896) to June 11 (1907). Most nests of this species contain two eggs but on May 17, 1953 Harold Lancaster found a nest with three eggs about 2 miles east of Port Glasgow, Eglin Co. (Brooman, 1954: 22). Speirs (1938: 44) gave Apr. 29 as the spring peak for Toronto. G. Bryant found a nest with two eggs at Willowdale as early as Mar. 19, 1972 (Goodwin, 1972: 598) and Barry Ranford saw one incubating on Mar. 23, 1974 at Mississauga when the temperature was 12°F (Goodwin, 1974: 634). Devitt (1967: 86) gave Apr. 5 as the 18-year average arrival date at Barrie. Mills (1981: 68) gave Mar. 29 as the 13-year average arrival date at Huntsville, with the earliest on Mar. 1, 1958. Nicholson (1981: 116) had a high spring count of 16 on Manitoulin on Apr. 12, 1980. K. Morrison found an early nest with one egg at Poplar, Manitoulin, on Apr. 25, 1973 (Goodwin, 1973: 865). Mark Robinson noted one at Cache Lake, Algonquin Park, on May 14, 1932 (MacLulich, 1938: 17). Ricker & Clarke (1939: 11) saw two at North Bay migrating westward on Apr. 28, 1924 and D. MacLulich noted the species at Frank's Bay on May 23, 1934. Denis (1961: 3) gave Apr. 29 as the average arrival date at Thunder Bay, with the earliest on Apr. 13, 1960. Peruniak (1971: 17) gave May 17 as the earliest date for Atikokan. An Indian took one on May 11, 1934 about 90 miles NW of Sioux Lookout (Snyder, 1953: 60). Alan Wormington saw one at Moosonee on May 27, 1974 (Goodwin, 1974: 796).

SUMMER:   On Breeding Bird Surveys, Mourning Doves were common in the agricultural south, becoming fairly common to absent in the Precambrian country north to Hearst, Dryden and Eagle River. Lloyd (1923: 151) reported the first Ottawa occurrence on Aug. 20, 1903 by E.G. White and the first breeding record by R.M. Anderson on July 3, 1919. Since then they have become well established there. Ricker & Clarke (1939: 11) had a record near Sturgeon Falls on Aug. 26, 1935. Harry Graham found a new nest (no eggs) as late as Aug. 29, 1938 at Maclennan, near Sault Ste. Marie (Snyder, 1942: 129). Skeel & Bondrup-Nielsen (1978: 176) flushed one at Pukaskwa on June 15-16, 1977. John B. Miles saw one at Cochrane on July 18, 1972 (Goodwin, 1972: 854). Bondrup-Nielsen (1976: 42) reported the first one at Kapuskasing on June 7, 1974 and saw none there in 1975. Elder (1979: 34) considered it to be a rare summer visitor at Geraldton, with only single birds seen. Louis Lemieux collected a male at Ship Sands, near Moosonee, on July 19, 1947 and saw another at Sandy Is. on Aug. 30 (Manning, 1952: 62-63). Ross James found young of the year at Sutton Ridges, in far northern Ontario, during the summer of 1981 (Goodwin, 1981: 935).

AUTUMN: Manning (1952: 62-63) mentioned two seen at Attawapiskat on Oct. 13, 1948 by J.P. Kelsall and Louis Lemieux and one collected at Moose Factory by Sam Waller on Sept. 11, 1929. Snyder (1953: 60) reported an immature specimen in the ROM which was taken about 8 miles west of Sioux Lookout on Oct. 15, 1930. Shirley Peruniak noted the species at Atikokan on Sept. 29 and Oct. 1, 1976 (Goodwin, 1977: 171). On Oct. 3, 1977 Skeel & Bondrup-Nielsen (1978: 176) flushed a flock of five from the road near the mouth of the Pic River, Lake Superior. MacLulich (1938: 17) had records on Sept. 23 and 30, 1930 at Brent, Algonquin Park. Nicholson (1981: 116) gave 35 as the high fall count for Manitoulin on Sept. 1, 1974. C. Campbell saw four at Parry Sound as late as Oct. 12, 1974 (Mills, 1981: 69). Frances Westman found a nest with two young nearly ready to fly as late as Sept. 23, 1950 at Angus (Devitt, 1967: 86). Snyder (1941: 59) reported flocks in Prince Edward Co. as late as Nov. 16, 1934. Allin (1940: 99) noted a nest with young at Darlington as late as Sept. 7, 1930. We had two young in a nest in our Pickering garden as late as Sept. 23, 1975 (Speirs, 1976: 27). Speirs (1938: 52) gave Sept. 7 as the fall peak for Toronto. Stirrett (1973d: 20) had a maximum count of 200 at Pelee on Sept. 15.

**MEASUREMENTS:**
*Length:* 11 to 13.2 ins.
(Godfrey, 1966: 207)
*Wingspread:* 17-19 ins.
(Roberts, 1955: 601)
*Weight:* 3 to 4 3/4 oz.
(Roberts, 1955: 601):
♀ smaller than ♂.

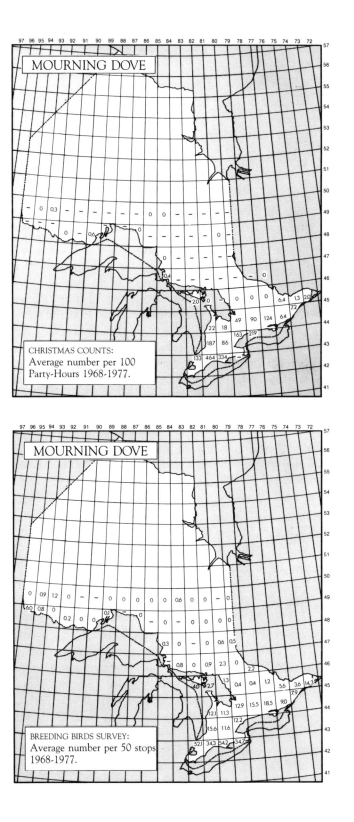

MOURNING DOVE

CHRISTMAS COUNTS:
Average number per 100
Party-Hours 1968-1977.

MOURNING DOVE

BREEDING BIRDS SURVEY:
Average number per 50 stops
1968-1977.

# PASSENGER PIGEON   *Ectopistes migratorius*   (Linnaeus)

This beauty used to breed abundantly in Ontario and wintered in southern U.S.A. It has been extinct since 1914 when the last bird died in the Cincinnati zoo. Mitchell (1935: 58) mapped its distribution in Ontario, from Glengarry Co. in the east to Lake-of-the Woods in the west, and from Long Point in the south to Ft. Severn in the north.

IDENTIFICATION:   The Passenger Pigeon was similar in shape to the Mourning Dove but larger and more colourful, with its redder breast, blue head and back. It lacked the black spot below the ear which is characteristic of the Mourning Dove.

WINTER:   R.B. Elgie reported seeing 17 in a cornfield at Dixie, near Toronto, on Jan. 1 about 1865 (Mitchell, 1935: 92). Manning (1952: 63) cited a December record for Moose Factory in the 1700's.

SPRING:   Saunders & Dale (1933: 201) reported two at Walker's Pond on Apr. 2, 1892 and 400 to 500 seen by R. Hedley over his farm in Middlesex Co. on May 22, 1902. Beardslee & Mitchell (1965: 272) cited Ontario records for Apr. 1-4, 1872 at Niagara, Mar. 20, 1883 at Niagara Falls, and Apr. 9, 1883 at Dunnville. Mitchell (1935: 89) listed Mar. 8 as the earliest date for Toronto. Fleming (1907: 72) reported an adult male taken at Toronto on May 12, 1890; a male on Apr. 13, 1891 and one on May 16, 1900. John Dutton saw one at Bowmanville on Apr. 15, 1881 (Tozer & Richards, 1974: 160). Allin (1940: 99) reported the last huge flock in Darlington Twp. in March, 1866. Quilliam (1973: 100) recorded a flock of 40-50 on March 20, 1858 at Kingston, with some on the 19th and "vast numbers" on the 21st. Devitt (1967: 87) gave Mar. 19, 1858, as the earliest date for Barrie, when a flock three miles long passed over to the west and northwest: 22 were shot near Barrie on Apr. 4, 1815 from another large flock. A.F. Young saw two at Penetanguishene on May 18, 1902 (Devitt, 1967: 89). Lloyd (1923: 151) noted 12 seen at McKay's Lake, near Ottawa, on Apr. 15, 1886, and one there on May 24, 1886.

SUMMER:   Brooman (1954: 22) reported a large nesting area in Elgin Co. about 1868-1870. Wm. Pope made a painting (dated June 30, 1860) of a young bird at Port Rowan (Snyder, 1931: 178). Fleming (1907: 71) reported that a bird seen on July 6, 1900, was the last reliable Toronto record. John Townson saw his last Passenger Pigeon on July 4, 1886 at Myrtle (Tozer & Richards, 1974: 160). The last known nesting colony (with about 12 nests) was at Rockwood, near Kingston, in 1898 (Quilliam, 1973: 99). Devitt (1967: 88) recounted tales of great nesting colonies in Simcoe Co. in the mid-1800's. Lloyd (1923: 151) had Ottawa records for June 6, 1884 (♂ shot): two females (adult & juvenal) shot on June 28, 1884; and single birds noted on Aug. 25, 1885 and on Aug. 23, 1887. Nicholson (1981: 116-117) recounted the history of the species on Manitoulin, largely as birds of passage. Snyder (1942: 129) cited Sault Ste. Marie records for the summer of 1762 and for June 30, 1848 when flocks were seen at Point aux Pins. Baillie & Hope (1947: 8) cited reports of "hundreds of thousands" at Gogama, some of which nested according to James Miller: one was seen as recently as late July, 1892 at Lake Kenogamissi. Snyder (1953: 68) cited old reports for the Lake of the Woods. Manning (1952: 63) cited evidence of former nesting at Moose Factory in June, 1888, where a specimen was collected on Aug. 16, 1860: he also mentioned a specimen from Ft. Severn, taken in 1771.

AUTUMN:    The last known specimen from the cottage country, where they were once plentiful, was taken at Pt. Sydney by A. Kay in the fall of 1880 (Mills, 1981: 69). Lloyd (1923: 151) reported one seen at Kettle Is., near Ottawa, on Sept. 3, 1887. John Townson saw a few at Carrying Place, Prince Edward Co. during October, 1876 and a male collected in the fall of 1874 at Huyck Pt. by Sam P. Morden is in the ROM. (Snyder, 1941: 59). Fleming (1907: 71) noted Toronto records for Sept. 20 and Oct. 4, 1890. Speirs (1938: 54) listed Oct. 22 as the latest Toronto date. Beardslee & Mitchell (1965: 272) gave fall records for Ft. Erie, where a pair was shot on Sept. 5, 1890, and for Niagara where a young male was taken in Sept., 1891. Godfrey (1966: 208) wrote that this specimen, taken at Skerkston, near Niagara, was the last one taken in Ontario—in mid-Sept., 1891. Wm. Pope shot one of three seen on Sept. 15, 1842 near Port Rowan and noted others on Sept. 18, Oct. 11 and Oct 14 (Snyder (1931: 178). Saunders & Dale (1933: 201) reported seeing four (of which a female and two young were collected) on Sept. 24, 1885, near London.

**MEASUREMENTS:**
*Length:* ♂ 17 1/4",
♀ 15 1/2" (Quilliam,
1973: 100) 15 to 18 ins.
(Roberts, 1955: 602)
*Wingspread:* ♀ 23 1/2"
(Quilliam, 1973: 100) 23
to 25 ins. (Roberts,
1955: 602)
*Weight:* about 12 oz.
(Roberts, 1955: 602).

**REFERENCES:**
Mitchell, Margaret H.
1935 The Passenger Pigeon
in Ontario. Univ. Toronto
Press: 1- 181.
    Schorger, A.W. 1955
The Passenger Pigeon. Its
natural history and
extinction. Univ.
Wisconsin Press: i-xiii;
1-424.

# COMMON GROUND-DOVE
## *Columbina passerina*   (Linneaus)

This is normally a bird of the tropics and subtropics, from southern U.S.A. to northern South America: accidental in Ontario.

**IDENTIFICATION:**  This is a sparrow-sized dove showing much reddish-brown in the primary wing feathers in flight.

**WINTER:**

**SPRING:**

**SUMMER:**

**AUTUMN:**   Mrs. John E. Freeman *et al* found a dead Ground Dove at Red Rock near Nipigon on Oct. 29, 1968 and sent the specimen to the ROM, where it is Specimen No. 103396 (Dick & James, 1969: 405-406).

**MEASUREMENTS:**
*Length:* 6 3/4 ins. (Pough,
1951: 313)
*Wingspread:*
*Weight:* 22.4 to 41.2 g.
(average 30.1 g.)
(Dunning, 1984: 13)

**REFERENCE:**
Dick, James A. and Ross
D. James 1969 The
Ground Dove in Canada.
Can. Field-Nat.,
83:(4): 405-406.

# CAROLINA PARAKEET   *Conuropsis carolinensis*   (Linnaeus)

This extinct parakeet once occurred over much of the eastern United States but was last reported in Florida in February, 1920.

IDENTIFICATION:   This colourful bird was about the size and shape of a Mourning Dove, except for the typical heavy parrotlike beak. The body was mainly green, with head and neck yellow, shading to orange or red on the forehead and cheeks. The tail was green above and yellow below.

WINTER:

SPRING:

SUMMER:

AUTUMN:   Saunders & Dale (1933: 201) listed this as a hypothetical species for the London region: "About 1877 Russell Burnett went up to the "Valley" at the head of Maitland St., London, and shot a yellow and green parrot out of a tree. The specimen was not preserved, and although it probably was a Carolina Paroquet, there is now no proof, and the species is therefore placed on the hypothetical list."

**MEASUREMENTS:**
*Length:* about 13 ins.
(Howell, 1932: 283)
*Wingspread:* 21 to 23 ins.
(Howell, 1932: 283)
Weight:

**REFERENCE:**
Howell, Arthur H., 1932
Florida bird life. Fla. Dept.
Game & Fresh Water Fish
& U.S. Dept. Agr., Bureau
Biological Survey: i-xxiv;
1-579. Account of
"Carolina Paroquet"
pp. 283- 286.

# BLACK-BILLED CUCKOO
*Coccyzus erythropthalmus*  (Wilson)

This is the more common cuckoo in Ontario, except in the Pelee vicinity. They winter in northwestern South America. Many observers have noted local increases in abundance when there have been outbreaks of tent caterpillars, a food source avoided by many birds but used by cuckoos.

IDENTIFICATION: These are grackle-sized birds, brown above and white below. From the Yellow-billed Cuckoo, this species is distinguished by its all dark bill, lack of the cinnamon flash on the wings in flight and lack of the big white spots on the tail (this species has narrow white bars instead). Young Yellow-billed Cuckoos many also lack the big white tail spots and may have green, instead of red eye rings, a conspicuous feature of adult Black-billed Cuckoos. The call of this species usually consists of paired notes "Cow-cow....cow-cow...cow-cow...etc." but single notes are sometimes uttered and it is best to try to actually see the bird to confirm identification.

WINTER:

SPRING:   Stirrett (1973b: 18) gave May 7 as the earliest Pelee record, with a maximum of 20 on May 13. Ussher (1965: 14) gave May 18 as the 17-year average arrival date at Rondeau, with the earliest on May 7. Saunders & Dale (1933: 202) gave May 22 as the 14-year average arrival date for London, with the earliest on May 9, 1913. Snyder (1931: 185) had his earliest Long Point arrival on May 19, 1928. Speirs (1938: 40) listed May 8 as the earliest Toronto date. Long (1966: 29) noted one at Pickering Beach as early as May 6, 1964. Ron Tozer watched one building as early as May 30, 1969 near Port Perry (Tozer & Richards, 1974: 31). Snyder (1941: 60) noted its return at Hallowell, Prince Edward Co., on May 24, 1930. Weir & Quilliam (1980: 36) gave May 18 as the 26-year average arrival date at Kingston with the earliest on May 5: E. Beaupré collected a set of 3 eggs on May 30, 1900 and described another found on May 31, 1896 (Quilliam, 1973: 101). Devitt (1967: 90) gave May 26 as the 15-year average arrival date at Barrie, with a very early one at the Holland River on May 5, 1939: a set of 4 eggs was collected at Barrie on May 30, 1938 by H.P. Bingham. Mills (1981: 70) gave May 18 as the 7-year average arrival date for Huntsville, with the earliest on May 7, 1972 by V. Heron: a window casualty on May 15, 1962, at Dwight contained an "egg in the yolk stage." Nicholson (1981: 117) gave May 22 as the 7-year average arrival date on Manitoulin, the earliest on May 13, 1978. Louise Lawrence noted one at Rutherglen on May 25, 1944 (Speirs & Speirs, 1947: 29). Skeel & Bondrup-Nielsen (1978: 176) noted one eating spiders on the beach at Pukaskwa on May 24, 1977. Denis (1961: 4) gave June 1 as the average arrival date at Thunder Bay, with the earliest on May 18, 1953. Smith (1957: 73) observed one near New Liskeard on May 30-31, 1954 and one at Hearst on May 31.

SUMMER:   On Breeding Bird Surveys it has been fairly common but well distributed from North Bay southward. North of there the occurrences have been rather spotty, absent on some routes and fairly common at others, probably reflecting local caterpillar outbreaks. Stirrett (1973c: 16-17) had records throughout the summer at Pelee, but somewhat fewer than for Yellow-billed Cuckoo. Saunders & Dale (1933: 202) noted sets of 3 eggs on June 19, 1891 and June 9, 1908 and a set of four on June 1, 1912 at London. Brooman (1954: 22) cited a record of a nest with two eggs at St. Thomas on June 7, 1887. John Edmonds found a nest with 4 eggs (and one egg of Yellow-billed Cuckoo) 2 1/2 ft. up in a buttonbush thicket on Long Point on June 24, 1927 (Snyder, 1931: 185-186). At Toronto, Thompson (1890: 193, 195) reported nests with 2 eggs as early as June 2, 1889 (by Wm. Brodie) and as late as Aug. 12, 1889 (by James R. Thurston): Atkinson (1892: 80) collected one after it flew off a Wood Pewee's nest in July 1885 and saw another come off a Yellow Warbler's nest in July, 1886 (both eggs taken). Paul Harrington found a nest with 3 eggs in King Twp. on June 19, 1926 (Snyder, 1930: 188). J.M. Richards found a nest with 2 eggs and one young as early as June 2, 1962 near Whitby and two adults building as late as Aug. 21, 1968 near Oshawa (Tozer & Richards, 1974: 161). Snyder (1941: 60) noted nest building on June 15, 1930 at Hallowell, Prince Edward Co.: this nest held two eggs (and one egg of a Yellow-billed Cuckoo) on June 23. E. Beaupré collected a set of 5 eggs on June 4, 1901 at Kingston and a nest with young was seen near Crow Lake on June 24, 1962 (Quilliam, 1973: 101). Devitt (1967: 90) detailed several nest records for Simcoe Co., including a late nest with 2 eggs on Aug. 6, 1933 that he found near Oakview. Lloyd (1923: 153-154) cited details of several nest records for the Ottawa region, including W. Anderson's nest with 3 eggs as early as June 3, 1899 near Cyrville. Mills (1981: 70-71) gave details of several nests in the cottage country, mostly in June and July, but one as late as Aug. 5, 1926 at Sundridge by J.M. Speirs. A nest with 2 eggs was found at Mindemoya, Manitoulin, on June 16, 1938 by J.L. Baillie (Nicholson, 1981: 117). At Rutherglen, L.L. Snyder collected a female which contained an egg on July 2, 1935 (Speirs & Speirs, 1947: 29). Ricker & Clarke (1939: 11) saw one carrying food to young at Frank's Bay, Lake Nipissing on June 26, 1933. Snyder (1942: 130) reported a nest with 5 eggs in a hazel shrub near Maclennan (vicinity of Sault Ste. Marie) on June 30, 1931. Fred A.E. Starr found a nest with 3 eggs and one young at Sudbury on June 20, 1936 (Baillie & Hope, 1947: 9), who found them common in parts of Sudbury District during an outbreak of forest tent caterpillars in 1937. Skeel & Bondrup-Nielsen (1978: 176) heard one calling on June 28, 1977 at Pukaskwa. Smith (1957: 173) found them "in greater numbers during 1953, a year of generally heavy tent caterpillar infestations" from Kapuskasing to Lake Abitibi. Elder (1979: 34) called it a rare summer resident at Geraldton. Dear (1940: 129) took a set of 3 eggs on July 12, 1931 near Thunder Bay. Peruniak (1971: 17) called it an uncommon summer resident at Atikokan from June 1 to Aug. 31, but commoner in 1962 and 1963 when a tent caterpillar outbreak was building up. Snyder (1938: 189) noted one at Rainy River on June 20, 1929. L.S. Paterson saw one at Kenora on June 10, 1932 (Baillie & Harrington, 1936: 44). Snyder (1953: 60-61) reported this species on 9 of 21 days between Ingolf and Savanne where a female collected on July 7, 1937 had an egg in the oviduct: this was during an outbreak of forest tent caterpillars: however, individuals were noted on July 5-6, 1947 at Sioux Lookout when there was no outbreak.

**AUTUMN:** Smith (1957: 173) heard one about 10 miles NW of Timmins on Sept. 6, 1953. Nicholson (1981: 117) gave Oct. 11, 1970 as the latest date for Manitoulin. The latest date for Parry Sound was Oct. 9, 1976 (Mills, 1981: 71). Devitt (1967: 90) gave Sept. 15, 1940 as the latest Simcoe Co. record (at Holland River). Weir & Quilliam (1980: 36) gave Sept. 10 as the 22-year average departure date from Kingston, with the latest on Oct. 25, 1959 at Amherst Is. Tozer & Richards (1974: 162) reported a window casualty in Whitby at late as Oct. 8, 1955. Saunders (1947: 367) listed Oct. 13 as his latest Toronto record. Snyder (1931: 185) mentioned one that struck the Long Point lighthouse between Sept. 24 and 29, 1929. Ussher (1965: 14) gave Sept. 21 as the 9-year average departure date from Rondeau, with the latest on Oct. 21. Stirrett (1973d: 21) gave Oct. 21 as his latest Pelee record. This species tends to migrate south earlier than the Yellow-billed, so examine late birds carefully!

**MEASUREMENTS:**
*Length:* 11 to 12.6 ins. (Godfrey, 1966: 210)
*Wingspread:* 15 to 16.75 ins. (Roberts, 1955: 603)
*Weight:* 34.7 to 40 grams (Terres, 1980: 146).

**REFERENCE:**
Nolan, Val Jr. and Charles F. Thompson 1975 The occurrence and significance of anomalous reproductive activities in two North American non-parasitic cuckoos *Coccyzus* sp. Ibis, 117: (4): 496-503. (As noted above they sometimes lay in other birds' nests, but not to the extent of Old World cuckoos.)

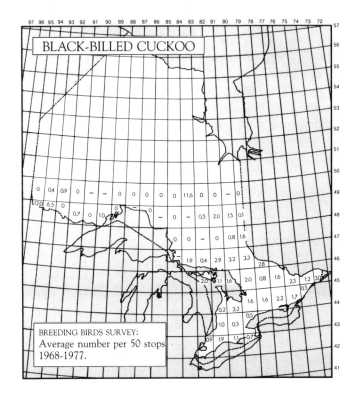

BLACK-BILLED CUCKOO

BREEDING BIRDS SURVEY:
Average number per 50 stops
1968-1977.

# YELLOW-BILLED CUCKOO
## *Coccyzus americanus* (Linnaeus)

Except along the north shore of Lake Erie this is generally the less common of our two cuckoos, in Ontario. Both are rather late spring arrivals, sometimes not showing up until June. They winter in South America.

IDENTIFICATION: From the Black-billed Cuckoo it is separated by its yellow lower mandible, the cinnamon flash in the wing in flight, the large white spots on the tail and the green, rather than red eye ring. The calls are not always separable but the call of the Yellow-bill usually starts with a gargle, followed by single, not double, series of "cows", rather than the double Cow-cow—-cow-cow—-cow-cow—- of the Black-bill. The notes of this species often have a guttural ending "Cowug—-cowug—-".

WINTER:

SPRING: Stirrett (1973b: 18) considered it fairly common at Pelee, with the earliest arrival on May 4 and a maximum of 12 on May 17. Ussher (1965: 14) gave May 18 as the 12-year average arrival date for Rondeau, with the earliest on May 5. Saunders & Dale (1933: 201) gave May 22 as the 17-year average arrival date for London, with the earliest on May 8, 1912. Speirs (1938: 40) gave May 17 as the earliest Toronto date. Pearson (1892: 77) was given a female caught roosting in Toronto's Union Station at 4 am. on May 29, 1890. Naomi LeVay noted one at Eastbourne, Whitby, as early as May 12, 1957 (Tozer & Richards, 1974: 160). Frank Brimley noted one as early as May 27, 1913 in Prince Edward Co. (Snyder, 1941: 60). Weir & Quilliam (1980: 36) gave May 20 as the 23-year average arrival date for Kingston, with the earliest on May 2: nests with 3 eggs each were found there on May 23, 1897 and May 29, 1898 (Quilliam, 1973: 101). One was recorded on Manitoulin as early as May 21, 1979 (Nicholson, 1981: 117).

SUMMER: On Breeding Bird Surveys it has been most plentiful on routes near the north shores of Lake Erie and Lake Ontario, becoming rare north to Haileybury, Suomi (Thunder Bay) and Eagle River. On our 1970 study of a 25-acre quadrat in hackberry forest at Pelee we found 1.5 territories (one competely in the quadrat and two others on its borders). Saunders & Dale (1933: 201) reported one set of 5 eggs at London on June 7, 1902 and four sets of 3 eggs from June 8 (1912) to June 26 (1895). Brooman (1954: 22) reported a set of two eggs found at St. Thomas on June 3, 1885 and a nest with young as late as August in 1949. At Long Point, John Edmonds collected a nestling from a nest with three young on July 6, 1927 and Snyder (1931: 185) described the curious pin-feathered appearance of the young and its unbirdlike behaviour: he also remarked that an egg of this species was found in a Black-billed Cuckoo's nest there. William Brodie discovered a pair nesting in Toronto during the summer of 1884 and specimens were taken there in June, 1896; 2 on June 12, 1889 and one on June 17, 1889 and one on July 29, 1889 (Thompson, 1890: 183, 184, 194). One was seen in King Twp. on June 14, 1925 by H.H. Brown *et al* (Snyder, 1930: 188). Synder (1941: 60) reported first arrivals in Prince Edward Co. on June 12, 1930 when five were noted: Frank Brimley found a nest near Consecon on June 29, 1930: and again an egg of this species was found in a Black-billed Cuckoo's nest on June 23, 1930. Quilliam (1973: 101) saw one carrying food on July 1, 1967 near Kingston. Devitt (1967: 89) cited several nest records for Simcoe Co.

from June 17 (1954) to Aug. 4 (1939): and A.J. Mitchener found a nest with 4 eggs in summer, 1957, only 20 yards from a nesting Black-billed Cuckoo! Lloyd (1923: 153) had only one specimen record from Ottawa, taken June 27, 1890 from a nesting pair. J.L. Baillie found a nest with one egg on July 5, 1946 which held 3 eggs on July 7, at Franklin Is. north of Parry Sound (Mills, 1981: 69) who cited a few other records from the cottage country, including one collected by R. Anderson at Go Home Bay on June 3, 1903. L. Dyer observed one carefully on June 15, 1963 at Atikokan (Peruniak, 1971: 17).

AUTUMN: Denis (1961: 6) gave Sept. 24, 1958 as the first record for Thunder Bay. Snyder (1942: 130) mentioned a specimen from Michipicoten Is., Lake Superior, dated Sept. 10, 1901. Nicholson (1981: 117) saw one on Manitoulin as late as Oct. 6, 1978. On Sept. 25, 1965, T. Kilner reported two at Huntsville (Mills, 1981: 70). Frances Westman picked up a highway casualty near Barrie on Oct. 13, 1954 (Devitt, 1967: 89). Weir & Quilliam (1980: 36) gave Sept. 22 as the 17-year average departure date from Kingston, with the latest on Nov. 2: a pair was noted feeding young there as late as Sept. 23, 1960 (Quilliam, 1973: 101). Naomi LeVay had late observations at Eastbourne on Oct. 21, 1961 and Nov. 20, 1954 (Tozer & Richards, 1974: 161). Speirs (1938: 54) gave Oct. 3 as the latest Toronto date. After "Hurricane Hazel" on Oct 24, 1954, one was seen at Rockhouse Point and one at Stromness (Beardslee & Mitchell, 1965: 274). Ussher (1965: 14) gave Sept. 18 as the 8-year average departure date from Rondeau with the latest on Oct. 16. Stirrett (1973d: 20) had a maximum of 10 at Pelee on Sept. 10 and saw his latest there on Nov. 1.

**MEASUREMENTS:**
*Length:* 11 to 12.6 ins.
(Godfrey, 1966: 209)
*Wingspread:* 15.5 to 17
ins. (Roberts, 1955: 603)
*Weight:* 2 1/8 oz.
(Roberts, 1955: 603)

**REFERENCE:**
Pearson, Chas E. 1892
*Coccyzus americanus* in
Union Station. Trans. Can.
Inst., 3: Part 1: (5): 77.

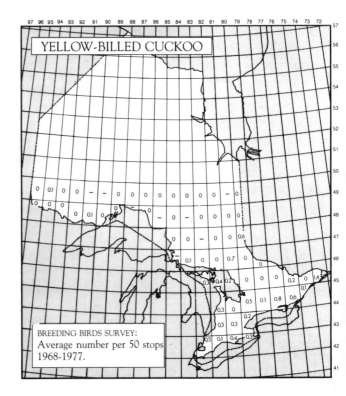

YELLOW-BILLED CUCKOO

BREEDING BIRDS SURVEY:
Average number per 50 stops
1968-1977.

# GROOVE-BILLED ANI   *Crotophaga sulcirostris*   Swainson

This relative of the cuckoos normally lives in the tropics and subtropics, from southern Texas south into South America. In Ontario it is an accidental.

IDENTIFICATION:   The big, laterally compressed bill with prominent grooves (if you are close enough) distinguishes this bird from the Smooth-billed Ani and from grackles, which it resembles in colour and size and large tail.

WINTER:

SPRING:

SUMMER:

AUTUMN:   The first specimen was found at Sundridge on Oct. 27, 1978 and sent to the ROM, *fide* Ross James (Goodwin, 1979: 278). The only other Ontario record was by R. Wagner who carefully studied one at Stromness on Oct. 12, 1969 (Goodwin, 1970: 42).

**MEASUREMENTS:**
*Length:* 12 to 12 1/2 ins.
(Terres, 1980: 146)
*Wingspread:* 16 ins.
(Terres, 1980: 146)
*Weight:* 6 ♂ from 69.5 to 98.4 g. 3 ♀ from 72.1 to 75.2 g. (Terres, 1980: 146).

# COMMON BARN-OWL   *Tyto alba*   (Scopoli)

This cosmopolitan species is quite rare in Ontario. It is most likely to be found in old church steeples or barn silos. Their ability to find mice by hearing on dark nights is well known. They breed well in some captive conditions.

IDENTIFICATION: They are pale buffy brown above and whitish below, dotted with dark "freckles". The heart-shaped face and dark eyes have earned them the nickname of "monkey-faced owls". The notes that I have heard are an explosive hiss (reminding me of steam from the safety valve of a steam radiator when overheated).

WINTER: Stirrett (1973a: 16) had two winter records from Pelee, on Dec. 1 and Dec. 10. Saunders & Dale (1933: 202) had two winter records for London; one in 1901-1902 and the other taken on Dec. 18, 1925 by G.F. Kennedy. One was shot in St. Thomas on Feb. 10, 1952 (Brooman, 1954: 23). Fleming (1930: 68) had two records of Barn Owls taken near Brantford: one on Dec. 21, 1927 and the other prior to Dec. 15th, 1927: he also mentioned one captured at St. Catharines about Feb. 17, 1928 which was sent to the Toronto Zoo. One was killed at Kingston Mills in Dec., 1911 (Quilliam, 1973: 102).

SPRING: Stirrett (1973b: 18) considered it very rare at Pelee, from Apr. 1 to May 25. Ussher (1965: 14) had only one Rondeau record: on May 18, 1942. E. Boug shot one in his barn in London in Apr., 1923 (Saunders & Dale, 1933: 202). One was found in South Aldborough Twp., Elgin Co., on Apr. 6, 1953 (Brooman, 1954: 23). F. Salisbury found a nest with two young at Thorold on Apr. 5, 1955 (Beardslee & Mitchell, 1965: 277). McIlwraith (1894: 223) mentioned a specimen taken in Hamilton in May, 1882 and two seen near Sault Ste. Marie by C.J. Bampton (no date). Speirs (1938: 40) listed an Apr. 24 record for Toronto. Saunders (1947: 160, 367) wrote about an encounter with one on the Toronto lakefront on May 24, 1940 and cited a May 13 record by J.L. Baillie. Speirs (1976: 32) cited four records for the Pickering-Oshawa lakefront: Apr. 24, 1956 (found dead at Oshawa); May 12-13, 1962 near Whitby (photographed by G. Norris); Apr. 24, 1966 (photographed at Corner Marsh, Pickering by G. Norris and Bob Wood); and another at Oshawa on May 5, 1973. Quilliam (1965: 101) reported one seen at Kingston on Apr. 20, 1949 and another on May 12, 1958. One was found dead at Kingston on May 3, 1966 and one raised two young there in 1970 and returned on Apr. 12, 1971 but died on Apr. 19 (Quilliam, 1973: 102). Carmen Douglas sent an adult male weighing 317 g. taken at Michipicoten Harbour, Algoma on Mar. 25, 1957 to the ROM where it is Skin No. 91704.

SUMMER: Stirrett (1973c: 17) had one summer record for Pelee, on Aug. 5. Kelley (1978: 43) reported one at Bradley's Marsh in 1968. Gertrude Selby noted three young "about ready to fly" in a nest at Queenston on Aug. 20, 1950 and a nest with 5 young there in the first week of June, 1951 (Beardslee & Mitchell, 1965: 277). "Nesting has taken place within recent years in a church belfry in St. Catharines" (Sheppard, 1960: 29). C.E. Cantelon took one alive at Norval on June 13, 1923 (Fleming, 1930: 68). One was observed at Kingston on Aug. 21, 1955, in a collegiate belfry (Quilliam, 1965: 101).

AUTUMN: Johnson (1934: 82) wrote about one that was first noted in captivity in the southern outskirts of Ottawa in the latter part of Oct., 1933 by H.L. Bailey and the mounted skin was confirmed by Johnson in Jan., 1934. L. Beamer reported one taken

alive from an Owen Sound grain elevator on Nov. 15, 1940 and sent alive to the ROM.
The Kingston bird first noted on Aug. 21, 1955 was last seen on Oct. 20, 1955 (Quilliam,
1965: 101). Margaret Houlding reported one north of Oshawa on Nov. 22, 1971 (Tozer
& Richards, 1974: 32). Fleming (1907: 74) noted one taken at Toronto on Sept. 7, 1899.
Saunders (1947: 367) listed Oct. 15 and Nov. 5 dates for Toronto. F. Salisbury noted
five at Thorold on Sept. 5, 1955 (Beardslee & Mitchell, 1965: 277). Harold Lancaster
reported one shot during the fall of 1946 in South Dunwich Twp., Elgin Co. (Brooman,
1954: 22). Fleming (1930: 68) examined one taken near Kingsville on Sept. 3, 1919.
Stirrett (1973d: 21) had four fall records for Pelee: Oct. 12, 1936; Oct. 31, 1945; Nov.
4, 1918 and Nov. 13, 1936; all single birds.

**MEASUREMENTS:**
*Length:* 14.5 to 17.5 ins.
(Godfrey, 1966: 211)
*Wingspread:* 43.25 to
47.0 ins. (Roberts,
1955: 606)
*Weight:* ♂ 20 oz. ♀ 18 to
24 oz. (Roberts,
1955: 606)

**REFERENCE:**
Johnson, C.E. 1934
American Barn Owl (*Tyto
alba*) at Ottawa. Can.
Field-Nat., 48:(5):82.

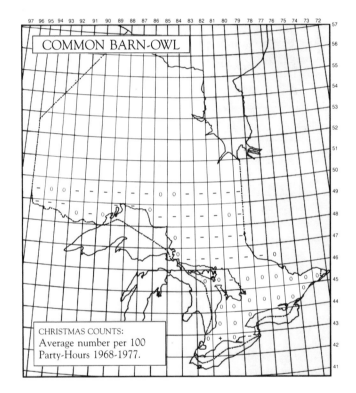

COMMON BARN-OWL

CHRISTMAS COUNTS:
Average number per 100
Party-Hours 1968-1977.

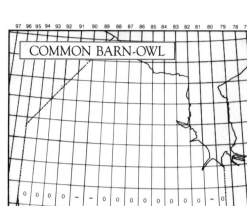

COMMON BARN-OWL

BREEDING BIRDS SURVEY:
Average number per 50 stops
1968-1977.

# EASTERN SCREECH-OWL   *Otus asio*   (Linnaeus)

The Screech Owl nests in tree cavities (or nest boxes) in southern Ontario and tends to be resident wherever found.

IDENTIFICATION: This is the smallest of the Ontario owls which have prominent ear tufts. They may be rufous (or red) or more likely gray: there are two colour phases. Owls, being nocturnal are more likely to be heard than seen: the call of this species is a tremulous whistle (not a screech by any stretch of the imagination): sometimes all the notes are on one pitch but usually rise and then fall away. The summer food is largely big insects but mice and small birds make up the winter diet.

WINTER: On Christmas counts they have been fairly common in southerwestern Ontario, becoming rare north to Ottawa and Meaford. Stirrett (1973a: 16) had records of single birds at Pelee throughout the winter. We had a Screech Owl at our home in Pickering on 9 of 28 winters, roosting in an old flicker hole (Speirs, 1976: 33) Snyder (1941: 60) gave specimen records for Wellington, Prince Edward Co., on Feb. 2, 1937 and Feb. 10, 1934 (a female intermediate between the red and gray phases). The 10 noted at Kingston on Dec. 19, 1971 was the high Christmas count for Canada that year (Quilliam, 1973: 102-103). A red phase male was found dead at Barrie on Dec. 8, 1945 (Devitt, 1967: 90). L. Beamer had winter records at Meaford during 8 winters, pellets collected at a roost site at the town hall on Feb. 15, 1947, contained the beak and foot of a Starling (a bird almost as large as a Screech Owl). Mills (1981: 71) reported Hunstville records on Jan. 11 and 18, 1960 and a specimen taken at Emsdale in January, 1895.

SPRING: Stirrett (1973b: 18) had Pelee records from Apr. 4 to May 25. Kelley (1978: 43) reported a nest with eggs in a barn in Gosfield Twp., Essex Co. as early as Apr. 17, 1964. Saunders & Dale (1933: 202) mentioned four nests in or near London, including a nest with 4 eggs on May 5, 1900 and a nest with 4 young on May 22, 1921 both by W.A. Balkwill. Marshall Field found a nest with two young at St. Thomas on May 30, 1949 (Brooman, 1954: 23). John L. Jackson found a nest with 5 eggs about 5 miles east of Victoria Park, Toronto, on Apr. 27, 1890 (Fleming, 1907: 74 and Trans. Can. Inst., 3: Part 1: (5): 73). J.M. Richards found a nest with 2 eggs as early as Apr. 5, 1967 near Oshawa and another there on May 2, 1964 (Tozer & Richards, 1974: 162-163), they also reported a headless one found on the edge of a Great Horned Owl's nest in Whitby on Mar. 29, 1958. E. Beaupré found a nest with 5 eggs on Apr. 21, 1926 at Kingston (Quilliam, 1973: 103). H.P. Bingham collected a set of 5 eggs on May 24, 1918 near Barrie (Devitt, 1967: 90). At Honey Harbour, D. Sutherland and G. Gemmell heard one regularly from March 19 to Apr. 1, 1977 (Mills, 1981: 71). Gerry McKeating heard one near Gore May, Manitoulin, on May 21, 1972 (Nicholson, 1981: 118). Robert Fraser noted one at North Bay on Apr. 9, 1944 (Speirs & Speirs, 1947: 29).

SUMMER: Stirrett (1973c: 17) had a nest record for Pelee and recorded single birds or pairs through the summer months. Ussher (1965: 14) gave it as a nesting resident at Rondeau. James R. Thurston reported a brood of four young (1 red, 3 gray) at Toronto on June 20, 1889 (Thompson, 1890: 194). Snyder (1930: 188) noted a brood of flying young with adult in King Twp., near Toronto, on June 16, 1926. On June 21, 1949, we saw four by the road in front of our Pickering home which we considered to be adults with flying young; and R.C. Long had a late July, 1973 record for Cannington (Speirs,

1976: 33). On June 17, 1950 George North and R.B. Stewart found two adults and four young at Kingston (Quilliam, 1973: 103). Paul Harrington saw five young recently out of the nest at Wasaga Beach on July 17, 1920 (Devitt, 1967: 90). Lloyd (1923: 153) banded two young at Ottawa on June 7, 1922. D. MacDonald heard one at Ahmic Lake on Aug. 9, 1967 (Mills, 1981: 71). A. Kay listed this as a resident species at Pt. Sydney, Muskoka (Trans. Can. Inst., 3: Part 1:(5):79). Nicholson (1981: 118) heard Screech Owls on Manitoulin on June 29, 1969 and July 15, 1972. J.W. Aldrich noted one in mid-June, 1938 at Fish Bay, Lake Nipissing (Ricker & Clarke, 1939: 11). Snyder (1942: 130) mentioned summer records at Sault Ste. Marie by Harry Graham. Snyder (1938: 190) cited two records from the Rainy River region: one at Emo and one at Sabaskong Bay, Lake of the Woods.

AUTUMN: D.B. Ferguson noted one at Spring Bay, Manitoulin, on Nov. 1, 1980 (Nicholson, 1981: 118). Devitt (1967: 91) reported one female taken at Collingwood on Nov. 2, 1947. We have noted both red and gray phase birds at our Pickering home (Speirs, 1976: 33). Saunders (1947: 321) described the banding of a red-phased bird by H. Southam on Nov. 20, 1938 at Toronto: the bird "played dead" when handled. Stirrett (1973d: 21) saw single birds or sometimes two at Pelee throughout the fall months.

BANDING: (See above). Paul Catling banded a red phase bird at Ajax on Jan. 18, 1970 which was recovered by J. Treffers near Whitby on Feb. 1, 1970. He also banded another red phase bird at Ajax on Oct. 10, 1968 that was recovered at the same place on Dec. 26, 1969 (Speirs, 1976: 33). One banded at Toronto on May 30, 1944 was shot in October, 1950 at Toronto (about 6 1/2 years later). Many others banded at Toronto have returned to the banding site.

**MEASUREMENTS:**
*Length:* 7 to 10 ins.
(Godfrey, 1966: 212)
*Wingspread:* 18 to 24 ins.
(Roberts, 1955: 606)
*Weight:* ♂ 4 to 6 oz.
♀ 5 to 7 oz. (Roberts, 1955: 606).

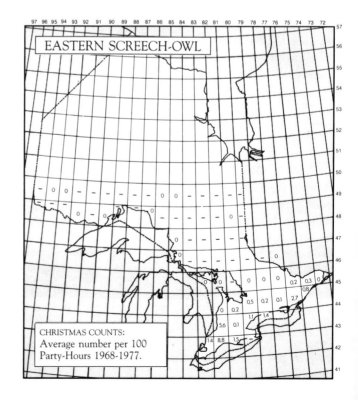

EASTERN SCREECH-OWL

CHRISTMAS COUNTS:
Average number per 100
Party-Hours 1968-1977.

# GREAT HORNED OWL   *Bubo virginianus*   (Gmelin)

This is the most frequently noted Ontario owl, occurring at all seasons throughout much of the province, wherever there are trees. There have been periodic invasions of the pale northern race associated with fluctuations in Varying Hare populations (Speirs, 1939: 412-413).

**IDENTIFICATION:** This is the largest of our owls that have ear tufts, much larger than a crow. In southern Ontario they are usually a rich tawny colour but from James Bay westward in the north they are often almost as white as Snowy Owls. This is a very early nester, often beginning in February in the southern part of Ontario. A mob of heckling crows will often lead you to a Great Horned Owl. At night listen for their "hoo-hoohoo-hoo-hoo".

**WINTER:** On Christmas counts they have been fairly common in the Kingston-Thousand Island region, uncommon at most localities south of Ottawa and Manitoulin Island and rather scattered in the north to Hornepayne and Manitouwadge. Fleming (1930: 69) reported a specimen of the pale Arctic race taken at Pelee Island a few days before Jan. 21, 1901 (when he examined it). Kelley (1978: 44) cited a nest record for Lambton Co. as early as Feb. 5, 1967. Saunders & Dale (1933: 203) had a set of two eggs taken at London on Feb. 25, 1915. Harold Lancaster found a nest on Feb. 27, 1948 in Aldborough Twp., Elgin Co. some forty ft. up in a maple in a nest which has been used in previous years by crows and Red-tailed Hawks: young were first noted in this nest on March 25 (Brooman, 1954: 23). Wm. Cross reported receiving one male from Weston on Feb. 7, 1889 (Thompson, 1890: 188). Ron Tozer saw an adult on a nest (built previously by Red-shouldered Hawks) on Feb. 15, 1964 which held two eggs on Feb. 22: J.A. Edwards found a nest with three eggs in an old Great Blue Heron nest on Thorah Is. in Lake Simcoe on Feb. 27, 1931 (Speirs, 1976: 34). Jim Bayly noted an incubating bird at Abbey Dawn, near Kingston, on Feb. 24, 1968 (Quilliam, 1973: 103). Louise Lawrence heard one at Rutherglen on Feb. 15, 1945 (Speirs & Speirs, 1947: 29). Skeel & Bondrup-Nielsen (1978: 176) heard only one at Pukaskwa, on Jan. 2, 1977.

**SPRING:** Saunders & Dale (1933: 203) cited several sets of eggs taken near London: 2 eggs on March 19, 1901; three eggs on March 21, 1902 almost hatched; two almost hatched on March 26, 1903; and two almost hatched on Apr. 1, 1909. A.A. Wood found a young one in a Great Blue Heron nest, nearly ready to fly on Apr. 28, 1914. A.R. Muma found three young in old heron nests in Welland Co.: two in spring, 1948 and one half grown on Apr. 23, 1949 (Sheppard, 1960: 29). Fleming (1907: 74) reported nests in Vaughan Twp. on Mar. 25, 1889 and in Scarborough on Apr. 2, 1897. On May 11, 1928, E. Beaupré found a nest with two young in an old heron nest at Narboro Lake, near Kingston (Quilliam, 1973: 103). Devitt (1967: 91) found a half-grown young in a nest 60 ft. up in a sugar maple near Barrie on Apr. 24, 1938: the nest contained one house rat, one partly eaten cottontail and many Starling feathers. On Mar. 28, 1909, E. Norman found a nest with three eggs 85 ft. up in a pine at Doe Lake, one of several nests reported from the cottage country (Mills, 1981: 71). Dear (1940: 129) reported a nest with 2 eggs near Thunder Bay on Mar. 8, 1933 and a nest with 3 eggs on Mar. 24, 1935 and Denis (1961: 5) noted a nest with 2 young there on May 23, 1951.

SUMMER: On Breeding Bird Surveys it has been uncommon to rare but present on most southern routes, more scattered in the north to Cochrane, Kapuskasing and Nipigon. P.A. Taverner saw one near Kemptville in mid-July, 1918 (Lloyd, 1923: 153). Nicholson (1981: 118) indicated a recent decline in the Manitoulin population, but saw an immature bird there on July 19, 1980. Ricker & Clarke (1939: 12) found a well-grown young near North Bay on June 11, 1924. C.H.D. Clarke saw two well-grown young at Batchawana Bay on July 12, 1935 (Baillie & Harrington, 1936: 46). Snyder (1928: 261) secured two juvenile specimens at Macdiarmid, Lake Nipigon, on June 23, 1923. Peruniak (1971: 17) had Atikokan records on Aug. 14 and 26, 1961. Snyder (1953: 61) heard three at Savanne on the night of July 6, 1937. Hope (1938: 22) collected two juveniles not long out of the nest at Favourable Lake on July 29, 1938. R.V. Whelan found a nest at Smoky Falls on July 22, 1933 and took a juvenile specimen on June 15, 1933 there (Baillie & Harrington 1936: 46). Cringan (1953d: 3) saw one at Kasabonika Lake on June 5, 1953. Cringan (1950: 11) heard this species at Nikip Lake twice in June, 1950 and Elsey reported a nest with young on the Muzhikoba Creek. Schueler, Baldwin & Rising (1974: 143) noted this species only at Cochrane and Hawley Lake, not at any of their James Bay or Hudson Bay localities. McLaren & McLaren (1981: 4) found a nest with three young in a spruce forest along the Severn River on June 17, 1977 (between 53° and 54° North).

AUTUMN: Cringan (1950: 11) saw one beside Magiss Lake on Sept. 2, 1950. D. McRae and A. Wormington noted this species at Netitishi Point on James Bay, on Oct. 22 and 26, 1981. Peruniak (1971: 17) had Atikokan records on Sept. 22, 1962 and Sept. 19, 1965. W. Wyett saw one at Pukaskwa on Sept. 18, 1971 (Skeel & Bondrup-Nielsen, 1978: 176). Nicholson (1981: 118) reported a pale bird of the Arctic race on Manitoulin on Nov. 18, 1972. Devitt (1967: 91) reported three fall specimens from Barrie and an immature male taken at Stayner on Nov. 10, 1946. In 1967, from 5 p.m. Nov. 18 to 5 p.m. Nov. 19, some 57 were noted by Kingston Field Naturalists (Quilliam, 1973: 103). Saunders (1947: 280) described the mobbing by crows of two Great Horned Owls found near Holland River on Oct. 3, 1943. James R. Thurston noted stomach contents of two shot near Toronto: a mouse (*Peromyscus leucopus*) in one on Oct. 10, 1889 and skunk flesh in one on Nov. 12, 1889 (Thompson, 1890: 196 and 198).

**MEASUREMENTS:**
*Length:* ♂ 18 to 23 ins.
♀ 22 to 25 ins. (Godfrey, 1966: 213)
*Wingspread:* ♂ 51.5 to 56.0 ins. ♀ 52.5 to 56.0 ins. (Roberts, 1955: 608)
*Weight:* 2 ♂ av. 1256 g. 4 ♀ av. 1505 g. (Hope, 1938: 22).

**REFERENCES:**
Speirs, J. Murray 1961 Courtship of Great Horned Owls. Can. Field-Nat., 75: (1): 52.
   Taverner, P.A. 1942 Canadian races of the Great Horned Owls. Auk, 59:(2):234-245.

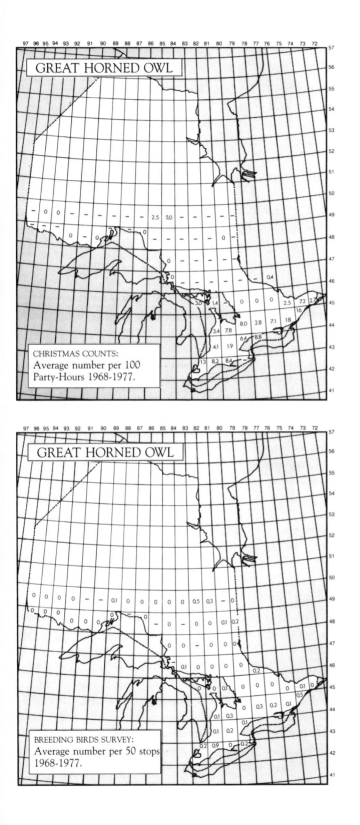

GREAT HORNED OWL

CHRISTMAS COUNTS:
Average number per 100
Party-Hours 1968-1977.

GREAT HORNED OWL

BREEDING BIRDS SURVEY:
Average number per 50 stops
1968-1977.

# SNOWY OWL   *Nyctea scandiaca*   (Linnaeus)

In Ontario this is a favourite among winter bird watchers, rare enough in most winters to require a special search. It may be found conspicuously perched on an icy breakwater along the shores of the Great Lakes or on a fence post beside a farm field, even sometimes on a TV aerial, or again it may look like a piece of newspaper or a small patch of snow far out on an early spring field.

IDENTIFICATION: Males are often almost pure white, with just a few dark flecks on the flight feathers while females may be heavily barred with dark brown. The white face with big yellow eyes may be swiveled around to face any direction. Some of the northern race of the Great Horned Owl may be almost as white, but the conspicuous ear tufts denote it as a Horned Owl and not this species which has only minute ear tufts or none at all.

WINTER: On the 1968-1977 Christmas counts, Snowy Owls were noted at most localities south of Thunder Bay and Marathon, uncommon to rare at most localities except at Sault Ste. Marie and Kingston where they were almost common in some winters. Big flights occurred in 1971 and 1974 with smaller numbers in other years. Saunders & Dale (1933: 203) cited London invasions in the winters of 1890-91, 1926-27 and 1930-31. Beardslee & Mitchell (1965: 280) mentioned Niagara invasions in the winters of 1930-31, 1933-34, 1937-38, 1941-42, 1945-46, 1949-50, 1953-54 and 1960-61. Fleming (1907: 75) gave dates of Toronto influxes in winters beginning in 1833, 1837, 1839, 1853, 1862, 1884, 1888, 1889, 1896 and 1901. Speirs (1939: 411-419) correlated these invasions with those of other animals with a 3 to 4 year cycle of abudance. Speirs (1976: 35) gave flight years for Ontario Co. in the winters of 1960-61, 1964-65, 1966-67, 1971-72 and 1974-75. Devitt (1967: 91-92) reported Barrie invasions in 1930-31, 1937-38, 1941-42, 1945-46, 1949-50, 1954-55, 1960-61 and 1964-65; one shot at Collingwood on Jan. 29, 1941 had two rats in its stomach. Lloyd (1923: 153) reported that some 300 were received by Ottawa taxidermists in the big flight in 1901-02. From 1938 to 1956 L. Beamer had winter records for Meaford in every winter except 1948-49 and recounted many interesting experiences. A. Kay reported that one wintered at Pt. Sydney, Muskoka in 1889-90 (where they are less common than about the Great Lakes shores). Dennison (1980: 147) reported the species at Sault Ste. Marie on 15 of 25 Christmas counts with a high of 11 in 1974. Elder (1979: 34) called it a rare fall and winter visitor at Geraldton.

SPRING: Stirrett (1973b: 19) had one at Pelee as late as May 15, 1950. Ussher (1965: 14) gave Apr. 25 as the latest Rondeau record. J.L. Baillie gave May 22 as his latest Toronto date (Saunders, 1947: 367). Dennis Barry saw one near Bowmanville as late as Apr. 27, 1973 (Tozer & Richards, 1974: 165). Frances Westman saw one on May 13, 1967 near Barrie (Devitt, 1967: 92). L. Beamer reported that one shot at Mountain Lake, near Meaford on Apr. 22, 1938 "had been in an argument with a skunk": his latest Meaford sighting was on Apr. 22, 1947: he examined 8 pellets found near Meaford Harbour on Mar. 30, 1942 "all contained rat bones"—this bird stayed until Apr. 15, 1942: Wm. Linn, in conversation with Beamer told him that he had mounted 17 during the winter of 1945-46, the last shot on Apr. 3 "had as many eggs in it as an ordinary hen".

SUMMER: At a Nov., 1902 meeting, Fred V. Langford spoke of one that spent part of the summer near London (Saunders & Dale, 1933: 203). Beardslee & Mitchell (1965: 280) reported one observed at Ft. Erie on June 5 and June 8, 1938. Fleming (1907: 75) noted one taken at Toronto on June 7, 1902. Weir & Quilliam (1980: 36) had Kingston records as late as June 15 and one was seen at the dump there from July 30 to Aug. 13, 1968 (Quilliam, 1973: 105). Manning saw one at Cape Henrietta Maria on July 20, 21 and 22, 1947 and Peck (1972: 345) cited several other records from the Cape Henrietta Maria region during the summer months. There is still no nesting record from Ontario but this is the most likely place for nesting to occur, with its tundra habitat resembling that of the normal nesting grounds farther north in the Arctic.

AUTUMN: H. Lumsden saw one at Hook Point (south of Cape Henrietta Maria) on Oct. 16, 1971 (Peck, 1972: 345). Doug. McRae and A. Wormington saw from one to seven almost daily from Oct. 19 to Nov. 22, 1981 at Netitishi Point, James Bay. E.S. Covett took one at the mouth of the Moose River on Nov. 6, 1933 (Manning, 1952: 64). Peruniak (1971: 17) gave Oct. 25 as the earliest fall record for Atikokan. K. Boschoff saw one at Pukaskwa as early as Oct. 3, 1973 (Skeel & Bondrup-Nielsen, 1978: 177). Nicholson (1981: 119) gave Nov. 4, 1972 as the earliest Manitoulin fall record. Mills (1981: 72) reported one on Nov. 4, 1958 near Huntsville. L. Beamer had a note under the date Oct. 7, 1944 "Snowy Owl reported earlier in the week". R. Charles Long saw one at Cannington as early as Sept. 30, 1974 (Speirs, 1976: 35). Speirs (1938: 48) had an Oct. 12 record for Toronto. Fred Bodsworth reported one at Port Burwell on Nov. 8, 1942 (Brooman, 1954: 23). Saunders & Dale (1933: 203) mentioned one shot by Mack Whillans at Vanneck on Nov. 6, 1918. Ussher (1965: 14) gave Oct. 20 as the earliest fall record for Rondeau. Stirrett (1973d: 21) had three late October records at Pelee, the earliest on Oct. 27, 1905.

**MEASUREMENTS:**
*Length:* 22 to 27 ins.
(Godfrey, 1966: 214)
♀ larger than ♂.
*Wingspread:* 54 to 66 ins.
(Roberts, 1955: 609).
*Weight:* ♂ 2 lb. 4 1/2 oz.
to 4 lbs. ♀ 4 lb. 10 oz. to
5 lbs. 5 oz. (Roberts,
1955: 609)

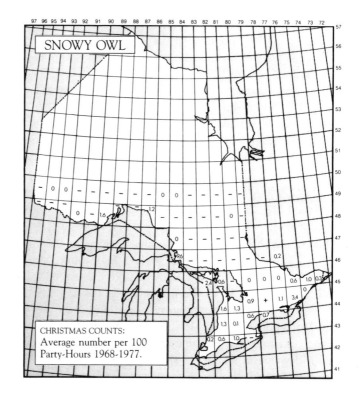

SNOWY OWL

CHRISTMAS COUNTS:
Average number per 100
Party-Hours 1968-1977.

# NORTHERN HAWK-OWL   *Surnia ulula*   (Linnaeus)

This is a circumpolar breeder in the northern coniferous forests. It comes as far south as southern Ontario some winters. Some individuals set up hunting territories where they may be found day after day, to the delight of bird watchers. They often hunt by day, plunging into roadside snowdrifts and emerging with some luckless mouse, oblivious to the presence of onlookers.

IDENTIFICATION: This is a pigeon-sized owl, with a long tail which it frequently raises up and down, in the manner of a perching Kestrel. It is heavily barred on the breast. Its facial disc, surrounding the yellow eyes, is heavily outlined with black.

WINTER: On the 1968-1977 Christmas counts it was noted only at Thunder Bay, Sault Ste. Marie, Ottawa, Pakenham, Manitoulin, Peterborough, Georgian Bay Is. and Oshawa (mostly on the 1976 counts). Fleming (1907: 75) cited a Toronto record for Jan. 10. Speirs (1976: 36) gave details of Ontario Co. sightings on Dec. 4, 1944; Jan. 19, 1958; Dec. 2, 1962 to Jan. 1, 1963; Dec. 22 and 26, 1963; Feb. 1, 1964; Dec. 26, 1964 to Feb. 21, 1965; Jan. 29, 1966; Dec. 28, 1967 and Jan. 1 to 11, 1970. Tozer & Richards (1974: 165) reported one in Darlington Twp. from Dec. 29, 1962 to Jan. 6, 1963. Quilliam (1973: 105) reported 8 in the Kingston region during the 1962-63 invasion of southern Ontario. Weir & Quilliam (1980: 16) listed subsequent records at Kingston every year from 1973 to 1979. Devitt (1967: 92) noted that S. Hughes took one at Collingwood during the winter to 1918: single birds were seen on Barrie Christmas counts on Dec. 30, 1961 and Jan. 9, 1964: Alf Mitchener saw six during the 1962-63 invasion at Collingwood: another was seen at Guthrie from Feb. 2 to 19, 1966. Mills (1981: 72-73) reported one shot at Scotia on Dec. 9, 1898; one seen at Hunstville in Jan., 1962, another there to Dec. 22, 1966 and another there on Dec. 11, 1977: one at Honey Harbour showed up on Dec. 16, 1976 and remained until March. Nicholson (1981: 119) had winter records on Manitoulin from Dec. 8 to 16, 1973; Dec. 15, 1974; Dec. 6, 1978 and Dec. 17, 1978. Mark Robinson reported one at Canoe Lake, Algonquin Park, at Christmas 1913 (MacLulich, 1938: 17). Dennison (1980: 148) reported six on five of 25 Christmas counts at Sault Ste. Marie. Peruniak (1971: 18) had Atikokan records from Dec. 10 to 31. Goodwin (1963: 33) received well over 100 reports (including some duplications) from the big 1962-63 invasion of southern Ontario.

SPRING: James R. Thurston saw one in St. James Cemetery, Toronto, on Apr. 14, 1889 (Thompson, 1890: 191). Speirs (1976: 36) cited a record by Alf Bunker at Pickering on March 15, 1962. During the big owl invasion of Amherst Is. in 1978-79 only one Hawk-Owl appeared, which was last seen on May 3, 1979 (Weir & Quilliam, 1980: 16). The Honey Harbour bird mentioned above was last reported on Mar. 19, 1977 (Mills, 1981: 73) Nicholson (1981: 119) had Manitoulin records for Mar. 22, 1975; Mar. 12, 1976 and Mar. 20, 1978. Goodwin (1963: 33) mentioned a Mar. 31, 1963 record from Killarney by W.R. Lowe. Peruniak (1971: 18) had Atikokan records from Mar. 30 to May 2, 1965. D. Fillman *et al* reported a nest and saw five adults (representing 4 pairs) during late May and early June, 1980 near Hillsport (Goodwin, 1980:772). The Owl Rehabilitation and Research Foundation received young from Gogama, Chapleau, Kapuskasing and Moosonee in spring, 1981 (their first young of this species) (Goodwin, 1981: 819).

SUMMER: Ewart Brereton identified one at Rebecca lake, Muskoka on Aug. 18, 1942 (Mills, 1981: 73). Skeel & Bondrup-Nielsen (1978: 172) reported one seen at Pukaskwa in July, 1976 by Rob. Hall. Baillie & Hope (1943: 10) collected one at Peninsula (Marathon) on June 12, 1936. Dear (1940: 129) was threatened by adults near Thunder Bay on June 28, 1926, when he approached their young. Smith (1957: 174) reported that F. Cowell had sightings in summer in the vicinity of Timmins. Snyder (1928: 22-24) saw and collected several along Lake Abitibi shores, including dependent young. Bondrup-Nielsen (1975: 42) listed this as a rare permanent resident near Kapuskasing as did Elder (1979: 34) for the Geraldton region. Shirley Peruniak et al found two young, out of the nest, at Quetico on July 5, 1979 (Goodwin, 1979: 859). James (1980: 86) noted one on June 4 and two hunting over a beaver meadow at Pickle Lake on June 6, 1977. Schueler, Baldwin & Rising (1974: 146) took the male of a pair seen 8 miles NE of Hawley Lake on June 16, 1962 (at the junction of the Sutton and Warchescu rivers). C.E. Hope collected individuals at Ft. Severn on June 22 and July 1, 1940.

AUTUMN: Lewis & Peters (1941: 113) reported one at Albany on Sept. 22, 1940. Hope (1938: 22) mentioned a male collected at Favourable Lake on Nov. 12, 1938, that weighed 295 g. Peruniak (1971: 18) had records through November in 1962 at Atikokan. Ricker & Clarke (1939: 12) cited specimen records for North Bay on Oct. 29, 1924; Nov. 18, 1924 and Oct. 5, 1925 and we saw one there on Nov. 25, 1944 (Speirs & Speirs, 1947: 29). J. Hughes Samuel collected one near Whitney on Nov. 23, 1898 (MacLulich, 1938: 17). Nicholson (1981: 119) noted one at Little Current from Nov. 22, into December, 1978. Mills (1981: 72) cited dates of four ROM specimens taken by A. Kay in the cottage country: one at Port Sydney on Nov. 5, 1898; one between there and Bracebridge on Nov. 12, 1895 and others on Nov. 25, 1906 and Nov. 1, 1925; two were seen near Huntsville on Oct. 13 and 14, 1962 and another there from Nov. 28 into December. E.G. White shot one at Stittsville on Nov. 6, 1922 (Lloyd, 1923: 153). Devitt (1967: 92) noted one shot at New Lowell on Nov. 3, 1933; one seen at Wyevale by F. Bodsworth on Nov. 3, 1962; one at Waubaushene on Nov. 12, 1962 and one at the mouth of the Holland River on Nov. 2, 1962. The Amherst Is. bird showed up on Nov. 5, 1978 and stayed until spring (Weir & Quilliam, 1980: 16). Snyder (1941: 61) had two specimens from Prince Edward Co.: a male on Oct. 24, 1935 at Hillier and a female on Nov. 23, 1935 at Bloomfield. Black (1934: 148) cited Charles Fothergill's observations of this species at Rice Lake, including one shot on Nov. 29, 1821 and many taken in Nov., 1817 as well as descriptions of the daylight hunting activities. E.W. Calvert found one by Scugog's East Causeway on Nov. 18, 1962 while E.G. and Ron Tozer located another there on Nov. 25, 1967 which stayed into the winter. (Tozer & Richards, 1974: 165). R.V. Lindsay took one alive from a barn near Sebright, Ontario Co., on Nov. 1, 1934 (Speirs, 1976: 36). Fleming (1907: 75) had an Oct. 22 record for Toronto and Saunders (1947: 367) listed an Oct. 18 date there.

**MEASUREMENTS:**
*Length:* 14 1/2 to 17 ins.
(Godfrey, 1966: 214)
*Wingspread:* 31-34 ins.
(Roberts, 1955: 613)
*Weight:* ♂ 10 1/2 to
11 oz. ♀ 11 1/2 oz.
(Roberts, 1955: 613)
♂ 295 g. (Hope,
1938: 22).

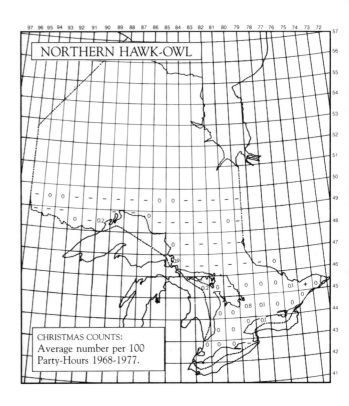

NORTHERN HAWK-OWL

CHRISTMAS COUNTS:
Average number per 100
Party-Hours 1968-1977.

# BURROWING OWL   *Athene cunicularia*   (Molina)

This is a bird of the plains, accidental in Ontario. They live in burrows made by burrowing mammals and are often seen at the entrance of such burrows or perched on fence posts overlooking fields.

IDENTIFICATION:   This is a small, sandy-coloured owl with white eyebrows and throat and long slim legs and bright yellow eyes. They have a habit of bobbing up and down and gazing at the observer as if they could not believe their eyes.

WINTER:

SPRING:   The one that created such excitement near Maple in the spring of 1982 was probably released from the Ontario Owl Rehabilitation and Research Foundation. Nicholson (1981: 119) observed one at Mississagi Light, Manitoulin on May 18, 1977. One was found by Mrs. Cassells at Iroquois Falls on May 8, 1976 and seen the next day by J. Young *et al* (Goodwin, 1976: 835).

SUMMER:   One appeared at Erieau from June 14 to July 1, 1977 where it was seen by K.J. Burk and many others (Goodwin, 1977: 1133). George W. North found one at Aldershot on June 3, 1940 (Baillie, 1964: 8).

AUTUMN:   The first Ontario record was one taken alive on Wolfe Is., near Kingston, in the fall of 1894 by D. Breakey and later preserved by W. Stratford (Baillie, 1964: 8). The authenticity of this record has been questioned (Quilliam, 1965: 105). A male was collected at Ajax on Oct. 15, 1963 by D.H. Baldwin (ROM 93589).

**MEASUREMENTS:**
*Length:* 9 to 10 ins.
(Godfrey, 1966: 216)
*Wingspread:* 24 1/4 to
25 1/2 ins. (Roberts,
1955: 610)
*Weight:* ♂ 5 1/4 to 6 1/4
oz. ♀ 5 1/2 oz.
(Roberts, 1955: 610)

# BARRED OWL   *Strix varia*   Barton

This is one of the more familiar owls throughout much of Ontario, though not as frequently noted as the Great Horned Owl. Some have wintered even in the heart of Toronto, but most retire to the forests of the cottage country to breed.

IDENTIFICATION: Other large owls in Ontario have yellow or orange eyes (except for the unmistakable Barn Owl): the Barred Owl has dark eyes. Except for the streaked breast, most of its plumage is barred (as its name suggests), barred with dark brown on buffy gray background. Its call has been rendered as "Who cooks, who cooks, who cooks for you-aaal" (the beginning has the quality of a dog's bark, the ending is a descending gargle (often omitted): it may be given in broad daylight in its nesting habitats.

WINTER: On the 1968-1977 Christmas counts this was an uncommon to rare species from Lake Erie north to Deep River and Manitoulin. E. Deacon noted one at Toronto on Jan. 4, 1891 (Trans. Can. Inst., 3: Part 1: (5): 92). Speirs (1976: 38) cited several winter records for Ontario Co., including Christmas counts at Pickering, Oshawa and Columbus. Snyder (1941: 61) noted a female collected at Hillier, Prince Edward Co. on Jan. 23, 1937. A. Kay considered it resident at Pt. Sydney, Muskoka (Trans. Can. Inst., 3: Part 1: (5): 79). Mills (1981: 73) called this the most common owl in the cottage country: it was noted on 7 of 29 Christmas counts at Huntsville. One was taken near North Bay on Jan. 7, 1923 (Ricker & Clarke, 1939: 12). Three were noted on one of 25 Christmas counts at Sault Ste. Marie (Dennison, 1980: 148). F. Cowell has noted this species at Timmins in both winter and spring (Smith, 1957: 174).

SPRING: Sheppard (1960: 29) had one record for Stamford, near Niagara Falls, on Apr. 5, 1954. Saunders (1947: 367) gave Apr. 9 as the latest spring date for Toronto. Speirs (1976: 38) cited several spring records for Ontario Co. (from Mar. 8 in 1960 to Apr. 10 in 1975). Snyder (1941: 61) noted a female collected in Prince Edward Co. on Mar. 8, 1890. Quilliam (1973: 106) gave details of Kingston region nestings in 1970 and 1972. J. Jennings showed J. Goltz a nest hole near Bala, 20 ft. up in a maple, from which an adult flew, in mid-Apr. 1975 (Mills, 1981: 73). Douglas Elliott noted adults with a downy young at Mindemoya, Manitoulin, in May, 1969 (Nicholson, 1981: 177). Ricker & Clarke (1939: 12) saw one at North Bay on Apr. 1, 1924. Skeel & Bondrup-Nielsen (1978: 177) heard one calling at Pukaskwa on May 19, 28 and 31, 1977. Dear (1940: 129) found a nest with one young and one infertile egg on May 3, 1940 near Thunder Bay. Bondrup-Nielsen (1976: 42) noted this species at Kapuskasing in 1975.

SUMMER: On the 1968-1977 Breeding Bird Survey, individuals showed up on the Mt. Julian, Gore Bay, Thessalon, Thunder Bay, Atikokan and Dryden routes. Kelley (1978: 44) wrote that it may breed at Rondeau (but gave no details). Speirs (1976: 38) gave breeding records for 3 of 11 townships in Ontario Co.: on July 10, 1968 Dennis Barry saw an adult with young in East Whitby Twp.: and with Ron Tozer he found an adult with two young in Scugog Twp. on June 1, 1968: on June 9, 1967 in Rama Twp. I found a half-grown young in "wooly" plumage on the ground with its back to a tree, while a concerned parent fluttered about overhead in the canopy with calls resembling those of a Ruffed Grouse with threatened young. J.M. Richards noted agitated adults in Darlington Twp. from May, 1965 to Sept., 1967 (Tozer & Richards, 1974: 166). Devitt (1967: 93) reported a male taken by an ROM party at Penetanguishene on June 12, 1935.

L. Beamer noted one at Meaford on June 18, 1949. R.J. Rutter found two adults with one young (down still in evidence) at Katrine in June, 1933 (Baillie & Harrington, 1936: 48). C.H.D. Clarke and D. MacLulich sometimes heard as many as five calling at Biggar Lake, Algonquin Park, in July, 1933 (MacLulich, 1938: 18). One was seen at Sault Ste. Marie in the summer of 1848 and C.H.D. Clarke noted one at Batchawana Bay on July 31, 1931 (Snyder, 1942: 130). John Walty noted the species from June 7-18, 1937 at Washagami, Sudbury Dist. and Paul Harrington found a carcass near Chapleau on June 13, 1937 (Baillie & Hope, 1947: 9). Baillie & Hope (1943: 10) found a fresh feather at Amyot on June 27, 1936. Peruniak (1971: 18) called it fairly common in Quetico in summer. I noted them on Breeding Bird Surveys at Manitouwadge on June 22, 1980 and June 19, 1982. Snyder (1953: 61) collected one at Ingolf on June 11, 1937 and also reported one at Dinorwic Lake in early July, 1940. Manning (1952: 64) mentioned several specimens taken at Moose Factory.

AUTUMN:    Ottelyn Addison heard calls each night during the first two weeks of September, 1964 near the Georgian Bay shore of Conc. 14, Tiny Twp., Simcoe Co. (Devitt, 1967: 93). R.W. Smith took a male at Kingston on Nov. 30, 1939 (Quilliam, 1973: 106). Snyder (1941: 61) had two female specimens from Prince Edward Co.: one taken about Oct. 28, 1935 at Weller Bay and the other taken Nov. 23, 1935 at Bloomfield. Speirs (1938: 48) had an early fall record for Toronto on Sept. 28 and Fleming (1907: 74) called it abundant there from Oct. 1-10, 1902. Speirs (1976: 38) cited several fall records from Ontario Co. (from Oct. 27, 1957 to Nov. 22, 1963). Sheppard (1960: 29) had a Stamford record on Sept. 24, 1956. W.E. Saunders saw one near London on Oct. 22, 1918: none since (Saunders & Dale, 1933: 204).

**MEASUREMENTS:**
*Length:* 18 to 23 ins.
(Godfrey, 1966: 216)
*Wingspread:* 40 to 50 ins.
(Roberts, 1955: 613)
*Weight:* ♂ 1 lb. 6 oz. to 1
lb. 11 1/2 oz. ♀ 1 lb.
11 1/2 oz. (Roberts,
1955: 613)

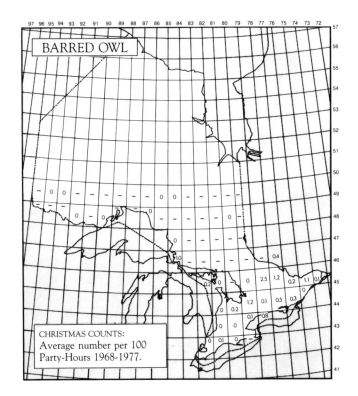

BARRED OWL

CHRISTMAS COUNTS:
Average number per 100
Party-Hours 1968-1977.

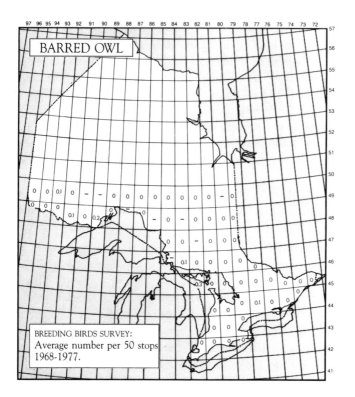

BARRED OWL

BREEDING BIRDS SURVEY:
Average number per 50 stops
1968-1977.

# GREAT GRAY OWL   *Strix nebulosa*   Forster

This has usually been a great rarity anywhere in Ontario but there have been some winters when numbers have been found in southern Ontario and more are being found in northern Ontario during the breeding season. The studies of Robert W. Nero and Robert R. Taylor in Manitoba and Minnesota have greatly enhanced our knowledge and appreciation of these birds.

IDENTIFICATION:   This is our largest owl (although Great Horned Owls are heavier). They are distinguished from the Great Horned Owl by lack of ear tufts and by the yellow eyes from the somewhat similar but much smaller Barred Owl (which has dark eyes). The big half-dome-shaped head and concentric dark rings around the yellow eyes are characteristic. At close range the white "cravat" is conspicuous.

WINTER:   None were seen on the 1968-1977 Christmas counts except at Hornepayne in 1975 but in 1978 they were reported at Hamilton, Pickering, Pakenham and Marathon, the beginning of the major influx that winter. Speirs (1938: 48) listed an early record on Dec. 1 at Toronto. Fleming (1907: 74) noted a great flight at Toronto in 1889-90 when Wm. Cross received 23 specimens from various parts of Ontario and an acquaintance in Barrie received 26: he also recorded specimens taken in Dec., 1890, Jan. 1894, Jan., 1895 and Jan.-Feb., 1896. One shot at Beaverton on Jan. 29, 1890 had a white-footed mouse and four meadow mice in its stomach (Speirs, 1976: 39). Tozer & Richards (1974: 166) reported one shot in Darlington Twp. on Feb. 27, 1972. Quilliam (1973: 106) cited Kingston records on Dec. 27, 1968 and Feb. 14, 1971. Devitt (1967: 93) reported that 9 were shot at Lake Simcoe in 1894-95; another at Collingwood in 1918-19; one collected by H.B. Haugh at Oro Station on Feb. 17, 1943 and one shot at Orillia on Jan. 14, 1956. Lloyd (1923: 153) cited a report of four near Ottawa in 1906-07. Mills (1981: 74) cited several Huntsville records including one taken on Feb. 25, 1951; also one at Melissa on Jan. 15, 1966 and one on Beausoleil Is. on Feb. 1, 1974. Nicholson (1981: 120) had Manitoulin records for South Baymouth on Feb. 21, 1971 and Tehkummah on Feb. 14, 1973. Dennison (1980: 149) reported that 8 were seen on the Christmas, 1978 count at Sault Ste. Marie. Denis (1961: 6) noted a heavy flight at Thunder Bay in 1950-51 with 14 records before Dec. 30 and the last noted on Jan. 14, 1951. A. Wormington saw two at Moosonee on Jan. 9-10, 1974 (Goodwin, 1974: 634). Goodwin (1971: 573) gave details of the 1970-71 invasion "the heaviest since the huge invasion of 1965-66". Goodwin (1979: 278) chronicled the 1978-79 influx.

SPRING:   Speirs (1938: 46) gave Apr. 28 as the latest spring date for Toronto. Tozer & Richards (1974: 166) cited a report from Darlington Twp. on Mar. 19, 1972. Charles Fothergill called it "very common in the woods about the Otonibee where it breeds" and reported a male taken there in March, 1821 and a female on Apr. 30, 1921: he also mentioned one shot at Toronto in May, 1826 (Black, 1934: 148). Jim Bayly found one at Abbey Dawn, near Kingston, on Apr. 29, 1966 (Quilliam, 1973: 106). On Mar. 10, 1979 an estimate of 34 on Amherst Is. was made by G.A. Bell and the last was seen there on Apr. 4 (Weir & Quilliam, 1980: 16). Lloyd (1923: 153) noted one taken on Apr. 3, 1896 near Ottawa. Mills (1981: 74) gave an Apr. 17 record for the Huntsville area. Nicholson (1981: 120) reported one at Providence Bay, Manitoulin, from Mar. 18 to Apr. 7, 1979. Ricker & Clarke (1939: 12) cited a record by Mrs. Edgar Hobbs at Little Sturgeon

River, near North Bay, on Apr. 20, 1935. Skeel & Bondrup-Nielsen (1978: 177) noted that two were seen in May, 1973 at Pukaskwa by W. Wyett. Bondrup-Nielsen (1976: 42) listed it as rare at Kapuskasing in 1975, as did Elder (1979: 34) for Geraldton. S. Peruniak saw one at Atikokan from Apr. 11 to May 4, 1977. (Goodwin, 1977: 995). The Thunder Bay area had five reports to May 3 in 1973 according to K. Denis (Goodwin, 1973: 767). B. Hunter and T. Perrons saw three young at Thunder Bay on Apr. 15, 1979 (Goodwin, 1979: 767). T. Perrons saw one at Savanne on Mar. 7 and 15, 1974 (Goodwin, 1974: 634).

SUMMER: On the 1968-1977 Breeding Bird Surveys, they were noted only at Atikokan, in 1970 and 1973: since then I have noted them on the Longlac route in 1981 and 1982 and Dann Lee found one on the Kenora route in 1982. Janice Robinson noted two on Main Duck Is., Lake Ontario, in Aug., 1979 (Weir & Quilliam, 1980: 16). Mayor Kelly of Powassan took two juveniles in Chisholm Twp. on July 31, 1911 (NMC and ROM). Baillie & Harrington (1936: 48) mentioned one noted on the Michipicoten River on Aug. 19 and 21, 1928. On June 25, 1981, Len Hanna showed me a young bird at Manitouwadge, still with some fuzz about the head, calling and being answered by another young out of sight back in the forest: other observers reported seeing several adults in that vicinity during the summer. Dear (1940: 130) saw and heard this species during the breeding season at Thunder Bay. Goodwin (1973: 865) had reports from June 14 to Aug. 15, 1973 at Longlac, Sibley, Upsala and Atikokan. James (1977: 55) photographed an adult and downy young in a nest near Pickle Lake on June 6, 1977, to establish the first proof of nesting in Ontario. Cringan (1950: 11) saw one in a mature Jack pine stand east of Nikip Lake on June 25, 1950. Sam Waller took specimens at Moose Factory in 1927 (ROM) and the original description was based on a specimen from Severn River (Baillie & Harrington, 1936: 48).

AUTUMN: J.P. Kelsall and G.M. Stirrett saw one near Moose Factory on Oct. 2, 1948 (Manning, 1952: 64). Doug. McRae and Alan Wormington noted one at Netitishi Point, James Bay on Nov. 20, 1981. A heavy flight in 1950-51 at Thunder Bay started on Oct. 7, 1950 (Denis, 1961: 6). J.B. Miles saw three at Hornepayne between late November and late January, 1973 (Goodwin, 1974: 634). Ricker & Clarke (1939: 12) reported one taken at North Bay in fall, 1927. J.R. Thurston received one on Oct. 29, 1889 from North Bay whose stomach contained field mice and a shrew: another was received by Wm. Cross from Powassan on Nov. 12, 1889 (Thompson, 1890: 197, 198). Mark Robinson saw a few in Algonquin Park in the fall of 1913 (MacLulich, 1938: 18). A. Kay listed it as a resident of Port Sydney, Muskoka (Trans. Can. Inst., 3: Part 1: (5): 79). E. Cole saw one at Kingston on Nov. 4, 1973 (Goodwin, 1974: 47). Lloyd (1923: 153) reported one at Constance Bay, near Ottawa, on Oct. 1, 1917. Fleming (1907: 74) mentioned that the 1889-90 influx began in November.

**MEASUREMENTS:**
*Length:* 25 to 33 ins.
(Godfrey, 1966: 217)
*Wingspread:* 48 1/2 to 60
ins. (Roberts, 1955: 614)
*Weight:* ♂ 1 lb. 15 oz. to
2 lbs. 11 oz. ♀ 2 lbs. 2 oz
to 2 lbs. 14 oz. (Roberts.
1955: 614).

**REFERENCES:**
James, Ross D. 1977 First nesting of the Great Gray Owl in Ontario. Ont. Field Biologist, 31:(2): 55. The nest was 20 m. up in an aspen in an old Common Raven nest. Adults seen June 4 and 6, 1977. Photo of adult and yg. in nest on June 6, 1977: nest empty June 14.

Nero, Robert W. (illustrations by Robert R. Taylor) 1980 The Great Gray Owl, phantom of the northern forest. Washington, D.C. Smithsonian Institution Press: 1-167.

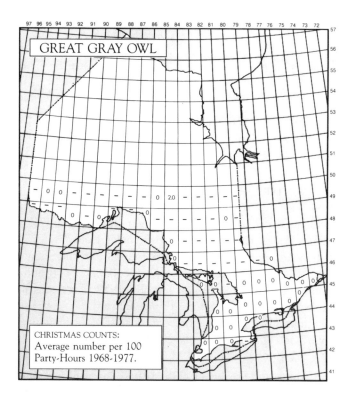

GREAT GRAY OWL

CHRISTMAS COUNTS:
Average number per 100
Party-Hours 1968-1977.

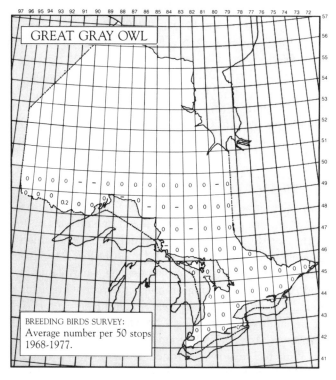

GREAT GRAY OWL

BREEDING BIRDS SURVEY:
Average number per 50 stops
1968-1977.

# LONG-EARED OWL   *Asio otus*   (Linnaeus)

This owl is found in the forested areas of both the Old World and America. In Ontario they are most frequently found in fall and winter, when they roost together in dense conifers. They nest here in spring, often taking over old crow's nests.

IDENTIFICATION:   The Long-eared Owl looks like a small, slim, edition of the Great Horned Owl, but with relatively long ear tufts, placed closer together near the centre of the head. Saunders & Dale (1933: 205) noted a gnatcatcher-like squeal "sweah, sweah" by adults when their nest was approached.

WINTER:   Long-eared Owls were uncommon on the 1968-1977 Christmas counts from Toronto to Pelee and rare north of there to Ottawa and Meaford. On Jan. 25, 1942 about a dozen were flushed from a heavy cedar swamp near St. Thomas (Brooman, 1954: 23). A.R. Muma sent two males from Niagara to the ROM on Dec. 26, 1947 (Sheppard, 1960: 29). Earl Stark found 30 in the Shoal Point cedar woods, Pickering, on Dec. 18, 1960 (Speirs, 1976: 40). George A. Scott and Ron Tozer counted 21 in willows bordering Oshawa Creek on Jan. 18, 1959 (Tozer & Richards, 1974: 167). A female was collected near Wellington, Prince Edward Co., on Dec. 28, 1937 (Snyder, 1941: 62). Quilliam (1973: 107) reported a roost of 10 at Kingston on Jan. 31, 1971. E.L. Brereton found one at Barrie on Feb. 29, 1936 (Devitt, 1967: 94). One was seen at Huntsville on Dec. 1, 1969 (Mills, 1981: 74).

SPRING:   Stirrett (1973b: 19) had just one spring record at Pelee, on May 21, 1961. Saunders & Dale (1933: 204-205) had several spring nest records near London: the earliest on Mar. 30 with 2 eggs and the latest on May 17, 1907 with 4 eggs: A.A. Wood had a set of 5 eggs taken on May 1, 1916. Brooman (1954: 23) reported a nest with 4 eggs in an old crow's nest near St. Thomas on Apr. 18, 1889 and Harold Lancaster had a nest on Apr. 4, 1941 at his sanctuary. Snyder (1931: 183) collected a female at Long Point on May 22, 1928. A.E. Schaffner noted one young out of the nest at Morgan's Point, Lake Erie, on May 11, 1956 (Beardslee & Mitchell, 1965: 283-284). Fleming (1907: 74) had a breeding record at Toronto on May 24, 1894. Speirs (1976: 40) cited several nest records for Ontario Co.: Cyril Peake found a nest with 5 eggs at Ajax on Apr. 19, 1958 about 60 ft. up in an old crow's nest; two nests in Pickering Twp. contained young as early as Apr. 24, 1966; J.A. Edwards found a nest with 6 eggs on Thorah Is. on Apr. 28, 1929 also in a crow's nest but 18 ft. up; Paul Catling found a nest with 5 young there on May 19, 1968. On May 17, 1969 J. Kamstra found a nest with 5 large young in Darlington Twp. (Tozer & Richards, 1974: 167). C.K. Clarke found two nests with 5 eggs each near Kingston, one on Apr. 28, 1902 and one on May 5, 1902; Richard Norman found a nest with 3 eggs on Wolfe Is. on March 30, 1970 which produced 3 young seen there all summer (Quilliam, 1973: 107). Devitt (1967: 94) cited four nest records for Simcoe Co.: a nest with 5 eggs in an old crow's nest near Barrie on May 24, 1918 found by H.P. Bingham and A. Pratt; P. Harrington found them breeding near Bradford on May 23, 1920; Devitt found a nest with 4 eggs near Bradford on Apr. 17, 1938 which contained two small young and two infertile eggs on May 15: and a nest with 3 eggs about 10 miles south of Barrie on May 24, 1943 found by E.L. Brereton. Baillie & Harrington (1936: 49) cited breeding records for Pt. Sydney, Muskoka by A. Kay and at Katrine, Parry Sound by R.J. Rutter. Ron Tasker found individuals in Burpee Twp., Manitoulin, on May 17, 1970;

May 21, 1971 and May 9 to 19, 1976 (Nicholson, 1981: 120-121). Dear (1940: 130) reported a nest with 4 eggs near Thunder Bay on May 20, 1924.

SUMMER: Snyder (1931: 183) found fresh feathers at Long Point on June 25, 1927. A female was collected in King Twp. on Aug. 20, 1928 (Snyder, 1930: 188). Naomi LeVay noted one at Whitby on July 14, 1957, one of the few summer records for Ontario Co. (Speirs, 1976: 40). F.A. Saunders took one at Ottawa on July 7, 1890 (Lloyd, 1923: 153). Mark Robinson noted the species in Algonquin Park during the summers of 1912 and 1918 (MacLulich, 1938: 18). Ron Tasker saw one in Burpee Twp. Manitoulin, on Aug. 7, 1971 (Nicholson, 1981: 120). Snyder (1928: 260) collected a male at Lake Nipigon on June 24, 1924. Elder (1979: 34) had only one Geraldton record, a road kill on June 7, 1972. Manning (1952: 65) cited an old (1782) breeding record from Severn, which Baillie & Harrington (1936: 48) considered in need of confirmation.

AUTUMN: One shot near Corbeil (in the North Bay vicinity) on Oct. 9, 1934 had been banded at Escondido, California, on Apr. 22, 1934 (Ricker & Clarke, 1939: 12). Ron Tasker found one in Burpee Twp., Manitoulin, on Sept. 9, 1971 and Nicholson (1981: 120-121) noted two at Mississagi Light between Sept. 18 and Oct. 19, 1975: he also found one at Great Duck Is. on Oct. 14, 1978. On Nov. 15, 1963, Frances Westman examined a Hwy. 400 roadkill near Cookstown (Devitt, 1967: 94). George A. Scott found one at Oshawa's Second Marsh on Sept. 29, 1963 (Speirs, 1976: 40). Fleming (1907: 74) called it a common fall migrant at Toronto from Oct. 2 to Nov. 7 and they are still frequently taken by banders during this period, working with Saw-whet Owls. Stirrett (1973d: 21) had a few fall records at Pelee, the earliest on Oct. 12.

BANDING: (See the remarkable recovery under autumn above.) One banded by Gordon Lambert near Toronto on Feb. 5, 1954 was recovered on June 10, 1962 between Englehart and Virginiatown. Another banded by R.R. Taylor near Toronto on Nov. 8, 1958 was recovered on Jan. 6, 1959 in Maryland. Todd (1963: 447) cited a report that one banded in Michigan in May was recovered near Lake Abitibi the following September.

**MEASUREMENTS:**
Length: 13 to 16 ins.
(Godfrey, 1966: 218)
Wingspread: 36 to 42 ins.
(Roberts, 1955: 607)
Weight: ♂ 9 1/2 to 11 oz.
♀ 10 1/8 oz. (Roberts,
1955: 607)

**REFERENCE:**
Speirs, Doris Huestis 1957
The notes of the Long-
eared Owl. Ont. Field
Biologist, No. 11: 19, 21.

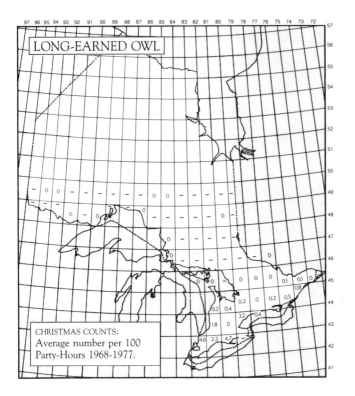

LONG-EARNED OWL

CHRISTMAS COUNTS:
Average number per 100
Party-Hours 1968-1977.

# SHORT-EARED OWL   *Asio flammeus*   (Pontoppidan)

This is an almost cosmopolitan species. It has occurred throughout Ontario but is most familiar to southern Ontario bird watchers in winter, where it may be seen flying over old fields in the evening.

IDENTIFICATION: When milk was still sold in quart bottles we used to call this owl the "flying milk bottle" because of its rounded head and whitish colouration. The wing beats are very deep, giving it a very buoyant, almost tern-like, flight. During the day we often flushed a group of them from groups of evergreens on the York Downs Golf Club. The ear tufts are very small. The general colourations is sandy buff (paler than the woodland Long-eared Owl). In flight these two species look much alike as the Long-eared depresses its ear tufts in flight, but the Short-eared lacks the breast barring of the Long-eared. Snyder (1931: 183) mentioned the sooty facial mask of a juvenile bird and its "rich reddish-buff coloured wooly feathers of the belly and flanks".

WINTER: On the 1968-1977 Christmas counts they were uncommon in the London area and rare elsewhere north to Ottawa and Kettle Point. Stirrett (1973a: 16) had Pelee records for Dec. 21 and Jan. 18. Saunders & Dale (1933: 205) mentioned flushing a group of 10 about 10 miles north of London on Dec. 26, 1931. A group of 10 was noted 4 miles east of St. Thomas in late Feb. and early March, 1952 (Brooman, 1954: 23). Wm. Cross reported that a flock of over 50 was seen at Ashbridge's Bay, Toronto, on Dec. 5, 1889: "Seven specimens were killed at three shots and brought to me" (Thompson, 1890:200). Speirs (1976: 41) cited several winter records from Ajax to Oshawa: the largest flock noted consisted of 9 birds seen by Ken Adcoe and Audrey Russ at Ajax on Jan. 12, 1966. Quilliam (1973: 108) gave 19 on Wolfe Is. on Dec. 26, 1967 as the highest count for the Kingston region. Devitt (1967: 94) mentioned one seen at Angus on Dec. 30, 1951 by F. Munro. Nicholson (1981: 121) saw one on Barrie Is., Manitoulin, on Dec. 3, 1972 and Donald B. Ferguson saw one at Providence Bay on Dec. 10, 1978.

SPRING: Stirrett (1973b: 19) had Pelee sightings on Apr. 15 and May 10-11. Harold Lancaster, with Earl and Bob Lemon, flushed a pair from a nest with one egg in the Dunwich Marsh, Elgin Co., on Apr. 14, 1946 (Brooman, 1954: 23). Fleming (1907: 74) called it a regular spring migrant at Toronto from Mar. 5 to 15. Doris Speirs and I saw one in Scott Twp., Ontario Co., on Apr. 23, 1971 and James Kamstra noted one at the south end of Lake Scugog on May 20, 1972 (Speirs, 1976: 41). Quilliam (1973: 107-108) gave details of nests in the Kingston region: one with 7 eggs was found by E. Beaupré on May 23, 1902: he also found a nest with two young on May 30, 1906: on May 27, 1970 a nest with four young was found by Elizabeth Hughes and Helen Quilliam. W. Hahn collected a male at Waubaushene on Apr. 16, 1934 and Alf. Mitchener saw one at Collingwood on Apr. 20, 1957 (Devitt, 1967: 94). L. Beamer had Meaford records on Apr. 13, 1941; Apr. 14, 1942 and May 4, 1947. Nicholson (1981: 121) had several spring obsrvations from Manitoulin, from Apr. 18 (1980) to May 5 (1979). Denis (1961: 2) gave Apr. 23 as the average arrival date at Thunder Bay, with the earliest on Apr. 17, 1941. Elder (1979: 34) called it a rare spring migrant at Geraldton. Sam Waller took one at Moosonee on Apr. 29, 1930 (Manning, 1952: 65).

SUMMER:   On the 1968-1977 Breeding Bird Survey it was seen only on the Swastika route, in 1971. Stirrett (1973c: 17) had only one summer record at Pelee, on July 25. Kelley (1978: 44) reported one at Rondeau on June 25, 1950. Saunders & Dale (1933: 205) wrote that they were fairly common near Duncrief in the summer of 1925 and a farmer's boy there reported seeing downy young. John Edmonds secured a "virtually flightless" young at Long Point on June 15, 1927 and a male was collected there on July 14, 1927 (Snyder, 1938: 190). Speirs (1938: 48) listed an Aug. 3 record for Toronto. Calvert (1925: 51) reported one near Port Perry frequently during the summers of 1956 and 1957. Jim Richards saw adults regularly over the Camp X Marsh (Tozer & Richards, 1974: 168). Ray and M. Pannell noted one at Port Sydney between June 25 and July 8, 1960 and on July 11, 1959, B. Geale saw one at Foote's Bay, Lake Joseph (Mills, 1981: 75). Dear (1940: 130) saw adults with several fully fledged young on July 26, 1938 in Neebing Twp., Thunder Bay. Snyder (1938; 190) took an adult male at Emo on June 19, 1929, and noted a family of four various-sized young on June 24 (one female collected): another immature female was collected by J.L. Baillie at Rainy River on July 31, 1929. Manning (1952: 65) called this the common owl of the James Bay and southern Hudson Bay coasts and cited several records to support this view: he saw one at North Point on June 6, 1947 and one at Big Piskwanish on June 12: M.Y. Williams, reported six on Aug. 19 and 10 on Aug. 21, 1920 at Ft. Albany, etc. Peck (1972: 345) cited several records for the Cape Henrietta Maria region: he saw one there on June 27, 1970 and the 1948 ROM party saw at least a dozen and collected two. Schueler, Baldwin & Rising (1974: 143) reported the species at Ft. Albany and Winisk. C.E. Hope noted them regularly during the summer of 1940 at Ft. Severn and collected 5 young there on July 19, 1940.

AUTUMN:   H. Lewis and H.S. Peters reported it in Sept. or Oct., 1940 near the Moose River Estuary (Manning, 1952: 65). Elder (1979: 34) called it a rare fall migrant at Geraldton. We saw one flying south parallel to the east shore of Lake Nipissing on Oct. 14, 1944 (Speirs & Speirs, 1947: 29). Nicholson (1981: 121) had fall sightings on Great Duck Is., Manitoulin, on Sept. 22, 1975 and Oct. 5, 22 and 24, 1978. Chris Harris saw one at Go Home Bay on Oct. 7, 1977 (Mills, 1981: 75). L. Beamer had Meaford records for Sept. 25, 1949, Oct. 1, 1939 and Oct. 22, 1945. Lloyd (1923: 153) mentioned "a good number" of fall specimens from Ottawa. Devitt (1967: 94) reported an ROM female at Bradford on Sept. 27, 1907 and another female taken at Wasaga Beach on Oct. 13, 1941. Snyder (1941: 62) gave fall records for Prince Edward Co. on Oct. 13, 1934 and Nov. 13, 1939: also a female taken about Oct. 22, 1938 and a male about Nov. 16, 1938. I saw four at Ajax flats on Nov. 27, 1965 (Speirs, 1976: 41). Four were received by Wm. Cross on Oct. 10, 1889 (Thompson, 1890: 196). Stirrett (1973d: 21) had several fall records for Pelee, the earliest on Sept. 1.

**MEASUREMENTS:**
*Length:* 13 to 17 ins.
(Godfrey, 1966: 219)
*Wingspread:* 38 to 44 ins.
(Roberts, 1955: 612)
*Weight:* ♂ 10 3/4 to 12
oz. ♀ 14 oz. (Roberts,
1955: 612).

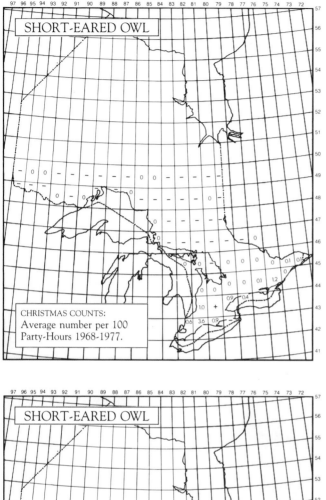

SHORT-EARED OWL

CHRISTMAS COUNTS:
Average number per 100
Party-Hours 1968-1977.

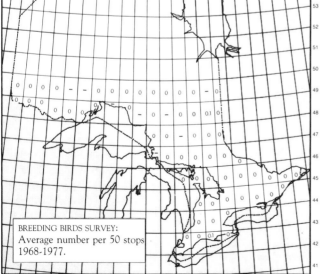

SHORT-EARED OWL

BREEDING BIRDS SURVEY:
Average number per 50 stops
1968-1977.

# BOREAL OWL   *Aegolius funereus*   (Linnaeus)

This is a circumpolar bird found in coniferous forests. It breeds in northern Ontario and is found in southern Ontario in winter and early spring. It is sufficiently rare to excite much interest wherever found. One that turned up at our home on Christmas morning in 1958 was a highlight of that day.

IDENTIFICATION: It is distinguished from its smaller relative, the Saw-whet Owl by its spotted forehead (streaked in the Saw-whet), by its yellow instead of blackish bill and by the black outline around its facial discs (like a small Hawk-Owl). The Screech Owl is about the same size but has conspicuous ear tufts, missing in this species.

WINTER: On the 1968-1977 Christmas counts it was noted only at Ottawa, in 1973 and 1976. H. Clemens *et al* saw one at Ailsa Craig, near London, from Feb. 6 to Mar. 23, 1973 (Goodwin, 1973: 610). Grant Hawes photographed one near St. Catharines on Feb. 16, 1963 (Beardslee & Mitchell, 1965: 285). Speirs (1976: 42) gave details of Ontario Co. sightings from Jan. 15-29, 1955; Dec. 25, 1958; Jan. 22, 1966; Feb. 26, 1969; Jan. 8-14, 1973 and Dec. 24, 1973. Tozer & Richards (1974: 168) gave Darlington Twp. records for Feb. 22, 1963; Feb. 8, 1969 and Feb. 25, 1971. Quilliam (1973: 108) had Kingston area records for Dec. 15, 1957; Jan. 20, 1963 and Jan. 23, 1969: Weir & Quilliam (1980: 16) added Jan. 7-8, 1973 and Feb. 25, 1979. Specimens were collected near Barrie on Feb. 15, 1940 and during the winter of 1961-62 (Devitt, 1967: 94-95). Lloyd (1923: 153) cited Ottawa records for Jan. 1, 1884, Dec. 17, 1903 and Dec., 1922: B. Barrett noted one there on Dec. 1 and 19, 1976 (Goodwin, 1977: 327). Mrs. Kettle noted one at Meaford on Feb. 11, 1972 (Goodwin, 1972: 599). Mills (1981: 75) cited winter records from Muskoka on Jan. 25, Jan. 30 and Feb., 1963; Feb. 27-28, 1960; Feb. 1, 1955 and A. Kay's Port Sydney specimen taken on Feb. 15, 1895. Individuals were noted on the Sault Ste. Marie Christmas counts in 1961 and 1962 (Dennison, 1980: 149). J. Miles noted one at Hornepayne on Dec. 16, 1973 (Goodwin, 1974: 634). D. Elder reported three caught in traps near Geraldton in winter, 1972 (Goodwin, 1972: 599). S. Peruniak heard one calling as early as Feb. 13, 1981 at French Lake, Quetico (Goodwin, 1981: 297).

SPRING: Grant Hawes *et al* found one near St. Catharines on March 24, 1963, seen later that day by many bird watchers from Buffalo (Beardslee & Mitchell, 1965: 285). Fleming (1907: 74) gave Apr. 3 as his latest spring date for Toronto. Saunders (1947: 65-66) recounted the experience of some ten observers converging on one found at Ashbridge's "jungle", Toronto, on March 15, 1942, and finally caught for banding by Herb. Southam. Speirs (1976: 42) gave details of Ontario Co. records for March 2-4, 1974; Mar. 11-17, 1961; Mar. 8, 1969 and the latest banded on Apr. 12, 1969. Black (1934: 148) mentioned one shot at Port Hope on Mar. 14, 1817 and described in detail by Charles Fothergill. Quilliam (1973: 108) mentioned one photographed on Wolfe Is. on Apr. 5, 1970. Weir & Quilliam (1980: 16-17) heard one calling at Abbey Dawn, near Kingston, on Mar. 11, 1977 and four were found on Amherst Is. during the big owl invasion on March 7, 1979 and one remained as late as Apr. 1. L. Beamer had Meaford records for Apr. 14, 1940; March 23, 1946 and Apr. 12, 1947: all found dead. An emaciated bird was collected at Huntsville on March 16, 1950 (Mills, 1981: 75). Nicholson (1981: 121) had Manitoulin records on March 14, 1976 at Providence Bay and one on March 15, 1980 in Gordon Twp. by the Taskers. Skeel & Bondrup-Nielsen (1978: 177) heard one at Pukaskwa on

March 2, 1977: D. Hoy and W. Wyett heard one there on May 29, 1974 and W. Wyett heard another there on May 9 and 10, 1975. N.G. Escott heard one at Marathon on March 28, 1976 (Goodwin, 1976: 835). Bondrup-Nielsen (1976: 46) located eleven calling males near Kapuskasing in spring, 1974 and seven in 1975: he found a nest in a cavity in a live trembling aspen on May 2, 1975. On May 23, 1971, David Elder showed me one that was picked up injured about 6 miles north of Geraldton about May 9 (he was taking care of it): he saw another at Sapawe, Rainy River, on March 9, 1981. S. Peruniak heard one calling at Quetico on May 30-31, 1979 (Goodwin, 1979: 767).

SUMMER: Skeel & Bondrup-Nielsen (1978: 177) reported one heard at Pukaskwa on June 17, 1975 by W. Wyett. D. Fillman noted one at Hillsport, near Manitouwadge, on June 11, 1980 (Goodwin, 1980: 772).

AUTUMN: A.E. Grimme found one at Hymers, Thunder Bay on Nov. 11, 1972 (Goodwin, 1973: 53). A. Kay found one dead in a barn at Port Sydney, Muskoka, on Nov. 21, 1904 (Mills, 1981: 75). Lloyd (1923: 153) reported a "considerable flight" at Ottawa during the fall of 1922 and mentioned others collected on Nov. 29, 1884 and Nov. 16, 1906. Paul Harrington shot one at the mouth of the Nottawasaga River on Oct. 12, 1922 (Devitt, 1967: 94). On Nov. 2, 1976 a female was killed on Hwy. 401 near Kingston and anoter was netted at Prince Edward Point on Oct. 24, 1978 (Weir & Quilliam, 1980: 16-17). Snyder (1941: 62) listed a Picton specimen taken on Oct. 27, 1931. Fleming (1907: 74) gave Nov. 8 as his earliest fall record for Toronto, but J.R. Thurston received one on Oct. 23, 1889 and Wm. Cross another on Nov. 12, 1889 (Thompson, 1890: 191, 198). One was photographed by Grant Hawes near Fonthill on Nov. 25, 1961 (Beardslee & Mitchell, 1965: 285).

**MEASUREMENTS:**
*Length:* 8.5 to 11.5 ins. (Godfrey, 1966: 219)
*Wingspread:* 19 to 24 1/4 ins. (Roberts, 1955: 611)
*Weight:* ♂ 3 1/2 - 4 oz. ♀ 5 oz. (Roberts, 1955: 611)

**REFERENCE:**
Catling, Paul M. 1972 A study of the Boreal Owl in southern Ontario with particular reference to the irruption of 1968-69. Can. Field-Nat., 86:(3): 223-232.

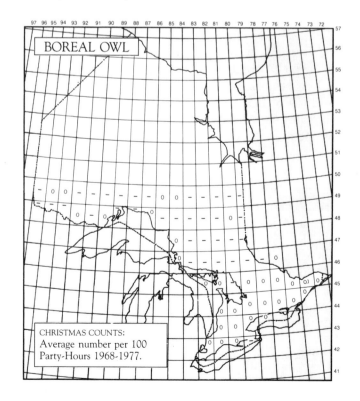

BOREAL OWL

CHRISTMAS COUNTS: Average number per 100 Party-Hours 1968-1977.

# NORTHERN SAW-WHET OWL
*Aegolius acadicus*   (Gmelin)

In Ontario this endearing wee owl is most often encountered in evergreens or dense willow scrub near the shores of Lake Ontario or Lake Erie during its fall migration. Once found it often allows very close approach. During the breeding season it may be located by its call notes.

IDENTIFICATION:   This is our smallest owl (about the same length as a cowbird). It is smaller than a Boreal Owl (see distinctions under that species). Young Screech Owls may depress their ear tufts and look a bit like this species in poor light. Young Saw-whet Owls go through a plumage when they are a rather uniform dark brown colour but with conspicuous white "eyebrows" and blackish faces, this is generally lost by the time of the fall migration but birds of the year can still be distinguished from adults in most cases by banders by their unworn, uniformly coloured wings while adults have two-toned, worn flight feathers in the fall (see Weir *et al*, 1980 for details). The notes uttered in the breeding season are distinctive. One kept me awake for several nights between May 14 and June 9, 1973 by its persistent rather musical whistling., on a note near high C, repeated about twice per second all night long.

WINTER:   On the 1968-1977 Christmas counts Saw-whet Owls were noted, but rarely, at most localities south of a line from Ottawa to Kettle Point, Lake Huron. Brooman (1954: 24) cited winter records for Elgin Co. on Jan. 19, 1953 and Dec. 19, 1953. Speirs (1976: 43) documented several winter records from Pickering to Oshawa. Charles Fothergill described one that was caught alive at Port Hope on Feb. 29, 1824 (Black, 1934: 148). E.L. Brereton found one at Barrie on Feb. 3, 1940 and James Knights saw one being attacked by a Northern Shrike near Collingwood on Feb. 18, 1967 (Devitt, 1967: 95). Ken Kerr brought in a starved individual to L. Beamer on Feb. 18, 1939 "too far gone to eat anything": another was found dead and emaciated on Feb. 21, 1941 and another found dead on Feb. 22, 1942—all victims of deep snow at Meaford, covering up their food. Lloyd (1923: 153) reported Ottawa specimens taken on Feb. 9, 1887 and Jan. 18, 1896. Wm. Cross received a pair from Bardsville, Muskoka, on Feb. 24, 1891 and Phil Bailey saw one near Dorset on Jan. 27, 1961 (Mills, 1981: 75).

SPRING:   Stirrett (1973b: 19) had just two spring records for Pelee: March 14, 1953 and May 6 to 13, 1954. Ussher (1965: 14) had a March 29 record for Rondeau. Saunders and Dale (1933: 206) heard his first at Komoka on March 8, 1888 and took a party there again to hear them on March 14, 1914: he also had a specimen taken March 30, 1908. Brooman (1954: 24) cited records near St. Thomas in May, 1889 and on Apr. 4, 1942. James R. Thurston found one grasping a mouse, west of the Humber River, Toronto, on March 5, 1889 (Thompson, 1890: 188). Fleming (1907: 74) reported a young bird taken at Toronto on May 15, 1889. Catling (1971: 110) found that the spring migration at Toronto begins about March 24, peaks between Apr. 12 and 20 and ends about Apr. 25: the chief influxes occurred on clear nights with light winds. Between Apr. 7 and Apr. 16, 1929 J.A. Edwards located 4 nests with 6 eggs each and two with five eggs each, on Thorah Is., Lake Simcoe: he also found two other nests on the island, the latest on May 4, 1936 with 6 eggs (Speirs, 1976: 43). One pair nested in a Wood Duck nest-box on Amherst Is. where the 6 young were banded on May 22, 1976 (Weir & Quilliam,

1980: 17): the 15-year average arrival date at Kingston was on March 26 (Weir & Quilliam, 1980: 36). E.L. Brereton found one dead at Barrie on Apr. 2, 1940 and he saw a nest with young there in 1931 (Devitt, 1967: 95). L. Beamer recorded one that was caught alive at Meaford on Apr. 6, 1944 with an injured upper mandible: it died emaciated very shortly afterwards: Al. Lowe brought one to his school on Apr. 18, 1955. Lloyd (1923: 153) reported Ottawa specimens taken on March 9, 1885 and on Apr. 11, 1901; the latter with a fully developed egg in its ovary. Mills (1981: 75-76) documented several spring observations in the cottage country, including one collected at Lake Muskoka on Apr. 8, 1892. Nicholson (1981: 122) had several Manitoulin records from Apr. 27 (1974) to May 22 (1974) and one was found dead in March, 1976. Ricker & Clarke (1939: 12) reported a North Bay specimen brought in on Apr. 17, 1926. Skeel & Bondrup-Nielsen (1978: 178) recorded them at Pukaskwa from Apr. 25 (1974) to May 10 (1975). Denis (1961: 5) reported a nest with 3 eggs at Thunder Bay on May 24, 1954. Elder (1979: 34) had only one record for Geraldton: May 16, 1971.

SUMMER: W.E. Saunders reported young taken near St. Thomas in July (Brooman, 1954: 24). John Edmonds collected a juvenile male, not long out of the nest, at Long Point (Snyder, 1931: 183). A.R. Muma sent a specimen to the ROM in July, 1949 (Sheppard, 1960: 30). Fleming (1907: 74) reported a young bird taken at Toronto in August. One sang in our woods in Pickering Twp. until June 9, 1973 and LGL reported two heard on June 12, 1973 (Speirs, 1976: 43). One newley fledged bird was banded on July 21, 1979 at Prince Edward Point (Weir & Quilliam, 1980: 17). Lloyd (1923: 153) reported Ottawa specimens taken on July 14, 1885 and June 27, 1921, the latter in juvenile plumage "which lasts but a short time". Mills (1981: 76) reported one at Ahmic Lake on June 30, 1948 and one on a Georgian Bay island near Twelve Mile Bay, on July 8, 1974. Nicholson (1981: 122) found one at Mississagi Light, Manitoulin, on Aug. 18, 1979. Snyder (1928: 260-261) noted that a nest with two young was taken by Walter Koelz at Lake Nipigon on July 21, 1922. Dear (1940: 130) found a nest with 4 eggs near Thunder Bay on June 26, 1926. Peruniak (1971: 18) had just two records at Atikokan: June 4, 1964 and June 13, 1965. Snyder (1953: 61-62) mentioned a road-killed female (with enlarged ovaries) found 8 miles west of Kenora on June 23, 1951.

AUTUMN: Olaus J. Murie saw a small owl that he took to be this species at Moose Factory on Oct. 10, 1915 and James Mackenzie collected one there (no date) (Todd, 1963: 451). W. Wyett observed one at Pukaskwa on Sept. 26, 1973 (Skeel & Bondrup-Nielsen, 1978: 178). A. Kay collected two young at Port Sydney, Muskoka, on Sept. 12, 1891 (Mills, 1981: 75). Lloyd (1923: 153) reported an Ottawa specimen taken on Oct. 11, 1920. L. Beamer reported one caught at Meaford on Oct. 22, 1945. R.A. Smith saw one at Bradford on Nov. 18, 1946 and A.J. Mitchener noted one at Collingwood on Nov. 20, 1948 (Devitt, 1967: 95). Weir & Quilliam (1980: 36) gave Oct. 6 and Nov. 5 as average arrival and departure dates for Kingston: several hundred have been banded each recent fall at Prince Edward Point. Allin (1940: 99) reported one in Darlington Twp. on Oct 31, 1920. Long (1968b: 19) had observations in the Shoal Point cedar woods as late as Nov. 27. At the Toronto Bird Observatory (on Mugg's Island) these owls have been taken for banding through October and the first half of November, with one peak about Oct. 15 and a later one about Oct. 26: this pattern has been about the same at the Lynde Shores, Whitby, banding substation according to Rob Nisbet. Speirs (1938: 48, 52) gave Sept. 22 as the earliest fall date for Toronto, with the peak on Oct. 28. Beardslee &

Mitchell (1965: 286-287) reported one at Point Abino, Lake Erie, on Nov. 26, 1945. Saunders & Dale (1933: 205) reported Middlesex Co. specimens taken on Nov. 13, 1909 and on Nov. 1 and 2, 1913. Ussher (1965: 14) gave a Nov. 1 record for Rondeau. Stirrett (1973a: 16) gave Nov. 22 as the latest fall date for Pelee: one was banded there as early as Oct. 5 and 26 were banded on Oct. 17 (Stirrett, 1973d: 21).

BANDING:    Several thousand have been banded at the various bird observatories in Ontario. Woodford (1959: 23) noted that 791 had been banded at Toronto between 1953 and 1957. Holroyd and Woods (1975) mapped the recoveries over their whole range: one banded in southern Indiana in spring was recovered near Ottawa, Ont. Weir *et al* (1980) summarized work at the Prince Edward Point Bird Observatory during the fall migration. They found that most owls arrived following cold fronts, with clear skies and NW winds. Females generally preceded the males. The peak of the flight there was generally in the second and third weeks of October. One bird banded there in Oct., 1977 was found dead in Arkansas in Apr., 1978: another banded there in Oct., 1978 was netted and released at Whitby in Oct., 1979 (Weir & Quilliam, 1980: 17). One banded at Toronto on Oct. 14, 1949 was recovered at White Plains, Kentucky, on Dec. 24, 1949: 4 others were taken in Ohio and one in Pennsylvania: one banded at Toronto on Nov. 3, 1950 was recovered at Sudbury, Ont. on Nov. 11, 1951. Five others banded at Toronto were taken later at Bowmanville (2), London, St. Catharines and Jeanettes Creek (Woodford (1959)).

**MEASUREMENTS:**
*Length:* 7 to 8.5 ins.
(Godfrey, 1966: 220)
*Wingspread:* 17 to 20.5
ins. (Roberts, 1955: 611)
*Weight:* ♂ 2 1/2 oz.
♀ 2 1/8 to 2 1/2 oz.
(Roberts, 1955: 611)

**REFERENCES:**
Catling, Paul M. 1971
Spring migration of Saw-
whet Owls at Toronto,
Ontario. Bird-Banding,
42: (2): 110-114.
   Holroyd, Geoffrey L.
and John G. Woods 1975
Migration of the Saw-whet
Owl in eastern North
America. Bird-Banding,
46:(2): 101-105.
   Weir, R.D.; F. Cooke;
M.H. Edwards and R.B.
Stewart 1980 Fall
migration of Saw-whet
Owls at Prince Edward
Point, Ontario. Wilson
Bull., 92:(4):475-488.
   Woodford, J. 1959
Returns and recoveries of
Saw-whet Owls banded at
Toronto, Ontario. Ont.
Field Biologist, No.
13: 19, 21-23.

Woods, John G. 1972
An introduction to the
literature on the Saw-whet
Owl. Ont. Bird Banding,
8:(1): 8-23.

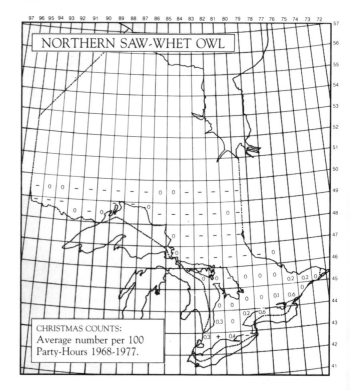

NORTHERN SAW-WHET OWL

CHRISTMAS COUNTS:
Average number per 100
Party-Hours 1968-1977.

# LESSER NIGHTHAWK   *Chordeiles acutipennis*   (Hermann)

This is normally a bird of southwestern United States, and Central and South America. Accidental in Ontario.

IDENTIFICATION:  Smaller and browner than the Common Nighthawk, with a call note resembling a trilling toad. Males have the white spot on the wing closer to its tip: females have this spot buff-coloured while immatures have no such spot. The wings appear to be narrower and more pointed than those of the Common Nighthawk.

WINTER:

SPRING:   A. Wormington photographed one at Pelee on Apr. 29, 1974 (very early for any nighthawk) and the identity was confirmed by W.E. Godfrey. This is the first Canadian record.

SUMMER:

AUTUMN:

**MEASUREMENTS:**
*Length:* 8 to 9 ins. (Terres, 1980: 634)
Wingspread:
*Weight:* ♂ 58 g. (Terres, 1980: 634)

# COMMON NIGHTHAWK   *Chordeiles minor*   (Forster)

As a boy living in Toronto, I took great delight in watching the Common Nighthawks on summer evenings, mounting stepwise into the sky, uttering their "geep" note as they climbed higher and higher, then plunging in a spectacular dive and pulling up with a great "whirr" of wings in a great J-shaped arc, only to repeat the performance all through the evening. When I learned that their diet included many mosquitoes I was even more pleased. They nest on gravel roofs in cities or on bare ground or rocks or pine needles in northern Ontario.

IDENTIFICATION:   The long, dark, angled wings with the rectangular white patch as well as the manner of flight and notes mentioned above, are diagnostic. As they are frequently abroad in the afternoon on dark days before a storm and as they lack the hooked beak and talons of true hawks, their name is not very appropriate.

WINTER:

SPRING:   Stirrett (1973b: 19) had a maximum of 10 at Pelee on May 20 and his earliest one on May 1. Ussher (1965: 15) gave May 13 as the earliest date for Rondeau with a 23-year average arrival date on May 19. Saunders & Dale (1933: 206) gave May 15 as the 17-year average arrival date for London, with the earliest on May 5, 1917. Fleming (1907: 76) gave May 1 as the earliest Toronto date while Saunders (1947: 367) listed May 17 as his 13-year average arrival date there. Long (1966: 30) saw one at Pickering Beach as early as May 8, 1965. Ron Tozer saw a flock of 40 over Oshawa on May 23, 1960 (Tozer & Richards, 1974: 170). Snyder (1941: 62) gave May 7, 1913 as the earliest date for Prince Edward Co. Weir & Quilliam (1980: 36) gave May 2 as the earliest Kingston record with the 30-year average arrival on May 15. Quilliam (1973: 110) mentioned a nest on the parade ground of the Royal Military College on May 26, 1958. Devitt (1967: 96) gave May 13, 1962 as the earliest Barrie record with the 17-year average arrival on May 23. C. Harris saw five at Go Home Bay as early as May 10, 1974 (Mills, 1981: 77). Nicholson (1981: 123) gave May 21 as the 11-year average arrival date for Manitoulin, with the earliest on May 19 (on 5 years). MacLulich (1938: 18) had an arrival date for Algonquin Park on May 23, 1912. Ricker & Clarke (1939: 12) saw their first near Lake Nipissing on May 19 in both 1933 and 1934. Skeel & Bondrup-Nielsen (1978: 178) saw their first at Pukaskwa on May 21, 1977. Denis (1961: 4) gave May 25 as the average arrival date for Thunder Bay, with the earliest on May 16, 1951. Bondrup-Nielsen (1976: 42) saw his first near Kapuskasing on May 20, 1975. The earliest Atikokan date was on May 15 (Peruniak, 1971: 18).

SUMMER:   This species was noted on many of the Breeding Bird Survey routes from Port Dover north to Smooth Rock Falls and Dryden, and was most numerous near Sudbury. Stirrett (1973c: 17) had Pelee records throughout the summer. Kelley (1978: 45) reported a nest with 2 eggs at Chatham on June 6, 1952. Saunders & Dale (1933: 206) noted two nests with 2 eggs each, one on the ground on June 22, 1902 and the other on the roof of the Grand Opera House, London, on June 26, 1909. Speirs (1938: 44) gave June 7 as the "spring peak" for Toronto. Charles Fothergill noted "Upwards of a thousand seen over Toronto, 30th Aug., 1817" (Black, 1934: 149). Snyder (1930: 190) noted a female feeding almost fully grown young in King Twp. on Aug. 20, 1928. J.M. Richards found a nest with 2 eggs on an apartment roof in Oshawa on June 17, 1961 and another nest with 2 eggs was found in Uxbridge on June 16, 1896 (Speirs, 1976: 45). The peak of the southward flight near Pickering is about the end of August, e.g. 40 on Aug. 31, 1961 (Speirs, 1976: 45). Charles Fothergill described one shot at Rice Lake on Aug. 3, 1821 (Black, 1934: 149). Quilliam (1973: 110) mentioned two Kingston nestings: one with two young on June 29, 1961 and the other with 2 eggs as late as Aug. 13, 1960. In Simcoe Co., Devitt (1967: 96) reported a set of eggs in a sandy pasture in Innisfil Twp. on June 24, 1936; a nest with 2 eggs at Camp Borden in 1950 that hatched two young on Aug. 7 and two nests with eggs on rock outcropings in Matchedash Twp. on July 5, 1963. Lloyd (1923: 154) reported a nest on the roof of the Museum in Ottawa on June 29, 1917. Egg dates for the cottage country ranged from May 26 to July 27, with nests on rock, lichens and pine needles (Mills, 1981: 77). D.B. Ferguson found a nest with one young at Silverwater, Manitoulin, on July 18, 1979 (Nicholson, 1981: 123). Speirs & Speirs (1947: 29) noted 60 at North Bay on Aug. 1, 1944. Ricker & Clarke (1939: 12) saw them catching cockroaches on the bare rocks at Frank's Bay, Lake Nipissing and found a nest near there on June 14, 1921 with 2 eggs, also on June 21, 1932 and June 10, 1933; also a nest on the Normal School roof in North Bay on June 27, 1925. Snyder (1942: 131) noted two nests with 2 eggs each on June 9, 1931 near Sault Ste. Marie and flushed a female brooding two newly hatched young on June 29 at Maclennan. Baillie & Hope (1947: 9) found two nests with 2 eggs each, on needles under Jack pines, one at Chapleau on June 11, 1937 and the other at Bigwood on July 22, 1937. Skeel & Bondrup-Nielsen (1978: 178) saw their last at Pukaskwa on Aug. 27, 1977. Baillie & Hope (1943: 10) collected two females in 1936, one at Rossport on June 3 and the other at Peninsula (Marathon) on June 15. Dear (1940: 130) found two nests with 2 eggs each on gravel roofs in Ft. William (Thunder Bay) on June 24, 1924. Elder (1979: 34) called this a common summer resident at Geraldton, with his earliest record on June 1. Snyder (1928: 263) collected two young at Lake Nipigon on Aug. 19, 1923. Snyder (1928: 25) saw 20 feeding over the mouth of the Ghost River, Lake Abitibi, on July 1, 1925. Snyder (1938: 190) found a fresh egg and collected a female in north central Rainy River Dist. on July 1, 1929. Snyder (1953: 62) found a clutch of 2 eggs near Dryden on July 3, 1939 and two young on July 20, 1939 as well as a group of about 200 at Malachi on Aug. 4, 1947. James (1980: 86-87) found 3 nests with 2 eggs each near Pickle Lake on June 15, 1977, two on June 19, 1979 and a nest with one egg on June 1, 1979. Hope (1938: 22) found them very common near Favourable Lake and took a newly hatched young there on July 7, 1938. Cringan (1950: 11) saw them regularly from June 10 to early Aug., 1950 near Nikip Lake with a maximum of 30 on June 24 at Petownikip Lake. Cringan (1953b: 3) saw his first at Kasabonika Lake on June 1, 1953. Manning (1952: 65-66) frequently saw two or three over Moosonee in late June and early July, 1949 and cited other records for the area, including one at the head of the Albany Eastuary on Aug. 18, 1920. Lee (1978: 24) saw them at Big Trout Lake from June 3 to Aug. 10, 1975 and a family group on Aug. 4. Peck (1972: 345) tape recorded one at Cape Henrietta Maria on June 28, 1970 as it flew about overhead. Schueler, Baldwin & Rising (1974: 143) noted the species as far north as Hawley Lake and Winisk.

AUTUMN: Peruniak (1971: 18) gave Sept. 8 as her latest date for Atikokan. Speirs & Speirs (1947: 29) saw one at North Bay as late as Sept. 11, 1944. Nicholson (1981: 123) had his latest Manitoulin record on Sept. 21, 1975. C. Harris saw 30 at Go Home Bay on Aug. 31, 1979, the latest date for the cottage country (Mills, 1981: 77). Frances Westman noted one at Barrie as late as Sept. 30, 1965 (Devitt, 1967: 96). Weir & Quilliam

(1980: 36) gave Sept. 16 as the 22-year average departure date from Kingston, with the latest on Oct. 24. Tozer & Richards (1974: 170) noted one flying around in one of the General Motors buildings in Oshawa as late as Oct. 23, 1973. Fleming (1907: 76) gave Oct. 11 as the latest Toronto date and Speirs (1938: 54) gave Sept. 3 as the fall peak there. Ussher (1965: 15) gave Oct. 20 as the latest Rondeau date, with the 7-year average departure on Oct. 10. Stirrett (1973d: 21) had a maximum of 50 on Sept. 7 at Pelee, with the latest one on Oct. 15.

**MEASUREMENTS:**

*Length:* 8.3 to 10 ins. (Godfrey, 1966: 225)
*Wingspread:* 21 to 23 3/4 ins. (Roberts, 1955: 616)
*Weight:* 3 ♂ averaged 74 g. 5 ♀ averaged 78 g. (Hope, 1938: 22).

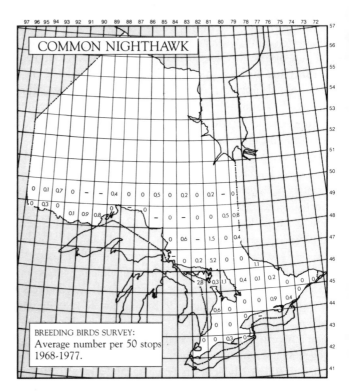

COMMON NIGHTHAWK

BREEDING BIRDS SURVEY:
Average number per 50 stops
1968-1977.

# COMMON POORWILL   *Phalaenoptilus nuttallii*   (Audubon)

The Common Poorwill is a bird of semiarid regions in the rain shadows of the western mountains, accidental in Ontario. This is the only bird known to go into protracted hibernation, though some related species and hummingbirds save precious energy by going into a state of torpor for short periods.

IDENTIFICATION: The Common Poorwill looks like a small Whip-poor-will, with its black face and crown, but has just a small white tip to the outer tail feathers, not completely white outer tail feathers as in the Whip-poor-will. The call is given as "poor-will" or at close range "poor-will-uck".

WINTER:

SPRING:

SUMMER:   Chris. Rimmer collected one at North Point, James Bay, on June 4, 1982 for the National Museum of Canada.

AUTUMN:

**MEASUREMENTS:**
*Length:* 7.0 to 8.5 ins.
(Godfrey, 1966: 224)
*Wingspread:*
*Weight:* The weight of a banded, hibernating, bird decreased from 45.61 g. on Jan. 4, 1948 to 44.56 g. of Feb. 14, 1948. On Dec. 5, 1948 it weighed 52.68 g. (Jaeger, 1949: 106).

**REFERENCE:**
Jaeger, Edmund C. 1949 Further observations on the hibernation of the Poor-will. Condor, 51: (3): 105-109. A bird was found hibernating in a rocky cavity in a Colorado canyon on Dec. 29, 1946; banded on Dec. 6, 1947 and found there again on Dec. 5, 1948. Rectal temperatures varied from 19.8°C on Dec. 30, 1947 to 18.0°C in the period up to Feb. 14, 1948.

# CHUCK-WILL'S-WIDOW
*Caprimulgus carolinensis*  Gmelin

I associate this bird with the coastal forests of South Carolina, where we heard about 20 calling on the night of May 5, 1953 and saw three with their red eyes shining in the car's headlights. There are a few Ontario records from the forests along the shores of Lake Erie and Lake Ontario.

IDENTIFICATION: This bird, like its relative the Whip-poor-will, is usually identified by its call, its 4-syllabled call distinguishing it from the 3-syllabled Whip-poor-will. It is a somewhat larger bird than the Whip-poor-will and a paler, more buffy colour. The male has only the inner webs of its outer tail feathers white: both webs are white in the male Whip-poor-will (females of both have no white in the tail). With the bird in the hand it will be seen that the bristles around the mouth are branched in this species and unbranched in the Whip-poor-will. The Common Nighthawk differs from both these species in having white patches in the wings and having a forked, rather than a rounded tail.

WINTER:

SPRING:    Stirrett (1973b: 19) had only one Pelee record: on May 21, 1906. From 1975 to 1980 one or two were heard each spring at Pelee, calling as early as May 3 in 1980 (Goodwin, 1980: 772). P.A. Woodliffe heard one or more at Rondeau from May 16, 1980 (Goodwin, 1980: 772) and again during May in 1981 when none were heard at Pelee (Goodwin, 1981: 819). Weir & Quilliam (1980: 17) had records at Prince Edward Point, Lake Ontario, for three springs: May 23 to June 2, 1976; May 21-25, 1977 and May 20-21, 1978.

SUMMER:    C.A. Campbell heard one calling on Pelee Is. on June 24, 1975 and two were heard calling at Point Pelee during the summer of 1975 (Goodwin, 1975: 965). The first Ontario nest was found at Pelee on June 5, 1977 by A. Wormington *et al* (Goodwin, 1977: 1134), where they were heard each summer from 1975 to 1979. P.A. Woodliffe reported one or more from Rondeau during the summers of 1976, 1979 and 1980 (Goodwin, 1976: 950; 1979: 859 and 1980: 891). B. Jones heard one at St. Williams throughout June, 1978 (Goodwin, 1978: 1155).

AUTUMN:

**MEASUREMENTS:**
*Length:* 11-13 ins.
(Godfrey, 1966: 223)
*Wingspread:* 24 1/2 to
25 1/2 ins. (Terres, 1980:
633)
*Weight:* 12 averaged
120 g. (Dunning,
1984: 14)

# WHIP-POOR-WILL   *Caprimulgus vociferus*   Wilson

One of the joys of summer evenings in the resort country of Ontario is being serenaded by Whip-poor-wills, seemingly endlessly repeating their name, perhaps with responses from others echoing across the lakes, from hill to hill.

**IDENTIFICATION:**   See distinctions from the very rare Chuck-will's-widow and the Common Nighthawk under those species. Doris H. Speirs claims that the Whip-poor-will really says "Purple-rib": see what you think when you next hear the species.

**WINTER:**

**SPRING:**   Stirrett (1973b: 19) gave Apr. 16 his earliest date for Pelee, with a maximum of 8 on May 13 and the latest spring bird on May 30. Ussher (1965: 15) gave May 3 as the 16-year average arrival date at Rondeau, with the earliest on Apr. 24. Saunders & Dale (1933: 206) had their earliest London record on Apr. 23, 1925 with Apr. 28 as the 11-year average arrival date. Fleming (1907: 76) gave Apr. 14 as the earliest Toronto record and had a breeding record on May 21, 1888: Speirs (1938: 44) had a Toronto peak on May 19. Naomi LeVay heard one at Eastbourne, Whitby, as early as Apr. 15, 1967 but the spring peak is during the second week of May (Speirs, 1976: 44). Charles Fothergill heard his first on May 6, 1821 at Rice Lake (Black, 1934: 148). Weir & Quilliam (1980: 36) gave Apr. 30 as the 29-year average arrival date for Kingston, with the earliest on Apr. 19. May 9 was the 16-year average arrival date at Barrie, and the earliest Simcoe Co. record was on Apr. 18, 1959 at Collingwood (Devitt, 1967: 96): H.P. Bingham located two nests with two eggs each at Barrie on May 26, 1933 and May 30, 1938. Mills (1981: 76) gave May 6 as the 11-year average arrival date at Huntsville, with the earliest in the cottage country at Port Sydney on Apr. 19, 1973. Nicholson (1981: 123) noted one as early as Apr. 29, 1979 on Manitoulin. MacLulich (1938: 18) noted his earliest Algonquin Park bird on Apr. 26, 1913. Ricker & Clarke (1939: 12) gave May 3, 1934 as their earliest date for Frank's Bay, Lake Nipissing. Denis (1961: 3) had his earliest Thunder Bay record on Apr. 28, 1951 and the average arrival date there was May 12.

**SUMMER:**   On the 1968-1977 Breeding Bird Surveys, they were rare on many routes from Port Dover on Lake Erie north to Massey and Haileybury, absent north of there as well as in the agricultural southwest and southeast parts of Ontario. Stirrett (1973c: 17) had the earliest returning two at Pelee on Aug. 11. Kelley (1978: 45) reported two nests, each with two young: at Ipperwash Beach on June 16, 1964 and at Kettle Point on June 25, 1974. Ussher (1965: 15) listed this as a breeding species at Rondeau. Saunders & Dale (1933: 206) mentioned two nests: one set taken at Komoka in June, 1883 and the other with two eggs, seen about 5 miles east of London about 1912. On June 5, 1949, Fred Bodsworth heard many calling at Springwater Park, Elgin Co., and Marshall Field found two fledglings there on July 16, 1950 (Brooman, 1954: 24). Silas Tool found a nest in Pickering Twp. on Aug. 21, 1934 (Baillie & Harrington, 1936: 199). Devitt (1967: 96) cited three nest records for northern Simcoe Co.: a nest with two eggs on June 12, 1923; another with two eggs at Wasaga Beach on July 4, 1922 and the third on June 4, 1966, again with two eggs. D. Blakely took a set of two eggs near Ottawa on June 2, 1916 (Lloyd, 1923: 154). On June 20, 1975 C. Harris counted 46 calling birds along a four mile stretch of shoreline near Honey Harbour and I found a nest with two young near Torrance on July 7, 1936 (Mills, 1981: 76). Snyder (1942: 131) collected a calling bird

448

at Maclennan, near Sault Ste. Marie on July 25, 1931 and to his surprise it proved to be a female. Baillie & Hope (1947: 9) collected three males at Bigwood, Sudbury Dist., on July 18, 25 and 27, 1937. Claude Garton heard one in Pukaskwa in June, 1974 (Skeel & Bondrup-Nielsen, 1978: 178). W.K.W. Baldwin heard them at Matheson and Larder Lake in summer, 1953 (Smith, 1957: 174). Peruniak (1971: 18) had just one record near Atikokan, on June 30, 1966 at French Lake. Snyder (1938: 190) heard it at Off Lake, Rainy River Dist., on four nights from July 5-11, 1929.

AUTUMN: Louise Lawrence heard one calling as late as Sept. 7, 1944 at Pimisi Bay (Speirs & Speirs, 1947: 29). MacLulich (1938: 18) gave Sept. 26 as the latest date for Algonquin Park. Nicholson (1981: 123) found one killed at the lighthouse on Great Duck Is. as late as Sept. 21, 1977. Katherine Ketchum noted one off Pointe au Baril on Sept. 21, 1962 (Mills, 1981: 77). Devitt (1967: 76) mentioned one heard as late as Oct. 27, 1965 at Orillia by W.E. Cattley. Weir & Quilliam (1980: 36) listed Sept. 22 as the 16-year average departure date from Kingston, with the latest on Oct. 18. I flushed one from the floor of our woods in Pickering on Oct. 8, 1972 (Speirs, 1976: 44). Speirs (1938: 54) gave Oct. 20 as the latest Toronto date. Ussher (1965: 15) had his latest Rondeau record on Oct. 17. Stirrett (1973d: 21) had a maximum of 30 at Pelee on Sept. 13 and his latest on Nov. 5.

**MEASUREMENTS:**
*Length:* 9.0 to 10.2 ins.
(Godfrey, 1966: 223)
*Wingspread:* 16.0 to 19.4
ins. (Roberts, 1955: 616)
*Weight:* 2 1/4 oz.
(Roberts, 1955: 616)

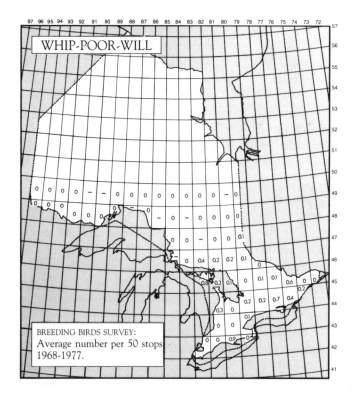

WHIP-POOR-WILL

BREEDING BIRDS SURVEY:
Average number per 50 stops
1968-1977.

# CHIMNEY SWIFT   *Chaetura pelagica*   (Linnaeus)

Chimney Swifts not only nest in chimneys but often use them as communal roost sites during migration. Several hundreds or even thousands may go to roost in a big chimney (or ventilation shaft) and sometimes it looks as if smoke is pouring into the chimney so used, instead of coming out, as they retire in the evening dusk. During the nesting season you frequently see three of them circling together over town and Ralph Dexter has shown that a pair often has a "helper at the nest" in his banding studies in Ohio. Banding also finally solved the problem of where they go in the winter; several banded in U.S.A. and at Kingston, Ont., showed up in Peru.

IDENTIFICATION:   In flight, as usually seen, they look a bit like swallows lacking the swallow tail, but with a very fast wing beat. They have been described as "flying cigars". The "tit'tit'tit——" call note is also diagnostic.

WINTER:

SPRING:   Stirrett (1973b: 19) gave Apr. 12 as the earliest one seen at Pelee, with a maximum of 200 on May 17. Ussher (1965: 15) had his earliest Rondeau record on Apr. 17, with the 24-year average arrival on May 3. Saunders & Dale (1933: 206) gave Apr. 24 as the 17-year average arrival date for London, with the earliest on Apr. 16, 1912. Fleming (1907: 76) gave Apr. 18, 1891 as the earliest Toronto record while Saunders (1947: 367) listed May 3 as his 13-year average arrival date and Speirs (1938: 44) had spring peaks on May 23 and June 1. Speirs (1976: 46) cited a sighting at Squires Beach on Apr. 17, 1966 as the earliest for Ontario Co., with the peak in early June. Snyder (1941: 63) gave Apr. 30 as his earliest arrivals in Prince Edward Co. (in 1934 and 1936). Quilliam (1973: 111) gave Apr. 17 (1952 and 1963) as the earliest arrival date for Kingston, with the 23-year average on Apr. 28. The 16-year average arrival date at Barrie was on May 4, with the earliest on Apr. 10, 1953 (Devitt, 1967: 97): and S.H. Henry noted 200 to 300 flying about the Catholic Church there on May 18, 1917. L. Beamer's earliest date for Meaford was Apr. 24 and the median arrival date was May 2. The earliest record for Huntsville was Apr. 27, 1964 (Mills, 1981:78). Nicholson (1981: 123) gave May 1, 1977 as the earliest Manitoulin record, with the 12-year average arrival on May 8. MacLulich (1938: 18) gave May 7, 1912 as an arrival date for Algonquin Park. Speirs & Speirs (1947: 29) saw one at North Bay as early as Apr. 30, 1944 and estimated 5000 entering a chimney on the evening of May 16, 1944: they took 50 minutes for all to enter. Baillie & Hope (1943: 11) saw one at White River on May 26, 1936. Skeel & Bondrup-Nielsen (1978: 179) saw one at Pukaskwa on May 16, 1977. Denis (1961: 3) gave May 17 as the average arrival date at Thunder Bay, with the earliest on May 5, 1952. Peruniak (1971: 18) found them uncommon at Atikokan and the earliest date was May 11.

SUMMER:   On the 1968-1977 Breeding Bird Survey they were seen on most routes south of Haileybury and Thessalon: north of there only on the Atikokan and Nipigon routes. Stirrett (1973c: 17) listed this as a nesting species at Pelee. Saunders & Dale (1933: 206) had three nesting records for London: a set of 3 eggs on June 29, 1896; a set of 5 on June 24, 1900 and a set of 4 on July 9, 1912. Baillie & Harrington (1937: 200) reported a set of 4 eggs taken at Aylmer by R.T. Anderson. Snyder (1931: 188) discovered a pair nesting at Long Point in July, 1927. Fleming (1907: 76) mentioned a Toronto breeding record on June 7, 1892. Speirs (1976: 46) reported that 17 sets with a total of

76 eggs had been found in Ontario Co.; the earliest on June 8, 1914 and the latest on July 17, 1934 (most of these were on Thorah Is.: the numbers peaked in late July and decreased through August: on urban censuses in Ontario Co. this species ranked fifth in abundance. Allin (1940: 100) mentioned that more than 650 used the chimney of Bowmanville Public School for roosting on Aug. 30, 1921. Snyder (1941: 63) reported nesting at Milford, Prince Edward Co. on July 3, 1930. E. Beaupré took a set of 5 eggs at Kingston on June 27, 1918 (Quilliam 1973: 111). Devitt (1967: 97) gave details of three nestings in Simcoe Co.: a nest with 4 eggs on June 23, 1894 at Barrie; a nest with 3 eggs at Wasaga Beach on July 4, 1914 and a nest with 4 eggs at Barrie on June 29, 1915. Mills (1981: 78) reported several nests in the cottage country, with egg dates from May 24 to July 15. Stuart Thompson found a nest with 5 eggs in a shack in Algonquin Park on July 14, 1910 (Baillie & Harrington, 1937: 201). Speirs & Speirs (1947: 29) saw ten gathering twigs in flight from the dead tops of elm trees at North Bay on June 13, 1945 and saw their latest two there on Aug. 19, 1944. Baillie & Hope (1947: 10) discovered a new nest at Biscotasing on June 21, 1937. Smith (1957: 174) had few records from the Clay Belt: 3 at Judge on July 21, 1953; 3 or 4 at Gogama on July 23-24, 1954 and one reported at Cochrane by A.N. Boissonneau on June 14, 1950. Baillie & Hope (1943: 11) collected one on June 10, 1936 at Peninsula (Marathon). Elder (1979: 34) had only one Geraldton record, on June 28, 1966. Dear (1940: 130) reported a nest with 4 eggs at North Lake, Thunder Bay. Snyder (1953: 62-63) noted six at Wabigoon on June 23, 1937: one female with a fully developed egg was collected in mid-July, 1937 at Savanne: also one was noted near Redditt on June 3, 1949. Cringan (1953a: 2) observed one at Sioux Lookout on June 23, 1953.

AUTUMN: Nicholson (1981: 124) noted two at Mississagi Light, Manitoulin, on Sept. 23, 1975. The latest Muskoka sighting was on Sept. 4, 1904 (Mills, 1981: 78). The latest one at Barrie was noted on Sept. 15, 1940 (Devitt, 1967: 97). Weir & Quilliam, (1980: 36) gave Oct. 5 as the 20-year average departure date from Kingston, with the latest on Nov. 22. Stuart Thompson noted the species in Prince Edward Co. on Sept. 1, 1930 (Snyder, 1941: 63). My latest personal record at our Pickering home was on Sept. 29, 1952. Speirs (1938: 52) gave Sept. 3 as the fall peak for Toronto, while Saunders (1947: 367) gave Sept. 29 as his latest date and Sept. 15 as his 12-year average departure date. Marshall Field found three as late as Sept. 26, 1949 at Aylmer (Brooman, 1954: 24). Ussher (1965: 15) gave Oct. 4 as the latest Rondeau record, with his 6-year average departure date on Sept. 17. Stirrett (1973d: 21) had two as late as Nov. 14 at Pelee and a fall maximum of 100 on Sept. 30.

BANDING: One banded in Rome, Georgia, on Sept. 21, 1952 was captured and released at Aylmer in June, 1953 (Brooman, 1954: 24). One banded at Toronto on Aug. 21, 1938 was recovered in New York state on May 15, 1940; another banded on July 24, 1940 was later found in Tennessee, on Sept. 1, 1941 and one banded on Aug. 11, 1941 was also found on Sept. 1, 1941 in Tennessee. Several banded in Tennessee in fall have been recovered in the Toronto region in summer, e.g. one banded on Sept. 16, 1944 was recovered on July 14, 1952 (about 8 years later).

Bowman (1952: 151-164) summarized the results from banding 21,930 at Kingston from 1923 to 1947. About 10% returned to Kingston or were recovered elsewhere. The age record was about 12 years. Recoveries were from as far south as Peru, from 15 states in U.S., and as far north in Ontario as Blind River and in Quebec at Kamouraska. Most of the U.S. recoveries were in Tennessee, Georgia and Alabama. One banded at Nashville, Tenn. on Sept. 13, 1941 was found dead at Barrie on July 1, 1942 (Devitt, 1967: 97). One banded on Oct. 16, 1928 at Chattanooga, Tenn. was captured at Trout Lake, near North Bay, (Ricker & Clarke, 1939: 13). Another banded at Chattanooga on Oct. 16, 1928 was captured at Markstay, near Sudbury, (Baillie & Hope, 1947: 10).

**MEASUREMENTS:**
*Length:* 4.8 to 5.7 ins. (Godfrey, 1966: 228)
*Wingspread:* 11.98 to 12.65 ins. (Roberts, 1955: 617)
*Weight:* 0.88 to 1.00 oz. (Roberts, 1955: 617)

**REFERENCES:**
Bowman, R.I. 1952 Chimney Swift banding at Kingston, Ontario from 1928 to 1947. Can. Field-Nat., 66: (6): 151-164.

Dexter, Ralph W. 1960 Storm damage and renesting behavior by the Chimney Swift. Auk, 77: (3): 352-354.

Dexter, Ralph W. 1979 Fourteen-year life history of a banded Chimney Swift. Bird- Banding, 50:(1): 30-33.

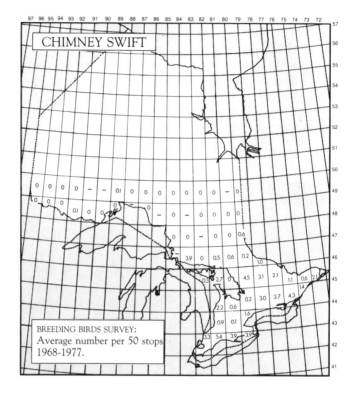

CHIMNEY SWIFT

BREEDING BIRDS SURVEY: Average number per 50 stops 1968-1977.

# RUBY-THROATED HUMMINGBIRD
## Archilochus colubris   (Linnaeus)

These tiny sprites leave the tropics where they spend the winter with other hummingbirds, to come north and breed in Ontario, then migrate back again, many crossing the Gulf of Mexico en route. I have watched them gathering spider webs to bind together the lichens with which they construct their miniscule nests, usually atop a horizontal branch where it looks like a cup-shaped knot on the branch. They usually lay two pea-sized white eggs. In courtship the males display in a spectacular "pendulum flight" back and forth, up and down. Their ability to hover in front of a flower to sip its nectar and fly backwards away when satisfied, is well known. They are also frequent visitors to the sap wells of sapsuckers. They may be attracted by putting out hummingbird feeders filled with a sweet solution or by planting such flowers as trumpet vines. I well remember one that perched so often on the same spot on a hydro wire that it had worn the insulation smooth and I could confidently focus my telescope on the spot and show the perched bird to boys at a camp in Muskoka.

IDENTIFICATION: This is the only hummingbird you are likely to see in Ontario. Some hawk moths fly in a similar manner and have been confused with hummingbirds. Males are distinguished by their flash of red on the throat (which appears black at certain angles of view) from the females which have a whitish throat. Both have whitish breasts, with some buffy red on the sides and irridescent green back and white terminal spots on the outer tail feathers. Young males on their way south have a few black or reddish spots on the mainly white throat.

WINTER:

SPRING: Stirrett (1973b: 19) gave Apr. 30 as the earliest Pelee record and had a maximum of about 200 there on May 11, 1963. Ussher (1965: 15) gave May 3 as the earliest Rondeau record with the 25-year average arrival date on May 14. Saunders & Dale (1933: 207) had their earliest one at London on May 6, 1916 and their 17-year average arrival on May 14. A nest with 2 eggs was taken by R.T. Anderson at Alymer on May 28, 1898 (Baillie & Harrington, 1937: 201). Snyder (1931: 188) gave May 9, 1928 as his arrival date at Long Point. Sheppard (1960: 30) cited May 3 as the earliest date for the Niagara region. Fleming (1907: 76) reported one at Toronto on Apr. 12, 1890 and the peak of the spring migration there is about May 19 (Speirs, 1938: 44). Naomi LeVay saw one at Eastbourne, Whitby, as early as Apr. 25, 1952 (Tozer & Richards, 1974: 172). Snyder (1941: 63) gave May 7, 1912 as the earliest date in Prince Edward Co. Weir & Quilliam (1980: 36) gave May 9 as the 30-year average arrival date at Kingston, with the earliest on May 1: Quilliam (1973: 113) reported a nest found on Wolfe Is. as early as May 19, 1963. Devitt (1967: 97-98) gave May 16 as the 14-year average arrival date at Barrie, with the earliest on May 8, 1938. The earliest Muskoka date appears to be one seen at Bala by Jim Goltz on May 7, 1972 (Mills, 1981: 78). Nicholson (1981: 124) gave May 13 as the 12-year average arrival date on Manitoulin, with the earliest on May 6, 1976. Ricker & Clarke (1939: 13) had their earliest Lake Nipissing sighting on May 16, 1933. Skeel & Bondrup-Nielsen (1978: 179) saw one at Pukaskwa on May 30, 1977. Denis (1961: 4) gave May 26 as the average arrival date at Thunder Bay, with the earliest on May 19, 1951. Elder (1979: 34) had his earliest Geraldton record on May 26. Peruniak (1971: 19) gave May 19 as the earliest date for Atikokan.

SUMMER:  On the 1968-1977 Breeding Bird Survey routes they were rare but present on most southern Ontario routes but absent from most northern ones, especially NE of Lake Superior; they were most numerous near Algonquin Park. Stirrett (1973c: 17) had a few at Pelee through the summer months and reported nesting there. Kelley (1978: 46) reported a late nest with 2 young in Kent Co. on Aug. 20, 1966. Saunders & Dale (1933: 207) reported a nest with one egg on June 21, 1902; one with 2 eggs on June 11, 1907 and another with 2 eggs on June 5, 1923, all at London. Fleming (1907: 76) gave June 1, 1904 as a breeding date for Toronto. J.A. Edwards found 15 nests on Thorah Is. between 1929 and 1938, the earliest on June 8, 1935 and the latest on Aug. 1, 1929: all but one were in white cedars (Speirs, 1976: 47). Quilliam (1973: 111-112) cited several nest records for the Kingston region, one watched as late as from Aug. 21 to Sept. 3, 1931 on Wellesley Is. H.P. Bingham found nests in cedar, spruce, beech, maple, apple and elm trees: a female on a nest in a willow was noted at Couchiching Beach Park on Aug. 8, 1963 and a nest was watched in a red pine during the summer of 1964 in Conc. 14, Tiny Twp: a nest with 2 eggs was found at Wasaga Beach on June 19, 1921 and another at Stayner on July 10, 1937 (Devitt, 1967: 97). Lloyd (1923: 154) reported an Ottawa nest found by W.E. and F.A. Saunders on July 12, 1890. Mills (1981: 79) summarized data from 10 nests found in the cottage country: one with eggs as early as June 10 and two young still in a nest as late as Aug. 31. A nest with 2 young was found at Windfall Lake, Manitoulin, on July 1, 1979 (Nicholson, 1981: 124). R.R. Langford found a nest 5 ft. up, at Lake Opeongo in Algonquin Park in early June, 1937 (MacLulich, 1938: 19). On June 21, 1945 we saw a female collecting spider web and building 30 ft. up in a white birch near Eau Claire: Louise Lawrence watched another collecting spider web on June 25, 1944 near Rutherglen and followed its fortunes until Aug. 9 when the young were seen out of the nest with the female (Speirs & Speirs, 1947: 29). Snyder (1942: 132) reported a female with 2 young near Maclennan on July 19, 1939 and he watched one catching minute insects flycatcher fashion on July 15, 1931. Baillie & Hope (1947: 10) collected an immature male at Bigwood on Aug. 4, 1937. Skeel & Bondrup-Nielsen (1978: 179) cited several summer records for Pukaskwa, but considered it rare there. Snyder (1928: 263) saw them about Macdiarmid, Lake Nipigon, and collected a juvenile male there on Aug. 11, 1923. Snyder (1938: 191) found a nest with 2 eggs at Aylesworth, Rainy River, on June 25, 1929 about 15 ft. up on a horizontal branch of a bur oak. Baillie & Harrington (1937: 201) reported a nest with 2 eggs about 20 ft. up in a white birch at Wabigoon on June 19, 1937. Snyder (1953: 63) cited several summer records from western Ontario between Ingolf and Sioux Lookout where Cringan (1953a: 2) saw one on June 8, 1953. Snyder (1928: 25) collected a male on June 23, 1925 at Lake Abitibi and T.F. McIlwraith saw one at Cochrane on Aug. 25, 1931 (Baillie & Harrington, 1937: 201). Hope (1938: 23) collected a female at Favourable Lake on July 18, 1938 and saw another there the same day. Mr. & Mrs. A.H. Mitchell reported one at Attawapiskat in late July, 1940 (Lewis & Peters, 1941: 114). Keith Reynolds encountered two at Fort Severn and one at Hawley Lake around July 31, 1975: one was also reported at Big Trout Lake in summer of 1974 by Mike McKay (Lee, 1978: 24).

AUTUMN:  George Stirrett saw one at Moose Factory on Sept. 27, 1948 (Manning, 1952: 66). Peruniak (1971: 19) gave Sept. 6 as the latest Atikokan record. The latest Pukaskwa sighting was on Sept. 2, 1977 (Skeel & Bondrup-Nielsen, 1978: 179). One was reported at Tehkummah, Manitoulin, as late as Oct. 26, 1971 (Nicholson, 1981: 124). Devitt (1967: 77) gave Sept. 21, 1942 at his latest date for Barrie. Weir & Quilliam

(1980: 36) gave Sept. 19 as the 26-year average departure date from Kingston, with the latest on Nov. 12. David O'Brien saw one at his delphiniums at Frenchman Bay as late as Oct. 15, 1972 but the fall peak is about Sept. 10 (Speirs, 1976: 47). Speirs (1938: 52, 54) found the Toronto peak to be about Sept. 3 with the latest on Oct. 6. Beardslee & Mitchell (1965: 290) reported one seen at Lorraine on Oct. 20, 1947. Sheppard (1960: 30) gave Oct. 3 as his latest Niagara record. Saunders (1942: 588) with the help of E.M.S. Dale and Kathleen Fetherston, counted 170 in less than an hour migrating past Hawk Cliff, Lake Erie, on Aug. 30, 1936. Brooman (1954: 24) cited one seen by Wm. Girling at Port Stanley as late as Oct. 11, 1953. Ussher (1965: 15) gave Sept. 24 as the 13-year average departure date from Rondeau, the latest on Oct. 16. Stirrett (1973d: 21) noted the latest one at Pelee on Oct. 12, with "hundreds" on Sept. 2: Kelley (1978: 46) mentioned a maximum of 350 there on Sept. 14, 1952.

BANDING: The legs are too small to accept ordinary bird bands. Al. Selby of Fonthill made special bands from gold chain links. Of 22 banded in 1949, one female returned each year until 1953 and two males until 1952 and several others banded in subsequent years returned in the following years.

**MEASUREMENTS:**
*Length:* 3.0 to 3.7 ins. (Godfrey, 1966: 230)
*Wingspread:* 4 to 4 3/4 ins. (Roberts, 1955: 618)
*Weight:* ♀ 3.3 g. (Hope, 1938: 23)

**REFERENCES:**
Saunders, W.E. 1942 A hummingbird migration. Auk, 59:(4): 587-589.
    Selby, Gertrude and James A. Selby 1955 Ruby-throated Hummingbirds at Lookout Point. F.O.N. Bull., No. 70: 9-20. One arrived at Fonthill as early as May 7, 1954 and one lingered until Sept. 24, 1949. Fourteen nests were found there in 1950 and studies included their territories, courtship and displays, nests, food consumption, the young as well as banding methods and results.

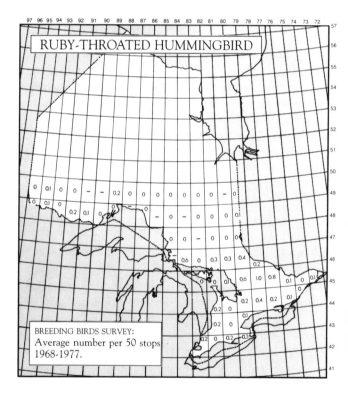

RUBY-THROATED HUMMINGBIRD

BREEDING BIRDS SURVEY:
Average number per 50 stops
1968-1977.

# RUFOUS HUMMINGBIRD   *Selasphorus rufus*   (Gmelin)

In Canada this is essentially a British Columbia bird, with some in the Rocky Mountain portion of Alberta. It is accidental east of there. They winter in Mexico.

IDENTIFICATION:   They differ from the Ruby-throated Hummingbird in showing much rufous colour at the base of the tail. Males are largely rufous except for some green on the head and a little in the back and a pale breast. Females show the rufous in the tail and on the sides (which are largely green in the Ruby-throat). The males show much red on the throat in certain light conditions.

WINTER:

SPRING:

SUMMER:   There is a sight record from Wheatley in August, 1972 (Goodwin, 1972: 36).

AUTUMN:   Daniel Kostachin collected one at Winisk on Sept. 8, 1966. This is now in the ROM collection (Barlow, 1967: 148: 149).

**MEASUREMENTS:**
*Length:* 3.3 to 3.8 ins.
(Godfrey, 1966: 231)
*Wingspread:* about 4 1/2
ins. (Terres, 1980: 547)
*Weight:* ♂ average 3.2 g.
♀ average 3.4 g. (Terres,
1980: 547)

**REFERENCE:**
Barlow, Jon C. 1967
Rufous Hummingbird in
Ontario. Can. Field-Nat.,
81:(2): 148-149.

# BELTED KINGFISHER    *Ceryle alcyon*    (Linnaeus)

Belted Kingfishers may be found throughout Ontario, wherever there are small fish to catch and sand banks to tunnel into for nesting purposes. The tunnels may be six to seven feet long. They winter as far south as Panama and Trinidad but some may be found in winter in Ontario where there is open water.

IDENTIFICATION:    This is the only kingfisher to be expected in Ontario. Its rattling cry is a familiar sound along streams and lake borders. The rusty-sided individuals are females. Both sexes are generally blue above and white below and have ragged crests. The huge beaks distinguish them from similarly coloured Blue Jays. They are often seen hovering over one spot in the manner of Kestrels.

WINTER:    On the 1968-1977 Christmas counts they were present but uncommon at most localities north to Ottawa and Manitoulin. Speirs (1976: 48) had winter records for Pickering Twp. on Dec. 13, 1972, Jan. 20, 1973 and Feb. 2, 1974, and they were noted on more than half of the Pickering Christmas counts. Mills (1981: 80) cited a few January records from the cottage country. Dennison (1980: 148) listed one on one of 25 Christmas counts at Sault Ste. Marie.

SPRING:    Stirrett (1973b: 19) gave March 28 as his earliest Pelee record with a maximum of 7 on May 3. Ussher (1965: 15) had his earliest at Rondeau on March 21 and his 16-year average arrival on Apr. 4. Spring birds usually arrived at London about Apr. 3 and nests with eggs were found near there from May 12 (7 eggs in 1906) to May 24 (6 eggs in 1901) according to Saunders & Dale (1933: 207). Beardslee & Mitchell (1965: 291) noted one at Thorold as early as March 8, 1959. J. Hughes Samuel saw one at Toronto as early as March 6, 1894 (Fleming, 1907: 75): Speirs (1938: 44) gave Apr. 29 as the spring peak there, while Saunders (1947: 367) listed Apr. 2 as his 13-year average arrival date. My earliest spring arrival in Pickering was on March 24, 1973, with peaks about Apr. 23 and May 13 (Speirs, 1976: 48). J.L. Baillie saw an adult at its nest hole at Caesarea, Lake Scugog, as early as May 7, 1933 (Tozer & Richards, 1974: 174). Charles Fothergill saw his first at Rice Lake on Apr. 19, 1821 and described one taken there a week later: he mentioned a nest in a saw pit where two men were working daily with a whip saw (Black, 1934: 149). Weir & Quilliam (1980: 36) listed Apr. 2 as the 30-year average arrival date for Kingston. Devitt (1967: 98) gave Apr. 3 as the 19-year average arrival date for Barrie: a set of 7 eggs was taken by H.P. Bingham at Crownhill on May 18, 1939. Mills (1981: 79) gave Apr. 11 as the 13-year average arrival date at Huntsville, with the earliest on March 25, 1965. MacLulich (1938: 19) noted one in Algonquin Park as early as Apr. 11, 1933. Louise Lawrence noted one at Pimisi Bay as early as Apr. 9, 1945 (Speirs & Speirs, 1947: 29). Harry Graham found a nest with 5 eggs on the Root River, near Sault Ste. Marie, on May 29, 1937 (Snyder, 1942: 132). Skeel & Bondrup-Nielsen (1978: 179) noted their first at Pukaskwa on Apr. 14, 1977 and found a nest with 3 eggs on May 22, 1977. Baillie & Hope (1943: 11) found two nests at Rossport on May 31, 1936: one held 4 eggs and the other 7 eggs and an incubating male: the nest tunnels were only about 3 ft. long, perhaps because the sandy ground was frozen at that date. Denis (1961: 2) gave Apr. 10, 1954 as the earliest Thunder Bay record with the average arrival on Apr. 23. Bondrup-Nielsen (1976: 42, 46) saw his first near Kapuskasing on Apr. 28, 1975 and found a nest with 7 eggs on May 30, 1974 (from which 4 young fledged). Elder (1979: 34) gave Apr. 25 as the earliest date for Geraldton. Peruniak (1971: 19) listed Apr. 23 as the earliest date for Atikokan. Cringan (1953a: 2) saw his first at Sioux Lookout on May 4, 1953. His first in the Asheweig area was noted on May 21, 1950 (Cringan, 1950: 11).

SUMMER:    On the 1968-1977 Breeding Bird Surveys they were uncommon to fairly common on almost all routes from Lake Erie north to Kenora. Stirrett (1973c: 17) listed this as a nesting species at Pelee. Kelley (1978: 46) reported an adult with three recently fledged young in Lambton Co. on July 8, 1954. J.A. Edwards found two nests with 6 eggs each on Thorah Is. (one on June 5, 1939, the other on June 11, 1938): also one with 7 eggs near Beaverton on June 17, 1912 (Speirs, 1976: 48). Ron Tozer saw an adult with four fledged young at Lake Scugog on July 5, 1960. Allin (1940: 100) reported a nest with 6 eggs collected on June 7, 1933 in Darlington Twp. E. Beaupré took a set of 7 eggs on Simcoe Is., near Kingston, on June 8, 1898 (Quilliam, 1973: 112). Lloyd (1923: 152) reported a nest with 7 young at Black Rapids, near Ottawa, on June 5, 1918. D.B. Ferguson found a nest with 5 young at Michael's Bay, Manitoulin, on June 26, 1940 (Nicholson, 1981: 124). We saw a scolding adult by two nest holes near Eau Claire on June 19, 1945 (Speirs & Speirs, 1947: 29). Snyder (1942: 132) noted a nesting tunnel in a gravel pit at Island Lake, near Sault Ste. Marie on June 30, 1931. Baillie & Hope (1947: 10) found a nest with 6 eggs about 40 miles south of Chapleau, with the incubating male about 4 ft. in from the entrance to the nest tunnel. On July 2, 1936, at Amyot, a nest with 7 young was found in a tunnel 6 to 7 ft. long (Baillie & Hope, 1943: 11). Snyder (1928: 261) reported a nest with 7 partly feathered young at Lake Nipigon on June 3, 1923. Dear (1940: 131) reported two Thunder Bay nests: one with 6 eggs on June 18, 1926 and the other with 7 eggs on June 17, 1937. Snyder (1928: 24) found them scarce about Lake Abitibi but collected a male on June 28, 1925 at Ghost River. Snyder (1953: 63) found a nest tunnel near Kenora on June 20, 1930 and cited other records throughout western Ontario. James (1980: 87) found two nests near Pickle Lake: one with 3 eggs on June 1, 1977 and the other with 5 eggs on June 16, 1979. Manning (1952: 66) had records at Sandy Is. on June 19, 1949 and at Haysey Is. on June 27, 1949, both near Moosonee. Schueler, Baldwin & Rising (1974: 146) found a nest with 7 eggs on June 17, 1962 along the Sutton River about 20 miles NE of Hawley Lake and saw individuals entering nest holes along the Winisk River: they also had records from Moosonee and Cochrane. Lee (1978: 25) noted the species at Big Trout Lake.

AUTUMN:    George Stirrett saw one at Ship Sands, near Moosonee, on Oct. 2, 1948 (Manning, 1952: 16). Hope (1938: 23) mentioned a female collected at Favourable Lake on Oct. 9, 1938. Peruniak (1971: 19) gave Oct. 15 as her latest Atikokan record. Skeel & Bondrup-Neilsen (1978: 179) saw their last at Pukaskwa on Oct. 2, 1977. Mills (1981: 80) gave Nov. 17 as the 6-year average departure date from Huntsville. Weir & Quilliam (1980: 36) gave Oct. 24 as the 26-year average departure date from Kingston. Long (1966: 30) gave Nov. 29, 1963 as his latest date for Pickering Beach. Saunders (1947: 367) listed Oct. 20 as his 13-year average departure date from Toronto. Ussher (1965: 15) had his latest Rondeau sighting on Nov. 2 with the 7-year average departure date on Oct. 20. Stirrett (1973a: 16) had one at Pelee as late as Nov. 22.

BANDING:    One banded near Toronto on July 2, 1939 was recovered near Long Point on Sept. 9, 1939.

## MEASUREMENTS:

*Length:* 11.0 to 14.8 ins.
(Godfrey, 1966: 234)
*Wingspread:* 21 to 23 ins.
(Roberts, 1955: 619)
*Weight:* 2 ♂ averaged
137.3 g. one ♀ weighed
190 g. (Hope, 1938: 23)

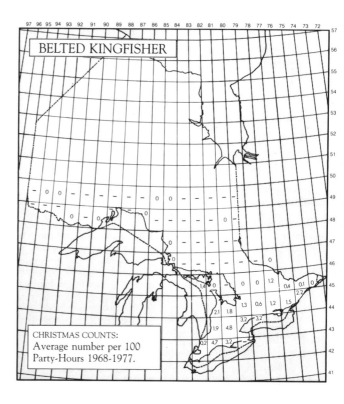

BELTED KINGFISHER

CHRISTMAS COUNTS:
Average number per 100
Party-Hours 1968-1977.

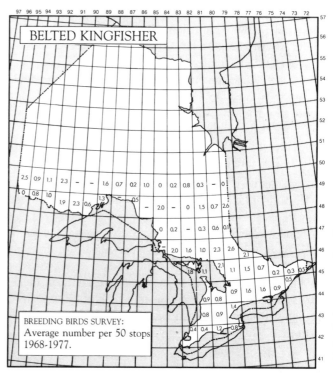

BELTED KINGFISHER

BREEDING BIRDS SURVEY:
Average number per 50 stops
1968-1977.

# LEWIS'S WOODPECKER   *Melanerpes lewis*   (Gray)

Lewis's Woodpecker is a bird of southern British Columbia and Alberta, accidental in Ontario.

**IDENTIFICATION:**   This woodpecker is somewhat larger than a Robin, iridescent greenish black on the back, with a gray collar and breast and a reddish face and belly.

**WINTER:**   James W. Wilson identified and photographed one at Windsor: it was seen by many observers from Feb. 6 to March 10, 1973 (Goodwin, 1973: 610).

**SPRING:**   Edgar Sullivan reported seeing one at Emo, Rainy River, on May 27, 1929 (Snyder, 1938: 192).

**SUMMER:**

**AUTUMN:**   Dennis Rupert saw one with a flock of Blue Jays at Pelee on Oct. 27, 1972 (Goodwin, 1973: 50).

**MEASUREMENTS:**
*Length:* 10.5 to 11.5 ins.
(Godfrey, 1966: 242)
*Wingspread:* 20 to 21 ins.
(Terres, 1980: 1022)
*Weight:* about 3 3/4 oz.
(Terres, 1980: 1023).

# RED-HEADED WOODPECKER
## *Melanerpes erythrocephalus*   (Linnaeus)

The spectacular Red-headed Woodpecker favours large large dead trees for making its nest holes, so it tends to increase at times of large scale die-offs, e.g. of elms in the 1970's and oaks in the 1920's. The advent of Starlings, which tend to usurp their nesting holes, and of automobiles which have been responsible for many roadside casulties have also been held responsible for the general decrease since the 1800's. Most migrate south in fall and return again in May, but a few may be found in winter in southern Ontario.

**IDENTIFICATION:**   This is a Robin-sized woodpecker. The whole head is red in adults (dirty gray in the young), not just the red nape spots of the Hairy and Downy Woodpeckers that are often erroneously called red-headed. The back is an iridescent blue-black and the breast white. They have large white wing patches, very conspicuous in flight (these white patches have black cross bars in the young). They often utter a diagnostic "hrrr" note. At feeding stations they can be very pugnacious and drive off even jays and grackles with spectacular power dives.

**WINTER:**   On the 1968-1977 Christmas counts they were uncommon along the shore of Lake Erie north to Kettle Point and Niagara, and rare farther north to Kingston and Barrie. Stirrett (1973a: 16) had just three December records for Pelee, the latest on Dec. 27. Saunders & Dale (1933: 208) remarked that they often wintered at London, especially when beechnuts were plentiful. Fleming (1907: 76) had one winter record for Toronto, on Jan. 28, 1905. Speirs (1976: 52) cited several winter records for Ontario Co. including five seen on the 1967 Christmas count near Claremont, by Tom Hassall. Charles Fothergill noted one during the severe winter of 1831 on Feb. 10 in Clarke Twp., Durham Co. (Black, 1934: 149). Devitt (1967: 100) reported an immature bird that was seen just west of Barrie from Dec. 21, 1962 to Jan. 6, 1963. In 1974, a very aggressive one patronized a feeder at Bala throughout the winter: Donald Sutherland saw two at Honey Harbour on Jan. 10, 1977 (Mills, 1981: 83). Dennison (1980: 149) reported one on the 1973 Christmas count at Sault Ste. Marie.

SPRING: Stirrett (1973b: 19) called it a common transient at Pelee, with a maximum of 123 on May 8 and the earliest one on Apr. 20. Ussher (1965: 16) gave May 5 as the 20-year average arrival date at Rondeau, with the earliest on Apr. 15. Saunders & Dale (1933: 208) gave May 2 as the 17-year average arrival date at London, with the earliest on Apr. 6, 1918. The average arrival date in Elgin Co. was May 7 according to Harold Lancaster (Brooman, 1954: 25). Snyder (1931: 187) noted the first migrants at Long Point on May 4, 1928. E. Reinecke took a set of 5 eggs at Sherkston on May 31, 1895 (Baillie & Harrington, 1937: 205). Speirs (1938: 44) gave May 19 as the spring peak at Toronto: while Saunders (1947: 368) listed May 8 as his 12-year average arrival there. Snyder (1930: 189) found a nest in a tall dead elm stub in King Twp. on May 25, 1924 (with Starling, House Sparrow and American Kestrel pairs also nesting in the same stub). Speirs (1976: 52) had his earliest spring sighting at Rouge Hills on March 31, 1973, with the peak of the spring flight about May 24. Charles Fothergill wrote: "it may generally be seen about the 2nd week in May" and considered it "one of the commonest and most noisy birds of Canada" (Black, 1934: 149). Snyder (1941: 64) gave May 7, 1912 as his earliest Prince Edward Co. record. Weir & Quilliam (1980: 36) gave May 7 as the 31-year average arrival date at Kingston: M. Grimshaw took a set of 7 eggs on May 29, 1898 on Wolfe Is. and C.K. Clarke took one young there on May 14, 1898— specimens in ROM (Quilliam, 1973: 115). Devitt (1967: 100) gave May 19 as the 9-year average arrival date at Collingwood, with the earliest there on May 5, 1914: among the several nesting records was one he found at Midland Point on May 26, 1956. L. Beamer saw one at Meaford on May 15, 1949 and recorded a pair seen by Bill Linn, busy in a tree near Meaford on May 26, 1943. Chris Harris saw one at Go Home Bay as early as May 4, 1977 (Mills, 1981: 82). Nicholson (1981: 126) gave May 8 as the 12-year average arrival date on Manitoulin, with the earliest on Apr. 26, 1970 and the high total for a day of 26 (at two localities) on May 9, 1979. Denis (1961: 4) gave May 26 as the average arrival date at Thunder Bay, with the earliest on May 22, 1949. Elder (1979: 35) noted one at Castlebar Lake, near Longlac, on May 20, 1970.

SUMMER: On the 1968-1977 Breeding Bird Surveys, the western race was found on the Rainy River routes and the eastern race north to Thessalon, Manitoulin and Picton. They were uncommon to rare on all routes except those near the north shore of Lake Erie, where they were fairly common. This was listed as a nesting species at Pelee, with a maximum summer count of 18 on June 30 (Stirrett, 1973c: 17). Saunders & Dale (1933: 208) listed nest records for London from May 31 (1899) to June 8 (1902). Marshall Field reported that a St. Thomas pair raised two broods in the summer of 1949: the young of the first brood left the nest on July 15. (Brooman, 1954: 25). Snyder (1931: 187) collected four nestlings (1 male, 3 females) at Long Point on June 29, 1927. C. Christy and J.M. Richards found a nest with 4 eggs near Oshawa on June 18, 1957 (Speirs, 1976: 52) who cited several other breeding records for Ontario Co. including one as far north as Mara Twp. where, with Ron Orenstein, I saw one fly to a nest hole 30 ft. up in a dead stub on June 17, 1965. Allin (1940: 100) reported a set of 6 eggs taken by O. Byers at Enniskillen (in NMC) and told of a pair that dispossessed a pair of Flickers, then deposited their 5 eggs. Snyder (1941: 64) noted a nest with young at Hallowell on July 9, 1930. C.M.Clarke took 3 eggs (now in ROM) on July 10, 1897 at Kingston (Quilliam, 1973: 115). W.E. Cattley found a nest at Wilson's Point, Lake Couchiching, in July, 1964 (Devitt, 1967: 100). Lloyd (1923: 154) saw one by the Rideau River, near Ottawa, during the summer of 1922. On July 22, 1962 A. May saw two adults and at least two young flying over a field at Huntsville; and Hazel Petty saw one south of Callander on July 28, 1970 (Mills, 1981: 82-83). Chris Bell saw young being fed in a nest near Pike Lake, Manitoulin, from July 9-17, 1977 (Nicholson, 1981: 126). MacLulich (1938: 192) cited a few summer records from Algonquin Park, including one seen on July 8, 1912 and two seen on June 9 and 10, 1918. Snyder (1942: 133) collected a male at Laird on June 6, 1931. S.C. Downing saw one at Peninsula (Marathon) on June 19, 1936 (Baillie & Hope, 1943: 12). Elder (1979: 35) observed one at Neys Provincial Park on June 8, 1969. Dear (1940: 131) reported a nest with 3 eggs on June 21, 1927 and a nest with 4 eggs on June 27 in Paipoonge Twp., Thunder Bay. Snyder (1938: 192) saw 7 near Emo on June 25, 1929 and an occupied nest was found on June 20. Snyder (1953: 64) called it a "rare summer resident in the Kenora region, pairs noted at Malachi".

AUTUMN: Dorothy Mackenzie saw one that frequented a pole by her home at Eau Claire from Sept. 20-22, 1944 (Speirs & Speirs, 1947: 30). Nicholson (1981: 126) gave Nov. 27, 1975 as the latest date for Manitoulin, with high counts of 10 on Oct. 13 and 14, 1973. Marion Hill had a juvenile at her feeder at Solitaire Lake, Muskoka, from Nov. 2-4, 1971 (Mills, 1981: 83). Weir & Quilliam (1980: 36) gave Oct. 1 as the 25-year average departure date from Kingston. Saunders (1947: 368) listed Sept. 18 as his 7-year average departure date from Toronto. Beardslee & Mitchell (1965: 295) noted a maximum of 15 at Ft. George, Niagara, on Nov. 28, 1954. Ussher (1965: 16) gave Oct. 26 as the latest date at Rondeau. The maximum fall count at Pelee was 60 on Oct. 12, with the latest on Nov. 3 (Stirrett, 1973d: 21).

**MEASUREMENTS:**
*Length:* 8.7 to 9.7 ins. (Godfrey, 1966: 241)
*Wingspread:* 16.36 to 18.50 ins. (Roberts, 1955: 622)
*Weight:* 2 to 3 oz. (Roberts, 1955: 622)

462

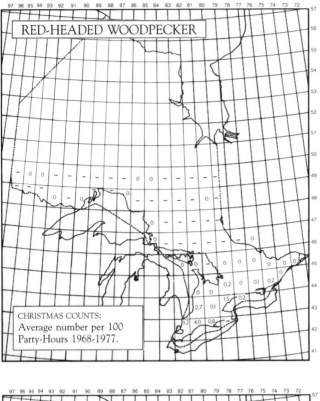

RED-HEADED WOODPECKER

CHRISTMAS COUNTS:
Average number per 100
Party-Hours 1968-1977.

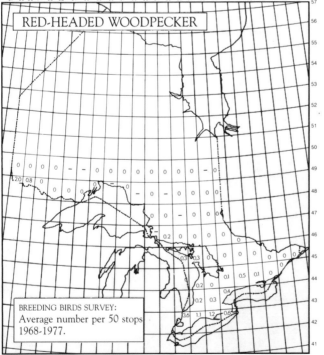

RED-HEADED WOODPECKER

BREEDING BIRDS SURVEY:
Average number per 50 stops
1968-1977.

# RED-BELLIED WOODPECKER
## *Melanerpes carolinus*   (Linnaeus)

This is a southern species, fairly common in the oak forests of eastern U.S.A. but rare in Ontario, except in the extreme southwestern portion. When one shows up elsewhere in Ontario, word soon spreads and birdwatchers flock in to gaze at the beautiful bird.

IDENTIFICATION: The Red-bellied Woodpecker has a hoarse note, like a person clearing the throat "khh-khh-khh" which may alert the observer of its presence before it is seen. This is a robin-sized woodpecker with a barred black and white back, vermilion on the top and back of the head, pale buff cheeks and underparts. The rosy blush on the underparts, from which it gets its name, is hard to see. The crown is gray in the female but red in the male.

WINTER: On the 1968-1977 Christmas counts it was uncommon in the London and Kettle Point regions and rare elsewhere north to Barrie and Kingston, with one outlier at Sault Ste. Marie. Stirrett (1973a: 16) had records of single birds at Pelee throughout the winter months. Brooman (1954: 25) reported one seen in North Dunwich Twp. Elgin Co., on Jan. 24, 1951. Three individuals were noted in Ontario Co: one male at Frank Barkey's feeder near Cherrywood during the winter of 1965-1966; another male at M. Wood's feeder near Brooklin in 1968-1969 and a female at our Pickering feeder in 1969-1970 (Speirs, 1976: 51): there have also been a few more recent records. A.E. Wilson noted one at a Grafton feeder on Dec. 4, 1971 and for several weeks thereafter (Goodwin, 1972: 58). Cliff MacFayden saw one in Barrie from Dec. 6, 1975 to Jan. 4, 1976 (Goodwin, 1976: 713). One was seen by many observers at Ottawa up to Jan. 21, 1978 (Goodwin, 1979: 278). Nicholson (1981: 126) reported one that wintered at Mindemoya in 1959-1960 and again the following winter, and one at an Evansville feeder in 1980-81: these stayed into the following springs.

SPRING: A pair defended a nest site on Pelee Island in late April, 1972 according to Paul Pratt and Craig Campbell (Goodwin, 1972: 854). Stirrett (1973b: 19) had a few spring records at Point Pelee. A.A. Wood took one egg from a nest at Coldstream, Middlesex Co., on May 7, 1913 (Saunders & Dale, 1933: 208). Earl Lemon *et al* saw one near West Lorne in April, 1932 and R.T. Anderson collected two eggs near Alymer and sent them to the ROM (Brooman, 1954: 25). A nest with 7 eggs was found at Sherkston by Ottomar Reinecke on May 1, 1891 (Beardslee & Mitchell, 1965: 293). Fleming (1907: 76) reported one taken at Toronto on May 19, 1885 and another on May 24, 1890. Frank Barkey saw the bird at his feeder near Cherrywood as late as Apr. 9, 1966 and again on May 21 and 22, 1967: our female stayed as late as Apr. 19, 1970 (Speirs, 1976: 51). N. Parks saw one at East Lake, Prince Edward Co., on March 21, 1971 (Goodwin, 1971: 573). K.F. Edwards observed two at Squaw Point, Kingston: one on May 16, 1965 and the other on May 21, 1967 (Quilliam, 1973: 114). Ron Tasker banded and photographed one in Burpee Twp., Manitoulin, on May 17, 1976 and another was noted at South Baymouth by C. Bell on May 12, 1979 (Nicholson, 1981: 126).

SUMMER: on the 1968-1977 Breeding Bird Surveys, individuals were noted only on the London and Sarnia routes. Kelley (1978: 47) wrote that it was first reported nesting at Pelee in 1967. Ussher (1965: 15) gave a June 25 date for Rondeau. Harold Axtell saw one at Fort Erie on June 4, 1973 (Goodwin, 1973: 865). S. Connop reported nesting at

The Pinery in 1978 (Goodwin, 1978: 1155). Goodwin (1979: 859) recorded one in King Twp. on June 2, 1979. Bruce Parker reported one at Sibbald Point, Lake Simcoe, on June 4, 1980 (Goodwin, 1980: 891).

AUTUMN: J. Miller observed one at Sault Ste. Marie from Nov. 16-30, 1973 (Goodwin, 1974: 47). Chris Bell and John Lemon saw one in Mills Twp., Manitoulin, on Oct. 16, 1977 (Nicholson, 1981: 126). B. DiLabio et al saw one at Ottawa on Sept. 1, 1974 (Goodwin, 1975: 52). G. Carpentier noted one at Haultain on Oct. 28, 1976 (Goodwin, 1977: 171). One arrived on Nov. 11, 1969 at a feeder on the Shore Rd., east of Kingston and stayed until the following March (Quilliam, 1973: 114). A female came to a big dead elm stub at our Pickering home on Nov. 9 and 10, 1958: another arrived at our feeder on Oct. 23, 1969 and stayed until the following spring: M. Wood's male was first noted at his feeder on Nov. 11, 1968 and stayed until the following Feb. 1: the male at Frank Barkey's feeder was first noted on Nov. 5, 1965 and stayed until Apr. 11 (Speirs, 1976: 51). Two were taken at Toronto on Nov. 27, 1899 (Fleming, 1907: 76). Ussher (1965: 15) had a Nov. 8 record at Rondeau.

**MEASUREMENTS:**
*Length:* 8.8 to 10 ins. (Godfrey, 1966: 240)
*Wingspread:* 16 to 17 1/2 ins. (Roberts, 1955: 622)
*Weight:* 72.5 g. (Terres, 1980: 1025)

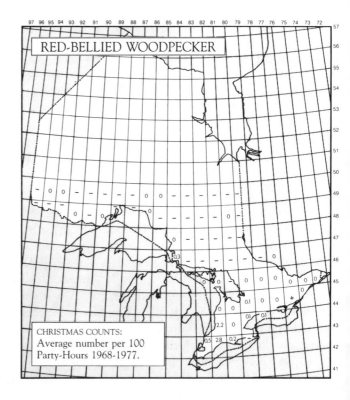

RED-BELLIED WOODPECKER

CHRISTMAS COUNTS:
Average number per 100
Party-Hours 1968-1977.

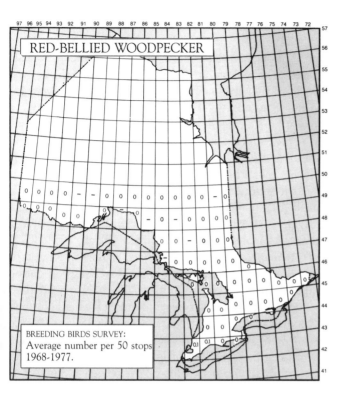

97 96 95 94 93 92 91 90 89 88 87 86 85 84 83 82 81 80 79 78 77 76 75 74 73 72

RED-BELLIED WOODPECKER

BREEDING BIRDS SURVEY:
Average number per 50 stops
1968-1977.

# YELLOW-BELLIED SAPSUCKER
*Sphyrapicus varius*   (Linnaeus)

Sapsuckers enliven the cottage country in summer with their "Morse code" tapping, their whining calls and excited activity near their nests. They create "birch beer" from the fermentation of sap which oozes from their sap wells drilled with rectangular precision on the larger branches of birch trees. These "bars" are popular, not only with sapsuckers that sometimes get a bit tipsy from imbibing the fermented juice but also with other customers, especially Ruby-throated Hummingbirds, Red Squirrels and White-faced Hornets. Most sapsuckers migrate south in winter to southern U.S.A. and Central America.

IDENTIFICATION: Yellow-bellied Sapsuckers are medium-sized woodpeckers, a bit smaller than Hairy Woodpeckers. The best field mark is the broad white stripe along the wing, contrasting with the general darkish background of the bird. Males have a red throat as well as red on the top of the head: the throat is whitish in females. The yellowish wash on the belly is hard to see in most light conditions. The "Morse code" drumming is diagnostic "dat—didat—dat—dat".

WINTER: On the 1968-1977 Christmas counts they were rare in southwestern Ontario and extreme southeastern Ontario, absent north of Peterborough and Wiarton. Stirrett (1973a: 16) had just one winter record for Pelee, on Dec. 23. A.A. Wood collected one in an orchard at Vanneck on Dec. 12, 1933 (Saunders & Dale, 1933: 208). A.J. Mitchener saw one at his Collingwood feeder on Dec. 24, 1963 (Devitt, 1967: 101).

SPRING:   Stirrett (1973b: 19) had his earliest Pelee record on Apr. 2 and his maximum count of 25 on Apr. 15. Ussher (1965: 16) had Rondeau records from March 19 to May 22 with the average arrival on Apr. 11 and departure on May 7. Saunders & Dale (1933: 208) gave Apr. 7 as the 17-year average arrival date at London, with the earliest on March 26, 1925: Robert Elliott saw a nest in a nearby black ash swamp on May 24, 1900. Snyder (1931: 187) reported that 8 struck the Long Point light on Apr. 17-18 and 4 on Apr. 20-21, 1930: he collected a female there on May 12, 1928. Speirs (1938: 40, 44) gave March 16 as the earliest Toronto record with the peak of the spring flight on Apr. 21: Saunders (1947: 368) listed Apr. 12 as his 13-year average arrival there. Speirs (1976: 53) found the peak of the spring migration at Pickering during the third week of April: Tozer & Richards (1974: 178) mentioned one at Whitby as early as March 22, 1952. Allin (1940: 100) wrote that it usually arrives about Apr. 11 in Darlington Twp. Charles Fothergill noted spring arrival at Rice Lake on Apr. 21, 1821 and compared a female taken there on Apr. 25, 1817 with a male taken Apr. 23, 1821 (Black, 1934: 150). Weir & Quilliam (1980: 36) gave Apr. 9 as the 32-year average arrival date at Kingston, with the earliest on March 15: A.B. Klugh estimated a total of 5000 in Kingston during a phenomenal flight on the morning of Apr. 17, 1909 (Quilliam, 1973: 116) who cited a few nesting records for the region, including a nest with 4 eggs found by Richard Norman at Bell's Swamp on May 26, 1968. Devitt (1967: 101) gave Apr. 18 as the 28-year average arrival date at Barrie, the earliest on Apr. 1, 1945: H.P. Bingham collected a set of 4 eggs near Barrie on May 7, 1941. Apr. 8 was the earliest of 17 spring arrivals at Meaford and Apr. 17 was the median date given by L. Beamer. Mills (1981: 83) gave Apr. 13 as the 13-year average arrival date at Huntsville, the earliest on Apr. 2. The 12-year average arrival on Manitoulin was Apr. 16, with the earliest on Apr. 1, 1971 and the high count of 20 on May1, 1976 at Mississagi Light (Nicholson, 1981: 127). MacLulich (1938: 20) had his earliest arrival in Algonquin Park on Apr. 17, 1913. Louise Lawrence noted one as early as Apr. 8, 1945 at Pimisi Bay and observed one excavating there on May 6, 1945 (Speirs & Speirs, 1947: 30). Skeel & Bondrup-Nielsen (1978: 181) saw their first at Pukaskwa on Apr. 16, 1977. Denis (1961: 2) gave Apr. 15 as the average arrival date at Thunder Bay, with one as early as March 31, 1948. Bondrup-Nielsen (1976: 43) saw his first at Kapuskasing on Apr. 21 in both 1974 and 1975. Elder (1979: 25) had his earliest Geraldton record on Apr. 15. Peruniak (1971: 19) gave Apr. 15 as her earliest Atikokan record. Cringan (1953a: 2) saw his first at Sioux Lookout on May 3 in 1953. On May 30, 1947 Manning (1952: 67) collected two females at Sandy Is., near Moosonee: he cited a few other records for the region.

SUMMER:   On the 1968-1977 Breeding Bird Surveys, they were rare or absent in southwestern Ontario, common from Larder Lake to Foleyet, and fairy common on most other routes. Stirrett (1973c: 17) had a few June and August records at Pelee, none in July. Snyder (1930: 189) collected two young in King Twp. on July 23, 1926 and found two occupied nests there. Speirs (1976: 53) cited nest records for most townships in Ontario Co., from Pickering north to Rama. Snyder (1941: 64) collected two females on July 7, 1930 at Hallowell and a young female on July 14, 1930 at Ferow Gore, Prince Edward Co. Two nests at Severn Falls contained young on June 17, 1938 (Devitt, 1967: 101). Lloyd (1923: 154) reported nests found by F.A. Saunders on June 15 and June 24 and two other nests found near Ottawa in the summers of 1921 and 1922. This has been the most common woodpecker in the cottage country with about 50 nests reported (Mills,

1981: 83). Young were seen being fed by adults on Manitoulin Is. on July 11, 1935 and July 1, 1979 (Nicholson, 1981: 127). MacLulich (1938: 20) found a nest with young in Algonquin Park on June 29, 1930 about 40 ft. up in a trembling aspen and C.H.D. Clarke found two nests there on June 15, 1934. D. MacLulich found a nest at Frank's Bay, Lake Nipissing, on June 1, 1932 (Ricker & Clarke, 1939: 13). Snyder (1942: 133) collected four nestlings on June 17 and five on June 25, 1931 at Maclennan. Baillie & Hope (1947: 11) collected four young at Bigwood from July 14-22, 1937 and several adults both there and at Chapleau. Skeel & Bondrup-Nielsen (1978: 181) found a nest with young at Pukaskwa about 14 m. up in a trembling aspen on June 27, 1977 and two later (one on July 9 about 7 m. up in an aspen and the other on July 10 about 6 m. up in an aspen). Baillie & Hope (1943: 12) found a nest hole about 35 ft. up in a poplar at Amyot on June 27, 1936. Dear (1940: 131) reported two nests, each with 5 eggs, in Paipoonge Twp., Thunder Bay, on June 6, 1928 and June 27, 1938. Snyder (1938: 193) collected a male at Emo on June 17, 1929 and found a nest with young on July 1. Snyder (1928: 25) noted three nests at Lake Abitibi during the summer of 1925, all in dead trees, and 30 to 50 ft. up. Snyder (1953: 64) found them breeding at Malachi, Kenora and Wabigoon and on July 16, 1924 a juvenile male was collected at Lake Nipigon (Snyder, 1928: 262). James (1980: 87) found a nest with young 17 km. northeast of Pickle Lake on June 4, 1977. Hope (1938: 24) found many nests with noisy young at Favourable Lake in summer of 1938. Schueler, Baldwin & Rising (1974: 146) found the characteristic drillings of the species at Attawapiskat in mid-June, 1971. McLaren & McLaren (1981: 4) found a nest about 25 km. east of Little Sachigo Lake on June 15, 1977.

AUTUMN:   Frits Johansen collected one at Sandy Is., near Moosonee, on Oct. 4, 1920 (Manning. 1952: 67). Peruniak (1971: 19) had her latest at Atikokan on Oct. 12. Louise Lawrence noted one as late as Sept. 25, 1944 at Pimisi Bay (Speirs & Speirs, 1947: 30). Nicholson (1981: 127) gave Oct. 11, 1970 as the latest Manitoulin record. A. Kay collected one on Oct. 18, 1890, the latest date for the cottage country (Mills, 1981: 84). Devitt (1967: 101) gave Oct. 4, 1965 as the latest Barrie TV tower kill. Weir & Quilliam (1980: 36) gave Oct. 10 as the 25-year average departure date from Kingston, the latest on Nov. 5. Tozer & Richards (1974: 179) noted one as late as Nov. 25, 1971 at Scugog. The peak of the fall migration at Pickering has been in the last week of September (Speirs, 1976: 53). Speirs (1938: 52, 54) gave Oct. 3 as the fall peak for Toronto, with the latest on Oct. 30: Saunders (1947: 368) listed Oct. 5 as his 11-year average departure date from Toronto. Beardslee & Mitchell (1965: 295-296) reported one on the Canadian shore of the Niagara River as late as Nov. 26, 1949. Ussher (1965: 16) had Rondeau records from Sept. 17 to Oct. 21, with the average arrival on Sept. 27 and departure on Oct. 11. Stirrett (1973d: 21) had his maximum count of 100 at Pelee on Sept. 21 and his latest on Nov. 5.

**MEASUREMENTS:**
*Length:* 8 to 9 ins.
(Godfrey, 1966: 242)
*Wingspread:* 14.62 to
15.30 ins. (Roberts,
1955: 621)
*Weight:* 3 ♂ averaged
47 g. 2 ♀ averaged
46.5 g. (Hope, 1938: 24)

## REFERENCES:

Lawrence, Louise de Kiriline 1976 Mar Clarke, Irwin & Co. Ltd. Toronto i-vii, 1-103. A beautifully written account of the behaviour on its nesting territory of a colour banded male sapsucker.

Lawrence, Louise de Kiriline, 1967 A comparative life history study of four species of Woodpeckers. Ornithological Monographs, 5: 1-156. A more technical account of the sapsucker's life history as compared with other local species.

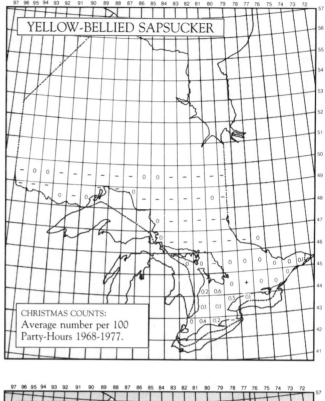

YELLOW-BELLIED SAPSUCKER

CHRISTMAS COUNTS:
Average number per 100
Party-Hours 1968-1977.

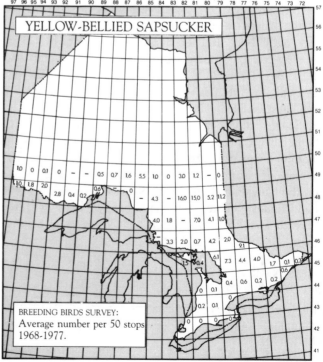

YELLOW-BELLIED SAPSUCKER

BREEDING BIRDS SURVEY:
Average number per 50 stops
1968-1977.

# DOWNY WOODPECKER   *Picoides pubescens*   (Linnaeus)

The Downy Woodpecker is the common woodpecker at feeding stations in southern Ontario, where it comes for suet and sometimes for sunflower seeds. If our feeder is empty our male will tap on the window to bring this to our attention, while our female will fly past our face and then perch by the empty feeder, expostulating loudly. Their range in Ontario is much like that of the Hairy Woodpecker though they are usually more common in the south and less common in the north.

IDENTIFICATION:   The Downy Woodpecker is separated from the Hairy by its smaller size, more stubby bill and by the spots or bars on its white outer tail feathers. They also have a descending series of notes in their "whinny" call and a dull "pec" note rather than the loud "peek" of the Hairy.

WINTER:   On the 1968-1977 Christmas counts the Downy Woodpecker was fairly common at most localities, common in the southwest near London. Stirrett (1973a: 17) had a maximum of 70 at Pelee on Dec. 27. Marshall Field banded 13 at Union, Elgin Co., during the winter of 1948-1949, one of which was recaptured there on Feb. 24, 1952 (Brooman, 1954: 25). Speirs (1976: 55) listed the Downy on all Pickering, Oshawa and Scugog Christmas counts. A 16-year sample of Christmas counts at Hunstville averaged 33.6 with a high of 72 on Jan. 10, 1971 (Mills, 1981: 85). The highest Christmas count on Manitoulin was 23 on Dec. 21, 1975 (Nicholson, 1981: 128). One of our few winter records at North Bay was on Dec. 23, 1944 (Speirs & Speirs, 1947: 30). Dennison (1980: 146) listed this as a species always seen on the Sault Ste. Marie Christmas counts, averaging 21 but with only 2 in 1967. Skeel & Bondrup-Nielsen (1978: 182) found this to be the second most common winter resident bird at Pukaskwa, where it also occurred throughout the year. Elder (1979: 35) called it a common permanent resident at Geraldton, but much scarcer in winter. David Elder saw one at Atikokan on Jan. 1, 1981 although Peruniak (1971: 19) did not list it.

SPRING:   Stirrett (1973b: 19) had a spring maximum of 22 at Pelee on March 14. Saunders & Dale (1933: 208) reported several nest records at London, including a set of four as early as May 4, 1892 and a set of 6 eggs on May 17, 1916. Beardslee & Mitchell (1965: 297-298) cited a nest with 4 eggs at Ft. Erie on May 20, 1905. R. Charles Long noted courtship activity in Cannington from March 5-29, 1973 and Ron Tozer watched nest excavation at Scugog as early as Apr. 27, 1963: an adult was seen at its nest hole at our Pickering home on May 6, 1967 but the hole was usurped by a Red-headed Woodpecker on May 21 (Speirs, 1976: 55): four nests with eggs have been noted in Ontario Co.: 3 in Thorah Twp. (6 eggs on May 30, 1913, 5 eggs on May 31, 1928 and 5 eggs on May 26, 1931) and a nest with 5 eggs in Whitby Twp. on May 26, 1962. Charles Fothergill shot one at Rice Lake as long ago as Apr. 23, 1817 (Black, 1934: 150). H. Clarke collected a set of 4 eggs at Rockwood on May 21, 1898 and Richard Norman found 2 eggs near Kingston on May 24, 1969 (Quilliam, 1973: 118). H.P. Bingham found a set of 6 eggs at Barrie on May 23, 1915 (Devitt, 1967: 102). Lloyd (1923: 154) reported an early nest with 5 eggs at Ottawa on May 6, 1915.

SUMMER:   On the 1968-1977 Breeding Bird Surveys they were noted on all southern Ontario routes but were uncommon to fairly common (most numerous around Georgian

Bay): they were absent from several routes north and east of Lake Superior. Stirrett (1973c: 17) found this species nesting in Pelee, but his maximum summer count was six on June 27. Snyder (1931: 186) collected young from July 4 (the earliest date that young were seen out of the nest) to July 23, 1927 at Long Point. Snyder (1930: 189) collected a young male in King Twp. on Aug. 17, 1926 and found several nesting cavities. Allin (1940: 100) saw adults with young on July 1, 1930 at Hampton. Snyder (1941: 65) collected young in Prince Edward Co. from July 2-10, 1930 and reported a nest 50 ft. up found on July 3, 1938 by H.H. Southam. Nests with 2 to 6 eggs were found in Simcoe Co. from May 22 to June 14: young in the nest were noted at Sparrow Lake on June 14, 1938 and young out of the nest at Severn Falls on June 18, 1938 (Devitt, 1967: 102). Mills (1981: 85) reported 8 nests with young in the cottage country from May 25 to July 3; and nest heights from 6 to 40 ft. up. MacLulich (1938: 20) saw two young with an adult female at Biggar Lake, Algonquin Park, on July 27, 1933. Ron Tasker found a nest with 5 eggs in Burpee Twp., Manitoulin, on June 17, 1974 (Nicholson, 1981: 128). Louise Lawrence found a nest with young at Pimisi Bay on June 8, 1945: they left on July 4 (Speirs & Speirs, 1947: 30). Ricker & Clarke (1939: 14) reported a nest at Lake Nipissing on June 16, 1924. Snyder (1942: 133-134) collected four nestlings at Maclennan on June 17, 1931 and saw the first young out of the nest there on July 2: other young and adults were noted from June 4 to July 28. Four young were collected at Bigwood from July 16-22, 1937 (Baillie & Hope, 1947: 11). Baillie & Hope (1943: 12) found nests at Rossport on June 1, at Marathon on June 27 and at Amyot on June 25, 1936 (the last with 3 eggs). Snyder (1928: 262) found this to be the most common woodpecker at Lake Nipigon, where a number of nests were found and 4 young collected from July 16-24, 1924. Dear (1940: 131) found a nest with 5 eggs in Paipoonge Twp. on June 12, 1927 and another nest with 5 eggs at Whitefish Lake on June 16, 1929, both near Thunder Bay. Young were first noted on July 2 and collected on July 6 at Off Lake and on July 30 at Rainy River (Snyder, 1938: 193). Snyder (1928: 24) collected a male at Lowbush, Lake Abitibi, on June 6, 1925. P.A. Taverner and C.E. Johnson saw adults with young at Kapuskasing on July 5, 1919 (Baillie & Harrington, 1937: 206). Snyder (1953: 65-66) found them to be uncommon in western Ontario with only one at Sioux Lookout on June 26, 1947: others noted from Lake of the Woods to Dinorwic Lake. Cringan (1950: 12) saw a few at Nikip Lake during the summer of 1950. Hope (1938: 25) found them uncommon at Favourable Lake but collected three juveniles from July 19-26, 1938 to confirm breeding there. Manning (1952: 67) collected a female near Moosonee on June 24, 1949 and a male at Big Piskwanish on June 11, 1947. Surveys at Pickle Lake, Big Trout Lake, Fort Severn and along the Hudson Bay lowlands did not turn up any.

AUTUMN: D. McRae and A. Wormington saw one or two almost daily at Netitishi Point, James Bay from Oct. 14-27, 1981 but only one thereafter to Nov. 22 (one on Nov. 14). Nicholson (1981: 128) had a maximum count of probable migrants at Mississagi Light, Manitoulin, on Oct. 27, 1974. Mills (1981: 85) recorded his greatest number in the cottage country in late September and October, suggesting a southward movement at that time. G.E. Atkinson recorded several at the Holland River on Oct. 21, 1890 (Devitt, 1967: 102). Speirs (1938: 52) had a fall peak at Toronto on Nov. 3. Stirrett (1973d: 22) had a fall maximum at Pelee on Oct. 14, of 8 birds.

**MEASUREMENTS:**
*Length:* 157 to 168 mm.
(Snyder, 1953: 66)
*Wingspread:* 300 mm.
(Snyder, 1953: 66)
*Weight:* 4 ♂ averaged
27 g. (Hope, 1938: 25)

**REFERENCE:**
Snyder, L.L. 1923 On the
crown markings of juvenile
Hairy and Downy
Woodpeckers. Can. Field-
Nat., 37:(9): 167-168.

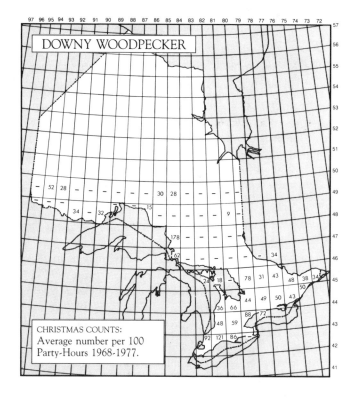

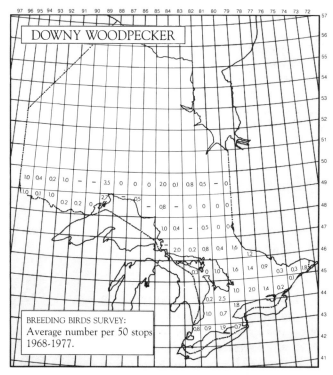

# HAIRY WOODPECKER   *Picoides villosus*   (Linnaeus)

This big, boisterous woodpecker is familiar to most people with feeding stations near wooded areas. It is found as a resident species throughout the wooded portions of Ontario, though some appear to shift to the south in fall.

IDENTIFICATION: From the similar Downy Woodpecker it is distinguished by its much larger size, relatively long bill and unspotted white outer tail feathers. Its calls are similar to those of the Downy Woodpecker but the single "keep" note of the Hairy is higher pitched and louder (and given more often) than the "kut" note of the Downy, while the "whinny" note of the Hairy tends to be more on one pitch rather than a descending series of notes as in the Downy. In both species the female lacks the red nape patch of the male. Young males have the whole crown pinkish red while young females have a blackish crown.

WINTER: On the 1968-1977 Christmas counts this was a fairly common species at all localities from Pelee north to Dryden. Stirrett (1973a: 17) had Pelee records throughout the winter, with a maximum count of 20 on Dec. 26. Numbers on the Pickering Christmas counts from 1961 to 1970 varied from 3 to 59, averaging 24. Similar notable variations have occurred at other localities. Charles Fothergill collected one at Port Hope as long ago as Feb. 28, 1817 (Black, 1934: 150).

SPRING: Stirrett (1973b: 19) had a spring maximum of 3 at Pelee on May 7. Kelley (1978: 48) noted adults bringing food to a nest with young at Thamesville, Kent co., on May 11, 1952. Saunders & Dale (1933: 208) reported a nest with 3 eggs near London on May 9, 1903 and a nest with 4 eggs on May 2, 1904. Snyder (1930: 188) found a nest with young in King Twp. on May 31, 1926. J.A. Edwards found a nest with 5 eggs on Thorah Is., Lake Simcoe, on May 2, 1927 and a nest with 4 eggs there on May 2, 1929: I saw a nest with young on May 29, 1967 in Whitby Twp. and Ken Carmichael located a nest with 5 young in Reach Twp. on May 28, 1971 (Speirs, 1976: 54). E. Beaupré took two nests of eggs near Kingston, one on May 4, 1897 and one on May 5, 1898 (Quilliam, 1973: 117). Baillie & Harrington (1937: 206) reported a nest with 5 eggs at Wasaga Beach on May 3, 1922 and a nest with young at Minesing on May 9, 1925. C.E. Johnson found a nest with young at Ottawa on May 24, 1921 (Lloyd, 1923: 154). Fred Bodsworth found a brood leaving a nest at Lake Muskoka as early as May 23, 1976 and in 1969, D. Brunton found 7 nests in Killbear Park and saw 34 individuals there on May 25 (Mills, 1981: 84). Dear (1940: 131) found a nest with 5 eggs at Whitefish Lake, Thunder Bay, on May 22, 1932.

SUMMER: On the 1968-1977 Breeding Bird Surveys Hairy Woodpeckers were noted on most routes except some, mainly agricultural routes, in the south where they were rare or absent: they were most plentiful on the most northerly routes from Hornepayne to Ignace. Stirrett (1973c: 17) had some summer records at Pelee but no nest record. Brooman (1954: 25) located a nest with young on June 8, 1942 about 7 miles SW of St. Thomas. Snyder (1931: 186) collected 8 young at Long Point from June 29 to July 11, 1927. He collected a juvenile female at Hallowell, Prince Edward Co., on July 7, 1930 (Snyder, 1941: 64). Tozer & Richards (1974: 179) noted a nest with young in Whitby Twp. in late June, 1963 and an adult with young in Scugog on July 18, 1954. Charles Fothergill shot a pair at Rice Lake on June 16 (Black, 1934: 150). Quilliam (1973: 117) found a nest with young on June 27, 1965 at Otter Lake, near Kingston. Devitt (1967: 101) reported a nest with young at Buckskin Lake, Simcoe Co., found by R.D. Ussher on June 17, 1938 and another found at Holland River on June 12, 1939. D.B. Ferguson saw a nest with young on Manitoulin Is. on June 11, 1978 (Nicholson, 1981: 127). MacLulich (1938: 20) noted a nest with young 20 ft. up in ash tree in Algonquin Park on June 16, 1909. Louise Lawrence watched an adult feeding young at Rutherglen on June 20, 1944 (Speirs & Speirs, 1947: 30). Baillie & Hope (1947: 11) found a nest with young 50 ft. up in a live aspen at Chapleau on June 2, 1937: they collected a young female at Biscotasing on July 6 and 3 young at Bigwood on July 14-15, 1937. Skeel & Bondrup-Nielsen (1978: 182) found a nest with 4 eggs in a dead birch at Pukaskwa on June 7, 1977, about 6 m. up. Baillie & Hope (1943: 12) collected two young males at Amyot, on June 30 and July 3, 1936. Snyder (1928: 261) saw a scattered brood at Lake Nipigon on July 26, 1923. Snyder (1938: 193) collected a young male at Emo on June 12, 1929 and young females at Off Lake on July 3 and 7, 1929. Snyder (1953: 65) reported breeding at Indian Bay, Kenora, Ingolf and Wabigoon and saw some as far north at Sioux Lookout. Snyder (1928: 24) collected 3 young males and one young female at Lowbush, Lake Abitibi, on June 11, 1925. James (1980: 87) found a nest with 4 young about 17 km. NE of Pickle Lake on June 20, 1979. Cringan (1950: 12) saw single birds a few times during the summer of 1950 at Nikip Lake. Hope (1938: 25) took young at Favourable Lake from July 8 to Aug. 1, 1938. Manning (1952: 67) collected a female at Big Piskwanish on June 9, 1947 and cited other records from the Moosonee region. Lee (1978: 25) saw single birds at Big Trout Lake during the summer of 1975. Schueler, Baldwin & Rising (1974: 146) saw 4 and collected two young at Hawley Lake on July 13, 1965 ("the most northerly record in Ontario").

AUTUMN: D. McRae and A. Wormington saw from one to three frequently at Netitishi Point, James Bay, from Oct. 17 to Nov. 17, 1981. Oliver Hewitt saw one at Ship Sands, Moosonee, on Sept. 24, 1947 (Manning, 1952: 67). Nicholson (1981: 127) saw 15 probable migrants at Mississagi Light, Manitoulin, on Oct. 13 and 10 there on Oct. 26, 1974. By mid-October they have frequently been seen migrating west or SW in Ontario Co. and some become established at feeding stations (Speirs, 1976: 54). Speirs (1938: 52) listed Oct. 21 as a peak date for fall migrants at Toronto. Stirrett (1973d: 22) had a fall maximum of 7 on Oct. 7 at Pelee.

**MEASUREMENTS:**
*Length:* 8.5 to 10.5 ins.
(Godfrey, 1966: 244)
*Wingspread:* 15 to 17 ins.
(Roberts, 1955: 622)
*Weight:* 2 ♂ averaged
87 g. 2 ♀ averaged 72 g.
(Hope, 1938: 25)
1 ♂ 84 g. 3 ♀ averaged
74.5 g. (Snyder, 1953: 65).

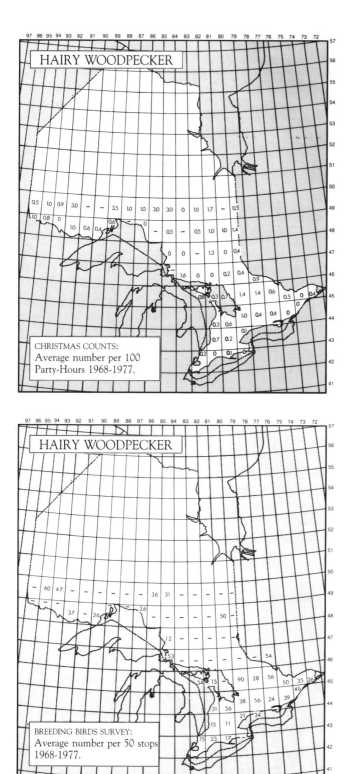

HAIRY WOODPECKER

CHRISTMAS COUNTS:
Average number per 100
Party-Hours 1968-1977.

HAIRY WOODPECKER

BREEDING BIRDS SURVEY:
Average number per 50 stops
1968-1977.

# THREE-TOED WOODPECKER
## *Picoides tridactylus* (Linnaeus)

This is a circumpolar bird of coniferous forests: unlike the Black-backed Woodpecker it occurs in the Old World as well as in Canada. Most observers in southern Ontario had not seen this species until the advent of Dutch elm disease when some came south in 1956-1957 and again in 1963-1966.

IDENTIFICATION: This "ladder-backed" woodpecker with three toes is somewhat smaller than the Black-backed Woodpecker, our other species with three toes and a glance at the back pattern easily distinguishes one from the other. It is more likely to be confused with the Yellow-bellied Sapsucker which is about the same size and shares much the same range in northern Ontario but the prominent white wing stripe of the sapsucker distinguishes it from this black-winged species. The yellow crown of the male and solid black crown of the female separate it from all but the Black-backed Woodpecker.

WINTER: On the 1968-1977 Christmas counts they were rare or absent at most southern Ontario localities, uncommon at some northern places and absent from others: Deep River, Manitouwadge and Atikokan usually had the largest numbers. Norman Chesterfield reported one at Pelee on Dec. 24, 1974 where it remained throughout the winter (Kelley, 1978: 49). Speirs (1976: 57) gave details of several sightings in southern Ontario Co. during the winters of 1963-1964 and 1965-1966 (7 were noted on the Pickering Christmas count on Dec. 26, 1965). Tozer & Richards (1974: 182) cited Darlington Twp. records from Dec. 31, 1969 to Jan. 17, 1970 by Dennis Barry *et al* and on Feb. 13, 1973 by J. Kamstra. Two were seen on the Napanee Christmas count on Dec. 27, 1965, the year of the most sightings in the Kingston region (Quilliam, 1973: 119). Devitt (1967: 103) reported individuals in Simcoe Co. on Feb. 1 and 4, 1964, Feb. 4, 1965 and Jan. 1-2, 1966. L. Beamer reported one at Meaford on Jan. 19, 1949. One was noted on the Huntsville Christmas count on Dec. 28, 1956 and another near there on Feb. 11 and 25, 1962 (Mills, 1981: 87) who cited several other winter records for the cottage country. They were noted on Manitoulin Christmas counts, in Gordon Twp., in 1974, 1975 (2) and 1976 (Nicholson, 1981: 128). Dennison (1980: 149) listed one on the 1963 Christmas count at Sault Ste. Marie and 2 on the 1978 count there. Skeel & Bondrup-Nielsen (1978: 183) saw two at Pukaskwa during the winter of 1976: 1977.

SPRING: G.W. Knechtel collected a male at Long Point on May 19, 1928 (Snyder, 1931: 186). J.M. Richards saw one on March 6, 1966 in Reach Twp. and one was killed hitting Judith Symons' window near Claremont on May 15, 1965 (Speirs, 1976: 57). Weir & Quilliam (1980: 36) gave Apr. 11 as the 7-year average departure date from Kingston: the latest was noted on May 13, 1963. Donald R. Gunn found the first Simcoe Co. bird near Orillia on May 12, 1963 (Devitt, 1967: 103). Shirley Black saw one at Melissa on March 19, 1972 (Mills, 1981: 87). K.P. Morrison saw one in Gordon Twp., Manitoulin, on May 2, 1974 (Nicholson, 1981: 128). Skeel & Bondrup-Nielsen (1978: 183) saw one at Pukaskwa on May 29, 1977. J. Jacobs found a nest with 4 eggs in O'Connor Twp., Thunder Bay, on May 27, 1904 (Dear, 1940: 132).

SUMMER: The only report on the 1968-1977 Breeding Bird Survey was on the Manitowaning route, Manitoulin, in 1969. J.E. Cabot noted one at Pic, Lake Superior, on July 13, 1848 (Baillie & Hope, 1943: 13). J.L. Baillie collected a female at Big Fork, Rainy River, on July 16, 1929 (Snyder, 1938: 194). Snyder (1928: 24) collected 3 males, an adult and a young female at Lake Abitibi from June 5 to July 18, 1925. Bondrup-Nielsen (1976: 46) found a nest with young near Kapuskasing on July 8, 1974 in a dead spruce stub. Snyder (1953: 66-67) found a nest with young 25 ft. up in a black spruce at Savanne on July 14, 1937: others were noted at Wabigoon on June 29, 1937 and at Malachi in July, 1947 (including young of the year). Ross James saw individuals near Pickle Lake on June 2 and 9, 1977. Hope (1938: 26) found a nest with 5 eggs at Favourable Lake on June 6, 1936 in a dead birch stub. On July 13, 1947, Manning (1952: 68) saw two together (and collected the female) at Raft River, James Bay: he also reported records near Ft. Albany on Aug. 19 and 21, 1920. Schueler, Baldwin & Rising (1974: 143) noted this species only at Hawley Lake.

AUTUMN:    D. McRae and A. Wormington frequently saw one or two per day at Netitishi Point, James Bay, from Oct. 21 to Nov. 22, 1981. Skeel & Bondrup-Nielsen (1978: 183) saw three at Pukaskwa on Sept. 30 and one on Oct. 14, 1977. We watched one scaling the bark from a black spruce in the Bonfield Bog on Oct. 18, 1944 (Speirs & Speirs, 1947: 30). Nicholson (1981: 128) had Manitoulin reports: one at Sheguiandah on Oct. 24, 1971 and one at South Baymouth on Oct. 30, 1971. M. Hill found a female at Solitaire Lake, Muskoka, on Oct. 13, 1963 (Mills, 1981: 87). Lloyd (1923: 154) considered this a rare fall migrant at Ottawa. Weir & Quilliam (1980: 36) gave Nov. 10 as the 7-year average arrival date at Kingston, with the earliest on Oct. 13. The major flight into southern Ontario was during the winter of 1956-1957 (West & Speirs, 1959: 354) when Wishart Campbell saw one as early as Nov. 11, 1956 at Ajax: there were also several sightings during the autumns of 1963, 1964 and 1965 including one at our Pickering home on Nov. 5, 1963, one by E. Damude at Whitby on Nov. 1, 1964 and another at Whitby on Oct. 20, 1965 by T. Hassall (Speirs, 1976: 57). Fleming (1907: 76) had a male in his collection taken at Toronto on Nov. 16, 1901. On Nov. 28, 1963 a female was found at Thunder Bay, Bertie Twp. Welland Co., by Mr. & Mrs. George Letchworth: this was collected on Dec. 12, 1963 by R.F. Andrle and H.H. Axtell (Beardslee & Mitchell, 1965: 300).

**MEASUREMENTS:**
*Length:* 8.0 to 9.6 ins.
(Godfrey, 1966: 247)
*Wingspread:* 13 3/4 to
14 1/4 ins. (Roberts,
1955: 624)
*Weight:* 2 ♂ averaged
56.5 g. 2 ♀ averaged
53.2 g. (Hope, 1938: 26)

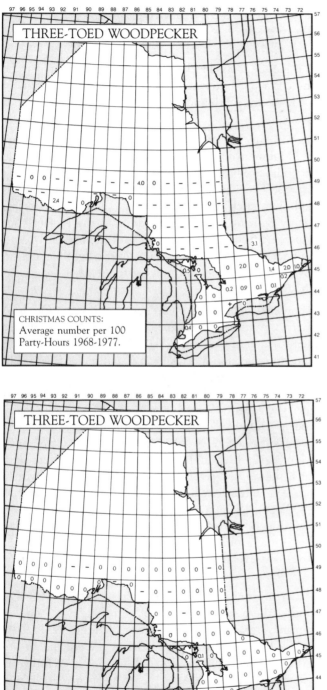

THREE-TOED WOODPECKER

CHRISTMAS COUNTS:
Average number per 100
Party-Hours 1968-1977.

THREE-TOED WOODPECKER

BREEDING BIRDS SURVEY:
Average number per 50 stops
1968-1977.

# BLACK-BACKED WOODPECKER
*Picoides arcticus*    (Swainson)

This is the more common of the three-toed woodpeckers in Ontario where it may be found throughout the year from the cottage country north into the coniferous forests of northern Ontario. In some winters a few come south and delight bird watchers in southern Ontario.

IDENTIFICATION:    This species is about the size of a Hairy Woodpecker but is easily distinguished by its solid black back. Males have a yellow crown patch as do males of the Three-toed Woodpecker: females of both have black crowns. However young of both sexes and both species have yellowish crowns. The Three-toed Woodpecker is smaller and has a prominently barred back. The explosive "click" note is diagnostic (you can imitate this note by pursing the lips and suddenly drawing back the tongue from the roof of your mouth). Both the three-toed woodpeckers feed by chipping the bark from recently dead trees to get at the larvae of beetles under the bark, leaving characteristic light patches on the dead trees. They sometimes invade recently burned forests or forests that have been logged over with the dead trees left standing.

WINTER:    They have been recorded at most Christmas count localities in Ontario, but irregularly and rarely in southern Ontario and uncommonly in northern Ontario. Kelley (1978: 48-49) reported some in Lambton Co. in 1953-1954 and three at Rondeau in December, 1974. One in the Saunders collection was taken at Appin on Dec. 14, 1899 (Saunders & Dale, 1933: 209). Fleming (1907: 76) had a Toronto record on Dec. 4, 1893 and Saunders (1947: 368) listed Dec. 23 and Dec. 31 dates for Toronto: there have been numerous winter sightings there since the advent of Dutch elm disease. There were many records in the decade 1956 to 1966 in Ontario Co. (the period of the rapid spread of Dutch elm disease) and a few later records (Speirs, 1976: 56). Tozer & Richards (1974: 181) gave Darlington Twp. records for Jan. 1-17, 1970 and Feb. 18, 1973. Three were seen on the Dec. 19 Christmas count at Kingston in 1971 but 1965-1966 was the big winter there (Quilliam, 1973: 118). Devitt (1967: 102) cited several winter records for Simcoe Co., including individuals on the 1965 and 1966 Christmas counts at Barrie. Nicholson (1981: 128) reported a Manitoulin bird seen by Ross Lowe and Grant Pilkey on Dec. 21, 1975. Dennison (1980: 148) listed one on one of 25 Christmas counts at Sault Ste. Marie. Skeel & Bondrup-Nielsen (1978: 182) saw several at Pukaskwa during the winter of 1976-1977.

SPRING:    Stirrett (1973b: 19) had only one spring record for Pelee, on May 16, 1954 but Kelley (1978: 48) reported another there on Apr. 7, 1973. A female was found at London on May 15, 1928 where it remained for about a week (Saunders & Dale, 1933: 209). Speirs (1938: 46) gave May 23 as the latest spring date at Toronto. West and Speirs (1959: 362) reported one at Pickering as late as June 2, 1957. I saw one at Whitby on May 3, 1967 and one was seen at Cannington as late as May 17, 1973 (Speirs, 1976: 56). Weir & Quilliam (1980: 36) gave March 7 as the 14-year average departure date from Kingston, with the latest on May 15, 1966. One of the "Dutch elm invasion" birds stayed at Barrie as late as May 18, 1957 (Devitt, 1967: 102). W. Raine found a nest 15 ft. up in a decayed pine at Lake Joseph on May 30, 1899 (Mills, 1981: 86). Nicholson (1981: 128) saw one at Little Current on Apr. 20, 1969. MacLulich (1938: 20) found one occupying a hole in a telephone pole at Cache Lake, Algonquin Park, on May 31, 1938. Dear (1940: 132) found three nests with 4 eggs each in Paipoonge Twp., Thunder Bay, on May 18, 1930. David Elder saw one at Atikokan on May 25, 1981.

SUMMER: On the 1968-1977 Breeding Bird Surveys, they were present but uncommon on several routes north and east of Lake Superior, absent from routes in northwestern Ontario and in southern Ontario. Paul Harrington saw one at Wasaga Beach on June 13, 1924 (Devitt, 1967: 102). R.E. DeLury saw one at Ottawa on Aug. 28, 1922 (Lloyd, 1923: 154). Iris Mills found a nest with young at Bella Lake, Muskoka, on July 5, 1940 and R. Taylor found another nest there, observed from July 1-10, 1958 (Mills, 1981: 86). MacLulich (1938: 20) collected four in Algonquin Park during the summers of 1933 and 1934. Snyder (1942: 134) saw a scattered family group at Point aux Pins, near Sault Ste. Marie, on July 18, 1931. Baillie & Hope (1947: 12) collected a female on June 11, 1937 and a male on June 12 at Chapleau and F.A.E. Starr reported a nest with young at Cartier in July, 1946. Skeel & Bondrup-Nielsen (1978: 182) saw one at Pukaskwa on July 25, 1977. Baillie & Hope (1943: 13) collected a female at Peninsula (Marathon) on June 10, 1936. Snyder (1928: 262) found two nests at Lake Nipigon during the summers of 1923 and 1924. Snyder (1938: 194) collected a male on July 9, 1929 at Off Lake and a juvenile female on July 8, 1929 at Clearwater Lake, Rainy River. Snyder (1928: 24) collected a male, 2 females and 3 young at Lake Abitibi from June 1 to July 22, 1925: two of the young with yellow crowns proved to be females! Smith (1957: 175) saw one north of Remi Lake, near Kapuskasing, on June 26, 1953. C.E. Hope and T.M. Shortt noted 50 in a recently burned forest at Malachi on July 24, 1947 but saw none in a healthy forest at Sioux Lookout from June 22 to July 9, 1947: on June 11, 1937 a nest with young was found 20 ft. up in a live Jack pine and another nest was found on June 16, 1937 at Wabigoon (Snyder, 1953: 66). Hope (1938: 25) took a female with incubation patches and exhibiting alarmed behavior as if near a nest, at Favourable Lake on June 29, 1938. Cringan (1950: 12) saw one by the Petownikip River in June, 1950. Manning (1952: 68) collected a female in the Sandy Island spruce stand near Moosonee on June 16, 1949 and mentioned several earlier specimens from Moose Factory in the U.S. National Museum. Schueler, Baldwin & Rising (1974: 146) collected a male on June 15, 1962 at Hawley Lake, found a nest with 2 young and one infertile egg at Aquatuk Lake on July 11, 1964 and a nest with young at Sutton Lake on June 28, 1964.

AUTUMN: Cringan (1950: 12) saw one by the Windigo River in September. D. McRae and A. Wormington had frequent sightings at Netitishi Point, James Bay from Oct. 20 to Nov. 16, 1981. Skeel & Bondrup-Nielsen (1978: 182) saw birds at Pukaskwa from Sept. 27 to Oct. 13, 1977. Louise Lawrence saw one at Pimisi Bay on Oct. 25, 1944 (Speirs & Speirs, 1947: 30). Nicholson (1981: 128) saw one on Manitoulin on Sept. 24, 1975 and 9 at Mississagi Light on Oct. 13, 1974. Another large flight (with Hairy Woodpeckers) was seen by Paul Harrington at Commanda, south of Lake Nipissing, from Oct. 6-13, 1956 (Speirs, 1957: 29). Devitt (1967: 102) found a male at Midhurst on Nov. 25, 1945 and reported another at Barrie as early as Sept. 25, 1956. Weir & Quilliam (1980: 36) gave Oct. 21 as the 16-year average arrival date at Kingston, with the earliest on Sept. 18, 1968. J.M. Richards collected a male in Darlington Twp. on Oct. 30, 1964 (Tozer & Richards, 1974: 181). The earliest fall record for Ontario Co. was one seen by Miles Hearn at Whitby on Oct. 4, 1974 (Speirs, 1976: 56). Fleming (1907: 76) had Toronto records on Oct. 21, 1893, Oct. 19, 1896 and Nov. 1 and 4, 1899. Speirs (1938: 48) gave

Sept. 22 as the earliest fall date for Toronto. A.A. Wood took a female near London on Nov. 20, 1918 and another was collected in the fall of 1875 (Saunders & Dale, 1933: 209). Kelley (1978: 49) reported one in Lambton Co. on Oct. 27, 1974. Stirrett (1973d: 22) had just one fall record for Pelee, on Oct. 27, 1956.

**MEASUREMENTS:**
*Length:* 9 to 10 ins.
(Godfrey, 1966: 246)
*Wingspread:* 14 3/4 to
16 1/2 ins. (Roberts,
1955: 624)
*Weight:* ♂ 82 g. 2
♀ averaged 70.5 g.
(Hope, 1938: 26)

**REFERENCE:**
West, J. David and J.
Murray Speirs 1959 The
1956-1957 invasion of
three-toed woodpeckers.
Wilson Bull., 71:(4): 348-
363.

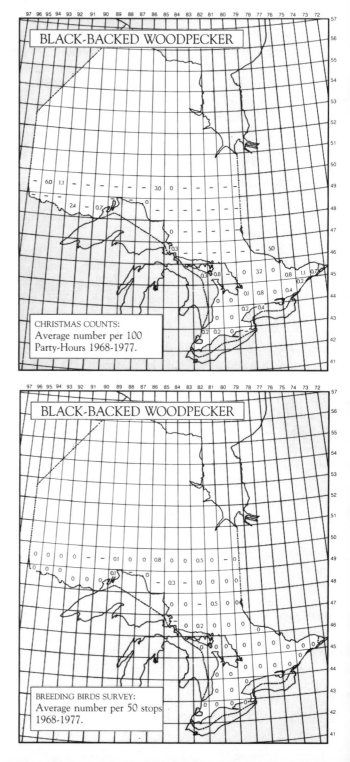

BLACK-BACKED WOODPECKER

CHRISTMAS COUNTS:
Average number per 100
Party-Hours 1968-1977.

BLACK-BACKED WOODPECKER

BREEDING BIRDS SURVEY:
Average number per 50 stops
1968-1977.

# NORTHERN FLICKER   *Colaptes auratus*   (Linnaeus)

Flickers are seen on the ground more often than other woodpeckers, investigating ant hills for their preferred food, ants. Their nest holes are frequently usurped by Starlings but they have been known to throw out the usurpers, and by laying many eggs they maintain their population, and in most parts of Ontario are our most numerous woodpecker during the warmer months.

IDENTIFICATION:   In flight this robin-sized woodpecker displays golden wing-linings and a white rump. On closer inspection you see the spotted buffy breast, with the black crescent across the breast and the red nape patch. Adult males have a black mustache mark absent in adult females, but Snyder (1930: 189) found that nestling females possess this black mustache, losing it in the post-juvenal moult. In western Canada (and rarely in Ontario) the yellow is replaced by red in the wing-linings and I have seen intermediates with orange replacing the yellow in Manitoulin. They drum like other woodpeckers and have a number of characteristic calls: "kee-ah" and one that might be interpreted as "flicker-flicker-flicker" and various "yaruping" calls during the mating displays.

WINTER:   On the 1968-1977 Christmas counts they were fairly common at Pelee, uncommon from there north to Oshawa and Kettle Point, and rare from that line north to Ottawa and Manitoulin. Stirrett (1973a: 16) noted as many as 20 at Pelee on Feb. 11. Fleming, (1907: 76) cited winter records for Toronto, on Jan. 28, 1905 and Feb. 3, 1906. They were found on 9 of 14 Christmas counts at Pickering (Speirs, 1976: 49). L. Beamer had several winter records at Meaford, including Feb. 25, 1943 and Feb. 8, 1945. Nicholson (1981: 125) had two winter records on Manitoulin: Dec. 20, 1969 at Gore Bay and Jan 22 to late March at Mindemoya. Dennison (1980: 148) reported three on one of 25 Christmas counts at Sault Ste. Marie.

SPRING:   Stirrett (1973b: 19) estimated 250 at Pelee on Apr. 16, his maximum there. Ussher (1965: 15) gave March 28 as the 23-year average arrival date at Rondeau, with the earliest spring bird on March 4. Saunders & Dale (1933: 207) wrote that they generally arrived at London about March 27: he gave several nest records from May 13 (7 eggs, 1901) to June 4 (7 eggs in 1912) and one set of 9 eggs on May 18, 1915. Beardslee & Mitchell (1965: 291-292) reported a nest with young at Erie Beach as early as May 22, 1955. Saunders (1947: 367) listed Apr. 4 as his 13-year average arrival date at Toronto, while Speirs (1938: 44) gave May 3 as the spring peak date at Toronto. I saw my earliest spring bird in Pickering Twp. on March 4, 1973 but the peak there is generally about Apr. 25: nesting activity was noted as early as Apr. 3, 1963 and on Apr. 9, 1968 we watched one tossing Starling nest material out of this hole: Paul Harrington found a nest with 8 eggs on Thorah Is. as early as May 14, 1915 (Speirs, 1976: 49). Allin (1940: 100) reported a nest with 7 eggs in Darlington Twp. on May 26, 1927. Weir & Quilliam (1980: 36) gave March 31 as the 32-year average arrival date at Kingston. Quilliam (1973: 113) noted 47 on May 9, 1971 as the spring maximum for Kingston. Devitt (1967: 98) gave Apr. 11 as the 17-year average arrival date at Barrie, with the earliest on March 19, 1945: D.S. Miller saw one excavating at Oro Station on May 2, 1938 and W.W. Smith found a nest with 8 eggs at Big Cedar Point on May 11, 1941. L. Beamer's median arrival date at Meaford was on Apr. 6. Mills (1981: 80) gave Apr. 12 as the 15-year average arrival date at Huntsville, with one as early as March 27, 1976. Nicholson

(1981: 125) found Apr. 3 to be the 11-year average arrival date on Manitoulin, with the earliest on March 19, 1973 and a high count of 450 on Apr. 18, 1976 at Mississagi Light. MacLulich (1938: 19) gave Apr. 14, 1934 as his earliest date in Algonquin Park. We saw one at North Bay as early as March 29, 1945 and saw one emerging from a hole in a pole there on May 30, 1944 (Speirs & Speirs, 1947: 29). Skeel & Bondrup-Nielsen (1978: 180) saw their first at Pukaskwa on Apr. 12, 1977, then 66 on 25 days to May 29. Denis (1961: 2) gave Apr. 16 as the average arrival date at Thunder Bay, with the earliest on Apr. 7, 1953. Bondrup-Nielsen (1976: 43) saw his first near Kapuskasing on Apr. 21, 1974. Elder (1979: 34) had his earliest sighting at Geraldton on Apr. 23. Peruniak (1971: 19) gave Apr. 16 as her earliest Atikokan record. Cringan (1953a: 2) saw his first at Sioux Lookout on Apr. 26, 1953. Cringan (1950: 12) gave May 17 as the average arrival date in the Asheweig area.

SUMMER: On the 1968-1977 Breeding Bird Surveys they were found on every route, and were fairly common on most routes: they were most numerous on a few surveys near Georgian Bay and in the Rainy River region. F. Starr took a set of 5 eggs at Port Burwell on June 18, 1924 (Baillie & Harrington, 1937: 203). Beardslee & Mitchell (1965: 291-292) reported a nest with 7 eggs at Fort Erie as late as July 20, 1904. J.A. Edwards found a nest with 6 eggs on Thorah Is. as late as June 29, 1936 and noisy young were heard at our Pickering home as late as Aug. 2, 1975: this was by far the commonest breeding woodpecker in Ontario Co. and was found on 7 of 11 field quadrats, 6 of 10 urban plots and all 11 forest quadrats surveyed (Speirs, 1976: 49). Allin (1940: 100) noted a nest with 9 young in Darlington Twp. on June 9, 1930. F.A.E. Starr found a nest with 6 eggs at Wasaga Beach on June 9, 1923 and W.E. Cattley found a nest with 6 young on June 25, 1966 in Matchedash Twp. (Devitt, 1967: 98). In the cottage country, young in the nest have been noted from June 12 to July 25 (Mills, 1981: 80). D.B. Ferguson found a nest with 3 young at Providence Bay, Manitoulin, on July 3, 1976 (Nicholson, 1981: 125). Ricker & Clarke (1939: 13) found a nest with 6 eggs at Lake Nipissing on June 3, 1924. Snyder (1942: 132) collected a set of 6 eggs at Laird on June 11, 1931. Skeel & Bondrup-Nielsen (1978: 180) found a nest with 5 young on June 15, 1977 at Pukaskwa in a nest about 18 m. up in a live trembling aspen. Baillie & Hope (1943: 11) found a nest with 6 young at Amyot on June 23, 1936 and a nest with 7 eggs there on June 27, 1936. Snyder (1928: 263) found a number of nests at Lake Nipigon, one with young only 18 inches above ground. Dear (1940: 131) found two nests with 6 eggs each at Thunder Bay: one on June 17, 1923, the other on June 4, 1928. Snyder (1953: 63-64) collected 11 adults and 3 juveniles in western Ontario (Ingolf to Wabigoon, north to Sioux Lookout) from 1937 to 1947. He found them breeding at two Lake Abitibi localities during the summer of 1925 (Snyder, 1928: 25). James (1980: 87) noted nests near Pickle Lake on June 4, 1977 and June 15, 1979. Cringan (1950: 12) found an occupied cavity in a dead black spruce on July 7, 1950 near Nikip Lake. Hope (1938: 24) collected 6 males and 5 females at Favourable Lake from June 1 to Aug. 6, 1938: he found many nests and noted the first young out of the nest on June 28. Manning (1952: 66) collected a female near Moosonee on June 1, 1947 and saw one as far north as Raft River on July 13, 1947. Schueler, Baldwin & Rising (1974: 146) collected a female in active breeding condition at Moosonee on June 4, 1972: they found a nest with 7 eggs at Sutton Gorge on June 15, 1962, a nest with 4 young at Hawley Lake on June 17, 1964 and saw adults visiting a nest there from June 9-15, 1965: they also noted the species at Attawapiskat and Winisk.

Lee (1978: 25) found two pairs at Big Trout Lake in summer of 1975. On July 7, 1940, C.E. Hope found a nest with 6 young at Ft. Severn and collected two of the young.

AUTUMN: Oliver Hewitt saw one at Moose Factory on Sept. 21, 1947 (Manning, 1952: 66). Peruniak (1971: 19) gave Oct. 18 as her latest date for Atikokan. We saw one at North Bay on Oct. 7, 1944 (Speirs & Speirs, 1947: 31). The high fall count for Manitoulin was 300 on Sept. 12, 1970 (Nicholson, 1981: 125). C. Harris saw one at Go Home Bay on Oct. 6, 1973 (Mills, 1981: 81). The highest fall count for Kingston was 170 noted by Jean Baxter on Oct. 6, 1960 (Quilliam , 1973: 113): the 29-year average departure date there was Oct. 19 (Weir & Quilliam, 1980: 36). The peak of the fall flight in Pickering Twp. is in mid-September and the latest fall bird was on Nov. 25, 1967 (Speirs, 1976: 49). Speirs (1938: 52) gave Sept. 15 as the fall peak date for Toronto, while Saunders (1947: 367) listed Oct. 18 as his 13-year average departure date there. James Savage witnessed a migration at Long Point on Sept. 30, 1930 when a steady steam of flickers passed by all morning (Snyder, 1931: 187). Ussher (1965: 15) gave Nov. 3 as the 11-year average departure date from Rondeau, with the latest on Nov. 20. Stirrett (1973d: 21) estimated maxima of 400 at Pelee on Sept. 21 and Sept. 29.

BANDING: One banded near Toronto on Apr. 24, 1948 was recovered in North Carolina on Nov. 25, 1948 and another banded near Toronto was also recovered in North Carolina on Feb. 17, 1960 about 5 1/2 years after being banded on Apr. 14, 1955. Another banded near Toronto on May 3, 1952 was recovered in Alabama on Oct. 21, 1952. One banded in north central Lower Michigan on June 30, 1967 was recovered near Toronto in April, 1968.

**MEASUREMENTS:**
*Length:* 12 to 13 ins.
(Godfrey, 1966: 238)
*Wingspread:* 19 3/4 to
21 1/2 ins. (Roberts,
1955: 621)
*Weight:* 4 ♂ averaged
144 g. 5 ♀ averaged
142 g. (Hope, 1938: 24).

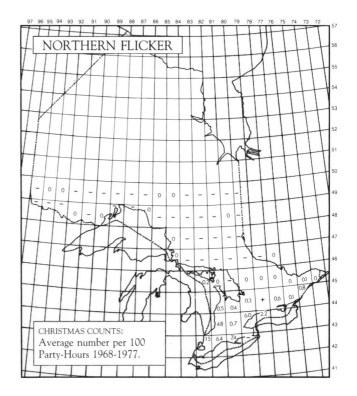

NORTHERN FLICKER

CHRISTMAS COUNTS:
Average number per 100
Party-Hours 1968-1977.

484

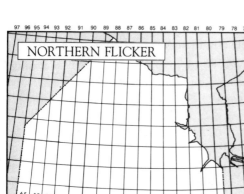

NORTHERN FLICKER

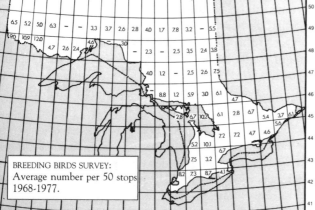

BREEDING BIRDS SURVEY:
Average number per 50 stops
1968-1977.

# PILEATED WOODPECKER   *Dryocopus pileatus*   (Linneaus)

Several writers have documented the decline of this species with the clearing of forests during the 1800's and their recent increase as the forests have grown back. It is now resident across the forested portions of Ontario. Small woodlots will not support these big birds: they require at least 100 acres of forest, with dead trees left standing, to satisfy their needs.

IDENTIFICATION:   This is a crow-sized woodpecker, mainly black but with a prominent white flash in the wings in flight and a fiery red crest. Males have red mustache marks: these are black in females. When feeding they sound like someone shingling a roof and slivers about the size of a finger come away at each peck so that big oblong holes are made rapidly in their search for the carpenter ants on which they feed. They also strip the bark off dead trees in search of beetle larvae. Their drumming signals are distinctive, loud and resonant with a characteristic crescendo and diminuendo. They also utter a flicker-like "kyuk-kyuk-kyuk. . ."

WINTER:   On the 1968-1977 Christmas counts they were found on all but a few counts but were uncommon at most. Speirs (1976: 50) reported a total of 25 tallied on 9 of 14 Pickering Christmas counts. Charles Fothergill described one taken at Rice Lake on Feb. 26, 1822 (Black, 1934: 149). Devitt (1967: 99) reported them on 13 of 16 Christmas counts at Barrie, with a maximum of seven on Dec. 28, 1957. Dennison (1980: 146) listed from one to five on most Christmas counts at Sault Ste. Marie. Skeel & Bondrup-Nielsen (1978: 180) heard it at Pukaskwa on Dec. 29 and Jan. 20 during the winter of 1976-1977. David Elder saw his first at Atikokan on Feb. 19 in 1981.

SPRING:   A nest was found in Middlesex Co. by Robert Elliot in May, 1885 and Dr. Macallum noted breeding near Dunnville (McIlwraith, 1894: 250). We have been privleged to watch their courtship on an old elm stub near our Pickering home and have watched as they excavated big oblong feeding cavities in other dead trees as we read nearby. C. Christy and J.M. Richards found a nest with 4 eggs on May 4, 1957 near Whitby and another there on May 7, 1964 (Speirs, 1976: 50). Charles Fothergill took one at Rice Lake on May 23, 1821 and mentioned having seen one take off as much hemlock bark as would fill a half bushel basket in 10 to 15 mins. (Black, 1934: 149). A specimen was taken near Kingston on Apr. 4, 1944 by W.H. Robb (Quilliam, 1973: 114). Devitt (1967: 99) reported several nests in Simcoe Co.: one with 1 egg on May 29, 1932; one with 3 eggs on May 15, 1940 and another with 3 eggs on May 21, 1940. We watched one at Rutherglen on Apr. 23, 1945 (Speirs & Speirs, 1947: 30). Skeel & Bondrup-Nielsen (1978: 180) heard two at Pukaskwa on Apr. 19 and May 26, 1977. Dear (1940: 131) cited two nest records near Thunder Bay, a nest with 4 eggs on May 13, 1930 and one at Saganaga Lake with 3 eggs on May 28, 1933.

SUMMER:   On the 1968-1977 Breeding Bird Surveys they were found on most routes except in southwestern Ontario where they were rare or absent: numbers were greatest on routes northeast of Lake Superior. Kelley (1978: 47) knew of only one breeding record in southwestern Ontario, at Camlachie, Lambton Co. in 1969. However, Ussher (1965: 15) listed it as a resident species at Rondeau. In June, 1970, we noted one several times in our study quadrat in Springwater Park, Elgin Co. (Speirs & Frank, 1970: 741-742). Saunders (1947: 190-192) described the activities of a pair stripping bark from dead trees near

Orangeville to obtain carpenter ants from the rotten wood beneath. Speirs (1976: 50) found breeding pairs on his Whitby and Scugog forest quadrats. On June 8, 1963 adults were seen feeding young at a nest in the Otter Lake sanctuary of the Kingston Field Naturalists (Quilliam, 1973: 114). Devitt (1967: 99) saw a nest with large young on June 9, 1941 near Edward Lake, Simcoe Co. Lloyd (1923: 154) considered it rare near Ottawa and cited only two rather indefinite breeding reports. Mills (1981: 81) reported several nests in the cottage country, including one with 6 eggs on June 2, 1899 at Lake Joseph and one with 7 eggs on June 17, 1920 near Kearney. D.B. Ferguson watched adults feeding young at a nest near Providence Bay, Manitoulin, on June 23, 1974 (Nicholson, 1981: 125). Ricker & Clarke (1939: 13) reported a nest found by C. Ramsay near North Bay. Snyder (1942: 133) discovered a nest 35 ft. up in a red pine at Maclennan, near Sault Ste. Marie, on July 25, 1931 and collected one young. Baillie & Hope (1947: 10) found a nest with young about 25 ft. up in a dead stub, some 40 miles south of Chapleau on June 9, 1937. Skeel & Bondrup-Nielsen (1978: 180) had 5 records in Pukaskwa from June 5 to July 20, 1977. P.A. Taverner and C.E. Johnson collected a young bird from a nest near Kapuskasing on July 3, 1919 (Baillie & Harrington, 1937: 203). Snyder (1928: 262-263) collected two young from a nest on St. Paul Is., Lake Nipigon, on July 14, 1924 and saw another nest in Macdiarmid. Snyder (1953: 64) reported breeding at Indian Bay and Malachi near the Manitoba border and noted the species from there east to Sioux Lookout and Savanne. C.A. Elsey saw the species in the Asheweig area in 1950 (Cringan, 1950: 12). Manning (1952: 67) cited a report of four specimens in the U.S. National Museum taken at Moose Factory.

AUTUMN: Doug McRae and A. Wormington had records at Netitishi Point, James Bay, on Oct. 24, Oct. 31, Nov. 15 and Nov. 17, 1981. Hope (1938: 24) recorded a few at Favourable Lake, and received one taken by Indians on Oct. 31, 1938. Skeel & Bondrup-Nielsen (1978: 180) had several fall records from Pukaskwa between Sept. 14 and Oct. 6, 1977. Louise Lawrence observed one at Pimisi Bay on Nov. 21, 1944 (Speirs & Speirs, 1947: 30). J.A. Bradley took a specimen at Landsdowne on Nov. 2, 1934 (Quilliam, 1973: 114). Naomi LeVay noted one at Cranberry Marsh on Oct. 6, 1968 (Tozer & Richards, 1974: 176). Stirrett (1973d: 21) had only one Pelee record, on Sept. 17, 1963.

**MEASUREMENTS:**
*Length:* 16 to 19.5 ins.
(Godfrey, 1966: 240)
*Wingspread:* 27.15 to
30.00 ins. (Roberts,
1955: 620)
*Weight:* ♀ 311 g. (Hope,
1938: 24)

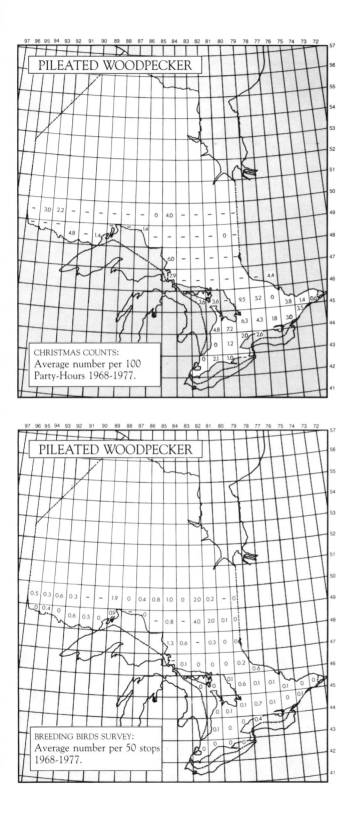

PILEATED WOODPECKER

CHRISTMAS COUNTS:
Average number per 100
Party-Hours 1968-1977.

PILEATED WOODPECKER

BREEDING BIRDS SURVEY:
Average number per 50 stops
1968-1977.

# OLIVE-SIDED FLYCATCHER
*Contopus borealis*   (Swainson)

When Olive-sided Flycatchers are mentioned I think at once of lonely northern Ontario bogs with tall dead tamaracks. During migration they sometimes pause on dead snags even in southern Ontario. One August day I watched one sally forth from the dead top of a big poplar near our home, snap up a big fly about 200 ft. from its perch, then return to resume its post: I was impressed with its keen vision (I was using binoculars to try to see why it flew so far from its perch). They go south to northern South America for the winter.

IDENTIFICATION:   This is a big-headed, short-tailed medium sized flycatcher (a little smaller than an Eastern Kingbird). Its dirty-olive sides are separated by a creamy white central strip down the breast. White puffs on each side of the rump may show above or below the wing tips. The rear of the head is sharply angled, suggesting a crest. On its breeding grounds its clear call is sometimes rendered as "quick, three beers"(emphasis on the bee).

WINTER:

SPRING:   Stirrett (1973b: 20) considered them irregular and rare at Pelee, from May 10, to June 6. Ussher (1965: 17) gave the 14-year average arrival date for Rondeau as May 23, with the earliest on May 15 and latest on May 30. Saunders & Dale (1933: 211) had their earliest record on May 7, 1924 at London, and May 20 as their 11-year average arrival date there. Brooman (1954: 26) cited three spring records for Elgin Co.: May 21, 1939; May 24, 1923 and May 29, 1949. J.L. Baillie's 11-year average arrival date at Toronto was May 21 (Saunders, 1947: 368). Fleming (1907: 77) gave May 10 as his earliest Toronto record while Speirs (1938: 44) considered May 22 the peak of the spring flight. George A. Scott had Oshawa records as early as May 7, 1961 and as late as June 4, 1961 (Speirs, 1975: 12). Weir & Quilliam (1980: 37) gave May 24 as the 14-year average arrival date at Kingston, with the earliest on May 14. Devitt (1967: 107) gave May 16 as the 6-year average arrival date at Barrie, the earliest on May 8, 1938. D. Brunton noted a very early one on May 7, 1969 at Killbear Park (Mills, 1981: 94). Nicholson (1981: 135) had a 9-year average arrival date for Manitoulin on May 20, with the earliest on May 14, 1978. MacLulich (1938: 22) gave May 20, 1932 as his earliest arrival date for Algonquin Park. Ricker & Clarke (1939: 14) saw one at Lake Nipissing as early as May 18, 1934. Skeel & Bondrup-Nielsen (1978: 185) heard one at Pukaskwa on May 30, 1977. Denis (1961: 4) gave May 27 as the average arrival date at Thunder Bay, with the earliest on May 9, 1959. Elder (1979: 35) had his earliest Geraldton arrival on May 23. At Atikokan the earliest record was on May 26 (Peruniak, 1971: 20). Todd (1963: 489) noted one at Kapuskasing on May 27, 1912.

SUMMER:   On the 1968-1977 Breeding Bird Surveys, it was uncommon to rare on routes south to Orillia, fairly common on the Cochrane and Smooth Rock Falls routes. Stirrett (1973c: 18) noted two southbound birds at Pelee on Aug. 15 and single birds on Aug. 22 and 29. Ussher (1965: 17) gave Aug. 26 as his 6-year average fall arrival date for Rondeau, the earliest on Aug. 20. Brooman (1954: 26) had one as early as Aug. 6, 1950 in Elgin Co. Speirs (1938: 52) gave Aug. 20 as the peak of the fall flight at Toronto.

Speirs (1975: 12) noted one in a tamarack bog in Brock Twp. on June 4 and 8, 1968: another was observed in a swamp forest in northern Mara Twp. on June 28 and July 6, 1963: I have seen migrants at our Pickering home as early as Aug.5, 1956. Weir & Quilliam (1980: 37) had Kingston records as late as June 13 and as early as July 14, but no breeding record. Devitt (1967: 106) cited several summer records for Simcoe Co.: he found a nest with 2 eggs about 4 miles SW of Bradford on June 15, 1940 and E.L. Brereton saw an adult feeding two young out of the nest at Wasaga Beach on Aug. 18, 1941. Mills (1981: 94) cited several records of nests with young in the cottage country. C.H.D. Clarke saw young being fed at Brule Lake, Algonquin Park, on July 26, 1934 (MacLulich, 1938: 22). T.M. Shortt saw two young of the year with an adult near Sault Ste. Marie (Snyder, 1942: 135). Baillie & Hope (1947: 13) collectted a juvenile female at Bigwood on July 27, 1937 and John Walty considered this the commonest flycatcher at Washagami in 1936. Baillie & Hope (1943: 14) found a nest with 3 eggs near Marathon on June 21, 1936 about 30 ft. up in a leaning dead spruce. Snyder (1928: 264) found them "well distributed through the stands of black spruce" at the north end of Lake Nipigon. Dear (1940: 133) found a nest with 3 eggs on June 24, 1934 and a nest with 3 young on July 1, 1932 near Thunder Bay. Snyder (1938: 196) collected a female at Off Lake, Rainy River, on July 5, 1929. Snyder (1953: 68) found them in the spruce country from Kenora to Sioux Lookout, with as many as 20 on July 24, 1947 at Malachi. Smith (1957: 175) had only two records for the Clay Belt, both near Gogama, on July 26, 1954 and Aug. 2, 1954. Snyder (1928: 25) collected partly feathered young at Lowbush, Lake Abitibi, on July 30, 1925. Cringan (1953a: 3) saw his first in 1953 at Perrault Falls, on June 16. From June to August, 1950, he noted one or two daily in the Nikip Lake region (Cringan, 1950: 13). James (1980: 87) watched one nest building near Lysander Lake (north of Pickle Lake). Hope (1938: 29) frequently noted pairs in black spruce bogs at Favourable Lake during the summer of 1938. Todd (1963: 489-490) listed and mapped over two dozen records from his travels between North Bay and Moose Factory, where he found them fairly common. Lee (1978: 26) recorded the species at Big Trout Lake on June 16, July 30 and Aug. 10, 1975. James, Nash & Peck (1981: 91) confirmed breeding at Kiruna Lake, Sutton Ridges, in 1981. McLaren & McLaren (1981: 4) found them present north to Little Sachigo Lake near the Manitoba border.

AUTUMN: We noted one at Nipissing Junction on Sept. 2, 1944 (Speirs & Speirs, 1947: 30). Nicholson (1981: 133) gave Sept. 21, 1974 as his latest Manitoulin record. The latest record from the cottage country was one seen by W. Mansell at Rebecca Lake on Sept. 3, 1939 (Mills 1981: 95). Frances Westman noted one at Barrie as late as Sept. 24, 1962 (Devitt, 1967: 107). Weir & Quilliam (1980: 37) listed Sept. 6 as the 13-year average departure date from Kingston, with the latest on Sept. 26. Naomi LeVay noted one at Eastbourne, Whitby, as late as Oct. 4, 1952 (Speirs, 1975: 12). Speirs (1938: 54) listed Sept. 30 as the latest Toronto record. Beardslee & Mitchell (1965: 308-309) mentioned one seen on the Canadian shore of Lake Erie on Sept. 17, 1942. Ussher (1965: 17) gave Sept. 14 as a 4-year average departure date from Rondeau, the latest on Oct. 1. Stirrett (1973d: 22) had individuals at Pelee on Sept. 1, 5 and 22.

**MEASUREMENTS:**
*Length:* 7.1 to 7.8 ins.
(Godfrey, 1966: 261)
*Wingspread:* 12 1/4 to
13 1/2 ins. (Roberts,
1955: 635)
*Weight:* 4 ♂ averaged
31.1 g. (Hope, 1938: 29)

**REFERENCE:**
Devitt, O.E. 1941 The
Olive-sided Flycatcher
nesting in the Toronto
region. Canadian Field-
Nat., 55:(3): 46. This nest
contained 2 eggs when
found on June 15, 3 eggs a
week later. The nest was
about 35 ft. up in a black
spruce, in the Holland
Marsh portion of King
Twp.

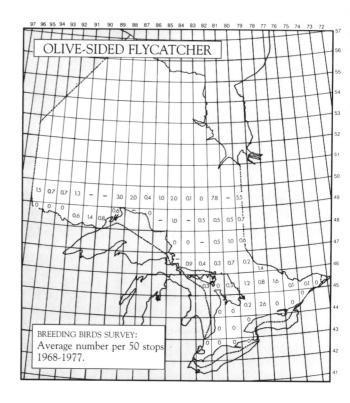

OLIVE-SIDED FLYCATCHER

BREEDING BIRDS SURVEY:
Average number per 50 stops
1968-1977.

# WESTERN WOOD-PEWEE   *Contopus sordidulus*   Sclater

This is the western counterpart of our Eastern Wood-Pewee, usually found from south-western Manitoba to the Pacific shores, accidental in Ontario.

**IDENTIFICATION:**   It is not safely distinguished from our Eastern Wood-Pewee except by song. Its lazy, nasal "Zee-ur" is diagnostic.

**WINTER:**

**SPRING:**   Stirrett (1973b: 20) reported one at Pelee on May 17, 1968. J.L. Baillie recorded one there on May 15, 1969 (Goodwin, 1969: 585).

**SUMMER:**

**AUTUMN:**

**MEASUREMENTS:**
*Length:* 6.0 to 6.6 ins.
(Godfrey, 1966: 260)
Wingspread:
*Weight:* 15 averaged
12.8 g. (Dunning,
1984: 16)

# EASTERN WOOD-PEWEE  *Contopus virens*  (Linnaeus)

The evening song of the Eastern Wood-Pewee is one of the delights of the deciduous forests of southern Ontario. It is a bird of mature, mosquito-infested forests, where the nests are saddled on horizontal limbs, high above the ground. The winter quarters are usually in southern Central America and northern South America.

IDENTIFICATION:  From the Eastern Phoebe it is distinguished by its yellowish lower mandible and the presence of wing bars and an eye ring. From the somewhat smaller *Empidonax* flycatchers the song is the safest character: "pee-ah-wee" or sometimes just "pee-ah" or "ah-wee" (or all three, usually given in sequence, in the evensong).

WINTER:

SPRING:  Stirrett (1973b: 20) gave Apr. 28 as the earliest record for Pelee, where 23 were banded on May 23. The earliest Rondeau bird was noted on May 8 and the 25-year average arrival date there was May 16 (Ussher, 1965: 17). Saunders & Dale (1933: 211) gave May 19 as the 17-year average arrival date at London, with the earliest on May 11, 1912. Snyder (1931: 189) mentioned a lighthouse kill at Long Point about May 14 but noted his first there on May 19 in 1928. Beardslee & Mitchell (1965: 308) reported one at Fort Erie as early as May 6, 1951. Saunders (1947: 368) gave May 15 as his 13-year average arrival date at Toronto and his earliest was on May 5. Tozer & Richards (1974: 191) cited Whitby and Oshawa records as early as May 4 but it is usually the fourth week of May before I see my first and the peak of the spring flight is in the first week of June (Speirs, 1975: 11). Weir & Quilliam (1980: 37) listed May 12 as the 32-year average arrival date for Kingston: a very early one was noted on Apr. 22. Devitt (1967: 106) gave May 12 as the 17-year average arrival date for Barrie, with the earliest on Apr. 22, 1959. Mills (1981: 93) gave May 19 as the 7-year average arrival date at Huntsville, with the earliest for the cottage country at Arrowhead Park on May 13, 1979. The 10-year average arrival date for Manitoulin was May 16, with the earliest on May 7, 1977 (Nicholson, 1981: 132). MacLulich (1938: 22) mentioned May 20, 1932 as an arrival date for Algonquin Park. Ricker & Clarke (1939: 14) noted one as early as May 22, 1933 at Lake Nipissing. Denis (1961: 4) listed May 30 as the average arrival date at Thunder Bay: the earliest was on May 15, 1949. Peruniak (1971: 20) considered them rare at Atikokan and gave May 30 as her earliest record.

SUMMER:  On the 1968-1977 Breeding Bird Survey routes they were fairly common on all routes south of North Bay (but most numerous north of Lake Ontario and east of Georgian Bay), becoming uncommon to absent on routes north of North Bay. During the breeding season Stirrett (1973c: 18) had a maximum count of 7 at Pelee but migrants had swelled the daily count to 100 by Aug. 21. Saunders & Dale (1933: 211) reported 5 nests near London, each with 3 eggs: the earliest was found on June 9, 1902 and the last on July 10, 1900. Snyder (1930: 191) noted a nest with 3 eggs about 50 ft. up on a horizontal oak branch in King Twp. on June 22, 1926. Of 32 sets of eggs reported for Ontario Co., 24 contained 3 eggs and 8 had 2 eggs: only one of these contained a cowbird egg: J.A. Edwards found 23 of these sets on Thorah Is., the earliest on June 10, 1939 and the latest on Aug. 14, 1932 (both high in elms—40 to 45 ft): all nine quadrats in mature forests in Ontario Co. had this species, with an average density of 20 birds per 100 acres and a maximum of 43 birds per 100 acres in the Scugog forest (Speirs, 1975: 11). Allin (1940: 101) reported finding several nests in Darlington Twp. made entirely of wool, which swelled up during the first rain and spilled all the eggs on the ground: another nest at Hampton contained young on July 25, 1930. Quilliam (1973: 123) reported 3 sets of eggs for Kingston, the earliest with 2 eggs on June 26, 1897, another with 4 eggs on July 6, 1898 and the latest with 3 eggs on July 7, 1901: a more recent nest was under construction June 8, 1963 and young were being fed in it by June 23. Devitt (1967: 106) reported nest building at Wasaga Beach on June 9, 1935: a nest with 2 eggs was collected by H.P. Bingham at Nottawaga Beach on June 12, 1938 and one with 4 eggs was found at Oro Station by D.S. Miller on Aug. 1, 1936. Lloyd (1923: 155) reported a nest with 2 eggs at Ottawa found by A.G. Kingston in June, 1892. Mills (1981: 93-94) cited several nest records for the cottage country, including a nest with 4 eggs found by H.P. Bingham on June 8, 1942 at Whiteside, Muskoka. D.B. Ferguson found a nest with 3 eggs at Lake Manitou, Manitoulin, on June 22, 1977 (Nicholson, 1981: 133). C.H.D. Clarke noted young being fed at Brule Lake, Algonquin Park, on Aug. 14, 1934 (MacLulich, 1938:22). S.L. Thompson saw an adult at a nest near North Bay on June 10, 1904 (Baillie & Harrington, 1937: 212). Snyder (1942: 135) noted up to 10 per day near Sault Ste. Marie in the summer of 1931 and observed young of the year there. Baillie & Hope (1947: 13) collected a female with a shelled egg in the oviduct at Bigwood on July 14, 1937: they considered this species rare there. Dear (1940: 133) found a nest with 4 small young in Paipoonge Twp., Thunder Bay, on July 15, 1928 and observed an incubating female there on July 1, 1929. Snyder (1938: 195) found them fairly common in the Rainy River area in 1929, up to 6 per day being observed. Snyder (1953: 68) found them regularly near Ingolf and Malachi, but rare at Dryden and only once at Sioux Lookout (on July 5, 1947). Cringan (1953a: 3) noted one on June 13, 1953 at Perrault Falls.

AUTUMN:    Skeel & Bondrup-Nielsen (1978: 184) saw one at Pukaskwa on Sept. 18, 1977. Ricker & Clarke (1939: 14) had a fall record at Lake Nipissing on Sept. 16, 1927. Nicholson (1981: 133) noted one at Great Duck Is. as late as Oct. 16, 1978. Mills (1981: 94) cited a late record by C. Harris on one of the Pine Is., Muskoka, on Oct. 2, 1976. Two were killed at the Barrie TV tower on Sept. 24, 1960 (Devitt, 1967: 106). Weir & Quilliam (1980: 37) gave Sept. 29 as the 30-year average departure date from Kingston, with the latest on Oct. 21. E. Laird reported two as late as Oct. 15, 1970 in Darlington Twp. (Tozer & Richards, 1974: 191). Peter Satterly noted a nest with young as late as Sept. 15, 1966 and R. Charles Long noted one bird on Oct. 13, 1965 at Ontoro Beach (Speirs, 1975: 11). Saunders (1947: 368) listed Sept. 23 as his 13-year average departure date from Toronto, with his latest on Oct. 6. Ussher (1965: 17) gave Sept. 18 as his 14-year average departure date from Rondeau: his latest was on Oct. 30. Stirrett (1973d: 17) had individuals at Pelee as late as Nov. 25 and Nov. 27.

**MEASUREMENTS:**
*Length:* 6.0 to 6.5 ins.
(Godfrey, 1966: 260)
*Wingspread:* 9 3/4 to 11
ins. (Roberts, 1955: 634)
*Weight:* 19 ROM
specimens varied from
12.2 to 17 g. (average
14.4 g.)

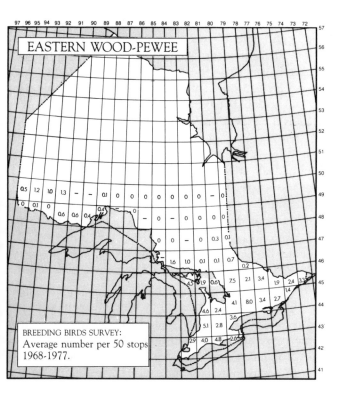

EASTERN WOOD-PEWEE

BREEDING BIRDS SURVEY:
Average number per 50 stops
1968-1977.

# YELLOW-BELLIED FLYCATCHER
*Empidonax flaviventris* (Baird and Baird)

I associate this flycatcher with pockets of alder bog in the black spruce forests of northern Ontario. In migration we sometimes find it in the shrubbery near our home. It winters in Central America.

**IDENTIFICATION:** This is one of several small flycatchers of the genus *Empidonax*, all very similar and best identified by their calls. This one utters a sad little "pu-wee" or "soo-wee", somewhat resembling the song of the Eastern Wood Pewee, but faster in tempo, less emphatic and lacking the middle syllable of the pewee's "pee-ah-wee" (sometimes the pewee omits this middle syllable too, so it is good to look up the singer to confirm your identification). Adults are quite yellow beneath, including the throat, and more green above than other common members of the genus. The Acadian Flycatcher is most likely to be confused with this species but the Acadian has a white throat and under tail converts and the yellow is mainly on the sides: it is also more southerly in distribution and has a quite different call, an explosive "pee-slip".

**WINTER:**

**SPRING:** Stirrett (1973b: 20) had an early record at Pelee on Apr. 26 and a maximum count of 20 on May 23. Ussher (1965: 16) had one at Rondeau as early as Apr. 24, and gave May 16 as the 13-year average arrival there. Saunders & Dale (1933: 209) had their earliest London bird on May 10, 1914 and their 12-year average arrival date was May 22. Speirs (1938: 40, 44) gave May 17 as the earliest spring date for Toronto, with the peak on May 31: Saunders (1947: 368) listed May 24 as the average arrival date there. A.A. Wood saw one at Oshawa as early as May 6, 1961 (Tozer & Richards, 1974: 188). Allin (1940: 101) reported a sighting by M.G. Gould at Bowmanville on May 14, 1921. Weir & Quilliam (1980: 37) gave May 19 as the 21-year average arrival date at Kingston, with the earliest on May 8. The earliest Barrie record was one seen by E.L. Brereton on May 16, 1943 (Devitt, 1967: 104). E.G. White took one at Ottawa on May 26, 1884 (Lloyd, 1923: 155). L. Beamer reported individuals at Meaford on May 15, 1949 and May 25, 1952. The earliest Huntsville date was May 13, 1975 (Mills, 1981: 90). Nicholson (1981: 131) cited several spring records from Manitoulin between May 21 and May 31. Ricker & Clarke (1939: 14) saw one at North Bay on May 31, 1925. Skeel & Bondrup-Nielsen (1978: 184) saw their first at Pukaskwa on May 30 in 1977. Denis (1961: 4) gave May 29 as the average arrival date at Thunder Bay, with the earliest on May 20, 1959. Bondrup-Neilsen (1976: 43) listed May 27, 1974 as his earliest near Kapuskasing. Elder saw his first at Flanders (near Atikokan) on May 25, 1981.

SUMMER: On the 1968-1977 Breeding Bird Surveys they were uncommon to rare on about half of the routes from Hwy. 11 south to Orillia and Mt. Julian (probably these latter were late spring migrants): they were most numerous from Thunder Bay westward. Stirrett (1973b: 20, 1973c: 17) had the latest northbound migrant on June 4 and the earliest returning 15 on Aug. 12, with a maximum of 50 on Aug. 29. Ussher (1965: 16) gave June 6 as the latest northbound bird at Rondeau and Aug. 13 as the earliest returning bird. Eames saw one at Rockhouse Point on July 17, 1938 (Beardslee & Mitchell, 1965: 304). Fleming (1907: 77) gave June 15, 1894 as the latest spring date for Toronto and July 27, 1893 as the earliest southbound date. Naomi LeVay noted individuals at Cranberry Marsh as late as June 20, 1963 and as early as Aug. 6, 1957 (Tozer & Richards, 1974: 188). Weir & Quilliam (1980: 37) gave June 5 as the average departure date for Kingston, with the latest northbound bird on June 17; the earliest returning bird on July 10 and Aug. 7 as the average arrival date for returning birds. E. Beaupré discovered a nest with 4 young on Amherst Is., near Kingston, on July 1, 1921 (Quilliam, 1973: 122). J.L. Baillie saw one near Mac Station, Simcoe Co., as late as June 7, 1929 (Devitt, 1967: 104). E.L. Brereton, O.E. Devitt and W. Smith found a pair building on the ground in a sphagnum bog at Bella Lake, Muskoka, on June 22, 1943: the nest held two eggs on June 26: the birds were also noted at Bella Lake in 1944, 1945 and 1948. Katherine Ketchum has noted southbound migrants off Point au Baril from July 29 (1965) to Aug. 28 (1967) (Mills, 1981: 90-91). Nicholson (1981: 131) had two summer records from Manitoulin: one on June 28, 1970 by John Lemon and one on July 21, 1976 by Ron Tasker. Louise Lawrence noted one at Pimisi Bay on June 2, 1945 (Speirs & Speirs, 1947: 30). Ricker & Clarke (1939: 14) saw one at Frank's Bay on June 9, 1932 and suggested that they probably bred in alder swamps there. Snyder (1942: 134) collected a male at Point aux Pins, near Sault Ste. Marie, on July 13, 1931. Skeel & Bondrup-Nielsen (1978: 184) noted 20 in 17 days at Pukaskwa, the latest on July 17, 1977. Snyder (1928: 264) collected a female on June 13, 1924 and a male on June 16, 1923 at Macdiarmid, Lake Nipigon. Dear (1940: 132) found two nests, each with 4 eggs, near Thunder Bay, one on June 24, 1934, the other on June 27, 1936. Smith (1957: 175) heard two singing near Kapuskasing during the summer of 1953. Elder (1979: 35) gave June 3 as his earliest record for Ger-

aldton, where he considered it uncommon and local. Peruniak (1971: 20) called it uncommon at Atikokan and gave only a June 3 record. Snyder (1953: 67, 68) found the
species at Malachi, Sioux Lookout, Ingolf, Kenora, Wabigoon and Savanne, with a nest
and 4 eggs at Wabigoon on July 1, 1937 in a hummock of deep moss in black spruce
forest. James (1980: 84, 87) found a population density of 15.2 per Km² at Pickle Lake
(the second most abundant species there). Cringan (1950: 13) noted a few at Nikip Lake
in June and early July 1, 1950. Hope (1938: 28) reported them "not uncommon" in the
black spruce bogs near Favourable Lake: he collected a male on June 1 and a female on
July 6 there. Schueler, Baldwin & Rising (1974: 143) noted the species at Hawley Lake
and Winisk. Lee (1978: 25) noted his first at Big Trout Lake on June 11, 1975: he found
them there in tamarack bogs and at the edge of clearings in the black spruce forest. C.E.
Hope found a nest with 5 eggs at Fort Severn on July 15, 1940 and noted as many as 7
individuals on July 5 there.

AUTUMN: Nicholson (1981: 131) cited fall reports from Manitoulin from Aug. 24
(1975) to Oct. 8 (1978). The latest Simcoe Co. bird was picked up dead under the Barrie
TV tower on Sept. 30, 1965 (Devitt, 1967: 105). Weir & Quilliam (1980: 37) gave Sept.
26 as the latest departure date from Kingston. Jack Sherrin saw one at Oshawa as late as
Sept. 28, 1958 (Speirs, 1975: 6). Speirs (1938: 54) gave Oct. 12 as the latest Toronto
date. James Savage noted one at Dufferin Is., Niagara Falls, on Oct. 3, 1937 (Beardslee
& Mitchell, 1965: 303-304). Ussher (1965: 16) had one at Rondeau as late as Oct. 17.
Stirrett (1973d: 22) had his latest at Pelee on Sept. 22.

**MEASUREMENTS:**
*Length:* 5.1 to 5.8 ins.
(Godfrey, 1966: 254)
*Wingspread:* 7.9 to 8.7
ins. (Roberts, 1955: 632)
*Weight:* ♂ 12.5 g.
♀ 11.4 g. (Hope,
1938: 28)

**REFERENCE:**
Hussell, David J.T. 1982
The timing of fall migration
in Yellow-bellied
Flycatchers. Journ. Field
Ornithology, 53:(1): 1-61.
"Immatures migrate about
24 days later than
adults,——"

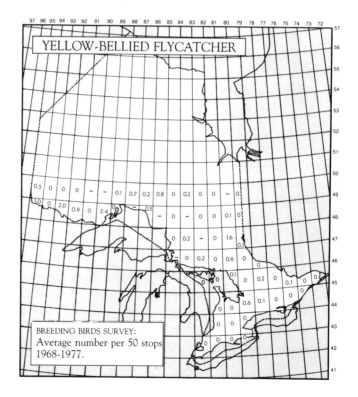

YELLOW-BELLIED FLYCATCHER

BREEDING BIRDS SURVEY:
Average number per 50 stops
1968-1977.

# ACADIAN FLYCATCHER   *Empidonax virescens*   (Vieillot)

This is a bird of the deciduous forests of the United States that just enters Ontario along the shores of Lake Erie and Lake Ontario. They usually build pensile nests in horizontal forks of trees in old forests, well out from the trunk and often quite low (the Pickering Twp. nest could be examined by pulling down the branch holding the nest). They winter in the tropics from Costa Rica south to Ecuador.

IDENTIFICATION: Males are best identified by their explosive "pee-slip" (sounding somewhat like a hungry baby robin). They often utter a wren-like series of twitters when disturbed near the nest. They are a somewhat paler green above and a much paler yellow below than the Yellow-bellied Flycatcher, and lack the yellow throat of that species.

WINTER:

SPRING:    Stirrett (1973b: 20) had a few Pelee records from May 6 to May 24: two were banded there on May 18. Ussher (1965: 16) gave May 21 as the 13-year average arrival date at Rondeau, with the earliest on May 10. A.A. Wood collected one at Coldstream on May 26, 1921 (Saunders & Dale 1933: 210). R.F. Andrle and H.H. Axtell collected one at Thunder Bay, Lake Erie, on May 28, 1959 (Beardslee & Mitchell 1965: 305). G. Bryant and R. Curry heard one at Hamilton on May 28, 1972 (Goodwin, 1972: 757). Ron. Weir heard one singing at Prince Edward Point on May 21, 1978: one was netted there on May 22, 1979 and others on May 23-24, 1980 (Weir & Quilliam 1980: 18).

SUMMER:    One was observed at Pelee from June 17 to July 8, 1951 (Stirrett, 1973c: 18) Baillie & Harrington (1937: 211) reported six nests at Rondeau, with 2 or 3 eggs each, from June 12-14 in 1931 and 1933: and W.E. Saunders collected a female at Renwick, Kent Co. on June 8, 1909, which contained an egg ready for extrusion. Ussher (1965: 16) gave Aug. 19 as his latest date for Rondeau. W.E. Saunders found one near Newbury, Middlesex Co., on June 23, 1930 (Saunders & Dale, 1933: 210). John Frank and I heard one in Springwater Park, Elgin Co., on June 2, 1970. G.A. MacCallum reported a nest with 3 eggs at Dunnville on June 24, 1884 (Baillie & Harrington, 1937: 210). A singing male was found at Abino Bay, Lake Erie, on July 15, 1956: H. Axtell found the nest on July 22: young were first seen being fed on Aug. 6 and on Aug. 17 the young bird left the nest (Beardslee & Mitchell 1965: 305). D. Bucknell noted one at Mud Lake, Oxford Co., on July 13, 1976: A. Wormington *et al* noted one at Millgrove on July 13 and observed a nest at Westover from July 7-31, 1976 (Goodwin, 1976: 950). Paul Eagles found birds on territory at Spottiswood, Waterloo Co. from July 4-16, 1979 (Goodwin, 1979: 859). Gerry Bennett and Dave Fidler heard one singing in King Twp. on June 27, 1971 (Goodwin, 1971: 853). One was found in the Eastbourne Woods, Whitby on June 13, 1959 by J.L. Baillie *et al* and seen there on several later occasions by Naomi LeVay: Edgerton Pegg found a nest on June 2, 1966 in Conc. 5-6, Lot 6-7, Uxbridge Twp.: Margaret McLaren found another nest in Conc. 4, Lot 26, Pickering Twp. on July 8, 1973 which she showed me on July 30 when it held young about 2 days old: after the young had left, the nest (with a cowbird egg embedded in the bottom) was given to the ROM (Speirs, 1975: 7). Gerry Bennett heard one singing on Amherst Is. on July 1, 1976: one was netted at Prince Edward Point on June 1, 1978 and another on June 19, 1979 (Weir & Quilliam, 1980: 18).

AUTUMN: A specimen in the National Museum, Ottawa, was collected by P.A. Taverner at Pelee on Sept. 21, 1906. Goodwin (1981: 178) reported that one was banded at Long Point on Sept. 16, 1980.

**MEASUREMENTS:**
Length: 5.6 to 6.3 ins.
(Godfrey, 1966: 254)
Wingspread:
Weight: ♂ 13.7 g. (Terres, 1980: 382)

# ALDER FLYCATCHER   Empidonax alnorum   Brewster

This is the more northerly of the species formerly known as Traill's Flycatcher now considered two species: its more southerly counterpart is now known as the Willow Flycatcher. Both are birds of the shrubby stage of forest succession and both winter in Central and South America.

IDENTIFICATION: Alder and Willow Flycatchers are not safely distinguished in the field except by their calls. The song of this species is often rendered as "fee-bee-o" though to me it sounds more like "wee-zhee'ah" (the final note only audible at close range so that I usually just hear the "wee-zhee" with the "zhee" somewhat higher pitched than the "wee" and more emphatic. The Willow Flycatcher's song is aptly rendered as "fitz'bew" the "bew" lower pitched and less emphatic than the "fitz". The single scold note of the Alder sounds to me like "pip" while the Willow scolds "fitz". The somewhat similar Least Flycatcher sings "che-bec" and scolds "chick". A third song type which I have called "zhwee-ur" was noted by Snyder (1928: 264) as "be-zee-oo" at Lake Nipigon. This note appears to be given by both species and may be an argument for lumping the two species. On two occasions I have heard the same bird giving both the "fitz-bew" song and the "wee-zhee" song alternately in succession (once in Illinois and once at Pickering in Ontario). In Ontario Co. both nest in alder bogs but Willow Flycatchers seem to prefer hawthorn or apple scrub where available.

WINTER:

SPRING: Long (1966: 32) reported a "wee-bee-o" near Pickering Beach as early as May 7, 1964. Weir & Quilliam (1980: 37) gave May 21 as the 21-year average arrival date at Kingston, with the earliest on May 9. A. Kay called the species abundant at Port Sydney, Muskoka, after May 16, 1888 (Mills, 1981: 91). Nicholson (1981: 132) noted one as early as May 18, 1975 on Manitoulin. Ricker & Clarke (1939: 14) had one on May 14, 1933 at Lake Nipissing. Denis (1961: 4) gave May 29 as the average arrival date at Thunder Bay, with the earliest on May 14, 1939. Baillie & Hope (1943: 13) noted their first at Rossport on May 30, 1936.

SUMMER: On Breeding Bird Surveys this has been a fairly common species from North Bay northward, uncommon to rare south of there, with the greatest abundance in the region from Hornepayne to Longlac. These are usually late migrants so birds heard in early June may be migrants rather than breeding birds. Speirs (1975: 9) mapped records of the various song types in Ontario Co. where they occurred in all 11 townships, but mainly Willows in the south and Alders in the north. On the Mara Twp. quadrat this was the second most common species, with a population density of 48 birds per 100 acres (Speirs & Orenstein, 1975: 11). I noted two at Sundridge on Aug. 20, 1932 and Wm. Mansell reported one at Rebecca Lake on Aug. 31, 1936 (Mills, 1981: 92). Ross James found a nest with 3 eggs at Evansville, Manitoulin, on June 30, 1977 (Nicholson, 1981: 132). Ricker & Clarke (1939: 14) observed a nest with 4 eggs at Lake Nipissing from June 21 to July 2, 1925. Speirs & Speirs (1947: 30) called them very common in alder bogs near North Bay in June and observed one in the Bonfield Bog as late as Aug. 11, 1944. Snyder (1942: 135) observed from one to 10 daily near Sault Ste. Marie in the summer of 1931. Baillie & Hope (1947: 12-13) found a nest with 4 eggs in a hazel bush at Biscotasing on June 25, 1937. Skeel & Bondrup-Nielsen (1978: 184) saw only one at Pukaskwa, on July 6, 1977, but remarked that it was common on the Marathon Breeding Bird Survey route. Baillie & Hope (1943: 13) considered them very common in summer along the northeast shore of Lake Superior. Snyder (1928: 264) noted them frequently at Lake Nipigon, but silent during the first 3 weeks of July, then vocal again. Dear (1940: 132) reported two nests at Fort William: one with 3 eggs on July 1, 1923 and the other with 4 eggs on July 1, 1924. Kendeigh (1947: 34) found this to be the third most common species in a cutover area at Black Sturgeon Lake, but absent from his quadrats in more mature forest. Smith (1957: 175) found them common in alder bogs throughout the Clay Belt and reported a nest found at Timmins by F. Cowell. Snyder (1928: 26) saw adults carrying food to young at Lake Abitibi in 1925 and reported them to be "fairly numerous" there. Bondrup-Nielsen (1976: 43) noted his first near Kapuskasing on June 1, 1975 and on June 8, 1974. Elder (1979: 35) gave June 2 as his earliest record for Geraldton and called it a common summer resident there. Peruniak (1971: 20) gave May 14 as the earliest Atikokan date. Snyder (1938: 195) collected a juvenile male at Rainy River on Aug. 3, 1929. In western Ontario Snyder (1953: 68) found them in alder-willow thickets and in new aspen stands from 5 to 10 ft. high after burns. James (1980: 84) found this species on only one of 12 transects studied in 1977 and 1979 at Pickle Lake. Cringan (1953a: 3) found his first in 1953 at Perrault Falls on June 16. In 1950 this was the most common *Empidonax* flycatcher in the Nikip Lake area with daily totals of 10 noted on several days in the latter half of June (Cringan, 1950: 13). Hope(1938: 28) noted his first at Favourable Lake on June 2, 1938 after which he heard them almost daily in wet alder-willow associations: singing ceased on July 6 and started again after July 28. Manning (1952: 68) noted 15 in 23 hours observing on Sandy Is., near Moosonee, from June 15-29, 1949: he collected a male farther north at the edge of spruce at Raft River on July 10, 1947. Lee (1978: 25-26) saw his first at Big Trout Lake on June 11, 1975: this was a common species in alder and willow thickets there, with a maximum of 7 noted on July 30 and Aug. 3. Schueler, Baldwin & Rising (1974: 143) found them common at Cochrane, Moosonee and Attawapiskat, uncommon at Winisk. C.E. Hope, in 1940, found a nest with one egg at Ft. Severn on July 19 and a nest with 3 eggs on July 22: he noted numbers up to 12 almost daily during his stay there.

AUTUMN: Manning (1952: 68) reported two at Sandy Is., near Moosonee, on Sept. 8, 1950. Nicholson (1981: 132) reported one as late as Oct. 12, 1974, on Manitoulin. Weir & Quilliam (1980: 37) gave Sept. 4 as the 12-year average departure date from Kingston, with the latest on Oct. 8.

**MEASUREMENTS:**
*Length:*
*Wingspread:*
*Weight:* 2 ♂ averaged
13.3 g. ♀ weighed 12.3 g.
(Hope, 1938: 28)

**REFERENCE:**
Stein, Robert Carrington
1958 The behavioral,
ecological and
morphological
characteristics of two
populations of the Alder
Flycatcher, *Empidonax
traillii* (Audubon). N.Y.
State Museum & Science
Service, Bull. 371: 1-63.

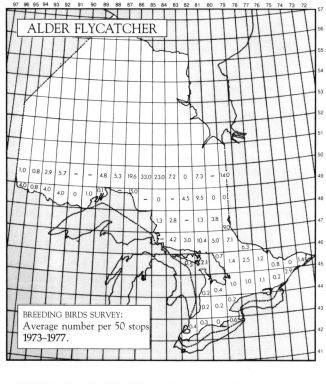

ALDER FLYCATCHER

BREEDING BIRDS SURVEY:
Average number per 50 stops
**1973–1977.**

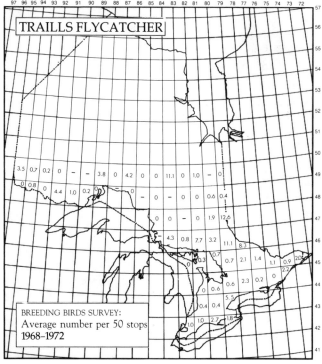

TRAILLS FLYCATCHER

BREEDING BIRDS SURVEY:
Average number per 50 stops
**1968–1972**

# WILLOW FLYCATCHER   *Empidonax traillii*   (Audubon)

Like the Alder Flycatcher, this is a bird of pioneer forests and shrubby vegetation. When the new growth exceeds about 10 ft. in height the Willow Flycatcher lose interest and move to younger growth. They build untidy nests in shrubs or low trees. They are late to arrive in spring and it is usually late May or early June before they are heard: when they stop singing in August they are almost impossible to identify, so only those bird watchers active during the summer months will make their acquaintance.

IDENTIFICATION:   Their "fitz-bew" song is the best means of separating this species from the Alder and Least Flycatchers. See discussion under these species.

WINTER:

SPRING:   Stirrett (1973b: 20) gave May 6 as the earliest Pelee date. Ussher (1965: 17) gave May 22 as the 16-year average arrival date for Rondeau, with the earliest on May 13. Saunders & Dale (1933: 210) gave May 27 as the 14-year average arrival date at London, earliest May 15, 1916. Long (1966: 8) heard a "fitz-bew" at Pickering Beach on May 13, 1964. Weir & Quilliam (1980: 37) gave May 23 as the 8-year average arrival date at Kingston, with the earliest on May 10. Nicholson (1981: 132) noted Willow Flycatchers at Great Duck Is. on May 20, 1977 and May 20, 1979.

SUMMER:   On the Breeding Bird Surveys they were reported mainly in southwestern Ontario, uncommon near the north shore of Lake Erie and rare elsewhere: outliers were reported from Byng Inlet, Ouelette and Atikokan. Stirrett (1973c: 18) reported nesting at Pelee. W.E. Saunders found a nest with 2 young and 1 egg on June 29, 1908 about 10 ins. up in a raspberry bush near London (Saunders & Dale, 1933: 210). McCracken, Bradstreet & Holroyd (1981: 56) noted some in alder and willow thickets near the base of Long Point and found an empty nest there in 1980. Stein (1958: 26) reported both Alder and Willow Flycatchers from Fort Erie west to Dunnville. Speirs (1975: 8, 9) found both Alder and Willow Flycatchers throughout Ontario Co., with Willows more numerous in townships fronting Lake Ontario and Alders more numerous in northern townships (I had 4 records of "fitz'bews" in Rama Twp., one of these near the Muskoka boundary) in the wild orchard quadrat in Pickering Twp. we found a population density of 29 birds per 100 acres. In 1982 Margaret Wilson found an empty nest in a clump of Red-osier Dogwood about 2 ft. above ground: this held 4 eggs on June 29 and July 9, and 4 young on July 14 and July 20. Joanne Dean found a nest low in a dogwood at Prince Edward Point on June 28, 1979: this contained 3 eggs as well as a cowbird egg on July 12 (Weir & Quilliam, 1980: 19). D. Sutherland and E. Van Ingen heard one singing on Beausoleil Is. on June 21, 1976: C. Harris heard both "fitz-bew" and "wee-bee-o" songs from a bog at Go Home Bay and believed that both were given by the same bird: Alex Mills heard birds in the cottage country which "sang a nice compromise between the two" (Mills, 1981: 91).

AUTUMN:   Weir & Quilliam (1980: 37) gave Sept. 2 as the latest Kingston date. Ussher (1965: 17) had a Sept. 29 record for Rondeau. Stirrett (1973d: 22) gave Sept. 10 as the latest Pelee record.

**MEASUREMENTS:**
*Length:*
*Wingspread:*
*Weight:* 13 ♂ averaged
13.1 g., 11 ♀ averaged
13.7 g. (Dunning,
1984: 16)

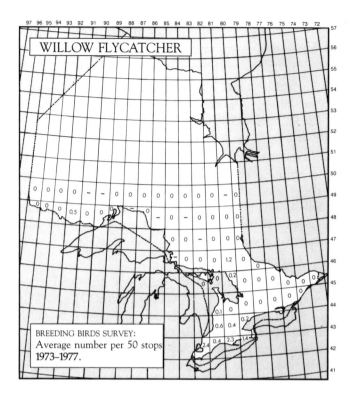

# LEAST FLYCATCHER
*Empidonax minimus*   (Baird and Baird)

The Least Flycatcher is the best known of the *Empidonax* flycatchers in Ontario. It usually appears earlier in spring and later in fall than its congeners. In northern Ontario it is one of the more conspicuous birds in mature aspen stands, usually rare in nearby spruces. It winters from Mexico south to Panama.

IDENTIFICATION:   From the other small flycatchers it is best identified by its "chebec" song: although smaller and less colourful than its congeners, this is not always apparent in the aspen shadows where it is usually found. Habitat is a useful clue: the congeners are usually found in bogs or bushes, while the Least Flycatcher is found in more mature forests. Immatures in fall have broad buffy wing bars while adults have narrow white wing bars and show a good deal of wear to flight feathers (Hussell, 1980: 65).

WINTER:

SPRING:   Stirrett (1973b: 20) noted his earliest at Pelee on Apr. 25 and had his maximum of 50 on May 15. Ussher (1965: 17) gave May 7 as the 21-year average arrival date at Rondeau, with the earliest on Apr. 27. Saunders & Dale (1933: 210) gave May 6 as the 17-year average arrival date at London, their earliest on May 2, 1914. Studies at Long Point in 1966, 1967 and 1968 found that 90% of the spring migrants passed between May 11 and June 1 with the median date on May 18 (Hussell, 1981: 100-101): the earliest was noted on May 2. Speirs (1938: 40, 44) listed Apr. 20 as the earliest Toronto record with the spring peak on May 23, while Saunders (1947: 368) gave May 6 as his 12-year average arrival there. J.M. Richards noted one as early as Apr. 29, 1965 at Oshawa (Tozer & Richards, 1974: 190). J. Satterly found one at Cedar Point, Lake Simcoe, as early as May 1, 1954, but the peak of the spring flight in Ontario Co. is during the third week of May (Speirs, 1975: 10). Weir & Quilliam (1980: 37) listed May 9 as the 31-year average arrival date at Kingston, the earliest on Apr. 27. Devitt (1967: 106) gave May 14 as the 16-year average arrival date at Barrie, with the earliest Simcoe Co. bird at Collingwood on May 1, 1954. Mills (1981: 92) gave May 9 as a 6-year average arrival date at Huntsville, with the earliest on Apr. 26, 1971. Nicholson (1981: 132) reported one on Manitoulin as early as Apr. 26, 1979. Speirs & Speirs (1947: 30) noted one at North Bay on May 13, 1944. Skeel & Bondrup-Nielsen (1978: 184) saw their first at Pukaskwa on May 19, 1977. Denis (1961: 4) gave May 20 as the average arrival date at Thunder Bay, with the earliest on May 14, 1958. Bondrup-Nielsen, (1976: 43) saw his first near Kapuskasing on May 21 in 1975. Elder (1979: 35) listed May 17 as his earliest Geraldton date. Peruniak (1971: 20) gave May 10 as her earliest Atikokan record. One was collected at Moose Factory on May 30, 1860 (Manning, 1952: 68).

SUMMER:   On the 1968-1977 Breeding Bird Surveys, the Least Flycatcher was uncommon in southwestern Ontario, fairly common on most other routes, becoming common on some routes north and east of Georgian Bay and Lake Superior and most numerous near Lake of the Woods. Stirrett (1973c: 18) listed this as a nesting species at Pelee and noted a maximum of 100 returning birds on Aug. 12. Ussher (1965: 17) called this a summer resident in the woods at Rondeau. Saunders & Dale (1933: 210) had only one nest record for London, on June 19, 1902 when a set of 4 eggs was taken. Snyder (1931: 191) collected a female at Long Point on July 16, 1927 which had been uttering the "chebec" note! At Long Point, 90% of southbound adults occurred between July 11 and Aug. 13, with a median date of July 22, whereas the corresponding dates for immatures were Aug. 17 to Sept. 13 with the median on Aug. 29, some 38 days later than for the adults (Hussell, 1981: 105). Beardslee & Mitchell (1965: 307) mentioned migrants at Morgan's Point, Lake Erie on Aug. 6, 1944. Snyder (1930: 192) found a nest with 4 eggs 15 ft. up in the crotch of an alder in King Twp. on June 9, 1926. J.A. Edwards found five nests with eggs on Thorah Is., Lake Simcoe, one as early as June 7, 1935 and one as late as July 5, 1927 (Speirs, 1975: 10). Devitt (1967: 105) reported several Simcoe Co. nests, one with 4 eggs at Barrie as early as June 3, 1915. Lloyd (1923: 155) called this a common breeding summer resident at Ottawa. Mills (1981: 93) reported that 24 nest record cards were on file at ROM for Muskoka and 10 for Parry Sound, with nests under construction as early as May 18 and as late as July 5: one held 3 eggs as late as July 23. D.B. Ferguson found a nest with 4 eggs at Windfall Lake, Manitoulin, on June 25, 1980 (Nicholson, 1981: 132). Ricker & Clarke (1939: 14) observed nest building at Frank's Bay, Lake Nipissing, on June 14, 1933. Fred A.E. Starr found a newly completed nest 10 miles south of Cartier on June 7, 1936 and young just out of the nest were seen on and after July 13, 1937 by Baillie & Hope (1941: 13). At Pukaskwa this was "by far the most common flycatcher and ranked 8 in relative abundance" of all species on their summer censuses there (Skeel & Bondrup-Nielsen, 1978: 184). Baillie & Hope (1943: 14) found 7 nests in dead trees after recent burns near Marathon on June 18 and 21, 1936: also a nest with 3 eggs at Amyot about 4 ft. up in a small white birch. Snyder (1928: 265) found a freshly completed nest at Lake Nipigon on June 9, 1924: it contained 2 eggs on June 16 and 4 on June 22 and was 20 ft. up in a white birch. Dear (1940: 132) found a nest with 4 eggs on June 25, 1924 at Port Arthur and a nest with 3 eggs on June 26, 1927 in Paipoonge Twp., Thunder Bay. Snyder (1938: 195) called this the commonest flycatcher in the Rainy River region and noted nest building on June 4, 1929. In our aspen forest quadrat at Lake of the Woods Provincial Park, this was the most abundant species, with 19 territories on the 25 acre plot (Price & Speirs, 1971: 977). In a 25-acre quadrat with tall aspens and birches among mature balsam fir and spruces, Kendeigh (1947: 12, 26) found a population of 5 pairs of Least Flycatchers: in 3 other plots with few or no aspens he had few or no Leasts. Snyder (1928: 26) found a nest with 2 eggs and 2 newly hatched young at Lake Abitibi on July 25, 1925. Snyder (1953: 68) found this to be the most common flycatcher in western Ontario from Kenora east to Dinorwic and north to Minaki: two nests with eggs at Kenora on June 12, 1930 were only 30 ft. apart. James (1980: 87) found a nest with 4 eggs at Pickle Lake on June 12, 1977. Cringan (1953b: 3) found one at Kasabonika Lake on June 1, 1953 and 4 there on June 3. He found them fairly common at Nikip Lake (Cringan, 1950: 13). Hope (1938: 28-29) collected a nest with 4 eggs on June 18, 1938 at Favourable Lake: he found many of their nests there during the latter half of June. Sam Waller found a nest at Moose Factory on June 18, 1930 and one female was collected at Big Piskwanish on June 10, 1947 (Manning, 1952: 69). Schueler, Baldwin & Rising (1974: 143) reported them as common at Cochrane, Moosonee and Attawa- piskat. Least Flycatchers were frequently seen carrying food at Big Trout Lake, where a maximum of 6 was noted on June 11, 1975: they were usually noted in spruce-aspen stands and were the commonest *Empidonax* there (Lee, 1978: 26). McLaren & McLaren (1981: 4) observed them north to the Manitoba border (at about 54°40'N). C.E. Hope noted only one at Ft. Severn during the summer of 1940, on July 19.

AUTUMN: Nicholson (1981: 132) recorded one on Manitoulin as late as Sept. 28, 1978. Frances Westman found two dead under the Barrie TV tower on Sept. 25, 1960 (Devitt, 1967: 105). Weir & Quilliam (1980: 37) gave Sept. 21 as the 21-year average departure date from Kingston, with the latest on Oct. 13. Audrey Russ found one as late as Oct. 21, 1966 at Ajax (Speirs, 1975: 10). Saunders (1947: 368) gave Sept. 20 as his 13-year average departure date from Toronto, and J.L. Baillie had his latest on Oct. 8. Ussher (1965: 17) gave Sept. 4 as the 7-year average departure date from Rondeau, with the latest on Oct. 10. Stirrett (1973d: 22) had two at Pelee as late as Oct. 25.

**MEASUREMENTS:**
*Length:* 5 to 5.5 ins.
(Godfrey, 1966: 256)
*Wingspread:* 7 3/4 to
8 1/2 ins. (Roberts,
1955: 634)
*Weight:* 2 ♂ averaged
10 g. (Hope, 1938: 29)

**REFERENCES:**
Hussell, D.J.T.; T. Davis
and R.D. Montgomerie
1967 Differential fall
migration of adult and
immature Least
Flycatchers. Bird-Banding,
38: (1): 61-66.
   Hussell, David J.T. 1980
The timing of fall migration
and molt in Least
Flycatchers. Journ. Field
Ornithology, 51:(1): 65-71.
   Hussell, David J.T.,
1981 Migration of the
Least Flycatcher in
southern Ontario. Journ.
Field Ornithology, 52: (2):
97-111.

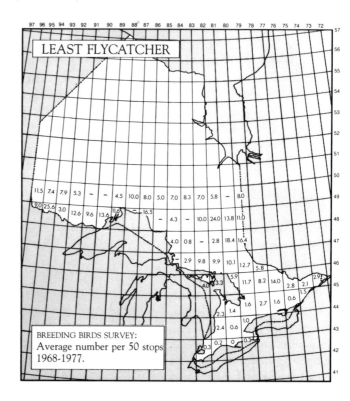

LEAST FLYCATCHER

BREEDING BIRDS SURVEY:
Average number per 50 stops
1968-1977.

# GRAY FLYCATCHER   *Empidonax wrightii*   Baird

One of the rewards of bird banding is the possibility of finding the unexpected. The first Gray Flycatcher for Canada turned up in the course of routine banding at the Toronto Bird Observatory's station on Mugg's Island, Toronto. It is normally a bird of the dry country from southern Idaho south to Arizona, wintering south to Mexico.

**IDENTIFICATION:** The back is gray with no brown or olive tint and the base of the lower mandible is flesh coloured. It is about the size of a Least Flycatcher and like that species has a conspicuous eye ring and wing bars. The outer web of the outer tail feathers as seen from above is definitely whitish and the tail is longer than that of a Least Flycatcher unless badly worn (Phillips & Lanyon, 1970: 196). The bill is long, straight-sided with the lower mandible pinkish with a dark tip.

**WINTER:**

**SPRING:**

**SUMMER:**

**AUTUMN:** David Broughton netted one at Mugg's Is., Toronto, on Sept. 11, 1981. His identification was confirmed by Ross James who made measurements, took photographs and preserved one of the diagnostic outer tail feathers in the ROM (James, 1982: 16).

**MEASUREMENTS:**
*Length:* 5 1/2 ins. (Terres, 1980: 384)
Wingspread:
*Weight:* 16 averaged 12.5 g. (Dunning, 1984: 16)

# EASTERN PHOEBE   *Sayornis phoebe*   (Latham)

The phoebe is the flycatcher most at home near human habitations, building its mossy nests under bridges and around summer cottages and outbuildings. Once quite common it has been undergoing a period of decline, perhaps brought on by a series of hard winters and late frosts in the 1950's and the advent of DDT in the 1960's. It is usually the first flycatcher to appear in spring and the last to leave in fall and it winters farther north than other flycatchers.

**IDENTIFICATION:** This is a medium-sized flycatcher, rather a dull gray bird, best identified by its call, when it asks "Phoebe??" and answers in the affirmative "Phoebe!" It has a diagnostic habit of wagging its tail as if stirring porridge with it, not just up and down or from side to side as do other birds.

**WINTER:** Individuals were noted on the 1968-1977 Christmas counts at Pelee, Long Point & Meaford. J.P. Kleiman saw one at Pelee on Dec. 24, 1972 (Goodwin, 1973: 610) and A.H. Kelley reported one there from Dec. 24 to February (Goodwin, 1975: 686). Ussher (1965: 16) had one linger at Rondeau until Dec. 4. T.D. Hayman and T. Patterson found one at Hyde Park, London, from Feb. 5 on (Goodwin, 1979: 278). R. Bateman *et al* saw one at Long Point on Dec. 19, 1971 (Goodwin, 1972: 599). J. ten Brugenkatte found one at Toronto Zoo on Dec. 22, 1974 (Goodwin, 1975: 686).

SPRING: Stirrett (1973b: 20) saw his earliest at Pelee on March 26 and his maximum count of 60 on Apr. 15. Ussher (1965: 16) had his earliest Rondeau record on March 21 and his 19-year average arrival date was Apr. 5. Saunders & Dale (1933: 209) gave March 24 as the 17-year average arrival date at London, with the earliest on March 12, 1923: one set of 5 eggs was noted as early as Apr. 29, 1915: a set of 6 on May 5, 1909; another set of 5 on May 10, 1901 and one with 4 eggs on May 24, 1902. Speirs (1938: 40, 44) gave March 17 as the earliest Toronto date, with the migration peak on Apr. 9: Saunders (1947: 368) listed Apr. 3 as his 13-year average arrival date there. Naomi LeVay had one at Cranberry Marsh, Whitby, as early as March 8, 1967 but the peak of the migration is mid-April: Ross James noted nest building in Pickering Twp. as early as Apr. 1, 1967: the nest contained one egg on Apr. 23 (Speirs, 1975: 5). Allin (1940: 101) reported nesting under overhanging banks in Darlington: one nest with 4 eggs on May 8, 1926. Quilliam (1973: 121) listed March 6, 1922 as the earliest Kingston date and March 29 as the 21-year average arrival date: a nest with 5 eggs was found on May 8, 1897; one with 6 eggs on May 19, 1897 and another with 5 eggs and 3 cowbird eggs on May 21, 1961. Devitt (1967: 104) gave Apr. 1 as the 18-year average arrival date at Barrie and one seen by T.J. Henderson on March 2, 1964 at Midland as the earliest in Simcoe Co: H.P. Bingham found a nest with 6 eggs as early as May 7, 1938 at Barrie. Lloyd (1923: 155) mentioned eggs found at Ottawa on May 14 and large young on May 24, 1921. L. Beamer's median arrival date at Meaford was Apr. 3, with the earliest on March 22, 1938. Mills (1981: 89) gave Apr. 8 as the 13-year average arrival date at Huntsville, with the earliest there on March 29, 1962 but he saw two at Magnetawan as early as March 24, 1979: nest building was noted as early as Apr. 21, 1972 at Go Home Bay and a full clutch of 5 eggs as early as May 4. Nicholson (1981: 130) gave Apr. 7 as the 12-year average arrival date on Manitoulin; the earliest on March 23, 1969. MacLulich (1938: 21) reported arrivals in Algonquin Park on Apr. 15 in both 1912 and 1913. Speirs & Speirs (1947: 30) saw one at North Bay on March 30, 1945 and observed nest building on Apr. 28, 1944. Denis (1961: 3) gave Apr. 27 as the average arrival date at Thunder Bay, with the earliest on Apr. 16, 1959. Dear (1940: 132) reported a nest with 5 eggs on May 21, 1911 in Neebing Twp., Thunder Bay. Smith (1957: 175) found phoebes rare in the Clay Belt: on May 27, 1954 he saw one on the NW side of Lake Timiskaming. Peruniak (1971: 20) gave Apr. 20 as her earliest Atikokan record. Cringan (1953a: 3) saw his first at Sioux Lookout on Apr. 27 in 1953.

SUMMER: On the 1968-1977 Breeding Bird Surveys they were present but uncommon to rare at all stations south of North Bay and Thessalon, and again at all stations NW of Lake Superior, but absent from most routes NE of Lake Superior, most numerous at stations just north of Lake Ontario and at Dryden. A few remained and nested at Pelee (Stirrett, 1973c: 17). Saunders & Dale (1933: 209) noted a set of 5 eggs (incubated about 3 days) on June 7, 1902, near London. F. Starr found a nest with 5 eggs on June 11, 1924 at Port Burwell (Baillie & Harrington, 1937: 209). Barry MacKay found a nest with 3 young in Thorah Twp. on June 2, 1967: this contained 5 eggs on July 7 and 4 young again on

July 26 (phoebes frequently have such second broods): some phoebes occurred on all but the three most populous urban quadrats studied in Ontario Co., with a maximum population of 8 per 100 acres in Atherley and Washago: of 47 sets of eggs reported in Ontario Co., 3 were parasitized by Brown-headed Cowbirds (Speirs, 1975: 5). Tozer & Richards (1974: 187) saw an adult with fledged young in Scugog Twp. as late as Aug. 16, 1963. Allin (1940: 101) found a nest with 2 young under an overhanging bank in Darlington Twp. on June 8, 1933. Second broods often hatch in late July, e.g. 4 young hatched on July 22, 1939 at Wasaga Beach (Devitt, 1967: 104). A total of 119 nest record cards had been turned in from the cottage country: young in the nest were noted as late as July 30 (Mills, 1981: 90). D.B. Ferguson found a nest with 4 eggs at Manitou River, Manitoulin, on June 19, 1977 (Nicholson, 1981: 130). Ricker & Clarke (1939: 14) reported a nest with 5 eggs at Frank's Bay, Lake Nipissing, on May 25, 1933. Harry Graham found a nest with 4 eggs at Sault Ste. Marie on June 1, 1937: nests with young were noted at Laird on June 15, 1931 and at Echo Lake on July 15, 1931 (Snyder, 1942: 134). Baillie & Hope (1947: 12) found a nest with 4 eggs on June 12, 1937 at Bigwood; this held 4 young on June 14: on June 9, 1937 they found a newly built nest in an abandoned shack about 40 miles south of Chapleau. Skeel & Bondrup-Nielsen (1978: 183) found phoebes rare at Pukaskwa, but noted single birds there on June 3, 1973 and Aug. 10, 1976. Baillie & Hope (1943: 131) also found them rare along the NE shore of Lake Superior: they collected a male at Rossport on June 3 and one at Amyot on June 30, 1936 and found an old nest at Amyot. Snyder (1928: 264) found nests with young at Macdiarmid, Lake Nipigon, on July 7 and July 12, 1924: none elsewhere in the region. Dear (1940: 132) found a nest with 5 eggs in O'Connor Twp., Thunder Bay, on June 5, 1927. Snyder (1938: 194) found an unusual nest below ground level in a root cellar at Emo on June 12, 1929. Snyder (1928: 25) collected a male at Lowbush, Lake Abitibi, on June 14 and a female there on July 16, 1925. Elder (1979: 35) had just two summer records for Geraldton. Snyder (1953: 67) reported breeding evidence for Wabigoon, Savanne, Shoal Lake, Black Sturgeon River, Indian Bay as well as a nest on a rock cliff at Chadwick Lake on Aug. 5, 1949: a female secured a new mate within 24 hours when her mate was collected at Ingolf on June 8, 1937. Hope (1938: 27) collected a female and her nest with 5 eggs at Favourable Lake on June 2, 1938: on June 13 the surviving male had secured another mate: this female was collected on June 20 but her nest with 3 eggs was not disturbed: by June 25 a third female had arrived and raised a brood of 4 young which left the nest on Aug. 5. Cringan (1950: 12) heard one at Round Lake on June 15, 1950.

AUTUMN: Peruniak (1971: 20) gave Sept. 5 as her latest Atikokan date. Smith (1957: 175) saw one south of Matheson on Sept. 3, 1953. Nicholson (1981: 130) gave Oct. 26, 1975 as the latest Manitoulin record. Mills (1981: 90) saw one at Magnetawan as late as Oct. 14, 1979. Devitt (1967: 104) cited a record late bird seen by Frances Westman at Barrie on Nov. 3, 1959. Weir & Quilliam (1980: 37) listed Oct. 21 as the 29-year average departure date from Kingston, with the latest on Nov. 12, 1972. Snyder (1941: 66) reported one in Prince Edward Co. on Oct. 20, 1934. The peak of the fall migration in Ontario Co. has been in the last week of September and my latest record was at the Jim Baillie Reserve in Scott Twp. on Oct. 31, 1970 (Speirs, 1975: 5). Saunders (1947: 368) listed Oct. 9 as his 13-year average departure date from Toronto: Speirs (1938: 52, 54) gave Oct. 2 as the peak of the fall migration there, with the latest on Nov. 3. Saunders (1930: 510) reported one killed at the Long Point light on Sept. 7, 1929. Ussher (1965: 16) gave Oct. 21 as the 14-year average departure date from Rondeau.

508

Stirrett (1973a: 17 and 1973d: 22) had one at Pelee as late as Nov. 26 and a maximum count of 200 on Sept. 27.

**MEASUREMENTS:**
*Length:* 6.3 to 7.2 ins.
(Godfrey, 1966: 251)
*Wingspread:* 10.52 to
11.25 ins. (Roberts,
1955: 635)
*Weight:* 2 ♀ averaged
19.7 g. (Hope, 1938: 28)

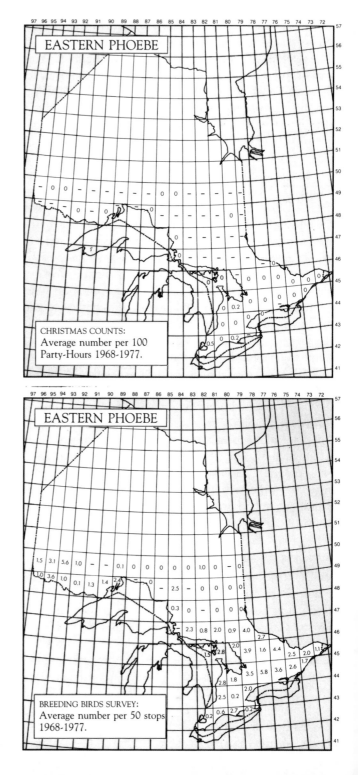

EASTERN PHOEBE

CHRISTMAS COUNTS:
Average number per 100
Party-Hours 1968-1977.

EASTERN PHOEBE

BREEDING BIRDS SURVEY:
Average number per 50 stops
1968-1977.

# SAY'S PHOEBE   *Sayornis saya*   (Bonaparte)

Say's Phoebe is a bird of the dry country in the rain shadow of the western mountains, from Alaska south to Mexico, accidental in Ontario.

**IDENTIFICATION:**   Say's Phoebe acts somewhat like our Eastern Phoebe, but is slightly larger and with warm colours befitting its chosen habitat. The cinnamon belly and undertail coverts are diagnostic.

**WINTER:**   One lived at Harry Clemens' orchard, near Nairn, Middlesex Co., through the winter of 1961-62 after being first noted there on Dec. 11, 1961: cluster flies were provided for it daily and it thrived, much to the edification of visiting bird watchers and photographers. H.G. Pickard identified one that stayed at Haileybury into December, 1948 (Baillie, 1964: 5).

**SPRING:**   The bird at Nairn was photographed as late as Apr. 15, 1962 by Donald Gunn (Baillie, 1964: 5). Nicholson (1981: 131) observed one near the lighthouse on Great Duck Island on May 11, 1979.

**SUMMER:**

**AUTUMN:**   The bird at Nairn was first noted on Oct. 2, 1961 (Baillie, 1964: 5). Laura Howe reported one at Dryden on Sept. 30, 1970 (James, McLaren & Barlow, 1976: 34).

**MEASUREMENTS:**
*Length:* 7 to 8 ins.
(Godfrey, 1966: 253)
Wingspread:
*Weight:* 8 averaged
21.2 g. (Dunning,
1984: 16)

# VERMILION FLYCATCHER
*Pyrocephalus rubinus*   (Boddaert)

This fiery-clad little flycatcher is usually found from southewestern United States south to South America. It was accidental in Ontario.

**IDENTIFICATION:** Except for a black patch through the eye and ear coverts the plumage of the male resembles that of a male Scarlet Tanager, but on a much smaller scale (it is not much bigger than our *Empidonax* flycatchers). The female is mostly brownish gray but has a salmon-coloured belly.

**WINTER:**

**SPRING:**

**SUMMER:**   Betty and John Broome reported an adult male in Brougham Twp., Renfrew Co., on July 25, 1972 (Goodwin, 1974: 10).

**AUTUMN:**   I well remember the excitement when Tom Swift announced his discovery of this bird in High Park, Toronto, on Oct. 29, 1949, during a southwesterly blow of warm air from the American southwest. Cliff Hope collected the bird on Nov. 1 after it had been observed by several bird watchers (Baillie, 1957: 1-2).

**MEASUREMENTS:**
*Length:* 5.5 to 6.5 ins.
(Godfrey, 1966: 262)
*Wingspread:* 263 mm.
(10 1/3 ins.) The Hope
specimen.
*Weight:* 20 g. (The Hope
specimen in ROM).

# ASH-THROATED FLYCATCHER
*Myiarchus cinerascens* (Lawrence)

This is a western United States and Mexican counterpart of our Great Crested Flycatcher, accidental in Ontario.

IDENTIFICATION: The Ash-throated Flycatcher looks like a 'washed out' version of a Great Crested Flycatcher, with very pale underparts, lacking the contrast between the gray throat and yellow belly of the Great Crested. Young birds of the Great Crested are paler below than adults but should have acquired adult plumage by September.

WINTER:

SPRING:

SUMMER:

AUTUMN: Wilfred Botham discovered one at Pelee on Nov. 24-25, 1962. Two other late fall birds showed up in 1982, the first at Cranberry Marsh, Whitby, on Oct. 29, observed and photographed by Jim Mountjoy and R.D. McRae, and the second observed at Prince Edward Point by M. Brown, R. Rogers, G. Vance and R.D. Weir (Weir, 1983: 176).

**MEASUREMENTS:**
*Length:* 8.0 to 8.5 ins.
(Godfrey, 1966: 251)
Wingspread:
*Weight:* 28.5 g. (Terres, 1980: 383)

# GREAT CRESTED FLYCATCHER
*Myiarchus crinitus* (Linnaeus)

This is a familiar resident of southern Ontario woodlots. It nests in old woodpecker holes, natural cavities in trees, in suitable nest boxes, even occasionally in rural mail boxes. It winters from southern United States to northern South America.

IDENTIFICATION: This is the largest of our common flycatchers, known by its rufous tail, and yellow belly contrasting with the gray upper breast. You are usually alerted to its presence by its loud "soo-weep" call.

WINTER: Stirrett (1973a: 17) reported one at Pelee on Dec. 25.

SPRING: Stirrett (1973b: 19) gave Apr. 23 as his earliest Pelee date, with his maximum count of 25 on May 14. The 21-year average arrival date at Rondeau was May 5, the earliest on Apr. 24 (Ussher, 1965: 16). Saunders & Dale (1933: 209) gave May 6 as the 17-year average arrival date at London, with the earliest on Apr. 29, 1915, they reported a set of 5 eggs on May 30, 1914. Speirs (1938: 40, 44) gave Apr. 29 as the earliest Toronto date, with the peak on May 27, while Saunders (1947: 368) listed May

8 as his 13-year average arrival date there. C. Christy saw one at Oshawa as early as Apr. 30, 1964: the spring peak at Pickering has been about May 21 (Speirs, 1975: 4). Weir & Quilliam (1980: 37) listed Apr. 28 as the earliest Kingston date, with May 7 as the 32-year average arrival date. Quilliam (1973: 121) mentioned two nests near Kingston: one with 4 eggs on May 30, 1898 and one with 5 eggs on May 30, 1970. Devitt (1967: 103-104) gave May 7 as the 17-year average arrival date at Barrie and H.P. Bingham collected a set of 6 eggs on May 30, 1936. L. Beamer's median arrival date at Meaford was on May 13. Mills (1981: 88) gave May 13 as the 7-year average arrival date at Huntsville, the earliest on May 9. Nicholson (1981: 130) found May 15 to be the 12-year average arrival date on Manitoulin with the earliest on May 9, 1979. Speirs & Speirs (1947: 30) noted two near North Bay on May 26, 1944.

SUMMER: On the 1968-1977 Breeding Bird Surveys this was a fairly common species just north of Lake Ontario, uncommon elsewhere in southern Ontario, rare north to North Bay and Thessalon, with a few south and west of Dryden and Atikokan; none on routes north and east of Lake Superior. Stirrett (1973c: 17 and 1973d: 22) had a June maximum of 10 at Pelee and a premigratory maximum of 20 on Aug. 21. Saunders & Dale (1933: 209) reported a set of 5 eggs near London on June 17, 1901. Fleming (1907: 76) gave June 22, 1892 as a breeding date for Toronto. I saw young at the entrance to a nest box at our Pickering home as late as July 15, 1973 (Speirs, 1975: 4). Tozer & Richards (1974: 185) listed a nest with 6 eggs as early as June 5,1970 in Scugog, while Chas. Christy found a nest with 4 eggs near Oshawa as late as June 25, 1956. The maximum density in our Ontario Co. forest quadrats was 26 birds per 100 acres in the Scugog forest, a mature, mainly deciduous plot (Speirs & Orenstein, 1975). Allin (1940: 101) found a nest with 4 young and two eggs on June 22, 1927 in Darlington Twp. E. Beaupré and C.J. Young found a nest with 5 small young on June 18, 1898 on Simcoe Is., near Kingston (Baillie & Harrington, 1937: 209). Paul Harrington collected a set of 4 eggs at Wasaga Beach as late as July 8, 1922 (Devitt, 1967: 103). Lloyd (1923: 155) cited two nest records for the Ottawa region: one on June 12, 1909 and another with 6 eggs on June 11, 1908. L. Beamer mentioned a nest with one egg at Meaford on June 1, 1941. Mills (1981: 89) reported 9 Muskoka and 7 Parry Sound nests, one in a Purple Martin house and one in a Wood Duck nest box: nest heights from 5 to 50 ft. up; young from June 21 to July 20: and the latest cottage country date on Aug. 29, 1904. D.B. Ferguson found a nest with 5 eggs near Mindemoya, Manitoulin, on June 2, 1977 (Nicholson, 1981: 130). Snyder (1942: 134) considered it rare near Sault Ste. Marie but collected a female on June 13, 1931 at Laird and reported an adult feeding young near Maclennan on July 16, 1939, seen by Harry Graham. Denis (1961: 6) called it a very rare summer resident at Thunder Bay. Smith (1957: 175) heard one at Dawson Point, Lake Timiskaming, on July 4, 1953 and mentioned one seen by A.N. Boissonneau at Cochrane on June 9, 1951. Peruniak (1971) had no Atikokan record but David Elder noted one there on May 25, 1981. J.L. Baillie observed two family groups near Rainy River on Aug. 5, 1929 (Snyder, 1938: 194). Snyder (1953: 67) observed one at Ingolf on June 4 and 5, 1937; another at Shoal Lake Narrows on June 17, 1947 and one during the summer of 1948 at Miles Bay, Lake of the Woods.

AUTUMN: Speirs & Speirs (1947: 30) noted one at North Bay on Sept. 3, 1944. Nicholson (1981: 130) reported a very late bird on Manitoulin, on Oct. 18, 1969. One seen at Holland River on Sept. 15, 1940 was the latest Simcoe Co. record (Devitt, 1967: 104). Weir & Quilliam (1980: 37) gave Sept. 17 as the 21-year average departure date from Kingston, the latest on Sept. 28, 1969. Long (1968b: 19) reported his latest at Pickering Beach on Sept. 25, 1963. Saunders (1947: 368) listed Sept. 15 as his 10-year average departure date from Toronto, while Speirs (1938: 54) gave Oct. 9 as the latest Toronto record. Beardslee & Mitchell (1965: 301-302) cited a Sept. 29, 1958 record by A. Smith in the Jordan Valley. Ussher (1965: 16) gave Sept. 6 as the 8-year average departure date from Rondeau, with the latest on Sept. 15. Stirrett (1973d: 22) gave Oct. 2 as his latest Pelee record.

**MEASUREMENTS:**

*Length:* 8.0 to 9.2 ins.
(Godfrey, 1966: 250)
*Wingspread:* 12.8 to 14.0
ins. (Roberts, 1955: 632)
*Weight:* 28.0 to 42.5 g.
(Terres, 1980: 385)

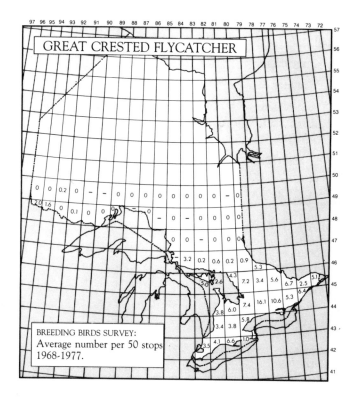

GREAT CRESTED FLYCATCHER

BREEDING BIRDS SURVEY:
Average number per 50 stops
1968-1977.

# CASSIN'S KINGBIRD   *Tyrannus vociferans*   Swainson

This is usually a summer resident of intermontane southwestern United States, accidental in Ontario.

**IDENTIFICATION:** Cassin's Kingbird is similar to the Western Kingbird but has a paler yellow belly and lacks the white outer tail feathers of that species, having an inconspicuous white tip to the tail instead. As its name suggests it is a noisy bird, with a lower pitched voice than the Western Kingbird which has a rather squeaky, grackle-like call.

**WINTER:**

**SPRING:**

**SUMMER:**   One was found by Alan Gordon at Achray in Algonquin Park on June 4, 1953 and collected the following day and sent to the ROM (No. 81283) (Snyder, 1954: 209).

**AUTUMN:**   One was reported at Pelee by Jack Sherrin, M. and R. McCleary on Sept. 16, 1963 (Woodford, 1964: 29). D. Brunton *et al* observed one at Ottawa from Sept. 19 to Oct. 8, 1970 (Goodwin, 1971: 573).

**MEASUREMENTS:**
*Length:* 8 3/4 to 9 ins.
(Godfrey, 1966: 250)
Wingspread:
*Weight:* 14 averaged
45.6 g. (Dunning,
1984: 17)

**REFERENCE:**
Snyder, L.L. 1954 Cassin's
Kingbird in Canada. Auk.
71:(2):209.

# WESTERN KINGBIRD   *Tyrannus verticalis*   Say

This is essentially a prairie bird, very rare in Ontario. Like the Eastern Kingbird it is a bird of open country, with some trees in which to build and wires from which it sallies forth to snap up passing insects.

**IDENTIFICATION:**   In this kingbird, the black tail has narrow white sides not a prominent white tip as in the Eastern Kingbird. The belly is yellow and the head and upper breast are gray (resembling the Great Crested Flycatcher in these respects but the rufous tail of that species is very different from the black tail bordered with white as in this species).

**WINTER:**

**SPRING:**   Stirrett (1973b: 19) reported single birds at Pelee on May 16, 1960; May

19 to 23, 1956 and May 20, 1967. John MacArthur *et al* found a pair at Cedar Springs, Kent Co. in May, 1942 (MacFayden 1945: 67). Speirs (1938: 40) listed a May 25 record for Toronto. Nicholson (1981: 129) had Manitoulin records on May 30, 1971; May 22, 1975 and May 17, 1980.

SUMMER: Stirrett (1973: 19) reported four at Pelee on June 1, 1937. On June 26, 1943, James Egan and Cliff MacFayden found a nest with 3 eggs about 15 ft. up in an apple tree at Port Alma, Kent Co. (MacFayden, 1945: 67). On June 23, 1937 I watched one at Van Wagner's Beach, Burlington, which George North had seen on several previous days: we noted the yellow belly, gray head, and black tail showing white edges when spread in flight. Speirs (1975: 2) reported four spring sightings in Ontario Co.: one seen at Ajax on June 3, 1961 by Gerry Bennett and Ron Scovell; one at Eastbourne, Whitby, on June 6, 1970 by Naomi LeVay: three there on July 16, 1968 and another there seen by Alan Telfer on July 31, 1960. One was found with a large concentration of Eastern Kingbirds at Prince Edward Point on Aug. 31, 1969 and watched by Fred Cooke, R.B. Stewart, A.E. Hughes and Helen Quilliam (Quilliam, 1973: 120). Mills (1981: 88) watched one for more than an hour at Emsdale on Aug. 6, 1980. Nicholson (1981: 129) reported one seen by Fred Cooke at Poplar, Manitoulin, on Aug. 29, 1972. Peruniak (1971: 19) cited a June 14, 1968 record for Atikokan. Snyder (1953: 67) collected the first Ontario specimen at Ingolf on June 4, 1937.

AUTUMN: Nicholson (1981: 129) reported Manitoulin sightings on Sept. 7, 1971; Sept. 13 and 15-16, 1975, and Sept. 21, 1979. J.L. Baillie and R.M. Saunders found one at Duffin Creek, Pickering, on Sept. 15, 1957; Elizabeth Forster spotted one near Pickering on Sept. 16, 1959 and showed it to us; perhaps the same bird was seen four days earlier by Naomi LeVay at Cranberry Marsh; the latest fall record in Ontario Co. was by Naomi LeVay at Cranberry Marsh on Sept. 27, 1960 (Speirs, 1975: 2). George A. Scott saw one near Oshawa's Second Marsh on Sept. 4, 1961 (Tozer & Richards, 1974: 184). Beardslee & Mitchell (1965: 301) reported one seen by the Axtells near Stromness on Sept. 3, 1956 and another by Brownstein, Salisbury *et al* on Sept. 11, 1960 on Niece Rd., Sherbrook Twp., Haldimand Co. E.M.S. Dale (1941: 4) reported one a mile east of Port Stanley as late as Oct. 1, 1939. Kelley (1978: 49) noted single birds at Big Creek on Sept. 15, 1957 and at Holiday Beach on Sept. 13, 1964. Stirrett (1973d: 22) had records of individuals at Pelee on Sept. 2, 1961 and Sept. 11, 1958.

**MEASUREMENTS:**
*Length:* 8.0 to 9.3 ins.
(Godfrey, 1966: 249)
*Wingspread:* 15.2 to 16.5
ins. (Roberts, 1955: 633)
*Weight:* 1.43 to 2 oz.
(Roberts, 1955: 633)
♂ larger than ♀.

**REFERENCE:**
MacFayden, Clifford J.
1945 Breeding of *Tyrannus
verticalis* in Ontario.
Can. Field-Nat.,
59:(2): 67.

# EASTERN KINGBIRD   *Tyrannus tyrannus*   (Linnaeus)

The Eastern Kingbird is a familiar roadside bird in Ontario during the warmer months. It frequently builds its nest out in the open and does not hesitate to attack any interloper, even much larger birds: hence its name.

IDENTIFICATION: This is a medium-sized flycatcher, smaller than a robin and larger than a House Sparrow. The white underparts, black upperparts and white tip to the tail are its distinguishing characteristics. It often perches on roadside wires or dead twigs and sallies forth to snap up a passing insect, returning again to its original perch. It utters a defiant "dickle-dickle-dickle" when defending its nest.

WINTER:

SPRING:   Stirrett (1973b: 19) noted 30 at Pelee as early as Apr. 16: his maximum spring count was 70 on May 22. Ussher (1965: 16) had his earliest arrival at Rondeau on May 3, with the 25-year average arrival date on May 6. Saunders & Dale (1933: 209) also gave May 6 as the 17-year average arrival date at London, with the earliest on Apr. 27, 1914. Snyder (1931: 188) saw the first at Long Point on May 6, 1928. Speirs (1938: 40-44) gave May 1 as the earliest Toronto date, with the spring peak on June 1, while Saunders (1947: 368) listed May 11 as his 13-year average arrival date there. Naomi LeVay saw one at Whitby as early as May 1, 1958 and J.M. Richards found a nest about 3/4 finished on May 23, 1970 north of Oshawa (Speirs, 1975: 1). Weir & Quilliam (1980: 37) listed May 3 as the 32-year average arrival date at Kingston, with the earliest on Apr. 14. Devitt (1967: 103) gave May 10 as the 19-year average arrival date at Barrie; the earliest on May 2, 1964. L. Beamer's median arrival date at Meaford was May 13: his earliest on May 1, 1942. Mills (1981: 87) gave May 11 as the 7-year average arrival date at Huntsville with the earliest on May 6, 1975. May 4, 1975 was the earliest Manitoulin date, May 10 the 12-year average arrival date and the maximum count of 100 was on May 15, 1978 (Nicholson, 1981: 129). MacLulich (1938: 21) gave May 9, 1912 as his earliest Algonquin Park date. We saw 5 at North Bay on May 15, 1944 (Speirs & Speirs, 1947: 30). Skeel & Bondrup-Nielsen (1978: 183) saw one at Pukaskwa on May 20, 1977. Denis (1961: 4) listed May 19 as the average arrival date at Thunder Bay with the earliest on May 10, 1959. The earliest Geraldton record was on May 22 (Elder, 1979: 35). Peruniak (1971: 19) had an Atikokan record as early as May 8. Cringan (1953a: 3) saw his first on May 16 in 1953 at Dryden.

SUMMER:   On the 1968-1977 Breeding Bird Surveys, this was a fairly common bird in the agricultural southern portion of Ontario, uncommon to rare on more northerly routes and absent from many routes northeast of Lake Superior. This is an early fall migrant and Stirrett (1973c: 17) had his maximum Pelee count of 600 on Aug. 15. Kelley (1978: 49) reported adults attending two fledglings at Bradley's Marsh as late as Aug. 20, 1950. Saunders & Dale (1933: 209) reported the earliest London set of 4 eggs on June 7, 1912 and the latest set of 4 on July 8, 1892. Beardslee & Mitchell (1965: 300-301) noted a nest with 2 young at Mud Lake, near Welland, on July 21, 1961. Fleming (1907: 76) had a Toronto breeding record on June 11, 1892. With Ron Orenstein and Barry MacKay I found a nest being built about 6 ft. over the water of John Creek, Rama Twp. on June 2, 1967: this held 3 eggs on June 9 and 4 on June 19: Peter Satterly saw young leaving the nest as late as July 25, 1962 at Cedar Point, Lake Simcoe (Speirs, 1975: 1). I found the maximum population density of 20 birds per 100 acres in a "wild orchard" in Pickering Twp. Snyder (1930: 190) noted a premigratory group of 70 near the Holland River on Aug. 28, 1928. J.M. Richards found a nest with 2 eggs in Darlington Twp. as late as July 19, 1968 (Tozer & Richards, 1974: 184). Allin (1940: 100) noted Darlington nests on June 12, 1927 and June 16, 1930. Charles Fothergill wrote: "I once saw one of these thrash a pair of large ravens - - -" (Black, 1934: 150). R.F. Smith found a nest with one egg near Kingston on May 23 which held 4 eggs on June 6 and 4 young on June 13 (Quilliam, 1973: 119). Paul Harrington found fresh eggs in nests at Wasaga Beach from June 6 to July 23 (Devitt, 1967: 103). Lloyd (1923: 155) found nests near Ottawa on June 3, 1919 and June 4, 1921. Egg dates in the cottage country ranged from June 1 to July 24 with young from June 20 to Aug. 2 (Mills, 1981: 88). D.B. Ferguson found a nest with 3 eggs at Big Lake, Manitoulin, on July 10, 1979 (Nicholson, 1981: 129) and the high count for the southward flight was 60 on Aug. 24, 1975. C.H.D. Clarke noted adults feeding young as late as Aug. 13, 1934 in Algonquin Park (MacLulich 1938: 21). Speirs & Speirs (1947: 30) reported nests near North Bay from June 4 (1944) to June 21 (1945). Snyder (1942: 134) collected a set of fresh eggs at Maclennan on June 16, 1931. Baillie & Hope (1947: 12) found a nest with 2 young at Bigwood on July 14, 1937 and F.A.E. Starr noted a nest at Cartier on July 5, 1946. In June, 1977, Skeel & Bondrup-Nielsen (1978: 183) found kingbirds scarce along the Lake Superior shore of Pukaskwa, but more common inland near drowned trees in shallow lakes. Baillie & Hope (1943: 13) found them rare along the NE shore of Lake Superior, but collected a male on June 13, 1936 at Peninsula (Marathon) and a female on June 26 at Amyot. Snyder (1928: 263) reported them as rare at Lake Nipigon and collected only one female on June 7, 1924 at Macdiarmid. Dear (1940: 132) called them common in burned over forest land near Thunder Bay and found a nest with 4 eggs on June 22, 1926 in Gorham Twp. Snyder (1938: 194) found a nearly completed nest in Rainy River Dist. on June 15, 1929. Snyder (1928: 25) collected a female on June 6, 1925 at Lowbush, Lake Abitibi, but found no nests. Smith (1957: 175) saw them commonly in the Clay Belt until Aug. 17 in 1953 and Aug. 21 in 1954. Snyder (1953: 67) found an occupied nest 12 ft. up in a Jack pine at Wabigoon on June 21, 1937 and a nest with 3 young about 9 ft. up in a black spruce at Malachi on June 20, 1947. James (1980: 87) found a pair building a nest near Central Patricia on June 17, 1977. Cringan (1950: 12) saw one at Nikip Lake on June 11, 1950 and five on June 28, 1950 along the North Caribou River. Hope (1938: 26) found them rare at Favourable Lake: he collected one on June 1, two on Aug. 4 and saw a brood of four flying young on July 31 in 1938. Manning (1952: 68) cited three old records: two for Moose Factory and one for Ft. Albany, but saw none himself. Lee (1978: 25) noted a single bird at Big Trout Lake present for one day only, on July 20, 1975.

AUTUMN: The latest Atikokan date was Sept. 27 (Peruniak, 1971: 19). We saw 3 between Cache Bay and North Bay on Sept. 4, 1944 (Speirs & Speirs 1947: 30). Nicholson (1981: 129) saw two on Great Duck Is. as late as Sept. 25, 1977. The latest report from the cottage country was one seen by K. Ketchum off Pointe au Baril on Sept. 13, 1958 (Mills, 1981: 88). Devitt (1967: 103) gave Sept. 12, 1937 as the latest Simcoe Co. record. Weir & Quilliam (1980: 37) gave Sept. 12 as the 26-year average departure date from Kingston, the latest on Oct. 19. My latest sighting at our Pickering home was on Sept. 20, 1952 (Speirs, 1975: 1). Speirs (1938: 54) listed Sept. 24 as the latest Toronto date.

518

Two were killed at the Long Point lighthouse on Sept. 7, 1929 (Snyder, 1931: 188). Ussher (1965: 16) gave Sept. 3 as the 11-year average departure date from Rondeau, with the latest on Sept. 16. Stirrett (1973d: 22) saw his latest one at Pelee on Sept. 21.

**MEASUREMENTS:**
*Length:* 7.8 to 8.7 ins.
(Godfrey, 1966: 248)
*Wingspread:* 14 to 15 ins.
(Roberts, 1955: 633)
Weigth: 3 ♂ averaged
42.7 g. (Hope, 1938: 26).

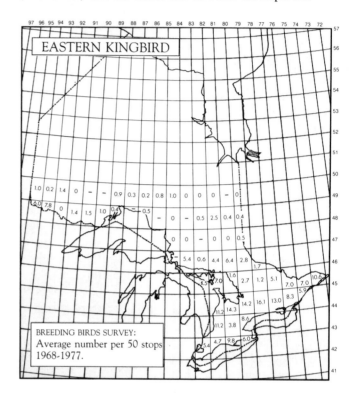

EASTERN KINGBIRD

BREEDING BIRDS SURVEY:
Average number per 50 stops
1968-1977.

# GRAY KINGBIRD   *Tyrannus dominicensis*   (Gmelin)

This kingbird is normally resident in the West Indies and elsewhere around the Caribbean Sea, with a few breeding in the southeastern United States. Three have shown up in Ontario, probably storm-blown waifs.

IDENTIFICATION: Gray Kingbirds average slightly larger and much paler than our common Eastern Kingbirds and lack the white tail tip of the latter. They have dark ear patches.

WINTER:

SPRING:   One was reported at Pelee on May 25, 1974, but rejected by the Ontario Ornithological Records Committee as a sight record of a new bird by a single observer (not named) (Goodwin, 1975: 32).

SUMMER:

AUTUMN:   Mary C. Edwards and Mrs. A.E. Hughes discovered one near Kingston on Oct. 29, 1970 (Quilliam, 1973: 120). Richard Blacquiere and Bruce Di Labio documented and photographed one near Ottawa on Oct. 31, 1982: this bird was also observed by E. LeBlanc and J. Wooley (Weir, 1983: 176).

**MEASUREMENTS:**
*Length:* 8.0 to 9.2 ins.
(Godfrey, 1966: 249)
*Wingspread:* 14 1/2 to 16
ins. (Terres, 1980: 390)
*Weight:* 37 to 51 g. (av.
44 g.). (Dunning,
1984: 17)

**REFERENCES:**
De Labio, Bruce M. and
Richard Blacquiere 1983
Gray Kingbird second
confirmed record for
Canada. Trail and
Landscape, 17:(2):
56-57.
   Hughes, A.E. 1971 A Gray
Kingbird in eastern
Ontario. Blue Bill,
18:(3): 45-46.

# SCISSOR-TAILED FLYCATCHER
*Tyrannus forficatus*   (Gmelin)

This is a fairly common species in southwestern United States. Some are great wanderers and have shown up in various parts of Ontario where their exotic beauty created great excitement wherever they appeared.

IDENTIFICATION:   The very long outer tail feathers, pearly white head and underparts, dark wings and tail with white edgings and the pink to scarlet shoulders, sides and underwing linings are diagnostic of this species: the somewhat similar Fork-tailed Flycatcher has a black head (dark brown in immatures).

WINTER:

SPRING:   Naomi, Bertrand and John LeVay watched one fly over Cranberry Marsh, Whitby, on May 21, 1966 "trailing a fabulous tail" (Tozer & Richards, 1974: 185). D. Reynolds found one at Dorland on Apr. 25, 1981 (Goodwin, 1981: 819). Nicholson (1981: 130) reported seeing one on Great Duck Is. on May 20, 1979. James, McLaren & Barlow (1976: 34) cited a photographic record of one at Streetsville on May 17, 1970.

SUMMER:   Stirrett (1973b: 19) had just one Pelee record, on June 3, 1961 (seen by Robert Mara). Harry Dowhaluk saw one at Oshawa on June 19, 1941 and sent a good description of the bird to J.L. Baillie (Tozer & Richards, 1974: 185). One at Dyer Bay, Bruce Co., was observed and photographed by P. & K. van Stamon June 1, 1974 (Goodwin, 1974: 796). Chris Blomme and Floyd Orford photographed one on Cockburn Is. on Aug. 10, 1978 (Nicholson, 1981: 130). J. Nicholson noted one at Copper Cliff on Aug. 29, 1975 (Goodwin, 1976: 62). C. Whitelaw reported one from nearby Hanmer on July 28, 1981 (Goodwin, 1981: 935). N. Juhtand saw one at Schreiber on June 13, 1978 and perhaps the same bird was photographed a few days later (on June 17) by O. Cearnes at Dorion about 70 miles to west (Goodwin, 1978: 1155). Lee (1978: 25) observed an adult female at Big Trout Lake on July 19-20, 1975, independently identified by others there at the same time.

AUTUMN:   One was picked up dead at Red Rock on Oct. 30, 1978 according to D. Freeman (Goodwin, 1979: 173). A. and J. Miles saw one on Oct. 8, 1973 at Lake Superior Provincial Park (Goodwin, 1974: 47). Ottawa's first was found by J. Dean *et al* on Oct. 27, 1980 (Goodwin, 1981: 178). One in Eastnor Twp., Bruce Co., on Nov. 5-6, 1972 was seen and photographed by M. Grant *et al* (Goodwin, 1973: 53). Baillie (1952: 14-15) reported one seen by Archie Reid at Toronto on Oct. 4, 1951 and mentioned previous records (without details) at Hamilton and Lucknow.

**MEASUREMENTS:**
*Length:* 12 to 15 ins.
including 8 to 10 inch tail
(Godfrey, 1966: 250)
Wingspread:
*Weight:* 33 averaged
43.2 g. (Dunning,
1984: 17).

# FORK-TAILED FLYCATCHER  *Tyrannus savana*  Vieillot

To find this bird of Central and South America in Ontario was most unexpected.

**IDENTIFICATION:** The entire head is black, which distinguishes it from the similar Scissor-tailed Flycatcher which has a pearly gray head: both have very long outer tail feathers.

**WINTER:**

**SPRING:**

**SUMMER:**

**AUTUMN:** Rita Taylor observed one from Oct. 28 to 30, 1977 at Dorion: the bird was photographed by A. Maki (Goodwin, 1978: 199).

**MEASUREMENTS:**
*Length:* ♂ 13 to 16 ins.
♀ 10 to 12 ins. (Terres, 1980: 384)
Wingspread:
*Weight:* 9 averaged 27.8 g. (Dunning, 1984: 17)

# HORNED LARK   *Eremophila alpestris*   (Linnaeus)

A few Horned Larks winter with flocks of Snow Buntings in southern Ontario, but it is usually February before they appear in numbers along roadsides and March before they set up territories in ploughed fields. Then their tinkling songs are one of the delights of early spring: these are sometimes given from the ground or from a fencepost, but frequently when the wind blows, the birds will ascend into the sky and hover over the territory facing into the wind and singing in the manner of skylarks. These are birds of barren fields, roadsides and lake shores.

IDENTIFICATION:   Several fairly well marked subspecies occur in Ontario but all share the black "horns", the black crescent on the breast and the unusual tail pattern where the outer feathers are darker than the inner ones (dark chocolate vs. milk chocolate). The "tseet'eet" flight notes are more musical than the "tsit'it" notes of Water Pipits with which they sometimese associate in fall. The Prairie Horned Lark *E. a. praticola* is the breeding bird in the southern portion of Ontario; the Northern Horned Lark *E. a. alpestris*, breeds around James Bay and east into Labrador and has bright yellow "eyebrows" and breast; while Hoyt's Horned Lark, with white "eyebrows" breeds from extreme north-western Ontario north along Hudson Bay. A bird of the prairie provinces just gets into western Ontario near Lake of the Woods *E. a. enthymia*. There are many other races both in the Old World and in America: I recall seeing one pale desert race in California that survived the blazing heat of a desert day by standing in the shade of roadside fenceposts during the hottest part of the day.

WINTER:   On the 1968-1977 Christmas counts they were common along the north shore of Lake Erie, fairly common north to Kettle Point and Kingston, uncommon north to Ottawa and Manitoulin and rare at Thunder Bay and Marathon. Stirrett (1973a: 17) had winter maxima of 150 on Dec. 19 and 100 on Feb. 20 but only single individuals in late January. Kelley (1978: 52) mentioned noting about 1000 along roadsides in Kent Co. on Jan. 14, 1968. On Jan. 30, 1949, Marshall Field banded 5 Northerns and one Prairie Horned Lark at St. Thomas (Brooman, 1954: 26). Saunders (1947: 368) listed Feb. 9 as his 13-year average arrival date at Toronto, while Speirs (1938: 44) gave Feb. 28 as the spring peak there. Weir & Quilliam (1980: 37) listed Feb. 14 as the 29-year average arrival date at Kingston. Devitt (1967: 107) gave Feb. 19 as the 22-year average arrival date at Barrie: he cited winter records at Barrie of two on Jan. 7, 1961, as well as Collingwood sightings of one on Jan. 1, 1954 and 12 on Dec. 21, 1958. L. Beamer's median arrival date at Meaford was Feb. 19, with the earliest on Feb. 1, 1951. E. Goltz saw 12 around a stable near Bracebridge on Dec. 24, 1972 while the earliest arrival at Huntsville was on Feb. 21 (Mills, 1981: 95-96). Speirs & Speirs (1947: 30) noted one at North Bay as early as Feb. 28, 1945. Dennison (1980: 148) listed a total of 46 on three Christmas counts at Sault Ste. Marie.

SPRING:   Stirrett (1973b: 20) had a spring maximum of 225 at Pelee on March 6. Saunders & Dale (1933: 212) noted 3 sets of eggs for the London region: 4 on Apr. 5, 1902: 3 on Apr. 1, 1904 and 5 on May 8, 1912: also a brood of young that left the nest on Apr. 25, 1900. Harold Lancaster reported that young had left the nest in Elgin Co. by Apr. 4, 1939 (Brooman, 1954: 26). George A. Scott noted nest construction at Oshawa on March 16, 1951; this was lined by March 24 and held 4 eggs on Apr. 1 (Tozer &

Richards, 1974: 191-192). Quilliam (1973: 124) mentioned a nest with 4 eggs at Kingston on Apr. 3, 1898 and a nest with 2 eggs on Apr. 24, 1900, as well as 22 other nests with eggs between Apr. 9 and 22. H.P. Bingham found a nest with 3 eggs at Barrie that hatched on Apr. 20, 1925 only to perish in a late snowfall: D. Butler found three nests at Esso Station on May 12, 1940 (Devitt, 1967: 107). C.W.G. Eifrig gave March 28 as the earliest breeding date for Ottawa and C.H. Young found a nest with 4 eggs there on Apr. 11, 1900 (Lloyd, 1923: 155). Mills (1981: 95) gave March 14 as a 5-year average arrival date at Huntsville and mentioned several early nesting records for the cottage country. Nicholson (1981: 134) gave March 12 as the 10-year average arrival date on Manitoulin with a maximum count of 350 on May 10, 1970. F.A.E. Starr found a nest with 4 eggs at Sudbury on May 26, 1935 (Baillie & Hope, 1947: 13). Skeel & Bondrup-Nielsen (1978: 185) saw 3 at Pukaskwa on Apr. 27, 1977 and one on May 15. Baillie & Hope (1943: 14) collected a male and a female at Rossport on May 29, 1936. Denis (1961: 3) gave May 7 as the average arrival date at Thunder Bay with the earliest on Apr. 8, 1939. Bondrup-Nielsen (1976: 43) noted a small number near Kapuskasing on May 13, 1974. Elder (1979: 35) gave March 3 as his earliest sighting at Geraldton. Cringan (1953a: 3) noted his first at Sioux Lookout on May 4, 1953. Oliver Hewitt reported them common in the Moose River estuary area from May 22 to 28, 1947 (Manning, 1952: 69).

SUMMER: On the 1968-1977 Breeding Bird Surveys, they were common on routes in the agricultural areas in southwestern and extreme southeastern Ontario: fairly common to uncommon north to Sudbury and absent on the routes in the forested Precambrian section of Ontario: there were outliers on the Swastika and Fort Frances routes. Stirrett (1973c: 18) reported this as a nesting bird at Pelee. W. Fox found a nest with 5 eggs at Long Point on June 15, 1967 (McCracken, Bradstreet & Holroyd, 1981: 57). W. Carrick observed a nest with 3 eggs near Uxbridge on June 30, 1957: in Ontario Co. we found maximum populations in ploughed fields—29 birds per 100 acres on our Scugog quadrat and 24 per 100 acres on our Thorah quadrat (Speirs, 1975: 13) A.E. Allin (1940: 101) found a nest with 4 eggs in Darlington Twp. as late as June 28, 1922. Nicholson (1981: 134) saw a young bird with adults near Mindemoya, Manitoulin, on June 28, 1969. Snyder (1942: 135) noted nuptial flights near Sault Ste. Marie as late as June 4 and saw young on the wing by July 19, 1931. Baillie & Hope (1947: 13) collected a juvenile male at Bigwood on July 20, 1937. K. Boshcoff saw one on June 5, 1973 at Pukaskwa Depot (Skeel & Bondrup-Nielsen, 1978: 185). Baillie & Hope (1943: 14) collected a male at Marathon on June 17, 1936. Snyder (1938: 196-197) collected a juvenile female and three adults of the *enthymia* race at Emo, Rainy River, from June 6 to 19, 1929. Manning (1952: 70) saw 300 in 6 hours at North Point, James Bay, from June 3 to 6, 1947 and smaller numbers at other points along the James Bay and Hudson Bay coasts: he collected 4 juveniles at Cape Henrietta Maria from July 20 to 24, 1947 and two at Little Cape, Hudson Bay, between July 29 and Aug. 1, 1947. Peck (1972: 345) found a nest with 3 young and one infertile egg at Cape Henrietta Maria on June 24, 1970 and a nest with 4 eggs on June 28, 1970: the ROM field party in 1948 saw several hundred there and collected 35 including 7 juveniles. Lee (1978: 26) saw only one at Big Trout Lake, killed by small boys on June 23, 1975. C.E. Hope saw 12 and collected 7 at Ft. Severn on July 9, 1940.

AUTUMN: Doug. McRae and Alan Wormington noted a maximum of 80 at Netitishi Point, James Bay, on Oct. 21 and noted the last one there on Nov. 20, 1981. Oliver Hewitt found them common near Moosonee from Sept. 21 to 25, 1947 (Manning, 1952: 69).

Peruniak (1971: 20) had fall records at Atikokan from Sept. 25 to Oct. 21. Skeel & Bondrup-Nielsen (1978: 185) saw 40 on Sept. 20 at Pukaskwa and one killed at the Otter Is. lighthouse on Oct. 14, 1977. Speirs & Speirs (1947: 31) observed one at North Bay on Sept. 26, 1944. Chris Bell noted a high count of 835 on Manitoulin on Oct. 8, 1972 (Nicholson, 1981: 134). Mills (1981: 96) cited several fall records of flocks seen in the cottage country during October and as late as Nov. 21, 1965 at Emsdale. Weir & Quilliam (1980: 37) listed Nov. 19 as the 29-year average departure date from Kingston. Snyder (1941: 67) gave Nov. 22, 1935 as the latest date for Prince Edward Co. Fall peaks in Ontario Co. were in the third week of October and second week of November (Speirs, 1975: 13). Speirs (1938: 52) listed Oct. 25 as the fall peak for Toronto, while Saunders (1947: 368) gave Nov. 9 as his 13-year average departure date. A.A. Wood collected two Hoyt's and two Northern Horned Larks on Nov. 11, 1926 near London (Saunders & Dale, 1933: 211). Stirrett (1973d: 22) had a maximum of 200 at Pelee on Oct. 19.

**MEASUREMENTS:**

*Length:* 6.8 to 8.0 ins. (Godfrey, 1966: 262)
*Wingspread:* 11.80 to 14.00 ins. (Roberts, 1955: 637)
*Weight:* ♂ 1.25 to 2.50 oz. ♀ 1.25 to 1.75 oz. (Roberts, 1955: 637)

**REFERENCES:**

Abbe, George 1974
The larks. Dublin, N.H.
William L. Bauhan
i-ix; 1-144. This is a lighthearted but very detailed account of the life history of Horned Larks.
    Saunders, W.E. 1927
The Horned Larks. Can. Field-Nat., 41: (4): 91.

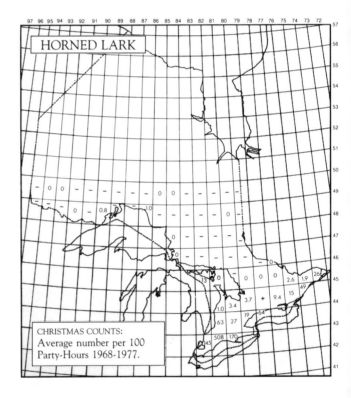

HORNED LARK

CHRISTMAS COUNTS:
Average number per 100
Party-Hours 1968-1977.

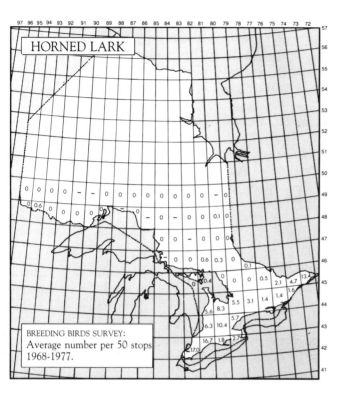

BREEDING BIRDS SURVEY:
Average number per 50 stops
1968-1977.

## PURPLE MARTIN  *Progne subis*  (Linnaeus)

Most Purple Martins in Ontario nest in multichamber houses on tall poles erected by people who enjoy their chatter and insect-eating activities: some nest in cavities about the eaves of old buildings, often on the main streets of old towns: a few nest in natural holes in trees. In winter they retire to South America.

**IDENTIFICATION:** This is the largest of our swallows. Old males are very dark blue, almost black. Females resemble oversize Tree Swallows, but with duller, less contrasting colours. The note is a loud whistle "tsew", with a curious resonant quality, as if given in a great hall or between tall buildings.

**WINTER:**

**SPRING:** Stirrett (1973b: 20) noted one at Pelee on March 26 and had maxima of 200 there on Apr. 25 and May 20. Kelley (1978: 54) reported birds at nest sites at Pelee as early as May 19, 1967. Ussher (1965: 18) gave Apr. 14 as the 28-year average arrival date at Rondeau, with the earliest on March 27. Saunders & Dale (1933: 214) gave Apr. 11 as the 17-year average arrival date at London, with the earliest on Apr. 3, 1913. Beardslee & Mitchell (1965: 316) noted a nest with young at Pt. Colborne as early as May 30, 1938. Speirs (1938: 40) listed March 29 as the earliest Toronto date, while Saunders (1947: 369) gave Apr. 28 as his 12-year average arrival date there. David O'Brien, who had several nest boxes at Frenchman Bay, gave Apr. 23 as the 17-year average arrival date there: birds may be seen hawking for emerging insects low over the waves of Lake Ontario before any are seen inland (Speirs, 1975: 19). The earliest Whitby report was by Naomi LeVay on Apr. 8, 1956 (Tozer & Richards, 1974: 197). Snyder (1941: 69) gave Apr. 6 as his earliest Prince Edward Co. record. Weir & Quilliam (1980: 37) listed Apr. 11 as the 31-year average arrival date for Kingston, with the earliest on March 28. Devitt (1967: 111) gave Apr. 25 as the 23-year average arrival date at Barrie, with the earliest Simcoe Co. bird at Collingwood on Apr. 6, 1955. A single male arrived at P.A. Taverner's Ottawa bird house on Apr. 7, 1922 (Lloyd, 1924: 12). L. Beamer's median arrival date at Meaford was Apr. 12, with the earliest on Apr. 1, 1956. Mills (1981: 101) gave Apr. 16, 1966 as his earliest date for the cottage country, when M. Ayres noted some at Huntsville. Nicholson (1981: 136) gave Apr. 23 as the 10-year average arrival date for Manitoulin, with the earliest on Apr. 17, 1976. Ricker & Clarke (1939: 15) noted as unusual a group of about 50 that rested under the eaves of the North Bay post office for a few days in spring, in 1920 or 1921.

SUMMER: On the 1968-1977 Breeding Bird Surveys, Purple Martins were common on routes near the Lake Erie shores, becoming rare north to Mattawa and uncommon at Rainy River. Stirrett (1973c: 18) had a maximum of 30 at Pelee during the nesting season but 1500 on Aug. 12 as they congregated before moving south. Kelley (1978: 54) reported adults with fledged young at nest sites at Ipperwash Beach as late as Aug. 12, 1951. McCracken, Bradstreet & Holroyd (1981: 58) reported over 200 nests from Long Point, including a few in natural tree cavities. J.A. Edwards found them nesting in the tower of the town hall in Beaverton for at least 20 years: one nest contained 4 eggs on June 9, 1927 and another held 5 eggs as late as June 30, 1946: David O'Brien gave Aug. 16 as the average departure date from his Frenchman Bay colony, with the latest on Aug. 31 (Speirs, 1975: 19). E. Beaupré collected a set of 5 eggs at Portsmouth on June 18, 1916, now in the ROM (Quilliam, 1973: 128). H.P. Bingham took a set of 5 eggs at Barrie on June 8, 1916 and R. Standfield found a nest with 4 young at Midland on July 17, 1935 (Baillie & Harrington, 1937: 218). Lloyd (1924: 12) banded several young from an Ottawa bird house on July 26, 1922. Mills (1981: 101) reported 29 nest record cards from the cottage country. Nicholson (1981: 136) had a maximum of 70 on Manitoulin on Aug. 30, 1969. Speirs & Speirs (1947: 31) had a few North Bay sightings between June 10 (1944) and June 25 (1945). Snyder (1942: 137) found them nesting about business buildings in Sault Ste. Marie in 1931 and mentioned that Harry Graham noted adults feeding fledged young on Aug. 2, 1939. Baillie & Hope (1947: 15) collected an immature male (of the previous year) at Biscotasing on June 26, 1937 (their only observation in Sudbury Dist.). My most northerly observation was at Latchford, where I saw 5 adults at nest boxes on June 18, 1980, but Percy Richter wrote me that they were noted nesting at Matachewan in 1982. Denis (1961: 6) called it an occasional summer resident at Thunder Bay. Snyder (1938: 198) found them nesting in an old woodpecker hole at Emo and J.L. Baillie saw a female feeding a young bird while both were on the wing at Rainy River. Peruniak (1971: 21) had just two records for Atikokan: June 3, 1956 and June 6, 1962 but David Elder noted the species at Lac La Croix on June 2, 1981. Snyder (1953: 69) noted nesting at Kenora, Ingolf, Wabigoon and Malachi with the most northerly pair breeding in a bird box at Minaki in summer of 1938. Cringan (1953a: 3) saw his first a Sioux Lookout on June 13, 1953. Hope (1938: 29) watched one for half an hour, circling the mine structure at Favourable Lake, calling frequently. The orginal description was based on a specimen presumed to have come from Ft. Severn though none have been noted there since (Manning, 1952: 71).

AUTUMN: Nicholson (1981: 136) gave Sept. 14 as the latest Manitoulin record. The latest date for the cottage country was Sept. 11, 1976 when Chris Harris saw two at Go Home Bay (Mills, 1981: 102). Devitt (1967: 111) gave Sept. 15, 1940 at Holland River as his latest Simcoe Co. record. Weir & Quilliam (1980: 37) gave Sept. 5 as the 19-year average departure date from Kingston, with the latest on Oct. 2. My latest record was on Sept. 22, 1956 near the mouth of Duffin Creek, Pickering (Speirs, 1975: 19). Speirs (1938: 54) gave Sept. 21 as the latest Toronto date. One was seen at Dunnville as late as Oct. 17, 1948 (Beardslee & Mitchell, 1965: 316). During the first week of September, 1946 up to 500 congregated in St. Thomas (Brooman, 1954: 27). Ussher (1965: 18) gave Sept. 1 as the 12-year average departure date from Rondeau, with the latest on Sept. 7. Stirrett (1973d: 23) saw his latest four at Pelee on Sept. 18.

**MEASUREMENTS:**
*Length:* 7.3 to 8.5 ins. (Godfrey, 1966: 270), about Starling size.
*Wingspread:* 15 1/2 to 16 3/4 ins. (Roberts, 1955: 638)
*Weight:* 2 to 2 1/4 oz. (Roberts, 1955: 638)

**REFERENCES:**
Gibson, George G. and Eric Broughton 1971 Death of Purple Martin nestlings apparently due to ingested mollusc shell. Can. Field-Nat., 85: (3): 257.
Mitchell, Margaret H. 1947 Fall migration of the Purple Martin. Auk, 64: (4): 627-628. She noted big invasions during late July or early August at Streetsville when her local birds were beginning to be fledged; all gone before the end of August.

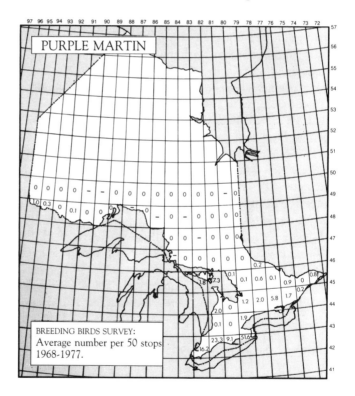

PURPLE MARTIN

BREEDING BIRDS SURVEY: Average number per 50 stops 1968-1977.

# TREE SWALLOW   *Tachycineta bicolor*   (Vieillot)

Tree Swallows nest in cavities of dead trees, especially those standing in water, but may be attracted to suitable nest boxes, even near houses. They are usually the first of our swallows to return in spring and the last to leave in fall. Most winter from southern U.S.A. to Central America.

IDENTIFICATION:   Males with their brilliant blue upper parts and snowy white breasts are unlike our other swallows. The young and some females are brownish gray above and might be confused with Bank Swallows (which however have a more pronounced dark breast band) and with Rough-winged Swallows (which have a dirty buff throat unlike the white throat of Tree Swallows in all plumages).

WINTER:   Stirrett (1973a: 17) reported one at Pelee as late as Dec. 1.

SPRING:   Stirrett (1973b: 20) had his earliest two at Pelee on March 26, with a maximum count of 300 on May 6. Ussher (1965: 17) gave Apr. 15 as the 21-year average arrival date at Rondeau, with the earliest on March 31. Apr. 13 was the 15-year average arrival date at London, with the earliest on March 25, 1929 (Saunders & Dale, 1933: 212). Median dates for laying the first egg in a clutch at Long Point varied from May 21 to 29 (De Steven & Hussell, 1977: 11-12). Speirs (1938: 40, 44) gave March 19 as the earliest Toronto date, with the spring peak on Apr. 25: Saunders (1947: 368) listed Apr. 20 as his 13-year average arrival date there. I saw two at Whitby as early as Apr. 3, 1971 and Dennis Barry estimated 600 near Oshawa's Second Marsh on Apr. 19, 1964 (Speirs, 1975: 14). J.M. Richards found a nest under construction in Darlington Twp. on May 5, 1964, which held 2 eggs on May 27, 6 eggs on June 4 and 5 young on June 25 (Tozer & Richards, 1974: 193). Snyder (1941: 68) reported the species in Prince Edward Co. as early as March 29. Weir & Quilliam (1980: 37) listed March 28 as the 32-year average arrival date at Kingston, the earliest on March 16, 1955. Devitt (1967: 108) gave Apr. 12 as the 18-year average arrival date at Barrie, with the earliest on March 31, 1962 and 500 at Little Lake on May 15, 1939 at the peak of migration: nest building was noted at Wasaga Beach on May 10, 1936 and a nest with 4 eggs was found at Little Lake on May 21, 1922. L. Beamer's median arrival date at Meaford was Apr. 11, the earliest on Apr. 3, 1956 when at least 5 were observed. At Huntsville the 14-year average arrival date was Apr. 11, the earliest on Apr. 4, 1974: C. Harris counted 260 at Go Home Bay on May 4, 1975 and individuals at bird houses were noted as early as Apr. 21, 1979 (Mills, 1981: 96). Nicholson (1981: 134) gave Apr. 11 as the 12-year average arrival date on Manitoulin, with the earliest on Apr. 2, 1978. MacLulich (1938: 23) gave Apr. 16, 1933 as his earliest date for Algonquin Park. I saw one at the North Bay airport as early as Apr. 9, 1945 (Speirs & Speirs, 1947: 31). Skeel & Bondrup-Nielsen (1978: 185) saw their first at Pukaskwa on Apr. 18, 1977: they found a nest with 4 eggs on May 29, 1977 and noted several other active nest holes there. Denis (1961: 3) gave May 1 as the average arrival date at Thunder Bay, the earliest on Apr. 17, 1952. Bondrup-Nielsen (1976: 43) saw his first near Kapuskasing on May 3, 1975. Elder (1979: 35) gave Apr. 27 as his earliest date for Geraldton. Peruniak (1971: 20) gave Apr. 20 as her earliest Atikokan record but David Elder noted his first on Apr. 16 in 1981. Cringan (1953a: 3) saw his first at Sioux Lookout on Apr. 24, 1953. Manning (1952: 70) frequently saw them near Moosonee in late May in 1947.

SUMMER:    On the 1968-1977 Breeding Bird Surveys, they were fairly common in agricultural southerwestern Ontario and northwest of Lake Superior, common elsewhere in Ontario. Stirrett (1973c: 18) reported summer maxima of 200 on June 16 and July 15 at Pelee. Bradstreet (1969: 69) found that 87% of successful female Tree Swallows at Long Point returned to breed the following year while only 14.4% of females whose nests were not successful returned the following year. McCracken, Bradstreet & Holroyd (1981: 57) found breeding densities as high as 299 territories per km² on Long Point: over 1300 nestings have been reported there, only 95 of these in natural cavities. See "References" below for some other results of long term studies of this species at Long Point. Speirs (1975: 14) reported that in Ontario Co. 78 sets of eggs totalled 369 eggs (6 sets has as many as 7 eggs but the mode was 5): the peak for nests with eggs was in the first week of June: the greatest population density in our study quadrats was in Washago with 38 birds per 100 acres. Allin (1940: 101) found a nest with 5 eggs in Darlington Twp. on June 9, 1930. Snyder (1941: 68) reported hundreds congregating for southward migration in Prince Edward Co. by July 10. Quilliam (1973: 125) mentioned a nest with 6 eggs found by E. Beaupré in a fencepost near Kingston on June 2, 1922 (and 3 other nests in the first half of June): she noted great flocks congregating on wires by mid-July. Young in the nest were noted as late as July 21, 1940 in Innisfil Twp., Simcoe Co. and on Aug. 3, 1936 a flock estimated at 3000 was observed near Wyevale (Devitt, 1967: 108). Lloyd (1924: 12) called this the most reliable occupant of Ottawa bird houses: young left one nest there on June 30, 1922. Mills (1981: 96) reported 36 Muskoka and 63 Parry Sound nest record cards: second broods are not common in this species so a pair whose first brood of 5 died in early June and who hatched 4 eggs on July 10 at Ahmic Lake is of interest. D.B. Ferguson found a nest with 5 eggs near Mindemoya, Manitoulin, on June 2, 1977: the fall maximum of 1000 was noted on Aug. 29, 1970 (Nicholson, 1981: 134). Ricker & Clarke (1939: 15) found a nest with 6 eggs on June 20, 1926 at Lake Nipissing. I saw my last at North Bay on Aug. 22, 1944 (Speirs & Speirs, 1947: 31). Snyder (1942: 138) reported a nest with 4 eggs in a fencepost near Sault Ste. Marie on June 11, 1931. Baillie & Hope (1947: 14) saw an occupied bird box in Chapleau on June 20, 1937 and found two nests at Biscotasing on June 21 and 22, 1937, one of which held 2 eggs on June 24, 4 eggs on June 30 and newly hatched young on July 7 and 8, 1937. W. Wyett saw one as late as Aug. 14, 1974 at Pukaskwa (Skeel & Bondrup-Nielsen, 1978: 185). Baillie & Hope (1943: 14) found them common at Amyot, Marathon and Rossport: they collected 6 nestlings at Amyot on June 25 and six more there on July 1. Dear (1940: 133) found a nest with 3 eggs on July 3, 1927 and a nest with 6 eggs on June 28, 1928 in Paipoonge Twp., Thunder Bay. Snyder (1938: 197) found a nest with eggs in Rainy River on June 7, 1929. Smith (1957: 175) called them very common in the Clay Belt and found nests at Timmins, Lake Abitibi and Kapuskasing. Snyder (1928: 29) observed a pair copulating on the wing at Lake Abitibi in 1925. Snyder (1953: 68-69) called this a common breeding species from Lake of the Woods east to Savanne and north to Sioux Lookout: (on June 23 and June 26, 1950) in a beaver meadow by the Petownikip River: he noted up to 40 in a day during June in that vicinity. Manning (1952: 71) saw 40 in 6 hours observing on June 30 and July 1, 1947 near Moosonee and saw several as far north as Raft River between July 7 and 13, 1947. H. Lumsden noted nesting in a pipe at a radar station on Cape Henrietta Maria on June 28, 1964 (Peck, 1972: 345). Ross James confirmed breeding at Kiruna Lake in the Sutton Ridges in 1981. Schueler, Baldwin & Rising (1974: 143) noted the species along the James Bay and Hudson Bay coasts as far north as Winisk: they found them breeding at Cochrane and Hawley Lake. Lee (1978: 27) called this one of the commonest birds at Big Trout Lake, where he observed them from June 1 to Aug. 3, with a maximum of 12 on July 5. C.E. Hope saw only two at Ft. Severn, on June 23, 1940.

AUTUMN: Nicholson (1981: 134) gave Oct. 9, 1972 as the latest Manitoulin date. T. Spratt reported one at Huntsville on Sept. 10, 1973—the latest date for the cottage country (Mills, 1981: 97). Alf. Mitchener saw one at Collingwood as late as Oct. 7, 1952 (Devitt, 1967: 108). Weir & Quilliam (1980: 37) listed Oct. 18 as the 27-year average departure date from Kingston, with the latest on Nov. 23. Snyder (1941:68) gave Oct. 15 as his latest date for Prince Edward Co. David O'Brien noted one as late as Nov. 11, 1963 at Frenchman Bay (Speirs, 1975: 14). J. Satterly had a fall peak of 2000 at Mara Provincial Park on Sept. 13, 1974 and Long (1968b: 11) estimated over 10,000 at Pickering Beach on Sept. 23, 1967. Speirs (1938: 52) gave Sept. 7 as the fall peak for Toronto and Fleming (1907: 82) cited a late record on Oct. 20, 1906 by H.H. Mitchell. J.L. Baillie et al noted 500 at Ft. Erie on Oct. 10, 1948 and the Brockners saw one at late as Nov. 23, 1958 at Port Robinson (Beardslee & Mitchell, 1965: 311). Ussher (1965: 17) gave Oct. 2 as the 11-year average departure date from Rondeau, with the latest on Nov. 4. Stirrett (1973d: 22) had a fall maximum of 400 at Pelee on Sept. 26.

BANDING: One banded at Levering, Mich., on June 14, 1964 was recovered about 257 miles SE, at Baptiste Creek Marsh, Ont. on Apr. 28, 1965 (Brewer & Salvadori, 1978: 67). One banded at Huntsville, Ont. on June 17, 1965 was recovered about 451 miles SE in New Jersey on March 29, 1966 (Mills, 1981: 97).

**MEASUREMENTS:**
Length: 5.0 to 6.2 ins.
(Godfrey, 1966: 265)
Wingspread: 12.25 to
13.62 ins. (Roberts,
1955: 638)
Weight: 14 one-year old
♀ averaged 20.50 g.,
while 57 adult ♀ averaged
21.50 g. (De Steven
1977: 13). 2 ♂ averaged
21.4 g. (Hope, 1938: 29).

**REFERENCES:**
Bradstreet, Michael S.W.
1969 Consecutive nesting
of female Tree Swallows at
Long Point, Ontario. Ont.
Bird Banding 5:(3): 68-71.
    De. Steven, Diane &
David J.T. Hussell 1977
The Tree Swallow breeding
season. Long Point Bird
Observatory Ann. Rept. for
1975: 11-12. Two
breeding ♀ were known to
be 6 years old and 3 others
at least 6 years old (or
older).

De Steven, Diane 1978 The influence of age on the breeding biology of the Tree Swallow, *Iridoprocne bicolor*. Ibis, 120:(4): 516-523. This gave statistics on clutch size, egg size, weights, productivity and survival from Long Poiont studies. The annual loss of adults was about 50%. The breeding performance improved with age (larger clutches laid and higher % young fledged).

Hussell, David J.T. 1974 Studies of breeding Tree Swallows, 1972. LPBO 1972 Ann. Rept.: 15-16. 143 completed clutches in 1972 averaged 5.55 eggs (in 1971 90 clutches had averaged 5.49 eggs).

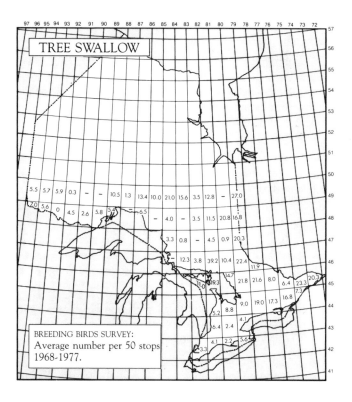

TREE SWALLOW

BREEDING BIRDS SURVEY: Average number per 50 stops 1968-1977.

# NORTHERN ROUGH-WINGED SWALLOW
## *Stelgidopteryx serripennis* (Audubon)

This species is often found with the more familiar Bank Swallow but I associate it with smaller sand banks and frequently find it perched on dead twigs beside quiet waters. It usually arrives about a week earlier in spring and stays longer in the fall than does the Bank Swallow. It is not found so far north as is the Bank Swallow in Ontario and is less common even in the south. Most go to Central America for the winter.

**IDENTIFICATION:** This is the brown backed swallow known by its "dirty chin" lacking the pure white throat of the Bank Swallow and some brownish backed plumages of the Tree Swallow. The Bank Swallow also sports a black "necklace" lacking in this species. When perched the Rough-wing shows a suggestion of a crest. The usual flight note is a single "bzzt" not the chittery series of "bzzt"s given by the Bank Swallow. In flight it glides frequently, with less fluttering than is usual with Bank Swallows. It usually nests in the low cut banks of small streams, or in low road cuts though it may nest with Bank Swallows in larger sand banks. Not infrequently it nests in drainage tiles under bridges. In the hand the leading edge of the outer primary shows a series of hooklets; hence its name.

**WINTER:** Three were found at the Greenvale sewage plant, London, on Dec. 3, 1979 and remained until it froze over on Jan. 6, 1980 (Goodwin, 1980: 268) and one was seen there again until Dec. 14, 1980 (Goodwin 1981: 297).

SPRING: Stirrett (1973b: 20) had his earliest one at Pelee on Apr. 2 and noted a maximum of 500 on May 17. Ussher (1965: 17) gave Apr. 26 as the 18-year average arrival date on Rondeau, with the earliest on Apr. 16. Saunders & Dale (1933: 213) gave Apr. 23 as the 17-year average arrival date at London, with the earliest on Apr. 17, 1914: he found a set of 7 eggs as early as May 30, 1899. Frank Farley collected a set of 7 eggs at St. Thomas on May 25, 1887 (Brooman 1954: 26). Saunders (1947: 369) listed Apr. 29 as the 19-year average arrival date at Toronto, with the earliest on Apr. 18, while Speirs (1938: 44) gave May 19 as the spring peak. Speirs (1975: 16) saw one as early as Apr. 11, 1965 in Pickering Twp. J.M. Richards found a completed nest in a bridge drain near Oshawa on May 23, 1970 and a nest with 2 eggs on May 26, 1957 at Oshawa (Tozer & Richards, 1974: 195). Allin (1940: 102) saw a pair carrying nest material into a stream-bank hole in Darlington Twp. on May 22, 1937. Weir & Quilliam (1980: 37) listed Apr. 25 as the 30-year average arrival date at Kingston, with the earliest on Apr. 10. Devitt (1967: 109) gave Apr. 29 as the 12-year average arrival date at Barrie, with the earliest on Apr. 19, 1938: H.P. Bingham found a nest with 5 eggs on May 27, 1933 at Hillsdale. The earliest date for the cottage country was one near Huntsville seen by P. and A. Bailey on May 2, 1976 (Mills, 1981: 98). Nicholson (1981: 135) gave May 6 as the 9-year average arrival date for Manitoulin, with the earliest on Apr. 26, 1970. Peruniak (1971: 20) had her earliest Atikokan record on May 24.

SUMMER: On the 1968-1977 Breeding Bird Survey it was fairly common on most routes near Lake Erie and Lake Ontario becoming rare to North Bay and Thessalon, with outliers only at Cochrane and Marathon. Stirrett (1973c: 18) reported none at Pelee from June 3 to July 8 but had a maximum of 500 by Aug. 14. Saunders & Dale (1933: 213) noted two sets of 5 eggs and two of 6 eggs near London, the latest on June 15, 1900. Fleming (1907: 82) collected a female that was nesting in an old kingfisher hole at Toronto on June 12, 1906. Snyder (1930: 197) found a nest with 5 eggs on June 17, 1926 in King Twp. We watched an adult feeding young on the wing at our home in Pickering Twp. on July 1, 1962 (Speirs, 1975: 16). Quilliam (1973: 126) cited details of several breeding records for the Kingston region. Devitt (1967: 109) reported a set of 4 eggs taken by Paul Harrington at Wasaga Beach on July 1, 1929 and a nest with 6 eggs located by G. Lambert in Innisfil Twp. on June 25, 1939. C.L. Patch found a nest with 6 eggs near Ottawa on June 5, 1918 (Lloyd, 1924: 12). J.L. Baillie observed nesting at Pickerel Lake on July 9, 1939 and G. Peck found a nest with 3 young and three pairs with young near Parry Sound on June 20, 1978 (Mills, 1981: 98). D.B. Ferguson found a nest with 6 eggs at High Falls, Manitoulin on June 20, 1976 (Nicholson, 1981: 135). Speirs & Speirs (1947: 31) saw two at the junction of Amable du Fond River and Smith's Lake, east of North Bay, on June 19, 1945. Denis (1961: 5) reported a nest with 5 eggs at Thunder Bay on June 28, 1953. J.L. Baillie noted 25, including young just out of the nest at Big Fork, Rainy River on July 20, 1929 "the most northerly record for the species in Ontario" (Snyder, 1938: 197).

AUTUMN: Three seen by C. Harris at Go Home Bay on Sept. 2, 1974 were the latest for the cottage country (Mills, 1981: 99). J.L. Baillie saw 60 at Big Cedar Point, Lake Simcoe as late as Sept. 12, 1943 (Devitt, 1967: 109). Weir & Quilliam (1980: 37) listed Oct. 1 as the 14-year average departure date from Kingston, with the latest on Oct. 30. David Calvert saw three at Cranberry Marsh as late at Oct. 1, 1972 (Tozer & Richards 1974: 195). Saunders (1947: 369) listed Sept. 15 as the latest Toronto date. Beardslee & Mitchell (1965: 314) noted 500 at Fort Erie on Oct. 10, 1948 and 10 at Chippewa as late as Nov. 1, 1959. Ussher (1965: 17) gave Sept. 12 as the 14-year average departure date from Rondeau, with the latest on Sept. 28. Several large flocks were noted at Pelee through September, with the latest on Oct. 12 when 11 were noted (Stirrett, 1973d: 22).

**MEASUREMENTS:**
*Length:* 5.0 to 5.7 ins. (Godfrey, 1966: 267)
*Wingspread:* 11 1/2 to 12 1/4 ins. (Roberts, 1955: 639)
*Weight:* 24 varied from 12.1 to 18.1 g. (Terres, 1980: 866)

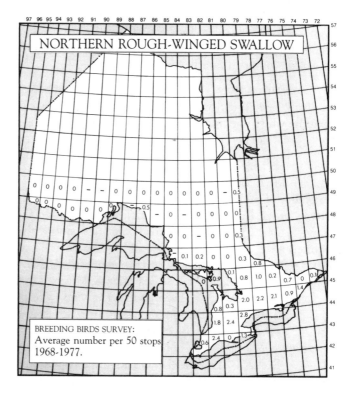

NORTHERN ROUGH-WINGED SWALLOW

BREEDING BIRDS SURVEY:
Average number per 50 stops
1968-1977.

# BANK SWALLOW   *Riparia riparia*   (Linnaeus)

Bank Swallows nest in burrows excavated into vertical banks of sand in such places as shore cliffs, eroded river banks, gravel pits and road cuts: in northern Ontario they have even used sawdust piles. In the Old World they are known as Sand Martins. These are usually the latest of our swallows to return in spring and the earliest to leave in autumn. Our birds winter in South America.

IDENTIFICATION:  This is the common brown backed swallow distinguished from the relatively rare Rough-winged Swallow by its blackish band separating the white throat from the white underparts. Rough-winged Swallows have a dingy buff throat and lack the breast band. (The breast band in young of the year is rather diffuse and brownish.)

WINTER:

SPRING:   Stirrett (1973b: 20) noted 20 at Pelee as early as Apr. 16 and had a maximum of 1000 on May 11. Ussher (1965: 17) gave Apr. 30 as the 25-year average arrival date at Rondeau, with his earliest on Apr. 19. Saunders & Dale (1933: 212) gave May 6 as the 17-year average arrival date at London with the earliest on Apr. 28, 1923: he reported a set of 4 eggs as early as May 25, 1901. Harold Lancaster gave May 4 as the average arrival date in Elgin Co. (Brooman, 1954: 26). Snyder (1931: 203) saw his first at Long Point on May 1, 1928. Beardslee & Mitchell (1965: 312) noted 10 at Rockhouse Pt. Lake Erie on Apr. 15, 1955 and two at Mud Lake the same day. Fleming (1907: 82) had an amazingly early Toronto record on Apr. 4, 1890, while Saunders (1947: 369) listed Apr. 30 as his 13-year average arrival date there and Speirs (1938: 44) gave May 9 as the spring peak. Naomi LeVay noted the species at Cranberry Marsh as early as Apr. 14, 1968 (Tozer & Richards, 1974: 193) but the spring peak in Ontario Co. has been in the fourth week of May (Speirs, 1975: 15). J. Satterly found a nesting colony in a roadside sand pit in Mara Twp. as early as May 19, 1968 (Speirs, 1975: 15). Allin (1940: 102) saw a nest with 7 eggs in Darlington Twp. on May 27, 1928. Weir & Quilliam (1980: 37) listed Apr. 30 as the 30-year average arrival date at Kingston, with the earliest on Apr. 15. Devitt (1967: 109) gave May 4 as the 16-year average arrival date at Barrie, the earliest on Apr. 23, 1958: H.P. Bingham took a set of 6 eggs at Little Lake as early as May 23, 1937. L. Beamer's median arrival date at Meaford was May 1, with the earliest on Apr. 24, 1953. Mills (1981: 97) mentioned a Huntsville record by A. Bailey as early as Apr. 18, 1973 but most arrive in the cottage country during May. Nicholson (1981: 135) gave May 4 as the 12-year average arrival date for Manitoulin, the earliest on Apr. 27, 1974. A flight of hundreds went through Algonquin Park on May 4, 1912 (MacLulich, 1938: 23). Ricker & Clarke (1939: 15) noted the species at Lake Nipissing on May 21, 1925. Skeel & Bondrup-Nielsen (1978: 186) saw 10 at Pukaskwa on May 23, 1977. Denis (1961: 4) listed May 21 as the average arrival date at Thunder Bay, with the earliest on May 1, 1941. Bondrup-Nielsen (1976: 43) noted some near Kapuskasing on May 19, 1974 (but saw none in 1975). Elder (1979: 35) gave May 25 as his earliest date for Geraldton: he noted his first at Atikokan on May 17 in 1981.

SUMMER:   On the 1968-1977 Breeding Bird Surveys they were abundant on the Port Dover route, common on other southern Ontario routes and uncommon to rare, even absent on some of the northern Precambrian routes. Stirrett (1973c: 18) had a premigratory maximum of 10,000 at Pelee on Aug. 12. Saunders & Dale (1933: 213) noted a set of 5 eggs as late as June 22, 1915 near London. J.L. Baillie and J. Edmonds estimated 20,000 flying north against a northerly gale over Long Point Bay on July 12, 1927 (Snyder, 1931: 204). McCracken, Bradstreet & Holroyd (1981: 57) estimated that 500 pairs nested in the Long Point dunes in 1967 and found nests with eggs as late as July 20 there. Beardslee & Mitchell (1965: 312) mentioned a colony of well over 2000 nests in the high banks bordering Lake Erie between Mohawk Point and Rockhouse Pt. On our June, 1962 roadside counts in Ontario Co. this was the fourth most numerous species with 789 tallied, some in each of the 11 townships (Speirs, 1975: 15). Long (1966: 33) saw an adult feeding 3 young as late as Aug. 6, 1965 at Pickering Beach. J.M. Richards found two nests with 5 eggs and one with 6 eggs among 22 active nests in Cartwright Twp. on June 10, 1968 (Tozer & Richards, 1974: 194). Snyder (1941: 68) estimated 5000 at Sand Banks, Prince Edward Co. on July 20, 1930. Devitt (1967: 108) mentioned a colony of 400 to 500 pairs at Oakview, Simcoe Co. and witnessed a premigratory flock of about 3000 at Bradford on Aug. 11, 1935. In the cottage country I noted about 120 holes in a sand bank at South River and Russell Rutter found a nest in a sawdust pile at Utterson: the latest date was Aug. 29, 1975 when Chris Harris saw 8 at Go Home Bay (Mills, 1981: 97-98). D.B. Ferguson found a nest with 6 eggs at Michael's Bay, Manitoulin on June 26, 1980 (Nicholson, 1981: 135). Speirs & Speirs (1947: 31) noted a few near North Bay between June 5 (in 1945) and July 29 (in 1944). Snyder (1942: 136) estimated 400 nest holes in a sand cliff at Gros Cap, near Sault Ste. Marie, on July 13, 1931. Baillie & Hope (1947: 14) mentioned a record of the species at Winnebago, Sudbury Dist. on June 30, 1906. Dear (1940: 133) found a nest with 4 eggs at Port Arthur on June 27, 1927. Snyder (1938: 197) found about 8 pairs nesting in a vertical bank of sawdust at Emo, Rainy River, on June 28, 1929 and naked young were found in one of these tunnels on that date. Smith (1957: 176) found a small nesting colony south of Kapuskasing on July 4, 1953 and noted a flock of 20 near Hearst on June 2, 1954. Snyder (1953: 69) reported breeding at Kenora and Malachi but found them relatively scarce in western Ontario. James (1980: 87) found a nest with 6 eggs in a gravel pit at Central Patricia on June 17, 1979. Sam Waller took a set of 4 eggs at Moose Factory on June 20, 1930 (Baillie & Harrington 1937: 215). Manning (1952: 71) saw about 30 occupied nest holes near Moosonee between June 27 and July 1, 1949 and mentioned an old Severn River record. Schueler, Baldwin & Rising (1974: 143, 146) found 11 active nest holes at Moosonee on June 4, 1972 and found them uncommon at Ft. Albany: they did not note any at other James Bay or Hudson Bay localities. Lee (1978: 27) saw a maximum of 7 at Big Trout Lake on July 5, 1975 and noted others from June 11 to July 25.

AUTUMN: Ron Tasker found a very late bird at Lorne Lake, Manitoulin, on Oct. 18, 1975 (Nicholson, 1981: 135). Weir & Quilliam (1980: 37) listed Aug. 31 as the 21-year average departure date from Kingston with the latest on Sept. 27. D. Calvert noted 11 in Whitby as late as Sept. 19, 1971 (Tozer & Richards, 1974: 194). Fleming (1907: 82) gave Oct. 9 as the latest Toronto date while Saunders (1947: 369) listed Sept. 7 as his 13-year average departure date there. Beardslee & Mitchell (1965: 312) reported 5 at Rockhouse Point, Lake Erie, as late as Sept. 30, 1942. Ussher (1965: 17) gave Sept. 2 as the 8-year average departure date from Rondeau, with the latest on Sept. 11. Numbers at Pelee fell off sharply during September and the latest 5 were noted on Oct. 5 (Stirrett, 1973d: 22).

BANDING:   One banded by B.N. Brouchoud at Manitowac, Wis. on May 24, 1964 was recovered at Gore Bay, Manitoulin on June 16, 1965 and another, banded at Gore Bay by F.E. Ludwig on June 12, 1967 was recovered at Orbisonia, Pa. on Aug. 18, 1969 (Brewer & Salvadori, 1978: 68). Well over 100 banded near Toronto returned in subsequent years to the banding locality.

**MEASUREMENTS:**
*Length:* 4.8 to 5.5 ins. (Godfrey, 1966: 266)
*Wingspread:* 10.1 to 11.0 ins. (Roberts, 1955: 639)
*Weight:* 0.5 oz. (Roberts, 1955: 639)

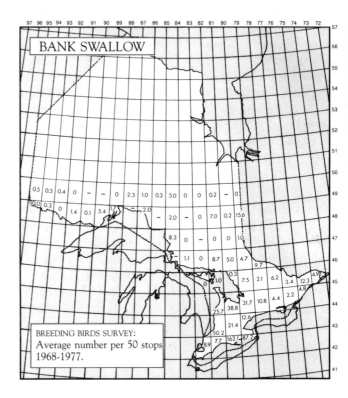

BANK SWALLOW

BREEDING BIRDS SURVEY:
Average number per 50 stops
1968-1977.

# CLIFF SWALLOW   *Hirundo pyrrhonota*   Vieillot

Cliff Swallows are uncommon or rare in most parts of southern Ontario but are perhaps the most frequently seen swallow around settlements and around highway bridges in northern Ontario. Several authors reported the former abundance of this species followed by a recent decline due to House Sparrows taking over their nests.

IDENTIFICATION:   This swallow is easily identified by its square tail and pinkish rump. After a rain you may see groups of them around mud puddles with fluttering wings raised aloft, gathering mud pellets which they use to fashion their elegant jug-shaped "pottery" nests. These are usually placed under eaves or gables of old barns, houses or under bridges.

WINTER:

SPRING:   Stirrett (1973b: 20) noted his first at Pelee on Apr. 19 and had a maximum of 25 on May 18. Ussher (1965: 18) gave May 11 as the 14-year average arrival date at Rondeau, with the earliest on Apr. 13. Saunders & Dale (1933: 214) called them "formerly abundant, now rare", with the 12-year average arrival date at London on Apr. 30 and the earliest on Apr. 20, 1916: a set of 4 eggs was found on May 27, 1898 and another set of 5 on May 31, 1916. J.L. Baillie had a Toronto record as early as Apr. 9 and gave May 7 as his 10-year average arrival date there (Saunders, 1947: 369). Ron Tozer saw two at Simcoe Pt., Pickering, as early as Apr. 15, 1960: Edgerton Pegg estimated 30 pairs nesting on his barn in Pickering Twp. on May 4, 1963, but none in 1967 and 20 pairs again on May 14, 1974 (Speirs, 1975: 18). Weir & Quilliam (1980: 37) listed May 2 as the 26-year average arrival date at Kingston with the earliest on Apr. 4. Devitt (1967: 110) gave May 15 as the 15-year average arrival date at Barrie, with the earliest on May 4, 1965. L. Beamer's median arrival date at Meaford was May 4, with the earliest on Apr. 10, 1941. Mills (1981: 100) gave Apr. 28, 1901 as the earliest date for the cottage country and reported 36 fresh nests on May 18, 1975. Nicholson (1981: 136) gave May 2 as the 10-year average arrival date for Manitoulin, the earliest on Apr. 26, 1970. MacLulich (1938: 23) gave May 6, 1913 as an arrival date for Algonquin Park. Louise Lawrence found 3 at Pimisi Bay on May 23, 1945 (Speirs & Speirs, 1947: 31). Skeel & Bondrup-Nielsen (1978: 187) saw 2 at Pukaskwa on May 23, 1977. Baillie & Hope (1943: 15) saw only one, at Rossport on May 27, 1936. Denis (1961: 3) listed May 16 as the average arrival date at Thunder Bay, with the earliest on Apr. 29, 1955. Bondrup-Nielsen (1976: 43) saw his first near Kapuskasing on May 20 in both 1974 and 1975. Elder (1979: 35) gave May 9 as the earliest Geraldton record for this common summer resident there. Peruniak (1971: 21) also considered this a common summer resident at Atikokan and had her earliest record on Apr. 28. Manning (1952: 71) cited an old record of a male in the Smithsonian Inst. collection that was taken at Moose Factory on May 17, 1860.

SUMMER:   On the 1968-1977 Breeding Bird Surveys, they were absent to uncommon on some southern Ontario routes becoming common on some northern routes (but absent on others) and most numerous in the Rainy River region. Stirrett (1973b: 20) had 50 at Pelee on June 5, but had no July record but one on Aug. 1 and 15 on Aug. 5 (Stirrett, 1973c: 18). Kelley (1978: 54) had an unusual record of 250 in Kent Co. on Aug. 18, 1969. Saunders & Dale (1933: 214) found a set of 7 eggs on June 15, 1891 and a set of 5 on June 2, 1915, near London. W.E. Clyde Todd saw an adult feeding a young bird near Pt. Rowan on July 13, 1907 (Snyder, 1931: 203). McCracken, Bradstreet & Holroyd (1981: 58) reported a nest with 3 eggs at the eastern end of Long Point on July 5, 1972 and reported other nests there and at Pt. Rowan with egg dates from May 21 to July 20. Twelve sets of eggs found in Ontario Co. totalled 49 eggs: J.A. Edwards found a nest with 4 eggs at Beaverton as late as July 20, 1926 (Speirs, 1975: 18). Allin (1940: 102) reported finding at least 5 colonies within a mile of Hampton, Darlington Twp. H.H. Southam found a nest with 1 egg and 1 small young at Pt. Traverse, Prince Edward Co., on July 3, 1938 (Snyder, 1941: 69). Weir & Quilliam (1980: 37) listed Aug. 28 as the 12-year average departure date from Kingston: Quilliam (1973: 127-128) gave details of some colonies near Kingston as well as the contents of 2 nests in the ROM: a set of 5 eggs on June 8, 1897 at Portsmouth by E. Beaupré and a set of 4 eggs on June 30, 1897 at Kingston by C.K. Clarke. Devitt (1967: 110) had information on 10 nesting colonies in Simcoe Co. Lloyd (1924: 12) found 2 nesting colonies near Ottawa in the summer of 1922. Mills (1981: 100) reported 27 nest record cards in the ROM from Muskoka and 14 from Parry Sound: I found occupied nests at Torrance as late as Aug. 3, 1937. D.B. Ferguson saw adults feeding young at Providence Bay, Manitoulin on June 30, 1977 (Nicholson, 1981: 136). Speirs & Speirs (1947: 31) noted 2 nests at Rutherglen on June 16, 1944. Louise Lawrence saw tremendous flocks that darkened the sky at Nosbonsing on Aug. 26, 1952 (Mills, 1981: 101). Snyder (1942: 136) estimated 150 at Sylvan Valley on July 20, 1931 and Harry Graham found 3 nests at Sault Ste. Marie on June 9, 1938. Baillie & Hope (1947: 14) found two nesting colonies at Bigwood on July 18 and 19, 1937 and collected 4 young from one nest. A.E. Allin found an occupied nest at Silver Islet on July 3, 1939 (Dear, 1940: 133). J.L. Baillie saw one at Big Fork, Rainy River, on July 21, 1929 and one set of eggs and one young were collected from a colony about 4 miles east of Emo on July 25, 1929 (Snyder, 1938: 198). Snyder (1953: 69) found them nesting between Kenora and Redditt on June 1, 1949, at Redditt on June 3, 1949 and at Wabigoon on June 10, 1952. James (1980: 88) found several colonies of up to 25 nests in both Pickle Lake and Central Patricia in June, 1977 and 1979. Schueler, Baldwin & Rising (1974: 146) reported 11 pairs nesting at Moosonee in 1972. C.E. Hope saw three and collected one at Ft. Severn on July 2, 1940: the one collected proved to be of a northwestern race (*Hirundo pyrrhonota hypopolia*) according to James, McLaren & Barlow (1976: 36). Manning (1952: 71) suggested the presence of a breeding colony at Ft. Severn in the late 1700's.

**AUTUMN:** Nicholson (1981: 136) saw his latest Manitoulin bird on Sept. 15, 1975. Devitt (1967: 110) gave Sept. 11, 1938 as the latest Simcoe Co. record (at Bradford by D.S. Miller and J.M. Speirs). Weir & Quilliam (1980: 37) listed Sept. 26 as the latest Kingston date. Long (1968b: 20) noted two at Pickering Beach as late as Sept. 27, 1967. Saunders (1947: 369) gave Sept. 29 as his latest Toronto sighting. Beardslee & Mitchell (1965: 315) mentioned one seen by H.H. Axtell at Ft. Erie on Sept. 24, 1954. Ussher (1965: 18) gave Sept. 26 as his latest Rondeau record. Stirrett (1973d: 23) had a fall maximum of 20 on Sept. 4 and his latest two at Pelee on Sept. 30.

**BANDING:** Marshall Field banded 50 from a colony just north of St. Thomas on June 12 and July 2, 1949: 8 were retaken there on July 16, 1950 and three in July, 1952 when 100 nests were occupied (Brooman, 1954: 27).

**MEASUREMENTS:**
*Length:* 5 to 6 ins.
(Godfrey, 1966: 269)
*Wingspread:* 11.5 to 12.3
ins. (Roberts, 1955: 639)
*Weight:* 0.75 oz. (Roberts,
1955: 639).

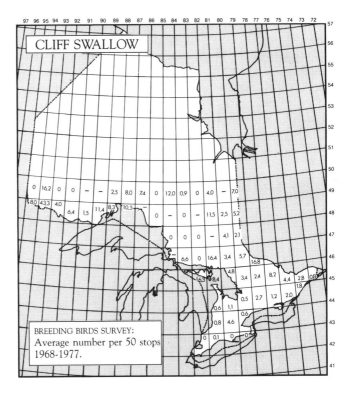

CLIFF SWALLOW

BREEDING BIRDS SURVEY:
Average number per 50 stops
1968-1977.

# BARN SWALLOW   *Hirundo rustica*   Linnaeus

The Barn Swallow is one of the most cosmopolitan of birds, at home wherever man and flying insects provide homesites and food. They frequently build on the beams in barns, on ledges under eaves or under bridges. Two broods are often raised in a season. Our Ontario birds winter as far south as Chile and Argentina.

**IDENTIFICATION:**   The long, trailing outer tail featuers distinguish this species from our other swallows: these feathers are shorter in young than in adults but still much more pronounced than in the somewhat similarly coloured Cliff Swallow which can always be distinguished by its pinkish rump.

**WINTER:**   One was found at the Greenvale sewage ponds near London on Dec. 3, 1979 and stayed until the cold snap on Jan.6, 1980: D. Murray found another at Melbourne as late as Jan. 21, 1980 (Goodwin, 1980: 268). J. Strickland reported one at the Greenvale ponds the following winter on Dec. 23 (Goodwin, 1981: 297).

**SPRING:**   Stirrett (1973b: 23) saw 31 at Pelee on Apr. 11, his earliest record there: his maximum estimate was 1000 on May 3-4. Ussher (1965: 17) gave Apr. 22 as the 21-year average arrival date at Rondeau, the earliest on Apr. 16. Saunders & Dale (1933: 213) gave Apr. 18 as the 17-year average arrival date at London, with the earliest on Apr. 13,

1916: a set of 5 eggs was noted on May 29, 1902. Fleming (1907: 82) gave Apr. 8, 1890, as his earliest Toronto date and Saunders (1947: 369) listed Apr. 23 as his 13-year average arrival date. Doris H. Speirs saw one as early as March 30, 1962 in Pickering Twp. and Edgerton Pegg reported 10 pairs nesting as early as May 10, 1974: the spring peak in Pickering is about May 16 (Speirs, 1975: 17). Tozer & Richards (1974: 195) saw four near Lake Scugog as early as Apr. 6, 1969 and about 1000 there on May 21, 1961: they also noted three active nests near there on May 15, 1965. Weir & Quilliam (1980: 37) listed Apr. 12 as the 29-year average arrival date at Kingston with the earliest on Apr. 3. Devitt (1967: 110) gave Apr. 24 as the 21-year average arrival date at Barrie, with the earliest on Apr. 15, 1964. L. Beamer's median arrival date at Meaford was Apr. 20 with one amazingly early pair seen at 6 ft. by E. Durkin on March 18, 1945 at Camperdown! A Port Sydney skin in the ROM is labelled Apr. 3, 1901, but the 8-year average arrival date at Bala was Apr. 26 (Mills, 1981: 99). The 12-year average arrival date on Manitoulin was Apr. 20, with the earliest on Apr. 13, 1969 (Nicholson, 1981: 135). MacLulich (1938: 23) gave Apr. 22, 1932 as his earliest date for Algonquin Park:C.H.D. Clarke noted a completed nest on a house at Brule Lake on May 26, 1934. Speirs & Speirs (1947: 31) saw two at North Bay on Apr. 29, 1944. Skeel & Bondrup-Nielsen (1978: 186) saw their first at Pukaskwa on May 10, 1977 and found the first nest with eggs on May 26. Denis (1961: 3) gave May 14 as the average arrival date at Thunder Bay, with the earliest on Apr. 29, 1955. Bondrup-Nielsen (1976: 43) saw his first near Kapuskasing on May 9, 1975. Elder (1979: 35) gave May 9 as his earliest Geraldton date for this common summer resident. Peruniak (1971: 21) gave Apr. 29 as her earliest Atikokan date. Cringan (1953a: 3) saw his first at Sioux Lookout on May 18 in 1953.

SUMMER:    On the 1968-1977 Breeding Bird Survey the Barn Swallow was common on all routes north to Mattawa and Sudbury and fairly common on most northerly routes. Stirrett (1973c: 18 and 1973d: 22) noted as many as 30 at Pelee during the nesting season with a southbound maximum of 1000 on Aug. 28. W.E. Saunders estimated that 20,000 left a roost in willows near London on Aug. 21, 1901 between 5:11 and 5:37 a.m. (Saunders & Dale, 1933: 213). Most sets of eggs in Ontario Co. contained 5 eggs: 52 sets totalled 249 eggs (Speirs, 1975: 17). Long (1966: 33) estimated 2000 at Pickering Beach on Aug. 17, 1963. Allin (1940: 102) followed a second brood in Darlington Twp. in which the eggs were laid on July 14, 15, 16 and 17, incubation began on July 18, the eggs hatched on July 31 and the young left on Aug. 23 but returned nightly for a week. Quilliam (1973: 127) reported two broods of 4 each that left her Kingston garage on June 24 and Aug. 15, 1971: also a set of 5 eggs taken by E. Beaupré on June 8, 1896 on Simcoe Is. In Simcoe Co. dates for fresh eggs ranged from May 21 (1922) to June 21 (1935) and young in the nest were noted as early as June 12 in 1935 and young fed by parents seen as late as Aug. 25, 1945 (Devitt, 1967: 109-110). Lloyd (1924: 12) reported a nest with 7 eggs found near Ottawa on May 29, 1909. More than 100 nests have been reported from the cottage country (Mills, 1981: 99). D.B. Ferguson found a nest with 5 eggs on June 30, 1977 at Providence Bay, Manitoulin (Nicholson, 1981: 135). Speirs & Speirs (1947: 31) reported a nest with 5 eggs on June 20, 1945 near Eau Claire and a nest with 3 young about 8 days old at Rutherglen on Aug. 12, 1944. Baillie & Hope (1947: 14) observed a nest with 4 eggs at Chapleau on June 16, 1937; a nest with 5 eggs on July 20, 1937 at Bigwood and a nest with 5 large young at Biscotasing on June 29, 1937. Skeel & Bondrup-Nielsen (1978: 187) found 10 nests with eggs at Pukaskwa in 1977, several of these in caves along the Lake Superior shore: the first nest with young was noted on

June 20, 1977. Baillie & Hope (1943: 15) found a nest with 5 eggs at Rossport on June 4, 1936. Dear (1940: 133) reported a nest with 5 eggs found on a rock ledge on Pie Is., off Thunder Bay, on June 23, 1935 and a nest with 4 eggs in McGregor Twp. on June 23, 1926. On June 25, 1929, Snyder (1938: 197-198) collected the male of an isolated pair nesting in a stable at Big Fork, Rainy River: in less than two hours another male was flying about with the resident female. Smith (1957: 176) found occupied nests at South Porcupine on June 19, 1953 and one at Hearst on June 2, 1954. Snyder (1953: 69) found them breeding at Kenora, Ingolf, Upsala, Wabigoon and Malachi: in this part of western Ontario they were restricted to such settlements. James (1980: 87) found nests with 3, 4, and 5 eggs about 43 km. NE of Pickle Lake on June 17, 1979 and a nest with 4 eggs in Central Patricia on June 11, 1977. Schueler, Baldwin & Rising (1974: 143) noted the species only at Cochrane and Moosonee. Sam Waller reported one killed by Clarence Hester at Moose Factory in 1924 (Baillie & Harrington, 1937: 216). Peck (1972: 345) saw an old nest in a shed at Cape Henrietta Maria where H. Lumsden had seen birds entering on June 25, 1964 and June 24, 1970. Lee (1978: 27) noted single males at Ft. Severn on June 19, 1975 and at Big Trout Lake on July 18, 1975.

AUTUMN: Peruniak (1971: 21) gave Sept. 25 as her latest Atikokan record. Skeel & Bondrup-Nielsen (1978: 186) saw two at Pukaskwa as late as Oct. 15, 1977. MacLulich (1938: 23) gave Sept. 3, 1934 as his latest Algonquin Park date. The latest Manitoulin record was on Oct. 2, 1971 (Nicholson, 1981: 135). The latest report from the cottage country was on Sept. 10, 1973 near Huntsville by T. Spratt (Mills, 1981: 100). Devitt (1967: 110) gave Sept. 15, 1940 as his latest Simcoe Co. record. Weir & Quilliam (1980: 37) listed Sept. 14 as the 25-year average departure date from Kingston, with the latest on Oct. 14. Speirs (1975: 17) reported one seen by R. Scovell at Whitby as late as Oct. 18, 1959. J.L. Baillie gave Sept. 4 as his 25-year average departure date from Toronto, with his latest on Sept. 28 (Saunders, 1947: 363). Beardslee & Mitchell (1965: 314) reported one at Sherkston, near Niagara, on Oct. 8, 1944. Saunders & Dale (1933: 213) noted a late bird at London on Oct. 14, 1917. Ussher (1965: 17) gave Sept. 12 as the 14-year average departure date from Rondeau, with the latest on Oct. 2. Stirrett (1973d: 23) had his latest 8 at Pelee on Oct. 4.

BANDING: Marshall Field banded 4 near St. Thomas on June 12, 1949 (Brooman, 1954: 27). One banded at Island Beach, N.J. on May 21, 1970 was recovered at Queensboro, Ont. on May 7, 1971 (Brewer & Salvadori, 1976: 83). One banded by J.B. Miles at Dundas Marsh on Sept. 3, 1966 was recovered at Macedon, N.Y. in May, 1967: during the period 1965-1970 some 1333 were banded in Ontario (Brewer & Salvadori, 1978: 34, 68).

**MEASUREMENTS:**
*Length:* 5.8 to 7.7 ins. (Godfrey, 1966: 267)
*Wingspread:* 11 3/4 to 13 1/2 ins. (Roberts, 1955: 639)
*Weight:* 0.56 to 0.75 oz. (Roberts, 1955: 639)

**REFERENCE:**
Ashdown, John F. 1970 An observation on the feeding

activities of Barn Swallows.
Ont. Field Biologist,
No. 24: 39.
On July 2, 1969 two adults
gave 1009 feedings to 5
young hatched 14 days
during an all day watch
from 0533 to 2125: max.
rate was 88/hr from 1800
to 1900.

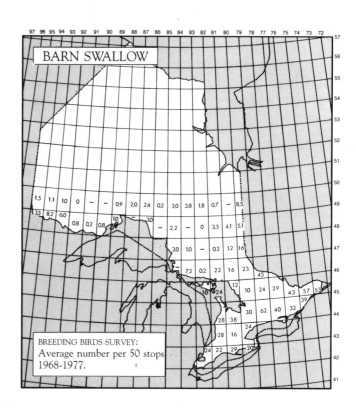

BARN SWALLOW

BREEDING BIRDS SURVEY:
Average number per 50 stops
1968-1977.

## GRAY JAY  *Perisoreus canadensis*  (Linnaeus)

This is a bird of coniferous forests, rarely seen in southern Ontario, except in winter when invasions sometimes occur from the north. In northern Ontario they are familiar to most outdoor enthusiasts, ever willing to share a meal with campers, or in summer, seen floating from tree to tree in family parties. I well remember being shown a March nest by Louise Lawrence, a bulky, well insulated structure, with two birds on the nest. See Rutter (1969) for an account of what was known about the biology of this fascinating species, their food storing habits, nesting and territoriality.

    **IDENTIFICATION:** This is a robin-or-grackle-sized jay with soft gray plumage, a black cap, white forehead and white ring around the back of the neck. The young are dull black and might be mistaken at first glance for grackles, but the floating flight from tree top to tree top with their parents will soon distinguish them. The Gray Jay has a great variety of calls from soft "whoo'whoo" to a grating "graak," reminiscent of Yellow-breasted Chat calls.

    **WINTER:** On the 1968-1977 Christmas counts this was a common species in northern Ontario, fairly common near Algonquin Park, becoming rare to absent in southern Ontario. George W. Allen wrote (*fide* Wm. Cross) that a great host appeared in Toronto in the winter of 1839-1840 and continued all winter "as common as House Sparrows are now" (Thompson, 1890: 184 and Fleming, 1907: 77). One was seen on the Toronto Christmas count in 1929 and two in 1939, but none on the other counts from 1925 to 1945 (Saunders, 1947: 379). Speirs (1975: 20) cited details of Pickering records during invasions in the winters of 1965-1966 and 1972-1973. W.H. Lunn noted them at Carrying Place during 1921-1922 and one near Wellington in December, 1925 (Snyder, 1941: 69). Quilliam (1973: 128) had a Kingston record on Dec. 31, 1964. Devitt (1967: 111) cited Barrie records on Dec. 26, 1941 and Dec. 18, 1965 and saw one as late as Feb. 24, 1952 at Midhurst. L. Beamer reported Meaford sightings on Dec. 27, 1948, Feb. 26, 1950 and five noted just east of Thornbury on Dec. 21, 1951. Wm. Melville found them "not uncommon" in Muskoka in 1888-1889 (Thompson, 1890: 190-191). The first Christmas count record for Manitoulin was on Dec. 20, 1975 when 5 were seen (Nicholson, 1981: 137). Strickland, Tozer & Rutter (1982) mentioned finding Gray Jays looking well fed and contented in the dead of winter in Algonquin Park miles from any visible food supply (thanks to food stored the previous summer). Dennison (1980: 147) reported the species on 18 of 25 Christmas counts at Sault Ste. Marie, with a high of 18 in 1968. Skeel & Bondrup-Nielsen (1978: 187) noted 22 on 15 days during the winter of 1976-1977 at Pukaskwa, where it ranked 7 in the relative abundance of winter birds.

SPRING: On March 15, 1942, Saunders (1947: 63), with Jim Baillie, Tom Murray and Art Smith, watched one stripping bark from a birch tree near Vandorf, but no further nesting evidence was forthcoming. One of the Pickering invaders lingered as late as Apr. 8, 1973 at Lorne Almack's feeder (Speirs, 1975: 20). Allin (1940: 102) noted one in Darlington Twp. on Apr. 21, 1922. Calvert (1925: 72) noted the last of the previous winter's influx at Lindsay in March, 1905. H.B. Haugh collected a male at Little Lake, Barrie, on Apr. 7, 1930, and three remained in Barrie until May 8, 1966 (Devitt, 1967: 112). By far the most southerly breeding record in Ontario was in the Mer Bleue Bog near Ottawa where nest building was noted as early as March 2, 1974; two eggs were noted in the nest early on March 23 and 3 eggs later in the day; still 3 eggs on Apr. 7 but one young and 2 eggs on Apr. 16: the young now out of the nest was banded on May 2 and the nest and two infertile eggs collected (Ouellet, O'Donell & Foxall, 1976: 5-10). Near the southern border of the usual breeding range Nicholson (1981: 137) cited records of adults with young on Manitoulin on May 21, 1970 (Ron Tasker) and May 20, 1980 (Nicholson). Speirs & Speirs (1947: 31) gave details of a nest at Talon Chute, near Rutherglen, from March 25, 1945 when it was being built to Apr. 23 when it held 5 eggs: on May 9 the one infertile egg was collected for the NMC by Louise Lawrence. Skeel & Bondrup-Nielsen (1978: 188) noted young with adults on May 26, 1977 and May 30, 1973 at Pukaskwa. Dear (1940: 134) found a nest with 4 eggs on March 13, 1933 and a nest with 3 eggs on March 14, 1934 near Thunder Bay. Bondrup-Nielsen (1976: 47) saw the first young of the year on May 11, 1975 near Kapuskasing. A nest at Sapawe, Rainy River, held 3 eggs on March 28, 1982 and 3 young in April according to N. Blogg (Weir, 1982: 848). Baillie & Harrington (1937: 219) reported a nest with 4 young at Wabigoon in April, 1928. Cringan (1953b: 4) saw 3 young at Kasabonika Lake on May 30, 1953.

SUMMER: On the 1968-1977 Breeding Bird Surveys Gray Jays were fairly common on most northern Ontario routes, becoming rare south to Algonquin Park with none in southern Ontario. Stirrett (1973c: 18) reported one at Pelee, collected by Wm. Wyett in July, 1969. Two were reported at the Mer Bleue Bog, near Ottawa, on June 23, 1973, fide G.R. Hanes (Goodwin, 1973: 865). Mills (1981: 102) cited several summer records for the Muskoka and Parry Sound regions, with August records in 1904 and 1972, perhaps precursors on invasions farther south in fall of those years. Nicholson (1981: 137) saw a pair with two young on Burnt Is., Manitoulin, on June 12, 1971. MacLulich (1938: 24) listed an adult male and juvenile female collected at Biggar Lake, Algonquin Park, on Aug. 27, 1932 and Aug. 21, 1932 respectively, and cited several records of young seen in the park in summer. Ricker & Clarke (1939: 15) saw young at Frank's Bay, Lake Nipissing, on June 3, 1932. Baillie & Hope (1947: 15) collected a juv. ♀ at Chapleau on June 3, 1937 and 2 juv. ♂ and 1 juv. ♀ there on June 9, 1937: they reported nests at Chapleau and Cartier and flying young at Biscotasing. Skeel & Bondrup-Nielsen (1978: 188) reported immatures at Pukaskwa on June 5, 1973 and June 17, 1975. Baillie & Hope (1943: 15) collected young at Marathon from June 10-18 and at Amyot from June 27 to July 4, 1936. Snyder (1928: 265) collected young at Lake Nipigon on July 16 and Aug. 5, 1924. In 1945, Kendeigh (1947: 26) found a breeding population of 4 pairs per 100 acres at Black Sturgeon Lake and Speirs (1949: 148) also noted one pair on each of three 25-acre plots at nearby Eaglehead Lake in 1946. Snyder (1938: 198) collected a juv. M at Off Lake, Rainy River, on July 2, 1929. Snyder (1928: 26) collected 8 young at Lake Abitibi from June 3 to 10, 1925. Elder (1979: 36) called this a common permanent resident at Geraldton. In western Ontario, Snyder (1953: 69) had his highest daily total of 20 at Savanne on July 8, 1937. James (1980: 88) encountered family groups at Pickle Lake on most days in June of 1977 and 1979. Hope (1938: 29) noted fully fledged young being fed by adults on June 2, 1938 at Favourable Lake. Ross James collected 2 young at Harricanaw River, near James Bay, on June 27 and July 6, 1982, where the species was noted daily. Manning (1952: 72) noted juveniles in spruce forests at Sandy Is., Raft River and as far north as Shagamu River, near Hudson Bay, in the summer of 1947. J. Satterly saw a juvenile at Stull Lake on the Manitoba border at 54° N on June 20, 1936 (Baillie & Harrington, 1937: 219). James, Ridges, in the summers of 1980 and 1981 and collected 10 adults and 1 young there. Schueler, Baldwin & Rising (1974: 146) reported 4 young at Winisk on June 22, 1971 and reported nesting evidence at Moosonee, Hawley Lake and Cochrane with a sighting at Attawapiskat. Lee (1978: 27) noted the species on all three study quadrats at Big Trout Lake in 1975. In 1940, C.E. Hope saw up to 7 in June and July, 1940 at Ft. Severn and collected a juvenile there on June 17.

AUTUMN: Doug. McRae and Alan Wormington noted from 1 to 12 each day from Oct. 14 to Nov. 22, 1981 at Netitishi Point, James Bay. Peruniak (1971: 21) observed a fall movement at Atikokan in October, 1961. Nicholson (1981: 137) noted an irruption on Manitoulin starting with the first on Sept. 6, 1975 and a maximum of 15 on Oct. 12. Devitt (1967: 111) gave several fall records for Barrie during invasion years, with the earliest on Oct. 25 in 1904 and on Sept. 21 in 1941. Quilliam (1973: 129, 198) mentioned the 1904 invasion at Kingston when the first was seen on Oct. 7: she also listed Kingston specimens taken on Nov. 3, 1929, Nov. 9, 1941 and 2 on Nov. 16, 1941: the 1972 invasion produced records near there on Oct. 21 and Nov. 5, J.H. Fleming reported a flight at Wellington, Prince Edward Co., on Oct. 21, 1904 (Snyder, 1941: 69). Calvert (1925: 72) called them "frequent" near Lindsay in November, 1904, R. Charles Long noted the first of the 1965 invasion at Pickering Beach on Oct. 13: see other Ontario Co. details in Speirs (1975: 20). The earliest Toronto record appears to be one noted by J.L. Baillie on Oct. 12 (Saunders, 1947: 369): York Edwards spotted 4 near Toronto's Eastern Gap on Oct. 19, 1941 and R.M. Saunders saw one at Purpleville on Nov. 16, 1941 (Saunders, 1947: 292). Fleming (1907: 77) mentioned the Toronto influx in October, 1904. R.A. Brooks saw one at Niagara Falls on Nov. 23, 1957 (Sheppard, 1960: 34).

T.D. Patterson added a new bird to the Middlesex Co. list when he found a Gray Jay in London on Oct. 26, 1929 (Saunders, 1930: 50). Kelley (1978: 54) reported two at Pelee on Oct. 11, 1972: one of these was banded.

BANDING: Gray Jays banded by R.J. Rutter in Algonquin Park on Dec. 11, 1968 were recovered at Barrie on a later date (found dead), another banded on Nov. 14, 1963 was recovered near Bracebridge on May 19, 1967 and another banded on Oct. 17, 1964 was recovered near Bracebridge on May 19, 1969 (Brewer & Salvadori, 1976: 84: Brewer & Salvadori, 1978: 68). Rutter (1969: 300-316) also did a good deal of colour banding in Algonquin Park to study territorial and other aspects of the life of Gray Jays.

**MEASUREMENTS:**
*Length* 10.8 to 12.2 ins. (Godfrey, 1966: 271)
*Wingspread:* 16 to 17 ins. (Roberts, 1955: 641)
*Weight:* 4 ♂ averaged 72.9 g. 2 ♀ averaged 67.1 g. (Hope, 1938: 29).

**REFERENCES:**
Campbell, J. Mitchell 1965 An impressive Gray Jay migration. Can. Field-Nat., 79:(2): 157-158.

Devitt, O.E. 1961 An example of the whisper song of the Gray Jay (*Perisoreus canadensis*) Auk, 78:(2): 265-266.

Dow, Douglas D. 1965 The role of saliva in food storage by the Gray Jay. Auk, 82:(2): 139-154.

Lawrence, Louise de Kiriline 1947 Five days with a pair of nesting Canada Jays. Can. Field-Nat., 61:(1): 1-11.

Lawrence, Louise de Kiriline 1957 Displacement singing in a Canada Jay (*Perisoreus canadensis*). Auk. 74: (2): 260-261.

Lawrence, Louise de Kiriline 1969 Notes on hoarding nesting material, display, and flycatching in the Gray Jay (*Perisoreus canadensis*). Auk. 85:(1): 139.

Ouelett, Henri; Stephen J. O'Donnell & Roger A. Foxall 1976 Gray Jay nesting in the Mer Bleue, Ottawa, Ontario. Can. Field-Nat., 90:(1): 5-10.

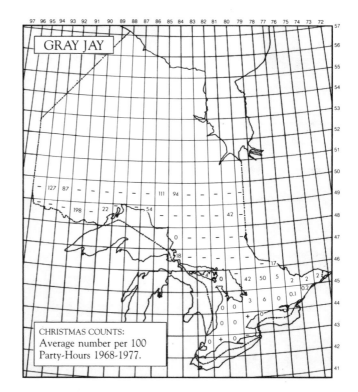

GRAY JAY

CHRISTMAS COUNTS:
Average number per 100
Party-Hours 1968-1977.

Rutter, Russell J. 1969 A contribution to the biology of the Gray Jay (*Perisoreus canadensis*). Can. Field-Nat., 83: (4): 300-316.

Saunders. W.E. 1930 The Whisky Jack. Can. Field-Nat., 44:(2) 50.

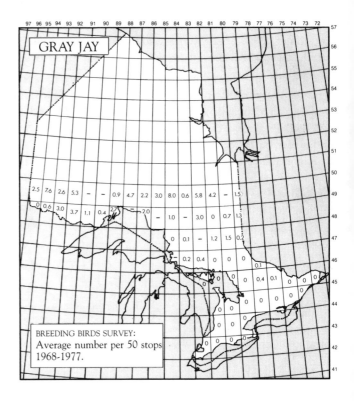

GRAY JAY

BREEDING BIRDS SURVEY:
Average number per 50 stops
1968-1977.

# BLUE JAY  *Cyanocitta cristata*  (Linnaeus)

Anyone with a bird feeder in Ontario will no doubt be familiar with the jaunty Blue Jay. Although some of our jays migrate as far south as Louisiana in winter, others stay with us all year (see banding section below). They are rare north of 50° N.

IDENTIFICATION: Most of its upper surface is a bright blue, with black and white accents; its under parts are gray, with a black "necklace". The conspicuous crest make them unmistakable even at quite a distance. Banders can distinguish young by the lack of black bars on the greater wing coverts: adults have conspicuous bars. The song is a musical yodel "kee-ookle-ook", calls include a raucous "jay-jay" and imitations of various hawks.

WINTER: On the 1968-1977 Christmas counts the Blue Jay was a common species from Lake Erie north to Dryden, with the highest numbers per 100 party-hours near Bancroft and the lowest northeast of Lake Superior. Stirrett (1973a: 17) had a winter maximum of 25 at Pelee. In 1981 David Elder noted it on Jan. 1 at Atikokan.

SPRING: Stirrett (1973b: 20) had a spring maximum of 1000 at Pelee on May 11. Saunders & Dale (1933: 215) reported five sets of eggs for the London area: a set of 6 on May 13, 1896; 5 on May 23, 1904; 4 on May 24, 1908; 4 on Apr. 29, 1915 and 4 on May 10, 1915. McCracken, Bradstreet & Holroyd (1981: 58) reported a nest with eggs at Backus Woods on May 10, 1955 (M. Porter) and another at Turkey Point on May 17, 1947 (George North) but no nests yet on Long Point though the species was found on three study quadrats on the point. Fleming (1907: 77) reported a nest at Toronto on May 15, 1892. Speirs (1938: 44) gave May 7 as the spring peak at Toronto. Paul Catling found a nest with 4 eggs at Amos Ponds, Pickering as early as Apr. 29, 1968, while I saw 100 migrants moving NE on May 11, 1958 (Speirs, 1975: 21). Quilliam (1973: 129, 130) noted Kingston nests on May 14, 1901, May 12, 1905 (4 eggs); May 12, 1960 (4 eggs) and May 20, 1965 (2 young): flocks of migrants were passing Prince Edward Point at this time of year during spring, 1971. At Big Cedar Point, Lake Simcoe, W.W. Smith noted a nest with eggs as early as May 1, 1938, while Paul Harrington reported enormous flocks passing Wasaga Beach from May 3 to 20, 1922 (Devitt, 1967: 112). Harry Graham found a nest with 4 eggs at Maclennan, near Sault Ste. Marie, on May 16, 1937 (Snyder, 1942: 137). Baillie & Hope (1943: 15) heard one at Rossport imitating the high whistle of the Broad-winged Hawk on May 28, 1936, just as they frequently imitate the Red-shouldered Hawk's scream in southern Ontario. Dear (1940: 134) found a nest with 4 eggs at Whitefish Lake, Thunder Bay, on May 31, 1929. Smith (1957: 176) saw one on May 27 and 2 on May 29 at New Liskeard. Ross James saw one at Pickle Lake on May 29, 1977. Cringan (1953a: 3) noted his first in 1953 at Perrault Falls on May 15 at the northern limit of the range.

SUMMER: On the 1968-1977 Breeding Bird Survey the Blue Jay was present and fairly common, on most routes in Ontario, common near Rainy River and uncommon to absent on many routes north and east of Lake Superior. Stirrett (1973c: 18) had a June maximum of 6 at Pelee but listed it as a nesting species. Snyder (1930: 192) reported two nests in King Twp.: one with 5 eggs on July 8, 1926 about 50 ft. up on a horizontal branch of an elm; the other with 4 young on July 20, 1926 in a more typical position, 10 ft. up in a hemlock. Populations in Ontario Co. forests averaged 15 birds per 100 acres, with a maximum of 36 per 100 acres in a mixed coniferous – deciduous forest in Scott Twp. (Speirs, 1975: 21). Tozer & Richards (1974: 199) reported a nest with 5 eggs in Darlington Twp. as late as June 19, 1967. W.W. Smith noted young in the nest at Big Cedar Point from June 2 (1935) to June 28, 1940 (Devitt, 1967: 112). Only 3 Muskoka and 5 Parry Sound nests have been reported although the Blue Jay has been noted on almost all the local Breeding Birds Surveys (Mills, 1981: 103). Kenneth Bennison found a nest with one young near Tehkummah, Manitoulin, in mid-June, 1979 (Nicholson, 1981: 137). C.H.D. Clarke noted young being fed at Brule Lake on July 15, 1934 (MacLulich, 1938: 24). Louise Lawrence saw a brood of flying young being fed at Pimisi Bay on July 26, 1944 (Speirs & Speirs, 1947: 31). Flying young were collected at Biscotasing on July 3 and 6, 1937 and at Bigwood on July 20, 1937 (Baillie & Hope, 1947: 15). Dear (1940: 134) saw 4 young on June 13, 1939 near Thunder Bay. Snyder (1938: 198) collected a male at Emo on June 5, 1929. Smith (1957: 176) found them "not common" in the Clay Belt but saw two on June 4, 1954 about 30 miles west of Hearst. Snyder (1928: 26) considered them rare at Lake Abitibi but collected a male there on June 19, 1925. Bondrup-Nielsen (1976: 43) found them uncommon in 1974 and 1975 near Kapuskasing. Elder (1979: 36) called this a fairly common species and a permanent resident at Geraldton. Snyder (1953: 70) found them common from Kenora to Wabigoon, less common north to Sioux Lookout. Ross James saw two on June 2, 1977 near Pickle Lake. Schueler, Baldwin & Rising (1974: 143) reported this species only at Cochrane and Fraserdale, not at any of their more northerly stations.

AUTUMN: George M. Sutton saw one at Long Portage, Mattagami River, about 3 miles north of Smoky Falls, on Oct. 9, 1923, the most northerly record known to Todd (1963: 514). Skeel & Bondrup-Nielsen (1978: 188) saw 16 on Sept. 2 and 13 on Sept. 20, 1977, flying overhead at Pukaskwa. At Mississagi Light, Manitoulin, about 800 were noted on Sept. 22, 1974 and again on Sept. 23, 1975 (Nicholson, 1981: 137). D. Sutherland noted about 175 on Beausoleil Is. on Sept. 15, 1976 and 500 the following day; and C. Harris counted 147 flying over Go Home Bay on Oct. 6, 1973 (Mills, 1981: 104). Fall flights of 25 to 30 birds were noted going SW at Holland River on Sept. 11 in both 1937 and 1938 (Devitt, 1967: 112). Adults were seen feeding fledged young at our feeding station at Pickering as late as Sept. 9, 1965 and the peak of the southwesterly fall flight there has been about Sept. 24 (Speirs, 1975: 21). Speirs (1938: 52) gave Sept. 10 as the fall peak date at Toronto. Dr. & Mrs. Williams counted 4000 passing Port Stanley in one hour on Sept. 29, 1952 (Brooman, 1954: 27). A.A. Wood reported them eating skunk cabbage seeds in cedar swamps near London in late fall (Saunders & Dale, 1933: 215). Stirrett (1973d: 23) had a fall maximum of 10,000 at Pelee on Sept. 16.

BANDING: The flocks that we see moving SW in fall appear to be headed for the Mississippi Valley: birds banded near Toronto have turned up near Port Burwell, Chatham, Detroit and Kentucky: one banded by Harold Richards on Aug. 6, 1968 ended up in northern Louisiana on Nov. 25, 1968. Some, however go the opposite direction. One banded near Port Huron, Mich. on July 5, 1964 turned up near Toronto on Dec. 27, 1964. One banded by Alf Bunker at Cherrywood, near Pickering, on May 17, 1958 was recovered in Nov., 1962 at St. Jerome, Que. (near Montreal) by J.G. Villeneuve. Brewer & Salvadori (1975: 84) listed one banded at Long Point on May 10, 1958 and recovered 64 miles west at London, Ont. on Apr. 12, 1971. Another Long Point bird banded on May 2, 1971 was recovered 121 miles west at Durham, Ont. on Nov. 5, 1971: one banded at Pt. Pelee on Oct. 1, 1970 was recovered 112 miles east at Girard, Pa. on Sept. 9, 1971. They also gave an interesting longevity record of one banded at Niagara Falls, Ont. on July 13, 1964 and retaken there on Sept. 19, 1971. Speirs (1975: 21) gave details of three colour-banded jays at our Pickering home: Lucie McDougall banded one there on March 17, 1950: we recaptured it on March 25, 1956 and added a gold band: it returned for a few days each spring and fall and was last seen on Feb. 19, 1963 (our oldest bird): another was banded with a blue band on Apr. 12, 1956 and was seen almost daily thereafter at all seasons until Oct. 2, 1961: the third with a red band was banded on Nov. 16, 1963: it came occasionally until Apr. 12, 1968.

**MEASUREMENTS:**

*Length:* 11.0 to 12.5 ins. (Godfrey, 1966: 272)
*Wingspread:* 15.7 to 17.5 ins. (Roberts, 1955: 641)
*Weight:* The average of 23 Ontario birds in ROM was 92 g. (80 to 108½ g.) Five we banded at our home weighed 82, 84, 88, 94 (Blue Left) and 94 (Red Left).

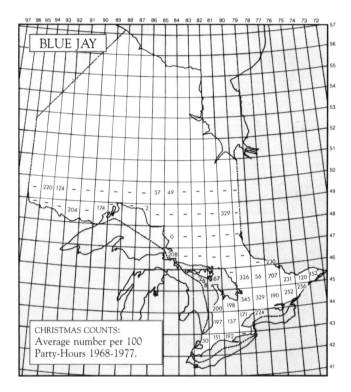

BLUE JAY

CHRISTMAS COUNTS: Average number per 100 Party-Hours 1968-1977.

550

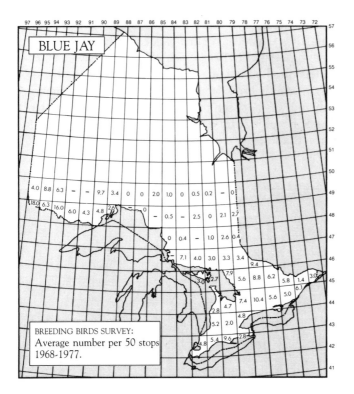

BLUE JAY

BREEDING BIRDS SURVEY:
Average number per 50 stops
1968-1977.

# CLARK'S NUTCRACKER  *Nucifraga columbiana*  (Wilson)

This is a bird of the coniferous forests of the Rocky Mountains, accidental in Ontario.

**IDENTIFICATION:** Nutcrackers are somewhat larger than robins but built more like Starlings, with a shortish tail and pointed bill. It is predominantly gray but with black wings and tail, edged with white, usually noisily uttering harsh "kraa-kraa-kraa" notes.

**WINTER:** Two were reported on the Dryden Christmas count held on Dec. 17, 1972.

**SPRING:** Rob Nisbet reported seeing one on Caribou Is., Lake Superior, on May 9, 1981 (Goodwin, 1981: 819).

**SUMMER:** The two at Oxdrift (near Dryden) were present until about June 19, 1973 (Goodwin, 1973: 865).

**AUTUMN:** Two were sighted and one photographed in Aubrey Twp., near Dryden, from Nov. 14 to 24, 1972 by C. Griffiths *et al* (Goodwin, 1973: 54). Another was reported near Thunder Bay (in Paipoonge Twp.) from Nov. 9 into December, 1972 but later proved to be a Mockingbird (Goodwin, 1973: 610).

**MEASUREMENTS:**
*Length:* 12 to 13 ins.
(Godfrey, 1966: 277)
*Wingspread:* about 22 ins.
(Roberts, 1955: 641)
*Weight:* about 5 oz.
(Terres, 1980: 144).

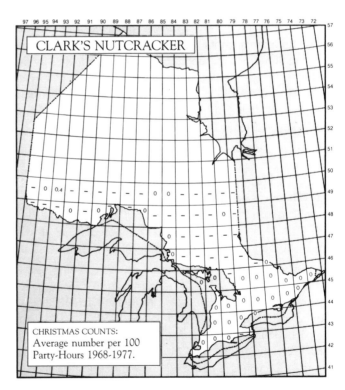

CLARK'S NUTCRACKER

CHRISTMAS COUNTS:
Average number per 100
Party-Hours 1968-1977.

# BLACK-BILLED MAGPIE  *Pica pica*  (Linnaeus)

This is a well-known bird of northern Europe, Asia and western North America, but is rare in Ontario. Those seen about southern Ontario cities are apt to be escaped cage birds. It is a spectacular big beauty with an enquiring mind and acquisitive habits, a builder of bulky stick nests, sometimes taken over by birds of prey as a basis for their nests.

IDENTIFICATION: This is a big black and white bird, as long as a crow but built more delicately, more like a jay. Its tapering tail may make up over half of its total length, streaming behind as it flies.

WINTER: On the 1968-1977 Christmas counts it was fairly common at Atikokan, uncommon at Dryden and rare at Thunder Bay, not seen elsewhere in Ontario. Kelley (1978: 55) reported one seen at Pelee by many observers from Jan. 12 into February, 1973. One was seen by many observers at a feeder on the estate of Dr. McGuire near St. Catharines until Jan. 1, 1960 (Beardslee & Mitchell, 1965: 319). I have two Toronto sightings, one where Cherry Beach is now situated, the other along the Don Valley north of Bloor St. on Feb. 3, 1935, probably one of two birds that escaped from the Riverdale Zoo the previous June. J. Kelley also noted one by Toronto's lakeshore from Dec. 25 to Jan. 3, 1982 (Weir, 1982: 290). Tozer & Richards (1974: 200) reported sightings of a bird raised in captivity and later released, in Darlington Twp. on Dec. 28, 1970 and Jan. 2, 1971. One showed up at a Peterborough feeder in early January, 1982 and perhaps the same bird was noted by T. Sprague at a feeder at Green Pt., Prince Edward Co. on Feb. 1, 1982 (Weir, 1982: 290). Four were seen at Crozier during the winter and N. Denis saw one at Ignace on Feb. 13, 1975 (Goodwin, 1975: 686).

SPRING: Stirrett (1973b: 20) had two Pelee records: May 28, 1946 and Apr. 21, 1957. My Feb. 3, 1935 bird was observed again up the Don Valley on Apr. 4, 1935, calling: "Char, char, char". B. and J. White reported another at Toronto on Apr. 30, 1978 (Goodwin, 1978: 1000). Quilliam (1965: 128-129) wrote of an invasion during 1898 when one was observed near Odessa by C.M. Clarke on May 12, 1898 and two were shot near Kingston later. P. Tapp reported one at Thunder Bay to March 25, 1973 (Goodwin, 1973: 767). Peruniak (1971: 21) reported one at Atikokan on March 4, 1959 and T. Nash found one there on March 13, 1978 (Goodwin, 1978: 1000).

SUMMER: H.H. Brown *et al* reported seeing one at Pt. Sydney, Muskoka, on June 20, 1897 (Mills, 1981: 104). One was noted in Burpee Twp., Manitoulin, by Wm. Koski on June 14, 1973 (Nicholson, 1981: 138). Denis (1961: 6) reported that specimens were collected at Thunder Bay in 1958, 1959 and 1960 but gave no dates or other details. Gordon Bellerby saw one at Rainy River on June 21, 1975 (Goodwin, 1975: 966). The first breeding record for Ontario was established by Lamey (1981: 40) who found two short-tailed young chasing adults and begging for food on July 4, 1980 in an aspen grove about 10 km. NE of Rainy River: with B. Duncan, A. Gray and W. Wilson 4 nests were located in this grove on July 6 and on July 9, three young with 4 adults were seen in the grove: one of the nests of a previous year contained two young Long-eared Owls on July 6. J.R. Dymond saw one bird at Kenora during June, 1947 (Snyder, 1953: 70). Ross James saw one on June 11 and June 17 and two on June 14, 1977 near Pickle Lake. Manning (1952: 72) reported an old specimen record from Ft. Albany, James Bay (no date given).

AUTUMN: Goodwin (1973: 54) had 40 reports for the fall of 1972 from Sioux Lookout and Nakina south to Atikokan and Terrace Bay (the greatest invasion in 50 years according to Keith Denis). N. Denis had sightings at Savant Lake from Oct. 18 to Nov. 16, 1976. Shirley Peruniak had 14 reports at Atikokan from Oct. 13 to Nov. 12 and one was noted at Markstay (near Sudbury) by E. Blomme on Sept. 19 (Goodwin, 1977: 172). T. Perrons saw single birds at Thunder Bay on Oct. 6 and 20, 1971 (Goodwin, 1972: 58). A. Wormington saw one at Manitouwadge on Oct. 5, 1970 (Goodwin, 1971: 52). On Oct. 11, 1975 C. and D. Campbell observed one at Parry Sound (Mills, 1981: 104). Penny and Bob Good noted one at Kingston on Oct. 24, 1976 (Weir & Quilliam, 1980: 19). J.E. Mason had one at Toronto on Nov. 1, 1970 (Goodwin, 1971: 53). D. Brewer noted one, possibly an escaped bird, at Puslinch, on Sept. 4, 1980 (Goodwin, 1981: 178). On Nov. 11, 1959 one showed up a few miles west of St. Catharines and remained into the winter (Beardslee & Mitchell, 1965: 319).

**MEASUREMENTS:**
*Length:* 18 to 22 ins.
(Godfrey, 1966: 273)
*Wingspread:* about 24 ins.
(Roberts, 1955: 641)
*Weight:* ♂ 6 to 7 oz.
♀ 4 3/4 to 6 1/3 oz.
(Terres, 1980: 142-143).

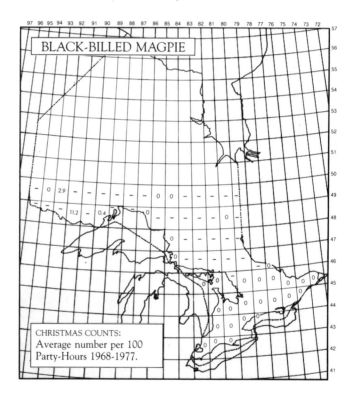

BLACK-BILLED MAGPIE

CHRISTMAS COUNTS:
Average number per 100
Party-Hours 1968-1977.

# AMERICAN CROW   *Corvus brachyrhynchos*   Brehm

Crows occur throughout Ontario. This is probably the most important species of bird in Ontario based on its energy requirements. Some of the smaller species are more numerous but because of its large size and overall abundance this is likely No. 1: near large cities and their garbage dumps such species as the Ring-billed Gull and the Common Raven may be locally more important. In fall you may see hundreds migrating southwestward to swell the ranks of crows in the cornfields of the midwestern U.S.A., but some stay with us all winter. In late February and early March we welcome their "caw" as a sign of returning spring. In summer they tend to be silent and furtive and we may forget them or take them for granted, but even then hundreds may gather at favourite roost sites and bedevil the local owls and hawks.

IDENTIFICATION: In southern Ontario everyone knows the crow with its familiar "caw" and deep flapping wing beats. In northern Ontario the Common Raven may be confused (see distinctions under that species). In southern Ontario in summer the blue-eyed young with a variety of raspy, gurgling notes may present some problems.

WINTER: On the 1968-1977 Christmas counts they were common to abundant south and west of Toronto, and north locally on Manitoulin and at Thunder Bay: they were fairly common north to Ottawa and Meaford, then rare to absent elsewhere in northern Ontario. Stirrett (1973a: 17) had a maximum of 3000 at Pelee on Dec. 30. Sheppard (1960: 34) mentioned large winter roosts in the Niagara Gorge. Snyder (1941: 70) gave Feb. 19, 1912 as an arrival date for Prince Edward Co. Weir & Quilliam (1980: 37) listed Feb. 20 as the 29-year average arrival date at Kingston, though some usually winter there at dumps and corn cribs. Devitt (1967: 113) gave Feb. 20 as the 14-year average arrival date at Barrie, though some winter there (34 on the Dec. 29, 1962 Christmas count was the maximum). During the winter of 1921-1922 about 200 wintered near Ottawa South (Lloyd, 1923: 155). L. Beamer's median arrival date for Meaford was Feb. 23. Dennison (1980: 146) listed this as species found on all 25 Christmas counts at Sault Ste. Marie: from 1 to 63 noted, averaging 15. David Elder had a Jan. 7 record for Atikokan in 1981.

SPRING: The spring maximum at Pelee was 400 on March 15 (Stirrett, 1973b: 21) but Kelley (1978: 55) estimated 20,000 along the Lake Huron shore on March 29, 1972. Saunders & Dale (1933: 215) mentioned 2 sets of 5 eggs found near London, one on Apr. 19, 1901 and another on Apr. 17, 1905 as well as 3 sets of 4 eggs, on Apr. 19, 1902. Apr. 27, 1904 and Apr. 24, 1906. McCracken, Bradstreet & Holroyd (1981: 55) found a nest with 6 eggs on Long Point on Apr. 12, 1968 which held young on May 21: they also noted a nest with 4 eggs on May 2, 1974 and a nest with 4 young on May 20, 1976. Saunders (1947: 43-44) described a nesting on the University of Toronto campus on Apr. 5, 1944. Speirs (1975: 23) gave the third week of March as the spring peak in Ontario Co. and tabulated 29 sets of eggs found there containing a total of 130 eggs. Tozer & Richards (1974: 201) reported a nest observed by C. Christy that was under construction near Oshawa as early as March 20, 1962. Allin (1940: 102) noted nests with 4 eggs found in Darlington Twp. on May 13, 1919 and on Apr. 30, 1927. Crows were seen incubating eggs on two Kingston nests on May 2, 1962 (Quilliam, 1973: 131). Crows carrying nesting material were noted as early as Apr. 7, 1940 at Holland River: W.W. Smith found a nest with eggs at Big Cedar Point on Apr. 15, 1938 and young in the nest were noted as early as May 11, 1941 (Devitt, 1967: 113). They nested on Parliament Hill, Ottawa in April, 1906 (Lloyd, 1923: 155). L. Beamer reported a nest with eggs at Meaford on Apr. 22, 1956. Mills (1981: 105) gave March 2 as the 10-year average arrival date at Huntsville. G. Lepp noted 2 young in a nest 50 ft. up on a cliff by the French River near Hwy. 69 on May 22, 1976. D. B. Ferguson found a nest with 5 eggs at Providence Bay, Manitoulin, on Apr. 19, 1980 (Nicholson, 1981: 138). MacLulich (1938: 25) cited 7 arrival dates for Algonquin Park: the median was March 5. Speirs & Speirs (1947: 31) noted two at North Bay as early as March 9, 1945 but the spring peak was in late March or early April. Skeel & Bondrup-Nielsen (1978: 189) saw 62 on 34 days from Apr. 6 to May 30, 1977 at Pukaskwa. S. Downing found a nest with 5 small, naked young at Rossport on May 29, 1936 (Baillie & Hope, 1943: 15). Denis (1961: 2) listed March 19 as the average arrival date at Thunder Bay, with the earliest on March 11, 1959. Dear (1940: 134) reported a nest with 4 eggs on May 11, 1928 and a nest with 3 eggs on May 24, 1934, near Thunder Bay, where he noted a great increase in numbers in recent years. Bondrup-Nielsen (1976: 43) saw his first near Kapuskasing on Apr. 1, 1975. Elder (1979: 36) gave March 2 as his earliest date for Geraldton. Peruniak (1971: 21) gave March 3 as her earliest date for Atikokan. Cringan (1953a: 3) listed March 20 as his first sighting at Sioux Lookout in 1953. Crows first appeared in the Asheweig area on Apr. 12 in 1950 (Cringan, 1950: 14).

SUMMER: On the 1968-1977 Breeding Bird Surveys they were common on most routes, and fairly common on a few of the northern routes where they tend to be concentrated at dump sites and rare in heavily forested regions. The summer maximum at Pelee was 70 on Aug. 14 (Stirrett, 1973c: 18). Snyder (1931: 191) found a nest with 4 young about 15 ft. up in a red cedar at Long Point on June 27, 1927. Speirs (1975: 23) found maximum populations of 23 and 24 birds per 100 acres in two rather mature mixed forests in Ontario Co. A nest with 3 young old enough to fly was found at Sand Banks, Prince Edward Co., on June 25, 1930 (Snyder, 1941: 70). Young in the nest were noted as late as July 3, 1939 in Innisfil Twp. Simcoe Co. (Devitt, 1967: 113). Mills (1981: 105) reported that C. Harris frightened a brood of young from a nest at Manitou Dock, Parry Sound on June 25, 1974. Speirs & Speirs (1947: 31) found a nest 35 ft. up in a white pine at Rutherglen on June 6, 1944, with young out of the nest by June 16. Young were noted at Chapleau on June 16 and 18 and at Biscotasing on June 23 and 24, 1937 (Baillie & Hope, 1947: 16). Snyder (1942: 137) noted the first young out of the nest near Sault Ste. Marie during the fourth week of June in 1931 and about 200 crows in a flock on July 30. Skeel & Bondrup-Nielsen (1978: 189) saw from 1 to 7 on a few summer days at Pukaskwa in 1977 but found none on any of their census routes. A juvenile not long out of the nest was taken at Amyot on July 1, 1936 (Baillie & Hope, 1943: 15). Snyder (1928: 266) collected two juveniles at Lake Nipigon on July 18, 1924. Snyder (1928: 26) found them rare and wary at Lake Nipigon, but observed an adult with flying young on July 26, 1925. Snyder (1953: 70) saw a nest with 4 young about 30 ft. up in a jack pine at Ingolf on June 3, 1937 and adults feeding flying young at Savanne on July 12, 1937: the maximum observed in western Ontario was 22 at Wabigoon on June 16, 1937: at Ingolf he noted with some surprise that adults recovered the buried carcasses of specimens that were collected at Ingolf. James (1980: 88) found a nest with 4 young near Central Patricia on June 19, 1979. Cringan (1950: 14) found a nest with 3 young about 30 ft. up in a balsam on the bank of the Windigo River, on July 5, 1950. Hope (1938: 30) collected two from a flock of 8 at Favourable Lake on June 3, 1938. Manning (1952: 73) saw 3 at

Attawapiskat, and collected a female there with an incubation patch, on July 5 and 6, 1947: he also noted the species at Moosonee, Raft River, Lake River on the James Bay coast and at Shagamu River on the Hudson Bay coast. Schueler, Baldwin & Rising (1974: 143) found crows at Winisk and at Hawley Lake as well as at the localities mentioned by Manning. Lee (1978: 27) noted crows on three occasions at Big Trout Lake in early August, 1975, including a family group of 2 adults with at least two young. C.E. Hope noted as many as 10 at Ft. Severn during the summer of 1940 and located a nest with 4 young on June 17 there.

AUTUMN: H. Lewis and H.S. Peters reported crows at Attawapiskat about Sept. 17, at Ft. Albany about Sept. 22 and near Moosonee about Sept. 15, 1940: George M. Stirrett also saw 4 at Moose Factory and 5 at Ship Sands about Oct. 2, 1948 (Manning, 1952: 73). Peruniak (1971: 21) gave Oct. 12 as her latest Atikokan date. Skeel & Bondrup-Nielsen (1978: 189) saw 27 on 8 days between Sept. 2 and Sept. 20, 1977 at Pukaskwa, with their latest record, 4 seen by W. Wyett on Oct. 3, 1975. Speirs & Speirs (1947: 31) observed 11 flying west near North Bay on Oct. 18, 1944. Nicholson (1981: 138) has observed large flocks moving *east* along the south shore of Manitoulin in October. K. Ketchum observed about 100 migrating off Point au Baril on Oct. 12, 1974 (Mills, 1981: 105). Crows reach their peak at Kingston in the latter half of October (Quilliam, 1973: 131). Speirs (1975: 23) estimated 2000 on Oct. 22, 1962 in Scarborough. Saunders (1947: 271) estimated 3000 to 4000 in sight at one time near Toronto airport where they continued moving west most of the day at about 25 to 30 miles per hour, on Oct. 14, 1945. Wm. Girling noted 1000 passing westward along the Lake Erie shore at Port Stanley in one hour on Oct. 24, 1948 (Brooman, 1954: 27). Stirrett (1973d: 23) had a fall maximum of 2000 at Pelee on Nov. 2.

BANDING: One banded near Toronto on March 22, 1940 was recovered in Indiana on Feb. 17, 1942: another banded near Toronto on Apr. 15, 1940 was recovered in Indiana on Jan. 30, 1942. Two banded near Toronto on March 27, 1940 were recovered in Ohio, one on Jan. 20, 1941, the other on Jan. 14, 1942. A third banded near Toronto on Apr. 27, 1941 was taken in Ohio on March 12, 1942.

**MEASUREMENTS:**
*Length:* 17 to 21 ins.
(Godfrey, 1966: 275)
*Wingspread:* 33.0 to 39.7
ins. (Roberts, 1955: 640)
*Weight:* 16 Ont. ♂ in
ROM averaged 507 g. 9
Ont. ♀ in ROM averaged
439.1 g.
(See comparison with
Common Raven under that
species.)

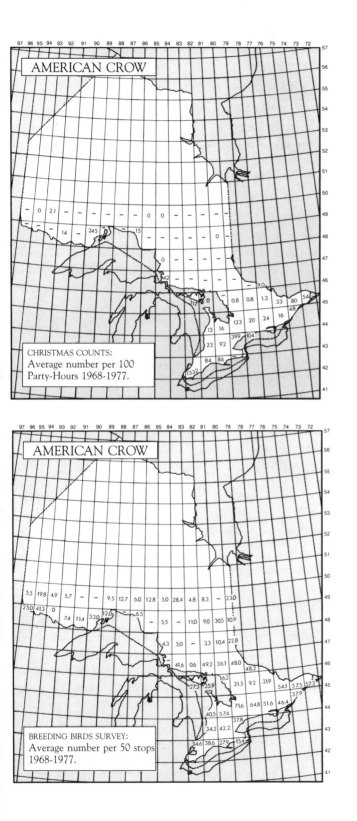

AMERICAN CROW

CHRISTMAS COUNTS:
Average number per 100
Party-Hours 1968-1977.

AMERICAN CROW

BREEDING BIRDS SURVEY:
Average number per 50 stops
1968-1977.

# FISH CROW   *Corvus ossifragus*   Wilson

The Fish Crow is primarily a bird of the seacoasts of the southeastern United States and inland along some of the major rivers: accidental in Ontario.

IDENTIFICATION:   Although generally described as a smaller, more slender bird than the American Crow, their measurements overlap considerably. The Fish Crow has more pointed wings, sometimes longer than those of some American Crows and the flight is more Accipiter-like with flaps and glides. The best field character appears to be the voice, nasal, high-pitched, sounding more like a night-heron than an American Crow.

WINTER:

SPRING:   On May 15, 1978 one was reported by M. Bentley and R. Ridout at Pelee and confirmed by A. Wormington *et al* (Goodwin, 1978: 1000). Donald A. Southerland reported another at Pelee on Apr. 21, 1982. D. Shepherd reported one at Long Point on May 20, 1983.

SUMMER:

AUTUMN:

**MEASUREMENTS:**
*Length:*  16 to 20 ins.
(Terres, 1980: 137)
*Wingspread:*  30 to 43 ins.
(Terres, 1980: 137)
*Weight:*  14 to 15 1/2 oz.
(Terres, 1980: 138)

# COMMON RAVEN   *Corvus corax*   Linnaeus

At North Bay airport I was entranced watching the local ravens showing the RAF trainees how to do loops and rolls and even "tumbling" with the best of tumbler pigeons, in their elaborate courtship displays. In more recent years their vocal prowess has delighted me: they give all sorts of sepulchral gurgles and croaks, to fine bell-like ringing notes. My wife and I well remember our visit with William Rowan who demonstrated that his ravens could "count up to nine". In spite of its evil reputation in folk lore we find this intelligent species a constant delight. Ravens are found in both the Old World and in North and South America: in Ontario it is one of the most prevalent species in the north but very rare in the south.

IDENTIFICATION:   The raven resembles a very large crow, but adults are distinguished by their wedge-shaped tails, very large deep bills and ragged feathers about the neck. In flight they often soar in the manner of *Buteo* hawks (crows sometimes do this in stormy weather too): in flapping flight they have much shallower wing beats than a crow and you will notice the "swept back" wing tips. Their usual call note is a harsh, guttural "Kraaa", deeper in pitch than the well-known "Caw" of the crow. They sometimes build big stick nests in trees but also often nest on rock ledges in the manner of peregrines and eagles. I often wondered how such big birds found enough food to survive our northern winters until I saw one eating poplar buds: although carrion and human garbage are more usual foods they will eat almost anything!

**WINTER:** On the 1968-1977 Christmas counts they were common to abundant from Deep River and Manitoulin northwards, fairly common south to Minden and Bancroft but rare to absent in southern Ontario. Brooman (1954: 27) reported one seen by Harley White at Springwater Pond during the winter 1947-1948. Quilliam (1973: 131) cited a record by W.E. Edwards on Feb. 3, 1938 near Gananoque as the first near Kingston in over 100 years but Betty Hughes found a dead one on Howe Is. on Feb. 27, 1963. W. Melville reported collecting one near Orillia in December, 1890 (Devitt, 1967: 112). Mills (1981: 104-105) cited several records for the cottage country where they have been increasing and seen throughout the year. Poisoned baits set out for wolves were often eaten by ravens, causing a decline in Algonquin Park in the 1930's (MacLulich, 1938: 25). Dennison (1980: 146) listed this as a species seen on all 25 Christmas counts at Sault Ste. Marie, averaging 27 (from 2 to 98). Peruniak (1971: 21) reported about 100 on winter censuses at Atikokan.

**SPRING:** Stirrett (1973b: 20) had just one spring record at Pelee, on May 9, 1962. Gordon Giles reported one at Port Union on Apr. 26, 1965 (Speirs, 1975: 22). In the early 1800's they were more plentiful in southern Ontario than at present and Charles Fothergill, on March 21, 1821, wrote that the ravens were paired and "give us their usual coarse love song of joy—" at Rice Lake (Black, 1934: 151). Quilliam (1973: 131) had records near Kingston from March 2 to Apr. 5, 1963 and March 5, 1971: more recent records there were on May 5, 1979, March 8, 1980 (2) and March 17, 1980 (6) (Weir & Quilliam, 1980: 19). H.P. Bingham saw two pursued by crows near Barrie in spring of 1929 (Devitt, 1967: 112). D.B. Ferguson found a nest with 3 young on Manitoulin on May 21, 1973 (Nicholson, 1981: 138). James (1980: 88) reported a juvenile at Pickle Lake on May 30, 1979, as well as about 100 birds at the town dump. Cringan (1953b: 4) observed one carrying food on May 31, 1953 at Kasabonika Lake.

**SUMMER:** On the 1968-1977 Breeding Bird Surveys they were common on northern routes, becoming fairly common south to Dorset and Manitoulin: none in southern Ontario. J.M. Richards identified one as it soared and called over Conc. 1, Lot 5, Cartwright Twp. on June 18, 1966 (Tozer & Richards, 1974: 200). On June 16, 1963, J. Simonyi found a nest with 4 young on a cliff at Skeleton Lake, Muskoka (Mills, 1981: 104), and Craig Campbell saw a brood of 3 young at Parry Sound on July 8, 1974. On June 10, 1954 I saw 4 birds at what appeared to be a nest site on a rocky ledge above the Haviland Hotel, north of Sault Ste. Marie. Skeel & Bondrup-Nielsen (1978: 189) noted a good deal of nesting evidence in Pukaskwa. Denis (1961: 5) reported a nest with young at Thunder Bay on June 2, 1955. Bondrup-Nielsen (1976: 47) reported finding 5 nests near Kapuskasing in 1974 and 1975, all in tall trembling aspens. Snyder (1953: 70) noted nesting at Gordon Lake (2), Minaki, Willard Lake, Ignace and Sioux Lookout. Cringan (1950: 14) saw as many as 8 one day in summer at Nikip Lake. Manning (1952: 73) collected a young bird not able to fly at Sandy Is., Moosonee, on June 15, 1949 and cited a record of two at the estuary of the Albany River on Aug. 18, 1920. James, Nash & Peck (1981: 91) noted breeding evidence at Kiruna Lake in 1980 and 1981. Peck (1972: 345) reported three nests at radar sites on Cape Henrietta Maria found by H.G. Lumsden in

1964, by G. O'Reilly in July, 1969 and by Peck on June 22, 1970. Schueler, Baldwin & Rising (1974: 146) took a flightless young male at Sutton Lake on June 29, 1964, and noted 4 young at Winisk in June, 1965 and one on June 28, 1971 there: they also found them common at Moosonee, Attawapiskat, and Cochrane but saw none at Ft. Albany. Lee (1978: 27) noted them at all three study plots at Big Trout Lake and as many as 16 around the dump there on June 11, 1975.

AUTUMN: Doug McRae and Alan Wormington noted from one to 22 almost daily from Oct. 14 to Nov. 2, 1981 at Netitishi Point, James Bay. One was collected west of Collingwood on Oct. 20, 1943 by E.L. Durkin and E. Hart (identified by L. Beamer): Bruce Falls observed 4 at Thunder Beach, Simcoe Co., on Sept. 25, 1948; and Alf. Mitchener identified one at the mouth of the Nottawasaga River on Oct. 26, 1952 (Devitt, 1967: 113). A dead raven was found by Betty Hughes on Howe Is. on Oct. 29, 1961 (Quilliam, 1973: 131). Three recent records near Kingston were on Sept. 23, Oct. 8 and Nov. 3, 1979 (Weir & Quilliam, 1980: 19). George A. Scott watched one soaring over Oshawa Harbour on Sept. 22, 1963 (Tozer & Richards, 1974: 200). Archie Reid collected an immature female at Floral Park, Rama Twp., on Oct. 4, 1952; Naomi LeVay saw two at Eastbourne, Whitby, on Oct. 12, 1953 and Doug. Scovell reported two at Pickering on Sept. 27, 1957 (Speirs, 1975: 22). Kelley (1978: 55) reported one at Pelee from Oct. 4 to 11, 1970; and from one to four at Ipperwash Beach from Oct. 19, 1969 and at Kettle Point on Oct. 20, 1974. Stirrett (1973a: 17 and 1973d: 23) had single birds at Pelee on Sept. 27, 1914; Oct. 7, 1911; Oct. 23, 1965 and Oct. 31, 1908 and as late as Nov. 22 and Nov. 28.

**MEASUREMENTS:**
*Length:* 22 to 26.5 ins.
(Godfrey, 1966: 274)
*Wingspread:* 50 to 52 ins.
(Roberts, 1955: 640)
*Weight:* 2 lbs. 5 oz.
to 2 lbs. 11 oz. (Roberts, 1955: 640)
Speirs (1975: 22)
compared measurements of ravens vs. crows:
*Length:* 610 mm.
495 mm.
*Wingspread:* 1215 mm.
945 mm.
*Weight:* 1055 g. 566 g.

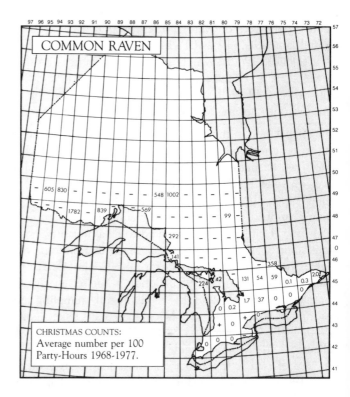

COMMON RAVEN

CHRISTMAS COUNTS:
Average number per 100
Party-Hours 1968-1977.

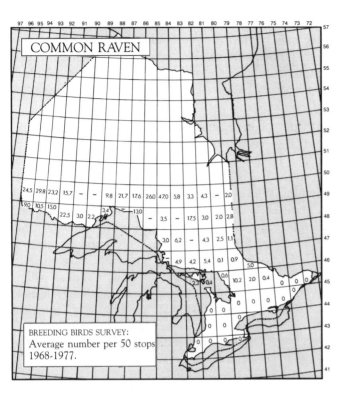

COMMON RAVEN

BREEDING BIRDS SURVEY:
Average number per 50 stops
1968-1977.

# BLACK-CAPPED CHICKADEE
## *Parus atricapillus*  Linnaeus

This is the most prevalent species at bird feeders in Ontario, quick to find new sources of food and giving constant delight with incessant activity and fearless behavior. In summer, most chickadees desert the bird feeders and retire to excavate nesting holes in rotten stubs in which they raise their big families: both adults help with the excavating, turn and turn about. Some may bring their families to feeders in late summer but it is generally October to November before they turn up in numbers: this is the time to be sure the feeders are well stocked and maintained through the winter. Bird banders find chickadees quite a problem as they tend to get hopelessly entangled in mist nests, and vent their displeasure at being extracted and during the banding process by pecking and pulling at hang nails! Drop traps are less stressful.

**IDENTIFICATION:** With their small size, black cap and throat, white cheeks, gray back and rufous-tinged sides the chickadee is known to all. They are named from their "chick-a-dee-dee" notes, and as spring approaches their clear, whistled "fee-be-be" whistle is often heard and betrays their presence in the forest before they are actually seen. The Boreal Chickadee is the only other similar species likely to be seen in Ontario, especially in northern Ontario (see distinctions under that species).

WINTER: On the 1968-1977 Christmas counts this was a common species throughout Ontario, from Dryden south to Lake Erie. Stirrett (1973a: 17) had a winter maximum of 325 at Pelee on Dec. 26. Dennison (1980: 146) reported from 9 to 259 on Christmas counts at Sault Ste. Marie, averaging 104: they were seen on all 25 counts there. Skeel & Bondrup-Nielsen (1978: 190) wrote from Pukaskwa that "in the winter it ranked by far the most abundant species in the park".

SPRING: Stirrett (1973b: 21) had a spring maximum of 1500 at Pelee on Apr. 15. Saunders & Dale (1933: 215) reported a set of 6 eggs taken near London on May 18, 1916. Saunders (1947: 94) watched a very tame pair of chickadees excavating a nest hole in a rotten elm stub about 3 ft. up, in the Rouge Valley, Scarborough. Long (1968a: 14) observed a west to east return migration through Pickering Beach from March 4 to 17, 1964 and I noted nest excavation as early as Apr. 14, 1968 in the Altona Forest, Pickering (Speirs, 1975: 24). J.M. Richards followed events at a nest in Darlington Twp. from construction on Apr. 29, 1970 to 5 eggs on May 9, 8 eggs on May 23 and 7 young on May 30 (Tozer & Richards, 1974: 203). Quilliam (1973: 132) saw a pair excavating on Apr. 28, 1961 and Richard Norman found young being fed in a hole in a dead willow stub near Kingston on May 24, 1970. E.L. Brereton watched a pair nest building near Barrie on Apr. 19, 1941: this nest contained 8 eggs on May 11: another set of 7 eggs was found by H.P. Bingham on May 9, 1915 (Devitt, 1967: 114). Mills (1981: 107) saw two pairs excavating near Magnetawan on Apr. 9, 1977 and reported 18 nest records for the cottage country. Speirs & Speirs (1947: 31-32) saw one excavating about 10 ft. up in a white birch stub at North Bay as early as March 11, 1945. Dear (1940: 134) reported a nest with 6 eggs at Saganaga Lake, Thunder Bay, on May 18, 1933.

SUMMER: On the 1968-1977 Breeding Bird Surveys this was a fairly common species on most routes, uncommon on a few routes in northeastern and southwestern Ontario. Stirrett (1973c: 18) had a summer maximum of 100 at Pelee on June 12. Marshall Field saw a pair feeding young in a hole in a dead willow stub at St. Thomas on June 17, 1952 (Brooman, 1954: 27). L.L. Snyder collected a juvenile on July 16, 1927 and J. McCracken found a nest with 5 young on June 6, 1980 at Long Point (McCracken, Bradstreet & Holroyd, 1981: 58). Snyder (1930: 201) found a nest with 6 eggs as late as July 14, 1926 in King Twp. We flushed an adult from a nest hole in Conc. 10, lot 20, Reach Twp. as late as July 17, 1967: 7 nests with eggs in Ontario Co. held 4, 6, 6, 6, 7, 7 and 8 eggs (Speirs, 1975: 24). All mid-and-late succession forests studied in Ontario Co. had populations of chickadees, with the maximum of 35 birds per 100 acres in the Scugog quadrat (Speirs & Orenstein, 1975: 19). Snyder (1941: 70) noted the first young of the year at Woodrous, Prince Edward Co., on June 28, 1930. Paul Harrington noted a nest with 6 eggs at Wasaga Beach on June 18, 1920 (Devitt, 1967: 114). C.H. Young took a nest with 6 eggs near Ottawa on June 1, 1908 (Lloyd, 1924: 15). D.B. Ferguson saw adults feeding young in a nest at Windfall Lake, Manitoulin, on July 8, 1980 (Nicholson, 1981: 139). Ricker & Clarke (1939: 15) observed young being fed at Frank's Bay, Lake Nipissing, on June 20, 1933. Baillie & Hope (1947: 16) found a nest with 6 young and one infertile egg on June 14, 1937 at Chapleau, about four ft. up in a rotten birch stub: flying young were also noted at Biscotasing on July 7 and at Bigwood on July 14. Snyder (1942: 137) found a nest with 4 young near Sault Ste. Marie on June 10, 1931. Baillie & Hope (1943: 16) found a nest with 6 young at Marathon on June 20, 1936: this was 12 ft. up in a dead birch stub. Snyder (1928: 276) found a nest at Lake Nipigon on

June 7, 1924 near the top of an 8 ft. stump standing in shallow water: family groups were seen by the second week of July. Dear (1940: 134) found a nest with large young on June 8, 1924 near Thunder Bay. Snyder (1938: 199) showed by collecting specimens on two occasions in the Rainy River Dist. that "adult males were found to be the family escort when family groups were met with". Snyder (1928: 33) found them "not plentiful" at Lake Abitibi but collected a young male on July 17, 1925. Snyder (1953: 71) established breeding for Wabigoon (family on June 28, 1937) Savanne (family on June 9, 1937), as well as at Malachi and Kenora. James (1980: 88) seldom encountered them at Pickle Lake and then usually single birds in disturbed woodlands. Cringan (1950: 14) recorded only a few at Nikip Lake in 1950 and none there until early July. Hope (1938: 30) found a nest with 6 young which flew from the nest when disturbed, at Favourable Lake on June 15, 1938. Ross James found adults feeding young in a nest cavity at Harricanaw River, near James Bay, on June 22, 1982: family groups were seen later on June 29 and July 3. Manning (1952: 74) cited records for Moosonee and Ft. Albany. At the northern edge of their range one was reported at Little Sachigo Lake on June 11, 1977 (McLaren & McLaren, 1981: 4). Schueler, Baldwin & Rising (1974: 143) called them uncommon at Attawapiskat and had none at Ft. Albany, Hawley Lake or Winisk. James, Nash & Peck (1972) saw none at Kiruna Lake, Sutton Ridges; Peck (1972) had none at Cape Henrietta Maria; Lee (1978) had none at Big Trout Lake and Cliff Hope saw none at Ft. Severn in 1940.

AUTUMN: Doug. McRae and Alan Wormington saw as many as 15 in a day in mid-October at Netistishi Pt., James Bay, but mainly singles after mid-November. Nicholson (1981: 139) observed an invasion at Mississagi Light, Manitoulin, from Sept. to Nov. 9, with a maximum of 900 on Sept. 24, 1975. Chris Harris saw 120 at Go Home Bay on Oct. 12, 1975 (Mills, 1981: 107). Devitt (1967: 114) reported that 1000 passed through Barrie in two hours on Oct. 3, 1941 and another such flight was seen there on Oct. 20, 1933. Quilliam (1973: 132) mentioned that over 200 were seen migrating on Amherst Is. on Oct. 6, 1968. Speirs (1975: 24) noted conspicuous fall migrations at Pickering every 2 to 4 years, with especially big ones in 1951 and 1965 (Ken Adcoe estimated over 100 at Pickering Beach on Oct. 16, 1965). Wm. Girling counted over 1400 in one hour at Pt. Stanley on Oct. 21, 1951 (Brooman, 1954: 27). Stirrett (1973d: 23) had a fall maximum of 1000 at Pelee on Oct. 30.

BANDING: One banded by Gordon Lambert near Toronto on Oct. 21, 1961 was recovered in Quebec (about 20 miles east of Cornwall, Ont.) about Feb. 25, 1963. One banded by V. Heron near Huntsville in 1962 was still there in 1970, an interesting longevity record (Mills, 1981: 107). During the big 1951 flight, Louise Lawrence showed by banding that transients began to arrive at her Pimisi Bay banding station during the first week of September and had all passed through by Sept. 27, leaving only her locally banded birds (Snyder, 1953: 72). On Jan. 20, 1959 we thought that we had about 8 chickadees coming to our feeders: then R.R. Taylor banded 21 there on that day and about as many unbanded birds remained: others have had similar experiences.

## MEASUREMENTS:

*Length:* 4.8 to 5.7 ins.
(Godfrey, 1966: 277)
*Wingspread:* 7.5 to 8.5
ins. (Roberts, 1955: 642)
*Weight:* 30 ♂ averaged
11.36 g. 33 ♀ averaged
10.59 g. (Speirs,
1975: 24).

## REFERENCES:

Speirs, J. Murray 1963
Survival and population
dynamics with particular
reference to Black-capped
Chickadees. Bird-banding,
34: (2): 87-93. A small
colour-banding project
suggested a first year
survival of about 11%
followed by a 60% survival
of adults each year. Of 13
banded on Nov. 17, 1957
the oldest survived for
about 4 1/2 years (only 4
were seen after the first
year).

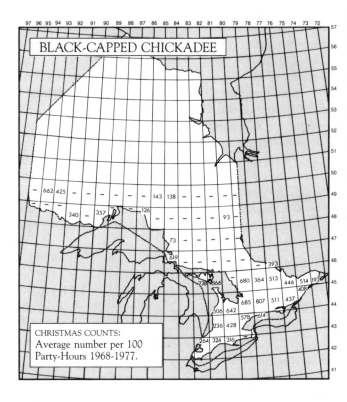

CHRISTMAS COUNTS:
Average number per 100
Party-Hours 1968-1977.

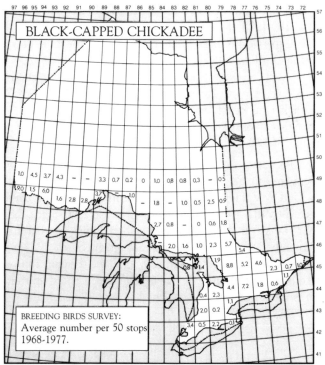

BREEDING BIRDS SURVEY:
Average number per 50 stops
1968-1977.

# CAROLINA CHICKADEE   *Parus carolinensis*   Audubon

The Carolina Chickadee is the southern counterpart of our Black-capped Chickadee, normally found in the southeastern United States and sometimes interbreeding with the Black-capped Chickadee where they co-exist.

IDENTIFICATION:   The 4-syllable song, higher pitched than that of the Black-capped Chickadee, is the best field identification feature:"see-saw-see-soo". The visual differences are not so obvious: smaller size, narrower white margins to the wing feathers, shorter tail, smaller bib are difficult to assess in the field.

WINTER:

SPRING:   One netted at the eastern tip of Long Point on May 18, 1983, was retained for confirmation of identity until May 19 when it died and was sent by D. Shepherd to the ROM (Weir, 1983: 42). This is the only Ontario specimen. Paul Harrington reported seeing one with a family of Black-capped Chickadees in Toronto on Apr. 10, 1914 (Harrington, 1915: 99).

SUMMER:   Jarvis (1965: 42) identified one in Rondeau on July 3, 1960 by its "dee-day, dee-day") song.

AUTUMN:

**MEASUREMENTS:**
*Length:* 4 1/4 to 4 3/4 ins.
(Terres, 1980: 926)
Wingspread:
*Weight:* The Long Point
bird weighed 9.1 g. at
capture. 9.6 to 12 g.
(Terres, 1980: 926)

**REFERENCE:**
Jarvis, John 1965 A
possible occurrence of the
Carolina Chickadee
(*Parus carolinensis*) in
southwestern Ontario.
Ont. Field Biologist,
No. 19: 42.

# MOUNTAIN CHICKADEE   *Parus gambeli*   Ridgway

This is a chickadee of the Rocky Mountains, accidental in Ontario.

**IDENTIFICATION:**  The white stripe over the eye separates it from the Black-capped Chickadee. The "chick-a-dee" call is harsher than in the Black-capped.

**WINTER:**

**SPRING:**  D.E. Perks documented his sighting of one in the Lorne Park woods west of Toronto, on Apr. 21, 1963 (Goodwin, 1963: 26) and Woodford (1963: 400).

**SUMMER:**

**AUTUMN:**

**MEASUREMENTS:**
*Length:*  5.0 to 5.7 ins.
(Godfrey, 1966: 278)
Wingspread:
*Weight:*  292 ♂ averaged
11.5 g., 164 ♀ averaged
10.1 g. (Dunning,
1984: 18).

# BOREAL CHICKADEE   *Parus hudsonicus*   Forster

In Ontario this is the chickadee of the northern bog forests, the only one to be expected in the Hudson Bay lowlands. They breed south to about Algonquin Park but are outnumbered by the Black-capped Chickadee south of about latitude 51°N. In southern Ontario there are occasional invasions with migrating flocks of Black-capped Chickadees during late October, with a few lingering at feeding stations during the winter: major invasions occurred in 1951 and 1972 with smaller ones in other years.

**IDENTIFICATION:**  Its nasal "pi-pi-tee-ee" is usually the first thing to alert you to its presence—the final notes have a nuthatch-like quality. The counterpart of the spring song of the Black-capped Chickadee (the "fee-bee" or "fee be-bee") is usually 4-syllabled but sometimes more: when I heard the song in the Bonfield bog by Hwy. 17 east of North Bay on March 16, 1945, I wrote it down as "peet-peet-teedle eedle". The brown cap and general more rufous colouration is often hard to see silhouetted against the sky in the tops of spruces.

**WINTER:**  On the 1968-1977 Christmas counts almost all stations reported them in 1972 and quite a few in 1975, as far south as Pelee: in the other years they were absent or very rare south of Algonquin Park: from there north they were fairly common and common at Hornepayne and Atikokan. Stirrett (1973a: 17) had Pelee records on Dec. 5 (5), with single birds on Dec. 22 and Feb. 28. Ussher (1965: 19) had just one Rondeau record: on Dec. 28, 1951. Saunders & Dale (1933: 215) reported one at London on Jan. 27, 1907 and two others that wintered there at feeders in 1919-1920. Brooman (1954: 28) reported one in Elgin Co. on Jan. 1, 1947. Sheppard (1960: 34) mentioned a Niagara Falls record for the winter of 1919, as well as some at Niagara Falls and Pt.Colborne in the winter of 1951-1952. Beardslee & Mitchell (1965: 324) noted one at Niagara Falls on Jan. 25, 1947. Speirs (1975: 25) noted records during the 1951 and 1972 invasions, including one by George A. Scott at Oshawa on Dec. 2, 1951 and 36 on the Dec. 26 Christmas count at Pickering in 1972, with a few records for intervening years. E.L.Brereton saw two at Barrie on Dec. 18, 1937 and Mark Robinson observed 3 at his feeders in Barrie on Dec. 25, 1937: one also was noted on the Barrie Christmas count on Dec. 18, 1965 (Devitt, 1967: 114). Louise Lawrence reported individuals at Pimisi Bay in mid-February, 1940 and on Feb. 25, 1945 (Speirs & Speirs, 1947: 32). Dennison (1980: 148) listed a total of 15 on four of 25 Christmas counts at Sault Ste. Marie. Skeel & Bondrup-Nielsen (1978: 190) found this to be the second most abundant species at Pukaskwa during the winter.

SPRING: Stirrett (1973b: 21) had single birds at Pelee on Apr. 18 and May 9, 1952 and on May 16, 1969. Sheppard (1960: 34) noted one at Niagara Falls early in March, 1958. Speirs (1975: 25) reported one seen at Whitby Hospital as late as March 21, 1966 and one that I saw near our Pickering home on Apr. 15, 1973. Quilliam (1973: 132) reported a small flock at Ivy Lea on March 22, 1938. Mills (1981: 107) cited Muskoka records for Apr. 9, 1912 and May 12, 1963. Louise Lawrence had 4 at Pimisi Bay on March 8, 1945 and two remained until Apr. 8: we saw one at the Bonfield bog on March 16, 1945 (Speirs & Speirs, 1947: 32). Skeel & Bondrup-Nielsen (1978: 190) found this species slightly more common than the Black-capped Chickadee at Pukaskwa in spring (109 on 21 days from Apr. 15 to May 30, 1977).

SUMMER: On the 1968-1977 Breeding Bird Surveys they were absent in southern Ontario, rare at Dorset and from Haileybury north, fairly common at Longlac and Jellicoe as well as at Farrington and Kenora. I saw one near Sundridge on June 24, 1932. Nicholson (1981: 139) cited Manitoulin records: 2 near South Baymouth on July 10, 1971 and 2 at Carroll Wood Bay on June 18, 1974. MacLulich (1938: 25) reported a young male collected for the ROM at Biggar Lake, Algonquin Park, on July 22, 1933: also young being fed at Brule Lake on July 16, 1934 and a nest with young there as late as Aug. 3, 1934. McLaren (1975 and 1976) made splendid studies of the breeding biology and vocalizations of this species at 8 nests in Algonquin Park in 1971 and 1972. Baillie & Hope (1947: 16) found a new nest in a rotten stub at Chapleau on June 7, 1937 and collected 10 adults there from June 1 to 18: they also collected a juvenile at Biscotasing on June 28. Snyder (1942: 138) found a brood just leaving a nest 5 ft. up in a dead aspen stub at Maclennan, near Sault Ste. Marie, on July 8, 1931. Skeel & Bondrup-Nielsen, (1978: 190) noted only 12 on 9 days in the summer of 1977 at Pukaskwa, when the birds were more quiet and solitary than at other seasons. Baillie & Hope (1943: 16) found two nests with 6 eggs each on June 12 and 13, 1936 near Marathon, both were in black spruce stubs 6 and 8 ft. up.: they also found a nest with 4 young ready for flight on July 1 at Amyot: this was 5 ft. up in a dead jack pine in a deserted woodpecker hole. Snyder (1928: 276) collected young at Macdiarmid, Lake Nipigon, on July 9 and July 22, 1923. Dear (1940: 134) found a nest with large young near Thunder Bay on June 18, 1936. Speirs (1949: 148) found 7 territories on 75 acres at Eaglehead Lake in June, 1946. Snyder (1938: 199) found them rare in the Rainy River area but collected 2 young males on July 16, 1929 and another young on July 21 in local boreal bogs at Big Fork. Snyder (1928: 33) collected a young male at Lake Abitibi on July 17, 1925. Snyder (1953: 72) secured breeding evidence at

Savanne in 1937, where 6 to 15 were noted almost daily: they were also observed at Kenora, Malachi, Minaki, Sioux Lookout and Wabigoon. At Pickle Lake, Ross James saw from 1 to 4 birds during most days in the first half of June, 1977. Hope (1938: 31) collected young at Favourable Lake on July 15, 21 and 25, 1938. Cringan (1950: 14) saw none at Nikip Lake until July 23, 1950 but after that date he saw it more regularly and frequently than the Black-capped Chickadee. James, Nash & Peck (1982: 64) saw young begging food from adults on July 6 and 10, 1982 near the mouth of the Harricanaw River (James Bay). Manning (1952: 74) collected 5 and saw 7 others at Raft River on July 10 and 12, 1947: on Aug. 11, 1947 he collected a juvenile and saw 6 others at Shagamu River (Hudson Bay). Ross James collected one young at Kiruna Lake, Sutton Ridges, in the summer of 1981. H. Lumsden saw the species at Cape Henrietta Maria on July 14, 1964 (Peck, 1972: 345). Schueler, Baldwin & Rising (1974: 143) noted the species as uncommon at Cochrane, Moosonee, Attawapiskat, Winisk and Hawley Lake. Lee (1978: 28) found them on all three study plots at Big Trout Lake in 1975: the maximum number seen in a day was 7 on June 26 and June 30. C.E. Hope collected several at Ft. Severn in 1940 including a juvenile on July 22: this is the type locality of the species.

AUTUMN: Doug. McRae and Alan Wormington noted a maximum of 30 at Netitishi Point, James Bay, on Nov. 1, 1981 and saw some almost every day during their stay from Oct. 14 to Nov. 23. George Stirrett saw 7 at Moose Factory on Oct. 2, 1948, as well as 7 at Attawapiskat between Oct. 7 and 10 Manning, (1952: 74): also H. Lewis observed a marked southward movement at Moosonee on Sept. 18 and 25, 1938. Skeel & Bondrup-Nielsen (1978: 190) saw them more often than Black-capped Chickadees at Puksaskwa in fall (133 on 28 days from Sept. 1 to Oct. 16, 1977). Ricker & Clarke (1939: 15) saw one at Lake Nipissing on Oct. 16, 1924. Nicholson (1981: 139) had a high count of 10 at Mississagi Light, Manitoulin, on Oct. 12, 1975. During the 1972 invasion, W. Mansell saw one at Rebecca Lake on Sept. 24; Vonnie Heron noted some in Huntsville in mid-October; Carmen Douglas found some at Parry Sound in November while C. Harris counted 15 at Go Home Bay over the Thanksgiving weekend (Mills, 1981: 108). Devitt (1967: 114) collected two at Holland River on Oct. 31, 1937 and Frances Westman saw one at Barrie in late October, 1963. Quilliam (1973: 132, 198) reported a maximum of 18 at Kingston on Nov. 18 during the 1951 invasion and 23 on Nov. 5, 1972 (when the earliest one was seen on Oct. 15). N. LeVay observed 31 at Cranberry Marsh, Whitby, on Oct. 20, 1951 and D. Scovell noted 20 or more during the 1972 influx between Whitby and Pickering (Tozer & Richards, 1974: 204). Speirs (1975: 25) saw his first 8 of the 1951 influx on Oct. 21 at our Pickering home with a maximum of 12 on Oct. 27 and the last on Nov. 5: Dave Calvert saw the first of the 1972 invasion on Oct. 1 near Oshawa. Saunders (1947: 293) had an Oct. 24, 1943 record of two at Scarborough Bluffs. R.F. Andrle collected one at Long Beach, Lake Erie, on Nov. 24, 1951 and the Axtells noted one at Rose Hill on Nov. 4, 1961 (Beardslee & Mitchell, 1965: 324-325). Brooman (1954: 28) reported two seen by Harold Lancaster on Oct. 30, ten near Hawk Cliff on Oct. 28 and several groups east of New Glasgow on Nov. 20 during the 1951 invasion. A.A. Wood collected two at Coldstream, near London, a male on Oct. 31, 1919 and a female on Nov. 28, 1919 (Saunders & Dale, 1933: 215). Kelley (1978: 56) reported that 69 were banded at Pelee from Oct. 11 to Nov.10 during the 1972 invasion, while 36 were reported in the Detroit region, during the 1951 influx, mainly from Ontario counties. Stirrett (1973a: 17 and 1973d: 23) had Pelee records on Oct. 27 (1); Oct. 28 (5); Oct. 29 (12); Nov. 4 (1); and Nov. 25 (1).

BANDING: A bird banded in 1961 came to a feeder in Nym until Apr. 9, 1966 (Peruniak, 1971: 22).

## MEASUREMENTS:
*Length:* 5.0 to 5.5 ins. (Godfrey, 1966: 279) *Wingspread:* 8.5 to 9.0 ins. (Roberts, 1955: 643) *Weight:* 2 ♂ averaged 11.2 g. 1 ♀ weighed 10.2 g. (Hope, 1938: 31).

## REFERENCES:
Dawe, Arnold 1952 Unusual fall migration of Brown-capped Chickadees. Toronto Field Naturalists, Newsletter 105: 1-6.

Hewitt, O.H. 1948 A local migration of Brown-headed Chickadee in James Bay. Can. Field-Nat., 62:(4): 123-124. On Sept. 20, 1947 150 to 200 were observed flying from north to south by the Kesogami River at the south end of Hannah Bay, James Bay.

Krug, Bruce A. 1947 Hudsonian Chickadee and Golden- winged Warbler in southern Ontario. Can. Field- Nat., 61: (2): 67.

McLaren, Margaret A. 1975 Breeding biology of the Boreal Chickadee. Wilson Bull., 87: (3): 344-354.
8 nests were studied in detail in Algonquin Park in 1971-1972. Hatching occurred about the 15th day of incubation and the young fledged after about 18 days in the nest. Behaviour of males and females was studied and the length of attentive periods was tabulated and the number of feedings per hour at different ages of the young.

McLaren, Margaret A. 1976 Vocalizations of the Boreal Chickadee. Auk, 93: (3): 451-465.
18 different calls were described in their

behavioural contexts and spectrograms were presented for 15 of them: at 7 nests in Algonquin Park.

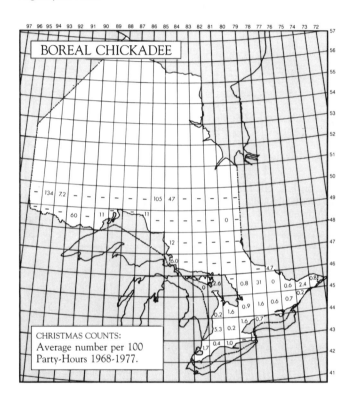

BOREAL CHICKADEE

CHRISTMAS COUNTS:
Average number per 100 Party-Hours 1968-1977.

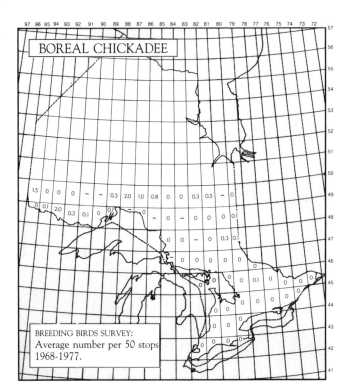

BOREAL CHICKADEE

BREEDING BIRDS SURVEY:
Average number per 50 stops
1968-1977.

# TUFTED TITMOUSE  *Parus bicolor*  Linnaeus

This species is well known and loved in the U.S.A., but just makes it into Ontario along its southern fringes. During our stay in Illinois we enjoyed its rollicking song and sprightly behaviour.

**IDENTIFICATION:** The first impression of the Tufted Titmouse is of a biggish chickadee with a prominent crest but lacking the black throat patch of the chickadee. The "peet-urr, peet-urr, peet-urr" song resembles the sweet whistles of the Cardinal and Carolina Wren but lacks their variety of phrasing.

**WINTER:** On the 1968-1977 Christmas counts, they were rare to uncommon south and west of Toronto, not reported elsewhere in Ontario. Stirrett (1973a: 17) had two winter records for Pelee, on Jan. 3 and Jan. 14. Brooman (1954: 28) observed from one to three in St. Thomas from Dec. 15 to Feb. 7, 1946, another there on Dec. 26, 1951 and one seen by Harold Lancaster in his woods on Jan. 31, 1952. Saunders (1947: 369) listed a Feb. 5 date for Toronto. Ruth Lamb's titmouse was seen at her Kingston feeder and that of John Meisel until about Jan. 14, 1962 (Quilliam, 1973: 133). Weir & Quilliam (1980: 20) reported that Bob Smith's bird stayed until Feb. 20, 1974 at Rockport and another came to Don Holman's feeder east of Kingston from Jan. 8 into spring.

**SPRING:** Stirrett (1973b: 21) gave 8 spring records for Pelee, of one or two birds, from March 4 to May 29. Ussher (1965: 18) had a March 31 record for Rondeau. Brooman (1954: 28) had spring records in Elgin Co. on May 5, 1929, Apr. 6, 1942, March 9, 1947 and Apr. 7, 1947. Saunders (1947: 78) described his encounter with this species at Ancaster on Apr. 7, 1946, where there have been many subsequent sightings including adults and young. Speirs (1938: 40) gave a March 29 date for Toronto and Saunders (1947: 369) listed an Apr. 28 date there. Don Holman's titmouse came to his feeder near Kingston until March 31, 1980 (Weir & Quilliam, 1980: 20).

**SUMMER:** Stirrett (1973c: 18) mentioned nesting at Pelee on July 29 and Aug. 4. Kelley (1978: 56) reported nest records from Lambton Co. in 1965 and in Essex Co. in 1967. Brooman (1954: 28) noted a record by Grant Cook at Pt. Stanley, reported by W.E. Saunders in his nature column on July 16, 1932.

**AUTUMN:** Stirrett (1973d: 23) had fall records of single birds at Pelee on Oct. 13, 22 and 30. Ussher (1965: 18) gave an Oct. 2 record for Rondeau. Fred Bodsworth and Douglas Bocking saw one on Oct. 18, 1942 at St. Thomas: other fall records there were on Nov. 1, 20 and 22, 1946 (Brooman, 1954: 28). Sheppard (1960: 24) cited a record for Point Abino, Lake Erie, on Nov. 15, 1953. J.L. Baillie had Nov. 19 and Nov. 27 records for Toronto (Saunders, 1947: 369). Catherine Cowman observed one at her Frenchman Bay feeder on Nov. 5, 1974 (Speirs, 1975: 26). Ruth Lamb watched one at her Kingston feeder on Nov. 1, 1961 and later from Nov. 16 into the winter (Quilliam, 1973: 133). Weir & Quilliam (1980: 20) reported one at Bob Smith's Rockport feeder from Nov. 16 into the winter.

**MEASUREMENTS:**
*Length:* 6.0 to 6.5 ins.
(Godfrey, 1966: 281)
*Wingspread:* 9 3/4 to

10 3/4 ins. (Roberts,
1955: 644)
*Weight:* 20.3 to 25.3 g.
(Terres, 1980: 928).

**REFERENCES:**
Thompson, Stuart L. 1927
The Tufted Titmouse at
Toronto. Can. Field-Nat.,
41: (8): 186-187.
  Thompson, Stuart L. 1930
A day with the Tufted
Titmouse at Toronto. Can.
Field-Nat., 44:(7):163-
164.
  Woodford, James 1962
The Tufted Titmouse
"invades" southern
Ontario. Fed. Ont.
Naturalists, Bull. 95:
18-20.
One was banded at
Bradley's Marsh by R.L.
Wright on Oct. 8, 1961.
From then until Jan., 1962
they were noted at
Ipperwash Beach, Owen
Sound, Rondeau, St.
Thomas, Ingersoll, Turkey
Point, Pt. Colborne,
Dundas, Hamilton, Stoney
Creek, Walkerton,
Clarkson, Toronto and
Kingston. Some historical
data was also
presented: First Canadian
record: May 2, 1914 - 2 at
Pelee by W.E. Saunders *et
al.* First summer
record: July 7, 1932 -
Fisher's Glen by W.E.
Saunders. First
breeding: Sept. 6, 1936 - 2
yg. with 2 adults -
Hamilton by George
North. First nest
record: mid-May, 1955 n/4
eggs at Sarnia by David
Johnston.

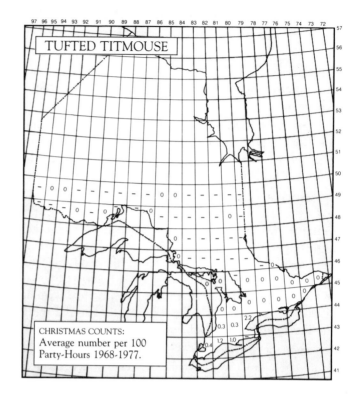

TUFTED TITMOUSE

CHRISTMAS COUNTS:
Average number per 100
Party-Hours 1968-1977.

# RED-BREASTED NUTHATCH   *Sitta canadensis*   Linnaeus

This charming little beauty may be found throughout Ontario at all seasons but is most likely to be seen in coniferous forests. It nests in cavities, often high up in dead trees or branches of live trees. It surrounds the entrance with sticky gum from pines or other conifers to keep out predators, but at least one adult got caught in its own pitch and died (Strickland, Tozer & Rutter, 1982). They are generally most numerous during migrations when they often accompany warbler "waves", but numbers vary considerably from year to year—hundreds may be seen some years and very few or none the next year, perhaps correlated with cone crops on northern conifers.

IDENTIFICATION: The Red-breasted Nuthatch differs from the more familiar White-breasted Nuthatch by its smaller size, the dark line through the eye and by the greater amount of reddish colouration on its underparts (the tawny red is restricted to the flanks and region around the vent in the White-breasted Nuthatch). The "nye-eh" call of the Red-breast has a rising inflection, unlike the "nya" of the White-breasted Nuthatch which is all on one pitch.

WINTER: On the 1968-1977 Christmas counts they were common in Algonquin Park and fairly common at most other localities in Ontario, but numbers varied from year to year as noted above. Stirrett (1973a: 17) had records of single birds at Pelee through the winter months. At Barrie the largest Christmas count was 22 on Jan. 7, 1961 (Devitt, 1967: 115). Numbers on the Huntsville count varied from 3 to 81, averaging 25 (Mills, 1981: 109). Nicholson (1981: 140) reported 18 on the Manitoulin count on Jan. 3, 1970, though most winters passed with no records. Louise Lawrence noted single birds at her Pimisi Bay home on Dec. 30, 1944 and Jan. 3, 1945 (Speirs & Speirs, 1947: 32). Dennison (1980: 147) reported from 1 to 4 on 14 of 25 Christmas counts at Sault Ste. Marie. Skeel & Bondrup-Nielsen (1978: 191) reported from 6 to 10 on the Marathon Christmas counts from 1975 to 1977: they saw one at Pukaskwa on Jan. 21, 1977. David Elder found one at Atikokan on Jan. 1, 1981.

SPRING: Stirrett (1973b: 21) had a high count of 12 at Pelee on May 7, but 17 there on June 1 (his latest date for northward bound birds). Ussher (1965: 18) had his earliest spring bird at Rondeau on Apr. 18 and gave May 6 to May 23 as the average stay there. Saunders & Dale (1933: 216) gave May 3 as the 12-year average arrival date for London, with the earliest on Apr. 13, 1910. W.E. Saunders at Long Point saw 5 as late as June 1, 1924 (Snyder, 1931: 219). Speirs (1938: 44) gave May 19 as the spring peak date for Toronto. Speirs (1975: 28) suggested a spring peak in Ontario Co. during the third week of May, accompanying migrating warblers. James M. Richards found a nest about 25 ft. up in a small dead limb of a basswood tree in the Uxbridge forest on May 26, 1966 (Speirs, 1975: 28). Dennis Barry watched nest excavation of two holes in Darlington Twp.: one on May 7, 1969 in a white pine 20 ft. up; the other in a white birch 25 ft. up on May 12, 1972 (Tozer & Richards, 1974: 205). Weir & Quilliam (1980: 37) listed Apr. 23 and May 23 as the average spring arrival and departure dates for Kingston. Richard Norman found a nest near Kingston on May 11, 1968 which contained 3 young on May 15 and one young on May 25, with the other two outside but nearby (Quilliam, 1973: 134). H.P. Bingham took a set of 6 eggs near Barrie on May 9, 1915 and E.L. Brereton found a nest with young there on May 24, 1938 (Devitt, 1967: 115). A. Kay found an unusually low nest with young only 5 ft. up in a stub at Port Sydney on May 24, 1889 (Mills, 1981: 109). Nicholson (1981: 140) gave 18 as a high spring count for Manitoulin on May 16, 1970. Louise Lawrence saw an adult at a nest hole about 40 ft. up in an aspen stub at Pimisi Bay on May 14, 1945 (Speirs & Speirs, 1947: 32). Skeel & Bondrup-Nielsen (1978: 191) noted 67 at Pukaskwa on 16 days from May 10 to May 31, with a maximum of 13 on May 19. Elder (1979: 36) gave Apr. 7 as his earliest date at Geraldton, and called it "A common summer resident that periodically winters". W.E. Saunders took a set of 6 eggs at Kenora on May 25, 1903 (Baillie & Harrington, 1937: 223). Cringan (1953a:3) noted his first at Sioux Lookout on May 6, 1953.

SUMMER: On the 1968-1977 Breeding Bird Surveys, they were rare to absent along the southern fringe of Ontario, fairly common on other routes but increasing from southeast to northwest. Stirrett (1973c: 19) reported his earliest returning bird on Aug. 13 with several later in August. Kelley (1978: 57) reported one at Rondeau on July 6, 1963 and Ussher (1965: 18) had June 23 and July 10 dates for Rondeau. The most southerly breeding record for Canada was at St. Williams Forestry Station where two pairs nested in nest boxes in 1974: on June 6 there were 5 eggs in one box and 6 in the other: 3 young from the first box and 5 from the second were banded on June 22 (Dunn, Howkins & Cartar, 1975: 467-468). Beardslee & Mitchell (1965: 328) mentioned one bird seen by the Axtells on July 13, 1961 in Bertie Twp. Gerry Bennett found a nest hole about 8 ft. up in a tree stub at Mud Lake, Scott Twp. on June 3, 1961 (Speirs, 1975: 28). Speirs & Orenstein (1975: 12) found a maximum population of 20 birds per 100 acres in the Uxbridge red pine plantation. Quilliam (1973: 134) saw an adult entering a nest hole near Kingston on June 5, 1969 (found earlier by Richard Norman). Paul Harrington found a nest with 4 young (just hatched) at Wasaga Beach on June 15, 1928 (Baillie & Harrington, 1937: 223). Ron Tasker watched two fledged young being fed on Manitoulin on July 17, 1976 (Nicholson, 1981: 140). C.H.D. Clarke saw adults feeding young at Brule Lake, Algonquin Park, on July 17, 1934 (Baillie & Harrington, 1937: 223). Louise Lawrence saw 6 young out of the nest at Pimisi Bay on June 14, 1945 (Speirs & Speirs, 1947: 32). Baillie & Hope (1943: 16) watched an adult feeding young not long out of the nest at Amyot on June 27, 1936. Dear (1940: 135) found a nest with 6 eggs on June 1, 1933 and a nest with young on June 7, 1935, both near Thunder Bay. Kendeigh (1947: 27) found a population of 3 pairs per 100 acres at Black Sturgeon Lake in 1945 while Speirs (1949: 148) found 11 territories on 75 acres at Eaglehead Lake in 1946. Snyder (1928: 32) found a pair nesting over 60 ft. up in a "tall dead rampike" at Lake Nipigon during the summer of 1925. At Pickle Lake, Ross James found only two on June 5 and single birds on June 12 and 13, 1977. Hope (1938: 31) had only one record near Favourable Lake, on July 23, 1938. Cringan (1950: 14) noted them through June and July at Nikip Lake. Todd (1963: 534-535) mapped and described its occurrence in northern Ontario with several records from North Bay north to Moosonee. Schueler, Baldwin & Rising (1974: 143) had no record north of Cochrane. Lee (1978: 28) found at least two pairs at Big Trout Lake in the summer of 1975, one strongly territorial pair in his mixed spruce-aspen study plot. McLaren & McLaren (1981: 4) found them north to the Manitoba border at about 54°30' N.

AUTUMN: J.P. Kelsall and George M. Stirrett saw one well at Moosonee on Oct. 2, 1948 (Manning, 1952: 74). Doug McRae & Alan Wormington noted one or two on 5 days from Oct. 15 to 22, 1981 at Netitishi Point, James Bay (but none later up to Nov. 22). Skeel & Bondrup-Nielsen (1978: 191) noted 165 on 36 days from Aug. 22 to Oct.

16, 1977 at Pukaskwa, one of the most common fall migrants there. Nicholson (1981: 140) had high counts of 40 on Manitoulin on Sept. 11, 1977 and Sept. 23, 1975. Weir & Quilliam (1980: 37) listed Aug. 26 and Oct. 15 as the average fall arrival and departure dates for Kingston. Speirs (1975: 28) mentioned two fall peaks for Ontario Co., one about mid-September and the other during the last week of September. Speirs (1938: 52) had fall peaks at Toronto on Sept. 10 and Sept. 25. Ussher (1965: 18) gave Sept. 3 and Oct. 18 as the average fall arrival and departure dates for Rondeau, the latest on Oct. 29. Stirrett (1973d: 23) had a fall maximum of 75 at Pelee on Sept. 30.

**MEASUREMENTS:**

*Length:* 4.1 to 4.8 ins. (Godfrey, 1966: 282) *Wingspread:* 8.0 to 8.5 ins. (Roberts, 1955: 646) *Weight:* 12 Ontario specimens in ROM averaged 10.6 g.

**REFERENCES:**

Dunn, Erica H.; Heather F. Howkins & Ralph V. Cartar 1975 Red-breasted Nuthatches breeding in nest boxes in pine plantations on the north shore of Lake Erie. Can. Field-Nat. 89: (4): 467-468.

Lawrence, Louise de Kiriline 1952 Red-breast makes a home. Audubon Magazine, 54: (1): 16-21. (First noted excavating at Pimisi Bay 15 ft. up in poplar stub on March 29, 1948: took over excavation from another female on Apr. 25 and raised a family. The male applied the seal of pine gum. [Lawrence] Louise de Kiriline 1954 Irrepressible nuthatch. Audubon Magazine, 56: (6): 264-267. (Mating behaviour and vocalizations described in detail. On March 15, 1953 the female started excavating and on June 5 the pair brought their fluffy children to the feeding station. On July 22 the last young of a *second brood* left the nest hole. The pitch was not applied at this hole until the young of

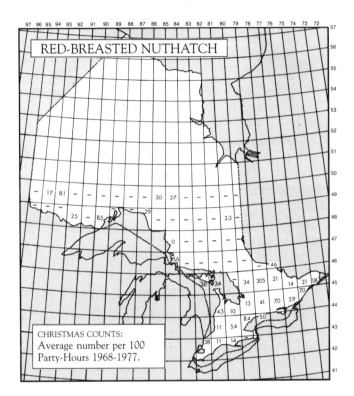

RED-BREASTED NUTHATCH

CHRISTMAS COUNTS:
Average number per 100
Party-Hours 1968-1977.

576

the first brood were
hatched.)

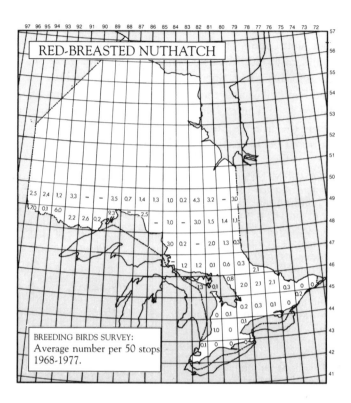

RED-BREASTED NUTHATCH

BREEDING BIRDS SURVEY:
Average number per 50 stops
1968-1977.

# WHITE-BREASTED NUTHATCH
### *Sitta carolinensis*   Latham

This is one of the favourite species at feeding stations, as perky as chickadees but less numerous and perhaps for this reason even more prized. One of the joys of visiting Roy Ivor's feeder at Erindale was watching his nuthatches fly out and catch in mid-air peanut pieces that he tossed up for them. They are present throughout the year in Ontario: fairly common south of North Bay but rare and scattered, north of there.

**IDENTIFICATION:** This is a bird the size of a House Sparrow, with blue gray back, blackish cap (navy in females), white breast and cheeks with contrasting beady black eyes, some rust colour on the flanks and under tail coverts and a longish slightly upturned bill. The call is a nasal "nya-nya: (not rising in pitch as in the smaller Red-breasted Nuthatch). In spring the song is a series of "nya's" that may sound like a distant Pileated Woodpecker. Their habit of clinging to tree bark with with head pointed down is characteristic.

**WINTER:** On the 1968-1977 Christmas counts they were fairly common at most localities north to Deep River and Sault Ste. Marie, absent from most localities north of this line, except at Kirkland Lake and a few places west from Thunder Bay. Stirrett (1973a: 17) had a winter maximum of 13 at Pelee on Dec. 26. Nicholson (1981: 140) gave 15 as a high count for Manitoulin on Dec. 18, 1976. Louise Lawrence observed single birds at her Pimisi Bay feeders rather frequently in winter (Speirs & Speirs, 1947: 32).

Dennison (1980: 146) listed this as a species noted on all 25 Christmas counts at Sault Ste. Marie. Denis (1961: 6) called it an uncommon visitant at Thunder Bay. Peruniak (1971: 22) had only one Atikokan record: a bird seen from Dec. 17, 1961 into March, 1962, but David Elder saw one on the Christmas count there on Dec. 27, 1981.

SPRING: Stirrett (1973b: 21) had a spring maximum of 5 at Pelee on Apr. 30. Saunders & Dale (1933: 216) reported the contents of four London nests: 8 eggs on Apr. 30, 1902; 8 eggs on May 9, 1904; 7 eggs on May 11, 1907 and 8 eggs on May 7, 1913. Snyder (1931: 218) noted a few migrating at Long Point in early May, 1928. A pair nested in a crack in a big white cedar at our Pickering home: I saw adults feeding young there on May 31, 1964 and watched one chip bark off a hop hornbeam tree and carry it into the cavity on Apr. 10, 1970 (Speirs, 1975: 27). Tozer & Richards (1974: 205) reported adults enlarging a nest cavity 20 ft. up in a red oak in Scugog Twp. on Apr. 19, 1971 and another nest under construction in Darlington Twp. on Apr. 25, 1970. E. Beaupré found a nest with young near Kingston on May 12, 1905 (Baillie & Harrington, 1937: 222). H.P. Bingham took a set of 8 eggs at Barrie on May 9, 1915 (Baillie & Harrington, 1937: 223). Lloyd (1924: 15) reported a nest with 11 eggs taken near Ottawa on May 19, 1911 by Taverner and Young. T. Armstrong saw adults feeding young at Bigwind Lake, Muskoka, as early as May 30, 1977 (Mills, 1981: 108). We saw one at Ernest Couchai's feeder just NW of North Bay on March 1, 1945, where it had been present during the previous winter (Speirs & Speirs, 1947: 32). Elder (1979: 36) had only one Geraldton record, at a feeder on March 1, 1969. Peruniak (1971: 22) noted her winter bird at Atikokan until March 29, 1962.

SUMMER: On the 1968-1977 Breeding Bird Surveys they were fairly common in the cottage country, uncommon at most southern Ontario localities and absent on most northern routes (rare at few places in northeastern and northwestern Ontario). Stirrett (1973c: 19) had a summer maximum of 4 at Pelee. Snyder (1931: 219) collected a young bird on Long Point on July 23, 1927. He also collected a young bird in King Twp. on July 23, 1926 (Snyder, 1930: 201). Speirs & Orenstein (1975: 19) listed this as a late succession species, with a maximum population of 15 birds per 100 acres in the Scugog quadrat. Snyder (1941: 70) saw young of the year at Woodrous, Prince Edward Co., on July 11, 1930. D.B. Ferguson saw adults feeding young at Windfall Lake, Manitoulin, on June 22, 1980 (Nicholson, 1981: 140). On June 16, 1944 we saw one near Rutherglen (Speirs & Speirs, 1947: 32). Snyder (1938: 199) found it only at Big Fork and considered it rare in the Rainy River region.

AUTUMN: David Elder saw one at Atikokan on Oct. 14, 1981. The only two noted at North Bay during a two year stay there were seen on Sept. 29, 1944 (Speirs & Speirs, 1947: 32). Stirrett (1973d: 23) had a fall maximum of 15 at Pelee on Oct. 31.

**MEASUREMENTS:**
Length: 5.2 to 6.2 ins.
(Godfrey, 1966: 281)
Wingspread: 9.2 to 11.5
ins. (Roberts, 1955: 645)
Weight: 2 ♂ averaged
22.5 g. 6 ♀ averaged
20.75 g. (ROM Ont.
specimens)

**REFERENCE:**
Cryer, Mary 1965 Nesting
record of the White-
breasted Nuthatch.
Newsletter, 19: (4): 36.
(Thunder Bay Nat. Club).

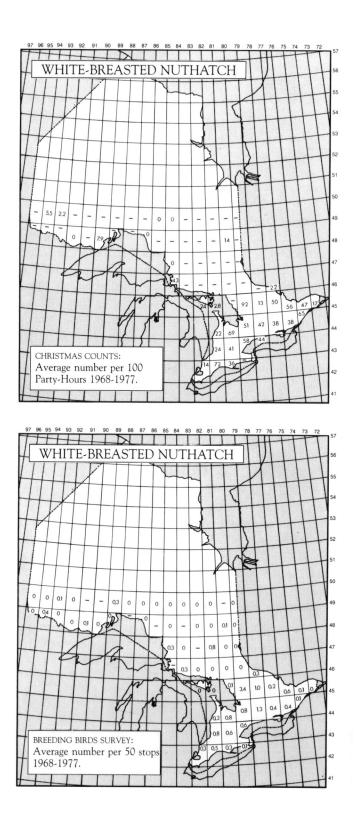

WHITE-BREASTED NUTHATCH

CHRISTMAS COUNTS:
Average number per 100
Party-Hours 1968-1977.

WHITE-BREASTED NUTHATCH

BREEDING BIRDS SURVEY:
Average number per 50 stops
1968-1977.

# BROWN CREEPER   *Certhia americana*   Bonaparte

This is the familiar "little brown bird" usually seen spiralling upward around trunks of big trees, then planing down to the base of the next tree, only to repeat the process. They build their fragile nests behind loose flakes of bark. During migration they are often seen in the big trees lining city streets, but they usually retire to the forests to breed.

IDENTIFICATION: They are smaller than House Sparrows, brown on the back and white below, with slender, down-curved beaks and stiff woodpecker-like tails used to prop them up as they creep up the rough bark of trees. The usual note heard is a high-pitched "pseeee", somewhat like the note of the Golden-crowned Kinglet but in this case a single long-drawn note, not repeated as in the kinglet. The high-pitched song reminds me (in rhythm) of the nursery jingle "fee-fie-fiddly-fum": Saunders (1947: 71) wrote the song as "Pee-e-see, pe-see, see see" (rising, falling, high, low).

WINTER: On the 1968-1977 Christmas counts they were common at Pelee, fairly common elsewhere along the north shore of Lake Erie, uncommon in most of southern Ontario, with a few north to Deep River and the north shore of Lake Superior. Stirrett (1973a: 17) had a winter maximum of 85 at Pelee on Jan. 2. Nicholson (1981: 141) reported one bird at Manitou River on Dec. 10, 1977 and one or two at Mindemoya during the winter of 1980-1981. Louise Lawrence noted one at Pimisi Bay on Jan. 4, 1945 (Speirs & Speirs, 1947: 32). Dennison (1980: 148) reported a total of 6 birds on 5 of 25 Christmas counts at Sault Ste. Marie. Skeel & Bondrup-Nielsen (1978: 191) encountered two late migrants at Pukaskwa on Dec. 7, 1976.

SPRING: Stirrett (1973b: 21) had a spring maximum of 100 at Pelee on Apr. 24. Ussher (1965: 19) gave May 4 as his 13-year average departure date from Rondeau. Snyder (1931: 218) gave May 3 as the peak of the spring migration at Long Point in 1928, when it was present in great numbers: his latest date was May 12 in 1928. Speirs (1938: 44) found spring peaks at Toronto on Apr. 15 and May 1. Saunders (1947: 369) gave May 8 as his 13-year average departure date from Toronto. Snyder (1930: 200) described a nest with 4 young found 9 ft. up in a large elm stub in King Twp. behind a loose sheet of bark on June 22, 1926, the first breeding record for the Toronto region. Speirs (1975: 29) gave Apr. 24 as the spring peak for Ontario Co., while Long (1968b: 20) gave March 30, 1968 and May 27, 1967 as his earliest and latest spring record for Pickering Beach. J.A. Edwards found a nest with 6 eggs on Thorah Is. on May 23, 1928, about 18 ft. up behind the loose bark of an elm (Speirs, 1975: 29). Tozer & Richards (1974: 207) reported a nest with 5 eggs (deserted) in Cartwright Twp. on May 27, 1972 and a nest with 7 young in Darlington Twp. on May 30, 1968. Weir & Quilliam (1980: 37) listed March 30 and May 5 as average arrival and departure dates for Kingston. Devitt (1967: 115-116) reported 3 nests for Simcoe Co.: one with 6 eggs on May 23, 1915 by H.P. Bingham at Barrie; one with 6 eggs near Wasaga Beach on May 24, 1958 by Alf Mitchener and one with young on May 25, 1959 at Willow Creek by Frances Westman. Birds were seen building a nest on May 25, 1978 at Lake Muskoka (Mills, 1981: 110). Nicholson (1981: 141) gave Apr. 13 as the 12-year average arrival date on Manitoulin, with the earliest on March 27, 1976 and a high count of 18 on May 4, 1975. Ricker & Clarke (1939: 16) saw their first at Lake Nipissing on Apr. 19, 1924: Apr. 25, 1925; Apr. 18, 1926 and Apr. 19, 1934. Skeel & Bondrup-Nielsen (1978: 191) noted 174 on 26 days from Apr. 11 to the end of May,

1977 (it ranked third as a spring migrant there). Dear (1940: 135) reported a nest with 6 eggs at Saganaga Lake, Thunder Bay, on May 29, 1937. Denis (1961: 2) gave Apr. 16 as the average arrival date at Thunder Bay, with the earliest on March 9, 1952. Bondrup-Nielsen (1976: 43) noted his first at Kapuskasing on May 3, 1975. Elder (1979: 36) gave Apr. 15 as his earliest Geraldton record. Peruniak (1971: 22) gave Apr. 6 as her earliest date for Atikokan. Cringan (1953a: 3) saw his first on May 7, 1953 at Perrault Falls.

SUMMER: On the 1968-1977 Breeding Bird Surveys they were uncommon to rare, but found as far south as Palgrave and as far north as Kenora and Longlac. Norman Chesterfield found two adults feeding young at a nest 18 ft. up in a high stump in wet woods at Pelee, on July 19, 1962 (Kelley, 1978: 57): she also mentioned recent summer records for Rondeau, where Ussher (1965: 19) had only one summer record (on Aug. 11). Saunders & Dale (1933: 216) reported a nest found near London in June, 1880 "but they nearly all go farther north to breed". J.A. Edwards found a nest with 5 eggs on July 3, 1935, about 6 ft. up in a slit in a cedar tree on Thorah Is. (Speirs, 1975: 29). They averaged about 7 birds per 100 acres in forest quadrats in Ontario Co., with a maximum population of 23 per 100 acres in the Whitby and Thorah plots (Speirs & Orenstein, 1975: 12). Charles Fothergill caught one alive at Rice Lake in the summer of 1820, that was so similar to the Creeper of England that he "did not think it worthwhile to give a particular description of it" (Black, 1934: 152). Quilliam (1973: 134) noted adults taking food to young in a nest near Kingston on July 12 and 16, 1970: five young left this nest on July 21. Frances Westman found a nest in a boathouse, behind a pillar, in July, 1965 (Devitt, 1967: 116). Mills (1981: 110) saw at least three young in a nest 18 ft. up in a drowned tree in an Ahmik Lake beaver pond on June 11, 1980. Nicholson (1981: 141) had only one summer record for Manitoulin: 2 at Pike Lake on July 18, 1971. MacLulich (1938: 26) watched a young bird being fed by adult at Biggar Lake, Algonquin Park on July 25, 1933. Baillie & Hope (1947: 17) had only one Sudbury region record, by John Walty at Wash-agami in June, 1936. Snyder (1942: 138) collected one young, of 8 seen, on July 3, 1931 at Laird. Baillie & Hope (1943: 16) found a nest with 5 eggs at Marathon on June 13, 1936, about 7 ft. up behind a slab of loosely-hanging bark on a dead white spruce. Snyder (1928: 275) collected young at Lake Nipigon on July 24, 1923 and July 8, 1924. Dear (1940: 135) found a nest with large young in Paipoonge Twp., Thunder Bay, on July 15, 1929. Kendeigh (1947: 27) found a breeding population of 9 pairs per 100 acres at Black Sturgeon Lake in 1945, while Speirs (1949: 148) found 6 pairs on 75 acres at Eaglehead Lake in 1946. In the Rainy River region Snyder (1938: 199) found only three during the summer of 1929: one at Off Lake and two at Big Fork. R.D. Ussher saw an adult with one young near Kapuskasing on July 10, 1925 (Baillie & Harrington, 1937: 223). Snyder (1928: 32) noted a few at Lake Abitibi in June and July, 1925. Snyder (1953: 72) collected young at Malachi and Sioux Lookout and saw a recently emerged family of young at Wabigoon on July 1, 1937. Hope (1938: 31) collected two males near Favourable Lake: one on July 14 and one on July 21, 1938. Ross James observed single birds near Pickle Lake on June 4 and 6, and four there on June 9, 1977. Cringan (1950: 15) saw one at Nikip Lake on July 10, 1950. James, Nash & Peck (1982: 64) found them upriver from James Bay along the Harricanaw River in dense coniferous forest during the summer of 1982. James, Nash & Peck (1981: 91) collected young at Kiruna Lake, Sutton Ridges, in the summer of 1981. Schueler, Baldwin & Rising (1974: 143) reported them as uncommon at Winisk in 1965. McLaren & McLaren (1981: 4) noted 3 singing males in the Wetiko

Hills at Lat. 55°N near the Manitoba border, about 150 km. north of the formerly known breeding range.

AUTUMN: D. McRae and A. Wormington observed only two at Netitishi Point, James Bay, in the fall of 1981: one on Oct. 21 and one on Nov. 12. Peruniak (1971: 22) gave Oct. 19 as her latest Atikokan date. Skeel & Bondrup-Nielsen (1978: 191) found only 19 from Sept. 14 to Oct. 10, 1977. MacLulich (1938: 26) gave Oct. 24, 1933 as a departure date from Algonquin Park. Nicholson (1981: 141) gave Sept. 23 as the 10-year average arrival date in fall on Manitoulin, with the earliest on Sept. 2, 1979 and high counts of 10 on Oct. 14, 1974 and on Sept. 23 and Oct. 11, 1975. The latest of 10 killed at the Barrie TV tower was found on Oct. 17, 1966 (Devitt, 1967: 116). Weir & Quilliam (1980: 37) gave Sept. 12 and Nov. 18 as average arrival and departure dates for Kingston. Speirs (1975: 29) gave the first week of October as the fall peak period in Ontario Co. Saunders (1947: 369) listed Sept. 25 as his 13-year average fall arrival date for Toronto while Speirs (1938: 52) gave Sept. 29 as the fall peak there. Ussher (1965: 19) gave Sept. 24 as his 8-year average arrival date for Rondeau. Stirrett (1973d: 23) had a fall maximum of 75 at Pelee on Oct. 3.

BANDING: One banded at Toronto by R.E. Dennis on Oct. 31, 1967 was recovered about 542 miles to the south at Garner, N.C. on Feb. 23, 1968 (Brewer & Salvadori, 1978: 70).

**MEASUREMENTS:**
*Length:* 5 to 5 3/4 ins.
(Godfrey, 1966: 283)
*Wingspread:* 7 to 8 ins.
(Roberts, 1955: 647)
*Weight:* 28 Ontario
specimens averaged 8.3 g.

582

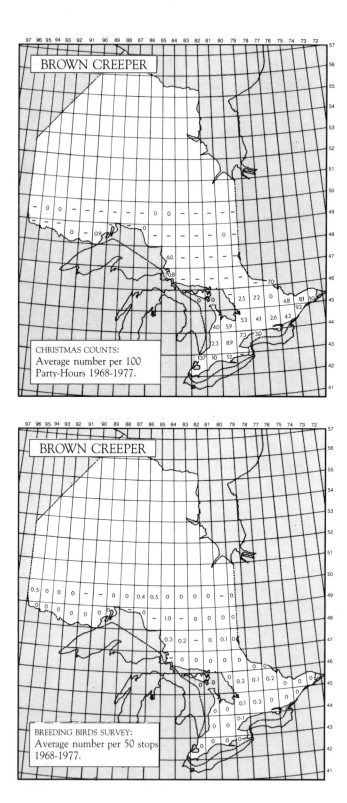

BROWN CREEPER

CHRISTMAS COUNTS:
Average number per 100
Party-Hours 1968-1977.

BROWN CREEPER

BREEDING BIRDS SURVEY:
Average number per 50 stops
1968-1977.

# ROCK WREN  *Salpinctes obsoletus*  (Say)

This is a wren of dry, rocky habitats, normally found from southern Saskatchewan and B.C., south into the U.S.A. Only two specimens have been taken in Ontario.

IDENTIFICATION:  This is a bird about the size of the Carolina Wren, but with more subdued colouration. It is brown above, with a whitish breast, buffy flanks and rump. It has a long dark bill and short, cocked tail which has buffy tips contrasting with a narrow black, subterminal bar. One field mark is the dark streaking on the whitish breast. Its song is loud and has repeated phrases, like the song of a Brown Thrasher.

WINTER:  David Salisbury found one at Port Weller, near St. Catharines, on Dec. 6, 1964: this bird was collected by Robert Andrle for the Buffalo Museum of Science on the following day (Baillie, 1964: 9).

SPRING:

SUMMER:

AUTUMN:  R. Gowler found one that was observed for about three weeks in October, 1972 at Ear Falls, after which it was found dead (Goodwin, 1973: 54).

**MEASUREMENTS:**
*Length:* 5.2 to 6.2 ins.
(Godfrey, 1966: 291)
*Wingspread:* about 9 ins.
(Terres, 1980: 1030)
*Weight:* 31 averaged
16.5 g. (Dunning,
1984: 18).

**REFERENCE:**
Burger, Joanna and
Richard Brownstein 1967
Rock Wren in Ontario.
Auk, 84:(4): 602.

# CAROLINA WREN   *Thryothorus ludovicianus*   (Latham)

In Ontario the Carolina Wren is rare enough to rejoice the bird watcher when found, but, at least in southern Ontario, common enough that you have a fair chance of finding one eventually. They may be found at any season but are most likely to be located in spring when their rollicking song is to be heard.

IDENTIFICATION: This is a biggish wren, with rich brown colouration and prominent white "eyebrows". It is fond of ravines but not entirely averse to human habitations. It has a variety of cardinal-like songs, usually of three syllables, sometimes written as "tea-kettle, tea-kettle, tea-kettle": it also gives a rolling chatter when disturbed.

WINTER: On the 1968-1977 Christmas counts they were fairly common at Pelee, becoming increasingly rare north to Ottawa and Owen Sound. Stirrett (1973a: 18) had a winter maximum of 20 at Pelee on Feb. 11. Brooman (1954: 29) cited Elgin Co. records for Feb. 6, 20-27, 1949 at Union and Dec. 16, 1950 at St. Thomas. Saunders (1947: 29) saw one at a feeding station in the northern outskirts of Toronto on Feb. 6, 1943. Sheldon McGregor showed us one at his Ajax feeder on Jan. 21, 1983, still there on Feb. 18. Tozer & Richards (1974: 210) cited records of four Oshawa birds seen in December by several observers. Walter Lamb reported the first at Kingston since the 1920's on Jan. 28, 1949 and another was found on the Christmas count on Dec. 21, 1957 (Quilliam, 1973: 136). Devitt (1967: 117) reported one at Oro Station, Simcoe Co., in January and February, 1960. Two were observed at Ottawa to Dec. 21, 1980 (Goodwin, 1981: 297) and one wintered there the following winter according to B.M. DiLabio (Weir, 1982: 290). J. Woodword observed one at Paudash Lake, Haliburton, from Dec. 28-31, 1975 (Goodwin, 1976: 713). C. Arnott first observed one at Huntsville on Feb. 17, 1972 which stayed into spring (Mills, 1981: 112). Goodwin (1975: 686) reported sightings north to Huntsville and Port Sydney in January, 1975, by D. Salmon and W. Teachman. One overwintered at Bruce Mines in 1979-1980 according to J. Keast (Goodwin, 1980: 891).

SPRING: Stirrett (1973b: 21) had a spring maximum of 10 at Pelee on March 14. Kelley (1978: 59) mentioned a nest with 5 eggs at Rondeau on May 6, 1955. Brooman (1954: 29) cited several spring records for Elgin Co. J. McInally found a nest in a wash basin on the wall of a building at the Big Creek Muskrat Farm at the base of Long Point on May 13, 1939 - the third known nesting in Ontario (McCracken, Bradstreet & Holroyd, 1981: 59). "Lenna found a nesting pair at Point Abino" on May 26, 1951 and "Mrs. Fisk discovered a nest containing five young at Rose Hill, Ontario, on May 30, 1953" (Beardslee & Mitchell, 1965: 331). Tozer & Richards (1974: 210) reported one seen by T. Norris in Darlington Twp. on May 17, 1973. Nora Mansfield found one in Kingston on Apr. 20, 1970 (Quilliam, 1973: 136). Frances Westman found one at Tollendal on May 12, 1953 and another at her feeding station there up to Apr. 26, 1957: W.E. Cattley found one in Conc. 6, Matchedash Twp. on May 16, 1964 (Devitt, 1967: 117). The Arnott bird at Huntsville, mentioned above, found a mate by May and was seen fighting over a nest box with Tree Swallows on May 29, 1972 (Mills, 1981: 112).

SUMMER: On the 1968-1977 Breeding Bird Surveys they were noted only on the Port Dover route. Baillie & Harrington (1937: 225) found a new nest on Pelee Is. on June 4, 1933. Stirrett (1973c: 19) reported Pelee maxima of 10 on July 16 and Aug. 13. Saunders (1927: 138) heard one singing a strange medley of songs in his London garden on June 26, 1927 "including Baltimore Oriole, Winter Wren, House Wren and Mourning Warbler". Snyder (1931: 217) heard one at Long Point on June 12 and July 26, 1927 and J.L. Baillie reported finding an egg shell on July 4 believed to belong to this species. On Aug. 5, 1961, a nest with one young was found at Port Colborne (Beardslee & Mitchell, 1965: 331-332). I heard one scolding at our Pickering home on Aug. 16, 1971 and another singing and scolding there from July 26 to Aug. 1, 1973: J. Satterly heard one singing at Cedar Point, Lake Simcoe, on Aug. 15 and 19, 1959 (Speirs, 1975: 32). A.E. Bell noted one at Napanee on Aug. 20, 1973 (Goodwin, 1974: 47). Weir & Quilliam, 1980: 20) reported hatch-year birds banded at Prince Edward Point in July, 1977 and July, 1980. Devitt (1967: 117) reported one seen by Norman Martin at Sandy Cove, Lake Simcoe, on June 30, 1939. Two were noted at Wasaga Beach on July 1, 1975 (Goodwin, 1975: 967). M. Brigham *et al* noted the species at Ottawa from Aug. 1-7, 1971 (Goodwin, 1972: 58). On Aug. 25, 1964, M. Hill found one at Solitaire Lake (Limberlost) near Huntsville (Mills, 1981: 112). T.C. Mackie observed one at North Bay on Aug. 3, 1972 (Goodwin, 1972: 854). Paul Harrington reported one about 15 miles east of Longlac on Aug. 6, 1957, a most remarkable occurrence (Bennett, Mitchell & Gunn, 1958: 29).

AUTUMN: J. Miller noted one on Squirrel Is., near Sault Ste. Marie, from Aug. 10 to Nov. 16, 1973 (Goodwin, 1974: 47). The Limberlost bird mentioned above was seen up to Nov. 22, 1964 (Mills, 1981: 112). Frances Westman had one at her Tollendal feeding station from Oct. 31, 1956 until the following spring (Devitt, 1967: 117). R.D. Weir saw one at Kingston on Sept. 24, 1972 (Goodwin, 1973: 54). Don Perks observed one at Greenwood Conservation Area on Nov. 28, 1971 (Speirs, 1975: 32). Fred Bodsworth found one at Springwater Pond, Elgin Co., on Nov. 8, 1942 (Brooman, 1954: 29). Stirrett (1973d: 24) had a fall maximum of 10 at Pelee on Oct. 15.

**MEASUREMENTS:**
*Length:* 5.2 to 6.0 ins. (Godfrey, 1966: 289)
*Wingspread:* 6.8 to 7.8 ins. (Roberts, 1955: 649)
*Weight:* 14.2 to 19.7 g. (Terres, 1980: 1029): one ♂ weighed 21.1 g.

**REFERENCE:**
Saunders, W.E. Sept., 1927 Unusual song from a Carolina Wren. Can. Field-Nat., 41: (6): 138.

586

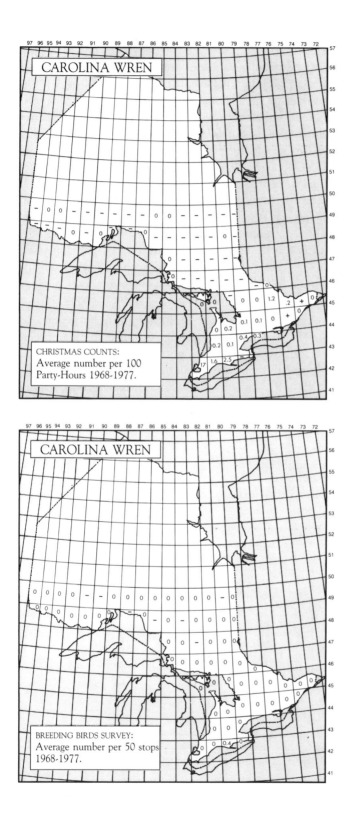

CAROLINA WREN

CHRISTMAS COUNTS:
Average number per 100
Party-Hours 1968-1977.

CAROLINA WREN

BREEDING BIRDS SURVEY:
Average number per 50 stops
1968-1977.

# BEWICK'S WREN    *Thryomanes bewickii*    (Audubon)

This wren is widespread but not very common in much of the U.S.A., but makes it into Ontario only in the southwestern portion. Most records have been at Pelee in spring.

IDENTIFICATION:  Bewick's Wren is somewhat larger than a House Wren, but with a distinct white line over the eye (as in the larger Carolina Wren) and with white spots at the end of all but the central tail feathers, showing when the tail is spread. The song reminded me of a Song Sparrow's song: Bent (1948: 180) wrote this as "chip, chip, chip, te-da-a, te-dee".

WINTER:  The first Canadian specimen "was taken by W.E. Saunders on Dec. 12, 1898, near Appin in a swampy area full of brush and fallen trees" (Saunders & Dale, 1933: 217).

SPRING:  Stirrett (1973b: 21) gave Apr. 1 as his earliest Pelee date, with a maximum of 6 on Apr. 25. The first nest was found at Pelee on May 20, 1950 by W.W.H. Gunn: it held 4 eggs: by May 24 it was deserted and 3 eggs collected for the ROM. John Crosby found another nest there on May 17, 1957, with one egg. On May 19, J.L. Baillie saw another nest there with 5 eggs, which held 6 eggs on May 25 (Baillie, 1962: 10). Several more recent sightings at Pelee have been published. Goodwin (1972: 757) also mentioned sightings at East Sister Is. on May 16, 1972 by S. Postapolsky and R. Simpson: also one at Erieau on May 2, 1975 by K.J. Burk (Goodwin, 1975: 846): and one at Rondeau on May 17 to May 20, 1981 by P.A. Woodliffe (Goodwin, 1981: 819). Brooman (1954: 29) cited three spring records by Marshall Field: one seen and heard singing at St. Thomas on May 15, 1950: one near Port Bruce on Apr. 20, 1952 and another at St. Thomas on Apr. 2, 1953. On Apr. 28, 1957, "Dr. & Mrs. Harold H. Axtell carefully studied a bird of this species near the base of Morgan's Point, Ontario" (Beardslee & Mitchell, 1965: 331). Saunders (1947: 108-109) described the discovery of the first Toronto Bewick's Wren by John MacArthur *et al* on Apr. 17, 1942.

SUMMER:  Stirrett (1973c: 19) had one summer record for Pelee, on Aug. 12, 1952. Another was seen there on Aug. 8, 1981 by D.A. Sutherland (Goodwin, 1982: 173). Gerald W. Knechtel found a pair at Port Franks in August, 1927 (Baillie, 1962: 10). R.M. Saunders noted his second one at Toronto on July 1, 1954 (Baillie, 1962: 10). A singing male was seen at Leith, Grey Co., on June 20, 1937 by D.B. and T.R. Murray and W.E. Saunders (Baillie, 1962: 10).

AUTUMN:  One was observed at the Long Point Bird Observatory from Sept. 28 to Oct. 23, 1976 (Goodwin, 1977: 172). Kelley (1978: 58) gave two fall records for Pelee: Sept. 17 and Oct. 7, 1950. Stirrett (1973d: 23) added a later record, on Oct. 22.

**MEASUREMENTS:**
*Length:* 5.0 to 5.5 ins.
(Godfrey, 1966: 288)
*Wingspread:* 6.90 to 7.15
ins. (Roberts, 1955: 648)
*Weight:* 56 averaged
9.9 g. (7.8 - 11.8 g.)
(Dunning, 1984: 18).

**REFERENCE:**
Saunders, W.E. Dec.,
1919 The status of
Bewick's Wren in Ontario.
Can. Field-Nat.,
33: (6): 118.

# HOUSE WREN   *Troglodytes aedon*   Vieillot

Though numbers vary from year to year, this is usually a fairly common bird in the built up part of southern Ontario, much appreciated by some for its cheerful song and activity, deplored by others when it takes over bird houses built for other species. If several bird boxes are available, the male will generally fill them all with sticks, while the female selects one to use for raising the family. They winter in southern U.S.A. and in Mexico. S. Charles Kendeigh, who made a special study of this species, showed that most had to migrate to avoid overnight starvation in our long winter nights.

IDENTIFICATION: This is the most plain of our wrens, lacking the back stripes of the marsh wrens, the white tip to the outer tail feathers of the Bewick's Wren and the barred flanks of the Winter Wren: a small, brown, very active little bird. Its song is a musical, bubbling chatter: "zhuh, whu-wee-wee-wah-wah-wah".

WINTER: On the 1968-1977 Christmas counts, they were rare at localities from Pelee to Long Point, along the north shore of Lake Erie, absent elsewhere in Ontario. Stirrett (1973a: 18) reported one at Pelee on Dec. 24, 1970: Kelley (1978: 58) gave the year as 1972. R.F. Andrle and J.F. Thill noted one at Thunder Bay, Lake Erie, on Dec. 6, 1959 (Beardslee & Mitchell, 1965: 329).

SPRING: Stirrett (1973b: 21) gave Apr. 22 as his earliest date for Pelee, with a maximum of 30 from May 14 to June 1. Ussher (1965: 19) had his earliest at Rondeau on Apr. 14, with his 26-year average arrival date on Apr. 30. Saunders & Dale (1933: 216) gave Apr. 26 as the 17-year average arrival date for London, with the earliest on Apr. 18, 1920: a set of 7 eggs was found on May 22, 1896. Fleming (1907: 85) gave Apr. 15, 1890 as his earliest date for Toronto, while Saunders (1947: 369) gave May 3 as his 13-year average arrival date there. Tozer & Richards (1974: 207) noted one singing at Lake Scugog as early as Apr. 20, 1969. J. Satterly found one nesting at Cedar Point, Lake Simcoe, as early as May 11, 1957 (Speirs, 1975: 30) and Kenneth Carmichael found a nest with 4 eggs in Uxbridge Twp. on May 21, 1966. Snyder (1941: 71) gave May 2, 1934 as his earliest Prince Edward Co. record. Weir & Quilliam (1980: 37) listed Apr. 29 as the 32-year average arrival date for Kingston, with the earliest on Apr. 4. Devitt (1967: 116) gave May 5 as the 20-year average arrival date at Barrie, with the earliest on Apr. 24, 1938: he observed nest building at Wasaga Beach as early as May 14, 1938 and reported a set of 6 eggs found near Barrie by D. Butler on May 21, 1938. L. Beamer's median arrival date at Meaford was May 1, with the earliest on Apr. 22 in 1941 and 1949. Wm. Mansell saw one at Peninsula Lake, Muskoka, on May 5, 1933 and on May 28, 1889, W. Melville caught one on a nest with 6 eggs at Gravenhurst (Mills, 1981: 110-111). Nicholson (1981: 142) gave May 9 as the 9-year average arrival date on Manitoulin, with the earliest on May 3. MacLulich (1938: 26) listed Algonquin Park arrival dates on May 14, 1912; May 19, 1933 and May 14, 1934. Speirs & Speirs (1947: 32) observed four at North Bay on May 6, 1944. Denis (1961: 3) gave May 13 as the average arrival date at Thunder Bay, with the earliest on Apr. 22, 1945. Peruniak (1971: 22) gave May 8 as her earliest Atikokan date. Cringan (1953a: 3) noted his first at Sioux Lookout on May 17, 1953.

SUMMER: On the 1968-1977 Breeding Bird Surveys they were common to fairly common along the southern fringe of Ontario, becoming uncommon north to Chapleau and Dryden. Stirrett (1973c: 19) had a summer maximum of 40 at Pelee on Aug. 17. Saunders & Dale (1933: 216) reported sets of 7 eggs at London on June 10, 1915 and June 4, 1916. Harold Lancaster found a nest with 3 eggs in Aldborough Twp., Elgin Co., on June 24, 1953 (Brooman, 1954: 28). McCracken, Bradstreet & Holroyd (1981: 59) reported that there were 18 records of active nests on Long Point, with more than one brood often raised in a season and populations as high as 175 territories per km². Charles Fothergill found a nest in Wm. Scadding's garden in Toronto on June 17, 1825 in a "large, hollow, pine, prostrate, partly burnt" (Black, 1934: 152). R.G. Tozer found a nest with 4 young as late as Aug. 26, 1963 at Scugog (Tozer & Richards, 1974: 209). Our highest Ontario Co. population was in a hurricane damaged forest plot in Whitby Twp. with 43 birds per 100 acres (Speirs & Orenstein, 1975: 12). Allin (1940: 103) found a nest with 6 eggs in Darlington Twp. on June 6, 1933. Young of the year were first noted at Woodrous on June 38, 1930 (Snyder, 1941: 71). Quilliam (1973: 135) saw adults feeding young in a nest at Kingston on June 29, 1961. G.L. Lambert found a nest with 7 eggs at Alcona Beach, Lake Simcoe as late as Aug. 1, 1939 (Devitt, 1967: 116). J.L. Baillie found a clutch hatching at Pickerel Lake on July 22, 1936 (Mills, 1981: 110). Ron Tasker found a nest with eggs in Burpee Twp., Manitoulin, on July 12, 1975 (Nicholson, 1981: 142). C.H.D. Clarke saw young being fed at Brule Lake, Algonquin Park, on July 9, 1934 (MacLulich, 1938: 26). Ricker & Clarke (1939: 16) found a nest with 5 eggs at Lake Nipissing on June 20, 1926. Baillie & Hope (1947: 17) watched one carrying nest material into a nest box at Chapleau on June 20, 1937: they saw the first flying young at Bigwood on July 14, a nest with 6 eggs on July 12 and a nest with 7 young there on July 26. Snyder (1942: 138) found a nest with 6 eggs on June 12, 1931 near Maclennan and reported them to be common near Sault Ste. Marie. Baillie & Hope (1943: 17) found a nest in a birch stub at Marathon and collected adults, both there and at Rossport, in June, 1936. Snyder (1928: 275) found a pair nesting near Weatherbe, Lake Nipigon, on June 27, 1924, the only ones noted in two summers there. Dear (1940: 135) found a nest with 6 eggs on July 22, 1922 at Ft. William (Thunder Bay). Snyder (1938: 200) found a completed nest as early as June 1, 1929 but young were not conspicuous until mid-July in the Rainy River region. Smith (1957: 176) found them to be uncommon in the Clay Belt, but noted some at New Liskeard, Kapuskasing, Hearst and Gogama. Snyder (1928: 32) found two nests near the southern shore of Lake Abitibi and collected an immature bird there on July 8. Elder (1979: 36) gave June 1 as his earliest date for Geraldton where he regarded this as an "uncommon summer resident". Snyder (1953: 73) had a maximum daily total of 50 (adults and young) at Malachi on July 24, 1947, but found some breeding at Ingolf, Kenora and Shoal Lake, with a few north to Sioux Lookout.

AUTUMN: Ricker & Clarke (1939: 16) recorded this species at Lake Nipissing up to Sept. 26, 1925. Speirs & Speirs (1947: 32) observed one at North Bay on Sept. 17, 1944. Nicholson (1981: 142) gave Sept. 24, 1979 as his latest Manitoulin date. A. Kay collected a male at Pt. Sydney, Muskoka, as late as Sept. 26, 1907 (Mills, 1981: 111). Bruce Falls saw one at Thunder Bay, Simcoe Co., as late as Oct. 11, 1947 (Devitt, 1967: 116) and E.L. Brereton saw an adult taking food to young in a nest at Balm Beach as late as Sept. 4, 1944. Weir & Quillima (1980: 37) listed Oct. 1 as the 26-year average departure date from Kingston, with the latest on Oct. 22. Tozer & Richards (1974: 209) gave Oct 19, 1969 as their latest Oshawa record. J.L. Baillie (in Saunders, 1947: 369) listed Oct. 29 as his latest Toronto date. Beardslee & Mitchell (1965: 329) reported one at Erie Beach on Nov. 10, 1957. Ussher (1965: 19) gave Sept. 27 as his 8-year average departure date from Rondeau, with the latest on Nov. 25. Stirrett (1973d: 23) had a fall maximum of 100 at Pelee on Sept. 27, with the latest on Nov. 11.

**MEASUREMENTS:**

*Length:* 4.5 to 5.3 ins. (Godfrey, 1966: 286)
*Wingspread:* 6.5 to 7.0 ins. (Roberts, 1955: 650)
*Weight:* Nine Ontario specimens averaged 11.3 g.

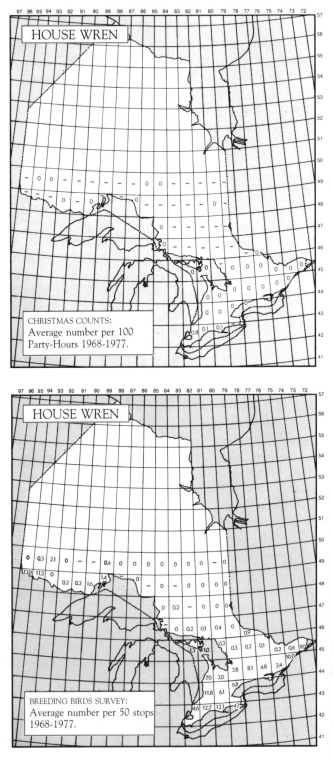

HOUSE WREN

CHRISTMAS COUNTS:
Average number per 100
Party-Hours 1968-1977.

HOUSE WREN

BREEDING BIRDS SURVEY:
Average number per 50 stops
1968-1977.

# WINTER WREN  *Troglodytes troglodytes*  (Linnaeus)

This is a bird of brush piles and fallen dead trees, a bird of cedar swamps and spruce bogs. From such places in the breeding season may issue an almost continuous stream of tinkling, silvery "fairy music", the song of the Winter Wren. In Ontario it is truly a winter wren only in the south: most of them migrate into the U.S.A. at that season, and even there an unusually severe winter, such as that of 1976-1977, may wipe out most of the population, so that even now they have not regained their former abundance in northern Ontario.

IDENTIFICATION: This is a tiny wren, differing from the familiar House Wren in its more heavily barred flanks and shorter tail, usually held at right angles to the body or even bending somewhat forward of the vertical. Its song goes on and on, often for 10 seconds or more, while the House Wren song is usually about 2 seconds (and lower in pitch). In migration you hear its "dick-dick" (pause) "dick-dick" (pause) "dick-dick" call from heavy cover. Although this is supposed to be the same bird as the wren of Europe and Asia, my impression is of quite a different bird, in disposition, habitat and vocalizations (their wren is a common garden bird, not a shy, retiring bird of dense coniferous forests: the ones that I have heard there had a shorter, less pleasing song than ours (perhaps the wilderness setting lends charm to our bird).

WINTER: On the 1968-1977 Christmas counts it was fairly common at Pelee and Long Point, becoming rare north to Thousand Islands and Wiarton. Stirrett (1973a: 18) had a winter maximum of 5 at Pelee on Dec. 27. Saunders & Dale (1933: 217) noted one at London on Jan. 7, 1911 and another there from Dec. 23, 1922 to Jan. 7, 1923. Fleming (1907: 85) mentioned a Toronto record for Jan. 15, 1892. Devitt (1967: 117) reported one collected near Barrie on Dec. 16, 1925, where it had been noted on 6 Christmas counts between 1951 and 1967. L. Beamer reported one on Dec. 26, 1951 at Meaford. C. Campbell found one near Parry Sound on Dec. 31, 1974 (Mills, 1981: 111).

SPRING: Stirrett (1973b: 21) had a spring maximum of 6 at Pelee on Apr. 18. Ussher (1965: 19) had Rondeau records from March 27 to May 13, with the average arrival on Apr. 15 and departure on May 5. Saunders & Dale (1933: 217) gave Apr. 11 as the 16-year average arrival date for London, with the earliest on March 31, 1913. Snyder (1931: 217) saw his latest three at Long Point on May 6 in 1928. Ada Diaz found a nest in Niagara Glen on Apr. 26, 1932 that was completed on Apr. 28 (Beardslee & Mitchell, 1965: 330). J.L. Baillie (in Saunders, 1947: 369) gave Apr. 12 as his 20-year average arrival date at Toronto, while Speirs (1938: 44) listed Apr. 15 as the spring peak there. Fleming (1907: 85) had a Toronto record as early as March 17, 1894. Speirs (1975: 31) gave May 2 as the spring peak for Ontario Co. with his earliest Pickering Twp. bird on Apr. 1, 1953. Snyder (1941: 71) gave March 22, 1938 as his earliest date for Prince Edward Co. Weir & Quilliam (1980: 37) listed Apr. 6 and May 16 as average spring arrival and departure dates for Kingston. Devitt (1967: 117) gave Apr. 19 as the 7-year average arrival date at Collingwood. L. Beamer's earliest arrival date at Meaford was March 26, 1948. Mills (1981: 111) reported a 13-year average arrival date at Huntsville as Apr. 14, with the earliest on Apr. 3, 1976; but A. Kay collected one at Pt. Sydney on March 3, 1900 that may have wintered there. Nicholson (1981: 142) gave Apr. 15 as the 8-year average arrival date for Manitoulin, with the earliest on Apr. 2, 1978 and a high count of 10 on May 23, 1976. MacLulich (1938: 26) gave May 4, 1932 as an arrival date for Algonquin Park. Louise

Lawrence noted one at Pimisi Bay as early as March 30, 1945 (Speirs & Speirs, 1947: 32). Skeel & Bondrup-Nielsen (1978: 192) noted 100 on 30 days at Pukaskwa from Apr. 14 to May 31, 1977. Denis (1961: 3) gave May 7 as the average arrival date at Thunder Bay, with the earliest on Apr. 19, 1952. Bondrup-Nielsen (1976: 44) saw his first at Kapuskasing on Apr. 25, 1974. Elder (1979: 36) gave May 3 as his earliest Geraldton date. Peruniak (1971: 22) noted her earliest at Atikokan on Apr. 22. Cringan (1953a: 3) noted his first at Sioux Lookout on May 6, 1953.

SUMMER: On the 1968-1977 Breeding Bird Surveys it was absent along the southern fringe of Ontario, becoming common east and north of Lake Superior. Stirrett (1973b: 21 and 1973d: 23) noted two at Pelee as late as June 9 but no others in summer until Aug. 27. Snyder (1930: 200) found families just capable of flight in the tangled woods bordering Holland Marsh, in King Twp., on June 25 and Aug. 2, 1926. In Ontario Co., Speirs & Orenstein (1975: 17) found a maximum population density of 21 birds per 100 acres in the Scott Twp. forest quadrat. Tozer & Richards (1974: 210) mentioned two observations of fledged young being fed by adults in Darlington Twp.: one on July 2, 1961, the other on July 9, 1965. Snyder (1941: 72) collected a young male at Woodrous, Prince Edward Co., on June 28, 1930. R.V. Lindsay saw young being fed by parents on July 8, 1926 at Mountain Grove, north of Kingston (Baillie & Harrington, 1937: 225). Devitt (1967: 116-117) saw a brood of 4 young in wet woods along the Holland River on July 1, 1936, and mentioned other broods observed in Simcoe Co. L. Beamer heard one singing in evergreen forest along the Georgian Bay shore near Meaford on July 16, 1952. K. Clark found a nest with young hidden in the roots of a fallen hemlock at Dotty Lake, Muskoka on June 20, 1978 (Mills, 1981: 111). C.H.D. Clarke noted young in Algonquin Park on Aug. 8, 1932 and Aug. 9, 1924 (MacLulich, 1938: 26). Ricker & Clarke (1939: 16) observed young being fed at Frank's Bay, Lake Nipissing, on June 19, 1933. Snyder (1942: 139) collected two young at Laird on July 3, 1931. From June 1 to July 17, 1977, Skeel & Bondrup-Nielsen (1978: 192) observed 36 on 21 days at Pukaskwa. A partially constructed nest was found at Marathon on June 12, 1936 under the roots of a fallen tree (Baillie & Hope, 1943: 17). Dear (1940: 135) found a nest with 6 eggs near Thunder Bay on June 1, 1933. Kendeigh (1947: 27) found a breeding density of 5 pairs per 100 acres at Black Sturgeon Lake in 1945. Speirs (1949: 148) found 3 territories per 75 acres at Eaglehead Lake in 1946. Snyder (1938: 200) found them to be very rare in the Rainy River region. Smith (1957: 176) called them "common songsters" in the Clay Belt. Snyder (1928: 32) collected a male at Lake Abitibi on June 2, 1925. James (1980: 88) reported small numbers at Pickle Lake in the summers of 1977 and 1979. Snyder (1953: 73) found them to be rare at Kenora, Malachi, Wabigoon and Savanne but noted from one to four on half of the days spent at Sioux Lookout from June 21 to July 8, 1947. Hope (1938: 31) saw young just out of the nest at Favourable Lake on July 6, 1938. Cringan (1950: 15) heard singing on four occasions in June and early July in the Nikip Lake region in 1950. James, Nash & Peck (1982: 64) found them daily but uncommon at Harricanaw River, near James Bay, in the summer of 1982. Lee (1978: 28) watched two adults feeding young barely able to fly at Big Trout Lake on July 11, 1975.

AUTUMN: D. McRae and A. Wormington noted their last (and only) Winter Wren at Netitishi Point, James Bay, on Oct. 18, 1981. Skeel & Bondrup-Nielsen (1978: 192) saw their last at Pukaskwa on Oct. 15, 1977. Louise Lawrence noted one at Pimisi Bay on Oct. 7, 1944 (Speirs & Speirs, 1947: 32). Ron Tasker had a high count of 30 on Oct.

11-12, 1974 on Manitoulin, with his latest on Nov. 28, 1976 in Burpee Twp. (Nicholson, 1981: 142). Devitt (1967: 117) reported a brood of 4 fledged young along the Holland River as late as Sept. 12, 1937 (probably a second brood). Weir & Quilliam (1980: 37) listed Sept. 14 and Oct. 30 as average fall arrival and departure dates for Kingston. Speirs (1975: 31) had fall records for Pickering from Sept. 7 (1952) to Nov. 5 (1967) with the fall peak about Oct. 10. Speirs (1938: 52) listed Oct. 7 as the fall peak at Toronto, while J.L. Baillie (in Saunders, 1947: 369) gave Oct. 13 as his 21-year average departure date. Ussher (1965: 19) had fall records at Rondeau from Sept. 6 to Nov. 25, with average arrival on Sept. 28 and departure on Nov. 3. Stirrett (1973d: 23) had a fall maximum of 60 at Pelee on Sept. 26.

**MEASUREMENTS:**
*Length:* 4.0 to 4.5 ins.
(Godfrey, 1966: 287)
*Wingspread:* 5.86 to 6.38
ins. (Roberts, 1955: 649)
*Weight:* 15 Ontario
specimens averaged 9.0 g.

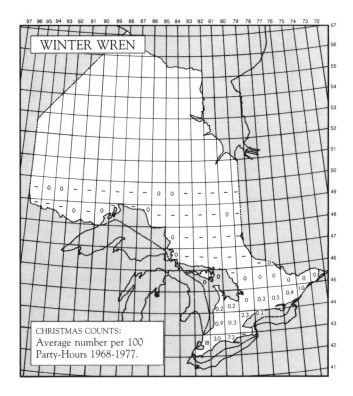

WINTER WREN

CHRISTMAS COUNTS:
Average number per 100
Party-Hours 1968-1977.

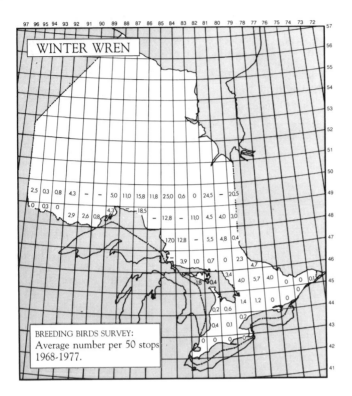

WINTER WREN

97 96 95 94 93 92 91 90 89 88 87 86 85 84 83 82 81 80 79 78 77 76 75 74 73 72

2.5 0.3 0.8 4.3 – – 5.0 11.0 15.8 11.8 25.0 0.6 0 24.5 – 20.5

0 0.3 0 2.9 2.6 0.8 4.3 18.5 – 12.8 – 11.0 4.5 4.0 3.0

170 12.8 – 5.5 4.8 0.4

3.9 1.0 0.7 0 2.3

3.4 4.7

1.8 0.4 4.0 5.7 4.0 0 0 0.1

1.4 1.2 0 0 0

0.2 0.6 0

0.4 0.1 0.2

0 0 0

BREEDING BIRDS SURVEY:
Average number per 50 stops
1968-1977.

# SEDGE WREN *Cistothorus platensis* (Latham)

Except in the big marshes bordering Lake Erie and Lake Ontario, the Sedge Wren is generally more numerous than the Marsh Wren in Ontario. It occurs in somewhat drier locations, in sedge meadows, old fields and around the edges of marshes where cat-tails give way to long grasses. Colonies move about frequently from year to year so they may be absent from locations where you found them common in a preceding year. They are usually found because of their loud, persistent singing in their breeding locations, so that migrants are not often located in spring and fall. In winter they go south to the southern U.S.A. Some races occur in Central and South America.

**IDENTIFICATION:** Like the Marsh Wren this tiny wren has a white-striped back, but unlike the Marsh Wren this species has also a streaked crown and a very inconspicuous eye stripe and a much shorter bill. The emphatic song "dick-dick-dick-shh-shh-shh-shh" is diagnostic (although somewhat similar to the song of the Dickcissel).

**WINTER:**

**SPRING:** Stirrett (1973b: 21) gave Apr. 13 as the earliest Pelee date, with his maximum of 10 found on May 27. Ussher (1965: 19) gave May 13 as the 17-year average arrival date at Rondeau, with his earliest on May 1. Earl Lemon had West Elgin records on May 15 in 1934 and 1938 (Brooman, 1954: 29). McCracken, Bradstreet & Holroyd (1981: 59) reported three singing near the base of Long Point on May 20, 1963. J.L.

Baillie had a Toronto record as early as May 8 and gave May 18 as his average arrival date (Saunders, 1947: 370). Edgerton Pegg noted one at the mouth of Duffin Creek, Pickering, on May 19, 1968 (Speirs, 1975: 34). Weir & Quilliam (1980: 37) listed May 17 as the 20-year average arrival date at Kingston, with the earliest on May 6. Devitt (1967: 118) gave May 19 as the average arrival date near Barrie, with the earliest on May 9, 1964. K. Ketchum saw one at Pointe au Baril on May 19, 1962 (Mills, 1981: 113). Nicholson (1981: 143) found May 14 to be the 9-year average arrival date on Manitoulin, with the earliest on May 1, 1976. MacLulich (1938: 27) mentioned a May 30, 1934 record for Algonquin Park. Ricker & Clarke (1939: 16) heard the species just south of North Bay on May 25, 1932. Peruniak (1971: 22) gave May 15 as her earliest date for Atikokan.

SUMMER: On the 1968-1977 Breeding Bird Surveys they were rare or uncommon from Lake Erie and Lake Ontario, north to Sudbury, fairly common in the Rainy River region and uncommon at Ignace. Stirrett (1973c: 19) reported four nests at Pelee from June 28 to July 8. Kelley (1978: 59) reported a nest with 8 eggs in Mersea Twp. (near Pelee) on June 21, 1958 and 4 pairs with 4 nests at Kettle Point on June 2, 1974. Saunders & Dale (1933: 218) watched an adult feeding young near London on July 3, 1915, and later found the nest which contained young and one addled egg. W.W.H. Gunn found two birds just north of Sparta, Elgin Co., on June 30, 1953 (Brooman, 1954: 29) W.E.C. Todd found a nest with 4 eggs near the base of Long Point on July 10, 1907 (McCracken, Bradstreet & Holroyd, 1981: 60). Snyder (1931: 218) saw as many as 10 on a single day on Long Point in the summer of 1927 and collected a young bird on July 16, 1927: numbers appear to have declined since then on the point. C.W. Nash collected a male on June 7, 1895 and a female on Aug. 29, 1891 at Toronto, the only records known to Fleming (1907: 85). D.M. Scott found a "dummy" nest during the field survey on York Downs, north of Toronto, on June 3, 1937 (Lawrie, 1937: 5). F.H. Emery and I spent the night of June 24-25, 1937, on York Downs and heard two of them singing each hour from 11 p.m. to 6 a.m., all night along. Snyder (1930: 200) reported a large colony scattered along the grassy flats bordering the Holland River in King Twp., where J.L. Baillie and W.P. Young saw an adult carrying food on July 4, 1926 and a female with an egg ready to be laid was collected on July 16. Otto Devitt found the first nest in the Toronto region in the Corner Marsh, Pickering, on June 30, 1935 (it contained 7 young then and again on July 5): George A. Scott found a nest with 6 eggs in Oshawa's Second Marsh on July 8, 1962, and Ronald Orenstein found a "dummy" nest in the Shoal Point Marsh, Pickering, on June 10, 1965: on roadside counts in Ontario Co. we tallied a few in each of Pickering, Reach, Brock, Mara and Rama Twps. in the early 1960's (Speirs, 1975: 34). Snyder (1941: 72) estimated 15 individuals in a colony near Wellington, Prince Edward Co., on July 17, 1930: W.H. Lunn found a nest with one egg there on June 6, which contained 7 eggs on June 17. On June 23, 1922, E. Beaupré found a nest with 7 eggs at Kingston (Quilliam, 1973: 137). H.P. Bingham found a nest with 6 eggs near Barrie about June 1, 1922: W.V. Crich and R.D. Ussher found a nest with 3 eggs in Holland Marsh, near Bradford, on June 9, 1938: Paul Harrington found a nest with 6 young near Phelpston on June 14, 1929 (Devitt, 1967: 118). Lloyd (1924: 15) reported specimens taken at the Mer Bleue, near Ottawa, on June 17, 1898 and June 16, 1905. B. McTavish estimated 75 at Richmond, also near Ottawa, on June 19, 1972 (Goodwin, 1972: 854). Mills (1981: 112-113) cited several summer records for the cottage country. C. Bell, K. Bennison and D. Ferguson found 45 pairs on Manitoulin on June 29, 1981 (Goodwin, 1981: 936). MacLulich (1938: 27) cited one Algonquin Park record, on July 18, 1933 at Pine River. Speirs &

Speirs (1947: 32) observed them frequently at Ferris, south of North Bay, between June 5 and Aug. 1, 1944. On July 18, 1937, two were frequenting an area of thick, long grass bordering the railway track near Bigwood and C.E. Hope found a "dummy" nest there on July 19 (Baillie & Hope, 1947: 17). Snyder (1942: 139) reported four colonies near Sault Ste. Marie during the summer of 1931 and one "dummy" nest was found near Maclennan. K. Boshcoff encountered one in early June, 1973, at Pukaskwa (Skeel & Bondrup-Nielsen, 1978: 192). N.G. Escott heard two singing at Heron Bay, near Marathon, throughout June, 1978 (Goodwin, 1978: 1115). Dear (1940: 135) found a nest with 7 eggs on June 16, 1929, at Whitefish Lake, Thunder Bay. Snyder (1938: 200) collected young at Rainy River on July 30 and Aug. 7, 1929. Snyder (1953: 73) found them at Malachi, Wabigoon, Savanne and three situations between Kenora and Redditt in June, 1949.

AUTUMN: C. Blomme noted one in Burpee Twp., Manitoulin, as late as Sept. 27, 1980 (Nicholson, 1981: 143). Devitt (1967: 118) still found 10 at the Holland River colony on Sept. 14, 1937. Quilliam (1973: 138) gave Oct. 10, 1971 as the latest date at Prince Edward Point. Naomi LeVay found one at Cranberry Marsh, Whitby, as late as Oct. 21, 1961 (Tozer & Richards, 1974: 212). Saunders (1947: 370) gave Oct. 9 as his latest date for Toronto. Beardslee & Mitchell (1965: 333-334) reported one at Black Creek, near Niagara Falls, on Oct. 31, 1954. A.A. Wood collected one near London on Sept. 2, 1916 (Saunders & Dale, 1933: 218). Ussher (1965: 19) gave Oct. 10 as the latest date for Rondeau. Stirrett (1973d: 24) gave Oct. 27 as the latest Pelee date.

**MEASUREMENTS:**
*Length:* 4.0 to 4.5 ins.
(Godfrey, 1966: 290)
*Wingspread:* 5.75 to 5.88
ins. (Roberts, 1955: 647)
*Weight:* 8.1 to 8.2 g.
(Terres, 1980: 1047).

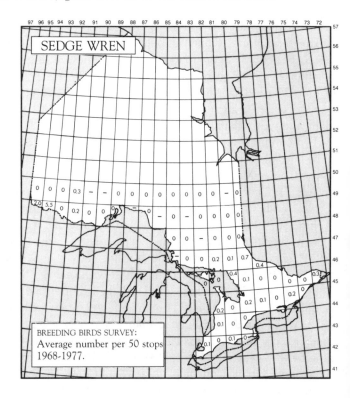

SEDGE WREN

BREEDING BIRDS SURVEY:
Average number per 50 stops
1968-1977.

# MARSH WREN   *Cistothorus palustris*   (Wilson)

This is a summer resident in cat-tail marshes in southern Ontario. In northern Ontario such marshes are widespread and only a few pioneer colonies have been found there. Males have a habit of making a number of "dummy" nests, one of which may be lined and used by the females to raise the family.

IDENTIFICATION:  This is a small wren, usually confined to cat-tail marshes, with a dark crown and prominent white line over the eye and white streaks on the back (a feature shared with the Sedge Wren, which differs in having a streaked crown, very inconspicuous eye line and much shorter bill). The song is a jerky "zhuh-wee-wuh-wuh-wuh-wuh..."

WINTER:  On the 1968-1977 Christmas counts there were records at Kingston, Hamilton, and along the north shore of Lake Erie. Stirrett (1973a: 18) had records through December at Pelee, with the latest two noted on Jan. 26. Kelley (1978: 59) mentioned a winter maximum of 5 at Pelee on Dec. 24, 1972. J.L. Baillie had a Dec. 7 sighting for Toronto (Saunders, 1947: 370). George A. Scott saw one in Oshawa's Second Marsh on Jan. 14, 21 and 29 and Feb. 4, 1956, one of five winter records along the Lake Ontario shore of Ontario Co. (Speirs, 1975: 33). Quilliam (1973: 137) had two winter records for Kingston: Dec. 3, 1961 and Jan. 1, 1962: another was reported there on Dec. 15, 1974 (Goodwin, 1975: 686). E.L. McDonald observed one at Port Hope from Dec. 21-23, 1980 (Goodwin, 1981: 297).

SPRING:  Stirrett (1973b: 21) gave Apr. 11 as the earliest one at Pelee with a peak count of 40 on May 17. Ussher (1965: 19) gave Apr. 6 as his earliest Rondeau date, with his 17-year average arrival date on Apr. 25. Earl Lemon had five spring records in West Elgin, the earliest on May 7, 1943 and the latest on May 20, 1929 (Brooman, 1954: 29). Snyder (1931: 218) noted the first at Long Point on May 12 in 1928. Fleming (1907: 85) gave Apr. 14 as his earliest spring date for Toronto, while Saunders (1947: 370) listed May 17 as the average arrival date. David O'Brien heard one singing at Frenchman Bay as early as March 31, 1973 (Speirs, 1975: 33). George A. Scott found a nest with 4 eggs at Oshawa's Second Marsh as early as May 27, 1962 (Tozer & Richards, 1974: 211). Snyder (1941: 72) noted his first in Prince Edward Co. on Apr. 25 in 1934. Weir & Quilliam (1980: 37) listed May 7 as the 30-year average arrival date at Kingston, with the earliest on Apr. 16, 1952. Devitt (1967: 118) gave May 17 as the average arrival date near Barrie, the earliest on May 8, 1938 at Holland River: H.P. Bingham found nests with complete sets of eggs as early as May 28, 1938 near Barrie. C. Harris found a singing male in a cat-tail marsh at Go Home Bay on Apr. 18, 1976, one of the few records for the cottage country (Mills, 1981: 112). Nicholson (1981: 142) noted one at Great Duck Is. on May 8, 1979. Ricker & Clarke (1939: 16) reported one on May 4, 1925 in a cat-tail marsh "along the old Callander road". Denis (1961a: 54) found one at Pickerel Lake, Sibley Park, on May 23, 1959 and found two there the following day. Peruniak (1971: 22) gave May 6 as her earliest Atikokan record.

SUMMER:  On the 1968-1977 Breeding Bird Survey, there were frequently occurrences in southern Ontario from Dunnville north to Orillia and Cobden, with outliers at North Bay and Atikokan. Kelley (1978: 59) mentioned a late nest with 3 eggs at Pelee on July 20, 1952. Stirrett (1973c: 19) had a summer maximum of 35 at Pelee on July 14. Brooman

(1954: 29) heard them singing at St. Thomas on June 25 and Aug. 7, 1950. McCracken, Bradstreet & Holroyd (1981: 59) reported 88 active nests in Long Point marshes, most not with eggs until the first week of June but with second clutches in July: breeding densities of 150 to 330 territorial males per km² were found in suitable habitat. Snyder (1931: 218) gave June 4 as the earliest date for a set of 5 eggs on Long Point. A nest with 3 eggs was found by C.J. Clout at Niagara-on-the-Lake on July 11, 1936 (Baillie & Harrington, 1937: 226): they also reported a nest with 6 eggs at Grimsby taken by J.L. Jackson on June 10, 1889. Tozer & Richards (1974: 211) reported several nesting records for the Oshawa region, one with 4 eggs as late as July 21, 1962 in the Second Marsh. R.C. Long found population densities of 40 to 50 birds per 100 acres in the Shoal Point marshes in the summers of 1964, 1965 and 1966: 24 sets of eggs found in Ontario Co. contained a total of 107 eggs (Speirs, 1975: 33). Allin (1940: 103) found a dozen "dummy" nests of this species on June 10, 1933 in Darlington Twp. Snyder (1941: 72) found eggs in nests in Prince Edward Co. from June 10 to July 2 in 1930. Devitt (1967: 118) found 10 nests, including one with 6 eggs at Otter Lake, Simcoe Co., on June 17, 1935: H.P. Bingham found a nest with 5 eggs as late as Aug. 15, 1915 near Barrie. W.E. Saunders took a set of 6 eggs at Ottawa on June 13, 1898 (Lloyd, 1924: 15). Nicholson (1981: 142) found the remains of an egg in a nest at Marsh Lake, Manitoulin, on July 12, 1970. Fifteen pairs were reported on Manitoulin on June 29, 1981 by C. Bell, K. Bennison and D. Ferguson (Goodwin, 1981: 936). Ricker & Clarke (1939: 16) noted one near Callander on June 8, 1924. On June 21, 1980, Len Hanna and I noted 3 at the Prairie Bee marsh between Chapleau and Wawa by Hwy. 101. N. Rae Brown had sightings at Black Sturgeon Lake and Macdiarmid, Nipigon during the summers of 1944 to 1946. Denis (1961a: 54) saw one carrying nest material at Pickerel Lake, Sibley Park, on June 7, 1959, and located 24 nests (mostly "dummies") between June 14 and July 15: on Aug. 3 one was noted with food in its bill. Snyder (1953: 73) noted individuals at Malachi on July 11 and 14, 1947: he found a pair and a dummy nest at Wabigoon in 1937 and reported them as plentiful at Indian Bay, near Kenora, in 1920.

AUTUMN: Peruniak (1971: 22) gave Sept. 30 as her latest Atikokan date. Devitt (1967: 118) have Oct. 9, 1939 as the latest Simcoe Co. date, at Collingwood. Weir & Quilliam (1980: 37) listed Oct. 12 as the 22-year average departure date from Kingston. Speirs (1975: 33) cited two Nov. 13 records, for Oshawa and Ajax marshes, but there were subsequent winter sightings in both marshes. Speirs (1938: 54) gave Nov. 17 as the latest fall date for Toronto, while Saunders (1947: 370) listed Oct. 3 as the average departure date. B. Parker reported one in Dereham Twp., Oxford Co., on Nov. 2, 1975 (Goodwin, 1976: 62). Beardslee & Mitchell (1965: 332) reported six in a big marsh at Stromness on Nov. 26, 1960. Brooman (1954: 29) counted six and heard others at St. Thomas on Sept. 4, 1949. Ussher (1965: 19) gave Oct. 4 as the 12-year average departure date from Rondeau, with the latest on Oct. 28. Stirrett (1973d: 24) had a fall maximum of 20 at Pelee on Oct. 5.

**MEASUREMENTS:**
*Length:* 4.1 to 5.5 ins.
(Godfrey, 1966: 289)
*Wingspread:* 5.0 to 7.0
ins. (Roberts, 1955: 648)
*Weight:* 0.5 oz. (Roberts,
1955: 648)

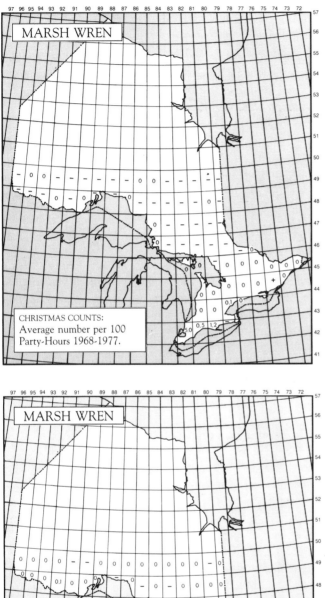

MARSH WREN

CHRISTMAS COUNTS:
Average number per 100
Party-Hours 1968-1977.

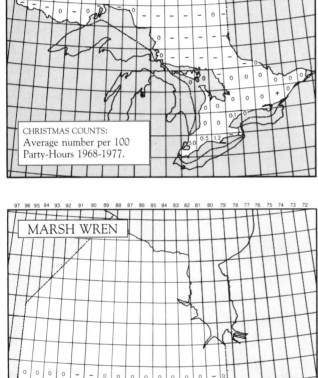

MARSH WREN

BREEDING BIRDS SURVEY:
Average number per 50 stops
1968-1977.

# GOLDEN-CROWNED KINGLET
## *Regulus satrapa*  Lichtenstein

Kinglets are partial to evergreen forests, but may be found almost anywhere during migration. In summer they may be found wherever suitable habitat occurs and some occur in winter in southern Ontario. Numbers vary considerably from year to year but this is frequently one of our most common birds during the migratory periods.

IDENTIFICATION: Kinglets are our smallest birds, apart from hummingbirds. This species is known by its orange crown (yellow in the female) , bordered by black stripes. The call is a frequently given, high-pitched "see-see-see". The song is a succession of "see"s, rising in pitch to a climax, followed by a series of "di-di-di" notes on a lower frequency (some Blackburnian Warblers sing a very similar song).

WINTER: On the 1968-1977 Christmas counts they were common at Pelee and fairly common north to Sault Ste. Marie and Deep River: noted at Thunder Bay in 1975 only. Stirrett (1973a: 18) had a maximum of 80 at Pelee on Dec. 27. Numbers on Pickering Christmas counts varied from 0 to 86, averaging 21 on 9 of 10 counts from 1961 to 1970 (Speirs, 1975: 47): similar extreme fluctuations occurred at other localities. Quilliam (1973: 144) reported a high Christmas count of 15 at Kingston on Dec. 21, 1963. Devitt (1967: 125) had a high of 26 at Barrie on the Jan. 3, 1954 count. L. Beamer had winter records at Meaford on 7 of 20 years, e.g. 3 on Jan. 2, 1948. Mills (1981: 121) reported them on 9 of 18 Christmas counts at Huntsville, with a maximum of 26 on Dec. 18, 1964. Nicholson (1981: 151) reported 9 at Providence Bay, Manitoulin, as late as Jan. 26, 1980. Dennison (1980: 148) listed a total of 14 on 3 of 25 Christmas counts at Sault Ste. Marie.

SPRING: Stirrett (1973b: 22) had a spring maximum of 250 at Pelee on Apr. 6, with the latest migrant on May 14. Ussher (1965: 21) gave Apr. 24 as the 10-year average departure date from Rondeau, with the latest on May 12. Snyder (1931: 219) gave May 6 as his latest Long Point date in 1928. Speirs (1938: 44) gave Apr. 11 as the peak date for spring migrants at Toronto. In Ontario Co., the spring peak had generally been during the second week of April (Speirs, 1975: 47). Long (1968b: 21) reported one at Pickering Beach as late as May 20, 1967. Weir & Quilliam (1980: 38) listed Apr. 3 and May 26 as the average arrival and departure dates for Kingston. Devitt (1967: 125) gave Apr. 8 as an average arrival date at Barrie. L. Beamer's median arrival date at Meaford was Apr. 22, with the earliest on March 31. Nicholson (1981: 151) gave Apr. 9 as the 11-year average arrival date on Manitoulin, with the earliest on March 15, 1980 and the maximum count of 60 on Apr. 20, 1980. Louise Lawrence saw one as early as March 27, 1945 at Pimisi Bay: mid-April was the peak of the spring migration at North Bay (Speirs & Speirs, 1947: 33). W. Wyett saw one at Pukaskwa as early as Apr. 10, 1974 and Skeel & Bondrup-Nielsen (1978: 196) ranked it sixth in spring abundance there after mid-April. Denis (1961: 2) gave Apr. 16 as the average arrival date at Thunder Bay, with the earliest on March 31, 1945. Dear (1940: 136) found a nest with 9 eggs near Thunder Bay on May 30, 1937. Peruniak (1971: 23) gave Apr. 20 as her earliest date for Atikokan, but David Elder found one there on Apr. 18, 1981. Elder (1979: 37) gave Apr. 25 as his earliest Geraldton record, where he considered it a common summer resident. Bondrup-Nielsen

(1976: 44) gave Apr. 27 as his earliest Kapuskasing date. Cringan (1953a: 3) saw his first on May 7, 1953 at Perrault Falls.

SUMMER: On the 1968-1977 Breeding Bird Surveys they were fairly common on some routes from Kenora to Thunder Bay and uncommon from there south to Manitoulin and Ottawa. Saunders & Dale (1933: 221) mentioned a nest found at London in 1915 and a flock of 12 or more in the Byron Bog on July 30, 1930. Beardslee & Mitchell reported a sighting at Abino Bay, Lake Erie, on July 27, 1957. Speirs (1975: 47) had no summer record for Ontario Co. after June 3 (1968) or before Aug. 18 (1958). Tozer & Richards (1974: 224) reported two in the Osler Tract, Lake Scugog, on July 20, 1968. Weir & Quilliam (1980: 21) discovered a nest with 4 young in the Harrowsmith Bog, near Kingston, on June 13, 1976. Paul Harrington found a recently completed, but empty, nest at Wasaga Beach on June 8, 1929 and Devitt (1967: 125) saw several young with parents northwest of Midhurst by Hwy. 20 on July 3, 1949. Mills (1981: 121) cited several breeding records (young with parents) for the cottage country. Ron Tasker found a brood of 5 young, barely able to fly, in Burpee Twp., Manitoulin, on July 2, 1970. C.H.C. Clarke saw adults feeding young at Brule Lake, Algonquin Park, on July 16, 1934 (Baillie & Harrington, 1937: 234). Baillie & Hope (1947: 20) found a brood of 4 young, not long out of the nest, at Biscotasing on June 30, 1937. J.L. Baillie noted young of the year near Sault Ste. Marie on July 18, 1931 (Snyder, 1942: 142). Baillie & Harrington (1943: 18) found a well-developed egg in the oviduct of one collected at Marathon on June 10, 1936. Snyder (1928: 276) collected a juvenile male at Macdiarmid, Lake Nipigon, on July 28, 1924. Dear (1940: 136) found a nest with young in McGregor Twp, Thunder Bay, on June 17, 1934. Kendeigh (1947: 27) found a population density of 8 pairs per 100 acres at Black Sturgeon Lake during the summer of 1945. Speirs (1949: 148) found 17 territories on 75 acres at Eaglehead Lake in 1946. Snyder (1953: 75) found young recently out of the nest at Malachi on July 15, 1947: he found them most common at Savanne, but some from the Manitoba border and north to Sioux Lookout. Smith (1957: 177) saw one at Gogama on July 26, 1954: he found them rare in the Clay Belt, as did Snyder (1928: 33) at Lake Abitibi (only one male collected, on June 11, 1925). James (1980: 84) found only 1.6 pairs per km$^2$ on 2 of 12 transects studied near Pickle Lake. Hope (1938: 33) found young not long out of the nest at Favourable Lake on July 7, 1938. James, Nash & Peck (1981: 92) confirmed breeding at Kiruna Lake, Sutton Ridges, during the summer of 1981. Schueler, Baldwin & Rising (1974: 143) reported the species only at Cochrane and Moosonee, not at any of the other James Bay or Hudson Bay localities visited. Lee (1978: 29) found two pairs at Big Trout Lake during the summer of 1975. McLaren & McLaren (1981: 4) found 7 singing males in the Wetiko Hills along the Manitoba-Ontario border at latitude 55°N.

AUTUMN: D. McRae and A. Wormington noted as many as 10 at Netitishi Point, James Bay, on Oct. 19, 1981 and the last one there on Nov. 5. Smith (1957: 177) noted only one female near Matheson on Sept. 2, 1953. Peruniak (1971: 23) gave Oct. 8 as her latest Atikokan date. Skeel & Bondrup-Nielsen (1978: 196) considered this to be an abundant fall migrant at Pukaskwa, with their latest on Oct. 10. Louise Lawrence saw 6 at Pimisi Bay on Oct. 26, 1944: the fall peak at North Bay was about mid-October (Speirs & Speirs, 1947: 33). Nicholson (1981: 151) gave Sept. 29 as the 10-year average fall arrival date at Manitoulin, with a high count of 58 on Oct. 10, 1970 and the earliest arrival on Sept. 6, 1975. Weir & Quilliam (1980: 38) listed Sept. 22 and Nov. 17 as average fall arrival and departure dates for Kingston. Returning migrants usually show up in Ontario Co. in late September and peak in mid-October (Speirs, 1975: 47). Speirs (1938: 52) gave Oct. 6 as the fall peak for Toronto. Ussher (1965: 21) gave Sept. 27 as the earliest fall date for Rondeau, with Oct. 7 as the 12-year average fall arrival date. Stirrett (1973d: 24 and 1973a: 18) gave Sept. 17 as the earliest fall date for Pelee (15 noted) with a maximum of 1000 on Nov. 23.

BANDING: One banded at Mitchell Bay, Ont. on Oct. 17, 1970 was recovered about a year later, on Oct. 29, 1971 at Kalamazoo, Mich. (Brewer & Salvadori, 1976: 84). One banded at Bayville, N.J. on Oct. 13, 1963, turned up at Long Point on Apr. 23, 1965 and one banded at Long Point was recovered near Perrine, Florida (1173 miles due south) on Jan. 11, 1966 (Brewer & Salvadori, 1978: 74).

**MEASUREMENTS:**
*Length:* 3.5 to 4.0 ins.
(Godfrey, 1966: 305)
*Wingspread:* 6.5 to 7.0
ins. (Roberts, 1955: 657)
*Weight:* 1 ♂ weighed
5.4 g. (Hope, 1938: 33).

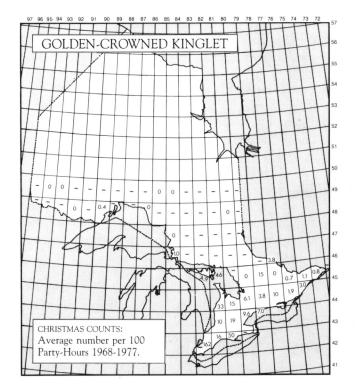

GOLDEN-CROWNED KINGLET

CHRISTMAS COUNTS:
Average number per 100
Party-Hours 1968-1977.

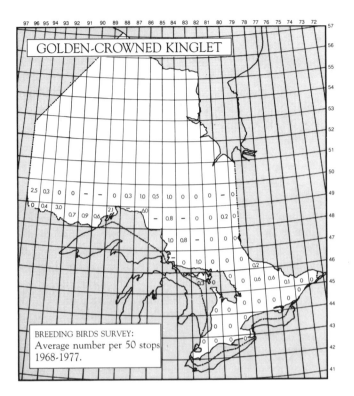

# RUBY-CROWNED KINGLET   *Regulus calendula*   (Linnaeus)

Numbers vary considerably from year to year, but this is normally one of the most characteristic birds of the spruce-moose biome of northern Ontario in summer. A few have wintered at feeding stations in southern Ontario in recent years but most go south, some as far at Guatemala.

**IDENTIFICATION:** Although one of our smallest birds, it is big in character, constantly flicking its wings and fluttering about. On its breeding grounds it has quite a loud song for so small a bird. Following one in the spruce forest north of Lake Superior to check the identity of the singer, it led me deeper into the forest until I was quite disoriented and it seemed to mock me as it sang:"ses-see-see-see; so-so-so-so: de-dibble, de-dibble-de-dibble". In migration all you usually hear is a rather buzzy "d'zup". Its ruby crown is generally concealed, showing up only in moments of excitement when its crown feathers are raised. With its plain, greenish gray plumage and prominent eye ring and wing bars, it resembles some of our small flycatchers and the white-eyed vireo, but it is even smaller than these birds and its habit of hovering and wing flicking is diagnostic.

**WINTER:** On the 1968-1977 Christmas counts they were fairly common at Pelee, becoming rare north to Cyprus Lake and Carleton Place, with outliers at Thunder Bay in 1969. Stirrett (1973a: 18) had a winter maximum of 5 at Pelee on Dec. 20. I saw one coming for suet at P.H. Currie's feeder in Pickering Twp. on Feb. 12, 1972 and J.M. Richards noted one as far north as Rama Twp. on Dec. 31, 1967: several others have been observed in Ontario Co. in recent winters (Speirs, 1975: 48). Mary L'Estrange reported one at Kingston on Feb. 3, 1957 and there were Christmas count reports there in 1959 and 1969 (Quilliam, 1973: 144). One was reported on the Huntsville Christmas count on Dec. 18, 1960 (Mills, 1981: 122). One lingered at a South Baymouth feeder until Feb. 8, 1975 (Nicholson, 1981: 152). Dennison (1980: 148) reported one on 1 of 25 Christmas counts at Sault Ste. Marie.

SPRING: Stirrett (1973b: 22) had a spring peak of 200 at Pelee on May 13, with the latest one on May 26. Ussher (1965: 21) had Rondeau birds from Apr. 5 to May 22, with average arrival on Apr. 18 and departure on May 15. Saunders & Dale (1933: 222) gave Apr. 15 as the 17-year average arrival date at London, with the earliest on Apr. 5, 1921. Snyder (1931: 219) found them common at Long Point on May 6, 1928 and noted the last one there on May 18. Speirs (1938: 40, 44, 46) had Toronto records from Apr. 7 to May 30, with the peak on Apr. 30. Saunders (1947: 370) gave Apr. 19 as the average arrival date at Toronto and May 21 as the average spring departure date. Fleming (1907: 86) had one as early as Apr. 4, 1890 there. Speirs (1975: 48) reported Ontario Co. records from Apr. 7 (1963) to May 22 (1967), with peak numbers at the end of April. Weir & Quilliam (1980: 38) listed Apr. 15 and May 17 as average spring arrival and departure dates for Kingston. Quilliam (1973: 144) mentioned a peak of 500 plus on May 2, 1972 at Prince Edward Point. Devitt (1967: 126) gave Apr. 19 as the 12-year average arrival date at Barrie, with the earliest on Apr. 1, 1959. L. Beamer's median arrival date at Meaford was Apr. 25, with the earliest two on March 31, 1950 (but no others before Apr. 19). Mills (1981: 122) gave Apr. 18 as the 9-year average arrival date at Huntsville: A. Kay noted one at Pt. Sydney as early as Apr. 4, 1889 and C. Harris counted 38 at Go Home Bay on May 4, 1975. Nicholson (1981: 151) gave Apr. 17 as the 11-year average arrival date on Manitoulin, with the earliest on Apr. 10, 1971 and the maximum count of 100 on May 4, 1975. MacLulich (1938: 29) saw his first in Algonquin Park on Apr. 29, 1932. Louise Lawrence noted two at Pimisi Bay on Apr. 9, 1945 but the peak in the North Bay region is in early May (Speirs & Speirs, 1947: 33). Skeel & Bondrup-Nielsen (1978: 196) ranked this as the 7th most abundant spring migrant at Pukaskwa (1982 seen on 35 days from Apr. 17 when first noted to May 31). Denis (1981: 2) gave Apr. 22 as the average arrival date at Thunder Bay, with the earliest on Apr. 12, 1945. Peruniak (1971: 25) gave Apr. 17 as her earliest Atikokan date. Elder (1979: 37) gave Apr. 25 as his earliest Geraldton record. Bondrup-Nielsen (1976: 44) listed Apr. 21, 1975 as his earliest near Kapuskasing. Cringan (1953a: 3) saw his first at Sioux Lookout on May 3, 1953. Oliver Hewitt saw several at Moosonee on May 22, 1947 (Manning, 1952: 77).

SUMMER: On the 1968-1977 Breeding Bird Surveys they were common on routes northeast of Lake Superior, becoming uncommon south to Orillia and Ottawa. Stirrett (1973d: 25) had the earliest 8 returning migrants at Pelee on Aug. 16. Beardslee & Mitchell (1965: 349-350) reported one at Sugarloaf, near Lake Erie, as early as Aug. 25, 1959. Doris H. Speirs noted a returning bird at our Pickering home as early as Aug. 16, 1951 (Speirs, 1975: 48). Richards (1983: 36) watched adults feeding 5 young in a nest at Sandbanks Provincial Park on July 25, 1976, the first breeding record for Prince Edward Co. Singing males have been reported in Simcoe Co. in June, but no nesting evidence had been found (Devitt, 1967: 125). Mills (1981: 122) found a pair building at Magnetawan on May 19, 1975 and an adult was on this nest on June 14: W. Mansell found a nest at Rebecca Lake on July 13, 1945. Nicholson (1981: 151-152) cited a few summer, but no breeding records, for Manitoulin. Baillie & Hope (1947: 20) observed young just out of the nest at Biscotasing on July 9, 1937 while Paul Harrington collected a nest with 8 eggs at Chapleau on June 10, 1937. Skeel & Bondrup-Nielsen (1978: 197) reported only 20 on 14 days from June 1 to July 11 at Pukaskwa. Baillie & Hope (1943: 18-19) found a nest with 9 eggs at Marathon on June 18, 1936 "a beautiful structure of moss, lined with feathers—". Snyder (1928: 276) collected a male at Lake Nipigon on June 25, 1924: "not seen in 1923 and at only one locality in 1924". Dear (1940: 136) found a nest with 8 eggs on June 3, 1934 and a nest with young on June 19, 1934, near Thunder Bay. Kendeigh (1947: 27) found 2 pairs per 100 acres at Black Sturgeon Lake in 1945 and Speirs (1949: 148) had 2 territories on 75 acres at Eaglehead Lake in 1946. Snyder (1953: 75) reported young of the year at Malachi, with "regular occurrences" at Minaki, Sioux Lookout, Ingolf, Kenora, Wabigoon and Savanne. L. Paterson watched a female feeding 5 young, out of the nest, on July 18, 1932 at Kenora (Baillie & Harrington, 1937: 235). R.D. Ussher saw a pair feeding young out of the nest on July 13, 1925 near Kapuskasing (Baillie & Harrington, 1937: 235). James (1980: 84) found a density of 25.6 pairs per km² on 10 of 12 transects censused at Pickle Lake in 1977 and 1979, making it "the most frequently encountered" bird there. Hope (1938: 33) noted young not long out of the nest at Favourable Lake on July 15, 1938 where he reported them to be common in spruce bogs. Cringan (1953b: 4) noted from 1 to 5 on 9 of 10 days at Kasabonika Lake in 1953. Manning (1952: 76) saw 3 at Big Piskwanish on June 9, 1947; one at Long Ridge Point on June 14, 1947 and 7 at Raft River on July 12-13, 1947. James, Nash & Peck (1982: 64) found a nest with at least 7 young which fled as the nest was approached on July 9, 1982 near the mouth of the Harricanaw River, James Bay. James, Nash & Peck (1981: 92) confirmed breeding at Kiruna Lake in 1981. Schueler, Baldwin & Rising (1974: 143) observed nesting at Moosonee and observed the species at Attawapiskat, Winisk, Hawley Lake and Cochrane, but not at Ft. Albany. Lee (1978: 29) found this species on all three study quadrats at Big Trout Lake and found family groups on two of them in late July, 1975: a maximum number of 12 was noted on June 26. C.E. Hope saw from 1 to 3 frequently from June 24 to July 23, 1940 at Ft. Severn: one was collected on July 15.

AUTUMN: D. McRae and A. Wormington saw single birds at Netitishi Point, James Bay, on Oct. 15, 16 and 22, 1981. Oliver Hewitt saw 4 at Ship Sands, near Moosonee, on Sept. 24, 1947 (Manning, 1952: 77). Peruniak (1971: 23) gave Oct. 11 as her latest Atikokan date. Skeel & Bondrup-Nielsen (1978: 197) saw their last at Pukaskwa on Oct. 14, 1977. Speirs & Speirs (1947: 33) observed one at North Bay as late as Oct. 19, 1944 and gave early October as the fall peak. MacLulich (1938: 29) saw one as late as Oct. 5, 1930 at Achray, Algonquin Park. Nicholson (1981: 152) had a high count of 250 on Manitoulin on Oct. 4, 1978, with the latest on Nov. 21, 1976. The latest fall record at Wasaga Beach was on Nov. 11, 1934 (Devitt, 1967: 126). Weir & Quilliam (1980: 38) listed Sept. 12 and Nov. 5 as average fall arrival and departure dates for Kingston. Quilliam (1973: 144) had a fall peak of 60 plus at Wolfe Is. on Sept. 30, 1962. Tozer & Richards (1974: 226) reported one at Oshawa as late as Nov. 29, 1959. The fall peak in the Pickering region is usually in the first week of October (Speirs, 1975: 48). Speirs (1938: 48, 52) listed Aug. 31 as the earliest fall migrant at Toronto, with the peak on Oct. 7.

Saunders (1947: 370) gave Sept. 29 and Oct. 26 as average fall arrival and departure dates for Toronto, with his latest on Nov.16. Beardslee & Mitchell (1965: 349-350) reported two at Queenston on Nov. 30, 1947. Ussher (1965: 21) had fall birds at Rondeau from Sept. 13 to Nov. 30 with average arrival on Sept. 27 and departure on Nov. 5. Stirrett (1973d: 25) had a fall maximum of 250 at Pelee on Oct. 22.

BANDING: One banded at Long Point on Oct. 23, 1965 was recovered at Cayce, South Carolina, on Feb. 3, 1966, about 600 miles to the south (Brewer & Salvadori, 1978: 75).

**MEASUREMENTS:**
*Length:* 3.7 to 4.5 ins. (Godfrey, 1966: 306)
*Wingspread:* 6 3/4 to 7 1/2 ins. (Roberts, 1955: 657)
*Weight:* one ♂ weighed 6.1 g. (Hope, 1938: 33).

**REFERENCES:**
Andrle, Robert F. 1978 Ruby-crowned Kinglet breeding in Regional Municipality of Niagara, Ontario. Ont. Field Biologist, 32: (1): 43-44.

Mark Jennings found the nest at Ft. Erie on June 11, 1977. On June 5, Andrle found the pair feeding a yg. Brown-headed Cowbird and on June 10, he collected the nest which contained one infertile kinglet egg: he mentioned nestings at Guelph, Kingston and in Halton Co., *fide* G.K. Peck.

Richards, James M. 1983 An addition to the breeding birds of Prince Edward Country, Ontario. Ont. Birds, 1: (1): 36.

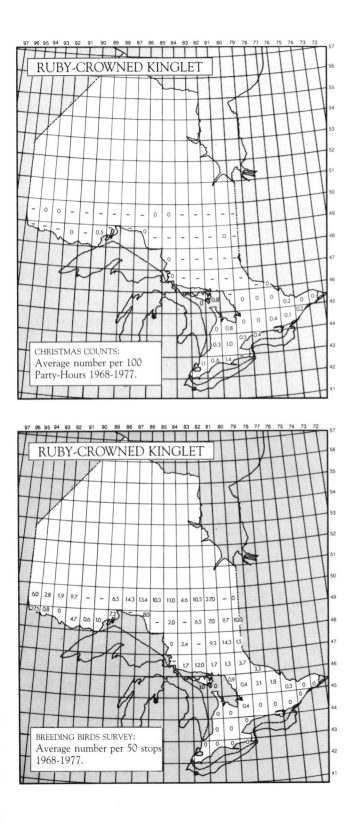

RUBY-CROWNED KINGLET

CHRISTMAS COUNTS:
Average number per 100
Party-Hours 1968-1977.

RUBY-CROWNED KINGLET

BREEDING BIRDS SURVEY:
Average number per 50 stops
1968-1977.

# BLUE-GRAY GNATCATCHER
*Polioptila caerulea* (Linnaeus)

This is a southern species, reaching its northern limit in southern Ontario and wintering from southern U.S.A. to Cuba and Guatemala. Everything about this restless sprite spells excitement, constantly flitting about, fanning and cocking its tail, uttering high-pitched squeals like a high soprano catbird, busily gathering lichens and spider webs to decorate its two-inch cup-shaped nest.

IDENTIFICATION: It reminds me of a diminutive mockingbird in colouration: blue gray above and whitish below, with flashes of white in the wings and edges of the tail, but with its black eye set in a white face.

WINTER:

SPRING: Stirrett (1973b: 22) gave Apr. 10 as the earliest Pelee date and Kelley (1978: 63) reported a maximum of 40 there on May 20, 1971. Ussher (1965: 21) gave May 2 as the 15-year average arrival date at Rondeau, with the earliest on Apr. 10. Saunders & Dale (1933: 221) gave May 11 as the 12-year average arrival date at London, with the earliest on May 2, 1913: a set of 4 eggs was found as early as May 19, 1903 and a set of 5 eggs on May 28, 1900. Brooman (1954: 30) reported one as early as Apr. 23, 1939 in West Elgin, as well as several May records. R.T. Anderson took a nest with 3 eggs at Aylmer on May 14, 1897 (Baillie & Harrington, 1937: 234). George North recorded the first nest for Long Point on May 14, 1949: subsequent nests were found there on May 19, 1975 and May 20, 1979 (McCracken, Bradstreet & Holroyd, 1981: 61). Beardslee & Mitchell (1965: 347-348) reported one at Point Abino, Lake Erie, on Apr. 15, 1960 where R.F. Andrle found a nest later. J.L. Baillie had an early one at Toronto on Apr. 22 but R.M. Saunders gave May 9 as his 6-year average arrival there (Saunders, 1947: 370). Fleming (1907: 86) had only three Toronto records, birds collected on May 9, 1885; May 5, 1891 and May 10, 1900. Speirs (1975: 46) gave Apr. 16, 1967 as the earliest Whitby record, by J. Smith: two nests were found in the Altona forest, Pickering, on May 14, 1972 and one there on May 20, 1973. George A. Scott observed nest building at Oshawa as early as May 9, 1965 (Tozer & Richards, 1974: 46). Allin (1940: 104) reported a nest found by J.H. Jennings in an orchard at Bowmanville on May 24, 1932, in which a brood was later raised. Weir & Quilliam (1980: 21, 38) listed May 6 as the 20-year average arrival date at Kingston, with the earliest on Apr. 21: Mary and Ken Edwards saw as many as 9 at Prince Edward Point on May 18, 1979 and Michele Goosens observed nest building there on May 29, 1979. Devitt (1967: 125) had just two Simcoe Co. records: one on May 8, 1953 by A.J. Mitchener at Collingwood and the other on May 8, 1966 by Frances Westman where Willow Creek crosses Hwy. 400. Mills (1981: 127) reported one seen by J. Goltz in extreme southwestern Muskoka on May 24, 1980. Nicholson (1981: 150) had several spring sightings on Manitoulin, the earliest on Apr. 28, 1979 and the latest on May 26, 1974. Declan Troy noted one at Killarney on May 14, 1975 (Goodwin, 1975: 846). R.J. Pittaway saw one at Lake of Two Rivers, Algonquin Park, on May 15, 1978 (Goodwin, 1978: 1000).

SUMMER: The only one observed on the 1968-1977 Breeding Bird Surveys was at Sarnia in 1974. Speirs & Frank (1970: 777) found 2 territories on their 25-acre Pelee quadrat in 1970. Stirrett (1973d: 24) reported a maximum of 20 at Pelee on Aug. 25. Saunders & Dale (1933: 221) found a set of 4 eggs plus one cowbird egg near London on June 7, 1902. Marshall Field saw one at Port Burwell on Aug. 24, 1982 (Brooman, 1954: 30). Incubating birds were seen on Long Point nests on June 13, 1979 and June 19 and 23, 1980 (McCracken, Bradstreet & Holroyd, 1981: 61). We saw one flitting about the top of a willow at our Pickering home on July 21, 1970 and J. Satterly saw one at Cedar Point, Lake Simcoe, on Aug. 21, 1963 (Speirs, 1975: 46). The nest at Prince Edward Point held 2 eggs and 2 young on June 11, 1979 (Weir & Quilliam, 1980: 21). Alex Mills reported a nest at Wasaga Beach on June 3, 1976 (Goodwin, 1976: 951). One was reported at Rainy River on July 12-13, 1980 by K.J. Burk, P.D. Pratt and A. McTavish (Goodwin, 1980: 892).

AUTUMN: Doug McRae and Alan Wormington reported one at Netitishi Point, James Bay, as late as Oct. 16, 1981. Alan Wormington noted one on Caribou Island, Lake Superior, from Oct. 1-3, 1979 (Goodwin, 1980: 157). Nicholson (1981: 150) had visitors at Great Duck Island on Oct. 2, 1978 and Sept. 14, 1979: also one at Cape Robert, Manitoulin, on Sept. 15, 1975. One settled for a few minutes on a feeder in Huntsville on Sept. 12, 1959 (Mills, 1981: 121). Weir & Quilliam (1980: 38) listed Sept. 27 as the 9-year average departure date from Kingston, with the latest on Nov. 12. George Fairfield saw one at Whitby as late as Oct. 18, 1958 (Speirs, 1975: 46). Speirs (1938: 54) gave Sept. 7 as the latest Toronto date. H.H. Axtell saw one at Erie Beach on Sept. 23, 1952 (Beardslee & Mitchell, 1965: 347-348). Ussher (1965: 21) gave Sept. 8 as the 11-year average departure date from Rondeau, with the latest on Oct. 14. Stirrett (1973d: 24) gave Nov. 1 as the latest one at Pelee.

**MEASUREMENTS:**
*Length:* 4 to 5 ins. (half of this tail) (Godfrey, 1966: 305)
*Wingspread:* 5.8 to 6.6 ins. (Roberts, 1955: 656)
*Weight:* 5.7 to 7.2 g. (Terres, 1980: 1000).

**REFERENCES:**
Parker, Bruce D. The Blue-gray Gnatcatcher in the Toronto region. Toronto Field Naturalist, No. 344: 26. Gives earliest Toronto region date as Apr. 13, 1980 and latest date at Oct. 27, 1976.
Saunders, W.E. 1917 Disappearance of the Blue Gray Gnat-catcher. Ottawa Naturalist, 31: (93-4): 45-46.
Thompson, Stuart L. 1929 Blue-gray Gnatcatcher at Toronto, Ontario. Can. Field-Naturalist, 43: (4): 85.

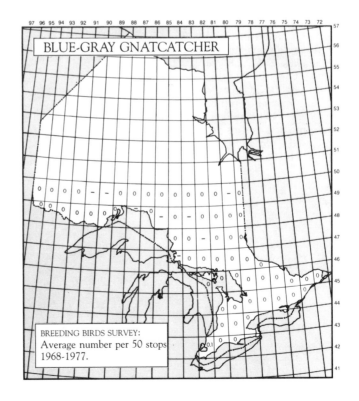

BLUE-GRAY GNATCATCHER

BREEDING BIRDS SURVEY:
Average number per 50 stops
1968-1977.

# SIBERIAN RUBYTHROAT   *Luscinia calliope*   (Pallas)

The Siberian Rubythroat is a bird of shrubby areas, breeding in Siberia: accidental in Ontario. This is a popular cage bird in China through which it migrates.

IDENTIFICATION:   This is a brown backed, gray breasted thrush, with a bright scarlet throat, bordered with black and with white"eyebrows" and "mustache marks". Females lack the scarlet throat and have buffy face markings, rather than white.

WINTER:   One was found dead on Dec. 26, 1983 by Mia Lane, at Hornby, Halton Co. The specimen, turned over to the Royal Ontario Museum, showed no signs of the wear usually associated with cage life.

SPRING:

SUMMER:

AUTUMN:

**MEASUREMENTS:**
*Length:* 6 ins. (Terres, 1980: 920)
*Wingspread:*
*Weight:*

**REFERENCES:**
Bent, Arthur Cleveland 1949 Greater Kamchatka Nightingale. *Calliope calliope camtschatkensis* (Gmelin), in Life histories of North American thrushes, kinglets, and their allies. U.S. National Mus., Bull. 196: 313-317.
   Brewer, David; Mia A.W. Lane and Martin L. Wernaart 1984 Siberian Rubythroat: a species new to Canada. Ont. Birds, 2: (2): 66-69.

# NORTHERN WHEATER    *Oenanthe oenanthe*    (Linnaeus)

This is a circumpolar high Arctic breeder, rarely reaching Ontario in migration. A few banding recoveries suggest that birds breeding in the Canadian Arctic migrate mainly to Europe across the North Atlantic.

**IDENTIFICATION:** The Northern Wheatear is about the size of a House Sparrow, largely gray above, with a conspicuous white rump and a buffy breast. The tail pattern is distinctive, mainly white with black central tail feathers and a black terminal bar. Males have blackish ear patches outlined with white and black wings. Females lack the black ear patches and the upper parts are brownish.

**WINTER:**

**SPRING:** One was seen at Amherstburg, Essex Co., on Apr. 22, 1978, by B. Eaton (Goodwin, 1978: 1155-1156). Two were noted at Prescott on March 19, 1954 by Robert Compton (Baillie, 1954: 343).

**SUMMER:** J. Krasnay found one at Whitby on Aug. 26, 1977, later seen by George A. Scott and many others into the autumn (Goodwin, 1978: 199). George A. Scott found another one at Ferland, north of Lake Nipigon, on June 6, 1941 (pers. comm. to Ross James, ROM). A McTavish and A. Wormington noted one at Winisk on June 2, 1981 (Goodwin, 1981: 936).

**AUTUMN:** A. Wormington saw one at Moosonee on Oct. 1, 1976 (Goodwin, 1977: 172) and another there on Sept. 26, 1980 (Goodwin, 1981: 178): he photographed one in the Abitibi Canyon on Oct. 6, 1972 (Goodwin, 1973: 54-55). D.B. McKillop picked up a dead one at Nipigon on Sept. 29, 1970 (Goodwin, 1971: 53). A. Wormington observed one at Marathon on Oct. 11-12, 1980 (Goodwin, 1981: 178). One was collected at Thunder Bay on Sept. 28, 1965 by A.E. Allin (Goodwin, 1966: 38). One was reported from Kirkland Lake by James McLanahan, *fide* F. Helleiner (Baillie, 1952: 15). P. Whelan reported one at Deep River from Oct. 16-18, 1976 and A. Wormington reported another there on Oct. 15, 1978 (Goodwin, 1977: 172 and 1979: 174). M. Runtz and many others observed one at Ottawa from Sept. 8-14, 1980 (Goodwin, 1981: 178). P.A. Taverner collected one at Beaumaris, Muskoka, on Sept. 25, 1894 (Mills, 1981: 120-121).H. Lumsden found one at Hainesville, Dundas Co., on Sept. 25, 1952 (*fide* R. James). The Whitby bird mentioned above was noted until Sept. 8, 1977 (Goodwin, 1978: 199). Beardslee & Mitchell (1965: 346-347) reported one seen near Ridgeway on Sept. 24, 1949 by B. Nathan and A.J. Wright.

NOTE: Two other specimens have been reported: one now in the British Museum taken on the Albany River (no data available) and one taken at Chatham by J.A. Jermyn and subsequently seen by W.E. Saunders, but apparently now lost (*fide* R. James).

**MEASUREMENTS:**
*Length:* 5.5 to 6.0 ins. (Godfrey, 1966: 303)
Wingspread:
*Weight:* 2 ♂'s weighed 29.1 and 29.8 g. and 2 ♀ weighed 27.6 and 36.8 g. (Terres, 1980: 923).

**REFERENCE:**
Wright, A.J. 1949
Greenland Wheatear in southern Ontario.
Prothonotary, 15: 60-61.

# EASTERN BLUEBIRD   *Sialia sialis*   (Linnaeus)

In the days of my youth this was a common bird around Toronto, with good-sized flocks migrating over in March and October, and many staying to nest in surrounding farmland. With the advent of starlings, wire fences and urbanization they are now rare in most parts of Ontario. A few very cold winters in the 1950's were also implicated in their decline. Various nest-box projects have been successful in maintaining populations in some areas. Our birds winter mainly in the southern U.S.A.

IDENTIFICATION: The Eastern Bluebirds are somewhat larger than House Sparrows, which are therefore able to occupy bluebird nest-boxes. With its blue back and reddish breast the bluebird is unmistakable. Mountain Bluebirds have a blue breast and paler blue back. Western Bluebirds have a rusty upper back (blue in our Eastern Bluebird). The song of the Eastern Bluebird is a mellow, usually 3-syllabled warble, sometimes given as "pur-i-ty". As well as in nest-boxes, they often nest in hollow fence posts, and in natural cavities in trees, etc.

WINTER: On the 1968-1977 Christmas counts they were uncommon along the north shore of Lake Erie and rare from there north to Meaford and the Thousand Islands. Stirrett (1973a: 18) had Pelee records throughout the winter, with a maximum of 40 on Jan. 30. Ussher (1965: 20) reported one lingering at Rondeau until Dec. 3. Saunders & Dale (1933: 221) had a Feb. 21, 1915 record at London, perhaps an early migrant. Brooman (1954: 30) had Elgin Co. records for Jan. 1, 1947; Dec. 21, 1952 (3) and Dec. 26, 1953 (6). Fleming (1907: 87) had one as early as Feb. 26, 1906 at Toronto and Speirs (1938: 40) had a Feb. 23 record. J.L. Baillie had a Dec. 19 record for Toronto (Saunders, 1947: 370). Speirs (1975: 40) had two winter records: one in Pickering on Dec. 12, 1964 and one in Oshawa on Jan. 2, 1954. L. Beamer reported two heard at Meaford on Jan. 16, 1949.

SPRING: Stirrett (1973b: 22) had a maximum of 300 at Pelee on March 15. Ussher (1965: 20) gave March 21 as his 19-year average arrival date at Rondeau, with his earliest on March 1. Saunders & Dale (1933: 221) gave March 10 as the 17-year average arrival date at London. J.R. McLeod found a nest with 4 eggs as early as March 27, 1893 and a set of 5 eggs was found on Apr. 30, 1902. Brooman (1954: 30) saw an adult carrying food to a nest in the Kettle Creek valley, Elgin Co., on May 24, 1948. Fleming (1907: 87) called it an abundant migrant and summer resident at Toronto from March 3: Speirs (1938: 44) gave March 25 as the spring peak at Toronto. My earliest record at our Pickering home was on March 12, 1955, with the spring peak during the second week of April: I noted a male entering one of our nest-boxes as early as March 22, 1953 (Speirs, 1975: 45). Allin (1940: 104) found a nest with 4 eggs on May 15, 1928 in Darlington Twp. Snyder (1941: 74) gave March 19, 1938 as his earliest record for Prince Edward Co. Weir & Quilliam (1980: 38) listed March 29 as the 32-year average arrival date at Kingston, with the earliest on March 5. E. Beaupré took a set of 5 eggs at Portsmouth, near Kingston, on May 14, 1902 (Quilliam, 1973: 143). Devitt (1967: 124) gave Apr. 9 as the 15-year average arrival date at Barrie, with the earliest on March 11, 1921 at Collingwood and about 100 seen near Orillia on Apr. 11, 1904: a set of 4 eggs was found as early as May 5, 1915 at Wasaga Beach. L. Beamer's median arrival date at Meaford was March 23, with the earliest one heard on Feb. 26, 1951 (a very mild day). Mills (1981: 119) gave Apr. 13 as the 8-year average arrival date at Huntsville, with March 22, 1889 as A. Kay's earliest record at Port Sydney. Nicholson (1981: 149) gave Apr. 11 as the 10-year average arrival date for Manitoulin, with the earliest on March 22, 1972. D.B. Ferguson found a nest with 4 eggs near Mindemoya on May 29, 1979. MacLulich (1938: 29) gave Apr. 9, 1934 as his earliest arrival date for Algonquin Park. Ricker & Clarke (1939: 17) had their earliest Lake Nipissing arrival on Apr. 4, 1925. Denis (1961: 3) gave Apr. 30 as the average arrival date for Thunder Bay, with the earliest on Apr. 11, 1955. Peruniak (1971: 23) gave Apr. 24 as her earliest record for Atikokan. Elder (1979: 37) mentioned May 21 as his earliest date for Geraldton, where it was "very uncommon". Smith (1957: 177) noted 3 at New Liskeard on May 29, 1954 and one at Kapuskasing on May 31. Sam Waller noted 5 at Moose Factory on May 11, 1930 (Todd, 1963: 562).

SUMMER: On the 1968-1977 Breeding Bird Surveys they were rare on most routes from Pelee north to Hearst and Nipigon but absent on heavily forested routes, and most plentiful along the Interlobate Moraine, on Manitoulin and in the Rainy River region. Stirrett (1973c: 19) had records at Pelee throughout the summer, with a maximum of 16 on June 30. Saunders & Dale (1933: 221) reported a set of 5 eggs found near London on June 12, 1917. McCracken, Bradstreet & Holroyd (1981: 60-61) chronicled the varying populations on Long Point, with 20 nests reported from 1965 to 1972, and with egg dates from May 28 to July 20. Alf. Bunker found a nest with 4 eggs as late as July 28, 1962 at his Pickering home and saw a female feeding young on Aug. 25 of that year: his only nest parasitized by a cowbird held two eggs and a cowbird egg on June 14, 1967 (Speirs, 1975: 45). We averaged about one per 100 acres in field quadrats in Uxbridge, Scott and Thorah Twps. (Speirs & Orenstein, 1967: 182). Barry (1974: 347-354) reported on a nest box project in the Oshawa region from 1967 to 1971, with a peak year with over 600 eggs laid and up to 340 banded in 1969. Allin (1940: 104) reported a nest with 3 young in Darlington Twp. on June 3, 1927. On July 3, 1938, H.H. Southam noted 12 family groups in a 20 mile drive in Prince Edward Co. (Snyder, 1941: 74). Quilliam (1973: 143) chronicled changes in abundance at Kingston. Paul Harrington took a set of 3 eggs on June 21, 1924 at Wasaga Beach (Baillie & Harrington, 1937: 233). Lloyd (1924: 16) reported a nest found by C.E. Johnson near Ottawa on June 3, 1921. Speirs & Speirs (1947: 33) watched a male take food into a nest hole near North Bay on June 13, 1945. Baillie & Hope (1947: 19) reported two nests at Chapleau in 1937: one with 5 eggs on June 16 and one with 3 eggs on June 18. Snyder (1942: 141) found a nest with 4 eggs as late as July 22, 1931 near Sault Ste. Marie. W. Wyett saw a male at Pukaskwa Depot on June 22, 1973 (Skeel & Bondrup-Nielsen, 1978: 196). Baillie & Hope (1943: 18) collected a female at Rossport on June 1 and 3 males and a female at Marathon from June 13-18, 1936. Dear (1940: 136) found a nest with 5 eggs in Paipoonge Twp., Thunder Bay, on June 24, 1928. Snyder (1938: 201) found a nest with small young at Emo, Rainy River, on June 20, 1929. L. Paterson found a nest with 4 eggs at Kenora on July 1, 1931 (Baillie & Harrington, 1937: 232). Snyder (1953: 75) reported an occupied nest at Wabigoon on June 18, 1937 and two young collected at Malachi: birds were also noted at Sioux Lookout and at Dinorwic. Smith (1957: 177) saw 3 at Hearst on June 5, 1954 and had summer records at Porcupine Lake, two at Nellie Lake near Iroquois Falls, 2 at Brethour near Lake Timiskaming on July 22 and one on Aug. 31 near Matheson. Snyder (1928: 33) saw two pairs at Lowbush and a nesting pair on the south side of Lake Abitibi in June, 1925. Hope (1938: 33) saw two pairs at Favourable Lake: one collected on June 5 and the other noted on June 11. Sam Waller collected one at Moose Factory on June 5, 1930 and Samuel S. Decker saw a female there on June 9, 1934 (Todd, 1963: 562).

AUTUMN: Smith (1957: 177) saw two on Sept. 2, 1953 near Matheson. Peruniak (1971: 23) gave Sept. 29 as her latest Atikokan record. Speirs & Speirs (1947: 33) had one at North Bay as late as Oct. 18, 1944. MacLulich (1938: 29) gave Oct. 4, 1930 as his latest date for Algonquin Park. Nicholson (1981: 149) gave Oct. 23, 1971 as the latest Manitoulin record with a maximum of 68 on Sept. 20, 1972. D.A. Sutherland saw 5 at Beausoleil Is. as late as Oct. 14, 1976 (Mills, 1981: 120). Five seen near Cranberry Lake, on Oct. 17, 1937 was the latest Simcoe Co. record (Devitt, 1967: 124). Weir & Quilliam (1980: 38) listed Oct. 25 as the 27-year average departure date from Kingston. I noted a flock of 11 flying over our Pickering home on Nov. 15, 1970 (Speirs, 1975: 45). Speirs (1938: 52) gave Oct. 20 as the peak of the fall migration at Toronto. Beardslee & Mitchell (1965: 345-346) reported 100 at Point Abino, Lake Erie, on Nov. 13, 1941 and two there on Nov. 25, 1948. Marshall Field counted 93 migrating past "Hawk Cliff", Elgin Co., on Oct. 12, 1953 (Brooman, 1954: 30). Ussher (1965: 20) gave Nov. 9 as his 10-year average departure date from Rondeau. Stirrett (1973d: 24) had a maximum of 800 at Pelee on Oct. 14.

BANDING: One banded near Bowmanville by Dennis Barry on June 11, 1969 was recovered at Pavo, Georgia, in January, 1970, some 951 miles to the south (Brewer & Salvadori, 1978: 74).

**MEASUREMENTS:**
*Length:* 6.5 to 7.7 ins. (Godfrey, 1966: 301)
*Wingspread:* 11.40 to 13.25 ins. (Roberts, 1955: 653)
*Weight:* ♂ 31.5 g. ♀ 31.8 g. (Hope, 1938: 33).

**REFERENCES:**
Barry, Dennis 1974 Eastern Bluebird nest-box project (in Tozer & Richards, 1974: 347-354).
   Woodford, J. 1957 The Bluebird in Ontario. Federation of Ont. Naturalists, Bull. No. 78: 7-10.
*Note:* Several other references were listed in the Toronto Field Naturalists, No. 354: 31 (mainly dealing with local nest-box projects).

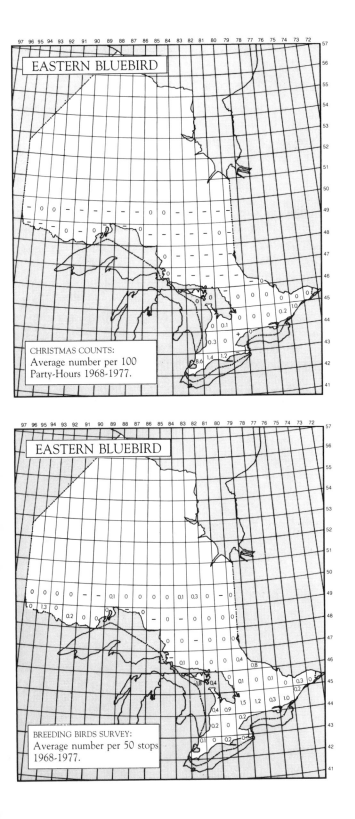

EASTERN BLUEBIRD

CHRISTMAS COUNTS:
Average number per 100
Party-Hours 1968-1977.

EASTERN BLUEBIRD

BREEDING BIRDS SURVEY:
Average number per 50 stops
1968-1977.

# MOUNTAIN BLUEBIRD   *Sialia currucoides*   (Bechstein)

This is a bird of the Rocky Mountains, and the Prairie Provinces where nest box projects have increased its numbers in recent years. In Ontario it is accidental. They winter south to Mexico.

IDENTIFICATION: This bluebird has a blue breast as well as a blue back and is somewhat paler in colour than our Eastern Bluebird: it is all blue except for white on the lower belly and undertail coverts. Females are mainly gray but with some blue on the wings and rump.

WINTER: Wyett (1966: 42) collected a female at Pelee on Dec. 6, 1965: this was one of two females first seen there by W. Botham on Dec. 4. J. Wilson saw another there on Dec. 29, 1971 (Goodwin, 1972: 599). D. Fidler, A. Wormington and many others saw one at Pelee from Nov. 28 to Jan. 6 during the winter of 1979-1980 (Goodwin, 1980: 270). J.W. Johnson found one at Colpoys Bay, Bruce Co., from Dec. 20-22, 1979 (Goodwin, 1980: 270). A.E. Allin saw a male at Thunder Bay on Dec. 22, 1962 (Wyett, 1966: 42).

SPRING: One was observed and photographed at Thunder Bay by D. Asquith, Mrs. W.P. Hogarth and Mr. & Mrs. T. Perrons from Apr. 4-7, 1968 (Goodwin, 1968: 522). Peruniak (1971: 23) reported one at Atikokan from May 19-20, 1967.

SUMMER: Jack Satterly (pers. comm.) found a male in Carden Twp., Victoria Co., about 3 miles east of Lake Dalrymple, on July 7, 1980: this bird was observed by him and several other observers to Aug. 18.

AUTUMN: Jack Satterly's bird was seen as late as Sept. 15, 1980 by Carl and Elaine Parsons and Ernie and Fidelle Johns (*fide* J. Satterly).

**MEASUREMENTS:**
*Length:* 6 1/2 to 7 3/4 ins.
(Godfrey, 1966: 302)
Wingspread:
*Weight:* 28.3 g (Wyett,
1966: 42).

**REFERENCE:**
Wyett, William R. 1966
First Ontario specimen of
Mountain Bluebird
collected at Point Pelee.
Ont. Field Biologist, No.
20: 42.

# TOWNSEND'S SOLITAIRE
*Myadestes townsendi*   (Audubon)

This is a Rocky Mountain species, with only rare stragglers to Ontario in the colder months of the year. I heard about one in a bit of forest on Shoal Point Rd. in Pickering one day in February: when I arrived there the next morning the bird was already surrounded by a busload of observers from Cleveland, Ohio, a vivid illustration of the efficiency of the "hot line" in finding rare birds!

IDENTIFICATION:   This is a bird about the size and general colouration of our Gray Catbird, but lacking the reddish undertail coverts of that species, and having instead a white eye ring, a white border to the tail and broad buffy edgings to some wing coverts, forming a conspicuous patch in flight. On its breeding grounds in the Rockies it is an accomplished singer, but all that is generally heard in Ontario is a rather loud "tsee-ah" (reminiscent of the Pine Grosbeak call but more slurred together).

WINTER:   W. Jarmain saw one at London on Dec. 10, 1965 (Goodwin, 1966: 418). S. Wood noted one at Ancaster on Feb. 16, 1976 (Goodwin, 1976: 714). J. Rising had one at his feeder for about a week; first noted on Dec. 8, 1975 and photographed on Dec. 10 (Goodwin, 1976: 714). Ray Gerras found the Shoal Point, Pickering bird on Feb. 25, 1981: I saw it later in the day as did many others until last seen in the spring.

SPRING:   Kelley (1978: 63) reported one found at Pelee on March 3, 1962 by Helen M. Horton and Robert E. Mara: Baldwin & Woodford (1962: 706) collected it there on March 8, 1962. Another was observed there by many observers from Apr. 26-28, 1981 (Goodwin, 1981: 819). One was seen at Cedar Springs, Kent Co., on March 25, 1976 by K.J. Burk (Goodwin, 1976: 714). S. Bond noted one at Toronto for a few days from March 11, 1976 (Goodwin, 1976: 714). The Shoal Point bird, Pickering, was last reported on Apr. 19, 1981 by A. Dobson (Goodwin, 1981: 819). Nicholson (1981: 149), with Christopher Bell and John Lemon, saw one at Little Current, Manitoulin, on March 22, 1970.

SUMMER:

AUTUMN:   A. Wormington found one on Caribou Island, Lake Superior, on Oct. 2, 1979 and also at Marathon on Oct. 25 and 29, 1979 (Goodwin, 1980: 157). J. Nicholson saw one about 21 miles north of Killarney on Nov. 16, 1975 (Goodwin, 1976: 63). One was noted at Whitby on Nov. 21, 1981 according to R. Nisbet (Goodwin, 1982: 174). One was noted on Sept. 29, 1960 at Toronto (Snyder, MSS). Doug. Scovell found one at Hamilton on Sept. 18, 1960, later seen by Ron Scovell *et al* (Speirs, 1960: 21).

**MEASUREMENTS:**
*Length:* 8.0 to 9.5 ins.
(Godfrey, 1966: 304)
Wingspread:
*Weight:* 40 g. (Baldwin &
Woodford, 1962: 706).

**REFERENCE:**
Baldwin, D.H. and James
Woodford 1962 First
Townsend's Solitaire
collected in Ontario. Auk,
79: (4): 706.

# VEERY   *Catharus fuscescens*   (Stephens)

I associate the Veery with fern covered floors of deciduous forests: in such places they may be one of the most abundant birds. Our birds retire to Central America and northern South America in winter.

IDENTIFICATION: Our southern Ontario Veery is a tawny bird, but those west of Lake Superior have much the same back colour as Swainson's Thrush. Both subspecies lack the distinct breast spots of our other thrushes, having rather faint streaks on the buffy or tawny upper breast instead. The "descending spiral" song: "zwee-ur, zwee-ur, zwaa-ur, zwah-ur" is characteristic and the questioning "veer-ee" call gives it its name, often interspersed with a more matter of fact "vee-ur" (slurred downward). These calls will identify overhead migrants in the night sky.

WINTER:

SPRING: Stirrett (1973b: 22) gave Apr. 15 as his earliest Pelee record: Kelley (1978: 62) estimated 500 there on May 10, 1952. Ussher (1965: 20) gave May 4 as the 23-year average arrival date at Rondeau, with the earliest on Apr. 17. Saunders & Dale (1933: 220-221) gave May 6 as the 17-year average arrival date at London, with the earliest on May 2, 1912: he reported a set of 4 eggs and one cowbird egg as early as May 22, 1905: also a set of 3 on May 23, 1904 and a set of 4 on May 31, 1912. Snyder (1931: 220) noted them at Long Point from May 6 to May 27, 1928, with peak numbers about May 18. J.L. Baillie had a very early one at Toronto on Apr. 10, but gave May 7 as his 27-year average arrival date (Saunders, 1947: 370): Speirs (1938: 44) gave May 19 as the spring peak at Toronto. Chas. Christy saw one at Oshawa as early as Apr. 30, 1964 (Tozer & Richards, 1974: 220). Speirs (1975: 44) gave May 17 as the spring peak in Ontario Co. and mentioned a nest with 2 eggs and 3 cowbird eggs at Whitby as early as May 26, 1962. Tozer & Richards (1974: 220) cited an early Apr. 29, 1963 record for Darlington Twp.: Allin (1940: 103) found a nest with 2 eggs and a cowbird egg on May 27, 1928 in Darlington. Weir & Quilliam (1980: 28) listed May 5 as the 31-year average arrival date at Kingston, with the earliest on Apr. 22: C.K. Clarke took a set of 3 eggs there on May 8, 1897 (Quilliam, 1973: 142). Devitt (1967: 123) gave May 12 as the 17-year average arrival date at Barrie, with the earliest on Apr. 25, 1941. L. Beamer's median arrival date at Meaford was May 16, with the earliest on May 6, 1949. Mills (1981: 119) gave May 24, 1930 as the earliest nest with a full clutch of eggs in the cottage country, at Peters Lake. Nicholson (1981: 148) gave May 11 as the 11-year average arrival date on Manitoulin, with the earliest on Apr. 22, 1972, and a maximum of 250 grounded at South Baymouth on May 13, 1978: at the Great Duck Is. tower 77 were killed between May 19-28, 1979. Speirs & Speirs (1947: 33) observed two at North Bay on May 10, 1944. Denis (1961: 3) gave May 16 as the average arrival date at Thunder Bay, with the earliest on May 4, 1954. Peruniak (1971: 23) gave May 16 as her earliest Atikokan date. Smith (1957: 177) noted three near New Liskeard on May 27, 1954.

SUMMER: On the 1968-1977 Breeding Bird Surveys they were common in the cottage country and from Rainy River to Lake of the Woods, becoming fairly common north to Larder Lake and Longlac, and rare south to Pelee and Long Point, with none from Cochrane to Hearst. Stirrett (1973c: 19) had records of single birds at Pelee throughout the summer but no nesting report. Saunders & Dale (1933: 220-221) found a set of 2 eggs and 2 cowbird eggs at London on June 26, 1902 and a set of 3 eggs on June 4, 1906. Speirs & Frank (1970: 742) found only one pair on their 25-acre quadrat in Springwater Park, Elgin Co., in the summer of 1970. Beardslee & Mitchell (1965: 344-345) reported a nest with 3 young at Cook's Mills on June 1, 1953. Speirs (1938: 52) gave Aug. 25 as the peak of the southward migration at Toronto. J. Satterly found a nest with 1 egg at Cedar Point, Mara Twp., as late as July 6, 1957 (Speirs, 1975: 44). Speirs & Orenstein (1975: 13) found the species in 5 of 11 forest quadrats in Ontario Co., mainly in mid-succession forests, with the maximum population of 49 birds per 100 acres in the Scott Twp. plot. Allin (1940: 104) found a nest with 2 eggs and 1 young on June 19, 1927 and a nest with 1 egg and 1 cowbird egg on June 22, 1930, in Darlington Twp. E. Beaupré took a set of 3 eggs at Portsmouth, near Kingston, on June 2, 1901 (Quilliam, 1973: 142). Devitt (1967: 123) cited several nest records for Simcoe Co., the earliest found by W.W. Smith at Big Cedar Point on June 2, 1940. Mills (1981: 118) reported this to be the most common bird on the Lake Rosseau and Byng Inlet Breeding Bird Survey routes: 46 nests have been reported in the cottage country. D.B. Ferguson found a nest with 2 eggs and 2 cowbird eggs at Windfall Lake, Manitoulin, on June 18, 1973 (Nicholson, 1981: 148). In a 4-year study of a beech-maple forest near Dorset, Veery populations varied from 26 to 38 territories per 100 acres and the Veery ranked from first to fifth in abundance. C.H.D. Clarke saw young being fed at Brule Lake, Algonquin Park on July 17, 1934 (MacLulich, 1938: 28). Speirs & Speirs (1947: 33) cited details of several nests in the North Bay region; two with 4 eggs each were discovered as early as June 8, 1944 at Pimisi Bay by Louise Lawrence. Baillie & Hope (1947: 19) collected 5 young at Bigwood from July 15-22, 1937 but saw none at Chapleau or Biscotasing. Snyder (1942: 140) observed two broods of flying young at Lake George, near Sault Ste. Marie, on July 9, 1931. Skeel & Bondrup-Nielsen (1978: 195) considered it rare at Pukaskwa but had a few records from June 3 (1973) to July 9 (1977). Baillie & Hope (1943: 18) took only one specimen along the north shore of Lake Superior, a male at Rossport on June 4, 1936. Dear (1940: 136) found two Thunder Bay nests, one with 4 eggs on July 1, 1924 and one with 3 eggs on July 1, 1928. Snyder (1938: 201) called this a common breeding species in the Rainy River region. Elder (1979: 37) had only one Geraldton record, on June 1, 1972: I heard one singing there on June 8, 1971 and another at Black Sands Provincial Park and one near Pearl on June 11, 1972. L. Paterson found a nest with 4 eggs at Kenora on July 1, 1931 (Baillie & Harrington, 1937: 232). Snyder (1953: 74) reported one on June 29 and 3 on July 5 at Sioux Lookout and found them "not uncommon" from Ingolf to Wabigoon.

AUTUMN: Louise Lawrence noted one at Pimisi Bay as late as Sept. 19, 1944 (Speirs & Speirs, 1947: 33). Nicholson (1981: 148) reported a very late one on Manitoulin on Nov. 13, 1976. Mills (1981: 119) had his latest cottage country bird on Sept. 25, 1976 at Magnetawan. At the Barrie TV tower 7 were killed in 4 of 7 years, the latest two on Sept. 27, 1962 (Devitt, 1967: 123). Weir & Quilliam (1980: 38) listed Sept. 14 as the 18-year average departure date from Kingston, the latest on Oct. 20. Long (1968a: 16) reported a late migrant on Oct. 14, 1964 at Pickering Beach. Saunders (1947: 370) gave Sept. 15 as his 11-year average departure date from Toronto, with his latest on Oct. 6: Speirs (1938: 54) gave Oct. 24 as the latest Toronto date. Saunders (1930: 511) found 6 casualties at the Long Point lighthouse on Sept. 7, 1929, one on Sept. 9 and none from Sept. 24-29. Ussher (1965: 20) gave Sept. 4 as his latest date for Rondeau. Stirrett (1973d: 24) gave Oct. 7 as his latest Pelee record, with a maximum of 8 on Sept. 6.

BANDING: Brewer & Salvadori (1978: 74) reported two interesting recoveries. One banded at Long Point on May 11, 1962 was recovered at Bronte lighthouse on May 7, 1965 about 63 miles to the northeast. Another banded at Muskegon State Park (about half way up the east shore of Lake Michigan in Michigan) was recovered at Fort William (Thunder Bay) on June 29, 1970, about 382 miles to the northwest.

**MEASUREMENTS:**
*Length:* 6.5 to 7.7 ins. (Godfrey, 1966: 299)
*Wingspread:* 11 1/4 to 12 1/2 ins. (Roberts, 1955: 652)
*Weight:* 25 Ontario specimens weighed an average of 32.26 g.

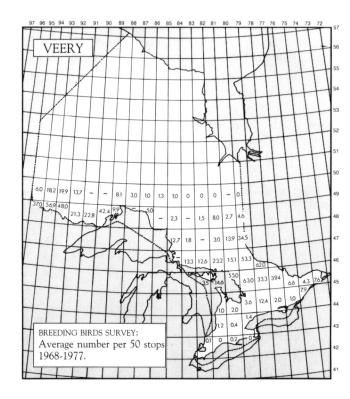

VEERY

BREEDING BIRDS SURVEY:
Average number per 50 stops
1968-1977.

# GRAY-CHEEKED THRUSH   *Catharus minimus*   (Lafresnaye)

Most observers have difficulty finding one for their year's list in Ontario, where it appears to breed only in the "land of little sticks" near the Hudson Bay coast. In southern Ontario a few may be found in late May and late September in migration. Surprising numbers are sometimes found in tower and lighthouse kills, and banders sometimes encounter numbers in migration. They winter in Central America and South America.

IDENTIFICATION: I think of this as the thrush with no good field marks except "dirty pants" (grayish-olive flanks). It lacks the rufous tail of the Hermit Thrush, the reddish brown head of the Wood Thrush, the orangy-buff cheeks of the Swainson's and tawny back of the Veery. Some Hermit Thrushes have grayish cheeks, so you are left with the "dirty pants". The song has the quality of the Veery's song, but does not consistently descend in pitch like the Veery or ascend like Swainson's, but tends to vary around one pitch. Its rhythm reminds me of the old saying "shave and a haircut, two bits".

WINTER: One was reported on the 1977 Christmas count at Kingston (Dec. 18).

SPRING: Stirrett (1973b: 22) had Pelee records from Apr. 25 to June 2, with a maximum of 25 on May 30. Ussher (1965: 20) had Rondeau records from May 3 to June 4, with average arrival on May 14 and departure on May 27. Saunders & Dale (1933: 220) gave May 20 as the 11-year average arrival date at London, with the earliest on May 11, 1924. Snyder (1931: 220) had Long Point records as early as May 4, 1928 and as late as June 4, 1927. J.L. Baillie had Toronto records from May 3 to June 7, with average arrival on May 12 and departure on May 26 (Saunders, 1947: 370). Speirs (1938: 40, 44) reported one as early as Apr. 28 at Toronto, with the peak on May 20. Speirs (1975: 43) had Pickering dates from May 13 to June 4. Snyder (1941: 74) had a May 27, 1930 record for Prince Edward Co. Weir & Quilliam (1980: 38) had Kingston records from May 3 to June 19, with the average arrival on May 14 and departure on May 27. Devitt (1967: 123) had Simcoe Co. records from May 20 to June 2. Mills (1981: 118) cited a May 22, 1962 record for Fairy Lake, Muskoka. Nicholson (1981: 148) had spring records for Manitoulin from May 18 to May 28. Speirs & Speirs (1947: 33) mentioned one noted by Louise Lawrence at Pimisi Bay on May 22, 1945 and another that they saw at North Bay on June 1, 1944. W. Wyett saw one on May 30, 1974 at Pukaskwa (Skeel & Bondrup-Nielsen, 1978: 195). Baillie & Hope (1943: 18) took one in a mouse trap at Rossport on May 31, 1936. Denis (1961: 4) gave May 19 as the average arrival date at Thunder Bay, with the earliest on May 4, 1954.

SUMMER: See late spring and early fall records of migrants above and below. Schueler, Baldwin & Rising (1974: 143, 147) reported them to be uncommon at Winisk and common at Hawley Lake, where they collected a female with brood patch on June 25, 1964: they found a nest with 3 young at Aquatuk Lake on July 6, 1964. C.E. Hope saw them almost daily at Ft. Severn during the summer of 1940 and saw as many as ten there on June 25: he found a nest with 3 eggs on July 2 and collected a young bird on July 15.

AUTUMN: Skeel & Bondrup-Nielsen (1978: 195) saw one on Sept. 18, 1977 in Pukaskwa and W. Wyett saw another one there on Sept. 17, 1971. Speirs & Speirs (1947: 33) saw one eating crumbs at their North Bay feeder on Sept. 22, 1944 and reported one seen at Pimisi Bay by Louise Lawrence on Sept. 29, 1944. Nicholson (1981: 148) reported big kills of this species at the Great Duck Island tower: 962 from Sept. 18-23, 1977; 126 on Sept. 21, 1979 and 174 on Sept. 16, 1980. C. Harris saw two at Go Home Bay on Sept. 14, 1975 and D. Sutherland saw two at Beausoleil Island on Sept. 16, 1976 (Mills, 1981: 118). Devitt (1967: 123) had fall records from Simcoe Co. from Sept. 12 to Oct. 3: he reported 15 killed at the Barrie TV tower in 3 of 7 years. Quilliam (1973: 142) gave Oct. 22, 1961 as her latest Kingston date. Weir & Quilliam (1980: 38) listed Sept. 7 as the average arrival date at Kingston and Oct. 13 as the average departure date, with one as early as July 29. Snyder (1941: 74) collected a male at Hillier, Prince Edward Co. on Sept. 19, 1936. Speirs (1975: 43) had Ontario Co. records from Aug. 20, 1959 (at Cedar Point, Mara Twp. by J. Satterly) to Oct. 22, 1973 (at Cannington by R. Charles Long) with most records in the latter half of September. Saunders (1947: 370) listed Toronto records from Sept. 4 to Oct. 10 with average arrival on Sept. 18 and departure on Sept. 28: Fleming (1907: 86) had one there as late as Oct. 18 and Speirs (1938: 52) gave Sept. 27 as the fall peak for Toronto. Saunders (1930: 511) reported Long Point lighthouse casualties in the fall of 1929: 1 on Sept. 7; 2 on Sept. 9 and 150 between Sept. 24-29. Ussher (1965: 20) had Rondeau records from Aug. 31 to Oct. 15 with average arrival on Sept. 11 and departure on Oct. 2. Stirrett (1973d: 24) had Pelee records from Aug. 31 to Oct. 19 with a maximum of 50 on Sept. 28.

**MEASUREMENTS:**

*Length:* 6.5 to 8.0 ins. (Godfrey, 1966: 299)
*Wingspread:* 12.3 to 13.5 ins. (Roberts, 1955: 653)
*Weight:* 23.9 to 35.3 g. (Terres, 1980: 921).

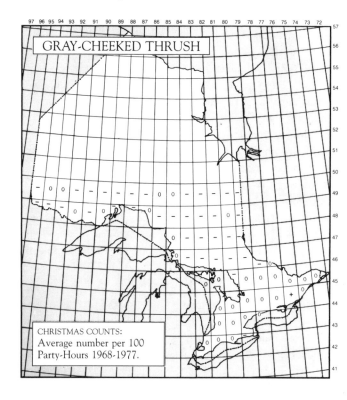

GRAY-CHEEKED THRUSH

CHRISTMAS COUNTS:
Average number per 100
Party-Hours 1968-1977.

# SWAINSON'S THRUSH  *Catharus ustulatus*  (Nuttall)

In summer this is the common thrush of the spruce forests of northern Ontario. Migrants are rather late to arrive in spring and early to depart in autumn. They winter in Central America and South America.

IDENTIFICATION: This is the thrush with orangy-buff cheeks and prominent eye-rings. Otherwise they are rather dull coloured, lacking the rufous tail of the Hermit Thrush, the reddish-brown crown of the Wood Thrush and general bright colour of the Veery. Note that Veeries west of Lake Superior may be as dull as Swainson's but lack the heavily spotted breast of Swainson's, and sing the typical Veery song. The song of Swainson's Thrush has been described as an "upward spiral" contrasting with the "downward spiral" of the Veery. The song lacks the long, sweet, introductory note of the Hermit Thrush, but is often introduced instead by the "quoit" call note that is so characteristic of the species (often heard overhead at night during migration as well as from the depths of the forest on its nesting grounds).

WINTER: A well-documented individual was reported on the Hamilton Christmas count on Dec. 26, 1976.

SPRING: Stirrett (1973b: 22) had Pelee records from Apr. 24 to May 29 (when 18 were noted), with a maximum of 200 on May 19. Ussher (1965: 20) had his earliest at Rondeau on Apr. 23, with average arrival on May 6 and departure on May 24. Saunders & Dale (1933: 220) gave May 10 as the 17-year average arrival date at London, with the earliest on Apr. 24, 1926. Snyder (1931: 220) had Long Point birds as early as May 4, 1928 and as late as May 28, 1927. J.L. Baillie's 25-year average arrival date at Toronto was May 13, with his earliest on May 2, but Fleming (1907: 370) reported a very early one on Apr. 13, 1890: Baillie's average departure date was May 28 (Saunders, 1947: 370). Speirs (1938: 44) gave May 25 as the spring peak at Toronto. The earliest Ontario Co. record was by Edgerton Pegg at Thickson's Point woods on May 3, 1970 and the peak date is about May 26 (Speirs, 1975: 42). Snyder (1941: 73) collected a male on May 30, 1930 at Hallowell, Prince Edward Co. Weir & Quilliam (1980: 38) listed May 10 and May 28 as average arrival and departure dates at Kingston, with the earliest on Apr. 27. Devitt (1967: 122) gave May 19 as the 12-year average arrival date at Barrie, with the earliest on May 8, 1965. L. Beamer's average arrival date at Meaford was May 17, with the earliest on May 7 (in both 1939 and 1949). Mills (1981: 118) gave May 9, 1965 as the earliest Huntsville date. Nicholson (1981: 147) gave May 12 as the 8-year average arrival date on Manitoulin, with the earliest on May 3, 1975 and the maximum count of 50 on Great Duck Island on May 23, 1976. Louise Lawrence heard one singing as early as May 10, 1945 at Pimisi Bay (Speirs & Speirs, 1947: 33). Skeel & Bondrup-Nielsen (1978: 195) noted their first at Pukaskwa on Apr. 25, 1977. Denis (1961: 3) gave May 11 as the average arrival date at Thunder Bay, with the earliest on Apr. 24, 1957. Peruniak (1971: 23) noted her earliest at Atikokan on Apr. 24. Elder (1979: 36) gave May 21 as his earliest Geraldton date. Bondrup-Nielsen (1976: 44) saw his first near Kapuskasing on May 6, 1975.

SUMMER: On the 1968-1977 Breeding Bird Surveys they were common from Wawa and Elk Lake northward, with a few south to Manitoulin and Barry's Bay, with outliers at Mt. Julian and Listowel. Ussher (1965: 20) had a northbound bird at Rondeau as late as June 6 and a southbound bird as early as July 15, with the average arrival on Aug. 22. Saunders (1947: 370) had a spring bird as late as June 10 and a returning one as early as Aug. 16 at Toronto. We had one at our Pickering home as late as June 3, 1961 and a returning bird on July 30, 1972: birds singing north of Sebright in Rama Twp. on June 17 and 26, 1963 were probably on breeding territory (Speirs, 1975: 42). Weir & Quilliam (1980: 38) had a spring bird as late as June 18 and a returning bird as early as July 6 at Kingston, with the average date for southbound arrivals on Aug. 9. Devitt (1967: 122) had only one definite breeding record for Simcoe Co.: a nest with 3 eggs found by L.A. Campbell at Barrie on June 17, 1915, though he has heard singing birds in mid-June elsewhere. Mills (1981: 118) reported 16 nest records for the cottage country. Ron Tasker found a nest in Burpee Twp., Manitoulin, on July 13, 1975 (Nicholson, 1981: 147). MacLulich (1938: 28) called this "probably the most abundant thrush in the park as a whole" (Algonquin Park). C.E. Hope collected a nest with 3 eggs at Eau Claire on July 1, 1935 (Baillie & Harrington, 1937: 232). C.E. Hope found 14 occupied nests at Chapleau and Biscotasing from June 8 to July 9, 1937: details have been tabulated in Baillie & Hope (1947: 19). Snyder (1942: 140) collected two males at Maclennan, near Sault Ste. Marie, on July 2 and 8, 1931. Skeel & Bondrup-Nielsen (1978: 195) wrote that this "was unquestionably the most abundant summer resident" at Pukaskwa: they found a nest with 4 eggs on June 9, 1977 and reported a nest with 3 eggs found on June 28, 1973 by W. Wyett et al. Baillie & Hope (1943: 17, 18) reported nests at Marathon, Amyot and Franz and called this the commonest thrush of the region. Snyder (1928: 277) found a nest with 4 eggs at Lake Nipigon on June 23, 1924. Dear (1940: 136) found two nests with 4 eggs each near Thunder Bay, one on June 13, 1931, the other on June 19, 1932. Kendeigh (1947: 27) found a population of 4 pairs per 100 acres at Black Sturgeon Lake in 1945 while Speirs (1949: 148) found 8 territories on 75 acres at nearby Eaglehead Lake in 1946. Snyder (1938: 201) noted a nest with 4 eggs at Off Lake, Rainy River, on July 4, 1929. Snyder (1953: 74) considered this to be the most plentiful thrush in western Ontario: he noted young of the year at Malachi and observed nest building at Wabigoon on June 18, 1937. Snyder (1928: 33) found a nest with 3 eggs on July 11, 1925 near the south shore of Lake Abitibi. James (1980: 88) found several nests with eggs near Pickle Lake, one with 4 eggs as early as June 18, 1977 and another with 4 eggs as late as June 23, 1979. Hope (1938: 33) encountered many nests at Favourable Lake, one found on June 17, 1938 held 4 eggs: it was 3 1/2 ft. up in a small balsam fir. Cringan (1953a: 3) saw one on June 17, 1953 at Perrault Falls: he saw another on June 4, 1953 at Kasabonika Lake (Cringan, 1953b: 4). Cringan (1950: 15) recorded it regularly in early summer, 1950, at Nikip Lake. Sam Waller collected a nest with 3 eggs at Moose Factory on June 27, 1930 and Manning (1952: 77) collected a male at Attawapiskat on June 22, 1947. James, Nash & Peck (1982: 64, 65) considered this one of the three most abundant species along the Harricanaw River, near James Bay, where they found several nests from June 23 to July 5, 1982, mostly very low in deciduous shrubs (not typical of the species). James, Nash & Peck (1981: 91) considered breeding probable at Kiruna Lake, Sutton Ridges, but found no definite evidence. Schueler, Baldwin & Rising (1974: 147) found a nest with 3 eggs at Winisk on July 5, 1971 and collected young at Hawley Lake on July 16, 1964: they also found them common at Cochrane, Moosonee and Attawapiskat. Lee (1978: 29) had a daily maximum count of 17 on June 26, 1975 at Big Trout Lake and had some on each of his three study quadrats there. C.E. Hope found a nest with 4 eggs on July 7, 1940 at Ft. Severn and noted up to 6 birds almost daily there.

AUTUMN: D. McRae and A. Wormington saw individuals from Oct. 18-23, 1981 at Netitishi Point, James Bay. Oliver Hewitt saw 4 on Ship Sands Is., near Moosonee, on Sept. 24, 1947 (Manning, 1952: 77). Skeel & Bondrup-Nielsen (1978: 195) noted their last at Pukaskwa on Oct. 15, 1977. Speirs & Speirs (1947: 33) observed one at North Bay on Sept. 26, 1944. Nicholson (1981: 147) reported 1954 killed at the Great Duck Island tower between Sept. 18-25, 1977: his latest Manitoulin record was on Oct. 27, 1973. Mills (1981: 118) gave Oct. 9, 1938 as the latest date for the cottage country. Devitt (1967: 122) reported 48 killed at the Barrie TV tower from Sept. 24-26, 1960: his latest Simcoe Co. record was on Oct. 21, 1945 at Belle Ewart. Weir & Quilliam (1980: 38) listed Oct. 13 as the average departure date from Kingston, with the latest on Nov. 11. Monica Connally observed one at a feeder in Oshawa as late as Nov. 22, 1970 (Tozer & Richards, 1974: 220). The peak of the fall migration at Pickering is mid-Sept. (Speirs, 1975: 42). Saunders (1947: 370) listed Sept. 10 and Sept. 27 as his average fall arrival and departure dates at Toronto, with the latest on Oct. 16. Speirs (1938: 52) had fall peaks at Toronto on Sept. 15 and Sept. 21. Beardslee & Mitchell (1965: 341-342) noted one at Point Abino, Lake Erie, on Oct. 21, 1945. Saunders (1930: 511) reported that 18 of 654 birds killed at the Long Point lighthouse on Sept. 7, 1929 were Swainson's Thrushes, as well as 10 of 169 on Sept. 9 and 140 of 1237 from Sept. 24-29. Ussher (1965: 20) gave Oct. 10 as the average departure date from Rondeau, with the latest on Oct. 18. Stirrett (1973d: 24) had southbound birds at Pelee from Aug. 21 to Nov. 5, with the maximum of 1000 on Sept. 16.

BANDING: Brewer & Salvadori (1978: 74) reported one banded at Balmoral Marsh, Lake St. Clair, on Sept. 10, 1967 and recovered about 1080 miles to the west at Gering, Nebraska in Oct., 1969.

**MEASUREMENTS:**
Length: 6.4 to 7.7 ins. (Godfrey, 1966: 298)
Wingspread: 10.5 to 13.0 ins. (Roberts, 1955: 653)
Weight: 3 ♂ averaged 30.3 g. 2 ♀ averaged 27.6 g. (Hope, 1938: 33).

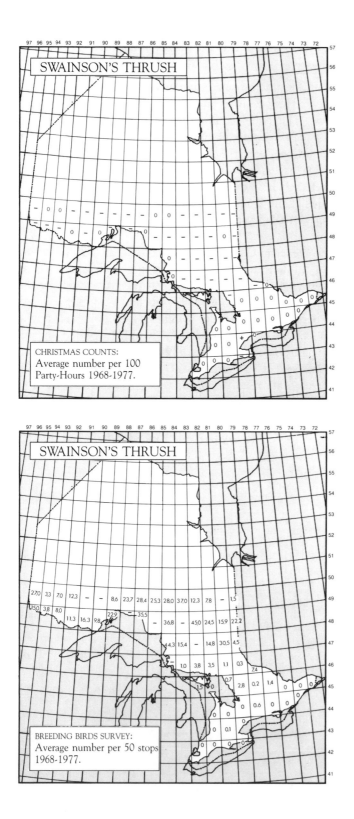

SWAINSON'S THRUSH

CHRISTMAS COUNTS:
Average number per 100
Party-Hours 1968-1977.

SWAINSON'S THRUSH

BREEDING BIRDS SURVEY:
Average number per 50 stops
1968-1977.

# HERMIT THRUSH   *Catharus guttatus*   (Pallas)

This is Canada's finest bird songster: from the rocky, pine-clad hills of northern Ontario, pure unhurried melody pours forth, evoking an almost religious feeling of ecstacy, at least in this listener. The Hermit Thrush is usually the first of our forest-dwelling thrushes to appear in spring and the last to leave in the fall: a few even linger into the winter though most go south to winter in the southern U.S.A.

IDENTIFICATION:   Of our brown-backed thrushes this is the one with the rufous tail, which it habitually raises as it perches near the forest floor. In migration the note usually heard is a soft "prrt". On its breeding grounds it may give an angry "meee" if disturbed near its nest. Its song begins with a single prolonged theme note, followed by a short note about a fifth higher on the piano scale, then a series of bell-like or flute-like rolling phrases. Each succeeding song tends to begin on a different theme note, sometimes higher, sometimes lower than the previous song. Although the pre-dawn period is favoured for singing, some birds may sing all day long.

WINTER:   On the 1968-1977 Christmas counts they were fairly common at Pelee, uncommon at Long Point, and rare elsewhere north to Barrie and Ottawa. Stirrett (1973a: 18) had records throughout the winter months at Pelee with a maximum of 15 on Feb. 26. Brooman (1954: 30) mentioned Elgin Co. records on Dec. 13, 1878, Dec. 10, 1890 and Dec. 26, 1952. Beardslee & Mitchell (1965: 340-341) had a Dec. 2, 1944 observation at Point Abino, Lake Erie. Saunders (1947: 378) had only one Christmas count bird listed for Toronto, on the 1939 count, for the 1925-1945 period. We had individuals at our home during five winters: there have also been several other winter records for the Pickering-Oshawa region (Speirs, 1975: 41). Weir & Quilliam (1980: 38) gave a Jan. 25 record for Kingston and Quilliam (1973: 141) cited three other winter records there.

SPRING:   Stirrett (1973b: 22) had maxima of 50 at Pelee on Apr. 16 and May 10, with his latest on May 21. Ussher (1965: 20) had Rondeau records from March 28 to May 1 with the average arrival on Apr. 11 and departure on May 6. Saunders & Dale (1933: 220) gave Apr. 6 as the 17-year average arrival date at London, with the earliest on March 26, 1925. Snyder (1931: 220) mentioned 8 Long Point lighthouse casualties between Apr. 17-21, 1930: he noted his last northbound bird on May 6, 1928. Beardslee & Mitchell (1965: 340-341) noted 15 at Point Abino, Lake Erie, on Apr. 25, 1961 and reported one as late as May 27, 1945 at Morgan's Point. Speirs (1938: 44) gave May 1 as the spring peak for Toronto. Saunders (1947: 370) had spring records at Toronto from Apr. 4 to May 26, with average arrival on Apr. 15 and departure on May 12. Speirs (1975: 41) had spring records for Pickering from March 23 to May 14, with a peak about Apr. 25. Snyder (1941: 73) noted his latest in Prince Edward Co. on May 23, 1930. Weir & Quilliam (1980: 38) listed Apr. 15 and May 15 as average arrival and departure dates for Kingston, with the earliest on March 27. Devitt (1967: 122) gave Apr. 27 as the 12-year average arrival date at Barrie, with the earliest on Apr. 7, 1921 at Collingwood. L. Beamer's median arrival date at Meaford was Apr. 12, with the earliest on Apr. 1, 1938. Mills (1981: 117) gave Apr. 15 as the 12-year average arrival date at Huntsville, with the earliest on March 28, 1961: the earliest clutch of eggs was found on May 17. Nicholson (1981: 146) gave Apr. 16 as the 8-year average arrival date for Manitoulin, with the earliest on March 27, 1976: D.B. Ferguson found a nest with 4 eggs on May 14, 1977 at

Kagawong (this also held 2 cowbird eggs). Speirs & Speirs (1947: 33) reported one singing and calling at North Bay airport on Apr. 10, 1945. Ricker & Clarke (1939: 17) found a nest with 4 eggs at Frank's Bay, Lake Nipissing, on May 31, 1933. Baillie & Hope (1947: 18) found a nest with 4 eggs at Chapleau on May 31, 1937 and F.A.E. Starr also found a nest with 4 eggs at Cartier on May 25, 1936. Skeel & Bondrup-Nielsen (1978: 194) heard them regularly from Apr. 23, 1977 at Pukaskwa. Denis (1961: 2) gave Apr. 24 as the average arrival date at Thunder Bay, with the earliest on Apr. 15, 1956. Dear (1940: 135) found a nest with 3 eggs in MacGregor Twp., Thunder Bay, on May 26, 1935. Elder (1979: 36) gave Apr. 25 as his earliest date for Geraldton. Peruniak (1971: 23) gave Apr. 22 as her earliest Atikokan record. J.A. Edwards took a set of 4 eggs at North Cobalt on May 21, 1919 (Baillie & Harrington, 1937: 231). Cringan (1953a: 3) saw his first at Sioux Lookout on May 4, 1953. Sam Waller collected two at Moose Factory on May 17, 1930 and Oliver Hewitt saw three on nearby Sandy Island on May 27, 1947 (Manning, 1952: 76-77).

SUMMER: On the 1968-1977 Breeding Bird Surveys they were common north and east of Lake Superior, fairly common elsewhere in northern Ontario, and rare south to Orillia and Avonmore. Saunders & Dale (1933: 220) mentioned singing birds in the Komoka Swamp in June, 1882. J.A. Edwards found a nest with 3 eggs and a cowbird egg on Thorah Is., on June 28, 1936, the only definite breeding record for Ontario Co., though birds have been heard singing in Uxbridge and Rama Twps. in June and July (Speirs, 1975: 41). Devitt (1967: 121-122) cited several nest records for Simcoe Co.: the young left one nest at Wasaga Beach on Aug. 15 from a nest with 4 eggs found on July 27, 1943. Mills (1981: 117) reported 15 nests found in the cottage country, one with eggs as late as July 14. MacLulich (1938: 28) caught a young bird in a mouse trap in Algonquin Park on July 16, 1933 and C.H.D. Clarke saw an adult feeding young at Brule Lake on July 4, 1934. Baillie & Hope (1947: 18) found two nests with 4 eggs each at Chapleau on June 4 and 6, 1937: they saw the first flying young at Biscotasing on June 30. Snyder (1942: 140) reported a nest with 4 eggs near Sault Ste. Marie on June 4, 1931 and another with 3 eggs on July 24, 1931 (perhaps a second brood). Skeel & Bondrup-Nielsen (1978: 194) noted 29 on 11 days from June 22 to July 28, 1977 in Pukaskwa. Baillie & Hope (1943: 17) found a nest with 3 newly-hatched young at Marathon on June 18, 1936 and collected a juvenile not long out of the nest at Amyot on July 3. Snyder (1928: 277) collected a male on July 7, 1923 at Macdiarmid and three others at Lake Nipigon in June and July, 1924. Dear (1940: 135) found a nest with 4 eggs at Thunder Bay on June 3, 1924. Snyder (1938: 201) collected two young at Off Lake, Rainy River, one on July 6 and the other on July 7, 1929. Snyder (1953: 74) reported the first young out of the nest at Wabigoon on June 19, 1937: he also had breeding evidence for Sioux Lookout. Baillie & Harrington (1937: 231) reported a nest with 4 eggs on July 1, 1931 at Minaki. Hope (1938: 32) found a nest with 4 eggs at Favourable Lake on June 5, 1938. Cringan (1953b: 4) noted two at Kasabonika Lake on June 1, 1953. Cringan (1950: 15) noted as many as 10 in a day at Nikip Lake during June, 1950. James, Nash & Peck (1982: 65) collected only one adult male along the Harricanaw River, near James Bay on June 27, 1982. Manning (1952: 79) collected a female at North Point, James Bay, on June 4, 1947. James, Nash & Peck (1981: 91) collected 4 adults and 2 young at Kiruna Lake, Sutton Ridges, in the summer of 1981. Schueler, Baldwin & Rising (1974: 143, 147) noted the species at Cochrane and Moosonee and collected a female with a brood patch at Hawley Lake on July 16, 1964. Lee (1978: 29) found the species on two of his three study plots at Big Trout Lake in the summer of 1975 and had a daily maximum of 4 there on June 26. C.E. Hope noted one during the summer of 1940 at Ft. Severn (James, McLaren & Barlow, 1976: 39).

AUTUMN: During their fall sojourn at Netitishi Point, James Bay, D. McRae and Alan Wormington saw only one, on Oct. 18, 1981. Peruniak (1971: 23) gave Oct. 12 as her latest Atikokan date. Skeel & Bondrup-Nielsen (1978: 194) saw three together at Pukaskwa on Sept. 18, 1977, their only fall date. Louise Lawrence observed one at Pimisi Bay until Oct. 14, 1944 (Speirs & Speirs, 1947: 33). Ron Tasker had one in Burpee Twp., Manitoulin, as late as Nov. 22, 1973 (Nicholson, 1981: 146). Mills (1981: 117) had a Huntsville record as late as Oct. 25, 1962. Frances Westman saw one at Barrie as late at Nov. 6, 1963 (Devitt, 1967: 122). Weir & Quilliam (1980: 38) listed Sept. 18 and Nov. 5 as average arrival and departure dates at Kingston. Speirs (1975: 41) cited fall records for Pickering as early as Aug. 14, 1964 and as late as Nov. 29, 1959, with a peak in mid-October. J.L. Baillie had fall records at Toronto from Sept. 10 to Nov. 10, with average arrival on Oct. 5 and departure on Oct. 22 (Saunders, 1947: 370). Speirs (1938: 52) had fall peaks at Toronto on Oct. 7 and Oct. 20. Snyder (1931: 221) had only one fall record for Long Point, a lighthouse casualty between Sept. 24-29, 1929. Ussher (1965: 20) had fall records at Rondeau from Sept. 16 to Nov. 30, with average arrival on Oct. 2 and departure on Nov. 9. Stirrett(1973d: 24) had his earliest returning migrant at Pelee on Sept. 6 and a maximum of 300 on Oct. 5.

**MEASUREMENTS:**
*Length:* 6.3 to 7.6 ins.
(Godfrey, 1966: 297)
*Wingspread:* 11 to 12 ins.
(Roberts, 1955: 652)
*Weight:* 2 ♂ averaged
29.8 g. 2 ♀ averaged
31.0 g. (Hope, 1938: 32).

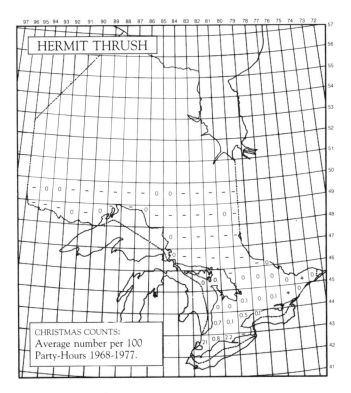

HERMIT THRUSH

CHRISTMAS COUNTS:
Average number per 100
Party-Hours 1968-1977.

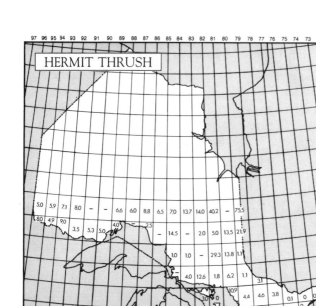

HERMIT THRUSH

BREEDING BIRDS SURVEY:
Average number per 50 stops
1968-1977.

# WOOD THRUSH   *Hylocichla mustelina*   (Gmelin)

The Wood Thrush is a bird of the deciduous forests in Ontario, going south to Central America in winter. You may find its nest of dead brown leaves in a crotch of a sapling, often in a shady ravine or an isolated woodlot in southern Ontario. It is one of our finest songsters.

**IDENTIFICATION:** The Wood Thrush is distinguished from our other brown-backed thrushes by the large, round, black dots on its white breast, by its reddish-brown crown and larger size. The somewhat similar Brown Thrasher has a much longer tail and is a bird of the forest edge, not the shady interior favoured by the Wood Thrush. The song of the Wood Thrush is usually introduced by a few yodelled notes "Oudle-ee" followed by a very complex vibrato "churrr-eee" (sonograms show that the bird may simultaneously sing an upward slur, a downward slur with various harmonics). The common scold note is a lip-smacking "plat-plat-plat-plat".

**WINTER:**

**SPRING:** Stirrett (1973b: 22) gave Apr. 28 as the earliest Pelee bird, with a maximum of 50 on May 10. May 1 was the earliest Rondeau record, with the 24-year average arrival date on May 7 (Ussher, 1965: 20). Saunders & Dale (1933: 220) gave May 9 as the 16-year average arrival date at London, with the earliest on May 3, 1913: one set of 3 eggs was found on May 18, 1901 and a set of 4 on May 31, 1906. Harold Lancaster's average arrival date in Elgin Co. was on May 9 (Brooman, 1954: 30). J.L. Baillie found one at Toronto as early as Apr. 30 but gave May 12 as his 18-year average arrival date (Saunders, 1947: 370). Speirs (1938: 44) listed May 27 as the spring peak at Toronto. Tozer & Richards (1974: 219) had an Oshawa bird as early as Apr. 29, 1956. Speirs (1975: 40) gave May 17 as the peak date at Pickering. Weir & Quilliam (1980: 38) listed May 8 as the 30-year average arrival date for Kingston, with the earliest on Apr. 27. W.J. Miller found a nest with 3 eggs at Gananoque as early as May 18, 1925 (Quilliam, 1973: 140). Devitt (1967: 121) gave May 13 as the 22-year average arrival date at Barrie, with the earliest on Apr. 30, 1938, while H.P. Bingham found completed sets of eggs near Barrie as early as May 29, 1927. Lloyd (1924: 16) considered the Wood Thrush rare at Ottawa but mentioned a specimen taken on May 14, 1889. L. Beamer's median arrival date at Meaford was May 15, with the earliest on May 3, 1953. Mills (1981: 116) gave May 13 as a 6-year average arrival date at Kearney: Jim Goltz found one at Bala on May 7, 1972. Nicholson (1981: 146) mentioned May 17 as the 10-year average arrival date on Manitoulin, with the earliest on May 8, 1979 and a maximum count of 12 on May 13, 1978. MacLulich (1938: 27) gave May 19, 1932 as an arrival date in Algonquin Park. Louise Lawrence heard one singing at Pimisi Bay on May 27, 1948 (Speirs & Speirs, 1947: 32). I heard one singing at the Dorion Fish Hatchery on May 25, 1957 and again on May 28, my most northerly personal record.

SUMMER: On the 1968-1977 Breeding Bird Surveys, they were common in the Dorset-Mattawa-Port Carling triangle, fairly common but widely distributed from there southwards, and with outliers north to Haileybury, Wawa and Dryden; absent on the more northerly routes. Stirrett (1973c: 19) reported a June 28 nest at Pelee. Saunders & Dale (1933: 220) reported a set of 3 eggs on June 14, 1905, a set of 4 eggs on June 7, 1912 and a set of 4, plus one cowbird egg, on June 2, 1915. We found this to be the most abundant species on our Springwater Park quadrat in 1970, with 22 territories per 100 acres: we found three nests there in May, one with 3 eggs plus 2 cowbird eggs on May 27, another the same day too high to examine the contents and another the next day with 2 eggs and 3 cowbird eggs. Beardslee & Mitchell (1965: 339) reported a nest with one young at Rose Hill, near Ft. Erie, on June 3, 1955. Chas. Christy found a nest with 4 eggs near Oshawa on June 3, 1957 (Tozer & Richards, 1974: 219). Speirs (1975: 40) cited details of nests found in Pickering, Reach and Scott Twps. and heard one singing as late as Aug. 4, 1957. Speirs & Orenstein (1975: 12) found populations in most Ontario Co. quadrats, with the highest density of 29 birds per 100 acres in the Rama one. Tozer & Richards (1974: 219) found a nest with two large young in Cartwright Twp. on June 15, 1968. Elizabeth Hughes found one on a nest near Kingston on June 21, 1966 (Quilliam, 1973: 140). Devitt (1967: 121) cited several June nest records for Simcoe Co., with one set of 2 eggs at Wasaga Beach taken by Paul Harrington as late as July 13, 1914. L. Beamer reported a nest with 4 eggs found at Meaford on June 9, 1947: the first egg hatched on June 10 and all four by June 11. Mills (1981: 116) found a nest with 3 young at Ahmic Lake about 15 ft. up in a cedar. Ron Tasker found a nest with 4 eggs in Burpee Twp., Manitoulin, on July 3, 1979 (Nicholson, 1981: 146). C.H.D. Clarke saw adults feeding young at Brule Lake, Algonquin Park, on July 4, 1934 (MacLulich, 1938: 28). Gerry Bennett on a trip north in late June, 1974, noted outliers east of Wawa and north of Rainy River (Goodwin, 1974: 898).

AUTUMN: Nicholson (1981: 146) reported 33 killed at the microwave tower on Great

Duck Is. between Sept. 19-23, 1977. Mills (1981: 117) saw his latest cottage country bird at Ahmic Lake on Sept. 26, 1976. The latest Simcoe Co. bird was seen at Wasaga Beach on Oct. 9, 1933 (Devitt, 1967: 121). Weir & Quilliam (1980: 38) listed Oct. 2 as the 19-year average departure date from Kingston, with the latest on Nov. 7. Speirs (1975: 40) gave Oct. 6 as the latest Pickering date. D. Scovell saw a very late bird on Nov. 14, 1975 in Scarborough (Goodwin, 1976: 63). Speirs (1938: 52, 54) gave Sept. 26 as the fall peak at Toronto, with the latest on Oct. 4. Snyder (1931: 219) had only one Long Point record, one that struck the lighthouse on Sept. 26. Ussher (1965: 20) gave Sept. 16 as a 6-year average departure date from Rondeau, with the latest on Oct. 26. Stirrett (1973d: 24) had a fall maximum of 8 at Pelee on Sept. 1 with his latest on Nov. 8.

BANDING: Gordon Lambert mist netted and banded one at Scarborough, Ont. on Aug. 10, 1965 that was recovered at Chicago, Ill. on Sept. 29, 1965 (seven weeks later and about 441 miles to the west): another banded at Long Point on May 12, 1966 turned up near Frankford, Ont. about 184 miles to the NE on May 16, 1969.

**MEASUREMENTS:**
*Length:* 7.5 to 8.5 ins.
(Godfrey, 1966: 296)
*Wingspread:* 13 to 14 ins.
(Roberts, 1955: 652)
*Weight:* 10 Ontario
specimens averaged
49.7 g.

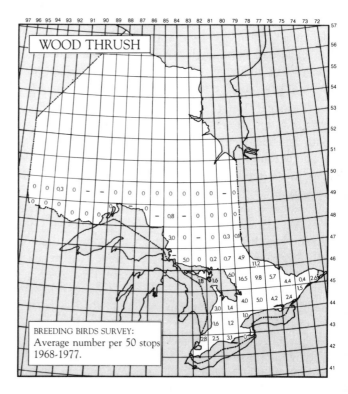

WOOD THRUSH

BREEDING BIRDS SURVEY:
Average number per 50 stops
1968-1977.

# EURASIAN BLACKBIRD   *Turdus merula*   Linnaeus

The Eurasian Blackbird is the Old World counterpart of our American Robin, a big thrush found in parks and gardens in close association with people: accidental in Ontario.

**IDENTIFICATION:** This is a bird about the size of our American Robin, with very similar habits, but jet black except for the yellow bill and eye ring.

**WINTER:**

**SPRING:** K.J. Burk found one at Erieau, Lake Erie, on Apr. 12, 1981. Most observations of this bird are of escaped cage birds, but this one showed no evidence of cage wear. Roy Ivor, who kept many birds in captivity at his Erindale home had one mated to an albino American Robin, an unusual pair.

**SUMMER:**

**AUTUMN:**

**MEASUREMENTS:**
*Length:*
*Wingspread:*
*Weight:*

# FIELDFARE   *Turdus pilaris*   Linnaeus

This is a bird of northern climes from Greenland east to Siberia, accidental in Ontario: so rare anywhere in North America that the one that wintered near Toronto attracted hordes of bird watchers, some from as far away as California.

IDENTIFICATION:   This is a big thrush, about the size of an American Robin, with a gray head and rump, contrasting with blackish tail and chestnut back. The breast and throat are buffy, belly white and sides heavily streaked with black.

WINTER:   One identified by Barry Kent MacKay turned up in a western suburb of Toronto on Jan. 1, 1981, and was observed eating mountain ash (rowan) berries for at least two months thereafter by many observers (Goodwin, 1981: 297). MacKenzie (1968: 51) gave a good description of one that he saw in Rockcliffe Park, Ottawa, on Jan. 8, 1967.

SPRING:   One was captured, photographed, banded and released at Long Point on May 24, 1975, by M. Porter *et al* (Goodwin, 1975: 846).

SUMMER:

AUTUMN:

**MEASUREMENTS:**
*Length:* 9.5 to 10.5 ins.
(Godfrey, 1966: 296)
*Wingspread:*
*Weight:* 89.4 g. (the Long Point bird - *fide* Erica Dunn).

**REFERENCES:**
Hussell, D.J.T. 1975 First Fieldfare banded in North America. Nature Canada, 4: (4): 27.
  Hussel, David J.T. and Michael J. Porter 1977 Fieldfare in Ontario. Can. Field-Naturalist, 91: (1): 91-92. Includes black and white reproduction of colour photograph by Isabel Smaller, first identification by Porter from call note, taken from mist net by Alex Steele, taken to mainland where it was measured, weighed and examined by Hussell, Bradstreet, Erica Dunn, G.W. Miller, Jim & Pat Woodford before release.
  MacKenzie, H.N. (Hue) 1968 A possible Fieldfare observation near Ottawa, Ontario. Can. Field-Nat., 82: (1): 51.

# AMERICAN ROBIN   *Turdus migratorius*   Linnaeus

The American Robin is probably our best known Ontario bird, the harbinger of spring to most people (though many spend the winter with us where fruits remain on the trees). It is a great consumer of worms and insects in our gardens during the summer and it nests on our houses and in trees and shrubs nearby. We tend to think of robins as strongly territorial birds, intolerant of other robins in their chosen acre, but every night the males go off to a chosen roost where hundreds may gather to spend the night in close proximity. In the southern U.S.A. where most of our robins go for the winter, such roosts may contain over a million birds, males and females, young and old. Here they are highly social birds, going about in great flocks, but shy of people. They may be driven far south by outbursts of polar air or come part way north again when the tropical air prevails. In spite of much study there are still many things to learn about robins, e.g. nobody seems to know in any detail how long the young retain their spotted plumage!

IDENTIFICATION: Adults have reddish breasts, slaty backs, blackish heads, prominent white eye rings, a white throat with blackish stripes and white spots terminating the outer tail feathers. Males generally have darker rufous breasts than females, but some (older?) females are as richly coloured as males. The young have a spotted plumage, like other young thrushes. The well known carolling song does not seem to have much territorial significance (it is often heard at roosts and out of the breeding season): the territorial song is a high-pitched "whisper song" and the "peep-toop-toop" given from roof top and tree tops when the birds arrive in spring may be territorial. A loud "teep-teep-teep" announces the presence of cats and other potential predators and a lisping "tsi-ip" precedes flight.

WINTER: On the 1968-1977 Christmas counts they were fairly common near Toronto, Pelee and Thunder Bay, uncommon elsewhere north to Ottawa, Meaford and Marathon, and rare to absent elsewhere in Ontario. The winter population north of Lake Superior depends on the crop of mountain ash fruits (Elder, 1979: 36). Stirrett (1973a: 18) had several estimates of 100 at Pelee during the winter months. W.H. Lunn noted single birds in Prince Edward Co. on Dec. 11, 1934 and Dec. 18, 1938 (Snyder, 1941: 73). Lloyd (1924: 16) cited several winter records for Ottawa. L. Beamer reported his first bird of the year at Meaford 8 times in January and 5 times in February. Mills (1981: 116) cited several winter records for the cottage country, one as late as Feb. 21, 1974. Nicholson (1981: 146) gave several winter records for Manitoulin, but Chris Bell noted the only one in February on Feb. 23, 1980. Dennison (1980: 147) listed them on 9 of 25 Christmas counts at Sault Ste. Marie. W. Wyett noted 2 at Pukaskwa on Jan. 23, 1974 (Skeel & Bondrup-Nielsen, 1978: 193).

SPRING: Stirrett (1973b: 22) had a spring maximum of 300 at Pelee on March 16. Ussher (1965: 20) gave March 11 as his 23-year average arrival date at Rondeau. Saunders & Dale (1933: 219) gave March 9 as the 17-year average arrival date at London: his earliest set of 4 eggs was found on Apr. 28, 1905: A.A. Wood reported two albinos hatched from the same nest during the spring of 1915. Brooman (1954: 29) followed a nesting at St. Thomas, begun on May 4; the young hatched on May 23 and left on June 4, 1946. McCracken, Bradstreet & Holroyd (1981: 60) mentioned Apr. 17 as the earliest of 20 nests with eggs found on Long Point: two broods and rarely three, may be raised in a season there. Speirs (1938: 44) gave Apr. 9 as the spring peak at Toronto, while Saunders

(1947: 370) listed March 18 as his 13-year average arrival date. Returning migrants at Pickering have arrived as early as the last week of February (1951 and 1961) or as late as the last week of March (1958, 1960 and 1970), depending on the weather (Speirs, 1975: 38). Charles Fothergill noted one at Rice Lake on March 1, 1822 (Black, 1934: 152). Weir & Quilliam (1980: 38) listed March 9 as the 32-year average arrival date at Kingston: C.K. Clarke found a nest with 4 eggs there as early as Apr. 28, 1897 and Owen Woods found two young hatched by May 8, 1962 (Quilliam, 1973: 140). Devitt (1967: 121) gave March 18 as the 17-year average arrival date for Barrie: W.W. Smith found a nest with 4 eggs at Big Cedar Point on Apr. 15, 1945 and well-feathered young were noted by May 9, 1945. For years with non-wintering birds, L. Beamer had a median for returning birds on March 12, at Meaford. Mills (1981: 115) gave March 20 as the 14-year average arrival date at Huntsville, with the earliest on March 7, 1973. Nicholson (1981: 145) gave March 17 as the 10-year average arrival date on Manitoulin, with the earliest on March 3, 1973 and a high count of 800 flying north at Mississagi Light on Apr. 18, 1976. MacLulich (1938: 27) gave March 20, 1913 as his earliest arrival date for Algonquin Park. Louise Lawrence observed two at Pimisi Bay as early as March 18, 1945 and on Apr. 11, 1945 we watched a female relining a 1944 nest in North Bay (Speirs & Speirs, 1947: 32). Ricker & Clarke (1939: 16) noted migrating flocks at Lake Nipissing as late as mid-May. Skeel & Bondrup-Nielsen (1978: 193) saw their first at Pukaskwa on Apr. 15, 1977 and had a maximum of 10 there on Apr. 23. Baillie & Hope (1943: 17) found two nests at Rossport on May 30, 1936: one with 2 eggs and one with 4. Denis (1961: 2) gave Apr. 4 as the average arrival date at Thunder Bay, with the earliest on March 11, 1946: Dear (1940: 135) found a nest with 3 eggs there as early as May 7, 1933. Peruniak (1971: 23) gave Apr. 8 as her earliest at Atikokan but David Elder saw one there on Apr. 2, 1981. Bondrup-Nielsen (1976: 44) saw his first near Kapuskasing on Apr. 20, 1974. Elder (1979: 36) gave Apr. 9 as his earliest Geraldton date. Wm. Dennis noted one at Sioux Lookout on Apr. 15, 1953 (Cringan, 1953a: 3).

SUMMER: On the 1968-1977 Breeding Bird Surveys they were common on all Ontario routes. Stirrett (1973c: 19) estimated 130 at Pelee on June 30. R.C. Long has been making special studies of robins and found a nest with 3 young at late as Aug. 22, 1965 at Pickering Beach. Population densities in quadrats in Ontario Co. varied from 0 to 20 per 100 acres in fields, 0 to 50 per 100 acres in forests and 18 to 222 per 100 acres in urban areas: it was outranked only by Starling and House Sparrow in abundance but only by the Starling in ecological impact: of 291 sets of eggs in Ontario Co. most held 3 or 4 eggs, but one as many as 7 (Speirs, 1975: 38). Allin (1940: 103) found a nest with 5 eggs in Darlington Twp. as late as Aug. 7, 1930. Paul Harrington saw one still incubating on Aug. 25, 1943 at Wasaga Beach (Devitt, 1967: 120). James (1979: 16) found this to be the most common breeding bird in Jack pine forests in western Parry Sound Dist. in 1978, averaging 8.5 males per 10 hectares. Snyder (1928: 33) found a nest with 3 eggs at Lake Abitibi on June 13, 1925. James (1980: 88) saw an adult feeding a stubby-tailed young at Pickle Lake on June 17, 1977. Hope (1938: 32) found a nest with 3 eggs at Favourable Lake on June 1, 1938. Cringan (1953b: 4) saw from 2 to 10 on five days during the summer of 1953 at Kasabonika Lake. Cringan (1950: 15) saw them regularly into August at Nikip Lake in 1950. James, Nash & Peck (1982: 65) found several nests along the Harricanaw River near James Bay, including a nest with 3 young on June 29 and a nest with 4 eggs on July 4, 1982. Manning (1952: 76) saw 28 in 6 hours on June 30 and July 1, 1949 at Moosonee; 2 in 5 hours at Attawapiskat on July 5, 1947; 13 in 20 hours at Raft River from July 8-

12, 1947 and 12 in 11 hours at Shagamu River on Aug. 10, 1947 where he collected 5 young: he also found a nest with 4 eggs on June 29, 1949 at Sandy Is., near Moosonee. James, Nash & Peck (1981: 91) found two nests with eggs and one nest with young at Kiruna Lake, Sutton Ridges, in summer of 1981. Schueler, Baldwin & Rising (1974: 143, 146) reported them to be common at Attawapiskat, and cited nesting evidence for Cochrane, Moosonee, Hawley Lake and Winisk. Peck (1972: 345) had sightings at Cape Henrietta Maria and cited other records but no nests there. Lee (1978: 29) saw 8 young at Big Trout Lake on July 29, 1975: he saw adults carrying food to nests and had a maximum of 15 on July 28: he suggested that two broods were attempted, even that far north. C.E. Hope saw from one to 10 almost daily at Ft. Severn in the summer of 1940.

AUTUMN: D. McRae and A. Wormington saw robins regularly through October at Netitishi Point, James Bay, with the latest on Nov. 2, 1981. Peruniak (1971: 23) gave Nov. 14 as her latest Atikokan date. Louise Lawrence saw two at Bonfield as late as Oct. 29, 1944 (Speirs & Speirs, 1947: 32), while Ricker & Clarke (1939: 16) saw migrating flocks at Lake Nipissing to Oct. 31, 1925. Mark Robinson saw one in Algonquin Park as late as Nov. 5, 1908 (MacLulich, 1938: 27). Nicholson (1981: 146) reported a high count of 250 for Manitoulin on Oct. 12, 1970. Weir & Quilliam (1980: 38) listed Nov. 3 as the 28-year average departure date from Kingston. Speirs (1938: 52) gave Sept. 9 as the fall peak at Toronto, while Saunders (1947: 370) listed Nov. 27 as his 13-year average departure date. Ussher (1965: 20) gave Nov. 14 as his 11-year average departure date from Rondeau. Stirrett (1973d: 24) had a fall maximum of 1000 at Pelee on Nov. 1.

BANDING: Banding studies have shown that over 90% of all eastern robins winter in the Gulf States, north to Tennessee and the Carolinas: most Ontario robins go south to Florida, Georgia, Alabama and Mississippi (Brewer & Salvadori, 1978: 71-73). Earlier winter recoveries include one banded by H.H. Southam on Apr. 28, 1939 near Toronto, recovered in South Carolina on Feb. 24, 1940 and another by him banded on Sept. 18, 1944 recovered in Florida in Jan., 1946; one banded by Gordon Lambert on May 10, 1951 was recovered in Georgia in Feb., 1954. Frank Lovesy banded two near Toronto; one on Aug. 3, 1959 went to Alabama on Jan. 24, 1960; the other banded on Sept. 1, 1962 went to North Carolina on Feb. 13, 1963. Gary Page banded one near Toronto on June 10, 1962 recovered in Georgia in January, 1964. Two others banded near Toronto by banders now inactive, one on June 25, 1957 was taken in South Carolina on Jan. 18, 1959, the other banded on Oct. 13, 1960 went to Mississippi by Jan. 21, 1963. An interesting longevity record is given by Brewer & Salvadori (1978: 73): one banded near Thorold, Ont. on July 19, 1956 was recovered at Don Mills, Ont. on May 24, 1969 (about 13 years later). Speirs (1946: 268) included a recovery at Lake Pontchartrain, La. on Dec. 21, 1934 of a bird banded by M.C. Baker at Kingston on July 22, 1934.

**MEASUREMENTS:**
Length: 9.0 to 10.8 ins.
(Godfrey, 1966: 294)
Wingspread: 14.8 to 16.5
ins. (Roberts, 1955: 653)
Weight: 40 Ontario
specimens averaged
80.2 g.

638

**REFERENCES:**

Burton, Donald E. 1963 Nestling Robin fed Red-bellied Snake. Ont. Field Biologist, No. 17: 34-35.

Putnam, William 1961 Starling feeds nestling Robins. Can. Field-Nat., 75:(1): 52-53.

Speirs, John Murray 1946 Local and migratory movements of the American Robin in eastern North America. Univ. of Illinois, Ph D Thesis: 1-342.

Speirs, J. Murray 1953 Winter distribution of Robins east of the Rocky Mountains. Wilson Bull. 65: (3): 175-183.

Speirs, J. Murray 1956 The migratory phase of Robin behaviour. Fed. Ont. Naturalists, Bull. 72: 20-27.

Speirs, J. Murray 1957 Robin roosts. Fed. Ont. Naturalists, Bull. 76: 18-23.

Taylor, Robert R. 1959 Robin nesting in tree cavity. Ont. Field Biologist, No. 13: 34.

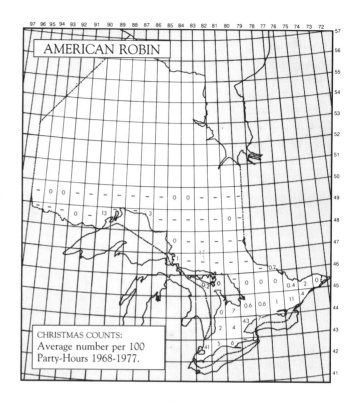

AMERICAN ROBIN

CHRISTMAS COUNTS: Average number per 100 Party-Hours 1968-1977.

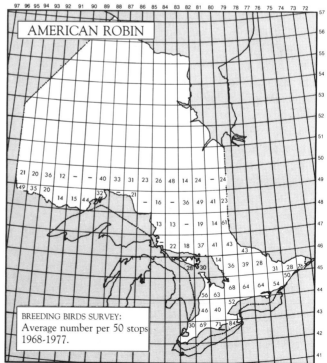

AMERICAN ROBIN

BREEDING BIRDS SURVEY: Average number per 50 stops 1968-1977.

# VARIED THRUSH   *Ixoreus naevius*   (Gmelin)

This is normally a bird of the western mountains and valleys. None were reported in Ontario until December, 1962, but in recent years a few have shown up almost every winter, usually at feeders. Our neighbour, Dagmar Borchert, kept her visitors happy during two winters on a diet of peanut butter sandwiches!

IDENTIFICATION:   Varied Thrushes superficially resemble American Robins, but have orange underparts including the throat, orange wing patches, an orange line over the eye and surrounding the dark ear patches and a black bar crossing the upper breast. I have not heard its song in Ontario but in B.C. it struck me as very appropriate for its wilderness setting: the two notes resemble the two introductory notes of the Hermit Thrush, changing pitch from one utterance to the next, but having the buzzy quality of a tanager song: "zurr-zreee...zarr-zrii....."

WINTER:   On the 1968-1977 Christmas counts, individuals were noted at Hamilton, Pickering, Sault Ste. Marie and Thunder Bay. H. Vibert observed one at Rosslyn, Essex Co., from Dec. 15-28, 1971 (Goodwin, 1972: 599). Kelley (1978: 61) reported one seen by R.D. Ussher *et al* from Jan. 23, 1965 (the third Ontario record): another was seen at Sarnia during the winter of 1968-1969. Weir (1982: 291) reported two Elgin Co. birds: a male at Wallacetown on Jan. 4, 1982 by R. Pokraka *et al* and a more dull plumaged bird at Port Burwell on Feb. 1, 1982 seen by D. Axford *et al*. The first for the Toronto region and second for Ontario was found by Ronald Tasker at Maple on Dec. 25, 1963 and collected for the ROM by D.H. Baldwin on Jan. 7, 1964 (Baillie, 1964: 7). Speirs (1975: 39) cited details of one at Henry Lowndes feeder in Pickering Twp. on Dec. 28, 1968 and from Dec. 23,1969 into spring, 1970: another showed up at C. Bowden's feeder in Pickering Twp. on Feb. 14, 1970 that Doris and I saw there on Feb. 17. I saw the bird (or birds) at Dagmar Borchert's Pickering feeder on Feb. 13, 1979 and on Dec. 15 and 28, 1980. The first Ontario record was one photographed at Mrs. E.E. Valentine's feeder at Norland from late December, 1962 (Baillie, 1964: 7). The first near Ottawa showed up at Braeside, Renfew Co., on Jan. 26, 1972, seen by M. Runtz, R.A. Foxall, *et al* (Goodwin, 1972: 599). There have been several recent Ottawa reports. Goodwin (1981: 297) reported sightings during the 1980-1981 winter at Buckhorn, by W. & E. Smith; at Parry Sound by H. & M. Burgess and at Sturgeon Falls, *fide* J. Nicholson. Helen Atkinson observed one at Hurkett on Dec. 14, 1978 (Goodwin, 1979: 278).

SPRING:   The 1965 Rondeau bird lingered until March 24 (Kelley, 1978: 61). Arnold Dawe saw one at Nobleton as late as Apr. 12, 1978 (Goodwin, 1978: 1000). T.R. Scovell saw one near Toronto to Apr. 7, 1981 and R. Gairdner noted one at Cheltenham on May 13 and 14, 1981 (Goodwin, 1981: 819). V. Trojek saw the bird at the Lowndes feeder, Pickering, as late as March 8, 1970 (Speirs, 1975: 39). Douglas Sadler obtained colour photographs of the first Ontario bird at Norland on March 16, 1963 (Baillie, 1964: 7). R.A. Foxall noted one at Ottawa to mid-March, 1980 (Goodwin, 1980: 772).

SUMMER:

AUTUMN:   I. Park noted one at Crozier, near Ft. Frances, as early as Oct. 8, 1974 (Goodwin, 1975: 52). Peruniak (1971: 23) noted an immature at Atikokan on Sept. 26, 1965, her only record. One was found at Thunder Bay on Nov. 12, 1974 by J. Merrifield (*fide* K. Denis) (Goodwin, 1975: 52). Helen Atikinson saw her Hurkett bird as early as Nov. 20, 1978 (Goodwin, 1979: 174). W.J. Clarke *et al* observed one at Ottawa from Nov. 14, 1977 (Goodwin, 1978: 199).

**MEASUREMENTS:**
*Length:* 9 to 10 ins.
(Godfrey, 1966: 296)
*Wingspread:*
*Weight:* 50 averaged
78.4 g. (Dunning,
1984: 19).

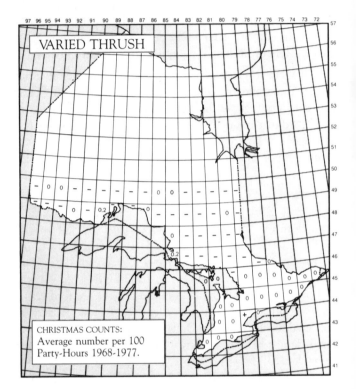

VARIED THRUSH

CHRISTMAS COUNTS:
Average number per 100
Party-Hours 1968-1977.

# GRAY CATBIRD *Dumetella carolinensis* (Linnaeus)

This is a familiar bird about suburban hedges in southern Ontario, rare in northern Ontario. A few sometimes winter in the southern parts of Ontario but most go south to southern U.S.A. and Central America.

**IDENTIFICATION:** Slightly smaller than the American Robin, the Gray Catbird is all gray except for rufous undertail coverts and a black cap. Its call is a catlike "meuw" and its song a muscial medley with few repeated phrases such as characterize the songs of the Brown Thrasher and Northern Mockingbird.

**WINTER:** On the 1968-1977 Christmas counts they were rare at Presqu'ile and from Toronto southwest to Pelee. Stirrett (1973a: 18) had five Pelee records of single birds from Dec. 27 to Jan. 3. Ussher (1965: 19) had a Dec. 5 record at Rondeau. Beardslee & Mitchell (1965: 336) reported wintering birds at Pt. Abino, Lake Erie, as late as Jan. 14, 1946 and Dec. 5, 1948: also one in Louth Twp. to Jan. 17, 1960. On Jan. 14, 1932, with A.L. Beldan, I saw one up the Don Valley in Toronto. There were Oshawa records on Dec. 23, 1967 and Feb. 7, 1969; also one at Frenchman Bay on Feb. 7, 1969 (Speirs, 1975: 36).

SPRING: Stirrett (1973b: 21) had his earliest returning bird at Pelee on Apr. 24 and his maximum of 200 on May 10. Ussher (1965: 19) had his earliest at Rondeau on Apr. 25 with the 23-year average arrival on May 3. Saunders & Dale (1933: 219) gave May 3 as the 17-year average arrival date at London, with the earliest on Apr. 24, 1921: a set of 5 eggs was found on May 25, 1901 and a set of 4 on May 31, 1915. C. Risley found two nests, both with young, at the base of Long Point as early as May 14, 1977 (McCracken, Bradstreet & Holroyd, 1981: 60). Snyder (1931: 216) noted his first on Long Point on May 6 in 1928. Beardslee & Mitchell (1965: 336) reported a nest with 3 eggs at Chippawa on May 20, 1904. Fleming (1907: 85) gave May 1, 1899 as his earliest Toronto record: Saunders (1947: 370) listed May 9 as his 13-year average arrival date and Speirs (1938: 44) gave May 20 as the spring peak there. Speirs (1975: 36) gave May 2 as the earliest Ontario Co. record but J.M. Richards found a nest with 5 eggs as early as May 3, 1958 near Oshawa: the spring peak is about May 18: I observed a Red Squirrel take two eggs from a nest with 3 eggs in a barberry bush at our Pickering home on May 18, 1964; the third egg vanished on May 22. J. Kamstra noted a very early bird on March 8, 1973 in Darlington Twp. (Tozer & Richards, 1974: 214) and A.E. Allin found a nest with one egg at Bowmanville Beach on May 30, 1940. Snyder (1941: 72) gave May 1, 1934 as his earliest Prince Edward Co. record, with the first complete set of eggs on May 25. Weir & Quilliam (1980: 37) listed May 4 as the 32-year average arrival date for Kingston, with the earliest on Apr. 22: E. Beaupré found a nest with 4 eggs as early as May 12, 1895 at nearby Portsmouth (Quilliam, 1973: 139). Devitt (1967: 119) gave May 3 as the 13-year average arrival date at Barrie, with the earliest on Apr. 11, 1954: H.P. Bingham found a nest with 4 eggs near Barrie on May 28, 1919. L. Beamer's median arrival date at Meaford was May 12, with the earliest on Apr. 25, 1942. Mills (1981: 113) gave May 14 as the average arrival date at Huntsville, the earliest on May 9, 1965. Nicholson (1981: 144) gave May 13 as the 11-year average arrival date on Manitoulin, the earliest on May 3, 1970 and a high count of 21 on May 20, 1977. MacLulich (1938: 27) had arrival dates in Algonquin Park from May 18 (1932) to May 25 (in 1912 and 1934). Speirs & Speirs (1947: 32) noted one at North Bay on May 14, 1944. Skeel & Bondrup-Nielsen (1978: 193) saw one at Pukaskwa from May 17 to 19, 1977. Denis (1961: 4) listed May 26 as the average arrival date at Thunder Bay, with the earliest on May 21, 1955. Peruniak (1971: 22) gave May 7 as her earliest Atikokan record. Smith (1957: 176) reported one seen at Gogama by J. Coyne in late May, 1954 and another noted at Cochrane on May 21, 1950 by A.N. Boissonneau.

SUMMER: On the 1968-1977 Breeding Bird Surveys they were fairly common from Lake Erie and Lake Ontario north to North Bay and Manitoulin, uncommon to rare from there north to Larder Lake and Kenora, with none on most northern routes. Stirrett (1973c: 19) had a summer maximum of 20 on July 27 at Pelee. Saunders & Dale (1933: 219) found a set of 4 eggs on June 4, 1906 and a set of 4 on June 11, 1913: night singing was observed when the moon was full around June 9, 1914. McCracken, Bradstreet & Holroyd (1981: 60) gave details of six summer nests on Long Point, most with young, but two with eggs on June 17 and 18, 1980. Speirs (1975: 36) tabulated 31 sets of eggs found in Ontario Co., with a total of 106 eggs (5 of these were cowbird eggs): in quadrat studies in Ontario Co. they were most abundant in a thorn-apple plot in Pickering with 27 birds per 100 acres: they were also found in 8 of 10 urban plots with a maximum of 12 birds per 100 acres in Washago. Quilliam (1973: 138) found a second nesting with 3 eggs at Kingston on July 11, 1965: this held 3 young on July 21. Baillie & Harrington (1937: 228) found a nest with 4 eggs at Wasaga Beach as late as July 27, 1915. Mills (1981: 144) reported active nests in the cottage country from June 5 to July 7: he heard an adult mimic the call of an Olive-sided Flycatcher in June, 1976. D.B. Ferguson found a nest with 3 eggs at Providence Bay, Manitoulin, on June 26, 1976 (Nicholson, 1981: 114). C.H.D. Clarke saw young being fed at Brule Lake, Algonquin Park, on June 29, 1934 (MacLulich, 1938: 27). Ricker & Clarke (1939: 16) observed nest building at Frank's Bay, Lake Nipissing, on June 1, 1932. Baillie & Hope (1947: 18) collected young at Bigwood on July 16 and 27, 1937. Snyder (1942: 139) collected a female with incubation patch at Echo Bay, near Sault Ste. Marie, on July 15, 1931. Skeel & Bondrup-Nielsen (1978: 193) heard two birds singing in Pukaskwa, on June 27 and from July 5 to 11, 1977. Dear (1940: 135) had only one Thunder Bay record: a nest with young on July 3, 1939. Snyder (1938: 200) collected a nest with 3 eggs near Emo, Rainy River, on June 5, 1929. L. Paterson found a nest with 4 eggs at Kenora on July 20, 1932 (Baillie & Harrington, 1937: 227). William C. Baker and his wife saw one at Moose Factory on July 5, 1951 (Baillie, 1951: 287). Lee (1978: 28) noted one singing near the cemetery at Big Trout Lake seven times in six weeks during the summer of 1975.

AUTUMN: P.D. Pratt observed one at Moosonee on Sept. 26, 1981 (Goodwin, 1982: 174). Peruniak (1971: 22) gave Sept. 29 as her latest Atikokan record. Skeel & Bondrup-Nielsen (1978: 193) saw their latest at Pukaskwa on Oct. 2, 1977. Speirs & Speirs (1947: 32) observed one at North Bay on Sept. 26, 1944. Nicholson (1981: 144) saw one at Mississagi Light, Manitoulin, as late as Nov. 2, 1975. C. Harris found one at Go Home Bay as late as Oct. 3, 1976 (Mills, 1981: 114). Devitt (1967: 119) gave Oct. 9, 1939 as his latest record for Simcoe Co., at Collingwood. Weir & Quilliam (1980: 37) listed Oct. 5 as the 30-year average departure date from Kingston, with the latest on Nov. 18. Ron Tozer saw one in Oshawa as late as Nov. 8, 1963 (Speirs, 1975: 36). Speirs (1938: 52) listed Sept. 2 as the fall peak at Toronto: Saunders (1947: 370) gave Oct. 14 as his 13-year average departure date with the latest on Nov. 30. Beardslee & Mitchell (1965: 336) reported one at Erie Beach on Nov. 23, 1960. Ussher (1965: 19) gave Oct. 10 as the 10-year average departure date from Rondeau. Stirrett (1973d: 24) had fall maxima of 20 at Pelee on Sept. 22 and Oct 2, with the latest on Oct. 22.

BANDING: One banded by Harold Richards near Toronto on July 4, 1959, was recovered in Pennsylvania on May 14, 1964 (almost 5 years later). Another banded near Toronto on Aug. 10, 1962 was recovered near Long Point on Oct. 9, 1962. One banded at Bellona, N.Y. on Sept. 12, 1970 was recovered at Dean Lake, Algoma, about 384 miles N.W. on May 21, 1971 (Brewer & Salvadori, 1976: 84). Another banded at Bayville, N.C. on Oct. 6, 1968 was recovered at Agincourt, Ont., in June, 1970, about 375 miles NW (Brewer & Salvadori, 1978: 70).

**MEASUREMENTS:**
*Length:* 8.4 to 9.4 ins.
(Godfrey, 1966: 292)
*Wingspread:* 11 to 12 ins.
(Roberts, 1955: 651)
*Weight:* 1.37 to 1.50 oz.
(Roberts, 1955: 651) 24
Ontario specimens
averaged 38.5 g.

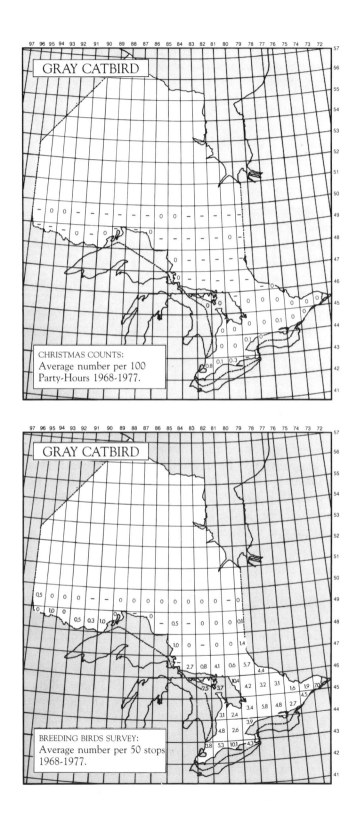

GRAY CATBIRD

CHRISTMAS COUNTS:
Average number per 100
Party-Hours 1968-1977.

GRAY CATBIRD

BREEDING BIRDS SURVEY:
Average number per 50 stops
1968-1977.

# NORTHERN MOCKINGBIRD
## Mimus polyglottos    (Linnaeus)

This is a common bird in much of the southern U.S.A. but it has been rare in Ontario (except around Niagara Falls and perhaps Pelee). It appears to be more common now than formerly and keeps turning up in most unexpected places. It occupies somewhat the same niche as the American Robin, eating insects and fruits and nesting about human habitations. Both are bold, aggressive birds. The mockingbird tends to outcompete the robin in southern U.S.A., with the reverse in more northerly climes.

IDENTIFICATION: This is a robin-sized bird, mostly gray with flashes of white in wings and edge of the tail and whitish underparts. It looks a bit like the shrikes but lacks their black masks. The song is a loud medley, with repeated phrases. Its scold note is a loud "tak" (like striking stones together).

WINTER: On the 1968-1977 Christmas counts it was fairly common at Niagara Falls, rare elsewhere north to Ottawa, Sault Ste. Marie and Thunder Bay. Stirrett (1973a: 18) had several December and January records of single birds at Pelee. A.A. Wood collected one at Duncrief on Jan. 6, 1921: another came to a London feeder in December, 1922 and disappeared in January, 1923 (Saunders & Dale, 1933: 218). Speirs (1931: 205) saw one at Toronto up to Dec. 1, 1927, and Fleming (1936: 340) had one coming for currant loaf at his Toronto home on Jan. 1, Feb. 12 and Feb. 13, 1936, when it died and became a female specimen in his collection. Speirs (1975: 35) gave details of three birds that wintered in the Whitby-Oshawa region between 1962 and 1972. Quilliam (1973: 138) mentioned one that spent from Jan. 7 to March 28 near Napanee. A.J. Mitchener saw one in Collingwood that frequented a feeder from Feb. 1-9, 1965 (Devitt, 1967: 119). K. May reported one in Huntsville in January, 1974 and birds wintered there in 1963-1964 and 1964-1965 (Mills, 1981: 113). Nicholson (1981: 143-144) had Manitoulin records on Dec. 17, 1972 and Dec. 16 and 25, 1973. Dennison (1980: 149) listed one on the Sault Ste. Marie Christmas count in 1970. Skeel & Bondrup-Nielsen (1978: 192) reported one wintering at Thunder Bay in 1976-1977.

SPRING: Stirrett (1973b: 21) gave Apr. 9 as his earliest spring record at Pelee, with several on May 10. Ross Anderson found one at Long Point on May 12, 1957 (Speirs, 1957: 30). Speirs (1938: 46) gave May 27 as the latest spring date for Toronto. Speirs (1975: 35) cited spring records from Pickering, East Whitby and Scugog Twps. from 1960 to 1974, one chasing an American Robin and another chased by one. Tozer & Richards (1974: 213) noted one in Darlington Twp. on May 15, 1968. Weir & Quilliam (1980: 37) listed May 3 as the 16-year average arrival date at Kingston. Devitt (1967: 119) cited three spring records for Simcoe Co.: May 24, 1941 at Big Cedar Point, May 16, 1959 in Conc. 4, Vespra Twp. and Apr. 24, 1963 near Barrie. Spencer (1957: 81) reported the first Ottawa record on May 16-17, 1956. The first report from the cottage country was at Go Home Bay on May 23, 1959 by G. Clark (Mills, 1981: 113). Nicholson (1981: 143) postulated a 10-year average arrival date for Manitoulin on May 8. Skeel & Bondrup-Nielsen (1978: 192-193) reported a May, 1977 sighting in Lake Superior Provincial Park and one at Pukaskwa on May 1, 1977: they also observed one in Marathon in May, 1977. On May 25, 1971 I was amazed to see one huddled up in a brush pile in Longlac during a cold northeasterly blow with wet snow. Elder (1979: 36) noted one at Geraldton on

May 30, 1969 and one at Middleton (east of Terrace Bay) on May 16, 1972. Peruniak (1971: 22) reported four at Atikokan on May 20, 1959 and one there on May 24, 1960. D.W. Simkin observed one at Sioux Lookout in spring, 1960 (De Vos, 1964: 491). Gunn (1958: 350-351) reported several birds in northern Ontario in spring of 1955: Paul Harrington saw one at Thor Lake, about 50 miles north of Sudbury on May 16; C.E. Garton noted one at Ft. William on May 24; and Donald and Bill Gunn saw individuals at Lillabelle Lake, Cochrane on May 21 and at Moosonee from May 26 to May 30.

SUMMER: On the 1968-1977 Breeding Bird Surveys, it was rare and scattered from Kingsville in the south to Hearst and Stratton in the north; absent on most routes. Kelley (1978: 60) reported nesting in Kent Co. and 3 well-grown young in a nest in Lambton Co. as late as July 29, 1973. John Frank and I saw one at the edge of our Pelee field quadrat on June 4, 1970 and Stirrett (1973c: 19) listed it as a nesting species there. Ussher (1965: 19) listed it as a rare breeder at Rondeau. J. Dwight Jr. saw one at Strathroy on July 1, 1880 (Saunders & Dale, 1933: 218). McCracken, Bradstreet & Holroyd (1981: 60) gave three nest records for Long Point: a nest with 4 eggs on June 16, 1966 which hatched June 22; a nest with 3 eggs on June 30, 1967 and a nest with 5 eggs on June 23, 1972 which hatched on June 25. Beardslee & Mitchell (1965: 335) gave details of a pair with two broods that nested about 3 miles west of Ft. Erie in 1961: the nest had 3 eggs on May 31 and June 11 and young on June 12 and three young of the second brood left on July 21. Donald Gunn and Don Perks found a nest with 4 eggs in Pickering Twp. on July 16, 1957 (Speirs, 1975: 35). Fred Cooke found a nest with 3 well-fledged young near Kingston on Aug. 13, 1966 (Quilliam, 1973: 138). M. Gold found a nest with 5 eggs at Novar on June 9, 1975: two young left this nest on July 27 (Mills, 1981: 113). Miles D. Pirnie found a nest with 4 eggs, one mile east of Spring Bay, Manitoulin, in the summer of 1955 (Nicholson, 1981: 143). Strickland, Tozer & Rutter (1982) wrote that at least one has turned up in Algonquin Park every year since 1967 and in 1975 a pair nested in Whitney. Allin & Dear (1949: 236) observed one about 5 miles west of Ft. William at the Mental Hospital on July 20, 1948. Elder (1979: 36) noted one at Geraldton on July 19, 1967. Sam Waller collected one at Moose Factory on June 4, 1928 (Manning, 1952: 75). Lee (1978: 28) observed one for five days (July 15-19, 1975) hopping about on the freshly cut grass of the cemetery at Big Trout Lake!

AUTUMN: Nicholson (1981: 143-144) had fall records on Manitoulin, on Sept. 30 and Nov. 30, 1972; Nov. 2, 1975 and Nov. 13-22, 1980. Hazel Petty found one at Wasi Falls, near Callander, on Sept. 6, 1973 and two were discovered in Huntsville on Nov. 1, 1963 (Mills, 1981: 113). M.G. Gould observed one repeatedly in Bowmanville from Oct. 20 to Nov. 12, 1921 (Allin, 1940: 103). Long (1968a: 15) reported one at Pickering Beach from Oct. 12 to Nov. 2, 1963. J.L. Baillie had a Toronto record as early as Sept. 16 (Saunders, 1947: 370). The first Toronto record was of one that I observed from Nov. 20 to Dec. 1, 1927 (Speirs, 1931: 205) and the second was noted from Nov. 8 and Nov. 25, 1935 (Fleming, 1936: 340). Sheppard (1960: 35) mentioned a record for Chippawa in November, 1959. Harold Lancaster found one in his garden in Elgin Co. on Nov. 2, 1948 (Brooman, 1954: 29). Stirrett (1973d: 24) had only one fall record at Pelee, on Sept. 16, 1911.

**MEASUREMENTS:**
*Length:* 9 to 11 ins.
(Godfrey, 1966: 292)
*Wingspread:* 13 to 15 ins.
(Roberts, 1955: 651)
*Weight:* 45.1 to 60.9 g.
(Terres, 1980: 612).

**REFERENCE:**
Spencer, Michael 1957 A
Mockingbird in Ottawa.
Can. Field-Naturalist,
71:(2): 81.

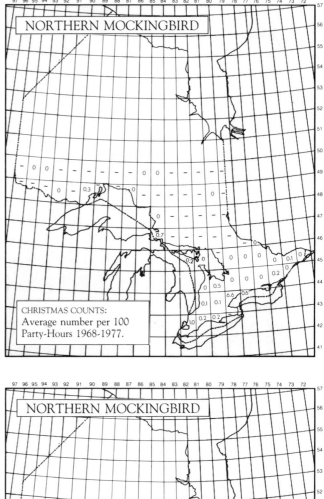

NORTHERN MOCKINGBIRD

CHRISTMAS COUNTS:
Average number per 100
Party-Hours 1968-1977.

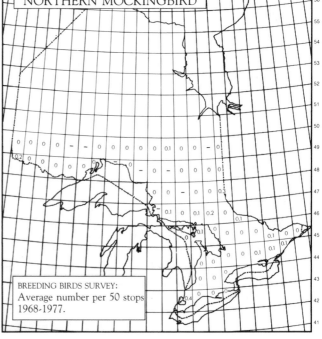

NORTHERN MOCKINGBIRD

BREEDING BIRDS SURVEY:
Average number per 50 stops
1968-1977.

# SAGE THRASHER   *Oreoscoptes montanus*   (Townsend)

This is a bird of the arid sagebrush country of western North America, accidental in Ontario.

IDENTIFICATION:   The Sage Thrasher looks like a small mockingbird, but with heavily steaked underparts, prominent white lines over the eyes, and with less white in the wings and tail.

WINTER:

SPRING:   One was discovered by Norman Chesterfield and photographed by Thomas Hayman at Pelee on May 12, 1965 (Baillie, 1965: 41). P.A. Woodliffe and many others observed one at Rondeau from Apr. 27 to May 16, 1981 (Goodwin, 1981: 819).

SUMMER:

AUTUMN:   J. Nicholson gave a good description of one he saw on Great Duck Is., Manitoulin, on Oct. 22, 1978 (Goodwin, 1979: 174). One was collected on Oct. 20, 1966 at Welland (Goodwin, 1967: 28).

**MEASUREMENTS:**
*Length:* 8 to 9 ins.
(Godfrey, 1966: 294)
*Wingspread:*
*Weight:* 14 ♂ averaged
41.1 g.; 8 ♀ averaged
45.5 g. (Dunning,
1984: 19).

# BROWN THRASHER   *Toxostoma rufum*   (Linnaeus)

Like the other mimids, the Brown Thrasher is a bird with a strong personality, shouting its couplets from the tree tops in spring, or slipping surreptitiously into your feeder when least expected, in winter. Our Illinois friends, the Satterthwaites, delighted in banding them and found that the eye colour changed from pale straw yellow to a fiery reddish orange as the birds aged. Most of our birds go to the southern U.S.A. to winter but a few may be found at feeders in southern Ontario.

IDENTIFICATION:   This is a long-tailed bird about the size of a Common Grackle, somewhat larger than an American Robin. It is a rich rufous brown above and with white underparts with bold streaking. The song is delivered in couplets: "Yes-yes-siree-siree, sirah, sirah, oh-oh——etc". The call note is an emphatic, smacking "tak".

WINTER:   On the 1968-1977 Christmas counts they were uncommon at Pelee, rare north to Barrie and Ottawa, with outliers at Deep River, Sault Ste. Marie and Thunder Bay. Stirrett (1973a: 18) had Pelee records of one or two birds throughout the winter. Ussher (1965: 19) had a Dec. 8 record at Rondeau. R.F. Andrle observed one at Niagara Falls, Ont., from Jan. 5 to Feb. 1, 1958 (Beardslee & Mitchell, 1965: 337). One came to our Pickering feeder from Jan. 1 to 28, 1960 and another spent the whole winter with us in 1972-1973: there have been several other winter records from Pickering to Oshawa (Speirs, 1975: 37). Quilliam (1973: 139) had Kingston records on Jan. 2 in 1965, 1966 and 1972. W.J. Jacklin saw one at his Midland feeder on Jan. 2, 1966 (Devitt, 1967: 120). One arrived at the feeder of P. Bailey in Huntsville on Dec. 26, 1967 and spent the winter there (Mills, 1981: 114). Nicholson (1981: 145) cited Manitoulin records during four winters. Dennison (1980: 148) noted one at Sault Ste. Marie on one of 25 Christmas counts there.

SPRING: Stirrett (1973b: 21) had his earliest spring bird at Pelee on Apr. 6 and a maximum of 30 on May 1. Ussher (1965: 19) gave Apr. 24 as his 24-year average arrival date at Rondeau, with the earliest on Apr. 13. Saunders & Dale (1933: 219) gave Apr. 17 as the 17-year average arrival date at London, with the earliest on Apr. 3, 1922: a set of 4 eggs was found as early as May 10, 1913 and a set of 5 was noted on May 25, 1901. Earl Lemon discovered a very early one in Elgin Co. on March 8, 1929 (Brooman, 1954: 29). H.H. Axtell saw one nest building near Ft. Erie on Apr. 29, 1961 and incubation was under way by May 4 (Beardslee & Mitchell, 1965: 337). Speirs (1938: 44) gave May 3 as the spring peak date at Toronto, where Saunders (1947: 370) listed Apr. 29 as his 12-year average arrival date. The peak of the spring migration at Pickering has been about May 14: W. Carrick found a nest in Uxbridge Twp. as early as Apr. 15, 1956, which held 2 eggs on May 1 (Speirs, 1975: 37). Weir & Quilliam (1980: 37) listed Apr. 22 as the 32-year average arrival date at Kingston, where Shirley Peruniak saw one as early as Apr. 9, 1969 (Quilliam, 1973: 139). Devitt (1967: 120) gave Apr. 25 as the 18-year average arrival date at Barrie: J.J. Baker found a nest with one egg at Big Cedar Point on May 17, 1936 and G. Holroyd found a nest with 4 eggs, 4 miles west of Loretto on May 28, 1966. L. Beamer's median arrival date at Meaford was May 6, with the earliest on Apr. 17, 1955. Mills (1981: 114) gave Apr. 26 as the 7-year average arrival date at Hunstville: C. Harris noted one as early as Apr. 18, 1976 at Go Home Bay, but one that had wintered at Huntsville broke into song on Apr. 11, 1968: of 7 nest records for the cottage country the earliest was on May 24. Nicholson (1981: 144) gave Apr. 29 as the 12-year average arrival date on Manitoulin, with the earliest on Apr. 21 in 1971 and 1974. MacLulich (1938: 27) gave May 7, 1912 as the earliest arrival date for Algonquin Park. Ricker & Clarke (1939: 16) had a Frank's Bay, Lake Nipissing, record as early as May 2, 1925. Skeel & Bondrup-Nielsen (1978: 193) saw just one live Brown Thrasher at Pukaskwa, on May 19, 1977, but picked up a dead one on an offshore island on May 25. Denis (1961: 4) listed May 18 as the average arrival date at Thunder Bay, with the earliest on May 9, 1955. Peruniak (1971: 23) gave May 5 as her earliest Atikokan date. In two years at Kapuskasing, Bondrup-Nielsen (1976: 44, 47) saw only one, on May 22, 1975.

SUMMER: On the 1968-1977 Breeding Bird Surveys, they were common around Kingston, fairly common on other southern Ontario routes, north to North Bay and Rainy River, uncommon west of Lake Superior and absent from most northeastern routes. Stirrett (1973c: 19) reported a maximum of 12 at Pelee on Aug. 22, with some nesting there. Saunders & Dale (1933: 219) found a nest with 4 eggs on June 21, 1901 near London and another nest with 4 eggs on June 8, 1912. McCracken, Bradstreet & Holroyd (1981: 60) gave details of 5 Long Point nests, 3 on the ground; one contained 4 young on June 1, 1974 and another had 3 young on July 3, 1965. Frank Lovesy found a late nest in Pickering on July 14, 1957 which still held 2 eggs on July 18: 29 Ontario Co. nests held a total of 100 eggs (9 of them cowbird eggs): the maximum population density of 16 birds per 100 acres was found in a hawthorn-apple quadrat in Pickering Twp. (Speirs, 1975: 37). Devitt (1967: 120) cited details of three Simcoe Co. nests in June. Lloyd (1924: 15) reported two Ottawa nests: one with 3 thrasher eggs and 1 cowbird egg on June 14, 1884 and another on June 16, 1898. The latest nest with eggs in the cottage country was found on July 7 (Mills, 1981: 114). D.B. Ferguson found a nest with 4 eggs at Providence Bay, Manitoulin, on June 12, 1976 (Nicholson, 1981: 144). D. MacLulich saw adults with young at Frank's Bay, Lake Nipissing, on July 23, 1934 (Ricker & Clarke, 1939: 16). Baillie & Hope (1947: 18) collected two young, not long out of the nest, at Bigwood on July 17, 1937. Snyder (1942: 139) had only one report of this species near Sault Ste. Marie, on June 9, 1931. Snyder (1938: 200) collected a male at Emo on June 12, 1929. Smith (1957: 176) saw one near Gogama on July 25, 1954. Elder (1979: 36) had only one Geraldton record, on June 2, 1967. L. Paterson observed it rarely in summer at Kenora (Snyder, 1953: 73). R. Charles Long observed one at Moosonee on June 17, 1967 (Goodwin, 1967: 563). McLaren & McLaren (1981: 4) heard two singing in the Pickle Lake region in summer (1976 or 1977), well north of the usual summer range.

AUTUMN: A. Wormington noted one on Oct. 16, 1981 at Netitishi Point, James Bay (the second record for the Moosonee region). Peruniak (1971: 23) gave Oct. 2 as her latest record for Atikokan. Speirs & Speirs (1947: 32) observed one at North Bay on Sept. 18, 1944. Nicholson (1981: 144) reported Oct. 18 as the latest fall record for Manitoulin. Mills (1981: 114) had his latest on Sept. 26, 1979, at Magnetawan. Weir & Quilliam (1980: 37) listed Oct. 27 as the 26-year average departure date from Kingston: there were two records there as late as Nov. 20 (Quilliam, 1973: 139). The fall peak at Pickering has been about Sept. 18 (Speirs, 1975: 37). Speirs (1938: 52) gave Sept. 21 as the fall peak at Toronto, while Saunders (1947: 370) listed Oct. 6 as his 13-year average departure date there. Ussher (1965: 19) gave Oct. 21 as his 9-year average departure date from Rondeau. Stirrett (1973d: 24) had a maximum of 30 at Pelee on Oct. 2.

BANDING: One banded at Long Point on May 14, 1966 was recovered at Toronto on Apr. 30, 1970 (almost 4 years later). Brewer & Salvadori (1978: 71) reported one banded near Olivehill, Tenn. on Oct. 11, 1968 that turned up at Coboconk, Ont. (about 810 miles north) on May 24, 1969. Three banded at Long Point were recovered some years later: one banded May 18, 1964 was recovered at Braintree, Mass., on Nov. 15, 1968; a second bird banded Oct. 1, 1962 went to Barwick, Ga. by March, 1966 and the third banded May 16, 1966 turned up near Plainwell, Mich., on Aug. 6, 1969.

**MEASUREMENTS:**
*Length:* 10.5 to 12.0 ins.
(Godfrey, 1966: 293)
*Wingspread:* 12.5 to 14.6
ins. (Roberts, 1955: 651)
*Weight:* 2.32 to 2.50 oz.
(Roberts, 1955: 651) 5
Ontario specimens
averaged 70.5 g.

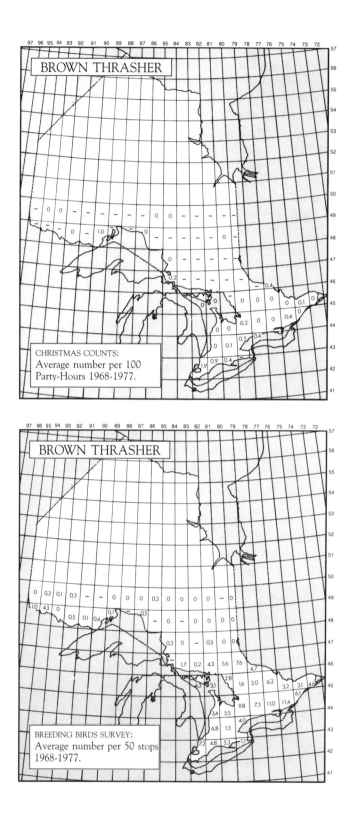

BROWN THRASHER

CHRISTMAS COUNTS:
Average number per 100
Party-Hours 1968-1977.

BROWN THRASHER

BREEDING BIRDS SURVEY:
Average number per 50 stops
1968-1977.

# WATER PIPIT   *Anthus spinoletta*   (Linnaeus)

In Ontario this is chiefly a fall migrant, though some may be found in spring and a few have lingered into winter. It is a tundra breeder and a few have been found in summer along Ontario's Hudson Bay strip of tundra. They winter in southern U.S.A. and in the mountains south to Guatemala. I usually see them in fall on ploughed fields or on mudflats with shorebirds.

IDENTIFICATION: Its general colouration reminds me of a dull, immature Yellow-rumped Warbler, but without the yellow rump of that species. It shows narrow white edges to the tail, which is pumps up and down like a waterthrush or Spotted Sandpiper. The flight is *very* erratic, birds of a flock rising high in the air, then falling, weaving in and out, uttering "pip-it" or "tsit-it" notes somewhat resembling the flight notes of Horned Larks (with which they often associate).

WINTER: On the 1968-1977 Christmas counts, they were uncommon along the north shore of Lake Erie, with outliers at Hamilton and Toronto. Stirrett (1973a: 18) had a few December records at Pelee, the latest on Dec. 30. Speirs (1975: 49) cited several winter records for the Pickering-Oshawa waterfront, one by George A. Scott as late as Feb. 26, 1961. Devitt (1967: 126) reported three on the Barrie Christmas count on Dec. 17, 1966.

SPRING: Stirrett (1973b: 22) had Pelee records from March 28 (4) to May 28. Ussher (1965: 21) gave Apr. 10 as the 7-year average arrival date at Rondeau and had spring records from March 19 to May 13. Saunders & Dale (1933: 222) gave May 5 as the 10-year average arrival date at London, with the earliest on Apr. 10, 1924. Harold Lancaster gave May 13 as the average arrival date in Elgin Co. (Brooman, 1954: 30). J.L. Baillie had spring records at Toronto from Apr. 23 to May 24 (Saunders, 1947: 370) and Speirs (1938: 44) gave May 21 as the spring peak there. Long (1968a: 16) saw two at Pickering Beach as early as Apr. 4, 1964 and J. Satterly saw 20 at Cedar Point, Lake Simcoe, as late as May 18, 1968 (Speirs, 1975: 49). Snyder (1941: 75) reported northbound migrants in Prince Edward Co. during the second and third week of May. Weir & Quilliam (1980: 38) listed Apr. 3 and May 31 as spring extremes at Kingston, with average arrival on Apr. 30 and departure on May 20. Devitt (1967: 126) gave May 4 as the 9-year average arrival date at Barrie, with the earliest on Apr. 18, 1959 and latest on May 23. Mills (1981: 123) had spring records for the cottage country on May 9, 1925 and May 20, 1973 (two birds in each case). Nicholson (1981: 152) had Manitoulin records between Apr. 26 (1970) and May 28 (1979) with a high count of 80 on May 10, 1969. Ricker & Clarke (1939: 17) had Lake Nipissing sightings on May 14, 1925; May 15, 1926 and May 25, 1933 while Speirs & Speirs (1947: 33) saw 21 near North Bay on May 11, 1944 and 15 on May 21, 1945 with others between these dates. Skeel & Bondrup-Nielsen (1978: 197) saw 3 on May 10 and one on May 12, 1977 at Pukaskwa. Baillie & Hope (1943: 19) collected one at Rossport on May 27, 1936 and two there on May 29. Denis (1961: 3) gave May 12 as the average arrival date at Thunder Bay, with the earliest on Apr. 18, 1959. Peruniak (1971: 24) had spring records at Atikokan from May 11 to June 1. Elder (1979: 37) gave May 8 as his earliest Geraldton date. Bondrup-Nielsen (1976: 44) saw his first near Kapuskasing on May 20 in 1974 and May 7 in 1975. Manning (1952: 78) saw a few feeding along the beach at Sandy Is., near Moosonee, on May 29 and 30, 1947 and collected two.

SUMMER: Speirs (1938: 46) gave June 5 as the latest Toronto date for northbound migrants. Weir & Quilliam (1980: 38) had a returning bird at Kingston as early as Aug. 14. Mills (1981: 123) had two August records for the cottage country: Aug. 15, 1890 at Port Stanley by A. Kay and Aug. 17, 1972 near Huntsville by V. Heron. Ron Tasker noted one in Burpee Twp., Manitoulin, on July 2, 1979 (Nicholson, 1981: 152). Manning (1952: 78) collected 4 adults and 5 juveniles of 22 seen at Little Cape, Hudson Bay, in 9 hours afield between July 29 and Aug. 1, 1947: later he collected one juvenile at Shagamu River, where he saw 11 in 7 hours between Aug. 6 and 10, 1947. L. Walden found a nest with 6 eggs at Cape Henrietta Maria on June 29, 1948 (the first Ontario nest record): there have been several subsequent reports from the same region (Peck, 1972: 345-346). Lee (1978: 29) saw one at Ft. Severn on June 19, 1975 and C.E. Hope collected 3 and saw another there between June 28 and July 7, 1940.

AUTUMN: Lewis & Peters (1941: 114) noted the species at Attawapiskat about Sept. 16, 1940. D. McRae and A. Wormington saw individuals at Netitishi Point, James Bay, on Oct. 18 and 25, 1981. Oliver Hewitt saw several near the Moose River Estuary between Sept. 22 and 25, 1947, and on Oct. 2, 1948, George M. Stirrett saw 6 at Ship Sands (Manning, 1952: 78). Peruniak (1971: 24) had fall records at Atikokan from Sept. 20 to Oct. 15. This was the most common non-resident bird on Pukaskwa beaches from Sept. 12 to Oct. 13, 1977, with a maximum of 23 on Sept. 22 (Skeel & Bondrup-Nielsen, 1978: 197). Speirs & Speirs (1947: 33) had fall records at North Bay between Sept. 13 and Oct. 20, 1944 with a peak in late September. MacLulich (1938: 29) saw one with Horned Larks at Achray, Algonquin Park, on Oct. 18, 1930. Nicholson (1981: 152) had fall birds on Manitoulin as early as Aug. 30, 1975 and as late as Nov. 20, 1976: Ron Tasker had a high count of 300 on Oct. 12, 1974. The largest fall flock for the cottage country was 44 on the Pine Islands, Georgian Bay, on Oct. 2, 1976 by C. Harris: the latest one was at Interlaken on Oct. 30, 1976 by M. and G. Withers (Mills, 1981: 123). Devitt (1967: 126) had fall birds in Simcoe Co. from Sept. 5 (1937) to Nov. 7 (1948), where J.L. Baillie & Paul Harrington had a maximum count of 273 on Oct. 2, 1927 at Wasaga Beach. Weir & Quilliam (1980: 38) listed Sept. 19 as the average fall arrival date for Kingston, with the average departure on Nov. 4 and the latest on Nov. 20, 1966: Quilliam (1973: 145) estimated 200 on Wolfe Is. on Nov. 3, 1963. Snyder (1941: 75) gave Sept. 24, 1934 as his earliest Prince Edward Co. record, with large numbers noted by W.H. Lunn from Oct. 16 to Nov. 11, and the latest on Nov. 15. Long (1968a: 16) saw two at Pickering Beach as early as Aug. 31, 1964 and tallied 240 there on Nov. 9, 1963: one flew over our Pickering home as late as Nov. 16, 1968 (Speirs, 1975: 49). Speirs (1938: 48, 52) gave Sept. 2 as the earliest fall date for Toronto, with the peak on Oct. 13: Saunders (1947: 370) had fall records there from Oct. 4 to Nov. 20. Sheppard (1960: 37) cited a record of 60 at Dufferin Is., Niagara Falls, on Nov. 3, 1951. Beardslee & Mitchell (1965: 350-351) reported 3 at Jaeger Rocks, Lake Erie, on Nov. 27, 1959. Wm. Girling reported 500 on Oct. 16, 1948 going west between St. Thomas and Port Stanley (Brooman, 1954: 30). Saunders & Dale (1933: 222) estimated that 50 to 75 passed by "The Ponds", London, during the morning of Oct. 12, 1924. Ussher (1965: 21) had Rondeau records from Sept. 27 to Nov. 30, with average arrival on Oct. 10 and departure on Nov. 7. Stirrett (1973d: 25) gave Sept. 16 as his earliest fall record (4 birds) at Pelee, with a maximum of 200 on Oct. 20.

**MEASUREMENTS:**
*Length:* 6 to 7 ins.
(Godfrey, 1966: 307)
*Wingspread:* 9.95 to 11.0
ins. (Roberts, 1955: 659)
*Weight:* 0.88 oz. (Roberts,
1955: 659)

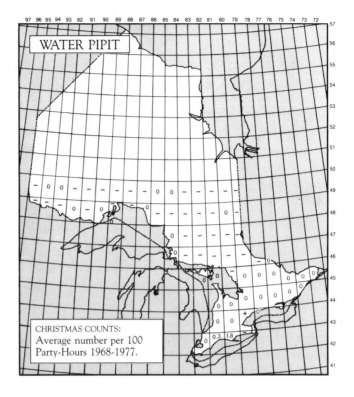

WATER PIPIT

CHRISTMAS COUNTS:
Average number per 100
Party-Hours 1968-1977.

# SPRAGUE'S PIPIT   *Anthus spragueii*   (Audubon)

Sprague's Pipit is a bird of the short grass prairies, accidental in Ontario.

**IDENTIFICATION:** Sprague's Pipit looks like a Water Pipit but has pale legs (black in the Water Pipit) and is buffy on the back, rather than slaty as in the Water Pipit. The Vesper Sparrow is somewhat similar but has a much shorter, more conical bill: both have white outer tail feathers. Like the Skylark and Horned Lark, the male sings for long periods, high in the sky, a tinkling descending song.

**WINTER:**

**SPRING:**

**SUMMER:** John Lamey found one on July 3, 1980 at Rainy River: the bird was also observed by several other observers and tape recorded by J.G. Kennleyside on July 12. (Goodwin, 1980: 892).

**AUTUMN:**

**MEASUREMENTS:**
*Length:* 6.0 to 6.9 ins.      *Weight:* 20 averaged
(Godfrey, 1966: 308)      25.3 g. (22.3 - 29.2 g.)
*Wingspread:*      (Dunning, 1984: 20).

# BOHEMIAN WAXWING   *Bombycilla garrulus*   (Linnaeus)

Waxwings are always a joy to behold, dressed in the most elegant attire and with impeccable manners. Add to this a touch of rarity, and these Bohemians are sought after by all avid bird watchers. In Ontario we find them mainly in winter, in multiflora rose hedges or groves of mountain ash (or the exotic relative in cities, the rowan tree). At our home, highbush cranberry has sometimes attracted them, and other persistent fruits are also used.

IDENTIFICATION:   Bohemian Waxwings are somewhat larger than their more familiar relatives, the Cedar Waxwings. The rufous-orange undertail coverts is the best way of distinguishing them from Cedar Waxwings, which have creamy-white undertail coverts. Bohemians show more white in the wing than Cedar Waxwings and their underparts are mainly gray, not brown as in Cedar Waxings. The face and base of the crest is a rich vinaceous colour, not uniform brown as in Cedar Waxwings. Both species may have the tiny red tips to some feathers which give them the name "waxwing" but some individuals lack these appendages, perhaps from wear. The voice of the Bohemian is more "beady" or chattery, than the more uniform, sibilant call of the Cedar Waxwing.

WINTER:   On the 1968-1977 Christmas counts they were fairly common from Napanee, Ottawa and Wiarton, north to Thunder Bay and Dryden, rare in most southerly localities. Stirrett (1973a: 18) saw 22 at Pelee on Dec. 16 (his earliest record) with a few January and February reports. A.A. Wood collected two males at Coldstream on Jan. 30, 1920 and others were seen nearby the same day and on Feb. 3: "a very rare winter visitor" at London (Saunders & Dale, 1933: 222). On Dec. 31, 1961 four were noted on a Christmas count at St. Catharines (Beardslee & Mitchell, 1965: 352). H.L. Lancaster reported one at Niagara-on-the-Lake on Jan. 10, 1959 (Sheppard, 1960: 37). Geo. E. Atkinson noted the arrival at Toronto on Feb. 3, 1895 and several flocks were observed into March (Fleming, 1907: 82). J.L. Baillie had a Dec. 18 record at Toronto and showed another one to R.M. Saunders on Feb. 1, 1941, who described it in detail (Saunders, 1947: 19, 20, 370). Speirs (1938: 48) gave Dec. 7 as the earliest Toronto date. Speirs (1975: 50) had winter records in Ontario Co. on 8 of 25 winters, the earliest on Dec. 5, 1964, at our Pickering home and the latest on Feb. 22, 1970 at Whitby, with one flock of 50 at Whitevale on Jan. 1, 1962. Wei· & Quilliam (1980: 38) listed Feb. 3 as the 10-year average departure date from Kingston. Quilliam (1973: 146) mentioned a flock of 432 on the Napanee Christmas count on Dec. 30, 1964. Devitt (1967: 126-127) cited several winter reports, with major invasions at Barrie of 400 on Jan. 4, 1959 and 60 at Collingwood on Jan. 11 the same year. W.E. Macoun called them abundant at Ottawa from January to April, 1897 (Lloyd, 1924: 12). Craig Campbell saw about 60 at Parry Sound on Dec. 23, 1972: the 1958 invasion peaked at about 250 at Huntsville on Dec. 13 (Mills, 1981: 123). The high count for Manitoulin was 120 on Dec. 21, 1980 (Nicholson, 1981: 153). E.M. Ricker reported some in North Bay during the winter of 1921-1922 (Ricker & Clarke, 1939: 17). Denis (1961: 6) called this a "regular very common winter visitant" at Thunder Bay, "usually appear about Dec. 15". David Elder saw his first at Atikokan on Jan. 3, 1981. Elder (1979: 37) called this a rare winter visitor at Geraldton.

SPRING:   Stirrett (1973b: 22) had Pelee records for March 18, 1911 and March 8, 1962 (3). R.T. Hedley reported about a dozen near London on Apr. 12, 1923 (Saunders & Dale, 1933: 222). Mr. & Mrs. Fred Bell saw 6 near Port Stanley on May 18, 1952

(Brooman, 1954: 31). C.W. Nash took one in eastern Toronto on March 20, 1895 (Fleming, 1907: 82). Speirs (1938: 46) gave May 11 as the latest Toronto date. David Calvert saw some eating crabapples at Ajax as late as Apr. 24, 1965 (Speirs, 1975: 50). Weir & Quilliam (1980: 38) listed March 25 as the latest spring record for Kingston. Frances Westman saw a small flock at Barrie on March 16, 1959 (Devitt, 1967: 127). Lloyd (1924: 12) cited Ottawa records from March 19-23, 1912 and into April in 1897. Mills (1981: 123) reported 8 seen by Aubrey May at Huntsville as late as March 23, 1962. Nicholson (1981: 153) gave Apr. 10, 1980 as the latest Manitoulin record. Peruniak (1971: 24) had only one Atikokan record, on Apr. 30, 1966.

SUMMER: On the 1968-1977 Breeding Bird Survey, they were reported only at Kapuskasing, in 1976. Schueler, Baldwin & Rising (1974: 147) collected a female with a brood patch near the junction of the Sutton and Warchesku rivers on July 19, 1964, where they found them during three summers (the first breeding evidence for Ontario).

AUTUMN: D. McRae and A. Wormington noted 3 at Netitishi Point, James Bay, on Nov. 15, 1981 and single birds there on Nov. 20, 21 and 22. As we were returning home from the A.O.U. meeting in Regina in three cars, Dorothy Bordner spotted a Bohemian Waxwing near Klotz Lake on Sept. 4, 1959 and showed it to us and to George and Laurel North. Nicholson (1981: 153) gave Nov. 7, 1971 as the earliest Manitoulin fall bird. The vanguard of the 1958 invasion was noted at Huntsville on Nov. 24 (Mills, (1981: 123). Lloyd (1924: 12) reported 5 at Ottawa on Nov. 11, 1883. E.L. Brereton saw 17 at Barrie on Nov. 27, 1944 (Devitt, 1967: 127). Weir & Quilliam (1980: 38) listed Nov. 27 as the 11-year average arrival date at Kingston, with the earliest on Nov. 4. Harry Gould took one at London in September, 1890 (Saunders & Dale, 1933: 222). Pelee had one fall record, on Nov. 10, 1968 (Kelley, 1978: 64).

**MEASUREMENTS:**
*Length:* 7.5 to 8.7 ins.
(Godfrey, 1966: 309)
*Wingspread:* 13.15 to
14.25 ins. (Roberts,
1955: 660)
*Weight:* ♂ av. 2.22 oz. ♀
av. 2.21 oz. (Roberts,
1955: 660).

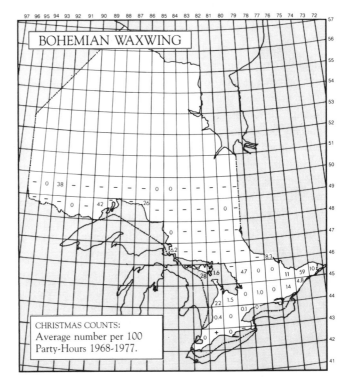

BOHEMIAN WAXWING

CHRISTMAS COUNTS:
Average number per 100
Party-Hours 1968-1977.

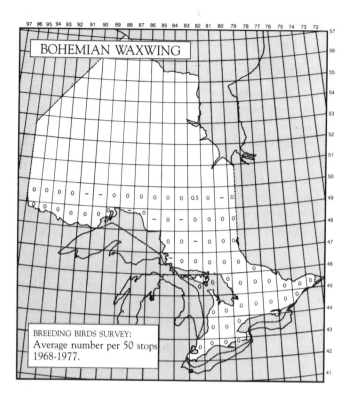

BOHEMIAN WAXWING

BREEDING BIRDS SURVEY:
Average number per 50 stops
1968-1977.

# CEDAR WAXWING  *Bombycilla cedrorum*  Vieillot

I remember my excitement as a schoolboy in witnessing the berry-passing ritual of several Cedar Waxwings as they perched side by side on a slender horizontal branch, each one in turn accepting the berry from its neighbour and passing it to the next bird in line, "politely" refraining from eating it. Almost equally astonishing is watching the adult disgorging berry after berry to feed its hungry offspring in the nest. Waxwing numbers are highly unpredictable, here in numbers one day, then gone for days or months. I usually see them in apple blossom time in spring (devouring the petals), again when the honey-suckle berries are ripe in summer, or busy flycatching over some northern stream. During some winters they descend en masse to clean up a stand of mountain ash, multiflora rose or other bushes with persistent winter fruits.

IDENTIFICATION: This is our only brown, sparrow-sized bird, with prominent crest, yellow-tipped tail and whitish undertail coverts.

WINTER: On the 1968-1977 Christmas counts they were fairly common at most southern Ontario localities as well as north of Lake Superior, absent elsewhere, with numbers varying greatly from year to year. Stirrett (1973a: 18) had a winter maximum of 200 at Pelee on Jan. 26. They were seen on about half of the Christmas counts in Ontario Co. (Speirs, 1975: 51). Ron. Weir estimated 1000 to 2000 in a cedar woods at Hay Bay, near Kingston, on Jan. 29, 1972 (Quilliam, 1973: 147). Frances Westman saw over 100 at Barrie on Dec. 31, 1958 (Devitt, 1967: 128). Lloyd (1924: 12) had a Feb. 22, 1908 record at Ottawa. They were seen on two of 28 Christmas counts at Huntsville (two on Dec. 30, 1962) and Craig Campbell saw 200 at Parry Sound from Dec. 25-27, 1964 (Mills, 1981: 124-25). Nicholson (1981: 153) reported 18 on Manitoulin on Feb. 9-10, 1980.

SPRING: Stirrett (1973b: 22) had a spring maximum of 500 at Pelee on May 30. Ussher (1965: 21) gave Apr. 6 as his earliest Rondeau record. Snyder (1931: 204) saw his first on May 15 in 1928 at Long Point. Saunders (1947: 370) gave May 17 as his 13-year average arrival date at Toronto, while Speirs (1938: 44) gave May 9 as the spring peak there. In Ontario Co. there have been peak numbers noted in the second week of March, again in mid-April and at apple blossom time in May (Speirs, 1975: 51). Mills (1981: 124) reported an early Huntsville sighting on March 21, 1959, but it was usually the fourth week of May before they turned up there. Nicholson (1981: 153) gave May 21 as the 10-year average arrival date on Manitoulin, with the earliest on May 14, 1972 (until 1979 when 10 showed up at South Baymouth on March 13 and 1980 when 30 turned up at Sheguiandah on March 8). Louise Lawrence saw 6 at Pimisi Bay as early as May 22, 1945 (Speirs & Speirs, 1947: 33). W. Wyett saw 3 at Pukaskwa on Apr. 11, 1974 (Skeel & Bondrup-Nielsen, 1978: 198). Peruniak (1971: 24) gave May 26 as her earliest Atikokan date but David Elder had one on May 22 in 1981. Elder (1979: 37) gave May 29 as his earliest Geraldton date.

SUMMER: On the 1968-1977 Breeding Bird Surveys they were uncommon to common on all routes. Stirrett (1973d: 25) had a summer maximum of 1000 on Aug. 27. Saunders & Dale (1933: 222) had London nest records from June 15 (1901 - 3 eggs) to Aug. 23 (1890 - 5 eggs). F. Starr took a set of 3 eggs at Port Burwell on June 23, 1924 (Baillie & Harrington, 1937: 235). McCracken, Bradstreet & Holroyd (1981: 61) had only three nest records for Long Point: nest with 5 eggs on July 3, 1965; nest with 5 eggs that hatched on July 14, 1974 and a nest being built on July 4, 1979. Fleming (1907: 82) mentioned a Toronto breeding record on June 20, 1898. Snyder (1930: 197) found the earliest eggs in King Twp. on July 3, 1926. I saw one on its nest in Zephyr as early as June 9, 1969: 41 sets found in Ontario Co. held a total of 155 eggs, including 3 sets with 2 cowbird eggs and two with one cowbird egg (Speirs, 1975: 51): they occurred in 8 of 10 urban quadrats with a maximum population density of 35 birds per 100 acres in Port Perry, but only in 4 of 11 forest quadrats with a maximum of 12 birds per 100 acres in the Thorah plot (a cedar woods). In Prince Edward Co., T.B. Kurata reported the first young on July 15, 1930 at Hallowell (Snyder, 1941: 75). Quilliam (1973: 147) reported several nests near Kingston; one as early as July 6, 1897 held 3 eggs and another with 5 eggs on July23, 1965 held 4 young and 1 egg on Aug. 2. W.W. Smith found a nest with 4 eggs at Big Cedar Point on June 15, 1940; Paul Harrington found one with 4 eggs at Wasaga Beach on July 31, 1914 and E.L. Brereton found a nest with young at Little Lake, Barrie as late as Aug. 30, 1941 (Devitt, 1967: 127). C.L. Patch found a nest with eggs near Ottawa on June 23, 1914 (Lloyd, 1924: 12). Mills (1980: 124) reported 47 nests in the cottage country. Nicholson (1981: 153) reported Manitoulin nests on June 14, 1920 and July 1, 1980 (4 eggs). MacLulich (1938: 30) noted his earliest Algonquin Park bird on June 3, 1934 but later found them common along lakes, rivers and brules: C.H.D. Clarke collected a young female at Brule Lake on Aug. 30, 1934. Speirs & Speirs (1947: 33) gave details of several North Bay region nestings: one bird collecting nest material as early as June 1, 1944: another completed a nest on July 10, 1945 that held an incubating bird from July

14 to Aug. 1; this was empty on Aug. 18 but a flying young was seen Aug. 22. Baillie & Hope (1947: 20) collected a nest with 5 young at Bigwood on July 22, 1937 and 3 young just out of the nest on July 27: some of these young showed "wax" shaft tips even at this early age. Snyder (1942: 142) found a nest with 5 eggs at Iron Bridge on July 15, 1931. Skeel & Bondrup-Nielsen (1978: 198) saw their first one at Pukaskwa on June 6 and found a nest with 5 eggs on June 16, 1977. Baillie & Hope (1943: 19) saw their first at Rossport on June 1, 1936 but by June 6 a flock of 100 or more was noted. Dear (1940: 136) found a nest with 4 eggs on June 19, 1914 and a nest with 5 eggs on July 12, 1931 near Thunder Bay. Snyder (1938: 201) found them "abundant" in the Rainy River region feeding on mayflies during the first week of July, 1929. Snyder (1953: 75) reported a nest being built in the Dryden area on June 18, 1939 and cited breeding evidence for Wabigoon and Kenora. Smith (1957: 177) found 4 occupied nests at Kapuskasing and a nest with 5 young at Gogama. Hope (1938: 34) found a nest with 5 eggs at Favourable Lake on July 5, 1938 and young just able to fly on July 24. Cringan (1953a: 3) saw his first at Sioux Lookout on June 23. Cringan (1950: 16) saw his first at Nikip Lake on June 19, 1950. Manning (1952: 78) saw 8 on June 23, 1949 and 10 on June 26, near Moosonee: and reported that Sam Waller found a nest there with 7 eggs in 1929. James, Nash & Peck (1982: 65) found two nests near the mouth of Harricanaw River, James Bay: a nest with 5 eggs on July 10 and a nest with 4 eggs on July 2, 1982. Schueler, Baldwin & Rising (1974: 143, 147) noted the species at Cochrane, Moosonee, Attawapiskat and Winisk: they collected a female with enlarged ovary at Aquatuk Lake on July 6, 1964. Lee (1978: 29) saw his first at Big Trout Lake on June 11, 1975, with small flocks about the settlement after July 1.

AUTUMN: D. McRae and A. Wormington saw individuals at Netitishi Point, James Bay, on Oct. 15, 21 and 24, 1981. Peruniak (1971: 24) gave Sept. 28 as her latest Atikokan date. Skeel & Bondrup-Nielsen (1978: 198) saw their last at Pukaskwa on Sept. 10, 1977. Speirs & Speirs (1947: 33) saw one at North Bay on Oct. 7, 1944. Nicholson (1981: 153) gave Oct. 9, 1978 as the latest Manitoulin date. J. Rogers saw several at Huntsville on Nov. 16, 1958 (Mills, 1981: 124). Allin (1940: 104) noted a bird leaving the nest in Darlington Twp. as late as Sept. 5, 1931. Speirs (1975: 51) found a fall peak in mid-September in Ontario Co. George A. Scott and Ron Tozer found a nest with 3 eggs as late as Sept. 16, 1962 at Oshawa (Tozer & Richards, 1974: 227). Saunders (1947: 370) gave Oct. 13 as his 13-year average departure date from Toronto, while Speirs (1938: 52) had a fall peak on Sept. 15 there. Ussher (1965: 21) gave Nov. 26 as his latest fall date for Rondeau. Stirrett (1973d: 25) had a fall maximum of 300 on Sept. 18 at Pelee.

BANDING: One banded near Cheboygan, Mich. on Aug. 25, 1936 was recovered near Toronto on July 5, 1937. Two others banded at Ferron Point, near Alpena, Mich. were later taken in Ontario: one banded on June 3, 1964 was recovered at Guelph on July 8, 1966: the other banded on June 11, 1968 was recovered at Don Mills, on June 28, 1970. Another banded at Dorset, Ohio on May 25, 1968, was recovered the following winter on Feb. 9, 1969 at Georgetown, Ont. One banded by John Miles at Dundas Marsh on Aug. 29, 1965, was recovered some 1263 miles to the southwest at Bellaire, Texas, on Aug. 12, 1966 (Brewer & Salvadori, 1978: 75).

**MEASUREMENTS:**

*Length:* 6.5 to 8.0 ins. (Godfrey, 1966: 310)
*Wingspread:* 11 to 12 1/4 ins. (Roberts, 1955: 660)
*Weight:* 35 Ontario specimens averaged 33.8 g. (25.0 to 41.2 g.).

**REFERENCE:**

Burton, D.E. 1958 Nesting of the Cedar Waxwing in southern Ontario. Ont. Field Biologist, No. 12: 19-22.

Of 41 nests found in the Toronto region, 33 were in hawthorns: these averaged 7 ft. above ground. Four early nests were parasitized by cowbirds. Occupied nests were reported from June 8 to Sept. 20.

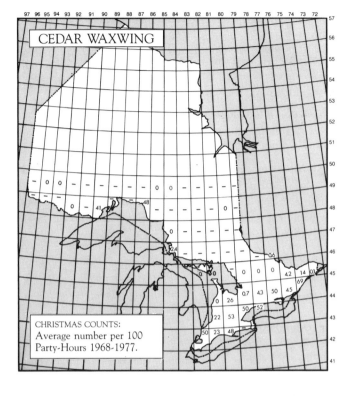

CEDAR WAXWING

CHRISTMAS COUNTS:
Average number per 100
Party-Hours 1968-1977.

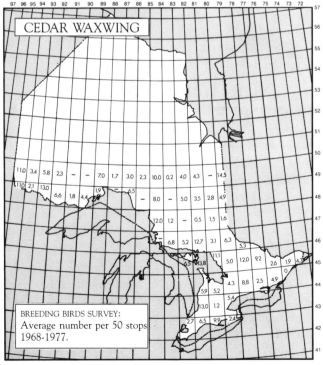

CEDAR WAXWING

BREEDING BIRDS SURVEY:
Average number per 50 stops
1968-1977.

## PHAINOPEPLA    *Phainopepla nitens*    (Swainson)

Accidental in Ontario. The occurrence of this bird of the southwestern United States in Ontario, *in winter*, is one of those unusual events, perhaps only to be explained by the fact that birds have wings; will travel.

IDENTIFICATION: This is a black bird with shiny, silky, plumage and conspicuous crest, a bright red eye, and white wing patches that show only in flight. They are about the size of a Cedar Waxwing.

WINTER: One showed up in an orchard at Wallacetown, Elgin Co., found on Dec. 27, 1975 by L.D. Auckland, Marshall H. Field and R. Pokraka. It was seen by many observers there until Jan. 17 (see photo by Marshall Field in American Birds, 30:(3): 714). Probably the same bird was reported at London on Feb. 29 and March 1 by K.C. Hulley and S.C. Somerville (Goodwin, 1976: 714).

SPRING:

SUMMER:

AUTUMN:

**MEASUREMENTS:**
*Length:* 7 to 7 3/4 ins.
(Terres, 1980: 822)
*Wingspread:*
*Weight:* 33 averaged
24.0 g. (22 - 28 g.)
(Dunning, 1984: 20).

## NORTHERN SHRIKE    *Lanius excubitor*    Linnaeus

This is the winter shrike in Ontario, occurring in summer only in the Hudson Bay and James Bay lowlands. It is usually seen conspicuously perched on top of an isolated tree overlooking open country (or bird feeders). From this lofty perch it drops down, levels off and flies with determination low over the field and rises with an upward swoop to perch again, occasionally flicking its tail like a small kestrel. When hunting has been good it sometimes caches extra prey (mouse or small bird) impaled on a thorn or hung up in the crotch of a small sapling.

IDENTIFICATION: The Northern Shrike is about the size and general colouration of a Mockingbird (smaller than an American Robin), gray with a black mask, black on the wings and tail which show white flashes in flight. Our very similar summer shrike, the Loggerhead Shrike, is somewhat smaller, with darker somewhat blue-gray upperparts and an all black bill (the base of the lower mandible of the Northern Shrike is creamy white). Northern Shrikes generally show wavy dark lines across the breast (vermiculations) while adult Loggerheads lack these markings: young of both species are brownish and both show the vermiculations in this plumage. In Northern Shrikes the gray of the forehead extends to the base of the bill, while in the Loggerhead the black of the masks extends as a narrow bar of black above the bill. (See James, 1983: 18-21 for more detail.) In spring a catbird-like rather musical song may be heard.

WINTER: On the 1968-1977 Christmas counts they were fairly common from Lake Ontario north to Minden, Barrie and Manitoulin, uncommon at most other Ontario localities and rare to absent at some of the northernmost places. Stirrett (1973a: 19) saw one or two throughout the winter at Pelee. Harold Lancaster found one in Elgin Co. as late as Feb. 21, 1952 (Brooman, 1954: 31). Numbers tallied on Pickering Christmas counts varied from 1 to 34 and at Oshawa from 0 to 35 (Speirs, 1975: 52). Quilliam (1973: 147) reported a maximum of 20 on the Dec. 20, 1970 Christmas count at Kingston: she mentioned them taking Black-capped Chickadees, Chipping Sparrows, Dark-eyed Juncos and House Sparrows at feeding stations. Devitt (1967: 128) gave 9 as the maximum daily total for Barrie, on Jan. 9, 1965. James Knights watched a Saw-whet Owl being attacked by a Northern Shrike near Collingwood on Feb. 18, 1967 (Devitt, 1967: 95). Lloyd (1924: 12) heard one singing at Ottawa in February, 1922. Mills (1981: 125) cited several winter records for the cottage country. Speirs & Speirs (1947: 33) saw one at North Bay on Feb. 20, 1945: the House Sparrows in the city formed a great defensive ball in the sky above the city whenever a shrike appeared. Dennison (1980: 147) reported from 1 to 4 on 10 of 25 Christmas counts at Sault Ste. Marie. Skeel & Bondrup-Nielsen (1978: 198) saw one at Pukaskwa on Dec. 30, 1976. David Elder saw one in Atikokan on Feb. 14, 1981.

SPRING: Stirrett (1973a: 19) gave March 8 as his latest Pelee date. Ussher (1965: 21) gave March 11 as his latest date for Rondeau. Saunders (1947: 371) listed March 4 as his average departure date from Toronto, while Fleming (1907: 82) gave Apr. 11, 1898 as his latest Toronto record. My latest personal Pickering record was on Apr. 5, 1964 when one perched on a lilac above our bird feeder. Ron Tozer saw one near Thickson's Woods, Whitby, as late as Apr. 12, 1963 (Tozer & Richards, 1974: 230). Frank Brimley saw one in Prince Edward Co. on Apr. 6, 1912 (Snyder, 1941: 75). Weir & Quilliam (1980: 38) listed March 18 as the 20-year average departure date from Kingston, with the latest on Apr. 25. Devitt (1967: 128) gave Apr. 4, 1947 as his latest Barrie date. R. Morgan saw a shrike, probably this species, at Huntsville on Apr. 19, 1972 (Mills, 1981: 125). Nicholson (1981: 154) gave Apr. 16 as the latest Manitoulin date. Ricker & Clarke (1939: 17) observed one singing at Lake Nipissing on Apr. 21, 1926. Skeel & Bondrup-Nielsen (1978: 198) reported one or two at Pukaskwa on Apr. 16-17, 1977. Peruniak (1971: 24) had a March 7 record for Atikokan. K. Powell found them especially frequent at Cochrane in early spring, 1954. Bondrup-Nielsen (1976: 44) saw one at Kapuskasing at late as May 1, 1975.

SUMMER: The only one reported on the 1968-1977 Breeding Bird Survey was at Larder Lake, probably a tardy migrant. Schueler, Baldwin & Rising (1974: 147) collected one with 6 enlarged ova at Moosonee on May 26, 1972: this bird had a White-throated Sparrow in its stomach: they also saw one at Winisk on June 22, 1971. The first confirmed breeding evidence for Ontario was obtained at Kiruna Lake, Sutton Ridges, on July 12, 1981 where a family of 4 begging young was found: a female was also collected nearby. H. Lumsden found the mummified body of one at a fox den at the mouth of the Brant River, near Cape Henrietta Maria, on July 17, 1969 (Peck, 1972: 346).

AUTUMN: Manning (1952: 79) reported one taken at Ft. Severn on Sept. 24, 1930 by Hugh Conn. D. McRae and A. Wormington saw individuals fairly regularly from Oct. 14 to Nov. 1 (3 noted) at Netitishi Point, James Bay, and one at Moosonee on Nov. 25, 1981. Peruniak (1971: 24) had an Oct. 23 record at Atikokan. Denis (1961: 6) gave Oct. 19 as the 12-year average arrival date at Thunder Bay. Speirs & Speirs (1947: 33) saw one at North Bay on Oct. 17, 1944, while Ricker & Clarke (1939: 17) saw one as early as Oct. 8, 1925 at Lake Nipissing. MacLulich (1938: 30) saw one at Achray, Algonquin Park, on Oct. 17, 1930. Nicholson (1981: 154) gave Oct. 16 as the 11-year average arrival date on Manitoulin with the earliest on Oct. 9, 1971. Mills (1981: 125) mentioned one collected at Pt. Sydney, Muskoka, as early as Oct. 12, 1898, and one (probably this species) at Pointe au Baril on Oct. 10, 1954. Devitt (1967: 128) gave Oct. 31, 1953 as the earliest Barrie record. Weir & Quilliam (1980: 38) listed Oct. 27 as the 25-year average arrival date at Kingston, with the earliest on Oct. 15. Charles Fothergill saw a great many and shot one male at Rice Lake in the fall of 1820 (Black, 1934: 153). Long (1968a: 17) noted one as early as Oct. 15, 1964 at Pickering Beach, trying to catch an American Robin. Fleming (1907: 82) gave Oct. 3, 1896 as his earliest Toronto date and J.L. Baillie gave Nov. 21 as his 11-year average arrival date there (Saunders, 1947: 371). H.H. Axtell collected one at Stromness Marsh as early as Oct. 12, 1954 and another was observed at McNab on Oct. 18, 1953 (Beardslee & Mitchell, 1965: 353-354). Marshall Field collected one near St. Thomas on Nov. 20, 1949 (Brooman, 1954: 31). Ussher (1965: 21) gave Oct. 18 as his earliest Rondeau record. Stirrett (1973d: 25) reported them common at Pelee on Sept. 5-6, 1909 (?JMS) with single birds on Oct. 16 and Nov. 3.

FLUCTUATIONS IN ABUNDANCE: Speirs (1938: 89) presented evidence for a 3 to 6 years "cycle" (usually 4 to 5 years) at Toronto from 1889 to 1935 (winters will be designated by the beginning year, e.g. 1935-1936, will be given as 1935). Speirs (1975: 52) had Ontario Co. peaks in 1949, 1953, 1958, 1961, 1965 and 1970. Beardslee & Mitchell (1965: 353) suggested peaks near Buffalo - Ft. Erie in 1934, 1938, 1945, 1949, 1953, 1960 and 1961. The 1953 peak was also noted in SW Ontario by Kelley (1978: 65) and Brooman (1954: 31). Saunders & Dale (1933: 222) mentioned the 1930 peak near London.

**MEASUREMENTS:**
Length: 9 to 10.7 ins.
(Godfrey, 1966: 311)
Wingspread: 13 1/2 to 14
3/4 ins. (Roberts,
1955: 661)
Weight: 2 to 2.63 oz.
(Roberts, 1955: 661).

**REFERENCE:**
James, R.D. 1983 Field
identification of shrikes.
Ont. Birds, 1: (1): 18-21.

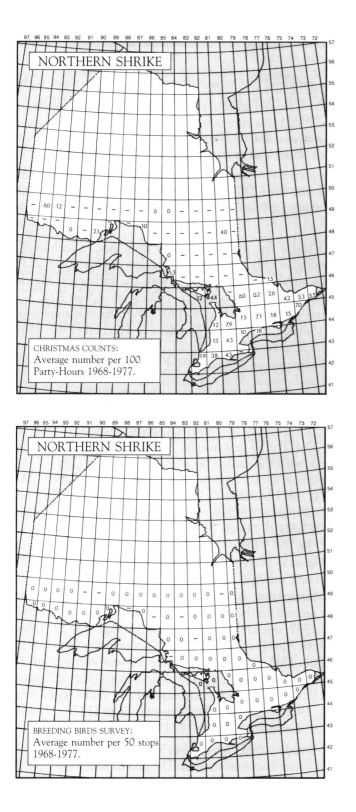

NORTHERN SHRIKE

CHRISTMAS COUNTS:
Average number per 100
Party-Hours 1968-1977.

NORTHERN SHRIKE

BREEDING BIRDS SURVEY:
Average number per 50 stops
1968-1977.

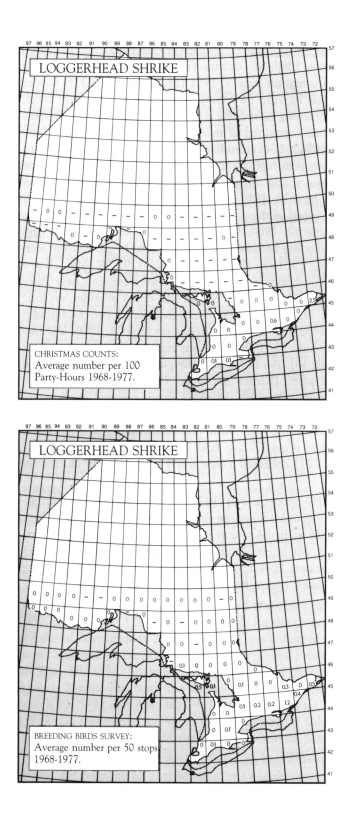

LOGGERHEAD SHRIKE

CHRISTMAS COUNTS:
Average number per 100
Party-Hours 1968-1977.

LOGGERHEAD SHRIKE

BREEDING BIRDS SURVEY:
Average number per 50 stops
1968-1977.

# EUROPEAN STARLING  *Sturnus vulgaris*  Linnaeus

This Old World species was introduced at New York in 1890 and spread rapidly, reaching Ontario at Niagara Falls in 1914 and Brockville in 1919. I saw my first at Toronto on March 24, 1925. Saunders (1930: 22) estimated 10,000 at a Brantford roost on March 21, 1929 and Snyder & Baillie (1930: 198) estimated 5000 at the Lawrence Park roost in Toronto by Sept. 3, 1929. Since that time they have occupied most of Ontario though rare in the far north, especially in winter. They are most common about cities and towns, but frequently nest in old fence posts in farmland and in cavities in old trees in forests. Some of our hole-nesting native birds have suffered from competition with starlings: such species as the Eastern Bluebird, Red-headed Woodpecker and Northern Flicker have been reduced in numbers. In an all day watch at a nest with young at our home they fed the young every few minutes all day, totalling several hundred feedings: most of the identified items proved to be cutworm larvae. In some European countries they are encouraged to nest about fields to reduce the cutworm damage. On the other hand they are also fond of cherries and other soft fruits, compete with native species and when they gather in great roosts their droppings and noise can create a nuisance. Banding recoveries have shown that many of our birds winter in the Mississippi Valley, from Ohio south to Alabama, but large numbers remain near cities, gathering at refuse dumps during the day and congregating at heating plants for the night (to protect their tender feet from the frost).

WINTER: On the 1968-1977 Christmas counts they were abundant at southern Ontario localities and locally at Thunder Bay: they were fairly common about northern cities and towns. Stirrett (1973a: 19) had a winter maximum of 2000 at Pelee on Dec. 26. Saunders & Dale (1933: 223) gave Feb. 17, 1923 as the first record for London. Earl Lemon had his first in Elgin Co. at West Lorne on Feb. 20, 1928 (Brooman, 1954: 31). Snyder (1941: 76) reported the first Prince Edward Co. record in Feb., 1925, though there was a Trenton record in 1922. E. Beaupré saw 150 near Kingston as early as Dec. 5, 1925 and the high count of 4300 there was tallied on Dec. 21, 1963 (Quilliam, 1973: 149), who reported large flocks of returning migrants flying north all morning on Feb. 26, 1961. E.L. Brereton saw his first at Barrie on Feb. 12, 1921 (Devitt, 1967: 129). C. Campbell saw 26 at Parry Sound on Feb. 13, 1973 (Mills, 1981: 127). Speirs & Speirs (1947: 34) saw 35 at the North Bay dump on Jan. 1, 1945 but Louise Lawrence saw none at Rutherglen from Oct. 25, 1944 to March 12, 1945. The first record for Thessalon was on Feb. 10, 1927 (Snyder, 1942: 142). Dennison (1980: 146) reported the species on all 25 Christmas counts at Sault Ste. Marie, with 6 to 334 noted, averaging 129 per count. Dear (1940: 137) reported that the first Thunder Bay record was one picked up dead in the winter of 1930-1931. Peruniak (1971: 24) mentioned that 5 to 15 have been seen at Atikokan in winter since 1964. L. Paterson reported a pair seen at Kenora during two weeks in the winter of 1935-1936 (Snyder, 1953: 75).

SPRING: Stirrett (1973b: 23) had a spring maximum of 1000 at Pelee on May 8 to 10. Eli Davis secured a set of 6 eggs near Komoka on May 6, 1928 (Saunders & Dale, 1933: 224). A.W. Preston noted them for the first time at Port Dover on March 11, 1923, while G. Bennett found a nest under construction in a mailbox at Port Rowan as early as March 31, 1973 (McCracken, Bradstreet & Holroyd, 1981: 61). Speirs (1974) reported spring migration peaks in Ontario Co. during the third week of March and first week of April. J.M. Richards saw a nest under construction in a Purple Martin house as early as March 20, 1958: this held 2 eggs on Apr. 22 and 4 eggs on Apr. 26 (Tozer & Richards, 1974: 233). Allin (1940: 104) reported the first in Darlington Twp. on March 7, 1925 and found a nest with 5 eggs there on May 8, 1928. E. Beaupré took a set of 7 eggs at Kingston on May 9, 1926 (Quilliam, 1973: 149). D. Butler collected 5 eggs at Barrie as early as May 7, 1938 and G.L. Lambert noted a nest with young by May 24, 1939 (Devitt, 1967: 130). A. Kay found his first at Port Sydney, Muskoka, in 1926 and Mills (1981: 126-127) summarized the subsequent spread and increase in the cottage country. D.B. Ferguson found a nest with 5 eggs on May 27, 1978 on Manitoulin (Nicholson, 1981: 155). MacLulich (1938: 30) gave March 30, 1933 as his earliest arrival date in Algonquin Park, and C.H.D. Clarke found occupied nests at Brule Lake on May 24, 1934. Ricker & Clarke (1939: 18) gave the spring of 1927 as the first North Bay record, when C. Ramsay found 7 nesting pairs there. Speirs & Speirs (1947: 34) found a nest with young in a gable roof in North Bay on May 16, 1945. Skeel & Bondrup-Nielsen (1978: 198) saw their first at Pukaskwa on March 15, another on Apr. 23 and 14 on May 13, 1977 (their only spring records that year). Dear (1940: 137) found a nest with 5 eggs at Thunder Bay on May 18, 1934. Peruniak (1971: 24) reported up to 30 in April at Atikokan, with migrants appearing near the end of March and adults feeding young in May. Bondrup-Nielsen (1976: 44) noted his first at Kapuskasing on March 20 in 1975. Cringan (1953a: 3) saw his first at Sioux Lookout on Apr. 1 in 1953.

SUMMER: On the 1968-1977 Breeding Bird Surveys they were abundant north to Ottawa and Manitoulin, fairly common farther north except common near the larger cities. Stirrett (1973c: 20) had several maxima of 100 at Pelee from June to August. McCracken, Bradstreet & Holroyd (1981: 61) found their maximum breeding density of 133 territorial males per km² in their red oak - basswood savannah quadrat at Long Point. With Christopher Plowright we estimated 2975 coming to roost in the Lynde Creek marshes near Whitby during the evening of Aug. 1, 1972 and in our urban quadrats we found population densities of 51 to 188 birds per 100 acres: on roadside counts in Ontario Co. this was the second most abundant species (after the Ring-billed Gull) (Speirs, 1974). Speirs & Orenstein (1975: 13) found this to be the most abundant breeding passerine in old forests in Ontario Co. but several early succession forests had none (no suitable nesting cavities in young trees): the maximum population density of 148 birds per 100 acres was found in a forest of old beech trees with many natural cavities, near Oshawa. Allin (1940: 104) found a nest with 6 eggs on June 12, 1930 in Darlington Twp. and saw young on June 26, 1927. L. Campbell collected a set of 5 eggs at Camp Borden on June 2, 1927 (Devitt, 1967: 129). Mills (1981: 127) mentioned 28 nest records for the cottage country between May 10 and July 21. Speirs & Speirs (1947: 34) reported summer nests near North Bay from June 4 (1944) to July 2 (1935). Baillie & Hope (1947: 20-21) found a nest with 4 eggs at Chapleau on June 16, a nest with 3 young at Biscotasing on June 21 and a nest with 2 young a Bigwood on July 20, 1937. Snyder (1942: 142) noted the first young of the year in the Sault Ste. Marie region on June 14, 1931. Skeel & Bondrup-Nielsen (1978: 198) reported only one at Pukaskwa in summer, on June 17, 1977. Baillie & Hope (1943: 19) found a nest with 2 eggs at Marathon, a nest with 4 eggs at Rossport on June 4 and two nests at Amyot on June 23, 1936, one with 5 young and one with 3 young. Snyder (1938: 202) saw none at Rainy River in the summer of 1929 but reported the first arrivals there in 1935. Snyder (1953: 76) reported 20 at Kenora on June 19, 1947 and the first young out of the nest there on June 15, 1947 and on June 13, 1949: he also found up to 25 at Malachi and Sioux Lookout in 1947. James (1980: 89) saw an adult carrying food into a building at Pickle Lake on June 11, 1977. Manning (1952: 79) saw a pair carrying nest material into the Hudson's Bay warehouse at Moosonee on June 14, 1949. Schueler, Baldwin & Rising (1974: 144, 147) collected a female at Winisk on June 25, 1971 and saw young being fed there: they reported that they had been seen there since 1965: they also found a dead young bird about 10 miles south of Smooth Rock Falls on July 4, 1973: they found them common at Cochrane and Moosonee and noted the species at Hawley Lake. H. Lumsden saw 2 at Cape Henrietta Maria on June 25, 1964 and 5 there on July 13 (Peck, 1972: 346). Lee (1978: 30) saw a maximum of 11 (adults and immatures) at Big Trout Lake on June 29, 1975. C.E. Hope found one dead at Ft. Severn on June 17, 1940.

AUTUMN: D. McRae and A. Wormington saw single birds at Netitishi Point, James Bay, on Nov. 1 and 5, 1981. Manning (1952: 79) reported that Harrison Lewis saw 7 at Moose Factory on Oct. 11, 1931 and 12 at Albany on Sept. 22, 1940. Flocks up to 100 have been seen at Atikokan in September (Peruniak, 1971: 24). Skeel & Bondrup-Nielsen (1978: 199) saw 15 at Pukaskwa on Oct. 15 and 3 on Oct. 16, 1977. Mills (1981: 127) saw 550 near Magnetawan on Oct. 14, 1979. Devitt (1967: 130) estimated 2000 to 3000 near Collingwood on Sept. 6, 1937. Harley C. White found large numbers breeding on Wolfe Is. and collected one on Oct. 10, 1921, the first definite record for the Kingston region (Quilliam, 1973: 148). Tozer & Richards (1974: 234) found 5000 roosting in Oshawa'a Second Marsh on Sept. 15, 1966. Speirs (1974) reported fall peaks in Ontario Co. during the first and third weeks of October. Sheppard (1960: 38) saw 4 or 5 at Niagara Falls in October, 1914 (the first Ontario sighting). Brooman (1954: 31) reported thousands migrating westward along the Lake Erie shore of Elgin Co. during October and early November. Saunders & Dale (1933: 224) recorded a flock of 3000 at London by Oct. 16, 1927. Stirrett (1973d: 25) had a fall maximum of 5000 at Pelee on Oct. 12.

BANDING: Fourteeen banded in the Toronto region up to 1958 were recovered elsewhere as follows: Arkansas - 4; Tennessee - 3; Kentucky - 3; and one each in Ohio, Mississippi, Illinois, Missouri, New York and Nova Scotia.

Of 28 banded in the U.S.A. and recovered in the Toronto region, 17 came from Ohio; 4 from Tennessee, 3 from Indiana, 2 from Michigan and one each from Arkansas and Kentucky.

Brewer & Salvadori (1978: 75-76) showed that of 23 banded in Ontario, 11 were taken in Ohio; and of 129 banded out of Ontario and recovered in Ontario, 89 came from Ohio, 5 from Tennessee and 5 from Arkansas: almost all winter recoveries were in states bordering the Mississippi Valley. Two rather distant recoveries of Ontario banded birds were as follows: One banded at Balmoral Marsh, Ont. on Aug. 9, 1966 was recovered at Sycamore, Georgia on Dec. 12, 1967, 751 miles to the south. Another banded at Dundas Marsh, Ont. on Apr. 23, 1966 was recovered at Culman, Alabama on Jan. 28, 1968, 740 miles SW.

**MEASUREMENTS:**
*Length:* 7.5 to 8.5 ins.
(Godfrey, 1966: 312)
*Wingspread:* 15 1/2 ins.
(Roberts, 1955: 631)
*Weight:* 43 Ontario
specimens averaged
81.8 g.

**REFERENCES:**
Saunders, W.E. 1930 The
increase of the Starling.
Can. Field-Naturalist,
44:(1):22.
    Snyder, L.L. and J.L.
Baillie 1930 The increase
and present status of the
Starling at Toronto, 1930.
Can. Field-Naturalist,
44:(8):197-198.

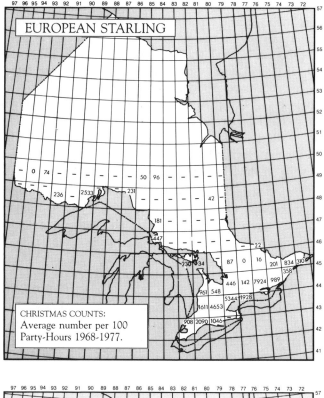

EUROPEAN STARLING

CHRISTMAS COUNTS:
Average number per 100
Party-Hours 1968-1977.

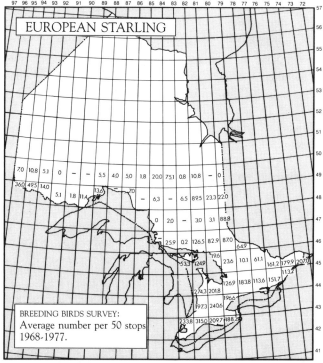

EUROPEAN STARLING

BREEDING BIRDS SURVEY:
Average number per 50 stops
1968-1977.

# WHITE-EYED VIREO   *Vireo griseus*   (Boddaert)

This perky little vireo is rare along the southern fringe of Ontario, occurring fairly regularly at Pelee, sporadically elsewhere. They winter from southern U.S.A. south to Guatemala and Cuba.

**IDENTIFICATION:** Superficially the White-eyed Vireo looks like a Ruby-crowned Kinglet, with its small size, general greenish colour, wing bars and eye ring. At close range the diagnostic white eye, yellow eye ring and yellow bar between eye and bill may be discerned. The song has been given as "*kiss* me Charlie, *quick*", with emphatic beginning and ending and somewhat more musical mid-section. It also utters a typical descending "mew" like other vireos and more characteristically, repeated "chat-chat-chat..."

**WINTER:**

**SPRING:** Stirrett (1973b: 23) gave Apr. 18 as the earliest Pelee date. Harold Lancaster saw one in his Elgin Co. woods on May 21, 1950 (Brooman, 1954: 31). W.D. Hobson collected one near Woodstock on Apr. 25, 1902 (Macoun, 1904: 579). One was observed at Rockhouse Point, Lake Erie, from May 5 to 10, 1962 (Beardslee & Mitchell, 1965: 358). On Apr. 27, 1938, with Henry Barnett, A.F. Coventry and Doris Mills, I found my first Toronto bird at Ashbridge's Bay (see Saunders, 1947: 122): this bird was subsequently collected by Farley Mowat for the ROM collection. Speirs (1974) cited several records for the Lynde Shores woodlot, Whitby and records from Oshawa and the Shoal Point woods, Pickering, all between May 6 and May 17: I saw one there on May 17, 1974 and described the song as "Gyp, me Charlie, Gyp". Weir Quilliam (1980: 21-22) had Kingston records from May 1 to May 30, during 9 seasons. Savile (1957: 33) had Ottawa records on May 14, 1946 and May 14, 1955: one was picked up dead on Apr. 7, 1947 nearby (Lloyd, 1949: 34).

**SUMMER:** During the summer of 1971, two active nests were reported at Rondeau, both unsuccessful (Kelley, 1978: 66). Speirs & Frank (1970: 777) reported a visitor on their Pelee forest quadrat (noted on June 16, 1970). Beardslee & Mitchell (1965: 357-358) reported a nest with 2 eggs at Sherkston on July 1, 1890: another was noted at Silver Bay on June 2, 1936. A.S. Goss found a nest in the Rosedale ravine, Toronto, during the first week of June, 1898 (Macoun, 1904: 579). My most northerly observation was hearing one sing near Wilfrid on our Breeding Bird Survey on June 10, 1979 (with Rob Nisbet).

**AUTUMN:** Nicholson (1981: 156) had a brief glimpse of one on Great Duck Is. on Sept. 22, 1978. Weir & Quilliam (1980: 22) had three fall records for Kingston: Aug. 30 to Sept. 2, 1980; Oct. 11, 1969 (Quilliam, 1973: 149) and Oct. 15, 1980. H.H. Axtell collected a male at Erie Beach on Oct. 5, 1954: sight records included one at Brock's Monument on Sept. 8, 1946 and one at Crescent Beach on Nov. 13, 1955 (Beardslee & Mitchell, 1965: 357-358). One was banded at Bradley's Marsh as late as Oct. 28, 1962 (Kelley, 1978: 66). Stirrett (1973d: 25) had one fall record for Pelee, on Oct. 16, 1964.

**MEASUREMENTS:**
*Length:* 4.5 to 5.5 ins.
(Godfrey, 1966: 314)
*Wingspread:* 7.50 to 8.45

ins. (Roberts, 1955: 664)
*Weight:* 153 averaged
11.4 g. (10.0 - 14.3 g.)
(Dunning, 1984: 20).

# BELL'S VIREO  *Vireo bellii*  Audubon

My only experience with this little vireo was on the Urbana campus of the University of Illinois, where a pair nested in a small orchard, part of my study area for observing American Robins. They are usually found in southwestern United States, wintering in Central America. A few have been found along the southern fringe of Ontario in recent years.

IDENTIFICATION:  This is another kinglet-sized vireo with wing bars, but it lacks the white eye and yellow "spectacles" of the White-eyed Vireo. In Illinois I found the dry, bubbling song to be its best means of identification: "De-bzzhhee, de, de bzzhhee, de-de-bzzhhee".

WINTER:

SPRING:  One was reported at Pelee on May 14, 15 and 22, 1972 by R. Burrows, R.E. Mason and D. Rupert (Goodwin, 1972: 757). Goodwin (1980: 772) *et al* saw one at Pelee on May 15, 1980. One was identified at Bradley's Marsh by J.G. Keenleyside on May 14, 1976 (Goodwin, 1976: 835). J. Kelly, R.E. Mason and R. Simpson reported one at Rondeau on May 16, 1971 (Goodwin, 1971: 738). Others have been reported in May north and east to Presqu'ile, the first identified at Toronto on May 18, 1940, by Henry Barnett *et al*; the first acceptable photograph by Ron Scovell taken at Pelee on May 19, 1963 (Baillie, 1964: 7-8).

SUMMER:  W. Wyett collected one at Pelee on June 23, 1970 (Wyett, 1971: 327-328).

AUTUMN:

**MEASUREMENTS:**
*Length:* 4 3/4 to 5 ins.
(Roberts, 1955: 664)
*Wingspread:* 7 to 8 ins.
(Roberts, 1955: 664)
*Weight:* 10.2 g. (Terres, 1980: 950).

**REFERENCE:**
Wyett, Bill 1971 First Canadian specimen of Bell's Vireo. Can. Field-Nat., 85:(4): 327-328.

# SOLITARY VIREO   *Vireo solitarius*   (Wilson)

This is generally the first of our vireos to show up in spring and the last to leave in autumn. In summer, it is a bird of coniferous forest and may occur anywhere that conifers are found, but is seldom common anywhere. In winter they go south to southern United States, Central America and Cuba.

**IDENTIFICATION:** This is one of our vireos with wing bars. For obvious reasons it was formerly known as the Blue-headed Vireo. It has white "spectacles", white throat and underparts, except for yellowish sides. Its song is similar to that of the Red-eyed Vireo but sung in a minor key and with characteristic "too-wee-choo" phrases like the "wolf-whistles" used by young men to attract the attention of girls.

**WINTER:**

**SPRING:** Stirrett (1973b: 23) had spring records at Pelee from Apr. 26 to June 1 with a maximum of 20 on May 10. Ussher (1965: 22) had Rondeau records from Apr. 25 to May 24, with average arrival on May 9 and departure on May 17. Saunders & Dale (1933: 224) gave the 17-year average arrival for London as May 6, with the earliest on Apr. 27, 1921. Snyder (1931: 205) had Long Point migrants from May 10 to 27, 1928. Speirs (1938: 40) gave Apr. 28 as the earliest Toronto date. Saunders (1947: 371) listed May 7 as the average arrival and May 16 as the average departure date for Toronto, with the latest on May 27. Doris H. Speirs had an early one at our Pickering home on Apr. 20, 1948, where the peak is generally in the second week of May: our latest was on June 3, 1951 (Speirs, 1974). Snyder (1941: 75) collected one at Hillier, Prince Edward Co. on May 3, 1938. Weir & Quilliam (1980: 38) had Kingston records from Apr. 19 to May 30 with the average arrival on May 5 and departure on May 22. Devitt (1967: 131) gave May 10 as the 9-year average arrival date for Barrie, with one at Collingwood as early as May 2, 1916 and the latest at Wasaga Beach on May 24, 1937. L. Beamer had Meaford records from May 9 to May 27. Mills (1981: 128) gave Apr. 29, 1972 as the earliest Huntsville date. Nicholson (1981: 156) found one on Manitoulin as early as Apr. 27, 1974: his high count was 10 on Great Duck Is. on May 23, 1976. MacLulich (1938: 30) gave May 15, 1912 as an arrival date for Algonquin Park. Ricker and Clarke (1939: 18) had one at Lake Nipissing on Apr. 3, 1934. Denis (1961: 4) listed May 19 as the average arrival date at Thunder Bay, with the earliest on May 14, 1944. Peruniak (1971: 24) gave May 5 as her earliest Atikokan date. The earliest at Geraldton was on May 13 (Elder, 1979: 37). Bondrup-Nielsen (1976: 44) gave May 16, 1975 as his earliest Kapuskasing record.

**SUMMER:** On the 1968-1977 Breeding Bird Surveys they were uncommon south to Ottawa, Mt. Julian and Manitoulin, becoming fairly common on the most northerly routes. Two noted singing in the conifer plantations at St. Williams by R. Curry on July 1, 1973 were well south of their normal range (Goodwin, 1973: 866). George A. Scott heard one singing in the Ghost Rd. bush, Oshawa, as late as June 14, 1964 and we heard one in a red pine plantation in Uxbridge Twp. on June 21, 1966 (Speirs, 1974). C.E. Hope collected one at Penetanguishene on June 14, 1935, the only summer record for Simcoe Co. (Devitt, 1967: 131). Mills (1981: 128) mentioned 30 nest records in the cottage country, 16 in balsam firs from 4 to 26 ft. up, with nest building noted as early as May 18 and young in the nest seen as late as Aug. 3. Ross James reported a nest with 4 eggs near Mindemoya, Manitoulin, on July 5, 1977 (Nicholson, 1981: 156). MacLulich (1938: 30) saw an adult with young at Biggar Lake, Algonquin Park, on July 25, 1933. Ricker & Clarke (1939: 18) saw a pair feeding a fledgling at Lake Nipissing on Aug. 23, 1925: they considered the species "quite common". Paul Harrington found a nest with 4 eggs about 6 ft. up in a small jack pine at Chapleau on June 7, 1937: another nest just completed was found 3 1/2 ft. up in a black spruce there on June 9, 1937 (Baillie & Hope, 1947: 21). Snyder (1942: 142) collected a male at Laird on June 6,1931 and saw others at Iron River and Point aux Pins, near Sault Ste. Marie. Baillie & Hope (1943: 20) collected a juvenile not long out of the nest at Amyot on July 4, 1936. Dear (1940: 137) found a nest with 3 eggs on June 18, 1936 and a nest with 4 small young on July 1, 1934 near Thunder Bay. Kendeigh (1947: 27) found 2 pairs per 100 acres at Black Sturgeon Lake in 1945, while Speirs (1949: 148) had 8 territories on 75 acres at nearby Eaglehead Lake in 1946. Snyder (1938: 203) found them rare in the Rainy River region, with only one record on July 10, 1929 at Off Lake. Snyder (1953: 76) found them fairly common in far western Ontario, from Savanne west to Ingolf. Smith (1957: 177) considered them to be uncommon in the Clay Belt, but had records from Hearst, Gogama and Lake Abitibi where Snyder (1928: 30) saw only five all summer in 1925. James (1980: 89) found two nests near Pickle Lake, one with 4 young on June 14, 1977 and the other with 4 eggs on June 15, 1979. Hope (1938: 34) found a nest with 5 young on June 23, 1938 at Favourable Lake about 7 ft. up in a small jack pine: another nest found the same day 4 ft. up in a small black spruce held 4 eggs. James, Nash & Peck (1982: 66) found a nest with 4 eggs on June 22, 1982 and another nest with 4 young on June 24 and 26, near James Bay by the Harricanaw River. George M. Sutton believed there were two pairs on Moose Island in the summer of 1956 (Todd, 1963: 584). C.E. Hope and T.M. Shortt listed this species at Ft. Albany during their stay between June 7 and July 4, 1942. Lee (1978: 30) found three singing males at Big Trout Lake, two of these on July 24, 1975.

AUTUMN: Peruniak (1971: 24) gave Sept. 19 as her latest Atikokan record. Louise Lawrence heard one singing at Pimisi Bay as late as Oct. 5, 1945 (Speirs & Speirs, 1947: 34). Nicholson (1981: 156) noted fall birds on Manitoulin from Sept. 4 (1977) to Oct. 27 (1973). K. Ketchum saw one off Pointe au Baril on Oct. 7, 1967 (Mills, 1981: 129). Devitt (1967: 131) had Simcoe Co. records from Sept. 4, 1938 at Wasaga Beach to Oct. 21, 1945 at DeGrassi Point. Weir & Quilliam (1980: 38) had Kingston records from Aug. 14 to Nov. 12, with average arrival on Sept. 5 and departure on Oct. 16. J. Satterly noted one as early as Aug. 23, 1959 at Cedar Point, Mara Twp. and George A. Scott observed one at Oshawa as late as Nov. 12, 1972 (Speirs, 1974). Saunders (1947: 371) listed Aug. 25 and Oct. 28 as his earliest and latest Toronto dates with Sept. 17 and Oct. 5 as average arrival and departure dates. Speirs (1938: 54) gave Nov. 8 as the latest Toronto record. Beardslee & Mitchell (1965: 359) had Ontario records near Buffalo on Aug. 25, 1946 and Nov. 7, 1954. Stirrett (1973a: 19) had one at Pelee as late as Nov. 17: the first showed up on Aug. 31 and the maximum of 10 was noted on Oct. 5 (Stirrett, 1973d: 25).

**MEASUREMENTS:**
*Length:* 5 to 6 ins.
(Godfrey, 1966: 316)
*Wingspread:* 8.35 to 9.75
ins. (Roberts, 1955: 663)
*Weight:* 2 ♂ averaged
16.5 g. (Hope, 1938: 34)
12.3 to 21.6 g. (a very fat
migrant) (Terres,
1980: 953).

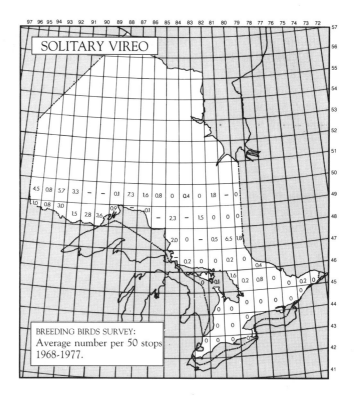

SOLITARY VIREO

BREEDING BIRDS SURVEY:
Average number per 50 stops
1968-1977.

# YELLOW-THROATED VIREO   *Vireo flavifrons*   Vieillot

The Yellow-throated Vireo is quite rare in most of southern Ontario and absent from most of the north, but there are traditional "pockets" where they may be found year after year: the one that I know best is just south of Washago, another is the Minesing Swamp. They retire to southern Central America in winter.

**IDENTIFICATION:** This vireo is known by its bright yellow throat, yellow "spectacles" and wing bars. Like most vireos it is more often heard than seen: its song is quite loud, similar to the song of the Red-eyed Vireo, but with a husky tanager-like quality that is distinctive.

**WINTER:**

**SPRING:** Stirrett (1973b: 23) had Pelee records from Apr. 30 to May 24, with a maximum of 10 on May 10. Ussher (1965: 22) gave May 15 as his 17-year average arrival date at Rondeau, with the earliest on May 4. Saunders & Dale (1933: 224) gave May 6 as the 16-year average arrival date at London, with the earliest on Apr. 29, 1921: a nest with 4 eggs was found on May 21, 1902. C.E. Hearn and D.G. Wake had an early one at Dorchester on Apr. 24, 1976. Earl Lemon found a nest at West Lorne on May 20, 1951, some 25 ft. up in an elm (Brooman, 1954: 31). Snyder (1931: 205) saw just one at Long Point, on May 30, 1927. Fleming (1907: 83) gave May 2 as his earliest Toronto date, while Saunders (1947: 371) listed May 21 as his 11-year average arrival date there.

Speirs (1974) saw one in his Pickering woods as early as Apr. 30, 1957 and four at the north end of Lake St. John, Rama Twp. on May 22, 1967. Weir & Quilliam (1980: 38) listed May 15 as the 34-year average arrival date at Kingston, with the earliest on May 4. Devitt (1967: 131) gave May 20 as a 4-year average arrival date at Minesing Swamp, with the earliest on May 17. Lloyd (1924: 13) cited a few Ottawa records from May 11 (1906) to May 26 (1884). Nicholson (1981: 156) had just two spring records for Manitoulin: May 20, 1975 at Mississagi Light and May 10, 1980 at Bass Lake. Louise Lawrence noted one at Pimisi Bay on May 20, 1972 (Goodwin, 1972: 757). Ross James reported a pair nest building at Rainy River on May 26, 1977 (Goodwin, 1977: 1134).

SUMMER: On the 1968-1977 Breeding Bird Surveys they were uncommon and spotty in southern Ontario, with northern outliers from Mattawa and Ouelette in the east to Silver Islet, Dryden and Eagle River in the west. Saunders & Dale (1933: 224) reported a nest with 4 eggs plus one cowbird egg at London on June 11, 1900. Frank Farley took a nest with 4 eggs in Elgin Co. about 40 ft. up in a large maple on June 18, 1887 (Brooman, 1954: 31). W.E. Clyde Todd found one at Pt. Rowan on July 15, 1907 (Snyder, 1931: 205). I watched a pair in Washago on June 21-22, 1969, building a nest 20 ft. up in an ash tree and Ron Tozer saw one carrying food in Scugog Twp. on July 2, 1968 (Speirs, 1974). Allin (1940: 104) had a Darlington Twp. sighting on June 18, 1933. Quilliam (1973: 150) detailed several summer records near Kingston, including an adult seen carrying food on June 25, 1925, by E. Beaupré . H.P. Bingham found a nest with 3 eggs plus 2 cowbird eggs on July 3, 1942 (Devitt, 1967: 130). Mills (1981: 128) cited details of several summer sightings in and around the cottage country. D.B. Ferguson found a pair building at Windfall Lake, Manitoulin, on June 22, 1930, with young being fed in the nest by July 13 (Nicholson, 1981: 156). Ricker and Clarke (1939: 18) reported one at Lake Nipissing on June 3, 1924. Snyder (1953: 76) reported one at Shoal Lake on June 15, 1949; one at Thunder Lake between Dryden and Wabigoon in August, 1939, and a summer record from Kenora. More recent records from this part of Ontario include one noted at Crozier on July 18, 1977 (Goodwin, 1977: 1134) and one observed at Rainy River by M. Robson and A. Wormington on July 2, 1979 (Goodwin, 1979: 860).

AUTUMN: J. Foster and C. Garton reported one at Slate River, near Thunder Bay, on Sept. 19, 1981 (Goodwin, 1982: 174). Nicholson (1981: 156) found one dead on Great Duck Is. on Sept. 22, 1977 and sent the specimen to the ROM. Two were reported at Huntsville on Oct. 2, 1961 (Mills, 1981: 128). Devitt (1967: 131) gave Oct. 13, 1966 as his latest Barrie date, a TV tower casualty. Weir & Quilliam (1980: 38) listed Sept. 11 as the 14-year average departure date from Kingston, with the latest on Sept. 25. E. Laird reported one in Darlington Twp. as late as Oct. 13, 1971 (Tozer & Richards, 1974: 235). Saunders (1947: 371) gave Sept. 21 as his 7-year average departure date from Toronto, his latest on Oct. 16. A very late one was noted at London on Nov. 19, 1972 by M. Larmour and R. Pukraka (Goodwin, 1973: 56). Ussher (1965: 22) gave Sept. 4 as his latest Rondeau date. Stirrett (1973d: 25) had just 7 fall records of single birds at Pelee, from Aug. 29 to Sept. 29.

**MEASUREMENTS:**
*Length:* 5 to 6 ins.
(Godfrey, 1966: 315)
*Wingspread:* 9.12 to
10.00 ins. (Roberts,
1955: 663)
*Weight:* 0.69 oz. (Roberts,
1955: 663).

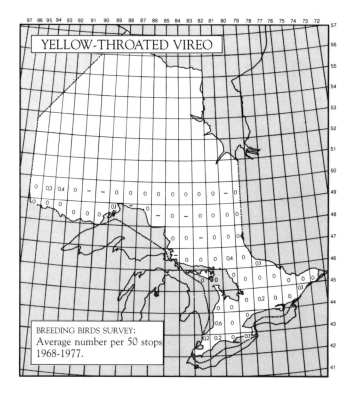

YELLOW-THROATED VIREO

BREEDING BIRDS SURVEY:
Average number per 50 stops
1968-1977.

# WARBLING VIREO   *Vireo gilvus*   (Vieillot)

In Ontario this is a bird of village shade trees or by rural roadsides, not a dweller in forest tree tops like the Red-eyed Vireo. In winter they go south to Central America.

IDENTIFICATION: This is a small vireo with no wing bars. The pale line over its eye is not bordered above and below with dark lines as in the Red-eyed and Philadelphia Vireos. It is best identified by its song which is a long warble, much like the song of the Purple Finch but always ending with a question (a rising pitch). In the fall the young may be quite yellowish below (see the account of the Philadelphia Vireo for distinction from that species).

WINTER:

SPRING: Stirrett (1973b: 23) had his earliest one at Pelee on May 2 and a maximum of 12 on May 10. Ussher (1965: 22) had a 24-year average arrival at Rondeau on May 9 with the earliest on Apr. 27. Saunders & Dale (1933: 225) gave May 6 as the 17-year average arrival date at London, with the earliest on Apr. 27, 1915. Frank Farley collected a set of 3 eggs plus one cowbird egg at St. Thomas on May 30, 1887 about 20 ft. up in a beech tree. Snyder (1931: 205) heard one on Long Point on May 5, 1928. J.L. Baillie (in Saunders, 1947: 371) gave May 14 as his 21-year average arrival date at Toronto, with the earliest on May 1: Speirs (1938: 44) gave May 19 as the spring peak there. Edgerton Pegg saw one as early as Apr. 29, 1969 at his Pickering Twp. home: I saw one at its nest in Washago on May 30, 1969 (Speirs, 1974). Weir & Quilliam (1980: 38) gave May 4 as the 29-year average arrival date at Kingston, with the earliest on Apr. 28. Devitt (1967: 133) gave May 18 as the 24-year average arrival date at Barrie, the earliest on May 2, 1955: J.J. Baker found a nest with 3 eggs at Big Cedar Point as early as May 21, 1933. Lloyd (1924: 13) gave May 23, 1891 as his earliest Ottawa date. L. Beamer's median arrival date at Meaford was May 17 and his earliest was on May 7, 1949. May 11 was the 5-year average arrival date at Huntsville, the earliest on May 5, 1965 (Mills, 1981: 131). Nicholson (1981: 158) gave May 19 as the 11-year average arrival date for Manitoulin, with the earliest on May 8, 1979 and a high count of 4 on May 22, 1977. Ricker & Clarke (1939: 18) noted one at North Bay on May 29, 1925. R.W. Trowern reported two seen at Cobalt on May 24, 1950 (Todd, 1963: 587).

SUMMER: On the 1968-1977 Breeding Bird Surveys they were common along the northeast shore of Lake Erie, fairly common elsewhere in southern Ontario and near Lake of the Woods, becoming uncommon north to Gogama and east to Thunder Bay, with one outlier at Smooth Rock Falls. Stirrett (1973c: 20) had records throughout the summer at Pelee but his maximum was only 6 on June 25. Saunders & Dale (1933: 225) had a nest with 4 eggs at London as early as June 4, 1877 and another set of 4 eggs as late as June 18, 1892: also one set of 3 eggs plus 2 cowbird eggs on June 14, 1916, all nests more than 25 ft. up. McCracken, Bradstreet & Holroyd (1981: 62) reported a nest with young on Long Point on July 4, 1977 and an adult on another nest on June 1, 1980, both in maples. J. Satterly located a nest 30 ft. up in a birch at Cedar Point, Mara Twp. on July 1, 1963 (Speirs, 1974). Populations of 6 to 27 birds per 100 acres were found in 6 of 10 urban quadrats studied in Ontario Co., in 1969: none in the most heavily populated centres nor in any of the 11 forest or field plots (Speirs, 1974). Tozer & Richards (1974: 238) followed a nesting on the Cartwright-Manvers townline at Hwy. 7A: it was 28 ft. up in a poplar and under construction on June 1, 1968; on July 1 it held 3 young. A.E. Hughes found a nest on Howe Is. near Kingston on May 17, 1954: this held one egg on May 23, 3 eggs hatching on June 8 and by June 30 the young were almost fully fledged (Quilliam, 1973: 152). Devitt (1967: 133) found a nest with 4 eggs at Big Cedar Point on June 13, 1943 about 25 ft. up in a maple and H.P. Bingham collected a set of 4 eggs at Barrie on June 14, 1928. Mills (1981: 131) cited about half a dozen breeding records for the cottage country, the earliest on June 2, 1979 at Port Sydney. Ross James found an empty nest at Evansville, Manitoulin on July 5, 1977 and Ron Tasker observed 10 in Burpee Twp. on June 25, 1974 (Nicholson, 1981: 158). Speirs & Speirs (1947: 34) heard two singing at North Bay on June 5 and one there on June 30 in 1944.

AUTUMN: One was killed at the Great Duck Is. tower on Sept. 21, 1977 (Nicholson, 1981: 158). Jim Goltz saw one at Bala on Sept. 1, 1970 (Mills, 1981: 131). At the Barrie TV tower two were killed in 2 of 7 years, the latest on Oct. 9, 1966 (Devitt, 1967: 133). Weir & Quilliam (1980: 38) gave Sept. 17 as the 23-year average departure date from Kingston, the latest on Oct. 20. My latest fall record for Pickering Twp. was on Sept. 24, 1956 (Speirs, 1974). Fleming (1907: 83) gave Sept. 24 as his latest Toronto date. Beardslee & Mitchell (1965: 361) had an Oct. 25, 1953 record for Rockhouse Point, Lake Erie. Ussher (1965: 22) had his latest at Rondeau on Sept. 7. Kelley (1978: 67) mentioned one as late as Nov. 19, 1974 at Pelee: Stirrett (1973d: 25) had a maximum of 10 there on Sept. 26.

**MEASUREMENTS:**
*Length:* 5 to 6 ins.
(Godfrey, 1966: 319)
*Wingspread:* 8 1/2 to 9 1/
4 ins. (Roberts, 1955: 664)
*Weight:* 0.56 oz. (Roberts,
1955: 664)
   13.4 to 18 g. (very fat)
(Terres, 1980: 953).

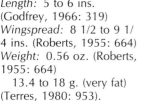

WARBLING VIREO

BREEDING BIRDS SURVEY:
Average number per 50 stops
1968-1977.

# PHILADELPHIA VIREO   *Vireo philadelphicus*   (Cassin)

In summer this is a bird of the Precambrian region of Ontario, where it is often overlooked because of its retiring habits and the similarity of its song to that of the common Red-eyed Vireo. Although often said to inhabit alders and other wetland deciduous growth, the one that I knew best (at Dorion north of Lake Superior) spent most of its time high in big aspens. They go south to winter in southern Central America and northern South America.

IDENTIFICATION: This is a small vireo with no wing bars, yellowish breast and with an "eyebrow line" bordered above and below with dusky (like a Red-eyed Vireo but less distinctly bordered). In fall, young Warbling Vireos may have quite yellowish sides; at this season be sure to look for the dark borders to the line over the eye that distinguishes the Philadelphia from the Warbling. The song is very similar to that of the Red-eyed Vireo but tends to be higher pitched, slower, with longer pauses between phrases. (Identification by song alone is risky.)

WINTER:

SPRING: Stirrett (1973b: 23) had Pelee records from May 2 to June 1, with a maximum of 14 on May 20. Ussher (1965: 22) had observations at Rondeau from May 4 to May 28, with average arrival on May 14 and departure on May 24. Saunders & Dale (1933: 225) gave May 20 as the 12-year average arrival date at London, with the earliest on May 11, 1924. Snyder (1931: 205) reported 14 killed at the Long Point light on May 14, 1925, and one collected at Turkey Point by D.A. MacLulich on May 27, 1931. J.L. Baillie (in Saunders, 1947: 371) had Toronto records from May 11 to June 7, with average arrival on May 18 and departure on May 27: Speirs (1938: 40) listed a May 7 date for Toronto. My earliest record at our Pickering home was May 10, 1970 (Speirs, 1974). Long (1968b: 21) observed one as late as June 3, 1968 at Pickering Beach. Tozer & Richards (1974: 237) observed one at Thickson's Woods, Whitby, on May 9, 1962. Allin (1940: 105) reported one seen by M.G. Gould in Darlington Twp. on May 14, 1921. Weir & Quilliam (1980: 38) had Kingston records from May 2 to June 6, with average arrival on May 13 and departure on May 27. Devitt (1967: 132) gave May 22 as the 6-year average arrival date at Barrie, with one at Collingwood as early as May 6, 1950, and one at Tollendal as late as June 5. Lloyd (1924: 12) reported Ottawa specimens taken on May 13, 1886 and May 30, 1906. Mills (1981: 130) reported spring migrants in the cottage country from May 16, 1964 at Point au Baril to June 1, 1974 along the Gibson River. Nicholson (1981: 158) gave May 21 as the 11-year average arrival date on Manitoulin, with the earliest on May 9, 1979 and 10 found dead by the Great Duck Is. tower on May 28, 1979. Louise Lawrence observed one at Pimisi Bay on May 18, 1945 (Speirs & Speirs, 1947: 34). Skeel & Bondrup-Nielsen (1978: 200) saw their first of 5 spring birds at Pukaskwa on May 21, 1977. Denis (1961: 4) listed May 26 as the average arrival date at Thunder Bay, with the earliest on May 23, 1952. Peruniak (1971: 24) gave May 21 as her earliest Atikokan date. Elder (1979: 37) had his earliest at Geraldton on May 24: he considered it "fairly common" there in summer. Cringan (1953a: 3) saw his first at Sioux Lookout on May 21, 1953.

SUMMER: On the 1968-1977 Bird Breeding Surveys they were fairly common from Kenora and Cochrane to rare south to Cobden and Byng Inlet. Stirrett (1973c: 20) had an Aug. 5 record of 3 at Pelee and others from Aug. 18 to 31. Ussher (1965: 22) gave Aug. 17 as his earliest southbound bird at Rondeau, with average arrival on Aug. 28. Beardslee & Mitchell (1965: 360-361) had their earliest returning migrant at Morgan's Point, Lake Erie, on Aug. 15, 1959. Saunders (1947: 371) reported a July 22 bird at Toronto. Speirs (1974) reported a very late northbound bird noted by Naomi LeVay at Eastbourne, Whitby, on June 25, 1972: our earliest returning bird at our Pickering home was on Aug. 12, 1972. Weir & Quilliam (1980: 38) listed the earliest returning bird at Kingston on July 19, with average arrival on Aug. 20. A.A. Outram reported seeing an adult feeding a young bird two miles NE of Washago on July 25, 1948 (Devitt, 1967: 132). Mills (1981: 130) cited details of breeding records at Lake Joseph, Huntsville, Doe Lake and Solitaire Lake and one nest record at Dickie Lake, near Baysville: a southbound bird was noted as early as July 26, 1977, at Ahmic Lake by J. Meritt. Ricker & Clarke (1939: 18) collected individuals at Frank's Bay, Lake Nipissing, on June 9 and 15, 1932, and noted others throughout June. Baillie & Hope (1947: 20) saw a male feeding a young cowbird at Bigwood on July 18, 1937 and they collected a female and young there on July 27, 1939. Snyder (1942: 142) saw only one near Sault Ste. Marie (on June 9, 1931 near Maclennan). Skeel & Bondrup-Nielsen (1978: 200) had Pukaskwa records from June 9 to Aug. 18. Baillie & Hope (1943: 20) collected two at Rossport on June 2 and 4 and two at Marathon on June 11 and 13, 1936. Snyder (1928: 271) considered this species almost as common at Lake Nipigon as the Red-eyed Vireo, with its song a musical fifth higher in pitch than the Red-eyed Vireo's and with slightly longer pauses between phrases: a pair was seen carrying nest material on June 19, 1923. Snyder (1935: 203) collected a male at Emo on June 13 and another male at Off Lake on July 5, 1929, in the Rainy River region. Peruniak (1971: 24) saw one carrying nesting material on June 8, 1961, at Atikokan. David Elder saw one there on Aug. 22, 1981. Snyder (1953: 76) found them "rather scarce" at Ingolf and Wagiboon in 1937 and at Malachi and Sioux Lookout in 1947 (his maximum was 8 at Sioux Lookout on July 5). Smith (1957: 177) called this "the voice of the wet alder thickets" in the Clay Belt: he saw an adult feeding a young bird at Lake Timiskaming on July 31, 1953 and one 8 miles north of Hearst on June 3, 1954. Snyder (1928: 30) found it at all three camps on Lake Abitibi in 1925. Bondrup-Nielsen (1976: 47) found a nest in an alder thicket near Kapuskasing on June 16, 1974. James (1980: 89) found a nest with 4 eggs about 13 km. NE of Pickle Lake on June 15, 1977 and a nest with 4 eggs at Central Patricia on June 18, 1979. The first Ontario nest was collected at Favourable Lake by Hope (1938: 35): it contained 3 young several days old on June 27, 1938. Manning (1952: 80) saw 12 and collected two of these near Moosonee from June 15 to 29, 1949. James, Nash & Peck (1982: 66) found three nests with 4 eggs each and one nest with 3 eggs from June 20 to July 7 near James Bay by the Harricanaw River. Schueler, Baldwin & Rising (1974: 144, 147) found them at Cochrane, Moosonee and "fairly common" at Attawapiskat in tall stands of balsam poplar. Lee (1978: 30) noted them at Big Trout Lake from June 8 to 26, 1975; one bird 6 times in about 2 weeks in thickets and deciduous trees around the cemetery.

AUTUMN: Nicholson (1981: 158) reported Manitoulin birds from Aug. 26 (1973) to Sept. 28 (1979) with 48 killed at the Great Duck Is. tower from Sept. 19 to 23, 1977. D. Sutherland saw one at Beausoleil Is. as late as Sept. 16, 1976 (Mills, 1981: 131). Devitt (1967: 132) reported one seen at Wasaga Beach on Aug. 27, 1942 as the earliest Simcoe Co. record: 37 were killed in 6 of 7 years at the Barrie TV tower, the latest two on Oct. 2, 1965. Quilliam (1973: 198) reported 46 killed at the Ontario Hydro Lennox station on Sept. 19, 1972. Weir & Quilliam (1980: 38) listed Sept. 27 as the average departure date from Kingston, with the latest on Nov. 6. George A. Scott saw one at the Oshawa lakefront on Oct. 17, 1954 following hurricane "Hazel". Saunders (1947: 371) saw his latest at Toronto on Sept. 30. Beardslee & Mitchell (1965: 360-361) had their latest fall bird at Rockhouse Pt., Lake Erie, on Oct. 19, 1958. Snyder (1931: 205) mentioned Long Point light casualties from Sept. 7 to 29, 1929. Ussher (1965: 22) gave Sept. 12 as the average departure date from Rondeau, the latest on Sept. 28. Stirrett (1973d: 25) gave Oct. 30 as his latest Pelee record.

BANDING: One banded at Bewdley, Ont. on Aug. 28, 1962 was recovered at Chiquimulilla, Guatemala on Apr. 13, 1970 about 2179 miles to the south and 7 1/2 yrs. after banding as an adult.

**MEASUREMENTS:**
*Length:* 4.5 to 5.0 ins.
(Godfrey, 1966: 318)
*Wingspread:* 8 to 9 ins.
(Roberts, 1955: 664)
*Weight:* 8.9 to 15.9 g. (a
fat migrant) (Terres,
1980: 952)
♂ 11.5 g. 2 ♀ averaged
11.3 g. (Hope, 1938: 35).

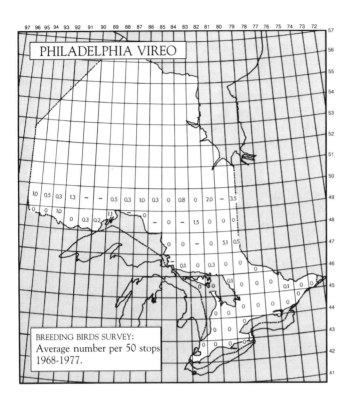

PHILADELPHIA VIREO

BREEDING BIRDS SURVEY:
Average number per 50 stops
1968-1977.

# RED-EYED VIREO   *Vireo olivaceus*   (Linnaeus)

In Ontario this is a warm weather bird, seldom plentiful until mid-May and most leaving by the end of September. In summer it is one of our most common birds, busy in the tops of deciduous trees where they are hard to see though their presence is betrayed by persistent singing. They often build their nests suspended from a fork low in the understory in a tall shrub or small sapling, lovely cup-shaped nests usually decorated with strips of birch bark. In winter they go south to northern South America.

**IDENTIFICATION:** This is one of our vireos without wing bars, greenish above and whitish below, with red eyes and prominent white stripe over each eye bordered with blackish lines above and below. The Philadelphia Vireo has yellow underparts while the Warbling Vireo lacks the blackish border above and below its eye stripes: both are much smaller than the Red-eyed Vireo. This species is a very persistent singer "Vireo-veery-veery-ee" something like a very slow-paced robin song.

**WINTER:**

**SPRING:** Stirrett (1973b: 23) had one at Pelee as early as Apr. 26, with a maximum of 30 on May 18. Ussher (1965: 22) gave May 11 as the 17-year average arrival date at Rondeau, with the earliest on May 4. Saunders & Dale (1933: 224) gave May 14 as the 17-year average arrival date at London, with the earliest on May 4, 1916: a set of 4 eggs was found on May 29, 1914. Snyder (1931: 204) mentioned 32 killed at the Long Point light, on May 14, 1925. Saunders (1947: 371) listed May 17 as his 13-year average arrival date at Toronto, with one as early as Apr. 23. Long (1968a: 17) had his earliest Pickering Beach record on May 7, 1967. Speirs (1974) gave May 25 as the peak for spring migration in Ontario Co.: George A. Scott noted 35 on that date in 1959 at Oshawa. J.M. Richards found a nest under construction in Darlington Twp. as early as May 23, 1970 (Tozer & Richards, 1974: 237). Weir & Quilliam (1980: 38) listed May 13 as the 31-year average arrival date at Kingston, with the earliest on Apr. 30. Devitt (1967: 132) gave May 20 as the 21-year average arrival date at Barrie, the earliest at Collingwood on May 11, 1955. L. Beamer reported one "just killed" on Apr. 9, 1947 at Meaford (specimen sent to the ROM): his next earliest record was a more usual May 19, 1939 and the median arrival date was May 25. Mills (1981: 129) gave May 15 as the 7-year average arrival date at Huntsville, with the earliest on May 12: in the ROM is a Muskoka skin dated May 4, 1897. Nicholson (1981: 157) gave May 18 as the 12-year average arrival date on Manitoulin, with the earliest on May 11, 1978 and a high count of 360 on May 20, 1977. MacLulich (1938: 31) gave May 19, 1933 as his earliest Algonquin Park record. Louise Lawrence noted one at Rutherglen on May 1, 1942 (Lawrence, 1953: 49). Skeel & Bondrup-Nielsen (1978: 199) saw only 12 on 7 days from May 15 to 31, 1977 at Pukaskwa. Denis (1961: 4) gave May 23 as the average arrival date at Thunder Bay, with the earliest on May 13, 1956. Peruniak (1971: 24) saw her earliest at Atikokan on May 14. Elder (1979: 37) gave June 2 as his earliest date for Geraldton. Bondrup-Nielsen (1976: 44) saw his first near Kapuskasing on May 29 in 1975.

SUMMER: In the Precambrian forest of Ontario this is probably our most common species. In the north they show a pronounced preference for stands of aspen and are relatively scarce in pure spruce forests. In the agricultural south it is confined to scattered woodlots which gave it a fairly common status on Breeding Bird Surveys there. Stirrett (1973c: 20) had a June 15 maximum of 8 at Pelee, increasing to 18 by Aug. 13. Saunders & Dale (1933: 224) cited several nest records for the London region: A.A. Wood described a nest found on June 8, 1918 which held one vireo egg and 4 cowbird eggs; a chipmunk approaching the nest was knocked to the ground by the defending vireo. McCracken, Bradstreet & Holroyd (1981: 61) reported two Long Point nests in 1978: one with young on June 28 and one with 2 eggs on July 1. Speirs & Orenstein (1975: 13) found populations in 9 of 11 forest plots in Ontario Co. (missing in two early succession plots) with a maximum of 77 birds per 100 acres in the Rama quadrat; exceeded in total abundance by Great Blue Heron (in the Scugog plot only), the Starling (found only in the 5 oldest plots) and by the Ovenbird (in the same 9 plots as the Red-eyed Vireo). J.A. Edwards found an early nest on Thorah Is. with 2 eggs and 2 cowbird eggs on June 6, 1933 and a late nest there on July 22, 1928 with one vireo egg and 3 cowbird eggs: of 14 sets of eggs found in Ontario Co. only 3 sets with a total of 11 eggs lacked cowbird eggs of which 21 were found in 11 other sets (Speirs, 1974). Quilliam (1973: 151) mentioned two nests, each with 4 eggs, found in the Kingston region: one by E. Beaupré on June 10, 1903; the other on June 16, 1963 at the Otter Lake Sanctuary. Dates for nests with fresh eggs in Simcoe Co. ranged from June 6 (1919) to July 17 (1918) (Devitt, 1967: 131). C.E. Johnson took a nest near Ottawa on June 23, 1916 (Lloyd, 1924: 12). Mills (1981: 129) reported 97 nest records for the cottage country: in a maple forest near Dorset I found a population of about 40 territories per 100 acres. M.Y. Williams found a nest with 4 eggs at Lake Manitou on June 24, 1920 and D.B. Ferguson found a nest with 3 eggs at Pike Lake, Manitoulin, on July 14, 1973 (Nicholson, 1981: 157). MacLulich (1938: 31) saw an adult feeding young in Algonquin Park on July 18, 1930. Ricker & Clarke (1938: 18) reported a nest with 4 eggs at Frank's Bay, Lake Nipissing, on June 14, 1933 and J.R. Dymond took a young cowbird from a nest with two young vireos there on July 7, 1930. Baillie & Hope (1947: 21) found two nests at Chapleau on June 7, 1937, one just completed and the other with 2 eggs: they found another nest with 3 eggs at Bigwood on July 19. This species ranked fifth in abundance at Pukaskwa in summer (Skeel & Bondrup-Nielsen, 1978: 199). Snyder (1928: 271) found a nest with 2 eggs and 2 newly-hatched young at Lake Nipigon on July 18, 1923. Dear (1940: 137) found a nest with 4 small young on July 1, 1934 and a nest with 3 eggs on June 18, 1936, both near Thunder Bay. Kendeigh (1947: 27) found 7 pairs on 100 acres at Black Sturgeon Lake in 1945 and Speirs (1949: 148) had 7 territories on 75 acres in 1946 at nearby Eaglehead Lake. Snyder (1938: 203) found a completed nest at Off Lake, Rainy River, on June 1, 1929. On July 11, 1962 one was incubating 2 eggs in a nest in a white pine at Atikokan (Peruniak, 1971: 24). Snyder (1953: 75) saw one nest building at Kenora on June 18, 1930 and a nest with 2 eggs at Wabigoon on June 17, 1937: his maximum daily total was 50 at Malachi on July 16, 1947. Hope (1938: 34) considered them abundant at Favourable Lake. Cringan (1953a: 3) noted his first at Sioux Lookout on June 10, 1953. Cringan (1950: 16) heard his first in the Nikip Lake area on June 5, 1950. James (1980: 84) had a population density of 8 per km² at Pickle Lake and saw a female building a nest on June 16, 1979 about 35 km. northeast of there. Manning (1952: 79) saw 16 in the Moosonee region from June 15 to July 1, 1949. James, Nash & Peck (1982: 66) found a nest with 3 eggs on June 29, 1982, near James Bay by the Harricanaw River. C.E. Hope and T.M. Shortt listed this species at Ft. Albany during their stay from June 7 to July 4, 1942. Lee (1978: 30) noted a maximum of 5 at Big Trout Lake on July 24, 1975, where it was the most common vireo in aspen stands: he saw his first there on June 13.

AUTUMN: Peruniak (1971: 24) gave Sept. 22 as her latest Atikokan date. Skeel & Bondrup-Nielsen (1978: 199) had only 5 on Sept. 5 in the fall of 1977 at Pukaskwa. Lawrence (1953: 74) gave Sept. 28 as her latest date for Pimisi Bay. Nicholson (1981: 157) reported 106 killed at the Great Duck Is. tower between Sept. 17 and 24, 1977, with his latest Manitoulin record on Nov. 2, 1975. J. Goltz found one at Arrowhead Park, Muskoka, as late as Oct. 12, 1980 (Mills, 1981: 130). Lloyd (1924: 12) watched one at close range in Ottawa on Nov. 4, 1922. Frances Westman found 230 killed at the Barrie TV tower in 7 years, the latest on Oct. 17, 1966 (Devitt, 1967: 132). Weir & Quilliam (1980: 38) listed Oct. 3 as the 27-year average departure date from Kingston, the latest on Oct. 22. Ross James collected a juvenile male near Brougham as late as Oct. 26, 1968 (Speirs, 1974). J.L. Baillie (in Saunders, 1947: 371) gave Sept. 22 as his 19-year average departure date from Toronto, with the latest on Oct. 21. Snyder (1931: 204) reported 109 picked up about the Long Point light after the night of Sept. 7, 1929 with smaller numbers after Sept. 9, 24 and 29. Ussher (1965: 22) gave Sept. 14 as the 9-year average departure date from Rondeau, the latest on Oct. 2. Stirrett (1973d: 25) had a fall maximum of 20 at Pelee on Oct. 3, and his latest on Nov. 9.

**MEASUREMENTS:**

*Length:* 5.3 to 6.5 ins. (Godfrey, 1966: 317)
*Wingspread:* 9 3/4 to 10 3/4 ins. (Roberts, 1955: 664)
*Weight:* 149 Ontario specimens averaged 17.67 g.

**REFERENCES:**

Lawrence, Louise de Kiriline 1953 Nesting life and behaviour of the Red-eyed Vireo. Can. Field-Nat., 67: (2): 47-77. Of 44 nests found, 34 were in deciduous trees, 10 in conifers, ranging from 3 to 55 ft. up; males sang from 21 to 52 phrases per minute during incubation (by the female); females spent from 58 to 88% of their time incubating; females did about 63% of the feeding of the young, males 37%; 30 nests contained 98 eggs of which 80% hatched and 60% produced fledged young; singing continued to Sept. 5, but with a 21-day lapse during moult. A very thorough study.

(Lawrence), Louise de Kiriline 1954 The voluble singer of the tree-tops. Audubon Magazine, 56:(3): 109-111. On May 27, 1952 a male at Pimisi Bay sang 22,197 songs from 4:22 a.m. to 6:13 p.m., singing about 10 hours and silent about 4 hours during this period.

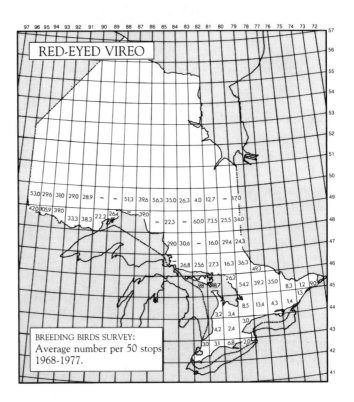

RED-EYED VIREO

BREEDING BIRDS SURVEY:
Average number per 50 stops
1968-1977.

# BLUE-WINGED WARBLER   *Vermivora pinus*   (Linnaeus)

Like the Golden-winged Warbler (with which it sometimes hybridizes), this is a bird of early to mid-succession forests, and occupies much the same places in Ontario, although it tends to be more confined to the southern fringe and is generally less common. They winter in southern Central America.

IDENTIFICATION: This is a mainly yellow warbler with bluish wings and a narrow black line through the eye: like a small Prothonotary Warbler but with white wing bars and the black line through the eye. Its song is a wheezy, high-pitched "zee-zah" as if inhaling then exhaling (but sometimes with more than two syllables).

WINTER: Harry Kerr, David Ruch and Margaret Wilson had excellent views of a lingering migrant at Lynde Shores Conservation Area, Whitby, on Dec. 1, 1982 (Weir, 1983: 298).

SPRING: Stirrett (1973b: 23) had Pelee records from Apr. 28 to May 24. A. Wormington saw an early one at Pelee on Apr. 19, 1977 (Goodwin, 1977: 995). Ussher (1965: 23) had Rondeau records from May 1 to May 28, with an 8-year average arrival on May 9. A.A. Wood collected a male in the Sydenham River valley on May 16, 1932 (Saunders & Dale, 1933: 248). G.E. Maddeford reported seven at Newbury on May 28, 1977 (Goodwin, 1977: 995). J.B. Miles noted one on territory at Wingham from May 12, 1974 (Goodwin, 1974: 797). J.L. Baillie had Toronto sightings on May 7 and May 12 (Saunders, 1947: 371). The earliest Ontario Co. record was on May 3, 1963 at Oshawa by Ora Sands, George A. Scott and Ron Tozer. I saw a fine male at our home in Pickering Twp. on May 19, 1958 and on May 21, 1961, I watched a mixed pair about a mile southwest of our home (see Brewster's Warbler) (Speirs, 1974). T. Norris observed one in Darlington Twp. from May 15-17, 1973 (Tozer & Richards, 1974: 240). Snyder (1941: 77) collected a male at Hallowell, Prince Edward Co., on May 23, 1930 (and reported the first Ontario specimen collected at Pelee before 1908 and a later one at Strathroy in 1932). Weir & Quilliam (1980: 22, 23, 38) gave May 14 as the 17-year average arrival date for Kingston, with the earliest on May 8. E.L. Brereton saw one at Wasaga Beach on May 16, 1941 (Devitt, 1967: 134-135). The only report from the cottage country was one at Bala seen on May 10, 1970 by J. Goltz (Mills, 1981: 133).

SUMMER: Ussher (1965: 23) had an Aug. 25 record at Rondeau. W. McCord noted one at Tillsonburg from June 6 to June 25, 1978 (Goodwin, 1979: 174). B.D. Parker had Oxford Co. sightings at Ingersoll and Lockhart Pond on June 13, 1981 (Goodwin, 1981: 936). P.A. Read noted nesting at Kilworth on July 17, 1981 (Goodwin, 1981: 936). C.A. Campbell found them in numerous locations near Waterloo on June 16, 1979, even more numerous than Golden-winged Warblers (Goodwin, 1979: 860). Saunders (1947: 235) described seeing his first in the Humber River valley, Toronto, on Aug. 13, 1944. C.J. MacFayden found them in Minesing Swamp on June 4 and 11, 1978 (Goodwin, 1978: 1156). Ron Orenstein and I saw three in Mara Twp. on June 10 and 17, 1966 (Speirs, 1974). One was seen at Kingston on June 4, 1972 according to R.D. Weir (Goodwin, 1972: 854) and one at the Otter Lake Sanctuary of the Kingston Field Naturalists on June 2 and 9, 1974 (Goodwin, 1974: 899). E. Elligsen found one in the Ellice Swamp, Perth Co. on June 9, 1974 (Goodwin, 1974: 899).

AUTUMN: Nicholson (1981: 159) saw one at Great Duck Is. on Sept. 23, 1977. Weir & Quilliam (1980: 22) reported fall records for Kingston from Aug. 20 to Sept. 25. J. and L. Fazio observed a very late one at Hamilton on Nov. 4, 1979 (Goodwin, 1980: 157). R. Erickson and H.J. Wolcott banded one at Bradley's Marsh on Sept. 25, 1971 (Goodwin, 1972: 58). Stirrett (1973d: 25) had Pelee records from Aug. 27 to Sept. 30.

**MEASUREMENTS:**
*Length:* 4.5 to 5.0 ins.
(Godfrey, 1966: 322)
*Wingspread:* 6.85 to 7.50
ins. (Roberts, 1955: 667)
*Weight:* 8.3 to 11.0 g.
(Terres, 1980: 967).

# BREWSTER'S WARBLER
*Vermivora chrysoptera x V. pinus*   (Hybrid)

This is the relatively common dominant hybrid between the Golden-winged and Blue-winged Warblers. They may show up wherever the parent species occur.

IDENTIFICATION: This hybrid usually shows the white underparts of the Golden-winged and the yellow wing bars, but the breast may show some yellow and the wing bars may be mainly white in some individuals. The face pattern is as in the Blue-winged with the black line through the eye but no black bib or ear patches. See Pough (1949: 153) for more details.

WINTER:

SPRING: Stirrett (1973b: 23) had records from May 4 to May 20 at Pelee. Goodwin (1978: 1000) reported several in mid-May, 1978, at Pelee. Beardslee & Mitchell (1965: 367-368) reported one at Rose Hill, Lake Erie, on May 6, 1955. On May 21, 1961, I watched a pair in Range 3, Lot 35, Pickering Twp.: the male sang like a typical Blue-winged while the female looked like a Brewster's. John A. Livingston observed one in the Lynde Shore woods, Whitby, on May 18, 1964. Mrs. Ora Sands and Mrs. F. Stephens noted one in the Osler Tract, south of Lake Scugog, on May 13, 1959 (Speirs, 1974). Tozer & Richards (1974: 240) discovered one in Darlington Twp. from May 10 to 13, 1965. Ken Edwards noted two singing by the Canoe Lake road, near Kingston, from May 19 to 24, 1977: another was observed at Prince Edward Point May 20-21, 1978 (Weir & Quilliam, 1980: 22-23). One was reported in Vespra Twp., Simcoe Co., on May 15, 1955 and another near Barrie on May 23, 1956 (Devitt, 1967: 134-135). A most unexpected sighting was made by Rob. Nisbet on Caribou Is., Lake Superior, on May 20, 1981 (Goodwin, 1981: 820).

SUMMER: J. Murray saw one at Palgrave on July 7, 1974 (Goodwin, 1974: 899). J.M. Richards saw a male Brewster's and female Golden-winged feeding a young cowbird in Darlington Twp. on June 26, 1965 and presumably the same male there again on June 5, 1966 (Tozer & Richards, 1974: 240). J. Satterly noted a bird with some Brewster characteristics in Mara Twp. during the summer of 1964 (Speirs, 1974). Weir & Quilliam (1980: 23) mentioned several records in the Kingston region, including one by Frank Phelan on Aug. 26, 1977 at Opinicon.

AUTUMN: Beardslee & Mitchell (1965: 367-368) reported one at Port Colborne on Sept. 1, 1944.

# LAWRENCE'S WARBLER
*Vermivora chrysoptera x V. pinus* (Hybrid)

This is the relatively rare recessive hybrid between the Golden-winged and Blue-winged Warblers.

IDENTIFICATION: This is the recessive hybrid, showing the yellow underparts and usually white wing bars as in Blue-winged Warblers and the black bib and ear patches as in Golden-winged Warblers. See Pough (1949: 153) for a more detailed explanation of the genetics of these hybrids.

WINTER:

SPRING: Stirrett (1973b: 23) had only one record of this hybrid at Pelee, on May 14, 1949. Kelley (1978: 68) had another Pelee record on May 20, 1967. Subsequent records there include one on May 12, 1976 by P.D. Pratt (Goodwin, 1976: 835) and one in mid-May, 1978 by D. Baker *et al* (Goodwin, 1978: 1000). Doris H. Speirs observed one carefully at our Pickering home on May 28, 1963 (Speirs, 1974). R.D. Weir found one at the Otter Lake Sanctuary of the Kingston Field Naturalists on May 23, 1981 (Goodwin, 1981: 820).

SUMMER: George Stirrett found one at Morton, near Kingston, on July 20, 1947 (Quilliam, 1973: 153).

AUTUMN:

# GOLDEN-WINGED WARBLER
*Vermivora chrysoptera*   (Linnaeus)

This species sometimes mates with the Blue-winged Warbler (see Brewster's and Lawrence's Warbler accounts): all are birds of early to mid-succession forests, usually with some dead trees to serve as singing posts: as the trees reach maturity the familiar sites are deserted. In suitable habitat they may be found north to Muskoka and stragglers farther north. They winter in southern Central America and northern South America.

IDENTIFICATION: The males have black throats and ear patches, golden-yellow wing patches and crowns: the black is replaced by gray in females. The song is a very high-pitched "zee-dzz-dzz-dzz". I can no longer hear such high-pitched songs but when I could, my tape-recorder could not pick up the song though to me at that time it sounded loud and clear.

WINTER:

SPRING: Stirrett (1973b: 23) had Pelee records from Apr. 21 to two as late as June 7, with a maximum of 6 on May 10. Ussher (1965: 22) had Rondeau birds from May 1 to May 31, with the 17-year average arrival on May 10. Saunders & Dale (1933: 226) gave May 11 as the 17-year average arrival date at London, with the earliest on Apr. 28, 1915. Snyder (1931: 206) noted one seen by W.E. Saunders at Turkey Point on May 17, 1925 and one collected there by D.A. MacLulich on May 26, 1931. J.L. Baillie (in Saunders, 1947: 371) had Toronto records from May 7 to May 17: Speirs (1938: 40) listed a May 6 record there. Speirs (1974) reported three traditional localities for this species in Ontario Co.: one in Pickering Twp. where I saw my earliest on May 5, 1964: one near Oshawa where George A. Scott had two May 7 dates (1950 and 1959) and one in northeastern Mara Twp. where Jack Satterly saw five on May 19, 1968. J.H. Jennings saw one at Bowmanville on May 10, 1934 (Baille & Harrington, 1937: 241). Weir & Quilliam (1980: 38) listed May 11 as the 24-year average arrival date at Kingston, with the earliest on Apr. 30, 1970. Devitt (1967: 134) gave May 16 as the 13-year average arrival date at Barrie, with the earliest on May 2, 1942. The earliest spring dates for Muskoka were at Bala, by Jim Goltz on May 10 in 1968 and again in 1970 (Mills, 1981: 133). Nicholson (1981: 159) gave May 17 as the 10-year average arrival date on Manitoulin, with the earliest on May 9, 1979.

SUMMER: On the 1968-1977 Breeding Bird Surveys they were rare from Port Dover north to Barry's Bay and Port Carling, absent on other routes. Stirrett (1973d: 25) had returning migrants at Pelee from Aug. 21 to 31. Ussher (1965: 22) had one as early as Aug. 7 at Rondeau. Saunders & Dale (1933: 226) reported a set of 4 eggs at London on June 8, 1912 and a set of 5 on June 2, 1914. J.L. Baillie (in Saunders, 1947: 371) had an Aug. 19 record for Toronto. Speirs & Orenstein (1975: 13) found a population of 16 birds per 100 acres in their Whitby forest quadrat, an area recovering from hurricane damage. George A. Scott observed one in the Osler tract south of Lake Scugog on June 13, 1958: Jack Satterly has seen birds in June and July, summer after summer, in Mara Twp., one male as late as Aug. 27, 1959: I saw 13 in roadside counts in Rama Twp. in June, 1963 (Speirs, 1974). Lewis H. Lowther found a nest with 4 well-feathered young at Canoe Lake, near Kingston, on June 14, 1961 (Quilliam, 1973: 153). W.E. Cattley found a nest with 4 young in Matchedash Twp., Simcoe Co., on June 18, 1966 (Devitt, 1967: 134). Mills (1981: 133) found a nest with 5 young a few inches off the ground in alder-spruce forest at Gibson Lake, Muskoka, on June 11, 1976: he cited a few other summer records for the cottage country. Nicholson (1981: 159) had four June records for Manitoulin, from June 4 to June 30 (but none later). D. Brunton and T. Pratt noted 5 singing birds at Colton Lake, Algonquin Park, on June 29, 1972 and a female was seen at Dahlia Station on June 9 (Goodwin, 1972: 854). Denis (1961: 7) listed this as a species for which there was an acceptable Thunder Bay record, but gave no details. David Elder banded one at Rainy River on Aug. 2, 1980 (Goodwin, 1980: 892).

AUTUMN: Chris Harris saw one at Go Home Bay on Aug. 31, 1975 (Mills, 1981: 133). Only one was killed at the Barrie TV tower, on Sept. 12, 1961 (Devitt, 1967: 134). Weir & Quilliam (1980: 38) listed Aug. 27 as the 5-year average departure date from Kingston, the latest on Sept. 6, 1957. Tozer & Richards (1974: 239) reported one as late as Sept. 29, 1962 in Darlington Provincial Park. R.M. Saunders saw one on Sept. 3, 1960 at Eastbourne, Whitby (Speirs, 1974). Speirs (1938: 54) listed a Sept. 13 record for Toronto. Beardslee & Mitchell (1965: 365-366) reported birds at Erie Beach on Sept. 21, 1940 and at Crescent Beach, Lake Erie, on Sept. 27, 1953. One was killed at the Long Point light on Sept. 7, 1929 (Snyder, 1931: 206). Ussher (1965: 22) gave Oct. 1 as his latest Rondeau record. Stirrett (1973d: 25) gave Sept. 23 as his latest at Pelee.

**MEASUREMENTS:**
*Length:* 4.9 to 5.3 ins.
(Godfrey, 1966: 321)
*Wingspread:* 6.50 to 8.16
ins. (Roberts, 1955: 678)
*Weight:* Three Ontario
specimens averaged 8.8 g.

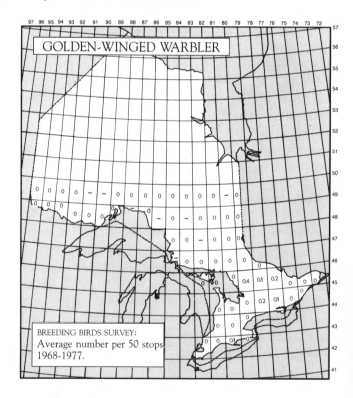

GOLDEN-WINGED WARBLER

BREEDING BIRDS SURVEY:
Average number per 50 stops
1968-1977.

# TENNESSEE WARBLER   *Vermivora peregrina*   (Wilson)

This is largely a bird of the tall spruces of northern Ontario. One summer we heard three or four singing every place we stopped between Timmins and Foleyet: this year we heard none there, but found it to be the most numerous warbler farther north, near Manitou-wadge. In the accounts below you will note similar year to year fluctuations in populations in other parts of northern Ontario, perhaps related to outbreaks of spruce budworm and other food species. They tend to be rather late in arriving in spring in Ontario from their winter homes in Central America (south to northern South America and north to Mexico).

**IDENTIFICATION:**   The Red-eyed Vireo has much the same colour pattern in spring and the Philadelphia Vireo in fall, but the fine pointed bill of the Tennessee will distinguish it from these species: it is also a more active bird than the vireos and lacks the blackish borders to the white line above its eye of these vireos. The song always reminds me of a steam locomotive starting up, with its emphatic accelerating beginning and smooth-running ending "tch-dee-tch-dee-tch-dee - di-di-di-di-di".

**WINTER:**

**SPRING:**   Stirrett (1973b: 23) had Pelee records from Apr. 22 to June 2, with a maximum of 100 on May 11. At Rondeau, Ussher (1965: 23) had reports from Apr. 29 to June 2, with average arrival on May 12 and departure on May 25. Saunders & Dale (1933: 226) gave May 14 as the 16-year average arrival date at London, with the earliest on May 9, 1916. Snyder (1931: 206-207) reported 22 killed at the Long Point light on May 14, 1925. Saunders (1947: 371) had Toronto records from May 2 to June 3, with average arrival on May 13 and departure on May 21: Speirs (1938: 44, 46) listed May 21 as the spring peak there and had a June 7 record. My earliest Pickering Twp. record was May 8, 1951 and latest on May 29 (1949 and 1960): George A. Scott saw one at Oshawa on May 7, 1950 (Speirs, 1974). Weir & Quilliam (1980: 38) had Kingston records from May 2 to June 3 with average arrival on May 13 and departure on May 27. Devitt (1967: 135) gave May 16 as the 16-year average arrival date at Barrie, with the earliest on May 7, 1964. Mills (1981: 134) noted spring migrants in the cottage country from May 16 to May 28. Nicholson (1981: 160) had Manitoulin records from Apr. 27 (1974) to May 31 (1979): he estimated 1500 during a phenomenal reverse migration at Great Duck Is. on May 19, 1979 with 168 killed at the tower there when returning on May 28. E.L. Brereton noted one as early as May 12, 1936 at Cache Lake, Algonquin Park (MacLulich, 1938: 31). Speirs & Speirs (1947: 34) saw three near North Bay on May 19, 1944. Skeel & Bondrup-Nielsen (1978: 201) saw only one in spring at Pukaskwa, on May 24, 1977. Denis (1961: 4) listed May 19 as the average arrival date at Thunder Bay, with the earliest on May 10, 1953. Peruniak (1971: 25) gave May 14 as her earliest Atikokan date. Elder (1979: 37) gave May 21 as his earliest date for Geraldton. Bondrup-Nielsen (1976: 44) listed May 19 as his earliest near Kapuskasing in 1975. Cringan (1953a: 3) found his first at Sioux Lookout on May 24 in 1953.

**SUMMER:**   On the 1968-1977 Breeding Bird Surveys it was rare south to Kemptville and Byng Inlet, becoming common on some of the more northerly routes. Stirrett (1973c: 20 and 1973d: 26) had a returning bird at Pelee as early as Aug. 12, with the fall maximum of 25 on Aug. 30. Ussher (1965: 23) had one as early as Aug. 1 at Rondeau, with Aug. 25 as the average date of return there. Beardslee & Mitchell (1965: 369) reported one at

Morgan's Point, Lake Erie, as early as Aug. 6, 1944. Saunders (1947: 371) gave Aug. 12 as his earliest date for a returning bird at Toronto. On July 5, 1963 one was singing at our Pickering Twp. home, perhaps "driven south by forest fires in the north?" but Aug. 12 was my earliest date for an ordinary returning migrant (Speirs, 1974). Weir & Quilliam (1980: 38) gave Aug. 14 as the 20-year average arrival date for southbound birds at Kingston, but had one as early as July 3. Mills (1981: 134) had cottage country records as late as June 5, 1941 and as early as July 5, 1941; some of these perhaps breeding birds though he had no definite record of breeding. Ron Tasker had summer birds in Burpee Twp., Manitoulin, on July 2, 1970, July 12, 1976 and banded one there on July 28, 1972. Louise Lawrence observed two young at Pimisi Bay on July 11, 1945 (Speirs & Speirs, 1947: 34). A.E. Allin and Paul Harrington found 4 nests in sphagnum at Biscotasing in 1941: a nest with 6 eggs on June 9, a nest with 5 eggs on June 10 and a nest with 4 small young also on June 10 and a nest with 4 eggs on June 11 (Baillie & Hope, 1947: 22). Snyder (1942: 143) identified one at Laird and one at Maclennan during the summer of 1931. Skeel & Bondrup-Nielsen (1978: 201) saw one on June 27 and two on July 1, 1977 at Pukaskwa. Baillie & Hope (1943: 20) also found it rare along the northeast shore of Lake Superior in 1936 but I noted 20 between Dorion and Marathon on June 15, 1956 and considered it one of the more common warblers that year, as did Snyder (1928: 271-272) who found a nest with 4 eggs on June 21, 1929 at Lake Nipigon. Dear (1940: 137) found a nest with 4 eggs at Whitefish Lake, Thunder Bay, on June 8, 1935. Kendeigh (1947: 27) found a population of 59 pairs on 100 acres at Black Sturgeon Lake in 1945: it ranked second in abundance there that year. Speirs (1949: 148) had just 7 territories on 75 acres at Eaglehead Lake in 1946: where it ranked 7th in abundance of the warblers that summer. Snyder (1938: 205) found them fairly common in the black spruce forest at Big Fork, but rare elsewhere in the Rainy River region in 1929. Peruniak (1971: 25) reported them to be fairly common at Atikokan and noted one carrying nest material there. Snyder (1953: 77) called this "Primarily a bird of the black spruce country" in western Ontario, commonly observed at Savanne, Sioux Lookout and Malachi. James (1980: 84) found 1.6 pairs per km. in one of 12 transects at Pickle Lake. Hope (1938: 35) called this "the commonest warbler" of the Favourable Lake region where he found a nest with 7 eggs on June 16 and a nest with 6 eggs on June 18, and many broods later in the season. Cringan (1950: 16) noted them throughout June and July, 1950 in the Nikip Lake area. Manning (1952: 80) reported them from Moosonee north along the James Bay coast to Raft River and collected two juveniles at Shagamu River on the Hudson Bay coast. James, Nash & Peck (1982: 69) found a nest with 6 eggs on June 24 and nests with 6 young on June 25 and again on June 27, 1982 at the Harricanaw River, near James Bay. James, Nash & Peck (1981: 92) found a nest at Kiruna Lake, Sutton Ridges, in the summer of 1981. Schueler, Baldwin & Rising (1974: 147) collected a female with two large ova at Attawapiskat on June 20, 1971 and breeding males near Hawley Lake on June 29, 1962 and July 3, 1964: they found them common at Winisk. Lee (1978: 31) had a maximum daily count of 4 on July 25, 1975 at Big Trout Lake where he found them on two of the three quadrats studied: he saw his first there on June 8. C.E. Hope noted them almost daily at Fort Severn in 1940 with a maximum of 20 on July 7.

AUTUMN: Speirs & Speirs (1947: 34) were surprised to see them for several weeks on broccoli plants in their North Bay garden, the last on Oct. 4, 1944. Nicholson (1981: 160) had fall migrants on Manitoulin from Aug. 25 (1974) to Oct. 13 (1973): 143

were killed at a tower there in Sept., 1977. The latest fall migrant in the cottage country was seen at Go Home Bay by Chris Harris on Oct. 12, 1975 (Mills, 1981: 134). A. Tyler reported one at Ottawa as late as Nov. 10, 1973 (Goodwin, 1974: 48). Devitt (1967: 135) reported 80 killed at the Barrie TV tower in 7 years from Sept. 9 to Oct. 2: Frances Westman saw a late one at Tollendal on Oct. 14, 1959. Weir & Quilliam (1980: 38) listed Oct. 5 as the 19-year average departure date from Kingston, the latest on Oct. 29. George A. Scott saw two as late as Oct. 19, 1958 at Oshawa (Speirs, 1974). Saunders (1947: 371) listed J.L. Baillie's latest Toronto date as Oct. 24, with Aug. 30 and Sept. 27 as average arrival and departure dates: Speirs (1938: 52) gave Sept. 23 as the fall peak there. Ussher (1965: 23) gave Oct. 7 as his average departure date from Rondeau, with the latest on Oct. 23. Stirrett (1973d: 26) had his latest Pelee bird on Oct. 14.

**MEASUREMENTS:**
*Length:* 4.5 to 5.0 ins. (Godfrey, 1966: 322)
*Wingspread:* 7.40 to 8.30 ins. (Roberts, 1955: 684)
*Weight:* 7 females averaged 9.3 g. (Hope, 1938: 36).

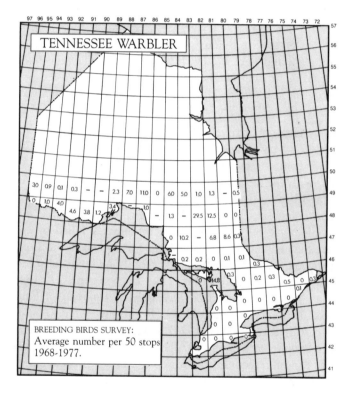

TENNESSEE WARBLER

BREEDING BIRDS SURVEY: Average number per 50 stops 1968-1977.

# ORANGE-CROWNED WARBLER   *Vermivora celata*   (Say)

In Ontario this is usually a rare warbler, breeding only in the far north. It tends to be a rather late fall migrant, after most other warblers have gone. It winters from Central America north to southern United States.

IDENTIFICATION: This is "the warbler with no field marks": no bright colours, no wingbars, no eye ring; only a very indistinct line over the eye, faint greenish streaks on the yellowish breast and yellow undertail coverts. The orange crown is seldom visible. The fall immature Blackpoll Warbler is somewhat similar but does have wing bars and white, not yellow, undertail coverts. This was a common songster on Vancouver Island, where I learned to recognize its trill, something like a Chipping Sparrow's trill, but descending in pitch and fading out at the end.

WINTER: Individuals were reported on the Long Point Christmas counts on Dec. 16, 1972 and Dec. 17, 1977. "Dr. White had one at his feeding station at Port Colborne, Ontario, from December 5 to 10, 1960" (Beardslee & Mitchell, 1965: 370). A. Wormington saw one at Hamilton on Dec. 6, 1977 (Goodwin, 1978: 345). Earl Stark and Doug. Scovell observed one at Whitby on Dec. 16, 1962 (Speirs, 1974).

SPRING: Stirrett (1973b: 23) had Pelee records from Apr. 20 to June 1, with maxima of 10 on May 10 and May 14. P.D. Pratt noted one at Windsor as early as Apr. 22, 1976 (Goodwin, 1976: 836). Ussher (1965: 23) had sightings at Rondeau from May 3 to May 22, with the 14-year average arrival date on May 11. Saunders & Dale (1933: 226) gave May 16 as the 12-year average arrival date at London, with the earliest on May 11, 1921. Earl Lemon noted one in West Elgin on May 27, 1934 and Harold Lancaster found one at his home on May 14, 1950, presumably killed by a grackle that was seen harrassing the bird earlier in the day. One was killed at the Long Point light on May 14, 1925 (Snyder, 1931: 206) who noted 8 on Long Point from May 20 - 27, 1928. A.E. Schaffner saw one at Morgan's Point, Lake Erie on Apr. 22, 1945 and one at Port Colborne on May 25, 1952 (Beardslee & Mitchell, 1965: 370). Saunders (1947: 371) had Toronto records from Apr. 30 to May 29 but gave May 11 and May 14 as average arrival and departure dates. Speirs (1974) had just six spring observations in 26 years in Ontario Co., the earliest on May 3, 1970 and latest on May 22, 1967. Weir & Quilliam (1980: 38) had Kingston records from May 3 to May 28, with average arrival on May 11 and departure on May 21. Devitt (1967: 135) gave May 17 as the 4-year average arrival date at Barrie: T.M. Shortt collected one at Minesing on May 16, 1931. G.R. White observed one at Ottawa on May 18, 1898 and collected one there on May 28, 1909 (Lloyd, 1924: 13). Mills (1981: 134) had just two records for Muskoka: one at Arrowhead Park on May 13, 1979 and one by D. Wilkins on May 20, 1956 at Go Home Bay. Nicholson (1981: 160) had Manitoulin records from May 1 (1977) to May 29 (1979), with a high count of 4 on May 23, 1976 and a 10-year average arrival date on May 12. Ricker & Clarke (1939: 18) noted two at Lake Nipissing on May 18, 1926. Denis (1961: 4) gave May 19 as the average arrival date at Thunder Bay, with the earliest on May 14, 1950. Peruniak (1971: 25) had just 3 spring records at Atikokan, from May 8 to May 17, in 1961, 1962 and 1963. She observed one at Quetico from May 14 in 1975 (Goodwin, 1975: 847). Elder (1979: 37) called it a rare spring migrant at Geraldton but cited no definite record.

SUMMER: On the 1968-1977 Breeding Bird Surveys they were reported only at Elk Lake and at Stratton. Saunders (1947: 371) had an early Aug. 16 record for Toronto: G. Bennett saw another there on Aug. 24, 1976 (Goodwin, 1977: 172). R.C. Long noted one on Wolfe Is., near Kingston, on Aug. 18, 1972 (Goodwin, 1973: 55). Devitt (1967: 135) saw one at Wasaga Beach as early as Aug. 21, 1938. Wm. Mansell reported one at Rebecca Lake on Aug. 10, 1939 and K. Ketchum saw one at Pointe au Baril on Aug. 22, 1973 (Mills, 1981: 134). Ron Tasker banded one in Burpee Twp., Manitoulin, on Aug. 27, 1979 (Nicholson, 1981: 160). Speirs & Speirs (1947: 34) found one at North Bay on Aug. 7, 1944. K. Boshcoff reported one at Pukaskwa on Aug. 11, 1973 (Skeel & Bondrup-Nielsen, 1978: 201). Snyder (1928: 271) noted a few pairs at Lake Nipigon and collected a male there on June 24, 1924, the most southerly record for the breeding season. David Elder saw one at Atikokan on Aug. 23, 1981. One was observed at Minaki on Aug. 16, 1937 by Cartwright (Snyder, 1953: 77). On July 19, 1953 I heard two singing between Kenora and Dryden (having become familiar with the song on Vancouver Is. earlier). James (1980: 89) found small numbers in scrub habitat at Pickle Lake from June 7 to 9, 1977. Hope (1938: 36) found this to be a "not uncommon summer resident" at Favourable Lake where he found Ontario's only nest, with 4 eggs, on June 14 and saw juveniles with parents on July 12, 1938. Manning (1952: 81) collected a male at Moosonee on July 1, 1949 and two females at Big Piskwanish on June 11, 1947. James, Nash & Peck (1981: 46) found 5 pairs per km² in black spruce forest at Kiruna Lake, Sutton Ridges, during the summer of 1981. Schueler, Baldwin & Rising (1974: 144) listed them as common in suitable habitat at Winisk, uncommon at Hawley Lake and noted at Cochrane. Lee (1978: 31) found at least 5 singing males at Big Trout Lake in the summer of 1975. C.E. Hope saw them frequently at Fort Severn from June 21 to July 15, 1940, and collected two there.

AUTUMN: Speirs & Speirs (1947: 34) noted individuals at North Bay on Sept. 16 and 18, 1944. Nicholson (1981: 160) had fall records for Manitoulin from Sept. 19 (1977) to Oct. 25 (1975) with the 11-year average departure date on Sept. 30 and a high count of 8 on Great Duck Is. on Oct. 15, 1978. One was collected in Ryde Twp. southern Muskoka, on Oct. 15, 1936 (Mills, 1981: 134). E.G. White shot one at Ottawa on Sept. 27, 1885: examined later by Lloyd (1924: 13). Frances Westman found only 5 killed at the Barrie TV tower in 7 years, the latest on Oct. 13, 1966 (Devitt, 1967: 135). Weir & Quilliam (1980: 38) had Kingston records from Aug. 24 to Oct. 28, with average arrival on Sept. 18 and departure on Oct. 11. George A. Scott saw an early one at Oshawa on Aug. 29, 1971 and Eric Nasmith reported one at Whitby as late as Nov. 13, 1966 (Speirs, 1974). Saunders (1947: 371) listed Sept. 10 and Oct. 11 as average fall arrival and departure dates for Toronto. Speirs (1938: 54) had a Nov. 25 date there. D.K. Powell noted one at Hamilton as early as Sept. 3, 1974 (Goodwin, 1975: 52) and A. Wormington observed one there from Nov. 9 to 12, 1971 (Goodwin, 1972: 58). B. Nathan observed one at Crescent Beach, Lake Erie, as early as Sept. 1, 1958 (Beardslee & Mitchell, 1965: 370). Ussher (1965: 23) had fall records at Rondeau from Oct. 8 to Nov. 2. Stirrett (1973d: 26) had Pelee records from Sept. 5 to Oct. 12.

**MEASUREMENTS:**
*Length:* 4.8 to 5.3 ins.
(Godfrey, 1966: 323)
*Wingspread:* 7.10 to 8.25
ins. (Roberts, 1955: 670)
*Weight:* 4 ♂ averaged 8.5
g and 1 ♀ weighed 9.8 g.
(Hope, 1938: 36).

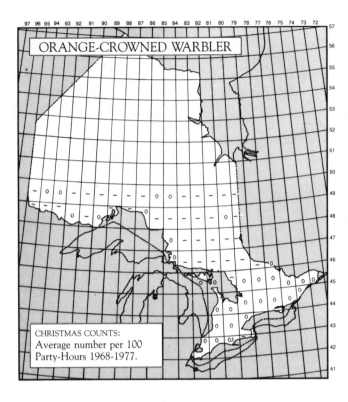

ORANGE-CROWNED WARBLER

CHRISTMAS COUNTS:
Average number per 100
Party-Hours 1968-1977.

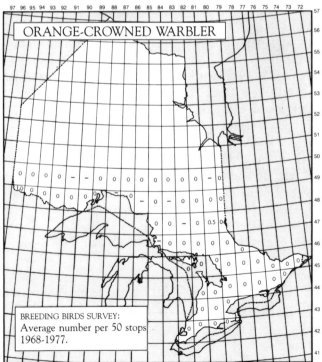

ORANGE-CROWNED WARBLER

BREEDING BIRDS SURVEY:
Average number per 50 stops
1968-1977.

# NASHVILLE WARBLER  *Vermivora ruficapilla*  (Wilson)

In southern Ontario Nashville Warblers are rather scattered, mostly in cedar swamps or relict tamarack-spruce bogs. In northern Ontario this is a fairly common bird of the coniferous forests. They winter from Mexico to Guatemala.

IDENTIFICATION: This is a warbler with no wing bars, a yellow throat and breast, a bluish-gray head with prominent white eye-rings. The rufous crown, from which it gets its scientific name, is seldom seen in life. The song is an enthusiastic, two-part ditty:"tee-da, tee-da, tee-da, du-du-du-du-du".

WINTER: Goodwin (1968: 435) reported one seen by N. Randall at Pinery Provincial Park on Dec. 23, 1967. Kelley (1978: 70) mentioned a straggler in Lambton Co. on Dec. 30, 1967 (the following week). Eli Davis found one near London on Jan. 10, 1932 (Saunders & Dale, 1933: 227).

SPRING: Stirrett (1973b: 23) had Pelee records from Apr. 21 to May 23, with a maximum of 200 on May 12. Ussher (1965: 23) had Rondeau reports from Apr. 5 to May 30. Saunders & Dale (1933: 226) gave May 5 as the 17-year average date for arrival at London, with the earliest on Apr. 28, 1915. Snyder (1931: 206) had Long Point records from May 6 to May 30 in 1928. Saunders (1947: 371) listed Apr. 23 as his earliest Toronto date, with the 13-year average arrival on May 3: Speirs (1938: 44) gave May 11 as the spring peak there. Speirs (1974) had spring birds in Pickering Twp. from Apr. 28 (1957) to May 30 (1968). Allin (1940: 105) found a nest with 3 eggs and a cowbird egg at Hampton, Darlington Twp., on May 24, 1930. Snyder (1941: 77) reported migrants in Prince Edward Co. from May 6 to May 25, 1930. Weir & Quilliam (1980: 38) listed May 3 as the 31-year average arrival date at Kingston, with the earliest on Apr. 23 and the 24-year average departure date on May 23. Devitt (1967: 136) gave May 8 as the 27-year average arrival date at Barrie, the earliest on Apr. 29, 1963: he reported three Simcoe Co. nests found during the last week of May; one with 5 eggs at Barrie on May 26, 1922; another there with 4 eggs and a cowbird egg on May 31, 1952 and another with 4 eggs and a cowbird egg in Conc. 10, Vespra Twp. on May 25, 1963. L. Beamer's median arrival date at Meaford was May 12, the earliest on May 7, 1939. The 7-year average arrival date at Huntsville was May 6, the earliest on Apr. 30, 1962 (Mills, 1981: 135). Nicholson (1981: 161) gave May 4 as the 12-year average date for arrival on Manitoulin with the earliest on Apr. 23, 1977 and a high count of 200 on May 11, 1974 (but 500 on May 19, 1979 on Great Duck Is.). MacLulich (1938: 31) gave May 17, 1932 as his earliest Algonquin Park date. Ricker & Clarke (1939: 18) gave May 4 as their earliest dates at Lake Nipissing (in 1925 and 1934). Skeel & Bondrup-Nielsen (1978: 201) noted their first at Pukaskwa on May 12, 1977, with 49 on 13 days up to May 31. Denis (1961: 3) gave May 15 as the average arrival date at Thunder Bay, with the earliest on May 7, 1950. Peruniak (1971: 25) gave Apr. 28 as her earliest Atikokan record. Elder (1979: 37) gave May 8 as his earliest at Geraldton. Cringan (1953a: 3) saw his first in 1953 at Perrault Falls on May 6.

SUMMER: On the 1968-1977 Breeding Bird Surveys they were common from Algonquin Park northwards, becoming rare and scattered south to Palgrave and Auburn. Stirrett (1973d: 26) had his earliest southbound bird at Pelee on Aug. 24. Ussher (1965: 23) also gave Aug. 24 as his earliest fall date at Rondeau, with Aug. 30 as his 8-year average arrival date. Saunders & Dale (1933: 226-227) mentioned an 1882 nesting in a spruce swamp near London. W.E. Saunders noted two at Long Point as late as June 7 or 8, 1925 (Snyder, 1931: 206). Beardslee & Mitchell (1965: 370-371) reported two at Morgan's Point, Lake Erie, as early as Aug. 6, 1944. Fleming (1907: 83) reported a male taken at Toronto on June 6, 1891 and a female on June 14, 1895. Snyder (1930: 198) collected a young male by a King Twp. swamp on July 14, 1926. Speirs & Orenstein (1975: 13) found populations in 5 of 11 Ontario Co. forest quadrats with a maximum density of 34 birds per 100 acres in the Brock Twp. black spruce-tamarack bog. I saw one in heavy moult at our Pickering Twp. home on Aug. 13, 1962 (Speirs, 1974). Tozer & Richards (1974: 242) cited several cases of adults seen feeding young in Darlington and Cartwright Twps. Snyder (1941: 77) collected a young male at Rednersville, Prince Edward Co., on July 16, 1930. Weir & Quilliam (1980: 38) listed Aug. 18 as the 22-year average arrival date in fall at Kingston: Richard Norman found a nest with 3 eggs and 2 cowbird eggs near Kingston on July 11, 1967 (Quilliam, 1973: 154). Baillie & Harrington (1937: 243) found a nest with 3 eggs and 2 cowbird eggs at Orr Lake, Simcoe Co. Lloyd (1924: 13) cited several breeding records for the Ottawa region. James (1979: 16) found this to be the second most abundant bird in short Jack pine forests of western Parry Sound with an average population density of 8.2 males per 10 hectares. H. Mueller found a nest with 4 eggs on July 25, 1976 in Burpee Twp., Manitoulin (Nicholson, 1981: 161); there was a high count of 60 there as early as Aug. 24, 1975. Louise Lawrence saw a young begging from an adult at Pimisi Bay on July 29, 1945 (Speirs & Speirs, 1947: 34). Baillie & Hope (1947: 22) found two nests, one with 5 eggs, the other with 3 eggs, on June 14, 1937 at Chapleau: they collected two young just out of the nest at Biscotasing on July 3 and saw flying young at Bigwood on July 17. Snyder (1942: 143) collected a young male at Maclennan on July 7 and a young female at Echo Bay on July 15, in 1931 (both near Sault Ste. Marie). Skeel & Bondrup-Nielsen (1978: 201) found this to be the fourth most numerous species at Pukaskwa in the summer of 1977, with 80 recorded on 25 days and found on all transects in all habitats there. Baillie & Hope (1943: 20) noted 35 in a big black spruce bog at Marathon on June 13, 1936. On several occasions, Snyder (1928: 271) saw young being fed by parents at Macdiarmid, Lake Nipigon, in late July, 1924. Dear (1940: 138) found a nest with 5 eggs at Whitefish Lake, on June 8, 1935 and a nest with 4 young, just hatched, in MacGregor Twp., Thunder Bay, on June 13, 1937. Kendeigh (1947: 27) found a breeding density of 8 pairs per 100 acres at Black Sturgeon Lake in 1945 while Speirs (1949: 148) had just 2 pairs on 75 acres at nearby Eaglehead Lake in 1946. J.L. Baillie found a nest with 3 eggs and a cowbird egg at Big Fork, Rainy River, on July 18, 1929 (Snyder, 1938: 203). Snyder (153: 77) called this the most common warbler of western Ontario, from Ingolf and Malachi to Wabigoon where a nest with young was observed on July 9, 1937. Price & Speirs (1971: 977) found a population of 10 pairs per 100 acres, confined to rocky Jack pine ridges in the predominantly aspen forest plot at Lake of the Woods Provincial Park in 1971. Erskine (1971: 985) found a population density of 13 territories per 100 acres in a black spruce quadrat near Matheson in 1971 and about 3 per 100 acres in a Jack pine quadrat nearby (1971: 987). Snyder (1928: 30) collected 2 males at Lake Abitibi, one on June 19 and one on July 17, 1925. Bondrup-Nielsen (1976: 44) saw his first near Kapuskasing on June 8 in 1974 and found none in 1975. James (1980: 84) found a breeding density of 10.4 pairs per km² at Pickle Lake on 8 of 12 transects studied (it ranked fourth of the species studied there). Hope

(1938: 36-37) found them much less common at Favourable Lake than farther south, but collected a young bird there to establish a breeding record. Cringan (1950: 16) noted just two in June, 1950, at Nikip Lake. James, Nash & Peck (1982: 67) saw single birds on 4 days and collected an adult female on July 9, 1982, at Harricanaw River, near James Bay. McLaren & McLaren (1981: 4) found singing males common in the Wetiko Hills, on the Manitoba border in the summer of 1977.

AUTUMN: Peruniak (1971: 25) gave Sept. 17 as her latest date for Atikokan. Skeel & Bondrup-Nielsen (1978: 201) noted their last at Pukaskwa on Sept. 8 in 1977. Speirs & Speirs (1947: 34) saw two as late as Sept. 29, 1944 at North Bay. Nicholson (1981: 161) gave Nov. 5, 1972 as the latest Manitoulin date. Mills (1981: 135) saw one at Ahmic Lake as late as Oct. 12, 1974. Devitt (1967: 136) reported 142 killed at the Barrie TV tower in 7 years, the latest on Oct. 16, 1966. Weir & Quilliam (1980: 38) listed Oct. 16 as the 24-year average departure date from Kingston, with the latest on Nov. 11. George A. Scott noted one at Oshawa as late as Nov. 9, 1952 (Speirs, 1974). Saunders (1947: 371) gave Oct. 24 as his latest Toronot date, with his 13-year average departure date on Sept. 27: Speirs (1938: 52) gave Sept. 17 as the fall peak there. Snyder (1931: 206) mentioned one killed at the Long Point light on Sept. 7, 1929 and 9 between Sept. 24 and 29, 1929. Ussher (1965: 23) gave Oct. 26 as his latest fall date at Rondeau with the 8-year average departure on Oct. 11. Stirrett (1973d: 26) had a maximum of 20 at Pelee on Sept. 1, with the latest on Oct. 18.

**MEASUREMENTS:**
*Length:* 4.5 to 5.0 ins.
(Godfrey, 1966: 324)
*Wingspread:* 7.30 to 7.75
ins. (Roberts, 1955: 669)
*Weight:* 69 Ontario
specimens averaged 8.8 g.

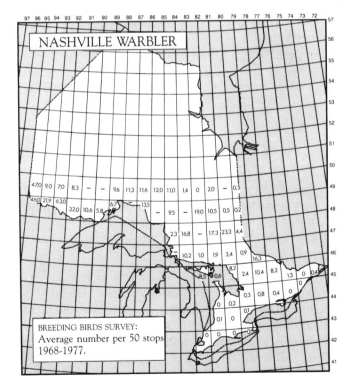

NASHVILLE WARBLER

BREEDING BIRDS SURVEY:
Average number per 50 stops
1968-1977.

# VIRGINIA'S WARBLER   *Vermivora virginiae*   (Baird)

This straggler to the Pelee area is normally a bird of the Rocky Mountains from Colorado south to Arizona, wintering in Mexico.

**IDENTIFICATION:** This is predominantly a gray bird with conspicuously yellow-green upper and lower tail coverts and a prominent white eye ring. It has a concealed chestnut crown patch like its congeners and no white wing bars or tail patches. Some have yellow on the throat and centre of the breast.

**WINTER:**

**SPRING:** One was seen on Pelee Is. from May 9 to 11, 1974 by David Broughton *et al* and photographed (Goodwin, 1974: 797). Douglas Dow and Leslie Gray saw one fluttering up in the tree tops at Pelee on May 16, 1958, identified it as this species but had it collected by George M. Stirrett. The specimen was made up by A.A. Wood and sent to the National Museum (No. 41430) where the identify was confirmed. Another was seen at Pelee on May 5, 1975 by J.A. Greenhouse *et al* (Goodwin, 1975: 847).

**SUMMER:**

**AUTUMN·**

**MEASUREMENTS:**
*Length:* 4.3 to 4.7 ins.
(Godfrey, 1966: 325)
Wingspread:
*Weight:* 8 averaged 7.8 g.
(7.0 - 9.0 g.) (Dunning,
1984: 21).

**REFERENCE:**
Dow, Douglas D. 1962
First Canadian record of
Virginia's Warbler. Auk,
79: (4): 715.

# NORTHERN PARULA   *Parula americana*   (Linnaeus)

This is an uncommon to rare warbler in Ontario, although apparently much more common in times past. They breed where Usnea (lichen) drapes the trees, chiefly near the influence of Lake Superior. They winter from Florida and Mexico south to the West Indies and Central America.

**IDENTIFICATION:** The field marks to look for are the "rainbow" on the chest and the vivid green patch on bluish back. The "rainbow" is a blackish arc, fading to red that merges with the yellow breast. This is one of many warblers with white wing bars and yellow throat and breast. It also has a white eye ring. The somewhat similar Nashville Warbler lacks the breast band, and wing bars and has completely yellow underparts: the Parula has a white belly and undertail coverts. The usual song is a buzzy trill, rising in pitch to an emphatic ending, but some have a song resembling the Cerulean Warbler's.

**WINTER:**

**SPRING:** Stirrett (1973b: 23) had Pelee records from May 3 to June 1, with a maximum of 10 on May 10. Ussher (1965: 23) had Rondeau records from May 4 to May 24 with average arrival on May 12 and departure on May 21. Saunders & Dale (1933: 227) gave May 11 as the 16-year average arrival date at London, with the earliest on May 4, 1912. Marshall Field found one at Port Burwell on May 25, 1952 (Brooman, 1954: 32). Saunders (1947: 371) listed an almost unbelievably early record by J.L. Baillie, on Apr. 6 at Toronto (his own earliest was on May 2 and latest on June 3): Fleming (1907: 83) called this an abundant migrant at Toronto, though it is now hard to find one in most years. Speirs (1974) cited Ontario Co. records from May 7, 1939, when T.L. Walker collected one at Claremont, to June 2, 1953 when Naomi Le Vay noted one at Whitby. Weir & Quilliam (1980: 38) listed May 10 and May 23 as average arrival and departure dates for Kingston, earliest Apr. 22 and latest May 30. Devitt (1967: 136) gave May 15 as a 5-year average arrival date at Collingwood: the earliest was a male collected at Orillia on May 6, 1888. Mills (1981: 135) cited an old 10-year average arrival date at Parry Sound as May 10, with the earliest on May 7, 1896, but most recent arrivals have been about May 20. Nicholson (1981: 161) gave May 13 as the 9-year average arrival date on Manitoulin, with the earliest on Apr. 26, 1979. MacLulich (1938: 31) gave May 19, 1932 as an arrival date for Algonquin Park. Ricker & Clarke (1939: 18) noted one as early as May 17, 1925 at Lake Nipissing. Skeel & Bondrup-Nielsen (1978: 202) noted 15 on 4 days from May 18 to May 26 in 1977 at Pukaskwa. Denis (1961: 4) gave May 24 as the average arrival date at Thunder Bay, with the earliest on May 18, 1951. Peruniak (1971: 25) gave May 16 as her earliest at Atikokan.

SUMMER: On the 1968-1977 Breeding Bird Surveys, they were fairly common on the Montreal Falls and Farrington routes, rare south to Algonquin Park and on northern routes away from the Lake Superior influence, absent in the agricultural south. Saunders & Dale (1933: 227) reported birds singing in June in the Komoka swamp. J.L. Baillie reported one singing on Long Point on June 29, 1927 and L.L. Snyder collected two singing males there on July 8, 1927 (McCracken, Bradstreet & Holroyd, 1981: 62). Weir & Quilliam (1980: 38) listed a returning bird at Kingston as early as Aug. 11. Devitt (1967: 136) observed a singing bird near Severn Falls on June 18, 1935 and Frances Westman noted one at Tollendal from June 17 to 26, 1956: a southbound bird was noted at Wasaga Beach as early as Aug. 4. Mills (1981: 136) cited several summer records from the cottage country, including breeding reports from Mud Lake, Port Sydney and Hunts-ville. Nicholson (1981: 162) cited several records of males singing on Manitoulin in June and July in suitable nesting habitat. MacLulich (1938: 31) cited three cases of adults observed feeding young in Algonquin Park: July 15 and July 26, 1933, at Biggar Lake, and July 9, 1934, at Brule Lake. Speirs & Speirs (1947: 34) noted two at Kaibuskong Bay, near North Bay, on June 22, 1944. Snyder (1942: 143) collected a singing male at Laird on June 9, 1931. Skeel & Bondrup-Nielsen (1978: 202) noted just 5 on 3 days from June 9 to 23, 1977, in Pukaskwa. Baillie & Hope (1943: 20) collected a female at Rossport on June 6, 1936 (their only record along the NE shore of Lake Superior). J.L. Baillie observed one at Whitefish Lake, Thunder Bay, in June, 1935 (Dear, 1940: 138). Snyder (1938: 204) collected a young female at Off Lake, Rainy River, on July 9, 1929 and the parents on July 6 and 9. Snyder (1953: 77) collected one at Malachi (no date given). Smith (1957: 178) heard one 8 miles north of Hearst on June 3, 1954. Snyder (1928: 30) collected 4 males at Lake Abitibi between June 3 and 27, 1925. Bondrup-Nielsen (1976: 44) noted the species near Kapuskasing on June 22, 1974 and June 8, 1975.

AUTUMN: Peruniak (1971: 25) gave Sept. 13 as her latest Atikokan date. Skeel & Bondrup-Nielsen (1978: 202) had only one fall record for Pukaskwa, on Oct. 9, 1977. Ricker & Clarke (1939: 18) saw one as late as Oct. 6, 1924 at Lake Nipissing. Nicholson (1981: 162) reported one killed at the Great Duck Is. tower on Sept. 22, 1972. B. Geale saw one at Lake Joseph as late as Sept. 26, 1937 (Mills, 1981: 136). Only three were killed at the Barrie TV tower in 7 years, the latest on Oct. 13, 1966 (Devitt, 1967: 136). Weir & Quilliam (1980: 38) listed Sept. 6 and Oct. 2 as average arrival and departure dates for Kingston, the latest on Oct. 22. Speirs (1974) had fall records from Pickering Twp. from Aug. 27, 1964 (R.C. Long) to Oct. 13, 1958. Saunders (1947: 371) had Toronto records from Aug. 11 to Oct. 16: Speirs (1938: 54) listed an Oct. 28 record for Toronto. Snyder (1931: 207) mentioned 8 killed at the Long Point light between Sept. 24 to 29, 1929. Ussher (1965: 23) had Rondeau records from Sept. 13 to Sept. 19. Stirrett (1973d: 26) had Pelee records from Aug. 28 to Oct. 23, with a maximum of 3 on Sept. 15: Kelley (1978: 70) gave a Nov. 23 record for Pelee.

**MEASUREMENTS:**
*Length:* 4.3 to 4.9 ins.
(Godfrey, 1966: 325)
*Wingspread:* 7.0 to 7.25
ins. (Roberts, 1955: 671)
*Weight:* 8.4 g. (Terres,
1980: 963).

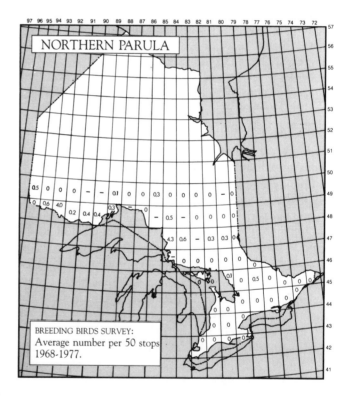

NORTHERN PARULA

BREEDING BIRDS SURVEY:
Average number per 50 stops
1968-1977.

# YELLOW WARBLER   *Dendroica petechia*   (Linnaeus)

The Yellow Warbler usually nests low down in shrubbery around houses, or in willow scrub or alders or other shrubby growth by rivers or lakeshores. In the Precambrian country it is usually confined to urban areas. Brown-headed Cowbirds frequently parasitize this species but some warblers defeat this parasite by building over the intruding egg and laying again on the new floor: some even build multiple layers as each cowbird egg is laid. This is a very early fall migrant, most leaving for winter quarters in Central and South America by August, with only a few stragglers remaining in September.

IDENTIFICATION: This is a familiar small yellow bird. The Wilson's Warbler is distinguished by its black cap and the American Goldfinch by its black wings, tail and cap (with some white patches here and there). Males have red streaks on the breast, lacking in the females. The song is a sprightly "sweet, sweet, sweet, cheery and sweet".

SPRING: Stirrett (1973b: 24) gave Apr. 22 as the earliest Pelee record, with a maximum of 500 on May 14 and 23. Ussher (1965: 23) gave May 1 as the 22-year average arrival date at Rondeau, with the earliest on Apr. 21. Saunders & Dale (1933: 227) gave Apr. 29 as the 17-year average arrival date at London, with the earliest on Apr. 20, 1919: his earliest nest (with 4 eggs on May 24, 1902) was eclipsed by one with 5 eggs and two cowbird eggs on May 27, 1915. Fleming (1907: 83) reported one at Toronto as early as Apr. 18: Speirs (1938: 44) gave May 23 as the spring peak there. Jack Satterly noted one as early as May 1, 1954 at Cedar Point, Mara Twp., where he found a nest under construction on May 16, 1953 (Speirs, 1974). Snyder (1941: 78) gave May 1, 1933 as his earliest date for Prince Edward Co.: Frank Brimley found a nest with 5 eggs there on May 31, 1912. Weir & Quilliam (1980: 38) listed May 3 as the 31-year average arrival date for Kingston, the earliest on Apr. 27: three nests were observed being built there on May 24, 1962 (Quilliam, 1973: 155). Devitt (1967: 137) gave May 10 as the 17-year average arrival date at Barrie, the earliest on Apr. 25, 1938. Lloyd (1924: 13) reported Ottawa nests on May 12, 1888 and May 23, 1904. L. Beamer's median arrival date at Meaford was May 8, with the earliest on Apr. 30, 1949. Mills (1981: 137) gave May 11 as a 6-year average arrival date at Huntsville, with the earliest on May 5, 1974 at Bala. Nicholson (1981: 162) gave May 8 as the 12-year average arrival date on Manitoulin, with the earliest on May 2, 1970 and a maximum of 40 on May 20, 1979. MacLulich (1938: 32) gave May 19, 1932 as an arrival date in Algonquin Park. Louise Lawrence saw one as early as May 4, 1944 at Pimisi Bay (Speirs & Speirs, 1947: 34). Ricker & Clarke (1939: 19) found a nest with one egg at Lake Nipissing on May 30, 1933: it held 4 eggs on June 2. Skeel & Bondrup-Nielsen (1978: 202) heard two singing at Pukaskwa on May 14, 1977 (their only spring record there). Baillie & Hope (1943: 21) collected a male at Rossport on May 28, and five more before the end of May, 1936. Denis (1961: 3) listed May 17 as the average arrival date at Thunder Bay, with the earliest on May 5, 1941. Peruniak (1971: 25) gave May 11 as her earliest Atikokan record. Elder (1979: 38) had his earliest at Geraldton on May 19. Bondrup-Nielsen (1976: 44) gave May 26 as his earliest date for Kapuskasing in 1975. Cringan (1953a: 3) saw his first on May 22 in 1953 at Perrault Falls. C.A. Elsey saw his first in the Asheweig area on May 29 in 1950 (Cringan, 1950: 16).

SUMMER: On the 1968-1977 Breeding Bird Surveys they were common near the northeast shores of Lake Erie and Lake Ontario and near Lake of the Woods, fairly common on most other routes, and uncommon to absent on many routes in the spruce forest northeast of Lake Superior. Stirrett (1973c: 20) had a summer maximum of 100 at Pelee on Aug. 14, after which the population fell off rapidly. Ussher (1965: 23) gave Aug. 26 as the 10-year average departure date from Rondeau. McCracken, Bradstreet & Holroyd (1981: 62) reported a population density of 120 pairs per km$^2$ in a study area on Long Point: they found 9 nests in one button bush swamp near Cedar Creek in June, 1980 and cited several other nestings. Snyder (1930: 198) saw adults carrying food to young in King Twp. in June, 1926. Speirs & Orenstein (1975: 16) found population densities of 44 and 56 birds per 100 acres in the two pioneer forest plots in Ontario Co., none in the more mature forests. Populations were found in half of our urban quadrats in Ontario Co. with a maximum of 31 birds per 100 acres in the Atherley plot: on our road and riverside counts in June, 1963 in Ontario Co. this was the most common warbler, with 205 tallied (Speirs, 1974). J.M. Richards found a nest under construction in Darlington Twp. as late as July 14, 1969 and a nest with 3 young there on July 18, 1968 (Tozer & Richards, 1974: 244). Allin (1940: 105) found a nest with 3 eggs in Darlington on June 8, 1933. A.J. Erskine found a breeding density of 50 males per 100 acres on a Wolfe Is. quadrat and a nest with 4 eggs was located there on June 6, 1954 (Quilliam, 1973: 155). Paul Harrington found a nest with 4 eggs and 3 imbedded cowbird eggs at Marl Lake on June 11, 1927 (Baillie & Harrington, 1937: 244). K. Ketchum saw a wave of migrants off Pointe au Baril on Aug. 12, 1974 and her latest there was on Aug. 31, 1961 (Mills, 1981: 137). D.B. Ferguson found a nest with 4 young at Providence Bay, Manitoulin, on June 30, 1977. Louise Lawrence found a nest with 5 eggs at Pimisi Bay on June 10, 1944 (Speirs & Speirs, 1947: 34). Paul Harrington found a nest with 4 eggs at Chapleau on June 15, 1937: a nest with 4 newly-hatched young and one egg was found at Biscotasing on June 25 (Baillie & Hope, 1947: 22). Harry Graham found a nest near Sault Ste. Marie on June 30, 1939 (Snyder, 1942: 143). W. Wyett reported one on June 23, 1973 in Pukaskwa, the only summer record there (Skeel & Bondrup-Nielsen, 1978: 202). Baillie & Hope (1943: 21) found a partially constructed nest at Rossport on June 7, 1936. Snyder (1928: 272) called them "not common" at Lake Nipigon but observed young being fed there. Dear (1940: 138) found a nest with 5 eggs at Thunder Bay on June 21, 1924. Snyder (1938: 204) found them nesting at Emo and noted family groups at Rainy River. Snyder (1953: 77) reported a newly completed nest at Kenora on June 15, 1947 and saw some birds at Sioux Lookout and Wabigoon. Snyder (1928: 30) found a newly completed nest at Lake Abitibi on June 26, 1925. James (1980: 89) encountered only two pairs near Pickle Lake and found a nest with one egg there on June 22, 1979. Hope (1938: 37) found a few near Favourable Lake but had no breeding data. Cringan (1953b: 4) saw single birds on 4 days at Kasabonika Lake, the first on June 1, 1953. Manning (1952: 81) found them "common" in willow and alder scrub along the James Bay and Hudson Bay coasts in the summers of 1947 and 1949 with records at Moosonee, Albany River, Attawapiskat, and Shagamu River. James, Nash & Peck (1982: 67) found a nest with 4 eggs on June 28, 1982 in deciduous thickets by the Harricanaw River, near James Bay. James, Nash & Peck (1981: 84) reported the species in the Sutton Ridges in 1980 but had no breeding record. Schueler, Baldwin & Rising (1974: 147) found a nest at Winisk, empty on June 18, 1965 and with 2 eggs on June 23. Peck (1972: 346) found one or two in dense willow borders of tundra sloughs at Cape Henrietta Maria from June 27 to July 3, 1970 (the only warbler in the region). Lee (1978: 31) noted as many as 16 at Big Trout Lake settlement on June 11, 1975 and saw several young birds around the cemetery there in late July and early August. C.E. Hope reported 30 at Ft. Severn on June 27, 1940 and found two nests there: a nest with 2 eggs on July 6 and a nest with 4 eggs on July 11.

AUTUMN: Peruniak (1971: 25) saw her latest at Atikokan on Sept. 1. Speirs & Speirs (1947: 34) had their latest one at North Bay on Sept. 11, 1944. Nicholson (1981: 162) reported only 10 killed at the Great Duck Is. tower during September, the latest on Sept. 26, 1980. C. Harris saw a very late bird in the cottage country on Sept. 29, 1979 (Mills, 1981: 137). Only 4 were found killed in 7 Septembers at the Barrie TV tower, the latest on Sept. 30, 1965 (Devitt, 1967: 137). Weir & Quilliam (1980: 38) listed Sept. 8 as the 24-year average departure date from Kingston, the latest on Sept. 28. George A. Scott noted one as late as Sept. 23, 1962 at Oshawa (Speirs, 1974). Speirs (1938: 54) gave Sept. 18 as the latest Toronto date. Beardslee & Mitchell (1965: 373) reported one as late as Sept. 28, 1958 at Erie Beach. Snyder (1931: 208) reported 7 killed at the Long Point light on Sept. 7 and two on Sept. 9, 1929, none later. Ussher (1965: 23) gave Sept. 8 as his latest date for Rondeau. Kelley (1978: 70) reported a very late one banded at Bradley's Marsh on Oct. 22, 1966.

**MEASUREMENTS:**

*Length:* 4.75 to 5.25 ins. (Godfrey, 1966: 326)
*Wingspread:* 7.12 to 8.00 ins. (Roberts, 1955: 672)
*Weight:* 23 Ontario specimens averaged 10.2 g.

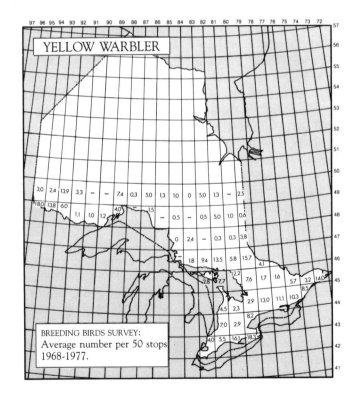

# CHESTNUT-SIDED WARBLER
*Dendroica pensylvanica*   (Linnaeus)

This is a bird of the shrubby edges of Ontario's Precambrian forests, much increased by such human activities as road building and tree cutting. They often nest in forest-edge raspberry canes and hazel clumps. They winter in southern Central America and the West Indies.

IDENTIFICATION: The male with its chestnut sides, yellow cap, green back, white underparts and black mask is easily identified. Adult females are similar but with more subdued colours. Young birds in the autumn lack the chestnut sides and black mask and yellow crown: They are bright green above and dirty white below, with pronounced eye rings and yellowish wing bars. The song is an emphatic "swee-swee-swee-ta- weecha". By mid-summer some get lazy and leave out the diagnostic terminal "weecha". (I call these the "undecided chestnut-sideds"—one of the challenges of identifying warblers by song alone).

WINTER:

SPRING:  Stirrett (1973b: 24) had Pelee records from Apr. 30 to June 6, with a maximum of 150 on June 1. Ussher (1965: 24) had Rondeau records from May 2 to May 30, with average arrival on May 9 and departure on May 25. Saunders & Dale (1933: 229) gave May 10 as the 17-year average arrival date at London, with the earliest on May 1, 1916: a set of 4 eggs plus 3 cowbird eggs was found on May 27, 1896. Speirs (1938: 39, 43) gave May 1 as the earliest Toronto date with May 21 as the spring peak date. Saunders (1947: 372) listed May 10 as his 13-year average arrival date at Toronto. Speirs (1974) gave May 2 as the earliest Pickering date with the peak about May 16 or 17: Naomi LeVay had May 1 records at Cranberry Marsh, Whitby, in 1952 and 1954 (Tozer & Richards, 1974: 249). Weir & Quilliam (1980: 39) gave May 10 as the 32-year average arrival date at Kingston, with the earliest on May 2. Devitt (1967: 142) gave May 12 as the 18-year average arrival date at Barrie, with the earliest on May 1, 1954: a nest with 4 eggs was found in Oro Twp. as early as May 30, 1955 by H.P. Bingham. L. Beamer's median arrival date at Meaford was May 17, the earliest on May 5, 1938. Mills (1981: 143) gave May 12 as a 7-year average arrival date for Huntsville, with the earliest on May 9, 1965, though A. Kay had a May 6 date. Nicholson (1981: 167) gave May 13 as the 12-year average arrival date on Manitoulin, with the earliest on May 6, 1972 and a peak about May 19 or 20. MacLulich (1938: 33) gave May 5, 1932 as his earliest arrival date for Algonquin Park. Louise Lawrence saw one at Rutherglen on May 13, 1944 (Speirs & Speirs, 1947: 35). Skeel & Bondrup-Nielsen (1978: 205) saw their first at Pukaskwa on May 21, 1977: 10 altogether on 4 days until May 29. Denis (1961: 4) listed May 21 as the average arrival date at Thunder Bay, with the earliest on May 2, 1954. Peruniak (1971: 26) gave May 11 as her earliest Atikokan date. Bondrup-Nielsen (1976: 44) saw his first near Kapuskasing on May 16, 1975. Elder (1979: 38) gave May 24 as his earliest date for Geraldton.

SUMMER:  On the 1968-1977 Breeding Bird Surveys, they were rare or uncommon on routes in the agricultural southern part of Ontario and on some of the Clay Belt routes, but were common on all of the routes on the Precambrian Shield. Stirrett (1973c: 20) had one at Pelee on July 3, and the first "fall migrant" on Aug. 11, with a maximum of 7 on Aug. 13. Ussher (1965: 24) had his earliest fall bird at Rondeau on Aug. 7, with the average arrival on Aug. 22. Saunders & Dale (1933: 229) reported a nest with 4 eggs on June 18, 1879 at Hyde Park, London. Snyder (1930: 198) reported two nests in King Twp. in 1926: one with 3 eggs on June 28 was 3 ft. up in a small choke-cherry. Speirs & Orenstein (1975: 13) found a population density of 6 birds per 100 acres in a disturbed forest in Whitby Twp. in 1967. Speirs (1974) cited several summer records for Ontario Co., especially in the northern townships of Mara and Rama. Tozer & Richards (1974: 249) reported two nests, each one foot up: one found by George Peck in raspberry canes on June 10, 1964 in Reach Twp. held 3 eggs and a cowbird egg: the other held 4 young on June 13, 1972 in Darlington Twp.: it was photographed by J.M. Richards and Dennis Barry. Kenneth Edwards found a nest with 4 eggs near Kingston on June 6, 1979 (Weir & Quilliam, 1980: 23). H.P. Bingham found a nest with 3 eggs as late as July 22, 1917 near Barrie (Devitt, 1967: 142). C.E. Johnson found a nest with 4 eggs at Ottawa on June 23, 1916 (Lloyd, 1924: 14). Mills (1981: 143) suggested that this might be the most common warbler of the cottage country, with 27 nests reported. Paul Harrington found a nest with 4 eggs near Mindemoya, Manitoulin, on June 16, 1938 (Nicholson, 1981: 167). C.H.D. Clarke saw one carrying food at Brule Lake, Algonquin Park, on June 30, 1934 (MacLulich, 1938: 33). Louise Lawrence followed the fortunes of a nest at Pimisi Bay in 1945: under construction 2 1/2 ft. up in raspberry canes on May 27; the first egg on June 4; the fourth egg on June 7; 3 young and one egg that did not hatch on June 19: the 3 young left on June 27 and one young was still being fed by the female on July 25 (Speirs & Speirs, 1947: 35). Baillie & Hope (1947: 24) collected 3 young at Bigwood from July 13-21, 1937. Snyder (1942: 144) collected a young female at Gros Cap on July 13, 1931 and reported Harry Graham's find of a nest with one cowbird egg in a hazel shrub near Sault Ste. Marie on June 25, 1939. Skeel & Bondrup-Nielsen (1978: 205) heard only 17 on 10 days at Pukaskwa from June 9 to July 9, 1977. Baillie & Hope (1943: 22) found them present, but not common, at all camps along the NE shore of Lake Superior. Snyder (1928: 273) found them common at the south end of Lake Nipigon but none at the north end. Dear (1940: 139) found two nests with 4 eggs each near Thunder Bay, one on June 29, 1924, the other on June 13, 1930. The earliest young in the nest at Rainy River were noted on June 27, 1929 (Snyder, 1938: 204). Snyder (1953: 78) ranked this species 8th in abundance of the warblers of western Ontario. L. Paterson saw adults feeding young at Kenora on July 27, 1931 and J. Satterly saw an adult feeding young at Ney Lake (54° 37'N) on Aug. 7, 1936 (Baillie & Harrington, 1937: 248). Smith (1957: 178) found them common at New Liskeard but found none farther north, though "A.N. Boissonneau has seen the species at Cochrane". Snyder (1928: 31) took only a single specimen at Lake Abitibi, on July 24, 1925. James (1980: 89) reported a few near Pickle Lake. McLaren & McLaren (1981: 4) noted four singing males near Pickle Lake from June 2 to 6, 1977 "about 140 km north of the known breeding range." Schueler, Baldwin & Rising (1974: 144) listed them as common at Cochrane, but found none farther north.

AUTUMN: Peruniak (1971: 26) gave Sept. 26 as her latest date for Atikokan. Skeel & Bondrup-Nielsen (1978: 205) saw their latest at Pukaskwa on Sept. 8 in 1977. Speirs & Speirs (1947: 35) saw one at North Bay on Sept. 29, 1944. Nicholson (1981: 167) gave Sept. 25, 1977 as his latest Manitoulin date, with 82 casualties at the Great Duck Is. tower from Sept. 18-23, 1977. Mills (1981: 144) gave a sighting by C. MacFayden at Glen Orchard on Sept. 29, 1979 as the latest for the cottage country. Devitt (1967: 142) reported that 222 were killed at the Barrie TV tower in 7 years, the greatest total of 90 on Sept. 12, 1961 and the latest on Oct. 3, 1965. Weir & Quilliam (1980: 39) gave Sept. 22 as the 20-year average departure date from Kingston, the latest on Oct. 16. The fall peak has been in mid-September in Ontario Co., with the latest on Oct. 19, 1952 at Amos Ponds, Pickering (Speirs, 1974). Saunders (1947: 372) listed Sept. 20 as his 12-year average departure date from Toronto, with the latest on Oct. 10: Speirs (1938: 51) gave Sept. 6 as the fall peak there. Ussher (1965: 24) gave Sept. 15 as his average departure date from Rondeau, with the latest on Oct. 2. Kelley (1978: 73) mentioned a very late one at Pelee on Nov. 23, 1974.

**MEASUREMENTS:**

*Length:* 4.5 to 5.3 ins. (Godfrey, 1966: 335)
*Wingspread:* 7.40 to 8.25 ins. (Roberts, 1955: 680)
*Weight:* 64 Ontario specimens averaged 10.0 g.

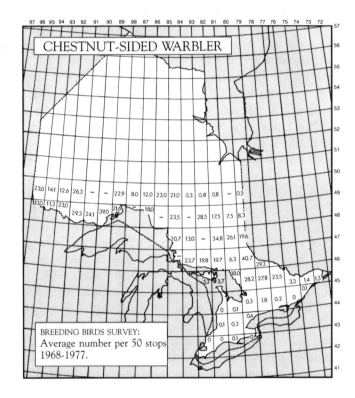

CHESTNUT-SIDED WARBLER

BREEDING BIRDS SURVEY:
Average number per 50 stops
1968-1977.

# MAGNOLIA WARBLER  *Dendroica magnolia*  (Wilson)

I associate this pretty warbler with stands of young balsam firs (Christmas tree size) along roads through the coniferous forests in Ontario's Precambrian country. In winter they go south from southern United States and the West Indies to Panama.

**IDENTIFICATION:** Look for the "flag tail" and tiger striped breast. Listen for the "weezy-weezy-wee-chee" song and "meggy" call note. The undertail pattern is a good field mark at all seasons: the basal 2/3 white and terminal 1/3 black. In fall only a hint of the black stripes on the yellow breast may remain to distinguish it from a fall Nashville (though the Nashville lacks wing bars and the distinctive black and white tail pattern). Like the

Yellow-rumped and Cape May Warblers, the Magnolia has a yellow rump, but it does not flaunt it the way the real Yellow-rumped Warbler does.

WINTER: Sheppard (1960: 40) reported a bright male, seen at Niagara Falls on Dec. 10, 1947.

SPRING: Stirrett (1973b: 24) had Pelee records from Apr. 21 to June 5, with a maximum of 250 on May 23. Ussher (1965: 23) gave May 8 as the average arrival date at Rondeau and May 24 as the average departure date, with the earliest on May 1. Saunders & Dale (1933: 227) gave May 10 as the 17-year average arrival date at London, with the earliest on May 5, 1912. Snyder (1931: 209) cited Long Point records from May 9 (1928) to June 1 (1924). Beardslee & Mitchell (1965: 374) reported two at Beaverdam, Ont., as early as Apr. 28, 1956. Fleming (1907: 84) gave Toronto records from Apr. 15 to June 1: Speirs (1938: 44) gave May 21 as the spring peak there; and Saunders (1947: 372) listed May 9 as his 13-year average arrival date. Speirs (1974) cited Ontario Co. records from May 1 to June 1, with a peak date about May 17. J.M. Richards noted one in Darlington Twp. on May 1, 1971 and Naomi LeVay had one at Cranberry Marsh as late as June 2, 1953 (Tozer & Richards, 1974: 244-245). Snyder (1941: 78) had spring records for Prince Edward Co. from May 12 (1912) to June 2 (1930). Weir & Quilliam (1980: 38) listed May 9 and May 30 as average arrival and departure dates for Kingston, with the earliest on Apr. 22. Devitt (1967: 138) gave May 14 as the 16-year average arrival date at Barrie, the earliest on Apr. 30, 1938. L. Beamer's median arrival date at Meaford was May 18, the earliest on May 7, 1939. Alfred Kay reported one at Port Sydney, Muskoka, on May 1, 1901, but an 11-year average arrival date for Parry Sound was May 13 (Mills, 1981: 137). Nicholson (1981: 162) gave May 14 as the 11-year average arrival date on Manitoulin, with the earliest on May 9, 1970 and the high count of 800 on Great Duck Is. on May 19, 1979. MacLulich (1938: 32) gave May 4, 1932 as his earliest Algonquin Park record. Louise Lawrence also saw one at Rutherglen on May 4, 1944 (Speirs & Speirs, 1947: 34). Skeel & Bondrup-Nielsen (1978: 202) ranked this warbler as the 5th most abundant spring migrant at Pukaskwa, first seen on May 15, 1977. Denis (1961: 4) gave May 17 as the average arrival date at Thunder Bay, with the earliest on May 9, 1958. Peruniak (1971: 25) gave May 9 as her earliest Atikokan date. Elder (1979: 38) gave May 22 as his earliest date for this "common summer resident" at Geraldton. Bondrup-Nielsen (1976: 44) saw his first at Kapuskasing on May 21 in 1975. Cringan (1953a: 3) saw his first on May 24 in 1953 at Sioux Lookout. Manning (1952: 82) cited an old record of one taken at Moose Factory on May 28, 1860.

SUMMER: On the 1968-1977 Breeding Bird Surveys, they were common on many routes northeast of Lake Superior, fairly common on other northern routes and rare south to Roblin and Port Bolster, with outliers on the London and Sarnia routes. Stirrett (1973c: 20 and 1973d: 26) had a migrant at Pelee as early as Aug. 12, and his fall peak there on Aug. 29. Ussher (1965: 23) had a summer record for Rondeau on June 27, with his earliest returning migrant on Aug. 19 and average arrival date on Aug. 25. Saunders & Dale (1933: 227) reported a male taken at London on June 8, 1882. McCracken, Bradstreet & Holroyd (1981: 63) cited several June and July records from Long Point and the adjacent "mainland". Speirs (1974) had two summer records for Ontario Co.: one at Chalk Lake, Uxbridge Twp. on June 14, 1963 and a July 26, 1963 record in Rama Twp. Long (1968a: 19) noted a returning bird at Pickering Beach as early as Aug. 2, 1963: there are many fall records for the latter half of August. Dennis Barry heard two singing males in the Osler Tract, Cartwright Twp. on June 17, 1973 (Tozer & Richards, 1974: 245). Quilliam (1973: 156) observed a singing male at Harrowsmith Bog on June 27 and 30, 1968: Weir & Quilliam (1980: 38) listed Aug. 17 as the 25-year average fall arrival date for Kingston. Devitt (1967: 138) cited several breeding records for Simcoe Co.: a nest with 4 eggs at Wasaga Beach on June 12, 1923; a nest with 3 eggs and a cowbird egg there on June 11, 1927; a nest with 3 newly hatched young and a young cowbird at Severn Falls on June 12, 1941 and young out of the nest, attended by parents, at Allenwood Beach on July 3, 1949. Lloyd (1924: 13) called this "probably a regular breeder" at Ottawa. Mills (1981: 137) reported 8 nest cards for the cottage country, including a nest with 4 eggs at Pt. Sydney as early as June 5, 1902. Ron Tasker found a nest with 2 infertile eggs and a young cowbird in Burpee Twp., Manitoulin, on July 26, 1976 (Nicholson, 1981: 163). MacLulich (1938: 32) cited several observations of young birds in Algonquin Park. Louise Lawrence followed a nesting at Pimisi Bay from June 12, 1945 when being built 6 ft. up in a balsam fir; first egg on June 16, second on June 17, third on June 18; 3 young on June 30 and 3 young left by July 9 (Speirs & Speirs, 1947: 34-35). D. MacLulich found a nest with 5 eggs at Frank's Bay, Lake Nipissing, on June 9, 1933 (Ricker & Clarke, 1939: 19). Baillie & Hope (1947: 23) found 5 nests in spruces (1 to 6 ft. up) at Chapleau from June 7 to 17, 1937 and 5 more at Biscotasing (1 to 4 ft. up) in spruces, from June 23 to July 3; also one recently vacated nest at Bigwood 3 1/2 ft. up in a spruce on July 18, 1937. Snyder (1942: 143) found them "not uncommon" in the Sault Ste. Marie region in 1931. Skeel & Bondrup-Nielsen (1978: 202) found this to be the second most abundant summer resident in Pukaskwa, seeing 111 on 29 days in June and the first half of July, 1977. Baillie & Hope (1943: 21) collected males at Rossport, Marathon and Amyot in 1936. Snyder (1928: 272) called this the "most abundant" warbler in the Lake Nipigon region in 1923 and 1924 and collected one young there on July 24, 1924. Dear (1940: 138) found a nest with 4 eggs on June 29, 1922 and a nest with 3 eggs and a cowbird egg on June 22, 1928 at Thunder Bay. Kendeigh (1947: 28) found 6 pairs on 100 acres at Black Sturgeon Lake in 1945 and Speirs (1949: 148) had 10 territories on 75 acres at nearby Eaglehead Lake in 1946. Snyder (1938: 204) collected a young male at Off Lake, Rainy River, on July 9, 1929. Snyder (1953: 77) ranked this sixth of the 23 resident warblers of western Ontario from Malachi and Kenora east to Sioux Lookout and Wabigoon. Snyder (1928: 31) noted young just out of the nest at Lake Abitibi in 1925. Baillie & Harrington (1937: 244) reported flightless young at Kapuskasing in the summer of 1919 according to P.A. Taverner. James (1980: 89) reported 3 nests, each with 4 eggs, near Pickle Lake: on June 11, 1977 and on June 18 and 22, 1979. Hope (1938: 37) found several nests at Favourable Lake in 1938, including a nest with 5 eggs on June 8 and a nest with 2 eggs on July 6. Cringan (1953b: 4) found as many as 10 in a day near Kasabonika Lake in June, 1953. Manning (1952: 82) took a female at Moosonee on June 27, 1949 and a male on July 1. James, Nash & Peck (1982: 67) found 3 nests by the Harricanaw River, near James Bay: a nest with 3 eggs on July 7; a nest with 4 young on July 7 and a nest with 5 young on July 10, 1982. James, Nash & Peck (1981: 84) found the species in the Sutton Ridges area in the summer of 1980 but obtained no breeding evidence. Schueler, Baldwin & Rising (1974: 144) had no record north of Cochrane. Lee (1978: 31) reported 9 or 10 singing males in the Big Trout Lake region, with populations on two of three census plots there. McLaren & McLaren (1981: 4) reported "singing males common in the Wetiko Hills."

AUTUMN: Peruniak (1971: 25) had one as late as Oct. 2 at Atikokan. In the fall, only 7 were found in 5 days from Sept. 4 to 8, 1977 in Pukaskwa (Skeel & Bondrup-Nielsen, 1978: 202). Louise Lawrence saw one at Pimisi Bay on Sept. 21, 1944 (Speirs & Speirs, 1947: 35). Nicholson (1981: 163) gave Oct. 20, 1973 as his latest Manitoulin record, with 135 killed at the Great Duck Is. tower from Sept. 18 to 23, 1977. Mills (1981: 138) saw one at Magnetawan as late as Sept. 26, 1979 and Vonnie Heron found a dead one at Huntsville on Nov. 12, 1961. Devitt (1967: 138) reported 112 killed at the Barrie TV tower in 7 years: 2 seen at Little Lake on Oct. 11, 1941 were his latest for Simcoe Co. Weir & Quilliam (1980: 38) listed Oct. 4 as the 27-year average departure date from Kingston, the latest on Oct. 20. The peak of the fall migration in Ontario Co. is about Sept. 15, with the latest two observed by George A. Scott at Oshawa's Second Marsh on Oct. 18, 1959 (Speirs, 1974). Saunders (1947: 372) listed Sept. 16 as his average departure date from Toronto, while Speirs (1938: 54) gave Oct. 16 as the latest Toronto date. Snyder (1931: 209) reported casualties at the Long Point light in 1929: 32 on Sept. 7, 6 on Sept. 9 and 36 from Sept. 24 to 29. Ussher (1965: 23) gave Sept. 23 as the average departure date from Rondeau, the latest on Oct. 3. Stirrett (1973d: 26) had his latest 2 at Pelee on Oct. 12.

**MEASUREMENTS:**

*Length:* 4.4 to 5.1 ins.
(Godfrey, 1966: 327)
*Wingspread:* 7.0 to 7.8
ins. (Roberts, 1955: 675)
*Weight:* ♂ 8.0 g. ♀ 8.9 g.
(Hope, 1938: 37)

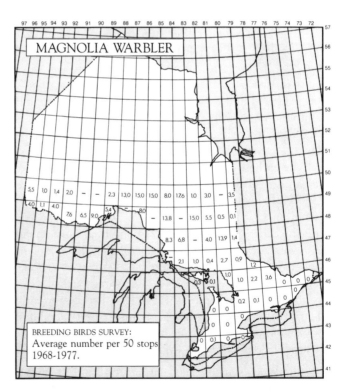

MAGNOLIA WARBLER

BREEDING BIRDS SURVEY:
Average number per 50 stops
1968-1977.

# CAPE MAY WARBLER   *Dendroica tigrina*   (Gmelin)

This is a bird of the treetops, occurring sparingly throughout the spruce country of Ontario, often concentrating where outbreaks of spruce budworm occur. They winter in the West Indies.

IDENTIFICATION:   Adult males, with their rufous ear patches contrasting with yellow "jowls", are unmistakable. Females and young still show some yellow below and behind the dusky cheeks, which together with the yellowish rump will distinguish them from fall Blackpolls, Black-throated Greens and dingy fall Yellow-rumped Warblers. The high-pitched "swee-swee-swee" song is characteristic, but the alternate "see-wee—see-wee-see-wee" is much like the song of a Bay-breasted Warbler.

WINTER:

SPRING:   Stirrett (1973b: 24) had Pelee records from Apr. 27 to May 25, with a maximum of 40 on May 17. Ussher (1965: 23) had birds at Rondeau from May 3 to May 24, with average arrival on May 10 and departure on May 21. Saunders & Dale (1933: 227) gave May 7 as the 15-year average arrival at London, with the earliest on Apr. 26, 1918. Snyder (1931: 207) cited Long Point records from May 14 (1925) to June 1 (1924). Beardslee & Mitchell (1965: 375) reported two at Point Abino, Lake Erie, on June 1, 1947. Speirs (1938: 40, 46) listed Toronto records from May 3 to May 31, while Saunders (1947: 372) gave May 10 and May 22 as his average arrival and departure dates there. Speirs (1974) cited George A. Scott records for the Whitby-Oshawa region as early as May 5 (1973) and as late as May 30 (1973). Dennis Barry saw 4 in Thickson's woods, Whitby, on May 2 in 1970 (Tozer & Richards, 1974: 245). Weir & Quilliam (1980: 38) listed Kingston records from Apr. 29 to May 30, with average arrival May 7 and departure May 21. Devitt (1967: 138) gave May 17 as the 12-year average arrival date at Barrie, with the earliest on Apr. 30, 1960 at Collingwood and the latest on May 29. L. Beamer's median arrival date at Meaford was May 15, with the earliest on May 7, 1939. Mills (1981: 139) had spring dates for the cottage country from May 7 (1972) to May 23. Nicholson (1981: 163) gave May 6 as the 11-year average arrival date on Manitoulin, with the earliest on Apr. 27, 1974 and high estimates of 500 on May 19 and 210 on May 20. Speirs & Speirs (1947: 35) saw one at North Bay on May 6, 1944. Skeel & Bondrup-Nielsen (1978: 203) encountered 12 on 6 days at Pukaskwa from May 19 to 31, 1977. Denis (1961: 4) gave May 19 as the average arrival date at Thunder Bay, with the earliest on May 13, 1952. Peruniak (1971: 25) had a very early record at Atikokan on Apr. 24. Elder (1979: 38) gave May 17 as his earliest Geraldton date. Cringan (1953a: 3) listed May 24 as his first 1953 record at Sioux Lookout. "Drexler collected a male" at Moose Factory on May 28, 1868 (Manning, 1952: 82).

SUMMER:   On the 1968-1977 Breeding Bird Surveys they were uncommon or rare, south to Kemptville and Byng Inlet. Stirrett (1973c: 20) noted two returning migrants at Pelee as early as Aug. 12. Ussher (1965: 23) gave Aug. 19 as his earliest fall bird at Rondeau, with average arrival on Aug. 28. Beardslee & Mitchell (1965: 375) reported 4 at Morgan's Point, Lake Erie, as early as Aug. 6, 1944. J.L. Baillie (in Saunders, 1947: 372) had a returning bird at Toronto on Aug. 8. Jack Satterly saw one as early as Aug. 3, 1959 at Cedar Point, Mara Twp. (Speirs, 1974). Weir & Quilliam (1980: 38) gave Aug. 2 as the earliest fall date for Kingston, with the average arrival on Aug. 19. On July 3, 1948 I observed one singing the "swee-swee-swee" song on Beckwith Is., Georgian Bay and Doris H. Speirs noted young there on July 27 and 30 the same summer. Baillie & Harrington (1937: 245) found a nest with 6 eggs at Dorcas Bay, Bruce Peninsula, on June 12, 1934 and collected an agitated female there on July 15, 1933. Mills (1981: 138) saw an agitated pair carrying food near Ahmic Lake on June 19, 1979 and reported a few other summer records for the cottage country, where migrants were frequently observed during August. D.B. Ferguson found a nest with 3 young at Providence Bay, Manitoulin, on June 26, 1977 and Ron Tasker saw a female feeding young in Burpee Twp. from June 9 to 12, 1975 (Nicholson, 1981: 164). Baillie & Hope (1947: 23) saw a pair at Chapleau on June 3, 1937 and young with parents at Biscotasing on July 1 and 3, 1937. Skeel & Bondrup-Nielsen (1978: 203) recorded 12 at Pukaskwa from June 1 to July 10, 1977, where it ranked 20 in abundance of the birds noted there. Kendeigh (1947: 28) found 28 pairs on 100 acres at Black Sturgeon Lake in 1945 (the third ranking bird there) while Speirs (1949: 148) found 19 territories on 75 acres at nearby Eaglehead Lake in 1946 (ranking fourth of the birds there): both were noted during a spruce budworm infestation. Peruniak (1971: 25) saw a female feeding two young at Atikokan on July 14, 1962. Snyder (1953: 78) reported just two summer records for western Ontario: one at Dinorwic Lake in early June, 1940 and two at Sioux Lookout on July 6, 1947. Snyder (1928: 30) collected two males at Lake Abitibi: one on June 27, the other on July 2, 1925: he considered the species rare there. D. Blakely took two juveniles at Lac Seul, on June 28 and Aug. 1, 1919 (Baillie & Harrington, 1937: 245). Hope (1938: 38) collected 2 males and a female at Favourable Lake between July 3 and 9, 1938. Lee (1978: 31) observed only one at Big Trout Lake, on June 27, 1975. McLaren & McLaren (1981: 4) reported one singing at Little Sachigo Lake on June 11, 1977.

AUTUMN: Peruniak (1971: 25) gave Sept. 23 as her latest fall record for Atikokan. Ricker & Clarke (1939: 19) had a Sept. 14, 1925 record for Lake Nipissing. MacLulich (1938: 32) reported several at Brent on Sept. 27, 1930. The latest Manitoulin report was on Oct. 12, 1974 (Nicholson, 1981: 164). Cliff MacFayden saw one as late as Sept. 29, 1929 at Glen Orchard, Muskoka (Mills, 1981: 139). Only six were killed at the Barrie TV tower in seven years: Frances Westman saw one at Tollendal as late as Oct. 18, 1955 (Devitt, 1967: 138). Weir & Quilliam (1980: 38) listed Sept. 22 as the average departure date from Kingston, the latest on Oct. 23. Long (1968b: 12) noted one at Pickering Beach on Oct. 14, 1968. Saunders (1947: 372) listed Aug. 31 as the average fall arrival date at Toronto, with average departure on Sept. 17 and latest on Oct. 8. Snyder (1931: 207) reported 14 casualties at the Long Point light on Sept. 7, one on Sept. 9 and 15 from Sept. 24 to 29, 1929. D. Currie *et al* reported a very late one at London on Nov. 29, 1974 (Goodwin, 1975: 52). Ussher (1965: 23) gave Oct. 1 as his average departure date from Rondeau, with the latest on Oct. 18. Stirrett (1973d: 26) had a maximum fall count of 25 at Pelee on Sept. 6, his latest on Oct. 6.

**MEASUREMENTS:**
*Length:* 4.7 to 5.6 ins.
(Godfrey, 1966: 327)
*Wingspread:* 7.6 to 8.5
ins. (Roberts, 1955: 675)
*Weight:* 2 ♂ averaged
9.5 g. one ♀ 10.2 g.
(Hope, 1938: 38).

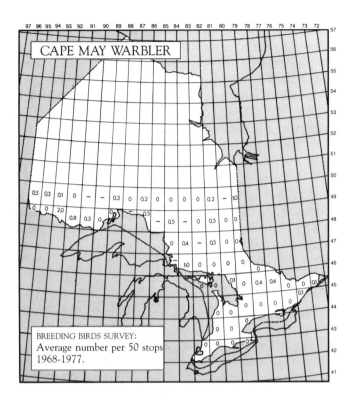

CAPE MAY WARBLER

BREEDING BIRDS SURVEY:
Average number per 50 stops
1968-1977.

# BLACK-THROATED BLUE WARBLER
## *Dendroica caerulescens* (Gmelin)

This natty little warbler I associate with openings in and around mature deciduous forests, north from the cottage country. They winter in the West Indies.

IDENTIFICATION: The male, with its black throat and sides, contrasting with the remaining white underparts and bright blue upperparts, is easily identified. Females are dull brownish birds, with only the little white square on the middle of the wings, the "trademark" of the species, to help identify them. The usual song is a rising, buzzy: "zwah–zwee-zwii" (sometimes with more than three phrases).

WINTER:

SPRING: Stirrett (1973b: 24) had Pelee records from May 3 to six on June 5, with maxima of 10 on May 10 and May 17. Rondeau dates ranged from May 4 to May 31, with average arrival on May 11 and departure on May 19 (Ussher, 1965: 24). Saunders & Dale (1933: 228) gave May 10 as the 17-year average arrival date at London, with the earliest on May 3, 1914. Snyder (1931: 208) had Long Point records from May 9 (1928) to June 1 (1924). Speirs (1938: 40, 44) gave May 1 as the earliest Toronto date, with spring peaks on May 11 and May 21: Saunders (1947: 372) listed May 9 as his average arrival date and May 24 as the average departure date from Toronto, with one as late as June 4. George A. Scott had Oshawa records from May 2 to June 3, and the spring peak is mid-May there (Speirs, 1974). Naomi LeVay had an early one at Cranberry Marsh on May 1, 1959 and J.M. Richards tallied as many as 40 in Darlington Twp. on May 9, 1970 (Tozer & Richards, 1974: 245). Charles Fothergill collected a male in the first week of June, 1821, by the Otonibee River (Black, 1934: 154). Weir & Quilliam (1980: 38) listed May 6 and May 27 as average arrival and departure dates at Kingston, with the earliest on Apr. 28. Devitt (1967: 139) gave May 15 as the 17-year average arrival date at Barrie, with the earliest at Collingwood on May 2, 1959. L. Beamer's median arrival date at Meaford was May 17, with his earliest on May 4, 1956. Mills (1981: 139) gave May 9 as a 6-year arrival date at Huntsville, the earliest on May 4, 1974. Nicholson (1981: 164) gave May 15 as the 10-year average arrival date on Manitoulin, the earliest on May 6, 1979 and a high count of 27 on Great Duck Is. on May 23, 1976. MacLulich (1938: 32) gave May 13, 1912 as his earliest Algonquin Park date. Louise Lawrence noted one on May 3, 1944 at Rutherglen (Speirs & Speirs, 1947: 35). Denis (1961: 4) gave May 20 as the average arrival date at Thunder Bay, with the earliest on May 12, 1952. Peruniak (1971: 25) had just two Atikokan records, the earliest on May 27, 1962. Bondrup-Nielsen (1976: 44) observed one near Kapuskasing on May 22, 1974.

SUMMER: On the 1968-1977 Breeding Bird Surveys they were uncommon to rare north to Hornepayne and Eagle River, and south to Fraserville and Mount Julian, fairly common in the Algonquin region and near Lake Superior at Montreal Falls and Silver Islet. Stirrett (1973c: 20) had his earliest fall bird at Pelee on Aug. 12. Saunders & Dale (1933: 228) reported a male taken near London on June 22, 1882. Beardslee & Mitchell (1965: 377) reported one at Morgan's Point, Lake Erie, as early as Aug. 6, 1944. J.L. Baillie (in Saunders, 1947: 372) had June 24 and Aug. 21 dates for Toronto. Bruce Parker heard one singing in McRae Provincial Park, Mara Twp., on June 19, 1973 (Speirs, 1974). Dennis Barry saw a female lining a nest in Darlington Twp. on June 16, 1973; the nest was 16 ins. up in a maple-leaved viburnum. Snyder (1941: 78) collected a male near Wellington, Prince Edward Co., on June 2, 1930 and another male of a pair established in a "dense, dry mixed forest near Woodrous" on June 27, 1930. Michael Evans found one singing by the Canoe Lake road, near Kingston, on June 27, 1971 (Quilliam, 1973: 157). H.P. Bingham collected a nest and 4 eggs at Little Lake, Barrie, on July 4, 1913 and there have been several summer records near the Georgian Bay shore of Simcoe Co. (Devitt, 1967: 138-139). W.E. Saunders took a set of 4 eggs and a cowbird egg at Durham, Grey Co., on June 22, 1909 (Baillie & Harrington, 1937: 249). D.B. Ferguson noted 7 singing males on the Cup and Saucer Trail, Manitoulin, on June 11, 1978 (Nicholson, 1981: 164). MacLulich (1938: 32) found a nest with 4 eggs at Little Nipissing River, Algonquin Park, on June 25, 1930, and C.H.D. Clarke saw young being fed at Brule Lake on July 9, 1934. Speirs & Speirs (1947: 35) cited details of several nestings in the Rutherglen - Eau Claire region. Paul Harrington found a nest with 4 eggs in a small balsam fir about a foot above ground at Chapleau on June 17, 1937: a young bird just out of the nest was taken at Biscotasing on July 8, 1937 (Baillie & Hope, 1947: 23). Skeel & Bondrup-Nielsen (1978: 203) had a few records at Pukaskwa from June 8 to July 9, 1977 in parts of the mature deciduous forest with shrubby undergrowth. Snyder (1953: 78) had only two records for western Ontario, both at Wabigoon, on June 17 and July 1, 1947. Smith (1957: 178) had Clay Belt records as follows: several near Lake Abitibi on June 19, 1953; a few near Kapuskasing from June 22 to July 6, 1953; and one at Forde Lake, about 30 miles west of Hearst on June 4, 1954. R.D. Ussher found a nest with 3 eggs near Kapuskasing on July 8, 1925 (Baillie & Harrington, 1937: 245).

AUTUMN: The only records from the James Bay region were two noted at Netitishi Point on Oct. 15, 1981 and one at Moose Factory on Oct. 6 by D. McRae and A. Wormington (one of the Netitishi Point birds was collected). Louise Lawrence saw 3 at Pimisi Bay on Sept. 21, 1944 (Speirs & Speirs, 1947: 35). Nicholson (1981: 164) had fall records on Manitoulin from Aug. 31 (1975) to Oct. 4 (1978), with a kill at the Great Duck Is. tower of 68 birds from Sept. 18 to 22, 1977. William Mansell saw one as late as Oct. 9, 1939 at Rebecca Lake, Muskoka (Mills, 1981: 140). At the Barrie TV tower 59 were killed in 6 of 7 years, the latest on Oct. 11, 1962 (Devitt, 1967: 139). Weir & Quilliam (1980: 38) listed Aug. 22 and Oct. 8 as average arrival and departure dates at Kingston, with a late one on Oct. 28. Tozer & Richards (1974: 246) saw one at Oshawa as late as Oct. 29, 1956. George A. Scott observed two males and two females at Oshawa as early as Aug. 20, 1972 (Speirs, 1974). Saunders (1947: 372) had Toronto dates from Aug. 29 to Oct. 17, with average arrival on Sept. 13 and departure on Sept. 29: Speirs (1938: 52, 56) listed Sept. 15 as the fall peak, with a very late one on Nov. 15. Beardslee & Mitchell (1965: 377) reported birds along the Lake Erie shores on Oct. 21, 1945 and Oct. 24, 1943 and one picked up dead at Lorraine, Ont. on Oct. 28, 1950. Snyder (1931: 208) cited Long Point casualties: 3 on Sept. 7, 4 on Sept. 9 and 35 from Sept. 24 to 29, 1929. Ussher (1965: 24) had fall dates at Rondeau from Aug. 24 to Oct. 11 with average arrival Sept. 1 and departure Sept. 23. Stirrett (1973d: 26) had a maximum of 20 at Pelee on Sept. 6, with the latest on Oct. 20.

**MEASUREMENTS:**

*Length:* 4.8 to 5.5 ins. (Godfrey, 1966: 328)
*Wingspread:* 7.12 to 7.88 ins. (Roberts, 1955: 677)
*Weight:* 7.5 to 14.1 g (very fat bird) (Terres, 1980: 967)

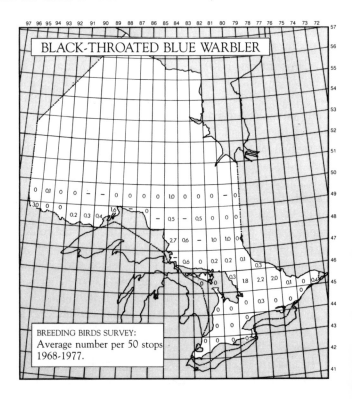

BLACK-THROATED BLUE WARBLER

BREEDING BIRDS SURVEY: Average number per 50 stops 1968-1977.

# YELLOW-RUMPED WARBLER
*Dendroica coronata* (Linnaeus)

This is usually the first warbler to appear in Ontario in spring and the last to leave in fall. The white-throated variety, the Myrtle Warbler, is the common one in Ontario. A few of the yellow-throated form, known as Audubon's Warbler, have wandered east into the province. Some individuals are found almost every winter in southern Ontario, but most go south to southern United States and some as far as the West Indies and Panama.

IDENTIFICATION: The bright yellow rump identifies this species in all plumages, and the loud "kissing note" when just heard. The song is a dreamy "see-see-see-soo-soo-soo".

WINTER: On the 1968-1977 Christmas counts they were rare at Pelee and Long Point, with outliers as far north as Deep River and Sault Ste. Marie. Stirrett (1973a: 19) reported a winter maximum of 35 at Pelee on Dec. 30. Harold Lancaster noted one at West Lorne on Dec. 27, 1946 (Brooman, 1954: 33). Beardslee & Mitchell (1965: 376) reported one at Dufferin Is., Niagara Falls, on Dec. 29, 1950. J. Lamey observed one on the Pickering Twp. Christmas count on Dec. 26, 1970 (Speirs, 1974). One visited R.C. Lunney's feeder at Bowmanville for three weeks up to Dec. 30, 1962 (Tozer & Richards, 1974: 247). Weir & Quilliam (1980: 23) wrote "Some have wintered each year since 1975" at Kingston, with records from December through to March. The A. Conway's had one at their Huntsville feeder up to Dec. 7, 1960 (Mills, 1981: 140). Chris Bell and Mick Throssell saw one on Dec. 15, 1973, at Gore Bay (Nicholson, 1981: 65). Dennison (1980: 149) reported one on the Sault Ste. Marie Christmas count in 1974.

SPRING: Stirrett (1973b: 24) had spring maxima of 500 at Pelee on May 5 and May 10. Ussher (1965: 24) had Rondeau records from March 24 to May 28, with average arrival on Apr. 18 and departure on May 17. Saunders & Dale (1933: 228) gave Apr. 19 as the 17-year average arrival date at London, with the earliest on Apr. 9, 1921. Snyder (1931: 208-209) was surprised to have only one record (spring or fall) of one killed at the Long Point light: this was on May 19, 1926: his latest spring bird there was on May 27, 1927. Saunders (1947: 372) had one as early as Apr. 4 at Toronto, but his average arrival date there was Apr. 23 and average departure May 25: the spring peak at Toronto has been about May 5 (Speirs, 1938: 44). J. Satterly noted one as early as Apr. 12, 1953 at Cedar Point, Mara Twp.: the spring peak in Ontario Co. was usually in the first week of May (Speirs, 1974). M.G. Gould noted one at Bowmanville on Apr. 14, 1922 (Allin, 1940: 105). Weir & Quilliam (1980: 23, 32) gave Apr. 16 and May 23 as average arrival and departure dates for Kingston, with a maximum of 2000 on May 11, 1975 at Prince Edward Point. Devitt (1962: 140) gave Apr. 24 as the 20-year average arrival date at Barrie: the earliest on Apr. 10, 1952: H.P. Bingham found a nest with one egg and a cowbird egg at Little Lake, Barrie, as early as May 24, 1920. L. Beamer's earliest date for Meaford was Apr. 10, 1954 and his median arrival date was Apr. 23. Mills (1981: 140) gave Apr. 22 as the 13-year average arrival date at Huntsville, with an early one at M. Hill's feeder there on March 31, 1960 and a nest as early as May 12, 1976 on Beausoleil Is. Nicholson (1981: 165) gave Apr. 19 as the 10-year average arrival date on Manitoulin, the earliest on Apr. 12, 1980 and a maximum of 400 on May 20, 1975. MacLulich (1938: 33) gave May 2, 1934 as his earliest Algonquin Park date. Louise Lawrence saw three at Pimisi Bay on Apr. 24, 1945 (Speirs & Speirs, 1947: 35). Skeel & Bondrup-

Nielsen (1978: 203) noted their first at Pukaskwa on Apr. 11, 1977, where they ranked it as the second most abundant spring migrant. Denis (1961: 2) gave Apr. 22 as the average arrival date for Thunder Bay, with the earliest on March 31, 1945. Peruniak (1971: 26) gave Apr. 17 as her earliest Atikokan date. Elder (1979: 38) gave Apr. 25 as his earliest date for Geraldton. Bondrup-Nielsen (1976: 44) saw his first near Kapuskasing on May 5, 1975. Cringan (1953a: 3) saw his first at Sioux Lookout on May 5 in 1953. C.A. Elsey reported a "big wave" in the Asheweig area on May 17, 1950 (Cringan, 1950: 17). Oliver Hewitt saw four at Moose Factory on May 24, 1947 (Manning, 1952: 82).

SUMMER: On the 1968-1977 Breeding Bird Surveys they were common on some of the more northerly routes becoming uncommon south to Flesherton, Orillia and Mt. Julian. Stirrett (1973b: 24 & 1973c: 20) had 8 at Pelee as late as June 5 and one as early as Aug. 5. Ussher (1965: 24) noted one at Rondeau as early as July 30. Beardslee & Mitchell (1965: 375, 376) had a record at Dunnville as late as June 4, 1950 and about 100 along the Canadian shore of Lake Erie on Aug. 24, 1952. Saunders (1947: 372) had a June 17 record for Toronto and Speirs (1938: 48) listed an Aug. 12 record. Snyder (1930: 198) collected a male on July 16, 1926 in the swamp bordering the Holland River in King Twp. I had June records in the summers of 1962, 1963 and 1969 in the Precambrian strip in northern Rama Twp. (Speirs, 1974). D. Barry and J. Richards saw a male and female together in the Osler Tract, Cartwright Twp., on July 20, 1968 (Tozer & Richards, 1974: 247). Richard Norman found a nest with 2 eggs and 3 cowbird eggs at Chaffey's Lock, near Kingston, on June 9, 1975 and Frank Phelan found a nest with 4 eggs at Lake Opinicon on June 11, 1976 (Weir & Quilliam, 1980: 23). Of 39 nests at Wasaga Beach examined by Paul Harrington, no less than 25 contained cowbird eggs (Devitt, 1967: 139). Katherine Ketchum saw an early wave off Pointe au Baril on Aug. 12, 1974 (Mills, 1981: 140), who also reported 29 nestings in the cottage country, one with 4 eggs as late as July 29, 1974 at Twelve-mile Bay, Muskoka. D.B. Ferguson watched adults feeding young at a nest near Windfall Lake, Manitoulin, on June 7, 1980 (Nicholson, 1981: 165). MacLulich (1938: 33) observed young being fed in Lister Twp., Algonquin Park on July 3, 1930 and cited other breeding records for the region. Speirs & Speirs (1947: 35) watched an adult feeding young at Lake Nipissing on Aug. 2, 1944. Baillie & Hope (1947: 24) reported a nest with 3 eggs in a black spruce at Chapleau on June 10; young out of the nest at Biscotasing on July 5 and two nests at Bigwood on July 22, 1937. Snyder (1942: 144) saw adults carrying food to young at Maclennan on July 27, 1931. This species ranked 8th in abundance on the summer censuses at Pukaskwa in 1977 (Skeel & Bondrup-Nielsen, 1978: 203). Baillie & Hope (1943: 21) found a nest with 4 eggs at Rossport on June 7, 1936 and collected several adults at Marathon and Amyot. Snyder (1928: 272) collected young at Lake Nipigon on Aug. 8 and 9, 1924. Dear (1940: 138) found a nest with 3 eggs and a cowbird egg at Thunder Bay on June 11, 1929 and a nest with 4 eggs there on June 12, 1938. Kendeigh (1947: 28) had a population of 3 pairs on 100 acres at Black Sturgeon Lake in 1945 while Speirs (1949: 148) had 25 pairs on 75 acres at nearby Eaglehead Lake in 1946 (it ranked third of the birds there). Snyder (1938: 204) collected a male at Off Lake, Rainy River, on July 9, 1929. Snyder (1953: 78) rated this to be the second most common warbler in western Ontario, with breeding established at Kenora, Wabigoon, Sioux Lookout and Malachi. Snyder (1928: 31) called this "the commonest warbler of the region" at Lake Abitibi in 1925: a nest was located 20 ft. up in a young white spruce on June 28. James (1980: 84) found this to be the most common warbler at Pickle Lake, with a population of 11.2 pairs per km $^2$ found on 7 of 12 transects there: a nest with one young was found nearby on June 12, 1977. Hope (1938: 38) found a nest with 5 eggs on June 26, 1938 at Favourable Lake: it was 4 ft. up in a small white spruce. Cringan (1953b: 4) found this to be the second most common warbler at Kasabonika Lake in early June, 1953. Manning (1952: 82) found them from Moosonee north along the James Bay coast to Big Piskwanish and Raft River: on the Hudson Bay coast he noted 21 (mostly juveniles) at Shagamu River. James, Nash & Peck (1982: 67-68) located a nest with young being fed by adults, by the Harricanaw River, James Bay, on June 22, 1982. James, Nash & Peck (1981: 46) found a population density of 40 pairs per km $^2$ in black spruce forest on dry ridges at Kiruna Lake, Sutton Ridges. Schueler, Baldwin & Rising (1974: 144, 147) listed them as uncommon at Winisk but common at Hawley Lake where a nest with 3 eggs was found on June 20, 1962. Lee (1975: 31) had populations on all three study plots at Big Trout Lake in 1975: he had a maximum of 12 there on July 2. C.E. Hope collected a nest with 5 eggs at Ft. Severn on July 2, 1940.

AUTUMN: D. McRae and A. Wormington noted them almost daily from Oct. 15 to 23, 1981 at Netitishi Point, James Bay. Peruniak (1971: 26) gave Oct. 18 as her latest date for Atikokan. Skeel & Bondrup-Nielsen (1978: 203) found this to be the most common warbler migrant at Pukaskwa in 1977, last seen on Oct. 1. Speirs & Speirs (1947: 35) saw one at North Bay on Oct. 17, 1944. E.L. Brereton saw one in Algonquin Park on Oct. 5, 1936 (MacLulich, 1938: 33). Ron Tasker reported "thousands" on Manitoulin on Oct. 13, 1974 and Chris Bell found one there as late as Nov. 11, 1973 (Nicholson, 1981: 165). At the Barrie TV tower 37 were killed in 4 of 7 years: one was observed at Collingwood as late as Nov. 14, 1953 (Devitt, 1967: 139-140). Weir & Quilliam (1980: 38) listed Aug. 18 and Nov. 9 as average fall arrival and departure dates for Kingston. Speirs (1974) had fall records from Aug. 11 to Dec. 8 in Ontario Co., with a maximum count of 52 on Oct. 8, 1955. Saunders (1947: 372) gave Sept. 18 and Oct. 31 as his average fall arrival and departure dates for Toronto, with the latest on Nov. 14: the fall peak there is about Oct. 1 (Speirs, 1938: 52). Ussher (1965: 24) gave Aug. 30 and Oct. 31 as average arrival and departure dates for Rondeau, with the latest on Nov. 22 (but also "rare in winter"). Stirrett (1973d: 26) had fall maxima of 250 at Pelee on Oct. 14 and Oct. 16.

BANDING: One banded at Long Point on Nov. 1, 1970 turned up the following fall on Oct. 22, 1971 at Sheridan, N.Y. (about 49 miles to the east) (Brewer & Salvadori, 1976: 85). Brewer & Salvadori (1978: 77 - 78) reported four more distant recoveries: one banded at Bewdley, Ont. on Sept. 25, 1963 was recovered at Geneva, Alabama, on Jan. 31, 1965 (about 989 miles southwest): another banded at Bewdley on Sept. 22, 1964 was recovered at Nahunta, Georgia on Jan. 15, 1965 (about 907 miles somewhat west of south). Another banded near Wolsey Lake, Ont. on May 19, 1967 was recovered near Sarnia on Oct. 18, 1967 (about 196 miles to the south): finally one banded at the Balmoral Marsh on Oct. 14, 1967 was recovered at Long Point on Oct. 6, 1968 (about 119 miles to the east).

**MEASUREMENTS:**
*Length:* 5 to 6 ins.
(Godfrey, 1966: 329)
*Wingspread:* 8.0 to 9.4
ins. (Roberts, 1955: 681)
*Weight:* 0.44 to 0.50 oz.
(Roberts, 1955: 681)
3 ♀ averaged 12 g. (Hope,
1938: 38).

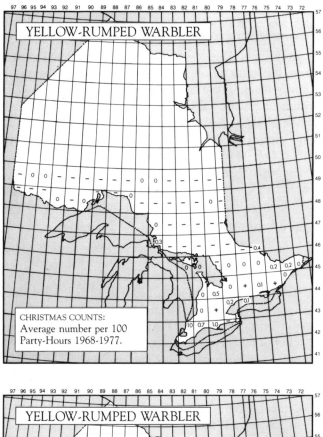

YELLOW-RUMPED WARBLER

CHRISTMAS COUNTS:
Average number per 100
Party-Hours 1968-1977.

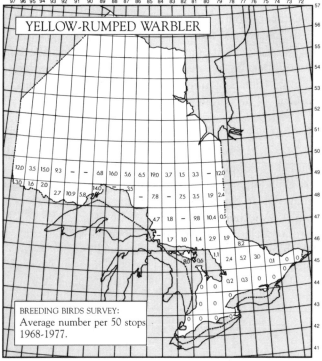

YELLOW-RUMPED WARBLER

BREEDING BIRDS SURVEY:
Average number per 50 stops
1968-1977.

# BLACK-THROATED GRAY WARBLER
## *Dendroica nigrescens* (Townsend)

This warbler of the Pacific coast has wandered a few times as far as Ontario.

**IDENTIFICATION:** Superficially it resembles a Black-and-white Warbler, but it has a blue back with black streaks, not white with black stripes as in the Black-and-white Warbler. It has a solid black crown, with no median white stripe. A small yellow spot in front of the eye is diagnostic but hard to see. The Blackpoll Warbler lacks the black cheeks and throat of this species and has a green back, not blue.

**WINTER:** Bristol Foster discovered one at Glendon Hall, Toronto, on Dec. 7, 1952. It was seen by many others and photographed by Charles Molony: last seen on Dec. 15 (Baillie, 1957: 2).

**SPRING:** One was seen at Rattray's Marsh, near Clarkson, on May 5, 1962 by T. Mason *et al* (Woodford, 1962: 408). Don Perks *et al* found one at Toronto on May 3, 1969 (Goodwin, 1969: 585).

**SUMMER:**

**AUTUMN:** Horace Dahmer and Willard Schaefer reported one at Pelee on Sept. 11, 1955 (Baillie, 1957: 2). H.H. Axtell and many others saw one at Niagara-on-the-Lake on Nov. 13, 1980 (Goodwin, 1981: 178).

**MEASUREMENTS:**
Length: 4.6 to 5.2 ins.
(Godfrey, 1966: 331)
Wingspread:
Weight: 11 ♂ averaged
8.8 g.; 13 ♀ averaged
7.9 g. (Dunning,
1984: 21).

# TOWNSEND'S WARBLER
## *Dendroica townsendi* (Townsend)

This Pacific coast warbler is usually found high in B.C. conifers. To date there have been five Ontario sightings.

IDENTIFICATION: This is the west coast counterpart of our Black-throated Green Warbler and looks much like it but has a black cap, black ear patches and much yellow on the breast and sides. Its song is buzzy like that of the Black-throated Green.

WINTER:

SPRING: There have been three records from Pelee: the first on May 1, 1966 (Stirrett, 1973b: 24). Norman Chesterfield *et al* saw another at Pelee on May 10, 1972 (Goodwin, 1972: 757) and the third was noted there by D.E. Perks *et al* on May 13, 1979 (Goodwin, 1979: 767). The most recent record was at Sarnia, where D. Johnston, D. Rupert *et al* saw one on May 18-19, 1981 (Goodwin, 1981: 820). J.P. Kleiman saw a male at Bradley's Marsh on May 15, 1966 (Kelley, 1978: 72).

SUMMER:

AUTUMN:

**MEASUREMENTS:**
*Length:* 4.5 to 5.0 ins.  9.1 g.; 48 ♀ averaged
(Godfrey, 1966: 331)  8.6 g. (Dunning,
Wingspread:  1984: 21).
*Weight:* 48 ♂ averaged


# HERMIT WARBLER   *Dendroica occidentalis*   (Townsend)

This is another tree top bird, normally found in conifers near the Pacific coast of the United States: only one Ontario record to date.

IDENTIFICATION: This warbler has a completely yellow head, two prominent white wing bars, white outer tail feather, a gray back with black streaks and white underparts with gray streaks on the sides. The male has a black chin and throat.

WINTER:

SPRING: One was seen at Pelee from May 2 to 6, 1981 by T. Hince and many others (Goodwin, 1981: 820). This bird was photographed by James Flynn.

SUMMER:

AUTUMN:

**MEASUREMENTS:**
*Length:* 4.5 to 5.0 ins.  9.5 g.; 18 ♀ averaged
(Terres, 1980: 978)  8.8 g. (Dunning,
Wingspread:  1984: 21).
*Weight:* 36 ♂ averaged

# BLACK-THROATED GREEN WARBLER
*Dendroica virens* (Gmelin)

This dainty little warbler is often seen fluttering about, part way up trees, picking off insects from the outer branches. In the breeding season it is often found in pine stands or hemlock groves: in migration it often favours birches and willows. It winters from southern United States to Panama and the West Indies.

IDENTIFICATION: With its black throat, green back, yellow cheeks, white underparts and white wing bars, the male is unmistakable. Females and young often lack the black throat but the yellow cheeks, green back and black streaks on the white lower parts identify them: some Pine Warblers are similar but they have yellow breasts. The buzzy song is often rendered "cheese, cheese, little more cheese" or "zhree-zhree-zhree-zu-shrii". The call note resembles the "kissing" note of the Yellow-rumped Warbler but it is a somewhat less "juicy" kiss.

WINTER:

SPRING: Stirrett (1973b: 24) had spring migrants at Pelee from Apr. 28 to May 24, with a maximum of 100 on May 9. Ussher (1965: 24) reported Rondeau birds from Apr. 23 to summer, with average arrival Apr. 30 and departure May 25. Saunders & Dale (1933: 228) gave May 2 as the 17-year average arrival date at London, with the earliest on Apr. 24, 1925. Snyder (1931: 211) noted his first at Long Point on May 3 in 1928, with many there by May 22. Speirs (1938: 40, 44) gave Apr. 20 as the earliest Toronto date, with peaks on May 11 and May 21. Saunders (1947: 372) listed May 4 as his 13-year average arrival date there. Speirs (1974) noted his earliest in Pickering Twp. on Apr. 26, 1964 and a well-defined peak on May 17. Weir & Quilliam (1980: 38) listed Apr. 26 as the earliest Kingston record with May 3 as the 29-year average arrival date. Devitt (1967: 140) gave May 6 as the 17-year arrival date at Barrie, with the earliest on Apr. 29, 1963. L. Beamer's median arrival date at Meaford was May 18, earliest May 6, 1945. C. Harris found a very early one at Go Home Bay on Apr. 18, 1976 but a 6-year average arrival date at Huntsville was May 11 (Mills, 1981: 141). Nicholson (1981: 165) gave May 6 as the 12-year average date on Manitoulin, with the earliest on Apr. 27, 1974 and a maximum estimate of 400 on Great Duck Is. on May 19, 1979. MacLulich (1938: 33) gave May 6, 1913 as his earliest Algonquin Park date. Louise Lawrence saw two at Pimisi Bay on May 8, 1945 (Speirs & Speirs, 1947: 35). Skeel & Bondrup-Nielsen (1978: 204) saw their first at Pukaskwa on May 13 in 1977 and heard 91 on 14 days later in May. Denis (1961: 3) gave May 15 as the average arrival date at Thunder Bay, with the earliest on May 7, 1952. Peruniak (1971: 26) gave May 20 as her earliest Atikokan date. May 16 was the earliest Geraldton date (Elder, 1979: 38). Bondrup-Nielsen (1976: 44) had his first on May 23 in 1974 near Kapuskasing. Cringan (1953a: 3) saw his first in 1953 at Perrault Falls on May 14.

SUMMER: On the 1968-1977 Breeding Bird Surveys, they were common on some routes near the north and east shores of Lake Superior, fairly common in the Algonquin Park region, becoming uncommon south to Lake Erie and north to Longlac and Kenora, absent from many routes in southeastern and northeastern Ontario. Stirrett (1973c: 20) had Pelee records on June 15 and June 25 and again as early as Aug. 12. Ussher (1965: 24) had Rondeau records as late as June 19 and returning birds as early as Aug. 21. Saunders

& Dale (1933: 228) reported a male in full song collected on June 12, 1882, near London. Snyder (1931: 211) reported an occupied nest on Long Point on June 21, 1927: there were several other summer records on Long Point (McCracken, Bradstreet & Holroyd, 1981: 63). Snyder (1930: 199) reported two nests in King Twp. in 1926; one on June 19 and the other on Aug. 9: both held 3 eggs and were situated about 30 ft. up in hemlocks. Speirs & Orenstein (1975: 13) found a population density of 54 birds per 100 acres in a pine plantation in Uxbridge Twp. in 1966: this was the most abundant bird in that quadrat: young were noted following parents on June 13: smaller numbers were noted in summer in 7 of 11 Ontario Co. townships (Speirs, 1974). Ken Carmichael found a nest with 4 young only five ft. up in a white cedar in Reach Twp. on June 22, 1966 (Tozer & Richards, 1974: 248). Snyder noted as many as 12 in Prince Edward Co. on June 28, 1930. E. Beaupré took a set of 4 eggs at Murvale, near Kingston, on June 12, 1905; and young out of the nest were seen being fed near the Otter Lake sanctuary on July 7, 1963 (Quilliam, 1973: 158). Devitt (1967: 140) cited several breeding records for Simcoe Co., from Holland River north to Wasaga Beach: most were parasitized by cowbirds. J.H. Fleming saw a pair feeding young at Rockcliffe on Aug. 16, 1900 (Lloyd, 1924: 14). This is a familiar summer bird in the cottage country: E. Miller found a nest with 4 eggs near Spider Bay, Parry Sound (Mills, 1981: 141). Nicholson (1981: 165) considered this to be the most common warbler on Manitoulin: Ron Tasker found a nest with 3 eggs and a young cowbird in Burpee Twp. on July 19, 1976. Louise Lawrence watched flying young being fed at Pimisi Bay on July 15, 1944 (Speirs & Speirs, 1947: 35). Baillie & Hope (1947: 24) collected 2 males and a female at Chapleau on June 3 and 5, 1937 and 2 young females at Bigwood on July 14. Snyder (1942: 144) saw as many as 24 near Sault Ste. Marie on July 7 and collected a young male at Maclennan on July 28, 1931. Skeel & Bondrup-Nielsen (1978: 204) found this species to rank third in abundance of the summer birds at Pukaskwa in 1977. Baillie & Hope (1943: 21) designated them as "not uncommon" at Rossport and Marathon, but "Rather rare at Amyot" in 1936. Snyder (1928: 273) saw young being fed by adults at Macdiarmid, Lake Nipigon, on July 25 and Aug. 3, 1924. Dear (1940: 138) found a nest with 4 eggs in MacGregor Twp., Thunder Bay, on June 24, 1934. Kendeigh (1947: 28) found 6 pairs on 100 acres at Black Sturgeon Lake in 1945 while Speirs (1949: 148) had 11 pairs on 75 acres at nearby Eaglehead Lake in 1946. Snyder (1938: 204) collected a male at Off Lake, where they were fairly common, on July 9, 1929. Snyder (1953: 78) noted up to 10 daily at Sioux Lookout and some at Kenora, but found them to be rare in most of western Ontario. Snyder (1928: 31) collected a male at Lake Abitibi on June 5, 1925, where they were "not very numerous". James (1980: 84) estimated 2.4 pairs per km $^2$ on 3 of 12 transects at Pickle Lake. Hope (1938: 38) saw a male feeding a young bird near Favourable Lake on July 21, 1938. Todd (1963: 607) had Moose Factory observations on June 26, 1908 and June 7, 1926.

AUTUMN: Peruniak (1971: 26) gave Sept. 26 as her latest Atikokan record. Skeel & Bondrup-Nielsen (1978: 204) saw their latest at Pukaskwa on Sept. 20 in 1977. Louise Lawrence saw 4 at Pimisi Bay on Sept. 12, 1944. Nicholson (1981: 166) gave Oct. 26, 1975 as the latest Manitoulin date and reported 112 killed at the Great Duck Is. tower from Sept. 18-22, 1977. C. Harris saw 3 at Go Home Bay on Oct. 2, 1976 (Mills, 1981: 142). At the Barrie TV tower 39 were killed in 5 of 7 years (Devitt, 1967: 140): A. Mills and T. Letson had a very late one in Simcoe Co. on Nov. 14, 1974 (Goodwin, 1975: 52). Weir & Quilliam (1980: 38) gave Oct. 5 as the 24-year average departure date from Kingston, with the latest on Oct. 23. George A. Scott found a female in pines by

Oshawa's Second Marsh as late as Oct. 27, 1973 (Speirs, 1974). Speirs (1938: 52, 54) gave Sept. 17 as the fall peak date for Toronto, with the latest on Nov. 1: Saunders (1947: 372) listed Sept. 26 as his 12-year average departure from Toronto. Seventeen were killed at the Long Point light from Sept. 24-29, 1929 (Snyder, 1931: 211). Ussher (1965: 24) gave Aug. 29 and Oct. 7 as average fall arrival and departure dates for Rondeau, his latest on Nov. 11. Stirrett (1973d: 26) had a fall maximum of 20 at Pelee on Sept. 16, the latest on Oct. 27.

**MEASUREMENTS:**
*Length:* 4.4 to 5.3 ins.
(Godfrey, 1966: 332)
*Wingspread:* 7.0 to 8.0
ins. (Roberts, 1955: 678)
*Weight:* 31 Ontario
specimens averaged 9.2 g.

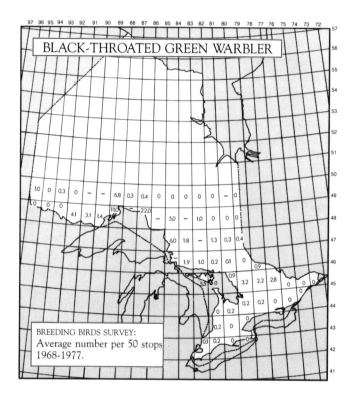

BLACK-THROATED GREEN WARBLER

BREEDING BIRDS SURVEY:
Average number per 50 stops
1968-1977.

# BLACKBURNIAN WARBLER  *Dendroica fusca*  (Müller)

Though brilliantly coloured, like a diminutive oriole, this warbler often escapes observation because of its fondness for the treetops and because of its weak, high-pitched song. They winter from Guatemala south to Peru.

IDENTIFICATION: The male, with its orange throat and upper breast, black and white wings and tail, and black ear patch outlined with orange, is easily identified. Females and young have a somewhat similar pattern with the orange replaced by yellow and with two white wing bars replacing the white wing patch of the male (these might be confused with Townsend's Warbler of B.C.). The song is an ascending series of "see-see-see" notes, ending very high (like a Golden-crowned Kinglet song).

WINTER:

SPRING: Stirrett (1973b: 24) had Pelee records from Apr. 28 to June 5, with a maximum of 100 on June 1. Kelley (1978: 72) mentioned a very early bird on Apr. 6, 1947 (but without definite locality—somewhere in SE Michigan or SW Ontario). Ussher (1965: 24) had Rondeau records from Apr. 29 to May 31, with average arrival on May 7 and departure on May 23. Saunders & Dale (1933: 228) gave May 6 as the 17-year average arrival date at London, with the earliest on Apr. 27, 1915. Harold Lancaster gave May 10 as his average arrival date in Elgin Co. (Brooman, 1954: 23). Snyder (1931: 210) reported Long Point dates from May 14, 1925 when 10 were killed at the light, to June 1, 1924 when W.E. Saunders saw five there. Saunders (1947: 372) gave May 9 as his 13-year average arrival date at Toronto, with the earliest on Apr. 27. Speirs (1938: 44) had two peaks at Toronto, on May 13 and May 23. George A. Scott saw one as early as May 4, 1952 at Oshawa but the spring peak is about May 17 (Speirs, 1974). Snyder (1941: 79) had Prince Edward Co. records from May 13 (1933) to May 27 (1925). Weir & Quilliam (1980: 39) listed May 8 as the 31-year average arrival date at Kingston, with the earliest on May 1. Devitt (1967: 141) gave May 10 as the 15-year average arrival date at Barrie, with one as early as May 3, 1955 at Collingwood. L. Beamer's median arrival date at Meaford was May 15, with his earliest on May 6, 1945. A 9-year average arrival date at Huntsville was May 11, with one as early as Apr. 26, 1959 (Mills, 1981: 142) who watched a female nest building at Ahmic Lake on May 21, 1977. Nicholson (1981: 166) gave May 10 as the 12-year average arrival date for Manitoulin, with the earliest on Apr. 26, 1979 and peak numbers around May 20. MacLulich (1938: 33) gave May 13, 1912 as an arrival date for Algonquin Park. Louise Lawrence saw one at Pimisi Bay on May 12, 1945 and watched one gathering nest material on May 27, 1944 (Speirs & Speirs, 1947: 35). Skeel & Bondrup-Nielsen (1978: 205) recorded 33 on 12 days in May after the first arrival on May 15 in 1977. Denis (1961: 3) listed May 17 as the average arrival date at Thunder Bay, with the earliest on May 10, 1953. Peruniak (1971: 26) gave May 9 as her earliest Atikokan date. Elder (1979: 38) gave May 23 as his earliest at Geraldton. Smith (1957: 178) saw one near New Liskeard on May 27, 1954 and two there the next day. Bondrup-Nielsen (1976: 44) saw one near Kapuskasing on May 28, 1974, none in 1975. Cringan (1953a: 3) saw his first in 1953 at Perrault Falls on May 6.

SUMMER: On the 1968-1977 Breeding Bird Surveys they were common on some western Ontario routes, fairly common in the cottage country, becoming uncommon in northeastern Ontario and south to Orillia. Stirrett (1973c: 20) had his earliest returning bird at Pelee on Aug. 6, but many from then through August, with a maximum of 60 on Aug. 12. Ussher (1965: 24) gave Aug. 22 as his 11-year average return date at Rondeau, with the earliest on Aug. 17. Snyder (1931: 210-211) collected a singing male on Long Point on June 29, 1927 and a female there on July 7; two singing males were observed on July 8, 1927: more recent records include a male and two females noted on June 22, 1972 and a male on June 27, 1975 (McCracken, Bradstreet & Holroyd, 1981: 63). Speirs (1938: 52) gave Aug. 23 as the fall peak date for Toronto. Snyder (1930: 199) collected males in King Twp. on June 5 and July 6, 1926. Speirs & Orenstein (1975: 20) found a population density of 9 birds per 100 acres in a pine plantation quadrat in Uxbridge Twp. in 1966. Quilliam (1973: 159) cited a few summer records for Kingston including one feeding a young cowbird on July 13, 1963 at the Otter Lake sanctuary. H.P. Bingham found a nest with 2 eggs at Barrie on June 9, 1923: the species is fairly common in the northern townships of Simcoe Co. (Devitt, 1967: 141). P.A. Taverner found a female feeding a young cowbird at Rockcliffe, Ottawa, in the summer of 1912 (Lloyd, 1924: 14). Mills (1981: 142-143) discovered two nests with "full clutches" on July 4, 1976 at Ahmic Lake, and a nest with one young there on July 18, 1974: adults were observed feeding fledged young there as late as Aug. 30, 1976. D.B. Ferguson saw a female feeding young in a nest at Providence Bay, Manitoulin, on June 26, 1976 and Ron Tasker saw recently fledged young in Burpee Twp. on July 10, 1972 (Nicholson, 1981: 166). C.H.D. Clarke observed an adult feeding young at Brule Lake, Algonquin Park, on July 9, 1934 (MacLulich, 1938: 33). Louise Lawrence watched adults feeding young at Pimisi Bay on July 26, 1945 (Speirs & Speirs, 1947: 35). Paul Harrington found a nest 40ft. up in a jack pine at Biscotasing on June 10, 1941 and collected the 4 eggs on June 13: breeding was also noted at Chapleau and Bigwood (Baillie & Hope, 1947: 24). T.M. Shortt found a nest 35 ft. up in a balsam fir near Sault Ste. Marie on June 15, 1931: it held 2 cowbird eggs (Snyder, 1942: 144). Skeel & Bondrup-Nielsen (1978: 205) found them most numerous on their mature evergreen transect in Pukaskwa in the summer of 1977. Baillie & Hope (1943: 21) found them "quite rare" along the northeast shore of Lake Superior, collecting one at Rossport on June 5 and one at Amyot on June 27, 1936. Snyder (1928: 273) saw a family of young at Macdiarmid, Lake Nipigon, in the summer of 1923 and collected 2 young there in 1924 (on July 24 and Aug. 9). Dear (1940: 138) found a nest with 4 eggs near Thunder Bay on June 17, 1934. Kendeigh (1947: 28) found 6 pairs on 100 acres at Black Sturgeon Lake in 1945 while Speirs (1949: 148) found 21 territories on 75 acres at nearby Eaglehead Lake in 1946. Snyder (1938: 204) saw young of the year at Off Lake and Rainy River in 1929. Snyder (1953: 78) noted adults feeding young at Savanne on July 8, 1937 and at Kenora in August, 1943: he ranked this as the fifth most numerous warbler in western Ontario. Snyder (1928: 31) considered them to be "rather rare" at Lake Abitibi in 1925, collecting a male on June 2 and a female on June 29. James (1980: 89) saw only one near Pickle Lake in the summer of 1979 and none in 1977. Hope (1938: 39) saw individuals on three occasions at Favourable Lake in 1938: a male was collected on July 8 and a young of the year on July 21. Robert H. Smith reported seeing one at Moose Factory on June 7, 1943 (Todd, 1963: 609). Manning (1952: 83) reported an old specimen record from Severn House.

AUTUMN: Peruniak (1971: 26) noted one as late as Sept. 29 at Atikokan. Nicholson (1981: 166) reported 24 killed at the Great Duck Is. tower from Sept. 18-23, 1977: he gave the latest Manitoulin date as Sept. 25, 1978. J.H. Fleming shot one east of Sand Lake, Parry Sound, as late as Nov. 2, 1889 (Mills, 1981: 142). Devitt (1967: 141) gave

Oct. 9, 1939 as the latest Collingwood date and reported 105 killed at the Barrie TV tower in 5 of 7 years (64 of them on Sept. 12, 1961). Weir & Quilliam (1980: 39) listed Sept. 29 as the 19-year average departure date from Kingston with the latest on Nov. 2. Long (1968b: 22) saw one at Pickering Beach on Oct. 13, 1967. Saunders (1947: 372) listed Sept. 7 as his average departure date from Toronto, with his latest on Oct. 21. Sheppard (1939: 341) had one in his Niagara Falls garden on Nov. 5, 6 and 11, 1938, apparently feeding on the numerous aphids on his willow trees. Ussher (1965: 24) gave Sept. 21 as his 8-year average departure date from Rondeau, with his latest on Nov. 11. Stirrett (1973d: 26) had his latest two at Pelee on Sept. 27: S. and J. Hughes had a very late one there on Nov. 15, 1981 (Goodwin, 1982: 174).

**MEASUREMENTS:**
*Length:* 4.5 to 5.5 ins. (Godfrey, 1966: 334)
*Wingspread:* 7.60 to 8.55 ins. (Roberts, 1955: 673)
*Weight:* 29 Ontario specimens averaged 9.8 g.

**REFERENCE:**
Sheppard, R.W. 1939 A very late Blackburnian Warbler. Auk., 56:(3):341.

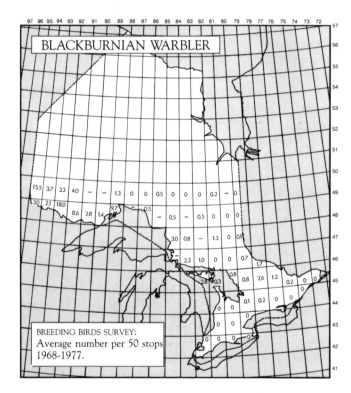

BLACKBURNIAN WARBLER

BREEDING BIRDS SURVEY:
Average number per 50 stops
1968-1977.

# YELLOW-THROATED WARBLER
*Dendroica dominica*   (Linnaeus)

This sweet singer of the United States bottomlands seldom gets as far north as Ontario. They winter from the southern United States to Central America and the West Indies.

IDENTIFICATION: This is a gray-backed warbler with two white wing bars: the throat and upper breast is yellow, the belly white with black stripes along the sides. The ear patches are black, broadly outlined with white behind and, as an eye stripe, above. The song is a rich series of descending whistles, somewhat like the song of the Louisiana Waterthrush. The species behaves something like a Black-and-white Warbler, creeping about along branches in search of its insect prey.

WINTER: One that turned up near Ottawa in late November finally disappeared on Dec. 6, 1977 according to S. Gawn (Goodwin, 1978: 345).

SPRING: Stirrett (1973b: 24) and Kelley (1978: 73) reported Pelee records on Apr. 25, 1962; May 2, 1962 (Botham): May 6, 1965 (2); May 13, 1965; May 19, 1946 (Zimmerman *et al*) and May 20, 1969 (Baillie): there have been a few more recent records there between the above dates. James W. Wilson reported one at Rondeau on Apr. 26, 1970 (Kelley, 1978: 73): P.A. Woodliffe *et al* observed one at Rondeau from Apr. 25 to May 16, 1981 (Goodwin, 1981: 820). Strauch (1974: 368) reported that one was banded and released at Long Point on May 2, 1970: he collected another there on May 25, 1970 (No. 216627 in Univ. Mich. Mus. Zool.): another was noted there on May 10, 1979 by P. Verburg *et al* (Goodwin, 1979: 767): and another on May 5-6, 1981 by C. Lemieux *et al* (Goodwin, 1981: 936). Sheppard (1944: 469) watched one in a garden at Stamford, near Niagara Falls, on May 20, 1943. Bartlett Wright and Albert J. Wright observed one at Rockhouse Point, Lake Erie, on May 18, 1958 (Beardslee & Mitchell, 1965: 381). One was photographed by R. Findlayson at Hamilton on May 2, 1974 (Goodwin, 1974: 797). A highlight of the TOC Spring Roundup on May 21, 1982 was the observation of one of these warblers at Unionville by Phyllis MacKay. Ken Edwards found the first Kingston bird at Squaw Point on Apr. 19, 1958: John Nicholson reported a second one at Cataraqui cemetery on May 9, 1968 (Quilliam, 1973: 160): a third was netted and banded on May 14, 1978 at Prince Edward Point and last seen there by Ken Edwards *et al* on May 16 (Weir & Quilliam, 1980: 23). T. Hince reported one at Ottawa on Apr. 29, 1974 (Goodwin, 1974: 899). Nicholson (1981: 167) found one at Great Duck Is. on May 22, 1977.

SUMMER:

AUTUMN: J. Wright *et al* found one at Ottawa on Nov. 19, 1977, which remained into December (see above) (Goodwin, 1978: 199). H.A.C. Jackson, with Mr. & Mrs. L.M. Terrill observed one on Nov. 4, 1957 in shrubbery at Manotick, about 15 miles south of Ottawa (Terrill, 1958: 171). One was noted at Port Britain on Oct. 30-31, 1972 by A.K. Sculthorpe, *fide* R. John and E.R. McDonald (Goodwin, 1973: 55). J.P. Prevett gave a good description of one noted at London from Oct. 7-10, 1971 (Goodwin, 1972: 59). Stirrett (1973d: 26) reported one at Pelee on Sept. 24, 1965.

**MEASUREMENTS:**
*Length:* 4 3/4 to 5 3/4 ins.
(Godfrey, 1966: 335)

Wingspread:
*Weight:* 6 averaged 9.4 g.
(8.8 - 10.0 g.) (Dunning,
1984: 21).

**REFERENCES:**
Sheppard, R.W. 1944
Sycamore Warbler in
Ontario. Auk.,
61: (3): 469.
    Strauch, Joseph G., Jr.
1974 First Ontario
specimen of the Yellow-
throated Warbler. Can.
Field-Nat., 88:(3): 368.
    Terrill, L.M. 1958 A
Yellow-throated Warbler at
Manotick, Ontario. Can.
Field-Nat., 72:(4):171.

# PINE WARBLER   *Dendroica pinus*   (Wilson)

The Pine Warbler is very aptly named, as it is usually to be found in the tallest pines available. They winter in the southern United States.

IDENTIFICATION:  This is another warbler with prominent white wing bars, much resembling fall Bay-breasted and Blackpoll Warblers but with yellow throat (and breast in males) and more white in the tail: it lacks the Blackpoll's streaks on the back. The song is diagnostic, like a very "juicy" Chipping Sparrow trill.

WINTER:  One was reported on the Blenheim Christmas count in 1972 (on Dec. 26, 1972 at Rondeau, according to Kelley (1978: 74). H. & S. Inch saw one at London on Dec. 16, 1980 (Goodwin, 1981: 297). One was reported at Chippewa as late as Jan. 1, 1974 by F.M. Rew (Goodwin, 1974: 635). J. Keenleyside saw one at Lorne Park on Dec. 1, 1963 and Harry Kerr found one in High Park, Toronto, on Jan 3, 1983 (Toronto Ornithological Club records). Catherine Cowman had one at her Frenchman Bay feeder from Nov. 28 to Dec. 1, 1974 (when I saw it there). Doug. Sadler *et al* found one at Peterborough on Dec. 15, 1981 (Weir, 1982: 291). J. Moore *et al* saw one at Angus on Dec. 10, 1972 (Goodwin, 1973: 610). R.A. Foxall and R. Poulin noted one at Ottawa on Dec. 4, 1971 (Goodwin, 1972: 600).

SPRING:  Stirrett (1973b: 24) had Pelee records from Apr. 23 to May 28, with a maximum of 8 on May 17. Ussher (1965: 25) gave Apr. 28 as his 12-year average arrival date at Rondeau, with the earliest on Apr. 6. Saunders & Dale (1933: 229) gave Apr. 29 as the 14-year average arrival date at London, with the earliest on Apr. 15, 1922: a female was observed gathering nest material on May 10, 1929 and carrying it to the top of a tall white pine about 6 miles west of London. Brooman (1954: 33) saw one 4 miles south of St. Thomas on Apr. 13, 1941. Beardslee & Mitchell (1965: 384) reported one seen at Thorold on Apr. 14, 1954 and another at Rockhouse Point, Lake Erie, on Apr. 17, 1949. Saunders (1947: 372) listed Apr. 28 as his 12-year average arrival date for

Toronto, with the earliest on March 30. Speirs (1974) cited two Whitby records for Apr. 22, 1967. Dennis Barry found one in Darlington Twp. on Apr. 19, 1968: a pair was observed using tent caterpillar web to build a nest in the Osler Tract in Cartwright Twp. on May 26, 1972, about 30ft. up in a red pine (Tozer & Richards, 1974: 250-251). Weir & Quilliam (1980: 39) listed Apr. 29 as the 27-year average arrival date at Kingston, with the earliest on Apr. 14. Devitt (1967: 143, 144) gave May 1 as the 20-year average arrival date at Barrie, with one seen at Angus as early as Apr. 10, 1945 by R.D. Ussher. E.G. White collected one at Ottawa on May 8, 1884 (Lloyd, 1924: 14). Chris Harris noted four at Go Home Bay on Apr. 17, 1976 (Mills, 1981: 145). Nicholson (1981: 168) had Manitoulin records from Apr. 24 (1979) to May 27 (1977). MacLulich (1938: 34) gave Apr. 23, 1913 as his earliest Algonquin Park record. Louise Lawrence heard one singing at Pimisi Bay on May 10, 1945 (Speirs & Speirs, 1947: 35).

SUMMER: On the 1968-1977 Breeding Bird Surveys they were uncommon to rare from Port Dover north to Swastika and Kenora, fairly common at Barry's Bay and Gogama. Stirrett (1973c: 20) had one summer record at Pelee, on June 20. Ussher (1965: 25) gave Aug. 28 as his latest fall date, at Rondeau. Brooman (1954: 33) heard them singing at Springwater Pond, Elgin Co., on June 6, 1949, as did John Frank and I on June 16, 1970, so they may breed in some of the tall pines there. Snyder (1931: 212) collected three young on Long Point from July 4-23, 1927. We were surprised to find two territorial males on our 25-acre quadrat in the Backus Woods in 1977 (Nol et al, 1978: 65). Speirs & Orenstein (1975: 20) found a breeding density of 5 birds per 100 acres in a pine plantation in Uxbridge Twp.: on July 1, 1969 I saw two adults feeding a young cowbird there (Speirs, 1974). Snyder (1941: 80) collected two females at Cherry Valley, Prince Edward Co., on July 2, 1930, both with brood patches. Quilliam (1973:162) cited several summer localities where Pine Warblers have summered in the Kingston region. Paul Harrington found a nest with 3 eggs at Wasaga Beach on June 16, 1922 and a nest with one young cowbird there on June 9, 1921 (Devitt, 1967: 143). F.A. Saunders reported breeding at the Experimental Farm, Ottawa, in June, 1898 (Lloyd, 1924: 14). Chris Harris found a nest with young about 50 ft. up in a white pine at Go Home Bay on June 26, 1972 (Mills, 1981: 145). Nicholson (1981: 169) had only one summer record for Manitoulin, at Carroll Wood Bay by Ross Lowe on June 18, 1974. Ricker & Clarke (1939: 30) saw adults carrying food to young at Frank's Bay, Lake Nipissing, and considered them "fairly common" along the French River. Baillie & Hope (1947: 25) collected two males at Bigwood on July 23 and 24, 1937. Tom Baxter had a breeding record for Lake Superior Provincial Park (Skeel & Bondrup-Nielsen, 1978: 206). Denis (1961: 7) listed the Pine Warbler as an "occasional, rare, visitant" at Thunder Bay. Snyder (1938: 205) collected two young at Rainy River on July 31, 1929. Snyder (1953: 79) cited summer records at Malachi, Ingolf and Kenora from 1937 to 1949.

AUTUMN: D. McRae and A. Wormington collected a male at Netitishi Point, James Bay, on Oct. 16, 1981 "the first Moosonee area record". Skeel & Bondrup-Nielsen (1978: 206) gave Sept. 5 as their latest Pukaskwa record. Nicholson (1981: 169) had fall records from Aug. 29 (1977) to Oct. 2 (1976) on Manitoulin. C. MacFayden saw one at Glen Orchard, Muskoka, on Sept. 29, 1979 (Mills, 1981: 145). Mrs. O'Brien-Saint saw one in her Barrie garden on Nov. 15, 1959: this was found dead on Nov. 22 and sent to the ROM. Weir & Quilliam (1980: 39) listed Sept. 26 as the 10-year average departure date from Kingston, the latest on Oct. 28. George A. Scott saw one at Oshawa on Oct. 17, 1954 (Speirs,

1974). Stirrett (1973d: 27) had 3 fall records of single birds at Pelee, on Aug. 31, Sept. 3 and one banded on Sept. 17.

**MEASUREMENTS:**

*Length:* 5. to 5 3/4 ins. (Godfrey, 1966: 338)
*Wingspread:* 8.4 to 9.6 ins. (Robserts, 1955: 667)
*Weight:* 15 Ontario specimens averaged 12.1 g.

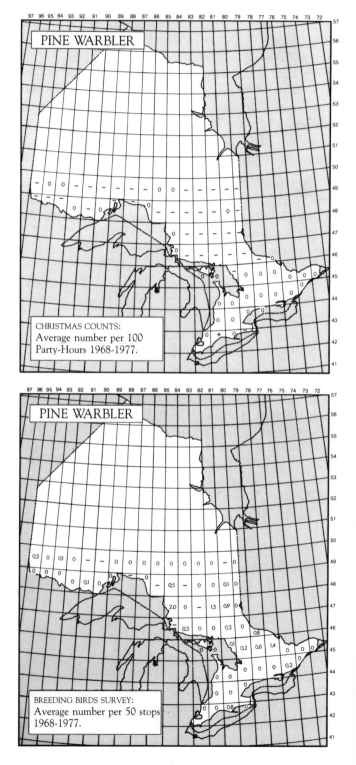

PINE WARBLER

CHRISTMAS COUNTS:
Average number per 100
Party-Hours 1968-1977.

PINE WARBLER

BREEDING BIRDS SURVEY:
Average number per 50 stops
1968-1977.

# KIRTLAND'S WARBLER   *Dendroica kirtlandii*   (Baird)

Kirtland's Warbler is a bird of sand country with scattered pines and an understory of sweet fern, blueberry or other small shrubs, normally summering in Michigan and wintering in the Bahamas. It is a very rare migrant through southern Ontario and should be looked for (but not expected) in summer in a strip from the Bruce Peninsula and Georgian Bay east to Petawawa.

**IDENTIFICATION:** The song is rich and loud, much like the song of a Northern Waterthrush: if you hear such a song away from water in pine barrens, look up the singer! Like the Palm Warbler it habitually pumps its tail up and down. It is bluish gray above with black streaks on the back, and yellow below with black streaks on the sides, and white undertail coverts.

**WINTER:**

**SPRING:** At least four have been reported at Pelee in spring migration: Baillie (1953: 271) reported a male there on May 10, 1953, seen by Frank Cook and Don Sutton: Kelley (1978: 74) added V. Miles and J. Parker as observers of this bird: Woodford (1959: 234) saw one with D. Dow, J. Lunn *et al* there on May 10, 1959; this bird was mist-netted and banded by W. Wasserfall: Stirrett (1973b: 24) reported another there on May 13, 1961: and most recently Goodwin (1979: 767) reported a dingy male there from May 14-19, 1979. The first Ontario specimen was taken at Toronto on May 16, 1900 by J. Hughes Samuel (Samuel, 1900: 391-392). Other Toronto records include one reported by C. Long on May 30, 1947; one found by G. Fairfield on May 16-18, 1958; another by J. Harrison and A. Sangster on May 24, 1959. Naomi LeVay noted birds at Eastbourne, Whitby, on May 19, 1962 and June 1, 1963 (Tozer & Richards, 1974: 251). Devitt (1967: 144) reported one found by Frances Westman near Midhurst on May 16, 1964 and seen by Devitt *et al* until May 21, 1964 and another found by H.B. Haugh at Little Lake, near Barrie on May 19, 1967. Paul Harrington reported them at Petawawa from May 24, 1916 into the summer.

**SUMMER:** A migrant turned up at Long Point on Aug. 31, 1941 according to H.A. Sivyer. Donald Campbell, John B. Miles and George W. North observed one singing in jack pines at Hamilton on June 17, 1960 (Speirs, 1960: 21): a tornado in Michigan the previous day may have been responsible for this displaced bird. Doris H. Speirs observed an agitated pair and at least one immature near Barrie from Aug. 9-15, 1945 and a single bird on Aug. 31. George A. Moore and C.R. Skelton observed one at McVicar, Bruce Peninsula, from June 8-30, 1958 (Gunn, 1958b: 410). Richard Savage found one dead near Pointe au Baril on June 17, 1961 (Woodford & Lunn, 1961: 467); a third Ontario specimen. Paul Harrington considered them "not uncommon" at Petawawa up to July 12, 1916: on June 5, 1939 he found a singing male there again and Paul Aird found a male singing there again in June, 1977 (Goodwin, 1978: 345).

**AUTUMN:** M. & T. Hendrick reported one at Morton, Leeds Co., on Sept. 9, 1981 (Goodwin, 1982: 174). Doris H. Speirs observed one at our home in Pickering Twp. on Sept. 14, 1948 (Speirs, 1974). The second Ontario specimen was taken by W.E. Saunders at Pelee on Oct. 2, 1915 and another was reported there on Sept. 22, 1962 (Stirrett, 1973d: 27).

**MEASUREMENTS:**
*Length:* 5.3 to 6.0 ins.
(Roberts, 1955: 673)
Wingspread:
*Weight:* 15.6 g.
(Woodford, 1960: 5).

**REFERENCES:**
Harrington, Paul 1929
Kirtland's Warbler in
Ontario. Jack-Pine
Warbler, 17: ( ): 195-197.
   Woodford, J. 1959
Migrant Kirtland's Warbler
mist- netted. Bird-Banding,
30: (4): 234.
   Woodford, James 1960
The Kirtland's Warbler in
Ontario. OBBA Contrs,
1:(1): 3-6.
   Mayfield, Harold 1960
The Kirtland's Warbler.
Cranbrook Inst. Sci., Bull.
40: i-xv; 1-242.
   Speirs, Doris Huestis
1984 The first breeding
record of Kirtland's
Warbler in Ontario. Ont.
Birds, 2: (2): 80-84.

# PRAIRIE WARBLER   *Dendroica discolor*   (Vieillot)

The Prairie Warbler is generally considered a rare bird in Ontario. It breeds in isolated pockets, usually associated with scattered junipers or with small pines in sand country. It winters in the West Indies.

IDENTIFICATION: This is a small, green-backed, yellow-breasted warbler, with diagnostic red flecks on the back and black streaks on the sides. The eyes are surrounded by rather large yellow eye rings, outlined with black and with a horizontal black line through the eyes. Females and young have a similar pattern but with less vivid colours. The song is a staccato series of notes, usually rising in pitch and in volume.

WINTER:

SPRING:  Stirrett (1973b: 24) had a few Pelee records from May 1 to May 17, with a maximum of 4 on May 9. R. Erickson and M.J. Wolcott saw one at Bradley's Marsh on May 22, 1971 (Goodwin, 1971: 738). Ussher (1965: 25) had Rondeau records from May 14 to May 20. Saunders & Dale (1933: 229-230) had a single bird near London on May 30, 1917 and reported one found by C.H. Zavitz at Coldstream on May 20, 1919 and collected by A.A. Wood on May 21. Snyder (1931: 212) reported one seen at Port Dover on May 7, 1914 by A. Preston and another back of Turkey Point on May 31, 1930 by W.E. Saunders. Fred Barratt made a field sketch of one of four singing males near the

St. Williams Forestry Station, as I watched on May 19, 1938. Beardslee & Mitchell (1965: 385) reported one seen by the Axtells and B. Nathan at Morgan's Point, Lake Erie, on May 2, 1954. I saw one in High Park, Toronto, on May 6, 1937, with J.L. Baillie *et al*. Speirs (1938: 39, 45) reported a Toronto record as early as Apr. 17 and one as late as May 26. Speirs (1974) had five spring records for Ontario Co. from May 10 (1962) to May 26 (1961). Goodwin (1972: 757) mentioned one at Prince Edward Point on Apr. 30, 1972. Weir & Quilliam (1980: 39) listed May 12 as the 21-year average arrival date for Kingston. Alden Strong found a nest under construction near Devil Lake (about 20 miles north of Kingston) on May 10, 1959: this held 2 warbler eggs and a cowbird egg on May 17: Eric Mills noted 7 by nearby Canoe Lake on May 17, 1964 (Quilliam, 1973: 162). Devitt (1967: 145) gave May 23 as the 15-year average arrival date at Wasaga Beach, with the earliest on May 14, 1933. D.N. Bucknell saw one at Thornbury on May 14, 1972 (Goodwin, 1972: 757). L. Sirois found one at Ottawa on May 13, 1978 (Goodwin, 1978: 1000). Mills (1981: 147) gave May 18, 1974 as the earliest Muskoka sighting, by C. Harris at Go Home Bay. Nicholson (1981: 169) reported Manitoulin birds on May 22, 1974 (3 ♂ ), May 24, 1976 (1 ♂ ) May 20-21, 1979. Hazel Petty reported one at North Bay on May 16, 1972 (Goodwin, 1976: 757).

SUMMER: Only one was reported on the 1968-1977 Breeding Bird Surveys, at Thessalon in 1970. Stirrett (1973c: 21) had records of individuals at Pelee on Aug. 12 and Aug. 15. Kelley (1978: 74) mentioned three breeding records along the Lake Huron shore of Lambton Co. in early July, 1954: C.G. Harris reported at least 11 singing males at The Pinery during the summer of 1978: others were noted there in 1979 and 1980 and a nest was found there in 1981, deserted after a cowbird laid in it (Goodwin, 1978: 1156; Goodwin, 1981: 936). Eli Davis heard one singing about 1/2 mile west of Mount Brydges on July 13, 1930 and one was heard near Springbank Hill from June 19 to July 1, 1931 (Saunders & Dale, 1933: 230). Four males were singing at the St. Williams colony on June 12, 1971 (Goodwin, 1971: 854). Saunders (1947: 372) had a Toronto record on Aug. 22. Speirs (1974) reported three August sightings in Ontario Co.: one at Whitby on Aug. 9, 1959; one at Oshawa on Aug. 21, 1949 and one at Cedar Point, Mara Twp. on Aug. 30, 1973. B.C. Olson reported two at Port Hope on Aug. 26, 1981 (Goodwin, 1982: 174). R.D. McRae and R.C. Tait found two new colonies in Prince Edward Co. on July 11-12, 1979 (Goodwin, 1979: 860). Herbert Blades heard two at Canoe Lake, north of Kingston, on June 25, 1961 (Quilliam, 1973: 162) and R. Rockwell found 22 there on June 10, 1973 (Goodwin, 1973: 866). M. Elsdon and G. White noted two at Apsley on June 19, 1976 (Goodwin, 1976: 951) and the first Peterborough region nest was found there on June 24, 1978 (Goodwin, 1979: 278). A new colony was located at Lake Mazinaw by M.J.B. Evans during the summer of 1971 (Goodwin, 1971: 864). Paul Harrington found three nests at Wasaga Beach: June 19, 1922 (2 young and 1 young cowbird); June 14, 1923 (3 eggs and 2 cowbird eggs) and June 9, 1927 (4 eggs): at nearby Allenwood Beach, O.E. Devitt found a nest with 4 young on June 24, 1934 and at Bluewater Beach he discovered a nest with 4 young on June 27, 1948 (Devitt, 1967: 144-145). B. MacTavish found one at Ottawa on Aug. 15, 1972 (Goodwin, 1973: 55); B. DiLabio had one there on Aug. 31, 1973 (Goodwin, 1974: 47) and R.A. Foxall reported another there on July 30, 1977 (Goodwin, 1977: 1135). Lord (1955: 24) found 8 nesting pairs in a half-mile radius near Go Home Bay in the summer of 1951. J. Francis and F. Phelan reported nestings in Georgian Bay National Park during the summer of 1980 (Goodwin, 1981: 936). Mills (1981: 146) cited several other breeding records for the

Georgian Bay shoreline. Ron Tasker noted two singing males in Burpee Twp., Manitoulin, from June 29 to July 16, 1970 (Nicholson, 1981: 169). C.H.D. Clarke saw one at Frank's Bay, Lake Nipissing, on June 24, 1933 (Ricker & Clarke, 1939: 20). Hazel Petty reported one at Wasi Falls, near Callander, on Aug. 19, 1970 (Mills, 1981: 147).

AUTUMN: Nicholson (1981: 169) recorded a very late female at Mississagi light, Manitoulin, on Oct. 12, 1975. Mills (1981: 147) cited records by J. Baillie at Gravenhurst on Sept. 29, 1956 and at Go Home Bay by C. Harris on Oct. 3, 1953. K.F. and R.K. Edwards saw a male at Squaw Point, Kingston, on Sept. 27, 1970 (Quilliam, 1973: 162). Naomi LeVay had records for Cranberry Marsh on Sept. 1, 1966 and Sept. 3, 1967 and R.C. Long noted one at Cannington on Sept. 17, 1973 (Speirs, 1974). R. Finlayson and D. Howes-Jones noted one at Hamilton from Sept. 18-24, 1971 (Goodwin, 1972: 59). Stirrett (1973d: 27) reported single birds at Pelee on Sept. 5-6, 1905, Sept. 20, 1906 and Sept. 20, 1907.

**MEASUREMENTS:**
*Length:* 4.3 to 5.2 ins.
(Godfrey, 1966: 339)
Wingspread:
*Weight:* 23 ♂ averaged
7.37 g. 41 ♀ averaged
7.74 g. (breeding adults)
(149 ad. ♂ av. 8.01 g.
imm. ♂ 25 av. 8.22
g: 110 ad ♀ av. 7.31 g. 73
imm. ♀ av. 7.62 g. Florida
tower kills: (Nolan,
1978: 446).

**REFERENCES:**
Lord, Dave 1955
Occurrence of the Prairie
Warbler at Georgian Bay,
Ontario. Ont. Field
Biologist, No. 9:23-24.
   Nolan, Val, Jr. 1978 The
ecology and behavior of
the Prairie Warbler,
*Dendroica discolor.*
A.O.U. Ornithological
Monographs, No. 26: i-
xvii, 1-595.

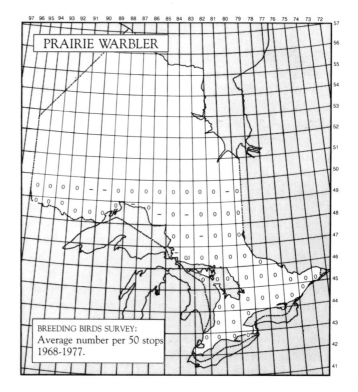

PRAIRIE WARBLER

BREEDING BIRDS SURVEY:
Average number per 50 stops
1968-1977.

# PALM WARBLER   *Dendroica palmarum*   (Gmelin)

The Palm Warbler sometimes migrates through Ontario with mixed flocks of other warblers but I have frequently encountered it alone along roadside hedgerows. They usually breed in bogs in the northern part of Ontario. They winter in the southern United States, Central America and the West Indies.

IDENTIFICATION: This is the most common of the tail-pumping warblers (Kirtland's and Prairie Warblers are the others). It has a reddish cap like a Chipping Sparrow but the tail pumping action and yellow undertail coverts will readily distinguish it: some have quite yellow underparts with fine streaks on the sides. The song is a dry trill, much like a Chipping Sparrow's song: Snyder (1953: 79) describes it as "weet-weet-weet-weet-weet" with a machine-like rhythm and a rattle-like quality."

WINTER: Only one was reported on the 1968-1977 Christmas counts, at Toronto, on Dec. 23, 1973. Kelley (1978: 74) gave three winter records for Pelee: Dec. 5, 1965; Dec. 31, 1966 and Jan. 3, 1966.

SPRING: Stirrett (1973b: 24) had Pelee records from one on Apr. 12 to 65 noted on May 26, with a maximum of 100 on May 11. Ussher (1965: 25) had Rondeau reports from Apr. 26 to May 24 with average arrival on May 2 and departure on May 20. Saunders & Dale (1933: 230) gave Apr. 30 as the 17-year average arrival date for London, with the earliest on Apr. 21, 1919. Snyder (1931: 212) had Long Point records from May 6 to May 30 in 1928, with peak numbers on May 9. Beardslee & Mitchell (1965: 385-386) reported one at Port Colborne on Apr. 12, 1953. Speirs (1938: 43, 45) gave May 5 as the spring peak at Toronto with the latest on May 27. J.L. Baillie (in Saunders, 1947: 372) listed May 5 and May 15 as average arrival and departure dates for Toronto, with the earliest on Apr. 28. George A. Scott saw one at Oshawa's Second Marsh on Apr. 23, 1960 and J. Satterly had one at Cedar Point, Mara Twp. on May 22 (Speirs, 1974). Charles Fothergill shot one in Darlington Twp. on May 6, 1824 (Black, 1934: 155). Weir & Quilliam (1980: 39) listed May 1 and May 17 as average arrival and departure dates for Kingston, with the earliest on Apr. 19 and latest on May 25. Devitt (1967: 145-146) gave May 9 as the 18-year average arrival date at Barrie, with the earliest on Apr. 27, 1938 and latest on May 26. L. Beamer's median arrival date at Meaford was May 6, with the earliest on Apr. 30, 1949. Lloyd (1924: 14) listed an Ottawa specimen taken on May 5, 1892 and a nest with 4 eggs collected at Mer Bleue by C.H. Young on May 25, 1908. The 7-year average arrival date at Huntsville was May 9, with the earliest on May 3, 1962 (Mills, 1981: 147). Nicholson (1981: 169) had Manitoulin records from Apr. 26 (1979) to May 28 (1979) with the 12-year average arrival on May 4 and a high count of 150 on May 16, 1970. Ricker & Clarke (1939: 20) gave May 6, 1934 as their earliest arrival date for Lake Nipissing. Skeel & Bondrup-Nielsen (1978: 207) had few spring records at Pukaskwa, from May 10 to May 15. Denis (1961: 3) gave May 12 as the average arrival date for Thunder Bay, with his earliest on May 2, 1954. Perunaik (1971: 26) had her earliest at Atikokan on May 8. Elder (1979: 38) gave May 8 as his earliest Geraldton record. Cringan (1953a: 3) saw his first in 1953 at Perrault Falls on May 13. Oliver Hewitt saw one at Moosonee on May 22, 1947 (Manning, 1952: 83).

SUMMER: On the 1968-1977 Breeding Bird Surveys they were uncommon on the

Gogama, Smooth Rock Falls, Manitouwadge and Longlac routes, fairly common on the Silver Islet route, none elsewhere. Long (1968b: 22) saw one at Pickering Beach as early as Aug. 3, 1966. E.L. Brereton noted fall transients at Wasaga Beach as early as Aug. 18, 1941 (Devitt, 1967: 145). Lloyd (1924: 14) mentioned a nest with 4 eggs taken by C.H. Young at Mer Bleue, Ottawa, on July 6, 1908: others have been collected there in summer, including young. Mills (1981: 147) reported summer records in the cottage country at Port Sydney, Go Home Bay and Ahmic Lake. J.L. Baillie collected a young female in a bog at Big Fork, Rainy River, on July 21, 1929 (Snyder, 1938: 205). Peruniak (1971: 26) wrote: "Found in bogs in summer" near Atikokan. Snyder (1953: 79) found them in stands of jack pine as well as in black spruce bogs in western Ontario, where breeding was established for Wabigoon, Savanne and Malachi, and birds observed in summer at Ingolf, Kenora and Sioux Lookout. We found 15 territories on our 25 acre quadrat in a bog at Geraldton in 1971 (Elder, Price & Speirs, 1971: 1006). Smith (1957: 178) saw an adult with two well-grown young in a bog near Cochrane on July 10, 1953. Ross James saw a maximum of 5 on June 9, 1977 at Pickle Lake. Hope (1938: 40) took a young bird "just recently out of the nest" at Favourable Lake on July 28, 1938. Cringan (1953b: 4) saw one at Kasabonika Lake on June 3, 1953. Cringan (1950: 17) found a nest with 4 eggs in spruce-tamarack muskeg near Nikip Lake on June 25, 1950. Manning (1952: 83) collected a pair at Moosonee on July 1, 1949 and a female at the mouth of the Attawapiskat River on July 5, 1947. James, Nash & Peck (1981: 92) listed the Palm Warbler as a breeding species at Kiruna Lake, Sutton Ridges. Schueler, Baldwin & Rising (1974: 147) collected a male on July 17, 1965, at the junction of Warcheska and Sutton Rivers. Lee (1978: 32) found an agitated pair carrying food in the spruce-tamarack bog plot at Big Trout Lake in 1975. C.E. Hope saw 3 and collected one at Fort Severn on July 3, 1940.

AUTUMN: D. McRae and A. Wormington saw an "astonishingly late" one at Netitishi Point, James Bay, on Nov. 13, 1981. Oliver Hewitt saw one at Ship Sands, near Moosonee, on Sept. 24, 1947 (Manning, 1952: 83). Smith (1957: 178) saw a few in early September, 1953 in jack pine forest just south of Matheson. Peruniak (1971: 26) gave Oct. 11 as her latest Atikokan record. This was the second most numerous migrant warbler at Pukaskwa in fall: 35 were noted on 7 days from Sept. 6 to Oct. 1, 1977 (Skeel & Bondrup-Nielsen, 1978: 207). Speirs & Speirs (1947: 35) mentioned one seen by Louise Lawrence at Pimisi Bay as late as Oct. 5, 1944: they saw 15 at North Bay on Sept. 26, 1944. C.H.D. Clarke saw one at Cache Lake, Algonquin Park, on Sept. 12, 1934 (MacLulich, 1938: 34). Nicholson (1981: 169) had fall records on Manitoulin from Aug. 23 (1975) to Oct. 29 (1968) with a 10-year average arrival on Sept. 9 and a high count of 100 on Oct. 8-9, 1967. Katherine Ketchum's 11 fall dates for Pointe au Baril ranged from Aug. 29, 1972 to Oct. 10, 1970 (Mills, 1981: 147). Eight were killed at the Barrie TV tower in 4 of 7 years, the latest on Oct. 13, 1966 (Devitt, 1967: 146). Weir & Quilliam (1980: 39) listed Sept. 10 and Oct. 9 as average arrival and departure dates for Kingston, the earliest on Aug. 20 and latest on Nov. 7. J. Satterly had single birds at Cedar Point, Mara Twp., on Aug. 28, 1955 and Aug. 29, 1959 and Grace Cole had Pickering Twp. birds as late as Nov. 21, 1964 (Speirs, 1974). J.L. Baillie (in Saunders, 1947: 372) listed Sept. 16 and Oct. 11 as average arrival and departure dates for Toronto, with the earliest on Sept. 5 and latest on Oct. 24. Speirs (1938: 51) gave Sept. 29 as the fall peak date for Toronto. Beardslee & Mitchell (1965: 385-386) reported one on the Canadian shore of Lake Erie as early as Aug. 24, 1942. Ussher (1965: 25) had Rondeau dates from Sept.

2 to Nov. 5, with average arrival on Sept. 13 and departure on Oct. 11. Stirrett (1973d: 27) had Pelee records from Aug. 23 to Nov. 7 with a maximum of 175 on Oct. 30.

**MEASUREMENTS:**

*Length:* 5 to 5 3/4 ins. (Godfrey, 1966: 339)
*Wingspread:* 7.5 to 8.4 ins. (Roberts, 1955: 672)
*Weight:* 3 ♂ averaged 10.2 g. 3 ♀ averaged 9.1 g. (Hope, 1938: 40) Speirs (1974) reported specimens weighing 9.5 and 12 g.

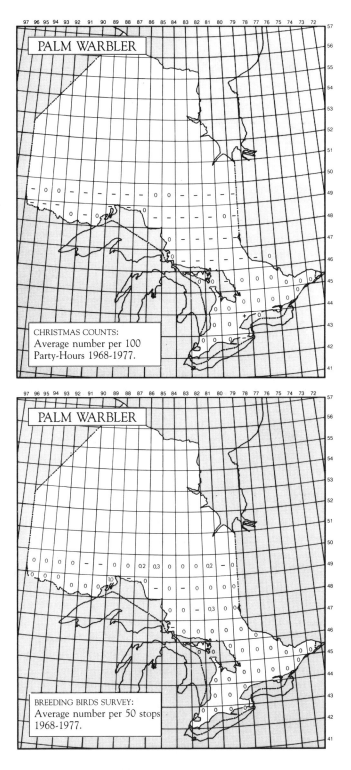

PALM WARBLER

CHRISTMAS COUNTS:
Average number per 100
Party-Hours 1968-1977.

PALM WARBLER

BREEDING BIRDS SURVEY:
Average number per 50 stops
1968-1977.

# BAY-BREASTED WARBLER   *Dendroica castanea*   (Wilson)

This handsome big warbler is usually one of the last to show up in Ontario in migration (the Blackpoll is often later). In summer they are found in mature stands of spruce and balsam firs where, especially at times of spruce budworm outbreaks, they may be the most abundant bird. However, because of their weak song, they are often hard to hear above highway noise so that roadside counts are usually low. They winter around the junction of Central America with South America.

IDENTIFICATION: Spring males with chestnut crown, throat and sides, contrasting with creamy cheeks and black mask, are easily identified: spring females are similar but with much paler colours. Fall birds usually show a hint of brown on the sides but are mainly green above and pale gray or buff below, with prominent white wing bars. Fall Chestnut-sided Warbers are brighter green above, and white below, have yellowish-wing bars and prominent eye rings. Fall Blackpoll Warblers are greenish above and below, with dark streaks on both back and breast and have pale legs and white undertail coverts (buff in Bay-breasted Warblers). In summer they work the dim interior of the big forest evergreens, singing their fast, high-pitched, rather weak "see-see, see-see, see" songs.

WINTER: John Jarvis reported one at Long Branch, near Toronto, from Nov. 29 to Dec. 2, 1964 (a Toronto Ornithological Club record).

SPRING: Stirrett (1973b: 24) had Pelee records from May 5 to May 31 with a maximum of 27 on May 23. Ussher (1965: 24) had birds at Rondeau from May 2 to May 31 with average arrival on May 13 and departure on May 23. Saunders & Dale (1933: 229) gave May 15 as the 17-year average arrival date at London, with the earliest on May 8, 1924. W.E. Saunders noted 9 at Long Point as late as June 1, 1924 (Snyder, 1931: 210). Saunders (1947: 372) listed Toronto records from May 7 to June 8, with average arrival on May 14 and departure on May 25. The peak of the spring migration at Pickering is about May 22: George A. Scott heard one singing at Oshawa as late as June 5, 1965 (Speirs, 1974). Dennis Barry noted one in Darlington Twp. on May 6, 1964 (Tozer & Richards, 1974: 250). Weir & Quilliam (1980: 39) had Kingston records from May 3 to June 12, with average arrival on May 13 and departure on May 27. Devitt (1967: 142) gave May 17 as the 16-year average arrival date for Barrie, with the earliest on May 9, 1938 and latest on June 1, 1932. L. Beamer's earliest Meaford record was May 14, 1956 and his median arrival date there May 21. Katherine Ketchum had Pointe au Baril records from May 16 (1964) to May 23 (1955) (Mills, 1980: 144). Nicholson (1981: 167) gave May 17 as the 12-year average arrival date for Manitoulin, with the earliest on May 9, 1979 and latest May 31, 1979: 59 were killed at the Great Duck Is. tower on May 28, 1979. E.L. Brereton had Cache Lake, Algonquin Park, records from May 12-16, 1936 (MacLulich, 1938: 34). Louise Lawrence noted the species at Rutherglen on May 13, 1944 (Speirs & Speirs, 1947: 35). Skeel & Bondrup-Nielsen (1978: 206) saw their first at Pukaskwa on May 13 in 1977 "the latest of the summer resident warblers to arrive". Denis (1961: 4) gave May 21 as the average arrival date at Thunder Bay, with the earliest on May 10, 1942. Peruniak (1971: 26) gave May 16 as her earliest Atikokan date. Elder (1979: 38) had his earliest at Geraldton on May 22. Bondrup-Nielsen (1976: 45) saw his first near Kapuskasing on May 28 in 1974.

SUMMER: On the 1968-1977 Breeding Bird Surveys, they were uncommon to fairly common on most routes in the Precambrian country, south to Barry's Bay and Eganville, with none in the agricultural south. Stirrett (1973c: 20) had one straggler at Pelee on June 30 and several in August starting on Aug. 11. Ussher (1965: 24) had the earliest fall bird at Rondeau on Aug. 5 with the average arrival on Aug. 28. J.L. Baillie (in Saunders, 1947: 372) had a returning bird at Toronto as early as Aug. 5, with his average arrival on Aug. 25. I noted one at our Pickering Twp. home as early as July 27, 1957, with others in early August (Speirs, 1974). Weir & Quilliam (1980: 39) gave Aug. 15 as the average fall arrival date at Kingston, with one as early as July 19. Southbound transients were noted at Wasaga Beach as early as Aug. 17 and by Aug. 24 were common (Devitt, 1967: 142). Baillie & Harrington (1937: 249) noted adults carrying nest material at Dorcas Bay on June 5, 1934. Mills (1981:144) cited a few summer records for the cottage country: K. Ketchum's earliest fall date for Pointe au Baril was Aug. 3, 1973. Nicholson (1981: 168) also cited a few summer records from Manitoulin. Speirs & Speirs (1947: 35) reported a singing male at Rutherglen on June 21, 1944 and a male was noted at Eau Claire on July 1, 1935 by T.M. Shortt. Baillie & Hope (1947: 25) collected young at Biscotasing on July 6 and 9, 1937 and commented that an adult female collected there on July 6 was in the plumage of an adult male. Snyder (1942: 144) considered the species rare near Sault Ste. Marie, but observed a pair in black spruce near Maclennan on July 8 and one at Point aux Pins on July 13, 1931. Skeel & Bondrup-Nielsen (1978: 206) ranked the species tenth in abundance at Pukaskwa and noted a strong preference for mature habitat: a male was seen carrying food on July 1, 1977. Along the northeast shore of Lake Superior, Baillie & Hope (1943: 22) found them only at Amyot where they collected 5 males from June 26 to July 4, 1936 "in the more mature mixed forest" but where they saw no females or nests. Snyder (1928: 273) collected 3 males and 3 females at Lake Nipigon from June 5, 1923 to Aug. 8, 1924: he compared the song to the notes of the Golden-crowned Kinglet but with "five whispered notes instead of three". Kendeigh (1947: 28) found 92 pairs on 100 acres at Black Sturgeon Lake in 1945 while Speirs (1949: 148) had 36 territories on 75 acres at nearby Eaglehead Lake in 1946 (by far the most abundant bird in both areas during a spruce budworm outbreak). Snyder (1938: 205) recorded it only once at Rainy River, on Aug. 3, 1929, but found them "commonly in the wild parts to the north". Peruniak (1971: 26) saw a male and a female with young at Atikokan on July 20. Snyder (1953: 79) reported from 3 to 12 daily at Sioux Lookout in the summer of 1947. Smith (1957: 178) had records at Timmins, Lake Abitibi, Kapuskasing and Hearst. Snyder (1928: 31) found young not long out of the nest with parents at Lake Abitibi in 1925. R.D. Ussher saw several feeding young on small islands in Bank's Lake, near Kapuskasing, on July 12, 1925 (Baillie & Harrington, 1937: 249). James (1980: 84) found 5.6 pairs per km $^2$ on 4 of 12 transects at Pickle Lake and found a nest with 4 eggs about 9.5 km. NE of Pickle Lake on June 18, 1979. Hope (1938: 39) found the first Ontario nests at Favourable Lake in 1938: a nest with 5 eggs on June 15 and a nest with 5 young on June 21, both in white spruces, 10 to 15 ft. up. Cringan (1950: 17) saw only one, an adult male, at Nikip Lake on June 12, 1950. Manning (1952: 83) reported one collected by Drexler at Moose Factory on June 2, 1860. James, Nash & Peck (1982: 68) found two nests, each with 5 eggs, one on June 23, the other on June 28: also 4 nests with young, on July 5, 7, 8 and 9, 1982, at Harricanaw River, near James Bay "the highest concentration we have encountered anywhere": the fourth in abundance of the species in open coniferous woods. McLaren & MacLaren (1981: 4) found singing males common in the Wetiko Hills, on the Manitoba border at 55 ° N.

AUTUMN: Peruniak (1971: 26) had her latest at Atikokan on Sept. 15. Skeel & Bondrup-Nielsen (1978: 206) saw their last at Pukaskwa on Sept. 3 in 1977. Nicholson (1981: 168) gave Oct. 4, 1978 as his latest Manitoulin record and reported 325 casualties at the Great Duck Is. tower from Sept. 18-24, 1977. K. Ketchum had her latest at Go Home Bay on Oct. 6, 1962 (Mills, 1981: 144). Devitt (1967: 142) reported 347 casualties at the Barrie TV tower in 5 of 7 years (152 on Sept. 24, 1960 and the latest on Oct. 11, (1962): the latest record near Barrie was at Little Lake on Oct. 16, 1938. Weir & Quilliam (1980: 39) listed Sept. 30 as the average fall departure date from Kingston, with a very late one on Nov. 20. I had one at our Pickering Twp. home as late as Oct. 13,1958 and George A. Scott observed a late female at Oshawa on Nov. 4, 1973 (Speirs, 1974). J.L. Baillie (in Saunders, 1947: 372) gave Sept. 20 as his average departure date for Toronto: Speirs (1938: 53) listed Oct. 7 as the latest Toronto date (but see the winter record above). Snyder (1931: 210) mentioned Long Point light casulties: 7 on Sept. 7; 7 on Sept. 9 and 31 from Sept. 24-29, 1929. Ussher (1965: 24) gave Sept. 29 as the average fall departure date from Rondeau, the latest on Nov. 7. Stirrett (1973d: 26) had a fall maximum of 15 on Sept. 20 at Pelee, with the latest on Oct. 15.

**MEASUREMENTS:**
*Length:* 5 to 6 ins.
(Godfrey, 1966: 336)
*Wingspread:* 8.25 to 9.30
ins. (Roberts, 1955: 676)
*Weight:* 9.3 to 19.2 g.
(Terres, 1980: 965)
♂ 11.8 g. ♀ 12.5 g.
(Hope, 1938: 39).

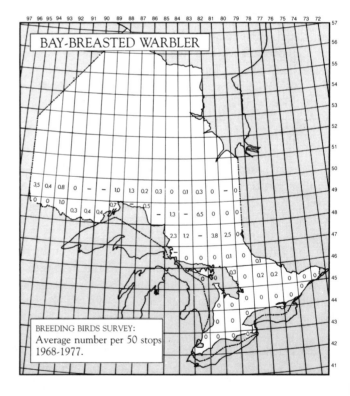

BAY-BREASTED WARBLER

BREEDING BIRDS SURVEY:
Average number per 50 stops
1968-1977.

# BLACKPOLL WARBLER   *Dendroica striata*   (Forster)

These warblers winter in western South America. They are usually our latest warbler to show up in migration, often in late May or even early June. In Ontario they nest in what Fred Bodsworth called "the land of little sticks" where stunted spruces push out into the tundra near the Hudson Bay lowlands. Winter is slow to release its grip in this country so there is no hurry for the Blackpolls to arrive there.

**IDENTIFICATION:** The trees are generally in full leaf by the time these warblers reach southern Ontario, so the observer must listen for their high-pitched, staccato, crescendo, then diminuendo, song: "ti,ti,ti,ti,TI,TI,TI,ti,ti,ti". When finally located the spring male with its black cap, white cheeks and underparts, with black streaks along the sides and on its greenish back, is easily identified: the female is green above and greenish white below, with white wing bars and white undertail coverts, streaked with black above and below. Fall birds have sometimes been confused with fall Bay-breasted Warblers but are much more streaked above and below than that species and have white undertail coverts, not buffy as in the Bay-breasted (which usually shows a hint of the brownish sides even in fall). (The pale legs of the Blackpoll are sometimes used to separate them from the darker-legged Bay-breasted Warblers.)

**WINTER:**

**SPRING:** Stirrett (1973b: 24) had Pelee records from May 2 to May 29: Kelley (1978: 73) reported a maximum of 35 there on May 25, 1974. Ussher (1965: 24) gave May 18 as the average arrival date for Rondeau and June 2 as the average departure date, with the earliest on May 10. Saunders & Dale (1933: 229) gave May 21 as the 16-year average arrival date at London, with the earliest on May 13, 1915. Harold Lancaster gave May 20 as the average date of arrival in Elgin Co. (Brooman, 1954: 33). Snyder (1931: 210) reported 18 casualties at the Long Point light on May 14, 1925 and collected one on June 2, 1927. Saunders (1947: 372) listed May 25 and May 28 as average arrival and departure dates for Toronto, with his earliest on May 14. Speirs (1938: 43) gave May 25 as the spring peak at Toronto. Naomi LeVay had one at Eastbourne, Whitby, as early as May 8, 1965 but the peak numbers are usually in the last week of May (Speirs, 1974). Weir & Quilliam (1980: 39) listed May 9 as the earliest Kingston record, with average arrival on May 20 and departure on May 31. Devitt (1967: 143) gave May 9, 1959 as the earliest one at Collingwood and May 25 as the 12-year average arrival date for Barrie. K. Ketchum noted one off Pointe au Baril on May 18, 1969 (Mills, 1981: 144). Nicholson (1981: 168) had Manitoulin records from May 17 to June 2, with average arrival on May 21 and a maximum of 20 on Great Duck Is. on May 23, 1976. Ricker and Clarke (1939: 20) cited several Lake Nipissing dates from May 21 (1934) to May 31 (1932). Denis (1961: 4) gave May 20 as the average arrival date at Thunder Bay, with the earliest on May 12, 1951. Peruniak (1971: 26) gave May 18 as her earliest Atikokan record. Elder (1979: 38) gave May 21 as his earliest Geraldton date.

**SUMMER:** A few were reported on the 1968-1977 Breeding Bird Surveys, but these were likely spring stragglers rather than breeding birds. Stirrett (1973c: 20) reported a returning bird at Pelee as early as Aug. 12. Ussher (1965: 24) had a northbound bird at Rondeau as late as June 17 and the earliest fall bird on Aug. 22, with average arrival on Aug. 30. Snyder (1931: 210) had a Long Point straggler as late as June 12, 1927. Beardslee

& Mitchell (1965: 383) reported 11 at Morgan's Point, Lake Erie, as early as Aug. 6, 1944. Speirs (1938: 45) gave June 13 as the latest spring date for Toronto. J.L. Baillie (in Saunders, 1947: 372) had a southbound bird at Toronto as early as Aug. 9, with Aug. 26 as his average arrival date. I noted one at our Pickering Twp. home as late as June 7, 1963 and as early as Aug. 13, 1972 (Speirs, 1974). Snyder (1941: 80) collected a male at Weller Bay, Prince Edward Co., on June 7, 1931 "a normal concluding date for the northward migration". A spring straggler was seen at Kingston as late as June 15 and an early fall bird showed up July 24, with average arrival Aug. 24 (Weir & Quilliam, 1980: 39): Arthur Bell observed one near Napanee from July 7-10, 1957 (Quilliam, 1973: 161). Devitt (1967: 143) reported a spring bird at Collingwood as late as June 12, 1917 and an early fall arrival at Wasaga Beach on Aug. 18, 1934. I saw single birds at Sundridge on June 10 and 11, 1933 and there were July records at Rebecca Lake and Go Home Bay (Mills, 1981: 144). MacLulich (1938: 34) cited several August records for Algonquin Park. K. Boshcoff saw one at Pukaskwa on June 25, 1973 (Skeel & Bondrup-Nielsen, 1978: 206). Snyder (1938: 205) had only one Rainy River record, a female collected on Aug. 5, 1929. David Elder had an Aug. 22 record for Atikokan in 1981. Ross James noted two at Pickle Lake on June 12, 1977. Hope (1938: 39) collected a singing male on June 14, 1938 at Favourable Lake. Cringan (1973b: 4) saw two on June 3 and another on June 4, 1953 at Kasabonika Lake. Manning (1952: 83) collected two immatures on Aug. 10 and 11, 1947 at Shagamu River, Hudson Bay and mentioned that the original description by Forster was based on a male and a female taken at Severn River. At Kiruna Lake, Sutton Ridges, in 1981, James, Nash & Peck (1981: 45) found a breeding density of 20 pairs per km $^2$ in open spruce lowlands (ranked third in this habitat): others were found in open fens (25.9 pairs per km $^2$ ); open spruce uplands (11.1 pairs per km $^2$ ); dense spruce lowlands (16.6 pairs per km $^2$). Schueler, Baldwin & Rising (1974: 144, 147) reported them as uncommon at Attawapiskat, abundant at Winisk where a nest with 4 eggs was found on July 3, 1965; and common at Hawley Lake where a nest with 2 eggs was found on June 23, 1964: this nest held 4 eggs from June 26 to July 3 and was empty on July 14. Lee (1978: 32) found the species on all three study quadrats at Big Trout Lake in 1975 and had a maximum of 10 on June 11 there. C.E. Hope collected a nest with 4 eggs at Ft. Severn on July 2, 1940 and saw a maximum of 15 there on June 17.

AUTUMN: Skeel & Bondrup-Nielsen (1978: 206) saw one on Sept. 5, 1977 at Pukaskwa. Speirs & Speirs (1947: 35) gave Sept. 19, 1944 as their latest North Bay record. Nicholson (1981: 168) had fall records from Aug. 31 (1980) to Oct. 4 (1975) on Manitoulin, with a maximum of 20 on Sept. 20, 1972. Mills (1981: 145) gave Sept. 26, 1907 as the latest fall record for the cottage country (a Port Sydney specimen). Devitt (1967: 143) reported 49 casualties at the Barrie TV tower in 7 years, the latest 3 on Oct. 2, 1965. Weir & Quilliam (1980: 39) listed Sept. 30 as the average departure date from Kingston: K.F. Edwards saw a very late bird at a feeder there on Nov. 20, 1970 (Quilliam, 1973: 161). George A. Scott saw one in weeds near the Oshawa shore on Oct. 23, 1972 (Speirs, 1974). Speirs (1938: 51) gave Sept. 15 as the fall peak at Toronto, where Saunders (1947: 372) listed Sept. 30 as his average departure date with his latest on Oct. 18. H.H. Axtell noted 90 at Erie Beach on Oct. 1, 1954 (Beardslee & Mitchell, 1965: 383-384). Fall casualties at the Long Point light included 31 on Sept. 7; 6 on Sept. 9 and 199 from Sept. 24-29, 1929 (Snyder, 1931: 210). Ussher (1965: 24) gave Sept. 31 (? !!) as the average departure date from Rondeau, with his latest on Oct. 18. Stirrett (1973d: 26) had a maximum of 500 at Pelee on Sept. 16 and his latest on Nov. 3.

**MEASUREMENTS:**

*Length:* 5 to 5 3/4 ins. (Godfrey, 1966: 337)
*Wingspread:* 8.32 to 9.70 ins. (Roberts, 1955: 680)
*Weight:* 0.50 to 0.56 oz. (Roberts, 1955: 680) one ♂ 13 g. (Hope, 1938: 39).

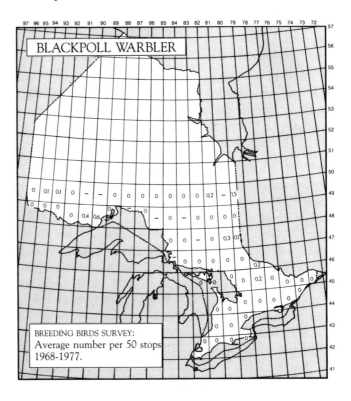

BLACKPOLL WARBLER

BREEDING BIRDS SURVEY:
Average number per 50 stops
1968-1977.

# CERULEAN WARBLER  *Dendroica cerulea*  (Wilson)

This "heavenly" warbler is associated with tall deciduous trees in the swamps of southern Ontario. We have had some success in luring them down from their tree tops by playing back tape recordings of their song. They winter in South America.

IDENTIFICATION: They are sky blue above, white below, with a black "necklace" and black streaks along the sides. This is another warbler with white wing bars. The song is a buzzy "zurree - zurree-zurree - zreeii" (some Parulas sing a similar song). Females have more subdued blue-gray above and a yellowish wash on the sides, and a more distinct whitish line over the eye (some males have this eyeline, others lack it).

WINTER:

SPRING: Stirrett (1973b: 24) gave Apr. 25 as the earliest Pelee record, with a maximum of 25 on May 13. Ussher (1965: 24) gave May 16 as the 18-year average arrival date at Rondeau, earliest on Apr. 30. Saunders & Dale (1933: 228) also had May 16 as their 17-year average arrival date at London, with the earliest on May 3, 1913. Beardslee & Mitchell (1965: 379-380) reported one at Morgan's Point, Lake Erie, on Apr. 24, 1954. Saunders (1947: 372) gave May 3 and May 31 as average arrival and departure dates at Toronto, with a very early one on Apr. 17. Tozer & Richards (1974: 248) reported one near Oshawa from Apr. 29 to May 1, 1962, and cited several later May records for the region. Speirs (1974) reported several records for the third week of May from Pickering to Oshawa and two males in Rama Twp. as early as May 20, 1967. Weir & Quilliam (1980: 39) listed May 15 as the 23-year average arrival date at Kingston, with the earliest on May 9. Devitt (1967: 140-141) reported 5 singing males in the Minesing Swamp as early as May 18, 1964. L. Beamer reported one at Meaford on May 14, 1950. R.E. DeLury reported finding two or three in the spring of 1922 about 22 miles south of Ottawa (Lloyd, 1924: 13). C. Campbell saw one at Parry Sound on May 9, 1970 (Mills, 1981: 142).

SUMMER: On the 1968-1977 Breeding Bird Surveys they were noted only on the Roblin and Port Carling routes. Stirrett (1973b: 24 and 1973c: 20) had Pelee records on June 8, July 8 and several August records, with a maximum of 6 on Aug. 26. Ussher (1965: 24) had a June 15 record for Rondeau. Saunders & Dale (1933: 228) cited details of 6 nestings in the London region, all from 25 to 60 ft. up, from June 7, 1902 (a nest with 4 eggs and a cowbird egg) to June 17, 1916 (a nest with 3 eggs). Brooman (1954: 33) reported nestings at Springwater Pond and McMurray's woods near St. Thomas. Snyder (1931: 209) collected a singing male on Long Point on June 27, 1927. John Frank and I heard two or three singing in Backus Woods, north of Long Point, on June 22-23, 1970 and Nol et al (1978: 65) reported a population of 4 per 100 acres there in 1977. Edward Reinecke found a nest with 4 eggs at Sherkston, Ont. on June 15, 1890, and birds were noted at Point Abino on July 26, 1942 and at Navy Island (Beardslee & Mitchell, 1965: 379). Toronto's first summer record was one collected by J.L. Baillie in King Twp. on June 7, 1926 (Snyder, 1930: 198). Speirs & Orenstein (1975: 13) were surprised to find a population of 50 birds per 100 acres on the Rama forest quadrat (the third most abundant bird on the plot). Speirs (1974) reported June records for two Pickering localities. Synder (1941: 79) collected a singing male at Hallowell, Prince Edward Co., on June 21, 1930. Weir & Quilliam (1980: 39) gave July 10 as the 10-year average departure date for Kingston, with the latest on July 16. W. Lamb found a pair nest building near Kingston on June 2, 1963 and saw the female on the nest on June 23: several other summer records have been established in the Kingston region (Quilliam, 1973: 158-159). Devitt (1967: 141) reported 12 singing males and one female on a trip through the Minesing Swamp on June 28, 1967. Mills (1981: 142) cited records for Beausoleil Is. on June 21, 1972; at Gibson Lake from June 21-24, 1976; near Port Sandfield on June 26, 1976 and another on the Port Carling BBS route on June 28, 1975. Nicholson (1981: 166) reported one near Wolsey Lake, Manitoulin, on June 5, 1960.

AUTUMN: Nicholson (1981: 166) saw one near Quarry Point, Manitoulin, on Sept. 6, 1975. Stirrett (1973d: 26) gave Sept. 22 as his latest Pelee date.

**MEASUREMENTS:**
*Length:* 4.0 to 5.0 ins. (Godfrey, 1966: 334)
*Wingspread:* 7.3 to 8.1 ins. (Roberts, 1955: 681)
*Weight:* Three Ontario specimens averaged 9.9 g.

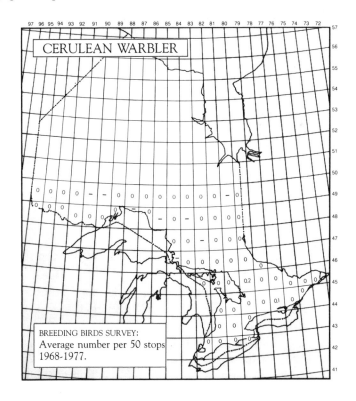

CERULEAN WARBLER

BREEDING BIRDS SURVEY:
Average number per 50 stops
1968-1977.

# BLACK-AND-WHITE WARBLER
*Mniotilta varia* (Linnaeus)

This warbler shares with our nuthatches and the Brown Creeper the care of our tree trunks. The creeper works from the bottom up, the nuthatches from the top down and this warbler from side to side. It is one of the early warblers to arrive in spring and occupies most of the forested area of Ontario during the summer. It winters from southern United States to northern South America.

IDENTIFICATION: With its black and white striped plumage and creeping habits this warbler is easily identified. Adult males have black throats, females have white throats. The song is a high-pitched, very rhythmic "wee-see—wee-see—wee-see. . ."

WINTER:

SPRING: Kelley (1978: 67-68) mentioned an unusual concentration (estimated 1000 birds) at Pelee on May 10, 1952. Stirrett (1973b: 23) had Pelee records from Apr. 12 to June 1: he gave May maximum as 200 on May 10. Ussher (1965: 22) had Rondeau birds from Apr. 23 to June 10, with average arrival on May 1 and departure on May 22. Saunders & Dale (1933: 225) gave Apr. 30 as the 17-year average arrival date at London, with the earliest on Apr. 24, 1925: a nest with 2 young and 2 cowbird young was found in May, 1881 in London. Seven were killed at the Long Point light on May 19, 1926 (Snyder, 1931: 205). Speirs (1938: 44) gave May 11 as the spring peak date at Toronto: Saunders (1947: 371) listed Apr. 25 as his earliest there with average arrival on May 3. Speirs (1974) gave Apr. 27, 1969 as the earliest Oshawa date with May 16 as the Ontario Co. peak. Tozer & Richards (1974: 238) had an Apr. 26, 1964 record for Whitby Twp. Snyder (1941: 77) collected his earliest Prince Edward Co. bird at Hillier on May 3, 1938. Weir & Quilliam (1980: 38) listed Apr. 30 as the 31-year average arrival date at Kingston, with the earliest on Apr. 9. A.E. Hyde found a nest with 5 eggs at Kingston Mills on May 31, 1959 (Quilliam, 1973: 152). Devitt (1967: 133) gave May 5 as the 26-year average arrival date at Barrie, the earliest on Apr. 29, 1963. L. Beamer's earliest at Meaford was Apr. 24, 1939, with median arrival on May 6. The 8-year average arrival date at Huntsville was May 8, with an early one at Port Sydney on Apr. 20, 1901: W. Mansell found a nest with 6 eggs as early as May 30, 1965 at Rebecca Lake (Mills, 1981: 132). Nicholson (1981: 158) gave May 5 as the 12-year average arrival date for Manitoulin, with the earliest on Apr. 27, 1974 and a high count of 20 on May 23, 1976. MacLulich (1938: 31) gave May 15, 1912 as his earliest Algonquin Park date. Louise Lawrence saw an early one at Rutherglen on Apr. 30, 1944 and watched one collecting nest material at Pimisi Bay on May 28, 1944 (Speirs & Speirs, 1947: 34). Skeel & Bondrup-Nielsen (1978: 200) saw their first at Pukaskwa on May 12, 1977, and 37 on 20 days from then until May 30. Denis (1961: 3) gave May 25 as the average arrival date at Thunder Bay, the earliest on May 2, 1942. Peruniak (1971: 25) gave Apr. 24 as her earliest Atikokan record. Elder (1979: 27) had his earliest at Geraldton on May 13. A.N. Boissonneau saw one at Cochrane on May 10, 1951 (Smith, 1957: 177). Bondrup-Nielsen (1976: 44) saw his first near Kapuskasing on May 10 in 1975. Manning (1952: 147) cited records for May 13 and May 31, 1860 at Moose Factory. Schueler, Baldwin & Rising (1974: 147) collected a female with a 2.5 mm. ovum at Moosonee on May 28, 1972.

SUMMER: On the 1968-1977 Breeding Bird Surveys they were rare south of the

Precambrian country and in the Clay Belt, fairly common on most of the Precambrian routes. Stirrett (1973c: 20) had his first returning bird at Pelee on July 28, with the high count of 75 on Aug. 13. Ussher (1965: 22) saw his first returning migrant at Rondeau on Aug. 15, with average arrival on Aug. 20. Saunders & Dale (1933: 225) reported a nest with 5 eggs plus one cowbird egg at Komoka on June 9, 1882 - "every cedar swamp having its quota". Snyder (1931: 205) cited several summer records for the mainland just north of Long Point. Snyder (1930: 198) found them "quite numerous" in King Twp. swamps, where a nest with 3 young and one infertile egg was found on June 19, 1926 on the ground under yew branches. Speirs & Orenstein (1975: 13) found populations of 2 to 28 birds per 100 acres in 5 of 11 forest quadrats in Ontario Co. where it was associated with cedar swamps. A.E. Edwards found a nest with 1 egg and 2 cowbird eggs on Thorah Is. on June 19, 1935 and Nancy Bellerby located a nest with 4 young in Greenwood Conservation Area on June 19, 1971 (Speirs, 1974). Long (1968a: 19) reported one at Pickering Beach on Aug. 2, 1963. George A. Scott found a nest with 1 egg and 4 cowbird eggs on June 4, 1961 in Darlington Twp. (Tozer & Richards, 1974: 238). Snyder (1941: 77) observed adults carrying food on June 28, 1930 at Woodrous, Prince Edward Co. Devitt (1967: 133) reported 3 nests in Simcoe Co.; a nest with 5 eggs at Barrie on June 5, 1897, a nest with 4 eggs there on June 10, 1923 and a nest with 3 eggs and a cowbird egg at Wasaga Beach on June 20, 1934. J.H. Fleming saw a pair feeding young at Ottawa as late as Aug. 16, 1900 and H. Groh found a nest with 5 eggs there on June 2, 1909 (Lloyd, 1924: 13). Mills (1981: 132) found this to be a common summer resident in the cottage country: he saw 4 young in a nest at Ahmic Lake on July 26, 1975. M.Y. Williams found a nest near Lake Manitou on June 27, 1912 and Ron Tasker a nest with 5 eggs in Burpee Twp. on July 28, 1971 (Nicholson, 1981: 158). C.H.D. Clarke observed young being fed in Algonquin Park on July 11, 1934 (MacLulich, 1938: 31). Ricker & Clarke (1939: 18) watched young being fed at Frank's Bay, Lake Nipissing, on July 24, 1933. Baillie & Hope (1947: 21-22) saw young, not long out of the nest, at Biscotasing on June 30 and flying young at Bigwood on July 15, 1937. Snyder (1942: 143) found a nest with 4 eggs near Sault Ste. Marie, 28 inches up in a fire-charred pine stub on June 7, 1931 and a second nest near Maclennan on June 23 with 4 young, also in a rotten stump but only 8 inches up from the ground (most nests of this species are ground nests). Skeel & Bondrup-Nielsen (1978: 200) flushed a female from a nest with 4 recently hatched young on June 11, 1977 at Pukaskwa. Baillie & Hope (1943: 20) considered them "rather uncommon" along the northeast shore of Lake Superior, but collected a male at Rossport on June 2 and another at Amyot on June 27, 1936. Snyder (1928: 271) found them common at Lake Nipigon in 1923 and 1924. Dear (1940: 137) saw young out of the nest fed by parents on July 1, 1929 near Thunder Bay. Snyder (1938: 203) found them fairly common in the Rainy River region, with a maximum of 6 noted in a day: a young bird in unusual plumage was described in detail. Peruniak (1971: 25) considered them uncommon in summer in the Atikokan region. Snyder (1953: 76-77) found them fairly common in most of western Ontario near Minaki, but comparatively rare near Savanne. L. Paterson saw young fed by adults at Kenora on July 18, 1932 (Baillie & Harrington, 1937: 240). Snyder (1928: 30) collected males at Lake Abitibi on June 23 and June 26, 1925. James (1980: 89) found "small numbers" at Pickle Lake. Hope (1938: 35) considered them rare at Favourable Lake but collected a young male there on July 19, 1938. Manning (1952: 80) collected one near the mouth of the Moose River on June 1, 1947. James, Nash & Peck (1982: 68) found a nest with 5 young near James Bay by the Harricanaw River on June 21, 1982.

Schueler, Baldwin & Rising (1974: 147) collected a male with enlarged testes at Atta-wapiskat on June 18, 1971. Lee (1978: 30) saw only one at Big Trout Lake, on July 30, 1975. McLaren & McLaren (1981: 4) reported "singing males common in the Wetiko Hills" (along the Manitoba border near 55 ° N).

AUTUMN: Peruniak (1971: 25) gave Sept. 23 as her latest Atikokan date. Skeel & Bondrup-Nielsen (1978: 200) saw their latest at Pukaskwa on Sept. 20, 1977. Louise Lawrence saw 3 at Pimisi Bay on Sept. 21, 1944 (Speirs & Speirs, 1947: 34). Some 81 were killed at the Great Duck Is. tower from Sept. 18 to 23, 1977 (Nicholson, 1981: 158). Mills (1981: 132) gave Sept. 18, 1975 at Interlaken as the latest record for the cottage country. At the Barrie TV tower 43 were killed in 6 of 7 years, the latest on Oct. 13, 1966 (Devitt, 1967: 133). Weir & Quilliam (1980: 38) listed Sept. 30 as the 25-year average departure date from Kingston, with the latest on Oct. 21. George A. Scott noted one in willows by Oshawa's Second Marsh as late as Oct. 27, 1973 (Speirs, 1974). Speirs (1938: 54) listed Oct. 20 as the latest Toronto date and Saunders (1947: 371) gave Sept. 10 as his average departure date. Ussher (1965: 22) had his latest at Rondeau on Oct. 11, with average departure date on Sept. 15. Stirrett (1973d: 25) had his latest at Pelee on Oct. 21.

**MEASUREMENTS:**

*Length:* 4.5 to 5.5 ins. (Godfrey, 1966: 320)
*Wingspread:* 8.2 to 9.0 ins. (Roberts, 1955: 677)
*Weight:* 34 Ontario specimens averaged 10.15 g.

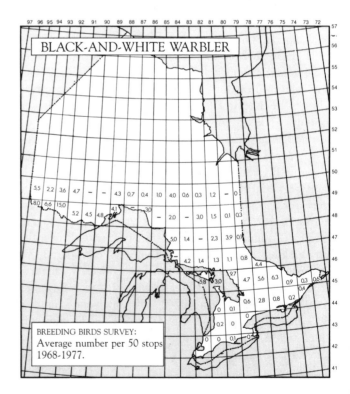

BLACK-AND-WHITE WARBLER

BREEDING BIRDS SURVEY:
Average number per 50 stops
1968-1977.

# AMERICAN REDSTART   *Setophaga ruticilla*   (Linnaeus)

American Redstarts are partial to saplings, in which the nests are usually placed in upright forks. They are exceedingly active sprites, constantly fanning the tail to display their bright colours, and often tumbling down from a high point to snatch prey far below. They winter from southern United States to northern South America.

**IDENTIFICATION:** Fully mature males are black above, with fiery orange wedges on the tail, wings and sides, with white belly and undertail coverts. Females and young have the black replaced with olive-gray, and the orange patches with yellow ones. Some of us facetiously call them "yellowstarts". Often they can be distinguished at a distance by their constant activity and tumbling displays. The typical song is "see-see-see-see, tsoo" (with emphatic emphasis on the final syllable). Young males often have a song like that of Black-and-white Warblers: "see-see see-see see-see-see" (without the final emphatic note).

**WINTER:**

**SPRING:** Stirrett (1973b: 25) gave Apr. 30 as the earliest one at Pelee, with peaks of 200 on May 14 and May 23. Ussher (1965: 26) gave May 10 as the 21-year average arrival date at Rondeau, with the earliest on May 3. Saunders & Dale (1933: 233) gave May 8 as the 17-year average arrival date at London, with the earliest on Apr. 28, 1915. Snyder (1931: 215) reported his first on Long Point on May 6, 1928: J.L. Baillie observed a nest under construction there as early as May 30, 1927 (McCracken, Bradstreet & Holroyd, 1980: 63). Speirs (1938: 39, 43) gave May 1 as the earliest Toronto record, with a peak on May 24: Saunders (1947: 373) listed May 11 as his average arrival date there. J.M. Richards found one near Oshawa as early as May 1, 1962 (Tozer & Richards, 1974: 259). Weir & Quilliam (1980: 39) listed May 8 as the 32-year average arrival date at Kingston, with the earliest on Apr. 30. Devitt (1967: 151) gave May 21 as the 21-year average arrival date at Barrie, with the earliest on May 5, 1938. L. Beamer's median arrival date at Meaford was May 14, with the earliest on May 3, 1953. C.E. Johnson found one nesting at Dow's Swamp, near Ottawa, as early as May 27, 1919 (Lloyd, 1924: 15). Mills (1981: 152-153) gave May 13 as a 9-year average arrival date at Huntsville, with the earliest on May 9, 1965 and birds seen nest building by May 22. Nicholson (1981: 174) gave May 15 as the 12-year average arrival date on Manitoulin, with the earliest on May 8, 1979 and a high count of 60 on May 20, 1975. MacLulich (1938: 36) gave May 4, 1932 as his earliest Algonquin Park date: H.C. Nunn watched a female gathering nest material there as early as May 30, 1934. Speirs & Speirs (1947: 36) saw one at North Bay on May 13, 1944. Skeel & Bondrup-Nielsen (1978: 210) noted their first at Pukaskwa on May 19 in 1977 with a total of 30 observed up to May 30. Denis (1961: 4) gave May 22 as the average arrival date at Thunder Bay, with the earliest on May 12, 1943. Peruniak (1971: 27) gave May 5 as her earliest Atikokan record. Elder (1979: 39) saw his earliest at Geraldton on May 24. Bondrup-Nielsen (1976: 45) saw his first at Kapuskasing on May 24 in 1974. One was collected by Drexler at Moose Factory on May 26, 1860 (Manning, 1952: 86).

**SUMMER:** On the 1968-1977 Breeding Bird Surveys, they were uncommon on a few routes in agricultural regions, fairly common on most routes in the Precambrian country, but common on routes near the north shores of Lake Huron and Lake Superior and up the Ottawa Valley from Mattawa to Haileybury. Stirrett (1973c: 21) had a June 22 peak of 30 at Pelee, with 100 on Aug. 12. Saunders & Dale (1933: 233) reported three sets of 4 eggs each, near London: on June 9, 1901, June 9, 1902 and June 15, 1907. McCracken, Bradstreet & Holroyd (1980: 63-64) reported several nests on Long Point, one as late as July 7, 1927. Speirs & Orenstein (1975: 14) found a population density of 43 birds per 100 acres on their Rama Twp. forest quadrat, the only one of 11 townships in Ontario Co. with any in the forest plots studied: although the Rama plot was in fairly mature forest there was a good understory of blue beech and juneberry for the nesting redstarts. J.A. Edwards found a nest with one egg and a cowbird egg on Thorah Is. on June 25, 1933 (Speirs, 1974). Snyder (1941: 82) observed the first young of the year at Cherry Valley, Prince Edward Co., on July 2, 1930. Quilliam (1973: 168) reported a nest with 4 eggs on June 7, 1904 and a nest with 4 young on June 13, 1965, near Kingston. Devitt (1967: 151) cited several nest records for Simcoe Co., including a nest with 5 eggs at Wasaga Beach on June 9, 1927 and a nest with 3 eggs there as late as July 17, 1938, from which the young left on July 31. G.E. White found a nest at Ottawa on June 24, 1894 (Lloyd, 1924: 15). Mills (1981: 152) reported 53 nests in the cottage country, some with eggs from June 3 to July 9. D.B. Ferguson found a nest with 4 young at Windfall Lake, Manitoulin, on July 9, 1979 (Nicholson, 1981: 174). D. MacLulich found a nest with 4 eggs at Franks Bay, Lake Nipissing, on June 15, 1932 (Ricker & Clarke, 1939: 21). Baillie & Hope (1947: 26) considered them common in Sudbury Dist. in 1937: they found a nest with 2 eggs at Chapleau on June 15 and a nest with 3 young at Bigwood on July 12. Snyder (1942: 145) considered this to be the most common warbler in the Sault Ste. Marie region in 1931: six nests were found in the first two weeks of June. Skeel & Bondrup-Nielsen (1978: 210) saw a male and a female gathering food at Pukaskwa on June 24, 1977. Baillie & Hope (1943: 23) found them common from Rossport to Amyot, with a nest under construction at Marathon on June 11, which held one egg on June 21, 1936. Snyder (1928: 275) collected a young male at Macdiarmid on July 31, 1924 and considered the species common about Lake Nipigon. Dear (1940: 140) found two nests, with 4 eggs each, one on June 17, 1925, the other on June 19, 1932, near Thunder Bay. Snyder (1953: 81) ranked the redstart 19th of the 23 resident warblers of western Ontario, but noted 5 as far north as Sioux Lookout. Snyder (1928: 32) called them "fairly common"— - "and known to breed" at Lake Abitibi, in 1925. Hope (1938: 42) encountered a few at Favourable Lake in 1938, where he collected a young of the year on Aug. 5. Sam Waller found a nest with 4 eggs at Moose Factory on June 25, 1930 (Baille & Harrington, 1937: 255).

AUTUMN: P.M. Holmes saw one at the head of Hannah Bay on Sept. 27, 1983 (Todd, 1963: 630). Peruniak (1971: 27) gave Oct. 2 as her latest Atikokan date. Skeel & Bondrup-Nielsen (1978: 210) noted their latest at Pukaskwa on Sept. 20, 1977. Louise Lawrence saw two at Pimisi Bay as late as Sept. 21, 1944 (Speirs & Speirs, 1947: 36). Nicholson (1981: 175) reported 49 casualties at the Great Duck Is. tower from Sept. 18-23, 1977, and a late bird was reported on Manitoulin on Oct. 27, 1973. Mills (1981: 153) gave Sept. 25, 1979 as his latest observation at Magnetawan. Devitt (1967: 151) gave Oct. 23, 1956 as the latest near Barrie, where 30 were killed at the TV tower in 7 years. Weir & Quilliam (1980: 39) listed Oct. 5 as the 25-year average departure date from Kingston, with the latest on Nov. 9. Long (1968b: 22) gave Oct. 18, 1967 as his latest date for Pickering Beach. Speirs (1938: 53) gave Oct. 24 as the latest Toronto date: Saunders (1947: 373) listed Sept. 22 as his average departure date. Snyder (1931: 216) reported

Long Point lighthouse casualties: one on Sept. 2, 1930; 23 on Sept. 7, 1929; 3 on Sept. 9, 1929 and 40 from Sept. 24-29, 1929. Ussher (1965: 26) gave Sept. 18 as the 11-year average departure date from Rondeau, with the latest on Oct. 6. Stirrett (1973d: 27) had a fall peak of 200 on Sept. 5 at Pelee, with the latest on Nov. 8.

**MEASUREMENTS:**
*Length:* 4.7 to 5.7 ins. (Godfrey, 1966: 349)
*Wingspread:* 7.15 to 7.75 ins. (Roberts, 1955: 676)
*Weight:* 38 Ontario specimens averaged 8.3 g.

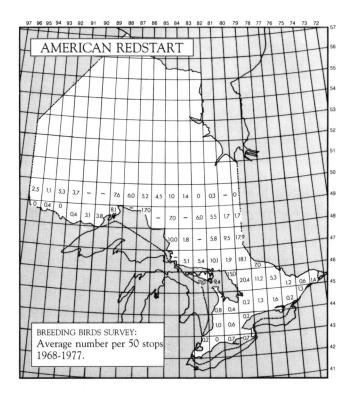

AMERICAN REDSTART

BREEDING BIRDS SURVEY: Average number per 50 stops 1968-1977.

# PROTHONOTARY WARBLER
## *Protonotaria citrea* (Boddaert)

This handsome, big warbler is a summer inhabitant of swamps along the southern fringe of Ontario, where it nests in holes, usually in dead trees standing in water. Wanderers have been reported as far north as North Bay and Quetico. They winter chiefly in Central America.

**IDENTIFICATION:** This is a biggish warbler, mostly yellow with a tinge of orange, bluish wings with no wing bars and a dark tail showing flashes of white in flight. The back is greenish. Its song is a loud, rich "sweet-sweet-sweet-sweet" (Some Swamp Sparrows have a similar song.)

**WINTER:**

**SPRING:** One was seen on Pelee Is. as early as Apr. 27, 1972 by P.D. Pratt (Goodwin, 1972: 757). Stirrett (1973b: 23) gave Apr. 30 as his earliest record at Point Pelee with a maximum of 6 on May 22. Kelley (1978: 68) noted a pair building at Pelee on May 16.

Ussher (1965: 22) gave May 8 as his earliest at Rondeau, with the 17-year average arrival on May 13. W.E. Saunders was "attracted by the notes of a Swamp Sparrow coming from a large elm tree" at London on May 20, 1920: investigation of this unusual occurrence disclosed the singer to be a Prothonotary Warbler (Saunders & Dale, 1933: 225). Brooman (1954: 32) had two Elgin Co. records: one at Copenhagen in May, 1941, the other on May 9, 1953 near Sparta. Beardslee & Mitchell (1965: 363) reported one singing about 2 1/2 miles west of Ridgeway on May 29, 1955 and again there on May 26, 1956. Gordon Bellerby reported a very early one at Toronto on Apr. 17, 1977 (Goodwin, 1977: 995). Speirs (1938: 46) gave May 19 as the latest Toronto record. Speirs (1974) had a good view of one singing at Amos Ponds, Pickering Twp., on May 25, 1963 and Long (1968b: 22) saw a male at Pickering Beach on May 13, 1968. Naomi LeVay carefully described a female seen at Cranberry Marsh, Whitby, on May 22, 1974 (Tozer & Richards, 1974: 310). Charles Francis banded a female at Prince Edward Point on May 23, 1980 (Weir & Quilliam, 1980: 22). P. Bridges saw one at Peterborough on May 23, 1980 (Goodwin, 1980: 772). Bruce Parker observed one at Sibbalds Point, Lake Simcoe, on May 13, 1978 (Goodwin, 1978: 1000). Devitt (1967: 133, 134) had three Simcoe Co. sightings, all along Willow Creek: the first on May 15, 1930 by E.L. Brereton; the second by Mrs. R. Freeman on May 24, 1959 and the third by Frances Westman, O.E. Devitt et al from May 8 to 13, 1966. The most unexpected was seen at Quetico by D. Haddow et al from Apr. 27 to May 3, 1976 (Goodwin, 1976: 835).

SUMMER: Stirrett (1973c: 20 and 1973d: 25) noted two on Aug. 15, single birds on Aug. 22 and 29 and three on Aug. 30, at Pelee. Ussher (1965: 22) gave Aug. 25 as his latest Rondeau record. McCracken, Bradstreet & Holroyd (1981: 62) cited several nest records for the Long Point region by George North from 1939 to 1963 and by McCracken who found 8 nests in 1979 and who emphasized the importance of dead trees for this hole-nesting species. A male was found helping at a Yellow Warbler nest, feeding two young on June 24, 1956, and 4 young on June 26, 1958 and at a nest with 4 eggs on June 14, 1959: Sheppard (1960: 39) and others gave the locality of this strange behaviour as Point Abino. The most northerly breeding record was at the Pinery in the summer of 1981 (Goodwin, 1982: 174). A. Wormington noted one at Campbellville on July 8, 1973 (Goodwin, 1973: 55). J. Hoskin reported two at Waubaushene on July 21, 1974 (Goodwin, 1974: 899). Pearl Rogers found one at Huntsville on July 24, 1977: this was seen and heard the following day by Anne Spratt: on June 14, 1972 one was noted on Beausoleil Is. by an FON group (Mills, 1981: 132). A female was found dead at Wye Marsh on the same day (June 14, 1972) according to C.J. MacFayden (Goodwin, 1972: 757). Hazel Petty saw one at West Ferris, near North Bay, on Aug. 17, 1950 (Baillie, 1951: 14) and Louise Lawrence noted one at Pimisi Bay on Aug. 14, 1981 (Goodwin, 1982: 174).

AUTUMN: H. MacKenzie reported one at Ottawa as late as Oct. 1, 1971 (Goodwin, 1972: 58). W. Fahey reported one at Durham on Sept. 15, 1976 (Goodwin, 1977: 172).

**MEASUREMENTS:**
*Length:* 5.3 to 5.8 ins.
(Godfrey, 1966: 320)
*Wingspread:* 7.88 to 9.12
ins. (Roberts, 1955: 668)
*Weight:* 14.4 to 17.8 g.
(Terres, 1980: 977).

# WORM-EATING WARBLER
*Helmintheros vermivorus*   (Gmelin)

This is a rare warbler along the southern fringe of Ontario, wintering mainly in Central America and the West Indies.

**IDENTIFICATION:** Illustrations seldom do justice to the vivid green of the back and orange blush on the breast of this ground lover. The somewhat similar Ovenbird has a white breast with blackish spots, not a clear buffy breast like this species. The Ovenbird also lacks the buffy stripe over the eyes of this species: both have a central crown stripe and share the same habitat, a forest floor with lots of dead leaf litter. The song of this species is similar to the Chipping Sparrow's trill.

**WINTER:**

**SPRING:** Stirrett (1973b: 23) had Pelee records from May 5 to May 20: there have been several more recent records there. A.H. Kelley reported one at Bradley's Marsh on May 1, 1976 (Goodwin, 1976: 835). One was seen at Rondeau on May 16, 1971 *fide* R. Simpson (Goodwin, 1971: 738): there have been several more recent records there. G.F. Bates noted one at Delaware on May 16, 1971 (Goodwin, 1971: 738). Saunders & Dale (1933: 226) collected one at London on May 28, 1908. One turned up at the Long Point Bird Observatory on May 4, 1972 (Goodwin, 1972: 757). Harold Axtell collected one at Morgan's Point, Lake Erie on Apr. 25, 1949, having seen it there the previous day: A.E. Schaffner saw another there on Apr. 22, 1954 (Beardslee & Mitchell, 1965: 639). M. Jennings, George W. North and J. Olmsted saw one at Bronte as early as Apr. 24, 1974 (Goodwin, 1974: 797). R. Barkely, J. White and P. Wukash found one at Toronto from May 9 to 13, 1979 (Goodwin, 1979: 767). Donald Pace reported one at Amos Ponds, Pickering Twp., on May 26, 1969 (Speirs, 1974). Margaret Bain found one in Thickson's Woods, Whitby, on May 9, 1978, which she showed to me: others have been noted there in subsequent Mays, including one she saw there on May 9, 1981. Weir & Quilliam (1980: 22) had five Kingston records from Apr. 19, 1976 (photographed by Ken Edwards) to May 26, 1979 (banded and also photographed by Ken Edwards). R.A. Foxall and R.M. Poulin discovered one at Ottawa on May 18, 1975 (Goodwin, 1975: 847) and H.N. MacKenzie found another there on May 11, 1980 (Goodwin, 1980: 772).

**SUMMER:** D. Wilkes and A. Wormington reported one at Pelee on Aug. 6 and 19, 1981 (Goodwin, 1982: 174). A. Wormington noted one at Dundas Marsh on June 7, 1971 (Goodwin, 1971: 738). Arnold Dawe found one at Woodbridge on Aug. 28, 1979 (Goodwin, 1980: 157). One frequented a woodlot at Ajax for a few days from July 1, 1974, seen by H. Kerr and many others (Goodwin, 1974: 899).

**AUTUMN:** Frank Smith reported one from the Rouge Valley, Pickering Twp., on Sept. 2, 1938 (Speirs, 1974). K.J. Burk had one at Rondeau as late as Sept. 19, 1975 (Goodwin, 1976: 63).

**MEASUREMENTS:**
*Length:* 5 to 5 3/4 ins.
(Godfrey, 1966: 321)
Wingspread:
*Weight:* 12.7 g. (Terres, 1980: 979).

# SWAINSON'S WARBLER
*Limnothlypis swainsonii* (Audubon)

This is normally a bird of cane thickets of coastal southeastern United States or tangles of various shrubs high in the mountains from West Virginia south to Tennessee. There has been one Ontario record, at Pelee.

**IDENTIFICATION:** This is a warbler with no wing bars, whitish below and olive brown above, with prominent white lines over each eye, a rusty cap like a Chipping Sparrow, with "dirty" face, sides and flanks. It has a loud, rich song somewhat like that of a Hooded Warbler.

**WINTER:**

**SPRING:** Stirrett (1973b: 23) reported one at Pelee from May 7 to 9, 1968.

**SUMMER:**

**AUTUMN:**

**MEASUREMENTS:**
*Length:* 5 to 6 1/2 ins.
(Terres, 1980: 977)
Wingspread:
*Weight:* 13.7 g. (Terres,
1980: 978).

# OVENBIRD *Seiurus aurocapillus* (Linnaeus)

In summer, the Ovenbird is one of the most common woodland birds in Ontario, building its domed nests (like little Dutch ovens) in the leaf litter on the forest floor. Its loud song is usually given from the understory, between the ground and the forest canopy, where the singer views interlopers with wide-eyed suspicion. When on the ground it *walks*, not hopping like many small birds. They winter from the southern United States to northern South America.

**IDENTIFICATION:** The Ovenbird is coloured like a small thrush, with olive-brown back and white breast with black spots. Unlike the thrushes the Ovenbird has an orange crown bordered with black. The rare Worm-eating Warbler shares the orange crown bordered with black, but has unspotted peach-coloured underparts and bright green upperparts. The song of the Ovenbird is the well-known "teacher-teacher-teacher-TEACHER-TEACHER" crescendo.

**WINTER:** B. Wilkes noted one at Pelee on Dec. 15, 1981 (Weir, 1982: 291). Ron Scovell had one at his home in Thistletown on Dec. 20, 1975 (Goodwin, 1976: 714). Parker (1983: 24) reported that the species was found on four Christmas bird counts in the Toronto region.

**SPRING:** Stirrett (1973b: 24) had Pelee transients from Apr. 30 to June 1, with a maximum of 100 on May 10. Ussher (1965: 25) gave May 7 as his 22-year average arrival date at Rondeau, with the earliest on Apr. 30. Saunders & Dale (1933: 230) gave May 4 as the 17-year average arrival date at London, with the earliest on Apr. 24, 1916: a set of 5 eggs was found as early as May 26, 1906. Sixteen struck the Long Point light on May 14, 1925 (Snyder, 1931: 212). Speirs (1938: 39, 43) gave Apr. 28 as the earliest Toronto date, with spring peaks on May 18 and May 25: Saunders (1947: 372) listed May 8 as his 13-year average arrival date there. Speirs (1974) reported the earliest Ontario Co. record as one seen by Dennis Barry in Thickson's woods, Whitby, on May 2, 1964: the spring peak is usually in the third week of May. Weir & Quilliam (1980: 39) listed May 6 as the 31-year average arrival date at Kingston, with the earliest on Apr. 26. Devitt (1967: 146) gave May 8 as the 19-year average arrival date at Barrie, with the earliest at Collingwood on Apr. 30, 1960: several hundred were noted by E.L. Brereton at Barrie on May 17, 1933: D.S. Miller found a nearly completed nest at Holland River as early as May 29, 1938, which held 5 eggs and 1 cowbird egg on June 5. L. Beamer's median arrival date at Meaford was May 16, with the earliest on May 8, 1938. Mills (1981: 148) gave May 8 as the 8-year average arrival date at Huntsville, the earliest on May 6, 1962. Nicholson (1981: 170) gave May 14 as the 11-year average arrival date on Manitoulin, with the earliest on May 8, 1977 and maximum of 150 at South Baymouth on May 13, 1978. Louise Lawrence noted one at Pimisi Bay on May 11, 1944 (Speirs & Speirs, 1947: 35). Skeel & Bondrup-Nielsen (1978: 207) saw their first at Pukaskwa on May 13 in 1977: they noted 69 on 14 days up to May 31. Peruniak (1971: 26) gave May 6 as her earliest Atikokan date. Elder (1979: 38) noted his earliest at Geraldton on May 21. Bondrup-Nielsen (1976: 45) gave May 18, 1975 as his earliest spring record for Kapuskasing.

SUMMER: On the 1968-1977 Breeding Bird Surveys, they were common throughout the forested part of Ontario, becoming uncommon in the agricultural south, and most numerous on routes north and west of Lake Superior. Speirs & Frank (1970: 777) had a partial territory on their Pelee forest quadrat in 1970: also one full territory in the beech forest plot in Springwater Park, Elgin Co. (Speirs & Frank, 1970: 742). Saunders & Dale (1933: 230) found a nest with 2 eggs near London on June 8, 1901. F. Starr took a set of 5 eggs and a cowbird egg at Port Burwell on June 11, 1924 (Baillie & Harrington, 1937: 251). On our 25-acre plot in Backus woods, north of Long Point, we had just one partial territory, perhaps due to the swampy nature of the quadrat (Nol et al, 1978: 65). Snyder (1930: 199) reported a nest with 4 eggs found in King Twp. on June 11, 1926. Speirs & Orenstein (1975: 13) found Ovenbirds in all 9 mid-and-late succession forest plots in Ontario Co.: they were second in abundance only to the European Starling (which occurred in just 5 of the late succession quadrats): my earliest nest, which held 4 eggs and 1 cowbird egg was in Brock Twp. on June 4, 1968. J.M. Richards found a nest with 5 eggs in Darlington Twp. on June 4, 1965 (Tozer & Richards, 1974: 252). Snyder (1941: 80) found young just out of the nest at Woodrous, Prince Edward Co., on June 27, 1930. Quilliam (1973: 163-164) reported 4 nests near Kingston: a nest with 4 eggs on June 2, 1965; a nest with 3 eggs and 1 young on June 9, 1971; a nest with 5 eggs in June, 1896 and a nest with 4 eggs on July 5, 1959. Devitt (1967: 146) cited several nest records for Simcoe Co., one as late as July 15, 1917, at Little Lake, Barrie. I found the Ovenbird to be the second commonest bird in a hardwood quadrat near Dorset in the 1960's, with a breeding density of 39 males per 100 acres: 27 cottage country nests held full sets of eggs between May 26 and July 17 (Mills, 1981: 148). D.B. Ferguson found a nest with 3 young at Windfall Lake, Manitoulin, on July 12, 1980 (Nicholson, 1981: 170).

Louise Lawrence found a nest with 5 eggs at Pimisi Bay on June 12, 1944 that held 4 young on June 17: they had left the nest by June 25 (Speirs & Speirs, 1947: 35). Baillie & Hope (1947: 25) noted young out of the nest at Biscotasing on July 5 and at Bigwood from July 19-23, 1937: they reported a nest with 4 young in Wanapitei Provincial Forest found by D. A. MacLulich on July 8, 1929. Snyder (1942: 144) noted young out of the nest at Maclennan on July 2 and at Laird on July 3, 1931. Skeel & Bondrup-Nielsen (1978: 207) found a nest with 5 eggs in Pukaskwa on June 7, 1977 and a nest with 4 young on June 25: the Ovenbird ranked sixth in abundance on their summer censuses. Snyder (1928: 273) found young at two localities near Lake Nipigon in July, 1924. Dear (1940: 139) found a nest with 4 eggs on July 6, 1926 and a nest with 2 eggs and 1 cowbird egg on July 8, 1928 near Thunder Bay. Kendeigh (1947: 28) found 10 pairs on 100 acres at Black Sturgeon Lake in 1945 while Speirs (1949: 148) found 4 territories on 75 acres at nearby Eaglehead Lake in 1946. Snyder (1938: 205) found them common in the Rainy River region in 1929, with the first young out of the nest noted on July 5. Snyder (1953: 79) ranked the Ovenbird third in abundance of the 23 species of warblers in western Ontario: a newly completed nest was found at Ingolf on June 3, 1937; two nests, each with 4 young, were found at Wabigoon on June 21, 1937 and a nest with 4 eggs near Dinorwic on July 5, 1937. We found the Ovenbird to rank third in abundance of the birds on an aspen forest quadrat at Lake of the Woods, with 56 territories per 100 acres (Price & Speirs, 1971: 977). James (1980: 84, 90) found 6.4 pairs per km $^2$ on 4 of his 12 transects near Pickle Lake and reported a nest with 5 eggs found by the McLarens just north of Lysander Lake on June 5, 1977. Hope (1938: 40) found a nest with 4 young at Favourable Lake on June 25, 1938. Manning (1952: 84) collected a male on Sandy Is., near Moosonee on June 24, 1949 and reported others there on June 19 and 29. James, Nash & Peck (1982: 69) found fledged young on June 29, 1982 in deciduous groves by the Harricanaw River, near James Bay. McLaren & McLaren (1981: 5) found singing males common in the Wetiko Hills along the Manitoba border at 56 ° N. Most observers in the Hudson Bay lowlands have failed to find the species there.

AUTUMN: Peruniak (1971: 26) gave Sept. 15 as her latest Atikokan record. Skeel & Bondrup-Nielsen (1978: 207) noted their last at Pukaskwa on Sept. 7 in 1977. Louise Lawrence observed one at Pimisi Bay on Sept. 12, 1944 (Speirs & Speirs, 1947: 35). Nicholson (1981: 170) gave Oct. 6, 1973 as the latest Manitoulin date, with 874 casualties at the Great Duck Is. tower from Sept. 18-23, 1977. Mills (1981: 148) saw his latest on Sept. 25, 1976, at Ahmic Lake. At the Barrie TV tower, 507 were killed in 7 years, the latest on Oct. 14, 1966. Weir & Quilliam (1980: 39) gave Oct. 2 as the 26-year average departure date from Kingston, with the latest on Oct. 17. George A. Scott noted a late one at Oshawa on Nov. 8, 1950 (Speirs, 1974). Speirs (1938: 51, 53) gave Sept. 13 as the fall peak at Toronto, the latest on Nov. 4. Snyder (1931: 213) reported Long Point casualties: 30 on Sept. 7; 9 on Sept. 9 and 107 from Sept. 24-29, 1929. Ussher (1965: 25) gave Oct. 7 as his 6-year average departure date from Rondeau, with the latest on Oct. 21. Stirrett (1973d: 27) had a fall maximum of 50 at Pelee on Sept. 5, and his latest on Nov. 1.

BANDING: One banded 11 miles north of Alpena, Mich. on May 17, 1970 was recovered at McFarlane Lake, Sudbury Dist., Ont. on May 24, 1971, 146 miles NE. (Brewer & Salvadori, 1976: 85). Another banded at Bay Delvan, Alabama, on Oct. 11,

1962 was recovered at Derry West, Ont. on Nov. 20, 1965 (found dead) about 992 miles NE. (Brewer & Salvadori, 1978: 78).

**MEASUREMENTS:**
*Length:* 5.5 to 6.5 ins. (Godfrey, 1966: 340)
*Wingspread:* 8.75 to 10.40 ins. (Roberts, 1955: 682)
*Weight:* 112 Ontario specimens averaged 20.73 g.

**REFERENCES:**
Falls, J. Bruce 1963 Properties of bird song eliciting responses from territorial males. Proc. 13th Internat. Ornithological Congress: 259-271. In the case of Ovenbirds, studied in Algonquin Park, the "cher" appeared to be more significant than the "tea-". Speed and spacing were also important, but not loudness.

Stenger, Judith 1958 Food habits and available food of Ovenbirds in relation to territory size. Auk, 75: (3): 335-346. Food consisted mainly of forest floor invertebrates, taken in proportion to their availability: this food reached maximum availability during the first two weeks of July in Algonquin Park, the nestling period of Ovenbird chicks. Small territories had a richer invertebrate fauna than did large territories.

Stenger, Judith and J. Bruce Falls 1959 The utilized territory of the Ovenbird. Wilson Bull., 71: (2): 125-139. Utilized territories varied from 0.8 to 4.3 acres, being larger in forests approaching climax: the size varied with the season, being largest early and late and smallest at the time of nest building and egg laying.

Weeden, Judith Stenger and J. Bruce Falls 1959 Differential responses of male Ovenbirds to recorded songs of neighboring and more distant individuals. Auk, 76: (3): 343-354. The Ovenbirds responded faster and more strongly to songs of non-adjacent birds than to songs of neighbors.

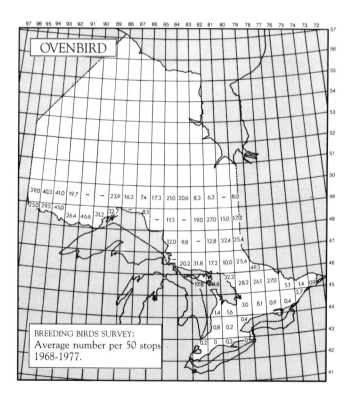

OVENBIRD

BREEDING BIRDS SURVEY:
Average number per 50 stops
1968-1977.

# NORTHERN WATERTHRUSH
*Seiurus noveboracensis* (Gmelin)

Each spring we look forward to the return of our resident waterthrushes, about the end of April, enlivening the leafless forest with their energetic songs. In summer they occur in swampy areas throughout Ontario, except for a strip along the north shore of Lake Erie. They winter from the Bahamas and Mexico south to northern South America.

IDENTIFICATION: Brown above and yellowish white below, with dark breast streaks. The Northern Waterthrush differs from the very similar Louisiana Waterthrush by having a buffy stripe over the eye (white in the Louisiana). Both waterthrushes bob the hind-quarters vigorously up and down (*Seiurus* translates as ""tail wagger"). The song is an emphatic "quoit - quoit-quoit - swee-wee-wee - wheat". They are very early fall migrants, when their loud "peenk" note may alert you to their presence.

WINTER: On the 1968-1977 Christmas counts they were tallied only once, at Long Point, in 1973.

SPRING: Stirrett (1973b: 24) had Pelee records from Apr. 22 to June 7, with a maximum of 10 on May 17. Ussher (1965: 25) had Rondeau reports from Apr. 25 to May 24, with average arrival on May 7 and departure on May 18. Saunders & Dale (1933: 230) gave May 1 as the 17-year average arrival date at London, with the earliest on Apr. 23, 1914: a set of 4 eggs was taken on May 30, 1879 at Hyde Park. Saunders (1947: 372) listed Apr. 25 as his earliest Toronto date with average arrival on May 2: Speirs (1938: 43) had spring peaks there on May 10 and May 23. My earliest singing bird in our Pickering Twp. forest was on Apr. 21, 1961 and J. Satterly noted one at Cedar Point, Mara Twp., as early as Apr. 25, 1954 (Speirs, 1974). Dennis Barry found a nest with 2 eggs and 5 cowbird eggs on May 28, 1967 in Darlington Twp. (Tozer & Richards, 1974: 253). Allin (1940: 106) found a nest with 6 eggs in Darlington Twp. on May 29, 1926. D.C. Sadler reported one at Peterborough as early as Apr. 11, 1974 (Goodwin, 1974: 797). Weir & Quilliam (1980: 39) listed May 1 as the 30-year average arrival date at Kingston, with the earliest on Apr. 22. Devitt (1967: 147) gave May 5 as the 25-year average arrival date at Barrie, with the earliest on Apr. 24, 1960: J.L. Baillie noted 20 singing males on May 16, 1931 in Minesing Swamp and H.P. Bingham took a set of 5 eggs at Barrie on May 24, 1924. J. Goltz saw one as early as Apr. 22 at Bala but May 7 was the 6-year average arrival date at Huntsville: a pair was observed nest building at Ahmic Lake on May 18, 1975 (Mills, 1981: 148). Nicholson (1981: 170) gave May 16 as the 10-year average arrival date on Manitoulin, with the earliest on May 9, 1970 and a high count of 8 on May 15, 1971. Louise Lawrence observed one at Rutherglen on May 3, 1944 (Speirs & Speirs, 1947: 35). Skeel & Bondrup-Nielsen (1978: 207) gave May 13 as their earliest Pukaskwa record. Denis (1961: 4) gave May 18 as the average arrival date at Thunder Bay, with the earliest on May 11, 1956. Peruniak (1971: 27) gave May 14 as her earliest Atikokan date. Elder (1979: 38) had his earliest at Geraldton on May 8. Cringan (1953a: 3) saw his first at Dryden on May 20 in 1953. Manning (1952: 84) mentioned one collected by Drexler at Moose Factory on May 26, 1860.

SUMMER: On the 1968-1977 Breeding Bird Surveys, they were absent on routes near Lake Erie, uncommon on most other routes, fairly common in the cottage country and on several of the most northerly routes. Stirrett (1973c: 21) had returning birds from July 22 through August at Pelee. Ussher (1965: 25) had his earliest return at Rondeau on July 30, with the average return on Aug. 14. Wm. Girling reported one at Port Bruce, Elgin Co. from July 15-18, 1934 (Brooman, 1954: 33). Beardslee & Mitchell (1965: 387-388) reported one from the Canadian shore of Lake Erie on July 24, 1949. Snyder (1930: 199) collected young in King Twp. on July 27 and 29, 1926. Speirs & Orenstein (1975: 14) had populations of 16 and 7 birds per 100 acres in their Scott and Reach Twp. forest quadrats in Ontario Co. A.E. Allin found a nest with 3 eggs in Darlington Twp. on June 6, 1934 (Baillie & Harrington, 1937: 252). Snyder (1941: 80-81) noted young in Prince Edward Co. on July 7 and 14, 1930 and July 2, 1938. Robert Stewart and George Stirrett estimated 75 singing birds during a 6 1/2 mile canoe trip down Cameron Creek, near Kingston on June 8, 1952 (Quilliam, 1973: 164). Devitt (1967: 147) reported several Simcoe Co. nests including a nest with 3 young and one egg at the Holland River, found by R.A. Smith on June 16, 1940. Mills (1981: 149) reported a nest with 4 young at Walker Lake, Muskoka, on June 3, 1977 found by M. Cadman: Katherine Ketchum noted an early migrant off Pointe au Baril on July 26, 1953: the latest date for the cottage country was one seen by M. Speirs at Sundridge on Aug. 21, 1932. Baillie & Hope (1947: 25) had July records at Chapleau, Bigwood and Washagami. Snyder (1942: 145) had just two records near Sault Ste. Marie, both on the shore of the St. Joseph Channel, on July 2 and July 21, 1931. At Pukaskwa, Skeel & Bondrup-Nielsen (1978: 207) had just 13 records on 9 days from June 9 to July 9, 1977, none later. Baillie & Hope (1943: 22) found them "quite scarce" along the northeast shore of Lake Superior, collecting a female at Rossport on June 4 and a male at Amyot on July 3, 1936. Snyder (1928: 274) collected only one at Lake Nipigon, on June 25, 1924. Dear (1940: 139) found a nest with 4 eggs on June 19, 1914 and a nest with 5 eggs on June 4, 1935 near Thunder Bay. Snyder (1938: 206) collected two males at Off Lake, Rainy River, on July 4 and July 5, 1929. Snyder (1953: 80) found them scarce in western Ontario, but noted a few at Kenora, Sioux Lookout, Wabigoon, Savanne and Minaki. Elder (1979: 38) considered them to be common summer residents at Geraldton. Smith (1957: 178) found a nest about 9 miles north of Hearst on June 2, 1954. Snyder (1928: 31) found them common about the flooded shores of Lake Abitibi in 1925, saw adults carrying food and collected 2 males and a female there in June, 1925. R.D. Ussher found a nest with 4 eggs near Kapuskasing on June 30, 1925 (Baillie & Harrington, 1937: 251). James (1980: 84) listed 2.4 pairs per km $^2$ on 3 of 12 transects near Pickle Lake. Hope (1938: 40) found two nests near Favourable Lake: a nest with 2 eggs on June 16 and a nest with 4 eggs on June 28, 1938. Cringan (1953b: 4) found them "very common" at Kasabonika Lake in 1953. Cringan (1950: 17) found them common in the Nikip Lake region in 1950. Manning (1952: 84) observed individuals from Moosonee north to Attawapiskat, Raft River and at Shagamu River on the Hudson Bay coast where he collected a young bird on Aug. 8, 1947. James, Nash & Peck (1982: 69) found a nest with 4 young on June 22 and a nest with 3 young on June 29, 1982 by the Harricanaw River, James Bay. James, Nash & Peck (1981: 44) estimated a breeding density of 10 pairs per km $^2$ in riparian thicket (willow) swamp at Kiruna Lake, Sutton Ridges, in 1981. Schueler, Baldwin & Rising (1974: 144, 1847) found them common at Moosonee, Attawapiskat and Hawley Lake, uncommon at Winisk: they collected a female with brood patch at Aquatuk Lake on July 9, 1964. Lee (1978: 32) described them as well-distributed in alder thickets and along streams in the Big Trout Lake region in 1975. C.E. Hope noted up to 10 per day at Ft. Severn in 1940 and located a nest with 4 young on June 29.

AUTUMN: Speirs & Speirs (1947: 36) noted one at North Bay on Sept. 13, 1944. Nicholson (1981: 170) reported 39 killed at the Great Duck Is. tower from Sept. 19-24, 1977. Devitt (1967: 147) reported 7 killed at the Barrie TV tower in 4 of 7 years, the latest on Sept. 19, 1964. Weir & Quilliam (1980: 39) listed Sept. 10 as the 26-year average departure date from Kingston, the latest on Oct. 12. George A. Scott found one in Oshawa's Second Marsh on Oct. 7, 1973 (Speirs, 1974). Saunders (1947: 372) gave Sept. 5 as his average departure date from Toronto, with his latest on Sept. 24. Snyder (1931: 213) reported casualties at the Long Point light: 36 on Sept. 7; 5 on Sept. 9 and 5 from Sept. 24-29, 1929. A very late one was reported at the Long Point Bird Observatory on Oct. 31, 1982 (Weir, 1983: 176). Ussher (1965: 25) gave Sept. 24 as the average departure date from Rondeau, the latest on Oct. 14. Stirrett (1973d: 27) had a Pelee maximum of 25 on Sept. 1, his latest on Oct. 1.

BANDING: One banded at Charleston, S.C. on Apr. 23, 1967 was recovered at Etobicoke, Ont. on May 4, 1968, about 750 miles to the north. Another banded at Stann Cr., Belize, on March 24, 1964 was recovered near Port Colborne, Ont. in November, 1966, about 1870 miles to the north. (Brewer & Salvadori, 1978: 78)

**MEASUREMENTS:**
*Length:* 5.0 to 6.0 ins.
(Godfrey, 1966: 341)
5.5 to 6.5 ins. (Roberts, 1955: 683)
*Wingspread:* 9.4 to 10.2 ins. (Roberts, 1955: 683)
*Weight:* 7 Ontario specimens averaged 16.9 g.
6 ♂ av. 15.8 g. 3 ♀ av. 16 g. (Hope, 1938: 41).

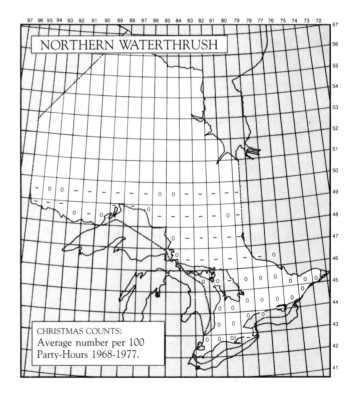

NORTHERN WATERTHRUSH

CHRISTMAS COUNTS:
Average number per 100
Party-Hours 1968-1977.

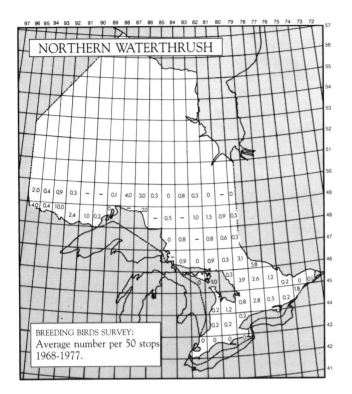

NORTHERN WATERTHRUSH

BREEDING BIRDS SURVEY:
Average number per 50 stops
1968-1977.

# LOUISIANA WATERTHRUSH  *Seiurus motacilla*  (Vieillot)

I associate this active tail bobber with the rapids below small waterfalls along the Niagara Cuesta. It is a rare bird in Ontario in the southern portion, retiring in winter to the region from the Bahamas and Mexico south to northern South America.

**IDENTIFICATION:** From the very similar Northern Waterthrush it is distinguished chiefly by the long *white* line over the eye (buffy in the Northern Waterthrush). The Louisiana is somewhat larger, whiter below and has an unspotted throat (as do some Northerns). The song is quite different, starting with a few sweet upslurred notes, followed by a generally descending jingle, in character with its habitat of tumbling waters (see Saunders, 1935: 207).

**WINTER:**

**SPRING:** C.A. Campbell and P.D. Pratt noted one on Pelee Is. on Apr. 28, 1972 (Goodwin, 1972: 757). Stirrett (1973b: 24) had individual transients at Pelee from Apr. 23 to May 28. J. Wilson had a very early one there on March 28, 1976 (Goodwin, 1976: 714). Ussher (1965: 25) gave May 6 as an 8-year average arrival date at Rondeau, with the earliest on Apr. 29. A. Rider noted one at Kettle Point, Lake Huron, on Apr. 16, 1976 (Goodwin, 1976: 836). Saunders & Dale (1933: 231) gave Apr. 25 as a 5-year average arrival date for the London vicinity, the earliest on Apr. 21, 1917: D. McLeod observed one at Dorchester on Apr. 18, 1979 (Goodwin, 1979: 767). W.J. Preston found a nest with 2 young and a young cowbird near Komoka on May 30, 1936 (Baillie & Harrington, 1937: 252). W.E. Saunders saw one at Turkey Point on May 17, 1925 (Snyder, 1931: 213). I noted one at Bulmer's Glen, near Ancaster, on May 22, 1938. D. Morton and A. Wormington saw a pair at Webster's Falls, near Dundas, as early as Apr. 17, 1971 (Goodwin, 1971: 738-739). C.W. Nash collected a female at Kew Beach, Toronto, on May 8, 1900 (Fleming, 1907: 85): Saunders (1947: 372) gave Apr. 24 as the earliest Toronto date. Weir & Quilliam (1980: 23) cited several spring records for the Kingston region, including one banded at Prince Edward Point on Apr. 22, 1979 and two singing from May 3-25, 1980 in a ravine between Desert Lake and Canoe Lake, where one sang in previous years. D.N. Bucknell found one at Collingwood on Apr. 29, 1972 (Goodwin, 1972: 757). Nicholson (1981: 171) reported one on Great Duck Is. on May 9, 1979.

SUMMER: Kelley (1978: 75) mentioned a nest found at Point Pelee in 1969, though Stirrett (1973c: 21 and 1973d: 27) had no June or July record, with the first fall bird on Aug. 8, and 6 there on Aug. 21. Baillie & Harrington (1937: 252) took a nest with 4 eggs and 3 cowbird eggs at Rondeau on June 2, 1933. Saunders & Dale (1933: 230) gave summer records for Longwood, Hyde Park and Wonnacott's farm, near Delaware, and reported a male collected 4 miles west of Coldstream on June 2, 1913 by W.R. Campbell. Baillie & Harrington, 1937: 252) reported that R.T. Anderson took a set of 3 eggs at Aylmer in 1895 and that Keith Reynolds reported young with adults at Komoka in July, 1935. A. Starling observed one at Long Point on Aug. 20, 1980 (Goodwin, 1981: 178). P. Eagles found one in the Oakland Swamp, Brant Co., in June, 1978 (Goodwin, 1978: 1156). I was present when A.H. Lawrie found a nest with 5 young at Webster's Falls on June 23, 1937 and observed that the adult was not only bobbing up and down but from side to side, so that the tail was swung about like the baton of an orchestra conductor. Brooman (1954: 34) identified one near St. Thomas on Aug. 10, 1947 and Marshall Field saw one there on July 29, 1950. J.B. Miles observed one along the Maitland River on June 8, 1979 (Goodwin, 1979: 860). Ernest Seton collected a female on the Credit River, west of Toronto, on Aug. 23, 1888 (Fleming, 1907: 85). D. McRae found one at Peterborough on July 7, 1976 (Goodwin, 1976: 951). Robert B. Stewart reported one at Kingston on Aug. 3, 1953 (Quilliam, 1973: 164). Chip Weseloh noted one on Wolfe Is. on Aug. 7, 1981 (Goodwin, 1982: 174) and Linda Weseloh had one there on Aug. 16, 1982 (Weir, 1983: 176).

AUTUMN: Quilliam (1973: 164) reported one seen at Squaw Point, Kingston, on Sept. 4, 1954 by Robert B. Stewart. Saunders (1947: 372) gave Sept. 3 and Sept. 11 dates for Toronto. Ussher (1965: 25) gave Oct. 2 as his latest Rondeau record. Stirrett (1973d: 27) had a maximum of 11 on Sept. 5 and his latest at Pelee on Sept. 29.

**MEASUREMENTS:**
*Length:* 5.9 to 6.3 ins.
(Godfrey, 1966: 342)
*Wingspread:* 9 3/4 to 10
3/4 ins. (Roberts,
1955: 683)
*Weight:* 22.4 g. (Terres,
1980: 980).

# KENTUCKY WARBLER   *Oporornis formosus*   (Wilson)

This inhabitant of shady ravines in southeastern United States occasionally overshoots in migration into southern Ontario, where it is much sought after by bird listers. Kentucky Warblers winter from southern Mexico to northern South America.

**IDENTIFICATION:** This is an olive backed warbler with yellow underparts, distinguished by its black crown and "sideburns" and the broad yellow stripe over the eyes and partly surrounding them. The Kentucky Warbler walks about the forest floor like an Ovenbird but bobs its tail like a waterthrush. The song consists of two-syllabled phrases (like an Ovenbird's song) but has the quality of a Carolina Wren's song.

**WINTER:**

**SPRING:** Stirrett (1973b: 24) had individuals at Pelee from Apr. 28 to May 26: a few usually turn up there each spring: T. Hince and B. MacTavish had an early one there on Apr. 22, 1973 (Goodwin, 1973: 768). Rondeau is another locality where they frequently show up in spring: Ussher (1965: 25) reported May 8 records there. G. Bennett and D. Fidler found one at Bradley's Marsh on Apr. 22, 1972 (Goodwin, 1972: 757). Saunders & Dale (1933: 23) reported two specimens taken in Middlesex Co.: the first by Robert Elliott near Bryanston on May 16, 1898 and the second by A.A. Wood two miles north of Strathroy on May 25, 1931. T. Hayman *et al* noted one at London on Apr. 23, 1973 (Goodwin, 1973: 768). At least half a dozen have shown up at Long Point, incluing three on May 11, 1979 according to M. Dyer (Goodwin, 1979: 767). Beardslee & Mitchell (1965: 389) reported individuals at Rockhouse Point on May 18, 1958 and at Morgan's Point, Lake Erie on May 27, 1962. D. Bucknell saw one at Mud Lake, Oxford Co., on May 23, 1978 (Goodwin, 1978: 1000). Individuals turned up at Ancaster on May 19, 1973, noted by R. Curry (Goodwin, 1973: 768) and again on May 26, 1981, seen by C. and S. Wood (Goodwin, 1981: 820). At nearby Hamilton many observers saw one on May 22, 1972 (Goodwin, 1972: 757). G. Bellerby found one on the Toronto Is. on May 17, 1971 (Goodwin, 1971: 739) and another at Downsview on May 10, 1972 (Goodwin, 1972: 757). Four were observed at Toronto between May 9 and 19, 1979, including one killed, noted by M. Butler, A. Dawe and R. & D. Scovell (Goodwin, 1979: 767). R. Powley found another at Toronto on May 12, 1981 (Goodwin, 1981: 820). R.C. Long saw one at Pickering Beach on May 30, 1964 (Speirs, 1974). Margaret Bain turned one up at Whitby on May 28, 1982 (Weir, 1982: 848). Weir & Quilliam (1980: 24) cited several records from Prince Edward Point: May 18 & 21, 1975; May 21 and 24 (2 banded) in 1977; May 11 and 13, 1979 (both netted and one photographed) and finally May 11, 1980 (netted). Devitt (1967: 147) reported one found by W.W. Smith about 4 miles southwest of Bradford, along the Holland River, on May 8, 1943: this bird was also seen by John Crosby, O.E. Devitt, R.M. Saunders and D. Sutherland and finally collected, the third Ontario specimen (Smith & Devitt, 1943: 247). Doris H. Speirs noted the diagnostic black and yellow face pattern of one at South Baymouth, Manitoulin, on May 28, 1947 and Nicholson (1981: 171) saw one on Great Duck Is. on May 9, 1979.

**SUMMER:** Ussher (1965: 25) had an Aug. 28 record for Rondeau. Erica Nol banded one at Long Point on Aug. 12, 1976 (Goodwin, 1977: 172). A. Rider reported birds at Kettle Point on June 1, 1979 (Goodwin, 1979: 860), June 6 and 10, 1982 (Goodwin, 1982: 174 and June 7-10, 1981 (Goodwin, 1981: 936). T. Hince observed a male at

Rockport, Leeds Co. on June 3, 1982 (Weir, 1982: 973) and R.D. Weir found one at Marlbank, Hastings Co. singing on June 13, 1981 (Goodwin, 1981: 936).

AUTUMN: Nicholson (1981: 171) saw a male on Great Duck Is. on Sept. 28, 1978. R.C. Long saw one at Pickering Beach on Sept. 22, 1967 (Speirs, 1974). One was noted at the Long Point Bird Observatory on Sept. 3, 1971 (Goodwin, 1972: 59) and another was killed at the lighthouse there on Oct. 25-26, 1976 (Goodwin, 1977: 172). R. Finlayson observed one at Pelee on Sept. 1, 1982 (Goodwin, 1982: 174).

**MEASUREMENTS:**
*Length:* 5.0 to 5.8 ins.
(Godfrey, 1966: 342)
Wingspread:
*Weight:* 12 averaged 14 g.
(Terres, 1980: 972).

**REFERENCE:**
Smith, W.W. and O.E. Devitt 1943 The Kentucky Warbler in the Toronto region. Wilson Bull., 55: (4): 247.
As well as the Bradford specimen noted above this article mentioned 4 spring sight records: one for Hamilton on May 3, 1942 and three for Toronto: on May 12, 1933; May 27, 1938 and May 10-12, 1943.

# CONNECTICUT WARBLER   *Oporornis agilis*   (Wilson)

This secretive warbler eludes most of us as it migrates through southern Ontario, though surprising numbers sometimes occur at tower kills. It is also rare in most of its breeding range in our northern bogs: only near Lake of the Woods have I found it at all common, and then in willow thickets rather than the open spruce bogs favoured elsewhere in northern Ontario. They retire to northern South America in winter.

IDENTIFICATION: Apart from its distinct eye ring, the Connecticut Warbler looks a great deal like a female Mourning Warbler, with green back, blue hood and yellow underparts. The smaller Nashville Warbler is distinguished by its yellow throat and tree-top habitat: the Connecticut is a skulker in thickets. The loud, emphatic, lip-smacking song has been variously rendered: I rather like the version in Smith (1950: 179) "spik-a spaka spik-a spaka spic-a spacka - spik" without change of emphasis, rather like the song of a Yellow throat."

WINTER:

SPRING: Stirrett (1973b: 25) had Pelee records from May 9 to June 1, with a maximum of 6 on May 27. Ussher (1965: 25) had Rondeau records from May 11 to June 4, with average arrival on May 20 and departure on May 29. Saunders & Dale (1933: 231) gave May 24 as a 14-year average arrival date at London, with the earliest on May 20, 1922. Earl Lemon had an extremely early record of one in West Elgin on Apr. 2, 1947: two specimens were collected in Elgin Co., one on May 30, 1888, the other on May 24, 1889 (Brooman, 1954: 34). Snyder (1931: 213) gave Long Point records for May 14, 1925 (a lighthouse casualty), June 1, 1924 and June 4, 1927 (a specimen). Speirs (1938: 39, 45) listed Toronto records from May 10 to June 3. Audrey Russ noted one at Ajax as early as May 9 in 1965 but most in this region were observed from May 19 to June 2 (Speirs, 1974). Weir & Quilliam (1980: 39) listed Kingston records from May 16 to May 31, with a 7-year average arrival on May 23. Devitt (1967: 147) had just five Simcoe Co. sightings in spring, from May 13 (1957) by Frances Westman to June 3 (1942) by W.W. Smith. Mills (1981: 149) cited Huntsville records for May 11, 1962 and May 15, 1974. One was killed at the Great Duck Is. tower on May 28, 1979 and Chip Weseloh saw one on Fitzwilliam Is. on May 22, 1980 (Nicholson, 1981: 171). Skeel & Bondrup-Nielsen (1978: 208) heard one at Pukaskwa on May 28, 1977. Denis (1961: 4) gave May 20 as the average arrival date at Thunder Bay, with the earliest on May 15, 1949. Peruniak (1971: 27) gave May 22 as her earliest Atikokan record.

SUMMER: On the 1968-1977 Breeding Bird Surveys, they were rare at Thessalon, uncommon north to Longlac and Jellicoe and fairly common locally at Elk Lake, Cochrane, Smooth Rock Falls and from Thunder Bay west to Kenora. Stirrett (1973c: 21) had a returning bird at Pelee on Aug. 12, with a few there later in August. Naomi LeVay noted one at Eastbourne, Whitby, as early as Aug. 5, 1963 (Speirs, 1974). J.H. Fleming reported a probable sighting at Rockcliffe, Ottawa, on Aug. 15, 1898 (Lloyd, 1924: 15). Mills (1981: 149) cited records of birds banded at Port Loring on July 1, 1974 and Aug. 24, 1975 and birds identified at Magnetawan on July 24, 1944 and July 24, 1979 by D. MacDonald. Skeel & Bondrup-Nielsen (1978: 208) heard two on June 7 and one on June 9, 1977 at Pukaskwa. Baillie & Hope (1943: 22) heard a few in spruce bogs near Amyot, where they collected two males, one on June 30 and one on July 1, 1936. Snyder (1928: 274) collected a male at Lake Nipigon on June 27, 1924: he rendered its song as "ca-chicka-chicka, chicka-chicka, chicka-chicka." Dear (1940: 139) reported several males in a large spruce bog at Whitefish Lake, near Thunder Bay, in June, 1935. Peruniak (1971: 27) called this a fairly common summer resident at Atikokan: David Elder noted one there on June 7, 1981. On June 18, 1971, Donald Price, Doris Speirs and I heard seven singing as we approached Lake of the Woods Provincial Park, mostly in willow scrub habitat. Snyder (1953: 80) reported up to 8 at Ingolf, 3 at Wabigoon, 3 at Savanne, 3 at Sioux Lookout, 2 at Malachi and 3 at Kenora, during summers from 1937 to 1949. Elder (1979: 38) gave June 1 as his earliest date for this uncommon, local summer resident at Geraldton. Smith (1957: 178-179) heard two singing near Kapuskasing on June 30, 1953, collected a male about 7 miles north of Hearst on June 2, 1954 and heard one 30 miles west of Hearst on June 4, 1954. Snyder (1928: 31) heard one at Lowbush, Lake Abitibi, on June 3, 1925. Ross James heard from one to three almost daily from June 2 to 14, 1977, near Pickle Lake. Hope (1938: 41) called this "a rare inhabitant of the dense black spruce bogs" at Favourable Lake, where he collected two males, one on June 11 and one on July 6, 1938. Cringan (1950: 17) heard individuals in the Nikip Lake area on June 12 and July 9, 1950. Wm. C. Baker found an adult attending a fully grown young bird on Aug. 9, 1949 about 25 miles west of Cochrane: W. Clyde Todd shot one at Moose Factory on Aug. 24, 1931 and his party noted one singing there on June 11, 1926 (Todd, 1963: 621-

622). McLaren & McLaren (1981: 5) recorded the species north to Little Sachigo Lake (about 100 km. north of their known breeding range).

AUTUMN: Louise Lawrence saw one at Pimisi Bay on Sept. 20, 1952 (Todd, 1963: 622). Nicholson (1981: 171) had half a dozen Manitoulin records from Aug. 30 (1975) to Sept. 28 (1969) including Great Duck Is. casualties: one on Sept. 18 and 2 on Sept. 22, 1977. Southbound migrants were noted in Simcoe Co. from Sept. 2 (1940) to Sept. 30 (1965): 16 were killed at the Barrie TV tower in 5 of 7 years (Devitt, 1967: 148). Weir & Quilliam (1981: 39) had fall records at Kingston from Aug. 24 to Oct. 2. David Calvert noted one near Oshawa on Oct. 4, 1970 (Tozer & Richards, 1974: 254). Saunders (1947: 373) listed Toronto records from Aug. 13 to Oct. 20. H.H. Axtell collected two at Erie Beach: one on Sept. 29, 1954, the other on Oct. 1, 1954 (Beardslee & Mitchell, 1965: 390). Snyder (1931: 213) cited Long Point casualties: 8 on Sept. 7, 6 on Sept. 9 and 35 from Sept. 24-29, 1929. Brooman (1954: 34) saw one at St. Thomas on Sept. 8, 1940. Ussher (1965: 25) had fall birds at Rondeau from Aug. 26 to Sept. 10. Stirrett (1973d: 27) had a maximum of 7 on Sept. 7 at Pelee.

**MEASUREMENTS:**
*Length:* 5.2 to 6.0 ins.
(Godfrey, 1966: 343)
*Wingspread:* 8.5 to 9.0
ins. (Roberts, 1955: 679)
*Weight:* 2 ♂ averaged
19.1 g. (Hope, 1938: 41).

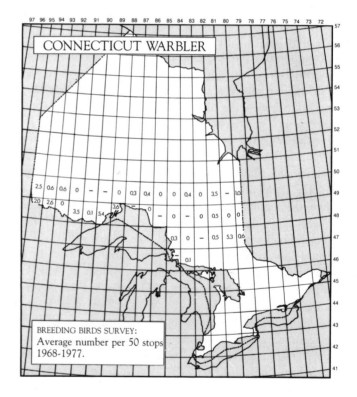

CONNECTICUT WARBLER

BREEDING BIRDS SURVEY:
Average number per 50 stops
1968-1977.

# MOURNING WARBLER   *Oporornis philadelphia*   (Wilson)

Mourning Warblers generally arrive in southern Ontario in spring after most other warblers have gone through, when trees are in full leaf and they are difficult to see. Fortunately they have an easily identifiable song. In the Precambrian portion of Ontario they are one of the more common warblers in summer, in shrubbery along roadsides and at the edge of clearings or burns. The more mature spruce forests they leave to the "budworm species". In winter they are found in southern Central America and northern South America.

**IDENTIFICATION:** This is a blue hooded, green backed warbler with no wing bars and with yellow underparts. Males have a blackish "bib". They lack the eye rings of Connecticut and MacGillivray's Warblers and lack the yellow throat of Nashville Warblers. The rich, liquid song reminds me of the phrases: "Chewy-chewy-choy-choy". Charles Fothergill wrote on July 8, 1821: "It was continually uttering a sharp snapping note by which I discovered it" (once learned this "fitz" note is a valuable field character).

**WINTER:**

**SPRING:** Stirrett (1973b: 25) had Pelee records from May 10 to June 1, with a maximum of 6 on May 17. Ussher (1965: 25) noted birds at Rondeau from May 6 to June 6, with average arrival on May 17 and departure on May 30. Saunders & Dale (1933: 231) gave May 19 as the 17-year average arrival date at London, with the earliest on May 12, 1915. Snyder (1931: 214) reported 23 casualties at the Long Point lighthouse on May 14, 1925 and one on May 19, 1926: he collected one there as late as June 4, 1927. Mrs. W.H. Marcy picked up a specimen at Abino Bay, Lake Erie, as early as May 5, 1938 (Beardslee & Mitchell, 1965: 391). J.L. Baillie (in Saunders, 1947: 373) had one at Toronto as early as May 6 but his 20-year average arrival date was May 20: Speirs (1938: 43) gave May 30 as the spring peak date for Toronto. Speirs (1974) had only one record before mid-May in Ontario Co., one seen by George A. Scott at Oshawa on May 2, 1944. Weir & Quilliam (1980: 39) listed May 17 as the 26-year average arrival date at Kingston, with the earliest on May 7. Devitt (1967: 148) gave May 23 as the 15-year average arrival date at Barrie, with the earliest on May 3, 1958. Mills (1981: 149) gave May 23 as the 7-year average arrival date at Huntsville, the earliest on May 12, 1963. Louise Lawrence noted 8 at Rutherglen on May 22, 1945 (Speirs & Speirs, 1947: 36). Skeel & Bondrup-Nielsen (1978: 208) heard their first at Pukaskwa on May 30, 1977. Denis (1961: 4) gave May 27 as the average arrival date at Thunder Bay, with the earliest on May 24, 1942. Peruniak (1971: 27) had one very early one at Atikokan on Apr. 30, 1965 but the next earliest was on May 11.

**SUMMER:** On the 1968-1977 Breeding Bird Surveys they were common on most northern routes, becoming rare in agricultural areas in the south. Stirrett (1973c: 21) had 6 returning birds at Pelee as early as Aug. 12. Ussher (1965: 25) had his earliest fall bird at Rondeau on Aug. 20. A nest with eggs was found at Pleasant Beach, Lake Erie, on June 28, 1941 and a returning bird was noted at Morgan's Point as early as Aug. 19, 1945 (Beardslee & Mitchell, 1965: 391). C.W. Nash took a young bird from the nest at Toronto on July 1, 1893 and J. Hughes Samuel saw adults feeding young there on July 30, 1895 (Fleming, 1907: 85). C.E. Hope collected 3 eggs and a cowbird egg from a nest at Mt. Dennis, Toronto, on June 15, 1930 (Baillie & Harrington, 1937: 253). Speirs & Orenstein

(1975: 14) reported population densities of 8 birds per 100 acres in their Brock and Scott Twp. quadrats and 23 birds per 100 acres in the Whitby Twp. plot, all wet, mid-succession forests: they had none in the two pioneer forests and none in the more mature forest quadrats in Ontario Co. Don Sands found a nest with 2 eggs on July 9, 1967 near Oshawa: this nest still held 2 eggs on July 19; one young hatched by July 20 and both by July 21 (Tozer & Richards, 1974: 255). An adult was observed carrying food on June 28, 1930 at Woodrous, Prince Edward Co. (Snyder, 1941: 81). R.V. Lindsay saw a female carrying food at Mountain Grove, Frontenac Co., on July 6, 1926 (Baillie & Harrington, 1937: 253). Devitt (1967: 148) counted 25 singing males along 4 miles of the Nottawasaga River through the Minesing Swamp on June 28, 1967: a set of 2 eggs and a cowbird egg was taken there on June 9, 1929. Mills (1981: 150) found a nest with one egg at Ahmic Lake on June 18, 1975: this held 5 eggs on June 22. C.H.D. Clarke watched an adult carrying food at Brule Lake, Algonquin Park, on July 3, 1934 (MacLulich, 1938: 35). Louise Lawrence saw young being fed at Pimisi Bay on July 15 and 21, 1944 (Speirs & Speirs, 1947: 36). Baillie & Hope (1947: 25) collected a young female at Bigwood on July 24, 1937 but found them more common at their Chapleau and Biscotasing camps. Snyder (1942: 145) collected a young male at Maclennan on July 6, 1931 and considered them common in the Sault Ste. Marie region. Skeel & Bondrup-Nielsen (1978: 208) found them rare in summer at Pukaskwa from lack of suitable habitat. Baillie & Hope (1943: 22) collected males at Rossport, Marathon and Amyot where they called them "not uncommon". Snyder (1928: 274) found them common in clearings at Lake Nipigon: found a partial set of eggs at Macdiarmid on June 29, 1923 and collected a young female just out of the nest there on July 24, 1924. Dear (1940: 139) found a nest with 4 eggs on July 1, 1923 and a nest with 4 eggs on June 19, 1927 at Thunder Bay. Kendeigh (1947: 28, 34) had a density of 2 pairs per 100 acres on his forested plots at Black Sturgeon Lake in 1945 but 9 pairs per 100 acres on a cutover area there. H.P. Stovell found a nest with 1 egg near Emo on June 16, 1929 (Snyder, 1938: 206). Snyder (1953: 80) ranked it 4th in abundance of the resident warblers in western Ontario from Savanne to Malachi, in clearings and edge conditions. Elder (1979: 38) had his earliest Geraldton bird on May 31, where it was a common summer resident. Bondrup-Nielsen (1976: 45) noted his first at Kapuskasing on June 3 in 1974 and on June 4 in 1975. Ross James had a maximum of 3 on June 5 at Pickle Lake in 1977 and just three other June records there. Hope (1938: 41) collected two males and a female at Favourable Lake in 1938 "in clearings in deciduous forests". Cringan (1953a: 3) noted his first at Sioux Lookout on June 9 in 1953. One was collected at Sandy Is., Moosonee, on June 20, 1949 (Manning, 1952: 85). James, Nash & Peck (1982: 69) found a nest with 5 eggs on June 24, 1982, by the Harricanaw River, near James Bay. Schueler, Baldwin & Rising (1974: 144) noted the species at Cochrane, Moosonee and Attawapiskat. Lee (1978: 32) noted a single singing male at Big Trout Lake on June 17, 23 and 27, 1975.

AUTUMN: One was seen at Albany on Sept. 22, 1940 (Lewis & Peters, 1941: 114). Peruniak (1971: 27) gave Sept. 16 as her latest Atikokan date. N.G. Escott saw a very late bird at Marathon on Oct. 17, 1975 (Skeel & Bondrup-Nielsen, 1978: 208). Nicholson (1981: 172) gave Oct. 6, 1973 as his latest Manitoulin record: 87 were killed at the Great Duck Is. tower from Sept. 18-23, 1977. The latest cottage country date was Oct. 6, 1885, a Port Sydney specimen in the ROM (Mills, 1981: 150). Two were killed at the Barrie TV tower on Sept. 24, 1960, the latest of 11 killed there in 5 of 7 years (Devitt, 1967: 148). Weir & Quilliam (1980: 39) listed Sept. 14 as the 20-year average departure date from

Kingston, the latest on Sept. 28. Saunders (1947: 373) had a late one at Toronto on Oct. 18. Snyder (1931: 214) cited Long Point lighthouse casualties: 20 on Sept. 7, 5 on Sept. 9 and 12 from Sept. 24-29, 1929. Ussher (1965: 25) gave Oct. 1 as his latest at Rondeau. Stirrett (1973d: 27) also reported one at Pelee as late as Oct. 1.

**MEASUREMENTS:**
*Length:* 5 to 5 3/4 ins.
(Godfrey, 1966: 343)
*Wingspread:* 7.60 to 8.15
ins. (Roberts, 1955: 679)
*Weight:* 29 Ontario
specimens averaged
12.2 g.

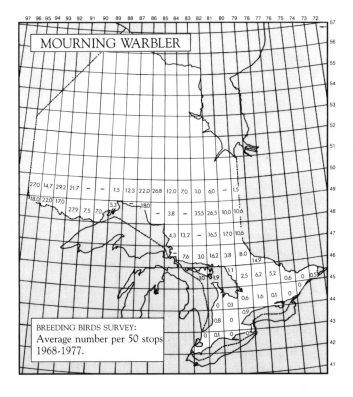

MOURNING WARBLER

BREEDING BIRDS SURVEY:
Average number per 50 stops
1968-1977.

# MACGILLIVRAY'S WARBLER
*Oporornis tolmiei* (Townsend)

MacGillivray's Warbler is the western counterpart of our Mourning Warbler: some authors suggest that they are conspecific, or form a superspecies. One stray turned up near Hamilton. They winter mainly in western Central America.

IDENTIFICATION: Adult males look very much like Mourning Warblers except that they have white spots above and below the eyes (incomplete eye rings) while Mourning Warblers have no eye rings (usually) and Connecticut Warblers have complete eye rings. Banders should consult Lanyon and Bull (1967: 189-190) for distinguishing measurements: the wing - tail formula for this species ranges from 2 to 11 mm., for Mourning Warblers it is 10 to 18 mm. and for Connecticut Warblers is 19-27 mm. (MacGillivrays have the longest tails and Connecticuts the longest wings of these three similar species).

WINTER:

SPRING: One specimen (# 507393) in the collection of the American Museum of Natural History was collected at Hamilton on May 20, 1890 (Lanyon & Bull., 1967: 188).

SUMMER:

AUTUMN:

**MEASUREMENTS:**
*Length:* 4.8 to 5.5 ins.
(Godfrey, 1966: 344)
Wingspread:
*Weight:* 26 averaged
10.4 g. (8.6 - 12.6 g.)
(Dunning, 1984: 22).

**REFERENCE:**
Lanyon, Wesley E. and
John Bull 1967
Identification of
Connecticut, Mourning
and MacGillivray's
Warblers. Bird-Banding,
38: (3): 187-194.

# COMMON YELLOWTHROAT   *Geothlypis trichas*   (Linnaeus)

In summer this is one of our most common warblers, usually found in thickets near wet areas. A few may linger in such areas until Christmas time in southern Ontario though most go south to Central America and the West Indies in winter.

IDENTIFICATION: Yellowthroats are more often heard than seen: their characteristic "wichety - wichety - wichety - witch" betraying their presence around marshes, bogs, and wet areas in fields and on roadsides. Local dialects differ chiefly in the emphasis placed on the various syllables in the song. In northern Ontario the rare Connecticut Warbler has a somewhat similar song, but is usually more emphatic and with a lip-smacking quality. Males, with their black masks, outlined above with blue, present no problem in identification. Females look a bit like the rare Kentucky Warbler but live in more open habitats.

WINTER: On the 1968-1977 Christmas counts they were uncommon to rare near the shores of Lake Erie and Lake Ontario, with outliers north to Peterborough and Wiarton. Stirrett (1973a: 19) had his latest one at Pelee on Dec. 16. Ussher (1965: 26) had one winter record at Rondeau, on Feb. 26. Saunders (1947: 378-379) listed Christmas count individuals at Toronto in 1927 and 1938. Parker (1983: 25) reported Toronto birds on six Christmas counts, with January and February records as well. Speirs (1974) had about a dozen winter records for Ontario Co., the latest at Eastbourne, Whitby, by Naomi LeVay on Jan. 30, 1967. Weir & Quilliam (1980: 39) listed Dec. 16 as the latest Kingston record.

SPRING: Stirrett (1973b: 25) had his earliest Pelee bird on Apr. 25, with a maximum of 100 on May 23. Ussher (1965: 26) gave May 5 as his 22-year average arrival date for Rondeau, with the earliest on Apr. 27. Saunders & Dale (1933: 232) gave May 7 as the 17-year average arrival date at London, with the earliest on Apr. 25, 1925. Snyder (1931: 214) had his earliest at Long Point on May 3 in 1928, with peak numbers from May 17 to May 22. McCracken, Bradstreet & Holroyd, (1981: 63) reported a nest with one egg at Long Point on May 26, 1974 and a nest with 4 eggs on May 31, 1979. J.L. Baillie (in Saunders, 1947: 373) gave May 3 as his earliest Toronto record with May 13 as his 27-year average arrival date. Speirs (1938: 43) gave May 24 as the spring peak at Toronto. Parker (1983: 25) indicated a March and an April record for Toronto. Naomi LeVay noted one at Cranberry Marsh as early as Apr. 27, 1953 (Tozer & Richards, 1974: 255). Weir & Quilliam (1980: 39) listed May 7 as the 32-year average arrival date at Kingston, with the earliest on Apr. 30. Devitt (1967: 149) gave May 13 as the 22-year average arrival date at Barrie, with the earliest on Apr. 28, 1938. L. Beamer's median arrival date at Meaford was May 16, with the earliest on May 11, 1944. Mills (1981: 151) gave May 9 as the 7-year average arrival date at Huntsville, with one very early one on Apr. 24, 1977; he observed a pair nest building at Magnetawan as early as May 23, 1976. Nicholson (1981: 172) gave May 12 as a 12-year average arrival date for Manitoulin, with the earliest on May 6, 1972 and a high count of 200 on Great Duck Is. on May 23, 1976. MacLulich (1938: 35) gave May 19, 1933 as his earliest Algonquin Park record. Louise Lawrence noted one as early as May 6, 1944 at Rutherglen (Speirs & Speirs, 1947: 36). Skeel & Bondrup-Nielsen (1978: 208) heard 3 at Pukaskwa on May 23, 1977. Baillie & Hope (1943: 22) had just one record at Rossport, on May 31, 1936. Denis (1961: 4) gave May 23 as his average arrival date at Thunder Bay, with the earliest on May 12, 1955. Peruniak (1971: 27) gave May 15 as her earliest Atikokan date. Elder (1979: 38) had his earliest at Geraldton on May 21. Bondrup-Nielsen (1976: 45) noted his first near Kapus-kasing on May 29, 1975. Oliver Hewitt saw two at Moosonee on May 22, 1947 (Manning, 1952: 85). Lee (1978: 32) saw two at Bearskin Lake on May 29, 1975.

SUMMER: On the 1968-1977 Breeding Bird Surveys they were fairly common on some routes in agricultural areas and along the north shore of Lake Superior, common on all other routes, and most nummerous in the North Bay region. Stirrett (1973c: 21) had a summer maximum of 15 at Pelee on June 27. Snyder (1931: 214) reported a nest with one egg at Long Point on June 8, 1927: other nests there included five nests with eggs found on June 7, 1969 and a nest with 3 young on June 17, 1960 (McCracken, Bradstreet & Holroyd, 1981: 63). Speirs & Orenstein (1975: 14) had a population density of 66 birds per 100 acres on their pioneer forest quadrat in Mara Twp. with smaller densities in 4 other early succession forests in Ontario Co. but none in the 6 more mature forest plots. J.M. Richards found a nest with 2 eggs and 6 cowbird eggs on June 12, 1965, near Whitby and I found a nest with 4 eggs in Mara Twp. on June 22, 1966 (Speirs, 1974). J.M.Richards found a nest with 4 eggs on July 14, 1968 which held 3 young on July 17, in Darlington Twp. (Tozer & Richards, 1974: 255). Quilliam (1973: 165) mentioned two nests, both with 4 eggs, found near Kingston: one by F. Starr on July 10, 1920 and the other by E. Beaupré on June 4, 1922. H.P. Bingham found a nest with 5 eggs near Barrie as early as June 2, 1933 and Frances Westman a nest with 3 eggs near Barrie as late as July 23, 1964 (Devitt, 1967: 149). Mills (1981: 160) reported 17 nests in the cottage country. Macoun (1904: 638) reported a nest with 4 young about a week old in Algonquin Park on June 26, 1900. Louise Lawrence watched a male feeding young at Pimisi Bay on July 15, 1944 (Speirs & Speirs, 1947: 36). Baillie & Hope (1947: 26) found a nest with 4 eggs at Chapleau on June 16, 1937 and collected 4 young at Bigwood from July 16 - 23, 1937. Snyder (1942: 145) found a nest with 4 eggs on June 29, 1931 near Sault Ste. Marie. Skeel & Bondrup-Nielsen (1978: 208) called it a "scarce summer resident" at Pukaskwa in 1977. Again emphasizing the scarcity along the north shore of Lake Superior, Baillie & Hope (1943: 22) found none at Marathon and recorded just two at Amyot (one collected) and heard one at Franz on July 7, 1936. Dear (1940: 139) found a nest with 5 eggs on June 14, 1937 near Thunder Bay. Snyder (1938: 206) saw a female carrying food near Rainy River on June 27. 1929 and collected young there on July 30 and Aug. 6. In western Ontario, Snyder (1953: 81) found them "rather plentiful" in the Kenora region, becoming scarce from Sioux Lookout to Savanne. We found this to be by far the most abundant species in a leatherleaf bog quadrat near Geraldton in 1971 with a breeding density of 80 territories per 100 acres (Elder, Price & Speirs, 1971: 1006). Smith (1957: 179) called them "Common on marshes and bogs throughout the Clay Belt". Ross James observed just two individuals near Pickle Lake, on June 1 and 12, 1977. Cringan (1953b: 4) recorded two at Kasabonika Lake on June 3, 1953. James, Nash & Peck (1982: 70) saw recently fledged young on July 4, 1982 by the Harricanaw River near James Bay. Manning (1952: 85) saw two and collected one of them at Albany River. James, Nash & Peck (1981: 92) noted a vagrant at Kiruna Lake in the summer of 1980. Lee (1978: 32) noted the species at Big Trout Lake only on June 6 and 12, 1975. McLaren & McLaren (1981: 5) heard singing males near Lysander Lake on June 4 and near Sachigo Lake on June 9, 1977.

AUTUMN: D. McRae and A. Wormington noted one at Netitishi Point, James Bay, as late as Oct. 22, 1981. Lewis and Peters, 1941: 114) noted one at Albany on Sept. 22,

1940. Oliver Hewitt observed 4 at Ship Sands, near Moosonee, on Sept. 24-25, 1947 (Manning, 1952: 85). Peruniak (1971: 27) gave Sept. 21 as her latest Atikokan date. Skeel & Bondrup-Nielsen (1978: 208) reported their latest at Pukaskwa on Sept. 7, 1977. Speirs & Speirs (1947: 36) had their latest at North Bay on Oct. 5, 1944. Nicholson (1981: 172) reported 277 casualties at the Great Duck Is. tower from Sept. 18-23, 1977 and his latest Manitoulin date was on Oct. 29, 1978. Mills (1981: 151) reported a late one at Huntsville on Oct. 14, 1963. Devitt (1967: 149) reported 133 killed at the Barrie TV tower in 7 years, the latest on Oct. 14, 1966. Weir & Quilliam (1980: 39) gave Oct. 16 as the 27-year average departure date from Kingston. I saw one as late as Oct. 24, 1972 at Glen Major, Uxbridge Twp. (Speirs, 1974). Saunders (1947: 373) gave Oct. 7 as his 13-year average departure date from Toronto, with his latest on Nov. 26. Snyder (1931: 214) reported very heavy casualties at the Long Point lighthouse: 111 on Sept. 7, 29 on Sept. 9 and 114 from Sept. 24-29, 1929. Ussher (1965: 26) gave Sept. 27 as his 9-year average departure date from Rondeau, with his latest on Oct. 21. Stirrett (1973d: 27) had a fall maximum of 10 at Pelee on Sept. 7.

BANDING: One banded at Chatham on May 26, 1968 was recovered at Christmas, Florida (about 965 miles to the south) on Oct. 8, 1971 (Brewer & Salvadori, 1976: 87). Brewer & Salvadori (1978: 79) reported two others: one banded at E. Tawas, Mich., on Sept. 16, 1961 was taken at Balmoral Marsh, Ont. (about 136 miles SE) on May 16, 1966: another banded at Long Point on Sept. 23, 1968 was recovered about a week later at Coolspring Reservoir, Pa. (185 miles to the south) on Oct. 1, 1968.

**MEASUREMENTS:**
*Length:* 4.5 to 5.7 ins. (Godfrey, 1966: 345)
*Wingspread:* 6.5 to 7.2 ins. (Roberts, 1955: 669)
*Weight:* 91 Ontario specimens averaged 11.61 g.

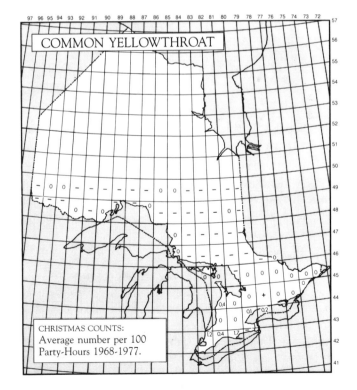

COMMON YELLOWTHROAT

CHRISTMAS COUNTS:
Average number per 100
Party-Hours 1968-1977.

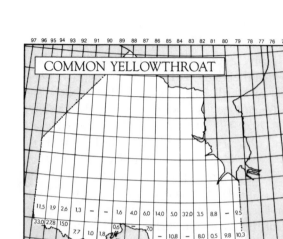

COMMON YELLOWTHROAT

BREEDING BIRDS SURVEY:
Average number per 50 stops
1968-1977.

# HOODED WARBLER  *Wilsonia citrina*  (Boddaert)

The Hooded Warbler is a Carolinian species that breeds in a few relict old forests along the southern fringe of Ontario. They winter in Central America.

**IDENTIFICATION:** The male with its black hood surrounding yellow face and forehead is easily identified. The female looks something like a big Wilson's Warbler but has much white in its tail (lacking in Wilson's). The song resembles the song of the Magnolia Warbler but is louder: if you hear a "Magnolia song" in a southern hardwood forest in summer, look for a Hooded!

**WINTER:**

**SPRING:** Stirrett (1973b: 25) had records of single birds at Pelee from Apr. 23 to May 31: Goodwin (1978: 1000) reported about 25 there on May 15, 1978. Ussher (1965: 26) gave May 15 as the 11-year average arrival date at Rondeau, with the earliest on Apr. 30. Saunders & Dale (1933: 232) saw one near London on May 24, 1931: there have been several more recent sightings at nearby Newbury, including one on May 15, 1980 by J.W. Leach (Goodwin, 1980: 772). Birds were reported at the Long Point Bird Observatory on May 13, 1972 (Goodwin, 1972: 757) and on May 16 and 23, 1971 (Goodwin, 1971: 739). Sheppard (1960: 43) reported one found dead at Niagara Falls as early as Apr. 14, 1950. M. Furber noted one at Cayuga on May 8, 1982 (Weir, 1982: 848). M. Jennings reported individuals at Burlington on Apr. 25, 1975 and at Bronte on June 1, 1975

(Goodwin, 1975: 847). Saunders (1947: 155, 373) gave details of a sighting in Cedarvale Ravine, Toronto, on May 15, 1946 and listed early birds on Apr. 6 and 13, 1947 - see Gunn & Crocker (1951: 145). Speirs (1974) had 10 spring records for the Whitby-Oshawa area, from May 8 (1965) to May 25 (1963): there have been several recent records in spring, chiefly from Thickson's Woods, Whitby. R. John spotted one at Willow Beach, near Cobourg, on May 24, 1980 (Goodwin, 1980: 772). Weir & Quilliam (1980: 39) listed Kingston records from May 3 to May 23, with an 8-year average arrival on May 13. Nicholson (1981: 73) noted individuals at Mississagi Light on May 18, 1976; at Great Duck Is. on Apr. 26, 1979 and again there on May 26, 1979.

SUMMER: Stirrett (1973c: 21, 1973d: 27) had probable migrants at Pelee on Aug. 12, 21 and 31. Ussher (1965: 26) had a July 6 record for Rondeau: R. Simpson noted one there on June 26, 1971 (Goodwin, 1971: 854). J. Grom and T.N. Hayman found a nest at Newbury, near London, on June 9, 1978 (Goodwin, 1978: 1156) and there have been several other summer records near London. On July 27, 1949, Fred Bodsworth found a nest with 3 eggs in Springwater Park, Elgin Co.: other nests were found there in 1950 and 1952 (Brooman, 1954: 34): Speirs & Frank (1970: 742) found a population density of 10 pairs per 100 acres in this mature beech forest in June, 1970, where they favoured ravines with an understory of spicebush: the Hooded Warbler ranked fifth in abundance of the 20 species found on their study quadrat. A. Rider reported one at Thedford in the summer of 1980 (Goodwin, 1980: 892). A. Epp heard one singing to mid-June, 1976 at Hamilton (Goodwin, 1976: 951) and R.H. Westmore noted another there on Aug. 25, 1978 (Goodwin, 1979: 174). Naomi LeVay noted one at Eastbourne, Whitby, on Aug. 25, 1955. Weir & Quilliam (1980: 24) had a Kingston record for Aug. 24, 1974. Frances Westman observed a singing male near Barrie on June 9, 1959 (Devitt, 1967: 149). B. DiLabio and J. Harris observed one at Ottawa on July 30, 1975 (Goodwin, 1975: 966). Gerald McKeating saw one at South Baymouth, Manitoulin, on Aug. 13, 1968 (Nicholson, 1981: 173).

AUTUMN: M. Jennings and A. Wormington had an amazing sighting at Moosonee on Sept. 27, 1976 (Goodwin, 1977: 172). Nicholson (1981: 173) saw one at Cape Robert, Manitouin, on Sept. 19, 1971 and reported a very late one observed by J. Smith, at Indian Point on Nov. 22, 1959. Weir & Quilliam (1980: 24) had Kingston records for Sept. 2, 1973 and Sept. 21, 1980. Naomi LeVay observed birds at Eastbourne, Whitby, on Sept. 1, 1959 and Sept. 11, 1964 (Speirs, 1974). J.L. Baillie and R.M. Saunders reported one at a TOC meeting, seen on Nov. 2, 1957 in Toronto. The Long Point Bird Observatory reported one on Sept. 15, 1982 (Weir, 1983: 176). J.E. Strickland *et al* saw one at Hawk Cliff on Sept. 18, 1978 (Goodwin, 1979: 174). Stirrett (1973d: 27) had Pelee records for Sept. 7, 21 and 23.

**MEASUREMENTS:**
*Length:* 5 to 5 3/4 ins.
(Godfrey, 1966: 346)
*Wingspread:* 8 to 8 1/4
ins. (Terres, 1980: 971)
*Weight:* 46 averaged
10.7 g. (Terres,
1980: 972).

# WILSON'S WARBLER   *Wilsonia pusilla*   (Wilson)

This active little warbler sings its jittery song from alder-willow thickets in northern Ontario bottomlands in summer, retiring to winter in Central America and southern United States.

**IDENTIFICATION:** Wilson's Warbler is a small, active, generally yellow bird with greenish back and black cap (olive-gray in some females). Hooded Warbler females look like female Wilson's but are much bigger and have much white in the tail (lacking in Wilson's). The song is an energetic "jit-jit-jit-jit-jetty-jit" with a rather wooden quality.

**WINTER:**

**SPRING:** This is usually one of the later warblers to arrive in Ontario. Stirrett (1973b: 25) had Pelee records from May 6 to June 5, with a maximum of 25 on May 21. Ussher (1965: 26) had Rondeau records from May 4 to June 4, with average arrival on May 14 and departure on May 26. Saunders & Dale (1933: 233) gave May 19 as the 16-year average arrival date at London with the earliest on May 11, 1922. Snyder (1931: 215) mentioned 15 casualties at the Long Point light on May 14, 1925 and one as late as June 1 there. Saunders (1947: 373) listed May 9 as his earliest Toronto date with average arrival on May 16 and departure on May 28: Speirs (1938: 43, 45) gave May 25 as the peak and June 7 as the latest Toronto date. Long (1968a: 21) reported one at Pickering Beach on May 7, 1964 and George A. Scott had one at Oshawa as late as June 6, 1948 (Speirs, 1974). Weir & Quilliam (1980: 39) listed May 16 as the 29-year average arrival date for Kingston, with the earliest on May 7. Devitt (1967: 150) gave May 21 as a 7-year average arrival date at Barrie, with the earliest on May 14, 1964. L. Beamer's median arrival date at Meaford was May 21, with the earliest on May 13, 1956. Mills (1981: 151) cited spring records for the cottage country from May 18 (1974) to May 28 (1978). Nicholson (1981: 173) gave May 18 as the 11-year average arrival date for Manitoulin, with the earliest on May 11, 1980 and a high count of 15 on May 31, 1979. MacLulich (1938: 35) reported one seen by Mark Robinson in Algonquin Park as early as May 15, 1933. Ricker & Clarke (1939: 20) gave May 18, 1933 as their earliest Lake Nipissing date. Skeel & Bondrup-Nielsen (1978: 209) noted only one at Pukaskwa, on May 26, 1977. Baillie & Hope (1943: 23) observed a few at Rossport from May 29 to June 1, 1936. Denis (1961: 4) gave May 25 as the average arrival date at Thunder Bay, with the earliest on May 17, 1958. Peruniak (1971: 27) gave May 11 as her earliest Atikokan date. Elder (1979: 38) gave May 20 as his earliest Geraldton record. Bondrup-Nielsen (1976: 45) saw his first near Kapuskasing on May 22, 1974. Hope (1938: 41) collected a female at Favourable Lake on May 31, 1938.

**SUMMER:** On the 1968-1977 Breeding Bird Surveys they were rare to fairly common from Sudbury north. Ussher (1965: 26) had a returning bird as early as Aug. 19 at Rondeau, with average arrival on Aug. 27. Saunders (1947: 373) had an early arrival at Toronto on Aug. 7. George A. Scott noted an early migrant at Oshawa on Aug. 13, 1967 (Speirs, 1974). Weir & Quilliam (1980: 39) listed June 26 and Aug. 10 dates for Kingston (which they treated as migrants). Devitt (1967: 149) reported a spring bird as late as June 7, 1942 at Belle Ewart and a returning bird as early as Aug. 21 at Wasaga Beach. I noted one at Sundridge on July 19, 1931 and single birds at Lake Muskoka on Aug. 11 and 18, 1937. Ron Tasker banded three in Burpee Twp., Manitoulin, on Aug. 25, 1974, presumably early fall migrants (Nicholson, 1981: 174). Speirs & Speirs (1947: 36) observed one in a willow-alder bog near North Bay, on June 5, 1944. Baillie & Harrington (1937: 254) reported a nest with 5 eggs, collected by F. Starr, at Sudbury on June 14, 1936. Baillie & Hope (1947: 26) collected males at Chapleau on June 9 and 12, 1937. I recorded 5 on a roadside count from Dorion to Marathon on June 15, 1956. At Lake Nipigon in 1924, Snyder (1928: 274) collected two males on June 7 and one on June 22. J. Jacob found a nest with 5 eggs in O'Connor Twp., Thunder Bay, on June 18, 1906 (Dear, 1940: 139). David Elder observed one at Atikokan on June 15, 1981. Snyder (1953: 81) reported 2 at Savanne on July 13 and one on July 15, 1937 and at Sioux Lookout 4 were noted on July 4 and 2 on July 5, 1947. Snyder (1928: 32) observed an adult carrying food to young at Lake Abitibi in the summer of 1925: a female collected there on June 3, 1925 had a black cap. Ross James noted single birds at Pickle Lake on June 2 and 11, 1977. Hope (1938: 41) collected males at Favourable Lake, one on June 9 and another on June 17, 1938. Cringan (1950: 17) called this "a prominent species of the streamside community" at Nikip Lake in 1950. James, Nash & Peck (1982: 70) found a nest with 5 young on June 29, 1982 at the Harricanaw River, James Bay. A.H. Macpherson found a nest with 5 young at Moosonee on July 2, 1949 (Manning, 1952: 85). Schueler, Baldwin & Rising (1974: 147) found a nest with 5 eggs at Hawley Lake on July 1, 1964: they noted the species also at Cochrane, Moosonee, Attawapiskat and Winisk. Lee (1978: 32) saw a maximum of 6 at Big Trout Lake on June 8, 1975 and called it "another of the more conspicuous warblers present"—"alongside streams and in alder-willow thickets". C.E. Hope had a daily maximum of 12 at Ft. Severn on July 9, 1940 and collected 3 of 10 seen on July 16, there.

AUTUMN: Peruniak (1971: 27) gave Sept. 7 as her latest Atikokan date. Skeel & Bondrup-Nielsen (1978: 209) had only one fall sighting at Pukaskwa, on Sept. 8, 1977. Louise Lawrence noted one at Pimisi Bay on Sept. 11, 1944 (Speirs & Speirs, 1947: 36). Nicholson (1981: 174) reported one on Manitoulin as late as Oct. 2, 1978 and 31 casualties at the Great Duck Is. tower from Sept. 18-23, 1977. Mills (1981: 151) observed one as late as Sept. 25, 1976 at Magnetawan. At the Barrie TV tower, 4 were killed in 1961 and 12 in 1965, none in other years studied: the latest was one Oct. 2, 1965 according to Frances Westman (Devitt, 1967: 150). Weir & Quilliam (1980: 39) listed Sept. 28 as the 23-year average departure date from Kingston, the latest on Oct. 7. George A. Scott noted one at Oshawa as late as Oct. 29, 1967 (Speirs, 1974). Speirs (1938: 53) gave Sept. 30 as the latest Toronto record, but Parker (1983: 25) shows one as late as November. Saunders (1947: 373) listed Sept. 4 and 22 as average fall arrival and departure dates for Toronto. Beardslee & Mitchell (1965: 395) had a record from the Canadian shore of Lake Erie on Oct. 16, 1955. Snyder (1931: 215) reported only 8 casualties at the Long Point light from Sept. 7-29, 1929. Ussher (1965: 26) gave Sept 17 as the average departure date from Rondeau, the latest on Oct. 31. Stirrett (1973d: 27) had Pelee records from Aug. 24 to Oct. 12, with a maximum of 15 on Sept. 4.

**MEASUREMENTS:**
*Length:* 4.25 to 5.1 ins.
(Godfrey, 1966: 347)
*Wingspread:* 6 1/4 to 7
ins. (Roberts, 1955: 668)
*Weight:* 2 ♂ averaged 7.2
g, one ♀ weighed 7.1 g.
(Hope, 1938: 41).

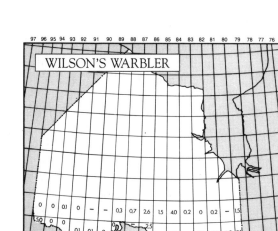

WILSON'S WARBLER

BREEDING BIRDS SURVEY:
Average number per 50 stops
1968-1977.

# CANADA WARBLER  *Wilsonia canadensis*  (Linnaeus)

In summer I have usually found Canada Warblers in central Ontario gullies with slopes covered with mountain maples or other shrubs, over gurgling rivulets. They winter in South America.

**IDENTIFICATION:** The Canada Warbler is identified by the "necklace" of black spots across its yellow breast. It is a gray-backed warbler with yellow "spectacles" and white undertail coverts. The song starts with an emphatic "tick" followed by a chattery, but sweet, series of ups and downs.

**WINTER:**

**SPRING:** Stirrett (1973b: 25) had Pelee records from May 4 to June 5, with a maximum of 15 on May 17. Ussher (1965: 26) had Rondeau birds from May 6 to June 3, with average arrival on May 14 and departure on May 29. Saunders & Dale (1933: 233) gave May 15 as the 17-year average arrival date at London, with the earliest on May 5, 1912. Snyder (1931: 215) cited Long Point records from May 14, 1925 (when 31 were killed at the Long Point lighthouse) to June 1, 1924. J.L. Baillie (in Saunders, 1947: 373) gave May 9 as his earliest Toronto date, with the 25-year average arrival on May 18: Speirs (1938: 42) gave May 25 as the spring peak at Toronto. Naomi LeVay and Doris H. Speirs saw one as early as May 7 at Eastbourne, Whitby (Speirs, 1974). Weir & Quilliam (1980: 39) listed May 4 as the earliest Kingston date, with average arrival on May 14 and departure on May 31. Devitt (1967: 150) gave May 19 as the 17-year average arrival at Barrie, with the earliest on May 8, 1965: A.J. Mitchener found a nest with 3 eggs about 3 miles west of Collingwood as early as May 26, 1961, which held 3 cowbird eggs on May 30 and was later deserted. L. Beamer's median arrival date at Meaford was May 23, with his earliest on May 14, 1956. Mills (1981: 151) gave May 16 as a 7-year average arrival date for Huntsville, with the earliest on May 12, 1963. Nicholson (1981: 174) gave May 20 as the 12-year average arrival date for Manitoulin, with the earliest on May 9, 1979, and a maximum of 20 on May 28, 1979: Ron Tasker banded 9 on May 27, 1973 in Burpee Twp. MacLulich (1938: 35) gave May 17, 1932 as an arrival date for Algonquin Park. Speirs & Speirs (1947: 36) noted one at North Bay as early as May 15, 1944. Skeel & Bondrup-Nielsen (1978: 209) saw their first six on May 23, 1977 at Pukaskwa. Denis (1961: 4) listed May 26 as the average arrival date at Thunder Bay, with the earliest on May 19, 1958. Peruniak (1971: 27) gave May 24 as her earliest Atikokan date. Elder (1979: 28) had one as early as May 23 at Geraldton. Bondrup-Nielsen (1976: 45) saw his first near Kapuskasing on May 29 in 1974.

SUMMER: On the 1968-1977 Breeding Bird Surveys they were rare in agricultural regions (southern Ontario and the Clay Belt), fairly common on most routes in the Precambrian region and common on the Mattawa route. Stirrett (1973c: 21) had the first returning migrant at Pelee on Aug. 7 and the fall maximum of 25 on Aug. 13. Ussher (1965: 26) had his earliest fall bird at Rondeau on Aug. 12, with the average arrival on Aug. 20. W.E. Saunders took a set of 3 eggs and a cowbird egg near London on June 5, 1914 (Saunders & Dale, 1933: 233). R.V. Lindsay noted four at Fishers Glen, Norfolk Co., during the first two weeks of July, 1927 (Snyder, 1931: 215). Beardslee & Mitchell (1965: 396) reported one at Morgan's Point, Lake Erie, as early as Aug. 6, 1944. Snyder (1930: 199) reported seeing young out of the nest in King Twp. in the summer of 1926. Speirs & Orenstein (1975: 14) reported population densities of 19, 2 and 13 birds per 100 acres in the forest quadrats in Scott, Brock and Reach Twps. of Ontario Co. Long (1968a: 21) saw a female feeding a young cowbird at Pickering Beach on Aug. 2, 1963. Tozer & Richards (1974: 259) saw an adult carrying food in the Osler Tract, Cartwright Twp., on June 15, 1968 and George A. Scott watched a pair feeding a young cowbird on June 20, 1965 in Darlington Twp. Charles Fothergill described one shot near Port Hope on July 8, 1821 (Black, 1934: 156). Snyder (1941: 82) noted parents carrying food at Woodrous, Prince Edward Co., on June 28, 1930. Quilliam (1973: 167) cited summer records from Bell's Swamp, Amherstview Bog and Harrowsmith Bog, near Kingston. Weir & Quilliam (1980: 39) gave Aug. 16 as the average fall arrival date at Kingston. Devitt (1967: 150) reported several nest records for Simcoe Co., including a set of 4 eggs collected by L. Campbell on June 15, 1918 at Ferndale, near Barrie. F.A. Saunders reported breeding in Dow's Swamp, near Ottawa, in June, 1898 (Lloyd, 1924: 15). B. Perrin and H. Halliday found 3 nests with young at Sand Lake, Parry Sound Dist., from June 23-29, 1945 (Mills, 1981: 152). Ron Tasker banded 43 in two weeks, beginning Aug. 24 (Nicholson, 1981: 174). MacLulich (1938: 35) saw a pair feeding young in Algonquin Park on July 20, 1930. T.M. Shortt saw young at Eau Claire from June 29-July 2, 1935 (Baillie & Harrington, 1937: 255). Baillie & Hope (1947: 26) collected young at Biscotasing on July 8 and at Bigwood on July 15 and 21, 1937. Snyder (1942: 145) collected males at Laird on June 4 and June 12, 1931. Skeel & Bondrup-Nielsen (1978: 209) found them common in shrubbery at Wolf Howl Lake, Pukaskwa in the summer of 1977. Baillie & Hope (1943: 23) collected males at Rossport, Marathon and Amyot from June 4 to July 1, 1936. Snyder (1928: 275) collected a partially-feathered young at Macdiarmid, Lake Nipigon, on July 25, 1924. Dear (1940: 140) found a nest with 5 eggs on June 14, 1936 and a nest with 2 small young on June 26, 1927, near Thunder Bay. Snyder (1938: 206) found them "fairly common" at Off Lake, Rainy River, in 1929. Snyder (1953: 81) noted 1 to 4 daily at Sioux Lookout and 1 to 6 daily at Ingolf: a few were also noted at Wabigoon and Malachi. Snyder (1928: 32) collected two males and a female at Lake Abitibi in 1925. Bondrup-Nielsen (1976: 47) was scolded by a pair as he searched for their nest near Kapuskasing in 1974. James (1980: 90) had only one bird each year near Pickle Lake, in alders at lake edges. Hope (1938: 42) considered this a rare species at Favourable Lake, where he collected two males, one on June 12 and the other on July 5, 1938. James, Nash & Peck (1982: 70) observed recently flying young by the Harricanaw River, near James Bay, on July 8 and 9, 1982. Manning (1952: 85) cited two old records for Moose Factory, one in 1881, the other on June 11, 1896. Schueler, Baldwin & Rising (1974: 144) listed them as present at Cochrane and Moosonee, but saw none farther north.

AUTUMN: Skeel & Bondrup-Nielsen (1978: 209) saw one, still singing, at Pukaskwa on Sept. 6, 1977. From Sept. 18-23, 1973, some 15 were killed at the Great Duck Is. tower (Nicholson, 1981: 174). Mills (1981: 152) found one as late as Sept. 25, 1971 at Ahmic Lake. Devitt (1967: 150) reported 34 casualties at the Barrie TV tower in 5 of 7 years, the latest on Oct. 2, 1965. Weir & Quilliam (1980: 39) listed Sept. 20 as the average departure date from Kingston, the latest on Oct. 11. My latest Pickering Twp. date was Sept. 27, 1962 (Speirs, 1974). Saunders (1947: 373) listed Sept. 8 as his average departure date from Toronto: Fleming (1907: 85) had one as late as Sept. 27 there. Casualties at the Long Point light were: 11 on Sept. 7, 7 on Sept. 9 and 3 from Sept. 24-29, 1929 (Snyder, 1931: 215). Ussher (1965: 26) gave Sept. 13 as the average departure date from Rondeau, the latest on Oct. 2. Stirrett (1973d: 27) had his latest one at Pelee on Sept. 30.

**MEASUREMENTS:**
*Length:* 5 to 5 3/4 ins. (Godfrey, 1966: 248)
*Wingspread:* 7.75 to 8.38 ins. (Roberts, 1955: 674)
*Weight:* 32 Ontario specimens averaged 10.1 g.

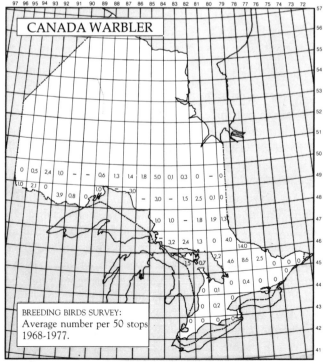

CANADA WARBLER

BREEDING BIRDS SURVEY: Average number per 50 stops 1968-1977.

# PAINTED REDSTART   *Myioborus pictus*   (Swainson)

To find one of these subtropical birds, native to southwestern United States and Central America, in Ontario in late fall, was totally unexpected.

**IDENTIFICATION:** The Painted Redstart is mainly a black bird, with red breast and prominent white splashes on the wings, outer tail feathers, undertail coverts and lower eyelid.

**WINTER:**

**SPRING:**

**SUMMER:**

**AUTUMN:** Mrs. Lindsay Death of Pickering Twp., first noticed this unusual bird at her home on Nov. 4, 1971. She notified Edgerton Pegg, who had a fleeting glimpse of it on Nov. 9. Mrs. Death captured it in her apple barn on Nov. 15 and turned it over to Edgerton Pegg, where it was photographed. They turned it over again to us and we notified Barry and Phyllis MacKay, who have had some experience keeping insectivorous birds. They kept it in their home for over six years (until June 24, 1978) picking specially raised flies from the walls and ceiling of their living room.

**MEASUREMENTS:**
*Length:* 5 to 5 3/4 ins.
(Terres, 1980: 964)
Wingspread:
*Weight:* 12 averaged
7.9 g. (5.9 - 9.6 g.)
(Dunning, 1984: 22).

**REFERENCE:**
Speirs, J. Murray and
Edgerton Pegg 1972 First
record of Painted Redstart
for Canada. Auk,
89: (4): 898.

# YELLOW-BREASTED CHAT   *Icteria virens*   (Linnaeus)

One of the reasons that bird watchers flock to Pelee is to see and hear the Yellow-breasted Chat, rare elsewhere in southern Ontario. It sounds more like a Gray Jay than a warbler and behaves more like a member of the Mockingbird family: although coloured like a warbler it seems out of place in this family. Most chats retire to Central America in winter.

IDENTIFICATION:   The song of the chat with its "Whoo-whoo crrk - crrk - swee - swee—" emanating from a dense thicket along the Lake Erie shore is diagnostic. The chat is big for a warbler, about the size of a Bobolink. It has an orange-yellow throat and breast fading to white on the lower belly and undertail coverts: it has a greenish back, bluish head and white "spectacles". Some of the vireos have similar colours, but they are smaller and are treetop lovers, not skulkers in thickets like the chat.

WINTER:   Stirrett (1973a: 19) mentioned a Dec. 26 record at Pelee.

SPRING:   Stirrett (1973b: 25) had one at Pelee as early as Apr. 25 and a maximum of 12 on May 12. Ussher (1965: 26) gave May 9 as his 19-year average arrival date at Rondeau, with the earliest on Apr. 27. Saunders & Dale (1933: 232) had a few records in the London region, from May 14 (1918 - one collected by Hoyes Lloyd at Coldstream) to May 31 (1923): an early one was found dead at London on Apr. 26, 1983 (Weir, 1983: 866). Earl and Bob Lemon found 6 near New Glasgow, Elgin Co., on May 24, 1948 (Brooman, 1954: 34). In 1983 near Long Point, 19 were reported from May 4-27: 10 of these were banded (Weir, 1983: 866). D. Bucknell observed one in Oxford Co. on May 16, 1975 (Goodwin, 1975: 847). Speirs (1974) cited about a dozen spring records for the Pickering-Oshawa waterfront: with my wife Doris, I saw one and heard another at Thickson's Woods, Whitby, on May 7, 1983. Dennis Barry noted one in Darlington Twp. on May 13, 1963 (Tozer & Richards, 1974: 257). E.R. McDonald saw one at Cobourg on May 16, 1971 (Goodwin, 1971: 739). A.E. Bell found one at Newburg on May 22, 1971 (Goodwin, 1971: 739). Weir & Quilliam (1980: 39) gave May 14 as a 13-year average arrival date at Kingston, with the earliest on May 8. G. Bennett noted one at Tiny Marsh on May 31, 1975 (Goodwin, 1975: 847). Two were spotted at Ottawa on May 9, 1979 by B. DiLabio and B. Bracken (Goodwin, 1979: 767). T. Kelner reported one at Huntsville on May 21, 1967 (Mills, 1981: 151). Nicholson (1981: 173) had a few spring records for Manitoulin, the earliest on May 8 (1976) and one as late as June 5 (1960). The most remarkable record was one found on Caribou Is., Lake Superior, by R. Nisbet on May 17, 1981 (Goodwin, 1981: 820).

SUMMER:   On the 1968-1977 Breeding Bird Surveys, they were noted on the Kingsville and Sarnia routes, with strays to Listowel and Fraserville. C.A. Campbell reported two or three pairs on Pelee Is. in summer of 1975 (Goodwin, 1975: 966). Stirrett (1973c: 21) had up to 3 birds at Pelee throughout the summer. A.H. Kelley reported the first Rondeau nest in the summer of 1980 (Goodwin, 1980: 892). R.W. Morris and B.B. Thompson heard one singing at Delaware from July 11-21, 1971 and later saw one carrying food (Goodwin, 1971: 854). F. Starr took a set of 3 eggs and a cowbird egg at Port Burwell on June 14, 1924 (Baillie & Harrington, 1937: 254). Marshall Field found one at St. Thomas on July 29, 1950 (Brooman, 1954: 34). Snyder (1931: 214) collected a female at Long Point on June 14, 1927. R.F. Andrle found one in the Wainfleet Bog on June 25, 1975 (Goodwin, 1975: 966). A. Dorst found a nest with 5 eggs near St. Catharines on June 3, 1962: one young had hatched by June 9 (Beardslee & Mitchell, 1965: 393). A. Wormington saw a pair feeding young at Ancaster on June 28, 1971 (Goodwin, 1971: 854). M. Jennings reported a nest at Bronte on July 19, 1976 (Goodwin, 1976: 951). H.R. Ivor, J.L. Baillie *et al* saw a pair at Erindale from June 17-27, 1934 (Baillie & Harrington, 1937: 254). Speirs (1974) reported a spring bird that lingered near Amos Ponds, Pickering, to June 7, 1969 and another near Oshawa seen as late as July 21, 1967 by J.M. Richards. E.R. McDonald saw one at Port Britain on Aug. 23, 1980 (Goodwin, 1981: 178). Snyder (1941: 81) shot one near Hallowell, Prince Edward Co., on June 20, 1930. E. Elligsen reported two in the Ellice Swamp, Perth Co., on June 9, 1974 (Goodwin, 1974: 899). Weir (1982: 973) observed a male on territory near Erinsville on June 12, 1982. W. Smith saw one at Jones Falls, Leeds Co., on June 6, 1971 (Goodwin, 1971: 854). S. Curtis reported one at Ottawa from June 25-29, 1976 (Goodwin, 1976: 951). Grace Malkin saw one at Fox Lake, near Huntsville, on Aug. 16, 1965 (Mills, 1981: 151).

AUTUMN: A. Wormington noted one at Caribou Is., Lake Superior, on Sept. 25, 1979 (Goodwin, 1980: 157). J.M. Glenday noted 2 at North Bay on Sept. 5, 1971 (Goodwin, 1972: 59). W. Crins and many others observed 2 in Algonquin Park on Oct. 11, 1981 (Goodwin, 1982: 174). Nicholson (1981: 173) reported one at Great Duck Is. on Sept. 23, 1973. L. Irwin and R. Ziefeld noted one as late as Oct. 30, 1973 at Orillia (Goodwin, 1974: 635). Weir & Quilliam (1980: 39) gave Sept. 30 as the latest Kingston record. W. Fahey reported one at Durham on Sept. 15, 1976 (Goodwin, 1977: 172). On Sept. 21, 1965 I was surprised to hear one singing and scolding near our Pickering Twp. home (Speirs, 1974). R. Curry had a very late one at Burlington on Nov. 11, 1973 (Goodwin, 1974: 47). Weir (1983: 176) reported one seen at Forest on Oct. 23, 1982 and 3 at the Long Point Bird Observatory, the latest on Sept. 12, 1982. Ussher (1965: 26) gave Sept. 19 as his latest Rondeau date. Stirrett (1973d: 27) had just one fall record at Pelee, on Oct. 12.

**MEASUREMENTS:**
*Length:* 6 3/4 to 7 1/2 ins. (Godfrey, 1966: 346)
*Wingspread:* 9 to 10 ins. (Roberts, 1955: 671)
*Weight:* 19.4 to 33.4 g. (Terres, 1980: 962).

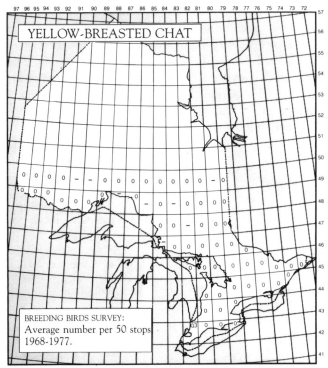

YELLOW-BREASTED CHAT

BREEDING BIRDS SURVEY: Average number per 50 stops 1968-1977.

# SUMMER TANAGER  *Piranga rubra*  (Linnaeus)

This is a bird of southeastern United States, rarely comming into southern Ontario and then mainly as storm-blown waifs in spring. They winter chiefly in Central and South America.

IDENTIFICATION: Males are all red, lacking the black wings and tail of Scarlet Tanagers and lacking the crest of the Northern Cardinal. Females are more yellow below than are female Scarlet Tanagers.

WINTER:

SPRING: Stirrett (1973b: 26) had 6 spring records at Pelee, from May 2 to May 27: there have been several more recent records there. Ussher (1965: 28) mentioned a May 24 record at Rondeau and P.A. Woodliffe reported two there from May 5 to 15, 1982 (Weir, 1982: 848). Marshall Field and W. Rayner saw one at St. Thomas on May 2, 1975: G. Bennett *et al* saw one at London from Apr. 23 to May 5, 1975 and W.G. Day *et al* had one at Thorndale (also in Middlesex Co.) on May 17, 1975 (Goodwin, 1975: 847). J. Black and L. Gollert saw a male at St. Catharines on May 10-11, 1983 and D. Garvin also noted a male at Burlington on May 10, 1983 (Weir, 1983: 866). T. Doubleday reported one at Long Point on May 22, 1980 and O. Oppertshauser one at Toronto on May 10-11, 1980 (Goodwin, 1980: 773). Fleming (1907: 82) mentioned a specimen taken at Toronto by Mr. Herring in May, 1890 (actually at Scarborough Heights nearby): Speirs (1938: 39, 45) listed May 17 and May 22 records for Toronto: the only one I personally saw at Toronto was on Apr. 19, 1947 at F.H. Emery's home above the Humber River, after a big storm which also brought several other southern birds into the region: this bird was also seen by York Edwards, Ian Halliday, Mary Jackson, Douglas Miller, Bill Smith *et al.* Weir & Quilliam (1980: 26) reported a female at Prince Edward Point on May 13, 1976 seen by Phil Little and Ron Weir and a male there from May 4 to 25,1979, seen by many observers and banded by Michele Goossens. More recent reports from Prince Edward Point involved one seen by G. Vance and Ron Weir on May 17, 1981 (Goodwin, 1981: 820) and one found by R.K. Edwards on May 16-17, 1982 (Weir, 1982: 848). Devitt (1967: 158) reported one seen at Holly, Simcoe Co., on May 9 and 11, 1962, by Gordon Johns, Frances Westman *et al.* Nicholson (1981: 181) had two Manitoulin records: one that he saw at Gore Bay on May 17, 1970 and another seen by D.B. Ferguson at Windfall Lake on May 20, 1979. The most unusual report was one reported by R. Taylor at Ouimet, north of Lake Superior, on Apr. 28, 1979 (Goodwin, 1979: 767).

SUMMER: Ussher (1965: 28) had a June 12 record for Rondeau.

AUTUMN: A. Wormington reported another bird north of Lake Superior, at Neys Provincial Park, on Oct. 21, 1979 (Goodwin, 1980: 158).

MEASUREMENTS:

*Length:* 7.0 to 7.8 ins. (Godfrey, 1966: 363) *Wingspread:* 11 1/4 to 12 1/8 ins. (Roberts, 1955: 697)

*Weight:* 45 North Carolina birds averaged 31 g. (Terres, 1980: 848).

**REFERENCES:**
Brunton, Dan 1967 First
record of the Summer
Tanager in Ottawa,
Ontario. Can. Field-
Naturalist, 81: (4): 274.
(Male found by D.B. on
May 24, 1967 and
confirmed by W.E.
Godfrey: collected May 25
by A.E. Bourguignon).
   Scott, David M. 1961
Summer Tanager at
London, Ontario. Can.
Field-Naturalist,
75: (4): 264. (Female
collected May 21, 1960.)

# SCARLET TANAGER  *Piranga olivacea*  (Gmelin)

Scarlet Tanagers often appear in southern Ontario in mid-May, before the trees are in leaf, when their brilliant plumage causes gasps of wonder in appreciative onlookers. On their breeding grounds, high in the maples in June, they are surprisingly hard to find and are usually located only by song or calls. By fall much of their spring finery has been replaced by green and most pass by unnoticed, to winter in the tropical forests of South America.

**IDENTIFICATION:** Males with their brilliant scarlet or vermilion bodies and contrasting black wings and tail, are easily identified. Females have green body plumage with dark brown wings and tail. The song is a hoarse, robin-like carol and the call an emphatic "tip-her".

**WINTER:** Sheppard (1960: 45) reported two seen as late as the first week of December on Navy Island, Niagara Falls. A.G. Carpentier reported a probable female-plumaged bird in Douro Twp., near Peterboroough, on Feb. 5, 1979 (Goodwin, 1979: 278).

**SPRING:** Stirrett (1973b: 26) had a spring maximum of 50 at Pelee on May 10, with the earliest group of 3 on Apr. 30. Ussher (1965: 28) gave May 9 as his 26-year average arrival date at Rondeau, with the earliest on May 1. Saunders & Dale (1933: 236) had their earliest London bird on May 2, 1915, with the 17-year average arrival date on May 11: they reported one set of 4 eggs as early as May 30, 1915. Snyder (1931: 202) mentioned 15 killed at the Long Point lighthouse on May 14, 1925. J.L. Baillie had one at Toronto as early as May 3 and his 25-year average arrival date was May 18 (Saunders, 1947: 374). Naomi LeVay noted her first at Cranberry Marsh on May 4 in 1954 and again in 1962: on May 31, 1970, Dennis Barry and J.M. Richards found a nest under construction 50 ft. up in a sugar maple in Darlington Twp. (Tozer & Richards, 1974: 275-276). Charles Fothergill noted individuals on May 6, 1817 at Port Hope and on May 21, 1821 at Rice Lake: he observed 3 notches on each side of the bill of the latter bird in place of the usual one (Black, 1934: 157). Snyder (1941: 85) found his first in Prince Edward Co. at Wellington on May 15, 1937. Weir & Quilliam (1980: 39) listed May 10 as the 32-year average arrival date at Kingston, with the earliest on Apr. 29. Devitt (1967: 158) gave May 15 as the 17-year average arrival date at Barrie, with the earliest on May 6, 1960. L. Beamer had no record during 12 of 20 springs at Meaford: the average arrival date for the other 8 years was May 21 and the earliest was on May 15, 1946. Mills (1981: 162) gave May 13 as a 9-year average arrival date at Huntsville, with the earliest on May 9, 1965. Nicholson (1981: 180-181) gave May 14 as the 11-year average arrival date on Manitoulin, with the earliest on May 8, 1979: 39 were killed at the Great Duck Is. tower from May 19-28, 1979 and some 150 were seen there on May 19, 1979. MacLulich (1938: 38) gave May 20, 1932 as his earliest Algonquin Park date. Louise Lawrence saw one at Rutherglen on May 14, 1944 (Speirs & Speirs, 1947: 37). Skeel & Bondrup-Nielsen (1978: 213) had three records from May 23 to May 27, 1977 at Pukaskwa. Denis (1961: 4) gave May 24 as the average arrival date at Thunder Bay, with the earliest on May 21, 1955. Peruniak (1971: 28) gave May 16 as her earliest Atikokan date. Smith (1957: 180) saw a male on May 30, 1954 at Lake Timiskaming.

SUMMER: On the 1968-1977 Breeding Bird Surveys, they were fairly common in the cottage country and uncommon elsewhere, missing on many northern routes but some as far north as Jellicoe and Kenora. Stirrett (1973c: 22) had a summer maximum of 6 at Pelee on July 27. Kelley (1978: 82) wrote: "may be fairly common locally in mature deciduous woodland such as Rondeau". Saunders & Dale (1933: 236) had nests near London; one with 3 eggs on June 5, 1902, one with one egg and 3 cowbird eggs on June 9, 1902 and another with one egg and 2 cowbird eggs on June 15, 1912. Speirs & Frank (1970: 742) found a breeding density of 12 territories per 100 acres in a beech forest at Springwater Park, Elgin Co. R.T. Anderson took a set of 4 eggs at Aylmer (Baillie & Harrington, 1937: 262). Brooman (1954: 36) watched both adults feeding young at a nest 15 ft. up, about 5 miles east of St. Thomas on June 21, 1941. R.V. Lindsay observed several birds at Fishers Glen, Lake Erie, in July, 1927 (Snyder, 1931: 202). Snyder (1930: 196) collected a male on June 12, 1926 in King Twp. Speirs & Orenstein (1975: 14) found populations in 5 of 11 forest plots in Ontario Co., with the maximum density of 22 birds pers 100 acres in the Rama quadrat. Snyder (1941: 85) collected 4 males and a female during June and July, 1930 in Prince Edward Co. Quilliam (1973: 175) recorded a pair building at the Kingston Field Naturalists' sanctuary at Otter Lake on June 7, 1964, and saw a male feeding a young bird out of the nest there on July 11, 1965: E. Beaupré took a set of 4 eggs at Murvale on June 12, 1905. Barry Ranford found a nest with 2 eggs at Baxter, Simcoe Co., on June 6, 1956 (Devitt, 1967: 157). J.H. Fleming found a nest with 2 eggs on June 4, 1892, at Emsdale (Mills, 1981: 163). D.B. Ferguson found a nest with 3 eggs near Windfall Lake, Manitoulin, on July 13, 1979 (Nicholson, 1981: 181). MacLulich (1938: 38) reported young collected in Algonquin Park on July 28, 1922, Aug. 11, 1934 and Aug. 23, 1934. Ricker & Clarke (1939: 22) reported young being fed at Frank's Bay, Lake Nipissing, on June 27, 1933 and a nest with one egg found there as late as Aug. 29, 1930. Baillie & Hope (1947: 28) collected a male at Biscotasing on June 25, 1937 and saw one at Bigwood on July 27. Snyder (1942: 148) collected males at Laird on June 6 and July 9, 1931. Skeel & Bondrup-Nielsen (1978: 213) heard males singing on the 4 mostly mature deciduous forest tracts in Pukaskwa in 1977. Speirs (1949: 148) had one territory on 75 acres at Eaglehead Lake in 1946. Snyder (1938: 209) collected a female on July 1 and a male on July 2, 1929, at Off Lake, Rainy River. David Elder noted one at Steep Rock Lake on June 3, 1981. Snyder (1953: 85) reported the species at

Kenora, Dinorwic, Ingolf, Malachi (the only breeding record), Wabigoon, Sioux Lookout and on Aug. 18, 1952 one as far north at 10 miles south of Perrault Falls. Smith (1957: 180) saw a female at Lake Timiskaming on July 31, 1953 and mentioned that Leonard Berry saw one at Timmins on June 3, 1936. McLaren & McLaren (1981: 5) heard one singing near Nakina on June 7, 1977. The most northerly record appears to be one reported at North Point, James Bay, on June 29, 1983 by C. Rimmer (Weir, 1983: 985).

AUTUMN: M. Jennings and A. Wormington reported 4 at Moose Factory on Sept. 25, 1976, one of which was still there on Oct. 2 (Goodwin, 1977: 176). N.G. Escott saw 3 at Marathon on Sept. 5, 1976 (Skeel & Bondrup-Nielsen, 1978: 213). Manitoulin birds were recorded as late as Oct. 13 in 1973 and 1975 (Nicholson, 1981: 181). Mervin Austin and B. Waters reported a late bird at Huntsville on Oct. 9, 1969 (Mills, 1981: 163). Ottelyn Addison found an adult feeding a young bird out of the nest in Tiny Twp., as late as Sept. 19, 1965: at the Barrie TV tower 22 were killed in 4 of 7 years, 16 of these on Sept. 24, 1960, and one as late as Oct. 2, 1965 (Devitt, 1967: 157-158). Weir & Quilliam (1980: 39) listed Oct. 1 as the 23-year average departure date from Kingston, with the latest on Oct. 18. One hit a window at our Pickering home on Nov. 22, 1970 and was examined by J.M. Richards and myself: we noted narrow white borders to the secondaries and greater coverts, before it recovered and flew off (Speirs, 1973). Saunders (1947: 374) gave Sept. 25 as his 8-year average departure date from Toronto: Fleming (1907: 81) had one as late as Oct. 13. Beardslee & Mitchell (1965: 411) saw one at the Sugar Loaf Hill, Welland Co. on Oct. 12, 1952 and another on the Canadian shore of Lake Erie on Oct. 16, 1949. One was killed at the Long Point lighthouse on Sept. 7 and 14 others from Sept. 24-29, 1929 (Snyder, 1931: 202). Ussher (1965: 28) gave Sept. 15 as his average departure date from Rondeau, with the latest on Sept. 30. The fall maximum at Pelee was 3 on Oct. 14 and one was noted there as late as Nov. 25 (Stirrett, 1973a: 19 and 1973d: 28).

**MEASUREMENTS:**
*Length:* 6.5 to 7.6 ins.
(Godfrey, 1966: 362)
*Wingspread:* 11 to 12 ins.
(Roberts, 1955: 698)
*Weight:* 40 Ontario
specimens averaged
29.7 g.

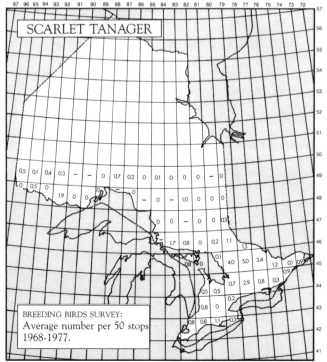

SCARLET TANAGER

BREEDING BIRDS SURVEY:
Average number per 50 stops
1968-1977.

# WESTERN TANAGER  *Piranga ludoviciana*  (Wilson)

This is mainly a bird of the western mountains, breeding in evergreens or aspens, some as far east as central Saskatchewan. Strays have wandered east to Ontario and shown up there at feeders in winter and spring. They normally winter in Central America.

IDENTIFICATION: Males are mainly yellow birds with black wings and tail and a red head. Females are greenish yellow with drab wings and tail. Both differ from our other tanagers in having *conspicuous* yellow or white wing bars (some Scarlet Tanagers have very narrow white wing bars). The song is a hoarse, robin-like carol, much like the song of a Scarlet Tanager: I noted a call note as "dee-deek".

WINTER: Baillie (1958: 28) reported one seen from Dec. 18, 1957 to Feb. 13, 1958 at Herb O'Reilly's feeder at Tintern (southwest of St. Catharines) and another at Mrs. Hugh Haughton's feeder at Cooksville from Dec. 1-4, 1957, trapped by Lucie McDougall and kept at Roy Ivor's sanctuary where it was photographed by Donald Gunn and eventually shipped by air to Arizona on Jan. 9, 1958. E.R. McDonald photographed one that was seen at Port Hope from Dec. 1 to 16, 1973 (Goodwin, 1974: 635).

SPRING: Stirrett (1973b: 26) had only one Pelee record, a male seen on May 18, 1969. N. and M. Richard reported a male at Amherstburg on May 1, 1982 (Weir, 1982: 848). Kelley (1978: 82) reported one at Bradley's Marsh on May 10, 1969, seen by William Pesold. Donald Bucknell saw a male at Ingersoll on Apr. 27, 1947 (Baillie, 1958: 28). J. McCauley saw one at The Pinery on May 11, 1981 (Goodwin, 1982: 174). Baillie (1964: 1) reported one in Leeds Co. on March 29, 1958. Mrs. W.P. Hogarth saw one on May 20, 1951 about 20 miles northeast of Thunder Bay (Baillie, 1958: 28).

SUMMER: Baillie (1964: 1) reported Lake Nipissing records on Aug. 7, 1961 and July 22, 1962. T.C. Mackie reported one at North Bay on Aug. 27, 1973 (Goodwin, 1974: 48).

AUTUMN: One was banded at Port Hope on Sept. 5, 1977 *fide* R.D. James (Goodwin, 1978: 1001).

**MEASUREMENTS:**
*Length:* 7 to 7 3/4 ins.
(Godfrey, 1966: 361)
*Wingspread:* 11 to 12 ins.
(Roberts, 1955: 697)
*Weight:* 109 averaged
28.1 g. (22.5 - 37.4 g.)
(Dunning, 1984: 23).

**REFERENCE:**
Baillie, J.L. 1958 Western Tanager an Ontario bird. Ont. Field Biologist, No. 12: 28-29.

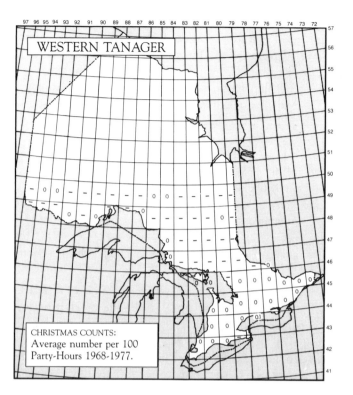

WESTERN TANAGER

CHRISTMAS COUNTS:
Average number per 100
Party-Hours 1968-1977.

# NORTHERN CARDINAL  *Cardinalis cardinalis*  (Linnaeus)

Northern Cardinals have been gradually spreading north and east into Ontario since about 1900. Adults drive the young out of their territories when they acquire the red beaks of adulthood (they are brown in the young). The young tend to wander and settle down in unoccupied areas, preferably near feeding stations which supply winter food and near shrubbery which will provide suitable nesting territories.

**IDENTIFICATION:** Males are all red except for some black surrounding the bill and have a prominent red crest. Females are brownish with bright red bill and some red in the flight feathers. The young look much like the adults but have brown beaks. Both sexes sing but it is usually the male that you hear with his rich, sweet: "what-cheer——cheer-cheer-cheer".

**WINTER:** Cardinals are most conspicuous against the white snowy background of winter. On the 1968-1977 Christmas counts they were common north and east to Richmond Hill, fairly common north to Georgian Bay, becoming rare to Ottawa and Sault Ste. Marie. Stirrett (1973a: 19) had a winter maximum of 75 at Pelee on Dec. 26. Harold Lancaster counted 35 along a short stretch of the Thames River in Essex Co. on Jan. 1, 1946 (Brooman, 1954: 36). Fleming (1907: 87) considered the species accidental at Toronto, but reported a female taken in February, 1900. From 1925 to 1930 single birds were seen on only 2 of the 6 Christmas counts, but they have been seen in increasing numbers on every count since (Saunders, 1947: 378). On the Pickering Christmas counts from 1961 to 1970, the numbers varied from 24 to 106, averaging 63 (Speirs, 1973). Snyder (1941: 85) reported two in Prince Edward Co. in January, 1939, following a massive influx into Ontario in the fall of 1938. Walter Lamb reported the first definite Kingston record at his feeder on Jan. 4, 1952. A.F. Young collected a female at Penetanguishene on Feb. 14, 1901 (Macoun, 1904: 527). L. Beamer reported one at Meaford on Jan. 29, 1938 and during most subsequent winters until Dec. 31, 1955. A Northern Strike killed one at Huntsville on Feb. 16, 1955, and C.A. Campbell reported overwintering birds at Parry Sound feeders since 1963-1964 (Mills, 1981: 164). Nicholson (1981: 181) reported a pair at a Gore Bay feeder on Dec. 22, 1968, with Manitoulin sightings annually since then. Louise Lawrence observed one daily at her Pimisi Bay feeder from Dec. 9, 1941 until the following spring: singing commenced on Feb. 25 (Speirs & Speirs, 1947: 37). Dennison (1980: 147) reported the species on 8 of 25 Christmas counts at Sault Ste. Marie, with a maximum of 3 in 1961). Denis (1961: 7) called the cardinal an irregular, very rare, visitant to Thunder Bay.

SPRING: Stirrett (1973b: 26) had a spring maximum of 30 at Pelee on May 7. Irla Flack found a nest with young at St. Thomas on May 6, 1932 (Baillie & Harrington, 1937: 263). Speirs (1973) noted courtship feeding as early as March 19, 1972 in Pickering Twp. and Dennis Barry found a nest with 3 eggs as early as April 13, 1968 in Whitby. Tozer & Richards (1974: 278) reported a nest with 3 eggs and 4 cowbird eggs in Darlington Twp. on May 20, 1971. One seen in Ottawa in the spring of 1888 may have been an escaped cage bird (Lloyd, 1924: 11).

SUMMER: On the 1968-1977 Breeding Bird Survey, they were common from London to Port Dover, fairly common north to Kincardine and east to Fraserville, and rare to Kingston and Manitoulin Island. Stirrett (1973c: 22) had a summer maximum of 12 at Pelee on June 19 and June 27. L.L. Snyder took a set of 3 eggs at Pelee on June 15, 1920 (Baillie & Harrington, 1937: 263). C.C. Bell found a nest with 3 eggs and a cowbird egg at Rondeau on June 2, 1933 (Baillie & Harrington, 1937: 263). R.V. Lindsay found a nest at Fishers Glen in July, 1927 (Snyder, 1931: 201). W. Joyce found a nest with 4 eggs on Long Point on July 12, 1973 (McCracken, Bradstreet & Holroyd, 1981: 65). I saw my first Toronto bird on Aug. 10, 1922, then no more until July 21, 1928, but have seen inceasing numbers every year since that time. Speirs & Orenstein (1975: 14) found a population density of 8 birds per 100 acres in the Whitby forest plot, but none in the other 10 forest quadrats in Ontario Co. Speirs, Markle & Tozer (1970: 5) found populations of 8, 6 and 7 birds per 100 acres in the Uxbridge, Port Perry and Whitby urban plots, none in the other 7 urban quadrats in Ontario Co. Richard Norman found the first Kingston nest, containing 3 eggs, on June 17, 1969, though Nora Mansfield had seen an adult feeding young on July 20, 1968 (Quilliam, 1973: 176). Devitt (1967: 158) found a nest with 3 young at Orillia on June 11, 1941. L. Beamer reported a juvenile feeding in a mulberry tree in Meaford on July 31 and Aug. 1, 1956. On June 1, 1974, C.A. Campbell found the remains of a nest and eggs at Parry Sound (Mills, 1981: 164). Kathleen Dinsmore found a nest with eggs at South Baymouth, Manitoulin, in the summer of 1973 (Nicholson, 1981: 181).

AUTUMN: David Elder saw a male at Atikokan on Nov. 6, 1981. F.W. McKee collected a female at Hardy Bay on the French River in autumn about 1930 (Baillie &

Harrington, 1937: 262-263). P. Tapley watched an adult feeding 2 young at Huntsville on Oct. 6, 1969 (Mills, 1981: 164). Devitt (1967: 159) reported adults feeding 2 young, out of the nest, at Barrie on Sept. 21, 1964. The first specimen from eastern Ontario was taken at Portsmouth, near Kingston, on Nov. 15, 1962 (Quilliam, 1973: 176). We saw our female feeding a young male on our Pickering Twp. feeder as late as Oct. 16, 1972. Fleming (1907: 81) reported a male seen in Toronto in November, 1902, as "accidental". Beardslee & Mitchell (1965: 413) reported a young bird, out of the nest but still not able to fly, at Morgan's Point, Lake Erie, as late as Sept. 16, 1962. Saunders & Dale (1933: 236) mentioned that the first London record was a bird observed on Nov. 30, 1896. Stirrett (1973d: 28) had a fall maximum of 15 at Pelee on Sept. 28.

**MEASUREMENTS:**
*Length:* 7.5 to 9.3 ins.
(Godfrey, 1966: 363)
*Wingspread:* 10 1/4 to 12
ins. (Roberts, 1955: 700)
*Weight:* 17 Ontario
specimens averaged
44.3 g.

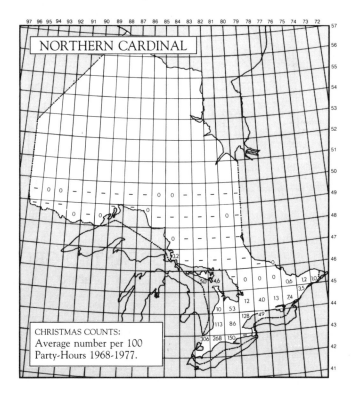

NORTHERN CARDINAL

CHRISTMAS COUNTS:
Average number per 100
Party-Hours 1968-1977.

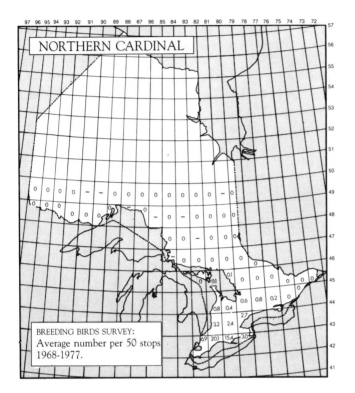

NORTHERN CARDINAL

BREEDING BIRDS SURVEY:
Average number per 50 stops
1968-1977.

# ROSE-BREASTED GROSBEAK
*Pheucticus ludovicianus*   (Linnaeus)

These colourful migrants may come to your feeders for sunflower seeds when they arrive in early May, but they soon retire to shrubs under the forest canopy to nest. The male shares incubation duties with its mate and may even sing while on the nest. Most go south to the tropical forests of Central and northern South America in winter.

IDENTIFICATION: Adult males are mainly black above and white below, with a big red triangular patch on the upper breast and on the wing linings. There are big white splotches on the black wings. Females are brown above with whitish wing bars and a white breast heavily streaked with brown (like an oversize female Purple Finch). Both sexes have big white beaks. The song is somewhat like a robin's, but faster, and may be interrupted by the "heek" call note (suggesting a slightly inebriated robin).

WINTER: On the 1968-1977 Christmas counts, individuals were reported at Port Hope, Wiarton, Ottawa and Deep River. A fine male was noted at the Gurtners' feeder on Rosebank Rd., Pickering, on the Dec. 26, 1979 Christmas count and was seen by many observers for the following weeks: I found it still there on Jan. 20, 1980. M.C. Edwards and W. Glover found a late bird at Wolfe Is., Kingston, on Dec. 2, 1969 (Quilliam, 1973: 176). J.W. Johnson had one to Dec. 20, 1977 at Wiarton (Goodwin, 1978: 346).

SPRING: Stirrett (1973b: 26) had 7 at Pelee as early as Apr. 20, and a maximum of 100 there on May 10. Ussher (1965: 28) gave May 7 as his 24-year average arrival date at Rondeau, with the earliest on Apr. 28. Saunders & Dale (1933: 237) gave May 8 as the 17-year average arrival date at London, with the earliest on May 3, 1913: their earliest nest was found on May 27, 1914, which held 3 eggs and two cowbird eggs. J.L. Baillie (in Saunders, 1947: 374) gave May 13 as his 24-year average arrival date at Toronto, with the earliest on May 2. Dennis Barry found one in Thickson's Woods, Whitby, as early as May 2, 1964 (Speirs, 1973) and counted an astonishing 190 there on May 13, 1972 (Tozer & Richards, 1974: 279). The earliest nest, with 5 eggs, near Oshawa was found on May 30, 1968 and the earliest in Darlington Twp., with 2 eggs, was found on May 30, 1970 (Tozer & Richards, 1974: 279). Weir & Quilliam (1980: 40) listed May 6 as the 32-year average arrival date at Kingston, with one very early bird on Apr. 11, 1969: Richard Norman located a nest with 3 eggs in Bell's Swamp, near Kingston, on May 26, 1968 (Quilliam, 1973: 176). Devitt (1967: 159) gave May 12 as the 21-year average arrival date at Barrie, with the earliest on May 4, 1964: W.W. Smith found a nest with one egg as early as May 25, 1941 at Big Cedar Point. L. Beamer's median arrival date at Meaford was May 18, with the earliest on May 3, 1953. On May 24, 1904, J.H. Fleming found a nest with 4 eggs at Rockcliffe, Ottawa (Lloyd, 1924: 11). Mills (1981: 164) gave May 10 as the 12-year average arrival date at Huntsville, with the earliest on Apr. 30, 1962. Nicholson (1981: 182) gave May 10 as the 11-year average arrival date on Manitoulin, with a maximum of 240 at the Mississagi Light on May 20, 1977 and an exceptionally early Apr. 15, 1977 record by Grant Garrette. MacLulich (1938: 39) reported May 19, 1932 as his earliest Algonquin Park record. Louise Lawrence observed one at Pimisi Bay on May 8, 1945 (Speirs & Speirs, 1947: 37). Skeel & Bondrup-Nielsen (1978: 213) heard their first at Pukaskwa on May 19, 1977. Denis (1961: 4) gave May 22 as the average arrival date at Thunder Bay, with the earliest on May 14, 1953. Peruniak (1971: 29) gave May 11 as her earliest Atikokan date. Elder (1979: 39) had his earliest at Geraldton on May 16.

SUMMER: On the 1968-1977 Breeding Bird Surveys, they were common from Fraserville north through the cottage country to Mattawa, as well as on some Rainy River routes: they were fairly common on most other routes but lacking on some of the more northeasterly routes. Stirrett (1973c: 22) had single birds at Pelee on July 18 and 31. Saunders & Dale (1933: 237) found a nest with 4 eggs as late as June 15, 1912, near London. Speirs & Frank (1970: 742) found a breeding density of 8 territories per 100 acres in the Springwater Forest, near Aylmer, in 1970. R.W. Johnson found a nest with 4 eggs at St. Thomas on May 10, 1905 (Baillie & Harrington, 1937: 263). Nol et al (1978: 65) found this to be the most common species in their quadrat in the Backus Woods, near Port Rowan, in 1977, with a density of 26 territories per 100 acres. Beardslee & Mitchell (1965: 415) reported a nest with eggs as late as June 26, 1897 (or 1898) at Sherkston, near Niagara Falls. Snyder (1930: 196) found a nest with 4 eggs in King Twp. on June 3, 1926. Speirs & Orenstein (1975: 14) found breeding populations in 8 of 11 forest quadrats in Ontario Co., with a maximum density of 39 birds per 100 acres in the Whibty plot. A.J. Mitchener found a female incubating as late as June 28, 1967 in the Minesing Swamp (Devitt, 1967: 159). I found a breeding density of 12 territories per 100 acres in a sugar maple forest near Dorset (Mills, 1981: 165). D.B. Ferguson found a nest with 2 eggs near Mindemoya, Manitoulin, on July 11, 1980 (Nicholson, 1981: 182). C.H.D. Clarke saw adults feeding young at Brule Lake, Algonquin Park, on July 4, 1934

(MacLulich, 1938: 39). Louise Lawrence found a nest with 4 eggs at Pimisi Bay on June 14, 1945, about 8 ft. up in a balsam fir (Speirs & Speirs, 1947: 37). Baillie & Hope (1947: 28) collected a young male on July 31 and a young female on July 29, 1937, at Bigwood. Snyder (1942: 148-149) found a nest with 4 young at Gordon Lake, near Sault Ste. Marie, on June 29, 1931. Skeel & Bondrup-Nielsen (1978: 213) heard a few on deciduous forest transects in Pukaskwa, the latest on July 6, 1977. Snyder (1928: 270) collected a male at Macdiarmid, Lake Nipigon, on June 10, 1924, the only one he observed there. Dear (1940: 141) found a nest with 4 eggs on July 4, 1928 in Paipoonge Twp. Thunder Bay. Snyder (1938: 209) collected a young bird at Big Fork, Rainy River, on June 19, 1929. Snyder (1953: 85) found them "Not uncommon" at Kenora, diminishing to the north and east to Perrault Falls and Dinorwic. Smith (1957: 180) saw one at New Liskeard on July 30, 1953. J.R. Dymond saw a male at Lake Abitibi on July 8, 1925 (Snyder, 1928: 29). James (1980: 90) noted two singing males at Shred Lake (northeast of Pickle Lake) during the summer of 1979. Cringan (1953a: 4) noted one at Perrault Falls on June 18, 1953. A. Wormington reported an immature at Moosonee on Aug. 8, 1972 (Goodwin, 1973: 55). James, McLaren & Barlow (1976: 49) described one noted at Winisk on June 15, 1970 as "accidental".

AUTUMN: Peruniak (1971: 29) gave Sept. 19 as her latest Atikokan date. Louise Lawrence noted one at Pimisi Bay on Sept. 4, 1944 (Speirs & Speirs, 1947: 37). Nicholson (1981: 182) had one as late as Oct. 6, 1978 on Manitoulin. At Ahmic Lake, Parry Sound Dist., Mills (1981: 165) noted 10 on Sept. 16, 1979 and Cliff MacFayden saw a late bird on Oct. 1, 1978 at Glen Orchard, Muskoka. At the Barrie TV tower 16 were killed in 5 of 7 years: A Helmsley saw two as late as Oct. 10, 1938 in the Minesing Swamp (Devitt, 1967: 159). Weir & Quilliam (1980: 40) gave Oct. 1 as the 27-year average departure date from Kingston. Doris H. Speirs saw one at our Pickering Twp. home as late as Oct. 9, 1967 (Speirs, 1973). Saunders (1947: 374) gave Sept. 24 as his 10-year average departure date from Toronto, with the latest on Oct. 28. Beardslee & Mitchell (1965: 414) reported one along the Ontario shore of the Niagara River as late as Oct. 16, 1949. Snyder (1931: 202) reported 4 lighthouse casualties at Long Point between Sept. 24-29, 1929. Ussher (1965: 28) gave Sept. 26 as his 10-year average departure date from Rondeau. Stirrett (1973d: 28) had a fall maximum of 5 at Pelee on Sept. 15 with the latest on Oct. 12.

BANDING: Brewer & Salvadori (1978: 79, 87, 88) reported a male banded at Long Point on Aug. 15, 1966 and recovered on Nov. 11, 1970 at Monteria, Colombia. Another banded at Long Point on May 14, 1970 turned up on June 25, 1970 at Bobcageon.

**MEASUREMENTS:**
*Length:* 7 to 8 1/2 ins.
(Godfrey, 1966: 364)
*Wingspread:* 12 1/4 to 13
3/4 ins. (Roberts,
1955: 704)
*Weight:* 32 Ontario
specimens averaged
45.9 g.

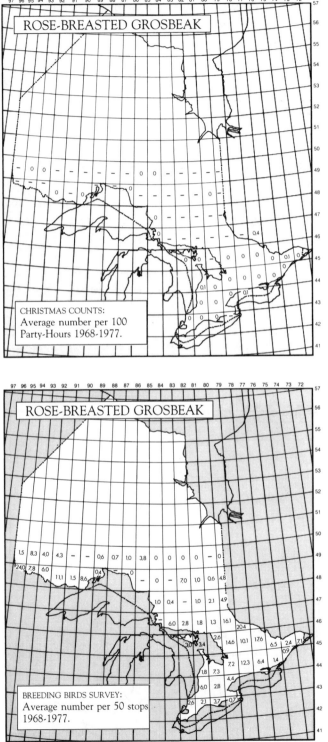

ROSE-BREASTED GROSBEAK

CHRISTMAS COUNTS:
Average number per 100
Party-Hours 1968-1977.

ROSE-BREASTED GROSBEAK

BREEDING BIRDS SURVEY:
Average number per 50 stops
1968-1977.

# BLACK-HEADED GROSBEAK
*Pheucticus melanocephalus* (Swainson)

This is the western counterpart of our Rose-breasted Grosbeak, with very similar habits, song, etc. and interbreeding where the ranges overlap. It is very rare in Ontario. They winter mainly in Mexico.

IDENTIFICATION: The body plumage of the male is a rusty orange colour. The wings and tail are black with white blotches and the head is mainly black with an orange stripe running back above the eye. Females resemble female Rose-breasted Grosbeaks but have a warm buffy breast. The song is similar to that of the Rose-breasted Grosbeak.

WINTER: G.E. Maddeford, W.R. Jarmain *et al* reported one at London from Jan. 27, 1979 to mid-April. (Goodwin, 1979: 278, 767). E.L. Griffin found one at Ancaster, where it was seen by many others and photographed by Don. Gunn, from Dec. 4-24, 1973 (Goodwin, 1974: 635).

SPRING: H. and M. Vibert photographed one at Rosslyn, Essex Co., on May 6, 1978 (Goodwin, 1978: 1001). B.C. Olson found a male at Port Hope on May 4, 1981 (Goodwin, 1981: 820). P. Tapp found one at Thunder Bay on May 20, 1979 and one was identified at Sibley nearby on May 23, 1979 by J. Crowe and J. Hebden (Goodwin, 1979: 767).

SUMMER: One was identified on Aug. 28, 1949 by Mrs. Ralph D. Baker and Mrs. F.G. Mather at Kenora, according to A.G. Lawrence (Baillie, 1950: 14).

AUTUMN:

**MEASUREMENTS:**
*Length:* 7 to 8 1/2 ins. (Godfrey, 1966: 365)
Wingspread:
*Weight:* 18 ♂ averaged 41.8 g., 15 ♀ averaged 47.2 g. (Dunning, 1984: 23).

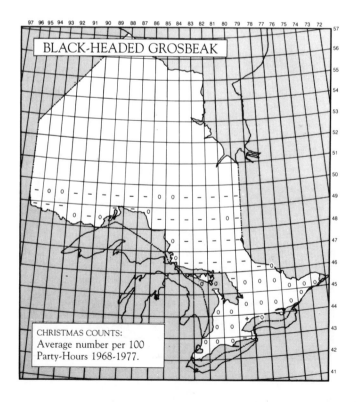

BLACK-HEADED GROSBEAK

CHRISTMAS COUNTS:
Average number per 100
Party-Hours 1968-1977.

# BLUE GROSBEAK  Guiraca caerulea  (Linnaeus)

This is normally a bird of the southern United States, rarely coming as far north as southern Ontario. They winter in Mexico and Central America.

IDENTIFICATION: Blue Grosbeaks look like oversize Indigo Buntings but with relatively heavy beaks and with constrastingly conspicuous rusty wing bars (Indigo Buntings may have a good deal of brown in the wings, but not as conspicuous wing bars).

WINTER:

SPRING: Stirrett (1973b: 26) had 4 Pelee records of single birds: May 13, 1961, May 15, 1964, May 6, 1966 and May 31, 1967. Goodwin (1972: 758) reported one seen there by Jeffrey A. Greenhouse et al from May 7-19, 1972. In 1979 there were 4 Pelee reports (one documented) from May 7-22 (Goodwin, 1979: 767): another showed up there from May 11-16, 1981 seen by M. Brown, P.D. Pratt and many others (Goodwin, 1981: 820). Miss I. Flach reported a male at Eagle on May 25, 1937 (Brooman, 1954: 36). An immature male was collected at Long Point on May 23, 1960 (Woodford & Baldwin, 1961: 97) and another was photographed there on May 24, 1975 (Goodwin, 1975: 847). A female was reported at Long Point on May 18, 1983 (Weir, 1983: 866). A female was reported at Fort Erie on May 21, 1913 by Mrs. G.M. Turner (Beardslee & Mitchell, 1965: 416). Allin (1942: 140) reported one seen at Bowmanville by Ralph H. Carruthers on May 26, 1923. Edith Hartman found two at Odessa on May 14, 1972 that remained until May 19 and were seen and documented by several other observers (Quilliam, 1973: 177). Another male showed up at Crow Lake, near Kingston, on Apr. 17 and 18, 1974 as documented by John Meisel (Weir & Quilliam, 1980: 26). T. Bigg reported a male at Lakefield on May 28, 1974 (Goodwin, 1974: 797). Louise Lawrence saw one at Pimisi Bay on May 8, 1965 (Goodwin, 1965: 34) and two were photographed at nearby Rutherglen on May 9, 1983 by Mr. & Mrs. B. LaFrance fide Ross James.

SUMMER: Stirrett (1973c: 22) reported one at Pelee on July 29. Mrs. G. Arnold saw a male near Aylmer on Aug. 31, 1937 (Brooman, 1954: 36). L.L. Snyder identified a male at Toronto in August, 1918 (Baillie, 1964: 4). R.C. Long saw an immature male in the Shoal Point woods, Pickering on July 15, 1969 (Speirs, 1973). J.B. Wallace found one in Eastnor Twp., Bruce Co., on June 30, 1980 (Goodwin, 1981: 178). The most remarkable record was of a male reported at Cliff Lake, about 25 miles north of Vermilion Bay, on June 25, 1949 (Marvel, 1950: 94).

AUTUMN: Gwendolen Lunn wrote to J.L. Baillie describing a male she saw at Richmond Hill on Sept. 17, 1968.

## MEASUREMENTS:

Length: 6 1/2 to 7 1/2 ins. (Godfrey, 1966: 366)
Wingspread:
Weight: 21 North Carolina birds averaged 28.4 g. (Terres, 1980: 331).

Ontario. Can. Field-Naturalist, 64: (2): 94.
　Woodford, James & D.H. Baldwin 1961 First Blue Grosbeak collected in Ontario. Auk, 78: (1): 97.

## REFERENCES:
Marvel, C.S. 1950 The Blue Grosbeak in western

# LAZULI BUNTING   *Passerina amoena*   (Say)

The Lazuli Bunting is a bird of arid brushy areas in western North America, accidental in Ontario.

**IDENTIFICATION:** Males resemble Indigo Buntings but have white wing bars and belly and brownish breast. Females are very similar to female Indigo Buntings apart from the white wing bars and generally paler colour. The two species sometimes interbreed where their ranges overlap in the prairies.

**WINTER:**

**SPRING:**   S.B. Terrill saw one at Pelee on May 23, 1982 and Don Koval photographed one at Pickle Lake on May 10, 1979.

**SUMMER:**

**AUTUMN:**

**MEASUREMENTS:**
*Length:* 5 to 5 3/4 ins.
(Godfrey, 1966: 367)
Wingspread:
*Weight:* 58 ♂ averaged
16.0 g.; 25 ♀ 15.0 g.
(Dunning, 1984: 23).

# INDIGO BUNTING   *Passerina cyanea*   (Linnaeus)

The Indigo Bunting is a forest-edge bird, where the demure brown female nests in raspberry thickets, while the brilliant blue male sings, silhouetted against the blue summer skies. In the days of my youth I associated them with unpaved roads along the Niagara Cuesta. I have sometimes found them more common in midsummer than during the first influx of migrants in late May, and wondered if some nest farther south and come north after the first brood, to nest in Ontario for the second brood, or perhaps just come north as the herons do after nesting in the south. In winter most of them go south to Mexico or Central America; some to the West Indies.

**IDENTIFICATION:** These are goldfinch-sized birds, not to be confused with the much larger Blue Grosbeaks, which are about the size of cowbirds. Adult males are rich blue with sometimes some brown in wings and tail, but lacking the rusty wing bars of Blue Grosbeaks. Females are inconspicuous dull brown little birds.

**WINTER:** Two were reported on the Meaford Christmas count in 1972, but without adequate documentation.

**SPRING:** Stirrett (1973b: 26) reported two at Pelee as early as Apr. 27 and had a maximum of 150 on May 21. Between 6:40 and 10:00 a.m. on May 21, 1938 we counted 40 flying south off the tip of Point Pelee, during a spectacular reverse migration involving several other species. Ussher (1965: 28) gave May 12 as his 23-year average arrival date at Rondeau, with the earliest on May 4. Saunders & Dale (1933: 237) gave May 16 as the 17-year average arrival date at London, with the earliest on May 10, 1916. Speirs (1938: 39) listed an Apr. 28 date for Toronto: Saunders (1947: 374) gave May 17 as his 11-year average arrival date there. Tozer & Richards (1974: 279) reported one as early as May 8, 1965 in Oshawa. Weir & Quilliam (1980: 40) listed May 13 as the 31-year average arrival date at Kingston, with the earliest on May 1. Devitt (1967: 160) gave May 22 as the 18-year average arrival date at Barrie, with the earliest on May 13, 1953. L. Beamer's median arrival date at Meaford was May 24, with the earliest on May 14, 1956. Mills (1981: 165) gave May 15, 1965 as the earliest Huntsville date. Nicholson (1981: 182) gave May 15 as the 10-year average arrival date on Manitoulin, with the earliest on May 1, 1976. On May 30, 1938, J.L. Baillie saw single males at North Bay and Beaucage (Ricker & Clarke, 1939: 22). Peruniak (1971: 29) gave May 26 as her earliest Atikokan date.

SUMMER: On the 1968-1977 Breeding Bird Surveys, they were common on the Port Dover route, fairly common elsewhere north to Mattawa and Montreal Falls and in the Rainy River region; rare north to Nipigon and Eagle River, and missing on northeastern routes. Stirrett (1973c: 22) had a summer maximum of 25 at Pelee on June 15, but had 30, including migrants, on Aug. 17 (Stirrett, 1973d: 28): Speirs & Frank (1970: 777) found a breeding density of 16 territories per 100 acres in the Pelee forest in 1970, where it ranked as the second most abundant species. Saunders & Dale (1933: 237) found a nest with 3 eggs on June 6, 1902 near London and a nest with 5 eggs and a cowbird egg on June 16, 1894, as well as three other June 11 sets. R.T. Anderson took a set of 2 eggs at Alymer on June 12, 1896 (Baillie & Harrington, 1937: 264). Snyder (1931: 202) reported a nest with one egg and 3 newly hatched young on Long Point on July 12, 1927. Fairfield & Nasmith (1978: 65) found a breeding density of 8 territorial males per 100 acres in the Moore Park Ravine, Toronto in 1977. Snyder (1930: 196) reported a nest with 4 eggs in King Twp. on June 19, 1926 about 3 ft. up in a hazelbush. Speirs & Orenstein (1975: 15) found populations in 5 of 11 forest quadrats in Ontario Co., with a maximum density of 17 birds per 100 acres in the Whitby plot. L.L. Snyder found a nest with 4 eggs at Rouge Hills, Pickering, on June 23, 1932 and J.A. Edwards found two nests, both with 3 eggs, on Thorah Is. one on July 3, 1909, the other on July 24, 1909 (Speirs, 1973). Charles Fothergill shot a male at Rice Lake on July 17, 1820 (Black, 1934: 158). W.H. Lunn collected a nest with 3 eggs as late as Aug. 15, 1938, in Prince Edward Co. (Snyder, 1941: 86). Quilliam (1973: 177) found a nest with 4 eggs at Otter Lake, near Kingston, on June 30, 1968. Devitt (1967: 160) reported several nest records for Simcoe Co., one nest with 4 eggs as early as June 7, 1933, found by H.P. Bingham at Barrie and another nest with 4 eggs there by the same observer as late as July 20, 1939. Lloyd (1924: 11) found a nest with 4 young near Ottawa on July 9, 1922, with C.L. Patch. Mills (1981: 166) reported two nests in Parry Sound Dist., one at Pickerel Lake held 3 eggs and a cowbird egg on July 14 and 22, 1939, the other at Rock Island Lake held 4 young on June 24, 1978: I saw young being fed by adults at Torrance, Muskoka, as late as Aug. 17, 1936. D.B. Ferguson found a nest with 3 eggs near Windfall Lake, Manitoulin, on July 2, 1979 (Nicholson, 1981: 182). MacLulich (1938: 39) noted a few summer records for Algonquin Park. Speirs & Speirs (1947: 37) heard singing males near Rutherglen from June 6 (1944) to June 20 (1945). Snyder (1942: 149) collected two young at Maclennan, near Sault Ste. Marie, on July 27, 1931. Dear (1940: 141) found a nest with 2 eggs at Whitefish

Lake, near Thunder Bay, on June 18, 1938. David Elder saw one at Lac La Croix on June 2, 1981. Snyder (1953: 86) found a pair at Wabigoon on June 22, 1937. On June 15, 1983, I heard two near Foleyet. Three observers saw a pair with at least two young about 12 miles northwest of Cochrane on July 10, 1955 (Todd, 1965: 644). Baillie & Harrington (1937: 264) mentioned a male seen at Sioux Lookout in June by Miss E. Keefe (*fide* A.G. Lawrence).

AUTUMN: James, McLaren & Barlow (1976: 50) mentioned an "accidental" at Winisk on Oct. 15, 1973. Nicholson (1981: 182) gave Oct. 5, 1978 as his latest record, at Great Duck Island. Mills (1981: 166) found 3 at Ahmic Lake as late as Sept. 26, 1979. L. Beamer noted one as late as Sept. 17, 1938, at Meaford. Devitt (1967: 160) gave Sept. 24, 1939, as the latest Barrie record. Weir & Quilliam (1980: 40) listed Sept. 19 as the 21-year average departure date from Kingston, with the latest on Oct. 19. Harold Richards noted a very late bird at Leaside on Nov. 27, 1972 (Parker, 1983: 25). LGL (1974: 213) noted migrants along the Lake Ontario shore as late as Oct. 15, 16 and 17, 1973. R.C. Long saw 15 at Pickering Beach on Sept. 21, 1963 and one there as late as Oct. 11, 1968 (Speirs, 1973). Speirs (1938: 53) gave Oct. 4 as the latest Toronto date. Beardslee & Mitchell (1965: 416) reported one as late as Oct. 12, 1958, at Morgan's Point, Lake Erie. Snyder (1931: 202) reported 5 lighthouse casualties at Long Point from Sept. 24-29, 1929. Ussher (1965: 28) gave Oct. 4 as a 5-year average departure date from Rondeau, with the latest on Oct. 14. Stirrett (1973d: 28) had a fall maximum of 20 at Pelee on Sept. 17, with the latest on Oct. 14.

**MEASUREMENTS:**
*Length:* 5 1/4 to 5 3/4 ins.
(Godfrey, 1966: 366)
*Wingspread:* 8.25 to 8.62
ins. (Roberts, 1955: 705)
*Weight:* 26 Ontario
specimens averaged
15.2 g.

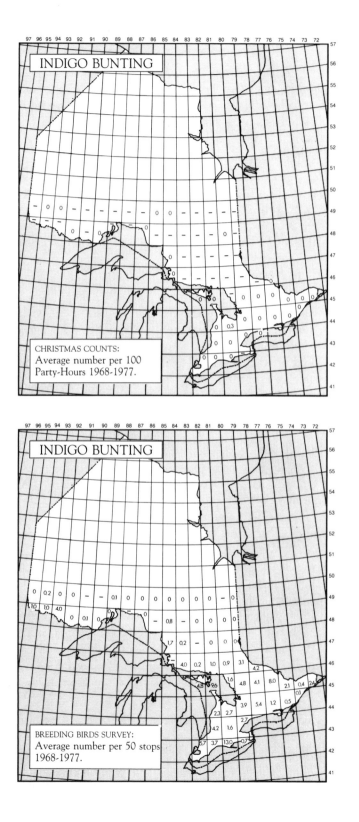

INDIGO BUNTING

CHRISTMAS COUNTS:
Average number per 100
Party-Hours 1968-1977.

INDIGO BUNTING

BREEDING BIRDS SURVEY:
Average number per 50 stops
1968-1977.

# DICKCISSEL   *Spiza americana*   (Gmelin)

The Dickcissel is a rare bird in Ontario, but a few breed near the Lake Erie shore and stragglers show up in most unexpected places farther north. It is a fairly common bird in the midwestern United States, along roadsides. Most winter from Mexico south to northern South America.

IDENTIFICATION: The Dickcissel is much the size and build of a House Sparrow and often associates with them at feeders. The females are very similar indeed but the Dickcissel may show some yellow on the breast and on the bend of the wing. Adult males have a breast pattern like a meadowlark, with yellow breast crossed by a black V: they have chestnut wing coverts, like a Vesper Sparrow, but lack the white outer tail feathers of that species. The song resembles the song of the Sedge Wren: "dick-dick-dick-cis-cis-cisl".

WINTER: The only one reported on the 1968-1977 Christmas counts, was studied at 6 ft. range by Terry Sprague on the Belleville count on Dec. 21, 1969. H.H. Axtell noted one with a flock of House Sparrows at his Fort Erie feeder from Dec. 2-10, 1961 and another there from Feb. 1-26, 1964 (Beardslee & Mitchell, 1965: 418). W. Wagner and many others saw one at Streetsville from Feb. 17, 1980 (Goodwin, 1980: 270). L. Thomson and E. Kennedy reported one at Richmond Hill from Dec. 12 to early January, in the winter of 1973-1974 (Goodwin, 1974: 635). W. Osborn and many others observed one at Port Hope from Dec. 16-18, 1979 (Goodwin, 1980: 270). Quilliam (1973: 178) reported one at Kingston on Dec. 3, 1969. A.A. Buckingham found one at Ottawa on Dec. 27, 1974 (Goodwin, 1975: 687).

SPRING: Gus Yaki and G. Meyers found one on Pelee Island on May 10, 1971 (Goodwin, 1971: 739). Stirrett (1973b: 26) gave Apr. 26 as his earliest Pelee record, with a maximum of 10 on May 8: most Ontario sightings have been in the Pelee region. P.A. Woodliffe *et al* observed one at Rondeau on May 11 and 12, 1981 (Goodwin, 1981: 820). R.P. McLeod noted one at Hyde Park, near London, on Apr. 20, 1976 (Goodwin, 1976: 836). M.E. Foley found one at St. Catharines on May 8, 1983 (Weir, 1983: 866). L. Marsh and many others observed one at Weston to Apr. 13, 1974 (Goodwin, 1974: 797). Naomi LeVay had one at Cranberry Marsh on May 12, 1951 and David Ruch noted one at his Whitby home on Apr. 22, 1980 (Speirs, 1973, etc.). W. Osborn observed one at Port Hope from May 6-9, 1976 (Goodwin, 1976: 836). Quilliam (1973: 178) had May 31 records at Kingston in 1958 and 1971. Martin Parker *et al* noted one at Hay Bay, Bruce Co., on May 20, 1973 (Goodwin, 1973: 866). Nicholson (1981: 182) reported two strays on Manitoulin: a male on May 3, 1975 in Carnarvon Twp. and another male on Great Duck Is. on May 18, 1979. M. Gawn, B. Gorman *et al* observed one at Batchawana Point, Lake Superior, on May 10, 1980 (Goodwin, 1980: 773) and N.G. Escott found one farther north at Marathon on May 6 to 8, 1980.

SUMMER: The only one reported on the 1968-1977 Breeding Bird Surveys, was on the Woodford route in 1972. Stirrett (1973c: 22) had a summer maximum of 12 at Pelee on June 16. J.A. Greenhouse and J.P. Kleiman found one at Port Alma on July 6, 1974 (Goodwin, 1974: 899). Ussher (1965: 28) had a Rondeau record on June 16, 1934. Saunders & Dale (1933: 237) saw a nest with 5 eggs at Bryanston on June 21, 1895, found by Robert Elliott on June 17: others were noted near London and one near Port Stanley on July 3: A.A. Wood collected one on June 27, 1930 at Strathroy. Recent records near London have been near Melbourne by D. Murray *et al*; where 3 pairs and another male were noted in the summer of 1972 and one on June 24, 1973 (Goodwin, 1972: 855 and Goodwin, 1973: 866). Brooman (1954: 37) reported a pair 3 or 4 miles east of Port Bruce on July 27, 1930 and a nest with 4 eggs found by G. Kains at Union in 1885. G. Bennett reported a male in Puslinch Twp. in the summer of 1972 (Goodwin, 1972: 855). Farley Mowat observed a male at Consecon, Prince Edward Co., in midsummer of 1940 (Snyder, 1941: 86). R.D. Weir found one at Prince Edward Point on Aug. 24, 1974 (Goodwin, 1975: 53). Five (two males and 3 females) were reported at Gananoque on Aug. 7, 1949 and one on Wolfe Is. on July 23, 1972 (Quilliam, 1965: 176 and 1973: 178). Goodwin (1972: 855) saw two males at Wiarton on June 26, 1972. L. Robertson reported a small colony in Eastnor Twp., Bruce Co., in the summer of 1975 and J.W. Johnson saw one at Hope Ness on June 7, 1975 (Goodwin, 1975: 967). J. W. Johnson and Martin Parker saw one at Hope Bay, Bruce Co., from June 5-20, 1981 (Goodwin, 1981: 936). F.A. and W.E. Saunders identified a male that spent the summer of 1895 at the Experimental Farm, Ottawa (Lloyd, 1924: 11).

AUTUMN: A. Wormington reported a far northern stray at Fort Albany on Oct. 10, 1981 (Goodwin, 1982: 174). N.G. Escott noted one at Marathon on Oct. 6, 1979 (Goodwin, 1980: 158). Mills (1981: 166) reported two Huntsville records, both at feeders with House Sparrows: one from Nov. 2-14, 1967, the other from Nov. 14-26, 1969. M. Young noted one at Ottawa from Oct. 7-14, 1972 (Goodwin, 1973: 55). Weir & Quilliam (1980: 40) listed Oct. 10 as a 6-year average fall arrival date at Kingston. G. Carpentier, D. McRae and D.C. Sadler reported one at Peterborough from Nov. 9-11, 1975 (Goodwin, 1976: 63). We had a female with House Sparrows at our Pickering Twp. feeder from Oct. 30 to Nov. 1, 1954 (about two weeks after Hurricane Hazel) and George A. Scott saw one at Oshawa about the same time (Oct. 31, 1954): with Chris. Amos I saw one near Corner Marsh, Pickering, on Oct. 1, 1967 (Speirs, 1973). G. Bennett reported one at Toronto on Nov. 22, 1981 (Goodwin, 1982: 174). H.H. Axtell had two on Oct. 6, 1962 and one the next day, at Fort Erie and two again there on Oct. 26, 1963 (Beardslee & Mitchell, 1965: 418). Four were reported at Long Point on Sept. 26, 1982 (Weir, 1983: 176). P.A. Woodliffe had one at Rondeau on Oct. 19, 1982 and P. Wilson one at Aylmer, Nov. 30, 1982 (Weir, 1983: 176). Many observers observed one at Windsor from Nov. 1, 1976 (Goodwin, 1977: 172) and B. Eaton found one at Amherstberg on Nov. 30, 1981 (Goodwin, 1982: 174). Stirrett (1973d: 28) had two September records at Pelee, one in 1967, the other from Sept. 19-20, 1900.

**MEASUREMENTS:**
*Length:* 6 to 7 ins.
(Godfrey, 1966: 368)
*Wingspread:* 9.62 to
10.60 ins. (Roberts,
1955: 714)
*Weight:* 1 oz. (Roberts,
1955: 714).

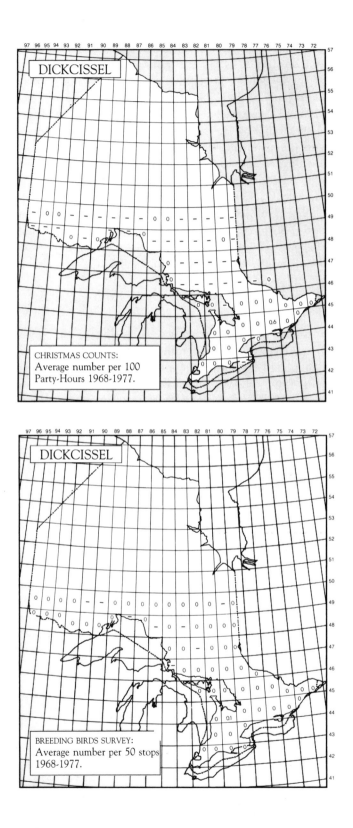

DICKCISSEL

CHRISTMAS COUNTS:
Average number per 100
Party-Hours 1968-1977.

DICKCISSEL

BREEDING BIRDS SURVEY:
Average number per 50 stops
1968-1977.

# GREEN-TAILED TOWHEE   *Pipilo chlorurus*   (Audubon)

This is normally a bird of scrubland in western United States mountains. A few have wandered east to Ontario in migration.

**IDENTIFICATION:**   The Green-tailed Towhee, as its name suggests, has a long greenish tail and wings. It is about the size and build of our common White-throated Sparrow, and like that species has a conspicuous white throat. The breast and face are gray and it has a big rufous cap.

**WINTER:**

**SPRING:**   On March 30, 1954 one turned up at the feeder of G.W.A. Aitken in London, who photographed it in colour. Another showed up, also in March, 1954, at John Young's feeder in Welland where it remained into April and was observed and described by Gertrude Selby, William W.H. Gunn, H.H. Axtell and others (Baillie, 1957: 2 and Beardslee & Mitchell, 1965: 429).

**SUMMER:**

**AUTUMN:**   On Nov. 24, 1956, L.E. Jaquith caught one in his garage at Terra Cotta and turned it over to H.R. Ivor's aviary where it was photographed (Baillie, 1957: 2). Mr. & Mrs. A.E. Robertson watched one feeding on the patio below their window in Whitby Twp. on Oct. 11 and 12, 1970 and gave me a good description of the bird (Speirs, 1973).

**MEASUREMENTS:**
*Length:* 6.5 to 7.0 ins.
(Godfrey, 1966: 380).
Wingspread:
*Weight:* 68 averaged
29.4 g. (21.5 - 37.3 g.)
(Dunning, 1984: 23).

# RUFOUS-SIDED TOWHEE
*Pipilo erythrophthalmus* (Linnaeus)

This colourful towhee is a fairly common bird in most of southern Ontario, usually found in dry shrubby vegetation, but sometimes coming to feeders in winter. Most go south in winter, some as far as the Gulf states.

IDENTIFICATION: Males superficially resemble small American Robins, with their black heads, rufous sides, but the belly is white and the outer tail feathers are much more broadly tipped with white. Females have a similar pattern to the males with the black replaced by brown. The common call is a loud "wheee" (rising in pitch) and the song gives it its name "Too-wheee-ti-ti-ti-ti", resembling some cardinal songs but more nasal, not as sweet and clear as the cardinal's song. Towhees are great scratchers, and often betray their presence scattering beds of fallen leaves.

WINTER: On the 1968-1977 Christmas counts, they were uncommon along the north shore of Lake Erie, becoming rare north to Sault Ste. Marie and Deep River. Stirrett (1973a: 20) had records throughout the winter at Pelee, with a maximum of 12 on Jan. 2. Ussher (1965: 29) wrote: "often occurs in winter" at Rondeau. Saunders & Dale (1933: 241) cited two wintering records for London and called them "rather unusual". Brooman (1954: 38) reported 17 on the St. Thomas Christmas count on Dec. 26, 1953. They were reported on 28 of 58 Christmas counts at Toronto (Parker, 1983: 25). They were seen on 4 of 10 Christmas counts at Pickering (1961-1970) and 5 of 16 Oshawa counts (1955-1970): other winter records were cited (Speirs, 1973). D.C. Sadler reported one at Peterborough to Jan. 7, 1978 (Goodwin, 1978: 346). Two were found on the Kingston count on Dec. 27, 1970 and one remained at a feeder throughout January and February (Quilliam, 1973: 184). A. Bain and R. Howie noted one at Summerstown, Glengarry Co., from Dec. 27, 1974 to Feb. 1, 1975 (Goodwin, 1975: 687). Frances Westman had a male at her feeder from Dec. 8, 1958 to the spring of 1959 and single birds were noted on 4 Barrie Christmas counts (Devitt, 1967: 166). The first successful wintering at Ottawa was reported in 1975-1976 by R.M. Poulin (Goodwin, 1976: 714). J. Goltz observed one at a Bala feeder to Jan. 31, 1971 and one seen on the Huntsville Christmas count on Dec. 20, 1964 remained until Jan. 14, 1965 (Mills, 1981: 176). Dennison (1980: 149) reported single birds on 2 of 25 Christmas counts at Sault Ste. Marie, in 1963 and 1966.

SPRING: Stirrett (1973b: 26) had a spring maximum of 32 at Pelee on Apr. 11. Ussher (1965: 29) gave Apr. 5 as his 23-year average arrival date at Rondeau. Saunders & Dale (1933: 241) gave March 31 as the 17-year average arrival date for London, with the earliest on March 15, 1915: a set of 3 eggs was found as early as May 15, 1907 and a nest with one egg and 3 cowbird eggs was found on May 25, 1909. McCracken, Bradstreet and Holroyd (1981: 66) reported a nest with 5 eggs near St. Williams, found by G. Bennett on May 15, 1959 and a nest with young at Backus Woods on May 28, 1976. Saunders (1947: 374) listed Apr. 21 as his 13-year average arrival date at Toronto and Speirs (1938: 43) gave May 3 as the peak of the spring migration there: Fleming (1907: 81) reported breeding on May 25, 1890. Mrs. Stuart L. Thompson found a nest with 4 eggs near Kelly Lake, King Twp., on May 25, 1926 (Snyder, 1930: 196). Weir & Quilliam (1980: 40) listed Apr. 16 as the 27-year average arrival date at Kingston with the earliest on March 23: Quilliam (1973: 184) reported 4 May nests near Kingston, one with 4 eggs in a ground nest as early as May 6 and another with 3 eggs and 3 cowbird eggs on May 3, 1968. Devitt (1967: 166) gave Apr. 23 as the 20-year average arrival date at Barrie, with the earliest on Apr. 5, 1963: H.P. Bingham found a nest with 4 eggs there on May 25, 1924. L. Beamer's median arrival date at Meaford was May 3, with his earliest on Apr. 20, 1938. Mills (1981: 176) gave Apr. 25 as an 8-year average arrival date at Huntsville, with the earliest on Apr. 8, 1971. D.B. Ferguson found a Manitoulin bird as early as Apr. 4, 1971 and Ron Tasker banded one in Burpee Twp. on May 25, 1971 (Nicholson, 1981: 187). Strickland, Tozer & Rutter (1982) listed May 14 as an average arrival date for Algonquin Park, with the earliest on Apr. 29. Ricker & Clarke (1939: 23) had four May records for Lake Nipissing: May 3 in 1925 and 1934, May 15 in 1926 and May 20 in 1929. Joan Hebden reported one at Thunder Bay on March 28, 1980 and N.G. Escott observed a wintering bird at Marathon up to March 15, 1980 (Goodwin, 1980: 773). A. Wormington had single birds at Harris Hill, Rainy River, on May 20, 1974 and Apr. 16, 1982 (Goodwin, 1974: 797 and Weir, 1982: 848).

SUMMER: On the 1968-1977 Breeding Bird Surveys, they were fairly common on most routes in the agricultural parts of southern Ontario, and rare north to Sudbury and Mattawa. Stirrett (1973c: 22) had Pelee records throughout the summer, with a maximum of 10 from Aug. 12-14. Speirs & Frank (1970: 777) had a breeding density of 6 territories per 100 acres in the Pelee forest plot and 4 per 100 acres in the Windsor prairie quadrat (1970: 765). Saunders & Dale (1933: 241) reported a set of 3 eggs as late as July 6, 1900 at London. R.V. Lindsay found a nest with 4 eggs at Fishers Glen in July, 1927 (Snyder, 1931: 201). We saw a striped young bird in our Pickering Twp. garden as late as Aug. 22, 1965 (Speirs, 1973). Speirs & Orenstein (1975: 15) had populations in two of 11 forest plots in Ontario Co.: 32 birds per 100 acres in the Whitby quadrat and 16 per 100 acres in the Brock Twp. plot. J.M. Richards found an interesting nest 4 ft. up in a Scots pine in a Christmas tree plantation in Cartwright Twp.: it held 3 young towhees, 1 young cowbird and 2 cowbird eggs on June 25, 1966: the 4 young were still in the nest on June 29 but the cowbird eggs had disappeared (Tozer & Richards, 1974: 288). Paul Harrington collected a set of 3 eggs at Wasaga Beach as late as Aug. 13, 1922 (Devitt, 1967: 166). Lloyd (1924: 11) had an Ottawa record for June 28, 1908 but never saw one there himself. C. Harris counted 17 at Go Home Bay on June 24, 1975 and E. Miller found a nest with 6 eggs hatching at Spider Bay on July 12, 1976: Hazel Petty saw one as far north as Wasi Falls on Lake Nipissing on July 9, 1972 (Mills, 1981: 176). Ron Tasker banded one on July 25, 1972 in Burpee Twp., Manitoulin (Nicholson, 1981: 187). On Aug. 3, 1930 MacLulich (1938: 42) saw a female in Algonquin Park and G.M. Meade noted one in the park on July 26, 1935. Snyder (1942: 150) had 8 summer records (3 collected) near Sault Ste. Marie 1931. Denis (1961: 7) listed this as a rare visitant at Thunder Bay but without details. James, McLaren & Barlow (1976: 51) mentioned one at Halfway Point, James Bay, again without details. C.E. Hope collected one far north of its usual range at Fort Severn on June 29, 1940.

AUTUMN: D. McRae & A. Wormington noted both a male and a female at Netitishi Point, James Bay, on Oct. 18, 1981: the female was seen again as late as Oct. 27 and the male to Nov. 5. O. Cearnes et al observed a bird of the "Spotted" race in the Red Rock Nipigon region from Nov. 16, which wintered at the feeder of T. Kukko (Weir, 1982: 174, 291). Mrs. I. Park reported one at Fort Frances in early Sept., 1972 (Goodwin,

1973: 55). O. Zarubik noted one at Sudbury on Nov. 27, 1976 (Goodwin, 1977: 172). Ricker & Clarke (1939: 23) had one fall record for Lake Nipissing, on Sept. 26, 1925. Strickland, Tozer & Rutter (1982) listed Oct. 20 as their latest Algonquin Park record. Nicholson (1981: 187) recorded a Manitoulin bird as late as Oct. 27, 1973. L. Vien saw two at Beausoleil Is. as late as Oct. 16, 1976 (Mills, 1981: 176). B. MacTavish observed one at Ottawa on Nov. 16, 1973 (Goodwin, 1974: 48). Weir & Quilliam (1980: 40) listed Oct. 20 as the 22-year average departure date from Kingston. Long (1968b: 23) gave Nov. 20, 1967 as his latest date for Pickering Beach. Saunders (1947: 374) listed Oct. 19 as his 13-year average departure date from Toronto: Speirs (1938: 51) gave Oct. 6 as the fall peak there. Beardslee & Mitchell (1965: 430) noted two at Erie Beach on Nov. 26, 1960. Ussher (1965: 29) gave Nov. 1 as his 9-year average departure date from Rondeau. Stirrett (1973d: 29) had a fall maximum of 15 at Pelee on Oct. 15.

**MEASUREMENTS:**
*Length:* 7.5 to 8.7 ins.
(Godfrey, 1966: 380)
*Wingspread:* 10.5 to 11.7
ins. (Roberts, 1955: 709)
*Weight:* 10 Ontario
specimens averaged
44.2 g.

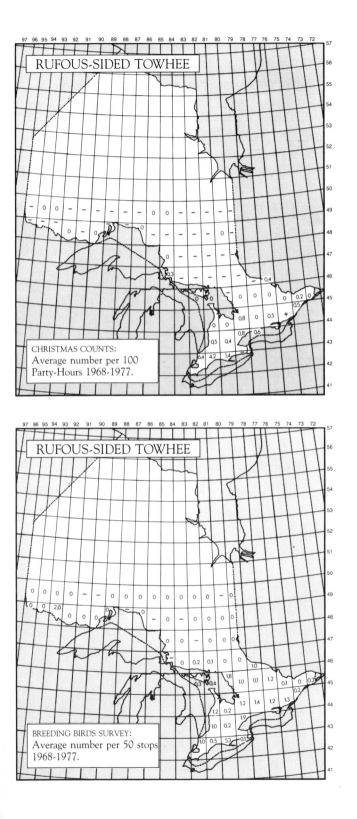

RUFOUS-SIDED TOWHEE

CHRISTMAS COUNTS:
Average number per 100
Party-Hours 1968-1977.

RUFOUS-SIDED TOWHEE

BREEDING BIRDS SURVEY:
Average number per 50 stops
1968-1977.

# BACHMAN'S SPARROW    *Aimophila aestivalis*    (Lichtenstein)

Bachman's Sparrow was once called the Pine-woods Sparrow, suggestive of its preference for sandy fields with scattered pines (or oaks). In Ontario this has been a very rare bird, with a few spring records along the Lake Erie shores. It is normally a permanent resident of the southeastern United States, where I learned its song during visits to the Carolinas.

IDENTIFICATION:   Bachman's Sparrow is a rather plain-looking sparrow with a buffy, unmarked breast. It is best identified by its lovely, clear song: "Sweeee-choo-choo-choo-choo...." The higher-pitched introductory note may be clear or somewhat trilled. It often occurs with Field Sparrows, from which it may be distinguished by its dark upper mandible (pink in the Field Sparrow), whitish "eyebrow" (not eye-ring as in the Field Sparrow) and a small yellow patch at the bend of the wing.

WINTER:

SPRING:   Saunders (1919: 118) collected one at Pelee on Apr. 16, 1917. Stirrett (1973b: 27) had six other records for Pelee: Apr. 17, 1960; May 10, 1965; May 12-14, 1963; May 13-14, 1961 and May 20, 1966; also two from May 7-10, 1964. Snyder (1929: 119) collected a female on Long Point on May 6, 1928.

SUMMER:

AUTUMN:

**MEASUREMENTS:**
*Length:* about 5 3/4 ins.
(Godfrey, 1966: 389)
Wingspread:
*Weight:* 12 ♂ averaged
20.2 g., one ♀ weighed
19.1 g.) (Dunning,
1984: 23).

**REFERENCES:**
Saunders, W.E. 1919
Bachman's Sparrow an
addition to the Canadian
fauna. Can. Field-
Naturalist, 33: (6): 118.
   Snyder, L.L. 1929
Second Canadian record of
Bachman's Sparrow. Auk,
46: (1): 119.

# CASSIN'S SPARROW   *Aimophila cassinii*   (Woodhouse)

Cassin's Sparrow is normally a bird of the sagebrush country of southwestern United States, accidental in Ontario. They winter mostly in Mexico.

**IDENTIFICATION:**   This is a predominantly gray sparrow, as befits a bird of short grass and sagebrush, with fine dark streaks on the crown and back and plain sandy gray breast.

**WINTER:**

**SPRING:**   Long (1968: 34) reported the first discovery of a Cassin's Sparrow in Canada, at Pelee on May 13, 1967, when it was watched at distances as close as 5 ft. by 40 or more observers and photographed by Vic. Crich and Ron. Scovell.

**SUMMER:**

**AUTUMN:**   A. McTavish and A. Wormington reported one at Marathon on Sept. 28, 1981 (Goodwin, 1982: 174).

**MEASUREMENTS:**
*Length:* 5 1/4 to 5 3/4 ins.
(Terres, 1980: 340)
Wingspread:
*Weight:* 92 averaged
18.9 g. (14.0 - 23.5 g.)
(Dunning, 1984: 23).

**REFERENCE:**
Long, R. Charles 1968 First
occurrence of Cassin's
Sparrow in Canada. Ont.
Field Biologist, No.
22: 34.

# AMERICAN TREE SPARROW   *Spizella arborea*   (Wilson)

In Ontario most of us think of the Tree Sparrow as a winter bird, or from the cottage country north, as a spring and fall migrant. Only near the Hudson Bay coast and the northern part of James Bay, is it known to breed. So, when one of our winter-banded birds came to us again the following winter and fed on our window sill feeder about 3 ft. from where were sat eating our meals, we marvelled at its navigational ability, finding our feeder again after spending the summer 1000 miles or so to the north. Others have had similar experiences.

IDENTIFICATION:   This is the cold weather sparrow with a blackish "stickpin" in the centre of an otherwise immaculate breast, with a tinkling "tsee-ooh-wee" call and, in the spring, a song like an octave-higher version of a Song Sparrow song. At close quarters it is a very colourful bird, with rich reddish-browns and contrasting black-centred buffy scapulars. The two-toned bill, yellow below and black above, will easily separate it from the pink-billed Field Sparrow and the all-black-billed Chipping Sparrow.

WINTER:   On the 1968-1977 Christmas counts they were abundant along the Lake Erie shores, common north to Ottawa and southern Georgian Bay, becoming rare or absent north of Deep River and Manitoulin. Stirrett (1973a: 20) had a winter maximum of 760 at Pelee on a Christmas count. On ten Christmas counts in Pickering Twp. 3908 were tallied, making this the most abundant of our winter sparrows there (Speirs, 1973). In Algonquin Park where they have been rare in winter, Mark Robinson had a record on Feb. 8, 1908. (MacLulich, 1938: 43). Speirs & Speirs (1947: 35) saw 3 birds at the North Bay dump on Dec. 23, 1944 and again on Jan. 1, 1945. Tree Sparrows were found on 14 of 25 Christmas counts at Sault Ste. Marie, with a high count of 96 in 1957 (Dennison, 1980: 147).

SPRING:   Stirrett (1973b: 27) had a spring maximum of 200 at Pelee on March 14, with the latest on May 13. Ussher (1965: 30) gave Apr. 19 as an 8-year average departure date from Rondeau, with the latest on May 10. Snyder (1931: 198) gave May 2 as his latest date for Long Point: 4 were killed at the lighthouse there on Apr. 17-18, 1930. One was noted at Long Beach, Lake Erie, as late as May 15, 1958 (Beardslee & Mitchell, 1965: 440). Speirs (1938: 43, 45) gave Apr. 5 as the spring peak date at Toronto, with the latest on May 24: Saunders (1947: 375) gave Apr. 30 as his 13-year average departure date for Toronto. R. Charles Long noted one at Pickering Beach as late as May 14, 1966 but most have left by the end of April (Speirs, 1973). Tozer & Richards (1974: 297) observed one in Darlington Twp. on May 15, 1966. Weir & Quilliam (1980: 40) listed Apr. 29 as the 29-year average departure date from Kingston. Devitt (1967: 172) cited an Orillia specimen taken on May 11, 1888. Pearl Rogers saw the latest Huntsville bird on May 15, 1977 (Mills, 1981: 181). Nicholson (1981: 191) gave May 23, 1976 as his latest Manitoulin date with the high count of 600 noted on Apr. 24, 1972. Strickland, Tozer & Rutter (1982) listed March 9 and May 14 as the earliest and latest spring dates for Algonquin Park, with the average arrival on Apr. 2 and departure on May 3. Ricker & Clarke (1939: 23) gave Apr. 7, 1925 as their earliest Lake Nipissing record: Speirs & Speirs (1947: 38) had two as late as May 13, 1945 at North Bay and found the peak in late April. Skeel & Bondrup-Nielsen (1978: 218) had records from Apr. 5 to May 14, 1977 at Pukaskwa. Denis (1961: 2) gave Apr. 19 as the average arrival date at Thunder

Bay, with the earliest on Apr. 6, 1946. Peruniak (1971: 30) had spring migrants at Atikokan from Apr. 14 to May 8. Elder (1979: 40) gave Apr. 16 as his earliest spring date for Geraldton. Bondrup-Nielsen (1976: 45) saw birds near Kapuskasing on Apr. 22, 1974 and May 11, 1975. Cringan (1953a: 4) saw his first at Sioux Lookout on Apr. 11 in 1953.

SUMMER: Weir & Quilliam (1980: 40) listed a Kingston straggler as late as June 10. Snyder (1928: 28) collected a singing male at Lake Abitibi on June 21, 1925, perhaps a bird delayed by injury. Cringan (1953b: 5) saw one at Kasabonika Lake on June 2, 1953, probably a late migrant. James (1980: 91) saw as many as 6 birds on 3 days in mid-June, 1977 about 15 km. northeast of Pickle Lake. McLaren & McLaren (1981: 5) recorded a singing male at Little Sachigo Lake on June 12, 1977. Peck (1972: 346) saw some at Cape Henrietta Maria on 7 days, from June 22 to July 3, 1970 and reported 14, including 6 young, collected on the 1948 ROM field party there. Manning (1952: 93-94) saw 35 or more and collected 9 from Sandy Island, near Moosonee, north to Long Ridge Point from June 1-14, 1947; from Raft River north to Lake River, along the James Bay coast he saw 17 and collected 3 from July 13-17, 1947; from Little Cape to Shagamu River, along the Hudson Bay coast, he tallied 81 and collected 14, including 7 young, from July 29-Aug. 10, 1947. Schueler, Baldwin & Rising (1974: 148) found two nests about 4 miles east of Winisk, both with 6 eggs, on June 26 and 27, 1971: they saw none at other northern localities visited. C.E. Hope noted 100 at Fort Severn on July 1, 1940 and found a nest with 5 young there that day: good numbers were noted almost daily during the summer there.

AUTUMN: George Stirrett saw 5 at Attawapiskat on Oct. 7, 1948 (Manning, 1952: 93). D. McRae and A. Wormington recorded up to 45 per day from Oct. 14-30, 1981 and saw the last one on Nov. 1. Peruniak (1971: 30) had fall migrants at Atikokan from Oct. 3 to Nov. 2. Skeel & Bondrup-Nielsen (1978: 218) saw one on Sept. 5 and 3 on Oct. 15 at Pukaskwa. Speirs & Speirs (1947: 38) reported a fall migration peak at North Bay in mid-October. Strickland, Tozer & Rutter (1982) listed Sept. 26 and Nov. 22 as the earliest and latest fall migrants in Algonquin Park, with average arrival on Oct. 9 and departure on Nov. 4. Nicholson (1981: 191) gave Oct. 9 as an 11-year average arrival date on Manitoulin, with the earliest on Sept. 26, 1975 and a high count of 400 on Oct. 29, 1968. Pearl Rogers noted the earliest Huntsville bird on Sept. 23, 1973 (Mills, 1981: 151). Devitt (1967: 171) saw a flock of 20 at Wasaga Beach as early as Sept. 17, 1938. Weir & Quilliam (1980: 40) listed Oct. 16 as the 28-year average arrival date at Kingston, with the earliest on Sept. 16. My earliest Pickering Twp. date was Sept. 20, 1957 (Speirs, 1973). Speirs (1938: 47, 51) gave Sept. 28 as the earliest Toronto record, with peaks on Oct. 31 and Nov. 9: Saunders (1947: 375) listed Oct. 16 as his 13-year average arrival date there. Ussher (1965: 30) gave Oct. 27 as his 13-year average arrival date at Rondeau, with the earliest on Oct. 14. Stirrett (1973d: 29) had his earliest 5 at Pelee on Oct. 7.

BANDING: Alfred Bunker banded 70 at his Pickering Twp. home from 1958 to 1964 (from Jan. 4 to Apr. 3: none in the fall when they seldom come to feeders): one returned 3 years later and 8 others one or two years after banding (Speirs, 1973). Of 189 banded at Kingston between 1956 and 1961, 34 returned the next winter, 9 the third winter and 3 the fourth winter (Quilliam, 1973: 189). One banded near Detroit, Mich. on Apr. 5, 1958 was recovered near Toronto on March 6, 1960. A most remarkable recovery involved a bird banded by E.T. Jones at Edmonton, Alberta on Sept. 14, 1957 and recovered near Toronto on Apr. 9, 1958. Brewer & Salvadori (1978: 94) cited five recoveries: one banded at Atholl Springs, N.Y. on Feb. 24, 1958 was recovered at Barrie on Sept. 23, 1967 (at least 10 yrs. old); another banded at Atholl Springs on Feb. 3, 1969 was recovered at Bridgenorth, near Peterborough, on Feb. 13, 1970: one banded at Dorset, Ohio, on Feb. 26, 1967 was taken the following year at Belwood Lake, Wellington Co.: one banded at Bennington, Vt. on Feb. 8, 1968 was recovered at Don Mills, Ont. on Apr. 4, 1969 and finally, one banded at Balmoral Marsh, Ont. was recovered near Sault Ste. Marie on May 11, 1966.

**MEASUREMENTS:**
*Length:* 5.8 to 6.5 ins. (Godfrey, 1966: 391)
*Wingspread:* 8.5 to 9.5 ins. (Roberts, (1955: 716)
*Weight:* 12 banded at our home averaged 21.3 g. (18.0 to 25.7 g.).

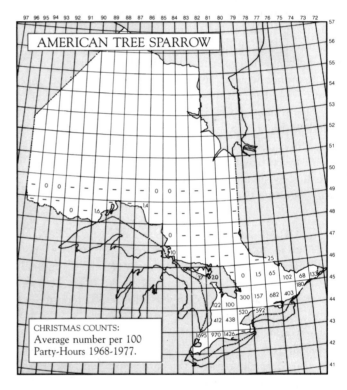

AMERICAN TREE SPARROW

CHRISTMAS COUNTS:
Average number per 100
Party-Hours 1968-1977.

# CHIPPING SPARROW   *Spizella passerina*   (Bechstein)

Chipping Sparrows are common birds through Ontario except for the Hudson Bay vicinity, often nesting close to our homes in ornamental evergreens or other shrubs, as well as along roadsides and forest openings in northern Ontario. When horsehair is available they line their nests with it. One of my most vivid boyhood memories was seeing a nest in the grapevine in our Toronto back yard, with four lovely tiny blue eggs resting on a lining of black horse hair. Most of our birds go south to winter in southern United States or Mexico, but a few have lingered in southern Ontario to show up on Christmas counts or at feeders.

IDENTIFICATION: The Chipping Sparrow is one of our smallest sparrows, known by its reddish-brown crown set off by conspicuous white "eyebrow" lines, and with a clear gray breast. The song is a dry, monotone trill and the call a definite "chip" (hence its name). The young have striped breasts.

WINTER: On the 1968-1977 Christmas counts they were rare north to Deep River and Owen Sound. Stirrett (1973a: 20) had a few records of single birds at Pelee throughout the winter months. Saunders & Dale (1933: 243) saw one at St. Thomas on Dec. 25, 1912: another was noted there on Dec. 21, 1952 (Brooman, 1954: 39). Beardslee & Mitchell (1965: 441) reported one at a Port Colborne feeder from Jan. 18 to March 10, 1951. One came to our Pickering Twp. feeder almost daily from Jan. 21 to Feb. 6, 1967: others were noted in Pickering Twp. on Dec. 26, 1961 and Dec. 16, 1967 (Speirs, 1973). Tozer & Richards (1974: 298-299) reported one near Oshawa on Dec. 27, 1948 and one at Port Perry on Jan. 10, 1972. One was found on the Kingston Christmas count on Dec. 27, 1970 (Quilliam, 1973: 190).

SPRING: Stirrett (1973b: 27) had a spring maximum of 125 at Pelee. Ussher (1965: 30) gave Apr. 21 as his 20-year average arrival date at Rondeau, with the earliest on Apr. 2. Saunders & Dale (1933: 243) gave Apr. 14 as the 17-year average arrival date at London, with the earliest on Apr. 1, 1910: the earliest of 3 May nests held 4 eggs on May 20, 1912. Fleming (1907: 81) gave March 16 as his earliest Toronto date: J.L. Baillie (in Saunders, 1947: 375) listed Apr. 22 as his 27-year average arrival date at Toronto and Speirs (1938: 43) gave May 8 as the spring peak there. Long (1968a: 23) noted one at Pickering Beach as early as Apr. 4, 1968. Tozer & Richards (1974: 298) found two nests near Oshawa as early as May 12, 1958 (both held a cowbird egg as well as one and 2 eggs of the host, respectively). Snyder (1941: 89) saw one carrying nesting material in Prince Edward Co. as early as Apr. 28, 1928. Weir & Quilliam (1980: 40) listed Apr. 19 as the 32-year average arrival date at Kingston, with the earliest on March 31. Devitt (1967: 172) gave Apr. 23 as the 24-year average arrival date at Barrie, with the earliest on Apr. 3, 1966: H.P. Bingham found a nest with 4 eggs there as early as May 16, 1913. L. Beamer's median arrival date at Meaford was Apr. 27, with the earliest on Apr. 13, 1941. Mills (1981: 182) gave Apr. 22 as the 14-year average arrival date at Huntsville, with the earliest on Apr. 13, 1874. Nicholson (1981: 192) gave Apr. 28 as the 11-year average arrival date on Manitoulin, with the earliest on Apr. 20, 1974 and a high count of 300 on May 23, 1976. Strickland, Tozer & Rutter (1982) listed May 1 as the average arrival date in Algonquin Park, with the earliest on Apr. 23 but MacLulich (1938: 43) gave an Apr. 11, 1934 date. Ricker & Clarke (1939: 24) noted one at Lake Nipissing as early as Apr. 18, 1934. Skeel & Bondrup-Nielsen (1978: 29) heard 82 on 16 days from May 5 to

31, 1977 at Pukaskwa. Denis (1961: 3) listed May 5 as the average arrival date at Thunder Bay, with the earliest on Apr. 27, 1948. Peruniak (1971: 31) gave Apr. 23 as her earliest Atikokan record. Elder (1979: 40) gave May 8 as his earliest at Geraldton. Bondrup-Nielsen (1976: 45) saw his first near Kapuskasing on May 12 in 1975. Cringan (1953a: 4) saw his first at Sioux Lookout on May 3 in 1953.

SUMMER: On the 1968-1977 Breeding Bird Surveys they were common on almost all routes from Lake Erie north to Cochrane and Kenora. Stirrett (1973c: 23) had a June maximum of 50 at Pelee. Saunders & Dale (1933: 243) reported two June nests at London, the latest held 4 eggs on June 6, 1908. McCracken, Bradstreet & Holroyd (1981: 66) considered this one of the most common birds on Long Point and reported 10 nest records, with eggs from May 31 to July 7. Speirs & Orenstein (1967: 182) found some on 3 of 11 field quadrats in Ontario Co., with a maximum of 16 birds per 100 acres on the Uxbridge plot: Speirs, Markle & Tozer (1970: 5) found populations on all 10 urban quadrats studied in Ontario Co., with a maximum of 95 birds per 100 acres in Port Perry: Speirs & Orenstein (1975: 15) found populations in 3 of 11 forest plots in Ontario Co., with a maximum of 34 birds per 100 acres in the Uxbridge quadrat: of 22 sets of eggs found in Ontario Co., 5 held one cowbird egg and two held 2 cowbird eggs (Speirs, 1973). Tozer & Richards (1974: 298) found a nest with 4 eggs and one cowbird egg as late as July 7, 1958, near Oshawa. Allin (1940: 109) found a nest with 3 eggs in Darlington Twp. on June 9, 1930 and a nest with large young there on July 19, 1927. Snyder (1941: 89) collected 5 young at various localities in Prince Edward Co. from June 30 to July 11, 1930. E. Beaupré found a nest with 4 eggs and a cowbird egg near Kingston on June 6, 1897 (Quilliam, 1973: 190). G.L. Lambert found a nest with 4 eggs at Glenwood Beach, Simcoe Co., as late as July 21, 1940 (Devitt, 1967: 172). C.L. Patch found a nest with eggs at Meach's Lake, near Ottawa, on June 23, 1914 (Lloyd, 1924: 11). James (1979: 16) found this to be the third commonest bird in jack pine forests in western Parry Sound Dist. averaging 27 males per 100 acres. Mills (1981: 181) reported 37 nests in the cottage country, with young as early as June 4 and as late as August: J.L. Baillie found a nest with 4 young at Brittania on June 11, 1961 being tended by a male Clay-colored Sparrow and a female Chipping Sparrow. D.B. Ferguson found a nest with 4 eggs at Windfall Lake, Manitoulin, on July 2, 1979 (Nicholson, 1981: 192). J.M.B. Corkill found a nest with 4 eggs at Lake Nipissing on June 2, 1933 (Ricker & Clarke, 1939: 24). Baillie & Hope (1947: 31) found the first nest with eggs at Chapleau on June 7, 1937 and the first flying young on June 28 at Biscotasing. Snyder (1942: 151) found two nests with 4 eggs each on June 7, 1931 near Sault Ste. Marie: the first young out of the nest were noted on June 20. Skeel & Bondrup-Nielsen (1978: 219) noted 12 on 7 days from June 1 to July 11, 1977, at Pukaskwa: 4 immatures were observed on Aug. 15; none were seen later. Baillie & Hope (1943: 25) found two nests, with 4 eggs each, at Marathon, on June 17 and June 20, 1936. Snyder (1928: 269) found partly fledged young at Macdiarmid, Lake Nipigon, after mid-July, in 1923 and 1924. Dear (1940: 142) found two nests, with 4 eggs each, near Thunder Bay, on June 2, 1911 and June 11, 1927. Snyder (1938: 212) reported a nest found at Fort Frances on June 7, 1929. Snyder (1953: 88) obtained breeding evidence from Malachi and Sioux Lookout and found the Chipping Sparrow to be the third most common sparrow in western Ontario. Smith (1957: 180) found nests at Kapuskasing and dependent young at Lake Abitibi. James (1980: 91) reported 3 nests, with 4 young in each, near Pickle Lake: 2 on June 17, 1977 and one on June 22, 1979. Cringan (1950: 18) saw a group in a spruce muskeg near Nikip Lake in mid-July, 1950. Hope (1938: 47) found a nest with

4 eggs about 1 foot up in a tiny white spruce at Favourable Lake on June 8, 1938. Sam. Waller took a nest with 4 eggs at Moose Factory on June 16, 1930 and J. Satterly found a nest with 4 young at Fry Lake (51 °14' N, 91 °19'W) on June 25, 1935 (Baillie & Harrington, 1937: 274). Schueler, Baldwin & Rising (1974: 144) reported them common at Cochrane and Moosonee, and present at Hawley Lake. Lee (1978: 34) saw a maximum of 10 at Big Trout Lake on June 12, 1975 and young were noted there during the latter part of July.

AUTUMN: D. McRae and A. Wormington saw individuals at Netitishi Point, James Bay, on Oct. 17, 19 and 21, 1981. Peruniak (1971: 31) gave Sept. 24 as her latest date at Atikokan. Speirs & Speirs (1947: 38) noted 3 at North Bay on Oct. 9, 1944. Strickland, Tozer & Rutter (1982) listed Oct. 3 as the average departure date from Algonquin Park, with the latest on Oct. 16. Nicholson (1981: 192) gave Oct. 21, 1978 as his latest Manitoulin date, with a high count of 200 on Sept. 30, 1972. R. Rutter collected an injured male at Huntsville as late as Oct. 28, 1957 (Mills, 1981: 182). Frances Westman saw two near Barrie as late as Oct. 20, 1954 (Devitt, 1967: 172). Weir & Quilliam (1980: 40) listed Oct. 28 as the 27-year average departure date from Kingston. My latest date for Pickering Twp. was Nov. 12, 1967 (Speirs, 1973). Speirs (1938: 51) gave Oct. 3 as the fall peak at Toronto and Saunders (1947: 375) listed Oct. 29 as his 13-year average departure date. Ussher (1965: 30) gave Oct. 28 as his 10-year average departure date from Rondeau, with the latest on Nov. 13. Stirrett (1973d: 29) had a fall maximum of 100 at Pelee on Sept. 15 and another on Oct. 3.

BANDING: Alfred Bunker banded 24 at his Pickering home from 1955 to 1963: three of these returned: one banded as a young bird on Sept. 17, 1958 returned on July 28, 1962. Brewer & Salvadori (1978: 95) listed three interesting recoveries: one banded at East Tawas, Michigan, on Sept. 12, 1963 was recovered at Long Point on May 17, 1966. The most distant recovery was one banded at Gainesville, Florida, on March 20, 1966 and recovered at Richmond, Ont. in 1968 (1148 miles to the north). One banded at Long Point was recovered at Hastings, Florida, 889 miles to the south: banded on June 2, 1967 and recovered, Jan. 3, 1969.

**MEASUREMENTS:**
*Length:* 5.0 to 5.8 ins.
(Godfrey, 1966: 392)
*Wingspread:* 8.0 to 9.0
ins. (Roberts, 1955: 717)
*Weight:* 46 Ontario
specimens averaged
12.5 g.

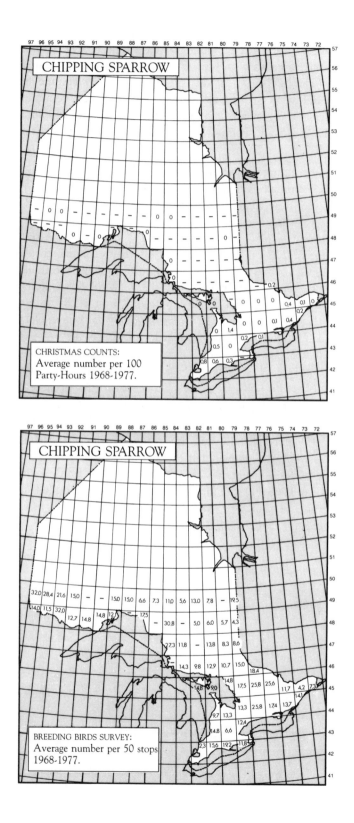

CHIPPING SPARROW

CHRISTMAS COUNTS:
Average number per 100
Party-Hours 1968-1977.

CHIPPING SPARROW

BREEDING BIRDS SURVEY:
Average number per 50 stops
1968-1977.

# CLAY-COLORED SPARROW  *Spizella pallida*  (Swainson)

The Clay-colored Sparrow is a common inhabitant of shrubby country in the prairies. In Ontario it is most numerous in the Rainy River region, but may turn up rarely almost anywhere where suitable habitat exists. In southern Ontario it is often associated with Christmas tree plantations. Hybridization with Chipping Sparrows is fairly frequent when appropriate mates cannot be located. They winter chiefly in Mexico.

**IDENTIFICATION:**  Clay-colored Sparrows are usually found by hearing the characteristic "office-buzzer" song: "dzzz-dzzz". The singer is then usually found at the tip of a shrub or small tree, a bird much the size and build of a Chipping Sparrow, but lacking the reddish crown and bright, white "eyebrow" of that species, instead having a crown of black and brown stripes, a buffy "eyebrow" and perhaps the best visual field mark, a brown ear patch, bordered with fine black lines. Immature Chipping Sparrows in fall look much like Clay-colored Sparrows but have gray rumps, buffy in Clay-colored Sparrows (I have yet to see either without the wings covering the rump).

**WINTER:**

**SPRING:**  Stirrett (1973b: 27) found them rare and irregular at Pelee, from May 3 to May 24. Ussher (1965: 32) had two Rondeau records: May 16, 1959 and May, 1968. W.E. Saunders collected the first Ontario specimen at Mount Brydges, near London, on May 9, 1894: others were found nearby on May 28, 1922, May 30, 1923 and May 28, 1924 (Saunders & Dale, 1933: 243). Saunders (1947: 375) listed spring records at Toronto from May 14 to May 30. Speirs (1973) cited some 8 spring records from Ontario Co., from Pickering Beach north to Mara Twp., between May 11 (1961) and May 31 (1962). Weir & Quilliam (1980: 40) listed May 21 as the 11-year average arrival date at Kingston, with the earliest on May 10. Devitt (1967: 173) observed six near Barrie on May 17, 1964. Hazel Petty reported one at Callander on May 9, 1971 (Mills, 1981: 182). Nicholson (1981: 192) reported 3 on Great Duck Is. between May 8 and May 29, 1979. Strickland, Tozer & Rutter (1982) listed May 21 as the average arrival date in Algonquin Park, with the earliest on May 16. Skeel & Bondrup-Nielsen (1978: 219) noted one at Pukaskwa on May 16, 1977. Baillie & Hope (1943: 26) heard single birds singing at Rossport on May 27 and June 4, 1936. Denis (1961: 3) gave May 14 as the average arrival date at Thunder Bay, with the earliest on May 6, 1943. Dear (1940: 143) found a nest with 4 eggs at Thunder Bay on May 29, 1938. Peruniak (1971: 31) noted one at Atikokan on May 15, 1963. Cringan (1953a: 4) observed his first at Sioux Lookout on May 24 in 1953. Three were reported by P.D. Pratt *et al* at Shipsands Is., near Moosonee, from May 24-28, 1981 (Goodwin, 1981: 820).

**SUMMER:**  On the 1968-1977 Breeding Bird Surveys,they were common at Fort Frances, fairly common at Stratton and Dryden: rare and widely scattered elsewhere in Ontario. Saunders & Dale (1933: 243-244) found a lingering bird in the summer of 1924 near Mount Brydges and another near London on June 26, 1931. Harold Lancaster saw one in Aldborough Twp., Elgin Co., in 1949 on June 19, July 3 and July 10 (Brooman, 1954: 39). Speirs (1973) cited several nest records for the Whitby-Oshawa region: one nest held 4 eggs on June 18, 1957: a hybrid pair ( ♂ Clay-colored and ♀ Chipping) had a nest with 2 eggs and 2 cowbird eggs on June 22, 1965. Tozer & Richards (1974: 299-300) cited several nestings in Cartwright Twp.: one nest held 3 eggs and a cowbird egg on June 18, 1966, all of which hatched the following day. Fred Cooke heard one singing near Kingston on July 29, 1968, the latest record there (Quilliam, 1973: 190). Devitt (1967: 172-173) cited Simcoe Co. records at Wasaga Beach, Medonte, Midhurst, Camp Borden, Penetanguishene, Collingwood and Barrie: Frank Munro found a nest with 4 young near Camp Borden on July 11, 1953. Mills (1981: 182) cited J.L. Baillie's find of a nest with 4 young at Brittania, Lake of Bays, on July 11, 1961, tended by a ♂ Clay-colored Sparrow and a ♀ Chipping Sparrow: on July 12, 1976 Alex Mills suspected a similar hybrid mating at Gibson Lake, Muskoka. Ross James et al found a nest with 4 eggs near Mindemoya, Manitoulin, on June 29, 1977 (Nicholson, 1981: 192). Strickland, Tozer & Rutter (1982) listed July 6 as the latest record for this rare species in Algonquin Park. Snyder (1942: 151) collected 3 males and 2 young of an estimated group of 15 at Little Rapids near Sault Ste. Marie, on July 20, 1931. Dear (1940: 143) found a nest with 4 eggs at Thunder Bay on June 10, 1938. Snyder (1938: 212) collected young at Rainy River on Aug. 1 and Aug. 4, 1929. Peruniak (1971: 31) reported one at Atikokan on June 14, 1967. Snyder (1953: 89) observed from one to 7 fairly regularly at Ingolf and from 1 to 10 daily at Wabigoon in 1937; also individuals at Savanne on July 10, 1937 and at Sioux Lookout on June 30, 1947. L. Paterson found them nesting fairly commonly at Kenora in 1932 (Baillie & Harrington, 1937: 275). Snyder (1953: 89) collected a male Chipping Sparrow at Ingolf on June 11, 1937 that was singing "a song indistinguishable from the song of a Clay-colored Sparrow" (perhaps the progeny of a hybrid breeding?? JMS). Schueler, Baldwin & Rising (1974: 148) collected a singing male at Attawapiskat on June 21, 1971. Keith Reynolds reported hearing a singing Clay-colored Sparrow at Bearskin Lake on July 30, 1975 (Lee, 1978: 35). McLaren & McLaren (1981: 5) heard one singing by the Severn River on June 12, 1977 (at about latitude 53 ° 40'N). D.C. Sadler reported one at Winisk on June 21, 1983 and D. Shepherd found 3 pairs at Fort Severn in June, 1983 (Weir, 1983: 985).

AUTUMN: Goodwin (1980: 158) reported a late one at Marathon on Oct. 30, 1979. Nicholson (1981: 192) reported one on Great Duck Is. on Oct. 5, 1978. Naomi LeVay reported birds at Cranberry Marsh, Whitby, on Sept. 22, 1962, Oct. 3, 1964 and Oct. 27, 1956 (Tozer & Richards, 1974: 300). Saunders (1947: 375) listed two fall records for Toronto: Oct. 3 and Nov. 7. One was killed at the Long Point lighthouse on Sept. 16-17, 1982 (Weir, 1983: 176). A. Rider noted one at Kettle Point on Oct. 20, 1980 (Goodwin, 1981: 179). Stirrett (1973d: 29) had two fall records for Pelee, with 2 birds noted on each occasion: Sept. 28, 1963 and Oct. 5, 1963.

**MEASUREMENTS:**
Length: 4.9 to 5.5 ins.
(Godfrey, 1966: 393)
Wingspread: 7.62 to 8.12
ins. (Roberts, 1955: 720)
Weight: 10.9 to 12.2 g.
(Terres, 1980: 341).

**REFERENCES:**
Dale, E.M.S. 1927 The
Clay-coloured Sparrow at
London, Ontario. Can.
Field-Naturalist,
41: (3): 64.

Godfrey, W. Earl 1966 Clay-colored Sparrow nesting at Ottawa, Ontario. Can. Field-Naturalist, 80: (4): 255-256. n/4e on June 4/66 Uplands.

Lloyd, Hoyes 1933 An occurrence of the Clay-coloured Sparrow, *Spizella pallida*, in Renfrew County, Ontario. Can. Field-Naturalist, 47: (2): 36.

Mitchener, A.J. 1956 Clay-coloured Sparrow nesting in Grey County, Ontario. Can. Field-Naturalist, 70: (3): 141. n/ 4e June 12/52 Craigleith.

Terrill, Lewis McI. 1952 The Clay-colored Sparrow in Southeastern Ontario. Can. Field-Naturalist, 66: (5): 145-147. At Merrickville, Lanark Co.

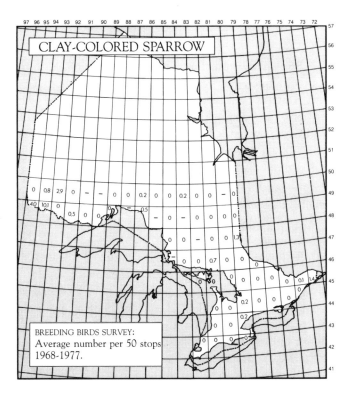

CLAY-COLORED SPARROW

BREEDING BIRDS SURVEY:
Average number per 50 stops
1968-1977.

---

# BREWER'S SPARROW   *Spizella breweri*   Cassin

Brewer's Sparrow is normally a bird of sagebrush scrub in the southwestern Canadian prairies, accidental in Ontario (one record).

**IDENTIFICATION:** Brewer's Sparrow looks like a very pale Clay-colored Sparrow but lacks the median crown stripe of that species. It has a much longer and more melodious song, with canary-like trills as well as buzzy notes.

**WINTER:**

**SPRING:** One showed up at a Port Stanley feeder on March 25, 1980, was well photographed by M.S. Smout, eventually captured and kept in a St. Thomas aviary where it was examined at leisure by Marshall Field and many others (Goodwin, 1980: 773).

**SUMMER:**

**AUTUMN:**

**MEASUREMENTS:**
*Length:* 5.0 to 5.4 ins.
(Godfrey, 1966: 394)
Wingspread:
*Weight:* 10 to 12 g.
(Terres, 1980: 340).

# FIELD SPARROW   *Spizella pusilla*   (Wilson)

Field Sparrows are usually found, in southern Ontario, in abandoned fields with scattered, small shrubs. A few remain to winter in southern Ontario, but most go south to the United States or Mexico. Our local bird has come to our feeder for a few days when it first returned in spring, sometimes coming briefly with its mate, but leaves to sing in nearby fields when it has regained its strength after migration.

IDENTIFICATION: The pink bill, conspicuous eye ring and lack of central breast spot distinguish it from the somewhat similar American Tree Sparrow, during the colder months. The song of the Field Sparrow consists of an accelerating series of sweet, whistled notes, sometimes ascending in pitch, sometimes descending, but often with all notes on the same pitch: one of the most delightful of our bird songs.

WINTER: On the 1968-1977 Christmas counts, they were fairly common near the Lake Erie shores, rare elsewhere north to Ottawa and Saulte Ste. Marie. Stirrett (1973a: 20) reported a winter maximum of 180 at Pelee on Dec. 24. Brooman (1954: 39) cited several winter records for Elgin Co., including a flock of 15 near Port Stanley on Jan. 18, 1953, noted by Marshall Field. Parker (1983: 26) recorded the species on 27 of 58 Christmas counts at Toronto. Speirs (1973) reported a total of 19 on 5 of 10 Pickering Christmas counts: one came to our Pickering Twp. feeder as late as Jan. 25, 1967 and George A. Scott had one at Oshawa as late as Feb. 11, 1951. Quilliam (1973: 191) had three December records at Kingston: Dec. 9, 1961, Dec. 21, 1957 and two on Dec. 19, 1971. L. Varley reported two wintering at Kearney, Parry Sound Dist., in 1970-1971 (Goodwin, 1971: 574). Dennison (1980: 149) reported single birds on the Sault Ste. Marie Christmas counts in 1975 and 1976 (i.e. on 2 of 25 counts there).

SPRING: Stirrett (1973b: 27) had a spring maximum of 300 at Pelee on Apr. 11. Ussher (1965: 30) gave Apr. 16 as the 19-year average arrival date at Rondeau, with the earliest on March 25. Saunders & Dale (1933: 244) gave Apr. 10 as the 17-year average arrival date at London, with the earliest on March 29, 1918: a set of 4 eggs was found on May 19, 1902 and another set of 3 and a cowbird egg on May 29, 1912. Beardslee & Mitchell (1965: 442) reported a nest with 4 eggs near St. Catharines on May 13, 1962. Fleming (1907: 81) gave Apr. 4, 1890 as his earliest Toronto record: J.L. Baillie (in Saunders, 1947: 375) listed Apr. 25 as his 22-year average arrival date there. Our earliest spring record at our Pickering Twp. home was on Apr. 3, 1955 (Speirs, 1973). Tozer & Richards (1974: 300) found a nest with 4 eggs in Darlington Twp. on May 23, 1965. Weir & Quilliam (1980: 40) listed Apr. 12 as the 31-year average arrival date at Kingston, with the earliest on March 25. Devitt (1967: 174) gave Apr. 22 as the 11-year average arrival date at Barrie, with the earliest on Apr. 2, 1962. Mills (1981: 183) reported a Huntsville arrival date as early as Apr. 10, 1971. Nicholson (1981: 193) gave May 5 as a 10-year average arrival date on Manitoulin, with the earliest on Apr. 12, 1980 and a high count of 7 on Great Duck Is. on May 8, 1979. Strickland, Tozer & Rutter (1982) listed May 1 as the average arrival date in Algonquin Park, with the earliest on Apr. 9. R. Nisbet found a stray on Caribou Is., Lake Superior, on May 17, 1981 (Goodwin, 1981: 820). T. Hince found one at Marathon on Apr. 17, 1983 (Weir, 1983: 866): this bird was at a feeder there.

SUMMER: On the 1968-1977 Breeding Bird Surveys they were fairly common from Lake Erie and Lake Ontario north to Kincardine and Barry's Bay, uncommon farther north to North Bay: one was reported on the Eagle River route in 1977 in far western Ontario. Stirrett (1973c: 23) had a late summer maximum of 50 at Pelee on Aug. 12. Speirs & Frank (1970: 764-765) found this to be the most common sparrow on the Pelee field plot (with a density of 10 territories per 100 acres) and the most common bird on the Windsor prairie quadrat (with a density of 30 territories per 100 acres). Saunders & Dale (1933: 244) found a nest with 4 eggs near London on June 3, 1916, a nest with 5 eggs on June 11, 1908 and a nest with 2 eggs and 2 cowbird eggs on June 19, 1902. F. Starr collected a nest with one egg and a cowbird egg at Port Burwell on June 7, 1925 (Baillie & Harrington, 1937: 275). McCracken, Bradstreet & Holroyd (1981: 67) found a population density of 42 territories per km $^2$ in juniper savannahs on Long Point: a nest with 3 eggs was found on June 19, 1965 and 11 subsequent nests held eggs from May 21 to July 27. Speirs & Orenstein (1975: 15) found populations of 47 birds per 100 acres in a young pine plantation in Mara Twp. and 9 birds per 100 acres in a thorn scrub plot in Pickering Twp., but none in older forests (nor in any of the field or urban plots in Ontario Co.). Tozer & Richards (1974: 300-302) cited details of 10 nestings in the Oshawa-Scugog region, four of which contained cowbird eggs: one on July 17, 1971 in Darlington Twp. held 3 cowbird eggs! E. Beaupré found a nest with 3 eggs at Kingston on June 20, 1905 (Quilliam, 1973: 191). Paul Harrington found a nest with 4 eggs and a nest with 3 eggs and a cowbird egg at Oakview Beach, Simcoe Co., on June 7, 1923 (Devitt, 1967: 173). C. Harris found a nest with 3 eggs at Gibson Lake, Muskoka, on June 22, 1976: this held 4 eggs on the following day and Mills (1981: 183) found a nest with 4 young at Ahmic Lake, Parry Sound Dist., on July 7, 1977. R. Tasker reported 3 birds at Manitowaning on July 4, 1976, the only Manitoulin summer record up to that time (Nicholson, 1981: 193) but J. Nicholson subsequently found one on Manitoulin on June 12, 1983 (Weir, 1983: 985). G. Henson et al found fledged young in Algonquin Park during the summer of 1982, the first confirmed nesting in the park (Weir, 1982: 974). J. Lemon observed one at Lively from June 16-20, 1974 (Goodwin, 1974: 900) and another one for the Sudbury region was found at Hanmer on June 24, 1975 (Goodwin, 1975: 967). The most remarkable summer sighting was one reported by H. Lumsden at the forks of the Brant River, Cape Henrietta Maria, on July 20, 1969 (Peck, 1972: 346).

AUTUMN: D. McRae and A. Wormington reported single birds at Netitishi Point, James Bay, on Oct. 14 and 18, 1981. J.B. Miles noted one at Hornepayne on Sept. 29, 1974 (Goodwin, 1975: 53). M.J. McCormick reported 2 at Thunder Bay on Sept. 26, 1982 (Weir, 1983: 176). N. Escott found a very late one at Marathon on Nov. 2, 1975 (Goodwin, 1976: 63). B. Crins found one in Algonquin Park on Oct. 9, 1982 (Weir, 1983: 176). Goodwin (1973: 56) reported one on the North Channel of Georgian Bay (Darch Is.) on Oct. 28, 1972. C. Bell noted one at Mindemoya on Oct. 17, 1976 (Nicholson, 1981: 193). C. Harris saw a late bird at Go Home Bay on Oct. 30, 1977 (Mills, 1981: 183). E.G. White collected one at Hurdman's Bridge, near Ottawa, on Oct. 20, 1905 (Lloyd, 1924: 11). Devitt (1967: 174) saw one near Anten Mills, Simcoe Co., as late as Oct. 18, 1952. Weir & Quilliam (1980: 40) listed Nov. 7 as the 24-year average departure date from Kingston. Saunders (1947: 375) listed Oct. 4 as his 10-year average departure date from Toronto: Speirs (1938: 53) gave Nov. 14 as the latest fall date there. Beardslee & Mitchell (1965: 442) reported 3 at Fort Erie on Nov. 24, 1960. Ussher (1965: 30) gave Oct. 28 as a 7-year average departure date from Rondeau, with the latest on Nov. 6 (though "a few winter"). Stirrett (1973d: 29) had a fall maximum of 25 at Pelee on Oct. 2.

BANDING:   One banded at Don Mills on May 2, 1967, turned up near Nacogdoches, Texas, on March 22, 1969 (Brewer & Salvadori, 1978: 95).

**MEASUREMENTS:**
*Length:* 5.1 to 6.0 ins. (Godfrey, 1966: 394)
*Wingspread:* 7.9 to 8.5 ins. (Roberts, 1955: 715)
*Weight:* 10 Ontario specimens averaged 13.8 g.

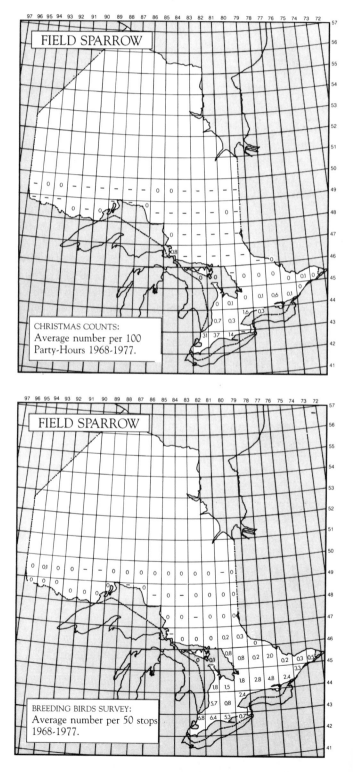

FIELD SPARROW

CHRISTMAS COUNTS:
Average number per 100
Party-Hours 1968-1977.

FIELD SPARROW

BREEDING BIRDS SURVEY:
Average number per 50 stops
1968-1977.

# VESPER SPARROW   *Pooecetes gramineus*   (Gmelin)

Although the sweet, dreamy song of the Vesper Sparrow may seem appropriate to the vesper hours, they sing quite happily at other hours of the day. They often sing from trees bordering dry, short grass fields with sandy patches, or fields ploughed for a late corn crop or for summer fallow, areas often favoured by Horned Larks or Grasshopper Sparrows, but not by Savannah Sparrows that prefer longer stemmed grasses. In winter most go to the southern United States or even into Mexico.

IDENTIFICATION: The Vesper Sparrow is the largest of our "grass sparrows", with conspicuous white outer tail feathers in flight. When perched, the white eye rings and bay coloured "shoulders" set it apart. The sweet, deliberate song begins with a few long, rising notes and trails off into warbling trills: "soo-swee' see - tiddle-iddle-iddle-reee".

WINTER: On the 1968-1977 Christmas counts they were uncommon at Pelee and Blenheim, becoming rare north to Presqu'ile. Stirrett (1973a: 20) had a winter maximum of 40 at Pelee on Dec. 2. Saunders & Dale (1933: 242) had two winter records for Middlesex Co.: one near Glanworth on Dec. 18, 1914 and the other at London on Jan. 3, 1915. Brooman (1954: 38-39) reported 2 at St. Thomas on Dec. 24, 1950 and single birds on Dec. 21, 1952 and Dec. 26, 1953. Beardslee & Mitchell (1965: 436) mentioned one at Fonthill on Dec. 17, 1956, one in Willoughby Twp. on Jan. 1, 1960 and 5 at Morgan's Point, Lake Erie, on Jan. 5, 1941. Parker (1983: 26) listed Vesper Sparrows on 4 of 58 Christmas counts at Toronto. Jack Sherrin saw one as late as Dec. 6, 1959 at Ajax and I saw one at Frank Barkey's feeder on the Scarborough-Pickering Townline on Jan. 13, 1962 (Speirs, 1973). Quilliam (1973: 187) reported one on the Napanee Christmas count on Dec. 27, 1965 and Weir & Quilliam (1980: 40) listed a Jan. 26 record for Kingston.

SPRING: Stirrett (1973b: 27) had a spring maximum of 25 at Pelee on Apr. 25. Ussher (1965: 30) gave Apr. 5 as his 19-year average arrival date at Rondeau, with the earliest on March 10. Saunders & Dale (1933: 242) gave Apr. 1 as the 17-year average arrival date at London, with the earliest on March 24, 1921: a set of 4 eggs taken on May 8, 1902 was the earliest of four May nest records cited. Marshall Field found a nest with 4 eggs at St. Thomas on May 18, 1946 (Brooman, 1954: 39). Snyder (1931: 196) mentioned three lighthouse casualties at Long Point on Apr. 17-18, 1930. J.L. Baillie (in Saunders, 1947: 375) listed Apr. 16 as his 27-year average arrival date at Toronto, with the earliest on March 25. My earliest spring record for Pickering Twp. was on March 31, 1948 (Speirs, 1973). Tozer & Richards (1974: 295) reported a nest with 4 eggs as early as May 12, 1956 near Oshawa and a nest with one egg and 2 cowbird eggs in Darlington Twp. on May 14, 1968. Allin (1940: 109) saw a nest with 4 eggs in Darlington Twp. on May 26, 1927. Snyder (1941: 88) reported a nest with 4 eggs taken at Hillier, Prince Edward Co., as early as May 6, 1912: his earliest spring record was on March 31, 1938. Weir & Quilliam (1980: 40) listed Apr. 9 as the 32-year average arrival date at Kingston, with the earliest on March 19. Devitt (1967: 170) gave Apr. 14 as the 26-year average arrival date at Barrie, with the earliest on March 30, 1945: the earliest nest, with 4 eggs, was found there by H.P. Bingham on May 22, 1938. Wm. Arundel reported one at Meaford as early as March 10, 1957 but the median arrival date there was Apr. 22. A 9-year average arrival date at Kearney, Parry Sound Dist., was Apr. 17, with the earliest on Apr. 15, 1897 (Mills, 1981: 179). Nicholson (1981: 190) gave Apr. 15 as a 12-year average arrival date on Manitoulin, with the earliest on Apr. 7, 1974. Strickland, Tozer & Rutter (1982) listed Apr. 25 as the average arrival date in Algonquin Park, with the earliest on Apr. 15. Speirs & Speirs (1947: 38) noted one at North Bay as early as Apr. 9, 1945. Skeel & Bondrup-Nielsen (1978: 217) saw one at Pukaskwa on Apr. 19, 1977 and found a dead one in a Herring Gull nest on May 25. Denis (1961: 3) gave Apr. 28 as the average arrival date at Thunder Bay, with the earliest on Apr. 18, 1945. Peruniak (1971: 30) had just one spring record for Atikokan, on May 20, 1956 but David Elder saw one at the airport there on Apr. 26, 1981. Elder (1979: 40) gave May 8 as his earliest Geraldton date. Cringan (1953a: 4) observed his first at Sioux Lookout on May 3 in 1953.

SUMMER: On the 1968-1977 Breeding Bird Surveys, they were common in the sandy fields of southern Ontario, becoming rare north to Larder Lake in the east and Nipigon in the northwest: they were fairly common in fields from Rainy River north to Dryden. Stirrett (1973c: 23) reported a summer maximum of 43 at Pelee on June 30. Saunders & Dale (1933: 242) had a nest with 4 eggs near London on June 22, 1915. R.V. Lindsay found two nests at Fisher's Glen, Lake Erie, during the first two weeks of July, 1927, one with 4 eggs and the other with 3 eggs (Snyder, 1931: 196). Snyder (1930: 194) saw young just out of the nest in King Twp. on July 9, 1926. Vesper Sparrows occurred on 7 of 11 field plots studied in 1965 in Ontario Co. and was the most abundant species in the Scott Twp. quadrat with 51 birds per 100 acres: Wm. Carrick found a nest with 2 eggs and a cowbird egg in Uxbridge Twp. on June 15, 1957 and Ken Adcoe found a nest with 4 eggs as late as July 4, 1965 in East Whitby Twp. (Speirs, 1973). Snyder (1941: 88) reported a nest with 3 young and 1 egg at Point Traverse, Prince Edward Co. on June 30, 1930. H.P. Bingham found a nest with 5 eggs as late as July 8, 1915 at Barrie (Devitt, 1967: 170). Young flew from two nests near Meaford on June 22, 1946, according to Lloyd Beamer. C.L. Patch took a nest at Ottawa on June 23, 1916 (Lloyd, 1924: 10). Dates for full sets of eggs in Muskoka ranged from June 18 to July 23 (Mills, 1981: 178). D.B. Ferguson found a nest with 4 eggs at Windfall Lake, Manitoulin, on July 8, 1980 (Nicholson, 1981: 190). A field party from the Royal Ontario Museum found a nest with eggs and young at Eau Claire, June 29-July 2, 1935 (Speirs & Speirs, 1947: 38). Baillie & Hope (1947: 30) found a nest with 4 small young at Chapleau on June 3, 1937 and flying young at Bigwood on July 19: males were collected at Biscotasing on June 26 and 29. Snyder (1942: 150) found them common in fields near Sault Ste. Marie: a nest with 6 eggs was found on July 5, 1931. Baillie & Hope (1943: 25) found them common at Marathon, where they located a nest with 2 eggs on June 21, 1936. Snyder (1928: 268) took a singing male at Macdiarmid, Lake Nipigon, on June 5, 1924. Dear (1940: 142) found a nest with 4 eggs at Thunder Bay on June 8, 1926 and another nest with 4 eggs there on June 11, 1927. Snyder (1938: 211) saw adults carrying food in the Rainy River region, beginning June 15, 1929. D. Strickland saw one at Atikokan in July, 1964 (Peruniak, 1971: 30). T.M. Shortt found a nest with 4 eggs at Wabigoon on June 21, 1937 (Baillie & Harrington, 1937: 272). Snyder (1953: 88) found birds breeding at Malachi in 1947 and reported others at Kenora, Redditt, Dryden and Sioux Lookout. Snyder (1928: 28) collected two males by Lake Abitibi, one on June 5, 1925, the other on July 24. Hope (1938: 46) heard two singing at Favourable Lake and collected one of them on June 3, 1938. Sam Waller took a nest with eggs at Moose Factory on June 16, 1930 (Baillie & Harrington, 1927: 271).

AUTUMN: Smith (1957: 180) reported several near Matheson in September, 1953. The only fall record for Pukaskwa was on Sept. 20, 1977 (Skeel & Bondrup-Nielsen, 1978: 217). Speirs & Speirs (1947: 38) observed one at North Bay on Oct. 19, 1944.

Strickland, Tozer & Rutter (1982) listed Sept. 30 as the average departure date from Algonquin Park, with the latest on Oct. 18. Nicholson (1981: 190) gave Oct. 31, 1976 as his latest Manitoulin record, with a high count of 16 on Oct. 2, 1971. Mills (1981: 179) saw one at Parry Sound on Oct. 13, 1979. The latest Simcoe Co. record was one seen by Frances Westman at Painswick on Nov. 16, 1947 (Devitt, 1967: 170). Weir & Quilliam (1980: 40) listed Nov. 3 as the 29-year average departure date from Kingston. Snyder (1941: 88) gave Oct. 27, 1935 as his latest date for Prince Edward Co. I saw one as late as Nov. 5, 1967 in Scott Twp., Ontario Co. (Speirs, 1973). J.L. Baillie (in Saunders, 1947: 375) listed Sept. 30 as his 18-year average departure date from Toronto, with the latest on Nov. 27. Ussher (1965: 30) gave Nov. 5 as his 8-year average departure date from Rondeau, with the latest on Dec. 1. Stirrett (1973d: 29) had fall maxima of 500 at Pelee on Oct. 14 and Oct. 21.

**MEASUREMENTS:**

*Length:* 5.5 to 6.7 ins. (Godfrey, 1966: 387)
*Wingspread:* 10.0 to 11.15 ins. (Roberts, 1955: 721)
*Weight:* 22.0 to 27.5 g. (Terres, 1980: 350).

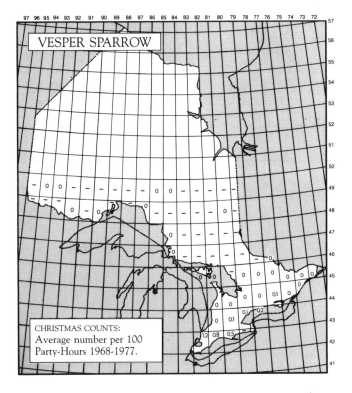

VESPER SPARROW

CHRISTMAS COUNTS:
Average number per 100
Party-Hours 1968-1977.

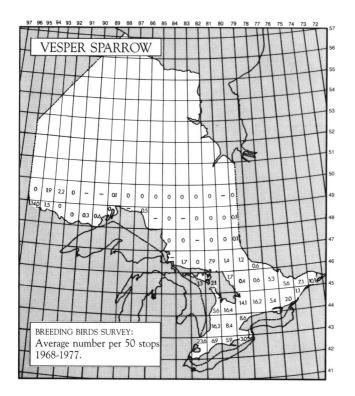

VESPER SPARROW

BREEDING BIRDS SURVEY:
Average number per 50 stops
1968-1977.

# LARK SPARROW   *Chondestes grammacus*   (Say)

The Lark Sparrow has rarely been found breeding in Ontario and then, chiefly, in the sand country of southwestern Ontario. Strays have appeared widely during spring and fall migrations. They winter mainly in southern United States and Mexico.

**IDENTIFICATION:**   The striking, bold face pattern of brown, white and black is quite unlike that of any other Ontario sparrow. The plain breast with a single central black spot may remind you of a Tree Sparrow and the white outer tail feathers of a towhee or Vesper Sparrow (though there is more white at the tips than in the Vesper Sparrow). I have not heard the song but it is said to resemble that of a Vesper Sparrow.

**WINTER:**

**SPRING:**   Stirrett (1973b: 27) reported single birds at Pelee on Apr. 18, Apr. 30, May 3, May 11 and May 15, with two there on May 14. Dennis Rupert *et al* saw a more recent one there on May 11-12, 1983 (Weir, 1983: 866). R. Simpson and N. Van Sickle saw one at Rondeau on Apr. 27, 1971 (Goodwin, 1971: 739). A. Rider noted one at Bright's Grove, Lambton Co., on May 9, 1981 (Goodwin, 1981: 820). Saunders & Dale (1933: 242-243) reported one seen on Apr. 3, 1897 at London and another collected there on Apr. 28, 1885. Brooman (1954: 39) reported one seen by Lloyd Auckland and Russell Foster on May 9, 1953 near St. Thomas. G. Matthews observed one at Long Point on May 28, 1976 (Goodwin, 1976: 836). Beardslee & Mitchell (1965: 437) reported one at Morgan's Point, Lake Erie, on May 11, 1956. J.L. Jackson took a set of 3 eggs at Toronto on May 31, 1892 (Baillie & Harrington, 1937: 272): Fleming (1907: 80) gave May 3, 1895 as his earliest Toronto record and mentioned breeding on May 15, 1899. G. Bennett and A. Dawe found one in Albion Twp. on Apr. 30, 1972 (Goodwin, 1972: 758). R. Charles Long noted one along the Shoal Point Rd., Pickering, on Apr. 22, 1967 (Long, 1968b: 23). W. Osborn reported one at Willow Beach, Lake Ontario, on Apr. 21, 1976 (Goodwin, 1976: 836). Chris. Bell found one in Campbell Twp., Manitoulin, on May 4, 1976 and another was seen on Great Duck Is. on May 24, 1977 by W.R. Lowe and J. Nicholson (Nicholson, 1981: 190). J. Nicholson also reported one in Blezard Valley, near Sudbury, on May 29, 1974 (Goodwin, 1974: 798). N.G. Escott observed one at Marathon on May 10-11, 1978 (Goodwin, 1978: 1001). Helen Atkinson reported two at Dorion on Apr. 14, 1976 (Goodwin, 1976: 836). Peruniak (1971: 30) reported one at Atikokan on May 21, 1966. J.B. Miles found one at Hornepayne from Apr. 20-22, 1974 (Goodwin, 1974: 798).

**SUMMER:**   The only one reported on the 1968-1977 Breeding Bird Survey was on the Avonmore route, near Montreal, in 1974. Stirrett (1973c: 23) had three June records for Pelee, 2 on June 17, one on June 21 and 3 on June 22 (perhaps these were the young, just out of the nest taken by P.A. Taverner on June 22, 1913 (Baillie & Harrington, 1937: 272). W.E. Saunders collected one at Fargo, Kent Co., on June 6, 1901 (Baillie & Harrington, 1937: 272). Saunders & Dale (1933: 242) reported one or two pairs each summer from 1878 to 1889 near London, in open sandy country between pine trees; others seen in 1891 and 1900: a single nest was found in 1890 a few miles west of London. Several nests have been found near Walsingham, Norfolk Co.: J.F. Calvert found a nest with 4 eggs there on May 24, 1930, which held 4 young on June 1: W.E. Saunders found another nest with 4 young there on June 16, 1935 (Baillie & Harrington, 1937: 272): more recently G.W. North and A. Wormington found a nest with small young in the summer of 1971 (Goodwin, 1971: 854): R. Copeland and David Hussell reported an unsuccessful nesting there, observed from June 16 to July 3, 1976 (Goodwin, 1976: 951). Paul Harrington had a set of 3 eggs and a cowbird egg in his collection that was taken originally by E.V. Rippon at Toronto on July 1, 1898 (Fleming, 1907: 80 and Baillie & Harrington, 1937: 272). J. Kamstra and M. Saunders reported one in Darlington Twp. on Aug. 18, 1973 (Tozer & Richards, 1974: 296). Joe Johnson reported one at Inverhuron Provincial Park on June 13, 1975 (Goodwin, 1975: 967). A. Badiuk *et al* observed nesting at Sudbury (2 sterile eggs and 2 fledged young) from July 5-21, 1973 (Goodwin, 1974: 48). Paul Harrington collected a singing male at Loon Lake, near Chapleau, on June 16, 1937 (Baillie & Hope, 1947: 30). D. Shepherd *et al* saw one at Moosonee on June 18, 1983 (Weir, 1983: 985).

AUTUMN: A. Wormington saw one at Moose Factory on Oct. 2, 1978 (Goodwin, 1979: 174). Peruniak (1971: 30) had one fall record for Atikokan, on Sept. 24, 1963. W.E. Saunders saw one at Sault Ste. Marie in September, 1880 (Baillie & Harrington, 1937: 272). Strickland, Tozer & Rutter (1982) listed an Oct. 8 record for Algonquin Park. The Kingston Field Naturalists had three fall records for Prince Edward Point: one on Aug. 31, 1969 (Quilliam, 1973: 188); one on Sept. 2, 1973 and another on Sept. 30, 1977 (Weir & Quilliam, 1980: 28). Rob. Nisbet reported one at Pickering on Oct. 18, 1981 (Goodwin, 1982: 174). Speirs (1938: 53) listed Oct. 29 as the latest Toronto date. E. Elligsen *et al* saw one at Stratford on Sept. 7, 1974 (Goodwin, 1975: 53).

**MEASUREMENTS:**
*Length:* 5.7 to 6.8 ins. (Godfrey, 1966: 388)
*Wingspread:* 10.25 to 11.38 ins. (Roberts, 1955: 722)
*Weight:* one weighed 27.1 g. (Terres, 1980: 345).

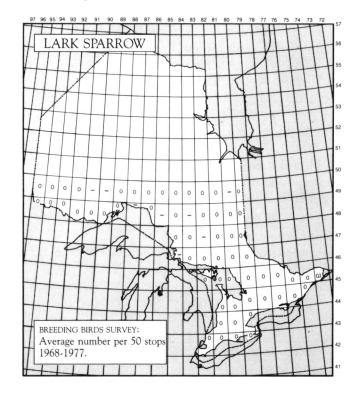

LARK SPARROW

BREEDING BIRDS SURVEY: Average number per 50 stops 1968-1977.

# LARK BUNTING   *Calamospiza melanocorys*   Stejneger

The Lark Bunting is a bird of the short grass prairies and sage brush country; accidental in Ontario. They winter in southwestern United States and Mexico.

IDENTIFICATION: Lark Buntings are a bit bigger than House Sparrows. Males in breeding plumage are all black except for a conspicuous white wing patch and a little white in the tail. Females and males in winter plumage look rather like female Purple Finches except for the whitish wing patch and white in the tail. On April 18, 1977 I described the song as "much like cardinal's, but with dry, canary-like trills added" and on Apr. 19 the singer was observed "following the singing ♂ cardinal from tree to tree, apparently intrigued by its similar song".

WINTER:   W.R. Jarmain and M. Comfort reported one at a London feeder from Dec. 24, 1970 to March 8, 1971 (Goodwin, 1971: 574).

SPRING:   A male was observed and photographed at Pelee by Dennis Rupert *et al* on May 17 and 18, 1974 (Kelley, 1978: 86). David Calvert found one on the northern edge of Thickson's Woods, Whitby, on Apr. 17, 1977: I saw it there on Apr. 18 and 19 as did many other observers (see notes above). Nicholson (1981: 187) reported a male at Mississagi Light, Manitoulin, on May 21, 1975.

SUMMER:   Joe Johnson noted one at Cape Chin, Bruce Co., from July 3-5, 1975 (Goodwin, 1975: 967). Snyder (1927: 375) collected a female in breeding condition at Lowbush, Lake Abitibi, on June 5, 1925, the first Ontario record.

AUTUMN:   Chris Rimmer observed an immature bird at North Point, James Bay, from Sept. 24-29, 1982 (Weir, 1983: 298-299). Kathleen Dinsmore had a male at her South Baymouth feeder from Oct. 14-21, 1974 (Nicholson, 1981: 187). One was spotted by Ron Scovell at Pickering Marsh on Oct. 5, 1958 and confirmed by Doug. Scovell and Earl Stark: John Crosby *et al* saw one at Sunnyside, Toronto, on Sept. 21, 1941 (Speirs, 1973).

**MEASUREMENTS:**
*Length:* 6.0 to 7.5 ins.
(Godfrey, 1966: 381)
*Wingspread:* 10.4 to 12.0
ins. (Roberts, 1955: 707)
*Weight:* 1.25 to 1.38 oz.
(Roberts, 1955: 707).

**REFERENCE:**
Snyder, L.L. 1927 First
record of the Lark bunting
for Ontario. Auk,
43: (3): 375.

# SAVANNAH SPARROW
## *Passerculus sandwichensis*   (Gmelin)

The Savannah Sparrow is probably the most abundant breeding bird in fields, bogs and other low growth, throughout Ontario. Most go to southern United States in winter. Even in fall after song has ceased they may be hard to find though they are then in their finest plumage.

IDENTIFICATION: Savannah Sparrows resemble the more familiar streaky Song Sparrows but have shorter, less rufous tails, and most show prominent yellow "eyebrows". The song is an insect-like "zip-zip-zip-zip-sav-annnnn-ah", usually given from a fence or a tall weed in an open field or bog.

WINTER: On the 1968-1977 Christmas counts they were rare along the north shore of Lake Erie and east to Oshawa, none farther north. Stirrett (1973a: 20) had single birds at Pelee on Dec. 23, Dec. 29 and 3 there on Jan. 1. Marshall Field found one near St. Thomas on Jan. 21, 1951 (Brooman, 1954: 38). Speirs (1938: 53) listed a Dec. 10 record for Toronto and Parker (1983: 26) reported it on 3 of 58 Toronto Christmas counts. Speirs (1973) cited about 10 winter records for Ontario Co., including one as late as Feb. 11, 1950 at Oshawa and one as far north as Lake Scugog on Dec. 30, 1966. One was found on the Moscow Christmas count near Kingston on Dec. 27, 1966 (Quilliam, 1973: 185).

SPRING: Stirrett (1973b: 26) had his earliest bird at Pelee on Apr. 3 and a high count of 30 on May 11. Ussher (1965: 29) gave Apr. 13 as his 18-year average arrival date at Rondeau, with the earliest on March 28. Saunders & Dale (1933: 241) gave Apr. 5 as the 17-year average arrival date at London, with the earliest on March 24, 1921: four May nests were reported of which the earliest, with 4 eggs, was found on May 15, 1913. Lorne Brown found 44 killed at the Long Point lighthouse from Apr. 17-19, 1930 (Snyder, 1931: 196). J.L. Baillie (in Saunders, 1947: 374) listed Apr. 14 as his 27-year average arrival date at Toronto: Speirs (1938: 39, 43) gave March 23 as the earliest spring record there with Apr. 30 as the peak of the spring migration. Doris H. Speirs noted one as early as March 26, 1968 at our Pickering Twp. feeding station (Speirs, 1973). LGL (1974: 222) found a spring peak on May 2 on the proposed Pickering airport site. Dennis Barry found one in Darlington Twp. as early as March 20, 1973 (Tozer & Richards, 1974: 289). Weir & Quilliam (1980: 40) listed May 8 (misprint for Apr. 8) as the 30-year average arrival date at Kingston, with the earliest on March 16: Quilliam (1973: 185) reported three May nests near Kingston; one with 4 eggs and 4 cowbird eggs on May 11, 1969 and another with 3 young and 2 eggs as early as May 14, 1898. Devitt (1967: 167) gave Apr. 18 as the 22-year average arrival date at Barrie, with the earliest on March 30, 1940: H.P. Bingham found a nest with 4 eggs and 3 cowbird eggs near Barrie as early as Apr. 29, 1938. L. Beamer's median arrival date at Meaford was Apr. 20, with the earliest on Apr. 2, 1948. Mills (1981: 177) gave Apr. 21 as a 10-year average arrival date at Huntsville, with the earliest on Apr. 10, 1964. Nicholson (1981: 188) gave Apr. 18 as the 12-year average arrival date on Manitoulin, with the earliest on Apr. 9, 1971 and a high count of 150 on Great Duck Island on May 20, 1977 where 50 were killed at the tower on May 28, 1979. Strickland, Tozer & Rutter (1982) listed Apr. 23 as the average arrival date in Algonquin Park, with the earliest on Apr. 8. Speirs & Speirs (1947: 38) saw one at North Bay on Apr. 9, 1945. Skeel & Bondrup-Nielsen (1978: 217) did not see their first at

Pukaskwa until May 10 in 1977. Denis (1961: 3) listed May 1 as the average arrival date at Thunder Bay, with the earliest on Apr. 12, 1945. David Elder saw one at Atikokan on Apr. 29, 1981. Elder (1979: 40) gave May 11 as his earliest Geraldton record. Bondrup-Nielsen (1976: 45) saw his first near Kapuskasing on May 4, 1974. Cringan (1953a: 4) saw his first in 1953 on May 6 at Dryden. Hope (1938: 45) collected a male at Favourable Lake on May 30, 1938.

SUMMER: On the 1968-1977 Breeding Bird Surveys they were common on routes in agricultural regions from Pelee north to Hearst and Dryden, but uncommon or absent in heavily forested routes in the Precambrian region. Stirrett (1973c: 22) had a summer maximum of 15 at Pelee on June 30. Speirs & Frank (1970: 765) had only 4 pairs per 100 acres on their field plot at Pelee and none on the Windsor prairie plot (the Field Sparrow was the common sparrow on these quadrats). Saunders & Dale (1933: 241) reported a nest with 5 eggs at London on June 8, 1917. Marshall Field found a nest with 4 eggs in Yarmouth Twp., Elgin Co., on June 21, 1953 (Brooman, 1954: 38). T. Dean found a nest with 3 eggs at Port Rowan on June 12, 1977 (McCracken, Bradstreet & Holroyd, 1981: 66). Lawrie (1937: 5) tabulated nests found on a 20-acre plot at York Downs, north of Toronto, in 1937, including a nest with 4 eggs on June 12, a nest with 3 young on June 12 and a nest with 2 young on June 13: nearby nests included a nest with 4 eggs on May 29, a nest with 4 eggs on May 30 and a nest with 2 young on June 10. Snyder (1930: 195) collected 2 young in King Twp. on July 23, 1926. Speirs & Orenstein (1967: 182) found this to be by far the most abundant species in fields in Ontario Co., averaging 71 birds per 100 acres in the 11 fields censused (in old fields and hay fields they averaged about 1 bird per acre, in pasture fields they were about half as common). Only one of 27 nests found in Ontario Co. contained cowbird eggs (2): the other 26 sets totalled 105 eggs (Speirs, 1973). LGL (1974: 222) estimated a density of 135 pairs per 100 acres in Pickering fields. Allin (1940: 108) saw adults feeding young in Darlington Twp. on July 12, 1927. Snyder (1941: 89) collected young at Hallowell, Prince Edward Co., on July 9 and July 26, 1930. H.P. Bingham found a nest with 3 eggs as late as July 16 near Barrie (Devitt, 1967: 167). C.E. Johnson reported adults feeding young at Ottawa on June 3, 1921 (Lloyd, 1924: 10). Mills (1981: 177) found a nest with 4 young on June 13, 1980 at Ahmic Lake and R. Ranford found a nest with 4 young in a Common Tern colony on the South Limestone Islands on June 9, 1968. Glen Murphy found a nest with 4 eggs near Little Current on July 1, 1977 (Nicholson, 1981: 188). MacLulich (1938: 42) saw young being fed by parents in Algonquin Park on June 23, 1938. Louise Lawrence saw young being fed at Rutherglen on July 9, 1944 (Speirs & Speirs, 1947: 38). Three young, just out of the nest, were seen at Biscotasing on June 26, 1937 and fully grown young at Bigwood on July 18 and 19 (Baillie & Hope, 1947: 29-30). Snyder (1942: 150) found a nest with 3 eggs on June 2, 1931 and a nest with 4 eggs on June 12, near Sault Ste. Marie and tallied 65 birds on July 8. Baillie & Hope (1943: 24) found a nest with 4 young at Amyot on June 23, 1936. Snyder (1928: 268) noted single birds or pairs at three localities on Lake Nipigon and collected single males on June 25 and July 2, 1924. Dear (1940: 142) found a nest with 4 eggs at Thunder Bay on June 11, 1924. Snyder (1938: 210) found a nest with 4 eggs near Emo on June 6, 1929 and a young female was collected at Big Fork on July 19. Snyder (1953: 87) found some from Malachi east to Savanne and north to Sioux Lookout: a nest with 4 eggs was found on June 21, 1937 at Wabigoon. Smith (1957: 180) considered this to be the most common bird about farms in the Clay Belt, but Snyder (1928: 28) observed only one at Lake Abitibi in 1925.

James (1980: 91) reported "small numbers in large open bogs" in the Pickle Lake region. Cringan (1953b: 5) saw one near Kasabonika Lake on June 3, 1953. Cringan (1950: 18) observed one carrying food on July 7, 1950 in the Nikip Lake region. Hope (1938: 45) collected a male at Favourable Lake on June 23, 1938. James, Nash & Peck (1982: 70) found them to be abundant in sedge meadows by the Harricanaw River near James Bay, where numerous recently fledged young were seen on July 3, 1982. Manning (1952: 90-91) found this to be the most common bird along the James Bay and Hudson Bay coasts, seeing over 1500 in 137 hours observing in open country along these coasts: Sam Waller found a nest with 6 eggs near Moose Factory. Schueler, Baldwin & Rising (1974: 144, 148) found them common to abundant at all their northern stations: 11 clutches at Moosonee all held 4 eggs; 29 at Attawapiskat averaged 4.1 and 12 at Winisk averaged 4.5 eggs per nest; dates of clutch completion ranged from June 6 to June 30. Harry Lumsden found a nest with 5 young near the mouth of the Brant River, Cape Henrietta Maria region, on July 17, 1969 and nests with 4 young each on July 14 and 17, 1970 (Peck, 1972: 346). James, Nash & Peck (1981: 43) found a density of 18.5 pairs per km $^2$ in open fens at Kiruna Lake in 1981. Lee (1978: 34) found them on grassy areas about Big Trout Lake settlements and saw young and adults carrying food in July, 1975. C.E. Hope estimated 75 at Fort Severn on July 1 and July 17, 1940 and found three nests: a nest with 5 eggs on June 25; a nest with 6 eggs on June 26 and a nest with 5 eggs on July 11.

AUTUMN: D. McRae and A. Wormington saw only one at Netitishi Point, James Bay, on Oct. 19, 1981. Peruniak (1971: 30) gave Oct. 5 as her latest Atikokan date. W. Wyett saw one at Pukaskwa on Sept. 27, 1973 (Skeel & Bondrup-Nielsen, 1978: 217). Speirs & Speirs (1947: 38) observed three on the shores of Lake Nipissing at North Bay on Oct. 11, 1944. Strickland, Tozer & Rutter (1982) listed Oct. 6 as the average departure date from Algonquin Park, with the latest on Oct. 13. Some 108 died at the Great Duck Island tower from Sept. 18-24, 1977: one at Gore Bay on Oct. 24, 1976 was the latest Manitoulin date (Nicholson, 1981: 188). Mills (1981: 177) saw 3 north of Magnetawan on Oct. 14, 1979. Devitt (1967: 167) reported 7 killed at the Barrie TV tower in 7 years, the latest on Oct. 16, 1960. Weir & Quilliam (1980: 40) listed Oct. 18 as the 26-year average departure date from Kingston. Saunders (1947: 374) gave Oct. 9 as his 13-year average departure date from Toronto: Speirs (1938: 51, 53) gave Sept. 15 as the fall peak for Toronto and Oct. 25 as the latest fall date. Snyder (1931: 196) reported 83 destroyed at the Long Point lighthouse between Sept. 24-29, 1929. Saunders & Dale (1933: 241) mentioned one at Strathroy on Nov. 19, 1927 and another a week later at London. Ussher (1965: 29) gave Oct. 14 as his latest Rondeau date. Stirrett (1973d: 29) had a fall maximum of 50 at Pelee on Sept. 29, with his latest one on Nov. 21.

**MEASUREMENTS:**
*Length:* 5.0 to 5.8 ins.
(Godfrey, 1966: 382)
*Wingspread:* 8.6 to 9.2
ins. (Roberts, 1955: 728)
*Weight:* 45 Ontario
specimens averaged
18.8 g.

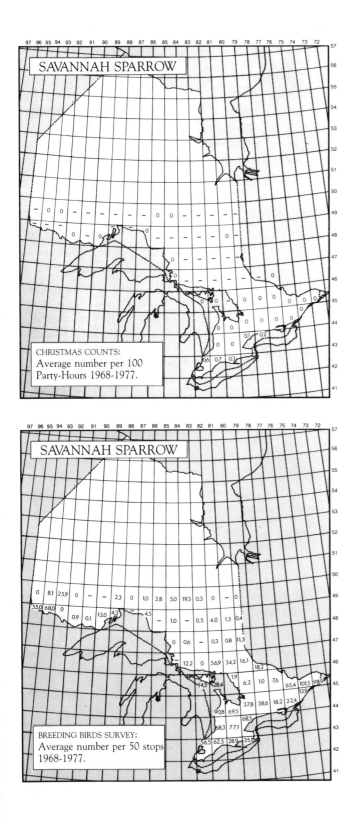

SAVANNAH SPARROW

CHRISTMAS COUNTS:
Average number per 100
Party-Hours 1968-1977.

SAVANNAH SPARROW

BREEDING BIRDS SURVEY:
Average number per 50 stops
1968-1977.

# BAIRD'S SPARROW   *Ammodramus bairdii*   (Audubon)

Baird's Sparrow is a bird of the prairies, accidental as storm-blown waifs in Ontario.

IDENTIFICATION: Baird's Sparrow looks like a washed-out Savannah Sparrow, but with more buff on the face and especially the nape: the outer tail feathers often show white in flight. The breast streaking is something like the Lincoln's Sparrow pattern, forming a "necklace" on a buffy background. Males often show a broad buffy median crown stripe.

WINTER:

SPRING: Baillie (1947: 172) reported the passage of a storm with winds of 80 M.P.H. over Toronto on Apr. 6, 1947, followed by the occurrence of numerous unusual birds the following day and up to early May, including 2 Baird's Sparrows at Toronto. He gave no further details of the sightings. Rob. Nisbet reported one on Caribou Island, Lake Superior, on the day when a major storm system passed, May 9, 1981. He noted "Head and neck generally light brown to buff in colour, black stripes on crown, rather wide, rich brown median crown stripe (immediately visible upon encountering the bird). Back brown marked with black and white; tail short and sharp with light outer feathers. Underparts white, with narrow breast band of fine streaks over a mild wash matching the colour of the head area. Throat white and clear . . . Hint of continuation of fine streaking down upper portions of flanks." The bird was viewed for 7 to 10 minutes with 7 x 50 binoculars and at times moved as close as 3 metres.

SUMMER:

AUTUMN:

**MEASUREMENTS:**
*Length:* 5.0 to 5.8 ins.
(Godfrey, 1966: 384)
*Wingspread:* 8.6 to 9.3
ins. (Roberts, 1955: 726)
*Weight:* 16.0 to 18.2 g.
(Terres, 1980: 339).

# GRASSHOPPER SPARROW
## *Ammodramus savannarum*   (Gmelin)

I associate the Grasshopper Sparrow with dry, sandy hillsides, with scattered dead mullein stalks from the top of which they sing on hot summer days. They have been generally rare north to North Bay and Sault Ste. Marie, but are sometimes locally common in their preferred habitat. They winter from Costa Rica north to the southern United States.

IDENTIFICATION: They are much the size of the more common Savannah Sparrow but have unstreaked underparts (except the young) and much heavier bills. The song is very distinctive (if not too high-pitched for your hearing): "pituck-dzzzzz": it also has a jumbled, ecstatic "flight song" of dry "pick" "tuck" and "dzzz" notes.

**WINTER:**

**SPRING:** Stirrett (1973b: 26) gave Apr. 14 as his earliest Pelee date, with a maximum of 12 on May 10. Ussher (1965: 29) gave May 3 as his 12-year average arrival date at Rondeau, with the earliest on Apr. 19. Saunders & Dale (1933: 241) gave May 10 as the 17-year average arrival date at London, with the earliest on Apr. 7, 1921. Snyder (1931: 197) collected one on Long Point on May 17, 1928 and one struck the lighthouse there on May 14, 1925. M. Furber found one at Hamilton as early as Apr. 20, 1982 (Weir 1982: 848). Speirs (1938: 39) listed Apr. 7 as the earliest Toronto record: this was a male noted by L.L. Snyder in 1928 (Speirs, 1973) who gave Apr. 18, 1960 as the earliest Pickering Twp. record and found a nest with 5 eggs on the East Whitby field quadrat on May 26, 1965. Tozer & Richards (1974: 291) reported a nest with 5 eggs in Cartwright Twp. on May 31, 1970. Weir & Quilliam (1980: 40) listed May 14 as the 29-year average arrival date at Kingston, with the earliest on Apr. 23, 1968. Weir (1982: 848) found one somewhat earlier at Prince Edward Point on Apr. 17, 1982. Devitt (1967: 168) gave May 16 as a 12-year average arrival date at Barrie, earliest observed in Tecumseth Twp. by C.E. Hope on Apr. 25, 1946. Nicholson (1981: 188) noted 7 on Great Duck Is. between May 9 and 28, 1979 and cited a few other Manitoulin records between these dates. Strickland, Tozer & Rutter (1982) listed May 28 as the earliest of very few Algonquin Park records. One was observed at Thunder Bay on May 30, 1982 by many observers (Weir, 1982: 848).

**SUMMER:** On the 1968-1977 Breeding Bird Surveys, they were fairly common at Sarnia (Dennis Rupert reported 33 on the Sarnia route in June, 1978), and on routes along the Lake Huron shore and in the Interlobate Moraine country from Orillia to Fraserville, and rare north to North Bay and Thessalon. Kelley (1978: 87) reported a nest with eggs at Pelee on June 16, 1969 (Stirrett gave the year as 1968). Speirs & Frank (1970: 765) reported a singing male on their Pelee field plot in the summer of 1970. A.H. Kelley mentioned the first Rondeau nesting in the summer of 1976 (Goodwin, 1976: 951). A.A. Wood collected a set of eggs a mile southwest of Strathroy on July 8, 1929 (Saunders & Dale, 1933: 241). F.H. Emery found a nest with 4 eggs as late as Aug. 12, 1930 at Copenhagen, Elgin Co. (Baillie & Harrington, 1937: 270). R.A. Smith found a nest with 3 young at Lowbanks on July 9, 1935 (Baillie & Harrington, 1937: 270). Speirs & Orenstein (1967: 182) found populations of 82 birds per 100 acres on their East Whitby plot and 55 per 100 acres in the Uxbridge quadrat, but none in the other 9 fields studied in Ontario Co.: in these two plots it was second only to the Savannah Sparrow in abundance. Dennis Barry and J.M. Richards found a nest with 5 eggs across the road from my May 26 nest on June 4, 1969: both these nests fledged young (see Speirs, 1973 for details). Tozer & Richards (1974: 291) reported several nests in the Oshawa region, including one with 1 egg plus 1 cowbird egg and 2 young cowbirds on June 11, 1966 in Cartwright Twp. and a nest with 5 newly-hatched young as late as July 14, 1967 in Darlington Twp. T.F. McIllwraith saw one near Bloomfield on July 24, 1940 and Farley Mowat noted 3 near Picton on Aug. 20, 1940 (Snyder, 1941: 88). Quilliam (1973: 186) saw an adult carrying food near Kingston on June 5, 1963 and K.F. Edwards saw a tailless young with 2 adults on June 19, 1966. Frank Munro found a nest with 4 eggs at Camp Borden on June 21, 1953 (Devitt, 1967: 167). One was shot at the Experimental Farm, Ottawa, on June 28, 1898 (Lloyd, 1924: 10). On Beausoleil Is., Doris Speirs and I saw one with food in its bill, scolding us, on Aug. 10 and 11, 1946 and saw one young there on Aug. 22. Mills (1981: 177) cited 3 records for the Parry Sound district: J.L. Baillie collected one at

Pickerel Lake on July 3, 1939; J. Meritt located a fledged young and the perturbed parents "executed a broken wing act" near Ahmic Lake on July 14, 1947. Nicholson (1981: 188) had a few summer records for Manitoulin: two were heard by John Lemon as late as July 16, 1972. Strickland, Tozer & Rutter (1982) listed June 17 as the latest Algonquin Park record. Between June 21 and July 8, 1974, John Lemon observed one at Lively, near Sudbury (Goodwin, 1974: 899). Jean Wallace found one in Ingram Twp., Timiskaming, on July 6, 1977 (Goodwin, 1977: 1135). C. Garton, N. Hordy and M. Roinila observed one at Thunder Bay on June 22, 1980 (Goodwin, 1980: 892).

AUTUMN: The only fall record for Simcoe Co. was one found dead on the Barrie TV tower by Frances Westman on Sept. 19, 1964 (Devitt, 1967: 168). The latest Kingston bird was one seen by K.F. Edwards on Amherst Is. on Oct. 18, 1978 (Quilliam, 1973: 186). R.D. Weir reported finding one killed at the Lennox Chimney on Sept. 19, 1972 (Goodwin, 1973: 56). Dennis Barry saw one in Darlington Twp. as late as Oct. 15, 1967 (Tozer & Richards, 1974: 291). J.L. Baillie (in Saunders, 1947: 374) had an Oct. 1 record for Toronto. Beardslee & Mitchell (1965: 432-433) reported one at Port Weller on Sept. 29, 1960. One was killed at the Long Point lighthouse between Sept. 24-29, 1929 (Snyder, 1931: 197). Ussher (1965: 29) had a Nov. 11 record for Rondeau.

**MEASUREMENTS:**
*Length:* 4.8 to 5.4 ins.
(Godfrey, 1966: 383)
*Wingspread:* 8 to 8 1/4
ins. (Roberts, 1955: 719)
*Weight:* 16.4 to 20.6 g.
(Terres, 1980: 344).

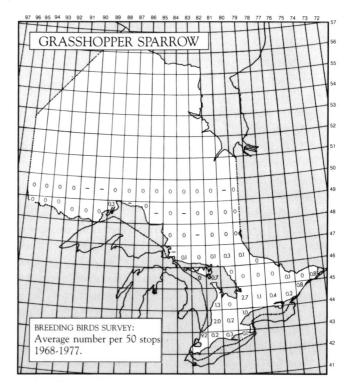

GRASSHOPPER SPARROW

BREEDING BIRDS SURVEY:
Average number per 50 stops
1968-1977.

# HENSLOW'S SPARROW   *Ammodramus henslowii*   (Audubon)

The Henslow's Sparrow is a bird of retiring habits, normally found deep in extensive damp meadows but sometimes in alfalfa or clover crops in southern Ontario. Numbers have fluctuated widely and appear to have decreased in recent years. They winter in southern United States.

IDENTIFICATION: They are best identified by the characteristic, brief "ti-slick" or "tzz-dick" song, given forth with head thrown back enthusiastically, often from a semi-concealed perch half way up a weed stalk, after which the singer drops down and disappears into the meadow grasses. If flushed, it flies a few feet displaying a ragged tail of pointed feathers, then drops into the grass again before a good view has been obtained. Sometimes a singing bird will stay in sight long enough to glimpse the necklace of dark streaks on the breast and the greenish face and back of the neck. The wings are a richer rufous brown than in other "grass sparrows".

WINTER:

SPRING: Stirrett (1973b: 26) had his earliest Pelee record on Apr. 14 and maxima of 5 on Apr. 30 and May 21. Ussher (1965: 30) gave May 11 as the 10-year average arrival date at Rondeau, with the earliest on Apr. 27. W.E. Saunders noted several at Jeannette's Creek, Kent Co., on May 24, 1898 (Macoun, 1904: 472). Saunders & Dale (1933: 242) had one near London on May 4, 1921 and "quite a number" at Komoka on May 16, 1931. D. Currie noted 4 at Byron from May 29, 1974 (Goodwin, 1974: 797). Goodwin (1972: 758) reported one at Long Point on May 6, 1972. I found a colony of 6 singers at Lowbanks, near Lake Erie, on May 15, 1932 (Speirs, 1933: 35). Saunders (1947: 375) listed March 24 as his earliest Toronto record. Weir & Quilliam (1980: 40) listed May 9 as the 24-year average arrival date at Kingston, with the earliest on Apr. 22, 1960: C.J. Young found a pair near Lansdowne, Leeds Co., in May, 1898, and later discovered the nest with 4 eggs (Quilliam, 1973: 186). C. Harris and C.J. MacFayden noted 3 at Barrie as early as May 5, 1974 (Goodwin, 1974: 797). M. Brigham reported 2 at North Gower, near Ottawa, on May 17, 1975 (Goodwin, 1975: 847). Nicholson (1981: 189) found one on Great Duck Is. on May 21, 1977. R.D. Ussher reported a singing bird at Obatanga Provincial Park, Algoma, from May 25-30, 1978 (Goodwin, 1979: 174).

SUMMER: On the 1968-1977 Breeding Bird Surveys there were single observations on the London, Palgrave and Auburn routes, none elsewhere. Stirrett (1973c: 23) had just one summer record at Pelee, on June 16, but G. Bennett and R. Curry heard 3 singing there on July 22, 1973 (Goodwin, 1973: 867). Saunders & Dale (1933: 242) heard one near London on June 15, 1920. F.H. Emery collected a nest with 3 eggs on Aug. 12, 1930, near Port Bruce, Elgin Co., and found another nest there the same month (Brooman, 1954: 38). Snyder (1931: 197) found an extensive colony on Long Point in 1927 and collected 5 ♂ and 1 ♀ there between June 24 and July 23: J.L. Baillie saw one carrying material in its beak on July 14, 1927. My first and most memorable acquaintance with Henslow's Sparrow was at Lowbanks on June 1 and later in 1931 and again at Erindale on July 3, 1932 (Speirs, 1933: 35). Doug. Miller found a nest with 5 young on the York Downs study plot on June 11, 1937 (Lawrie, 1937: 5). Speirs & Orenstein (1967: 182) found populations on 4 of 11 fields studied in Ontario Co. in 1965, with population densities of 20 birds per 100 acres in the East Whitby quadrat, 16 per 100 acres in the Uxbridge plot and 4 per 100 acres in the Pickering and Uxbridge fields. Speirs (1973) had records for 9 of the 11 townships in Ontario Co.: George A. Scott found two nests in Whitby Twp.: one with 5 eggs on June 5, 1960, the other with 2 eggs on June 1, 1960. Tozer & Richards (1974: 293) cited colonies near Oshawa in Cartwright, Darlington and Reach Twps. B. Morin located a bird near Cornwall on July 2, 1982 (Weir, 1982: 973). Devitt (1967: 169) heard one singing in the Holland River Marshes on July 10, 1937, where they were found for about 10 years until market gardens took over the area. C.J. MacFayden followed the fortunes of several Simcoe Co. colonies, the largest of which at Tiny Marsh, had 43 birds on July 14, 1978 (Goodwin, 1978: 1156). J.H. Fleming found a small colony at Port Sandfield, Muskoka, on July 14, 1902 (Macoun, 1904: 472). "Robbins heard one of these sparrows near Providence Bay, June 23, 1952" (Nicholson, 1981: 189).

AUTUMN: Devitt (1967: 169) gave Sept. 14, 1937, as his latest date for the Holland Marsh. Quilliam (1973: 187) listed Oct. 12, 1969, as the latest Kingston date. R.C. Long noted one at Shoal Point Marsh on Oct. 1, 1969 (Speirs, 1973). Saunders (1947: 268, 375) saw one at Holland Marsh on Sept. 13, 1942: he listed Oct. 3 as his latest Toronto date. R. Curry et al observed one at Long Point on Oct. 2, 1971 (Goodwin, 1972: 59). Saunders & Dale (1933: 242) noted one near London on Oct. 12, 1930. Ussher (1965: 30) had a Nov. 11 record at Rondeau. Stirrett (1973d: 29) had fall records at Pelee from Sept. 11 to Nov. 3 and P.D. Pratt observed a late one there on Nov. 10, 1979 (Goodwin, 1980: 158).

**MEASUREMENTS:**
*Length:* 4.7 to 5.3 ins. (Godfrey, 1966: 385)
*Wingspread:* 6.6 to 7.1 ins. (Roberts, 1955: 722)
*Weight:* 18 averaged 13.1 g. (11.1 - 14.9 g.) (Dunning, 1984: 24).

**REFERENCES:**
Knapton, Richard W. 1984 The Henslow's Sparrow in Ontario: a historical perspective. Ont. Birds, 2: (2): 70-74. This article cited several other references.
  Speirs, J. Murray 1933 Some notes on the Henslow Sparrow. Can. Field-Naturalist, 47: (2): 35.

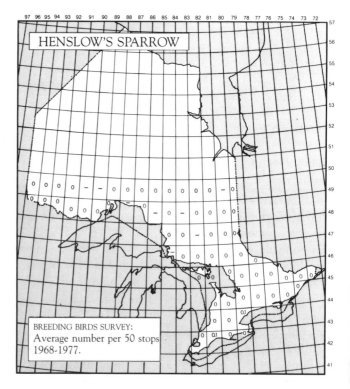

HENSLOW'S SPARROW

BREEDING BIRDS SURVEY: Average number per 50 stops 1968-1977.

# LE CONTE'S SPARROW  *Ammodramus leconteii*  (Audubon)

Le Conte's Sparrow is another denizen of wet meadows, seldom seen unless first heard singing. In Ontario, most breed in the northern and far western regions, but a few have been found, at long intervals, in southern Ontario. My first encounter was on the York Downs study plot near Toronto during the summer of 1937, where none had been found for about 40 years. These secretive sparrows winter in the southern United States.

**IDENTIFICATION:** Like the other "grass sparrows" this species is best identified by its song, a high-pitched buzzy song "like a bee in a bottle". If spotted singing from a weed top it proves to be a colourful little sprite, with yellow-buff face and underparts with a contrasting blue-gray ear patch and dark streaks along the sides: the hind neck is decorated with rows of pink dots, a good mark when it can be seen.

**WINTER:**

**SPRING:** Stirrett (1973b: 26) had a few Pelee records from Apr. 10 to May 20. Marshall Field found one at Springwater Park, Elgin Co., on May 14, 1950 (Brooman, 1954: 38). W.R. Jarmain spotted one at Melbourne, near London, on May 14, 1982 (Weir, 1982: 848). One was observed at the Long Point Bird Observatory on May 1, 1972 (Goodwin, 1972: 758). George Pierce collected one at Toronto on May 5, 1897 (Fleming, 1907: 80). I found two at York Downs about 40 years later, on May 27, 1937 where 6 territories were later located (Lawrie, 1937: 3). Saunders (1947: 140) found one at Highland Creek on May 29, 1943. David Calvert reported hearing two on May 29, 1971 and 3 on May 6, 1972 in Pickering Twp. (Speirs, 1973): he also reported them near Burketon, Cartwright Twp., as early as Apr. 27, 1970 (Tozer & Richards, 1974: 291). David Ruch observed one at Cranberry Marsh, Whitby, on May 8, 1982 and B. Olson reported one in the Port Hope - Cobourg marshes on May 4, 1982 (Weir, 1982: 848). R.D. Weir saw one at Prince Edward Point on May 12, 1975 (Goodwin, 1975: 847). N. and R.B. Stewart observed one on Amherst Is., near Kingston, on May 22, 1983 (Weir, 1983: 866). Devitt (1967: 168) heard one singing in the York Co. section of the Holland Marsh as recently as May 24, 1957. R.A. Foxall and R. Poulin noted 2 at Ottawa from May 19, 1974 (Goodwin, 1974: 899). Nicholson (1981: 189) found one at Mississagi light, Manitoulin, on May 9, 1976 and at least 4 on Great Duck Is. on May 25, 1976 and others there on May 15 and 18, 1979: an early one was also found there on Apr. 26, 1981 (Goodwin, 1981: 820). The first Algonquin Park record was on May 29, 1981 by J.D. Reynolds (Goodwin, 1981: 820). J. Lemon reported one at Worthington, near Sudbury, from May 25-31, 1975 (Goodwin, 1975: 847). Skeel & Bondrup-Nielsen (1978: 217) saw two at Pukaskwa on May 13, 1977. T. Hince noted one at Marathon on May 2, 1983 (Weir, 1983: 866). Denis (1961: 3) gave May 16 as the average arrival date at Thunder Bay, with the earliest on Apr. 24, 1957. A.J. Erskine observed one in the Abitibi area on May 27, 1971 (Goodwin, 1971: 739). M. Jennings, P.D. Pratt and J. Thompson estimated 30 or more on Shipsands Is., near Moosonee, from May 24-28, 1981 (Goodwin, 1981: 820).

**SUMMER:** On the 1968-1977 Breeding Bird Surveys they were rare at Atikokan and Hearst, uncommon at Fort Frances, fairly common at Dryden and absent on other routes. One was reported at the Long Point Bird Observatory on Aug. 18, 1982 (Weir, 1983: 176). Saunders (1947: 171-172) found 3 in the Holland River marshes on June 11, 1944 and 10 there on June 17, 1945. Devitt (1967: 168) reported that a female collected in the

Holland River marshes on July 10, 1937 had an egg in its oviduct almost ready for extrusion: on July 23, 1938 he found a young bird there: at least 15 singing males were heard there on July 4, 1948. One was seen and heard on Barrie Is., Manitoulin, on June 19, 1971 by Monty Brigham, D. Coskren and Ronald Pittaway (Nicholson, 1981: 189). J. Lemon noted one in the Blezard Valley on June 29, 1976 and one at Kelly Lake throughout June, 1978, both in Sudbury Dist. (Goodwin, 1976: 951 and 1978: 1156). C. Garton reported one at Onion Lake, Thunder Bay, on July 31, 1979 (Goodwin, 1979: 860). Koelz (1923: 118) collected a young female at Macdiarmid, Lake Nipigon, on July 27, 1922. Dear (1940: 142) reported two nests at Thunder Bay, both with 4 eggs: one on June 10, 1924, the other on June 17, 1924. Fargo & Trautman (1930: 31-33) collected a "male of the year" near Lake Manitowik (NE of Wawa) on Aug. 24, 1928. S. Peruniak noted one at Atikokan in June, 1977 (Goodwin, 1977: 1135). J. Wallace found one in Ingram Twp. Timiskaming, on June 5, 1977 (Goodwin, 1977: 1135). With a population density of 14 territories per 100 acres, this was the third most abundant species in a study plot in a hayfield at Dryden in 1971 (Price & Speirs, 1971: 1109). Snyder (1953: 87) reported singing males near Wabigoon on June 26, 1937 and another west of Sioux Lookout on June 29, 1947. G. Bennett and R. Curry noted 2 singing males at Smoky Falls on July 4-5, 1972 (Goodwin, 1973: 55). Todd (1963: 677) "picked up no fewer than five" at Partridge Creeks, near Moosonee, between June 11-16, 1941 and one at Nattabisha Point on June 17. Manning (1952: 92) reported one collected at Shipsands on June 18, 1949 and another at Big Piskwanish on June 11, 1947 (both near Moosonee). Schueler, Baldwin & Rising (1974: 147-148) collected 4 males at Whitetop Creek, near Moosonee, from June 11-14, 1971 and 4 females there on June 5, 1972: also 3 females at Attawapiskat on June 15 and 20, 1971. A. McTavish and A. Wormington noted one at Winisk on June 2, 1981 and D.C. Sadler heard one there on June 14, 1983 (Goodwin, 1981: 936 and Weir, 1983: 985). C.E. Hope collected one at Fort Severn on July 8 and observed 6 there on July 17 in 1940.

AUTUMN: George M. Sutton collected 8 near Moosonee from Sept. 1-22, 1923 (Todd, 1963: 677) and A. Wormington et al noted one there on Oct. 9, 1972 (Goodwin, 1973: 55). K. Denis reported one in Pearson Twp., Thunder Bay, on Sept. 12, 1976 (Goodwin, 1977: 172). N. Suhtand saw one at Schreiber on Sept. 10, 1977 (Goodwin, 1978: 200). Nicholson (1981: 189) had records from Great Duck Is. on Sept. 23, 1977, Oct. 5, 1978 and Sept. 18, 24 and 28, 1980. Mills (1981: 178) observed one at Ahmic Lake on Oct. 9, 1977 and C. Harris watched one near Go Home Bay on Sept. 29, 1979. The first Ottawa record was on Sept. 5, 1971 when B. MacTavish, M. McKie, and H. Williamson found one in the Mer Bleu Bog (Goodwin, 1972: 59). Devitt (1967: 168) gave Sept. 11, 1937 as his latest Simcoe Co. record. Gerry Bennett reported one at Prince Edward Point on Sept. 1, 1976 (Weir & Quilliam, 1980: 27). Saunders (1947: 267) noted one at Holland River on Sept. 13, 1942. D.T. Hussell et al noted one at Long Point on Sept. 13-14, 1980 (Goodwin, 1980: 158) and a very late one was seen there on Nov. 7, 1982 (Weir, 1983: 176). M. Jennings saw one at Bronte on Sept. 17, 1982 and A. Dobson noted one at Toronto on Oct. 16, 1982 (Weir, 1983: 176). H.H. Axtell observed one near the edge of the Dunnville marshes on Oct. 20, 1953 (Beardslee & Mitchell, 1965: 433). R. Marson with J. and M. Tabak reported one at London on Oct. 21, 1972 (Goodwin, 1973: 56). Kelley (1978: 87) reported two fall records for Pelee: one on Oct. 16, 1965 by J.P. Kleiman and S. Postupalski, the other on Oct. 27-28, 1973 by A. Maley and K. Overman.

**MEASUREMENTS:**
*Length:* 4.5 to 5.3 ins.
(Godfrey, 1966: 385)
*Wingspread:* 6 1/2 to 7 1/
4 ins. (Roberts, 1955: 724)
*Weight:* 11.2 and 12.2 g.
(Terres, 1981: 345)
12.3; 12.8 and 13.1 g.
(Walkinshaw, 1937: 314).

**REFERENCE:**
Walkinshaw, Lawrence H.
1937 Le Conte's Sparrow
breeding in Michigan and
South Dakota. Auk,
54: (3): 309-320. This
important paper
summarized what was
known about the species,
including distribution
records (two from Ontario)
and life history.

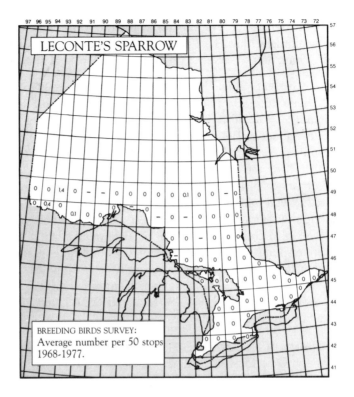

LECONTE'S SPARROW

BREEDING BIRDS SURVEY:
Average number per 50 stops
1968-1977.

# SHARP-TAILED SPARROW
*Ammodramus caudacutus* (Gmelin)

In Ontario the Sharp-tailed Sparrow has been known to breed only around James Bay,
though there have been several June records at Long Point and other southern Ontario
marshes. In migration they have been found by wading around in cattail marshes at the
appropriate seasons. In winter they have usually been found in coastal marshes along the
Atlantic and Gulf of Mexico.

IDENTIFICATION: The Sharp-tailed Sparrow is quite similar to Le Conte's Sparrow
but lacks the pink on the hind neck, has streaked breast and more contrasty black and
white striped back: also the median crown stripe is buffy in the Sharp-tailed Sparrow, not
gray as in Le Conte's. After hearing several in the Delta marshes in Manitoba, I described
the song as "psheeee-you!", mostly "shhh", with a "beady" quality.

WINTER: One was reported "with excellent details" on the Blenheim Christmas count
in 1973.

SPRING: Stirrett (1973b: 27) had three Pelee records: May 8, 1965; May 14, 1955
and May 20, 1956 (2 birds): Dennis Rupert saw one there on May 16 and 25, 1974 (Kelley,
1978: 87) and J. G. Keenleyside noted another there on May 15-16, 1976 (Goodwin,
1976: 836). A.H. Lawrie and H. Barnett reported one on the York Downs study plot,
north of Toronto, on May 29, 1937 (Lawrie, 1937: 3) and Saunders (1947: 375) listed a

May 31 record for Toronto (probably the York Downs bird). Ron Weir heard one that sang all night May 21-22, 1978 at Prince Edward Point (Weir & Quilliam, 1980: 27) and W. Grummett observed 3 on Amherst Is. on May 16, 1982 (Weir, 1982: 848).

SUMMER: Single birds were reported at Long Point on June 12, 1971; June 3, 1973 and June 16, 1982 (Goodwin, 1971: 737; Goodwin, 1973: 769 and Weir, 1982: 974). Fleming (1907: 80) reported a female collected at Toronto by C.W. Nash on June 10, 1898. Saunders (1947: 375) listed a Toronto record by J.L. Baillie on June 8 and a personal record on Aug. 2. George North and George M. Stirrett found one in the Little Cataraqui marsh, Kingston on June 3, 1950 (Quilliam, 1973: 187). M. Robson and A. Wormington observed over 5 at Rainy River on June 30, 1979 (Goodwin, 1979: 860). Manning (1952: 92) cited several summer records, from Moosonee, Fort Albany, Attawapiskat and Raft River along the James Bay coast, many of which were collected. Schueler, Baldwin & Rising (1974: 148) collected 3 females at Attawapiskat from June 16-20, 1971 and two males there on June 17, 1971; also 2 males about 4 miles east of Winisk on June 27, 1971 and one male at the mouth of the Sutton River on June 25, 1962. Peck (1972: 346) reported 2 collected by T.M. Shortt at Cape Henrietta Maria, on July 8 and 21, 1948: others were noted there on July 2 and 19. McLaren & McLaren (1981: 5) heard one singing along the Severn River on June 12, 1977.

AUTUMN: D. McRae and A. Wormington noted only one at Netitishi Point, James Bay, on Oct. 15, 1981. Oliver Hewitt saw several at Ship Sands, Moosonee, from Sept. 22-25, 1947 and others by George Stirrett on Oct. 2, 1948: 3 were taken there on Sept. 3, 1923 (Manning, 1952: 92). Nicholson (1981: 190) had 3 Manitoulin records: one observed by Ron Tasker at Lorne Lake on Oct. 9, 1967; a casualty at the Great Duck Is. tower on Sept. 22, 1977 and another seen there on Sept. 24, 1980. C. Griffiths *et al* mistnetted one at Ottawa, Oct. 2-3, 1976 (Goodwin, 1977: 172) and many observers saw one there on Oct. 16, 1977 (Goodwin, 1978: 200): B.M. DiLabio reported another there Sept. 29 - Oct. 2, 1979 (Goodwin, 1980: 158). E.L. Brereton identified one at Barrie on Sept. 19, 1945 (Devitt, 1967: 169). E. Beaupré noted numerous Sharp-tailed Sparrows on Snake Is. and Amherst Is., off Kingston, on Sept. 6, 1928 (Quilliam, 1973: 187) and Ron Weir noted one at Prince Edward Point on Oct. 28, 1972 (Goodwin, 1973: 56). H. McCormick reported one at Peterborough between Sept. 14 and Oct. 7, 1980 (Goodwin, 1981: 179). E.R. McDonald saw one at Willow Beach on Oct. 24 and Nov. 12, 1977 (Goodwin, 1978: 200). Speirs (1973) reported one seen by R. Charles Long at Pickering Beach as early as Aug. 31, 1966 and one as late as Nov. 30, 1958 at Oshawa's Second Marsh, seen by George A. Scott and W. Neal with 17 records totalling about 30 individuals, mostly in late September and early October in the Lake Ontario marshes from Pickering to Oshawa: there have been several more recent records in these marshes. Fleming (1907: 80) reported seeing 11 Toronto specimens, 2 taken on Sept. 22, 1894 and the latest on Oct. 28, 1896: Speirs (1938: 47) listed Sept. 16 as the earliest Toronto date and Oct. 29 as the latest: H. Kerr found one at Toronto as recently as Sept. 29, 1979 (Goodwin, 1980: 158). Three were observed at Dundas Marsh Oct. 17-22, 1976 by R. Curry, R.H. Westman and A. Wormington (Goodwin, 1977: 172) and 3 there again on Oct. 15, 1978, by V. Evans (Goodwin, 1979: 174). Beardslee & Mitchell (1965: 435) reported two at the Dunnville marsh on Oct. 18, 1953, 4 there on Oct. 19, 1958 and again on Oct. 7, 1961: R.F. Andrle collected one there on Oct. 21, 1957 and another on Oct. 1, 1970 (Goodwin, 1971: 53).

**MEASUREMENTS:**
*Length:* 5.0 to 5.8 ins.
(Godfrey, 1966: 386)
*Wingspread:* 6.9 to 7.1
ins. (Roberts, 1955: 723)
*Weight:* 13.3 to 19.3 g.
(Terres, 1980: 349).

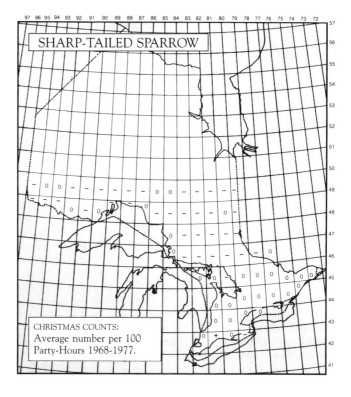

SHARP-TAILED SPARROW

CHRISTMAS COUNTS:
Average number per 100
Party-Hours 1968-1977.

# FOX SPARROW   *Passerella iliaca*   (Merrem)

Fox Sparrows are great scratchers, and the first evidence of their presence is often hearing dead leaves being showered aside by their vigorous activity. In Ontario they breed chiefly in the dryer parts of the Hudson Bay Lowlands and most go to the southern United States or northern Mexico to winter, so we see them rather briefly during the spring and fall migrations and then seldom in large numbers, so they are birds sought after by bird watchers.

**IDENTIFICATION:** Fox Sparrows are larger than most of our migrant sparrows. With their rich rufous tails and spotted breasts they may be confused with Hermit Thrushes though their scratching habit should readily separate them from the hop and pause behaviour of the Hermits, with frequent tail raising. The Fox Sparrow also has much gray on the face and hind neck with rufous ear coverts, while the Hermit has a fairly uniform brownish head with grayish ear coverts. The song of the Fox Sparrow is a series of "sliding" whistles "Soo-ee—swee—sa-sooee-swah", somewhat like the song of a Tree Sparrow but much lower in pitch.

**WINTER:** They were uncommon on the 1968-1977 Christmas counts at Pelee and rare on other counts near the Lake Erie and Lake Ontario shores, with outliers at Deep River and Dryden. Stirrett (1973a: 21) had records of one or two birds throughout the winter at Pelee. Saunders & Dale (1933: 245) reported one that came to a London feeder during the winter of 1919-1920. Brooman (1954: 40) reported 4 on the West Elgin Christmas count on Dec. 26, 1952. One was found at Port Colborne on Jan. 20, 1949

(Beardslee & Mitchell, 1965: 446). The Fox Sparrow was reported on 10 of 58 Christmas counts at Toronto (Parker, 1983: 26). Doris Speirs saw one at our feeder in Pickering Twp. on Dec. 6, 1968 and two were noted at feeders on the Oshawa Christmas count on Dec. 28, 1969 (Tozer & Richards, 1974: 304). Weir & Quilliam (1980: 40) had a Dec. 16 record at Kingston. Frances Westman saw one near Ivy, Simcoe Co., on Jan. 28, 1961 (Devitt, 1967: 176). Kathleen Dinsmore had one wintering at South Baymouth, Manitoulin, in 1969-1970 and again the following winter (Nicholson, 1981: 195).

SPRING: Stirrett (1973b: 27) had spring birds at Pelee from March 20 to May 13, with a maximum of 50 on Apr. 8. Ussher (1965: 31) had Rondeau migrants from March 15 to May 8, with average arrival on Apr. 4 and departure on Apr. 23. Saunders & Dale (1933: 245) gave Apr. 1 as the 17-year average arrival date at London, with the earliest on March 10, 1921. Snyder (1931: 201) reported 32 casualties at the Long Point lighthouse from Apr. 17-21, 1930: one was collected as late as May 4 in 1928. J.L. Baillie (in Saunders, 1947: 375) had Toronto records from March 13 to May 3, with average arrival on Apr. 15 and departure on Apr. 24. Grace Cole saw one in Pickering Twp. as early as March 7, 1964 and Naomi LeVay reported one as late as May 25, 1952 at Whitby: the peak for spring migrants in this region is usually in the third week of April (Speirs, 1973). Weir & Quilliam (1980: 40) listed March 24 and May 12 as the earliest and latest spring migrants at Kingston, with average arrival on Apr. 7 and departure on Apr. 27. Devitt (1967: 175-176) had spring records near Barrie from March 30 (1961) to May 8 (1966), with an 18-year average arrival on Apr. 13. L. Beamer had Meaford records for only 7 of 20 years, with the earliest on March 25, 1955 and a median arrival date on Apr. 8. Mills (1981: 185) gave Apr. 9 as the 12-year average arrival date at Huntsville, with the earliest on March 23, 1966: Alfred Kay had Port Sydney records from March 26 (1894) to May 3 (1890). Nicholson (1981: 194) gave Apr. 9 as the 10-year average arrival date on Manitoulin with the earliest on March 19, 1979 and latest on May 23, 1976: the high count was only 7, noted at South Baymouth on Apr. 18, 1971 by Kathleen Dinsmore. Strickland, Tozer & Rutter (1982) gave Apr. 4 and May 5 as the earliest and latest dates for Algonquin Park, with average arrival on Apr. 19 and departure on May 4. Louise Lawrence had records at Pimisi Bay in 1945 from Apr. 8 to Apr. 30 (Speirs & Speirs, 1947: 38). Skeel & Bondrup-Nielsen (1978: 220) noted 6 at Pukaskwa on Apr. 20 and 4 on Apr. 23 in 1977. Denis (1961: 2) listed Apr. 18 as the average arrival date at Thunder Bay, with the earliest on Apr. 9, 1956. Peruniak (1971: 31) had Atikokan records from Apr. 18 to May 3: David Elder noted one there as early as Apr. 13 in 1981. Cringan (1953a: 4) noted his first in 1953 at Sioux Lookout on May 12. Sam Waller recorded its arrival at Moose Factory on Apr. 22, 1930 (Todd, 1963: 702): Oliver Hewitt saw 2 at Moosonee on May 22 and one at Moose Factory on May 23, 1947 (Manning, 1952: 96).

SUMMER: The only one reported on the 1968-1977 Breeding Bird Surveys was on the 1968 Byng Inlet route, no doubt a belated migrant. James, Nash & Peck (1982: 70-71) observed them daily all summer along the Harricanaw River, near James Bay. Todd (1963: 702) mentioned a nest with eggs collected at Moose Factory on June 4, 1860 by Drexler and another nest, with 3 eggs, collected there on June 6, 1934 by Samuel S. Dickey. McLaren & McLaren (1981: 5) noted 7 in the Pickle Lake area from June 3-7, 1977. Hope (1938: 47-48) found them "not uncommon" at Favourable Lake from May 30 to July 13, 1938 and observed an agitated pair there on July 6. Cringan (1953b: 5) saw 3 at Kasabonika Lake on June 3, 1953. Manning (1952: 96-97) cited summer records for Moosonee, Fort Albany, Attawapiskat and Raft River, along the James Bay coast. Schueler, Baldwin & Rising (1974: 148) cited breeding evidence for Attawapiskat and Hawley Lake and found a nest with 3 eggs at Winisk on June 8, 1965 and a flying young there on July 1, 1971. James, Nash & Peck (1981: 93) confirmed breeding at Kiruna Lake, Sutton Ridges, in 1980. Lee & Speirs (1977: 50, 54) reported a territorial male on 2 of the 3 quadrats studied at Big Trout Lake in 1975. C.E. Hope noted as many as 14 at Fort Severn on June 17, 1940 and collected a nest with 3 eggs there on July 17.

AUTUMN: D. McRae and A. Wormington noted 2 on Oct. 15 and one the following day at Netitishi Point, James Bay in 1981. Elder (1979: 40) called it a "common regular fall migrant" at Geraldton, but had no spring record there. Peruniak (1971: 31) had fall migrants at Atikokan from Sept. 22 to Oct. 22. Louise Lawrence noted one at Pimisi Bay on Oct. 2, 1942 (Speirs, 1973). Ricker & Clarke (1939: 24) reported a North Bay specimen taken on Oct. 21, 1925. Strickland, Tozer & Rutter (1982) listed Oct. 4 and Nov. 4 as the earliest and latest fall dates for Algonquin Park, with average arrival on Oct. 8 and departure on Oct. 21. Nicholson (1981: 195) had just two fall records for Manitoulin: Oct. 15, 1971 at South Baymouth and Oct. 4 & 9, 1978 on Great Duck Is. Mills (1981: 185-186) cited Huntsville records from Sept. 23 (1978) to Nov. 30 (1959). Devitt (1967: 176) had fall records for Barrie from Sept. 30 (1963) to Nov. 2 (1955). Weir & Quilliam (1980: 40) gave Oct. 9 and Nov. 3 as average fall arrival and departure dates for Kingston, with one as early as Aug. 30. Snyder (1941: 90) gave Nov. 2, 1935 as his latest Prince Edward Co. record. Tozer & Richards (1974: 304) found as many as 15 feeding on dumped grain in an Oshawa woods on Nov. 3, 1963: one seen there on Sept. 11, 1957 was very early. Saunders (1947: 375) had fall records for Toronto from Sept. 30 to Nov. 13, with average arrival on Oct. 20 and departure on Nov. 1. Beardslee & Mitchell (1965: 445-446) noted one on Sept. 28, 1930 at Fort Erie. Ussher (1965: 31) reported fall birds at Rondeau from Oct. 5 to Nov. 24, with average arrival on Oct. 13 and departure on Nov. 13. Stirrett (1973d: 30) had his earliest fall migrant at Pelee on Sept. 30 and a maximum of 15 on Nov. 5.

BANDING: Quilliam (1973: 193) banded one at Kingston on Oct. 18, 1958 that stayed until Nov. 2.

## MEASUREMENTS:
*Length:* 6.7 to 7.5 ins.
(Godfrey, 1966: 399)
*Wingspread:* 10.12 to
11.25 ins. (Roberts,
1955: 715)
*Weight:* 1.25 oz. (Roberts,
1955: 715)
3 ♂ averaged 33.6 g. 1 ♀
weighed 28.7 g. (Hope,
1938: 48).

850

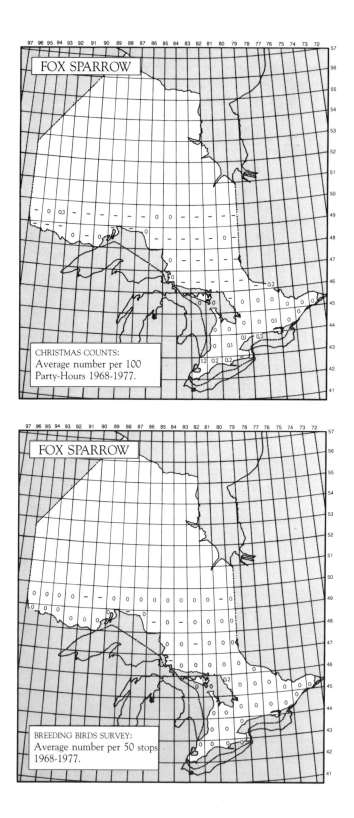

# SONG SPARROW   *Melospiza melodia*   (Wilson)

The Song Sparrow is probably the most widespread and best known of Ontario sparrows, nesting in suburban gardens, old fields, roadsides and forest edge throughout Ontario. Most go south to the United States in winter but a few linger at feeders and in weed patches in southern Ontario.

IDENTIFICATION:   The triangle of dark blotches, one on each side of the throat and one in the centre of the breast is the best field mark. In flight they pump the tail up and down more than most of our other sparrows. The song is diagnostic, once learned, but is difficult to paraphrase: it usually starts with three sweet emphatic notes, followed by a jumble of up and down phrases. The common call note is a diagnostic "chunk".

WINTER:   On the 1968-1977 Christmas counts they were common at most localities near the Lake Erie shore, fairly common along the southern Lake Huron and Lake Ontario shores, becoming rare north to Deep River, Sault Ste. Marie and the north shore of Lake Superior. Stirrett (1973a: 21) had a winter maximum of 46 at Pelee on Dec. 26. Ussher (1965: 31) reported Dec. 6 and Feb. 20 records at Rondeau: "a few winter". Marshall Field noted a group of at least 50 near Union, Elgin Co., in February, 1949 (Brooman, 1954: 40). The Song Sparrow was noted on all 58 Christmas counts at Toronto (Parker, 1983: 26). Individual males were collected at Wellington, Prince Edward Co., on Jan. 30, Feb. 12 and Feb. 28, 1937 (Snyder, 1941: 91). Quilliam (1973: 194) reported Song Sparrows on 17 Christmas counts at Kingston, with a high count of 31 on Dec. 27, 1970. Devitt (1967: 178) reported them on 6 Barrie Christmas counts since 1951: Frances Westman noted a midwinter bird there on Feb. 9, 1963. L. Beamer had four January records at Meaford, including one singing on a sunny day on Jan. 30, 1944. Mills (1981: 188) cited a few winter records for the cottage country, one as far north as Parry Sound on Dec. 25, 1972. Single birds wintered at South Baymouth, Manitoulin, in 1969-1970 and 1975-1976 (Nicholson, 1981: 196). Individual Song Sparrows were noted on 3 of 25 Christmas counts at Sault Ste. Marie (Dennison, 1980: 148). On the 1976 and 1977 Christmas counts at Marathon, 2 and 1 were recorded (Skeel & Bondrup-Nielsen, 1978: 221).

SPRING:   Stirrett (1973b: 27) estimated 5000 at Pelee on Apr. 6. Ussher (1965: 31) gave March 12 as his 17-year average arrival date at Rondeau. Saunders & Dale (1933: 246) found a nest with 4 eggs and 2 cowbird eggs as early as May 6, 1916, at London. Harold Lancaster found a nest with 7 eggs on May 10, 1942 in west Elgin Co. (Brooman, 1954: 40). Snyder (1931: 199) reported lighthouse casualties at Long Point, one on Apr. 18-19 and two on Apr. 20-21, 1930: a nest with 3 eggs was found on May 18, 1928. Speirs (1938: 43) gave Apr. 7 as the spring peak date for Toronto. A nest with 3 eggs was found in Ontario Co. as early as May 4 (Speirs, 1973). Allin (1940: 109) found a nest with 3 eggs on May 15, 1930 in Darlington Twp. Weir & Quilliam (1980: 40) listed March 15 as the 31-year average arrival date at Kingston; E. Beaupré found a nest with 6 eggs as early as May 4, 1897 at Portsmouth, near Kingston (Quilliam, 1973: 194). H.P. Bingham found a nest with 5 eggs near Barrie on May 5, 1935: the 21-year average arrival date there was March 20 (Devitt, 1967: 177-178). L. Beamer's median arrival date at Meaford was March 12, with the earliest on March 2, 1953. Lloyd (1924: 11) reported a nest with eggs at Ottawa on May 15, 1921. Mills (1981: 188) gave March 27 as the 14-year average arrival date at Huntsville, with the earliest on March 3, 1974. Nicholson (1981: 196) gave March

20 as the 11-year average arrival date on Manitoulin, with the earliest on March 5, 1973: a nest with 5 eggs was found at Lynn Point on May 25, 1980. Strickland, Tozer & Rutter (1982) listed Apr. 3 as the average arrival date in Algonquin Park, with the earliest on March 5. Speirs & Speirs (1947: 38) gave March 19, 1945 as their earliest North Bay record (2 observed): they found a nest with 3 eggs on May 19, 1945 there. W. Wyett recorded one as early as Apr. 14, 1974 at Pukaskwa (Skeel & Bondrup-Nielsen, 1978: 221). Denis (1961: 2) listed Apr. 16 as the average arrival date at Thunder Bay, with the earliest on March 31, 1945. Dear (1940: 143) found a nest with 4 eggs at Thunder Bay on May 25, 1930. Peruniak (1971: 32) gave Apr. 8 as her earliest Atikokan record. Elder (1979: 41) gave Apr. 22 as his earliest at Geraldton. Bondrup-Nielsen (1976: 45) saw his first at Kapuskasing on Apr. 27 in 1974. Cringan (1953a: 4) saw his first at Sioux Lookout on Apr. 28 in 1953.

SUMMER: On the 1968-1977 Breeding Bird Surveys there were common on southern Ontario routes and routes in far western Ontario, fairly common on most northern Ontario routes. Stirrett (1973c: 23) had a summer maximum of 40 at Pelee on June 30. Speirs & Frank (1970: 765) found a breeding density of 10 males per 100 acres on the Windsor prairie relict in 1970. Saunders & Dale (1933: 246) found a nest with 3 eggs at London as late as Aug. 1, 1901. McCracken, Bradstreet & Holroyd (1981: 67) reported 16 nest records for Long Point: the latest with eggs on July 10. Snyder (1930: 195) reported the "harsh rasping quality" of a young bird just beginning to sing in King Twp. I found a nest with 4 young on the York Downs study plot on June 10, 1937 (Lawrie, 1937: 5). The Song Sparrow was the fourth most common species in fields of Ontario Co., with a maximum breeding density of 50 birds per 100 acres on the Pickering Twp. plot (Speirs & Orenstein, 1967: 182): they were found in 9 of 10 urban plots, missing only in the downtown Oshawa quadrat, with a maximum density of 63 birds per 100 acres on the Zephyr quadrat (Speirs, Markel & Tozer, 1970: 5): they occurred on 9 of 11 forest plots with a maximum density of 65 birds per 100 acres in the thorn-apple plot in Pickering Twp. (Speirs & Orenstein, 1975: 15): of 67 nests found in Ontario Co., 23 contained cowbird eggs (35%); the latest nest with eggs was found on July 24 (Speirs, 1973). George A. Scott found a nest with 4 young as late as Aug. 11, 1956 in Oshawa's Second Marsh (Tozer & Richards, 1974: 307). Allin (1940: 109) found a nest with 3 eggs as late as Aug. 10, 1930. Paul Harrington found a nest with 3 eggs as late as July 27, 1914 at Wasaga Beach (Devitt, 1967: 177). W.A.D. Lees took a nest with eggs at Ottawa on June 16, 1889 (Lloyd, 1924: 11). Mills (1981: 188) reported 44 nests found in the cottage country, with egg dates from May 21 to July 27. C.H.D. Clarke found a nest with 4 eggs at Brule Lake, Algonquin Park, on June 2, 1934 (MacLulich, 1938: 45). Louise Lawrence found a nest with 5 eggs at Pimisi Bay on May 25, 1945: this held 5 young on June 4 and the young were out of the nest on June 11 (Speirs & Speirs, 1947: 38). Baillie & Hope (1947: 31) found two broods of young, just out of the nest, at Biscotasing on June 26, 1937. Snyder (1942: 152) reported a nest with 5 eggs near Sault Ste. Marie on June 11 and a nest with 4 eggs on July 8, 1931, with a young bird out of the nest as early as June 6 there. The Song Sparrow ranked 46th, among the less common summer residents of Pukaskwa (Skeel & Bondrup-Nielsen, 1978: 221). Baillie & Hope (1943: 27) found a nest with 5 eggs at Rossport on June 3 and a nest with 5 young at Amyot on June 25, 1936. Snyder (1928: 269) found them common in all suitable situations at Lake Nipigon, where both nests, eggs and young were collected. Dear (1940: 143) found a nest with 5 eggs at Thunder Bay on June 5, 1924. Snyder (1938: 213) collected a nest with 4 eggs and a cowbird egg at Off Lake, Rainy River, on July 5, 1929. Peruniak (1971: 32) found a number of nests at Atikokan "on the ground under blueberry and among lichen". Price & Speirs (1971: 1009) found just one male on their 25-acre study plot in a hayfield at Dryden. In western Ontario, Snyder (1953: 90) found breeding evidence at Malachi, Ingolf, Indian Bay, Kenora, Wabigoon and Savanne. Smith (1957: 181) found a nest near Gogama on July 25, 1954 and collected a young bird at Kapuskasing on Aug. 6, 1954. Snyder (1928: 29) found a nest with 5 eggs at Lake Abitibi on June 17, 1925. James (1980: 91) found "very small numbers" at Pickle Lake in bogs and at lake edges. Cringan (1953b: 5) noted individuals along streams near Kasabonika Lake on six days in late May and early June, 1953. Cringan (1950: 19) found a nest with 3 very small young in the Petownikip River beaver meadows on July 31, 1950. Hope (1938: 49) encountered only five individuals at Favourable Lake in the summer of 1938, but took a well-feathered young there on July 29. James, Nash & Peck (1982: 71) noted a few territorial males on islands in the Harricanaw River, near James Bay. Manning (1952: 78-79) noted 54 along the James Bay coast from Moosonee north to Raft River in 108 hours observing: a female collected at Raft River had an incubation patch. Schueler, Baldwin & Rising (1974: 144, 148) found Song Sparrows at Cochrane, Moosonee, Attawapiskat (one female with enlarged ova) and at Winisk. Lee & Speirs (1977: 54) had a breeding density of 6 males per 100 acres on one of three study plots at Big Trout Lake: Lee (1978: 35-36) noted a maximum of 11 there on June 13, 1975; young were noted in late July as well as adults carrying food. C.E. Hope found a nest with 5 eggs at Ft. Severn on June 27, 1940 and noted up to 10 individuals then and on July 9 and 19.

AUTUMN: D. McRae and A. Wormington saw 6 at Netitishi Point, James Bay, from Oct. 14-26, 1981. Oliver Hewitt saw several in the Moose River estuary from Sept. 22-25, 1949 (Manning, 1952: 98). Peruniak (1971: 32) gave Nov. 1 as her latest Atikokan date. Skeel & Bondrup-Nielsen (1978: 221) saw their last at Pukaskwa on Sept. 22, 1977. Ricker & Clarke (1939: 24) saw a stray as late as Nov. 18, 1924 at Lake Nipissing. Strickland, Tozer & Rutter (1982) listed Oct. 20 as the average departure date from Algonquin Park. Mills (1981: 188) tallied 24 at Magnetawan on Oct. 14, 1979 with his latest there on Oct. 30, 1978. Only 6 casualties were found at the Barrie TV tower in 3 of 7 years (Devitt, 1967: 177). An immature bird was collected at Hillier, Prince Edward Co., on Oct. 24, 1936 (Snyder, 1941: 91). Speirs (1938: 51) gave Oct. 13 as the fall peak date at Toronto. Ussher (1965: 31) gave Nov. 11 as a 7-year average departure date from Rondeau. Stirrett (1973d: 30) had a fall maximum of 200 at Pelee on Oct. 16.

BANDING: One banded near Toronto on Oct. 17, 1942 was recovered in North Carolina on Dec. 16, 1943. Brewer & Salvadori (1976: 93) reported one banded at Irondequoit Bay, N.Y. on Dec. 24, 1970 that was recovered at Coe Hill, Ont. on May 5, 1971. Brewer & Salvadori (1978: 97) reported one banded at Loganton, Pa. on March 29, 1963 that was recovered at Bewdley, Ont. on Apr. 7, 1968: another banded at Lakefield, Ont. on Sept. 13, 1959 was found near Walling, Tenn. in February, 1966. Two banded at Long Point in March were recovered the following spring in Ohio: another banded there on March 27, 1967 was found a year later (on Apr. 10, 1968) at Bancroft. The most distant recovery appears to be one banded near Ear Falls, in northwestern Ontario on July 20, 1965 and recovered at Blue Wing Lake, Ill. in February, 1966, some 907 miles to the south.

**MEASUREMENTS:**

*Length:* 6.0 to 7.0 ins.
(Godfrey, 1966: 402)
*Wingspread:* 7 3/4 to 9
ins. (Roberts, 1955: 727)
*Weight:* 26 Ontario
specimens averaged
21.5 g.

**REFERENCE:**

Fleming, J.H. and L.L.
Snyder 1939 On *Melospiza
melodia* in Ontario. Occ.
Pap. ROMZ, No. 5: 1-8.

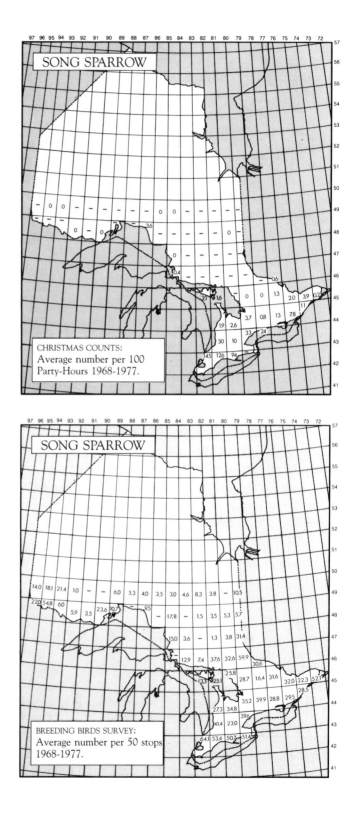

SONG SPARROW

CHRISTMAS COUNTS:
Average number per 100
Party-Hours 1968-1977.

SONG SPARROW

BREEDING BIRDS SURVEY:
Average number per 50 stops
1968-1977.

# LINCOLN'S SPARROW   *Melospiza lincolnii*   (Audubon)

Lincoln's Sparrows are fairly common breeders in northern Ontario and pass through southern Ontario in migration about the same time as the much more conspicuous White-crowned Sparrows, on their way south to winter in Central America. Because of their furtive habits they are frequently missed by casual bird watchers, but bird banders often catch good numbers.

IDENTIFICATION:   Lincoln's Sparrows look like small grayish Song Sparrows but with fine black streaking. The breast has a broad buffy band across it and down the sides. They may or may not show a central breast spot. I think of them as the little sparrow with orange "jowls" (malar stripes) and a scared expression caused by an eye-ring and somewhat raised crest, often emphasized by outstretched neck and crouched position, as they peek furtively out from a low bush and then silently steal away. The song sounds to me like "chur-chur-chur-ta-wee-wee-wee-wah-ah", but sonagrams show that the bird actually sings two notes for every one that I register: the song has a bubbly quality reminiscent of House Wren or Purple Finch songs. The call note is a dry "tick".

WINTER:   On the 1968-1977 Christmas counts they were rare at localities near the Lake Erie and Lake Ontario shores, none elsewhere. Kelley (1978: 90) reported one at Pelee on Dec. 14, 1966. Kingston's only winter record was a female specimen found by W.H. Robb at nearby Abbey Dawn on Jan. 4, 1932.

SPRING:   Stirrett (1973b: 27) had Pelee records from May 4 to May 25, with a maximum of 20 on May 10. Ussher (1965: 31) had Rondeau records from May 2 to May 25, with average arrival on May 9 and departure on May 21. Saunders & Dale (1933: 245) gave May 14 as the 8-year average arrival date at London, with the earliest on May 8, 1924. Snyder (1931: 200) noted 20 on Long Point from May 17-22, 1928 and reported two lighthouse casualties about May 14, 1925. Beardslee & Mitchell (1965: 447) reported 12 along the Canadian shore of Lake Erie on May 7, 1961 and at least 13 there on May 13, 1950. Speirs (1938: 39, 43) gave Apr. 29 as the earliest Toronto record with the peak on May 19: Saunders (1947: 375) listed May 10 and May 21 as average arrival and departure dates there. Long (1968a: 27) noted individuals at Pickering Beach as early as May 5, 1964 and as late as June 1, 1968. Doris Speirs heard a singing "duel" with a House Wren at our Pickering Twp. home on May 13, 1970, the songs evidently sufficiently alike to elicit responses (Speirs, 1973). Tozer & Richards (1974: 304) found 15 during a day's birding near Oshawa on May 19, 1963. Weir & Quilliam (1980: 40) listed May 7 and May 26 as average arrival and departure dates for Kingston, with one very early one on March 31. Devitt (1967: 176) had just 3 spring records for Simcoe Co.: one killed at the Collingwood grain elevator on May 12, 1956 and Barrie birds on May 20, 1956 and May 5, 1958. G.R. White collected one at Ottawa on May 16, 1884 (Lloyd, 1924: 11). Russell Rutter found one near Huntsville on May 11, 1958 and Mills (1981: 186) had records from May 17 (1980) to May 23 (1976) at Ahmic Lake. Nicholson (1981: 195) had spring records on Manitoulin from May 3 (1970) to June 4 (1979): there were 21 casualties at the Great Duck Is. tower on May 25, 1979. Strickland, Tozer & Rutter (1982) had Algonquin Park records from May 6 to May 18. Speirs & Speirs (1947: 38) noted one near North Bay on May 20, 1944. Baillie & Hope (1943: 26) collected 2 at Rossport on May 28 and 29, 1936 and 2 at Marathon on May 30. Denis (1961: 3) gave May 12 as the average arrival date at Thunder Bay, with the earliest on Apr. 28, 1945. Peruniak (1971: 31) gave May 8 as her earliest Atikokan date. Elder (1979: 41) also had his earliest at Geraldton on May 8. Drexler procured specimens at Moose Factory on May 23, 1860 (Manning, 1952: 97).

SUMMER: On the 1968-1977 Breeding Bird Surveys they were common on some northern Ontario routes: becoming rare south to Thessalon and Byng Inlet. Harold Lancaster found one singing along Big Creek, Elgin Co., on July 29, 1952 (Brooman, 1954: 40). Beardslee & Mitchell (1965: 446-447) cited evidence for breeding in the Wainfleet Bog: young out of the nest on Aug. 6, 1952; 16 birds there on July 13, 1935 and 6 there on July 17, 1958. Snyder (1930: 196) noted adults feeding young in the Holland River swamp, King Twp., on July 14 and 16, 1926. D.H. Baldwin noted 3 near the Shoal Point marsh, Pickering Twp., on July 27, 1965 (Long, 1968a: 27) and I saw one at Oshawa's Third Marsh on June 8, 1962 (Speirs, 1973). Weir & Quilliam (1980: 40) listed June 16 and July 24 records for Kingston. Paul Harrington reported a singing male in the Minesing Swamp on June 7, 1927 and B. Nathan *et al* found singing males in bogs near Midhurst and Bradford on July 4, 1948 (Devitt, 1967: 176). Eric Miller found a nest with 4 eggs at Spider Bay, near Parry Sound, on June 21, 1977: it held 3 young on June 29 (Mills, 1981: 186). MacLulich (1938: 44) reported one shot by Speadborough at Cache Lake, Algonquin Park, on July 10, 1900 and mentioned W.E. Saunders sightings of 4 to 8 seen from June 8-10, 1918. Baillie & Hope (1947: 31) collected a male at Chapleau on June 18, 1937 and 6 specimens at Biscotasing from June 21 to 26, 1937. Skeel & Bondrup-Nielsen (1978: 220) called it a scarce summer resident in Pukaskwa from May 31 to July 10, 1977. Baillie & Hope (1943: 26) collected 4 at Rossport from June 1-6, 1936; 4 at Marathon from June 10-17, 1936, and 10 at Amyot from June 29 to July 1, 1936, including a juvenile female just out of the nest. Snyder(1928: 270) collected 6 at Macdiarmid, Lake Nipigon, from June 14 to July 9, including a young bird just out of the nest on July 4, 1924. Paul Harrington found a nest with 4 eggs at Whitefish Lake, Thunder Bay, on June 13, 1935 (Dear, 1940: 143). Speirs & Speirs (1968: 1442-1447) determined the incubation period of the last marked egg of a 4 egg set found near Dorion on May 31, 1957, to be about 13 days and 6 hours and followed the development of the young for about a month from the day of hatching. Snyder (1953: 89) noted 2 to 12 daily at Savanne, 1 to 3 occasionally at Ingolf and Wabigoon, one on 3 occasions at Sioux Lookout, just one on July 14, 1947 at Malachi and one at Kenora on June 8, 1949. Elder, Price & Speirs (1971: 1006) found a breeding density of 12 males per 100 acres in a leatherleaf bog near Geraldton, where it ranked as the third most common species. Smith (1957: 181) found 3 pairs near the edge of a bog near Cochrane between July 6 and 20, 1953. Snyder (1928: 29) saw an adult feeding young at Lake Abitibi on July 24, 1925. Baillie & Harrington (1937: 276) reported a juvenile just able to fly collected by C.E. Johnson at Kapuskasing on June 25, 1919 and another young collected by R.V. Whelan at Smoky Falls on July 27, 1935. James (1980: 91) encountered small numbers in bogs near Pickle Lake. Hope (1938: 48) collected a juvenile male at Favourable Lake on July 19, 1938 and described a flight song heard there, where the species "was a common summer resident in all wet situations." James, Nash & Peck (1982: 71) saw a few on July 10, 1982 by the Harricanaw River near James Bay. Manning (1952: 97) reported 25 near Moosonee from June 25 to July 2, 1949 and saw one at North Point, 2 at Big Piskwanish and 3 at Raft River along the James Bay coast from June 4 to July 13, 1947. Schueler, Baldwin & Rising (1974: 144, 148) found them at all their northern stations except Ft. Albany: they found a nest with 3 young at Winisk on July 1, 1971 and watched a nest with 5 eggs at Hawley Lake from June 17-20, 1964: this held 4 eggs on June 23 and 2 young from June 26 to July 1. James, Nash & Peck (1981: 93) found a nest at Kiruna Lake, Sutton Ridges, and reported a breeding density of 25.9 pairs per km $^2$ in open fens there, in which it ranked 4th in abundance. Lee & Speirs (1977: 50) found one on the bog quadrat at Big Trout Lake in 1975. C.E. Hope collected a nest with 4 eggs at Ft. Severn on June 25, 1940 as well as one individual of 6 observed on July 3.

AUTUMN: Manning (1952: 97) saw 31 near Moosonee from Sept. 8-10, 1950 and cited records from Attawapiskat about Sept. 16 and from Ft. Albany about Sept. 22, 1940. Peruniak (1971: 31) gave Oct. 19 as her latest Atikokan record. Speirs & Speirs (1947: 38) cited fall records for the North Bay region from Sept. 11 to Oct. 16, 1944. Strickland, Tozer & Rutter (1982) listed Algonquin Park records from Sept. 24 to Oct. 7. Nicholson (1981: 195) had fall records on Manitoulin from Sept. 2 (1972) to Oct. 19 (1978), with 181 casualties at the Great Duck Is. tower from Sept. 18-23, 1977. Mills (1981: 186) cited fall records from the cottage country, from late summer to Oct. 5, 1974. Weir & Quilliam (1980: 40) listed Sept. 5 and Oct. 3 as average arrival and departure dates for Kingston, with the latest on Oct. 29. Snyder (1941: 90) reported one collected at Hillier, Prince Edward Co., on Sept. 19, 1936. Speirs (1973) had Pickering Twp. records from Sept. 9 (1962) to Oct. 22 (1963). Speirs (1938: 51, 53) had fall peaks at Toronto on Sept. 19 and 23, with the latest on Nov. 19: Saunders (1947: 375) listed Sept. 26 and Oct. 12 as average arrival and departure dates there. Snyder (1931: 200) reported 2 lighthouse casualties at Long Point on Sept. 9, 1929 and 10 from Sept. 24-29, 1929. Brooman (1954: 40) cited an Aylmer record on Sept. 18, 1941 and one at St. Thomas on Sept. 25, 1949. Saunders & Dale (1933: 245) reported one in a London garden on Oct. 7. Ussher (1965: 31) had Rondeau records from Sept. 20 to Nov. 11, with average arrival on Sept. 27 and departure on Oct. 22. Stirrett (1973d: 30) had Pelee records from Sept. 16 to Oct. 21, with a maximum of 20 on Oct. 12.

**MEASUREMENTS:**
*Length:* 5.3 to 6.0 ins.
(Godfrey, 1966: 400)
*Wingspread:* 7.9 to 8.4
ins. (Roberts, 1955: 725)
201 and 207 mm. (Speirs,
1973)
*Weight:* 15.1 to 17.3 g.
(Speirs & Speirs,
1968: 1446)

**REFERENCE:**
Speirs, J. Murray and Doris Huestis Speirs 1968 Melospiza lincolnii lincolnii (Audubon) Lincoln's Sparrow, in Life Histories of North American Cardinals, Grosbeaks, Buntings, Towhees, Finches, Sparrows, and allies. By Arthur Cleveland Bent and collaborators, compiled and edited by Oliver L. Austin, Jr. U.S. National Mus. Bull. 237: Part 3: 1434-1463.

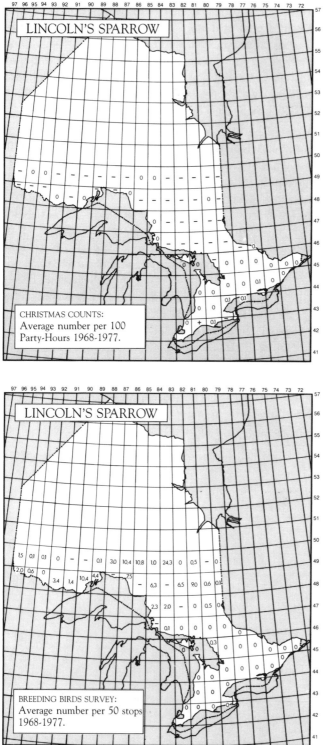

LINCOLN'S SPARROW

CHRISTMAS COUNTS:
Average number per 100
Party-Hours 1968-1977.

LINCOLN'S SPARROW

BREEDING BIRDS SURVEY:
Average number per 50 stops
1968-1977.

# SWAMP SPARROW   *Melospiza georgiana*   (Latham)

In southern Ontario the Swamp Sparrow is predominantly a bird of cattail marshes; farther north they occur chiefly in bogs or swamps along rivers. During migration they may be found in roadside hedges. A few linger in marshes in winter but most go south to the United States and a few reach Mexico.

IDENTIFICATION: Adults have a reddish crown (like our wintering Tree Sparrows and summering Chipping Sparrows). They have a white throat patch (like White-throated Sparrows but smaller) and a plain gray breast but they have rather rufous wings and tail (unlike the others mentioned above) and a strong preference for wet areas (also unlike the others mentioned). The song is a slow, sweet, "tsee-tsee-tsee-tsee-tsee-tsee" sometimes as sweet as a Prothonotary Warbler song, at other times almost as dry as a Chipping Sparrow trill (in a large breeding colony almost every bird seems to have its own distinctive song). The call note is a metallic "chink", resembling the call of a White-throated Sparrow but not as loud. Young in juvenal plumage have a blackish cap, distinguishing them from young Song Sparrows which have a brown cap with no black streaks and young Lincoln's Sparrows which have about 6 black, fine streaks on a brown background and a central gray stripe.

WINTER: On the 1968-1977 Christmas counts they were common near Pelee and Rondeau, uncommon in the Lake Ontario marshes and rare north to Ottawa and Manitoulin. Stirrett (1973a: 21) had a winter maximum of 25 at Pelee on Dec. 31. Brooman (1954: 40) reported one at St. Thomas on Dec. 24, 1950 and 4 there on Dec. 26, 1953. Parker (1983: 26) reported them on 46 of 58 Christmas counts at Toronto. Speirs (1973) reported a total of 9 individuals on 7 of 10 Christmas counts in Pickering Twp. Quilliam (1973: 193) reported 3 at Kingston on Dec. 28, 1968. One was noted at Barrie on Jan. 9, 1965 (Devitt, 1967: 177). Nicholson (1981: 196) had two winter records for Manitoulin: one at Pike Lake from Dec. 18-26, 1971 and one by the Manitou River on Dec. 18, 1976. Dennison (1980: 148) listed one on one of 25 Christmas counts at Sault Ste. Marie.

SPRING: Stirrett (1973b: 27) had a spring maximum of 100 at Pelee on May 10. Ussher (1965: 31) gave Apr. 10 as his 15-year average arrival date at Rondeau, with the earliest on March 8. Saunders & Dale (1933: 246) gave Apr. 8 as the 17-year average arrival date at London, with the earliest on March 21, 1918: a nest with 5 eggs was found on May 16, 1908 and a nest with 4 eggs on May 27, 1898. Snyder (1931: 201) reported 3 casualties at the Long Point lighthouse on Apr. 17-18, 1930 and 3 more on May 19, 1926. McCracken, Bradstreet & Holroyd (1981: 67) reported a nest with 5 eggs found by G. Peck at Long Point on May 24, 1959 and mentioned 7 other nests with eggs from May 14 to June 12. Saunders (1947: 375) listed Apr. 13 as his 13-year average arrival date for Toronto: Speirs (1938: 43) gave Apr. 30 as the spring peak date there. Speirs (1973) reported a Whitby nest with 4 eggs and 2 cowbird eggs found on May 14, 1955 and a nest with 4 young at Oshawa on May 28, 1968. Allin (1940: 109) found a nest with 3 eggs and a cowbird egg in Darlington Twp. on May 19, 1932. Weir & Quilliam (1980: 40) listed Apr. 17 as the 31-year average arrival date at Kingston. Devitt (1967: 177) gave Apr. 24 as the 17-year average arrival date at Barrie, with the earliest on Apr. 1, 1963: H.P. Bingham found a nest with 5 eggs near Barrie as early as May 19, 1918. L.

Beamer's earliest Meaford record was on Apr. 9, 1949. Mills (1981: 186) gave Apr. 22 as a 6-year average arrival date at Huntsville, with the earliest on Apr. 11, 1965. Nicholson (1981: 196) gave Apr. 27 as the 11-year average arrival date on Manitoulin, with the earliest on Apr. 20, 1974 and the high count of 20 on May 1, 1976. Strickland, Tozer & Rutter (1982) listed Apr. 27 as the average arrival date in Algonquin Park, with the earliest on Apr. 18. Louise Lawrence heard two singing at Pimisi Bay as early as Apr. 10, 1945 (Speirs & Speirs, 1947: 38). W. Wyett recorded one on May 10, 1975 at Pukaskwa (Skeel & Bondrup-Nielsen, 1978: 221). Denis (1961: 2) listed Apr. 27 as the average arrival date at Thunder Bay, with the earliest on Apr. 17, 1949. Peruniak (1971: 31) gave Apr. 25 as her earliest Atikokan date. Elder (1979: 41) had his earliest at Geraldton on May 2.

SUMMER: On the 1968-1977 Breeding Bird Surveys they were missing in southwestern Ontario, fairly common on most other routes but common on the Byng Inlet, North Bay and Kenora routes. Stirrett (1973c: 23) had a summer maximum of 10 at Pelee on July 26. Saunders & Dale (1933: 246) reported a nest with 3 eggs at London on June 2, 1907. McCracken, Bradstreet & Holroyd (1981: 67) reported a breeding density of 218 territories per km $^2$ in a dense grassy marsh - shrub carr quadrat on Long Point. W.P. Young found a nest with 4 eggs at Niagara-on-the Lake on June 23, 1926 (Baillie & Harrington, 1937: 277). Snyder (1930: 196) collected 2 young, not long out of the nest, in King Twp. on July 6 and 16, 1926. Speirs, Markle & Tozer (1970: 11) found a breeding density of 22 birds per 100 acres in marsh habitat in Ontario Co. J.M. Richards found a nest with 5 eggs and 4 cowbird eggs in a Whitby marsh on June 23, 1962 (Tozer & Richards, 1974: 305). Allin (1940: 109) found a nest with 2 eggs and 2 cowbird eggs on June 12, 1933 in Darlington Twp. Snyder (1941: 90) reported a nest with 3 eggs and 2 cowbird eggs at Hallowell, Prince Edward Co., on June 5, 1930. Richard Norman found a nest with 1 egg and 3 cowbird eggs on Wolfe Is., off Kingston, on June 14, 1968 (Quilliam, 1973: 193). H.P. Bingham found a nest with 4 eggs near Barrie on July 5, 1939 (Devitt, 1967: 176-177). James (1979: 16) found one singing male per 10 hectares on each of 5 transects through the jack pine country of western Parry Sound Dist. Ross James found a nest with 4 eggs on Manitoulin on July 5, 1977 (Nicholson, 1981: 196). MacLulich (1938: 44) saw an adult carrying food to several noisy young on June 22, 1930 and C.H.D. Clarke watched another adult carrying food on June 30, 1934 at Brule Lake, Algonquin Park. Ricker & Clarke (1939: 24) found a nest with 4 eggs at Frank's Bay, Lake Nipissing, on June 22, 1934. Baillie & Hope (1947: 31) noted flying young at Bigwood from July 16-24, 1937. Snyder (1942: 152) found a nest with 3 eggs near Sault Ste. Marie on June 11, 1931. Baillie & Hope (1943: 27) noted as many as 20 adults at Amyot on June 26, 1936 and collected a male at Rossport on June 3 and one at Marathon on June 13. Snyder (1928: 270) collected a young female at Orient Bay, Lake Nipigon, on July 31, 1923. Dear (1940: 143) found a nest with 4 eggs at Thunder Bay on June 9, 1924 and a nest with 5 eggs there on June 14, 1929. Snyder (1938: 43) collected 3 males in the Rainy River region from July 3-26, 1929. Elder, Price & Speirs (1971: 1006) found a breeding density of 44 males per 100 acres in a leatherleaf bog near Geraldton, where this was the second most common species. Snyder (1953: 90) found from 1 to 15 daily at Savanne and Malachi; from 1 to 10 frequently at Wabigoon and Sioux Lookout, with small numbers regularly at Ingolf and Kenora. Snyder (1928: 29) collected 4 males at Lake Abitibi from June 6-23, 1925. Hope (1938: 49) found a newly constructed nest at Favourable Lake on June 4, 1938: it held 2 eggs on June 13: a well-feathered young was collected there on

July 17. James, Nash & Peck (1982: 71) saw a young bird scarcely able to fly, on July 1, 1982 by the Harricanaw River, near James Bay. Manning (1952: 98) tallied 28 in 37 hours of observation between May 31 and June 14, 1947 from Moosonee north to Long Ridge Point, James Bay. Schueler, Baldwin & Rising (1974: 144, 148) noted Swamp Sparrows at all their northern stations, and collected laying females near Moosonee, Attawapiskat and Hawley Lake. James, Nash & Peck (1981: 93) found a nest at Kiruna Lake, Sutton Ridges, in 1981. Lee & Speirs (1977: 50, 54) reported a territorial male on two of three quadrats studied at Big Trout Lake in 1975. C.E. Hope found a nest with 3 eggs at Ft. Severn on June 25 and a nest with 2 eggs on July 3, 1940, with a maximum of 10 individuals on July 11.

AUTUMN: D. McRae and A. Wormington tallied 10 at Netitishi Point, James Bay, on Oct. 14, 1981 and decreasing numbers from then until the last one on Nov. 1. Oliver Hewitt saw several near Moosonee from Sept. 22-25, 1947 (Manning, 1952: 198). Peruniak (1971: 31) gave Oct. 19 as her latest Atikokan date. Speirs & Speirs (1947: 38) noted one at North Bay on Oct. 17, 1944. Strickland, Tozer & Rutter (1982) listed Oct. 7 as the average departure date from Algonquin Park, with the latest on Nov. 29. Nicholson (1981: 196) reported a high count of 75 on Great Duck Is. on Sept. 24, 1980. Mills (1981: 187) tallied 22 at Magnetawan on Sept. 16, 1979 and 6 there as late as Oct. 22, 1978. Devitt (1967: 177) reported 6 killed at the Barrie TV tower on 3 of 7 years: F.H. Emery observed two in the Holland River swamp as late as Nov. 7, 1937. Weir & Quilliam (1980: 40) listed Nov. 14 as the 25-year average departure date from Kington. Saunders (1947: 375) listed Oct. 29 as his 13-year average departure date from Toronto: Speirs (1938: 51) gave Oct. 13 as the fall peak there. Three were killed at the Long Point lighthouse between Sept. 24-29, 1929 (Snyder, 1931: 201). Ussher (1965: 31) gave Oct. 30 as a 4-year average departure date for Rondeau, with the latest on Nov. 6 but "a few winter". Stirrett (1973d: 30) had a fall maximum of 1000 at Pelee on Oct. 30.

BANDING: One banded at Balmoral Marsh (near Chatham) on Apr. 25, 1965 was recovered at Ocean View, Virginia, on Feb. 2, 1966 (about 501 miles to the southeast) (Brewer & Salvadori, 1978: 96).

**MEASUREMENTS:**
*Length:* 5.0 to 5.8 ins.
(Godfrey, 1966: 401)
*Wingspread:* 7 1/4 to 8
ins. (Roberts, 1955: 717)
*Weight:* 14.8 to 17.8 g.
(Terres, 1980: 350)
two males averaged
15.7 g. (Hope, 1938: 49).

**REFERENCE:**
Godfrey, W. Earl 1949
Distribution of the races of
the Swamp Sparrow. Auk,
66: (1): 35-38. (*georgiana*
north from Lake Erie to
Sault Ste. Marie in Ontario
and *ericrypta* from there
north to Hudson Bay).

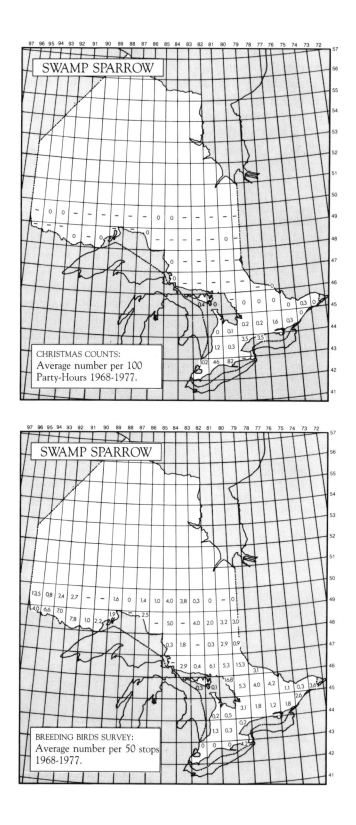

# WHITE-THROATED SPARROW
*Zonotrichia albicollis* (Gmelin)

The White-throated Sparrow is the most conspicuous bird summering in Ontario forests from the cottage country north to Hudson Bay, where its sweet song is familiar to most summer visitors and residents. A few may be found in bog relicts farther south. Quite a few linger at feeding stations in southern Ontario in winter and great numbers migrate through residential areas in May and October.

IDENTIFICATION: The white throat contrasting with otherwise gray underparts distinguish this from our other sparrows. There are two colour morphs: one has bright white "eyebrows" and median crown stripe, bordered with black and bright yellow in front and above the eye: the other has pale tan instead of white head markings, bordered with dark brown instead of black. It was formerly thought that the tan-striped birds were females and the white-striped birds were males, but it has been shown that either sex may be tan-striped or white-striped. In Canada we like to paraphrase the song as "Sweet-sweet-sweet-Canada - Canada - Canada" but south of the border other interpretations are more popular. The metallic "chink" call-note separates it from the "chunk" of Song Sparrows and "chip" of some other sparrows, though the call-note of the White-crowned Sparrow is very similar.

WINTER: On the 1968-1977 Christmas counts, they were common at Pelee, fairly common near the Lake Erie and Lake Ontario shores, becoming rare north to Manitoulin and Deep River and near the Lake Superior shores. Stirrett (1973a: 21) had a winter maximum of 60 at Pelee on Dec. 26. Parker (1983: 26) listed the species as occurring on 49 of 58 Christmas counts at Toronto. A.J. Mitchener noted one at Collingwood on Feb. 21, 1948 (Devitt, 1967: 175). L. Beamer had one at Meaford on Feb. 17, 1945. Lloyd (1924: 11) reported two at Ottawa on Dec. 24, 1922. Mills (1981: 185) cited several winter records for the cottage country, including one seen by Hazel Petty as far north as Wasi Falls from Jan. 21 to Feb. 4, 1975. Nicholson (1981: 194) reported birds to Dec. 21, 1974 at Mindemoya and Gore Bay, and one through January to March in 1980 at Providence Bay, Manitoulin. Dennison (1980: 148) listed 3 birds on 2 of 25 Christmas counts at Sault Ste. Marie.

SPRING: Stirrett (1973b: 27) had a high estimate of 20,000 at Pelee on May 10, with the latest three on May 26. Ussher (1965: 30) had spring migrants at Rondeau from March 21 to June 9, with average arrival on Apr. 24 and departure on May 20. Saunders & Dale (1933: 245) gave Apr. 18 as the 17-year average arrival date at London, with the earliest on Apr. 5, 1921. Snyder (1931: 198) reported 4 killed at the Long Point lighthouse from Apr. 17-19, 1930. Saunders (1947: 375) listed Apr. 22 as his 13-year average arrival date at Toronto: Speirs (1938: 43) gave May 3 as the spring peak there. Tozer & Richards (1974: 303) found a nest with 4 eggs in Cartwright Twp. on May 25, 1969 and another nest with 3 eggs and a cowbird egg there on May 31, 1969. Weir & Quilliam (1980: 40) listed Apr. 13 and May 21 as average arrival and departure dates for Kingston: Quilliam (1973: 192) mentioned a peak count of 1450 on May 2, 1972 at Prince Edward Point. Devitt (1967: 175) gave Apr. 22 as a 21-year average arrival date for Barrie: Mary Devitt found a nest with one egg and 3 newly-hatched young at Mac Station, Simcoe Co., as early as May 24, 1963. L. Beamer found a median arrival date of Apr. 26 at Meaford. Mills (1981: 184) gave Apr. 17 as a 14-year average arrival date at Huntsville. J.H. Fleming found a nest with 4 eggs near Sand Lake, Parry Sound Dist., on May 25, 1897. Nicholson (1981: 194) gave Apr. 20 as a 12-year average arrival date on Manitoulin, with the earliest on Apr. 16, 1977, excluding one very early bird on March 9, 1975: high counts of 300 were noted at Mississagi Light on May 1, 1976 and May 11, 1980. Strickland, Tozer & Rutter (1982) listed Apr. 23 as the average arrival date in Algonquin Park, with the earliest on Apr. 13. Speirs & Speirs (1947: 38) heard one singing at North Bay as early as Apr. 11, 1945, with the spring peak in mid-May. Skeel & Bondrup-Nielsen (1978: 22) found about 215 on 27 days from Apr. 20 to May 30, 1977 in Pukaskwa, the most abundant of the spring migrants. Denis (1961: 2) listed Apr. 26 as the average arrival date at Thunder Bay, with the earliest on Arp. 12, 1955. Peruniak (1971: 31) gave Apr. 26 as her earliest Atikokan date. Elder (1979: 40) gave May 3 as his earliest date for Geraldton. Bondrup-Nielsen (1976: 45) had his earliest at Kapuskasing on May 3 in 1975. Cringan (1953a: 4) saw his first in 1953 at Perrault Falls on May 7. Cringan (1950: 19) gave May 21 as the 1950 arrival date in the Asheweig area. Manning (1952: 94) saw several at Sandy Is., near Moosonee, from May 28-30, 1947.

SUMMER: On the 1968-1977 Breeding Bird Surveys, they were common on all northern Ontario routes, south to the cottage country, becoming uncommon on routes in the agricultural south. Snyder (1931: 198) reported a singing male on Long Point on July 16, 1927. Fleming (1907: 81) mentioned hearing singing males at several places near Toronto from June 6 to July 7, 1906. Snyder (1930: 195) reported two nests found in King Twp. in 1926: one held 3 eggs and a cowbird egg on June 3, the other held 3 eggs on July 4; both were in the Holland River swamp. Speirs & Orenstein (1975: 15) found populations in 4 of 11 forest plots in Ontario Co. (Whitby, Reach, Scott and Brock Twps.) with a maximum of 44 birds per 100 acres in the Scott quadrat. Allin (1940: 109) found a nest with 5 eggs at Hampton on June 22, 1927. Snyder(1941: 90) collected two males at Hallowell, Prince Edward Co., on June 21, 1930. E. Beaupré found a nest with 4 eggs and a cowbird egg at Portsmouth, near Kingston, on June 20, 1921 (Quilliam, 1973: 192). Devitt (1967: 175) found a nest with one egg and 2 small young as late as July 10, 1938 at the Holland River, Simcoe Co. Mills (1981: 184) reported 33 nests in the cottage country: young were seen in nests as early as June 1 and as late as Aug. 12: James (1979) found this to be the fifth most common species in the jack pine forests in Parry Sound, with 14 breeding males per 100 acres. D.B. Ferguson found a nest with 5 eggs at Windfall Lake, Manitoulin, on July 1, 1979 (Nicholson, 1981: 194). MacLulich (1938: 44) reported a nest with 4 eggs found by C.H.D. Clarke at Brule Lake, Algonquin Park, as early as June 1, 1934 and a nest with 4 eggs collected by W.E. Saunders as late as Aug. 5, 1908 at Cache Lake. Louise Lawrence found a nest with 4 eggs at Pimisi Bay, on June 14, 1945, 3 of which hatched on June 16 and the young left the nest on June 24 (Speirs & Speirs, 1947: 38). Baillie & Hope (1947: 31) found a nest with 4 eggs at Chapleau on June 2, 1937. Snyder (1942: 152) found a number of nests with eggs near Sault Ste. Marie in 1931: the first young out of the nest were seen on June 23. Skeel & Bondrup-Nielsen (1978: 220) found 100 on 29 days from June 2 to July 17, 1977 in Pukaskwa, where it ranked 9th in abundance as a summer resident. Baillie & Hope (1943: 26) found a nest with 4 eggs near Rossport on June 7, 1936 and a nest with 4 young at Amyot on June 27. Snyder (1928: 268) found this to be the commonest bird near clearings in the Lake Nipigon region, finding a number of nests each summer. Dear (1940: 143) reported a nest with 4 eggs at Thunder Bay on June 5, 1914 and a nest with 5 eggs on June 13, 1924. Kendeigh (1947: 28) found a breeding population of 18 pairs per 100 acres at Black

Sturgeon Lake in 1945 while Speirs (1949: 148) had just 5 territories on 75 acres at nearby Eaglehead Lake in 1946. Snyder (1938: 212) found a nest with 3 eggs near Emo on June 5, 1929, the first of several found in the Rainy River region. Snyder (1953: 89) wrote: "Probably the most plentiful of all species of birds in the region" (Western Ontario). Smith (1957: 180) found nests at Lake Timiskaming and at Cochrane. Snyder (1928: 28) called this the commonest bird of the Lake Abitibi region and collected a young female there on July 15, 1925. Bondrup-Nielsen (1976: 47) found a nest with 4 eggs on June 19, 1974 near Kapuskasing and a nest with 3 young on June 21, 1974. James (1980: 84, 91) found a population density of 4.8 pairs per km $^2$ near Pickle Lake and discovered a nest with 5 eggs on June 3, 1977 some 13 km. to the northeast. Cringan (1953b: 5) saw from 1 to 3 on 9 of 10 days at Kasabonika Lake, from May 27 to June 6, 1953. This was the commonest sparrow in the Nikip Lake region (Cringan, 1950: 19). Hope (1938: 47) found two nests at Favourable Lake: a nest with 4 eggs on June 15, 1938 and a nest with 5 eggs on July 2, 1938. James, Nash & Peck (1982: 50, 71) found a nest with 5 eggs on June 24, 1982 by the Harricanaw River, near James Bay: "This was undoubtedly the most abundant bird in the area" with 94.7 pairs per km $^2$ on the 11 plots censused. Manning (1952: 96) saw 89 from Moosonee to Raft River, along the James Bay coast in 1947 and 1949 and collected one young bird at Shagamu River, Hudson Bay, on Aug. 8, 1947: Sam Waller collected a nest with 4 eggs at Moose Factory on June 12, 1930. Schueler, Baldwin & Rising (1974: 144, 148) found them common at all their northern stations, except at Ft. Albany: they located a nest with 4 eggs on June 4, 1971 at Attawapiskat, a nest with 4 eggs on June 20, 1964 at Hawley Lake and a nest with 4 young there on June 23, 1964. James, Nash & Peck (1981: 23) found two nests in the Kiruna Lake region, Sutton Ridges. Lee (1978: 35) found this to be the commonest sparrow at Big Trout Lake, found on all three study plots, with 20 territorial males per 100 acres, 14 per 100 acres and 12 per 100 acres on the quadrats studied (Lee & Speirs, 1977: 50-54). C.E. Hope found 4 nests at Ft. Severn in 1940: one nest with 3 eggs as early as June 17 and a nest with 4 eggs as late as July 20.

AUTUMN: D. McRae and A. Wormington tallied single birds at Netitishi Point, James Bay, from Oct. 18-24, 1981. Peruniak (1971: 31) gave Oct. 21 as her latest Atikokan record. W. Wyett saw some at Pukaskwa as late as Oct. 2, 1975 (Skeel & Bondrup-Nielsen, 1978: 220). Speirs & Speirs (1947: 35) noted two at North Bay on Oct. 18, 1944, but the fall peak was in late September. Strickland, Tozer & Rutter (1982) listed Oct. 18 as the average departure date from Algonquin Park, with the latest on Nov. 24. Fall high counts of 150 were noted on Manitoulin on Sept. 23, 1975 and Sept. 28, 1980 (Nicholson, 1981: 194). At the Barrie TV tower 27 were killed in 6 of 7 years of study, 15 of these on Sept. 24, 1960 and the latest on Oct. 14, 1966 (Devitt, 1967: 175). Weir & Quilliam (1980: 40) listed Sept. 5 and Nov. 8 as the average fall arrival and departure dates for Kingston. Saunders (1947: 375) listed Oct. 31 as his 13-year average departure date from Toronto: Speirs (1938: 51) gave Oct. 3 as the fall peak there. Beardslee & Mitchell (1965: 444-445) reported two at Fort Erie as late as Nov. 27, 1953. Snyder (1931: 198) reported 16 killed at the Long Point lighthouse on Sept. 24-25, 1929. Ussher (1965: 30) had fall migrants at Rondeau from Sept. 11 to Nov. 11, with average arrival on Sept. 21 and departure on Nov. 2. Stirrett (1973d: 30) had his earliest 3 at Pelee on Sept. 7, with maxima of 300 on Sept. 25 and Sept. 29.

BANDING: Three birds banded in migration near Toronto were recovered in the colder months in the lower Mississippi valley: one banded May 11, 1946 was found in Arkansas on Jan. 26, 1947; another banded on Apr. 29, 1956 turned up in Tennessee on March 5, 1959 and one banded on Oct. 1, 1960 was recovered in Mississippi in late November, 1962. One banded near Toronto on Sept. 30, 1948 was recovered near Lake Abitibi during the latter half of August, 1949. One banded in Pennsylvania on Oct. 22, 1951 turned up about May 12, 1954 near Toronto. Brewer & Salvadori (1976: 93) reported one banded at Long Point on Apr. 21, 1968 and recovered at Thornhill, 87 miles to the north, on May 4, 1971. Brewer & Salvadori (1978: 96) mentioned four interesting recoveries: one banded at Clarksville, Pa. on Oct. 19, 1966 was recovered at Coniston, Ont. on Oct. 12, 1969 (3 years later and 462 miles to the north): one banded at Burlington, Ont. on Oct. 2, 1965 was retaken at Crisp, Pa. on Oct. 9, 1965 (a week later and 220 miles to the south). One banded at Long Point on Sept. 25, 1964 was recovered at Alexandria, Louisiana, 1035 miles to the southwest on about May 3, 1965: another Long Point bird, banded on Oct. 9, 1966 was recovered at Dickinson, Alabama, about 857 miles to the southwest on about Jan. 21, 1968.

**MEASUREMENTS:**
*Length:* 6.3 to 7.2 ins. (Godfrey, 1966: 398)
*Wingspread:* 9 to 9 3/4 ins. (Roberts, 1955: 726)
*Weight:* 66 Ontario specimens averaged 26.4 g.

**REFERENCES:**
Brooks, Ronald J. and J. Bruce Falls 1975 Individual recognition by song in White-throated Sparrows. I. Discrimination of songs of neighbors and strangers. Can. Journ. Zool., 53: (7): 879-888.

Brooks, Ronald J. and J. Bruce Falls 1975 Individual recognition by song in White-throated Sparrows. III. Song features used in individual recognition. Can. Journ. Zool., 53: (12): 1749- 1761.

Falls, J. Bruce 1963 Properties of bird song eliciting responses from territorial males. Proc. XIIIth International Ornithological Congress: 259- 271.

Falls, J. Bruce 1969 Functions of territorial song in the White-throated Sparrow. from Bird Vocalizations (editor R.A. Hinde) Cambridge Univ. Press: 207-232.

Falls, J. Bruce and Ronald J. Brooks 1975 Individual recognition by song in White-throated Sparrows. II. Effects of location. Can. Journ. Zool., 53: (10): 1412-1420.

Falls, J. Bruce 1981 Mapping territories with playback: an accurate census method for songbirds. In: Estimating the numbers of terrestrial birds (editors C.J. Ralph and J.M. Scott). Studies Avian Biol., 6: 86-91.

Knapton, Richard W. and J. Bruce Falls 1982 Polymorphism in the White-throated Sparrow: habitat occupancy and nest-site selection. Can. Journ. Zool., 60: (3): 452-459.

Knapton, R.W. and J.B. Falls 1983 Differences in parental contribution among pair types in the polymorphic White-throated Sparrow. Can. Journ. Zool., 61: (6): 1288-1292.

Knapton, Richard W.; Ralph V. Cartar and J. Bruce Falls 1984 A comparison of breeding ecology and reproductive success between morphs of

the White- throated Sparrow. Wilson Bull., 96: (1): 60-71.

Lainevool, Maire 1966 Some aspects of territorial behaviour in the White-throated Sparrow. Zonotrichia albicollis (Gmelin) Univ. Toronto, M.A. Thesis: i-iii; 1-97.

Loncke, Daniel J. and J. Bruce Falls 1973 An attempted third brood in the White-throated Sparrow. Auk, 90: (4): 904.

Lowther, James K. 1961 Polymorphism in the White- throated Sparrow, Zonotrichia albicollis (Gmelin). Can. Journ. Zool., 39: (3): 281-292.

Lowther, James K. and J. Bruce Falls 1968 Zonotrichia albicollis (Gmelin) White-throated Sparrow. in Life Histories of North American Cardinals, Grosbeaks, Buntings, Towhees, Finches, Sparrows, and allies. By Arthur Cleveland Bent and collaborators, compiled and edited by Oliver L. Austin, Jr. U.S. National Mus. Bull. 237: Part 3: 1364-1392.

Melemis, Steven M. and J. Bruce Falls 1982 The

defense function: a measure of territorial behavior. Can. Journ. Zool., 60: (4): 495-501.

Stefanski, Raymond A. and J. Bruce Falls 1972 A study of distress calls of Song, Swamp, and White-throated Sparrows (Aves: Fringillidae). I. Intraspecific responses and functions. II. interspecific responses and properties used in recognition. Can. Journ. Zool., 50: (12): 1501- 1512; 1513-1525.

Thorneycroft, H.B. 1966 Chromosomal polymorphism in the White-throated Sparrow, Zonotrichia albicollis (Gmelin). Science, 154: (3756): 1571-1572.

Thorneycroft, H.Bruce 1976 A cytogenetic study of the White-throated Sparrow, *Zonotrichia albicollis* (Gmelin). Evolution, 29: (4): 611-621.

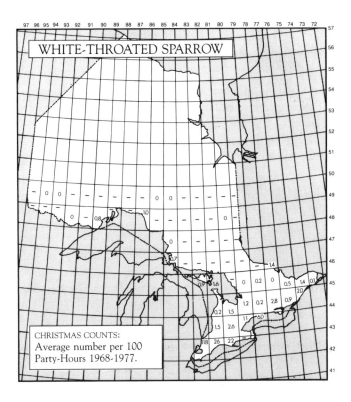

WHITE-THROATED SPARROW

CHRISTMAS COUNTS:
Average number per 100
Party-Hours 1968-1977.

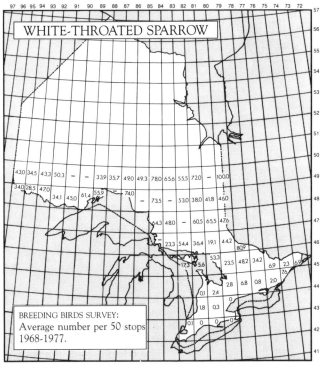

WHITE-THROATED SPARROW

BREEDING BIRDS SURVEY:
Average number per 50 stops
1968-1977.

# GOLDEN-CROWNED SPARROW
*Zonotrichia atricapilla* (Gmelin)

The Golden-crowned Sparrow is normally a bird of British Columbia, breeding north to the Yukon and Alaska in summer and wintering south to Baja California. There have been three Ontario reports to date, one that stayed near a feeding station for about two weeks in winter and was seen by many observers, the other two seen in migration with somewhat less satisfactory confirmation.

IDENTIFICATION: Golden-crowned Sparrows average slightly smaller than White-crowned Sparrows and have a mainly black cap but with a broad median yellow stripe: in young birds just the forehead is yellow.

WINTER: One stayed near a feeder at Gosport, near Brighton, from Jan. 3 to 15, 1982, where it was seen by C. Harris, F. Helleiner, Sheldon McGregor and many other observers (Weir, 1982: 291).

SPRING: Hazel Petty reported one at North Bay on Apr. 16, 1974 (Goodwin, 1974: 798).

SUMMER:

AUTUMN: R. Yukich reported seeing one on Toronto Island on Nov. 9, 1983 (Weir, 1984: 198).

**MEASUREMENTS:**
*Length:* 6.0 to 7.2 ins.
(Godfrey, 1966: 397)
Wingspread:
*Weight:* 1422 averaged
28.8 g. (21.2 - 42.2 g.)
(Dunning, 1984: 24).

# WHITE-CROWNED SPARROW
*Zonotrichia leucophrys* (Forster)

The White-crowned Sparrow is a fairly common migrant through Ontario but nesting has been mainly in the vicinity of Hudson and James Bays. Most go south in winter to southern United States and Mexico but in recent years a few have lingered near feeding stations in southern Ontario.

**IDENTIFICATION:** This is a big sparrow, with plain gray throat and underparts and a conspicuous white crown bordered on each side with broad black stripes. In young birds the crown is pale buff, bordered with dark brown stripes, which, with their mainly pink bills makes them look somewhat like oversize Field Sparrows. The song may be rendered as "zwee-za-za-zweezy-zoo", easily recognized, once learned.

**WINTER:** On the 1968-1977 Christmas counts they were fairly common at some localities near the Lake Erie shores, with strays north to Deep River and Thunder Bay. Stirrett (1973a: 21) had single birds at Pelee from Dec. 17 to Feb. 6, with a high count of 2 on Jan. 2. Ussher (1965: 30) had a Dec. 8 record at Rondeau. Brooman (1954: 40) reported 12 near Port Stanley on Dec. 21, 1952. A.E. Schaffner counted 32 individuals in February on a trip from Vineland to Beamsville (Beardslee & Mitchell, 1965: 444). Parker (1983: 27) reported the species on 15 of 58 Christmas counts at Toronto, mostly in recent years: Saunders (1947: 378) listed only 2 on the 1938 count, as the only record from 1925 to 1945. Speirs (1973) cited several winter records in the Pickering-Oshawa region, the first by Frank Lovesy at Ajax on Dec. 9, 1956. George A. Scott had several winter records for Oshawa and Darlington (Tozer & Richards, 1974: 305). Quilliam (1973: 191) reported single birds at Kingston on Jan. 2, 1967 and Dec. 28, 1968. Devitt (1967: 174) reported Barrie sightings on Dec. 27, 1958 and Dec. 15, 1959. Nicholson (1981: 193) cited winter records for Manitoulin at Mindemoya on Dec. 18, 1976 and at Little Current through January and February, 1978.

**SPRING:** Stirrett (1973b: 27) had his earliest one at Pelee on Apr. 11 and the latest 12 on May 23, with a maximum estimate of 12,000 on May 10, 1952. Ussher (1965: 30) had Rondeau birds from Apr. 21 to May 25, with average arrival on May 5 and departure on May 19. Saunders & Dale (1933: 244) gave May 9 as the 16-year average arrival date at London, with the earliest on May 3, 1913. Marshall Field banded 62 near St. Thomas between May 2 and May 27, 1949 (Brooman, 1954: 40). Snyder (1931: 198) reported a casualty at the Long Point lighthouse as early as Apr. 18-19, 1930. Saunders (1947: 375) listed May 6 and May 20 as his average spring arrival and departure dates for Toronto: Speirs (1938: 39, 43, 45) listed Toronto extremes as Apr. 13 and May 29, with peaks on May 13 and May 17. One came to our Pickering Twp. feeder as early as Apr. 25, 1967 (perhaps the one seen there on Jan. 22, 1967): others have been seen from May 1 to May 25, with a peak in mid-May (Speirs, 1973). Dennis Barry and George A. Scott found one in a Whitby garden on March 7 and 15, 1964, perhaps an overwintering bird (Tozer & Richards, 1974: 303). Snyder (1941: 89) had Prince Edward Co. records from Apr. 25 (1938) to May 23 (1930). Weir & Quilliam (1980: 40) listed May 2 and May 22 as average spring arrival and departure dates for Kingston, with the earliest March 25 and latest May 31. Devitt (1967: 174) gave May 9 as the 15-year average arrival date at Barrie, with the earliest on Apr. 29, 1961 and latest departure on May 31, 1948. L. Beamer's median arrival date at Meaford was May 6, with the earliest on Apr. 26, 1954. Early individuals were reported at Huntsville on Apr. 23 in both 1962 and 1974, and D. Brunton found them at Killbear Park as late as May 23, 1969 (Mills, 1981: 184). Nicholson (1981: 194) gave May 2 as the 12-year average arrival date on Manitoulin, with a high count of 500 on May 16, 1970: Chris. Bell reported one on March 9, 1975 (possibly a wintering bird). Strickland, Tozer & Rutter (1982) listed May 7 and May 23 as average spring arrival and departure dates for Algonquin Park, with the earliest on Apr. 29. Ricker & Clarke (1939: 24) had Lake Nipissing birds from May 5, 1925 to the last week in May. Skeel & Bondrup-Nielsen (1978: 219) saw 4 on May 12, 1977 at Pukaskwa and W. Wyett noted one there on May 31, 1973. Baillie & Hope (1943: 26) noted birds at Rossport as late as May 30, 1936. Denis (1961: 3) listed May 12 as the average arrival date at Thunder Bay, with the earliest on May 3, 1952. Peruniak (1971: 31) had Atikokan records from May 4 to May 24: David Elder saw one there as early as Apr. 30 in 1981. Elder (1979: 40) gave May 11 as his earliest at Geraldton. Bondrup-Nielsen (1976: 45) gave May 11, 1975 as his earliest at Kapuskasing. Cringan (1953a: 4) had his first at Sioux Lookout on May 10 in 1953. Cringan (1953b: 5) saw one at Kasabonika Lake on May 27, 1953. Manning (1952: 95) collected one at Moose River on May 28, 1947.

SUMMER: The only one reported on the 1968-1977 Breeding Bird Surveys was seen at Hornepayne in 1975, no doubt a lingering bird at a feeder there. A cripple came to our Pickering Twp. feeder as late as June 5, 1951 (Speirs, 1973). Chris Blomme noted 2 lingering birds on Great Duck Is. on June 16, 1973 (Nicholson, 1981: 194). Strickland, Tozer & Rutter (1982) listed June 23 as the latest spring migrant for Algonquin Park. Speirs & Speirs (1947: 38) had a lingering migrant at North Bay on June 6, 1945. John Walty noted one at Washagami, Sudbury Dist., as late as June 8 and June 17, 1938 (Baillie & Hope, 1947: 31). The most southerly nest record was by George M. Sutton, who found a nest with young on Moose Island on June 29, 1956 (Todd, 1963: 691). Manning (1952: 95) collected individuals at North Point, James Bay, on June 5, 1947 and at Big Piskwanish on June 9, 1947; also 3 at Shagamu River, Hudson Bay, from Aug. 8-10, 1947, where young birds were seen. Schueler, Baldwin & Rising (1974: 144, 148) noted the species at Moosonee and Attawapiskat and found nests at Hawley Lake (4 of them): also one nest at Sutton Lake and one at Winisk. Peck (1972: 347) found two nests, each with 4 eggs, on June 29 and June 30, 1970, at Cape Henrietta Maria. James, Nash & Peck (1981: 93) found nests with eggs and young at Kiruna Lake, Sutton Ridges, in 1981. Lee (1978: 35) noted at least 6 singing males at Big Trout Lake in the summer of 1975. C.E. Hope found a nest with 4 eggs on June 18, 1940 at Ft. Severn and a nest with 5 eggs there on June 25, 1940: he noted as many as 14 birds there on July 15.

AUTUMN: Peruniak (1971: 31) had fall records at Atikokan from Sept. 9 to Oct. 21. Skeel & Bondrup-Nielsen (1978: 219) encountered 38 on 5 days from Sept. 15 to Oct. 10 at Pukaskwa. Speirs & Speirs (1947: 38) saw two at North Bay as early as Sept. 17, 1944 and Louise Lawrence noted one at Pimisi Bay as late as Oct. 21, 1944. Strickland, Tozer & Rutter (1982) listed Sept. 21 and Oct. 16 as average fall arrival and departure dates for Algonquin Park, with the earliest on Sept. 11 and latest on Nov. 29. Nicholson (1981: 193) gave Sept. 20 as the 12-year average arrival date on Manitoulin, with the earliest on Sept. 6, 1975 and the high count of 800 on Sept. 26, 1976. Mills (1981: 184) reported Huntsville birds from Sept. 15 (1959) to Nov. 27 (also 1959), with a peak of over 300 at Ahmic Lake on Sept. 25, 1976. Devitt (1967: 174) reported Simcoe Co. birds as early as Sept. 18, 1938 and as late as Oct. 15, 1966. Weir & Quilliam (1980: 40) listed Sept. 24 and Oct. 29 as average fall arrival and departure dates for Kingston, with the earliest on Sept. 14. Snyder (1941: 89) collected one at Hillier, Prince Edward Co., as late as Oct. 24, 1936. Tozer & Richards (1974: 303) reported 6 at Oshawa as late as Nov. 16, 1963. My earliest fall record for Pickering was Sept. 22, 1952 and latest Nov. 10, 1968, with the fall peak in the second week of October (Speirs, 1973). Saunders (1947: 375) listed Oct. 2 and Oct. 15 as his average fall arrival and departure dates for Toronto: Speirs (1938: 47, 51, 53) had extreme fall records of Sept. 13 and Nov. 13, with the peak on Oct. 5. Gertrude Selby saw one at Fonthill on Nov. 5, 1951 (Beardslee & Mitchell, 1965: 443-444). Snyder (1931: 198) reported 17 casualties at the Long Point lighthouse from Sept. 24-29, 1929. Ussher (1965: 30) gave Oct. 4 and Nov. 2 as average fall arrival and departure dates at Rondeau, with the earliest on Sept. 27. Stirrett (1973d: 29) had fall maxima of 50 at Pelee from Oct. 9 to Oct. 19, with the earliest 5 on Sept. 17 and the latest 3 on Nov. 11 (but some wintered there).

BANDING: Brewer & Salvadori (1975: 93) reported one banded at Jefferson, Ohio, on Oct. 1, 1968 and recovered at Ottawa on May 13, 1971 (about 358 miles to the northeast). Brewer & Salvadori (1978: 95) had two interesting recoveries: one banded at Harlow Lake, Michigan, on Sept. 26, 1964 was recovered at Lillabelle Lake, near Cochrane, about 341 miles to the northeast, on May 17, 1968: another banded at Long Point on Oct. 13, 1967 was found at Bellair, Texas, on March 5, 1970 (about 1227 miles to the southwest).

**MEASUREMENTS:**
*Length:* 6.5 to 7.5 ins. (Godfrey, 1966: 396)
*Wingspread:* 9.6 to 10.6 ins. (Roberts, 1955: 719)
*Weight:* 1 oz. (Roberts, 1955: 719).

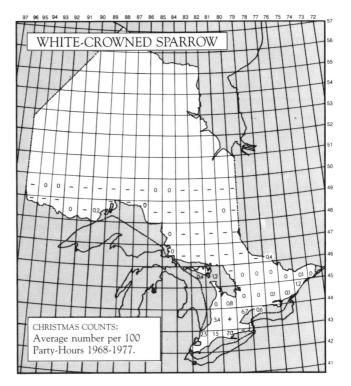

WHITE-CROWNED SPARROW

CHRISTMAS COUNTS:
Average number per 100 Party-Hours 1968-1977.

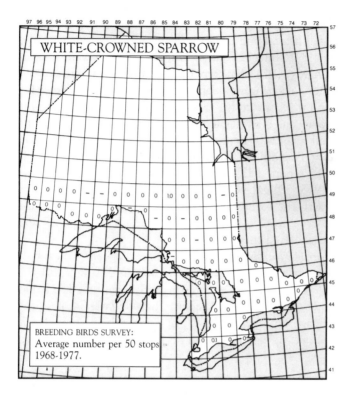

97 96 95 94 93 92 91 90 89 88 87 86 85 84 83 82 81 80 79 78 77 76 75 74 73 72

WHITE-CROWNED SPARROW

BREEDING BIRDS SURVEY:
Average number per 50 stops
1968-1977.

# HARRIS' SPARROW *Zonotrichia querula* (Nuttall)

Harris' Sparrow is seen chiefly as a migrant through the central prairies, but some stray eastward into Ontario, especially north of Lake Superior and a few show up in winter at Ontario feeders. They breed along the border between the tundra and the coniferous forest and were recently found for the first time in that zone in extreme northwestern Ontario. They winter in shrubby country in the central United States.

**IDENTIFICATION**: Harris' Sparrows average somewhat larger than White-crowned Sparrows and, like that species, have a pink bill. Adults, with their black throat, face and crown are unmistakable. The young have a heavy black "necklace" and streaked sides: their pink bill is darker on the upper mandible than in the adults. The song reminds me of the introductory two or three notes of a White-throated Sparrow song but is much lower in pitch.

**WINTER**: On the 1968-1977 Christmas counts there were reports at Long Point (1973): Pickering (1969), Meaford (1975), Thunder Bay (1971) and Horneypayne (1973). Stirrett (1973a: 21) had one winter record at Pelee: from Jan. 30 to late March in 1966. D. Murray *et al* saw one at Melbourne, near London, from Jan. 28 to Feb. 28, 1977 (Goodwin, 1977: 328) and again on Dec. 27, 1977 (Goodwin, 1978: 346). H. Lancaster found one at Welland on Jan. 1, 1975 (Goodwin, 1975: 687). Parker (1983: 27) reported one on 1 of 58 Christmas counts at Toronto, perhaps the one at Frank Barkey's feeder on Dec. 26, 1969 (Speirs, 1973). R. and A. Foster had one at their Darlington Twp. feeder from Jan. 11-14, 1963 (Tozer & Richards, 1974: 302). The bird on the Meaford Christmas count stayed until Jan. 31, 1976 according to M. Grant (Goodwin, 1976: 714) and another was found there on Feb. 16, 1980, seen by J.C. Clarke (Goodwin, 1980: 270). E.R. McDonald reported one at a feeder at Harwood, Northumberland Co. from Dec. 22, 1982 to Feb. 25, 1983, seen by many others (Weir, 1983: 298). A. Munro et al observed one at Ottawa until Jan. 20, 1978 (Goodwin, 1978: 346). Nicholson (1981: 193) reported one in Gordon Twp., Manitoulin, on Dec. 16, 1979. The bird on the Hornepayne Christmas count was seen until Jan. 9, 1974 (Goodwin, 1974: 635).

SPRING: Stirrett (1973b: 27) had four spring records of single birds at Pelee: March 28, 1968, May 8-14, 1965, May 9-10, 1953 and May 13, 1956: Peter Whelan and many others saw one there on May 17, 1974 (Goodwin, 1974: 798). Two were present at Rondeau on May 10 and 11, 1970 and were photographed by Dennis Rupert and Robert Simpson (Kelley, 1978: 89). W.E. Saunders collected one near London on March 18, 1907 (Saunders & Dale, 1933: 244). Individuals showed up at Long Point on Apr. 17, 1972 (Goodwin, 1972: 758) and on May 7, 1977 (Goodwin, 1977: 996). H.H. Axtell found one in Bertie Twp., Welland Co., seen by many others from Feb. 14 to March 31, 1972 (Goodwin, 1972: 600). P. Van Dyken noted one at Bronte to Apr. 17, 1972 (Goodwin, 1972: 758). Speirs (1938: 39) listed a May 13 record for Toronto. Speirs (1973) reported one seen by R. Charles Long at Pickering Beach on Apr. 27, 1964 and another at an Oshawa feeder on May 9, 1965 seen by George A. Scott et al. Edgerton Pegg telephoned us to report one at the Currie's Pickering Twp. feeder on Apr. 29, 1974: we had a splendid view of it, noting the pink bill, black throat and crown and the two-note song. P. Bridges and R. Fellows observed one at Bowmanville from Apr. 17 to May 11, 1978 (Goodwin, 1978: 1001). E.R. McDonald reported one near Port Hope from Apr. 22 to May 8, 1983 and one at Harwood to May 13, 1983 (Weir, 1983: 866). P. Hogenbirk et al had one at Peterborough to May 11, 1980 and B. Parker noted one at Sibbald Point on May 14, 1980 (Goodwin, 1980: 773). A.E. Wilson reported one at Cobourg from March 12-31, 1972 (Goodwin, 1972: 600). E.L. Brereton saw one at Barrie on Apr. 21, 1949 while P.W. Brown and S.H. Henry observed one at Collingwood on May 5, 1913 (Devitt, 1967: 174). The one on the 1975 Christmas count at Meaford left on Apr. 11, 1976 according to R. Milani (Goodwin, 1976: 836). J.W. Johnson noted one at Wiarton from May 11-19, 1983 (Weir, 1983: 298). Mills (1981: 192) cited Huntsville reports on March 10, 1962 and May 24, 1970. Skeel & Bondrup-Nielsen (1978: 219) saw one at Pukaskwa on May 13, 1977 and reported one seen by N.G. Escott at Marathon from May 7-11, 1976 (Escott noted birds at Marathon in 1977 and 1978 also). The bird seen on the Thunder Bay Christmas count in 1971, stayed there until March 20, 1972 according to W. Rosser (Goodwin, 1972: 600). Denis (1961: 3) gave May 12 as the average arrival date at Thunder Bay, with the earliest on May 4, 1954. We saw two at Dorion on May 19, 1956 and one the following day: Rita Taylor had 3 at her feeder there on May 24, 1957. Peruniak (1971: 31) called this a fairly common migrant at Atikokan from May 6 to May 23. M. and S. Gawn saw one at Manitouwadge on May 13, 1980 (Goodwin, 1980: 773). In 1971 we had 10 at Lake of the Woods Provincial Park on May 17, two at Kenora on May 19, one at Dryden on May 20 and one at Geraldton on May 27. Elder (1979: 40) gave May 21 as his earliest Geraldton record. J.B. Miles et al observed one at Hornepayne from May 16-17, 1975 (Goodwin, 1975: 847). Cringan (1953a: 4) saw his first at Sioux Lookout on May 10 in 1953.

**SUMMER:** Goodwin (1976: 63) saw one at Moosonee on Aug. 17, 1975. Tim & Doris Nowicki and R. & T. Thobaben found Ontario's first nest, with eggs, at Fort Severn on July 4, 1983: the young fledged on July 25 (Weir, 1983: 985) and (James, 1984: 28).

**AUTUMN:** Peruniak (1971: 31) had fall migrants at Atikokan from Sept. 13 to Oct. 23. K. Denis saw one at Thunder Bay on Sept. 22, 1971 (Goodwin, 1972: 59). J.B. Miles *et al* noted 2 at Hornepayne from Sept. 22-26 and on Oct. 5, 1974 (Goodwin, 1975: 53). A. Wormington had a maximum of 4 on Caribou Is., Lake Superior, on Sept. 25, 1979 (Goodwin, 1980: 158). Nicholson (1981: 193) had 2 fall records on Manitoulin: one at Kathleen Dinsmore's feeder at South Baymouth from Oct. 1-9, 1971 and the other on Great Duck Is. on Oct. 22, 1978. D. Prest reported one at Ottawa as late as Nov. 26, 1972 (Goodwin, 1973: 611). E.L. Brereton described one seen at Barrie on Oct. 12, 1935 and Mary Devitt found one at Allenwood Beach, near Wasaga Beach, that was later collected on Oct. 18, 1947 (Devitt, 1967: 174). Weir & Quilliam (1980: 28) had 3 sightings at Prince Edward Point from Sept. 13 to Oct. 10, 1980. G. Hamilton noted one at Kincardine on Sept. 20, 1976 (Goodwin, 1977: 172). R. Cubitt had one at Guelph on Oct. 25, 1975 (Goodwin, 1976: 63). G. Sutherland observed one at a West Hill feeder from Oct. 17-19, 1977 (Goodwin, 1978: 200). Speirs (1938: 53) listed an Oct. 14 record for Toronto. M. Jennings and P. Van Dyken noted birds at Bronte on Oct. 10 and 14, 1976 (Goodwin, 1977: 172). R.L. Sommerville reported one at Fort Erie from Nov. 4-8, 1973 (Goodwin, 1974: 48). Max Alton found one on Nov. 2, 1952 near Eden, Elgin Co., (Brooman, 1954: 39) and Marshall Field noted one at Hawk Cliff on Oct. 27, 1979 (Goodwin, 1980: 158). Stirrett (1973d: 29) had 3 fall records at Pelee: Oct. 12, 1936, Oct. 24, 1960 and Nov. 13, 1936.

**MEASUREMENTS:**

*Length:* 7 to 7 3/4 ins. (Godfrey, 1966: 395)
*Wingspread:* 10.15 to 11.62 ins. (Roberts, 1955: 710)
*Weight:* 1.44 to 1.75 oz. (Roberts, 1955: 710).

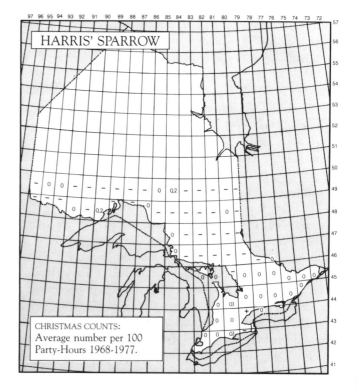

HARRIS' SPARROW

CHRISTMAS COUNTS:
Average number per 100
Party-Hours 1968-1977.

# DARK-EYED JUNCO    *Junco hyemalis*    (Linnaeus)

In Ontario juncos are familiar to most bird feeder operators during the colder months and to residents in the cottage country and northern Ontario in the summer.

IDENTIFICATION: Most of the juncos that we see in Ontario are slaty-black birds except for flashing white outer tail feathers in flight, with white bellies and pinkish-white bills. Females have the black replaced by dark brown. Occasionally one of the western races will show up with pink sides, rusty-brown back contrasting with the black hood. These were formerly considered to be a full species, the Oregon Junco, while our common form was known as the Slate-colored Junco. The song resembles the trill of a Chipping Sparrow but is usually somewhat more mellow.

WINTER: On the 1968-1977 Christmas counts, juncos were common north to Presqu'ile and fairly common north to the Thousand Islands and Wiarton, becoming rare at more northern localities. Stirrett (1973a: 20) had a winter maximum of 100 at Pelee on Dec. 26. Quilliam (1973: 188) reported them on 19 Christmas counts at Kingston since 1948, with a maximum of 50 on Dec. 19, 1971. Mills (1981: 180) reported some on 15 of 21 Christmas counts at Huntsville, but the maximum was 11 in 1960. Nicholson (1981: 191) mentioned birds wintering at South Baymouth in 1969-1970 and 1970-1971. Strickland, Tozer & Rutter (1982) considered it "very rare in winter" in Algonquin Park though earlier writers found it common there. Dennison (1980: 147) reported juncos on 8 of 25 Christmas counts as Sault Ste. Marie, with a maximum of 141 in 1957. David Elder saw one at Atikokan on Jan. 1, 1981.

SPRING: Stirrett (1973b: 27) had a peak of 1500 or more at Pelee on Apr. 15, with his latest there on May 21. Ussher (1965: 30) gave May 9 as his 11-year average departure date from Rondeau, with the latest on May 31. Saunders & Dale (1933: 243) reported several nests near London though they are seldom seen there recently in the nesting season: one nest, with 5 eggs, was found in a thicket of vines growing against a brick wall on Apr. 18, 1873; another nest was found on May 20, 1880 holding 4 eggs and one with 3 eggs was found on May 10, 1884. Snyder (1931: 199) collected an injured female at Long Point as late as May 27, 1927: lighthouse casualties there included 14 on Apr. 17-18, 7 on Apr. 18-19 and 8 on Apr. 20-21, 1930. Speirs (1938: 43) gave Apr. 9 as the spring peak at Toronto while Saunders (1947: 375) listed May 9 as his 13-year average departure date: J.H. Samuel found a nest with 4 or 5 young at Toronto on May 14, 1894 (Baillie & Harrington, 1937: 273). Weir & Quilliam (1980: 40) listed March 25 as the 32-year average arrival date at Kingston and May 13 as the 28-year average departure date in spring. Lloyd (1924: 11) reported a nest with 4 young at Rockcliffe, Ottawa, on May 24, 1920. Mills (1981: 180) gave March 30 as a 12-year average arrival date at Huntsville, with the earliest on March 16. Nicholson (1981: 191) gave Apr. 2 as a 12-year average arrival date on Manitoulin, with the earliest on March 12, 1977 and a high count of 1000 on Apr. 23, 1972. Strickland, Tozer & Rutter (1982) listed Apr. 4 as the average arrival date in Algonquin Park, with the earliest on March 12. Louise Lawrence noted 5 at Pimisi Bay as early as March 24, 1945 (Speirs & Speirs, 1947: 38). Juncos ranked 4th in abundance as spring migrants at Pukaskwa: the first was noted on Apr. 4 in 1977, with the peak from Apr. 18 to Apr. 25 (Skeel & Bondrup-Nielsen, 1978: 218). Denis (1961: 2) listed Apr. 10 as the average arrival date at Thunder Bay, with the earliest on March 20,

1958. Dear (1940: 142) found a nest with 5 eggs in Gorham Twp., Thunder Bay, as early as May 27, 1926. Peruniak (1971: 30) gave Apr. 5 as her earliest date for Atikokan and Elder (1979: 40) had his first at Geraldton on Apr. 16. Cringan (1953a: 4) saw his first at Sioux Lookout on Apr. 26 in 1953. C.A. Elsey saw his first in the Asheweig area on May 17 in 1950 (Cringan, 1950: 18). Manning (1952: 93) collected one at Sandy Is., near Moosonee, on May 30, 1947.

SUMMER: On the 1968-1977 Breeding Bird Surveys, juncos were fairly common to common on the northern routes, becoming uncommon south to the fringes of Algonquin Park. Stirrett (1973c: 23) had just one summer record at Pelee, on July 8, 1913, when 2 were seen. Kelley (1978: 88) reported a singing male at Rondeau on July 5, 1953. Saunders & Dale (1933: 243) mentioned a nest with 4 eggs at Komoka on June 16, 1894. Frank Farley recorded a set of eggs taken at Belmont on the Elgin-Middlesex border, on July 9, 1887 (Brooman, 1954: 39). At Toronto, J.L. Jackson took a set of four eggs on June 13, 1890, and a set of 3 eggs on July 7, 1887 (Baillie & Harrington, 1937: 273). Snyder (1930: 195) saw pairs along the height of land in King Twp. in midsummer: R.D. Ussher saw adults feeding young there on July 17, 1934 (Baillie & Harrington, 1937: 273). On July 15, 1984, we had an unexpected bird at our Pickering Twp. feeder for one day. Tozer & Richards (1974: 296) reported such a straggler in Scugog Twp. on June 30, 1960. Weir & Quilliam (1980: 40) had birds at Kingston as late as June 24 and as early as Aug. 13. Devitt (1967: 170) saw a young bird being fed by its parents near Wasaga Beach on June 21, 1934 and A.J. Mitchener found a nest with young in the Blue Mountains, near the Grey Co. border in June, 1964. Lloyd (1924: 11) reported a nest with 4 eggs found at Meach's Lake, near Ottawa, on July 6, 1908. Mills (1981: 179) reported 11 nests in the cottage country, with full clutches from May 4 to July 19. M.Y. Williams found a nest with 4 eggs at Tamarack Cove, Manitoulin, on July 22, 1915 (Nicholson, 1981: 191). C.H.D. Clarke found a nest with 4 eggs at Biggar Lake, Algonquin Park, on July 24, 1933 (MacLulich, 1938: 43). Ricker & Clarke (1939: 23) reported a nest with 4 eggs at Frank's Bay, Lake Nipissing, on June 1, 1932. Baillie & Hope (1947: 30) saw two young, just out of the nest, at Chapleau on June 14, 1937 and two fully-fledged young at Bigwood on July 14. Snyder (1942: 151) noted young out of the nest at Laird on June 9, 1931 and collected fresh eggs near Sault Ste. Marie as late as July 4. Skeel & Bondrup-Nielsen (1978: 218) ranked it 19th in relative abundance in summer at Pukaskwa (44 noted in 19 days from June 1 to July 16, but none later in July or in August). Baillie & Hope (1943: 25) found a nest with 5 eggs on June 18, 1936 at Marathon and a nest with 4 young at Amyot on June 29. Snyder (1928: 269) found a nest with 4 eggs at Lake Nipigon on June 26, 1924. Dear (1940: 142) found a nest with 4 eggs in Sibley Twp., Thunder Bay, on June 3, 1933. Kendeigh (1947: 28) found a density of 3 pairs per 100 acres at Black Sturgeon Lake in 1945 while Speirs (1949: 148) had 5 pairs per 75 acres at nearby Eaglehead Lake in 1946. Snyder (1938: 212) watched a female collecting deer hair for a nest on June 21, 1929, at Emo, Rainy River. Snyder (1953: 88) reported several nestings in western Ontario: a nest with 4 eggs at Ingolf on June 8, 1937; a nest with 5 eggs at Dryden on July 3, 1939; a nest with 3 eggs near Dinorwic on June 8 and another there with 2 eggs and 2 newly hatched young on June 20, 1946: birds were noted from Malachi east to Savanne and north to Sioux Lookout. R.D. Ussher found a nest with 3 eggs and a recently hatched young near Kapuskasing on July 14, 1925 and Mrs. G. Roach found a nest with young at Timmins in June, 1936 (Baillie & Harrington, 1937: 273). Snyder (1928: 28) found a nest with young at Lake Abitibi in the summer of 1925. Bondrup-

Nielsen (1976: 47) found a nest with 4 young near Kapuskasing on June 16, 1974. James (1980: 91) found two nests on June 18, 1979 about 11 km. northeast of Pickle Lake: one held 3 young, the other one egg. Cringan (1953b: 5) noted from 1 to 10 on 6 days at Kasabonika Lake in the summer of 1953. Cringan (1950: 18) found a nest with 3 young in a spruce swamp near Nikip Lake on July 8, 1950. Hope (1938: 46) found 3 nests near Favourable Lake in 1938: a nest with 3 eggs on June 3 in a sphagnum hummock, a nest with 4 eggs on June 9 in a dry clearing and a nest with 6 eggs on June 13 on a dry, wooded hillside. Sam Waller collected a nest with 4 eggs at Moose Factory on June 16, 1930 (Baillie & Harrington, 1937: 273). Manning (1952: 93) collected 2 at North Point, James Bay, on June 6, 1947; one at Big Piskwanish on June 11; 7 including 1 young at Raft River from July 10-12, 1947 and 5 young at Shagamu River, Hudson Bay, from Aug. 8-10, 1947. Schueler, Baldwin & Rising (1974: 144) found them uncommon at Winisk but abundant and breeding at Hawley Lake. James, Nash & Peck (1981) found this to be the most abundant bird in most habitats studied at Kiruna Lake, Sutton Ridges, with 83.3 pairs per km $^2$ in the most favoured habitat (moist conifer forest). Lee & Speirs (1977) found them in all 3 study quadrats at Big Trout Lake in 1975, and the most abundant species in black spruce - tamarack bog plot (35 territories per 100 acres, or 86 per km $^2$). C.E. Hope observed some on most days at Fort Severn in 1940, with a maximum of 10 on June 21.

AUTUMN: D. McRae and A. Wormington saw many up to Oct. 27 at Netitishi Point, James Bay, and a single bird as late as Nov. 15, 1981. George Stirrett saw 5 at Attawapiskat on Oct. 7, 1948 and 6 at Moose Factory on Oct. 2, 1948 (Manning, 1952: 92). Peruniak (1971: 30) reported her latest at Atikokan on Nov. 20, and one of the *oregonus* race on Oct. 14, 1958. Skeel & Bondrup-Nielsen (1978: 218) ranked it 3rd as a fall migrant at Pukaskwa, with 65 noted on 18 days, from Sept. 1 to Oct. 14, 1977. Speirs & Speirs (1947: 38) noted one at North Bay on Oct. 23, 1944. Strickland, Tozer & Rutter (1982) listed Nov. 10 as the average departure date from Algonquin Park, with the latest on Nov. 24. Nicholson (1981: 191) reported a high count of 250 on Manitoulin on Oct. 13, 1974. Weir & Quilliam (1980: 40) listed Sept. 11 as the 29-year average fall arrival date at Kingston, with Nov. 23 as the 28-year average departure date. Saunders (1947: 375) listed Sept. 24 as his 13-year average arrival date at Toronto and Speirs (1938: 51) gave Oct. 3 as the fall peak there. Brooman (1954: 39) reported a hybrid (with a White-throated Sparrow) collected by Marshall Field at St. Thomas on Oct. 8, 1953. Ussher (1965: 30) gave Sept. 29 as his 10-year average arrival date at Rondeau, with the earliest on Sept. 15. Stirrett (1973d: 29) had his earliest Pelee bird on Sept. 3 and a maximum of 500 on Oct. 30-Nov. 1.

BANDING: From 1955 to 1964, Alf. Bunker banded 309 at his Pickering Twp. home, between Sept. 26 and May 1: of these 9 returned the same winter, 3 the following winter and 3 the winter after that. Birds banded near Toronto have turned up in Ohio, Pennsylvania and Maryland during the colder months, while birds banded in Michigan, New Jersey and Pennsylvania have been recovered near Toronto. Brewer & Salvadori (1978: 93-94) cited some interesting recoveries: the long distance record was held by one banded at Dover, Pa. on Dec. 10, 1967 and recovered the following May at Geraldton, Ont. (a distance of 825 miles); another banded at Clarksville, Pa. on Feb. 22, 1965 turned up at Moonbeam, Ont. in April of the following year, a distance of 665 miles. The most southerly banding was at Cary, N.C. on March 20, 1969: this bird turned up at Long Point on

Apr. 4 of the same year, a flight of 477 miles. One banded at Long Point on Apr. 26, 1963 showed up 5 years later as far west as Elcho, Wisconsin, on May 5, 1968.

**MEASUREMENTS:**

*Length:* 5 3/4 to 6 1/2 ins. (Godfrey, 1966: 389)
*Wingspread:* 9.2 to 9.9 ins. (Roberts, 1955: 712)
*Weight:* 18 banded at our Pickering Twp. home between Jan. 31 and May 10 averaged 22.5 g. Hope (1938: 46) found that 5 ♂ averaged 18.2 g. and 1 ♀ weighed 18.9 g. at Favourable Lake in the breeding season.

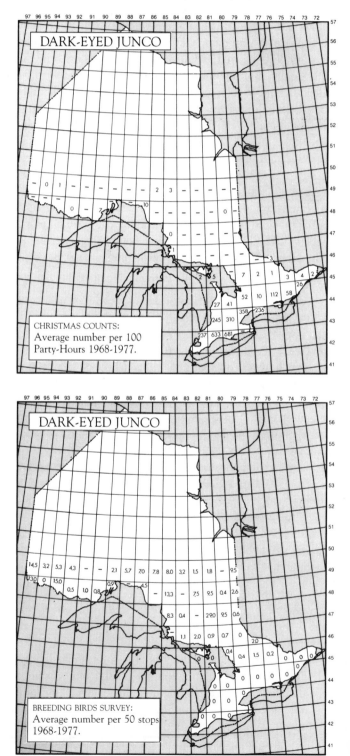

DARK-EYED JUNCO

CHRISTMAS COUNTS:
Average number per 100
Party-Hours 1968-1977.

DARK-EYED JUNCO

BREEDING BIRDS SURVEY:
Average number per 50 stops
1968-1977.

# LAPLAND LONGSPUR   *Calcarius lapponicus*   (Linnaeus)

The Lapland Longspur is a circumpolar breeder, chiefly in the Arctic tundra. In the colder months they may be found in Ontario with flocks of Snow Buntings and Horned Larks along roadsides and in weedy or manured fields. Some breed along the Hudson Bay vicinity in summer. Speirs (1973) contrasted the relative abundance of this species on Christmas counts in Ontario, where it is far outnumbered by Snow Buntings, with the condition in the midwestern United States; where it outnumbers the Snow Bunting.

IDENTIFICATION: In flocks of Snow Buntings watch for smaller, darker associates, ones that lack the dark outer tail feathers and characteristic markings of Horned Larks. Lapland Longspurs look more like some of our stripy sparrows, particularly Vesper Sparrows which also have white outer tail feathers, but the Longspurs are more heavily built and tend to hug the ground. On closer inspection the light brown hind neck and buffy ear patches outlined in black are diagnostic. In late spring you may come across adults in breeding plumage with chestnut hind neck and black crown, face and "bib" bordered behind with creamy white. Spring migrants may be heard uttering their delightful tinkling song, but winter birds share many of the Snow Bunting calls, notably a dry, rolling "r-r-r-r-" and a descending "teeee-ur".

WINTER: On the 1968-1977 Christmas counts they were fairly common at some localities near the Lake Erie and Lake Ontario shores, becoming rare north to Ottawa and Sault Ste. Marie. Stirrett (1973a: 21) had a winter maximum of 100 at Pelee on Jan. 21. Ussher (1965: 31) had a Rondeau record on Dec. 29. Saunders & Dale (1933: 246) cited Middlesex Co. records in January and February. Marshall Field banded one at St. Thomas on Jan. 30, 1949 (Brooman, 1954: 40). They were reported on only 18 of 58 Christmas counts at Toronto: none on 40 counts but an amazing 750 on the Dec. 24, 1939 count (Parker, 1983: 27 and Saunders, 1947: 378). Wishart Campbell reported 200 on the Ajax fields on Dec. 19, 1954 and George A. Scott found 40 in January and February, 1962 on fields near Oshawa's Second Marsh (Speirs, 1973). Quilliam (1973: 195) reported some on 15 Christmas counts at Kingston, with a high of 340 on Dec. 30, 1960. E.L. Brereton saw 7 at Barrie on Dec. 27, 1943 (Devitt, 1967: 178). Mills (1981: 189) spotted one in a group of 600 Snow Buntings at Lake Cecebe, Parry Sound Dist., on Dec. 31, 1979. Nicholson (1981: 197) saw 10 in Gordon Twp., Manitoulin, on Dec. 21, 1975. Dennison (1980: 148) reported 3 birds on 1 of 25 Christmas counts at Sault Ste. Marie.

SPRING: Stirrett (1973b: 27) had two March records at Pelee: 6 on March 6, 1954 and 25 on March 22, 1940. Ussher (1965: 31) gave March 23 as his average departure date from Rondeau, with one as late as May 16. Saunders & Dale (1933: 246) cited several spring records for Middlesex Co., where Tom Willis Jr. found a flock of about 100 as late as May 4, 1929, confirmed by others during the next few days. Harold Lancaster found 5 in spring plumage in the Dunwich Marsh, Elgin Co., as late as May 12, 1952 (Brooman, 1954: 40). Beardslee & Mitchell (1965: 449) reported one in breeding plumage at Rockhouse Point, Lake Erie, on May 15 and again on May 28, 1938. J.L. Baillie (in Saunders, 1947: 375) gave March 11 as his average departure date from Toronto but Speirs (1938: 43) listed March 27 as the spring peak there: Fleming (1907: 80) gave May 17, 1891 as his latest Toronto date. George Fairfield saw a flock of 20 in Pickering Twp. on Apr. 26, 1958 (Speirs, 1973). Paul Bridges found two at Bowmanville as late as Apr. 30, 1967

(Tozer & Richards, 1974: 308). Allin (1940: 110) saw a flock of 100 or more in Darlington Twp. fields on Apr. 11, 1921. Snyder (1941: 91) reported 7 specimens from Hillier, Prince Edward Co., from March 20 (1937) to May 18 (1934). Weir & Quilliam (1980: 40) listed March 2 as the 22-year average departure date from Kingston, with the latest on Apr. 19. A.J. Mitchener saw several at Collingwood in "bright spring plumage" as late as May 15, 1953 (Devitt, 1967: 178). On May 19, 1933, C. McInnis picked up a bird killed striking the forestry tower at Parry Sound and Katherine Ketchum saw the species off Point au Baril on May 22, 1961 (Mills, 1981: 189). Nicholson (1981: 197) had Manitoulin records from March 16 (1980) to May 22 (1978) with a high count of 150 on Apr. 25, 1971. James Foulds saw one near Cache Lake, Algonquin Park, on Apr. 4, 1934 (MacLulich, 1938: 45): Strickland, Tozer & Rutter (1982) listed Apr. 22 as the average arrival date there and May 29 as the average departure date, with one as late as June 4. Ricker & Clarke (1939: 24) reported 3 males at North Bay on May 6, 1926 and 2 males at Frank's Bay, Lake Nipissing, on May 16, 1933. Speirs & Speirs (1947: 38) had North Bay records from Apr. 29 to May 14, 1944. Skeel & Bondrup-Nielsen (1978: 222) saw single birds at Pukaskwa on May 2 and 3, 1977. Denis (1961: 3) gave Apr. 28 as the average arrival date at Thunder Bay, with the earliest on Apr. 11, 1949. Bondrup-Nielsen (1976: 45) noted a few at Kapuskasing on Apr. 22-23, 1974. Cringan (1953a: 4) saw his first at Sioux Lookout on May 4 in 1953. Sam Waller noted his first at Moose Factory on Apr. 18 in 1930 (Todd, 1963: 714). Manning (1952: 100) reported 200 near Moosonee on May 31, 1947 and 350 at North Point, James Bay, from June 3-6, 1947, all migrants.

SUMMER: Manning (1952: 100) saw 8 migrants at Big Piskwanish on June 11, 1947 and 3 at Long Ridge Point, James Bay on June 15, 1947: he saw 41 at Cape Henrietta Maria from July 20-24, 1947 and collected one young bird there, as well as another at Little Cape, Hudson Bay on Aug. 11 where 6 birds were seen. Schueler, Baldwin & Rising (1974: 144) had records at Moosonee and at Winisk. Peck (1972: 347) photographed a nest with 4 eggs at Cape Henrietta Maria on June 29, 1970, where he was almost never out of sight or hearing of the species: he cited several previous breeding records for the region.

AUTUMN: Todd (1963: 714) noted the first southbound bird at Partridge Creeks, near Moosonee, on Sept. 11, 1923. D. McRae and A. Wormington saw as many as 30 at Netitishi Point, James Bay, on Oct. 15, 1981 and flocks on most days until the end of October with single birds on Nov. 7 and Nov. 23. Peruniak (1971: 32) called this a very common fall migrant at Atikokan, from Sept. 22 to Oct. 19. Skeel & Bondrup-Nielsen (1978: 222) saw a flock of 12 at Pukaskwa on Sept. 30, 1977. Speirs & Speirs (1947: 38) watched 7 at North Bay on Oct. 4, 1944 and Louise Lawrence noted one at Pimisi Bay on Nov. 2, 1944. Strickland, Tozer & Rutter (1982) had Algonquin Park records from Sept. 15 to Nov. 15, with average arrival on Sept. 23 and departure on Oct. 16. Nicholson (1981: 196) gave Sept. 24 as the 10-year average arrival date at Manitoulin, with the earliest on Sept. 10, 1977 and the high count of 180 on Oct. 25, 1970. Mills (1981: 189) cited severral records from the cottage country from Oct. 6 (1973) to Nov. 3 (1959). A.J. Mitchener noted the species at Collingwood as early as Oct. 3, 1953 (Devitt, 1967: 178). Weir & Quilliam (1980: 40) listed Oct. 31 as the 19-year average arrival date at Kingston, with the earliest on Sept. 20. Speirs (1973) cited Oct. 3 records for Whitby in 1961 and for Ajax in 1970. Saunders (1947: 375) listed Sept. 26 as his earliest fall record for Toronto: C.W. Nash recorded "flocks" there from Oct. 10-26, 1891 (Fleming, 1907: 80).

W.E. Saunders collected one in Middlesex Co. on Nov. 16, 1901 (Saunders & Dale, 1933: 246). Stirrett (1973d: 30) had his earliest at Pelee on Oct. 10 and a maximum of 50 on Oct. 18.

**MEASUREMENTS:**
*Length:* 6.0 to 7.0 ins. (Godfrey, 1966: 404)
*Wingspread:* 10 3/4 to 11 1/2 ins. (Roberts, 1955: 712)
*Weight:* 1.00 to 1.87 oz. (Roberts, 1955: 712).

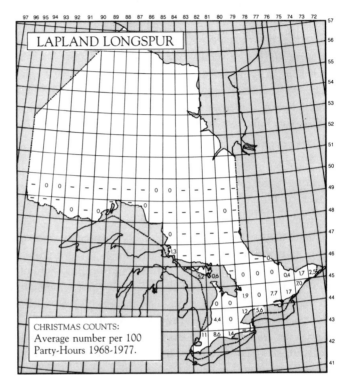

LAPLAND LONGSPUR

CHRISTMAS COUNTS:
Average number per 100
Party-Hours 1968-1977.

# SMITH'S LONGSPUR   *Calcarius pictus*   (Swainson)

Smith's Longspurs are tundra breeders, very rare in Ontario except along the Hudson Bay coast where they are locally common in summer.

**IDENTIFICATION:** Adult males in breeding plumage have a clear buff breast and a striking black and white face pattern, a black crown and a broad white stripe over the eye. Migrants, not in breeding plumage, resemble Lapland Longspurs in similar plumage, but have a blacker crown and ear patches, separated by a broad white stripe over the eye, and a breast pattern something like a Lincoln's Sparrow with fine streaks across a buffy breast band and down the sides.

**WINTER:**

**SPRING:** L.V. Marsh, A. Mason and T.R. Scovell carefully documented a sighting at Long Point on Apr. 20, 1980 (Goodwin, 1980: 773). Devitt (1967: 179) identified one near Elmvale, Simcoe Co., on May 22, 1949. T. Hince reported one at Marathon on Apr. 24, 1983 (Weir, 1983: 866).

**SUMMER:** Manning (1952: 100) counted 16 and collected 11 at Little Cape, Hudson Bay, between July 29 and Aug. 1, 1947: one of those collected was a juvenile bird: he also saw one bird at Shagamu River, Hudson Bay. Schueler, Baldwin & Rising (1974: 144, 148) had records at Sutton River and Winisk where 3 incubating females were collected on June 27, 1971. Peck (1972: 347) found a nest with 4 eggs on June 30, 1970 at Cape Henrietta Maria and cited previous breeding records for the region, including a nest with 4 eggs on June 29, 1948 and a nest with 5 eggs on July 7, 1948 found by the ROM expedition. C.E. Hope saw up to 10 individuals at Fort Severn on June 23, July 1 and July 19, 1940 and collected several birds there.

**AUTUMN:** George E. Atkinson collected an immature female at Port Arthur (now Thunder Bay) in September, 1892 (Fleming, 1913: 228). Skeel & Bondrup-Nielsen (1978: 222) saw 2 at Pukaskwa on Sept. 20, 1977, hopping on the ground at their feet, also one on Sept. 25, 4 on Sept. 28 and 30 on Sept. 29, 1977. E.L. Brereton detected one in a flock of Lapland Longspurs near Barrie on Nov. 2, 1947 (Devitt, 1967: 178-179). Ron Weir identified one at the Amherstview sewage lagoons on Sept. 24, 1973 (Weir & Quilliam, 1980: 29).

**MEASUREMENTS:**
*Length:* 5.7 to 6.5 ins.
(Godfrey, 1966: 405)
*Wingspread:* 10 to 11 ins.
(Roberts, 1955: 711)
*Weight:* 22 ♂ averaged
28.5 g.; 7 ♀ averaged
24.3 g. (Dunning,
1984: 25).

# CHESTNUT-COLLARED LONGSPUR
## *Calcarius ornatus*   (Townsend)

The Chestnut-collared Longspur is a bird of short grass prairies, accidental in Ontario.

**IDENTIFICATION:** The male in breeding plumage has a black breast and crown, a mainly creamy-white face and a bright chestnut hindneck. In all plumages the tail is mainly white with a central triangle of black, narrow in front and broad at the tip. Apart from the tail, the female is a dingy pale brown, heavily streaked above and below with dark brown.

**WINTER:**

**SPRING:** Weir, Quilliam & Norman (1972: 382-383) documented a sighting at Prince Edward Point on May 2, 1972. W.A. Este photographed one at Garson, near Sudbury, on Apr. 17-18, 1978 (Goodwin, 1978: 1001).

**SUMMER:**

**AUTUMN:** W. Wyett saw one at Pukaskwa on Sept. 2, 1975 (Skeel & Bondrup-Nielsen, 1978: 222).

**MEASUREMENTS:**
*Length:* 5.2 to 6.5 ins.
(Godfrey, 1966: 406)
*Wingspread:* 10.0 to
10.65 ins. (Roberts,
1955: 706)
*Weight:* 0.63 to 0.75 oz.
(Roberts, 1955: 706).

**REFERENCE:**
Weir, R.D.; H. Quilliam &
R. Norman 1972 First
record of Chestnut-collared
Longspur in Ontario. Can.
Field-Naturalist,
86: (4): 382-383.

# SNOW BUNTING   *Plectrophenax nivalis*   (Linnaeus)

Snow Buntings are circumpolar high Arctic breeders. They usually come into southern Ontario in large flocks that reach their greatest abundance in mid-winter though some appear along shores with Horned Larks in late autumn and some linger to go north with Lapland Longspurs in spring. Although a few have been seen in summer along the James Bay and Hudson Bay coasts they are not known to breed there.

IDENTIFICATION: Look for whirling flocks of mainly white birds the size of big sparrows along winter roads, or gleaning seeds in fields, especially well manured fields. The big flocks quickly exhaust the food supply in a field so the birds at the rear are constantly leapfrogging over those in the front. Along highways they rise and wheel away as cars approach, then cruise back to feed again before the next car comes along, flashing white or dark as the white undersides or darker upper parts are presented to view. The rolling chatter and sweet, descending whistles are characteristic, though somewhat similar to notes of the Lapland Longspur.

WINTER: On the 1968-1977 Christmas counts they were abundant to common north to Deep River and Sault Ste. Marie, with smaller numbers at certain northerly localities but absent at some. Stirrett (1973a: 21) had a winter maximum of 200 at Pelee on Jan. 7. Parker (1983: 27) reported them on 35 of 58 Christmas counts at Toronto. My wife, Doris, and I estimated 400 in a flock at Ajax on Feb. 6, 1965 (Speirs, 1973). Quilliam (1973: 196) estimated over 10,000 at Kingston on Jan. 2, 1967. They were noted on 15 of 16 Christmas counts at Barrie, with a high of 1475 on Dec. 30, 1961 (Devitt, 1967: 179). They were observed on 13 of 19 Christmas counts at Huntsville, with a high count of 145 in 1959 but "when the snow lies deep these birds are few or absent" (Mills, 1981: 190). Chris Bell noted 600 on Manitoulin on Feb. 10, 1980 (an open winter) though most go farther south in most winters (Nicholson, 1981: 197). James Foulds saw 12 on Dec. 17, 1937 at Cache Lake, Algonquin Park (MacLulich, 1938: 45). Dennison (1980: 146) reported them on all 25 Christmas counts at Sault Ste. Marie, with a high of 685 in 1979 and a low of 12 in 1970. Lee (1978: 36) cited reports of birds at Big Trout Lake during some winters.

SPRING: Stirrett (1973b: 28) had three March records at Pelee, single birds on March 14 and 17 and a flock of 2000 on March 22. Ussher (1965: 31) gave March 28 as his latest Rondeau date. One was seen at Ft. Erie as late as Apr. 14, 1960 (Beardslee & Mitchell, 1965: 450-451). Saunders (1947: 375) gave March 1 as his 13-year average departure date from Toronto: Speirs (1938: 45) listed Apr. 22 as the latest Toronto date. J.M. Richards saw one at Oshawa as late as Apr. 23, 1962 (Speirs, 1973). George A. Scott reported a flock of 5000 at Oshawa on March 1, 1970 (Tozer & Richards, 1974: 308). Charles Fothergill shot one at Rice Lake as late as Apr. 28, 1821 (Black, 1934: 160). Quilliam (1973: 196) reported a mixed flock (with Lapland Longspurs) of 200 birds at Prince Edward Point as late as Apr. 16, 1972: Weir & Quilliam (1980: 40) listed March 31 as the 26-year average departure date from Kingston, with the latest on May 8. E.L. Brereton estimated 2000 at Edenvale, Simcoe Co. on Apr. 7, 1941 and 10 near Stayner as late as May 3, 1941 (Devitt, 1967: 179). A. Kay saw 3 at Port Sydney, Muskoka, as late as May 14, 1890 (Mills, 1981: 190). D.V. Weseloh recorded the species on Manitoulin as late as May 19, 1980 (Nicholson, 1981: 197). Strickland, Tozer & Rutter (1982) had

Algonquin Park records from March 4 to May 13, with average arrival on March 8 and departure on Apr. 28. Speirs & Speirs (1947: 38) noted 5 at North Bay airport on Apr. 19, 1944 and a migration peak in mid-March. Skeel & Bondrup-Nielsen (1978: 222) had Pukaskwa records from March 30 to May 11. Denis (1961: 2) gave Apr. 5 as the average arrival date at Thunder Bay, with the earliest on March 13, 1949. Peruniak (1971: 32) gave Apr. 29 as her latest spring date for Atikokan. Elder (1979: 41) saw his earliest Geraldton migrant on March 28. Bondrup-Nielsen (1976: 45) saw his first at Kapuskasing on Apr. 20 in both 1974 and 1975. Cringan (1953a: 4) saw his first at Sioux Lookout on Apr. 24 in 1953. Oliver Hewitt saw several at Ship Sands, near Moosonee, between May 21 and May 30, 1947 (Manning, 1952: 100).

SUMMER: C.J. MacFayden and D. Scott had a very unusual summer sighting at Tiny Marsh, Simcoe Co., on July 24-25, 1975 (Goodwin, 1975: 967). In 1947 Manning (1952: 100) saw 3 at North Point, James Bay, between June 3-6; and 2 at Long Ridge Point on June 15-16 and one at Shagamu River, Hudson Bay, on July 15-16: D. MacKenzie saw one at Cape Henrietta Maria about July 20. Schueler, Baldwin & Rising (1974: 144) reported the species only at Winisk in 1965. Peck (1972: 347) saw single birds at Cape Henrietta Maria on June 23, 26 and July 3, 1970 and H. Lumsden saw a small flock at the forks of the Brant River on June 26, 1971. C.E. Hope collected individuals at Ft. Severn on June 16 and July 1, 1940.

AUTUMN: George Stirrett saw 25 at Attawapiskat on Oct. 13, 1948 (Manning, 1952: 100). D. McRae and A. Wormington had records on most days from Oct. 14 to Nov. 22, 1981 at Netitishi Point, James Bay, with a peak of 2500 on Oct. 21. In 1935 I saw my first 6 at Timmins on Oct. 24, 40 on Nov. 2, 20 on Nov. 3 and the last one on Nov. 5. Peruniak (1971: 32) gave Oct. 9 as her earliest fall record at Atikokan. W. Wyett had Pukaskwa records from Oct. 3 (1975) to Oct. 29 (1976) (Skeel & Bondrup-Nielsen, 1978: 222). Speirs & Speirs (1947: 38) noted their first at North Bay on Nov. 11, 1944 with the migration peak in late November. Strickland, Tozer & Rutter (1982) had Algonquin Park records from Sept. 21 to Dec. 9, with average arrival on Oct. 16 and departure on Nov. 11. Nicholson (1981: 197) gave Oct. 12 as a 12-year average arrival date on Manitoulin, with the earliest on Sept. 26, 1980 and the high count of 600 on Oct. 29, 1968. Mills (1981: 189) reported a sighting by M. Withers at Interlaken, Muskoka, as early as Oct. 10, 1974. Devitt (1967: 179) gave Oct. 13, 1936 as his earliest Wasaga Beach record. Weir & Quilliam (1980: 40) listed Oct. 22 as the 25-year average arrival date at Kingston, with the earliest on Sept. 16. Jack Satterly saw 6 at Atherly on Oct. 16, 1965 (Speirs, 1973). Fleming (1907: 80) gave Oct. 10 as his earliest Toronto record: Saunders (1947: 375) listed Nov. 7 as his 11-year average fall arrival date there. Wm. Girling noted 6 at Port Stanley as early as Oct. 14, 1934. (Brooman, 1954: 40). Ussher (1965: 31) gave Nov. 4 as his earliest Rondeau record. Stirrett (1973d: 30) had his earliest 2 at Pelee on Oct. 23.

BANDING: One banded by H.H. Southam near Toronto on March 22, 1940 was recovered near the western shore of the Strait of Belle Isle in Labrador on Apr. 4, 1942. Gordon Lambert banded another near Toronto on Feb. 4, 1961: this was recovered near St. Anthony, Newfoundland about Apr. 27, 1961. A third Toronto bird, banded by David Hussell on Jan. 25, 1976, also turned up near St. Anthony on May 1, 1977. One banded near Kapuskasing on May 11, 1936 turned up in Massachusetts in Dec., 1939. Two birds banded in the Upper Peninsula of Michigan wound up near Kapuskasing: one banded on

March 10, 1933 was recovered on Apr. 13, 1936 and the other banded on Feb. 7, 1947 was recovered on Apr. 6, 1947. One banded near Sorel, Quebec, on Nov. 3, 1950 was recovered near Ottawa on Dec. 31, 1950. Four other birds banded in the Upper Peninsula of Michigan no doubt passed through Ontario to be recovered on the west shore of Greenland. I am indebted to Peter Lockhart, who has banded a great many Snow Buntings, for some of this information.

**MEASUREMENTS:**
*Length:* 6.0 to 7.4 ins.
(Godfrey, 1966: 406)
*Wingspread:* 11.60 to
12.75 ins. (Roberts,
1955: 713)
*Weight:* 1.25 to. 1.50 oz.
(Roberts, 1955: 713).

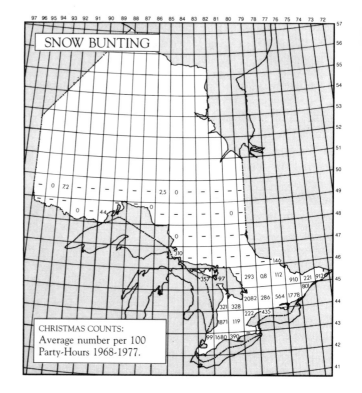

SNOW BUNTING

CHRISTMAS COUNTS:
Average number per 100
Party-Hours 1968-1977.

# BOBOLINK   *Dolichonyx oryzivorus*   (Linnaeus)

Bobolinks generally arrive in Ontario as small flocks of ecstatically musical males in early May. They breed in old fields and some cultivated crops where the males spend most of their time singing and chasing one another, or pouncing on any female that shows itself above the weed tops. They go south to southern Brazil or northern Argentina in winter. Southbound flocks used to be a menace to rice crops in the Carolinas (the specific name *oryzivorus* means *rice eater*). In Ontario where they eat many harmful insects and weed seeds, their food habits are considered beneficial.

IDENTIFICATION: Male Bobolinks with "their dress suits on backwards" are unmistakable. Females look like big yellow sparrows; as do the males after their mid-summer moult before leaving for the south. The song is an ecstatic outburst, often given from mid-air but frequently also from a weed top or fence and when arriving in spring from a fruit tree in bloom. The song reminds me of banjo music "de-gurgo-gingle, ting- tnago——". Migrants in spring and in August are often heard overhead giving their characteristic "pink" note.

WINTER: One bird, in the Fleming collection (now in ROM) was taken at Toronto on Dec. 20, 1896. James, McLaren & Barlow (1976: 47) mentioned a Dec. 5 date.

SPRING: Stirrett (1973b: 25) gave Apr. 25 for the earliest one at Pelee, with a maximum of 100 on May 15. Ussher (1965: 27) gave May 3 as the 18-year average arrival date at Rondeau, with the earliest on Apr. 29. Saunders & Dale (1933: 234) gave May 2 as the 17-year average arrival date at London, with the earliest on Apr. 25, 1913. Snyder (1931: 192) reported Long Point migrants from May 4 to 25, in 1928. Fleming (1907: 78) gave Apr. 19 as his earliest Toronto date, where Saunders (1947: 373) listed May 10 as his average arrival date and Speirs (1938: 43) gave May 23 as the spring peak date. My earliest Frenchman Bay record was on Apr. 28, 1935 (Speirs, 1974). R. Henry *et al* saw one in Darlington Twp. as early as Apr. 21, 1960: two early nests, both with 6 eggs, were reported, one near Oshawa on May 29, 1957 and the other near Whitby, on May 31, 1957 (Tozer & Richards, 1974: 263). Weir & Quilliam (1980: 39) listed May 4 as the 32-year average arrival date at Kingston, with the earliest on Apr. 27. Devitt (1967: 152) gave May 5 as the 16-year average arrival date at Barrie, with the earliest on May 1, 1954. L. Beamer's median arrival date at Meaford was May 13, with the earliest on Apr. 30, 1949. C.E. Johnson observed courtship behaviour at Ottawa on May 24, 1921 (Lloyd, 1923: 155). P. Taverner saw one at Beaumarais as early as May 7, 1898 but the 7-year average arrival date at Huntsville was May 14 (Mills, 1981: 154). Nicholson (1981: 175) gave May 12 as the 11-year average arrival date on Manitoulin, with the earliest on May 3, 1979. Speirs & Speirs (1947: 36) saw one at North Bay on May 11, 1944. Skeel & Bondrup-Nielsen (1978: 210) reported one singing at Pukaskwa on May 27, 1977. Denis (1961: 4) gave May 20 as the average arrival date at Thunder Bay, with the earliest on May 12, 1938.

SUMMER: On the 1968-1977 Breeding Bird Surveys, they were abundant on the Kincardine and Bourget routes, common elsewhere in the agricultural south, becoming uncommon to absent on most northern routes, except in western Rainy River, again in agricultural areas. Stirrett (1973c: 21) estimated 10,000 at Pelee on Aug. 14 at the peak of the southward migration. Kelley (1978: 79) mentioned a nest with eggs in Lambton Co. as early as June 3, 1972. Saunders & Dale (1933: 234) reported three sets of eggs taken near London: a set of 4 eggs on June 4, 1906; a set of 5 on June 6, 1907 and a set of 4 on June 11, 1917. Baillie & Harrington (1937: 256) reported a set of 6 eggs taken by F. Starr at Port Burwell on June 5, 1924. Snyder (1931: 193) reported the first two southbound birds at Long Point on July 11, 1927. McCracken, Bradstreet & Holroyd (1981: 64) noted singing males on Long Point from June 10 (1966) to July 7 (1978) but found no nests there. Beardslee & Mitchell (1965: 399) reported a nest with 4 eggs at Fort Erie on July 8, 1938. Speirs (1938: 51) gave Aug. 23 as the peak of the fall migration at Toronto. Bobolinks were found on 9 of 11 field quadrats studied in Ontario Co. in 1965 and were the second most abundant species, averaging 19.2 birds per 100 acres, with a high of 68 per 100 acres on the Pickering Twp. plot (Speirs & Orenstein, 1967: 182). George A. Scott found a nest with 5 eggs near Whitby as late as June 30, 1957 (Tozer & Richards, 1974: 263). Allin (1940: 106-107) saw fully-fledged young in Darlington Twp. on July 27, 1927. Snyder (1941: 82) reported 6 pairs in a 10 to 15 acre field at Hallowell, Prince Edward Co., in the summer of 1930. Lawrie (1937: 5) reported 4 nests on a 20-acre quadrat on York Downs, north of Toronto, from June 8 to 16, 1937, as well as three nearby nests from May 27 to June 13, 1937. Quilliam (1973: 169) reported two nests near Kingston, both with 5 eggs, one found on May 31, 1899 by C.K. Clarke, the other found June 12, 1922 by E. Beaupré . H.P. Bingham found a nest with 6 eggs near Barrie as early as June 1, 1922 and a nest with 5 eggs there as late as July 12, 1919 (Devitt, 1967: 152). C.E. Johnson observed young being fed at Ottawa on June 25, 1922 (Lloyd, 1923: 155). Mills (1981: 154) found a nest with 3 young at Magnetawan on June 19, 1975. Paul Harrington found a nest with 5 eggs at Perivale, Manitoulin, on June 9, 1938 (Nicholson, 1981: 175). Mark Robinson reported one of the few Algonquin Park sightings on June 2, 1932 (MacLulich, 1938: 36). Speirs & Speirs (1947: 36) saw a female with bill full of nesting material near North Bay on June 7, 1945. Baillie & Hope (1947: 27) saw flying young, just out of the nest, at Bigwood on July 20, 1937 and observed a pair at Biscotasing from June 9-14, 1941. Snyder (1942: 146-147) collected young birds, just out of the nest, at Maclennan, near Sault Ste. Marie, on July 18 and 25, 1931. Skeel & Bondrup-Nielsen (1978: 210) flushed 3 or 4 at Pukaskwa Depot on June 16, 1977. David Elder saw one at Atikokan on June 10, 1981. Elder (1979: 39) reported a pair in old fields at Neys, on Lake Superior east of Terrace Bay, in the summers of 1971 and 1972. I was surprised to find a male singing at White River during several June visits, up to 1982. Smith (1957: 179) reported birds at New Liskeard on July 22, 1954, at South Porcupine on June 19, 1953 and near Lillabelle Lake, Cochrane, on July 13, 1953. Sam Waller attested to the fact that one was shot at Moose Factory by Robert McLeod (Baillie & Harrington, 1937: 256). Lee (1978: 33) observed a singing male flying over Big Trout Lake settlement on June 28, 1975.

AUTUMN: Speirs & Speirs (1947: 36) saw their last two at Nipissing Junction, near North Bay, on Aug. 31, 1944. Nicholson (1981: 176) saw one on Manitoulin as late as Oct. 2, 1976. Donald Sutherland saw a very late one at Beausoleil Is. on Oct. 14, 1976, although most leave the cottage country by Sept. 1 (Mills, 1981: 155). Devitt (1967: 152) gave Sept. 14 as the latest Simcoe Co. record, at Holland River: only two casualties were found at the Barrie TV tower in 7 years, both on Sept. 12, 1961. Weir & Quilliam (1980: 39) listed Sept. 5 as the 26-year average departure date from Kingston, with the latest on Sept. 26. Doug. Scovell and Earl Stark found one lingering in the marshes at the mouth of Duffin Creek, Pickering, as late as Nov. 22, 1959 (Speirs, 1974). Saunders (1947: 373) listed Sept. 16 as his average departure date from Toronto, with a very late one on Nov. 12. Beardslee & Mitchell (1965: 399) reported one seen by many observers in the marsh at Dunnville as late as Oct. 25, 1953. Snyder (1931: 193) reported Long Point lighthouse casualties: 32 on Sept. 7, 5 on Sept. 9 and one between Sept. 24 and 29, 1929. Ussher (1965: 27) gave Sept. 6 as his 8-year average departure date from Rondeau, with the latest on Sept. 17. Stirrett (1973d: 27) reported 200 at Pelee as late as Sept. 18, with the latest one on Oct. 9.

**MEASUREMENTS:**

*Length:* 6.5 to 8.0 ins. (Godfrey, 1966: 351)
*Wingspread:* 10 1/4 to 12 1/2 ins. (Roberts, 1955: 689)
*Weight:* 20 Ontario specimens averaged 24.5 g. Males average larger than females.

**REFERENCE:**

Joyner, David E. 1978 Use of an old-field habitat by Bobolinks and Red-winged Blackbirds. Can Field-Naturalist, 92: (4): 383-386. 10 Bobolink nests were found on a 15.4 ha. field at Luther Marsh, from May 20 to June 30, 1977: tops of nests were flush with litter top: goldenrod, vetch, clover & dandelion were the chief cover.

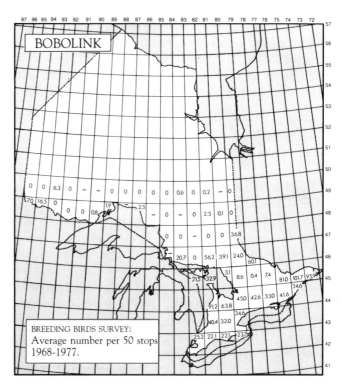

BOBOLINK

BREEDING BIRDS SURVEY:
Average number per 50 stops
1968-1977.

# RED-WINGED BLACKBIRD  *Agelaius phoeniceus*  (Linnaeus)

Cattail marshes are the preferred habitat of nesting Red-winged Blackbirds in Ontario, but this is an adaptable species and many now nest in old fields and shrubbery. Large flocks sometimes descend on corn crops in late summer and may do considerable damage if not frightened off. When our marshes freeze over in late fall, most of our birds go south to winter from South Carolina to northern Florida, but a few are found near feeding stations in southern Ontario through the winter and some glean corn after the harvest.

IDENTIFICATION: Males are mainly black with prominent scarlet "shoulder" patches, often bordered with yellow. Females are smaller than males and are striped birds with dull orange throats. The usual song of the territorial males is a rich "o-ka-lee". Both males and females have a rich vocabulary of shrill whistles and clucks and may vigorously attack when their nests are approached.

WINTER: On the 1968-1977 Christmas counts they were common along the north shore of Lake Erie, fairly common near the north shore of Lake Ontario, becoming rare north to Deep River and the shores of Lake Superior. Stirrett (1973a: 19) had a winter maximum of 1750 at Pelee on Dec. 13. Ussher (1965: 27) wrote: "often occurs in winter" at Rondeau. Beardslee & Mitchell (1965: 403) mentioned an early migration with 16 seen on the Canadian shore of Lake Erie on Feb. 21, 1954. Saunders (1947: 378) reported the species on 8 of 21 Christmas counts at Toronto, from 1925 to 1945, with a maximum of 13 on Dec. 22, 1935. Quilliam (1973: 171) reported some on 17 of 24 Christmas counts at Kingston, with a maximum of 105 birds on Jan. 2, 1967. Devitt (1967: 154) had a few winter records of single birds in Simcoe Co., one at a feeding station at Port Severn as late as Jan. 24, 1965. Mills (1981: 157) reported single birds on three Huntsville Christmas counts and six there on Feb. 1, 1972 and four on Feb. 2, 1973. Nicholson (1981: 177) gave Jan. 1, 1972 as his latest winter date for Manitoulin. Dennison (1980: 148) reported one on 1 of 25 Christmas counts at Sault Ste. Marie. One was recorded on the 1976 Christmas count at Marathon (Skeel & Bondrup-Nielsen, 1978: 211).

SPRING: Stirrett (1973b: 25) had a spring maximum of 25,000 at Pelee on Apr. 26. Kelley (1978: 80) gave Apr. 26, 1968, as her earliest nesting: a nest with 5 eggs in Lambton Co. Ussher (1965: 27) had his 22-year average arrival date at Rondeau on March 11. Saunders & Dale (1933: 234) gave March 14 as the 17-year average arrival date for London, with the earliest on March 5, 1921: a set of 4 eggs was found as early as May 12, 1914 and several other sets later in May. Beardslee & Mitchell (1965: 402-404) reported 4 young out of the nest at Mud Lake as early as May 22, 1954. Saunders (1947: 373) gave March 18 as the average arrival date at Toronto: Speirs (1938: 43) listed May 3 as the spring peak there. J.M. Richards found two nests, one with 1 egg and one with two eggs as early as May 6, 1963, near Oshawa (Tozer & Richards, 1974: 267). Allin (1940: 107) found a nest with 4 eggs in Darlington Twp. on May 28, 1928. Charles Fothergill reported them at Rice Lake as early as March 20, 1822 and gave a detailed description of their nest building habits (Black, 1934: 156). Snyder (1941: 83) gave March 16, 1936 as his earliest date for Prince Edward Co. and found the earliest nest, with 5 eggs, on May 28, 1930 at Hallowell. Lawrie (1937: 5) listed eight nests found at York Downs, north of Toronto, from May 28 to June 8, 1937: 4 with 3 eggs, 3 with 4 eggs and one with 5 young. Weir & Quilliam (1980: 39) gave March 9 as the 32-year average arrival date at

Kingston for males, with Apr. 5 for females. Devitt (1967: 154) gave March 22 as the 21-year average arrival date for Barrie, with the earliest full set of eggs found there on May 9, 1938, by H.P. Bingham. L. Beamer's median arrival date at Meaford was March 22, with the earliest on March 8, 1954. Mills (1981: 157) gave March 21 as the 16-year average arrival date at Huntsville, with the earliest on March 1, 1959. Nicholson (1981: 177) gave March 27 as a 10-year average arrival date for Manitoulin, with the earliest on March 5, 1973. MacLulich (1938: 37) gave March 25, 1913 as his earliest Algonquin Park record. Louise Lawernce saw two at Pimisi Bay on March 19, 1945 (Speirs & Speirs, 1947: 36). Ricker & Clarke (1939: 21) found a nest with 3 eggs at Frank's Bay, Lake Nipissing, on May 28, 1933. Skeel & Bondrup-Nielsen (1978: 211) saw their first at Pukaskwa on Apr. 12, 1977, then 17 on 11 days from Apr. 15, to May 28 along the Lake Superior shore: W. Wyett saw "many" at Soldier Lake on May 19, 1976. Denis (1961: 2) gave Apr. 13 as the average arrival date at Thunder Bay, with the earliest on March 24, 1946. Peruniak (1971: 28) gave March 29 as her earliest Atikokan date. Elder (1979: 39) gave Apr. 21 as his earliest at Geraldton. Bondrup-Nielsen (1976: 45) saw his first near Kapuskasing on Apr. 21, 1974. Cringan (1953a: 3) saw his first at Sioux Lookout on Apr. 15 in 1953. Cringan (1950: 17) gave May 17 as the 1950 arrival date in the Asheweig area. Sam Waller collected one at Moose Factory on May 30, 1930 (Manning, 1952: 86).

SUMMER: On the 1968-1977 Breeding Bird Surveys they were abundant in the agricultural part of southern Ontario, becoming fairly common on northern Ontario routes. The summer maximum at Pelee was 1000 (Stirrett, 1973c: 21). Saunders & Dale (1933: 234) found a nest with 4 eggs on June 3, 1914 at London. Brooman (1954: 35) found three nests on June 5, 1949 about 2 miles southeast of St. Thomas. McCracken, Bradstreet & Holroyd (1981: 64) reported a breeding density as high as 3607 territories per km $^2$ in a Long Point cattail marsh, were 50% of 636 nestings were found; 29% were in sedges and grasses; 14% in shrubs or small trees and 7% in weedy cover: two broods were sometimes raised and egg dates ranged from May 3 to July 12. R.F. Andrle found a nest with 4 young on July 8, 1944 at Sherkston (Beardslee & Mitchell, 1965: 402-403). This species ranked seventh as a nesting bird in fields of Ontario Co., with a maximum density of 53 birds per 100 acres in the Pickering quadrat (Speirs & Orenstein, 1967: 182). R. Tozer found a breeding density of 77 birds per 100 acres in Cranberry Marsh: of 259 sets reported in Ontario Co., only 3 contained cowbird eggs (11), with 790 eggs of the host (Speirs, 1974). Allin (1940: 107) found an unusual nest in Darlington Twp. on June 9, 1933, at least 15 ft. up in a red maple tree. Lawrie (1937: 5) listed five nests for the 20-acre quadrat on the York Downs field north of Toronto from June 8 to 18, 1937. Quilliam (1973: 171) wrote that this was the commonest bird on the breeding bird surveys near Kingston. H.P. Bingham found a nest with 4 eggs near Barrie as late as July 22, 1917. Lloyd (1923: 155) found a nest with 4 eggs at Black Rapids, near Ottawa, on June 4, 1921. Mills (1981: 155) reported 82 nests in the cottage country, some with eggs from May 22 to July 6. D.B. Ferguson found a nest with 4 eggs near Mindemoya on June 13, 1976 (Nicholson, 1981: 177). Stuart Thompson found a nest with 4 eggs at Hogan's Lake, Algonquin Park, on June 1, 1934 (MacLulich, 1938: 37). Louise Lawrence found 5 nests at Pimisi Bay on June 3, 1944: one with 4 young, one with 3 young and 1 egg, the other three with eggs (Speirs & Speirs, 1947: 36). Baillie & Hope (1947: 27) collected two young at Bigwood on July 15, 1937. Snyder (1942: 147) reported eggs as early as June 5, 1931 in the Sault Ste. Marie region. D. Hoy and W. Wyett reported 15 in early June, 1976 along the upper Swallow River lakes, Pukaskwa (Skeel & Bondrup-Nielsen, 1978: 211). Baillie & Hope

(1943: 23) saw only one or two at Rossport, on June 5, 1936. Snyder (1928: 266) collected a pair at Lake Nipigon that had just completed a nest on June 28, 1924. Dear (1940: 140) found a nest with 4 eggs at Thunder Bay on June 16, 1934 and a nest with 3 eggs at Whitefish Lake on June 17, 1938. Snyder (1938: 207) found a nest with 3 eggs at Off Lake, Rainy River, on July 1, 1927. Peruniak (1971: 28) banded nestlings at Atikokan from nests in cattail, willow, marsh grass and sweet gale. Snyder (1953: 84) reported scattered colonies from Malachi east to Savanne and north to Sioux Lookout. Snyder (1928: 26) saw females carrying food to young at Lake Abitibi in 1925 and Smith (1957: 179) found nests there. James (1980: 90) reported single males at Central Patricia in the summers of 1977 and 1979. Hope (1938: 42) found a nest with 3 eggs one foot up in a small willow at Favourable Lake on June 8, 1938: large flocks were encountered there in late July. Cringan (1950: 17) found a nest with 4 eggs and an empty nest on June 27, 1950 in the North Caribou River marsh, with up to 15 birds there. Manning (1952: 86) reported collecting birds at Sandy Is., near Moosonee, and north to Long Ridge Point, during the early part of June, 1947 and 1949, with 35 seen at North Point on June 3, 1947. Schueler, Baldwin & Rising (1974: 144) found them common at Cochrane and Moosonee, uncommon at Attawapiskat and Winisk. Peck (1972: 346) reported stragglers at Cape Henrietta Maria: a male collected by T.M. Shortt on July 20, 1948 and two females seen there by Harry Lumsden on June 28, 1964. Lee (1978: 33) saw a single male at Big Trout Lake on June 2, 1975.

AUTUMN: Peruniak (1971: 28) gave Sept. 6 as her latest Atikokan date. Speirs & Speirs (1947: 36) saw one near North Bay on Oct. 22, 1944. Nicholson (1981: 177) reported a high count of 900 on Manitoulin on Oct. 31, 1976. C. Harris counted 350 on Oct. 6, 1973 at Go Home Bay and 120 there on Oct. 30, 1977 (Mills, 1981: 157). Snyder (1941: 83) gave Nov. 23, 1935 as his latest Prince Edward Co. record. Saunders (1947: 373) gave Nov. 2 as his average departure date from Toronto: Speirs (1938: 51) listed Oct. 19 as the fall peak date there. Marshall Field counted at least 100 in small groups migrating near the Lake Erie shore of Elgin Co. on Nov. 12, 1950 (Brooman, 1954: 35). Ussher (1965: 27) gave Nov. 9 as his 8-year average departure date from Rondeau. Stirrett (1973d: 19) had a fall maximum of 250,000 at Pelee on Nov. 17.

BANDING: Brewer & Salvadori (1978: 80-82) documented and mapped recoveries of Ontario birds recovered over 1000 km. to the south in winter: 5 in South Carolina, 5 in Georgia, 2 in northwestern Florida and one in Alabama. The most distant recoveries (about 1400 km or 870 miles away) were in southern Georgia and northwestern Florida. The only distant recovery of a bird banded as a nestling was in western Virginia in early December. Many of our birds pass through Ohio: 18 of our birds were found there and 27 of their birds were later found in Ontario. One bird banded near Toronto on Apr. 22, 1966 was recovered two springs later near Montreal, on May 12, 1968. One banded near Toronto on Nov. 8, 1964 turned up in Maryland on Feb. 6, 1965, so they do not all go to the sunny south in winter.

## MEASUREMENTS:

*Length:* 7 1/2 to 10 ins.
(Godfrey, 1966: 355) ♂
larger than ♀
*Wingspread:* 12 to 14 1/2
ins. (Roberts, 1955: 690).
*Weight:* 20 Ontario males
averaged 66 g., 11 females
45 g.

## REFERENCES:

Blomme, Chris 1978 An
albino Red-winged
Blackbird at Burwash,
Ontario. Ont. Field
Biologist, 32: (1): 47.

Fairfield, George 1961 A
nesting study of Red-
winged Blackbirds. Ont.
Field Biologist, No.
15: 24-25.

Judd, W.W. 1960 Red-
winged Blackbird nesting
in a New England Aster.
Fed. Ont. Naturalists Bull.
88: 29.

Nero, Robert W. 1984
Redwings. Smithsonian
Institution Press.
Washington, D.C.: 1-100.
A fine study of the Red-
winged Blackbird:
behaviour, life history,
migrations, and control
measures.

Taylor, Robert R. 1959
Red-winged Blackbird's
nest with a roof. Ont. Field
Biologist, No. 13: 35.

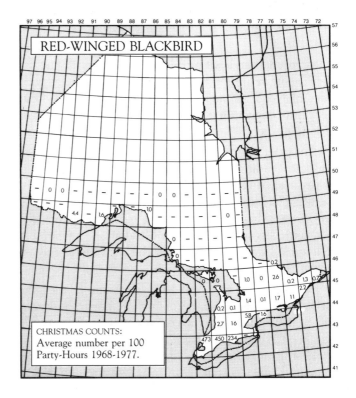

RED-WINGED BLACKBIRD

CHRISTMAS COUNTS:
Average number per 100
Party-Hours 1968-1977.

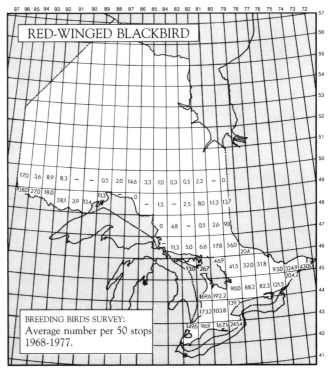

RED-WINGED BLACKBIRD

BREEDING BIRDS SURVEY:
Average number per 50 stops
1968-1977.

# EASTERN MEADOWLARK   *Sturnella magna*   (Linnaeus)

A few meadowlarks winter in southern Ontario but it is generally late March or early April before returning migrants brighten our fields with song. Savannah Sparrows and Bobolinks often are more numerous in our southern Ontario fields but meadowlarks rival them in frequency of occurrence: just about every large field has its quota. Most of our birds go to the southern United States in winter.

IDENTIFICATION:   The Eastern Meadowlark is much the same size and shape as the European Starling, but with prominent white outer tail feathers showing in flight. The breast is bright yellow with a black crescent across it. It is most easily distinguished from the Western Meadowlark by song and call. The song is a sweet, sliding whistle "see-ooh-tsee-iih: and the call a lip-smacking roll, very different from the "maids, maids, hold up your petticoats" of the Western Meadowlark song and its loud "klok" call note. (When we lived in Illinois we found that the birds there sang songs intermediate between typical eastern and western birds.)

WINTER:   On the 1968-1977 Christmas counts, they were fairly common near the north shore of Lake Erie, becoming rare north to Ottawa and Manitoulin Island. Stirrett (1973a: 19) had a winter maximum of 20 at Pelee on Feb. 20. Ussher (1965: 27) wrote that "it often occurs in winter" at Rondeau. Saunders & Dale (1933: 234) reported a flock of 7 near Bryanston on Dec. 23, 1922 and noted a few "almost every winter" near London. Brooman (1954: 35) reported wintering flocks (up to 50) in Elgin Co. Wishart Campbell and R.M. Saunders found a flock of 50 on the Ajax fields on Dec. 19, 1954 (Speirs, 1974). Charles Fothergill saw one on Feb. 10 during the severe winter of 1831 on the Lake Ontario shore in Clarke Twp., Durham Co. (Black, 1934: 156). Devitt (1967: 153) reported a Barrie Christmas count maximum of 13 on Jan. 3, 1960. L. Beamer found a bird with an injured wing near Meaford during the second week of January, 1957. Mills (1981: 156) mentioned one seen at Huntsville on Dec. 18, 1966 and two at Burks Falls on Dec. 2, 1968. Nicholson (1981: 176) found one as late as Jan. 8, 1972 on Manitoulin.

SPRING:   Stirrett (1973b: 25) had a spring maximum of 35 at Pelee on March 25. Ussher (1965: 27) gave March 17 as his 23-year average arrival date at Rondeau. Saunders & Dale (1933: 234) gave March 16 as the 17-year average arrival date at London: he mentioned five May nestings, one set of 5 eggs plus one cowbird egg as early as May 10, 1913. Saunders (1947: 373) listed March 23 as his average arrival date at Toronto, where the spring peak was Apr. 7 (Speirs, 1938: 43). Tozer & Richards (1974: 264) found a nest with 4 eggs near Whitby as early as May 16, 1965. Allin (1940: 107) took a set of 4 eggs in Darlington Twp. on May 18, 1932. Snyder (1941: 83) gave March 22, as his 1938 arrival date in Prince Edward Co. Lawrie (1937: 5) reported a nest with 5 young at York Downs, just north of Toronto, as early as May 27, 1937: also a nest with 4 eggs and another with 5 eggs there on May 28. Weir & Quilliam (1980: 39) listed March 18 as the 32-year average arrival date at Kingston. Quilliam (1973: 170) reported a nest with 4 eggs near Kingston on May 20, 1905 and two nests with eggs on May 22, 1963. Devitt (1967: 152) gave March 30 as the 23-year average arrival date for Barrie and Colling-wood: W.W. Smith found a nest with young as early as May 22, 1938 at Big Cedar Point. L. Beamer's median arrival date for Meaford was March 25, with the earliest on March 10, 1946. C.G. Eifrig found a nest with eggs at Ottawa as early as May 11 (Lloyd,

1923: 155). Mills (1981: 155) gave Apr. 5 as the 16-year average arrival date at Huntsville, with the earliest on March 12, 1973. Nicholson (1981: 176) gave March 13 as the 9-year average arrival date on Manitoulin, with the earliest on Feb. 27, 1971 and a maximum of 30 on Apr. 26, 1970. MacLulich (1938: 37) gave Apr. 13, 1912, as the earliest Algonquin Park date. Speirs & Speirs (1947: 36) cited a Rutherglen observation by Louise Lawrence as early as March 23, 1945. J. Coyne saw at least two at Gogama during May, 1954 and F. Cowell saw one at Timmins on May 11, 1954 (Smith, 1957: 179). Baillie (1925: 194) saw and heard one at Englehart, with L.L. Snyder, on May 31, 1925. Bondrup-Nielsen (1976: 45) reported one near Kapuskasing on Apr. 20, 1974.

SUMMER: On the 1968-1977 Breeding Bird Surveys they were common on routes in the agricultural parts of southern Ontario, most abundant on the Avonmore route in eastern Ontario, becoming uncommon north to Haileybury and absent on northern routes. Stirrett (1973c: 21) had a summer maximum of 27 at Pelee on June 30. Saunders & Dale (1933: 234) reported a nest with 5 eggs as late as June 28, 1907. McCracken, Bradstreet & Holroyd (1981: 64) reported a breeding density of 21 territories per km $^2$ in a dune-swale-savannah quadrat on Long Point and knew of 18 nest records with egg dates from May 14 to July 10. In our field studies in Ontario Co., this was the only species with appreciable populations on all eleven township quadrats, with an average population density of 15 birds per 100 acres (Speirs & Orenstein, 1967: 182). Of 17 nests found in Ontario Co., 3 held 3 eggs, 8 held 4 and 6 held 5: J.A. Edwards found a nest with 3 eggs on Thorah Is. as late as Aug. 3, 1939 (Speirs, 1974). Lawrie (1937: 5) reported a nest with 3 eggs on May 30 and a nest with 1 egg and 2 young on June 11 on a 20-acre quadrat on York Downs, north of Toronto, in 1937. E. Beaupré found a nest with 6 eggs near Kingston on June 10, 1898 (Quilliam, 1973: 170). Ottelyn Addison found a nest with 5 eggs at Wyevale on July 5, 1957 (Devitt, 1967: 152). W. Crins found a nest with 4 eggs at McKellar, Parry Sound Dist., on June 3, 1978 (Mills, 1981: 155), the only known nest for the cottage country. Kenneth Bennison found a nest with 5 eggs in mid-July,, 1979 on Manitoulin (Nicholson, 1981: 176). Ricker & Clarke (1939: 21) observed young just able to fly at Lake Nipissing on June 16, 1925. Baillie & Hope (1947: 27) encountered flying juveniles on July 18, 19 and 26, 1937 at Bigwood. Harry Graham found a nest with 4 eggs at Sault Ste. Marie on July 1, 1937 (Snyder, 1942: 147). Fred Helleiner et al noted three (two singing) about 6 miles south of Cochrane from July 9-12, 1955 (Baillie, 1955: 377). Schueler, Baldwin & Rising (1974: 147) heard about three singing at Attawapiskat on June 22, 1971.

AUTUMN: Vonnie Heron saw about 45 at Huntsville on Sept. 29, 1972 and D. Sutherland found 5 on Beausoleil Is. on Oct. 11, 1976 (Mills, 1981: 156). Weir & Quilliam (1980: 39) listed Nov. 30 as the 28-year average departure date from Kingston. Ken Adcoe reported at least 110 on the Ajax fields on Oct. 15, 1965 (Speirs, 1974). Speirs (1938: 51) gave Oct. 13 as the fall peak for Toronto. Saunders (1947: 373) listed Oct. 17 as his average departure date from Toronto. Ussher (1965: 27) gave Nov. 8 as his 8-year average departure date from Rondeau. Stirrett (1973d: 28) reported fall maxima of 500 at Pelee on Oct. 12 and Oct. 15.

BANDING: One banded near Toronto on Apr. 27, 1958 was recovered in South Carolina on Dec. 12, 1958.

## MEASUREMENTS:

*Length:* 8.5 to 11 ins.
(Godfrey, 1966: 352). ♂
larger than ♀ .
*Wingspread:* 15 1/4 to 16
1/2 ins. (Roberts,
1955: 693)
*Weight:* 5 Ontario males
averaged 120 g., 2 females
90 g.

## REFERENCES:

Baillie, Jas. L., Jr. 1925
Meadowlark at Englehart,
Ontario. Can. Field-Nat.,
39: (8): 194.

D'Agincourt, Lorraine
Gouges 1981 Aspects of
repertoire use in the
Eastern Meadowlark
(*Sturnella magna*). Univ.
Toronto, MSc Thesis: i-ix;
1-119.

D'Agincourt, Lorraine G.
& J. Bruce Falls 1983
Variation of repertoire use
in the Eastern Meadowlark,
*Sturnella magna.* Can.
Journ. Zool.,
61: (5): 1086-1093.

Falls, J. Bruce & Lorraine
G. D'Agincourt 1981 A
comparison of neighbor-
stranger discrimination in
Eastern and Western
Meadowlarks. Can. Journ.
Zool., 59: (12): 2380-
2385.

Falls, J. Bruce & Lorraine
G. D'Agincourt 1982 Why
do meadowlarks switch
song-types? Can. Journ.
Zool., 80: (12): 3400-
3408.

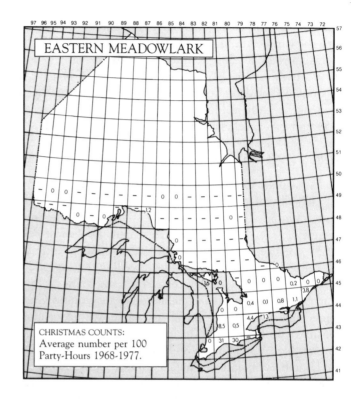

EASTERN MEADOWLARK

CHRISTMAS COUNTS:
Average number per 100
Party-Hours 1968-1977.

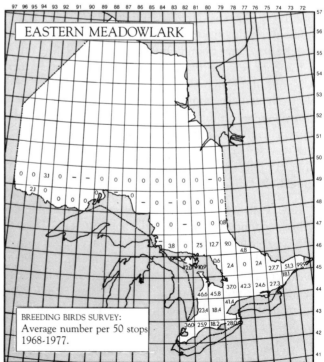

EASTERN MEADOWLARK

BREEDING BIRDS SURVEY:
Average number per 50 stops
1968-1977.

# WESTERN MEADOWLARK   *Sturnella neglecta*   Audubon

This is the meadowlark of western North America, including Ontario from Lake Superior to the Manitoba border. A few occur elsewhere in Ontario but are greatly outnumbered by the Eastern Meadowlark. The two are closely related and are considered to form a "superspecies".

IDENTIFICATION: For the vocal differences between this and the Eastern Meadowlark see that species. The visual differences are less obvious but the Western is a grayer bird with more obvious bars on the flight feathers. The Eastern Meadowlark has a yellow throat and in the Western this yellow extends up its cheeks almost to the eyes. (Movie goers will recognize the songs of Western Meadowlarks in almost all Hollywood movies made out of doors, even those supposed to represent scenes in India and other far away places.)

WINTER: Two were reported near St. Catharines on a Christmas count on Dec. 31, 1961 (Beardslee & Mitchell, 1965: 401).

SPRING: Stirrett (1973b: 25) had six spring records at Pelee, from Apr. 19 to May 14. Brooman (1954: 35) cited several spring records for Elgin Co., one as early as Apr. 9, 1950 near St. Thomas. Beardslee & Mitchell (1965: 401) cited several records near Rathfon Point, one as early as Apr. 8, 1962. Saunders (1947: 79-80) reported one at Barton, near Hamilton, on Apr. 7, 1946. George A. Scott observed one at Oshawa on Apr. 1, 1962 and Charles Long noted one at Pickering Beach on Apr. 4, 1969: several have been heard later in the spring, especially near Oshawa (Speirs, 1974). A.E. Hughes and F. Cooke found the first for the Kingston region, on Wolfe Is., on May 30, 1969: Weir & Quilliam (1980: 39) listed Apr. 30 as a 4-year average arrival date in subsequent years, with the earliest on Apr. 12. Frank Munro observed the first for Simcoe Co. on May 9, 1953: a pair located by Frances Westman on May 16, 1968 was seen the next day by Devitt (1967: 153). Mills (1981: 156) cited three Muskoka records: May 18, 1958 at Bracebridge, May 23, 1966 in Morrison Twp. and Apr. 27, 1967 at Huntsville. Nicholson (1981: 176) reported a Manitoulin bird as early as Apr. 11, 1970. Denis (1961: 2) gave Apr. 11 as the average arrival date at Thunder Bay, with the earliest on March 15, 1942. Dear (1940: 140) found a nest with 5 eggs in McIntyre Twp., Thunder Bay, on May 30, 1934 and considered them common in cultivated regions near there. Peruniak (1971: 27) found them rare at Atikokan: her earliest record was on May 10, 1957 and she had subsequent May records in 1959, 1962 and 1966: David Elder saw his first there on May 4 in 1981. Elder (1979: 39) had two spring records for Geraldton, on May 26, 1965 and Apr. 25, 1968, both singing birds. Hope (1938: 42) saw a single bird at Favourable Lake, on May 31, 1938. Cringan (1953a: 3) saw his first at Sioux Lookout on May 24 in 1953.

SUMMER: On the 1968-1977 Breeding Bird Surveys they were uncommon to absent on most routes, but were common in farmland in extreme western Ontario, from Rainy River to Lake of the Woods. Stirrett (1973c: 21) had two summer records for Pelee (July 4 and July 22). Kelley (1978: 79) reported nesting in Essex and Lambton Counties. Brooman (1954: 35) reported one near Wallacetown in late June, 1949 and another near St. Thomas on July 12, 1950. Beardslee & Mitchell (1965: 401) cited several summer records for the northeast shore on Lake Erie, including one at Mohawk Bay from July 12-27, 1958 and one at Gasline on June 19 and 21, 1959. Saunders (1947: 227-229, 373) reported hearing one on Toronto Is. on Aug. 1, 1944 where others observed it the following day: J.L. Baillie had a June 13 record for Toronto. George A. Scott saw one feeding young near Oshawa on July 2, 1961, while Ron Orenstein and I saw one carrying food north of Oshawa on June 22, 1965 (Speirs, 1974). Tozer & Richards (1974: 265) listed several localities in the Oshawa region where Western Meadowlarks have been observed in summer, including some breeding records. Quilliam (1973: 170) mentioned a June 15, 1969, observation by A.E. Hughes at Jackson Mills, near Kingston. Devitt (1967: 153) collected a young male, not long out of the nest, near Bradford on July 31, 1957. Nicholson (1981: 176) had summer records for Manitoulin at Little Current on June 19 and in Tehkummah Twp. on June 23, 1952. Snyder (1942: 147) collected a male at Maclennan on June 22, 1931 and noted a few others near Sault Ste. Marie. Snyder (1938: 207) reported a nest with 4 young near Emo on June 26, 1929 and called them "not uncommon" in farmland from Rainy River to Fort Frances. Fred Helleiner heard one singing at Val Gagne, 7 miles north of Matheson, from June 26 to July 8, 1955 (Baillie, 1955: 377). Snyder (1953: 83) found them scarce in western Ontario but had Kenora records and heard three singing near Dryden on June 28, 1937.

AUTUMN: David Calvert heard one singing at Oshawa on Oct. 24, 1971 (Speirs, 1974). Beardslee & Mitchell (1965: 401) reported three observed near Rockhouse Point, Lake Erie, on Oct. 16, 1960.

**MEASUREMENTS:**
(Same as Eastern Meadowlark).

**REFERENCES:**
Falls, J. Bruce and L.J. Szijj 1959 Reactions of Eastern and Western Meadowlarks in Ontario to each others' vocalizations. Anatomical Record, 134: (3): 560.

Szijj, Laszlo Jozef 1962 A comparative study of the sympatric species of meadowlarks (genus *Sturnella*) in Ontario. Univ. Toronto, PhD Thesis: i-vi; 1-145; vii-xxx.

Szijj, Laszlo Jozef 1963 A morphological analysis of the sympatric populations of meadowlarks in Ontario. Proc. 13th International Ornith. Congress: 176-188.

Szijj, Laszlo J. 1966 Hybridization and the nature of the isolating mechanism in sympatric populations of meadow-larks (*Sturnella*) in Ontario. Zeitschrift für Tierpsychologie, 23: 677-690.

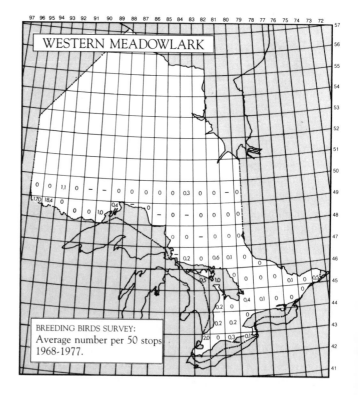

WESTERN MEADOWLARK

BREEDING BIRDS SURVEY: Average number per 50 stops 1968-1977.

# YELLOW-HEADED BLACKBIRD
*Xanthocephalus xanthocephalus* (Bonaparte)

This inhabitant of prairie marshes is rare in Ontario. They winter in southern United States and Mexico.

IDENTIFICATION: These are robin-sized birds. The males are mostly black, with vivid yellow-orange head and neck and conspicuous white wing patches. Females lack the white wing patches, the black is replaced by dusky brown and the yellow is confined mainly to the throat region. The song is a buzzy yodel which Godfrey (1966: 354) rendered as "kleep-kloop-a-ah-oo".

WINTER: Stirrett (1973a: 19) reported one at Pelee on Jan. 1 and 10, 1971.

SPRING: Stirrett (1973b: 25) had single birds at Pelee from May 8-15, 1955; on May 10, 1959 and May 21, 1960. Brooman (1954: 35) reported one seen at a small pond southwest of Jaffa, Elgin Co., on May 1, 1952. H.H. Axtell and B. Nathan saw one at Morgan's Point, Lake Erie, on May 6, 1956 (Beardslee & Mitchell, 1965: 402). H. Elliott and J. Kelley saw a male in High Park, Toronto, from May 3-5, 1977 (TOC record). Speirs (1974) reported three spring records for Ontario Co.: a female seen by John and Naomi LeVay at Cranberry Marsh, Whitby, on May 28, 1956; a male seen flying by Frenchman Bay on Apr. 28, 1962 by David O'Brien and a male seen by Sherri Richards in Conc. 6, Lot 24, Brock Twp. on May 31, 1964. The only Kingston record was a male seen by John and Evan Smith at Carruther's Point on Apr. 21, 1980 (Weir & Quilliam, 1980: 25). R. Campbell and A. Runnells saw a male on Barrie Island on May 1, 1973 (Nicholson, 1981: 176). Peruniak (1971: 28) had just two records for Atikokan: May 2, 1954 and May 4, 1967. John D. Jacob reported nesting near Quetico on May 14, 1931 (Baillie, 1961: 1). James, McLaren & Barlow (1976: 47) mentioned one photographed at Timmins in May , 1974.

SUMMER: On the 1968-1977 Breeding Bird Surveys, they were reported only at Dryden, in 1971. Stirrett (1973c: 21) had single birds at Pelee on June 18 and July 1. Four young fledged from a nest at Bradley's Marsh on June 25 and two young were still in a second nest there on June 30, 1966 (Kelley, 1978: 79). Fleming (1907: 79) had a Toronto specimen "a male taken about 1885". J. Russ *et al* saw one (possibly two) at Ajax from June 24-26, 1980 (Wilson, 1980: 118). Tozer & Richards (1974: 266) reported a male seen by three duck banders in Oshawa's Second Marsh on July 19, 1967 and another male seen by D. Martin in Darlington Twp. on June 23 and 25, 1970. Snyder (1928: 266) collected a male straggler at Macdiarmid, Lake Nipigon, on June 20, 1923. Denis (1961: 7) called this a "sporadic, rare, visitant" at Thunder Bay. David Elder saw 20 or more males and found two nests at Steep Rock Lake, near Atikokan, on June 3, 1981. C.S. Churcher collected a male of 35 counted, and a nest with 4 eggs two miles upstream from the mouth of Rainy River, on June 7, 1961 (Baillie, 1961: 1). Elder (1979: 39) saw an adult female collecting food in the Longlac marshes on July 15, 1967.

AUTUMN: Louise Lawrence noted one at Pimisi Bay on Sept. 14, 1980 (Goodwin, 1981: 178). G. Bennett and A. Dawe saw one at Nashville, near Toronto, on Nov. 2, 1980 (Goodwin, 1981: 178). Norman Mitchinson saw a group of about 15 including one full-plumaged male, every day for about a week in late October, 1955 at Stamford Centre, near Niagara Falls (Sheppard, 1960: 44).

**MEASUREMENTS:**
*Length:* 8 1/2 to 11 ins.
(Godfrey, 1966: 354)
*Wingspread:* 14 to 17 ins.
(Roberts, 1955: 688)
*Weight:* 1 3/4 to 3 oz.
(Roberts, 1955: 688) ♀
smaller than ♂.

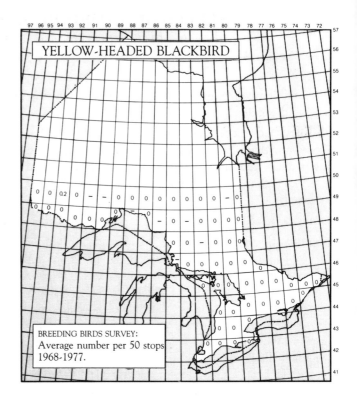

YELLOW-HEADED BLACKBIRD

BREEDING BIRDS SURVEY:
Average number per 50 stops
1968-1977.

# RUSTY BLACKBIRD   *Euphagus carolinus*   (Müller)

I associate Rusty Blackbirds with swamps, where they wade about in shallow water tossing leaves aside to find tidbits underneath, uttering gurgling whistles as they move about. In migration they are often found with mixed flocks of blackbirds and starlings, gleaning corn from harvested fields. They nest chiefly in remote areas of northern Ontario. Some may be found in southern Ontario in winter but most go south to the United States.

IDENTIFICATION: In winter plumage the white eyes and rusty feather edgings distinguish them from other blackbirds. In breeding plumage they lack the rusty markings and much resemble Brewer's Blackbirds but female Brewer's have dark eyes (still white in Rustys). The songs are very different with the musical gurgles of the Rusty constrasting with the "camera shutter" cluck of the Brewer's. The habitats preferred also differ, with the Rusty preferring swampland and the Brewer's along dry roadsides and farm fields. Grackles are bigger birds with the diagnostic boat-shaped tip to the tail (except in moult).

WINTER: On the 1968-1977 Christmas counts they were fairly common along the north shore of Lake Erie, becoming rare north to Ottawa and the Bruce Peninsula, with outliers at Thunder Bay. Stirrett (1973a: 19) had a winter maximum of 45 at Pelee on Dec. 13. Kelley (1978: 81) mentioned 30 at Bradley's Marsh on Jan. 23, 1960. Ussher (1965: 27) had Rondeau records on Dec. 9 and Feb. 25. Saunders & Dale (1933: 235) noted one at Byron, near London, on Jan. 1 and 3, 1920. Marshall Field saw two at St. Thomas on Dec. 20, 1953 and A.C. Steele one at Rodney on Feb. 9, 1948 (Brooman, 1954: 36). Dr. White had 1 to 3 at his Port Colborne feeder from Dec. 15, 1952 to Feb. 4, 1953 (Beardslee & Mitchell, 1965: 407). Parker (1983: 27) showed records at Toronto throughout the winter months, with some on 31 of 58 Christmas counts there. Speirs (1974) cited several winter records for Pickering, Whitby and Oshawa throughout the winter months. Dayton Murphy reported a flock of more than 100 in Prince Edward Co. on Dec. 1, 1937 (Snyder, 1941: 84). Weir & Quilliam (1980: 39) gave Dec. 17 as a 29-year average departure date from Kingston. One was observed on the Barrie Christmas count on Dec. 17, 1966 and 8 were seen near Barrie on Jan. 14, 1967 (Devitt, 1967: 155). L. Beamer watched one eating snow from the edge of a roof in Meaford on Feb. 15, 1947. C.A. Campbell saw one 7 miles south of Parry Sound on Dec. 26, 1965 and another in Parry Sound on Feb. 22, 1975: one was noted at Novar on Jan. 7, 1973 (Mills, 1981: 159). Nicholson (1981: 179) had three winter records for Manitoulin: one survived the 1971-1972 winter at Mindemoya and another was seen there on Feb. 9, 1980; the other was noted through January, 1973 at South Baymouth. Dennison (1980: 148) reported one on 1 of 25 Christmas counts at Sault Ste. Marie.

SPRING: Stirrett (1973b: 25) had a spring maximum of 500 at Pelee on March 30. Ussher (1965: 27) gave March 16 as the 14-year average arrival date at Rondeau, with Apr. 27 as the 8-year average departure date and the latest on May 12. Saunders & Dale (1933: 235) gave March 30 as the 14-year average arrival date at London, with the earliest on March 11, 1921. Snyder (1931: 195) reported casualties at the Long Point lighthouse: 4 on Apr. 17-18 and 2 on Apr. 20-21, 1930. Beardslee & Mitchell (1965: 406-407) reported one at Erie Beach as late as May 22, 1934. Saunders (1947: 373) listed March 26 as his average arrival date at Toronto, with his latest on May 24: Speirs (1938: 43) gave Apr. 19 as the spring peak there. Dennis Barry noted some at Oshawa's Second Marsh on

March 7, 1964 and Doris H. Speirs observed 33 in Pickering Twp. on March 18, 1957: I observed one in Scott Twp. on May 17, 1968 in swamp forest (Speirs, 1974). Weir & Quilliam (1980: 39) listed March 30 as the 27-year average arrival date at Kingston, with the average departure on May 8 and the latest on May 28. Quilliam (1973: 172) estimated 700 or more at Prince Edward Point on May 2, 1972. Devitt (1967: 155) gave Apr. 17 as the 16-year average arrival date at Barrie, with the earliest on March 25, 1962 and latest two at Minesing on May 16, 1931: one was collected near Barrie on March 10, 1930. Mills (1981: 159) gave Apr. 11 as an 11-year average arrival date in northeastern Muskoka, with the earliest on March 27, 1961. Nicholson (1981: 178) had his earliest on Manitoulin on March 13, 1977, with the average arrival on Apr. 6 and a high count of 160 on Apr. 27, 1980 with the latest on May 13, 1978. E.L. Brereton had an Algonquin Park record as early as May 12, 1936 (MacLulich, 1938: 37). Speirs & Speirs (1947: 36) had North Bay records from Apr. 11 to May 19, 1945. Skeel & Bondrup-Nielsen (1978: 211) reported a few at Pukaskwa from Apr. 18 to May 31. Denis (1961: 2) gave Apr. 24 as the average arrival date at Thunder Bay, with the earliest on Apr. 14, 1956. Peruniak (1971: 28) had migrants at Atikokan from Apr. 17 to May 2. Elder (1979: 39) gave Apr. 16 as his earliest Geraldton record, where it was a common migrant but scarce in summer. Bondrup-Nielsen (1976: 45) gave Apr. 27, 1974 as his earliest observation near Kapuskasing. Cringan (1953a: 3) saw his first at Sioux Lookout on May 4 in 1953. The first one was noted in the Asheweig area on May 18 in 1950 (Cringan, 1950: 18). Oliver Hewitt saw 3 at Sandy Is., Moosonee, on May 26, 1947 (Manning, 1952: 87).

SUMMER: On the 1968-1977 Breeding Bird Surveys, they were fairly common on some northern routes, becoming rare south to Mount Julian. Stirrett (1973c: 22) had individuals at Pelee as late as June 26 and as early as Aug. 10 returning. Doris H. Speirs recorded an immature at the mouth of Duffin Creek as early as Aug. 9, 1956 and Dennis Barry had one at Whitby on Aug. 14, 1967 (Speirs, 1974). Weir & Quilliam (1980: 39) had one at Kingston as early as Aug. 1. Quilliam (1973: 173) had three Kingston records for the summer of 1949: one on June 11, one on June 19 and 6 on July 5. C.G. Watson found a nest with 4 eggs at Durham, Grey Co., in early July, 1910 (Baillie & Harrington, 1937: 260). Mills (1981: 159) reported three breeding records for the cottage country: Maureen Sullivan found a nest with 2 young near Port Loring on June 18, 1978; Ross James found a nest with 4 eggs about 9 ft. up in a balsam fir 4 miles south of Dwight on May 28, 1970 which held 4 young on June 10; with Ron Orenstein I saw two fledged young being fed by adults near Dorset on June 8, 1967. Eleanor Thompson watched a parent feeding young at South Tea Lake, Algonquin Park, on July 7, 1926 and C.H.D. Clarke saw an adult feeding young on July 7, 1934 near Brule Lake (MacLulich, 1938: 37). T.F. McIlwraith saw two between North Bay and Sturgeon Falls on Aug. 18-19, 1931 (Ricker & Clarke, 1939: 21). Baillie & Hope (1947: 28) collected flying young at Bigwood on July 15 and July 25, 1937. Baillie & Hope (1943: 23) found a nest with 5 young at Marathon on June 18, 1936 about 18 ins. up in a small spruce and another nest about 28 ins. up in a willow with 4 young just out of the nest nearby, at Amyot on June 27, 1936. Snyder (1928: 266) took an injured female at Lake Nipigon on June 2, 1924. Snyder (1953: 84) discovered 22 birds, including young recently out of the nest, near Savanne on July 8, 1937 and about 25 at Perrault Falls from Aug. 17-19, 1952. Snyder (1928: 26) collected a female containing 4 eggs, one ready for deposition, on June 8, 1925 at Lake Abitibi: a young bird was also found there on July 30. I saw one carrying food near Klotz Lake on June 28, 1981. James (1980: 90) saw a few in wet places near Pickle Lake. Hope

(1938: 43) did not find any at Favourable Lake until Aug. 6, 1938 when 2 of 3 young were collected. Cringan (1953b: 4) encountered from 1 to 6 on three days in June at Kasabonika Lake. Cringan (1950: 18) considered them common at Nikip Lake, where daily totals up to 10 were observed and an adult carrying food was seen on July 2, 1950. James, Nash & Peck (1982: 72) saw recently fledged young and a used nest on June 26, 1982 at Harricanaw River, near James Bay. Manning (1952: 87) collected young at 53 ° 45'N on the James Bay coast on July 14 and at Shagamu River on the Hudson Bay coast on Aug. 10, 1947. Schueler, Baldwin & Rising (1974: 144, 147) had records for Ft. Albany and Winisk, collected a female with brood patch and enlarged ovary at Hawley Lake on June 29, 1962 and found a nest with 4 young on July 10, 1964 at Aquatuk Lake. James, Nash & Peck (1981: 44) found a breeding density of 10 pairs per km $^2$ at Kiruna Lake, Sutton Ridges in riparian thicket swamp habitat. Lee (1978: 33) saw a maximum of 9 birds at Big Trout Lake on July 24 and Aug. 8, 1975 and had birds on two of his three quadrats there. C.E. Hope saw 30 and collected 2 young at Fort Severn on July 14, 1940.

AUTUMN: George Stirrett noted 35 at Moose Factory on Sept. 27, 1948 (Manning, 1952: 87). Hope (1938: 43) received one collected at Favourable Lake as late as Oct. 24, 1938. Peruniak (1971: 28) had fall records at Atikokan from Sept. 25 to Oct. 27. Skeel & Bondrup-Nielsen (1978: 211) reported a few at Pukaskwa from Sept. 6 to Sept. 27. Speirs & Speirs (1947: 36) had fall records near North Bay from Sept. 16 to Oct. 13, 1944. MacLulich (1938: 38) saw migrating flocks at Brent, Algonquin Park, in late September, 1930. Nicholson (1981: 179) gave Sept. 18 as the 8-year average arrival date on Manitoulin in fall, with the earliest on Sept. 2, 1972: his high count was 400 on Oct. 12, 1970. Mills (1981: 159) saw about 400 at Ahmic Lake on Oct. 12, 1980. Devitt (1967: 155) gave Sept. 24, 1939 as his earliest fall record for Barrie: he reported 2000 to 3000 at Holland River on Oct. 15, 1944. Weir & Quilliam (1980: 39) gave Sept. 25 as the 26-year average arrival date at Kingston. LGL (1974: 205) reported flocks of 1119 on Oct. 9 and 1600 on Nov. 13 at Cranberry Marsh, Whitby, in 1973. Speirs (1974) estimated 600 in a flock on the Brock-Scott Townline on Nov. 7, 1971 and 150 the same day at Udney in Mara Twp. Saunders (1947: 373) gave Oct. 3 and Nov. 11 as his average arrival and departure dates for Toronto, with his earliest on Sept. 11 (J.L. Baillie had a Sept. 3 record): Speirs (1938: 51) gave Oct. 19 as the fall peak there. Marshall Field saw a flock of 100 at St. Thomas on Oct. 25, 1952 (Brooman, 1954: 36). Ussher (1965: 27) gave Oct. 10 and Nov. 9 as average arrival and departure dates for Rondeau, with the earliest on Sept. 21. Stirrett (1973d: 28) had a fall maximum of 2000 at Pelee on Oct. 17.

BANDING: One banded in North Carolina on Feb. 18, 1943 was recovered near Uphill, Victoria Co., on Apr. 24, 1944. One banded at Lewisburg, West Virginia, on Apr. 1, 1969 was recovered at Burwash, Ont. about 360 miles to the north, on Apr. 30, 1969 (Brewer & Salvadori, 1978: 83).

**MEASUREMENTS:**
*Length:* 8.5 to 9.8 ins.
(Godfrey, 1966: 358)
*Wingspread:* 13 to 15 ins.
(Roberts, 1955: 691)
*Weight:* ♂ 2 1/4 to 2 3/4
oz. ♀ 2 oz. (Roberts,
1955: 691).

**REFERENCE:**
Long, R. Charles and Audrey Russ 1968 Rusty Blackbird kills House Sparrow. Ont. Field Biologist, No. 22: 28. (At the Russ' Ajax feeder at 9:50 a.m. on Dec. 27, 1968, with the temperature 15 ° F and no food in the feeder at the time.)

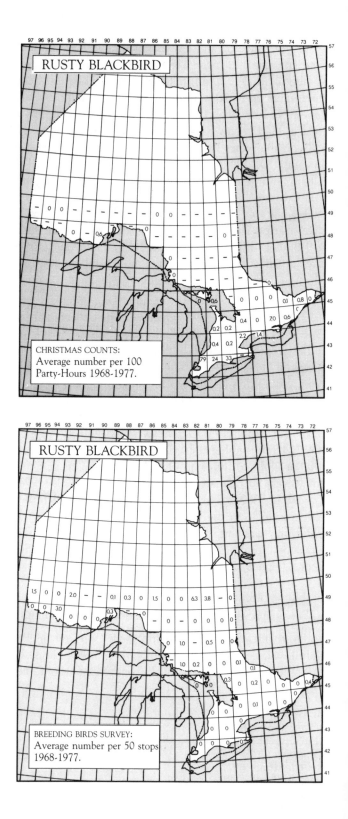

RUSTY BLACKBIRD

CHRISTMAS COUNTS:
Average number per 100
Party-Hours 1968-1977.

RUSTY BLACKBIRD

BREEDING BIRDS SURVEY:
Average number per 50 stops
1968-1977.

# BREWER'S BLACKBIRD   *Euphagus cyanocephalus*   (Wagler)

This bird of western farmlands and roadsides has been moving eastward into Ontario and is now fairly common from the Manitoba border to Thunder Bay and from Sault Ste. Marie to North Bay, with sporadic occurrences elsewhere. They winter in the United States and Mexico.

IDENTIFICATION: Brewer's Blackbirds greatly resemble the congeneric Rusty Blackbirds in size and general appearance during the breeding season except that female Brewer's have dark eyes while female Rustys have white eyes like the males of both species. Grackles are also black birds with white eyes, but are larger, have a much heavier, less pointed bill and have a boat-shaped tail (except when in moult). Cowbirds share the roadside habitat of Brewer's but are smaller, chunkier birds. During the breeding season Brewer's males have impressed me as very "starry-eyed" individuals. They are less vocal than other blackbirds, the males' call reminding me of the "schlupp" of a camera shutter.

WINTER: On the 1968-1977 Christmas counts they have been rare from as far south as Pelee and as far east as Carleton Place and as far north as Dryden. G. Hanagan and J.P. Kleiman saw one at Pelee on Dec. 13, 1980 and P.D. Pratt noted one there later on Feb. 14, 1981 (Goodwin, 1981: 297). Mrs. E. Allan described one seen at St. Thomas on Jan. 13, 1953 (Brooman, 1954: 36). D. Murray observed one at Melbourne on Jan. 27, 1978 (Goodwin, 1978: 345). R. Young reported one at Providence Bay, Manitoulin, on Dec. 20, 1975 and one was seen in Carnarvon Twp. on Feb. 10, 1980 by C. Bell and J. Lemon (Nicholson, 1981: 179). J. Nicholson noted another on Manitoulin on Dec. 19, 1981 and one at Sudbury on Jan. 3, 1982 (Weir, 1982: 291). Dennison (1980: 148) reported a total of 5 on 3 of 25 Christmas counts at Sault Ste. Marie. Elder (1979: 39) reported an injured bird that wintered at a feeder at Geraldton in 1972-1973, surviving temperatures as low as -45 ° C.

SPRING: A. Wormington *et al* saw some on Pelee Island on May 30, 1980 and as early as Apr. 13, 1980 at Erieau (Goodwin, 1980: 772): a nesting colony was noted at Erieau as early as 1977 (Goodwin, 1977: 1135). R. Curry and A.H. Kelley observed a pair at Lake St. Clair in spring, 1974 (Goodwin, 1974: 797). W.R. Jarmain saw one at Delaware on Apr. 14, 1975 (Goodwin, 1975: 847). G. Holroyd found a nest with 4 eggs in an open-faced bird box at Long Point on May 31, 1970 (McCracken, Bradstreet & Holroyd, 1981: 65). Speirs (1974) gave details of two nestings at Darlington Provincial Park in 1968 where 6 adults were found on May 13: J.M. Richards found a nest with 6 eggs there on May 13: the other nest held 2 eggs on May 15 and 4 eggs on May 27: further details of these were given in Richards and Peck (1968: 25). Robert B. Stewart reported 6 at Prince Edward Point on May 3, 1972 (Quilliam, 1973: 173) and there have been other sightings there since. Devitt (1967: 41) reported 3 nests in the Holland Marsh, King Twp.; two found on May 26, 1969, contained 4 young and 5 young; another found on May 30 held 3 young. J.W. Johnson observed a pair at Tobermory on May 28, 1974 (Goodwin, 1974: 899). C. and J. Campbell noted one at Parry Sound on May 1, 1975 (Mills, 1981: 160). Nicholson (1981: 179) reported the earliest Manitoulin record and the high count of 30 on Apr. 3, 1978 by Chris. Bell. Denis (1961: 3) gave Apr. 28 as the average arrival date at Thunder Bay, with the earliest on Apr. 18, 1959. Peruniak (1971: 28) gave Apr. 26 as her earliest Atikokan date but David Elder noted one there

906

on Apr. 22, 1981. D.C. Sadler reported a pair at Ferland, north of Lake Nipigon, from May 22-26, 1974 (Goodwin, 1974: 797).

SUMMER: On the 1968-1977 Breeding Bird Surveys, they were common near Sudbury and from Fort Frances west to Lake of the Woods, fairly common on Manitoulin and uncommon north of Lake Superior. Naomi LeVay reported an adult at Cranberry Marsh, Whitby, on July 25, 1957 (Tozer & Richards, 1974: 270). G.J. Yaki found a nest with 4 young at Luther Marsh on June 4, 1967 (Goodwin, 1967: 563). Devitt (1969: 41) found a nest with young about 5 miles north of Coldwater, Simcoe Co., on June 18, 1969: the young scattered when approached but one infertile egg remained in the nest. Mary and O.E. Devitt noted about 50 birds at Lovering, Simcoe Co., on Aug. 18, 1978 (Goodwin, 1979: 174). J.W. Johnson noted 6 or more from June 24, 1974 at Ferndale, Bruce Co., where they bred the previous year (Goodwin, 1974: 899) and three at Monument Corners, the site of the first Bruce breeding, on July 15, 1974 (Goodwin, 1974: 899). He found found another colony at Tobermory on June 15, 1978 (Goodwin, 1978: 1156). G. Bennett observed two at French River on Aug. 11, 1965 (Mills, 1981: 160). On June 22, 1975, an adult was seen carrying food on Manitoulin (Nicholson, 1981: 179). Devitt (1964: 44) noted birds at Echo Bay, east of Sault Ste. Marie, on June 17 and 19, 1953. Doris H. Speirs and D.M. Wood found 5 nests near Sault Ste. Marie in the summer of 1954 (Speirs, 1954: 29) and Wood (1955: 23). Devitt (1964: 45) flushed a female from a nest with 5 eggs at Rutter (37 miles south of Sudbury) on May 31, 1963 and 3 nests at McKerrow on June 1, 1963 (a nest with 1 egg and 4 young, a nest with 5 eggs and a nest with 5 young) I saw a bird at Blind River on Aug. 4, 1959 and individuals 7 miles east of Thessalon on July 31, 1959 and at Echo Bay the same day. Stepney (1975: 76) reported 8 nests at Warren (60 miles east of Sudbury) on June 9, 1974, from 4 1/2 to 6 ft. up in roadside pines. M. Gosselin saw 6 or more at Sturgeon Falls on June 16, 1979 (Goodwin, 1979: 860). N.G. Escott noted birds at Heron Bay on June 19 and July 16, 1977 (Goodwin, 1977: 1135). Allin & Dear (1947: 176) reported the first Ontario nest, with 4 young, on June 14, 1945, at Thunder Bay, having previously seen one bird there in the summer of 1943 and 8 there on June 13, 1945. A nest with 5 eggs was found at Thunder Bay on June 5, 1955 (Devitt, 1964: 44): and L.S. Dear collected a nest with 5 eggs there on May 22, 1949 (Baillie, 1961: 6). Two nests were located near Pass Lake (about 23 miles east of Thunder Bay on July 1, 1963: a nest with 1 egg and 3 young and another nest with 1 egg and 4 young (Devitt, 1964: 45). Leslie Paterson observed nesting at Fort Frances since 1957 (Baillie, 1961: 6). G.I. Park saw a flock of 50 blackbirds (mainly Brewer's) at Crozier on Aug. 15, 1977 (Goodwin, 1978: 199). A. Wormington saw one bird at Hearst on July 4, 1978 (Goodwin, 1978: 1156). On June 18, 1983 I saw 4 birds at Longlac, where we had seen birds the previous summer. The first Ontario specimen was collected by Clifford E. Hope at Lake Attawapiskat on June 5, 1939 (Baillie, 1953: 307).

AUTUMN: E.E. Kanaga noted 12 at Longlac on Sept. 1, 1948 (Devitt, 1964: 44). Peruniak (1971: 28) gave Sept. 17 as her latest Atikokan date. Skeel & Bondrup-Nielsen (1978: 212) reported a male at Pukaskwa on Sept. 19, 1977. One was observed on Manitoulin as late as Nov. 16, 1974 (Nicholson, 1981: 179). B.M. DiLabio saw one at Ottawa on Nov. 16, 1980 (Goodwin, 1981: 178). N. Dennys, J. Kearney and B.B. Weller reported 3 at Parry Sound on Nov. 2, 1980 (Goodwin, 1981: 178). A. Rider had one at Monument Corners, Bruce Co., on Oct. 24, 1975 (Goodwin, 1976: 62). T. Letson and C.J. MacFayden reported 10 at Coldwater on Oct. 3, 1976 (Goodwin, 1977: 172). The first for the Peterborough region was seen at Lakefield on Oct. 7, 1974 by T. Bigg (Goodwin,

1975: 52). Two were seen at Peterborough the following fall, on Sept. 28 and Nov. 29, by G. Carpentier, D. McRae and D.C. Sadler (Goodwin, 1976: 62). C.J. and E.A. MacFayden estimated 160 at Barrie on Nov. 11, 1979 (Goodwin, 1980: 158). Weir & Quilliam (1980: 25) reported one at Squaw Point, Kingston, on Sept. 15, 1973 by Ron Weir; another at Kingston on Oct. 7, 1976 by Marg. Brown and one at Prince Edward Point on Oct. 8, 1978 by Mark Gawn. A. Rider noted one at Kettle Point on Oct. 14, 1975 (Goodwin, 1976: 62). Stirrett (1973a: 19) reported one at Pelee on Nov. 16, 1969.

BANDING: One banded at McKerrow on June 13, 1970 was recovered at Thessalon (88 miles to the west) on Feb. 9, 1971 (Brewer & Salvadori, 1976: 88).

**MEASUREMENTS:**
*Length:* 8.0 to 10.3 ins. (Godfrey, 1966: 359)
*Wingspread:* ♂ 15 1/2 to 16 ins. ♀ 14 to 15 ins. (Roberts, 1955: 691)
*Weight:* 19 ♂ averaged 67.2 g.; 15 ♀ averaged 58.1 g. (Dunning, 1984: 25).

**REFERENCES:**
Allin, A.E. and L.S. Dear 1947 Brewer's Blackbird breeding in Ontario. Wilson Bull., 59: (3): 175-176.

Devitt, O.E. 1964 An extension in the breeding range of Brewer's Blackbird in Ontario. Can. Field- Nat., 78: (1): 42-46. (This includes a map of records to 1963)

Devitt, O.E. 1969 First nesting records of Brewer's Blackbird (*Euphagus cyanocephalus*) for King Township and Simcoe County, Ontario. Ont. Field Biologist, No. 23: 41-42.

Power, Dennis M. 1971 Range expansion of Brewer's Blackbird: phenetics of a new population. Can. Journ. Zool., 49: (2): 175-183.

Richards, J.M. and G.K. Peck 1968 Nesting of Brewer's Blackbird (*Euphagus cyanocephalus*) in Ontario and Durham Counties. Ont. Field Biologist, No. 22: 25-27

(includes photos of male, female and nest with eggs).

Speirs, J. Murray 1954 Brewer's Blackbird nesting at Sault Ste. Marie, Ontario. Fed. Ont. Naturalists Bull. 65: 29.

Stepney, P.H.R. and Dennis M. Power 1973 Analysis of the eastward breeding expansion of Brewer's Blackbird plus general aspects of avian expansions. Wilson Bull., 85: (4): 452-464. (includes a map showing dates of first appearances in Ontario and Great Lakes states).

Stepney, Philip H.R. 1975 Tree nesting sites and a breeding range extension of Brewer's Blackbird in the Great Lakes region. Can. Field Naturalist, 89: (1): 76-77.

Wood, D.M. 1955 Nesting of Brewer's Blackbird at Sault Ste. Marie, Ontario. Ont. Field Biologist, No. 9: 23.

908

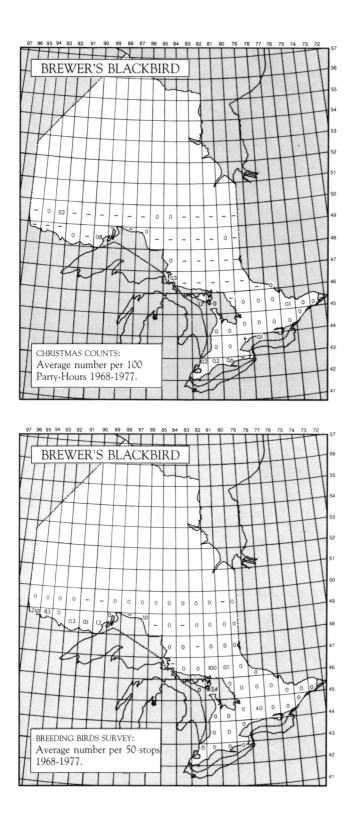

# COMMON GRACKLE  *Quiscalus quiscula*  (Linnaeus)

These are the "snooty" big blackbirds that waddle across the lawn with "their noses in the air", puffing themselves up with pride, then collapsing to expel love songs that sound like rusty hinges. They stay together in small groups, even in the nesting season, when they often nest in spruces, but sometimes in marshes with Red-winged Blackbirds or, in the north, in dead stumps in bogs or swamps. In the fall they congregate with other blackbirds, sometimes in immense numbers. Most retreat in winter to the United States.

IDENTIFICATION: Grackles are larger than our other white-eyed blackbirds (but not as large as crows). They sport many iridescent colours on their black coats, chiefly blues about the head and bronze shades on the body. The tail is somewhat boat shaped, bigger toward the rear than near the body with a V-shaped cross section, and (except during moult) will easily distinguish them from other blackbirds even at a distance. During moult the heavy bill, with its convex upper mandible, will distinguish grackles from the pointed-billed Rusty and Brewer's Blackbirds.

WINTER: On the 1968-1977 Christmas counts they were common along the north shore of Lake Erie, uncommon elsewhere in agricultural southern Ontario and along the north shore of Lake Superior, and generally absent in northeastern Ontario. Stirrett (1973a: 19) had a winter maximum of 500 at Pelee on Feb. 2 and Feb. 24. Ussher (1965: 27) had Dec. 3 and Feb. 22 records at Rondeau, and wrote: "often occur in winter". Beardslee & Mitchell (1965: 408) cited a record of two birds at Fort Erie on Dec. 19, 1955. Parker (1983: 27) listed grackles on 32 of 58 Christmas counts in the Toronto region. Speirs (1974) mentioned grackles on 7 of 10 Pickering Christmas counts and on 8 of 16 Oshawa counts. Devitt (1967: 156) reported 6 at Barrie on Jan. 3, 1960. C.L. Patch had one at Ottawa on Dec. 25, 1922 (Lloyd, 1923: 156). Mills (1981: 161) reported grackles on 4 of 28 Christmas counts at Huntsville, on 2 of 4 Georgian Bay counts and 2 of 3 Burk's Falls counts: C. Campbell saw 2 at Parry Sound on Jan. 2 and Feb. 22, 1975. Bruce Lord *et al* observed a wintering bird at North Bay on Jan. 7 and 10 and Feb. 5 and 6, 1945 (Speirs & Speirs, 1947: 36). Dennison (1980: 148) reported 3 birds on 1 of 25 Christmas counts at Sault Ste. Marie. A few were recorded on Christmas counts at Marathon from 1974 to 1977 (Skeel & Bondrup-Nielsen, 1978: 212). Elder (1979: 39) reported some overwintering at Geraldton feeders.

SPRING: Stirrett (1973b: 25) had spring maxima at Pelee of 3000 on March 26 and Apr. 26. Ussher (1965: 27) gave March 12 as his 21-year average arrival date at Rondeau. Saunders & Dale (1933: 235) gave March 15 as the 17-year average arrival date at London with the earliest on March 4, 1922: several sets of eggs were taken there, the earliest set of 6 eggs on Apr. 23, 1913. J.L. Baillie, in Saunders (1947: 373), listed March 23 as his 27-year average arrival date at Toronto: Speirs (1938: 43) gave Apr. 13 as the spring peak date for Toronto. Long (1968a: 24) observed nest building at Pickering Beach as early as Apr. 4, 1965. J.M. Richards found a nest with one egg at Oshawa on Apr. 21, 1962: this held 5 eggs on Apr. 25 (Speirs, 1974). H.F. Lewis saw one at Wellington as early as March 17, 1938 and a nest with 5 eggs was found at Hillier, Prince Edward Co., on May 6, 1931 (Snyder, 1941: 84). LGL (1974: 205) found a spring peak of 3435 on Apr. 23 on their roadside surveys on the site of the proposed Pickering airport. Quilliam (1973: 173-174) gave March 19 as the 24-year average arrival date at Kingston and C.M. Clarke found a nest with 4 eggs there as early as Apr. 27, 1898. R.A. Smith found a nest with 5 eggs at Bradford as early as Apr. 18, 1939: the 18-year average arrival date at Barrie was March 25 (Devitt, 1967: 155-156). L. Beamer's median arrival date at Meaford was March 26, with the earliest "about" March 11, 1957. Mills (1981: 160) gave March 28 as the 14-year average arrival date at Huntsville, with the earliest on March 11, 1973: Ross James saw birds nest building at Rosseau on Apr. 21, 1973. D.B. Ferguson found a nest with 5 eggs at Silverwater, Manitoulin, on May 20, 1979 (Nicholson, 1981: 180). MacLulich (1938: 38) gave Apr. 4, 1933 as his earliest Algonquin Park date. Speirs & Speirs (1947: 36) had a spring peak at North Bay in late April. Skeel & Bondrup-Nielsen (1978: 212) noted their first at Pukaskwa on Apr. 19 in 1977 and recorded 38 on 13 days from then until May 29. Denis (1961: 2) gave Apr. 11 as the average arrival date at Thunder Bay, with the earliest on March 31, 1945. Dear (1940: 140) reported a nest with 5 eggs on May 28, 1922 and a nest with 5 eggs on May 29, 1927 near Thunder Bay: these were probably the ones found by A.E. Allin (Allin, 1940: 140). Peruniak (1971: 28) gave Apr. 8 as her earliest Atikokan date but David Elder saw one there on Apr. 3, 1981. J.L. Baillie found a nest 20 ft. up in a spruce at Kenora on May 26, 1949 (Snyder, 1953: 84). Elder (1979: 39) gave Apr. 17 as his earliest Geraldton migrant. Bondrup-Nielsen (1976: 45) saw his first near Kapuskasing on Apr. 21 in 1974. Cringan (1953a: 3) gave Apr. 15 as his earliest record at Sioux Lookout in 1953.

SUMMER: On the 1968-1977 Breeding Bird Surveys they were abundant on routes near the north shore of Lake Erie, common in agricultural areas in southern Ontario, in the Clay Belt and from Lake of the Woods to Dryden, uncommon on some northern Ontario routes. Stirrett (1973c: 22) had a summer maximum of 2000 at Pelee on July 27. W.E. Saunders estimated 5000 in a Long Point flock on Aug. 25, 1918 (Snyder, 1931: 195). McCracken, Bradstreet & Holroyd (1981: 65) had breeding densities as high as 254 territories per km $^2$ on Long Point: they knew of 80 nest records there, with egg dates from Apr. 27 to June 19. Snyder (1930: 194) reported a nest in the top of a broken stub in a marshy clearing in a King Township swamp. Speirs (1974) reported a total of 363 eggs in 97 nests found in Ontario Co.: Speirs & Orenstein (1975: 14) found grackles in 8 of 11 forest quadrats in Ontario Co. with a maximum density of 24 birds per 100 acres in the Scugog plot: they were most abundant in urban quadrats in Ontario Co., occurring in all 10 urban plots with a maximum density of 81 birds per 100 acres in Uxbridge (Speirs, Markle & Tozer, 1970: 5). H.H. Southam found two nests in a Great Blue Heron colony at Gerow Gore, Prince Edward Co., on July 3, 1938 and J.L. Baillie watched one catching a fish by diving into the surf at Point Traverse on June 30, 1930 (Snyder, 1941: 84-85). M.H. Edwards found five nests with 4 eggs each near Kingston on June 5, 1963 (Quilliam, 1973: 173). Mills (1981: 160) reported 21 nest records for the cottage country, with egg dates from May 11 to July 3. C.H.D. Clarke saw young being fed at Brule Lake, Algonquin Park, on July 19, 1934 (MacLulich, 1938: 38). Ricker & Clarke (1939: 21) found a nest with 4 eggs at Frank's Bay, Lake Nipissing, on June 11, 1933 and reported other nests with eggs from May 30 to June 30. A nest with 4 young and one egg was found at Biscotasing on June 21, 1937 and young out of the nest were noted there and at Bigwood to July 23 (Baillie & Hope, 1947: 28). Snyder (1942: 148) found a nest with 3 young in an open shed near Sault Ste. Marie on June 2, 1931. Skeel & Bondrup-Nielsen (1978: 212) found grackles scarce (only 9 on 6 days) in summer at Pukaskwa. Baillie & Hope (1943: 24) noted a few at Rossport, none at Marathon, and found a nest with 2 young in a barn at Amyot on June 29, 1936. Many nests were found in early June, 1929 near Emo (Snyder,

1938: 208). Snyder (1953: 84) considered them "not uncommon" in western Ontario from Ingolf to Savanne and north to Sioux Lookout: a nest with young was observed at Ingolf on June 10, 1937 and two nests were found at Wabigoon on June 28 (one with 3 eggs and one with 4 eggs). Smith (1957: 179) noted birds with young at Kapuskasing. Snyder (1928: 27) found some nesting in cavities of dead trees at Lake Abitibi in 1925, where they were "quite numerous". James (1980: 90) found a nest with 3 young at Central Patricia on June 11, 1977. Cringan (1950: 18) regularly saw small numbers at Nikip Lake in summer, 1950. Hope (1938: 44) found a nest with 5 eggs at Favourable Lake on June 11, 1938. A.H. MacPherson collected a female on Haysey Island, near Moosonee, on June 27, 1949 (Manning, 1952: 87-88). Schueler, Baldwin & Rising (1974: 144, 147) listed a few at Cochrane and Moosonee: one was seen at Winisk on June 22, 1964 by D.H. Baldwin.

AUTUMN: D.H. Baldwin saw 3 at Fort Albany on Sept. 9, 1964 (Schueler, Baldwin & Rising, 1974: 147). Peruniak (1971: 28) reported a full albino at Atikokan on Sept. 5, 1968: her latest record there was on Oct. 31. Skeel & Bondrup-Nielsen (1978: 212) saw their latest at Pukaskwa on Sept. 26, 1977. Speirs & Speirs (1947: 36) had a fall peak at North Bay in early September and one there as late as Nov. 20, 1944. Naomi LeVay estimated 4000 at a Whitby Twp. roost on Oct. 9, 1966 (Speirs, 1974). LGL (1974: 207) had a fall peak of 10,000 on Sept. 24, 1973 on the proposed site of the Pickering airport and 25,000 there in the fall of 1972. Saunders (1947: 373) gave Oct. 24 as his 12-year average departure date from Toronto: Speirs (1938: 51) listed Oct. 3 as the fall peak there. Ussher (1965: 27) gave Nov. 6 as his 7-year average departure date from Rondeau. Stirrett (1973d: 28) had a fall maximum of 20,000 at Pelee on Oct. 31.

BANDING: Of 32 grackles banded near Toronto and recorded in the United States, 10 were found in Ohio, 7 in Kentucky, 5 in Alabama, 3 in Tennessee, 2 in West Virginia and one each in Georgia, Indiana, North Carolina, Pennsylvania and Virginia: in the same period (up to 1971) 2 banded in Alabama and one each in Delaware, Ohio, South Carolina and Tennessee were taken near Toronto.
Brewer & Salvadori (1978: 83-84) reported that 29 banded in Alabama had been recovered in Ontario, mostly between Windsor and Toronto, but one as far north as Algoma. As well as the Alabama birds 19 Ohio banded birds were recovered in Ontario, 11 from Michigan and one each from Minnesota, New Jersey and North Carolina. Between 1965 and 1970 birds banded in Ontario were taken as follows: 29 in Ohio, 11 in Michigan, 7 in Alabama, 4 in Kentucky, 4 in Pennsylvania, 2 in West Virginia, and one each in Florida, Georgia, Indiana and New York. The most distant recovery that they mention was of a grackle banded in Bowmanville on May 13, 1968 and found later at Cuthbert, Georgia on Dec. 30 of the same year, some 900 miles to the south.
Mills (1981: 161) mentioned one banded at Lake Manitouwabing, Muskoka, on Aug. 16, 1974 and recovered near Guelph on Aug. 15, 1977 (three years later). Brewer & Salvadori (1976: 88) reported one banded at Thornhill on Aug. 14, 1962 and recovered there again on July 23, 1971, when it must have been at least 9 years old.

**MEASUREMENTS:**

*Length:* 11 to 13 1/2 ins.
(Godfrey, 1966: 359)
*Wingspread:* 17 to 18 1/2
ins. (Roberts, 1955: 690)
*Weight:* 4 ♂ averaged
124.7 g. 2 ♀ averaged
98.3 g. (Hope, 1938: 44)
62 Ontario specimens
averaged 114.8 g.

**REFERENCES:**

Middleton, A.L.A. 1977
Predatory behaviour by
Common Grackles. Can.
Field-Naturalist,
91: (2): 187. Fifteen House
Sparrows were killed in 11
days at a Guelph feeder in
early July, 1975 and their
brains eaten.

Woodford, J. 1955
Grackle's feeding
behaviour. Ont. Field
Biologist, No. 9: 25. An
adult dunked bread in a
bird bath before feeding it
to young.

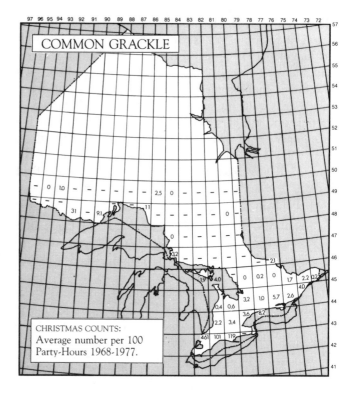

COMMON GRACKLE

CHRISTMAS COUNTS:
Average number per 100
Party-Hours 1968-1977.

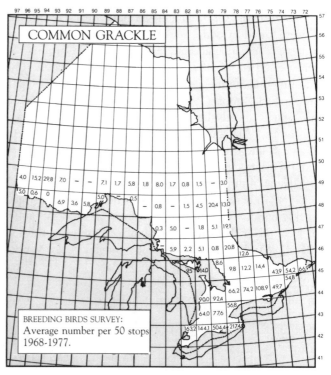

COMMON GRACKLE

BREEDING BIRDS SURVEY:
Average number per 50 stops
1968-1977.

# BROWN-HEADED COWBIRD  *Molothrus ater*  (Boddaert)

Cowbirds are fascinating birds, wholly dependent on other birds to incubate their eggs and raise their young. Then how do they come to know that they *are* cowbirds, having been raised by a Yellow Warbler or a Song Sparrow or some other species? Yet when fall comes they flock with their own kind and associate with other blackbirds. How do they know that they are blackbirds? when they have bills that might class them with finches or sparrows? Banding has shown that they have strong homing tendencies, but why, when other species raise their young and you might think they would have no need to establish a home base?

Most of our birds arrive with other blackbirds in early spring and the males are soon displaying, puffing themselves up, then bowing so low they almost overbalance. When other birds start nesting, the unobtrusive female cowbirds find many nests and deposit eggs in them, laying for several weeks. One lady, who had phenomenal success in finding nests, attributed her success to getting up early and following female cowbirds around. Most of our birds go south to the United States in winter but a few may be found in southern Ontario then. Peck (1981: 4-6) listed 84 species that have been parasitized in Ontario by cowbirds, with Yellow Warbler, Song Sparrow and Chipping Sparrow the chief hosts.

**IDENTIFICATION:** Males are black birds with brown heads, somewhat larger than House Sparrows, but quite similar in build. Females are blackish gray, the amount of black varying considerably. The young are gray, streaked with dusky: they make their presence known by incessant, loud, somewhat buzzy food calls. Adults utter "see-tu-tu" and have a lip-smacking sputter when they take off in flight.

**WINTER:** On the 1968-1977 Christmas counts they were common from Pelee to Guelph, fairly common from Oshawa to Kingston and on Manitoulin, uncommon to rare elsewhere, with none at many northern localities. Stirrett (1973a: 19) had a winter maximum of 700 at Pelee on Dec. 23. Kelley (1978: 87) reported 2000 at Rondeau on Dec. 28, 1970. A.A. Wood took a male near London on Dec. 4, 1917 (Saunders & Dale, 1933: 236). Marshall Field saw 50 at St. Thomas on Dec. 20, 1953 (Brooman, 1954: 36). Beardslee & Mitchell (1965: 409-410) reported 600 at a feed mill at Dunnville on Feb. 9, 1961 and 100 at Thorold on Dec. 26, 1961. Parker (1983: 27) listed cowbirds at Toronto on 25 of 58 Christmas counts there. Snyder (1941: 85) collected 4 adult males, one immature male and two females at Wellington on Dec. 2, 1937. Three came to W.E. Cattley's feeder at Orillia as late as Dec. 27-29, 1966 (Devitt, 1967: 157). Mills (1981: 162) cited several winter records for the cottage country: one visited a Huntsville feeder from Dec. 27, 1959 to Feb. 8, 1960. Two were recorded on the Marathon Christmas count in 1975 (Skeel & Bondrup-Nieslen, 1978: 212).

**SPRING:** Stirrett (1973b: 26) had a spring maximum of 200 at Pelee on Apr. 26. Ussher (1965: 28) gave March 21 as his 18-year average arrival date at Rondeau. Saunders & Dale (1933: 236) gave March 21 as the 17-year average arrival date at London, with the earliest on March 8, 1921. Saunders (1947: 374) listed March 30 as his average arrival date at Toronto: Speirs (1938: 43) gave May 3 as the spring peak there. Ross James found a Phoebe nest with one egg and 3 cowbird eggs as early as Apr. 30, 1967 in Pickering Township (Speirs, 1974). Weir & Quilliam (1980: 39) listed March 21 as the 27-year average arrival date at Kingston. Devitt (1967: 157) gave March 29 as the 14-year average arrival date at Barrie, with the earliest at Collingwood on March 23, 1957. Donald Sutherland found two eggs in a Song Sparrow nest at Holland River as early as May 8, 1938 (Devitt, 1967: 156). L. Beamer's median arrival date at Meaford was March 26, with the earliest in the last week of February during a mild spell in 1954. Mills (1981: 162) gave Apr. 1 as a 13-year average arrival date at Huntsville, with the earliest on March 21, 1959: C. Harris counted 50 at Go Home Bay on Apr. 30, 1977 and an egg was found in a Prairie Warbler nest at Go Home Bay as early as May 23, 1944. MacLulich (1938: 38) gave Apr. 14, 1933 as his earliest Algonquin Park date. Speirs & Speirs (1947: 36) saw one at North Bay on March 29, 1945. Skeel & Bondrup-Nielsen (1978: 212) noted their first at Pukaskwa on Apr. 15 in 1977 and observed 39 on 23 days to May 26. Baillie & Hope (1943: 24) saw a male at White River on May 26, 1936. Denis (1961: 2) gave Apr. 21 as the average arrival date at Thunder Bay, with the earliest on Apr. 7, 1957. Peruniak (1971: 28) gave Apr. 25 as her earliest date at Atikokan, but David Elder saw one there on Apr. 3, 1981. Elder (1979: 39) gave Apr. 10 as his earliest Geraldton record. Smith (1957: 180) saw three near New Liskeard on May 29, 1964. Bondrup-Nielsen (1976: 45) saw his first near Kapuskasing on Apr. 18 in 1975 and considered them rare there. Cringan (1953a: 3) had his first at Sioux Lookout on May 3 in 1953. Oliver Hewitt collected a female at the mouth of the Moose River on May 29, 1947 (Manning, 1952: 88).

SUMMER: On the 1968-1977 Breeding Bird Surveys, they were common throughout agricultural southern Ontario north to North Bay and Thessalon and in the Rainy River region but uncommon to fairly common in most of northern Ontario. Stirrett (1973c: 22) had a summer maximum of 200 at Pelee on July 16. McCracken, Bradstreet & Holroyd (1981: 65) reported finding eggs in nests of 10 species at Long Point, with Prothonotary Warbler (11 nests) and Red-winged Blackbird (9 nests) the chief hosts there. Beardslee & Mitchell (1965: 409) listed 50 species parasitized in the Niagara frontier region. Speirs & Orenstein (1975: 14) found populations on all forest plots in Ontario Co. with a maximum density of 39 birds per 100 acres on the Whitby quadrat: they were seen on 9 of 11 field plots, but only in the Scugog quadrat did they seem to be on territory and then only 4 birds per 100 acres: they were found on 9 of 10 urban plots (missing only on the downtown Oshawa plot), with a maximum density of 40 birds per 100 acres in Washago (Speirs, Markle & Tozer, 1970: 5). Speirs (1974) listed 27 species parasitized in Ontario Co. with Song Sparrow (28 nests) and Yellow Warbler (13 nests) the chief hosts: 67 of the 105 nests held only one cowbird egg; 30 held two; 6 held three and one each held 4 and 6 eggs: J.A. Edwards found an American Goldfinch nest with 2 eggs and 6 cowbird eggs as late as Aug. 5, 1926, at Beaverton. Tozer & Richards (1974: 355) listed 37 species parasitized by cowbirds in the Oshawa-Scugog region, with Song Sparrow (39 nests) and Chipping Sparrow (29 nests) the chief hosts. Paul Harrington found an egg in a Myrtle Warbler nest at Wasaga Beach as late as July 17, 1914: H.P. Bingham listed 30 speices victimized by cowbirds in the Barrie area, mainly Song Sparrows, Red-eyed Vireos, Yellow Warblers and Chipping Sparrows (Devitt, 1967: 156). An egg was found in the nest of an American Goldfinch at Spider Bay, Parry Sound, as late as Aug. 2, 1976 (Mills, 1981: 162). D.B. Ferguson found 3 cowbird eggs in a Veery's nest at Windfall Lake, Manitoulin, on June 18, 1977 (Nicholson, 1981: 180). C.H.D. Clarke saw a young cowbird with a Song Sparrow at Brule Lake, Algonquin Park, on June 30, 1934 (MacLulich, 1938: 38). T.M. Shortt collected a young female cowbird from the nest of a Black-throated Blue Warbler at Eau Claire on July 1, 1935 (Baillie & Harrington, 1937: 261). Baillie &

Hope (1947: 128) collected adults at Chapleau, Biscotasing and Bigwood: at Bigwood he saw a young cowbird attended by a male Philadelphia Vireo on July 18 and another young there left the nest of a Myrtle Warbler on July 22, 1937. Snyder (1942: 148) mentioned Blackburnian Warbler, Chestnut-sided Warbler and American Redstart as hosts near Sault Ste. Marie in 1931. Skeel & Bondrup-Nielsen (1978: 212) saw one male at Pukaskwa on June 16, 1977. Baillie & Hope (1943: 24) collected 3 males at Rossport from May 30 to June 5, 1936. Snyder (1928: 266) saw only one in two summers at Lake Nipigon, a male collected at Macdiarmid on June 11, 1923. Dear (1940: 141) reported finding eggs in nests of 8 species near Thunder Bay. Snyder (1938: 208) found them common about farmland in the Rainy River region. Snyder (1953: 85) saw up to 25 in a day at Kenora, and considered them rare east to Wabigoon and north to Sioux Lookout. Elder (1979: 39) called them common summer residents at Geraldton. James (1980: 90) had a daily maximum of 4 at Pickle Lake in 1977 and found none there in 1979. Schueler, Baldwin & Rising (1974: 144) listed them as uncommon at Cochrane, Moosonee, Attawapiskat and Winisk. Lee (1978: 33) saw two males and a female at Big Trout Lake on June 29, 1975.

AUTUMN: Peruniak (1971: 28) gave Sept. 21 as her latest Atikokan date. Louise Lawrence noted 30 at Eau Claire on Sept. 15, 1944 (Speirs & Speirs, 1947: 37). D. Sutherland saw 200 on Beausoleil Is. on Oct. 4, 1976 (Mills, 1981: 162). Devitt (1967: 157) saw 150 at Tiny Marsh, Simcoe Co., on Oct. 13, 1966. On Oct. 19, 1982 I watched a flock of about 300 on the Pickering-Whitby Townline using evasive tactics to thwart a harassing Merlin: first they formed a great whirling ball of birds in the sky; then they plummeted down, some settling close beside cows in a fairly close-packed group of cattle; others settled in a maze of twigs in an apple orchard; none were so silly as to try escape by free flight in the open. Saunders (1947: 374) gave Oct. 6 as his average departure date from Toronto, but Speirs (1938: 51) listed Oct. 10 as the fall peak there. Ussher (1965: 28) gave Oct. 26 as his average departure date from Rondeau. Stirrett (1973d: 28) had a fall maximum of 10,000 at Pelee on Oct. 30.

BANDING: Of the birds banded near Toronto up to 1966, 4 were recovered in Louisiana, one in Alabama, 2 in Kentucky, one in Georgia, 2 in Texas, one in Wisconsin and one in Illinois. Two banded in Alabama, one in Arkansaw and 7 in Ohio were recovered near Toronto. Brewer & Salvadori (1976: 89) reported a female banded at Mitchell Bay on Oct. 23, 1965 and recovered at Bemidji, Minnesota (704 miles NW) on Apr. 24, 1971. Brewer & Salvadori (1978: 85-87) listed and mapped several recoveries of Ontario birds in the Gulf States: 3 in eastern Texas, 8 in Louisiana, 4 in Alabama, 5 in Georgia and 6 in Florida, though most were found closer to home in Ohio (46) and Michigan (19) and some in intermediate states. One banded at Lake Manitouwabing, Muskoka, on July 27, 1974, was found dead in Louisiana in January, 1977 (Mills, 1981: 162).

MEASUREMENTS:
Males average larger than females.
*Length:* 7 to 8 1/4 ins. (Godfrey, 1966: 360)
*Wingspread:* 11.70 to 13.75 ins. (Roberts, 1955: 690)
*Weight:* 27 Ontario specimens averaged 44.3 g.

**REFERENCES:**
Scott, D.M. 1977 Cowbird parasitism on the Gray Catbird at London, Ontario. Auk, 94: (1): 18-27.

Scott, D.M. and C. Davison Ankney 1979 Evaluation of a method for estimating the laying rate of Brown-headed Cowbirds. Auk, 96: (3): 483-488.

Scott, D.M. and C. Davison Ankney 1983 The laying cycle of Brown-headed Cowbirds: passerine chickens? Auk, 100: (3): 583-592. "An average female cowbird lays about 40 eggs in an 8-week laying season in southern Ontario . . ." usually in successive clutches of 4 or 5 eggs, separated by one or two day intervals (as in chickens). This article has a good bibliography including other papers by these authors and many others.

Waltho, Ed 1970 Brown-headed Cowbird (*Molothrus ater*) gathering nesting material. Ont. Field Biologist, No. 24: 37.

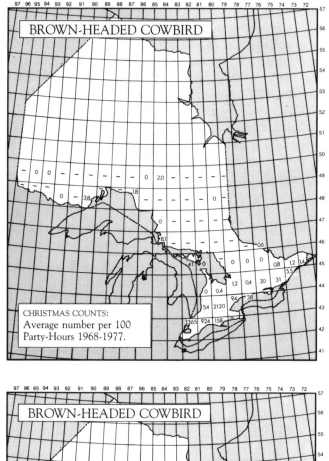

BROWN-HEADED COWBIRD

CHRISTMAS COUNTS:
Average number per 100
Party-Hours 1968-1977.

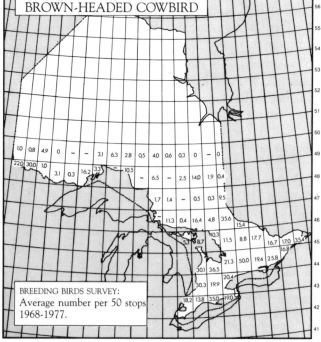

BROWN-HEADED COWBIRD

BREEDING BIRDS SURVEY:
Average number per 50 stops
1968-1977.

# ORCHARD ORIOLE   *Icterus spurius*   (Linnaeus)

This southern oriole is most likely to be found in Ontario at Pelee, or elsewhere along the Lake Erie shores: it is quite rare elsewhere in Ontario. They winter in Central America and northern South America.

IDENTIFICATION: Adult males are brick red, or chestnut, not orange in body plumage, with an all black tail. Young males are yellowish green with a prominent black throat patch. Females look like the young males but lack the throat patch: they are coloured something like female Scarlet Tanagers but have a more pointed bill and have white wing bars. The song is longer than that of the Northern Oriole and lacks the loud, sweet whistles of that species. When I heard an immature male at Lowbanks, near Lake Erie, on May 22, 1937, I wrote down its song as "chee-chee—hee-chee—he-che-che—hee-chee—ha-brrr-zhee-oo" (the somewhat buzzy, descending ending is characteristic).

WINTER:

SPRING: Stirrett (1973b: 25) gave Apr. 25 as his earliest Pelee record, with a maximum of 100 on May 23. Kelley (1978: 80) reported 129 at Pelee in May, 1949. Ussher (1965: 27) gave May 13 as his 17-year average arrival date at Rondeau, with the earliest on May 3. Saunders & Dale (1933: 235) mentioned one male collected near London on May 24, 1880 and another in song on May 31, 1917. W.E. Saunders noted one at Port Rowan on May 31, 1908 (Snyder, 1931: 195). Beardslee & Mitchell (1965: 404) reported one at Morgan's Point, Lake Erie, as early as Apr. 23, 1960. J.Hughes Samuel took an immature male at Toronto on May 20, 1900 (Fleming, 1907: 78) and J.L. Baillie had a Toronto record on May 29 (Saunders, 1947: 373). Don Perks and J. David West found a male Orchard Oriole at Lorne Park on Apr. 28, 1960 (Speirs, 1960: 34). The earliest Ontario Co. record was a male seen at Thickson's woods, Whitby, on May 4, 1970 by Ron Tozer: Speirs (1974) documented this and 8 other spring records for the Pickering to Oshawa waterfront area. Weir & Quilliam (1980: 39) gave May 14 as the 9-year average arrival date at Kingston, with the earliest on May 8. Nicholson (1981: 178) cited 8 spring records on Manitoulin from May 9 (1979) to May 20 (1969).

SUMMER: On the 1968-1977 Breeding Bird Surveys they were rare to fairly common on routes near the Lake Erie shore, absent elsewhere. Baillie & Harrington (1937: 259) took a set of 4 eggs on Pelee Is. on June 5, 1933 and L.L. Snyder collected a nest with 3 eggs and a cowbird egg at Pelee on June 14, 1920. Stirrett (1973c: 21) had a summer maximum of 150 at Pelee on June 16. T. Smith collected a set of 4 eggs at Chatham on June 30, 1887 (Baillie & Harrington, 1937: 259). W. McMillan took a set of 4 eggs at Hyde Park, near London, on June 5, 1889 (Saunders & Dale, 1933: 235). Brooman (1954: 36) mentioned a nest with 4 eggs and one young at St. Thomas on June 19, 1887 and a set of 5 eggs taken at Port Burwell on June 18, 1924 by F. Starr. Snyder (1931: 195) collected a male at Port Rowan on June 2, 1927. I saw adults at a nest at Port Dover on June 28, 1934 (Baillie & Harrington, 1937: 259). Beardslee & Mitchell (1965: 404) mentioned a nest with eggs at Fort Erie on June 19, 1904 and an unusual nest 30 ft. up in a farmyard spruce at Mohawk Point, Lake Erie, on June 24, 1956: also a nest with young on June 19, 1946 at Fort Erie: their latest record was one seen at Long Beach on Aug. 24, 1945. W.E. Hurlburt found a nest with young at Vineland on June 30, 1929 and I found a nest with young at Hamilton on June 23, 1937 (Baillie & Harrington,

918

1937: 259). J.H. Samuel found a pair nesting at Toronto on July 5, 1900 (Fleming, 1907: 78). The latest Toronto region record was one seen at Georgetown on Aug. 22, 1976 by M. and F. Helson (Goodwin, 1977: 172). Speirs (1974) mapped four summer records near the Lake Ontario shore from Pickering to Oshawa. Snyder (1941: 83) collected a male at Hallowell, Prince Edward Co., on June 12, 1930. Weir & Quilliam (1980: 25, 39) gave Aug. 20 as their latest record in the Kingston region: a mated pair was present at Prince Edward Point in 1973 and 1974 but no nest was found. Alice S. Dietrich reported one in Conc. 20, Tiny Twp. Simcoe Co., from June 17 to July 12, 1953 (Devitt, 1967: 154). Mills (1981: 157) found a singing male about 3 miles south of Magnetawan on June 11, 1977 and with C. Harris in 1976 observed breeding at Waubaushene.

AUTUMN: Stirrett (1973d: 28) gave Sept. 21 as his latest one at Pelee.

**MEASUREMENTS:**
*Length:* 6 to 7 1/4 ins.
(Godfrey, 1966: 356)
*Wingspread:* 9 1/4 to 10
1/4 ins. (Roberts,
1955: 688)
*Weight:* 3/4 oz. (Roberts,
1955: 688) ♂ larger than
♀ .

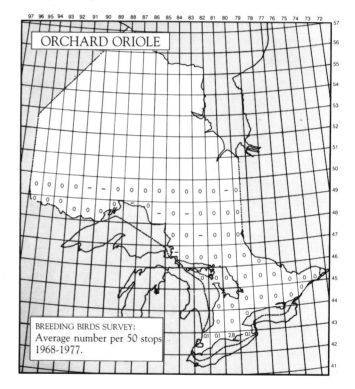

ORCHARD ORIOLE

BREEDING BIRDS SURVEY:
Average number per 50 stops
1968-1977.

# NORTHERN ORIOLE  *Icterus galbula*  (Linnaeus)

I always look forward to the arrival of the orioles when the fruit trees are in blossom in early May: their bright colours and lively songs add to this glad season. In summer they weave their pendant nests in the outermost twigs of drooping branches of such trees as elms and weeping willows: the male often sings nearby as the female incubates in her twine bag of a nest. When the young leave the nest, their incessant food calls help the parents to find them, well hidden in dense foliage, high in the canopy. They migrate early and few are to be found in Ontario after early September. They winter mainly in Central America and northern South America.

**IDENTIFICATION:**  Males are bright orange, with black head and upper back and black central tail feathers: the black wings have white flashes. Females are dull versions of the male, with the black reduced to spots or streaks. The song is a rich, whistled "too-hee-tew-tew-tew" (varying somewhat from bird to bird): they will often come to a whistled version of the final drooping "tew-tew-tew". They often utter a scolding lip-smacking sputter.

**WINTER:**  On the 1968-1977 Christmas counts, individuals were reported on the London (1971), Hamilton (1974) and Thousand Islands (1974) counts. Beardslee & Mitchell (1965: 405) reported one at Port Colborne from Dec. 3-29, 1956. Parker (1983: 28) showed Toronto records for every month of the year, including three on Christmas counts. Ron Tozer noted one at his Oshawa feeder on Dec. 23, 1960 and reported another at a Port Perry feeder the last two weeks of Dec., 1971 to Jan. 4, 1972 (Speirs, 1974). D. Calvert had one at his Oshawa feeder on Dec. 9 and 11, 1972 (Tozer & Richards, 1974: 269). Quilliam (1973: 172) reported two December (1963 and 1971) and two January (1964 and 1972) records for Kingston.

**SPRING:**  Stirrett (1973b: 25) had his earliest two at Pelee on Apr. 27 and his spring maximum of 150 on May 11. Ussher (1965: 27) gave May 4 as his 24-year average arrival date at Rondeau with the earliest on Apr. 27. Saunders & Dale (1933: 235) gave May 5 as the 17-year average arrival date at London, with the earliest on Apr. 28, 1915: a set of 5 eggs was found on May 29, 1914. Snyder (1931: 195) had his earliest at Long Point on May 7 in 1928. A nest with young was found as early as May 25, 1955 at Fort Erie (Beardslee & Mitchell, 1965: 405). Fleming (1907: 78) had a very early Toronto record, on Apr. 12. Saunders (1947: 373) listed May 9 as his average arrival date at Toronto, with his earliest on May 2, while Speirs (1938: 43) gave May 19 as the spring peak date there. Speirs (1974) noted one in Pickering Twp. on Apr. 30, 1964 and Joe Amos had one nesting at his Pickering Twp. home as early as May 21, 1967. Tozer & Richards (1974: 268) had a very early sighting in Scugog on Apr. 9, 1955 and reported a count of 70 in Thickson's Woods, Whitby, on May 13, 1972 by Dennis Barry. Allin (1940: 107) found a nest in Darlington Twp. as early as May 27, 1928. Snyder (1941: 89) reported a nest on May 31, 1917 at Wellington, Prince Edward Co. Weir & Quilliam (1980: 39) listed May 3 as the 31-year average arrival date at Kingston: an early arrival was noted there on Apr. 11, 1966 (Quilliam, 1973: 172). Devitt (1967: 155) gave May 6 as a 24-year average arrival date at Barrie, with one as early as May 1, 1954 at Collingwood: H.P. Bingham collected a set of 5 eggs near Barrie on May 31, 1933. L. Beamer's median arrival date at Meaford was May 6, with an early one in his garden on Apr. 27, 1957. Mills

(1981: 158-159) gave May 11 as a 7-year average arrival date at Huntsville, with the earliest on May 7, 1965: Paul Pratt observed nest building at Bracebridge as early as May 10, 1970. Nicholson (1981: 178) gave May 9 as the 11-year average arrival date on Manitoulin, with the earliest on May 2, 1973: a high count of some 330 flew south past the Great Duck Island lighthouse on May 19, 1979 and 90 were noted at South Baymouth the same day. The earliest Algonquin Park record was on May 12, 1936 at Cache Lake by E.L. Brereton (MacLulich, 1938: 37). Louise Lawrence noted one at Rutherglen on May 15, 1944 (Speirs & Speirs, 1947: 36). The only Pukaskwa record was a male seen by D. Hoy and W. Wyett on May 30, 1974 (Skeel & Bondrup-Nielsen, 1978: 211). Peruniak (1971: 28) had a few spring records for Atikokan, the earliest on May 18.

SUMMER: On the 1968-1977 Breeding Bird Surveys they were common north to Flesherton and Kemptville, becoming uncommon north to Mattawa, Thessalon, Thunder Bay and Dryden. Stirrett (1973c: 22) had a summer maximum of 125 at Pelee on July 24. Saunders & Dale (1933: 235) reported London nestings: with 5 eggs on June 5, 1892; 5 eggs on June 2, 1902; 4 eggs on June 3, 1914 and 5 eggs on June 4, 1916. Marshall Field found a nest at St. Thomas on June 2, 1946 (Brooman, 1954: 36). R. Hurst found a nest with 1 egg and 3 young at Long Point on June 18, 1978: one of 26 nest records there (McCracken, Bradstreet & Holroyd, 1981: 64-65). Snyder (1930: 193) collected a young male in King Twp. on July 3, 1926 and noted the preference for nesting in towering elms. Speirs & Orenstein (1975: 14) found orioles in 8 of 11 forest quadrats in Ontario Co. with a maximum density of 22 birds per 100 acres in the Scugog plot. Speirs, Markle & Tozer (1970: 5) found some in 9 of 10 urban quadrats in Ontario Co., with a maximum density of 25 birds per 100 acres in the Zephyr plot. J.A. Edwards found a nest with 6 eggs on Thorah Island on June 2, 1938 and another nest with 6 eggs there on June 17, 1926 (Speirs, 1974). Long (1968a: 22) observed adults feeding young in the nest as late as July 12, 1963 at Pickering Beach. Speirs (1974) reported 29 sets of eggs in Ontario Co. that held a total of 137 eggs: only two held cowbird eggs (one held 1 cowbird egg and 2 of the host, while the other held 2 cowbird eggs and 4 of the host). Allin (1940: 107) found an unusual nest, not more than 8 ft. up in a white spruce at Hampton, on June 18, 1927. While standing under an elm tree in Prince Edward Co. on June 30, 1930 during a heavy rain and wind storm a nest containing a female and 3 young fell at his feet (Snyder, 1941: 84). A.J. Erskine found a density of 14 males per 100 acres on his Wolfe Is. quadrat near Kingston: C.K. Clarke found a nest with 6 eggs near Kingston on June 4, 1898 (Quilliam, 1973: 172). Devitt (1967: 154) observed young out of the nest at Wasaga Beach being fed by parent on June 24, 1933. Mills (1981: 158) mentioned 16 nest records for the cottage country at heights from 18 to 58 ft. Ross James found a nest with 3 young near Poplar, Manitoulin, on July 5, 1977 (Nicholson, 1981: 178). J.L. Baillie & L.L. Snyder saw a male at Brent, Algonquin Park, on July 11, 1922 (MacLulich, 1938: 37). Speirs & Speirs (1947: 36) found a nest with young 20 ft. up in an aspen at Kaibuskong Bay, near Rutherglen, on June 21, 1944: their latest North Bay record was Aug. 15, 1944. S. Downing collected a male at Bigwood on July 31, 1937 (Baillie & Hope, 1947: 27). Elder (1979: 39) reported one captured on the Slate Islands, Lake Superior, on June 18, 1965. Denis (1961: 7) listed them as irregular, rare, visitants at Thunder Bay and no nests had been found there (Dear, 1940: 140). Baillie & Harrington (1937: 259) saw a male at Whitefish Lake on June 6, 1935. Snyder (1938: 208) noted the first brood out of the nest at Off Lake, Rainy River, on July 7, 1929. David Elder had a June 3, 1981, record at Atikokan. Snyder (1953: 84) had summer records in western Ontario from Ingolf, Malachi, Kenora and Redditt.

AUTUMN: Nicholson (1981: 178) had only two fall records for Manitoulin, both on Great Duck Is.: Sept. 22, 1973 and from Sept. 24 to Oct. 14, 1978. Devitt (1967: 155) gave Sept. 4, 1939 as his latest Simcoe Co. date. Weir & Quilliam (1980: 39) listed Sept. 12 as the 24-year average departure date from Kingston. Tozer & Richards (1974: 269) noted one at a feeder north of Oshawa for several days following Nov. 25,1965. Saunders (1947: 373) had a lingering bird at Toronto as late as Nov. 13, though J.L. Baillie gave Sept. 8 as his latest in 20 years there. Beardslee & Mitchell (1965: 405) reported one at Ft. Erie on Sept. 23, 1961. Ussher (1965: 27) gave Sept. 4 as his 14-year average departure date from Rondeau, with the latest on Oct. 12. Stirrett (1973d: 28) had two on Sept. 10 at Pelee, then none until a straggler on Nov. 9.

BANDING: One banded by Herb. Southam near Toronto on Aug. 4, 1936 was re-covered in Louisiana during the first ten days of May, 1937. Brewer & Salvadori (1978: 83) reported two recoveries: one banded at East Tawas, Mich. on May 16, 1968 was recovered at Dundas Marsh, Ont. on July 3, 1969 (about 188 miles to the east): the other, banded at Long Point on May 6, 1966, was recovered at Newberry, Pa. on June 7, 1968 (about 194 miles southeast).

**MEASUREMENTS:**
*Length:* 7.0 to 8.2 ins. (Godfrey, 1966: 356)
*Wingspread:* 11 to 12 1/4 ins. (Roberts, 1955: 694)
*Weight:* 17 Ontario specimens averaged 34.5 g.

**REFERENCE:**
Murray, H.W.H. 1962 A feeding habit of Baltimore Orioles. Fed. Ont. Naturalists, Bull 95: 11. (Observed taking nectar from flowering quince blossoms)

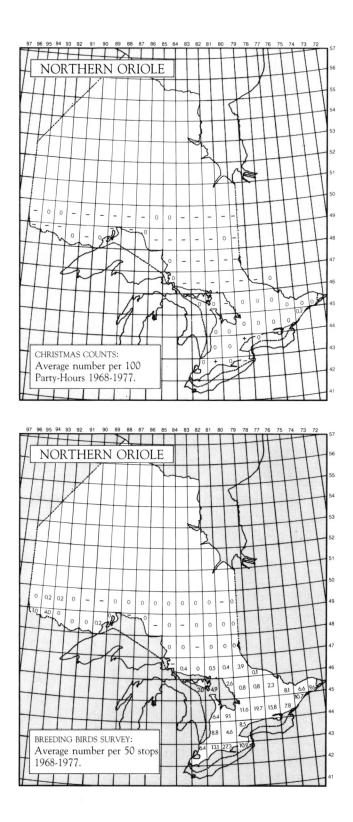

NORTHERN ORIOLE

CHRISTMAS COUNTS:
Average number per 100
Party-Hours 1968-1977.

NORTHERN ORIOLE

BREEDING BIRDS SURVEY:
Average number per 50 stops
1968-1977.

# SCOTT'S ORIOLE
## *Icterus parisorum*  Bonaparte

This is a bird of the southwestern United States, accidental in Canada, so when one showed up near Thunder Bay, in November, it caused quite a sensation.

IDENTIFICATION:  The front half of this oriole is black, the posterior (rump and belly) is mainly yellow. The wings are black except for yellow coverts and broad white wing bar. The tail is patterned like that of a yellow-plumaged redstart. Females look like a dingy version of other female orioles.

WINTER:

SPRING:

SUMMER:

AUTUMN:  An adult male was photographed by Arne Maki at Silver Islet, Sibley Provincial Park, about 30 km. east southeast of Thunder Bay, on Nov. 9, 1975. It was found and seen by about 7 other observers there the same day (Denis, 1976: 500). Although this was the first Ontario (and Canadian) record, one was banded not far away, at Duluth, Minn. on May 23, 1974 (Denis, 1976: 501).

**MEASUREMENTS:**
*Length:* 7 1/4 to 8 1/4 ins.
(Terres, 1980: 944)
Wingspread:
*Weight:* 39 averaged
37.4 g. (32.1 - 41.0 g.)
(Dunning, 1984: 26).

**REFERENCE:**
Denis, Keith 1976 Scott's
Oriole near Thunder Bay,
Ontario. Can. Field-Nat.
90: (4): 500-501.

# BRAMBLING   *Fringilla montifringilla*   Linnaeus

The Brambling is an Old World finch, accidental in Ontario.

**IDENTIFICATION:**   The Brambling has a black head and back, a white rump, orange breast and white belly. The forked tail is black. The wings are mainly black but with orange "shoulders" and white wing bars. It is about the size of a House Sparrow. It is usually found in forest edge habitat.

**WINTER:**

**SPRING:**

**SUMMER:**

**AUTUMN:**   Elder (1984: 38-39) described one that fed in his garden at Atikokan from Oct. 23-26, 1983. He took several photographs (on file at the ROM) and his identification was confirmed by several other observers during its stay at Atikokan.

**MEASUREMENTS:**
*Length:* 5³/₄ ins. (Peterson,
Mountford & Hollom,
1954: 282)
*Wingspread:*
*Weight:*

**REFERENCE:**
Elder, David H. 1984
Brambling: new to
Ontario. Ontario Birds, 2:
(1): 38-39.

# ROSY FINCH    *Leucosticte arctoa*    (Pallas)

This is a bird of rocky crags, high above timberline in the Rockies, windblown birds by glaciers where the oxygen supply is at risk for many human observers. However, in winter they come down to lower altitudes and some even come to feeding stations far from their mountain haunts. The few Ontario records have been at Thunder Bay feeders.

**IDENTIFICATION:**  These are about the size of House Sparrows, largely brown both above and below, with pinkish tinge on wings, rump and tail coverts, sometimes on the breast. There is a patch of gray running back and up from the eye to the top of the head.

**WINTER:**  B.J. Spenceley photographed one at his Thunder Bay feeder, where it was seen from Feb. 25 into March, 1973 (Goodwin, 1973: 611). H. Quackenbush also photographed one at Thunder Bay on Jan. 31, 1975 (Goodwin, 1975: 687).

**SPRING:**  Carl Rydholm photographed one at his feeder in Neebing Twp., Thunder Bay, on March 31, 1963 (Baillie, 1964: 7). The Spenceley bird remained until March 25, 1973 (Goodwin, 1973: 611).

**SUMMER:**

**AUTUMN:**

**MEASUREMENTS:**
*Length:*  5.8 to 6.8 ins.
(Godfrey, 1966: 373)
Wingspread:
*Weight:*  7 California birds
averaged 27.8 g., one as
much as 32.3 g. (Terres,
1980: 328).

# PINE GROSBEAK    *Pinicola enucleator*    (Linnaeus)

For southern Ontario bird watchers this is a winter bird, sometimes common but usually scarce: "good winters" occur about once in six years. Pine Grosbeaks are attracted to such winter foods as the seeds of ash trees, the "berries" of mountain ash and highbush cranberries and unpicked apples left hanging on the trees (they eat the seeds, not the pulp, of the apples). Farther north they are found during most winters and often eat buds of conifers as well as persistent wild fruits. Although some may be found as far south as Algonquin Park in summer, they are seldom seen in that season.

**IDENTIFICATION:**  The rosy males look at bit like robin-sized versions of Purple Finch males but the large bill, conspicuous wing bars and large size will easily distinguish them. Crossbills are also somewhat similar but smaller in size and with the distinctive crossed bills. Females and young males come in a variety of colours from gray-green to rusty-orange, but always with the distinctive wing bars and robin size. The common call note is a plaintive whistle "tee-choo" or "tee-choo-choo". The song, seldom heard in southern Ontario, is a continuous canary-like warble.

WINTER: On the 1968-1977 Christmas counts they were common at most northern localities (south to Wiarton and Kingston), becoming uncommon to rare in southwestern Ontario. Stirrett (1973a: 20) had single birds at Pelee on Dec. 14 and Jan. 4. Saunders & Dale (1933: 238) considered it "rare and irregular" at London, with the largest single flock of 32 on Dec. 24, 1921 and a combined Christmas count total of 51 on Dec. 28, 1929 (an "invasion year"). Saunders (1947: 379) gave Feb. 20 as his average departure date from Toronto. Speirs (1939: 417) presented evidence for a 5 to 6-year cycle in abundance in the Toronto region in winter. Speirs (1973) reported invasion years and years with no records, for Ontario Co. Snyder (1941: 86-87) reported one collected in Prince Edward Co. on Jan. 2, 1912 by Frank Brimley and another collected at Wellington by W.H. Lunn on Feb. 1, 1938. Quilliam (1973: 180) noted some invasion years at Kingston, but none in 1953. Devitt (1967: 162) reported 216 as the high Christmas count at Barrie on Dec. 30, 1961. Mills (1981: 170) cited some good winters for the cottage country, with a Huntsville Christmas count maximum of 179 in 1969. Dennison (1980: 146) listed this as a species found on all 25 Christmas counts at Sault Ste. Marie, in numbers varying from 2 to 164. This species ranked fourth as a winter bird in Pukaskwa: a flock of 13 was seen there on Dec. 20, 1976 (Skeel & Bondrup-Nielsen, 1978: 214). Elder (1979: 40) called it a common winter resident in Geraldton. Cringan (1953a: 4) listed it as a winter resident at Sioux Lookout in 1952-1953.

SPRING: Ussher (1965: 29) gave March 22 as his latest Rondeau record. Speirs (1938: 45) gave March 23 as the latest spring date for Toronto, but Saunders (1947: 374) had one as late as Apr. 12. Donald Price and I saw two in Uxbridge Twp. as late as March 31, 1972 (Speirs, 1973). Frank Brimley noted 3 in Prince Edward Co. on March 17, 1912 (Snyder, 1941: 86). Weir & Quilliam (1980: 40) listed March 6 as the 18-year average departure date from Kingston, with a very late one on May 25. Devitt (1967: 162) gave Apr. 27, 1938 as the latest Barrie record. Ross Lowe had a Manitoulin bird as late as Apr. 20, 1969 (Nicholson, 1981: 184). C.H.D. Clarke saw one at Brule Lake, Algonquin Park, on May 30, 1934 (MacLulich, 1938: 40). Speirs & Speirs (1947: 37) reported a peak at North Bay in mid-March, 1944: they observed courtship feeding on Apr. 15, 1944 (see Bent, 1968: 326-327 for details). Skeel & Bondrup-Nielsen (1978: 214) saw one at Pukaskwa on May 19, 1977. Peruniak (1971: 29) gave March 31 as her latest date for Atikokan.

SUMMER: On the 1968-1977 Breeding Bird Surveys they were uncommon south to Chapleau, but absent from most routes, even in the north. Charles Fothergill described one shot at Rice Lake on July 4, 1921, so perhaps they came further south in the old days (Black, 1934: 158). Percy Ghent reported a nest with young in late August, 1940 at Sundridge (Baillie, 1960: 17). Mills (1981: 170-171) mentioned a few other summer records for the cottage country. Robert and Virginia Rusk saw two at Gore Bay, Manitoulin, on Aug. 28, 1976 (Nicholson, 1981: 184). MacLulich (1938: 40) observed a singing male in Algonquin Park on Aug. 8, 1930. D. MacLulich heard a male singing at Frank's Bay, Lake Nipissing, on July 2, 1934 (Ricker & Clarke, 1939: 22). Hugh Funnell found a nest on an island in Lake Timagami in July, 1940 and saw adults with young there about 1935 (Baillie, 1960: 17). Skeel & Bondrup-Nielsen (1978: 214) saw single birds at Pukaskwa on June 6, 7, and 9, 1977. Snyder (1953: 86) reported one at Dinorwic Lake in early June, 1940 and one at Sioux Lookout on June 24, 1947. W. Earl Godfrey saw a small group between Longlac and Hearst, by Hwy. 11, on Aug. 11, 1953 (Smith, 1957: 180). Snyder (1928: 27) saw two at Lake Abitibi in summer, 1925, and collected a female there on June 20. Bondrup-Nielsen (1976: 45) listed this as an uncommon permanent resident near Kapuskasing in 1974 and 1975 (5 to 10 noted daily). Harry G. Lumsden collected a female with brood patch and a fully-formed egg, without shell, in its oviduct, at Hawley Lake on June 25, 1958 (Baillie, 1960: 17). James, Nash & Peck (1981: 93) collected two males and a female at Kiruna Lake, Sutton Ridges, in the summer of 1981. Lee (1978: 33) found a female "exhibiting strong territorial behaviour" in his black spruce quadrat at Big Trout Lake in the summer of 1975. C.E. Hope saw 5 (two collected) on July 3, 1940 at Fort Severn.

AUTUMN: Frits Johansen collected one on Moose Island on Oct. 3, 1930 (Manning, 1952: 88). Todd (1963: 649) took a number of specimens at Moose Factory in October and November. D. McRae and A. Wormington observed them daily (except on one bad day) from Oct. 15 to Nov. 23 at Netitishi Point, James Bay, with a maximum of 60 on their last day, Nov. 23. Peruniak (1971: 29) gave Oct. 19 as her earliest fall record for Atikokan. Denis (1961: 6) gave Nov. 17 as the 19-year average arrival date in fall at Thunder Bay. W. Wyett saw 20 at Pukaskwa on Oct. 2, 1975 (Skeel & Bondrup-Nielsen, 1978: 214). Nicholson (1981: 184) gave Oct. 13, 1979 as his earliest fall record for Manitoulin, and 500 seen by Ron Tasker in Burpee Twp. on Nov. 18, 1980, as the high count. Mills (1981: 170-171) reported a male seen by G. Thorn at Arrowhead Provincial Park as early as Sept. 30, 1977 and one collected at Port Sydney on Oct. 15, 1905. E.G. White saw 1500 in McKay's Woods, Ottawa, on Oct. 27, 1903 (Lloyd, 1923: 156). Devitt (1967: 162) gave Oct. 12, 1964 as the earliest Simcoe Co. date. Weir & Quilliam (1980: 40) listed Nov. 6 as the 18-year average arrival at Kingston, with the earliest on Sept. 14. Audrey Russ saw two at Ajax on Oct. 26, 1965 and I heard one at our Pickering home on Oct. 26, 1968 (Speirs, 1973). Speirs (1938: 47) gave Nov. 1 as the earliest Toronto date with a peak about Nov. 19. In 1951, an "invasion year", Marshall Field reported them at Port Burwell on Nov. 11 and at Port Stanley on Nov. 18 (Brooman, 1954: 37). Ussher (1965: 29) gave Nov. 15 as his earliest Rondeau record. Stirrett (1973a: 20) reported 5 at Pelee on Nov. 19 and 9 on Nov. 25 (just two records).

**MEASUREMENTS:**
*Length:* 9 to 9 3/4 ins.
(Godfrey, 1966: 372)
*Wingspread:* 13.75 to
14.87 ins. (Roberts,
1955: 701)
*Weight:* 2.00 to 2.31 oz.
(Roberts, 1955: 701).

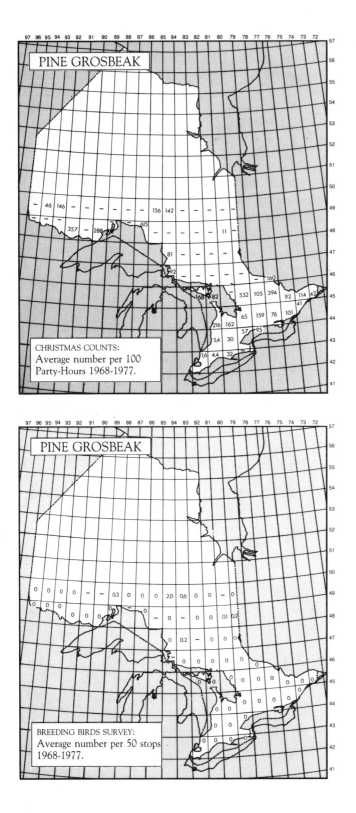

PINE GROSBEAK

CHRISTMAS COUNTS:
Average number per 100
Party-Hours 1968-1977.

PINE GROSBEAK

BREEDING BIRDS SURVEY:
Average number per 50 stops
1968-1977.

# PURPLE FINCH  *Carpodacus purpureus*  (Gmelin)

Like the Evening Grosbeak, the Purple Finch varies considerably in numbers from year to year and from place to place: the two are frequently found together at feeders in the south in winter and at roadside salt licks in summer in the north. The numbers coming to these attractions can be very deceiving as we found by banding: we thought about 8 were coming to a salt lick at Dorion one summer before we started banding but we banded 178 and then only about half of the birds coming were banded after all this effort! Although some occur in winter as far south as the southern U.S.A., most of our banding recoveries have come from farther north (North Carolina to Kansas) and many remain in Ontario all winter.

IDENTIFICATION: Adult males look at bit like female House Sparrows dipped in raspberry juice. Young males and females are also sparrowy looking birds, but with conspicuous white "eyebrows". The males usually take two or more years to acquire their reddish finery, but not the ecstatic, burbling, canary-like song. The common call note is a wooden "tic": once learned this will enable you to identify the birds at a considerable distance, even in flight. For distinctions from the House Finch, see that species.

WINTER: On the 1968-1977 Christmas counts they averaged fairly common along the north shore of Lake Erie, from Ottawa to Georgian Bay and at Manitouwadge, uncommon to rare elsewhere, but the numbers varied widely from year to year, especially in the north. Stirrett (1973a: 20) had winter maxima of 60 at Pelee on Jan. 4 and Jan. 30. Parker (1983: 28) reported the species on 50 of 58 Christmas counts at Toronto. Speirs (1973) reported Purple Finches during 22 of 24 winters in Pickering Twp. L. Beamer watched two eating ash seeds at Meaford on Jan. 24, 1938 and some in a mountain ash on Jan. 6, 1941. Some were reported on 14 of 21 Christmas counts at Huntsville, with a maximum of 53 on Dec. 20, 1964 (Mills, 1981: 169). Dennison (1980: 147) reported them on 11 of 25 Christmas counts at Sault Ste. Marie, with a maximum of 42 in 1960.

SPRING: Stirrett (1973b: 26) had a spring maximum of 50 at Pelee on March 15, with the latest group of 9 on May 29. Ussher (1965: 29) gave May 14 as his 7-year average departure date from Rondeau. Saunders & Dale (1933: 238) described the pleasure at hearing a chorus of about 25 singing near London in the latter half of March, 1914: he reported nesting there but without specific data. Harold Lancaster found a pair at his West Elgin sanctuary on May 19, 1946: a set of 3 eggs was taken at St. Thomas on May 25, 1886 (Brooman, 1954: 37). Speirs (1938: 43) gave March 15 as the peak of the spring migration at Toronto and the numbers at feeders in Pickering Twp. generally reached a maximum in March (Speirs, 1973). Dennis Barry estimated 1500 in a 3-acre woodlot of hemlock and yellow birch in Darlington Twp. on March 10, 1968 (Tozer & Richards, 1974: 283). H.P. Bingham found a nest with 5 eggs near Barrie as early as May 27, 1931 (Devitt, 1967: 161). L. Beamer had pairs nest in a spruce tree at his home at Meaford from 1941 to 1948: on May 15, 1941 a nest held 2 eggs plus 3 cowbird eggs: in 1946 he found three pairs apparently nesting, with little friction between the males. R. James found a nest under construction at Dwight on May 23, 1971 (Mills, 1981: 169). Louise Lawrence noted one as early as March 8, 1945 at Pimisi Bay (Speirs & Speirs, 1947: 37). Skeel & Bondrup-Nielsen (1978: 214) tallied 33 on 16 days from Apr. 16 to May 29, 1977 at Pukaskwa. Denis (1961: 2) gave Apr. 13 as an average arrival date at Thunder

Bay, though some have wintered there. Peruniak (1971: 29) gave Apr. 20 as her earliest Atikokan date, but David Elder saw one on Apr. 3 in 1981 there. Cringan (1953a: 4) noted his first at Sioux Lookout on May 2 in 1953.

SUMMER: On the 1968-1977 Breeding Bird Surveys they were absent from most routes in the agricultural south of Ontario, uncommon north from Ottawa to southern Georgian Bay and fairly common on most northern routes. Kelley (1978: 84) reported an adult feeding two fledged young in Bosanquet Twp., Lambton Co., on July 2, 1964. Ussher (1965: 29) had just two summer records for Rondeau: one on June 9, the other on July 31. Brooman (1954: 37) reported 3 sets of eggs taken at St. Thomas: 5 eggs on June 2, 1890, 4 eggs on June 25, 1887 and 3 eggs on July 6, 1887 (more recently they have occurred there mainly in winter). Fleming (1907: 79) mentioned a Toronto breeding record on July 13, 1895. Snyder (1930: 194) heard two singing males near his camp in King Twp. in the summer of 1926 and collected one on June 22. Speirs & Orenstein (1975: 15) had breeding densities of 12 birds per 100 acres in their Brock Twp. forest plot and 10 birds per 100 acres in the Reach Twp. quadrat, none in the other 9 forest plots: thirteen birds were tallied on the 1962 roadside counts in 7 of 11 townships in Ontario Co. (Speirs, 1973). D. Barry and J.M. Richards found a nest with 4 eggs about 7 ft. up in a Scots pine (Christmas tree) in Cartwright Twp. (Tozer & Richards, 1974: 283). Charles Fothergill observed a male with young at Rice Lake on July 17, 1820 (Black, 1934: 158). Quilliam (1973: 179) cited a few breeding records for the Kingston region. Devitt (1967: 161) reported several Simcoe Co. nestings: a nest with 4 eggs on July 15, 1915 and a nest with 5 eggs on June 18, 1916 at Barrie and a nest with 4 eggs on June 16, 1938 at Tea Lake. On June 1, 1947, L. Beamer watched many in his Meaford garden, eating the centres from plum blossoms, discarding the petals. Mills (1981: 169) reported 8 nests in evergreens in the cottage country, at heights from 5 1/2 to 60 ft. and with egg dates from June 14 to July 2. Ron Tasker found a nest with 2 young and one infertile egg in Burpee Twp., Manitoulin, on July 29, 1976 (Nicholson, 1981: 183). MacLulich (1938: 40) saw a young bird, able to fly, at Biggar Lake, Algonquin Park, on July 28, 1933 and C.H.D. Clarke observed young being fed at Brule Lake on July 2, 1934. Louise Lawrence watched a male feeding honeysuckle berries to young at Pimisi Bay on July 4, 1944 (Speirs & Speirs, 1947: 37). Baillie & Hope (1947: 29) saw young just out of the nest at Biscotasing on July 9, 1937 and flying young at Bigwood on July 22 and 27, 1937. Snyder (1942: 149) collected a young male at Maclennan, near Sault Ste. Marie, on July 27, 1931. Skeel & Bondrup-Nielsen (1978: 214) tallied 23 on 13 days from June 9 to July 16, 1977, at Pukaskwa. Baillie & Hope (1943: 24) found them common along the northeast shore of Lake Superior in 1936, with a high count of 20 on July 4 at Amyot. Snyder (1928: 267) collected young at Macdiarmid, Lake Nipigon, on July 18, 1923 and on July 12, 1924. Dear (1940: 141) reported a nest with 5 eggs at Whitefish Lake on June 10, 1935 and a nest with 3 eggs in MacGregor Twp., Thunder Bay, on June 18, 1936. Kendeigh (1947: 28) had just two territories per 100 acres at Black Sturgeon Lake in 1945, while Speirs (1949: 148) found 4 pairs on 75 acres at Eaglehead Lake in 1946. Snyder (1938: 209) found a nest with eggs, 35 ft. up in a balsam fir at Off Lake, Rainy River, on July 12, 1929. Snyder (1953: 86) mentioned breeding at Malachi and Kenora, with some birds as far north as Sioux Lookout and as far east as Savanne. Snyder (1928: 27) collected a young male at Lake Abitibi on July 16, 1925. R.V. Whelan collected an egg (in ROM collection) at Smoky Falls on June 16, 1934 (Baillie & Harrington, 1937: 266). James (1982: 72) collected a male on June 24 and a female on July 9, 1982 by the Harricanaw

River, near James Bay. Samuel S. Dickey found a nest with 3 eggs at Moose Factory on June 2, 1934 (Todd, 1963: 648). James (1980: 90) encountered just one at Pickle Lake in 1977 but small numbers in 1949 at Shred Lake (about 45 km to the northeast). Hope (1938: 44) collected a young female at Favourable Lake on July 18, 1938. Peck (1972: 346) reported one collected at Cape Henrietta Maria in August. 1968.

AUTUMN: George Stirrett saw 15 at Moose Factory on Oct. 2, 1948 (Manning, 1952: 88) and one was noted on Oct. 15, 1981 at Netitishi Point, James Bay, by D. McRae and A. Wormington. Peruniak (1971: 29) gave Oct. 9 as her latest Atikokan record. Louise Lawrence had 7 at Pimisi Bay as late as Nov. 2, 1944 (Speirs & Speirs, 1947: 37). Speirs (1973) reported an October peak in Pickering Twp. and Speirs (1938: 51) gave Oct. 23 as the fall peak at Toronto. Snyder (1931: 195) had only one Long Point record, one picked up dead about Nov. 7, 1929, by Munroe Landon. Ussher (1965: 29) gave Aug. 29 as the 17-year average arrival date at Rondeau, where they are winter residents. Stirrett (1973a: 20) had a fall maximum of 500 at Pelee on Nov. 23, with the earliest two on Aug. 17.

BANDING: One banded near Toronto on March 28, 1954 was recovered as far south as South Carolina on March 13, 1955. One banded in Connecticut on Feb. 27, 1953 was recovered near Toronto on Feb. 17, 1954 and one banded in Michigan on March 23, 1961 was recovered near Toronto on Feb. 21, 1963. Mills (1981: 169-170) reported that one banded at Rebecca Lake on July 8, 1952 was found dead in West Virginia in May, 1953 and one banded in New York State on Oct. 5, 1968 was recovered at Port Sydney, Muskoka on July 11, 1971. One banded at Sault Ste. Marie, Mich., on March 10, 1929 was killed by a cat at Cache Lake, Algonquin Park, on June 30, 1930 (MacLulich, 1938: 40). One banded at Byron, Indiana, on Apr. 13, 1971 was recovered at Terrace Bay, Ont. on June 10, 1971 (Brewer & Salvadori, 1976: 91). Brewer & Salvadori (1978: 91) mapped several recoveries of Purple Finches: one banded at Durham, N.C. on Feb. 25, 1966 was recovered near Larder Lake, Ont. on June 2, 1967. Another banded at Charlesbourg E., Que., on Sept. 8, 1967 was recovered at Minden, Ont. on Dec. 7 of the same year. Another remarkable flight was documented when one banded at Agincourt, Ont. on March 21, 1965 was recovered at Camp Towanyak, Kansas on Jan. 9, 1969 (almost 4 years later). The recovery rate is not high for this species: we had none from the 178 we banded at Dorion and none from 16 banded at our Pickering home: Alf Bunker had none from the 49 he banded at Cherrywood. However, other interesting information can result from the study of banded birds. We found that the average weight of 15 of our winter-banded birds in Pickering was 27 g., quite a bit heavier than the provincial average determined largely from birds collected in summer. M.J. Magee banded several thousand Purple Finches at Sault Ste. Marie, Mich. and made a significant contribution to the knowledge of their plumages: some birds did not acquire their full brilliance for 4 or 5 years, while some older females had a bit of reddish come into their plumage; others became yellowish or golden (as do birds kept in captivity).

**MEASUREMENTS:**
*Length:* 5.5 to 6.3 ins.
(Godfrey, 1966: 369)
*Wingspread:* 9.2 to 10.4
ins. (Roberts, 1955: 701)
*Weight:* 43 Ontario
specimens averaged
24.8 g.

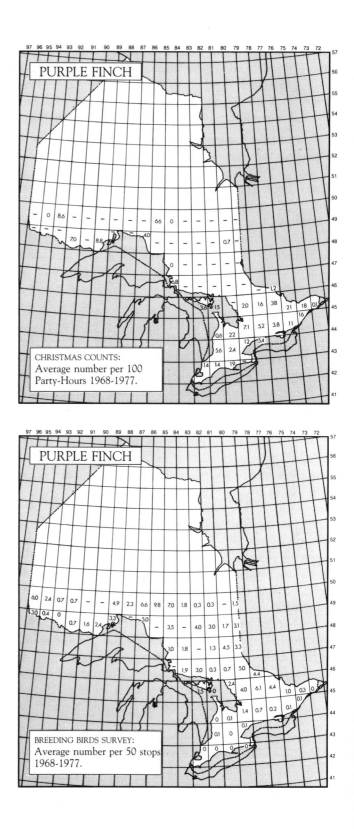

PURPLE FINCH

CHRISTMAS COUNTS:
Average number per 100
Party-Hours 1968-1977.

PURPLE FINCH

BREEDING BIRDS SURVEY:
Average number per 50 stops
1968-1977.

# HOUSE FINCH   *Carpodacus mexicanus*   (Müller)

The House Finch is a recent invader into Ontario. Originally a West Coast bird, caged birds were released on Long Island, N.Y., about 1940 and their progeny have since spread northwestward, reaching Ontario, near Kingston, about 1970 and becoming locally common in the south by 1980. Like the House Sparrow, this species adapts well to urban living, though somewhat more attractive in appearance, song and habits. They often nest in ornamental evergreens and shrubs near houses.

IDENTIFICATION: House Finches resemble Purple Finches but lack the prominent "eyebrow" stripes of that species and have shorter, stubbier, less pointed bills, the upper mandible (culmen) being distinctly convex. The adult males are a more orange red, not the raspberry red of Purple Finches. The call notes resemble the more musical calls of House Sparrows, quite unlike the wooden "tic" call of the Purple Finch. Yellow to orange-green plumages are more frequent than are such variations in Purple Finches. The reddish breast of a Purple Finch is continued down the flanks as pink stripes: in the House Finch the flank stripes are brown.

WINTER: Six were reported at St. Thomas from Jan. 10-23, 1980 by Marshall Field *et al* (Goodwin, 1980: 270). Arnold Dawe *et al* reported 12 during the winter of 1978-1979 at Niagara-on-the-Lake (Goodwin, 1979: 278), after 6 had been noted there the previous winter. St. Catharines has had a phenomenal increase in House Finch numbers and 250 were estimated there by mid-February, 1983 according to Richard Knapton (Weir, 1983: 298). A. Garrett reported one at Burlington on Jan. 29, 1980 (Goodwin, 1980: 270). Parker (1983: 28) reported it on 2 of 58 Toronto Christmas counts (in recent years). Weir & Quilliam (1980: 26) reported a possible House Finch at Mrs. Fellow's feeder at Reddendale, near Kingston, on Dec. 9, 1970, the first Ontario report. On Dec. 20, 1981 a total of 33 was reported in Kingston and F. Phelan noted 2 as far north as Chaffey's Lock (Weir, 1982: 291). A male wintered at Ottawa in 1979-1980 and again in 1980-1981 (Goodwin, 1981: 297).

SPRING: A female was spotted at Pelee on Apr. 16, 1976 by J.A. Greenhouse *et al* (Goodwin, 1976: 836). Goodwin (1978: 1001) reported one at St. Thomas, 2 at London, 2 at Toronto and one at Kingston in spring, 1978. A first for Stratford showed up on March 30, 1982 seen by M.P. Davis and a first for Long Point was reported by D. Shepherd on Apr. 7, 1982 (Weir, 1982: 848). A female was noted at Fort Erie from Apr. 8-16, 1976 by H.H. Axtell and many others (Goodwin, 1976: 836). G. Chapple found one at Dundas on Apr. 20, 1977 (Goodwin, 1977: 996). E.R. McDonald noted 10 at Port Hope-Cobourg from Apr. 1 to May 15, 1982 and G. Root had one at Belleville on May 23, 1982 (Weir, 1982: 848). Goodwin (1976: 836) found a female at Presqu'ile on May 22, 1976. The first feeder bird at Kingston, a male, was reported by Gwen Woods on March 21, 1977, since when they have appeared there annually: D. McRae reported as many as 13 at Prince Edward Point on Apr. 20, 1980 (Weir & Quilliam, 1980: 26). One was noted at Ottawa from Apr. 21-28, 1979, seen by R. Taylor and many others (Goodwin, 1979: 767). A nest was found at Peterborough on May 21, 1983 by R.D. McRae *et al* (Weir, 1983: 866) J. Bouvier noted two pairs at Pembroke in the spring of 1983 (Weir, 1983: 866). Nicholson (1981: 184) reported a male at Great Duck Island on May 3, 1979. L. and D.M. Ferguson reported one at Lively from Apr. 23 to May 9, 1979 and from May

23-31, 1980 (Goodwin, 1979: 767 and Goodwin, 1980: 773). The first substantiated Ontario record was a female, photographed at Marathon on the northeast shore of Lake Superior, on May 12, 1976 by N.G. Escott (Goodwin, 1976: 836).

SUMMER: The first nest for Sarnia was reported by D.F. Rupert in the summer of 1983 (Weir, 1983: 985). P.A. Woodliffe reported the first Rondeau nesting in the summer of 1982 (Weir, 1982: 773): three nests were found in London that summer. Marshall Field and R. Kingswood observed a pair raising several young at St. Thomas in the summer of 1980 (Goodwin, 1980: 892). T.N. Hayman reported birds at London on June 2 and July 2, 1977 (Goodwin, 1977: 1135) and more than 15 were noted there in the summer of 1981-1982 (Weir, 1982: 174). Birds were noted at Simcoe and Port Dover in the summer of 1982 (Weir, 1982: 773). Two nests were found at Niagara-on-the-Lake in the summer of 1978, the first nests for Ontario fide R.D. James (Goodwin, 1978: 1156). Several nests were found in St. Catharines in the summer of 1982 and 63 there in the summer of 1983 according to D. Koslovic (Weir, 1982: 773 and Weir, 1983: 985). Three nests were found in Hamilton and several in Toronto in the summer of 1982 (Weir, 1982: 773): birds were noted in Port Hope that summer. The first confirmed Ontario record came from Prince Edward Point, where a female was identified by A.E. Hughes, Helen Quilliam and R.D. Weir on Aug. 27, 1972: in 1980 some 27 were banded in the Kingston yard of Helen Quilliam from June 27 to Sept. 18 and breeding was first confirmed there that summer (Weir & Quilliam, 1980: 26-27). Five nests were found in Kingston in the summer of 1982 (Weir, 1982: 973). B. Morin found a pair at Cornwall in the summer of 1982 (Weir, 1982: 973). A male was found at Ottawa on July 3, 1977 by B. DiLabio and L. Murray (Goodwin, 1977: 1135) and B. Clark observed one there through the summer of 1980 (Goodwin, 1980: 892). J. Bouvier found the first Pembroke nest in the summer of 1983 (Weir, 1983: 985).

AUTUMN: H. Ferguson observed one at Ottawa from Oct. 10, 1979 (Goodwin, 1980: 158). One was banded as late as Sept. 18, 1980 at Helen Quilliam's home in Kingston (Weir & Quilliam, 1980: 26). On Nov. 20, 1982, M.E. Foley tallied 225 in St. Catharines (Weir, 1983: 176).

**MEASUREMENTS:**
*Length:* 5 to 5 3/4 ins.
(Godfrey, 1966: 371)
Wingspread:
*Weight:* about 21 g.
(Terres, 1980: 328).

**REFERENCE:**
James, Ross D. 1978
Nesting of the House Finch
(*Carpodacus mexicanus*) in
Ontario. Ont. Field
Biologist, 32: (2): 30-32.
This article chronicles the
spread of House Finches
from Long Island into
Ontario and details the two
Niagara on the Lake nests
found in 1978. There is
also a short bibliography.

# RED CROSSBILL   *Loxia curvirostra*   Linnaeus

Red Crossbills are among the most unpredictable of birds. They can be quite common one year, then absent or very rare for several years. They can occur far north or far south and have been found breeding in almost every month of the year. They can be quite shy of humans or very blasé (as we found them hopping about our feet at a salt lick at Montreal Falls by Lake Superior one summer). Two things are predictable: their passion for salt and their fondness for conifer seeds, especially pine seeds: White-winged Crossbills seem to prefer spruce cones, so occur farther north in Ontario.

IDENTIFICATION: Red Crossbills vary in colour from a rich brick red to dull olive green. The distinctive crossed mandibles separate them from other birds at close range, except from White-winged Crossbills, which have conspicuous white wing bars and sweeter voices than the Red Crossbill. The Red Crossbill has a wooden "yip-yip" call while the White-winged calls "treet'treet". The red of male White-wings is a bright rosy pink, not brick red as in Red Crossbills. However, both species are often seen high in the air as bouncy flocks, when only the call notes help to separate them.

WINTER: On the 1968-1977 Christmas counts they averaged fairly common at Long Point, Huntsville, Dryden and Deep River, uncommon to rare at other localities, but numbers varied considerably from year to year. Stirrett (1973a: 20) had a winter maximum of only 3 at Pelee, on Feb. 22 and Feb. 28. Ussher (1965: 29) had a Jan. 29 record at Rondeau. Max Alton reported 20 near Eden, Elgin Co., on Dec. 21, 1953 (Brooman, 1954: 38). Saunders (1947: 7-9) described the feeding of a mixed flock at Purpleville, near Toronto, on Jan. 21, 1940. Parker (1983: 28) reported Red Crossbills on only 16 of 58 Christmas counts at Toronto. In Ontario Co. Speirs (1973) reported major invasions in 1950-51, 1960-61, 1963-64, 1967-68 and 1969-70, with very few or none in intervening years. Several other authors noted these same invasions in other parts of Ontario. They were observed eating seeds from hemlock, white pine, Scots pine and late in the winter some elm buds. H.G. Lumsden collected a male at Joyceville, near Kingston, on Jan. 10, 1951 and E. Beaupré saw a flock on Jan. 29, 1912 (Quilliam, 1973: 183). E.L. Brereton found 13 killed on a road in Barrie on Feb. 8, 1938 and Frances Westman reported a dozen killed on a Midhurst road in January, 1966 and two dozen there in January, 1967 (Devitt, 1967: 165). They were observed on 6 of 20 Huntsville Christmas counts, with a high count of 16 on Dec. 18, 1960 (Mills, 1981: 174). Nicholson (1981: 186) had only one winter record for Manitoulin: 2 birds seen in Gordon Twp. on Dec. 21, 1980. Louise Lawrence noted 3 at Pimisi Bay on Jan. 18, 1945 (Speirs & Speirs, 1947: 37). Skeel & Bondrup-Nielsen (1978: 216) encountered only one flock in Pukaskwa: 15 birds feeding on spruce cones on Feb. 20, 1977. Denis (1961: 7) called them "irregular, rare visitants" at Thunder Bay. Peruniak (1971: 30) had one winter record at Atikokan, in December, 1969.

SPRING: Stirrett (1973b: 26) had just two spring records for Pelee: 13 from March 14-16 and one on May 16. Saunders & Dale (1933: 240) reported a nest with 3 eggs and a cowbird egg at London found on Apr. 29, 1909 about 45 ft. up in a maple: two individuals of a large race were collected at London on May 24, 1892 by F. Deeley: another female was collected on May 15, 1912. Brooman (1954: 38) found them quite common in Elgin Co. from March 10 to May 25 in 1951. R.V. Lindsay picked up a roadkill near Turkey

Point on May 10, 1931 (Snyder, 1931: 196). "In 1892 crossbills were here [Toronto] from March 30 to May 5"—"a male taken April 14, 1894, is in juvenile plumage"(Fleming, 1907: 79). Following the major invasions, many remained at feeders into late May or even early June (Speirs, 1973). Tozer & Richards (1974: 287) reported 150 feeding in hemlocks at Oshawa on March 19, 1961. Allin (1940: 108) reported Darlington Twp. records on March 3, 1881 and March 5, 1933. Weir & Quilliam (1980: 40) listed Apr. 28 as a 7-year average departure date from Kingston. A.J. Mitchener saw 4 as late as May 23, 1948 at Wasaga Beach (Devitt, 1967: 165). Jim Goltz saw some at Bala in the last half of April of both 1970 and 1973 (Mills, 1981: 174). Nicholson (1981: 186) reported 13 at Providence Bay on May 26, 1973 and 2 at Belanger Bay, Manitoulin, on May 27, 1974. Ricker & Clarke (1939: 23) saw a small flock in red pines at Lake Nipissing on March 17, 1923. Peruniak (1971: 30) had a May 20, 1961 record for Atikokan.

SUMMER: On the 1968-1977 Breeding Bird Surveys they occurred on only 6 routes, from London and Port Bolster in the south to Montreal Falls in the north. Kelley (1978: 85) had several June reports and three July ones from Rondeau and Lambton Co. Saunders & Dale (1933: 240) reported one shot at London on July 5, 1882, and 5 seen nearby on Aug. 27, 1908. On June 2, 1970 I observed one at Springwater Park, Elgin Co. Fleming (1907: 79) collected one at Toronto on July 17, 1892. Gerry Norris saw 4 immatures with an adult at Chalk Lake on Aug. 30, 1969 and a flock of 15 remained as late as June 22, 1961 and a single bird stayed until June 15 in 1970 at Pickering (Speirs, 1973). Tozer & Richards (1974: 287) reported 38 in the Osler tract in Cartwright Twp. on June 17, 1973 and Dennis Barry had six July and August records between Whitby and Oshawa during the summer of 1969. Charles Fothergill considered them very common at Rice Lake: he shot a female there on June 23, 1821 and a pair there on July 3. Weir & Quilliam (1980: 40) reported June 16 as the latest date for lingering Red Crossbills at Kingston. Devitt (1967: 165) saw 3 near Barrie on June 25, 1933 and I observed them on Beckwith Is. in Georgian Bay up to July 11 in 1948. Mills (1981: 174) saw a flock of 60 in a bog at Magnetawan on July 23, 1975. Nicholson (1981: 186) reported a high count of 50, seen in Burpee Twp., Manitoulin, on July 12, 1975 by Ron Tasker. W. Spreadborough found both old and young birds in Algonquin Park on July 2, 1900 (Baillie & Harrington, 1937: 268). Peruniak (1971: 30) observed an adult with young at Atikokan on June 6, 1965 and David Elder noted one on July 1, 1981 at Russell Lake to the southeast of Atikokan. Snyder (1953: 87) reported flocks of 4 to 20 at Malachi from July 24 to Aug. 6, 1947 and found them "not rare" in the pine country near Kenora in summer. Elder (1979: 40) called them uncommon and irregular both in summer and winter, at Geraldton.

AUTUMN: Peruniak (1971: 30) had a Nov. 17, 1963 record at Atikokan. G.S. Miller took a specimen at North Bay on Sept. 7, 1896 (Ricker & Clarke, 1939: 23). Nicholson (1981: 186) gave a Nov. 21, 1979 sighting by Ron Tasker as the latest fall date for Manitoulin. Weir & Quilliam (1980: 40) listed Nov. 15 as the 10-year average arrival date at Kingston, with the earliest on Sept. 13, 1969 when 50 were seen at the Otter Lake sanctuary (Quilliam, 1973: 183). Tozer & Richards (1974: 287) reported 75 in Scugog Twp. on Oct. 27, 1973. David Calvert noted a flock of 46 at Pickering on Oct. 25, 1970; my earliest fall report there (Speirs, 1973). Saunders & Dale (1933: 240) reported two seen near London on Sept. 9, 1908. Ussher (1965: 29) had a Sept. 2 record for Rondeau. Stirrett (1973d: 29) had a fall maximum of 35 at Pelee on Nov. 1.

## MEASUREMENTS:
*Length:* 5.5 to 6.5 ins. (Godfrey, 1966: 378)
*Wingspread:* 9 to 10 3/4 ins. (Roberts, 1955: 700)
*Weight:* 1.00 to 1.18 oz. (Roberts, 1955: 700).

## REFERENCE:
Lawrence, Louise de Kiriline 1949 The Red Crossbill at Pimisi Bay, Ontario. Can. Field-Naturalist, 63: (4): 147-160. Four nests were found between Apr. 3 and Apr. 9, 1948, after pairing was observed in mid-January and the first courtship feeding on Feb. 3. The nests were described in considerable detail: two were deserted and one was broken up by a predator, probably a crow. The male fed the female while incubating, both took part in feeding the young by regurgitation at rather long intervals. Songs and call notes were described in detail as well as the attentivity at the nest. An excellent study!

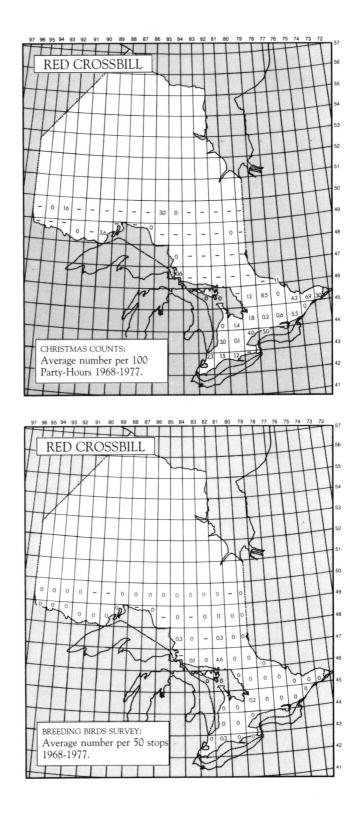

RED CROSSBILL

CHRISTMAS COUNTS:
Average number per 100 Party-Hours 1968-1977.

RED CROSSBILL

BREEDING BIRDS SURVEY:
Average number per 50 stops 1968-1977.

# WHITE-WINGED CROSSBILL   *Loxia leucoptera*   Gmelin

In Ontario the White-winged Crossbill is a more northerly breeder than is the Red Crossbill, occurring as far north as spruce trees do. Both species are very erratic as winter invaders into southern Ontario, but this species seldom lingers on into late spring or early summer as Red Crossbills sometimes do.

IDENTIFICATION: When the birds are seen well, there is no problem separating this species, with its conspicuous white wing bars and rosy-red males, from the brick red males with no wing bars of the Red Crossbill. So often, however, both species are often seen as bouncy flocks high overhead, when only the sweet "treet-treet" of this species separates it from the rather wooden "yip-yip" of Red Crossbills or the "cha'cha" of redpolls.

WINTER: On the 1968-1977 Christmas counts they averaged common to fairly common from Algonquin Park to the shores of Lake Superior, but elsewhere they have been uncommon to rare, except during "invasion years" when they may be numerous, even in southern Ontario. Stirrett (1973a: 20) had just two winter records of single birds at Pelee, on Jan. 30 and Feb. 28. Ussher (1965: 29) had a Dec. 6 record at Rondeau. Max Alton reported both species of crossbills near Eden, Elgin Co., in the winter of 1950-1951 (Brooman, 1954: 38). Parker (1983: 28) reported this species on 17 of 58 Christmas counts at Toronto. Speirs (1973) mentioned southern Ontario invasions in the winters of 1950-1951, 1955-1956, 1960-1961, 1963-1964 and 1971-1972. Tozer & Richards (1974: 287) reported 42 in the Osler tract, Cartwright Twp., on Jan. 27, 1972. The highest number tallied on a Kingston Christmas count was 237 on Dec. 21, 1955 (Quilliam, 1973: 184). Devitt (1967: 166) reported the species on 6 Christmas counts at Barrie since 1951, with a high count of 24 on Jan. 7, 1961. Mills (1981: 175) reported them on 11 of 20 Hunstville Christmas counts, with a maximum of 84 on Dec. 18, 1960. Chris. Bell had a Manitoulin record on Feb. 10, 1974 (Nicholson, 1981: 186). Skeel & Bondrup-Nielsen (1978: 216) reported up to 100 a day in Pukaskwa from Feb. 20-28, 1977. David Elder noted his first for 1981 at Atikokan on Jan. 10, where Peruniak (1971: 30) wrote that "the species winters when the cone crop is good." Elder (1979: 40) called this "an uncommon irregular summer and winter resident at Geraldton".

SPRING: Saunders & Dale (1933: 241) reported two shot near London on May 3, 1902 that "were in the mottled plumage and it is presumed they were young which had been bred there." O. Foster shot two males at St. Thomas on March 10, 1890, the first record for Elgin Co. (Brooman, 1954: 38). J.L. Baillie (in Saunders, 1947: 374) listed Apr. 17 as his latest spring record for Toronto. My latest spring date for Pickering Twp. was Apr. 18, 1951 (Speirs, 1973). Dennis Barry tallied 300 in a 3-acre hemlock grove in Darlington Twp. on March 10, 1968 (Tozer & Richards, 1974: 287). Weir & Quilliam (1980: 40) listed March 21 as the 11-year average departure date from Kingston, with the latest on May 30. Devitt (1967: 166) cited several spring records, from March 4 to Apr. 3, in Simcoe Co. J. Goltz saw 3 at a Bala feeder on Apr. 14, 1974 (Mills, 1981: 175). Nicholson (1981: 187) reported a pair at Belanger Bay, Manitoulin, on May 22, 1974. Ricker & Clarke (1939: 23) saw a few with Red Crossbills, at Lake Nipissing on March 17, 1923.

SUMMER: On the 1968-1977 Breeding Bird Surveys,they were absent on all routes south of Lake Superior, common at Kapuskasing and Longlac, and fairly common at

Marathon and Kenora. Beardslee & Mitchell (1965: 428-429) reported an immature bird at Morgan's Point, Lake Erie, on Aug. 25, 1959. Dennis Barry observed single birds in Darlington Twp. on July 4 and Aug. 2, 1972 (Tozer & Richards, 1974: 287). Paul Harrington watched a flock of about 30 at the mouth of the Nottawasaga River in June, 1921 and Frances Westman noted about 15 at Barrie on July 25, 1951 (Devitt, 1967: 165-166). Lloyd (1923: 156) mentioned an Ottawa record in June, 1882. D.A. MacLulich found a nest with eggs at Head Lake, Victoria Co., on Aug. 19, 1926 and A. Kay reported them breeding at Port Sydney, Muskoka (Baillie & Harrington, 1937: 268). Ron Tasker found 9 in Burpee Twp., Manitoulin, on Aug. 21, 1977 (Nicholson, 1981: 187). Two males were collected at Biggar Lake, Algonquin Park, on Aug. 28, 1932, one "mostly yellow" (MacLulich, 1938: 42). Snyder (1942: 150) reported single birds at Little Rapids on July 20 and at Echo Bay, near Sault Ste. Marie, on July 22, 1931. A flock of 45 was noted on July 15, 1977 in Pukaskwa and smaller flocks at intervals into the autumn (Skeel & Bondrup-Nielsen, 1978: 216-217). Baillie & Hope (1943: 24) collected a female at Amyot on July 5, 1936. T.M. Shortt collected an adult and flying young at Murillo, Thunder Bay Dist. on July 23, 1937 (Baillie & Harrington, 1937: 268). Peruniak (1971: 30) had "some July records" at Atikokan. Snyder (1953: 87) reported individuals and small flocks "noted daily at Savanne during the second week of July, 1937". Smith (1957: 180) saw 5 near Gogama on July 26, 1954. Snyder (1928: 27) saw a flock of 28 at Lake Abitibi on July 11 and 20 there on July 17 and again on Aug. 1. Cringan (1950: 18) saw up to 60 in flocks, almost daily, at Nikip Lake in late June and early July, 1950. After June 22, 1938 flocks of 3 to 150 were noted at Favourable Lake and 10 were collected there (Hope, 1938: 45). James, Nash & Peck (1982: 72) reported them common, daily at Harricanaw River, near James Bay, where they collected one male and tape recorded the song: stomach contents included spruce budworm (?) larvae. C.E. Hope saw a female at Cape Henrietta Maria on July 8, 1948 and H. Lumsden noted two juveniles in the willows at Brant River on July 28, 1969 (Peck, 1972: 346). James, Nash & Peck (1981: 93) collected a male and a young bird at Kiruna Lake, Sutton Ridges, in the summer of 1981. Lee (1978: 34) observed flocks up to 35 birds in spruce forests at Big Trout Lake until the first week of July, 1975: Lee & Speirs (1977: 52 and 54) reported them as "visitors" on two of the study quadrats there. C.E. Hope noted 200 at Fort Severn on July 6, 1940.

AUTUMN: D. McRae and A. Wormington frequently noted from 1 to 5 at Netitishi Point, James Bay, from Oct. 16 to Nov. 21, 1981. Skeel & Bondrup-Nielsen (1978: 217) encountered small flocks at Pukaskwa until they left on Oct. 16, 1977. Ron Tasker reported a high count of 150 in Burpee Twp., Manitoulin, on Nov. 18, 1973 (Nicholson, 1981: 186). J.H. Fleming collected two at Emsdale on Sept. 27, 1904 (Mills, 1981: 175). Devitt (1967: 165-166) reported about 150 on Nov. 26, 1939 at the Holland River, Simcoe Co., and A.J. Mitchener had three November records at Collingwood. Weir & Quilliam (1980: 40) listed Nov. 21 as the 18-year average arrival date at Kingston, with the earliest on Sept. 22. My earliest fall record was a flock of 8 at our Pickering Twp. home on Oct. 30, 1965 (Speirs, 1973). J.L. Baillie (in Saunders, 1947: 374) listed Oct. 31 as his earliest fall record at Toronto. Ussher (1965: 29) gave Nov. 4 as a 4-year average arrival date at Rondeau, with the earliest on Oct. 23. Stirrett (1973d: 29) had one as early as Nov. 7 at Pelee and a maximum of 30 on Nov. 9.

**MEASUREMENTS:**

*Length:* 6 to 6 3/4 ins.
(Godfrey, 1966: 379)
*Wingspread:* 9.2 to 10.7
ins. (Roberts, 1955: 700)
*Weight:* 3 ♂ averaged
26.4 g. 7 ♀ averaged
26.8 g. (Hope, 1938: 45)
Note on Singing: Lawrence
(1949: 290) observed
singing on Jan. 2, 9 and
13, 1948 at her Pimisi Bay
home (the Red Crossbill
was heard on Jan. 20).

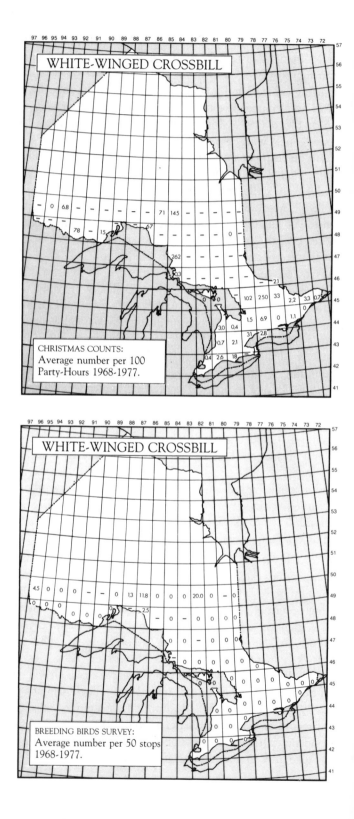

WHITE-WINGED CROSSBILL

CHRISTMAS COUNTS:
Average number per 100
Party-Hours 1968-1977.

WHITE-WINGED CROSSBILL

BREEDING BIRDS SURVEY:
Average number per 50 stops
1968-1977.

# COMMON REDPOLL   *Carduelis flammea*   (Linnaeus)

Common Redpolls are circumpolar breeders: in Ontario they breed chiefly in the Hudson Bay Lowlands. Great numbers invade southern Ontario during some winters, often followed by one to three winters with few or none. During invasions they are often attracted to "distlefink" feeders (with niger seed), even in city backyards. They frequently associate with Pine Siskins and American Goldfinches at these feeders, or on seed-laden birch trees as well as in fields of pigweeds.

IDENTIFICATION: These winter finches are about the size of goldfinches or chickadees, generally grayish-white, heavily streaked with dusky. The bright red cap when visible will easily identify them from all but the Hoary Redpoll (see distinctions under that species). In fast moving flocks they may often be distinguished by their characteristic wooden "cha-cha-cha" call from the similar Pine Siskins which have a more buzzy call note. Both are heavily streaked, bouncy, little birds and can be difficult to separate in poor seeing conditions (when back-lighted or in rapid flight). The more pointed bill and yellow wing flashes will help to identify the siskins in such conditions.

WINTER: On the 1968-1977 Christmas counts they were common in odd-numbered years and rare at most localities in even-numbered years, though the 1973 flight was poor at many southern localities and the 1968 flight good at some places. Redpolls are frequently at their maximum abundance in March so the Christmas counts do not always reflect the late winter condition. Stirrett (1973a: 20) reported a Pelee maximum of 510 on Dec. 27. Speirs (1973) cited major invasions of Ontario Co. as well as years when none were seen, illustrated by graphs: they were seen on 4 of 10 Christmas counts at Pickering from 1961 to 1970, in numbers varying from 0 to 764. Napanee reported 2691 on their Dec. 27, 1969 Christmas count, the high count for the continent that year (Quilliam, 1973: 181). They were reported on 16 of 20 Huntsville Christmas counts, with a maximum of 82 in 1963 and on all three Burk's Falls counts, with a maximum of 429 in 1978 (Mills, 1981: 172). G.W. Bartlett reported "hundreds of redpolls near Canoe Lake" on Feb. 25, 1909 (MacLulich, 1938: 41). Dennison (1980: 147) listed them on 13 of 25 Christmas counts at Sault Ste. Marie, with a high of 372 in 1977. David Elder reported 113 on the Atikokan Christmas count on Dec. 27, 1981.

SPRING: Stirrett (1973b: 26) gave Apr. 1 as the latest date for one at Pelee. Ussher (1965: 29) gave March 29 as his latest Rondeau date. Saunders & Dale (1933: 239) reported London birds as late as March 23, 1917. Speirs (1938: 45) listed one as late as May 5 at Toronto: J.L. Baillie (in Saunders, 1947: 374) listed March 17 as his 13-year average departure date from Toronto. My latest Pickering date was Apr. 9, 1960 when 4 were seen at our home (Speirs, 1973). D. Calvert saw one at Oshawa as late as Apr. 25, 1972 and D. Barry reported 1000 in Darlington Twp. on March 13, 1964 (Tozer & Richards, 1974: 284-285). Weir & Quilliam (1980: 40) listed Apr. 1 as the 19-year average departure date from Kingston, with the latest on May 22. Devitt (1967: 163) gave Apr. 22, 1939 as the latest Barrie record and estimated 3000 in a flock near Churchill, Simcoe Co., on March 27, 1938. P. Rogers had 150 as her Huntsville feeder on March 26, 1976 and A. Kay collected specimens at Port Sydney as late as Apr. 30 in 1897, 1901 and 1907 (Mills, 1981: 171-172). The spring maximum of 300 was noted on Manitoulin on March 18, 1978 and the latest, in Burpee Twp., by Ron Tasker, on May 17, 1966 (Nicholson,

1981: 185). Strickland, Tozer & Rutter (1982) listed Apr. 1 as the average departure date from Algonquin Park, with the latest on May 5. Speirs & Speirs (1947: 37) noted peak numbers at North Bay in early April, 1944 and one as late as Apr. 19. Skeel & Bondrup-Nielsen (1978: 215) noted up to 100 eating alder seeds at Pukaskwa on Apr. 12, 1977. Peruniak (1971: 29) gave Apr. 22 as her latest date for Atikokan. Cringan (1953b: 4) noted two at Kasabonika Post on May 27, 1953.

SUMMER: On the 1968-1977 Breeding Bird Surveys, individuals (probably tardy migrants) were reported at Larder Lake in 1969 and at Nipigon in 1976, none on any other route. Manning (1952: 89) reported specimens taken along the James Bay and Hudson Bay coasts from Shipsands (near Moosonee) on June 18, 1949 north to Shagamu River, from Aug. 8-10, 1947. Schueler, Baldwin & Rising (1974: 147) found a nest with 5 young at Winisk on July 7, 1965 and collected a laying female there on July 1, 1971. James, Nash & Peck (1981: 93) collected a male at Kiruna Lake, Sutton Ridges, in the summer of 1981. Peck (1972: 346) reported two nests at Cape Henrietta Maria: one nest with 4 young on July 20, 1948 and a nest with 4 eggs on June 16, 1965: he reported several sightings of the species in the vicinity also. Lee (1978: 33-34) saw flocks of up to 14 at Big Trout Lake, mainly after July 7 in the summer of 1975.

AUTUMN: On Sept. 25, 1938 from 7:15 to 8:30 a.m. Harrison Lewis recorded 241 at Moosonee, flying steadily southward in flocks of 5 to 60 (Manning, 1952: 89). D. McRae and A. Wormington noted them almost daily from Oct. 14 to Nov. 23, 1981 at Netitishi Point, James Bay, with a maximum of 120 on Nov. 5. Peruniak (1971: 29) gave Oct. 17 as her earliest fall date at Atikokan. Denis (1961: 6) listed Oct. 13 as his earliest fall date at Thunder Bay. Speirs & Speirs (1947: 37) saw 30 at North Bay on Nov. 22, 1944 but found them rare later in the winter of 1944-1945. MacLulich (1938: 41) reported 5 at Kiosk, Algonquin Park, as early as Oct. 30, 1930. Autumn arrival was noted on Manitoulin as early as Oct. 23, 1977 and the maximum of 300 was observed on Nov. 30, 1968 (Nicholson, 1981: 185). In 1964, the first was seen at Huntsville on Oct. 18 (Mills, 1981: 171). Devitt (1967: 163) reported one at Holland River as early as Oct. 20, 1935. Weir & Quilliam (1980: 40) listed Nov. 16 as the 20-year average arrival date at Kingston, with the earliest on Oct. 14. Snyder (1941: 87) mentioned a female collected at Hillier, Prince Edward Co., on Oct. 26, 1935. Rosemary MacKenzie noted one in Pickering Twp. on Oct. 18, 1962, the vanguard of a big influx the following winter. Speirs (1938: 47) listed one as early as Sept. 21 at Toronto: J.L. Baillie (in Saunders, 1947: 374) listed Nov. 19 as his 14-year average arrival date at Toronto. Ussher (1965: 29) gave Nov. 11 as his earliest Rondeau date. Stirrett (1973d: 29) gave Oct. 27 as his earliest for Pelee, when 17 were noted.

**MEASUREMENTS:**
Length 4 1/2 to 6 ins.
(Godfrey, 1966: 374)
*Wingspread:* 8.72 to 9.12
ins. (Roberts, 1955: 702)
*Weight:* 0.41 to 0.56 oz.
(Roberts, 1955: 702).

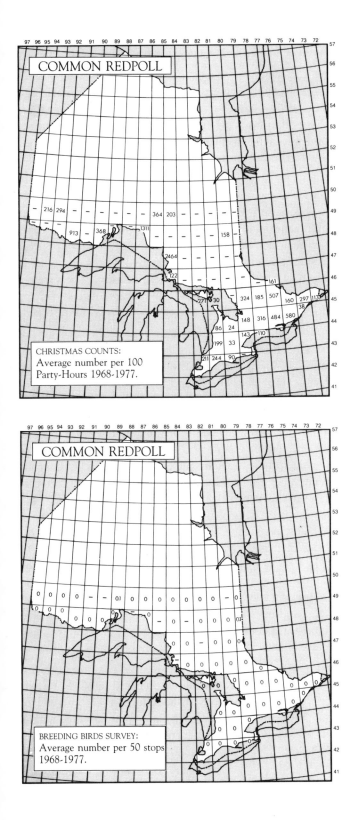

COMMON REDPOLL

CHRISTMAS COUNTS:
Average number per 100
Party-Hours 1968-1977.

COMMON REDPOLL

BREEDING BIRDS SURVEY:
Average number per 50 stops
1968-1977.

# HOARY REDPOLL   *Carduelis hornemanni*   Holböll

The Hoary Redpoll, like the Common Redpoll, is a circumpolar breeder. In Ontario it is chiefly a winter bird and much less numerous than the Common Redpoll. Whenever there is a major invasion of Common Redpolls into southern Ontario, a few of these snowy beauties are generally spotted by bird watchers. In my experience the percentage of these very white individuals is greater in northern Ontario than in the southern Ontario invasions.

IDENTIFICATION: Compared with the Common Redpoll this is a generally whiter bird, without pink on the sides or cheeks and with few or no dark streaks on the white rump. However, except in textbook illustrations, redpolls usually carefully cover the rump with the folded wings so that the critical lack of streaking on the rump is seldom visible in life: the amount of pink on the sides and cheeks of Common Redpolls is exceedingly variable, altogether a very unsatisfactory condition for field identification. The Greater Redpoll and some other types formerly recognized have already disappeared into synonymy and I will not be surprised if the Hoary is next to follow: the two "species" do interbreed.

WINTER: On the 1968-1977 Christmas counts, a few were reported as far south as St. Thomas and Long Point, but most localities, even in northern Ontario, reported none. They were reported as fairly common at Wawa and Marathon. Stirrett (1973a: 20) had three records of single birds at Pelee, on Jan. 22, Feb. 26 and Feb. 29. One was reported on the St. Catharines Christmas count of Dec. 31, 1961 (Beardslee & Mitchell, 1965: 423). Fleming (1907: 79) examined 9 specimens from a flock "that was about East Toronto from Feb. 10" into March, 1896 and another taken at Toronto on Jan. 8, 1904. J.L. Baillie (in Saunders, 1947: 374) had only one winter record at Toronto, on Feb. 1. Tozer & Richards (1974: 284, 310) cited several winter records, from Dec. 27, 1968 (in Darlington) to Feb. 20, 1960 (at Oshawa). Weir & Quilliam (1980: 40) gave Dec. 23 as a 5-year average arrival date at Kingston, with the earliest on Dec. 16: Quilliam (1973: 181) mentioned a female collected at Kingston by R.Y. Williams on Feb. 6, 1909. Two were reported on the Barrie Christmas count on Dec. 28, 1952 (Devitt, 1967: 162). Mills (1981: 171) cited a Port Sydney specimen and sight records at Huntsville on Jan. 26, 1969 (2); at Bracebridge on Feb. 27, 1972 (2); one at Bala on Feb. 24, 1974 and 2 to 5 at Parry Sound in February, 1974. Nicholson (1981: 184) reported Manitoulin birds on Feb. 5, 1972 and Jan. 27, 1974. Dennison (1980: 149) reported 5 at Sault Ste. Marie on the 1965 Christmas count. Skeel & Bondrup-Nielsen (1978: 215) reported one in 1976 and 7 in 1977 on the Marathon Christmas counts. David Elder noted one at Atikokan on Jan. 24, 1981: he listed it as a rare winter visitor at Geraldton (Elder, 1979: 40).

SPRING: Eleven were reported in a flock of 200 Common Redpolls at Point Abino, Lake Erie, on March 2, 1941 and one was still there on March 8 (Beardslee & Mitchell, 1965: 423). Fleming (1907: 79) reported specimens from his flock in East Toronto as late as March 23, 1896. Saunders (1947: 374) listed one as late as Apr. 3 at Toronto, with a 7-year average departure date on March 3. George A. Scott found 3 in a flock of 500 Common Redpolls at Oshawa on March 15, 1970 (Speirs, 1973). Tozer & Richards (1974: 284, 310) cited records from March 2, 1974 (at Oshawa) to March 28, 1966 (at Bowmanville). Weir & Quilliam (1980: 40) listed Apr. 3 as a 7-year average departure date from Kingston, with the latest on Apr. 11. Devitt (1967: 162) cited several spring records from Simcoe Co., including one collected at Barrie on March 6, 1939 and one at Collingwood as late as Apr. 29, 1949. Jim Goltz saw birds at Bala on March 23, 1970 and March 4, 1978 (Mills, 1981: 171). Nicholson (1981: 184) mentioned a high count of 6 by Ron Tasker on Manitoulin on March 19, 1974, with one as late as Apr. 7, 1974, noted by D.B. Ferguson. Strickland, Tozer & Rutter (1982) listed Apr. 7 as the latest Algonquin Park record. Speirs & Speirs (1947: 39) noted one at North Bay on March 17, 1944 and two there on Apr. 3, 1944. Denis (1961: 6) gave March 24 as the 6-year average arrival date at Thunder Bay.

SUMMER: D. MacKenzie collected a female at Shagamu River, Hudson Bay, on Aug. 9, 1947 (Manning, 1952: 89).

AUTUMN: R.D. McRae and A. Wormington saw one as early as Oct. 24, 1981 at Netitishi Point, James Bay, and noted them regularly during November, with a maximum of 27 on Nov. 17. Two specimens were collected by Wm. Goddard at Favourable Lake: a female on Nov. 6 and one, not sexed, on Nov. 9, 1938 (Hope, 1938: 44). Strickland, Tozer & Rutter (1982) listed Oct. 26 as the earliest Algonquin Park record. Nicholson (1981: 184) saw one at Spring Bay, Manitoulin, on Oct. 29, 1968. G.E. Atkinson collected one at Orillia in November, 1895 (Devitt, 1967: 163). W.H. Lunn collected one at Hillier, Prince Edward Co., on Nov. 23, 1935 (Snyder, 1941: 87). David Calvert noted one at Audley, Pickering Twp., on Nov. 15, 1965 (Speirs, 1973). Saunders (1947: 374) listed Oct. 29 as his earliest Toronto record, with his 6-year average arrival on Nov. 30. Dennis Rupert identified one at Sarnia on Oct. 23, 1968 and Roy John photographed one there on Nov. 23, 1968 (Kelley, 1978: 84).

**MEASUREMENTS:**
*Length:* 4.5 to 6.1 ins.
(Godfrey, 1966: 374)
*Wingspread:* 9.0 to 9.13 ins. (Roberts, 1955: 702)
*Weight:* 17.0 to 19.4 g.
(Terres, 1980: 337).

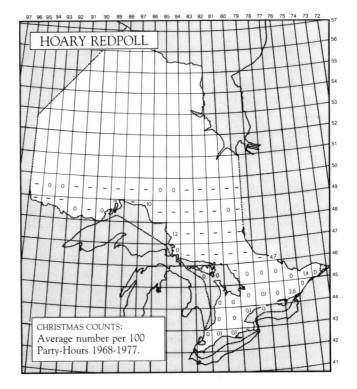

HOARY REDPOLL

CHRISTMAS COUNTS:
Average number per 100
Party-Hours 1968-1977.

# PINE SISKIN   *Carduelis pinus*   (Wilson)

Pine Siskins, like redpolls, are irruptive winter finches, very common some winters and rare other years. Sometimes their years of abundance coincide, other years one may be common, the other scarce. At feeders, Pine Siskins are very belligerent little birds, fighting with each other and with other small birds with heads down and wings raised to display their yellow wing flashes, uttering loud zizzy notes. Redpolls usually leave southern Ontario by early April but siskins may stay around until late May or even early June, greatly enlivening the scene. In years when they fail to appear they are greatly missed. In northern Ontario they may be found nesting high in firs or spruces.

IDENTIFICATION: Superficially they much resemble redpolls in size and behaviour but have more pointed bills and lack the scarlet crown and pink breast of the redpolls, making up for this by the yellow flashes in wings and tail. Instead of the "cha-cha-cha" call of the redpolls they say "zhe-zhe-zhe" and instead of the rising "seee-eeih" of goldfinches they say "zhee-eee-eee" also on a rising, but buzzy note. All three have ecstatic canary-like songs, but the siskin song is full of buzzy phrases.

WINTER: On the 1968-1977 Christmas counts they were common in Algonquin Park and fairly common at most other localities, but with numbers fluctuating widely from year to year. Stirrett (1973a: 20) had a winter maximum of 100 at Pelee on Dec. 21. Parker (1983: 28) reported some on 47 of 58 Christmas counts at Toronto. They were reported on 4 of 10 Christmas counts at Pickering, with numbers varying from 0 to 420 (Speirs, 1973). Snyder (1941: 87) mentioned a female collected at Wellington on Feb. 13, 1937 and two at Hillier, Prince Edward Co. on the following day. Devitt (1967: 164) reported them on 10 Barrie Christmas counts since 1951, with a maximum of 443 on Dec. 29, 1962. On the Dec. 24, 1922 Christmas count at Ottawa 900 were found, by far the most abundant species noted (Lloyd, 1923: 156). They were observed on 15 of 20 Christmas counts at Huntsville, with a maximum of 651 on Dec. 18, 1960 (Mills, 1981: 172). Dennison (1980: 147) listed them on 8 of 25 Christmas counts at Sault Ste. Marie, with a high of 49 in 1969. Skeel & Bondrup-Nielsen (1978: 216) saw up to 100 a day in late February in Pukaskwa, after seeing none in December or January. David Elder saw his first at Atikokan on Feb. 10 in 1981. Cringan (1953a: 4) listed them as winter residents as Sioux Lookout in 1952-1953.

SPRING: Stirrett (1973b: 26) had a spring maximum of 20 on May 14 at Pelee, the latest on May 24. Ussher (1965: 29) gave May 21 as a 5-year average departure date from Rondeau. Saunders & Dale (1933: 239) heard one singing its ecstatic song at daybreak on March 14, 1888, in the Komoka swamp, near London. J.L. Baillie (in Saunders, 1947: 374) listed March 26 as his 11-year average departure date from Toronto. Paul Harrington found a newly completed, but empty, nest in a tamarack bog by the Holland River in King Twp. on April 3, 1927 (Snyder, 1930: 194). Tozer & Richards (1974: 285) reported "hundreds" along the Oshawa-Whitby lake front on March 19, 1961. Weir & Quilliam (1980: 27, 40) listed May 13 as a 21-year average departure date from Kingston: Betty Hughes found a nest on Apr. 21, 1975 which held at least two young on May 18, according to Kenneth Edwards. Paul Harrington saw parents feeding two young at Wasaga Beach on May 24, 1951 (Devitt, 1967: 164). Mills (1981: 172-173) cited instances in the cottage country of pairs gathering nest material (mostly mammal hairs). Ron. Tasker reported a high count of 300 on Manitoulin on May 15, 1973 (Nicholson, 1981: 185). Louise Lawrence observed 3 at Pimisi Bay on March 27, 1945 (Speirs & Speirs, 1947: 37). In early March, 1977, up to 60 per day were noted at Pukaskwa (Skeel & Bondrup-Nielsen, 1978: 216). Denis (1961: 3) gave May 3 as the average arrival date at Thunder Bay, with the earliest on Apr. 17, 1949, although some occasionally winter there. Peruniak (1971: 29) saw a flock of about 300 at Atikokan in May, 1961.

SUMMER: On the 1968-1977 Breeding Bird Surveys, they were common on some routes near the shores of Lake Superior, becoming uncommon south to Barry's Bay and Eganville. Ussher (1965: 29) noted one at Rondeau as late as June 3. Kelley (1978: 85) reported 8 at Rondeau on the unusual date of Aug. 10, 1969. J.L. Baillie (in Saunders, 1947: 374) had one at Toronto as late as June 7. Speirs (1973) cited June records in Ontario Co. in Pickering and Mara Twps. Weir & Quilliam (1980: 27) found 7 on a Breeding Bird Survey at Crosby, near Kingston, on June 9, 1973. Lloyd (1923: 156) reported a single bird at Rockcliffe, Ottawa, on July 28, 1972. Nicholson (1981: 185) had a Manitoulin record on July 12, 1970. Snyder (1942: 149) collected a young male at Laird on July 9, 1931. Skeel & Bondrup-Nielsen (1978: 216) saw up to 14 per day in summer along the Lake Superior shore of Pukaskwa, until July 12, 1977. Baillie & Hope (1943: 24) noted up to 10 per day along the northeastern shore of Lake Superior: they collected males at Rossport on June 2 and 4 and at Marathon on June 15. Snyder (1928: 267) collected a male and two females at Macdiarmid, Lake Nipigon, on June 14, 1924 and a young male there on Aug. 1, 1923. On June 22, 1956, I found a nest about 35 ft. up in a 37 ft. balsam fir at the Dorion Fish Hatchery: this nest was still active on June 27. Kendeigh (1947: 28) had just one pair per 100 acres at Black Sturgeon Lake in 1945 while Speirs (1949: 148) had up to 11 pairs on 75 acres at nearby Eaglehead Lake in 1946. "Most years yield summer records" at Atikokan (Peruniak, 1971: 29). Snyder (1953: 86) found breeding evidence at Kenora and Savanne: noted from 3 to 50 daily at Malachi, 2 to 25 at Sioux Lookout, 2 to 47 at Ingolf, 4 to 18 at Savanne, 1 to 6 at Kenora and only 1 or 2 at Wabigoon. Elder (1979: 40) called it a common year-round resident at Geraldton. Smith (1957: 180) found 3 nests at Kapuskasing on June 24, 1953. Snyder (1928: 27) saw up to 50 at Lake Abitibi on June 15, 1925. Bondrup-Nielsen (1976: 45) saw none near Kapuskasing in 1974 and his first there on June 4 in 1975. James (1980: 90) found them uncommon at Pickle Lake in 1977 and noted them only twice in 1979. Hope (1938: 45) found them common in 1938 at Favourable Lake: "Juveniles not long out of the nest were met with frequency in late July." Schueler, Baldwin & Rising (1974: 144) listed the species only at Cochrane, none farther north. Lee (1978: 34) noted them regularly at Big Trout Lake after the second week of July in 1975.

AUTUMN: Skeel & Bondrup-Nielsen (1978: 216) saw up to 145 per day in Pukaskwa in late September, 1977. Speirs & Speirs (1947: 37) reported a peak in mid-October at North Bay, with 10 there as late as Nov. 22, 1944. A young bird, barely fledged was being fed by adults on Manitoulin on Oct. 11, 1969: Ron Tasker had high counts of 500 in Burpee Twp. from Nov. 18-22, 1975 and on Nov. 20, 1978 (Nicholson, 1981: 185). Mills (1981: 172) counted 39 at Magnetawan on Oct. 22, 1978. Frances Westman reported the earliest fall migrants at Barrie on Oct. 6, 1965 (Devitt, 1967: 163). Weir & Quilliam (1980: 27, 40) reported a high count of 300 at Prince Edward Point on Oct. 23, 1977 of which 28 were banded that day: they listed Oct. 23 as a 24-year average arrival date at Kingston, with the earliest on Sept. 23. Naomi LeVay had a Sept. 14, 1957 record at

948

Cranberry Marsh (Tozer & Richards, 1974: 285). My earliest fall record for Pickering Twp. was Sept. 27, 1951 (Speirs, 1973). Speirs (1938: 47) listed a Sept. 6 record for Toronto: Saunders (1947: 374) gave Oct. 29 as his 11-year average arrival date there. Beardslee & Mitchell (1965: 425-426) reported 4 at Port Maitland, Lake Erie, as early as Sept. 7, 1942. Brooman (1954: 37) observed 200 or more migrants at Hawk Cliff, near Port Stanley, Lake Erie, on Nov. 2, 1952. Ussher (1965: 29) had his earliest fall bird at Rondeau on Oct. 1, with a 12-year average arrival date on Oct. 23. Stirrett (1973d: 29) had a fall maximum of 200 at Pelee on Oct. 12 and Oct. 17.

BANDING: Brewer & Salvadori (1978: 92) reported three recoveries: one banded near Rochester, Minn., on Apr. 12, 1966 was recovered at Cambray, Ont. about 676 miles to the east on or about Feb. 20, 1970; one banded at Clarksille, Maryland, on Jan. 14, 1970 was recovered at Kashabowie, Ont. on May 15, 1970 about 934 miles to the northwest; one banded at Hubbard Lake, Mich. on Feb. 8, 1970 was recovered at South Baymouth, Manitoulin, on May 16, 1970, about 86 miles northeast. Weir & Quilliam (1980: 27) reported that one of the birds banded at Prince Edward Point on Oct. 23, 1977 was recovered in Maryland on Jan. 28, 1978. A most remarkable recovery was of a bird banded near Toronto on March 24, 1963 and recovered near San Francisco, California, on Feb. 14, 1964.

**MEASUREMENTS:**

*Length:* 4.5 to 5.2 ins. (Godfrey, 1966: 375)
*Wingspread:* 8.4 to 9.1 ins. (Roberts, 1955: 724)
*Weight:* 0.43 oz. (Roberts, 1955: 724)
3 ♂ averaged 12.4 g. 1 ♀ weighed 15.5 g. (Hope, 1938: 45).

**REFERENCE:**

Lowther, James K. and Robert E. Walker 1967 Sex ratios and wing chord lengths of Pine Siskins (*Spinus pinus*) in Algonquin Park, Ontario. Can. Field-Naturalist, 81: (3): 220-222. The sex ratio dropped from 230:100 on May 4 to 100:100 on May 8, 1961. The wing chord of males varied from 71 to 80 mm. (mean 74.22 mm): females varied from 68 to 75 mm. (mean 71.88 mm.) Some 222 males and 113 females were measured, of 371 caught.

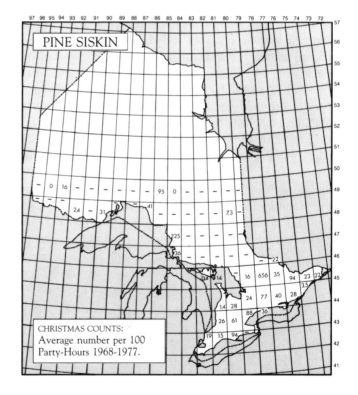

PINE SISKIN

CHRISTMAS COUNTS:
Average number per 100
Party-Hours 1968-1977.

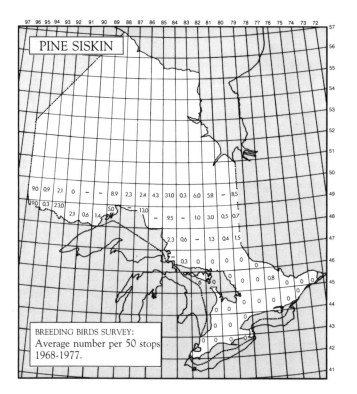

97 96 95 94 93 92 91 90 89 88 87 86 85 84 83 82 81 80 79 78 77 76 75 74 73 72

PINE SISKIN

BREEDING BIRDS SURVEY:
Average number per 50 stops
1968-1977.

# LESSER GOLDFINCH  *Carduelis psaltria*  (Say)

The Lesser Goldfinch is native in the western United States; accidental in Ontario.

**IDENTIFICATION:**  The Lesser Goldfinch resembles the American Goldfinch but has a black crown and olive-green upperparts and is smaller in size.

**WINTER:**

**SPRING:**

**SUMMER:**  Donald Fraser reported one on the Leslie St. Spit, Toronto, on Aug. 10, 1982 (James, 1983: 13).

**AUTUMN:**

**MEASUREMENTS:**
Length:  3.8 to 4.5 ins.
(Godfrey, 1966: 377)
Wingspread:
Weight:  202 averaged
9.5 g. (8.0-11.5 g.)
(Dunning, 1984: 26).

# AMERICAN GOLDFINCH   *Carduelis tristis*   (Linnaeus)

The American Goldfinch is a common bird at southern Ontario feeders where, like the redpolls and siskins, it is especially attracted to distlefink feeders filled with niger seed. It is a late nester, usually waiting for thistledown to use in nest construction, so the young are noisy and conspicuous in August and September, when cosmos seeds attract their parents into suburban gardens.

IDENTIFICATION: Males in summer are resplendent in brilliant yellow, accented with black cap, and with the black wing and tail with flashes of white. Females are more demurely dressed with dull olive-yellow body plumage, without the black cap of the male and with dusky wings and tail. Both sexes are dull olive in winter with dusky wings and tail. The adults have a sweet, rising, "see-eeee" call and a "per-chicory" flight note. The males have an esctatic canary-like song in late spring and summer. The young keep up a demanding "see-me—see-mee—" call throughout the late summer.

WINTER: On the 1968-1977 Christmas counts, they were common north to Deep River and the Bruce Peninsula, becoming uncommon to absent farther north. Stirrett (1973a: 20) had a winter maximum of 500 at Pelee on Dec. 2. They occurred on all Pickering Christmas counts (averaged 178 per count) and all Oshawa counts (averaging 205 per count) (Speirs, 1973). Quilliam (1973: 182) reported some on all but three Christmas counts at Kingston. Devitt reported some on every Barrie Christmas count since 1951, with a maximum of 534 on Dec. 29, 1962. Some were noted on 11 of 19 Christmas counts at Huntsville, with a high count of 209 on Dec. 20, 1964 (Mills, 1981: 174). Dennison (1980: 147) reported some on 10 of 25 Christmas counts at Sault Ste. Marie, with a maximum of 100 in 1969.

SPRING: Stirrett (1973b: 26) had a spring maximum of 350 at Pelee on May 21. Quilliam (1973: 183) followed the progress of the moult into breeding plumage at Kingston from its early beginnings on Apr. 2, 1970 to near completion by Apr. 27. Speirs & Speirs (1947: 37) observed one singing at North Bay as early as March 10, 1945, though Ricker and Clarke (1939: 23) gave May 14, 1923 as their earliest date there. Denis (1961: 4) gave May 18 as the average arrival date at Thunder Bay, with the earliest on Apr. 12, 1945 (but noted that some occasionally occur in winter). Peruniak (1971: 29) gave Apr. 13 as her earliest Atikokan date. Elder (1979: 40) gave May 24 as his earliest record for Geraldton. Cringan (1953a: 4) saw his first in 1953 at Dryden on May 13.

SUMMER: On the 1968-1977 Breeding Bird Surveys they were common north to Haileybury and Sudbury, becoming uncommon to absent on the northern routes. Stirrett (1973c: 22) had a summer maximum of 60 at Pelee on July 1. Saunders & Dale (1933: 240) found a set of 4 eggs at London on July 2, 1899 and a set of 5 on July 28, 1914. Brooman (1954: 38) found a nest 4 ft. up in a hawthorn by Kettle Creek, Elgin Co., on Aug. 11, 1946, from which the young hatched on Aug. 30. J.L. Baillie observed goldfinches gathering thistle down for nesting material on Long Point on July 10, 1927 (McCracken, Bradstreet & Holroyd, 1981: 66). Beardslee & Mitchell (1965: 426-427) reported a nest with 2 eggs at Fort Erie on July 8, 1938. G.J. Clout discovered a nest with 5 eggs and a cowbird egg at St. Catharines on July 10, 1936 and a nest with 4 eggs there on Aug. 28, 1934 which hatched on Sept. 1 (Baillie & Harrington, 1937: 267). Fleming (1907: 80) mentioned breeding at Toronto from July 23-30, 1893. Snyder (1930: 194) reported a nest with 3 eggs found 6 ft. up in a *Spiraea* shrub in King Twp. on Aug. 7, 1926. Speirs & Orenstein (1975: 15) found populations in all 11 forest plots in Ontario Co., with a maximum density of 41 birds per 100 acres in the thorn-apple wild orchard quadrat in Pickering Twp.: some were also found in all 11 field plots (Speirs & Orenstein, 1967: 182) and in all 10 urban quadrats (Speirs, Markle & Tozer, 1970: 5): this was the only species found in all 32 study plots. Of 35 sets found in Ontario Co. only one contained cowbird eggs (this nest, found at Beaverton by J.A. Edwards on Aug. 5, 1926 held 6 goldfinch eggs and 2 cowbird eggs: the other 34 sets held a total of 156 eggs (Speirs, 1973). J.M Richards found as many as 12 active nests in a 30-acre field overgrown with willow, birch and poplars in Darlington Twp. in August, 1965 (Tozer & Richards, 1974: 286). Allin (1940: 108) reported a nest with 1 egg and 2 cowbird eggs in Darlington Twp. on July 21, 1930. Quilliam (1973: 182) found a nest with 5 eggs on Aug. 27, 1962 about 5 ft. up in a hawthorn at Kingston: all had hatched by Aug. 31 and left the nest Sept. 11. Devitt (1967: 164) reported the earliest Simcoe Co. nest, with 5 eggs, found at Barrie by H.P. Bingham on July 13, 1915, and the latest nest with 5 eggs found at Wasaga Beach by Paul Harrington on Aug. 22, 1920. C.E. Johnson collected a nest with 6 eggs near Ottawa on July 31, 1916 (Lloyd, 1923: 156). Kurt Hoglund found 7 eggs hatching in a nest at Port Loring on Aug. 5, 1973 (Mills, 1981: 173). D.B. Ferguson watched a pair nest building at Providence Bay, Manitoulin, on July 31, 1976 (Nicholson, 1981: 186). Louise Lawrence observed a very high nest with young, 55 ft. up in a white pine at Pimisi Bay on Aug. 10, 1945 (Speirs & Speirs, 1947: 37). Baillie & Hope (1947: 29) found two nests, each with 5 eggs, at Bigwood on July 17, 1937. Snyder (1942: 150) reported three nests all under construction near Sault Ste. Marie on July 15, 1931. Baillie & Hope (1943: 24) reported a maximum of 14 at Rossport on June 4, 1936. Dear (1940: 141-142) located two nests, complete but unlined on June 30, 1929, at Thunder Bay: they appeared to be deserted for the next three weeks, but held 5 eggs and 6 eggs respectively on July 31. Snyder (1938: 210) found themcommon in the Rainy River region. Snyder (1953: 86-87) noted some from Malachi east to Savanne and north to Sioux Lookout. Smith (1957: 180) found them to be common throughout the Clay Belt, but Snyder (1928: 27) considered them "rather scarce" about Lake Abitibi. James (1980: 91) saw only one, in 1979, at Pickle Lake. James, Nash & Peck (1982: 72) saw only three by the Harricanaw River near James Bay, on June 23, 1982. Schueler, Baldwin & Rising (1974: 144) reported them as common at Cochrane, just noted at Moosonee and none farther north.

AUTUMN: George Stirrett saw 5 at Attawapiskat on Oct. 7, 1948 (Manning, 1952: 89). D. McRae and A. Wormington noted only one at Netitishi Point, James Bay: this came in off the bay on Oct. 31, 1981. Peruniak (1971: 29) gave Oct. 14 as her latest Atikokan record. Ricker & Clarke (1939: 23) observed young being fed at Lake Nipissing as late as Sept. 24, 1925. D.A. Sutherland reported 85 at Beausoleil Is., Georgian Bay, as late as Sept. 15, 1976 (Mills, 1981: 173-174). C.E. Hope found a nest with 2 young as late as Sept. 11 in Simcoe Co. (Devitt, 1967: 164). J.M. Richards found a nest with 4 eggs as late as Sept. 7, 1956 at Oshawa (Tozer & Richards, 1974: 286). Long (1968a: 25) found a nest with 3 young at Pickering Beach as late as Sept. 21, 1963. During the fall migration at Port Stanley, Lake Erie, 744 were counted in one hour on Sept. 26, 1948 (Brooman, 1954: 37-38). Stirrett (1973d: 29) had a fall maximum of 500 at Pelee on Nov. 8: Kelley (1978: 85) reported 1000 there on Oct. 5, 1974.

BANDING: One banded in Mass. on Jan. 24, 1930 turned up near Toronto during the second ten days of August, 1932. Another Mass. bird banded on Sept. 2, 1952 was recovered near Toronto on July 12, 1953. A Toronto bird banded on Feb. 25, 1960 was recovered in New York state on Apr. 18, 1961. Brewer & Salvadori (1976: 91) reported one banded at Bridgewater, Mich. on May 1, 1969 and recovered near Wallaceburg, Ont. on July 15, 1971. The most distant recovery was one banded at Guelph on March 2, 1971 and recovered at Ollah, Louisiana, about 1102 miles SW on Nov. 8, 1971. Another distant recovery was of one banded at Bellair, Florida, on Nov. 10, 1968 and found at Fort Erie, Ont. on July 6, 1969, about 911 miles to the north (Brewer & Salvadori, 1978: 92-93). Six others they reported were of exchanges from Ontario to or from Virginia, New York, Pennsylvania, New Jersey, Michigan and Ohio.

**MEASUREMENTS:**
*Length:* 4.5 to 5.5 ins. (Godfrey, 1966: 376)
*Wingspread:* 8 1/4 to 9 ins. (Roberts, 1955: 708)
*Weight:* 34 Ontario specimens averaged 13.1 g.

**REFERENCE:**
Middleton, A.L.A. 1977 Increase in overwintering by the American Goldfinch, *Carduelis tristis*, in Ontario. Can. Field-Naturalist, 91: (2): 165-172. Some 3433 were banded in Guelph in a 5-year study. Winter weights averaged about 15 g., dropping to about 12 g. in May (males averaged about 0.5 g. heavier than females).

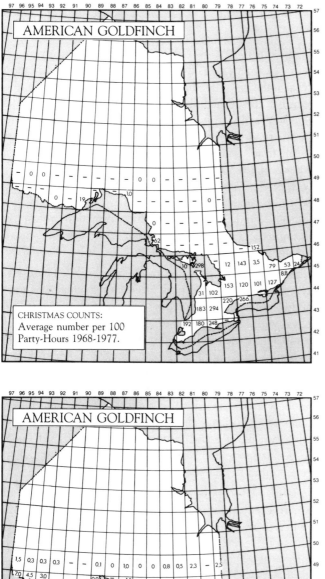

AMERICAN GOLDFINCH

CHRISTMAS COUNTS:
Average number per 100
Party-Hours 1968-1977.

AMERICAN GOLDFINCH

BREEDING BIRDS SURVEY:
Average number per 50 stops
1968-1977.

# EVENING GROSBEAK   *Coccothraustes vespertinus*   (Cooper)

When I became interested in birds in the 1920's and 1930's the Evening Grosbeak was regarded as a very rare bird in Ontario. In recent years it has become much more common, probably as a result of the increase in numbers of feeding stations. They are very fond of sunflower seeds and many have been banded at feeding stations, with fascinating results. Another weakness is their addiction for road salt: on several occasions I have had birds fly down underneath as I parked by the roadside, to pick salt off the underside of the car, and many are killed as they glean salt from roads. Their favourite wild food is the seeds of Manitoba maple, some of which we planted to attract them to our home. However, the young are fed insectivorous food, often the larvae of spruce budworm. They are very adept at concealing their nests, so that even where they are numerous in the breeding season, very few actual nests have been found. Numbers still fluctuate wildly from place to place and from year to year: this unpredictability, added to their natural beauty, makes them a fascinating species to watch and study (see Speirs, 1968: 206-256).

IDENTIFICATION: The huge beaks mark them as one of the grosbeaks. These bills vary in colour from white in winter (sometimes tinged pink after eating sumac) to green in spring and with the upper mandible blue in the breeding season. Adult males look somewhat like overgrown goldfinches, with their yellow bodies and black wings and tail, but the yellow stripe over the eyes and across the forehead and the big white wing patches (secondaries) distinguish them. Immature males are like the adults except that they lack the black cap, having golden heads. Adult females are generally gray-green, with touches of yellow, with a white throat and a small patch of white in the wing (which is very conspicuous in flight): they have more white in the tail than the males (in which the tail may be all black). Immature females resemble the adults. The usual notes are a loud, ringing "p'teer" and conversational "churr-churr"s and "chip-chip-choo-wee"s. The song is a very high pitched "wiz-wiz-teeee" (very seldom heard). The males do not defend nesting territories, just a small space around their mates.

WINTER: On the 1968-1977 Christmas counts this was a common species at all Ontario localities, except at Wawa, where none were seen on the one 1968 count, and in extreme southwestern Ontario where it was generally fairly common, but rare in some winters. The first Ontario report was on Dec. 25, 1854, at Toronto by Rev. Mr. Doel (McIlwraith, 1894: 291) although the original description was from a bird taken at Sault Ste. Marie, Michigan, in 1823. Cringan (1953a: 4) listed it as a winter resident as far north as Sioux Lookout during the winter of 1952-1953.

SPRING: Stirrett (1973b: 26) gave May 13 as the latest Pelee record. Apr. 26 was the 3-year average departure date from Rondeau, with the latest on May 3 (Ussher, 1965: 28). Saunders & Dale (1933: 298) still considered it a rare bird at London, except during 1920 when flocks were noted at intervals from Feb. 1 to May 21. Harold Lancaster noted three at West Lorne on Apr. 1, 1946 (Brooman, 1954: 37). A few were collected by Thomas Cottle from a flock of about 50 at Woodstock as early as May 7, 1855 (Fleming, 1906: 78). Tozer & Richards (1974: 310) saw two males at a Scugog feeder as late in the season as May 26, 1974. Weir & Quilliam (1980: 40) listed May 14 as the 25-year average departure date from Kingston. Mrs. F.E. Courtice reported a small flock lingering at

Collingwood until May 28, 1940 (Devitt, 1967: 161). Skeel & Bondrup-Nielsen (1978: 213) considered it a common spring migrant at Pukaskwa from May 13 to 29, 1975.

SUMMER: On the 1968-1977 Breeding Bird Surveys they were absent from southern Ontario routes, common in the Algonquin Park region and in northeastern Ontario from Gogama to Cochrane and west to Marathon, and generally present and uncommon to fairly common on other northern routes. Although young recently out of the nest have been frequently reported (Baillie, 1940: 15-25), actual nests have been very hard to find. Devitt (1944: 190-191) detailed the discovery of the first Ontario nest by Mrs. I.V. Earle about 7 miles south of Whitney, about 50 ft. up in a dead white cedar, on June 3, 1944: Devitt observed both adults feeding the young on June 20-21. Speirs & Speirs (1947: 37) gave some details of the second nest, 55 ft. up in a white pine, near Eau Claire, found on June 21, 1945 and containing at least three young. There are very few summer records from the northern half of Ontario, north of the Cochrane-Kenora line. Ross James had only five records of single birds at Pickle Lake from May 31 to June 17, 1977. McLaren & McLaren (1981: 5) commented that the three seen on June 5, 1977, near Postelnic Lake "were about 150 km. north of the known range". A male was seen singing in spruce woods at Moosonee on June 15, 1971 (Schueler, Baldwin & Rising, 1974: 147) but they noted none at Ft. Albany, Attawapiskat, Hawley Lake or Winisk. Manning (1952) had no James Bay or Hudson Bay records, nor did Peck (1972) have any at Cape Henrietta Maria. Cringan (1950) saw none in the Nikip Lake area and Hope had none at Favourable Lake and none at Ft. Severn. Lee (1978) had none at Big Trout Lake.

AUTUMN: Sam Waller collected one at Moose Factory on Oct. 27, 1924 (ROM spec.) D. Baldwin and R. Davis collected a male and a female at the Moose Factory dump on Nov. 26, 1965 (Schueler, Baldwin & Rising, 1974: 147). Skeel & Bondrup-Nielsen (1978: 214) saw 13 between Oct. 13 and Oct. 17, 1975, at Pukaskwa. Frances Westman reported one as early as Sept. 19, 1961 at Barrie (Devitt, 1967: 160). Weir & Quilliam (1980: 40) listed Oct. 10 as the 28-year average arrival date at Kingston. Allin (1940: 108) had his earliest arrival in Darlington Twp. on Oct. 20, 1921. On the 35 fall field days held in the Pickering-Whitby area by the Toronto Ornithological Club, Evening Grosbeaks turned up only twice: on Sept. 14, 1975 and Sept. 11, 1977. Earl Lemon saw one at West Lorne as early as Oct. 13, 1933 (Brooman, 1954: 37). E.L. Seeber *et al* saw two at Brock's Monument, Niagara, as early as Sept. 8, 1946 (Beardslee & Mitchell, 1965: 418-419). Ussher (1965: 28) had his earliest arrival at Rondeau on Oct. 16, with Oct. 26 as his 5-year average arrival date there. Stirrett (1973d: 28) noted a flock of 25 at Pelee as early as Oct. 12.

BANDING: Alf. Bunker banded over 2000 at Cherrywood (Pickering Twp.) and had recoveries from as far northwest as Winnipeg, east to the Gaspé Peninsula and Cape Cod, and south to New Jersey and Maryland (see maps in Speirs, 1973). Quilliam (1965: 177) listed recoveries from 118 banded at Kingston: one male banded Feb. 27, 1958 was recovered near Lac Humqui, mid-Gaspé , on Jan. 10, 1960. Several recoveries indicated an exchange of birds between Kingston and Watertown, N.Y. (one male banded on Apr. 16, 1958 was taken the next day at Watertown).

## MEASUREMENTS:

*Length:* 45 ♂ averaged 200 mm. (184-215); 42 ♀ averaged 200 also (187-216).

*Wingspread:* 10 ♂ av. 338 mm. (324-346); 7 ♀ av. 339 (320-350).

*Weight:* 14 ♂ av. 63 g. (55-70); 26 ♀ av. 62 g. (54-70).

Length & wingspread from museum specimens of Ontario birds: weights from birds banded and weighed at Pickering (DHS & JMS).

## REFERENCES:

Baillie, James L., Jr. 1940 The summer distribution of the Eastern Evening Grosbeak. Can. Field-Nat., 54: (2): 15-25.

Devitt, O.E. 1944 An Ontario nest of the Evening Grosbeak. Can. Field-Nat., 58: (6): 190-191.

Speirs, Doris Huestis 1968 Eastern Evening Grosbeak. in Bent, Arthur Cleveland et al. Life Histories of North American Cardinals, Grosbeaks, Buntings, Towhees, Finches, Sparrows and allies. U.S. National Mus. Bull. 237: Part 1: 206- 237. Plates 12, 13, 14.

Speirs, J. Murray 1972 Evening Grosbeak energetics. Ontario Field Biologist, No. 26: 16-19.

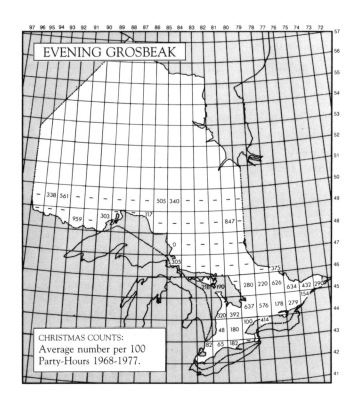

EVENING GROSBEAK

CHRISTMAS COUNTS:
Average number per 100 Party-Hours 1968-1977.

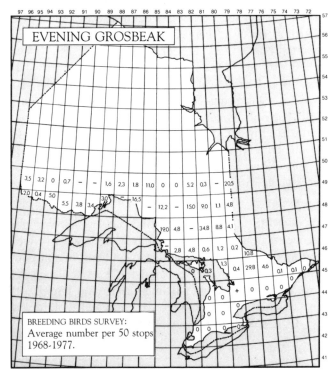

EVENING GROSBEAK

BREEDING BIRDS SURVEY:
Average number per 50 stops 1968-1977.

# HOUSE SPARROW   *Passer domesticus*   (Linnaeus)

This cosmopolitan species was introduced from Europe to Brooklyn, N.Y., in 1850 and into Ontario about 1870. It spread rapidly and was considered a pest by the end of the century. It was much more abundant in the days of horse-drawn transportation than it is now, living on waste grain and droppings, but it is still one of the most abundant species near human habitations, becoming increasingly rare in northern Ontario where it is found mainly near settlements and farms and absent from large, unsettled areas. Although usually considered nonmigratory I have witnessed flocks taking off over Lake Erie from Point Pelee. Nests are usually built in cavities under the eaves of houses or other buildings, or in bird boxes designed for other species but some build big globe-shaped nests about the size of a football in trees, more fitting for a member of the Ploceidae (the weaver finches).

IDENTIFICATION: Males with their gray crowns, chestnut napes, white cheeks and black bibs (reduced to the chin in winter) are easily identified, and their dingy mates by association with them. Males are sometimes confused with the rare Harris' Sparrow because both have black bibs (but the Harris' also has a black crown).

WINTER: On the 1968-1977 Christmas counts, they were abundant on most southern routes and near the larger northern cities. On northern counts they were common near the smaller towns but rare or absent away from settlements. Stirrett (1973a: 19) reported a winter maximum of 550 at Pelee on Feb. 21. House Sparrows were not counted on the early Brodie Club Christmas censuses until 1935 when 2839 were reported, exceeded in number only by Greater Scaup: in 1945 the total was 1357, then exceeded by Greater Scaup, Herring Gull and European Starling (Saunders, 1947: 378). Speirs (1974) gave this as the most abundant species on both Pickering and Oshawa Christmas counts, making up about 1/4 of all birds observed: R. Charles Long saw a male at a nest box at Pickering Beach as early as Feb. 20, 1966. Quilliam (1973: 168) noted a decrease on Kingston Christmas counts from 2190 in 1967 to 1008 in 1970. On March 1, 1935, J.S. Walker reported that only 2 of 14 survived the winter at Cache Lake, Algonquin Park (MacLulich, 1938: 36). Ricker & Clarke (1939: 21) cited a report of two seen at North Bay as early as the winter of 1885-1886 by John Bourk: by January, 1887 a flock of 100 was seen there: I noted 160 there on Jan. 1, 1945 and 140 on Feb. 20 when they reacted to the presence of a Northern Shrike by forming a great whirling ball of birds in the sky over the city. After the Mallard and Snow Bunting this was the most numerous species on the Sault Ste. Marie Christmas counts from 1954 to 1979 (Dennison, 1980: 146). Dear (1940: 140) reported them living at Thunder Bay in winter on grain spilled from railway cars at the grain elevators.

SPRING: Stirrett (1973b: 25) had a spring maximum of 250 at Pelee on May 7. Saunders & Dale (1933: 234) wrote that House Sparrows first arrived at London about 1874: the earliest of several spring nestings was a set of 5 eggs taken on Apr. 5, 1915. McCracken, Bradstreet & Holroyd (1980: 64) were aware of 40 nest records for Long Point: G. Bennett noted nest building at Port Rowan as early as Feb. 28 and eggs were found as early as Apr. 24. Tozer & Richards (1974: 261) found an Oshawa nest under construction by Feb. 28, 1960: this held 3 eggs and 2 young on Apr. 20 and 2 large young on May 4. Frank Brimley took a set of 5 eggs at Wellington, Prince Edward Co., on May 6, 1910 (Snyder, 1941: 82). E. Beaupré found a nest with 4 eggs at Portsmouth, near

Kingston, on Apr. 28, 1896, and another nest on Apr. 10, 1902 in a cavity in a tree below a Bald Eagle nest (Quilliam, 1973: 168). MacLulich (1938: 36) reported a first arrival in Algonquin Park at Canoe Lake on March 20, 1913. Baillie & Hope (1943: 23) saw three at Rossport on May 30, 1936, their only record for the northeast shore of Lake Superior. Barlow (1966: 1) reported a female collected at Smoky Falls on March 15, 1933: E.V. Goodwill noted House Sparrows at Red Lake in May (Barlow, 1966: 2).

SUMMER: On the 1968-1977 Breeding Bird Surveys, they were abundant on southern routes, common on urban routes in northern Ontario (Sudbury, Timmins, etc.) but rare or absent away from cities and towns. Stirrett (1973c: 21) had a summer maximum at Pelee of 300 on July 12. Saunders & Dale (1933: 234) reported three June nestings at London, the latest, a set of 6 eggs, taken on June 15, 1912. McCracken, Bradstreet & Holroyd (1980: 64) noted 3 Long Point nests in Barn Swallow nests and one in a Cliff Swallow nest: the latest nest with eggs was on July 19. R. Charles Long found a nest with 4 eggs as late as July 27, 1967 and a nest with 3 young on Aug. 27, 1965: of 29 sets found in Ontario Co., 9 held 5 eggs and 6 held 6 eggs; others had fewer eggs (Speirs, 1974). Speirs, Markle & Tozer (1970: 5) found population densities from a low of 20 birds per 100 acres in Washago to a high of 363 per 100 acres in Oshawa, in urban quadrats in Ontario Co.: it was the most numerous bird in the urban habitat, but ranked behind the European Starling, American Robin and Common Grackle in ecological impact. Tozer & Richards (1974: 26) followed several nestings in Darlington Twp., one still active as late as Aug. 24, 1964. Quilliam (1973: 168) reported a decline in House Sparrow populations on Kingston region Breeding Bird Surveys from 25.8 birds per route in 1968 to 10.9 in 1971, but increasing again to 17.3 in 1972. H.P. Bingham found one of the globe-shaped nests with 5 eggs in the top of a small spruce near Barrie on June 6, 1929 (Devitt, 1967: 152). Lloyd (1924: 10) reported that House Sparrows were introduced at Ottawa in 1870. Mills (1981: 153-154) cited several nest records for the cottage country, including one in a Cliff Swallow nest in a colony at Magnetawan in 1975. Gerry Bennett saw an adult feeding young at a nest in Little Current on June 21, 1973 (Nicholson, 1981: 175). Mark Robinson remarked "a few breed here" at Canoe Lake, Algonquin Park, in 1918 (MacLulich, 1938: 36). Louise Lawrence saw young being fed at Rutherglen on July 9, 1944 and we saw two nests with young in holes in a brick wall at North Bay on July 12, 1944 (Speirs & Speirs, 1947: 36). Baillie & Hope (1947: 27) observed a pair at a nest under the eaves of a farmhouse near Bigwood, and flying young, on July 19, 1937. Snyder (1942: 146) found nests with young by June 2, 1931, near Sault Ste. Marie. Snyder (1928: 267-268) saw 11 birds at Macdiarmid in 1923 and 26 there in 1924: nests were noted in the cupola of the ice house. Dear (1940: 140) called it a common permanent resident at Thunder Bay, nesting about habitations. Peruniak (1971: 27) reported a resident flock of 50 to 100 at Atikokan "where trains spill grain". Snyder (1953: 83) noted the first young out of the nest at Kenora on June 7, 1949: small populations were restricted to settlements in western Ontario: e.g. at Ingolf, Wabigoon, Redditt, Upsala, Sioux Lookout and Malachi. Elder (1979: 39) called it a common permanent resident at Geraldton. Smith (1957: 179) found them "common about settlements, but absent elsewhere" in the Clay Belt. Snyder (1928: 27) found them "numerous and nesting at Cochrane" but saw only three at Lowbush on Lake Abitibi. A male was collected at Fraserdale on June 21, 1939 (Barlow, 1966: 1). M.Y. Williams saw three at Moose Factory on Aug. 18, 1919 (Manning, 1952: 86). C.E. Hope took a female at Lansdowne House, Lake Attawapiskat, on June 5, 1939 and collected one of 3 seen at Fort Severn on June 30, 1940 (4 were seen there on June 17).

AUTUMN: D.H. Baldwin and R.A. Davis collected a male and two females at Moosonee on Nov. 25, 1965 (Barlow, 1966: 1). E.V. Goodwill reported House Sparrows at Red Lake in September (Barlow, 1966: 2). Mills (1981: 154) gave Nov. 13, 1977 as his latest date for Magnetawan. Stirrett (1973d: 27) had a fall maximum of 500 at Pelee on Sept. 12.

**MEASUREMENTS:**
*Length:* 5.8 to 6.7 ins. (Godfrey, 1966: 350)
*Wingspread:* 9.3 to 9.7 ins. (Roberts, 1955: 714)
*Weight:* 186 Ontario specimens averaged 30.9 g.

**REFERENCES:**
Barlow, Jon C. 1966 Extralimital occurrences of the House Sparrow in northern Ontario. Ont. Field Biologist, No. 20: 1-3.
Macintosh, James R. 1958 The English Sparrow. Fed. Ont. Naturalists Bull. No. 79: 13, 22.
(Introduced to U.S.A. at Brooklyn, N.Y. in 1850: legislation to try to annihilate them was brought in by 1885.)

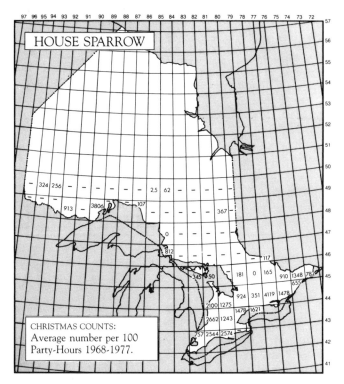

HOUSE SPARROW

CHRISTMAS COUNTS: Average number per 100 Party-Hours 1968-1977.

960

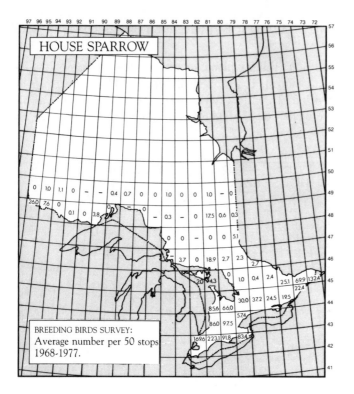

HOUSE SPARROW

BREEDING BIRDS SURVEY:
Average number per 50 stops
1968-1977.

# LITERATURE CITED*

ALISON, R.M. 1975 Some previously unpublished records of Trumpeter Swans in Ontario. Can. Field-Nat., 89: (3): 311-313.

ALLIN, A.E. 1940 The vertebrate fauna of Darlington Township, Durham County, Ontario. Trans. Royal Can. Inst., 23: Part 1: 83-118.

ALLIN, A.E. 1942 Some additions to the vertebrate fauna of Darlington Township, Durham County, Ontario. Can. Field-Naturalist, 56: (8&9): 140.

AMERICAN ORNITHOLOGISTS' UNION 1983 Check-list of North American birds. Sixth edition. i-xxix, 1-877.

ATKINSON, G.E. 1892 Nesting of Ontario birds. Trans. Can. Inst., 3: Part 1: (5): 80-84.

ATKINSON, G.E. 1894 A summer's collecting and observations at Port Arthur, Ont. Biological Review of Ontario, 1: (4): 94-101. Note: Denis (1961: 7) considered Atkinson's records of Caracara and Smith's Longspur as authentic but questioned his Arctic Loon, Great Black-backed Gull, Ivory Gull and Kittiwake records.

BAILLIE, JAMES L., JR. & PAUL HARRINGTON 1936-37 The distribution of breeding birds in Ontario. Trans. Royal Can. Inst., 21: Part 1: 1-50 (1936) Trans. Royal Can. Inst., 21: Part 2: 199-283 (1937)

BAILLIE, JAMES L., JR. 1939 Four additional breeding birds of Ontario. Can. Field-Nat., 42: (9): 130-131.

BAILLIE, J.L. JR. and C.E. HOPE 1943 The summer birds of the northeast shore of Lake Superior, Ontario. Royal Ont. Mus. Zool., Contr. No. 23: 1-27.

BAILLIE, JAS. L., JR. June, 1947 Stick insect is low animal form but cancer study aid. Birds blown by storms (subtitle). Forest & Outdoors, June, 1947: 171-172. For a period of a month following a storm passing Toronto, but originating in Oklahoma, some 19 unusual species were tallied at Toronto or other southern Ontario localities, including 2 Baird's Sparrows at Toronto and many Hooded Warblers (JMS noted one of these).

BAILLIE, JAMES L., JR. and CLIFFORD E. HOPE 1947 The summer birds of Sudbury District, Ontario. Royal Ont. Mus. Zool., Contrs. No. 28: 1-32.

BAILLIE, JAMES L., JR. 1948 Spring migration Ontario — western New York region. Audubon Field Notes, 2: (4): 174-175.

BAILLIE, JAMES L., JR. 1948 Nesting season Ontario — western New York region. Audubon Field Notes, 2: (5): 204-205.

BAILLIE, JAMES L. 1950 Fall migration. Ontario — western New York region. Audubon Field Notes, 4: (1): 12-14.

BAILLIE, JAMES L. 1950 Winter season. Ontario — western New York region. Audubon Field Notes, 4: (3): 199-200.

BAILLIE, JAMES L. 1950 Nesting season. Ontario — western New York region. Audubon Field Notes, 4: (5): 272-274.

BAILLIE, JAMES L. 1951 Fall migration. Ontario — western New York region. Audubon Field Notes, 5: (1): 12-14.

BAILLIE, JAMES L. 1951 Winter season. Ontario — western New York region. Audubon Field Notes, 5 (3): 201-203.

BAILLIE, JAMES L. 1951 Spring migration. Ontario — western New York region. Audubon Field Notes, 5: (4): 253-254.

BAILLIE, JAMES L. 1951 The nesting season. Ontario — western New York region. Audubon Field Notes: 5: (5): 286-287.

BAILLIE, JAMES L. 1952 Fall migration. Ontario — western New York region. Audubon Field Notes, 6: (1): 13-16.

BAILLIE, JAMES L. 1953 Spring migration. Ontario — western New York region. Audubon Field Notes, 7: (4): 270-272.

BAILLIE, JAMES L. 1953 Nesting season. Ontario — western New York region. Audubon Field Notes, 7: (5): 306-307.

BAILLIE, JAMES L. 1954 The nesting season. Ontario — western New York region. Audubon Field Notes, 8: (5): 342-344.

BAILLIE, J.L. 1955 Worth noting . . . FON Bull. 68: 33-35.

BAILLIE, J.L. 1955 Worth noting. Fed. Ont. Naturalists Bull. 70: 30-32.

BAILLIE, JAMES L. 1955 Winter season. Ontario — western New York region. Audubon Field Notes, 9: (3); 254-256.

BAILLIE, JAMES L., JR. 1955 Nesting season. Ontario — western New York region. Audubon Field Notes, 9: (5): 375-377.

BAILLIE, J.L. 1957 Recent additions to Ontario's bird list. Ont. Field Biologist, No. 11: 1-3.

BAILLIE, J.L. 1958 Six old yet new Ontario breeding birds. Ont. Field Biologist, No. 12: 1-7.

BAILLIE, J.L. 1960 New Ontario breeding birds. Ont. Field Biologist, No. 14: 14-23.

BAILLIE, J.L. 1961 More new Ontario breeding birds. Ont. Field Biologist, No. 15: 1-9.

BAILLIE, J.L. 1962 Fourteen additional Ontario breeding birds. Ont. Field Biol., No. 16: 1-15.

BAILLIE, J.L. 1963 Three bird immigrants from the Old World. Trans. Royal Can. Inst., 34: Part 2: 95-105.

BAILLIE, J.L. 1964 Ontario's newest birds. Ont. Field Biologist, No. 18: 1-13.

BAILLIE, JAMES L. 1965 Ontario's bird list: subtract one; add one. Ont. Field Biologist, No. 19: 41.

BAILLIE, JAMES L. 1969 Three additional Ontario birds. Ont. Field Biologist, No. 23: 34.

BAKER, WILLIAM C. 1932 Three unusual records for Ontario. Auk, 49: (1): 100-101.

BARLOW, JON C. 1966 Status of the Wood Ibis, the Fulvous Tree Duck, and the Wheatear in Ontario. Can. Field-Naturalist, 80: (4): 183-186.

BEARDSLEE, CLARK S. and HAROLD D. MITCHELL 1965 Birds of the Niagara Frontier region. Bull. Buffalo Soc. Natural Sciences, 22: i-xix; 1-478.

BELLROSE, FRANK C. and ARTHUR S. HAWKINS 1947 Duck weights in Illinois. Auk, 64: (3): 422-430.

BENT, ARTHUR CLEVELAND 1926 Life histories of North American marsh birds. U.S. National Mus., Bull. 135: i-xii; 1-392. Plates 1-98. (Dover reprint 1963)

BENT, ARTHUR CLEVELAND 1948 Life Histories of North American nuthatches, wrens, thrashers and their allies. U.S. National Mus., Bull. 195: i-xi; 1-475.

BENT, ARTHUR CLEVELAND (edited by Oliver L. Austin, Jr.) 1968 Life histories of North American Cardinals, Grosbeaks, Buntings, Towhees, Finches, Sparrows and Allies. U.S. National Mus., Bull. 237: Part 1: i-xxvii; 1-602; 32 Plates.

BLACK, R. DELAMERE 1934 Charles Fothergill's notes on the natural history of eastern Canada, 1816-1837. Trans. Royal Can. Inst., 20: Part 1: No. 43: 141-168.

BONDRUP-NIELSEN, SOREN 1976 Arrival dates and the status of birds near Kapuskasing, Ontario. Ont. Field Biol., 30: (1): 39-49.

BREWER. A.D. and A. SALVADORI 1976 First annual report of non-game bird banding in Ontario, 1971. Ont. Bird Banding, 10: (3): 52-96. Note: this vol. was No. 3 of the 1975 vol 10, but was actually published in Nov. 1976.

BREWER, A.D. and A. SALVADORI 1978 Bird banding in Ontario 1965 — 1970. Ont. Bird Banding, 11: (2 & 3): 30-99.

BROOMAN, R.C. 1954 Birds of Elgin County, Ontario. St. Thomas Gilbert Press: 1-41.

BRUUN, BERTEL (PAINTINGS BY ARTHUR SINGER) 1969 Birds of Europe. Golden Press New York: 1-321.

BUCKALEW, JOHN M. 1980 Distribution of mallards. North American Bird Bander, 5: (3): 104.

CALVERT, E.W. 1925 A preliminary list of the birds of the Lindsay district, Ontario. Can. Field-Naturalist, 39: (4): 72-74.

CRINGAN, A.T. 1950 Notes on the birds of the Nikip Lake area. Mimeo: 1-19.

CRINGAN, A.T. 1953a Some 1953 spring arrival dates of birds Sioux Lookout district. Mimeo: 1-4.

CRINGAN, A.T. 1953b Annotated list of birds seen at Kasabonika Lake, May 27th — June 5th, 1953. Mimeo: 1-5.

CURRY-LINDAHL, KAI 1963 Nordens djurvärld. Stockholm. Forum 1-464.

DALE, E.M.S. 1941 Bird notes from London, Ontario. Can. Field-Nat., 55: (1): 1-4.

DEAR, L.S. 1940 Breeding birds of the region of Thunder Bay, Lake Superior, Ontario. Trans. Royal Can. Inst., 23: Part 1: 119-143.

DENIS, K. 1961 Birds of the Canadian Lakehead area. Thunder Bay Field Naturalists' Club: Suppl. No. 2: 1-8.

DENNISON, RUSS 1980a Birds. Spring arrivals — fall departures. Sault Naturalists' Bulletin. 25th Anniversary: 14-16.

DENNISON, RUSS 1980b Analysis of Christmas bird counts by the Sault Naturalists, 1954-1979. Jack-Pine Warbler, 58: (4): 146-149.

DEVITT, O.E. 1967 The birds of Simcoe County, Ontario. Barrie. Brereton Field Naturalists Club: 1-192.

DE VOS, ANTOON 1964 Recent changes of birds in the Great Lakes region. Am. Midland Naturalist, 71: (2): 489-502.

DUNN, ERICA H.; HEATHER F. HOWKINS and RALPH V. CARTAR 1975 Red-breasted Nuthatches breeding in nest boxes in pine plantations on the north shore of Lake Erie. Can. Field-Nat., 89: (4): 467-468.

DUNNING, JOHN B., JR. 1984 Body weights of 686 species of North American birds. Western Bird Banding Association, Monograph No. 1: i-ii; 1-38.

ELDER, DAVID, DONALD PRICE & J. MURRAY SPEIRS 1971 Breeding bird census. Leatherleaf bog. Am. Birds, 25: (6): 1005-1006.

ELDER, DAVID H. 1979 Birds of the Geraldton district. Ont. Field Biol., 33: (1): 26-41.

ELSEY, C.A. 1950 Observations in the Asheweig-Winisk area during the breakup period in 1950. Fish & Wildlife Management Rept. #23.

ERSKINE, ANTHONY J. 1971 The thirty-fifth breeding bird census. Black spruce forest. Am. Birds, 25: (6): 985-986.

FAIRFIELD, GEORGE & ERIC NASMITH 1978 Forty-first breeding bird census. Wooded city ravine. Am. Birds, 32: (1): 65.

FALLA, R.A.; R.B. SIBSON & E.G. TURBOTT 1966 A field guide to the birds of New Zealand. London. Collins: 1-254.

FARGO, WILLIAM G. & MILTON B. TRAUTMAN 1930 Late summer bird notes along the upper Michipicoten River, Ontario. Can. Field-Naturalist, 44: (2): 30-33.

FIELD, MARSHALL & DOLLY FIELD 1979 Hawk Cliff raptor banding station seventh annual report: 1977. Ont. Bird Banding, 12: (1): 2-28.

FLEMING, JAMES H. 1900 Ontario bird notes. Auk, 17: (2): 176.

FLEMING, JAMES H. 1906 Birds of Toronto, Ontario. Part 1. Water birds. Auk, 23: (4): 437-453.

FLEMING, JAMES H. 1907 Birds of Toronto, Canada. Part II. Land birds. Auk, 24: (1): 71-89.

FLEMING, J.H. 1908 Ontario bird notes. Auk, 25: (4): 486.

FLEMING, J.H. 1913 Ontario bird notes. Auk, 30: (2): 225-228.

FLEMING, J.H. 1930 Ontario bird notes. Auk, 47: (1): 64-71.

FORBUSH, EDWARD HOWE 1925 Birds of Massachusetts and other New England States Part 1: Water birds, marsh birds and shore birds. Mass. Dept. Agriculture: i-xxxi; 1-481.

FORSTER, JOHN REINHOLD 1772 An account of the birds sent from Hudson's Bay, with observations relative to their natural history; and Latin desciptions of some of the most uncommon. Phil. Trans. Royal Soc., 62: 382-433. (citation from Manning, 1952: 103).

FOWLER, SHEILA 1983 Recoveries, foreign retraps, returns and repeats. Ontario Bird Banding, 16: (2): 14-19.

GODFREY, W. EARL 1966 The birds of Canada. Ottawa. Queen's Printer: 1-428.

GOODWIN, CLIVE E. 1962 Worth noting. Fed. Ont. Naturalists Bull. 98: 18-27.

GOODWIN, C.E. 1963 Worth noting. Ont. Naturalist, 1: (2): 31-34.

GOODWIN, CLIVE E. 1963 Worth noting. Ont. Naturalist, 1: (3): 23-26.

GOODWIN, CLIVE E. 1965 Worth noting. Ont. Naturalist, 3: (3): 31-34.

GOODWIN, CLIVE E. 1965 Nesting season. Ontario Audubon Field Notes, 19: (5): 537-540.

GOODWIN, CLIVE E. 1966 The fall migration. Ontario region. Audubon Field Notes, 20: (1): 35-38.

GOODWIN, CLIVE E. 1966 Winter season. Ontario. Audubon Field Notes, 20: (3): 416-418.

GOODWIN, C.E. 1966 Spring migration. Ontario — western New York region. Audubon Field Notes, 20: (4): 502-504.

GOODWIN, C.E. 1967 Fall migration. Ontario Audubon Field Notes, 21: (1): 25-29.

GOODWIN, C.E. 1967 Winter season. Ontario. Audubon Field Notes, 21: (3): 413-415.

GOODWIN, C.E. 1967 The nesting season. Ontario. Audubon Field Notes, 21: (5): 561-563.

GOODWIN, C.E. 1968 The winter season. Ontario. Audubon Field Notes, 22: (3): 434-436.

GOODWIN, C.E. 1968 The spring migration. Ontario. Audubon Field Notes, 22: (4): 520-523.

GOODWIN, C.E. 1969 Winter. Ontario — western New York region — Ontario. Audubon Field Notes, 23: (3): 473-476.

GOODWIN, CLIVE E. 1969 Spring migration. Ontario — western New York region. Audubon Field Notes, 23: (4): 583-586.

GOODWIN, CLIVE E. 1970 The fall migration. Ontario. Audubon Field Notes, 24: (1): 38-43.

GOODWIN, CLIVE E. 1970 Ontario ornithological records committee — report for 1970 Ont. Field Biologist, No. 24: 17-18.

GOODWIN, CLIVE E. 1971 The fall migration. Ontario. Am. Birds, 25: (1): 49-54.

GOODWIN, CLIVE E. 1971 The winter season. Ontario. Am. Birds, 25: (3): 570-575.

GOODWIN, CLIVE E. 1971 The spring migration. Ontario. Am. Birds, 25: (4): 735-739.

GOODWIN, CLIVE E. 1971 The nesting season. Ontario. Am. Birds, 25: (5): 851-854.

GOODWIN, CLIVE E. 1972 The fall migration. Ontario. Am. Birds, 26: (1): 54-59.

GOODWIN, CLIVE E. 1972 The winter season. Ontario. Am. Birds, 26: (3): 597-601.

GOODWIN, CLIVE E. 1972 The spring migration. Ontario. Am. Birds, 26: (4): 754-758.

GOODWIN, CLIVE E. 1972 The nesting season. Ontario. Am. Birds, 26: (5): 852-855.

GOODWIN, CLIVE E. 1972 Ontario ornithological records committee — report for 1972. Ont. Field Biologist, No. 26: 35-37.

GOODWIN, CLIVE E. 1973 The fall migration. Ontario. Am. Birds, 27: (1): 49-56.

GOODWIN, CLIVE E. 1973 The winter season. Ontario. Am. Birds, 27: (3): 608-611.

GOODWIN, CLIVE E. 1973 The spring migration. Ontario. Am. Birds, 27: (4): 765-769.

GOODWIN, CLIVE E. 1973 The nesting season. Ontario. Am. Birds, 27: (5): 863-867.

GOODWIN, CLIVE. E. 1974 The fall migration. Ontario. Am. Birds, 28: (1): 44-48.

GOODWIN, CLIVE E. 1974 The winter season. Ontario. Am. Birds, 28: (3): 632-635.

GOODWIN, CLIVE E. 1974 The spring migration. Ontario. Am. Birds, 28: (4): 794-798.

GOODWIN, CLIVE E. 1974 The nesting season. Ontario. Am. Birds, 28: (5): 896-900.

GOODWIN, CLIVE E. 1974 Ontario Ornithological Records Committee report for 1973. Ont. Field Biologist, 28: (1): 7-14.

GOODWIN, CLIVE E. 1975 The fall migration. Ontario region. Am. Birds, 29: (1): 48-53.

GOODWIN, CLIVE E. 1975 The winter season. Ontario region. Am. Birds, 29: (3): 683-688.

GOODWIN, CLIVE E. 1975 The spring migration. Ontario region. Am. Birds, 29: (4): 843-848.

GOODWIN, CLIVE E. 1975 The nesting season. Ontario region. Am. Birds, 29: (5): 963-967.

GOODWIN, CLIVE E. 1975 The Ontario Ornithological Records Committee report for 1974. Ont. Field Biologist, 29: (1): 29-39.

GOODWIN, CLIVE E. 1976 The fall migration. Ontario region. Am. Birds, 30: (1): 59-64.

GOODWIN, CLIVE E. 1976 The winter season. Ontario region. Am. Birds, 30: (3): 711-715.

GOODWIN, CLIVE E. 1976 The spring migration. Ontario region. Am. Birds, 30: (4): 832-836.

GOODWIN, CLIVE E. 1976 The nesting season. Ontario region. Am. Birds, 30: (5): 948-952.

GOODWIN, CLIVE E. 1977 The fall migration. Ontario region. Am. Birds, 31: (2): 169-173.

GOODWIN, CLIVE E. 1977 The winter season. Ontario region. Am. Birds, 31: (3): 325-328.

GOODWIN, CLIVE E. 1977 The spring migration. Ontario region. Am. Birds, 31: (5): 993-996.

GOODWIN, CLIVE E. 1977 The nesting season. Ontario region. Am. Birds, 31: (6): 1131-1135.

GOODWIN, C.E.; W. FREEDMAN & S.M. MCKAY 1977 Population trends in waterfowl wintering in the Toronto region. Ont. Field Biol., 31: (2): 1-28.

GOODWIN, CLIVE E. 1978 The autumn migration. Ontario region. Am. Birds, 32: (2): 197-200.

GOODWIN, CLIVE E. 1978 The winter season. Ontario region. Am. Birds, 32: (3): 342-346.

GOODWIN, CLIVE E. 1978 The spring migration. Ontario region. Am. Birds, 32: (5): 997-1001.

GOODWIN, CLIVE E. 1978 The nesting season. Ontario region. Am. Birds, 32: (6): 1153-1156.

GOODWIN, CLIVE E. 1979 The autumn migration. Ontario region. Am. Birds, 33: (2): 171-174.

GOODWIN, CLIVE E. 1979 The winter season. Ontario region. Am. Birds, 33: (3): 276-279.

GOODWIN, CLIVE E. 1979 The spring migration. Ontario region. Am. Birds, 33: (5): 765-768.

GOODWIN, CLIVE E. 1979 The nesting season. Ontario region. Am. Birds, 33: (6): 858-860.

GOODWIN, CLIVE E. 1980 The autumn migration. Ontario region. American Birds, 34: (2): 155-158.

GOODWIN, CLIVE E. 1980 The winter season. Ontario region. Am. Birds, 34: (3): 267-270.

GOODWIN, CLIVE E. 1980 The spring migration. Ontario region. Am. Birds, 34: (5): 770-773.

GOODWIN, CLIVE E. 1980 The nesting season. Ontario region. Am. Birds, 34: (6): 890-892.

GOODWIN, CLIVE E. 1981 The autumn migration. Ontario region. Am. Birds, 35: (2): 176-179.

GOODWIN, CLIVE E. 1981 The winter season. Ontario region. Am. Birds. 35: (3): 295-298.

GOODWIN, CLIVE E. 1981 The spring migration. Ontario region. Am. Birds, 35: (5): 817-820.

GOODWIN, CLIVE E. 1981 The nesting season. Ontario region. Am. Birds, 35: (6): 934-936.

GOODWIN, CLIVE E. 1982 The autumn migration. Ontario region. Am. Birds, 36: (2): 171-174.

GUNN, W.W.H. & A.M. CROCKER 1951 Analysis of unusual bird migration in North America during the storm of April 4-7, 1947. Auk, 68: (2): 139-163.

GUNN, WILLIAM W.H. 1957a The winter season. Ontario — western New York. Audubon Field Notes, 11: (3): 263-264.

GUNN, WILLIAM W.H. 1957b The nesting season. Ontario — western New York region. Audubon Field Notes, 11: (5): 402-403.

GUNN, WILLIAM W.H. 1958a Spring migration. Ontario — western New York. Audubon Field Notes, 12: (4): 348-352.

GUNN, WILLIAM W.H. 1958b The nesting season. Ontario — western New York. Audubon Field Notes, 12: (5): 408-410.

HARRINGTON, PAUL 1915 Ontario, 1914 nests. Oologist, 32: (6): 99.

HOPE, C.E. 1938 Birds of Favourable Lake Mine, Patricia portion of Kenora District, Ontario. Mimeo: 1-49.

HOPE, C.E. & T.M. SHORTT 1944 Southward migration of adult shorebirds on the west coast of James Bay, Ontario. Auk, 61: (4): 572-576.

IDEN, PETER Jan. 30, 1967 Toronto Birdfinding Bulletin, 3: (15): 1. (Mimeo).

JAMES, ROSS D. 1976 Changes in the list of birds known to occur in Ontario. Ont. Field Biol., 30: (2): 1-8.

JAMES, R.D.; P.L. MCLAREN & J.C. BARLOW 1976 Annotated checklist of the birds of Ontario. Royal Ont. Mus., Life Sciences Misc. Pubn. 1-75.

JAMES, ROSS D. 1979 Bird populations in short Jack pine woodlands of western Parry Sound District. Ont. Field Biologist, 33: (1): 12-18.

JAMES, ROSS D. 1980 Notes on the summer birds of Pickle Lake, Ontario. Ont. Field Biol., 34: (2): 80-92.

JAMES, ROSS D.; STEPHEN V. NASH & MARK K. PECK 1981 Distribution, abundance and natural history of birds at Kiruna Lake — 1981. Mimeo: 32-93. Royal Ont. Mus., Dept. Ornithology.

JAMES, ROSS D. 1982 Ontario Ornithological Records Committee report for 1981. Ont. Field Biologist, 36: (1): 16-18.

JAMES, ROSS D. 1983 Ontario Bird Records Committee report for 1982. Ontario Birds, 1: (1): 7-15.

JAMES, ROSS D. 1984 The breeding bird list for Ontario: additions and comments. Ontario Birds, 2: (1): 24-29.

JAMES, ROSS D. 1984 Ontario Bird Records Committee report for 1983. Ontario Birds, 2: (2): 53-65.

JOHNSGARD, PAUL A. 1978 Ducks, geese and swans of the world. Lincoln & London Univ. Nebraska Press: i-xxiii; 1-404.

KELLEY, ALICE H. 1978 Birds of southeastern Michigan and southwestern Ontario. Bloomfield Hills, Mich. Cranbrook Inst. Sci. i-vii; 1-99.

KENDEIGH, S. CHARLES 1947 Bird population studies in the coniferous forest biome during a spruce budworm outbreak. Ont. Dept. Lands & Forests, Div. Research, Biological Bull. No. 1: 1-100.

KOELZ, WALTER 1923 Some bird records for the Lake Superior region of Ontario. Can. Field-Naturalist, 37: (6): 118.

KORTRIGHT, FRANCIS H. 1942 The ducks, geese and swans of North America. Washington. Am. Wildlife Inst.: i-vii; 1-476.

LAMEY, JOHN 1981 Unusual records of birds for Ontario's Rainy River District. Ont. Bird Banding, 14: (1): 38-42.

LAWRENCE, LOUISE DE KIRILINE 1949 January singing in the black-capped chickadee and other species. Auk, 66: (3): 289-290.

LAWRIE, A.H. 1937 Field survey — York Downs. The Chat, 1: (4): 3-6.

LEE, D. & J.M. SPEIRS 1977 Breeding bird censuses at Big Trout Lake, 1975. Ont. Field Biol., 31: (2): 48-54.

LEE, DANN 1978 An annotated list of the birds of the Big Trout Lake area, Kenora District. Ont. Field Biol., 32: (1): 17-36.

LEWIS, HARRISON F. & HAROLD S. PETERS 1941 Notes on the birds of the James Bay region in the autumn of 1940. Can. Field-Nat., 55: (8): 111-117.

LGL LIMITED 1974 Bird populations and movements associated with the proposed site of the new Toronto International Airport. Final Report. Vol. 3: i-v; 1-261.

LLOYD, HOYES The birds of Ottawa, 1923. Can. Field Nat., 37: (6): 101-105. (Sept., 1923) 37: (7): 125-127 (Oct., 1923) 37: (8): 151-156 (Nov., 1923) 38: (1): 10-16 (Jan., 1924).

LLOYD, HOYES 1936 The birds of Ottawa. Addenda to February 28, 1935. Can. Field-Nat., 50: (9): 143-144.

LLOYD, HOYES 1949 Bird records for the Ottawa district. Can. Field-Nat., 63: (1): 31-34.

LONG, R. CHARLES 1965 An annotated list of the birds of Pickering Beach. Ont. Field Biologist, No. 19: 26-35.

LONG, R. CHARLES 1966 An annotated list of the birds of Pickering Beach. Part two. Ont. Field Biologist, No. 20: 25-35.

LONG, R. CHARLES 1968b An annotated list of the birds of Pickering Beach. Part 4. Ont. Field Biol., No. 22: 8-24.

LONG, R. CHARLES 1969 An annotated list of the birds of Pickering Beach. Part 5. Ont. Field Biol., No. 23: 14-23.

LONG, R. CHARLES 1970 An annotated list of the birds of Pickering Beach. Part 6. Ont. Field Biologist, No. 24: 19-22.

LONG, R. CHARLES 1972 An annotated list of the birds of Pickering Beach. Part 7. Ont. Field Biologist, No. 26: 38-45.

MACOUN, JOHN 1900 Catalogue of Canadian birds. Part I. Water birds, gallinaceous birds, and pigeons. Ottawa. Queen's Printer: i-vii; 1-218.

MACOUN, JOHN 1904 Catalogue of Canadian birds. Part III. Sparrows, swallows, vireos, warblers, wrens, titmice and thrushes. Ottawa. Queen's Printers: i-iv, 415-733.

MANNING, T.H. 1952 Birds of the west James Bay and southern Hudson Bay coasts. National Mus. Canada, Bull. No. 125: 1-114.

MAUGHAN, JOHN JR. 1897 Rare birds taken at Toronto. Proc. Can. Inst., 1: Part 1: No. 1: 2.

MCCRACKEN, JON D.; MICHAEL S.W. BRADSTREET & GEOFFREY L. HOLROYD 1981 Breeding birds of Long Point, Lake Erie. A study in succession. Can. Wildlife Service, Rept. Ser. No. 44: 1-74.

MCILWRAITH, THOMAS, 1894 The birds of Ontario. Toronto. William Briggs: i-ix; 11-426.

MCLAREN, PETER L. & MARGARET A. MCLAREN 1981 Bird observations in northwestern Ontario, 1976-77. Ont. Field Biologist, 35: (1): 1-6.

MILES, J.B. (compiler) 1965 Sixty-fifth Christmas bird count. Long Point. Ont. Audubon Field Notes, 19: (2): 93.

MILLS, ALEX 1981 A cottager's guide to the birds of Muskoka and Parry Sound. Toronto: i-xxiv; 1-209.

MITCHELL, HAROLD D. & ROBERT F. ANDRLE 1970 Birds of the Niagara Frontier Region. Supplement. Bull. Buffalo Soc. Natural Sciences, Vol. 22 Suppl.: 1-10.

MORDEN, J.A. & W.E. SAUNDERS 1883 The ornithology of western Ontario. Can. Sportsman and Naturalist, 3: 243. This gave the date of collection of J.H. Garnier's Sandwich Tern as autumn, 1881, not spring, 1882 as given in McIlwraith (1894: 52).

NICHOLSON, JOHN C. 1972 The birds of Manitoulin Island — a species accounts summary. Sudbury, Ont.: 1-46.

NICHOLSON, JOHN C. 1981 The birds of Manitoulin Island and adjacent islands within Manitoulin District. Sudbury, Ont. i-ix; 1-204. Map.

NOL, ERICA; CHRIS RISLEY; EDWARD RISLEY; ANN RIVERS; J. MURRAY SPEIRS (compiler); PHIL TAYLOR, SCOTT TRAQUAIR (Jan., 1978) Breeding Bird Census. Mixed forest (Backus woods) Am. Birds, 32: (1): 64-65.

PALMER, RALPH S. 1962 Handbook of North American birds. Vol. 1 Loons through flamingos: New Haven & London Yale Univ. Press i-xi; 1-567.

PALMER, RALPH S. 1976a Handbook of North American birds. Vol. 2 Waterfowl (Part 1): New Haven & London Yale Univ. Press i-xi; 1-521.

PALMER, RALPH S. 1976b Handbook of North American birds. Vol. 3 Waterfowl (Part 2): New Haven & London Yale Univ. Press i-vii; 1-560.

PARKER, BRUCE D. 1983 Toronto Region Bird Chart. Toronto Field Naturalists: i-ii; 1-31.

PECK, GEORGE K. 1972 Birds of the Cape Henrietta Maria region, Ontario. Can. Field-Nat., 86: (4): 333-348.

PECK, GEORGE K. 1976 Recent revisions to the list of Ontario's breeding birds. Ont. Field Biol., 20: (2): 9-16.

PECK, GEORGE K. 1981 Ontario nest records scheme. Sixteenth report (1956-1980) Mimeo: 1-26.

PERUNIAK, SHIRLEY 1971 The birds of the Atikokan area, Rainy River District, Ontario, Part 2. Ont. Field Biologist, No. 25: 15-33.

PETERSON, ROGER TORY; GUY MOUNTFORD & P.A.D. HOLLOM 1954 A field guilde to the birds of Britain and Europe. Boston. Houghton Mifflin Co.: i-xxxiv; 1-318.

PHILLIPS, ALLAN R.; MARSHALL A. HOWE & WESLEY E. LANYON 1966 Identification of the flycatchers of eastern North America, with special emphasis on the genus Empidonax. Bird-Banding, 37: (3): 153-171. For bird banders identifying flycatchers in the hand, this is a must!

PHILLIPS, ALLAN R. & WESLEY E. LANYON 1970 Additional notes on the flycatchers of eastern North America. Bird-banding, 41: (3): 190-197.

POUGH, RICHARD H. 1951 Audubon water bird guide. Garden City, N.Y. Doubleday & Co. i-xxviii; 1-352.

PRICE, DONALD & J. MURRAY SPEIRS 1971 Breeding-bird census. Aspen forest. Am. Birds, 25: (6): 976-977. At Lake of the Woods.

PRICE, DONALD & J. MURRAY SPEIRS 1971 Breeding-bird census. Hay field. Am. Birds, 25: (6): 1008-1009. Near Dryden, Ont.

QUILLIAM, HELEN R. 1965 The history of the birds of Kingston, Ontario. Kingston, Ont.: 1-216.

QUILLIAM, HELEN R. 1973 History of the birds of Kingston, Ontario. Kingston, Ont. Kingston Field Naturalists: 1-209. Map.

RICKER, WILLIAM E. & C.H.D. CLARKE 1939 The birds of the vicinity of Lake Nipissing, Ontario. Royal Ont. Mus. Zool., Contr. No. 16: 1-25.

ROBBINS, CHANDLER S.; BERTEL BRUUN & HERBERT S. ZIM 1966 Birds of North America. New York Golden Press: 1-340.

ROBERTS, THOMAS S. 1955 Manual for the identification of the birds of Minnesota and neighboring states. Univ. Minnesota Press: i-xiv; 459-738. (from Vol. 2 of the Birds of Minnesota 1936.).

SAMUEL, J. HUGHES 1900 List of the rare birds met with during the spring of 1900 in the immediate vicinity of Toronto. Auk, 17: (4): 391-392.

SAUNDERS, ARETAS A. 1935 A guide to bird songs. New York, London. D. Appleton-Century Co. i-xvii, 1-285.

SAUNDERS, RICHARD M. 1947 Flashing wings. Toronto. McClelland & Stewart: i-x; 1-388.

SAUNDERS, W.E. 1930 The destruction of birds at Long Point lighthouse, Ontario, on four nights in 1929. Auk, 47: (4): 507-511.

SAUNDERS, W.E. & E.M.S. DALE 1933 A history and list of the birds of Middlesex County, Ontario, Canada. Trans. Royal Can. Inst., 19: Part 2: 161-248. Index.

SAVILE, D.B.O. 1957 Some recent Ottawa bird records. Can. Field-Nat., 71: (1): 32-33.

SCHUELER, FREDERICK W.; DONALD H. BALDWIN & JAMES D. RISING 1974 The status of birds at selected sites in northern Ontario. Can. Field-Nat., 88: (2): 141-150.

SETON, ERNEST E.T. 1885 Interesting records from Toronto, Canada. Auk, 2: (4): 334-336.

SHEPPARD, R.W.; W.E. HURLBURT & G.H. DICKSON 1936 A preliminary list of the birds of Lincoln and Welland Counties, Ontario. Can. Field Nat., 50: (6): 95-102, (Sept.)50: (7): 118-122, (Oct.)50: (8): 131-140, (Nov.) 50: (9): 149-152. (Dec.)

SHEPPARD, R.W. 1945 Water birds of the Niagara. Can. Field-Nat., 59: (5): 151-169.

SHEPPARD, R.W. 1954 Phalaropes at Niagara Falls. Can. Field-Nat., 68: (3): 137-138.

SHEPPARD, R.W. 1960 Bird life of Canada's Niagara frontier. Mimeo: 1-50.

SKEEL, MARGARET & SOREN BONDRUP-NIELSEN 1978 Avifauna survey of Pukaskwa National Park. Mimeo: i-vii; 1-259.

SMITH, W. JOHN 1957 Birds of the Clay Belt of northern Ontario and Quebec. Can. Field-Nat., 71: (4): 163-181.

SNYDER, L.L. 1928 The summer birds of Lake Nipigon. Trans. Royal Can. Inst., 16: Part 2: 251-277.

SNYDER, L.L. 1928 The summer birds of Lake Abitibi. Univ. Toronto Studies: Biological Ser. No. 32: 17-34. (Royal Ont. Mus. Zool., Contr. No. 2)

SNYDER, L.L. 1931 The birds of Long Point and vicinity. Trans. Royal Can. Inst., 18: Part 1: 139-227.

SNYDER, L.L. 1938 The summer birds of western Rainy River District, Ontario. Trans. Royal Can. Inst. 22: Part 1: 181-213. (Royal Ont. Mus. Zool. Contr. No. 14.)

SNYDER, L.L. 1941 The birds of Prince Edward County, Ontario. Univ. Toronto, Biological Ser., No. 48: 25-92. (Royal Ont. Mus. Zool., Contr. No. 19).

SNYDER, L.L. 1942 Summer birds of the Sault Ste. Marie region, Ontario. Trans. Royal Can. Inst., 24: Part 1: 121-153.

SNYDER, L.L. 1953 Summer birds of western Ontario. Trans. Royal Can. Inst., 30: Part 1: 47-95.

SNYDER, L.L. 1957 Arctic birds of Canada. Univ. Toronto Press: i-x; 1-310.

SPEIRS, DORIS H. & J. MURRAY SPEIRS 1947 Birds of the vicinity of North Bay, Ontario. Can. Field-Nat., 61: (2): 23-38.

SPEIRS, DORIS H. & J. MURRAY SPEIRS 1960 Fall migration. Ontario — western New York region. Audubon Field Notes, 14: (1): 30-35.

SPEIRS, J. MURRAY 1938 Fluctuations in the numbers of birds in the Toronto region. Univ. Toronto M.A. Thesis: 1-99.

SPEIRS, J. MURRAY 1939 Fluctuations in the numbers of birds in the Toronto region. Auk, 56: (4): 411-419.

SPEIRS, J. MURRAY 1949 The relation of DDT spraying to the vertebrate life of the forest. In Forest spraying and some effects of DDT. Ont. Dept. Lands & Forests, Div. Research, Biological Bull. No. 2: 141-158.

SPEIRS, J. MURRAY 1956 Worth noting. Fed. Ont. Naturalists, Bull: 72: 29-32.

SPEIRS, J. MURRAY March, 1957 Worth noting. Fed. Ont. Naturalists, Bull. 75: 27-31.

SPEIRS, J. MURRAY, Sept. 1957 Worth noting. Fed. Ont. Nat. Bull. 77: 25-30.

SPEIRS, J. MURRAY 1958 Worth noting. Fed. Ont. Naturalists Bull. 82: 25-32.

SPEIRS, J. MURRAY Sept., 1959 Worth noting. Fed. Ont. Naturalists Bull. 85: 22-31.

SPEIRS, J. MURRAY June, 1960 Worth noting. Fed. Ont. Naturalists Bull. 88: 29-36.

SPEIRS, J. MURRAY Dec., 1960 Worth noting. Fed. Ont. Naturalists Bull. 90: 13-24.

SPEIRS, J. MURRAY & RONALD ORENSTEIN 1967 Bird populations in fields of Ontario County, 1965. Can. Field-Naturalist, 81: (3): 175-183.

SPEIRS, J. MURRAY & JOHN FRANK 1970 Thirty-fourth breeding bird census. Beech forest. Audubon Field Notes, 24: (6): 741-742.

SPEIRS, J. MURRAY & JOHN FRANK 1970 Breeding-bird census. Couch grass — downy brome grass field. Audubon Field Notes, 24: (6): 764-765.

SPEIRS, J. MURRAY & JOHN FRANK 1970 Breeding-bird census. Tall prairie relict. Audubon Field Notes, 24: (6): 765-766.

SPEIRS, J. MURRAY & JOHN FRANK 1970 Breeding-bird census. Pelee forest. Audubon Field Notes, 24: (6): 776-777.

SPEIRS, J. MURRAY; GRETCHEN MARKLE & RONALD G. TOZER 1970 Populations of birds in urban habitats, Ontario County, 1969. Ont. Field Biologist, No. 24: 1-12 (except pp. 3, 9)

SPEIRS, J. MURRAY; J.J.C. KANITZ & J. NOVAK 1971 Numbers, speeds, and directions of migrating geese from analysis of a radar display at Fort William, Ontario. Canadian Wildlife Service, Rept. Ser. No. 14: 69-76.

SPEIRS, J. MURRAY 1973 Birds of Ontario County. Scarlet Tanager to Snow Bunting. Fed. Ont. Naturalists: 40 species accounts. Maps & Graphs.

SPEIRS, J. MURRAY 1974 Birds of Ontario County. Starling to Brown-headed Cowbird. Fed. Ont. Naturalists: 55 species accounts. Maps and graphs.

SPEIRS, J. MURRAY 1975 Birds of Ontario County. Flycatchers to shrikes. Fed. Ont. Naturalists: 1-56. Maps & Graphs.

SPEIRS, J. MURRAY & RONALD ORENSTEIN 1975 Bird populations in forests of Ontario County, 1966-1968. Ont. Field Biologist, 29: (1): 1-24.

SPEIRS, J. MURRAY 1976 Birds of Ontario County. Jaegers to woodpeckers. Fed. Ont. Naturalists: 1-61. Maps & graphs.

SPEIRS, J. MURRAY 1977 Birds of Ontario County. Turkey Vulture to Northern Phalarope. Fed. Ont. Naturalists: 1-72. Maps & graphs.

NOL, ERICA; CHRIS RISLEY; EDWARD RISLEY; ANN RIVERS; J. MURRAY SPEIRS (compiler); PHIL TAYLOR, SCOTT TRAQUAIR. 1978 Forty-first Breeding Bird Census: Mixed forest. Am. Birds, 32: (1): 64-65.

SPEIRS, J. MURRAY 1979 Birds of Ontario County. Common Loon to Red-breasted Merganser. Fed. Ont. Naturalists: 1-62. Maps & Graphs.

STIRRETT, GEORGE M. 1973a The winter birds of Point Pelee National Park. Parks Canada: 1-22. Map.

STIRRETT, GEORGE M. 1973b The spring birds of Point Pelee National Park. Parks Canada: 1-28. Map.

STIRRETT, GEORGE M. 1973c The summer birds of Point Pelee National Park. Parks Canada: 1-24. Map.

STIRRETT, GEORGE M. 1973d The autumn birds of Point Pelee National Park. Parks Canada: 1-31. Map.

TERRES, JOHN K. 1980 The Audubon Society encyclopedia of North American birds. New York, Alfred A. Knoph 1-1109.

THOMPSON, ERNEST E. (ed.) 1890 Proceedings of the ornithological subsection of the biological section of the Canadian Institute. Proc. Can. Inst., 3rd Ser., Vol. 7, No. 2: 181-202.

TODD, W.E. CLYDE 1963 Birds of the Labrador Peninsula and adjacent areas. Carnegie Mus. and Univ. Toronto Press: i-xii; 1-819.

TOZER, RONALD G. & JAMES M. RICHARDS 1974 Birds of the Oshawa — Lake Scugog region, Ontario. Oshawa. Alger Press Ltd. i-vii; 1-383.

USSHER, R.D. 1965 Annotated check-list of the birds of Rondeau Provincial Park. Mimeo: 1-31.

WEIR, RON D. & HELEN R. QUILLIAM 1980 Supplement to History of the birds of Kingston, Ontario. Kingston Field Naturalists, Special Pubn.: 1-40.

WEIR, RON D. 1982 The winter season. Ontario region. Am. birds, 36: (3): 289-291.

WEIR, RON. D. 1982 The nesting season. Ontario region. Am. Birds, 36: (6): 970-974.

WEIR, RON D. 1983 The autumn migration. Ontario region. Am. Birds, 37: (2): 173-177.

WEIR, RON. D. 1983 The spring migration. Ontario region. Am. Birds. 37: (5): 863-867.

WEIR, RON. D. 1983 The nesting season. Ontario region. Am.Birds, 37: (6): 982-985.

WEIR, RON 1983 Arrivals and departures. Seasons, 23: (3): 42.

WEIR, RON D. 1984 The autumn migration. Ontario region. Am. Birds. 38: (2): 195-198.

WEIR, RON D. 1984 The winter season. Ontario region. Am. Birds, 38: (3): 310-314.

WEIR, RON D. 1984 The spring migration. Ontario region. Am. Birds, 38: (5): 903-907.

WILLIAMS, M.Y. 1942 Notes on the fauna of Bruce Peninsula, Manitoulin and adjacent islands. Can. Field-Naturalist, 56: (5): 70-81.

WILSON, REID 1980 Pickering birds — (April 16, 1980 to July 15, 1980). Pickering Naturalist, 5: (3): 116-118.

WITHERBY, H.F.; F.C.R. JOURDAIN; NORMAN F. TICEHURST & BERNARD W. TUCKER 1948 ed. The handbook of British birds. London. H.F. & G. Witherby Vol. 4: i-xiv; 1-461.

WOODFORD, JAMES & DONALD E. BURTON 1961 Ontario — western New York region. Spring. Audubon Field Notes, 15: (4): 405-409.

WOODFORD, JAMES & JOHN LUNN 1961 Ontario — western New York region. The nesting season. Audubon Field Notes, 15: (5): 464-467.

WOODFORD, JAMES & JOHN LUNN 1962 The winter season. Ontario — western New York region. Audubon Field Notes, 16: (3): 325-328.

WOODFORD, JAMES 1962 The spring migration. Ontario — western New York region. Audubon Field Notes, 16: (4): 404-408.

WOODFORD, JAMES 1962 The nesting season. Ontario — western New York region. Audubon Field Notes, 16: (5): 473-475.

WOODFORD, JAMES 1963 The spring migration. Ontario — western New York region. Audubon Field Notes, 17: (4): 399-401.

WOODFORD, JAMES 1963 The nesting season. Ontario — western New York region. Audubon Field Notes, 17: (5): 457-459.

WOODFORD, JAMES 1964 Fall migration. Ontario — western New York region. Audubon Field Notes, 18: (1): 28-30.

WORMINGTON, ALAN & ROSS D. JAMES 1984 Ontario Bird Records Committee, checklist of the birds of Ontario. Ontario Birds, 2: (1): 13-23.

# Explanatory Notes

ROM means Royal Ontario Museum; TOC – Toronto Ornithological Club

**Abbreviations:** Some of the localities have been abbreviated: e.g. Point Pelee National Park has been given as Pelee, Rondeau Provincial Park as Rondeau, Pukaskwa National Park as Pukaskwa, Presqu'ile Provincial Park as Presq'ile, etc.

**Measurements** have been given in metric units or in the English Units, as given in the original sources quoted. Some rough equivalents are given below for your convenience in translating to the measurements of your choice:

| | | | |
|---|---|---|---|
| 1 inch (in.) equals | | 25.4 | millimetres (mm.) or 2.54 centimetres (cm.) |
| 1 ounce (oz.) | '' | 28.3 | grams (g.) |
| 1 kilogram (kg.) | '' | 2.2 | pounds (lbs.) |
| 10 hectares (ha.) | '' | 25 | acres (24.7 is closer) |
| 1 km² | '' | 250 | acres (247 is closer) |
| 1 kilometre (km.) | '' | 1000 | metres |
| 1 mile (mi.) | '' | 1.609 | km. |

♂ means male and
♀ means female.

Most of the "quadrats" mentioned are areas of about 10 hectares or 25 acres (about 0.2 mile by 0.2 mile) or (0.32 by 0.32 km if your car odometer is calibrated in km.)

**Place names**: I have tried to follow the Gazetteer of Canada, Ontario. (1962 edition) for place names, in so far as they are given there. The end paper maps will locate some places frequently mentioned.

**Bird names**: I have followed the American Ornithologists Union (AOU) Check-List of North American Birds (Sixth edition 1983) for the names (nomenclature) and arrangement (taxonomy) of the birds mentioned in this publicaton.

The names of both the birds and the places mentioned are subject to change: e.g. the Common Moorhen was formerly known as the Florida Gallinule, then as the Common Gallinule and now as the Common Moorhen. And, greatly to my dismay, after studying the birds of Ontario County for many years the Ontario government saw fit to abolish that geographic entity, giving the two top townships to Simcoe County and the lower nine townships to the Regional Municipality of Durham (and lumping several of the townships).

The population figures given here will change. They will give a picture of the populations in the decade 1968 to 1977. Some birds rare in this decade are already showing signs of increasing abundance, e.g. the House Finch is rapidly spreading and increasing, as did the European Starling since I started bird watching in the 1920's when it was almost unknown in Ontario, until it is now one of our most abundant species. Other birds, e.g. the Eastern Bluebird, have greatly decreased. Almost every year sees new "accidentals" blown by storms or by pure wanderlust of adventurous individuals. The northern half of Ontario beyond the reach of roads will no doubt become much better known as roads develop and as "wilderness travel" becomes more available, and as bird atlassing becomes more popular.

**References** are given in two forms. References to a particular species are given following the account of the particular species, while references mentioning several species are given in the bibliography following the accounts of all species (in volume 2). These references contain much more information than can be given in a publication of this size and readers are encouraged to consult the original sources for more detail. Although we have been at some pains to check the references for accuracy there are bound to be some errors and the writer would be obliged to have these corrected.

**Explanation of map data**: On the Breeding Bird Survey maps there were generally 2 routes run in each degree squared in southern Ontario and only one (if any) in northern Ontario. The numbers given are the averages for all routes run in the square, a – indicates that no route was run in the square, while an 0 indicates that the route or routes were run but none of the given species was noted. The end paper map names the route (or routes) run in each square. The same procedure is followed in the case of Christmas counts, except that in southern Ontario several counts may have been made in a given square, not just one or two. Again an end paper map will indicate the Christmas counts made in each square. A third end paper map will show the locations of the quadrats I have mentioned and a final map will show the locations of localities frequently mentioned in the text, from Pelee in the south to Ft. Severn in the north. Most of the other localities will be found in the Gazeteer of Canada. Ontario section.

**Migration dates**: I have quoted the migration dates given by the different authors listed under each species. Some have given only "arrival" and "departure" dates: in some cases only the extreme dates when the earliest or latest birds were observed. Many have given the average, perhaps mentioning the number of years averaged, perhaps not. Some have indicated the date when the largest number were observed, or the "peak" dates (the best indicator of when to expect the species). Extreme dates are subject to rapid change, averages are better. I prefer median dates (i.e. the date when there have been equal numbers of records earlier and later than the given date). All these dates vary with the sex and age of the individuals concerned. Early migrants, like Red-winged Blackbirds or American Robins, may have most males arriving before most females, though there is generally some overlap and the date when they arrive varies greatly from year to year depending on temperature or other factors affecting the availability of food. A few members of the population may successfully overwinter and make the decision as to when the migrants arrive rather difficult to determine. In many species adults and young birds migrate at different times, e.g. most adult shorebirds go south before the young do. These differences are best determined by banders and much good work along this line has been done at the Long Point Bird Observatory.

**Weights**: The reader will note that the weights given for each species may cover quite a range. There are several reasons for these variations. For example female birds of prey are usually bigger than males. Some young birds may weigh more than the adults, just before leaving the nest: this is particularly true of sea birds. Birds tend to lay on a layer of fat before migrating (the fat is the fuel used for travel) and will weigh most heavily just before migrating. Birds also lay on fat during the cold seasons and may weigh 10% as much in winter as in summer. Birds may also weigh much more after a heavy meal than when near starvation.

Length and wingspread also vary with sex, age and degree of feather wear.

**For further information we can recommend the following:**

For life history data consult the volumes by Arthur Cleveland Bent, published by the Smithsonian Institution, U.S. National Museum. This series of some 20 volumes was a life work and is the foremost authority on life history matters.

For details of plumages not illustrated here we recommend the fine paintings by John Crosby in Godfrey's Birds of Canada. We have also mentioned the field guides by Peterson, Robbins *et al* and the recent National Geographic Field Guide. The various Audubon Society guides are also very useful. The Audubon Society Encyclopedia of North American Birds contains many fine photographs as well as general information on birds, this is the work by John K. Terres.

For more information on the structure and physiology of birds there is a good simple summary in a book by Lois and Louis Darling, simply called BIRD. This subject is covered in much greater detail in volumes by Marshall, *et al.*

If you wish to keep up to date on research on birds we recommend the periodicals The Auk, The Condor, The Ibis, The Wilson Bulletin and more locally Ontario Birds and The Ontario Field Biologist. Banders will especially want The Journal of Field Ornithology (formerly Bird Banding) and Ontario Bird Banding. For the general bird watcher we recommend American Birds, your local club publications, the FON publication Seasons and Nature Canada, its national counterpart.

*J. Murray Speirs*

# INDEX

English Names

*Names follow the AOU checklist of North American Birds, Sixth Edition, 1983.*

# INDEX

Scientific Names

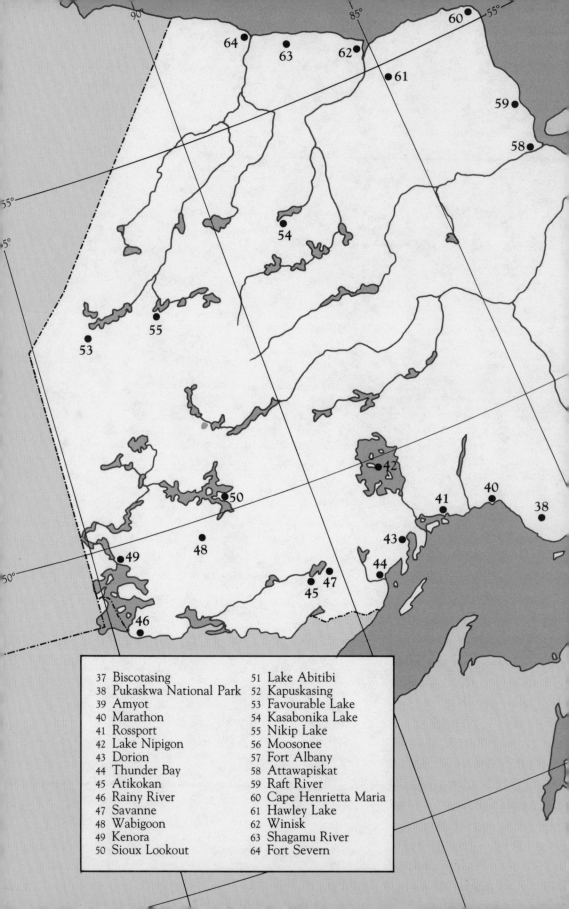

64

63

62

61

60

59

58

54

55

53

42

40

41

38

50

43

48

44

49

47

45

46